WHERE to SKI AND Snowboard 2003

The Reuters Guide
to the World's Best Winter Sports Resorts

Edited by
Chris Gill
and
Dave Watts

NortonWood

Published in Great Britain by
NortonWood Publishing
The Old Forge
Norton St Philip
Bath BA2 7LW
United Kingdom

tel 01373 835208
fax 01373 834106
e-mail mailbox@snow-zone.co.uk

This edition published 2002
Copyright (text and illustrations)
© Chris Gill and Dave Watts 2002

The right of Chris Gill and Dave Watts
to be identified as Authors of this
Work has been asserted by them in
accordance with the Copyright,
Design and Patents Act 1988.

10 9 8 7 6 5 4 3 2 1

ISBN 0 9536371 4 X

A CIP catalogue entry for this book is
available from the British Library.

Editors Chris Gill and Dave Watts
Assistant editors Martin Hall,
Mandy Crook, Catherine Weakley,
Emma Morris, Melanie Papworth,
Leigh Thompson, Robin Campbell,
Henry Druce
Australia/NZ editor Bronwen Gora
Contributors Chris Allan, Alan Coulson,
Nicky Holford, James Hooke,
Tim Perry, Adam Ruck,
Helena Wiesner, Ian Porter
Advertising manager Sam Palmer

Design by Fox Design Consultants
Production by Guide Editors
Contents photos
by Snowpix.com / Chris Gill
Production manager Ian Stratford
Proof-reader Sally Vince
Printed and bound in Spain
by Litografia Rosés

Although every care has been taken in
compiling this publication, using the
most up-to-date information available
at the time of going to press, all details
are liable to change and cannot be
guaranteed. Neither NortonWood
Publishing nor the Editors accept any
liability whatsoever arising from errors
or omissions, however caused.

Book trade sales are handled by
Portfolio Books Ltd
Unit 5 Perivale Industrial Park
Horsenden Lane South
Greenford UB6 7RL
tel 020 8997 9000
fax 020 8997 9097
e-mail sales@portfoliobooks.com

Individual copies of the book can be
bought by credit card from
www.amazon.co.uk or through our
own web site at:
www.snow-zone.co.uk
or by phoning:
01373 835208

WHERE *to* SKI
AND *SnoWboard* 2003

Contents

Resort chapters

7

About this book

it's simply the best

We believe that *Where to Ski and Snowboard* is the best guide to ski and snowboard resorts that you can buy. Here's why:

- By making the most of technology we were able to go to press later than ever this season (August as opposed to June a few editions ago) and get the late-breaking news to make the book **up to date for the 2002/03 season ahead**. To see what we mean, check out our What's new chapter, crammed with new resort developments, some announced only a few days before we went to press.

- We work hard to make our information **reader-friendly**, with clear cross-heads and verdicts for the main aspects of each resort.

- We don't hesitate to express **critical views**. We learned our craft at Consumers' Association, where Chris became editor of *Holiday Which?* magazine and Dave became editor of *Which?* itself – so a consumerist attitude comes naturally to us.

- Our resort chapters give an **unrivalled level of detail** – including scale plans showing the extent and layout of each major resort, as well as all the facts you need to have at your fingertips.

- We benefit enormously from the reports that hundreds of readers send in on the resorts they visit. The 100 best reports are rewarded by a free copy of the book, and many of **our best regular reporters get a free week's lift pass**. Prove your worth by sending us useful reports, and you could join the elite band who get to ski for free.

- We use **colour printing** fully, including not only piste maps for every major resort but also photographs, chosen not just to add colour but to allow you to see for yourself what the resorts are like.

Our ability to keep on improving *Where to Ski and Snowboard* is largely due to the support of our advertisers – many of whom have been with us since the first edition in 1994 – and of Reuters, our sponsor. We are grateful for that support, which has enabled us to **expand year after year**, allowing coverage of more resorts and more countries. In 1994 we had 500 pages; this year's expansion takes the book to just over 700.

We are uncompromising in our commitment to helping you, our readers, to make an informed choice; we're confident that you'll find this edition the best yet.

Enjoy your skiing and riding this season.

Chris Gill and Dave Watts
Norton St Philip, 2 August 2002

Get this edition FREE!

We reckon *Where to Ski and Snowboard* is a bargain at only £15.99. But if you plan to take a winter sports holiday this winter or the next, you can buy the book safe in the knowledge that you can get the cost of it refunded. See page 22.

Issues of the season

the editors have their say

GLOBAL WARMING – WHAT GLOBAL WARMING?

The greenhouse effect may or may not be at the root of it, but there's no doubt that global warming is taking its toll. Glaciers are melting, mountain villages are under threat of mud and ice slides, and lower resorts such as Kitzbühel, Grindelwald, Megève and Gstaad are in danger of eventually ceasing to function as ski resorts. The last two seasons have had very strange snowfall patterns. Winter in the Alps is certainly not the reliably cold and snowy affair that we remember fondly from our youth – when we always chose to take holidays in January for the reliable snow as well as low-season prices.

But if you choose the right resorts you can still have a great time on snow-sure slopes – with luck, for the rest of our lifetime. Last season, for example, is widely regarded as a terrible one for snow in the Alps. But we hit the slopes for the first time on 6 December along with 120 Daily Mail Ski & Snowboard readers with snow already piled high at Whistler in Canada. During the following ten days an amazing 1.5 metres (that's 5ft) of fresh powder fell. We finished the season on 24 April in Val-d'Isère in hot spring sunshine – but we were still able to ski from top to bottom of the mountain, and almost all pistes were still fully open.

The moral: choose resorts with a good snow record, and in Europe aim high – go for resorts with plenty of slopes above 2000m/6,500ft (or plenty of effectively used snowmaking).

SNOWMAKING SAVES THE DAY – DEPENDING WHERE YOU ARE

The start of the season was very dry in most of the Alps, except Austria, which had excellent early-season conditions. And it is true that we had to cancel a planned off-piste week in Italy in early January because of lack of snow. But snowmaking now means that you can have a good time on-piste even when natural snow is in short supply. We were in Courmayeur in mid-January before any real snow had fallen but still had an enjoyable weekend cruising man-made snowy pistes in the sunshine.

But most European resorts don't make good use of their snowmaking facilities. In North America, everywhere you go in early season you'll see snow-guns pumping out plumes of the white stuff to form a substantial base for the natural stuff to settle on. But in Europe it is a different matter. Italy seems to take number one position for snowmaking – we have ecstatic reports of great cruising on man-made strips of snow in the Selva area while all was green elsewhere and our own experiences of the Aosta valley resorts were very positive. On the other hand a reporter commented on Wengen in Switzerland, 'At least three machines were parked up and decorating the landscape at Kleine Scheidegg and never moved all week while the field below Wengernalp was 500 yards of sheet ice.' Another said, 'I was in St-Martin-de-Belleville in early January and the run home was excellent because of snowmaking. But the runs down to Méribel had stones coming through and the snow-guns there did not seem to be used.'

WEATHER: CHANGEABLE

Last season was one of Italy's worst in living memory for snowfall (some resorts never got a substantial snowfall) and tour operators have said they are worried about the effects on this season's bookings. But the previous season was one of the best for Italy – while the northern Alps suffered high temperatures and rain up to 3000m/10,000ft on occasion, Italy got dump after dump of powder. Similarly, in 2000/01 Western Canada suffered its worst season for many years. But in 2001/02 normal service was resumed and visitors wallowed in powder again through to late April. The moral: whatever you do, don't assume this season will be like the last.

LESSONS ABOUT SKI SCHOOLS

We continue to get a steady flow of complaints about standards of courtesy and care in European ski schools. This year's include a complete beginner in Mayrhofen 'in a class of 15 with an instructor who spoke no English – we got by on sign language' – and a five-year-old girl in the same resort being abandoned at the end of her ski lesson, 15 minutes before her father arrived to pick her up, despite previous assurances of supervision continuing until he arrived. And in Serre-Chevalier, a near beginner complained of 'appalling' treatment of herself and her friend in a French group: 'By Wednesday I was reduced to tears and we left our class halfway down a blue run.' These stories contrast strongly with the glowing reports we receive of lessons in North America. The one bright spot in Europe is the growing number of schools being run in the Alps by dynamic young British instructors. Unlike many of the locals, these people clearly understand what British pupils need, and know how to deliver it.

TERRAIN-PARK BOOM

Terrain-parks and half-pipes started off as playgrounds for snowboarders. But now they are as popular with 'new school' twin-tip skiers too. Even resorts which were slow to welcome snowboarders, such as Zermatt in Switzerland, now have excellent parks and pipes on offer. But America is leading the world in catering for this new demand. They are going to amazing lengths. Not only has 'exclusive' Aspen allowed boarders on to Aspen Mountain for the first time, but it has transformed the beginners' mountain, Buttermilk, by building a two-mile-long terrain-park from top to bottom, with a beginner and intermediate area, 30 rails and 25 jumps, a boarder-cross course and a 120m/400ft long super-pipe. Breckenridge will have a third terrain-park and half-pipe for 2002/03 – this new one aimed specifically at park and pipe novices. And Mammoth in California will go one better than a super pipe and build a super-duper pipe with 6.5m/22ft high walls for this season.

EXCLUSIVE RESORTS? NOT EXCLUSIVE ENOUGH

Once a resort gets known as a 'fashionable' or 'exclusive' place, the tag tends to stick. Normally, we're at pains to get across to our readers the fact that 'exclusive' resorts are not actually exclusive in any real sense: whether you're talking about Courchevel, Gstaad or Aspen, the fact is that the film stars and creative accountants make up a tiny proportion of the resort's visitors, most of whom are ordinary holidaymakers like you and us. There are, of course, hotels, restaurants and clubs where the price of entry is higher than most of us can manage, but there are always plenty of alternatives. In all

Millions rely on the net for information
but who does the net rely on?

REUTERS

three of the resorts I've mentioned we can point you to places where you can get egg and chips (or a close approximation).

And this year we have a new development to report: readers finding that the supposedly 'exclusive' resort they have chosen has turned out to be not nearly exclusive enough. A widely experienced visitor to Lech – famously fashionable with the Austrians and Germans, but also blessed with a good mix of snowy slopes and village charm – sent us this admonishment: 'Clientele now seems to be German car-workers and Russian mafia, with ski-wear dating from the 1980s. Expected somewhere smart and chi-chi, but it is the only ski resort I have ever visited where I have seen two men standing by a bus stop, in the middle of the village and the middle of the day, urinating into the road.' We also visited Lech last season, after an interval of a couple of years, and without witnessing any similar spectacle came to share our reporter's view that the place does seem less ... well, less exclusive than it did. We have changed the emphasis of our chapter as a result. More observations from readers on the real nature of supposedly exclusive resorts would be welcome.

REPORTING FOR DUTY, OR FOR A FREE LIFT PASS

In fact, reports from readers of any kind would be welcome. We rely heavily on readers' reports to assess aspects of resorts that are difficult to get to grips with when we are making a flying visit – ski schools, high-season lift queues, restaurants, nightlife – and to keep us in touch with resorts that we can't get to in a given season. Each year, we give free copies of the new edition to the authors of the 100 most useful reports. What's more, consistent book-winners are invited to become 'resort observers'. Observers notify us of their winter travel plans, and if those plans include resorts that we don't plan to visit, we arrange a lift-pass for the observer in exchange for a detailed review of the relevant chapter. Most observers seem to find this a worthwhile trade. If you like the idea, send us a report this season. There's more information about the kind of reports we want on page 40. We can send you a form if that helps, but many people these days prefer to use email, which we encourage.

PERILOUSLY PACKED PISTES

There are some excellent new lifts this season that should cut long queues in several key resorts. But we continue to be amazed by the way that resorts will add new lifts or upgrade old ones without thinking through the consequences – that is, without considering crowding on the pistes. This year, for example, Verbier is increasing the capacity of the jumbo Funitel gondola from Les Ruinettes to Les Attelas by 25%. The main red run it serves back down to Les Ruinettes was already one of the most dangerously overcrowded we have come across, and now it will be even worse.

Again, we ask: Why can't Europe learn from North America? Over there they have mountain planners who use computers to design networks of lifts and runs so that neither ends up crowded and everyone on the slopes has an enjoyable time. They have tried to sell their skills to European resorts, but have had few takers. Instead, millions of pounds are invested in new lifts to solve queue problems with apparently no thought given to the question of whether the runs can cope with the resulting crowds.

In some cases – Verbier may be an example – there are no easy solutions: the nature of the mountains prevents the creation of new

WINTER PARK SKIER'S CODE:

I PROMISE TO OBEY POSTED SIGNS.
I PROMISE TO SKI A MOUNTAIN THAT'S MADE FOR SKIING, NOT POSING.

The perfect skiing vacation is waiting for you deep in the Colorado Rockies. Once you arrive, you'll find Winter Park Resort is unlike the big, glitzy, presumptious, and most of all, pricey resorts. Here, you can find skiing like it used to be, along with prices like it used to be.

WINTER PARK RESORT®
colorado's favorite
skiwinterpark.com

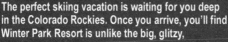

Find out more about Winter Park Resort:

Skiworld North American
Reservations ph: 0208 600 1799

Ski Safari
ph: 01273 223680

American Trails
ph: 029 2065 0752

American Ski Classics
ph: 020 83926660

Equity Travel
ph: 01273 299199

Skiersworld
ph: 0870 3333 620

AmericanSki
ph: 44-1892 511894

Lotus Supertravel
ph: 020 7962 9933

Oak Hall Skiing
ph: 01732 76131

Ski All America
ph: 08701 676 676

Worldskiers
ph: 0207 240 3113

Ski Independence
ph: 0870 555 0 555

Neilson
ph: 0870 33 33 347

Crystal Holidays
ph: 0870 848 7000

Thomson Ski Board Snow
ph: 0208 241 5129

United Vacations
ph: 0870 606 2222

Ski the American Dream
ph: 020 8552 1201

Virgin Holidays
ph: 0870 990 4212

runs. So cutting lift queues is always going to mean worse piste crowding. Or is it? What Verbier needs to look at is ways of getting people over to the less crowded slopes at La Chaux without riding the Funitel, and ways of getting people to spend time in the unjustly neglected Savoleyres sector. It also needs fewer visitor beds.

In other cases, the mountains are more amenable. Absolutely the most crowded piste in the Alps (and therefore the world) is the blue Steissbachtal run at St Anton. Everyone on the whole Galzig-Valluga-St Christoph sector has to use this run to get back to the village, along with people doing circuits on the upper mountain. The result is simply a nightmare. St Anton must establish other easy ways for people to get down the mountain. A start would be to develop a piste to St Anton from the slopes above St Christoph, following the route of the Maroi itinerary that was marked on the resort's piste map until 1998. Other steps might be needed. Until this problem is tackled, many people will rightly leave St Anton off their shortlist.

PISTE GRADING BLUES

We've complained before about the lack of uniformity in the way resorts classify pistes for difficulty. In an ideal world, international standards would ensure that skiers and boarders could identify the kind of run they want to spend time on, and avoid the kinds of run they dread. We don't hold out much hope of that. But it surely isn't too much to ask that there should be some consistency between resorts in a given country, at least.

Grumbles from readers this year remind us that this is a real problem that can spoil people's holidays. An example from Mayrhofen: 'To get on to most blues it was necessary to ski down a red. The only directly accessible blues were largely narrow tracks that have a steep drop or trees on one side and a rock face on the other, compounded by very variable snow conditions because of the trees and crowds of people because of the blue classification. They are much too narrow for most novices to be able to turn, and usually there was a long line of people in a permanent snowplough. Surely, tracks like this should really be graded red.' Indeed they should.

The essential problem is that run classification has marketing implications. Val-d'Isère gives a green classification to runs that should be blue so that novices don't steer away from the resort, perhaps taking 15 friends with them. Similarly, Gstaad has black runs so gentle that deep snow brings forward motion to a halt.

The problem is not confined to the Alps. Indeed, resorts in North America tend to be explicit about the fact that their classifications are relative – 'More difficult', 'Most difficult' and so on. And yet our experience is that American classification is more consistent than European classification. In particular, double-diamond blacks (the category above ordinary blacks) are always, but always, seriously steep expert terrain, and greens are always gentle. So it can be done.

What's new?

lifts and snow for 2003

The main news from the resorts of Europe and North America, plus key improvements from last season.

The Mont Blanc tunnel reopened in March 2002 after the tragic fire of 1999 – so Courmayeur and other resorts in the Aosta valley in Italy will again be quickly reachable from Geneva airport and for day-trips from Chamonix.

AUSTRIA

ALPBACH A new quad chair-lift will replace one of the Muldenlift drags behind Gmahkopf. An eight-seater gondola replaced the single-seater chair to the top of Reith last season.

BAD GASTEIN The old triple chair from the Angertal up towards Stubnerkogel is being replaced by a fast quad. Last season Schlossalm's Weitmoser T-bars were replaced by a new six-pack.

INNSBRUCK The Mutters ski area re-opens this season following construction of a new access gondola. New lifts have created an improved two-way link with Axamer Lizum's slopes.

ISCHGL A new chair-lift from Idalp to Pardatschgrat is planned for this season. Last season, a fast eight-seater chair replaced a slow quad to the border at Idjoch, a six-pack replaced two T-bars on Palinkopf and a quad chair was installed at Bodenalp. Samnaun has installed a new six-pack up to Alp Trida Sattel.

KAPRUN A 24-person gondola is replacing the funicular that suffered a tragic fire in autumn 2000. The first stage of the Gletscherjet opened last season and the upper section is due to be finished in October 2002.

KITZBÜHEL The Bärenbadkogel II T-bar between Jochberg and Pass Thurn will be replaced by a six-pack. In Pass Thurn an eight-seater chair will replace the two Hartkaser T-bars below Zweitausender.

OBERGURGL A four-seater chair-lift has replaced the Übungs drag-lift in the Gaisberg sector. A new six-pack replaces the Steinmann and Sattel drag-lifts. Last season an eight-seater gondola was built from Untergurgl via Hochgurgl to a point high on the Wurmkogl slopes.

OBERTAUERN Last season a new fast quad chair-lift, the Zentralbahn, replaced the old drag-lift.

PITZTAL At HochZeiger, a new six-pack is being installed. A run is being created from the glacier to the valley, giving a descent of an impressive 1700m/5,580ft vertical – and relieving any queues for the funicular at the end of the day.

SAALBACH-HINTERGLEMM The cable-car from Saalbach to Schattberg Ost is due to be replaced by a new eight-seater gondola.

SKIWELT A second gondola – an eight-seater – will run from Scheffau to the summit of Brandstadl, replacing the existing chair. A fast six-person chair-lift replaces a T-bar up from Brixen's mid-station.

SÖLDEN Last season the long Heidebahn chair up from Gaislachalm was replaced by a fast quad.

St Johann Last season an eight-seater gondola replaced the single-person chair from Oberndorf, greatly improving access for day trippers and taking pressure off the main village gondola.

Westendorf Two T-bars at the top, up to Fleiding and Gampen, were replaced by quad chairs last season.

Wildschönau More snowmaking is being installed. Last season the old Hahnkopf and Kothkaser drag-lifts on Schatzberg were replaced by a new six-pack.

Zillertal-Tux Valley Last season the Eggalm/Rastkogel area above Lanersbach was linked with Mayrhofen's Penken slopes, via a new fast six-seater chair from Rastkogel, with a new 150-person cable-car and a new piste to bring you back.

France

Alpe d'Huez A new fast quad chair-lift is planned on the Sarenne glacier. Last season the Glacier double chair was replaced by a quad starting lower down on the glacier. The capacity of the first stage of the Marmottes gondola was increased. A new drag-lift and nursery slope opened at Alpette, mid-station of the Vaujany cable-car.

Les Arcs A third chair-lift (a quad) will continue from the top of the second chair up from Le Pré, to allow a direct descent to Arc 2000. A new six-pack is planned to replace an existing chair and two drags from Arc 1800 towards Col des Frettes. For 2003/04 the long-awaited cable-car link between Les Arcs and La Plagne should be in place. Also opening for 2003/04 is a smart new village called Arc 1950, being built by Canadian company Intrawest – developer of many

attractive resorts in North America. It promises to be by far the most attractive of the Arcs villages, with pedestrian squares and buildings in sympathetic style built in local wood and stone. What's more, the apartments will be exceptionally spacious and comfortable.

AVORIAZ Last season a fast, six-seater chair replaced the double drag from Les Lindarets up to Avoriaz, cutting the queues at this bad bottleneck. A new piste built at the top joined the existing runs down to Les Lindarets.

CHÂTEL The triple Chaux des Rosées chair from Plaine Dranse will be replaced by a fast six-pack.

LA CLUSAZ In Le Grand-Bornand, the Lachat chair was upgraded to a new six-pack last season. This now accesses the new red Piste 2000 which runs from the top of Lachat, around the back of the mountain and down to the Maroly area above Chinaillon.

COURCHEVEL Last season a new fast six-seater chair replaced the long Pralong drag-lift from the beginner slopes above

What's new?

1850. Another fast six-pack replaced three drag-lifts in 1650.

LES DEUX-ALPES An eight-seater chair has replaced the old Jandri 3 gondola running from mid-mountain to the glacier, reducing queues on the second stage of the Jandri Express.

FLAINE A new eight-seater gondola – the Grand Massif Express – will finally open, linking Samoëns village to Samoëns 1600 at mid-mountain. Last season a new fast quad from Morillon 1100 opened to serve the Bergin run.

MEGÈVE There will be at least one new gondola in the Princesse area, we guess replacing the existing one. A major extension of the slopes of Le Jaillet will create a link with the village of La Giettaz, west of Megève on the road to La Clusaz.

LES MENUIRES The Tortollet chair, providing access from outlying accommodation to the main lifts, is being replaced by a fast quad. Last season two fast chairs from the centre gave faster access to Mont de la Chambre and the links with Méribel and Val Thorens.

MÉRIBEL A fast six-seat chair replaces the slow old Plan des Mains chair from the bottom of Mont Vallon to Plattières, relieving the bottleneck for those heading for Méribel or Courchevel from Mont Vallon or Val Thorens.

MONTGENÈVRE Another 5km/3 miles of snowmaking will be installed and a new boarder-cross course and a terrain-park will be built.

MORZINE A fast six-pack is due to replace the two Nauchets drag-lifts in the Les Chavannes-Le Ranfolly sector and a new fast quad is planned for the La Rosta slopes. The Mont Chéry gondola will be renovated and new six-seater bubbles installed. At Les Perrières, on the outskirts of Les Gets, a fast six-pack to take day visitors to the slopes is planned. Last season a fast quad replaced two drag-lifts from Grand Pré towards Chamossière.

LA PLAGNE Access to Roche de Mio and the glacier will be improved by two new fast six-packs. One will start from Plagne Bellecôte and go to the top of the ridge which leads to Champagny. The other starts a little below the ridge and takes you on up to Roche de Mio. See Les Arcs for details of a new link between the resorts.

PUY-ST-VINCENT Developments include, we're told, a new blue run – the Tournoux – and increased artificial snowmaking.

RISOUL Last season the first eight-seater chair in the southern Alps was built from the village to the middle of the slopes on Peyrefolle.

LA ROSIÈRE Last season a free drag-lift and a new green piste opened.

SERRE-CHEVALIER Last season a fast six-seater chair replaced the Prorel drag-lifts, linking the Chantemerle sector to the Briançon slopes.

ST-MARTIN-DE-BELLEVILLE A gondola is due to replace the chair out of the village. The drag-lift on the slope up from the church is being moved to the side and improved.

LA TANIA Snowmaking is being extended, allowing more visitors to ski back to their accommodation.

TIGNES-VAL-D'ISÈRE The slow Tommeuses chair-lifts – a major bottleneck on the way back from Val to Tignes – will at last be replaced, by a fast eight-seater. The old Bellevarde cable-car is being replaced by a jumbo gondola. Last season the triple Glacier chair, an essential link from Solaise towards the Col de l'Iseran and the Pissaillas glacier, was upgraded to a fast six-pack.

VAL-THORENS A third big Funitel gondola is to be installed, replacing the Bouquetin chair towards Méribel – not only cutting queues but also cutting the chance of closure by wind. This follows last season's construction of the Grand Fond Funitel towards the Maurienne valley. The nearby Plateau drags will be replaced by a chair.

ITALY

BORMIO A new fast quad replaces the Isabella chair from Bormio 2000, helping reduce the queues for the second stage of the cable-car. Bormio has been chosen to host the Alpine World Ski Championships in 2005, 20 years after it first staged them.

LIVIGNO A new six-pack from Valfin on the Mottolino slopes to the top of Monte Della Neve has opened up new black runs. A new quad chair from Teola to Pianoni Bassi takes skiers above the bottom station of the chairs to Monte Sponda and Monte della Neve.

SELVA/SELLA RONDA A new gondola is scheduled to replace the endless series of drag lifts from Colfosco towards Dantercëpies – the slowest part of the counterclockwise Sella Ronda circuit. The lift stations on either side of Ortisei are being linked by a series of moving walkways and escalators, so that skiers will be able to move between the Seceda and Alpe di Suisi areas without walking through the town.

LA THUILE The old chair from the Petit St Bernard Pass to Belvedere will be replaced by a new fast quad, speeding the link to France.

SWITZERLAND

CHAMPÉRY Two fast six-packs are planned to replace the old double chairs from Grand Paradis and at Planachaux – but final permission to build them had not been given when we went to press.

CRANS-MONTANA The Nationale and Barmaz lifts have been upgraded and now have loading carpets.

DAVOS The upgrading of the ancient Parsennbahn railway is back on track with provision of a bigger, faster train from the valley to the mid-station. The Schatzalp/Strela lift system is no longer included in the area lift pass and the link to Weissfluhjoch has been closed.

GRINDELWALD A new fast quad chair will replace the old Schilt T-bar at the top of the First area.

ST MORITZ The Alpine World Ski Championships are to be held in St Moritz from 1 to 16 February 2003 and the event has prompted improvements to road access, lift updating and more snowmaking. A faster 100-person cable-car from Corviglia to Piz Nair will replace the old queue-prone 40-person one. A fast six-pack will replace the FIS and Pitschen T-bars on Corviglia.

VERBIER The jumbo Funitel gondola from Les Ruinettes to Les Attelas will have an extra 25% capacity. Verbier's first six-pack will replace the Saxon chair and Nord drag on the back of the Savoleyres ridge. The two-stage gondola from Le Châble to Verbier and on to Les Ruinettes, has been upgraded – though the capacity remains modest.

VILLARS Last season a fast six-seater chair was installed between La Rasse and Chaux Ronde.

ZERMATT A new eight-seater gondola is to replace the old Zermatt-Furi gondola and Furi-Schwarzsee cable-car. It will go from Zermatt via Furi to Schwarzsee in just 10 minutes and be able to carry 3,000 people per hour.

UNITED STATES

CALIFORNIA

HEAVENLY The first phase of a 34-acre pedestrian 'village' around the base of the new gondola opens for this season.

MAMMOTH The first restaurants and shops in the Village at Mammoth are planned to open, along with a 15-person gondola linking it to Canyon Lodge lift base. A half-pipe with 7m/22ft walls is being built.

COLORADO

ASPEN 2001/02 was the first season that snowboarding was allowed on Aspen Mountain. For this season the Trenchtown terrain-park at Snowmass will double in size.

BRECKENRIDGE A new six-pack is being installed on Peak 7, serving new intermediate runs. A new fast quad will start above Beaver Run on Peak 9 and run to Peak 8, with a mid-station for boarding higher up. Peak 8 will have a third terrain-park and half-pipe aimed at novices.

TELLURIDE Three new fast chair-lifts opened up Prospect Bowl last season, giving another 733 acres of terrain and over 20 new runs.

WINTER PARK The terrain-parks and half-pipe are being expanded and improved. Intrawest has agreed to operate and develop the resort.

UTAH

ALTA-SNOWBIRD Last season neighbouring Alta and Snowbird finally got their act together, installing quad lifts to the ridge that separates them and offering a shared lift pass.

THE CANYONS There will be increased capacity on the gondola out of the village. Last season an additional chair-lift was installed, opening up new runs close to the existing Dreamscape area. A new terrain-park was built near the Red Hawk quad lift at the base area. The kids' nursery area at Red Pine Lodge has two new lifts, one a magic carpet.

DEER VALLEY The Ruby chair-lift will be replaced by a fast quad. Last season the Quincy triple chair was also replaced by a fast quad.

PARK CITY Last season a bridge was built linking the slopes directly to the base of the Town Lift, next to Main Street.

CANADA

WESTERN CANADA

BANFF In Sunshine village a sixth quad chair replaces the Wawa T-bar on Mount Standish. The eight-seater gondola to Sunshine Village installed last season is the world's fastest and longest single strand gondola. It has almost doubled capacity and cut the journey time by over 40% to under 13 minutes.

JASPER Last season the new Eagle Ridge quad chair opened up 20 new runs on either side of Eagle Ridge.

KICKING HORSE A new quad chair from Crystal Bowl to Blue Heaven is being built, opening up a further 20 marked runs and 150 acres of skiable terrain. Capacity on the main gondola has been doubled.

LAKE LOUISE Investment has been resumed with the construction of a new six-pack on the upper mountain, replacing the existing fast quad to the top of the front face.

SWEDEN

ÅRE A six-pack will be installed next to the main cable-car from town, replacing the slow double chair. This will feed a new four-seater chair, replacing a T-bar and two double chairs.

Banff's Best Snow!

skibanff.com

Deeper

Sunshine Village receives an average of 33 feet of dry, Canadian Rockies powder each season.

Bigger

Sunshine offers some of the best skiing and snowboarding in the Canadian Rockies, with three beautiful mountains, offering everything from groomed beginner slopes to steep and deep powder skiing. In addition, snowboarders can enjoy our permanent snowboard half-pipe, boarder–X course and terrain park!

More Convenient

The Sunshine Inn, a remarkable 84 room cozy alpine lodge located right in the middle of the ski area at 7200 feet, offers Banff's only ski-in, ski-out accommodation.

Faster

Sunshines's new state of the art 8 person gondola and recent $4m investment in high speed quads means queues are a thing of the past. Using world-leading technology, the new gondola will cut travel time by 40% and whisk skiers and riders up to the magnificent vistas in much greater comfort.

Airtours	Crystal	Frontier Ski	Neilson	Ski the American Dream
0870 608 1950	0870 848 7000	020 8776 8709	0870 333 3347	020 8552 1201
All Canada Ski	First Choice Ski	Inghams	Ski Independence	Thomson
01502 585825	0870 754 3477	020 8780 4444	0870 555 0555	0870 606 1470

Sunshine Village Ski & Snowboard Resort, Banff, Alberta, Canada. Tel 001 403 762 6500

Get your **money back**
When you book a holiday

You can reclaim the price of Where to Ski and Snowboard when you book a winter sports holiday for the 2002/03 or 2003/04 seasons. All you have to do is book the holiday through the specialist ski travel agency Ski Solutions.

Ski Solutions is Britain's original and leading ski travel agency. You can buy whatever kind of holiday you want through them.

Ski Solutions sells the package holidays offered by all the bonded tour operators in Britain (apart from the very few who are direct-sell only). And if that isn't enough choice, they can tailor-make a holiday, based on any form of travel and any kind of accommodation. No one is better placed to find you what you want than Ski Solutions.

Phone Ski Solutions on

020 7471 7700

Making a claim

Claiming your refund and free insurance is easy. When you make your definite booking, tell Ski Solutions that you want to take up this offer. They'll knock £15.99 off the cost of your holiday. That's all there is to it.

Get next year's edition **FREE** by reporting on your holiday

There are too many resorts for us to visit them all every year, and too many hotels, bars and mountain restaurants for us to see. So we are very keen to encourage more readers to send in reports on their holiday experiences. As usual, we'll be giving 100 copies of the next edition to the writers of the best reports.

There are five main kinds of feedback we need:
- what you particularly **liked and disliked** about the resort
- what aspects of the resort came as a **surprise** to you
- your other suggestions for **changes to our evaluation** of the resort – changes we should make to the ratings, verdicts, descriptions etc
- your experience of **queues** and other weaknesses in the lift system, and of the **ski school** and associated childcare arrangements
- your feedback on **individual facilities** in the resort – the hotels, bars, restaurants (including mountain restaurants), nightspots, equipment shops, sports facilities etc.

You can send your reports to us in three ways. In order of preference, they are:
- by e-mail to: reports@snow-zone.co.uk (don't forget to give us your postal address)
- word-processed and printed on paper
- handwritten on a form that we can provide.

Our postal address is:
Where to Ski and Snowboard, FREEPOST, The Old Forge, Norton St Philip, Bath BA2 7ZZ

All-inclusive holidays

come home on-budget

For anyone who wants to keep control of their holiday spending, there's nothing to beat an all-inclusive holiday. If you're heading for the beaches of the Caribbean, it's not difficult to find places where everything you're going to need is included in the crystal-clear upfront cost, from flights down to snorkel kit and all-day cocktails. When heading for the slopes, it's not so easy. Work through enough brochures and you'll track down a few package deals based on full board. But wine with meals? Not widely done, except in catered chalets that are only half-board. Ski equipment, tuition and a lift pass? Nope: perhaps surprisingly, no one sells packages that include absolutely everything. But there are a couple of companies that do roll most of these components into their packages: Club Med and Equity.

CLUB MED

Club Med is the big name in this game, and one it's difficult to escape, such is the scale of its operation. The brightly painted extension to Aime la Plagne? It's Club Med. The place with the swooping roofs in Arc 2000? The twin round tower blocks in Sestriere? The big old Palace hotel in Villars? Ditto Wengen? They're all Club Med 'villages'.

Some of these are grand hotels that had found their traditional markets disappearing, but some are purpose-built and some of the recently developed 'villages' – notably the trio of very smart chalet-style places they have in Méribel – are swanky, modern hotels that are impressive by any standard. The great majority of the ski properties are in France (it's a French company), but Club Med has taken over a handful of old hotels in Swiss resorts and also now has places in Italy (Sestriere and Cervinia).

The 'village' terminology is misleading to the beginner. It's presumably meant to strike a chord with Club Med's summer clientele. The company (which recently celebrated its 50th birthday) started out running all-inclusive summer holidays, and those holidays do take place in something like self-contained holiday villages. The ski villages are really hotels with ski shops in the basement (and crèches in most).

Club Med holidays are available with or without flights and transfers. They all include insurance. But perhaps the defining characteristic of the Club Med package is that it includes all meals, including beer and wine – and, because this is a French operation, lunch is just as serious a meal as dinner. In most villages, lunch is taken back at base (most are high resorts where this is not a problem) but in some – Chamonix and three Swiss resorts – Club Med has taken over a mountain restaurant where your 'free' lunch can be had.

Clearly, the full-board formula has its attractions. Well, it has one attraction: that your lunch (and accompanying drinks) are paid for. You have to weigh against this the fact that most of the villages are in resorts with big lift networks where, in the normal course of events, you wouldn't be heading back to base for lunch every day – beginners apart, many people would be planning on having lunch savouring the views on a remote mountaintop, or in some equally remote village in another valley.

Generally, Club Med prices include your lift pass and tuition (the Méribel villages are an exception). Some do only half-day tuition, but most do a full day. Skiing or boarding equipment costs extra, but is available on-site in all villages except Flaine – so at least you don't have to schlepp around the resort. They carry a range of kit, including performance skis.

Most villages have childcare facilities, and for many Club Med fans these are at the heart of the formula. There is a mini club in 20 of the villages (included in the holiday cost) for ages 4 to 13; the deal includes dinner and evening entertainment until 9pm. Of those 20, three have a petit club for ages 2 to 4, and two have a baby club for ages 4 months to 2 years; these facilities cost extra.

A handful of villages welcome children but make no special provision for them. Club Med recommends these for couples and singles. And two villages are 'Adults Only' – open only to those over 18, recommended for singles. It was to one of these – Val-Thorens – that a pal and I went, a few seasons back, for a taste of the Club Med recipe. (The other is in Alpe d'Huez.) We went in early December, when Val-Thorens was only half-open, Courchevel was just waking up and Méribel was pretty much still asleep. First clue as to how Club Med makes money: the place was apparently full, even at that early stage of the season.

There was a pretty international crowd, although naturally French-dominated. There were very few Brits – there were only five of us on the transfer minibus from Geneva, and the village has 180 rooms – a lot of Israelis, quite a few Dutch, the occasional Russian. So

Club Med in La Plagne: the red bit of Aime-la-Plagne, on the horizon ↓

it wasn't difficult to find dinner tables where English rather than French was the lingua franca. In what is apparently a standard Club Med arrangement, meals were taken at big round tables for eight people, and you just cruised around until you found a likely-looking bunch of companions. Bottles of house wine were freely distributed by waiters, and beer was on tap. All the food was served via buffets, the most popular bits of which generated queues at peak times. The food – with an exotic theme on some evenings – was pretty good, though not exactly a highlight of the day. We didn't hesitate to skip the lunch at base occasionally and splash out on a mountain restaurant meal, and when an invitation came our way late in the week to dine out in a smart restaurant elsewhere in the village, the change of scene was welcome.

We joined the free ski classes most days, and wound up in a friendly French-speaking advanced group with a Gitane-smoking ESF instructor who spoke good English – when his failing respiratory system permitted him to speak at all. We had a lot of fun. He took us off-piste in what I later discovered to be dangerous circumstances, but that's ESF instructors for you.

Val-Thorens is a 'three-trident' village, the most common kind on the Club Med three-point rating scale. Two-trident places are simpler, and generally have only half-day ski school. Single tridents aren't used. Four-trident places offer 'comfort of the highest standard'; there are three in Méribel, and others in Tignes, Val-d'Isère and St Moritz.

EQUITY SKI

The other major programme that can be described as all-inclusive is that of Equity Ski. This company's pricing is a lot simpler than Club Med's. All their holiday prices include the cost of your lift pass, equipment hire and insurance. And they all include either tuition or guiding around the slopes (it depends on where you are staying – you don't have a choice). On the other hand, they don't include lunch, and they include drinks with dinner only in catered chalets – so two serious budget variables are introduced into the equation.

The Equity accommodation is less uniform than Club Med's. The programme falls roughly into two halves. They offer a moderate number of Austrian and French resorts, in which they generally run their own chalets or hotels, and sometimes offer other hotels too. Then, in a larger number of Italian resorts, they offer two or three standard hotels that may be shared with other companies' clients. The resorts are a mix of established big names – Val-Thorens, Mayrhofen, Sauze d'Oulx – and smaller, less well-known places such as Le Corbier, St Michael and Sansicario. It's strong on 'back-door' resorts attached to major ski areas – St-Martin-de-Belleville for the Trois Vallées, Leogang for Saalbach-Hinterglemm, Valtournenche for Cervinia.

Equity this year has added a couple of new French resorts to its programme – Arc 1600 and La Plagne 1800, with hotels in each. In Austria, the company has taken over a sizeable hotel in Saalbach. Of more than academic interest to me is the fact that they have added Bristol flights.

by **Dave Watts**

New gear

to revolutionise your riding

Ski and snowboard equipment is changing more quickly than ever before. Every year major technical breakthroughs are made which make riding mountains easier and more fun. Over the last few years skis have got shorter, wider and more shaped. Free-ride skis have multiplied and New School twin-tip skiers are now outshining snowboarders in terrain-parks. Major advances in bindings and mounting systems have been made to give you a smoother ride and new skis have been developed to help you have more fun. This season will see the shops full of sexy new skiercross skis with radical graphics. And boots have improved beyond belief. Now nearly all boots have special custom fit liners that mould to the shape of your foot. And this season nearly all manufacturers are introducing a soft ski boot into their range.

Prices in the UK are now as competitive as in Europe. Readers used to get annoyed when they bought gear in the UK and then found it on sale significantly cheaper in ski resorts. That has changed as a result of manufacturers pricing in euros and UK retailers being determined to match European prices. And if you buy in North America, remember that you'll have to pay duty and VAT when you bring your gear back to the UK.

Some retailers have price-match guarantees. Snow + Rock, for example, offers a price pledge that it will refund the difference if you find you can buy something cheaper abroad (within time limits).

27

↑ Three of the new skiercross skis. From the top: Salomon Crossmax 10, Atomic SX11 Supercross and Dynastar Ski Cross 10

SKIERCROSS EXCITEMENT

Skiercross is the newest type of ski race and much more exciting for spectators than regular downhill and slalom races. Instead of racing one at a time against the clock, in a skiercross four or more skiers start from the same place at the same time as in an athletics track event. They then fly as fast as possible down a course that has bends, banks and jumps, and the only rule is that whoever crosses the finish line first wins. Collisions and falls are the norm and add to the fun.

To win races like this you need a GS-type race ski, and skiercross skis are based on those. They turn like a dream, hold an edge on the slickest ice, and absorb bumps and jumps superbly. For advanced and expert skiers they make hurtling down the pistes great fun, and because of their wide tips and tails, they float surprisingly well off-piste too. On a test of all the new season's skis that I went on last March everyone loved them. Salomon launched their funky-looking red, blue and silver Crossmax 10 last season. This season most manufacturers have a skiercross ski or three. Rossignol has its RPMs, Atomic its sensational SX11 Supercross and Dynastar its Ski Cross range.

Sponsored by

**SNOW
+
ROCK**

↑ Two great freestyle skis, ideal for the terrain-park and the half-pipe. From the left: K2 Enemy, Salomon Teneighty

There is also a great range of skis built primarily for skiers who like to stick to the pistes, aimed at ability ranges from first-time buyer to expert. And in a test of well over 100 skis we found hardly any poor skis left on the market. Some that stood out for excellence included the Volkl P50 Motion, K2 Axis Mod and Atomic 9.18.

FREE-RIDE AND NEW SCHOOL FUN

Free-ride has been the buzzword for the last few years and now there is a great range of skis that are wide underfoot as well as at tips and tails but which still have a carving shape. These are aimed at skiers who want to venture off-piste as well as on-piste and which ones you should choose depend on how much you want to go off-piste.

For an all round versatile free-ride ski that floats in powder, slices through the crud and grips well on-piste too, the classic Salomon X-Scream Series which started the free-ride trend several years ago is still on the market and still hard to beat. But it is now also available in a version with a Pilot binding system (see below) and other manufacturers are producing superb skis too – such as the Volkl Vertigo Motion, Rossignol Bandit XX and Head Monster 70.

There is an increasing number of twin-tip skis aimed at those who like to head for the half-pipe and the terrain-park and outdo the snowboarders for big air and tricks. The Salomon Teneighty has been redesigned this year to make it much wider throughout and uses a new Spaceframe technology; it works well off-piste as well as in the park – and on-piste if you ski it hard and are strong enough to make it carve. More specialist freestyle, terrain-park skis include the K2 Enemy and Rossignol Scratch FS.

Other skis are aimed at those who want to head to the backcountry most of the time and are super-wide to help flotation in deep powder and crud. These include the Salomon Pocket Rocket and AK Rocket Pilot, Rossignol Scratch BC, Volkl G4, Line Mothership and Nordica Beast 92.

SKIBOARDS

All the major manufacturers now have at least one pair of skiboards in their range – defined as less than a metre long and with fixed rather than releasing safety bindings. They take very little time to get to grips with and provide a totally different on-snow thrill. While all manufacturers have a cruisey carving skiboard that will take the first-time snow visitor around the mountain by the second day, there are also specialist skiboards aimed at in-line skaters and skiers who want to outdo snowboarders for flash tricks in the terrain-parks.

PERFECT TURNS

Traditional bindings are mounted on to the surface of the ski and prevent the ski from flexing naturally – they create a 'flat spot' under your boot. With the new shorter, wider and more shaped skis it is important that the ski flexes naturally if you are to get the best out of them. So nearly all manufacturers have now brought out integrated ski and binding systems that eliminate this flat spot.

Salomon started the trend in the 2000/01 season with its Pilot system – the binding is attached to the sides rather than the top of the skis through specially drilled holes, allowing the ski to flex naturally and giving quicker edge grip and transmission of power from boot to ski. For 2002/03 the Pilot system has been extended to most of the Salomon ski range.

SNOW + ROCK

Volkl's Motion System has rails on the ski that the Marker binding slides on to and is fixed by just one screw. I tried this system on their top free-ride ski, the Volkl Vertigo Motion, and thought it was phenomenal – perfect response and a really smooth ride. Head's Super Railflex system has a Tyrolia binding that slides on and is fixed by a single screw, and Atomic uses a single track that runs down the middle of its skis to attach its Device bindings.

Some of the other manufacturers' developments are based on plates that fit on to the skis and have various devices such as springs that allow the plate and therefore the ski to flex naturally. They have pre-drilled holes for bindings to fit into. Rossignol has a Power Propulsion System, Dynastar has an Autodrive floating plate and Fischer has its Accelerator plate that work in this way.

GOING SOFT

Over the last few years nearly every manufacturer has introduced custom-fit inner boots across all or part of its range. Normally, the inner boot is heated up and it then automatically moulds to the shape of your foot when you put it in. This has revolutionised boot comfort for a given level of performance. And this year Tecnica has boots with an inner boot that you can warm up yourself each day for greater comfort and better fit, using a home or car adaptor that you can buy for £15 to £20.

Another major development with boots in the last few years has been the development of softer plastic for parts such as the front cuff, to make getting them on and off easier, while retaining rigid plastic for the necessary sideways and rear support.

Last season, the first soft boots appeared on the market, aimed

↑ You can see how wide Salomon's Pocket Rocket (right) is compared with the classic X-Scream Series
Soft boots: from the left Rossignol SOFT, Atomic Softech, Salomon Verse

primarily at first-time buyers and intermediate skiers looking for comfort. Rossignol launched its SOFT range of three boots – your foot goes into a comfortable soft, leather-like boot that fits into a stiff 'Cockpit' frame, which gives good sideways and rear support but which does not confine you in a full traditional wrap-around plastic ski boot. The clips and buckles go over the soft boot, not the hard plastic. Salomon's Verse AF is a lace-up boot similar to lace-up snowboard boots, with just two buckles. It looks a bit like a convertible car with a hard lower chassis and soft top half. The other main soft boots available on the UK market for the 2002/03 season are the Atomic Softech and Nordica Smartech.

Lange continues with its revolutionary RRS (rear release system) designed to reduce lower leg injuries (especially anterior cruciate ligament damage). If you start to fall backwards a mechanism

SNOW +ROCK

↑ Two boards priced at £200 or less: Option GT (left) and K2 Satellite (right)

Hammer Twilight (top on left, base on right) back-country boards have a split tail, designed to make the tail sink and the nose rise in powder ↓

Flow bindings give the speed of a step-in with the flexibility of using a conventional boot →

attached to the lower shell and upper cuff at the back of the boot releases, allowing the upper cuff to move backwards 15°, therefore reducing potential injury occurring in backward falls. If you don't fall but regain your balance, the mechanism immediately re-engages so that there is no negative effect or loss of control. The RRS system has come down in price for this season and is fully adjustable to suit your weight and skiing ability and style.

Whatever boots you buy it is worth paying extra to have a customised footbed made to support your foot properly.

GET ON BOARD

One of the delights of snowboarding is the luxury of riding in soft boots, so whether you're racing down for the last chair of the day, hiking into the backcountry for fresh powder turns or dancing up on the bar at 3am your feet will be comfortable and warm. Don't expect a completely soft experience though; snowboard boots are becoming stiffer and more supportive, to satisfy the demands of riders wanting to push themselves to go bigger, faster and steeper. The inner liner and outer shell are both laced, making them easy to get on and off. Heat-mouldable liners that custom-mould to the shape of your foot lead to increased comfort and a more precise fit. And as with ski boots it is worth paying extra to have a customised footbed made to support your foot properly.

This coming season, manufacturers have crammed boots full of innovative features to make your life easier. Look out for lace locks that maintain lace tension at strategic points up the outer shell, for example. And Vans' innovative Boa lacing system replaces traditional laces with a cable and a tensioning dial; twisting the dial tightens the cable to provide a snug, effortless, pressure-free fit.

Two-strap bindings are by far the most popular style. Generally, the more you pay, the greater the comfort, response, support and adjustability. Step-in bindings are still the preferred choice for riders looking for a fast, convenient system and a dry backside (no sitting in the snow while you do your binding up after riding a lift). The quick entry is especially appreciated when you're riding with friends on skis. The sole of the boot clicks into the binding, and your support and heel retention are provided by the boot's ankle strap and the binding's high back.

Flow bindings provide the speed of a step-in system with the flexibility of using a conventional boot. A single large strap goes over the front of the boot, the high back drops back for you to slide your foot in. The high back is then raised and tensioned for a secure and powerful ride.

With boards my recommended type for relative beginners is a 'free-ride' board. These are designed for all-mountain use and most manufacturers offer boards aimed at first-time buyers for £200 or less – many have wide versions available specifically designed for all those size 11 wearers out there. They offer plenty of performance for intermediate riders too, having benefited from hand-me-down technology from previous seasons' high-end boards. Their softer flex makes them very forgiving and offers a confidence building ride.

SNOW
+
ROCK

New Superstore Opens October 2002

Port Solent, Portsmouth

Contact us now for your copy of our FREE Winter Sports 2003 Catalogue

↑ K2's Recon Riser system (top of board on right, base on left) integrates a 6mm riser plate into the deck, which gives increased leverage and so more powerful carving with no fear of toe-drag

Satisfying the demands of the advanced rider, K2's Recon Riser system integrates a 6mm riser plate into the board's deck. The rapid edge to edge performance of the narrow board, combined with greater toe and heel clearance and increased leverage lets you lay over powerful carves, no longer in fear of toe-drag or icy pistes. It's the big footed rider's dream. Palmer's Powerlink system is a version that can be used on any board. Salomon's revolutionary new F14 boot, has the shortest possible sole length for faster heel to toe response and minimal toe overhang.

Women-specific boards and boots have been around for a few seasons, and the choice continues to grow. This season there is a great range of female-specific bindings to complete the package. Designed with shorter, more flexible highbacks to alleviate the common complaint of painful calf muscles.

For advanced free-riders, the Hammer Twilight is a series (163, 167, 171) of backcountry boards with a split tail. The split lets the tail sink and the nose ride high above the powder. It's also indicative of a trend towards riding boards longer, especially if you're heading off piste, where they'll give you maximum flotation. There'll be plenty of boards over 170 out there, such as Nitro's Shogun, which goes up to 178. Lib Tech even have a 193 freestyle board.

SELF-PROTECTION
You want to have a great holiday and come back refreshed and healthy; the last thing you want is to be hurt or injured. So it is worth getting fit and working on some specific muscle groups; ideally ask a sports trainer or physio to give you a programme tailored to your own needs. Body Factor (part of Snow+Rock and contactable on 01932 564364) is a specialist in this field and has branches in London's Covent Garden and in Chertsey, Surrey (just off junction 11 of the M25).

↑ Helmets by Leedom (top) and Dainese (bottom) with Dainese body armour: from left, front and rear of gilet with back, lumber and lower neck protection; shorts protecting vital areas including hips, coccyx and buttocks; back and knee protectors

Also consider some protective measures. More and more people are now wearing helmets to prevent potentially lethal head injuries. And a wide range of body protection clothing is available. Back protection and a helmet are now compulsory in many free-ride competitions. And if you are going off-piste, don't even consider doing so without the proper equipment and a local mountain guide – see chapter on Off-piste delights on page 45.

AND FINALLY
If you own your own skis or board, have them serviced before you go away. And try on your old boots to make sure they still fit and aren't in need of repair. It also pays everyone to invest in some technical ski socks that wick away moisture and keep your feet warm and dry – and wear a clean pair daily.

by **Laura Gill**

introduction by
Chris Gill
(her dad)

Family holidays

which ones work best?

For several years now I've delivered in these pages an annual bulletin from the child-rearing front, principally for the benefit of that year's crop of parents contemplating family skiing for the first time. It's a heavy responsibility, in which I get no help from my co-editor, child-free Mr Watts. Maybe one year I'll persuade him to take over this slot for once (in which case I imagine you would be presented with the clear advice to leave the brats at home). But I'm not counting on it.

I have, however, come up with a way to give you a bit of a change from annual variants on my views of this business. As you may have read elsewhere, our ceaseless search for technological improvements in the production of *Where to Ski and Snowboard* has allowed us to push our final deadlines back until they fall well inside the school holidays. As a result, while we are finalising the book my kids are kicking their heels waiting for some sign of a summer trip abroad to materialise. Why not, I thought, ask them to use some of their abundant spare time to reflect on their various skiing trips and commit words to keyboard?

I'd forgotten, of course, that son Alex is now firmly a teenager, so after a token skirmish around the issue of payment per thousand words he has declined and gone off to play tennis. Daughter Laura, being a girl, is capable of responding with touching enthusiasm to parental suggestions (when she knows it is in her own interests), and has come up with what follows. At a price, of course. I hope you find Laura's observations shed some light on what does and does not make for a good family holiday. Ready availability of pizza appears to be crucial. CG

VERMONT, USA 1996 AGED 4

I learned to ski here, sort of by accident. We went to Killington first. The only reason I opted to go skiing was that I couldn't play outside in the snow if I went in the kindergarten, so it was slightly displeasing that I was forced to go skiing. Actually, I enjoyed it. Of course I was nervous, but having nerves somehow made it more exciting, and that made it even better. Mum apparently got frostbite, but I can't remember it, so it can't have been that bad.

In Smugglers' Notch I had a lot of fun. I really liked the slopes and I appreciated the food even when I was 4. I think it was fun for everyone, but I didn't like the fact that it was supposed to be a family holiday, yet Dad kept taking Alex and me to ski-school! I can't say I didn't enjoy it though.

Dad says we spent a fun day in Boston on the way back.

CHAMONIX, FRANCE 1997 AGED 5

Chamonix has quite a few bad memories for me. One thing I absolutely hated was my ski instructor. She was pure evil from my point of view. One time, my family was watching me on the nursery slope, and I skied down to them really well, but I still cried because of my instructor. She was horrible because she wore a horrible pair of blue-tinted glasses and she laughed at me when I fell over; I felt really embarrassed and she didn't even try to help me up. It wasn't fair – Alex got a really nice instructor.

Family holidays

34

The scenery was wonderful; I loved the view in the morning. The room in the hotel-chalet was a bit cramped, which didn't help. There were lots of other kids there, which made it a bit more bearable.

Some of the cable-cars here were a bit high though. Mum had to lie down at one point because she was feeling dizzy.

HINTERSTODER, AUSTRIA 1998 AGED 6

I liked the people in Hinterstoder more than any other thing. I went to a kind of ski school and the instructor was really nice, she didn't make fun of anyone and helped us all.

I was really excited when we went to see some husky dogs. That was extremely fun. The slopes were all just about right for me (apart from the one on the last day), though everyone else seemed to be having fun as well.

The food was all good; I liked the sausages a lot. I really liked Hinterstoder.

One night we went out to dinner to a kind of farm where they had sledges. Around the side of the house there was a steep hill and everyone's dads were pulling them right to the top and letting them go down on their sledges. I really wanted dad to help me and he did. But he only went three quarters of the way and then he wouldn't do any more, he was too old even then!

On the last day, dad said that we just had time to do the nice easy blue run all the way from the top of the mountain, but when we got there it was really steep and covered in ice! He still made me go down it though; I only fell over about sixteen times and then, three quarters of the way down, I got fed up and just went straight down. I never forgave him for that.

HEMSEDAL, NORWAY 1999 AGED 7

Norway's best point was the cosiness, warmth and friendliness of the place. We stayed in a sort of wooden block of flats.

I didn't really like the fact that it was desolate and you had to walk quite a way to get to the ski lifts. There wasn't any other extra activity apart from skiing going on, so it was a bit duller than the other holidays.

We ate twice in the restaurant across the road, in a cellar-like place. Then one night we were going to have a takeaway pizza, and (of course) Mum and Dad wanted a bottle of wine. Dad was furious because the nearest wine shop was 20 miles away. The mountain

SNOWPIX.COM / CHRIS GILL

← Laura misses a gate on her end-of-week slalom course at Smugglers' Notch, narrowly missing the photographer, who has been forced to take evasive action

restaurant had nothing but hot dogs and chips – which I thought was brilliant!

VERBIER, SWITZERLAND 2000 AGED 8

When we visited Verbier, we stayed in a chalet. I really liked that because you have much more room to relax and be yourself. We didn't really need to go out to eat because we had a chalet boy who cooked for us. It wasn't that hard to get to the slopes and they all lived up to their grading, not too hard or easy. That was good. Quite a few of them were steep though.

My room was a bit small for my liking and it would have been really annoying if two people had to sleep in it. One side of the double bed was up against the wall. It did test my patience that I had to use my bedside table as a desk.

LES ARCS, FRANCE 2001 AGED 9

The best thing about Les Arcs was that we could ski straight out of our apartment without having to do anything really! Though our apartment was small, I liked the interior and I always got a good night's sleep. I never had to get up early because there might be a queue at the gondola, because they were quick and efficient and the queues never stayed for long.

There was a pizza takeaway in the apartment block, which was good because my older brother and I could stay in the apartment while Mum and Dad got the food. The slopes are better for kids than adults in my view. There was one slope near our apartment that was half flat and half bumps that are really fun to go over. There is a really nice beginners' slope as well. I especially liked the evening,

Family holidays

37

01285 642 555
www.handmade-holidays.co.uk
AITO ATOL PROTECTED 4479

38

Laura and her mum, Val, leaving the horizontal rope tow that figured large in our 2002 holiday in Tignes-Val-Claret – we lived at one end, the Grande Motte lifts were at the other ↓

when the slopes were empty and everyone could go down on their toboggans.

We didn't really go to many different restaurants but one I remember was the Tex-Mex. I had ribs in a barbecue sauce. I didn't like that, but everyone else seemed to.

Les Arcs was okay, but I wouldn't put it at the top of my list of favourite places.

TIGNES, FRANCE 2002 AGED 10

One of my favourite things about Tignes is the amount of things you can do (not including skiing). I especially liked the swimming facilities and gym in our apartment block (MGM). There is also a jacuzzi, which was great for relaxing after a hard day's skiing. There is also a lake which in winter is frozen, and I enjoyed watching people cross-country ski and have snowball fights. There is also a cinema; you can see English films there, subtitled in French.

The food in Tignes was wonderful. They have a lot of pizza places, which I was tired of visiting by the end of the holiday. I loved the hot chocolate as well, and they do great pasta.

The slopes are quite nice, but I hated it when we went to the top of the Grande Motte and the snow was really icy; the wind was really harsh as well. But that only happened once, which was a relief. There were quite a lot of hard slopes but that didn't worry me – it might not be a good place for beginners though. All in all I liked the slopes in Tignes.

One of the things I didn't really like about Tignes was the amount of walking and climbing you have to do. There may have been an elevator up to the village next to MGM, but it didn't always work. It was very tricky to get to the MGM ski lockers because there was a slippery slope that was very hard to get up and down.

A good way to get to the ski lifts if you're staying at the far end of Val-Claret like we were is to use the Transcorde. You just grab on to the length of moving rope and are pulled along. I found it quite fun!

All in all, Tignes was a really nice place to stay for me.

Smugglers' Notch Vermont®
America's Family Resort℠

What's steeper –

the challenge of our mountains...

or the standard we set for family fun?

- Slopeside Resort Village Lodging within an easy walk or shuttle ride to lifts, shopping & dining

- Over 1,000 acres of terrain with the East's *only* triple black diamond run

- 3 big mountains, 72 trails with 796-metre vertical rise

- Terrain Parks & 122-metre Superpipe

- 27 km of cross-country trails and 20 km of snowshoe trails

- Internationally recognized *Snow Sport University*℠ – lessons for all abilities

- Professionally staffed Child Care in our *brand new,* slopeside Enrichment Centre, **Treasures,** with designated age group areas (6 weeks & older)

- All day *award-winning* children's ski & snowboard programs for ages 3-14 years

- *Endless fun* – indoor pool, hot tubs, snow tubing, ice skating, *FunZone,* family games, entertainment & more!

- Only 30 miles from Burlington, Vermont International Airport with shuttle service available!

Make your reservation today or call for a FREE brochure & video or DVD!

United Kingdom Free-Phone

0800-169-8219

001-802-644-8851 • FAX: 001-802-644-1230
E-Mail: smuggs@ smuggs.com   www.smuggs.com/wtsb

Get next year's edition **FREE**
by reporting on your holiday

There are too many resorts for us to visit them all every year, and too many hotels, bars and mountain restaurants for us to see. So we are very keen to encourage more readers to send in reports on their holiday experiences. As usual, we'll be giving 100 copies of the next edition to the writers of the best reports.

There are five main kinds of feedback we need:
- what you particularly **liked and disliked** about the resort
- what aspects of the resort came as a **surprise** to you
- your other suggestions for **changes to our evaluation** of the resort – changes we should make to the ratings, verdicts, descriptions etc
- your experience of **queues** and other weaknesses in the lift system, and the **ski school** and associated childcare arrangements
- your feedback on **individual facilities** in the resort – the hotels, bars, restaurants (including mountain restaurants), nightspots, equipment shops, sports facilities etc.

You can send your reports to us in three ways. In order of preference, they are:
- by e-mail to: reports@snow-zone.co.uk (don't forget to give us your postal address)
- word-processed and printed on paper
- handwritten on a form that we can provide.

Consistently helpful reporters are invited to become 'resort observers', which means that when possible we'll arrange free lift-passes in your holiday resorts, in exchange for detailed reports on those resorts.

Our postal address is:
Where to Ski and Snowboard, FREEPOST, The Old Forge, Norton St Philip, Bath BA2 7ZZ

Get your **money back**
when you book a holiday

You can reclaim the price of Where to Ski and Snowboard when you book a winter sports holiday for the 2002/03 or 2003/04 seasons. All you have to do is book the holiday through the specialist ski travel agency Ski Solutions.

Ski Solutions is Britain's original and leading ski travel agency. You can buy whatever kind of holiday you want through them.

Ski Solutions sells the package holidays offered by all the bonded tour operators in Britain (apart from the very few who are direct-sell only). And if that isn't enough choice, they can tailor-make a holiday, based on any form of travel and any kind of accommodation. No one is better placed to find you what you want than Ski Solutions.

Phone Ski Solutions on

020 7471 7700

Making a claim

Claiming your refund and free insurance is easy. When you make your definite booking, tell Ski Solutions that you want to take up this offer. They'll knock £15.99 off the cost of your holiday. That's all there is to it.

by **Dave Watts**

Weekend breaks

they become addictive

A weekend away with just one day off work can give you three great days on the slopes, leaving you with the feeling of having been away for ages and returning to work feeling really refreshed. And it does not need to cost you an arm and a leg.

'Go skiing for the weekend? You must be joking. A long journey each way. Crowded slopes when you get there. The weather might be bad. And it costs the same as a week away. Forget it.'

That was my attitude before I tried it. But now I'm a weekend addict. It's fantastic.

Picture this. Long hard day at work followed by a race to the airport for an 8pm flight to Geneva. Pick up your rental car and drive to Chamonix – arrive about midnight, check in to typically French two-star hotel, have a couple of beers and hit the sack. Wake in the morning and see it's snowing. Quick breakfast and head for the Les Houches area for a great day playing in the fresh powder in the trees. A few beers followed by dinner in a typical French restaurant and back to bed (plenty of bar and club options if you want them).

Next day it's still overcast, so you head through the Mont Blanc tunnel to Courmayeur in Italy, where it is a brilliant blue sky day. Head up and find fresh, untracked powder everywhere except for on the immaculately groomed virgin pistes. Spend the day whooping and hollering with delight, stopping only for an amazing Italian lunch including delightful fresh pasta at Maison Vieille in mid-mountain. Back to base for beers, dinner and bed.

Last day dawns. Perfect blue skies in Chamonix. Head up the Grands Montets to find it has been closed for two days and you (and hordes of rampant ski bums) compete for the best freshies for the first three runs before it is tracked out.

Exhausted, you persuade your mate to drive so you can have a few beers at 4pm before heading back to the airport for the 8pm flight home. Arrive at work the next morning grinning from ear to ear, with a healthy tan, having done half a week's skiing for one day off work and dying to tell your workmates stories of the weekend that they just will not be able to stand hearing.

Not a fantasy but a true account of my first weekend trip. No wonder I was hooked. Every weekend trip since has been a completely different experience and itinerary but they have all been wonderful fun. And I've since met many weekend addicts, including people who rent apartments for the season and go out every other weekend and others who book up 12 or so weekend flights well in advance and decide where to drive to nearer the time, depending on where the best snow is.

ARRANGING THE WEEKEND

The key to making the most of your time is to catch late flights each way – so it helps if you live near a suitable airport. Swiss has well-timed flights for both Geneva and Zürich from Heathrow and London City (but book early as the late flights are very popular).

41

EasyJet has suitable flights from both Gatwick and Luton to Geneva and Zürich and from Liverpool to Geneva. Alitalia has good flights to Milan.

We don't recommend flying to Munich if you are travelling out on a Friday or back on a Sunday – the queues on the motorway can be horrendous, as the whole of Munich seems to go weekend skiing and the airport is on the far side of the city from the Alps. Similarly, allow plenty of time if you are driving back to Lyon airport on a Sunday evening – we encountered very heavy traffic after leaving Courchevel in what we had thought was good time.

Booking a rental car or taxi in advance is usually cheaper than arranging one after you arrive. Several tour operators can arrange the rental as part of a complete weekend package. Taxis can be ridiculously expensive compared with the cost of renting a car. For example, you would expect to pay over £200 each way between Geneva airport and Courchevel by taxi if you book locally – but renting a small car for the weekend would be much less than the one-way taxi price. In our experience train and bus times between airports and resorts are more suitable for week-long visitors than for weekenders looking for maximum time on the slopes.

Using a weekend specialist, such as one of those advertising in this chapter, makes sense if you don't want the hassle of making your own arrangements. They know the best resorts to go to, can arrange transfers by their own staff or through local companies, and have special deals with hotels that do them good room rates or that might not otherwise take weekend bookings. Some arrange special weekend courses (eg with off-piste guides or even heli-skiing weekends). And local tour operator representatives and contacts can save you

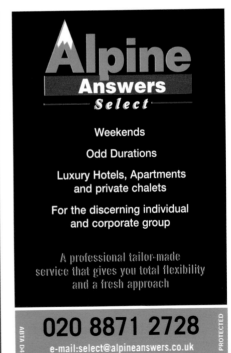

valuable time arranging lift passes (beware of big weekend queues on Saturday and Sunday mornings) and equipment hire and advise on local restaurants and other facilities.

CHOOSING A RESORT

As for choosing a resort, there are various considerations. Many people think they should go for a resort within a short drive of their arrival airport. But by definition, resorts close to major airports are close to large numbers of people poised to hit the slopes on fine weekends, which can mean queues for the lifts, crowds on the slopes and competition for hotel beds. These days most resorts are within striking distance of a major airport and an hour's extra transfer time is not really that much if it gets you to quieter slopes.

Resorts close to Geneva include Chamonix, St-Gervais, Megève and Les Contamines (all in the Mont Blanc area and sharing an area lift pass), Flaine and La Clusaz in France, and Villars and Les Diablerets in Switzerland. All these are within an hour or so of Geneva by car. Verbier and Crans-Montana in Switzerland are a bit further, as are the Three Valleys and other Tarentaise resorts – Val-d'Isère can be reached in under three hours now – and Morzine and the Portes du Soleil resorts in France.

Flying to Zürich opens up lots of other possibilities. Flims, Davos and Klosters are the nearest big resorts, and the less-well-known resorts of Engelberg and Andermatt are within easy reach. St Anton and Lech in Austria are within striking distance, as are the resorts of the Montafon valley.

In Italy, Courmayeur is a popular and attractive weekend destination. Now that the Mont Blanc tunnel is open again, it is

easily accessible from Geneva. Resorts such as Sauze d'Oulx and Sestriere are easily accessible from Milan or Turin.

Unless you are booking at short notice when you know the snow is good, we'd be tempted to avoid low resorts such as Megève and Villars – unless you have transport to get you to more snow-sure slopes. And because you don't want your whole weekend ruined by a white-out if it snows all the time, we'd also be tempted to avoid very high resorts where the skiing is entirely above the tree line – this rules out places such as Tignes and Val-Thorens in France, Obergurgl in Austria and Cervinia in Italy.

Another consideration is that hotels in big, popular winter resorts such as Verbier, St Anton and Val-d'Isère now often refuse to take weekend bookings except in very low season (eg early January or late March) because they can get week-long bookings which are more profitable. But many of the more summer-oriented resorts, which generally have accommodation spare in winter, are well worth considering – places such as Chamonix, Morzine, Engelberg, Villars and Mürren fall into this category.

WHAT ABOUT PRICE?

The cost can vary enormously. The flight and transfer or car hire are the expensive fixed costs and obviously make a weekend proportionately more expensive than a full week. But as we said before, you do get three days' skiing (half a full week) for only one day off work, and the three days makes a substantial break. A four-night break is, of course, even better – it only costs two days off work and means you can travel out and back on Thursday and Monday evenings (quieter than Fridays and Sundays).

In general, through a good specialist tour operator, you can expect to pay £300 to £350 a head for flights, car hire and a double room in a 3-star hotel for three nights, assuming two people sharing. With lift passes and meals you could be looking at £450 to £500. For a 4-star hotel add another £100 or so.

by **Dave Watts**

Off-piste delights

be aware of the risks

More and more people are enjoying the delights of heading off-piste (or free-riding to give it its trendy name) – untracked snow, stunning views, solitude. Compared with skiing, snowboarding off-piste is relatively easy because of the width and flotation of the board – even intermediates with only a couple of weeks under their belt can manage it. And the new shorter, fatter skis make off-piste much more accessible to skiers as well. All this is excellent news ... so long as you recognise the dangers of off-piste adventure and take sensible precautions to make sure you are not a victim and that you don't put other people in danger.

The main dangers of off-piste skiing are the terrain (cliffs you can fall off, gullies you have to climb out off, trees you can collide with, slopes you find too steep), finding your route, snow conditions (cruddy snow and breakable crust are the two we hate most) and the danger of being caught in an avalanche.

One of the reasons we enjoy skiing in North America so much is that American resorts take responsibility for a lot more steep, avalanche-prone terrain than European resorts do. They have clear resort boundaries – often marked by a rope, certainly by signs. Any slopes that are open within the boundary are controlled for avalanches and overseen by the ski patrollers; and dangers such as cliffs are normally marked. What's more the lifts are arranged so that wherever you go within the in-bounds territory you will end up at a lift. And within this territory are usually steep, ungroomed slopes that would be classed as off-piste in Europe.

As soon as you go off-piste in Europe, you take responsibility for your own safety – the slopes are not avalanche controlled or patrolled, and hazards such as cliff areas are rarely marked. Unless you know where you are going you could end up lost in the middle of nowhere.

If you are going off-piste in Europe (or backcountry outside the resort boundary in North America) we recommend you take some key precautions. First, hire a qualified local guide who knows the terrain, can take you to the best snow and slopes to suit your ability and can assess the avalanche danger. If possible, choose a guide (or group of off-piste guides such as exist in resorts like Val-d'Isère) whom you know or who has been recommended to you. We have

45

A Recco detector can pinpoint the location of an avalanche victim wearing Recco reflectors, even if he or she is buried under 10m/30ft of snow ➔

↑ Recco reflectors can easily be stuck on to your boots and could save your life if you were buried in an avalanche

Off-piste delights

46

been with guides in the past (usually ESF instructors, we have to say) in whom we have ended up having no faith. Some have taken us to terrain beyond the ability level of the group. Others have said the avalanche risk was low when it was high (there is a recognised avalanche warning scale used in resorts where 1 = Low and 5 = Very High, but it is not widely enough publicised in our view).

Second, always wear an avalanche transceiver compatible with those used by your guide and other members of your group – this emits a signal which allows you to be found if you are buried in an avalanche; and it can be turned on to receive mode if you are one of those who has to find a buried friend. But make sure that you and other members of your group are properly trained in how to use a transceiver. Too often we have been in groups that have been given no or very superficial training and have felt that only the guide would have a good chance of finding us if we were buried.

Third, wear a backpack containing an avalanche probe and a shovel (and make sure other members of your group do too). If someone is buried, these will be needed to locate them and dig them out. Also pack some water and emergency supplies of food and preferably a 'space blanket', which will preserve body heat if you get stuck on the mountain for some reason.

The importance of finding avalanche victims quickly cannot be overemphasised. 92% of those who are entirely buried are still alive after 15 minutes. But if it takes longer to dig them out, the chances of survival decline rapidly. After half an hour only around 50% of victims are alive, and after 45 minutes only 25%.

THE RECCO RESCUE SYSTEM

If you are going touring far away from a resort or area of lifts, you'll have to rely heavily on the above precautions. But most people go off-piste much nearer to resorts on a day or half-day trip. That's why everyone should wear Recco detectors. Even if you are just a few yards off-piste there is a danger of being buried – and a few incidents of being buried on-piste by avalanches have also occurred.

The Recco Rescue System is now in use at most resorts covered in this book – and we tell you whether it is in the Mountain Facts section in each resort. With this system, as soon as an avalanche is reported the ski patrol sends a rescue team equipped with Recco detectors (many resorts have several portable detectors distributed around the slopes for speedy rescue). Some helicopter rescue services, which cover many resorts, also carry Recco detectors.

The detectors emit a directional radio signal. When the signal hits a Recco reflector, even under 10m/30ft of snow, the frequency is doubled and sent back to the receiver in the detector. The trained operator can then instantly pinpoint the buried victim. Detectors can easily be used from helicopters searching for victims.

Recco reflectors are small, inconspicuous and cheap – and require no batteries or other maintenance. Reflectors are built in to some brands of clothing and boots. Failing that, you can buy self-adhesive ones to stick on your boots for only £12.95 a pair – a price not worth bothering about for something that may save your life. They are offered at half price when you buy a new pair of ski or snowboard boots from Snow+Rock.

The Swiss Alpine Club, Swiss Air Rescue and the Federal Institute for the Study of Snow and Avalanches in Davos recommend that all skiers and snowboarders should wear Recco reflectors. We agree.

by Chris Gill

Luxury chalets

the ultimate holiday

In the space of a couple of days last winter, I rode chair-lifts in Val-d'Isère and Tignes with two British skiers staying in Val who seemed similarly experienced, similarly affluent, similarly used to the good things in life. But their attitudes to holiday accommodation turned out to be quite different.

One was staying in one of the Ski Company's swanky chalets on the southern fringes of the resort; he'd stayed in dozens of chalets in Val and other big-name Alpine resorts, from Verbier to St Anton. 'We started with a chalet holiday and we've never done anything else,' he told me. 'The privacy and personal service you get in the best chalets is something I don't believe you can find in hotels.' The other was staying in the hotel Christiania, as he had done for years. 'Ever tried a chalet holiday?' 'Can't say I have,' he replied: 'not sure they would quite measure up to what I'm used to.'

Naturally I told the second guy about the first guy. And I gently suggested that he was way out of date. Sure, in the beginning the catered chalet business didn't do luxury. It was only in the late 1980s that one or two companies realised that there might be a market for a luxury experience without the fleets of bellboys and room-service waiters that hotels are obliged to lay on. All you had to do was provide comfortable and stylish accommodation, good food and wine, and a little bit of personal service – just enough to make the customer feel the staff are there to do something other than have a good time. The new formula worked, probably better than anyone would have expected.

FINDING YOUR DREAM CHALET

You can find isolated luxury chalets in all sorts of places, from Austria to Aspen, but the breed in general is still not widespread: most are concentrated in the more upmarket French mega-resorts of Méribel, Courchevel and Val-d'Isère.

The greatest concentration is found in Méribel, particularly in the hands of long-time local specialist Meriski. This company, more than any other, illustrates the transformation of the chalet business. In the 1980s it was a run-of-the-mill chalet operation, but then it successfully repositioned itself upmarket, and now has a range of 16 impressively comfortable chalets, most of which can be considered luxury properties.

The Ski Company Ltd is perhaps the most upmarket of all the established luxury chalet operators, and has an increasingly serious presence in Méribel. Its eight-bedroom Lodge is superb; its enormous, beautifully furnished living room has a wall of windows looking over to the pistes across the valley. The Génépi next door is very similar, but with a jacuzzi bath in every room and an outdoor hot-tub. The similarly smart five-bedroom chalets, Aurore and Boréale share an outdoor heated pool.

These last are in the Brames area of the resort, not far from the famously luxurious chalet Brames, these days marketed through Descent International. This is the grandest chalet I have visited in Méribel, with two-storey living room and some beautiful bedrooms, and a glorious view up the valley towards Mont Vallon.

If you like the idea of luxury but want to keep the cost down, consider staying with Bonne Neige down in the old village of Les Allues, served by the gondola linking Brides-les-Bains to Méribel. Les Allodis is a converted barn that makes a real change from the modern properties that dominate in Méribel – all beams and antique furniture, but with modern conveniences including underfloor heating, boot dryers, a sauna suite and an outdoor hot-tub.

Courchevel is well established as the smartest resort in France, and clearly doesn't lack smart chalets – but relatively few of them find their way on to the UK package market. My current favourite is Lotus Supertravel's five-bedroom chalet Founets, which has a lovely high-ceilinged sitting/dining room and a great position. Supertravel's Plein Sud chalet looks mighty impressive, too.

FlexiSki has two beautifully rustic five-bedroom chalets off the Bellecôte piste – Anemone, one of Courchevel's originals, and the recently built Vizelle.

THE CHALET HOLIDAY IN ITS ORIGINAL FORM

The catered chalet holiday is a uniquely British idea. Tour operators install their own cooks and housekeepers in private chalets which they take over for the season. They package them with travel on the UK market, normally offering half-board, sometimes with some provision for a snack lunch. Dinner is a no-choice affair at a communal table, including wine unlimited in quantity but not quality. You can either book a whole chalet (the smallest typically sleep around six or eight) or book space in a larger chalet that you share with whoever else turns up.

In the early days of the chalet, in the 1960s and 70s, taking a chalet holiday meant roughing it in creaky old buildings, putting up with spartan furniture and paper-thin walls, and with six or more people sharing a bathroom. And the chalet girl – always a girl, back then – was often straight out of college or finishing school, and more intent on having a fun season on the slopes than preparing gourmet meals. Happily, things have changed for the better in recent years.

Scott Dunn Ski has several properties. In a league of its own (and about 50% more expensive than anything else in the programme) is the five-bedroom Alaska, complete with indoor swimming pool.

Scott Dunn's properties include some exceptional ones in Val-d'Isère, too: the seven-bedroom Eagle's Nest – an extraordinary place complete with an indoor jetstream pool, sauna and steam room, and all four floors linked by lift – and the four-bedroom Abri du Houard.

The Ski Company Ltd has an impressive enclave of four modern luxury chalets – with a fifth being added for this season – right out at the southern extremity of the resort, with massive, well-furnished living rooms, huge windows and splendid views. YSE's Mountain Lodges are an old favourite, offering no picture windows but splendidly atmospheric and comfortable living rooms, with stone walls and ample leather sofas.

Verbier is said to be the chalet capital of the Alps but, here again, there are relatively few luxury properties on the UK market. The Ski Company Ltd's chalet Goodwood is much the best I have seen – a fabulously comfortable and stylish place in a great central position. Flexiski's Bouvreuil is not so grand, but is tastefully rustic, and close to Medran. Perhaps more of a rival is Septième Ciel, offered by Descent International. In a high position on the Savoleyres side of Verbier, it has two sitting rooms, study, sauna, steam room, massage room, cinema, games room, terrace with outdoor hot-tub, and a 'well-stocked' wine cellar.

Strangely, luxury chalets have never been common in Zermatt. But things are changing: the Ski Company will have three luxury properties for 2002/03 – a penthouse for six and two brand-new chalets for ten with jacuzzi, steam and fitness facilities.

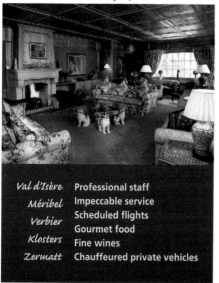

Get next year's edition **FREE**
by reporting on your holiday

There are too many resorts for us to visit them all every year, and too many hotels, bars and mountain restaurants for us to see. So we are very keen to encourage more readers to send in reports on their holiday experiences. As usual, we'll be giving 100 copies of the next edition to the writers of the best reports.

There are five main kinds of feedback we need:
- what you particularly **liked and disliked** about the resort
- what aspects of the resort came as a **surprise** to you
- your other suggestions for **changes to our evaluation** of the resort – changes we should make to the ratings, verdicts, descriptions etc
- your experience of **queues** and other weaknesses in the lift system, and the **ski school** and associated childcare arrangements
- your feedback on **individual facilities** in the resort – the hotels, bars, restaurants (including mountain restaurants), nightspots, equipment shops, sports facilities etc.

You can send your reports to us in three ways. In order of preference, they are:
- by e-mail to: reports@snow-zone.co.uk (don't forget to give us your postal address)
- word-processed and printed on paper
- handwritten on a form that we can provide.

Consistently helpful reporters are invited to become 'resort observers', which means that when possible we'll arrange free lift-passes in your holiday resorts, in exchange for detailed reports on those resorts.

Our postal address is:
Where to Ski and Snowboard, FREEPOST, The Old Forge, Norton St Philip, Bath BA2 7ZZ

Get your **money back**
when you book a holiday

You can reclaim the price of Where to Ski and Snowboard when you book a winter sports holiday for the 2002/03 or 2003/04 seasons. All you have to do is book the holiday through the specialist ski travel agency Ski Solutions.

Ski Solutions is Britain's original and leading ski travel agency. You can buy whatever kind of holiday you want through them.

Ski Solutions sells the package holidays offered by all the bonded tour operators in Britain (apart from the very few who are direct-sell only). And if that isn't enough choice, they can tailor-make a holiday, based on any form of travel and any kind of accommodation. No one is better placed to find you what you want than Ski Solutions.

Phone Ski Solutions on

020 7471 7700

Making a claim

Claiming your refund and free insurance is easy. When you make your definite booking, tell Ski Solutions that you want to take up this offer. They'll knock £15.99 off the cost of your holiday. That's all there is to it.

by **Chris Allan**

Drive to the Alps

and ski where you please

More and more people from Britain are doing what the French, the Germans and the Dutch have done for years, and driving to their Alpine resorts. For most people, it's just less hassle than checking in to Gatwick at dawn, and less tedious than sitting around waiting for a charter plane that's stuck in Majorca. For families (especially those going self-catering), it simplifies the job of moving half the household. For a few adventurous people, having a car makes moving around in the Alps much easier, and opens up exciting possibilities.

Cross-Channel ferries are faster and more comfortable than ever, and the shuttle-trains through the tunnel offer a painless alternative for those prone to mal de mer. The improved motorway networks in northern France and on the fringes of the Alps have removed most of the obstacles to smooth progress. You can now get to most resorts easily in a day, if you're based near the straits of Dover.

For us, the freedom factor is the key. If the snow's bad in your resort, if the lift queues are horrendous or if the resort you've plumped for is a let-down, car drivers can try somewhere else.

Another plus-point is that you can extend the standard six-day holiday by two days while taking only one extra day off work, crossing the Channel early on a Friday morning and returning nine days later on the Sunday evening. On the trip out, we often spend a day in a different resort before moving on to our final destination late on the Saturday. After a full day on the slopes on the final Saturday, driving for a few hours before stopping for the night means you won't find Sunday's journey too demanding, and you may even have time for a traditional French Sunday lunch.

51

AS YOU LIKE IT

If you fancy visiting several resorts, you can use one as a base and make day-trips to others when it suits you. This way, you can still take advantage of tour operator prices.

The key to turning this kind of holiday into a success is to go for a base that offers easy road access to other resorts. Our suggestions for France are in a separate chapter. A good choice in Austria is the Tirol: the resorts east of Innsbruck offer many options. Söll is a convenient base for exploring resorts such as Alpbach and Kitzbühel. Further east, you can use Zell am See as a base to visit Bad Gastein and Saalbach. Western Austria is not ideal for this sort of holiday, but from St Anton you could make day-trips to Zürs, Ischgl and Serfaus.

AROUND THE ALPS IN SEVEN DAYS

If you want to see as much of the Alps as possible, consider making a Grand Tour by car, moving every day or two to a different resort and enjoying the complete freedom of going where you want, when you want. Out of high season there's no need to book accommodation before you go, so you can decide at the last minute which part of the Alps and which countries to visit – where the snow is best, perhaps.

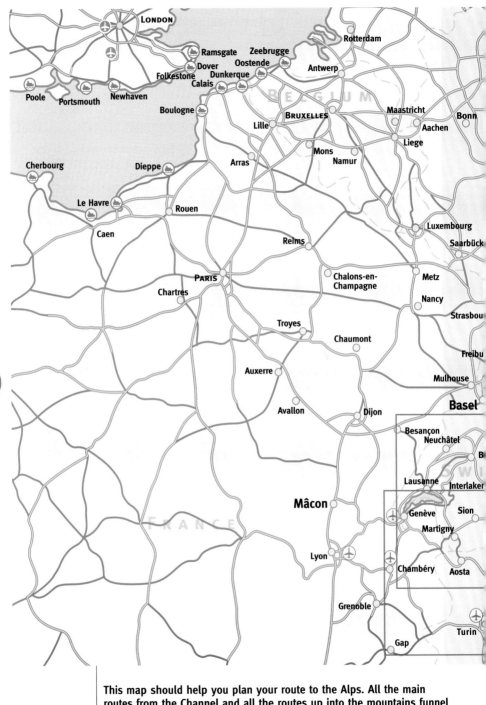

This map should help you plan your route to the Alps. All the main routes from the Channel and all the routes up into the mountains funnel through three 'gateways', picked out on the map in larger type – Mâcon, Basel and Ulm. Decide which gateway suits your destination, and pick a route to it. Occasionally, different Channel ports will lead you to use different gateways.

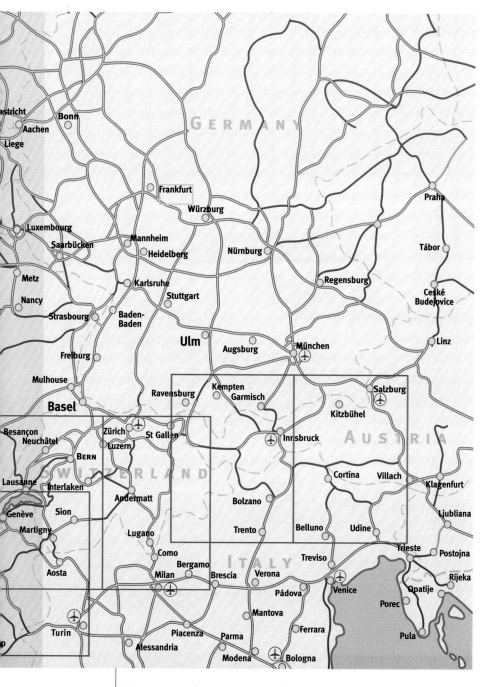

The boxes on the map correspond to the areas covered by the more detailed maps at the start of the main country sections of the book:
Austria page 95
France page 199
Italy page 361
Switzerland page 410

A touring holiday doesn't mean you'll be spending more time on the road than on the piste – provided you plan your route carefully. An hour's drive after the lifts have shut is all it need take.

Italy is far more suitable for tourers than day-trippers, provided you're prepared to put up with some slow drives on winding passes. You could start in Livigno, drive to Bormio and then to the Dolomites, visiting Madonna di Campiglio and Selva, and finish your Italian expedition in Cortina.

The major thing that you have to watch out for with a touring holiday is the cost of accommodation. Checking into a resort hotel as an independent traveller for a night or two doesn't come cheap. You can save money by staying down the valley – and you don't necessarily have to drive up to the slopes in the morning. For example, you can take the funicular from Bourg-St-Maurice to Les Arcs; a gondola links Brides-Les-Bains to Méribel.

THE COST OF A TICKET TO DRIVE

The cost of driving largely depends, of course, on how many passengers you cram into your car. You may find driving as cheap as flying even if there are only two or three of you. You'll pay from around £130 return to take your car with one passenger on a short Channel crossing – but look out for special offers (which may include travel insurance). Allow £100 to £200 for fuel, depending on where you're going and in what sort of car. Don't forget French motorway tolls – as much as £100. To use Swiss and Austrian motorways you need to buy permits (available at border points).

by **Chris Gill**

Drive to the French Alps

to make the most of them

If you've read the preceding chapter, you'll have gathered that we are keen on driving to the Alps. But we're particularly keen on driving to the French Alps. The drive is a relatively short one, whereas many of the transfers to major French resorts from Geneva airport are relatively long. And the route from the Channel is through France rather than Germany, which for Francophiles like us means it's a pleasant prospect rather than a grim one.

TRAVEL TIME

The French Alps are the number-one destination for British car-borne skiers. The journey time is surprisingly short. From Calais, for example, you can comfortably cover the 900km/560 miles to Chamonix in about nine hours plus stops – with the exception of the final few miles, the whole journey is on motorways. And except on peak weekends the traffic is relatively light. Look back at the map of Europe in the previous chapter to see what's involved.

With some southern exceptions, all the resorts of the French Alps are within a day's driving range, provided you cross the Channel early in the day (or overnight). And the weekend traffic jams that used to make such a nightmare (for drivers and coach passengers alike) of the journey from Albertville to the Tarentaise resorts are pretty much a thing of the past, except on peak-season Saturdays and in bad weather, thanks to road improvements.

DAY-TRIP BASES

Most people driving to the French Alps do it simply because they find it a more relaxing way to get themselves, their kit and perhaps their kids to their chosen resort. But, as we have explained in the previous chapter, having a car opens up different kinds of holiday for the more adventurous. Day-tripping, for example.

In the southern French Alps, Serre-Chevalier and Montgenèvre are ideal bases for day-tripping. They are within easy reach of one another, and Montgenèvre is at one end of the Milky Way lift network, which includes Sauze d'Oulx and Sestriere in Italy – you can drive on to these resorts, or reach them by lift and piste. On the French side of the border, a few miles south, Puy-St-Vincent is an underrated resort that is well worth a visit – as is Risoul, a little further south. The major resorts of Alpe-d'Huez and Les Deux-Alpes are also within range, as is the cult off-piste resort of La Grave. Getting to them involves crossing a high pass, but it's a major route linking Grenoble to Briançon and all points south, and is kept open pretty reliably. The Chamonix valley is an ideal destination for day-trippers. The Mont-Blanc lift pass covers Chamonix, Les Contamines, Megève and others. Flaine and its satellites are fairly accessible – and so are Verbier in Switzerland, if the intervening passes are open, and Courmayeur in Italy, now that the Mont Blanc tunnel is open once again. You could stay in a valley town, or base yourself in a relatively cheap resort such as St-Gervais.

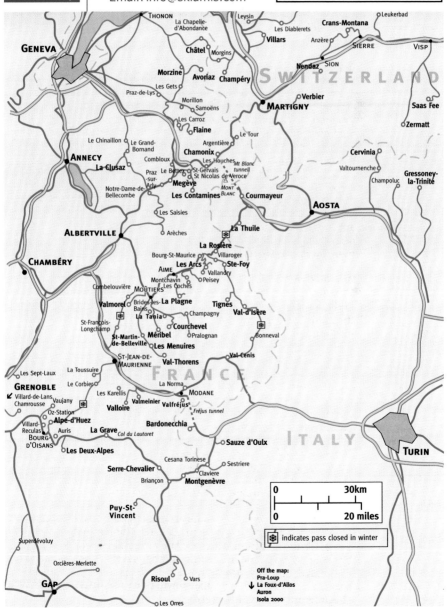

MOVING ON

A look at the map in this chapter shows that a different approach will pay dividends in the Tarentaise region of France. Practically all the resorts here – from Valmorel to Val-d'Isère – are found at the end of long winding roads up from the main valley. You could visit them all from a base such as Aime, but it would be hard work. If instead you stayed in a different resort each night, moving on from one to the next in the early evening, you could have the trip of a lifetime. Imagine a week in which you could explore the Three Valleys, La Plagne, Les Arcs and Val-d'Isère/Tignes.

GETTING THERE

The map in our Driving to the Alps chapter shows the main routes across France to the Alps. Whatever route you prefer across the Channel, the gateway to the French Alps is Mâcon and the initial target is Beaune. If you're taking the short crossing to Calais, Boulogne or Dunkirk, the route is via Reims, Troyes and Dijon. From Le Havre or Caen your route sounds even simpler: the A13 to Paris then the A6 south. But you have to get through or around Paris. The most direct way around the city is the notorious périphérique – a hectic, multi-lane urban motorway close to the centre, with exits every few hundred yards. But this is not the quickest route if it is jammed with traffic. The more reliable alternative is to take a series of motorways and dual carriageways through the south-west fringes of Greater Paris. One such route is signed, but with a detailed map and a good navigator you can take a more direct route from Versailles to the A10 near Orly.

by **Dave Watts**

Flying to the Alps

more budget options

EasyJet started the first cheap scheduled flights to the Alps by flying to Geneva five years ago. They still have the biggest range of flights to the key airports of Geneva and Zürich and were proposing to take over Go when we went to press. They have also been joined by other cut-price airlines, which offer different airport options. And all this competition has made the bigger, established airlines smarten up their acts and offer some competitive deals. This is great news for independent skiers and riders, who can now get flights for under £100 return, rent a car for a week for under £200 (£50 each between four) and have affordable holidays they arrange themselves.

I have used three of the cheap airlines quite often – EasyJet, Buzz and Go – over the last four seasons. All three were usually pretty much on time, and their no-frills service and pay-as-you-eat food is all you need on a short flight of 90 minutes or less. They are particularly convenient for me because I live only 20 minutes from Stansted and 40 minutes from Luton, the airports they mainly operate from. From Heathrow Swiss has well-timed flights for weekend or short-break trips and offers competitive fares through agents if you book a package. It may also be cheaper than the 'cheap' airlines when flights start to get full and 'cheap' prices rise.

When we went to press, EasyJet was almost certain to take over Go. But they plan to continue to operate Go flights under the Go brand until 31 March 2003.

All the cheap airlines are ticketless. None of them works through travel agents – you book direct with the airlines. They try to encourage bookings on the Internet rather than by telephone because it is cheaper for them, and there's usually a discount of a few pounds for booking on the Web. You pay by credit card (for which there is often an extra charge) or debit card and you either print out your own confirmation (if you book on the Web) or you receive it in the post or by fax or email. But all you need is a confirmation number; there are no tickets. Prices vary according to demand, and in general the cheapest flights (which they quote in their adverts) are for midweek flights early or late in the day, booked months in advance. As a flight fills up, the prices charged go up. But you may also get a bargain by booking at the last minute if the flight is not full. At their lowest, prices can be £40 return or less; at their peak they can be well over £200 return.

In general, flights have got more flexible. Although the budget airlines won't normally give you a refund if you decide not to travel, most will now allow you to change the flight time or route and the name of the passenger – but at a cost of perhaps £15 each way for each change (so £60 if you change both flights and passengers both ways). But check when you book because the airlines' policies change fairly frequently.

Policies on carrying skis and boards and on excess baggage vary. EasyJet has a 25kg baggage allowance to include any skis and boots. Buzz, on the other hand, charges an extra £15 return to guarantee

AIRLINE CONTACT DETAILS

Phone numbers for the major airlines are listed on page 672.

59

carrying your skis or board (which must be booked in advance) and then it still counts towards a baggage allowance of only 20kg. Ryanair charges £15 each way for skis or board and has a baggage allowance of only 15kg. Excess baggage is generally charged at £4/kg each way and can add up quickly. We have been told by some check-in staff that they have been told to enforce the baggage limits strictly as the airlines see this as a way of making money even if the fare is cheap.

Key airports for skiers include Geneva (for most French resorts and some Swiss and Italian), Zürich (for eastern Swiss and western Austrian resorts), Lyon (for many French resorts), Milan (for most Italian resorts except the Dolomites), Munich (for most Austrian resorts) and Barcelona (for Andorra and the Pyrenees), plus some smaller airports that we mention below.

For next season, EasyJet plans several flights a day from Luton, Gatwick and Liverpool to Geneva, Barcelona and Nice (only 90km/55 miles from Isola 2000) and from Luton and Gatwick to Zürich. Go will have flights from Stansted to Munich, Lyon, Milan, Barcelona, Nice, Malaga (for Sierra Nevada) and Venice (handy for the Dolomites); it will also go from Bristol to Barcelona, Malaga and Nice and from East Midlands to Malaga. Buzz (a subsidiary of KLM) plans to fly from Stansted to Geneva and Chambéry (nearer to many French resorts than Lyon or Geneva), Toulouse (for Andorra and the Pyrenees) and Grenoble (for the southern French Alps); but some of these routes may operate only certain days of the week such as Saturday. Ryanair looks likely to fly from Stansted to Turin (nearer than Milan for western Italian resorts), Venice, Salzburg (very convenient for most Austrian resorts), Friedrichshafen (just over the German border but handy for western Austrian resorts), Klagenfurt (handy for resorts in the Carinthia region of Austria), Carcassonne and Perpignan (both for Andorra and the Pyrenees) and St-Etienne (40 minutes south-west of Lyon and within striking distance of the French Alps).

A new airline called Swiss has now taken over many of the former Swissair and Crossair flights. They will operate several direct flights a day from Heathrow, London City, Birmingham, Manchester and Dublin to Zürich and from Heathrow and London City airport to Geneva. Late flights (8pm or so) to and from Heathrow and London City to both Geneva and Zürich make short breaks particularly easy if you live in the south-east – but book well in advance as these late flights are very popular. There is also a useful Saturday flight between Heathrow and Sion, less than half an hour's transfer to, for example, Nendaz (for Verbier's slopes) and Crans-Montana, and a bit further to Saas-Fee, Zermatt and Verbier.

Alitalia has eight flights a day direct from Heathrow to Milan (five to Malpensa airport and three to Linate), which give access to many of the Italian resorts. From Milan, you can get connecting flights to Venice and Verona (both handy for the Dolomites).

British Airways goes to Geneva, Zürich, Munich, Milan, Venice and Verona.

by **Dave Watts**

Travel by train

for eight days on snow

Taking the train to the Alps can be a great way to get more time on the slopes without taking more time off work. You can leave on Friday night, arriving in your resort on Saturday morning, and return on the following Saturday night, arriving back home on the Sunday – eight days' skiing for five days out of the office. Even if you opt for a different service that doesn't deliver the eight-day week, travelling by train is one of the most restful ways to get to the Alps – provided your journeys to and from the railway stations at either end are not too stressful.

The most popular train destination, with several different direct and indirect services, is the Tarentaise valley in France. You can step off the train in Bourg-St-Maurice and on to a funicular straight up to Arc 1600, and there are quick bus transfers to the other famous mega-resorts of this region – Val-d'Isère, Tignes, La Plagne, Courchevel and Méribel, with slightly longer transfers to Les Menuires and Val-Thorens.

But you can travel by train, one way or another, to many other resorts. And many traditional resorts, especially in Switzerland, are on the rail network and therefore reachable without resorting to buses. How many times you'll have to change trains is another matter.

DIRECT TRAIN SERVICES TO THE FRENCH ALPS

Since 1997, Eurostar has offered a truly direct service to the Alps – you board the train at London Waterloo or Ashford in Kent and disembark at Moûtiers or Bourg-St-Maurice in the Tarentaise valley, without changing trains en route. The special winter services will run from 20 December through to mid-April. Standard return tickets cost £179 for the overnight service and £199 for the daytime one (£260 and £295 for first class, which includes meals on board). Seats can also be booked as part of a package holiday. The overnight service affords you two extra days' skiing or boarding – it leaves on Friday night, arriving early on Saturday morning, and returns late Saturday evening, arriving back in London on Sunday morning. The service uses standard Eurostar carriages with no special sleeping arrangements – you just doze (or not) in your seat. The daytime service gives you no more than the standard six days on the slopes: both outward and return services leave on Saturday morning, arriving late afternoon. The outbound service also stops at Ashford, in Kent, and Aime (between Moûtiers and Bourg-St-Maurice). The return service doesn't stop at Aime.

All the other train services to the Alps involve a change somewhere along the line, but they can still be fairly convenient and also allow for extra time on the slopes. Unlike Eurostar, many of the other services are equipped with sleeping compartments.

The Snowtrain is another weekly overnight service to the Tarentaise giving an eight-day week on the slopes, but it starts from Calais. It runs from 27 December until 4 April, leaving Calais on Friday night and arriving in the Alps the following morning – first stop is Chambéry, then Albertville, Moûtiers, Aime, and finally Bourg-St-Maurice. For the return journey you leave the Alps on Saturday evening, arriving in Calais early on Sunday morning. You

cross the Channel by ferry from Dover (you can pay a supplement for a coach transfer from London or make your own arrangements and travel as a foot passenger). The train works on a charter basis and can be booked through UK tour operators – they have allocated spaces on each service. Overnight amenities include on-board couchettes (six drop-down berths to a compartment) and a disco/bar. Beware, it can get very noisy and crowded. It is possible to book a compartment for the exclusive use of four or five people on both legs of the journey. Booking independently costs from £135.

There is a similar Friday night sleeper service to the Tarentaise starting from Paris. You take the Eurostar to Paris from London Waterloo and change trains at Paris Gare du Nord for an overnight service to the Alps. The return journey leaves the Alps on Saturday evening, arriving in Paris early on Sunday morning. The service starts at £205 return including couchettes. Several tour operators offer this as part of an overall package.

There are a number of indirect services available on the French railway throughout the week, but most mean crossing Paris from the Gare du Nord to the Gare de Lyon or Gare d'Austerlitz – the change of station is not difficult, though, with a direct metro, regular buses and plenty of taxis at your disposal. Indirect services to many Alpine destinations via Brussels or Lille also run every day of the week and involve only a change of platform. This can be easier than going via Paris, and the timing of the slower overnight services via Brussels may be more suitable for some holidaymakers; the services tend to be less frequent and are often more expensive, but are worth considering at peak dates.

Motorail (or autotrain) is another option, getting your car to the Alps without having to drive it. These services have been cut back for the 2002/03 season and the main option is Paris to Lyon going out overnight on Friday and back overnight on Saturday (giving you eight days on the slopes). An alternative is using Belgian railways from Denderleeuw (between Gent and Brussels) to Milan. Motorail is not cheap and you still have a fair drive at the other end as destinations nearer to resorts have been axed; but the train will take some of the strain out the journey and save on hotel and petrol costs, as well as extra mileage on your car. Vehicles are usually loaded one hour before departure and are available for pick up half an hour after arrival. You should book your trip well in advance – at least 80 days in advance is recommended on most services.

For more details of rail services contact Rail Europe on 08701 244 646 for overnight ski trains or 08705 848 848 for Eurostar trains. Or visit www.raileurope.co.uk.

Corporate entertainment closer to home
Sailing in the Solent

by Chris Gill

Corporate ski trips

the ultimate way to get away

There are all kinds of reasons why companies find it valuable to get staff or clients together for a bit of a treat outside the usual business environment, ranging from sales incentives to strategic conference proceedings. And there are all kinds of places to do it, and all kinds of activities you can lay on, to act as a focus for your group or as light relief from the serious business. But few can rival ski resorts and skiing for sheer impact.

We do quite a bit of skiing, of course, but have never been involved in the corporate kind. We're well aware, though, that large numbers of people do it, and we thought it was time we found out more – so we've been talking to some experts to find out how it all works. If your sales force would benefit from some quality time together, if you want to bond more closely with the half-dozen customers who give you half your business, or if the managers of your various European offices really need to be introduced to your head office hymn sheet, read on.

Your starting point is likely to be to ask whether a ski trip is right for your corporate purposes, so we'll start there too.

WHAT'S THE ATTRACTION?

The mountain/skiing/boarding environment is one that has lots of advantages for corporate events. The clear air, sun and snowy landscape have a huge and immediate impact on people arriving from the European lowlands and their dreary winters. There is a great sense of fun and liberation – think how colourfully people dress, and how ready they are to let their hair down. And as Nicky Stephenson of Flexiski points out, 'A winter sports break need not appeal just to skiers. Non-skiing participants or partners will find it revitalising too.' The best resorts have a range of other activities, including ones that will fit naturally into the evening timetable. There are excellent and capacious hotels, many with conference facilities. The flights from northern Europe are short. And the perceived status of ski resorts is high – whoever it is you are inviting, they will be in no doubt that they are being given a bit of a treat.

WHAT'S THE COST?

The obvious answer is that it depends. Perhaps a more useful one is that it may be less than you'd think, and indeed less than some of the alternatives. Chris Scudds of Alpine Events reckons that 'a two-night ski trip including flight and ski hire could cost the same as a two-night stay in the UK', because UK hotel and restaurant costs are relatively high.

WHAT SORT OF CORPORATE EVENT WILL WORK?

The answer seems to be: more or less any event that is better done away from the office. Examples of events that have been successfully held in ski resorts include those with these objectives:
• communication to middle managers of a new business strategy
• concentrated attempt to crack a crucial business problem

- staff morale boost after recent business difficulties
- new product launches to sales staff or key customers
- gathering together of staff in related functions from geographically spread sites, to generate shared objectives
- team-building by giving groups shared objectives
- sales incentive 'prizes'
- client 'reward' to build business loyalty.

HOW LONG A TRIP?

Corporate trips of a few days are the norm. 'Most groups travel for four days from Thursday to Sunday,' says Annie Constantinou of The Ski Company, 'although some companies take over a cluster of chalets for a week or two and have different groups moving in and out, staying for a variety of durations.' But it is possible to cram a trip into just a weekend, says Harold Chrystal of White Roc: 'You can have two full, action-packed days in the Alps by leaving on Friday after work and returning late on Sunday night – arriving back at work on Monday morning refreshed, invigorated and remotivated.' And the Corporate Ski Company suggests that even one-night trips can be arranged, though it points out that in some cases it's only practical if you transfer to the resort by helicopter – not cheap.

HOW BIG A GROUP?

In principle, your group can be any size you like. In practice, the events that organisers like the Corporate Ski Company get involved in are for 30 to 50 guests, says the company's managing director John Denham. 'This size of event enables the programme to work well logistically, provides a good social "ambience" and is cost-effective. In general, we work on a minimum group size of 15 people; we can work with fewer, but the unit cost rises. On the other hand, we have managed plenty of events with numbers over 100.'

Someone else with plenty of experience of handling large groups is Amin Momen of Momentum Travel, who for the last few years has organised the City Ski Championships in Courmayeur. Last season this involved 150 racers, plus lots of hangers-on. 'Such a large group is quite a challenge,' says Amin, 'but it helps enormously that we have such good local contacts in the resort. If strings need to be pulled to solve a problem, we know exactly which strings.'

Some other companies operate in rather less exclusive markets: Skiworld's special events department, which is used to handling large groups of military personnel and students, cheerfully offers 'solutions for groups from 30 to 3,000'.

With really small groups, be aware that the social success is going to depend on how the individuals mesh – the group is likely to be relatively inflexible, whereas in a larger group people get some choice of who they spend time with.

WHERE TO GO?

How easy it is to settle on a resort for a corporate trip depends hugely on the nature of your project. If it's a dozen people travelling out together for a relaxed couple of days, you're really organising nothing more than a short holiday. If you are getting a large group together from all corners of the globe and need serious conference facilities, you're playing a different ballgame. Finding the right accommodation, meeting rooms and support services can be a real headache, and it's in dealing with this sort of challenge that the

Corporate ski trips

services of a tour operator or event management company will start to pay off.

Because corporate trips tend to be short, you'll want to keep the travel time to the minimum, so that it doesn't dominate the proceedings. Transfer times from airports to resorts generally range from one to four hours, and you'll probably want to operate at the lower end of that range if you can. You'll notice that a couple of our advertisers are based in Chamonix – a spectacular resort at the foot of Europe's highest mountain, but only an hour from Geneva airport.

You may of course have considerations other than practical ones. You may want to have a particular range of activities available. You may want your choice of resort to carry a message to your 'delegates'. Choosing Courchevel or St Moritz is effectively saying 'No expense spared – nothing but the best for you.' Choosing La Toussuire is stressing that you don't want to be extravagant with shareholders' money.

In focusing on the particular needs of a corporate trip, don't neglect the considerations that apply to any winter sports trip – in particular, snow. It's one thing for a family to have to fall back on Scrabble because there's no skiing, quite another for a group of 200 you've brought together in the hope of boosting their morale. You'll be fixing your trip a long time in advance, with no clue about the prevailing weather conditions, so go for resorts with a good snow record and/or extensive snowmaking. Be wary of low resorts.

On the other hand, you don't want to risk disruption of your plans by snow on the approach roads. Most resorts have this pretty much under control. But it would be tempting fate to organise an event in a resort like Lech or Zürs, which fairly frequently get cut off

from the outside world by avalanche risk on the Flexen pass.

Don't get hung up on size – you don't have to limit yourself to the Trois Vallées. As Chris Scudds of Alpine Events explains: 'For a corporate weekend you can consider a whole host of smaller resorts that might be disregarded for a week-long holiday. With only a couple of days to spend on the slopes, almost any resort has plenty of terrain, especially if you have good local guides to help you make the most of them.'

WHERE TO STAY?

Large groups really have no option: you'll need a large hotel (or two). Obviously, you and/or your event organiser will want to consider lots of angles to identify a place with the right blend of qualities. But for smaller groups there is the alternative of staying in one or more catered chalets – Alpine houses run by UK-based or at least UK-oriented companies, usually with native English-speaking staff. Some of these properties are very swanky and expensive, others less so. The Ski Company and Flexiski operate at the top of the market. They have properties in several resorts, as do Ski Olympic and Skiworld. Some chalets can accommodate quite a few people – including the Aravis Alpine Retreat, a one-off enterprise with 28 beds.

WHO TO GO WITH?

If you scan the ads in this chapter you'll see that the companies offering corporate trips are coming at this market from two main directions. On the one hand there are a couple of corporate event management companies that have developed special capabilities in the skiing area, and on the other quite a few ski holiday companies that have developed special capabilities in the corporate trip area. And in the latter category you can detect three special groups: companies that in their everyday business specialise in short trips (Ski Weekend and White Roc, for example); companies specialising in notably swanky accommodation (Ski Company and Flexiski, for example); and companies specialising in resorts that have particular attractions for the corporate market (Bigfoot and Huski, both based in Chamonix). The Aravis Alpine Retreat doesn't fit into any of these categories: it's an individual property, close to La Clusaz.

You'll doubtless want to consider a number of options. All the

Specialists in corporate incentives

luxury exclusive use ski lodge, resident event management team, 200km downhill skiing and all other options inc heli-ski, easy one hour transfer, luxury fleet 4x4 vehicles, team build potential.

T: 020 88 78 78 60

E: info@aravis-retreat.com W: www.aravis-retreat.co.uk

companies have websites that will help to give you a feel for how they deal with corporate event management.

ORGANISING THE SKIING

If you're a typical *Where to Ski and Snowboard* reader, you know what's involved in getting on to the slopes: clothing, equipment, lift passes. What you may not know is how to go about organising these elements for scores of people, many of them with no experience at all of the whole process.

A typical corporate group will naturally contain a mixture of experienced skiers and non-skiers. You'll want to organise tuition – perhaps setting up private group lessons as a good compromise between stuffing your guests in ski school classes and spending a fortune on private individual lessons.

Lunch in a mountain restaurant can be an opportunity to get your group together, but for a large and disparate group it can present some challenges. Another possibility, in good weather, is a swanky picnic, with plenty of champagne buried in the snow.

You might want to think about a race for delegates, though bear in mind that this won't appeal to the complete beginners in the group. Other forms of competition could be used to complement the ski racing, bringing in non-skiers too.

WHAT OTHER ACTIVITIES?

You need to be aware, of course, that not everyone will want to go skiing or boarding – so you'll need to be able to offer some other activities with a broad appeal. This may influence your choice of resort. Typical activities to consider would include dog-sledding,

NEWS

FINANCE

RESEARCH

All the information you need to follow every move in the equities markets.

We're more than just the world's most compelling information and news source. Together with Institutional Investor, we also bring you benchmark rankings for buy-side, sell-side and corporate players.

REUTERS :☷

snowmobiling, skating, curling, tobogganing, ballooning, swimming, flights in planes or helicopters. Bear in mind that activities like these tend to occupy relatively short, defined periods of time – in contrast to skiing and boarding which of course soak up any number of days. So you may need quite a range of activities to keep people busy all day. Walking and snow-shoeing, of course, can also fill whole days, but do require an energetic approach. Having brought people to a resort, excursions outside it may seem perverse, but they can work.

WHAT ABOUT THE EVENINGS?

The days of your event may be spent in a variety of ways – maybe all skiing or other activities on the snow, maybe some business sessions mixed in. While people are out being active, they are to an extent doing their own thing – separated to a degree by skiing competence and other factors. But the evenings are a time when every group can be brought together, so it's important to think about how you're going to use those opportunities to best effect. You can organise activities with more of a team emphasis, and you can create social events that reinforce your message – perhaps taking over a whole bar or a mountain restaurant, for example. In the right resort, dinner in a mountain restaurant could be followed by dangerous descents on skis or toboggans.

WHEN TO GO?

You're going to want to avoid peak times, for all sorts of reasons: congestion at airports and on approach roads, queues for lifts, crowded pistes, shortage of ski instructors, shortage of hotel rooms – and, of course, high prices.

French school holidays are a notorious problem period, and in the introduction to France on page 199 you'll find a summary of this year's dates. The impact of school holidays in other countries is less well defined, but the school holidays do exist and they do have an impact, so check them out when you know which country you're going to. Remember that it's German holidays that determine how crowded resorts get in the Austrian Alps and Italian Dolomites.

MANAGEMENT ISSUES

Like any business project, a skiing trip brings its own administrative burdens. As well as making it all happen smoothly – which means managing the delegates as tightly as the suppliers of all the components making up the trip – someone has to control expenditure, and provide clear, always up-to-date information. This is a key area to sort out with your organising company.

Corporate entertainment closer to home
Yacht racing in the Solent

- Reward your hard-working staff
- Weld your managers into a real team
- Get the attention of key journalists
- Entertain your most valued clients

Yacht Ventures

www.yachtventures.com
info@yachtventures.com
t 01373 835201

Take them out for a day's racing in the Solent on our big, sleek, powerful yachts – three identical 48ft First 47.7s, with space for up to 36 people in total. Your guests will find the day an exciting and memorable experience – quite unlike other, less absorbing forms of corporate entertainment. And you'll have an unrivalled opportunity to get to know them better.

Choosing your resort

get it right first time

Most people get to go skiing or boarding only once or twice a year – and then only for a week at a time. So choosing the right resort is crucially important. This book is designed to help you get it right first time. Here is some advice on how to use our information to best effect – particularly for the benefit of readers with relatively narrow experience of different resorts. Chamonix, Châtel and Courchevel are all French resorts, but they are as similar as chalk and Camembert.

Lots of factors need to be taken into account. The weight you attach to each of them depends on your own personal preferences, and on the make-up of the group you are going on holiday with. On page 91 you'll find 20 shortlists of resorts which are outstanding in various key respects.

Each resort chapter is organised in the same way, to help you choose the right resort. This short introduction takes you through the structure and what you will find under each heading we use.

WHICH RESORT?

We start each chapter with a one-line verdict, in which we aim to sum up the resort in a few words. If you like the sound of it, you might want to go next to our What it costs rating, in the margin. These ratings, ranging from ① to ⑥, reflect the total cost of a week's holiday from Britain, including a typical package of flights plus half-board accommodation, a lift pass and meals and drinks on the spot. As you might expect with a six-point scale, three means on the low side of average, four means on the high side. Further on in the margin copy we give the cost of lift passes in local currency; these are for the 2002/03 season if the resort had decided prices by the time we went to press, otherwise we use the 2001/02 prices. Below the What it costs rating, in the How it rates section, we rate each resort from 11 points of view – the more stars the better. (All these star ratings are brought together in one chart, which follows this chapter.) Still looking at the information in the margin, in most chapters we have a What's new section; this is likely to be of most use and interest in resorts you already know.

For major resorts, the next things to look at are our lists of the main good and bad points about the resort and its slopes, picked out with ➊ and ➋. These lists are followed by a summary in **bold type**, in which we've aimed to weigh up the pros and cons, coming off the fence and giving our view of who might like it. These sections should give you a good idea of whether the resort is likely to suit *you*, and whether you should read our detailed analysis of it.

You'll know by now whether this is, for example, a high, hideous, convenient, purpose-built resort with superb, snow-sure slopes for all standards of skier or boarder but absolutely no nightlife, or whether it's a pretty, traditional village with gentle wooded skiing, ideal for beginners if only there was some snow. We then look at each aspect in more detail.

Get online to find the best holiday deals to Europe's most popular ski destinations. Go on, it's not hard - book direct and save.

directski.com™

Freefone: 0800 587 0945

First Choice SKI

Over 73 resorts in 11 countries with the biggest selection of ClubHotel and Chalet holidays in France!

Over 17 new quality **Chalets & ClubHotels** For Winter 2002/3 in Verbier, Meribel, Courchevel, Val Thorens, Les Arcs, Val d'Isere, Les 2 Alpes Sauze d'Oulx. For the best piste side locations in **BRAND NEW chalets** with en suite bathrooms look no further than FIRST CHOICE SKI!

SAVE UP TO **25%** AND TAKE YOUR KIDS FOR FREE ON SELECTED HOLIDAYS NEXT WINTER

SALOMON

RIDE SALOMON TO THE MAX and test the latest Salomon skis for **FREE** with FIRST CHOICE SKI in Alpe d'Huez, Les Deux Alpes, Les Menuires, Tignes, Val d'Isere, Kitzbühel & Saalbach.

SKI Weekends & Shortbreaks

CALL:

0870 754 3477

or visit: **www.fcski.co.uk** or email: **sales@fcski.co.uk**
or see your local travel agent.

THE RESORT

Resorts vary enormously in character and charm. At the extremes of the range are the handful of really hideous modern apartment-block resorts thrown up in France in the 1960s – step forward, Les Menuires and Flaine – and the captivating old traffic-free mountain villages of which Switzerland has an unfair number. But it isn't simply a question of old versus new. Some purpose-built places (such as Valmorel) can have a much friendlier feel than some traditional resorts with big blocky buildings (eg Davos). And some places can be remarkably strung out (eg Vail) whereas others are surprisingly compact (eg Wengen).

The landscape can have an important impact – whether the resort is at the bottom of a narrow, shady valley (eg Ischgl) or on a sunny shelf with panoramic views (eg Crans-Montana). Some places are working towns as well as ski resorts (eg Bormio). Some are full of bars, discos and shops (eg St Anton). Others are peaceful backwaters (eg Arabba). Traffic may choke the streets (eg Sölden). Or the village may be traffic-free (eg Mürren).

In this first section of each chapter, we try to sort out the character of the place for you. Later, in the Staying there section, we tell you more about the hotels, restaurants, bars and so on.

THE MOUNTAINS

The slopes Some mountains and lift networks are vast and complex, while others are much smaller and lacking variation. The description here tells you how the area divides up into different sectors and how the links between them work.

Snow reliability This is a crucial factor for many people, and one which varies enormously. In some resorts you don't have to worry at all about a lack of snow, while others (including some very big names) are notorious for treating their paying guests to ice, mud and slush. Whether a resort is likely to have decent snow on its slopes normally depends on the height, the direction most of the slopes face (north good, south bad), its snow record and how much snowmaking it has. But bear in mind that in the Alps high resorts tend to have rocky terrain where the runs will need more snow than those on the pasture land of lower resorts. Many resorts have increased their snowmaking capacity in recent years and we list the latest amount they claim to have in the Mountain facts section and comment on it in the Snow reliability text. Bear in mind that snowmaking can operate only if temperatures are low enough (typically –2°C or less), so it's much more useful in midwinter than in spring.

For experts, intermediates, beginners Most (though not all) resorts have something to offer beginners, but relatively few will keep an expert happy for a week's holiday. As for intermediates, whether a resort will suit you really depends on your standard and inclinations. Places such as Cervinia and Obergurgl are ideal for those who want easy cruising runs, but have little to offer intermediates looking for more challenge. Others, such as Sölden and Val-d'Isère, may intimidate the less confident intermediate who doesn't know the area well. Some, such as the Trois Vallées and Portes du Soleil, have vast amounts of terrain so that you can cover different ground each day. But some other well-known names, such as Obergurgl, Courmayeur, Livigno, and many of the North American resorts, have surprisingly small areas of pistes.

For cross-country We don't pretend that this is a guide for avid cross-country skiers. But if you or one of your group wants to try it, our summary here will help you gauge whether the resort is worth considering or whether it is a washout. It looks not just at the amount of cross-country available but also at its scenic beauty and whether or not the tracks are likely to have decent snow (many are at low altitude).

Queues Another key factor. Most resorts have improved their lift systems enormously in the last 10 years, and monster queues are largely a thing of the past. Crowding on the pistes is more of a worry in many resorts, and we mention problems of this kind here. On our piste maps, note that we mark with a chair only high-speed chairs that shift large numbers of people. Lifts not marked with a symbol are slow chairs or drag-lifts.

Mountain restaurants Here's a subject that divides people clearly into two opposing camps. To some, having a decent lunch in civilised surroundings – either in the sun, contemplating amazing scenery, or in a cosy hut, sheltered from the elements – makes or breaks their holiday. Others regard a prolonged midday stop as a waste of valuable skiing time, as well as valuable spending money. We are firmly in the former camp. We get very disheartened by places with miserable restaurants and miserable food (eg some resorts in America); and there are some resorts that we go to regularly partly because of the cosy huts and excellent cuisine (eg Zermatt).

Schools and guides This is an area where we rely heavily on readers' reports of their own or their friends' experiences. The only way to judge a ski school is by trying it. Reports on schools are always extremely valuable and frequently record disappointment.

Facilities for children If you need nursery facilities, don't go to Italy. In other countries, facilities for looking after and teaching children can vary enormously between resorts. We say what is available in each resort, including what's on offer from UK tour operators – often the most attractive option for Brits. But, again, to be of real help we need reports from people who've used the facilities.

SNOWBOARDING

The Mountains section applies to both skiers and snowboarders. But because certain things are important to snowboarding that aren't relevant (or aren't as relevant) to skiing, we also include a special assessment for snowboarders. This covers issues such as whether the slopes present special attractions or problems (eg flat sections that snowboarders have to 'scoot' along), whether there is a good terrain-park and a half-pipe, how much you can expect to have to use drag-lifts and whether you'll find specialist snowboard schools and shops and lively snowboard bars in the resort.

STAYING THERE

How to go The basic choice is between catered chalets, hotels and self-catering accommodation. The catered chalet holiday remains a peculiarly British phenomenon. A tour operator takes over a chalet (or a hotel in some cases), staffs it with young Brits (or Antipodeans), fills it with British guests, provides half-board and free wine, and lets you drink your duty-free booze without hassle. You can take over a complete chalet, or share one with other groups. It is a relatively economical way of visiting the expensive top resorts.

Hotels, of course, can vary a lot but, especially in France and

Switzerland, can work out very expensive. In North America, watch out for supplements: rooms are often capable of sleeping four, and UK tour operators are inclined to base their standard brochure prices on the assumption that you fill all available bed spaces.

Apartments can be very economical but most French ones, in particular, tend to be very small. It's not unusual for brochure prices to be based on four people sleeping in a one-room studio, for example – to be comfortable, pay extra for under-occupancy. But some recently built French apartments are more spacious and comfortable – where we know of these we name them.

We also look at what's available for independent travellers who want to fix their own hotels or self-catering accommodation. With hotels we've given each a price rating from ① to ⓒⓒⓒⓒ⑤ – the more coins, the more expensive the hotel.

Staying up the mountain / down the valley If there are interesting options for staying on the slopes above the resort village or in valley towns below it, we've picked them out. The former is often good for avoiding early-morning scrums for the lifts, the latter for cutting costs considerably.

Eating out The range of restaurants varies widely. Even some big resorts, such as Les Arcs, may have little choice because most of the clientele stay in their apartments or chalets. Others, such as Val-d'Isère, have a huge range available, including national and regional cuisine, pizzas, fondues and international fare. American resorts generally have an excellent range of restaurants – most people eat out. This is an area where we rely a lot on reporters recommending restaurants that were good last season – and we are often able to recommend some out-of-the-way restaurants that you might not otherwise find (eg in the Les Arcs and Saas-Fee chapters).

Après-ski Tastes and styles vary enormously. Most resorts have pleasant places in which to have an immediate post-skiing beer or hot chocolate. Some then go dead. Others have noisy bars and discos until the early hours. And, especially in Austrian resorts, there may be a lot of events such as tobogganing and bowling that are organised by British tour operator reps. For this section we are largely dependent on hearing from reporters who are keen après-skiers.

Off the slopes This is largely aimed at assessing how suitable a resort is for someone who doesn't intend to use the slopes – a non-skiing spouse or elderly relative or friend, for example. In some resorts, such as most French purpose-built places, there is really nothing to amuse them. In others, such as Seefeld in Austria, there are more people walking, skating and swimming than there are people skiing or boarding. Excursion possibilities vary widely. And there are great variations in the practicality of meeting skiers and boarders for lunch up the mountain.

Get next year's edition free

There are too many hotels, nightspots and mountain restaurants for us to see them all every year – so we need reports on your holiday experiences. As usual, the 100 best reports will earn free copies of next year's edition.

We want to know:
• what you particularly **liked and disliked** about the resort
• what aspects of the resort came as a **surprise** to you
• your suggestions for **changes to our evaluation** of the resort
• your experience of lift **queues** and of the **ski school** and associated childcare
• your feedback on other **individual facilities** – hotels, bars, restaurants etc.

e-mail: reports@snow-zone.co.uk
mail: our address is at the front of the book; we'll send a form if you like.

Resort ratings at a glance

The following six pages bring together the ratings we give each resort for 11 key characteristics. You'll find these ratings at the start of each resort chapter too. Use the tables here to compare resorts directly for the aspects that are most important to you. You'll be able to see at a glance which resorts come out top and bottom of the pile.

AUSTRIA

	Alpbach	Bad Gastein	Ellmau	Hintertux	Ischgl	Kitzbühel	Lech
Page	102	104	111	114	123	128	134
Snow	**	***	**	*****	****	**	****
Extent	*	****	****	**	****	****	****
Experts	*	***	*	***	***	***	****
Intermediates	**	****	****	***	****	****	****
Beginners	****	**	****	*	**	**	****
Convenience	**	**	***	**	***	**	***
Queues	***	***	****	***	****	**	****
Restaurants	***	****	**	**	***	****	**
Scenery	***	***	***	***	***	***	***
Resort charm	*****	***	***	***	****	****	****
Off-slope	***	****	***	*	***	*****	***

	Mayrhofen	Obergurgl	Obertauern	Pitztal	Saalbach-Hinterglemm	Schladming	Sölden
Page	142	150	155	157	160	167	171
Snow	***	*****	****	*****	***	***	*****
Extent	***	**	**	***	***	***	***
Experts	*	**	***	***	**	**	***
Intermediates	***	***	****	****	****	****	****
Beginners	**	****	*****	***	***	****	**
Convenience	*	****	****	**	****	***	**
Queues	*	*****	****	***	***	****	***
Restaurants	****	**	***	**	****	****	***
Scenery	***	***	***	****	***	***	***
Resort charm	***	****	**	***	****	****	**
Off-slope	****	**	**	***	**	****	**

	Söll	St Anton	St Johann in Tirol	Westendorf	Wildschönau	Zell am See
Page	173	179	187	189	191	194
Snow	**	****	**	**	**	**
Extent	****	****	**	*	*	**
Experts	*	*****	*	*	*	**
Intermediates	****	***	***	**	**	***
Beginners	***	*	****	****	****	***
Convenience	**	***	***	***	***	**
Queues	***	**	***	****	****	**
Restaurants	**	***	****	***	**	***
Scenery	***	***	***	***	***	***
Resort charm	***	****	***	****	***	***
Off-slope	**	***	***	**	**	****

85

FRANCE

	Alpe-d'Huez	Les Arcs	Avoriaz	Chamonix	Châtel	La Clusaz	Les Contamines
Page	203	211	217	221	229	234	240
Snow	****	****	***	****	**	**	****
Extent	****	***	*****	***	*****	***	**
Experts	****	****	***	*****	***	***	**
Intermediates	****	****	****	**	****	****	***
Beginners	*****	****	****	*	**	****	***
Convenience	****	****	****	*	**	***	**
Queues	****	***	**	**	***	***	***
Restaurants	****	**	****	**	***	****	****
Scenery	****	***	***	*****	***	****	***
Resort charm	*	*	**	****	***	****	****
Off-slope	***	*	*	*****	**	***	**

	Courchevel	Les Deux-Alpes	Flaine	La Grave	Megève	Les Menuires	Méribel
Page	242	251	256	262	267	273	276
Snow	****	****	****	***	**	****	****
Extent	*****	***	****	**	*****	*****	*****
Experts	****	****	****	*****	**	****	****
Intermediates	*****	**	*****	*	****	*****	*****
Beginners	*****	***	*****	*	***	***	***
Convenience	****	***	*****	***	**	*****	***
Queues	****	**	****	****	****	****	****
Restaurants	****	**	**	**	*****	***	****
Scenery	***	****	****	****	***	***	***
Resort charm	**	**	*	***	****	*	***
Off-slope	***	**	*	*	****	*	***

	Montgenèvre	Morzine	La Plagne	Puy-St-Vincent	Risoul	La Rosière	Serre-Chevalier
Page	285	290	297	307	309	312	314
Snow	****	**	****	***	***	***	****
Extent	****	*****	****	**	***	***	****
Experts	**	***	***	***	**	**	***
Intermediates	****	****	*****	***	****	***	****
Beginners	*****	***	****	***	****	*****	****
Convenience	****	**	*****	*****	****	***	***
Queues	****	***	***	****	****	***	***
Restaurants	**	***	**	***	***	*	***
Scenery	***	***	****	***	***	***	****
Resort charm	***	***	*	**	**	***	***
Off-slope	*	***	*	*	*	*	**

	Ste-Foy	St-Martin-de-Belleville	La Tania	Tignes	Val-d'Isère	Valmorel	Val-Thorens
Page	320	322	325	329	338	350	355
Snow	***	***	***	*****	*****	***	*****
Extent	*	*****	*****	*****	*****	***	*****
Experts	****	****	****	*****	*****	**	****
Intermediates	***	*****	*****	*****	*****	****	*****
Beginners	**	***	**	**	***	*****	****
Convenience	***	***	****	****	***	*****	*****
Queues	*****	****	****	****	****	****	***
Restaurants	*	****	****	***	**	**	****
Scenery	***	***	***	***	***	***	***
Resort charm	***	****	***	**	***	****	**
Off-slope	*	*	*	*	**	**	**

	ITALY Bormio	Cervinia	Cortina d'Ampezzo	Courmayeur	Livigno	Madonna di Campiglio	Monterosa Ski
Page	366	368	373	378	383	387	389
Snow	***	*****	***	****	****	***	***
Extent	**	***	***	**	**	***	****
Experts	*	*	**	***	**	**	***
Intermediates	***	****	***	****	***	****	****
Beginners	**	*****	*****	**	****	****	**
Convenience	***	***	*	*	**	**	****
Queues	***	***	***	****	****	***	****
Restaurants	****	***	****	****	***	***	**
Scenery	***	****	*****	****	***	****	****
Resort charm	****	**	****	****	***	***	***
Off-slope	****	*	*****	***	**	***	*

	Sauze d'Oulx	Selva	Sestriere	La Thuile
Page	392	397	405	407
Snow	**	****	***	****
Extent	*****	*****	****	***
Experts	**	***	***	**
Intermediates	****	*****	****	****
Beginners	**	****	***	****
Convenience	**	***	****	***
Queues	***	***	***	****
Restaurants	***	****	**	*
Scenery	***	*****	***	***
Resort charm	**	***	*	***
Off-slope	*	***	*	**

SWITZERLAND – UNITED STATES

	Adelboden	Andermatt	Arosa	Champéry	Crans-Montana	Davos	Flims	Grindelwald
Page	415	417	419	421	423	428	435	440
Snow	**	****	***	**	**	****	***	**
Extent	***	*	**	*****	***	*****	****	***
Experts	**	****	*	***	**	****	***	**
Intermediates	***	**	***	****	****	*****	*****	*****
Beginners	****	*	****	**	***	**	****	***
Convenience	***	***	***	*	**	**	***	**
Queues	***	**	****	****	***	**	***	**
Restaurants	**	*	****	***	***	***	***	***
Scenery	***	***	***	****	****	****	***	*****
Resort charm	****	****	**	****	**	**	***	****
Off-slope	****	**	****	***	****	*****	***	****

	Gstaad	Mürren	Saas-Fee	St Moritz	Verbier	Villars	Wengen	Zermatt
Page	444	446	450	455	461	470	473	478
Snow	*	***	*****	****	***	**	**	****
Extent	****	*	**	*****	*****	***	***	****
Experts	**	***	***	****	*****	**	**	*****
Intermediates	***	***	****	****	***	***	****	****
Beginners	***	**	*****	**	**	****	***	*
Convenience	*	***	***	**	**	***	***	*
Queues	***	***	***	**	***	***	***	***
Restaurants	***	**	***	****	***	***	****	*****
Scenery	***	*****	****	****	****	***	*****	*****
Resort charm	****	*****	*****	*	***	****	*****	*****
Off-slope	****	***	****	*****	***	****	****	****

	CALIFORNIA		COLORADO			Copper	Crested
	Heavenly	Mammoth	Aspen	Beaver Cr'k	Breckenridge	Mountain	Butte
Page	490	499	504	511	513	518	520
Snow	****	****	*****	*****	*****	*****	****
Extent	***	***	****	***	**	**	**
Experts	***	****	*****	****	****	****	****
Intermediates	****	****	*****	****	****	****	***
Beginners	****	****	*****	*****	****	****	****
Convenience	*	**	**	****	***	****	***
Queues	****	****	****	*****	****	****	*****
Restaurants	*	*	****	**	**	*	*
Scenery	****	***	***	***	***	***	***
Resort charm	*	**	****	***	***	**	****
Off-slope	**	*	****	***	***	*	**

UNITED STATES (continued)

	Keystone	Steamboat	Telluride	Vail	Winter Park
Page	522	527	532	534	540
Snow	*****	****	****	*****	*****
Extent	**	***	**	****	***
Experts	***	***	****	****	****
Intermediates	****	****	***	*****	****
Beginners	****	*****	*****	****	*****
Convenience	**	***	****	***	***
Queues	****	****	*****	**	****
Restaurants	***	***	*	**	***
Scenery	***	***	****	***	***
Resort charm	**	**	****	***	**
Off-slope	**	**	**	***	*

UTAH

	Alta	The Canyons	Deer Valley	Park City	Snowbasin	Snowbird
Page	547	549	551	553	558	560
Snow	*****	****	****	****	*****	*****
Extent	***	***	**	***	***	***
Experts	*****	***	***	****	****	*****
Intermediates	***	***	****	****	****	***
Beginners	***	***	****	****	**	**
Convenience	****	****	****	***	*	*****
Queues	***	****	****	****	*****	**
Restaurants	**	***	****	**	**	*
Scenery	****	***	***	***	****	***
Resort charm	**	**	***	***	**	*
Off-slope	*	**	**	***	*	*

REST OF THE WEST / NEW ENGLAND

	Big Sky	Jackson Hole	Sun Valley	Killington	Smugglers'	Stowe	Sunday River
Page	564	566	571	576	580	582	584
Snow	****	****	***	***	***	***	***
Extent	***	***	***	**	*	*	**
Experts	*****	*****	***	***	***	***	**
Intermediates	****	**	****	***	***	****	****
Beginners	****	***	***	****	****	****	****
Convenience	****	***	**	*	*****	*	***
Queues	*****	***	****	****	****	****	****
Restaurants	*	*	****	*	*	**	***
Scenery	***	***	***	***	***	***	***
Resort charm	**	****	***	*	**	****	**
Off-slope	**	***	***	*	*	*	*

CANADA – AND THE REST

WESTERN CANADA

	Banff	Big White	Fernie	Jasper	Kicking Horse	Lake Louise	Panorama	Whistler
Page	591	597	599	603	605	607	612	614
Snow	****	*****	*****	***	*****	***	***	****
Extent	****	***	***	*	***	****	**	****
Experts	****	****	*****	**	****	****	****	*****
Intermediates	****	****	**	**	***	****	***	*****
Beginners	***	****	****	****	***	***	****	***
Convenience	*	****	****	*	*	*	****	****
Queues	****	*****	****	****	*****	****	****	***
Restaurants	***	*	*	**	**	**	*	**
Scenery	****	***	****	***	***	*****	***	***
Resort charm	***	**	**	***	*	***	**	***
Off-slope	*****	**	**	***	*	****	*	**

EASTERN CANADA / ANDORRA / SPAIN

	Tremblant	Arinsal	Pas de la Casa	Soldeu	Baqueira
Page	624	630	632	634	639
Snow	****	***	***	***	***
Extent	**	*	***	**	***
Experts	***	*	*	*	***
Intermediates	***	**	***	***	****
Beginners	****	***	****	****	**
Convenience	****	***	****	***	***
Queues	***	***	***	***	***
Restaurants	**	**	***	*	**
Scenery	***	***	**	***	***
Resort charm	****	*	*	*	**
Off-slope	***	*	*	*	*

NORWAY / SWEDEN / NEW ZEALAND

	Hemsedal	Åre	Queenstown
Page	650	653	661
Snow	****	***	**
Extent	*	**	*
Experts	**	**	***
Intermediates	****	****	***
Beginners	***	****	***
Convenience	**	***	*
Queues	****	****	***
Restaurants	*	***	*
Scenery	**	***	****
Resort charm	**	***	**
Off-slope	*	***	*****

Resort shortlists

To streamline the job of spotting the ideal resort for your own holiday, here are lists of the best ten or so resorts for 20 different categories. Some lists embrace European and North American resorts, but most we've confined to Europe, because America has too many qualifying resorts (eg for beginners) or because America does things differently, making comparisons invalid (eg for off-piste).

SOMETHING FOR EVERYONE
Resorts with everything from reassuring nursery slopes to real challenges for experts
Alpe-d'Huez, France p203
Les Arcs, France p211
Aspen-Snowmass, Colorado p504
Courchevel, France p242
Flaine, France p256
Mammoth, California p499
Vail, Colorado p534
Val-d'Isère, France p338
Whistler, Canada p614
Winter Park, Colorado p540

RELIABLE SNOW IN THE ALPS
Alpine resorts with good snow records or lots of snowmaking, and high or north-facing slopes
Argentière, France p221
Cervinia, Italy p368
Courchevel, France p242
Hintertux, Austria p114
Lech/Zürs, Austria p134
Obergurgl, Austria p150
Saas-Fee, Switzerland p450
Val-d'Isère/Tignes, France pp338/329
Val-Thorens, France p355
Zermatt, Switzerland p478

INTERNATIONAL OVERSIGHTS
Resorts that deserve as much attention as the ones we go back to every year, but don't seem to get it
Alta, Utah p547
Andermatt, Switzerland p517
Bad Gastein, Austria p104
Big Sky, Montana p564
Flims-Laax, Switzerland p435
Ischgl, Austria p123
Monterosa Ski, Italy p389
Risoul, France p309
Sun Valley, Idaho p571
Telluride, Colorado p532

OFF-PISTE WONDERS
Alpine resorts where, with the right guidance and equipment, you can have the time of your life
Alpe-d'Huez, France p203
Andermatt, Switzerland p417
Argentière/Chamonix, France p221
Davos/Klosters, Switzerland p428
La Grave, France p262
Lech/Zürs, Austria p134
Monterosa Ski, Italy p389
St Anton, Austria p179
Val-d'Isère/Tignes, France pp338/329
Verbier, Switzerland p461

SNOWPIX.COM / CHRIS GILL

Reliable snow in the Alps: this is Tignes (Val Claret) at Easter 2002, when the slopes of many lower resorts were as snowless as the Tignes car parks ➔

01285 642 555
www.handmade-holidays.co.uk
AITO ATOL PROTECTED 4479

POWDER PARADISES
Resorts with the snow, the terrain and (ideally) the lack of crowds that make for powder perfection
Alta/Snowbird, Utah pp547/560
Andermatt, Switzerland p417
Aspen-Snowmass, Colorado p504
Big Sky, Montana p564
Fernie, Canada p599
Grand Targhee, Wyoming p566
La Grave, France p262
Jackson Hole, Wyoming p566
Kicking Horse, Canada p605
Monterosa Ski, Italy, p389
Red Mountain, Canada, p589
Snowbasin, Utah p558
Ste-Foy, France p320

BLACK RUNS
Resorts with steep, mogully, lift-served slopes within the safety of the piste network
Alta/Snowbird, Utah pp547/560
Andermatt, Switzerland p417
Argentière/Chamonix, France p221
Aspen-Snowmass, Colorado p504
Beaver Creek, Colorado p511
Courchevel, France p242
Jackson Hole, Wyoming p566
Whistler, Canada p614
Winter Park, Colorado p540
Zermatt, Switzerland p478

CHOPAHOLICS
Resorts where you can quit the conventional lift network and have a day riding helicopters or cats
Aspen-Snowmass, Colorado p504
Crested Butte, Colorado p520
Fernie, Canada p599
Grand Targhee, Wyoming p566
Lech/Zürs, Austria p134
Monterosa Ski, Italy p389
Panorama, Canada p612
Verbier, Switzerland p461
Whistler, Canada p614
Zermatt, Switzerland p478

HIGH-MILEAGE PISTE-BASHING
Extensive intermediate slopes with big lift networks
Alpe-d'Huez, France p203
Davos/Klosters, Switzerland p428
Flims/Laax, Switzerland p435
Milky Way: Sauze d'Oulx (Italy), Montgenèvre (France) pp392/285
La Plagne, France p297
Portes du Soleil, France/Switz p305
Selva/Sella Ronda, Italy p397
Trois Vallées, France p336
Val-d'Isère/Tignes, France pp338/329
Whistler, Canada p614

MOTORWAY CRUISING
Long, gentle, super-smooth pistes to bolster the frail confidence of those not long off the nursery slope
Les Arcs, France p211
Aspen-Snowmass, Colorado p504
Breckenridge, Colorado p513
Cervinia, Italy p368
Cortina, Italy p373
Courchevel, France p242
Megève, France p267
La Plagne, France p297
La Thuile, Italy p407
Vail, Colorado p534

RESORTS FOR BEGINNERS
European resorts with gentle, snow-sure nursery slopes and easy longer runs to progress to
Alpe-d'Huez, France p203
Les Arcs, France p211
Cervinia, Italy p368
Courchevel, France p242
Flaine, France p256
Montgenèvre, France p285
Pamporovo, Bulgaria p641
La Plagne, France p297
Saas-Fee, Switzerland p450
Soldeu, Andorra p634

MODERN CONVENIENCE
Alpine resorts where there's plenty of slope-side accommodation to make life easy
Les Arcs, France p211
Avoriaz, France p217
Courchevel, France p242
Flaine, France p256
Les Menuires, France p273
Obertauern, Austria p155
La Plagne, France p297
Puy-St-Vincent, France, p307
Valmorel, France p350
Val-Thorens, France p355

WEATHERPROOF SLOPES
Alpine resorts with snow-sure slopes if the sun shines, and trees in case it doesn't
Les Arcs, France p211
Courchevel, France p242
Courmayeur, Italy p378
Flims, Switzerland p435
Montchavin/Les Coches, France p297
Schladming, Austria p167
Selva, Italy p397
Serre-Chevalier, France p314
Sestriere, Italy p405
La Thuile, Italy p407

BACK-DOOR RESORTS
Cute little Alpine villages linked to big, bold ski areas, giving you the best of two different worlds
Les Brévières (Tignes), France p329
Champagny (La Plagne), France p297
Leogang (Saalbach), Austria p160
Montchavin (La Plagne), France p297
Peisey (Les Arcs), France p211
Le Pré (Les Arcs), France p211
Samoëns (Flaine), France, p256
St-Martin (Three Valleys), France p322
Stuben (St Anton), Austria p134
Vaujany (Alpe-d'Huez), France p203

SNOW-SURE BUT SIMPATICO
Alpine resorts with high-rise slopes, but low-rise, traditional-style buildings
Andermatt, Switzerland p417
Arabba, Italy p397
Argentière, France p221
Les Contamines, France p240
Ischgl, Austria p123
Lech/Zürs, Austria p134
Monterosa Ski, Italy p389
Obergurgl, Austria p150
Saas-Fee, Switzerland p450
Zermatt, Switzerland p478

SPECIALLY FOR FAMILIES
Alpine resorts where you can easily find accommodation surrounded by snow, not by traffic and fumes
Les Arcs, France p211
Avoriaz, France p217
Flaine, France p256
Lech, Austria p134
Montchavin (La Plagne), France p297
Mürren, Switzerland p446
Risoul, France p309
Saas-Fee, Switzerland p450
Valmorel, France p350
Wengen, Switzerland p473

SPECIAL MOUNTAIN RESTAURANTS
Alpine resorts where the mountain restaurants can really add an extra dimension to your holiday
Alpe-d'Huez, France p203
La Clusaz, France p234
Courmayeur, Italy p378
Kitzbühel, Austria p128
Megève, France p267
St Johann in Tirol, Austria p187
St Moritz, Switzerland p455
Selva, Italy p397
Söll, Austria p173
Zermatt, Switzerland p478

DRAMATIC SCENERY
Resorts where the mountains are not just high and snowy, but spectacularly scenic too
Chamonix, France p221
Cortina, Italy p373
Courmayeur, Italy p378
Heavenly, California p490
Jungfrau resorts (Grindelwald, Mürren, Wengen), Switzerland pp440/446/473
Lake Louise, Canada p607
Saas-Fee, Switzerland p450
St Moritz, Switzerland p455
Selva, Italy p397
Zermatt, Switzerland p478

VILLAGE CHARM
Resorts with traditional character that enriches your holiday – from mountain villages to mining towns
Alpbach, Austria p102
Champéry, Switzerland p421
Courmayeur, Italy p378
Crested Butte, Colorado p520
Lech, Austria p134
Mürren, Switzerland p446
Saas-Fee, Switzerland p450
Telluride, Colorado p532
Wengen, Switzerland p473
Zermatt, Switzerland p478

LIVELY NIGHTLIFE
European resorts where you'll have no difficulty finding somewhere to boogy, and someone to do it with
Chamonix, France p221
Ischgl, Austria p123
Kitzbühel, Austria p128
Saalbach, Austria p160
St Anton, Austria p179
Sauze d'Oulx, Italy p392
Sölden, Austria p171
Pas de la Casa, Andorra p632
Val-d'Isère, France p338
Verbier, Switzerland p461

OTHER AMUSEMENTS
Alpine resorts where those not interested in skiing or boarding can still find plenty to do
Bad Gastein, Austria p104
Chamonix, France p221
Cortina, Italy p373
Davos, Switzerland p428
Gstaad, Switzerland p444
Innsbruck, Austria p119
Kitzbühel, Austria p128
Megève, France p267
St Moritz, Switzerland p455
Zell am See, Austria p194

Resort shortlists

93

Resort chapters explained

FINDING A RESORT

The bulk of the book consists of chapters devoted to individual major resorts, some also covering minor resorts that share the same lift system. These chapters are ordered alphabetically and grouped by country – first, the four major Alpine countries in alphabetical order; then the US and Canada (where resorts are grouped by states or regions); then Andorra, followed by minor European countries; then Australasia.

There's a **chapter-by-chapter listing** in the detailed Contents at the start of the book.

Short cuts to the resorts that might suit you are provided by a table of comparative **star-ratings** and a series of **shortlists** of resorts with particular merits. To find these, just turn back a few pages towards the front of the book.

At the back of the book is an **index** to the resort chapters, combined with a **directory** giving basic information on hundreds of other minor resorts. Where the resort you are looking up is a minor resort covered in a chapter devoted mainly to a bigger resort, the page reference will take you to the start of that chapter, not to the page on which the minor resort is described.

There's further guidance on using our information in the chapter on Choosing your resort – designed to be helpful particularly to people with narrow experience of resorts, who may not appreciate how big the differences can be.

READING A CHAPTER

The **cost** of visiting each resort is rated on a scale of one to six – ① to ⑥ – reflecting the typical cost of a one-week trip based on a half-board package from the UK, plus a lift pass and an allowance for lunch in mountain restaurants. We assume two people sharing a room – even in the US, where package prices are often based on four people sharing.

Star-ratings summarise our view of the resort in 11 respects, including how well it suits different standards of skier/boarder. The more stars, the better.

We give phone and fax numbers and Internet addresses of the **tourist office** and phone numbers for recommended **hotels.**

The UK tour operators offering **package holidays** in each resort are listed in the index at the back of the book, not in the main chapters.

Our **mountain maps** show the resorts' own gradings of runs – so those for the US and Canada show green, blue and black runs, and no red ones (unlike Europe). On some maps we also follow the North American convention of using black diamonds to indicate open expert terrain where the runs are not precisely defined. We do not distinguish single-diamond terrain from the steeper double-diamond terrain.

We show all the lifts on the mountain, including any definitely planned for construction for the coming seasons. We use the following symbols to identify **fast or high-capacity lifts**:

🚡 fast chair-lift

🚠 gondola

🚟 cable-car

🚋 funicular railway

Austria is a completely different holiday experience from the other Alpine countries. If you have never been there you will notice a huge difference – many people who discover it fall in love with it and never want to go anywhere else. One essential ingredient is that the partying is as important as the skiing or riding in most Austrian resorts – après-ski starts early and finishes late. The other essential ingredient is the nature of the villages. There are none of the monstrous purpose-built block resorts of France and few big resorts or places with steep, challenging slopes such as St Anton. Essentially Austria is the land of cute little villages clustered around onion-domed churches; of friendly wooded mountains, reassuring to beginners and timid intermediates in a way that bleak snowfields and craggy peaks will never be; of friendly, welcoming people who don't find it demeaning to speak their guests' language; and of jolly alcohol-fuelled après-ski action, starting in many resorts in mid-afternoon with dancing in on-mountain restaurants and going on as long as you have the legs for it. And Austrian resorts have made great strides in their attempt to catch up on the snowmaking front – most have radically increased their snowmaking capacity in recent years. In midwinter, especially, lack of snow generally goes hand in hand with low night-time temperatures, even at low altitudes, and snowmaking comes into its own. And last season was a bumper year for Austria – while many resorts elsewhere in the Alps suffered from bare slopes, Austria got some big early-season snowfalls.

It's the après-ski that strikes most first-time visitors as being Austria's unique selling point. The few French resorts that have lively après-ski are dominated by British or Scandinavian holidaymakers (and resort workers); the French themselves are noticeable by their absence and you could be in London or Stockholm rather than France.

But Austrian après-ski remains very Austrian. Huge quantities of beer and schnapps are drunk, German is the predominant language and German drinking songs are common. So is incredibly loud

95

HAUS IN ENNSTAL TO

Cheerful mountain restaurants are a key ingredient in the Austrian recipe ↓

Europop music. People pack into mountain restaurants at the end of the day and dance in their ski boots on the dance floor, on the tables, on the bar, on the roof beams, wherever there's room. There are open-air ice bars on the mountain, umbrella bars and countless transparent 'igloos' in which to shelter from bad weather. In many resorts the bands don't stop playing and the DJs don't stop working until darkness falls, when the happy punters slide off down the mountain in the dark to find another watering hole in town. After dinner the drinking and dancing starts again – for those who take time out for dinner, that is. Of course, not all Austrian resorts conform to this image. But lots of big-name ones with the best and most extensive slopes do. St Anton, Saalbach-Hinterglemm, Ischgl, Sölden and Zell am See, for example, fit this bill.

One thing that all Austrian resorts have in common is reliably comfortable accommodation – whether it's in 4-star hotels with pools, saunas and spas, or in great-value family-run guest houses, of which Austria has thousands. The accommodation scene is very much dominated by hotels and guest houses; catered chalets and self-catered apartments are in general much less widely available (though there are one or two resorts, such as St Anton and Kitzbühel, where catered chalets are more easily come by).

Most Austrian resorts are real, friendly villages on valley floors, with skiing and boarding on the wooded slopes above them. They have expanded enormously since the war, but practically all the development has been in traditional chalet style, and the villages generally look good even without the snow that is the saving grace

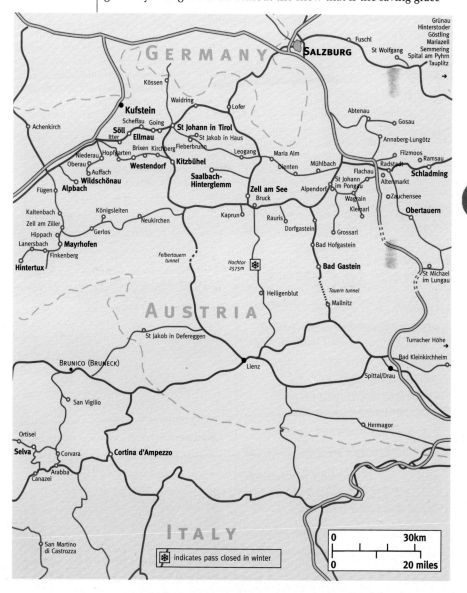

indicates pass closed in winter

of many French and even some Swiss resorts. Unlike Courchevel and Verbier, many Tirolean resorts are as busy in August as in February.

Outside the big-name resorts the skiing is often quite limited. There are many Austrian resorts that a keen skier could explore fully in half a day. Those who start their skiing careers in such resorts may not be worried by this; those who have tried the bigger areas of France and developed a taste for them may find the list of acceptable Austrian resorts quite a short one.

Unfortunately, several of the resorts on that shortlist bring you up against another problem – low altitude, and therefore poor snow conditions. Kitzbühel is at 760m/2,500ft and Söll at 700m/2,300ft, for example. The top heights of Austrian resorts are relatively low, too – typically 1800m to 2000m (5,900ft to 6,500ft); as we have noted above, snowmaking is becoming more widespread, but it works only when the conditions are right. The resorts of the Arlberg, at the western end of the Tirol – St Anton, Lech and Zürs – stand apart from these concerns, with excellent snow records and extensive skiing. And there are other resorts where you can be fairly confident of good snow, such as Obergurgl, Obertauern and Ischgl, not to mention the year-round slopes on glaciers such as those at Hintertux, Neustift, Kaprun and Sölden. But for many other resorts our advice is to book late, when you know what the snow conditions are like.

There are some extensive areas of slopes that are little-known in the UK and well worth considering. Bad Gastein, Schladming, Ischgl, Sölden and Lech spring to mind.

Snowboarders don't need big areas; and snowboarding in slushy snow is not as unpleasant as skiing in it. So it's not surprising that boarding in Austria is booming.

Nightlife is not limited to drinking and dancing. There are lots of floodlit toboggan runs and UK tour operator reps organise Tirolean, bowling, fondue, karaoke and other evenings. And not all resorts are raucous. Lech and Zürs, for example, are full of rich, cool, beautiful people enjoying the comfort of 4-star sophisticated hotels. And resorts such as Niederau in the Wildschönau and Westendorf and Alpbach in the Tirol are pretty, quiet, family resorts.

Austrian resorts are now easier to get to independently using cheap flights. Go (now taken over by EasyJet) has had flights from London Stansted to Munich for several years. Last season, Ryanair started flights from Stansted to Salzburg, giving very short transfer times to lots of Austrian resorts. In the summer it also started flights to Klagenfurt in Carinthia and to Friedrichshafen, just over the German border and handy for resorts in western Austria. These resorts can also be reached via Zürich, which EasyJet has regular flights to.

GETTING AROUND THE AUSTRIAN ALPS

The dominant feature of Austria for the ski driver is the thoroughfare of the Inn valley, which runs through the Tirol from Landeck via Innsbruck to Kufstein. The motorway along it extends, with one or two breaks, westwards to the Arlberg pass and on to Switzerland. This artery is relatively reliable except in exceptionally bad conditions – the altitude is low, and the road is a vital transport link.

The Arlberg – which divides Tirol from Vorarlberg, but which is also the watershed between Austria and Switzerland – is one of the few areas where driving plans are likely to be seriously affected by snow. The east–west Arlberg pass itself has a long tunnel underneath it; this isn't cheap, and you may want to take the high road when it's clear, through Stuben, St Christoph and St Anton. The Flexen pass road to Zürs and Lech (which may be closed by avalanche risk even when the Arlberg pass is open) branches off just to the west of the Arlberg summit.

At the eastern end of the Tirol, the Gerlos pass road from Zell am Ziller over into Salzburg province can be closed. Resorts in Carinthia, such as Bad Kleinkirchheim, are usually reached by motorway thanks to the Tauern and Katschberg tunnels. The alternative is to drive over the Radstädter Tauern pass through Obertauern, or use the car-carrying rail service from Böckstein to Mallnitz.

Get next year's edition free

There are too many hotels, nightspots and mountain restaurants for us to see them all every year – so we need reports on your holiday experiences. As usual, the 100 best reports will earn free copies of next year's edition.

We want to know:

- what you particularly **liked and disliked** about the resort
- what aspects of the resort came as a **surprise** to you
- your suggestions for **changes to our evaluation** of the resort
- your experience of lift **queues** and of the **ski school** and associated childcare
- your feedback on other **individual facilities** – hotels, bars, restaurants etc.

e-mail: reports@snow-zone.co.uk
mail: our address is at the front of the book; we'll send a form if you like.

The Heart of the Alps. The Soul of Winter. Quality holidays. Traditional hospitality.
Affordable prices. Discover Tirol's Premier Collection and more by visiting our website today:
www.livingroom.tirol.at

Traditional charm for those who like familiar slopes

WHAT IT COSTS

HOW IT RATES

The slopes
Snow	**
Extent	*
Experts	*
Intermediates	**
Beginners	****
Convenience	**
Queues	***
Restaurants	***

The rest
Scenery	***
Resort charm	*****
Off-slope	***

Premier Collection

102

➕ Charming traditional village with a relaxed atmosphere

➕ Good, varied, intermediate terrain, not without challenges for experts

➕ Handy central nursery slopes

➕ Short transfers from Innsbruck

➕ Several other worthwhile resorts within day-trip distance

➖ Limited slopes

➖ Main slopes are a shuttle-bus-ride away from the centre

➖ Few long easy runs for beginners to progress to

➖ Low altitude means lower slopes can suffer from poor snow – though a north-facing aspect and increased snowmaking have helped

Alpbach is an old British favourite – there is even a British club, the Alpbach Visitors. It is exceptionally pretty and friendly – 'It has great character and atmosphere,' says one visitor – and its small mountain is not without interest, even for experts. It's the kind of place that inspires loyalty in its visitors – a regular reporter who has been going for 20 years claims only junior status.

THE RESORT
Alpbach is near the head of a valley, looking south across it towards the Wiedersbergerhorn, where most of the slopes are to be found. It's captivating both in summer and winter, and has won awards for its outstanding beauty. Traditional chalets crowd around the pretty church (the graves are lit by candles every night), and the nursery slopes are only a few steps away.

Alpbach is small, but not necessarily convenient. The main village is the place to stay for atmosphere and après-ski, but involves using a free shuttle-bus to and from Achenwirt, a mile away, where the main gondola goes up to Hornboden. The backwater hamlet of Inneralpbach (about a mile south-east of Alpbach itself) is much more convenient for the slopes, with its own lifts up to the central ridge at Gmahkopf – just above Hornboden.

The Inn valley is a few miles north, and trips east to Kitzbühel or west to Innsbruck are possible. The Hintertux and Stubaier glaciers are within reach.

THE MOUNTAIN
Alpbach's slopes, on two flanks of the Wiedersbergerhorn, are small and simple. Piste grooming is excellent.
Slopes Chair-lifts and drags serve the open, north-facing slopes above the tree line, with black runs following the lift lines and reds (and a single blue) take less direct routes. The runs are mostly of 200m to 400m (650ft to 1,300ft) vertical, but you get 500m/1,650ft down the second stage of the gondola, and a full 1000m/3,300ft when snow is good enough to ski to valley level. Behind Gmahkopf is a short west-facing slope where a new quad chair-lift is due to replace one of the Muldenlift drags for 2002/3. The small area at Reith (about 3km/2 miles down the valley from Achenwirt) is on the lift pass and a new eight-seat gondola opened here for the 2001/02 season.
Snow reliability Alpbach cannot claim great snow reliability; but at least most slopes face north. The village nursery slope and, increasingly, other runs (including the home run

MOUNTAIN FACTS

Altitude	670m-2025m
	2,200ft-6,645ft
Lifts	19
Pistes	45km
	28 miles
Blue	15%
Red	70%
Black	15%
Snowmaking	25km
	16 miles

What's new

An eight-seater gondola replaced the single-seater chair to the top of Reith for 2001/02. More snowmaking has been installed on the main slopes down to the valley in recent years.

For 2002/3 a new four-person chair-lift is due to replace one of the Muldenlift drags behind Gmahkopf.

Plans for a lift link between Alpbach and Reith, and another one linking with Schatzberg in the Wildschönau area, are still on the drawing board.

Phone numbers

From elsewhere in Austria add the prefix 05336.
From abroad use the prefix +43 5336.

TOURIST OFFICE

Postcode A-6236
t 6000
f 600200
info@alpbach.at
www.alpbach.at

down to the gondola base station) have snowmaking.

Experts Alpbach isn't ideal, but the reds and the three blacks are not without challenge, and runs of 1000m/3,300ft vertical are not to be sniffed at. There are a number of off-piste routes to the valley, short tours are offered, and the schools apparently take the top classes off-piste.

Intermediates There is fine intermediate terrain; the problem is that it's limited. This resort is for practising technique on familiar slopes, not high mileage.

Beginners Beginners love the sunny nursery slopes beside the village. But the main slopes are not ideal for confidence-building: most are classified red (there are only a couple of blues).

Snowboarding There's some good free-riding terrain and a half-pipe near the top of the main gondola.

Cross-country 24km/15 miles of pretty cross-country trails rise up beyond Inneralpbach; the most challenging is about 8km/5 miles long and climbs 300m/1,000ft.

Queues Serious queues are rare, thanks to the efficient gondola and the recent chair-lift upgrades. At busy times, the Inneralpbach chair-lift is quieter than the Achenwirt gondola.

Mountain restaurants The area has squeezed in many mountain restaurants. Recommended are the Hornboden at the top of the gondola, the cosy Böglalm above Inneralpbach, the Kolberhof, and the Asthütte (Kafner Ast) for the sun. Achenwirt, at the lift base, doesn't really count as a mountain restaurant, but it is enthusiastically recommended.

Schools and guides Alpbach and Alpbach Aktiv are the two main ski schools. We have had excellent reports on both in the past, but the Alpbach school currently enjoys better support. Both take children.

Facilities for children Babysitters can be arranged by the tourist office.

STAYING THERE

How to go Hotels and pensions dominate in UK packages.

Hotels Of the smart 4-star places, the Alpbacherhof (5237) and ancient Böglerhof (52270) get most votes. But simpler Haus Thomas (5944) – 'very clean ... you feel like part of the family' – and Haus Angelika (5339) are recommended by visitors. The Alphof (5371) is 'excellent', as long as your room is not above the disco.

Self-catering Some self-catering is available via the tourist office and the Alpbach Visitors Club.

Eating out The Reblaus, and hotels Jakober, Berghof and Post ('superb', says a recent report) are popular, as is the Wiedersbergerhorn in Inneralpbach – worth a taxi-ride. The Rossmoos Inn is also recommended for its lively Tirolean evenings and 'superb' food.

Après-ski At peak times this is typically Tirolean, with lots of noisy tea-time beer-swilling in the bars of central hotels such as the Jakober and the Post. In the evening the Waschkuchl Pub is good for a drink. The Birdy Pub and Weinstadl disco have late-night dancing.

Off the slopes There are pretty walks and trips to Innsbruck and Salzburg. There's also an indoor swimming pool and an outdoor ice-skating rink.

Alpbach

103

Wiedersbergerhorn
2025m/6,640ft
Gmahkopf 1900m
Hornboden 1850m
1230m
Inneralpbach 1050m/3,440ft
1345m
1280m/4,200ft
Wölzenberg
Achenwirt 830m
Alpbach 1000m/3,280ft
Reith im Alpbachtal

Bad Gastein

1080m/3,540ft

Spa-town resort with extensive slopes and surprisingly few British visitors

104

WHAT IT COSTS

HOW IT RATES

The slopes

Snow	★★★
Extent	★★★★
Experts	★★★
Intermediates	★★★★
Beginners	★★
Convenience	★★
Queues	★★★
Restaurants	★★★★

The rest

Scenery	★★★
Resort charm	★★★
Off-slope	★★★★

What's new

Nightskiing is being introduced for 2002/03 with floodlights installed on the Bucheben piste near the Stubnerkogel valley station. It will be open every Wednesday from 6.30 to 9pm.

2002/03 will see the old triple chair from the Angertal up towards Stubnerkogel replaced by a high-speed quad – which will reduce queues here and speed the journey from Schlossalm to Stubnerkogel.

In 2001/02 both Schlossalm's Weitmoser parallel T-bars were replaced by a new six-pack and the old Gastein ski pass was replaced by the new Ski Alliance Amadé joint lift pass – see separate section on lift passes.

➕ Four separate, varied areas with a huge number of slopes both above and below the tree line

➕ Great for confident intermediates, with lots of long, challenging reds – and great cruising and carving in the Schlossalm sector

➕ More reliable snow than in most low-altitude Austrian resorts, with high Sportgastein area as back-up

➕ Lots of good, atmospheric, traditional mountain restaurants

➕ Plenty of off-slope facilities, many related to its origins as a spa resort

➕ Ski Alliance Amadé lift pass covers wide range of nearby resorts

➖ Unless you have a car, you need to choose your location with care or budget for a lot of taxi rides – the lift bases are widely spread and using the public transport can be time-consuming and frustrating

➖ Spa-town atmosphere is not to everyone's taste, and downtown Bad Gastein can suffer from local traffic on the narrow streets; more spacious Bad Hofgastein is a better base for many people

➖ Near-beginners and timid intermediates must be wary of leaving the Schlossalm sector

The Gastein valley isn't widely known internationally. It deserves better: it's a great resort for competent intermediates who are happy on genuine red runs, and the list of drawbacks we've identified above is short.

With its grand hotels, trinket shops and cramped, steep setting, central Bad Gastein itself is a far cry from your standard chalet-style Austrian village. You might prefer it. If not, staying out of the centre near the lifts offers a more normal winter-sports holiday experience, and both Bad Hofgastein and Dorfgastein, down the valley, are equally well worth considering as a base.

To make the most of the valley, you need a car. With five spread-out mountains, of which only two are linked, the valley needs a top-notch public transport system, and it doesn't have one – travelling from one end of the valley to the other can take over an hour and may involve a couple of changes.

MOUNTAIN FACTS

Figures relate to the
Gastein valley and
Grossarl areas only

Altitude 840m-2685m
          2,760ft-8,810ft
Lifts   51
Pistes   200km
                124 miles
Blue   24%
Red   66%
Black   10%
Snowmaking   93km
                 58 miles
Recco detectors used

LIFT PASSES

2002/03 prices in
euros

**Ski Alliance Amadé
Ski Pass**

The lift pass covers
over 275 lifts in more
than 30 ski resorts in
this part of Austria:
the Gastein valley and
Grossarl; Salzburger
Sportwelt (main
areas: Flachau/
Wagrain/ St Johann
and Zauchensee/
Kleinarl); Hochkönigs
Winterreich (Maria
Alm and neighbours).
Buses, trains and
road tolls between
the resorts are
covered by the pass.
Main pass
1-day pass 32.50
(low season 30)
6-day pass 156
(low-season 146)
Children
Under 6: free pass
6-15: 6-day pass 78
(low season 73)
15–18: 6-day pass 144
(low season 136)
Notes Morning and
afternoon tickets are
also available (as are
tickets from 11am,
1pm and 2pm on).
1½-day and 2½-day
tickets are also
possible.

BAD GASTEIN TOURIST OFFICE

← The block-like
buildings may not be
to everyone's taste
but the slopes are
great

The resort

Bad Gastein sits near the head of
eastern Austria's Gastein valley. It is an
old spa that had its heyday many years
ago; it has now spread widely, but still
has a compact core. Here, a bizarre
combination of buildings (smart,
modern, hotel-shopping-casino
complex; baroque town hall; concrete
multi-storey car park) are laid out in a
cramped horseshoe, set in what is
virtually a gorge, complete with
waterfall crashing beneath the main
street. It mainly attracts a quite formal
German/Austrian clientele. The main
road and railway bypass the centre –
though it can still get choked with
local traffic.

Up the hill above the centre of the
town, beside the railway, is a modern
suburb with more of a ski-resort feel.
For easy access to the slopes, this is
the place to be – a gondola gives
direct access to Stubnerkogel. On the
other side of the town is a second
mountain, Graukogel, accessed by a
chair-lift starting a bus-ride from the
centre.

A few miles down the valley is Bad
Hofgastein – also a spa, but a more
modern and less stuffy-feeling village
in an open setting on the wide valley
floor. The slopes of Schlossalm –
linked to Stubnerkogel via the
intervening valley of Angertal – are
accessed by a funicular from the
outskirts of Bad Hofgastein. But you
need a bus to get to it from the wrong
side of the sprawling resort.

Dorfgastein is a more relaxed and
rustic village a little further down the
valley. Dorfgastein has its own
extensive slopes, accessed by chair-
lifts starting well outside the village,
linked with the slopes of Grossarl in
the next valley to the east.

Sportgastein is a separate sector, at
the head of the Gastein valley, with
little in the way of resort development.

Buses and trains covered by the lift
pass run between the villages and lift
stations. There is a confusing range of
bus services running at least hourly
throughout the day, half-hourly on
some routes at peak times; this
sounds inadequate, and reporters
confirm that it is. A car is most
definitely an asset if you want to get
around easily.

The Ski Alliance Amadé lift pass
covers over 30 resorts in five areas in

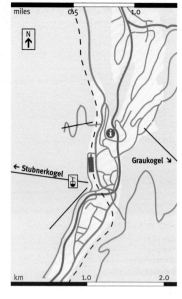

eastern Austria – see margin. The
linked resorts of Alpendorf, Wagrain
and Flachau are easily reached by a
regular train service to St Johann im
Pongau, near Alpendorf. From there it's
a short hop to the parallel linked area
of Kleinarl, Flachauwinkl and
Zauchensee. Further afield but worth a
visit is Schladming (also linked by rail
but involving at least one change).
Drivers can also visit Maria Alm, to the
north of the Gastein valley.

Also worth visiting but not included
on the lift pass are Zell am See (easily
reached by rail) and snow-sure
Obertauern and Kaprun.

The mountains

Most of the runs are on the open
slopes above the tree line, though
there are runs to the lift stations at
valley level. The terrain is generally
quite challenging without being at all
extreme – only on Schlossalm is there
a large area of genuinely easy slopes.

THE SLOPES
Extensive but fragmented
Most people based in Bad Gastein or
Bad Hofgastein naturally spend most
of their time on the extensive slopes of
the main mountains, Stubnerkogel and
Schlossalm.

Stubnerkogel is the more
challenging mountain, with blue runs
forced to take roundabout routes.
There are runs in all directions from

↑ Snow reliability is good for a low-altitude Austrian resort

BAD GASTEIN TOURIST OFFICE

Down the valley, the extensive slopes of **Dorfgastein** and **Grossarl**, linked via Kreuzkogel, offer a good choice of runs arranged in three tiers – though there is no easy run to the valley. This area is unjustly neglected by those staying further up the valley.

SNOW RELIABILITY
Good for a low-altitude resort
Although the area is of typically Austrian low altitude, this part of the Alps has a relatively good snow record and there is snowmaking on crucial sections. There are a lot of lifts and runs above mid-station height, and the higher sector of Sportgastein is an important fallback.

FOR EXPERTS
More fast cruises than challenge
There are few black runs but there are long, challenging reds with steepish terrain for fast cruising or mogul-bashing, depending on the conditions.

Graukogel has the World Cup slopes, and provides some challenge on its upper slopes. The other main sectors have plenty of opportunities to go off-piste, with or without hiking.

Sportgastein is worth the trip – there are off-piste possibilities on the front of the mountain, and a long off-piste trail off the back drops almost 1500m/4,900ft from Kreuzkogel to Heilstollen in the valley (on the bus route). Check the bus times carefully or a long wait (or walk) could await you at the bottom. On the sunny opposite shoulder a reader reports 'enormous' fields of corn snow in spring.

Dorfgastein has the least demanding slopes in the area, but there is a fine black from mid-mountain to the valley.

FOR INTERMEDIATES
Not for leisurely cruisers
Good intermediates will love all the areas on the lift pass – more than enough to keep you happy for a week. A particular delight is the beautiful 8km/5 mile red run, well away from the

the peak giving about 500m/1,600ft vertical on the open slopes above the tree line and rather more in the woods below it.

Schlossalm is better suited to timid skiers, with drags and chair-lifts serving a wide area of gentle runs above mid-mountain. But the top lifts lead to some challenging terrain, and the Kleine Scharte cable-car takes you up a serious 750m/2,500ft vertical. The runs from Schlossalm down into Angertal are south-facing and low, but well covered by snowmaking, and there is always the option of riding down in the gondola that serves this mountainside.

The separate and much smaller **Graukogel** is a steep, straightforward mountain. With pistes running through the forest, the area is a great asset in bad weather and quiet at other times.

The higher, more exposed slopes of **Sportgastein**, 9km/6 miles south of Bad Gastein, have the best snow in the area and are served by an eight-person two-stage gondola; the descent totals an impressive 1065m/3,500ft, but there are few pistes – basically, variants on the long run back down to the lift.

boarding The Gastein valley has started to embrace boarding, at least on the slopes. There's a snowboard park with a half-pipe on Schlossalm, and the valley plays host to lots of specialist snowboard events. The area is not ideal for beginners – there are few easy slopes and there's still a fairly high proportion of drag-lifts (unavoidable when making the link between Bad Hofgastein and Bad Gastein, and between Dorfgastein and Grossarl). There's a fair bit to do in the evenings, but it's not as lively and as boarder-friendly as a lot of other Austrian resorts.

lifts, from Höhe Scharte down to Bad Hofgastein. The open north-facing slopes of Stubnerkogel down into Angertal are good, for both interest and snow-cover – try the red down to Hartlgut at the end of the day and a train-ride home after a few beers. The same is true of the Graukogel runs.

For early intermediates, the area as a whole is uncomfortably challenging. But Grossarl (linked to Dorfgastein) and Schlossalm are less demanding than other sectors, and the open bowl around the main cluster of restaurants at Schlossalm is splendid cruising (and carving) territory.

FOR BEGINNERS
Unsuitable slopes
Nursery slopes are scattered around the valley, but none combines convenience with reassuringly gentle gradients. The transition to longer runs is not an easy one, either.

FOR CROSS-COUNTRY
Extensive, but low and scattered
There are an impressive 90km/56 miles of trails, but all are along the valley floor, making only the small loop at Sportgastein reasonably reliable for snow. Another drawback is the scattered nature of the loops. Bad Hofgastein is by far the best base for cross-country skiing, with long trails stretching almost to Bad Gastein.

QUEUES
Buses can be a problem
There are few problems outside the peak season in late February. The powerful gondola at Sportgastein put paid to the queues that used to arise when conditions were poor elsewhere. Morning queues to get out of the valley and for the Bad Hofgastein mid-station cable-car are the worst. Peak period queues for the valley buses may be the biggest problem.

MOUNTAIN RESTAURANTS
One of the pleasures of this area
Numerous atmospheric, traditional huts are scattered around. Good value and good food are the norm. Bad Gastein's restaurants are more expensive than those in the rest of the valley. The Jungerstube has been recommended for its 'atmosphere and traditional food'.

Bad Hofgastein's smart Kleine Scharte at Schlossalm has a large terrace, plus yodelling!

Jolly places include Aeroplanstadl on the 8km/5 mile Höhe Scharte run, Hamburger Skiheim again at Schlossalm (with 'barbecue in the snow') and the Panoramastube in Dorfgastein. The Wengeralm, also above Dorf, is a cosy, upmarket refuge with a good terrace.

We've had good reports of the restaurants at Sportgastein.

Bad Gastein

107

Kreuzkogel 2685m/8,810ft

Graukogel 2100m

Stubnerkogel 2245m

Sportgastein 1600m

Böckstein

Kötschachtal

Bad Gastein 1080m/3,540ft

Hohe Scharte 2300m/7,550ft

Angertal 1200m

Schlossalm 2050m

Kleine Scharte

Grossarl

Dorfgastein ski area

Bad Hofgastein 860m/2,820ft

Kitzsteinalm 1300m

Dorfgastein ↘

SCHOOLS/GUIDES

2001/02 prices in euros

Gastein
Managers Werner Pflaum and Luigi Kravanoa
Classes 6 days
5hr: 10am-3pm, 1hr lunch; 3hr: 1pm-4pm
6 full days: 135
Private lessons
1hr 40; each additional person 10

CHILDCARE

The ski school runs a ski kindergarten.

There is a kindergarten at the Relais & Châteaux Grüner Baum hotel in Kötschachtal, taking children aged 3 to 8, from 9.30 to 4pm. Skiing is available, with a special lift.

GETTING THERE

Air Salzburg, transfer 2hr. Linz or Munich, transfer 3½hr.

Rail Mainline station in resort.

SCHOOLS AND GUIDES
English widely spoken
The school has a good reputation. But we have a report this year of a beginner being told she was too slow and that she should pay for private lessons. She was very upset at the instructor's arrogant attitude.

FACILITIES FOR CHILDREN
Reasonable
With its fragmented areas and rather serious slopes, Bad Gastein hardly seems an ideal resort for small children, but there are facilities for all-day care, of which the ski kindergarten at the Grüner Baum sounds the most inviting. There's a 'Fun Centre' with a variety of activities for kids at the top of the Stubnerkogel gondola.

Staying there

HOW TO GO
Packages mainly to hotels
Although apartments make up nearly 15% of the total beds available, British tour operators sell mainly hotel-based packages.
Chalets The nearest thing to a catered chalet is Ski Miquel's Tannenburg, a traditional-style old hotel run as a chalet-hotel. It is a short walk from the gondola and we've had good reports of its 'good atmosphere, very pleasant communal rooms and bar, and large en-suite bedrooms'; one reporter 'couldn't praise the food highly enough' and 'would definitely return'.
Hotels This is an upmarket spa resort,

and it has lots of smart hotels with good spa facilities – there are almost as many 4-star places as 3-star ones.
((((5) **Elisabethpark** (25510) Luxury hotel popular with Brits looking for excellent facilities, style, comfort and formality. Poorly placed for the slopes, but does run a courtesy bus.
(((4) **Salzburger Hof** (20370) 4-star with excellent spa facilities, a longish walk from the village gondola.
(((4) **Wildbad** (3761) Luxurious 4-star within walking distance of the main lift. 'Wonderful, excellent food, great service, not for families with young children,' says a reporter this year.
(((4) **Schillerhof** (2581) Reliable 3-star in good position, opposite Graukogel lift.
((((4) **Grüner Baum** (25160) Splendidly secluded Relais & Châteaux place, tucked away in the Kötschachtal.
(((3) **Mozart** (26860) Well placed for buses. Good, filling food.
(((3) **Alpenblick** (20620) Good value, informal 3-star; well placed for slopes.
Self-catering Plenty of apartments are available if you book them directly.

EATING OUT
Something for most tastes
There is a fair range of restaurants, including surprisingly fine Chinese and seafood places. The Bellevue Alm, a short way up Stubnerkogel, is one of the liveliest places to eat at (it's a half-hour walk from the centre of Bad Gastein or you can take the private chair-lift up) – there's a weekly folklore evening with traditional food

---

Selected chalet hotels in Bad Gastein

ACTIVITIES

Indoor Fitness centre (swimming, sauna, gym), thermal baths, squash, tennis, bowling, indoor golf, darts, casino, museum, theatre, concerts

Outdoor Natural ice rinks (skating and curling), sleigh rides, horse-riding, ice-climbing, toboggan runs, snow bikes, 35km/22 miles cleared paths

Bad Gastein phone numbers
From elsewhere in Austria add the prefix 06434.
From abroad use the prefix +43 6434.

BAD GASTEIN TOURIST OFFICE

Postcode A-5640
t 25310
f 253137
info@gastein.com
www.gastein.com

and dancing. The à la carte menus at the 3-star hotels Nussdorferhof and Mozart are good value. The Medeterran in the town centre has also been recommended.

APRES-SKI
Varied, but no oom-pah-pah

There are elegant tea rooms, sophisticated dances, numerous bars, discos and casinos, but the general ambience is rather subdued. This part of Austria has not imported the informal Tirolean-style 'oom-pah-pah' jollity. There is tea-dancing at the Bellevue Alm though. The Elisabethpark, Salzburger Hof, Weismayr, Eden and Lindenhof bars are all pleasant for a quiet drink. The Hexenhaüsl is a more informal little wooden schnapps bar.

Haeggblom's has live music, gets full of young Swedes and is 'brilliant', says a reporter. The Bunny Bar is more sophisticated than its name suggests.

The Gatz and High Life are the main clubs. The casino gives you a generous amount of free chips, so those with will power and/or luck can have a surprisingly inexpensive couple of hours there. Bowling and a casino trip are likely to be organised by tour operator reps.

OFF THE SLOPES
Great variety of things to do

Provided you don't mind the style of the place, Bad Gastein has a lot to offer off the slopes, whether you're active or not. The spas are supposed to have a regenerative effect thanks to the high radon content. The Gastein Healing Gallery is a highlight – a train takes you down into an old gold-digging tunnel where you can lie on benches inhaling radon in steam-room-like heat and humidity for a couple of hours. We find all this a bit strange: radon is a radioactive, carcinogenic gas, and we spend a fortune keeping it out of our homes in the UK. The Rock Pool is a large indoor pool hewn out of the rock, heated naturally by hot springs.

Meeting up the mountain is no problem for pedestrians, though getting to the best mountain restaurants isn't easy.

There are organised coach trips to Kitzbühel, Salzburg and Goldegg Castle, and trains run to the resorts of Zell am See and St Johann im Pongau.

Bad Hofgastein
860m/2,820ft

Bad Hofgastein is a sizeable, quiet, old spa village set spaciously in a broad section of the valley. It has an impressive Gothic church, traditional-style buildings, elegant quiet hotels, narrow alleys and a babbling brook. Everything is kept in pristine order.

THE RESORT

Although rather sprawling, the village has a pleasant pedestrianised area which acts as a central focus. Because of the spa 'cures' there's a relatively high number of people just pottering about during the day, notably at the curling rinks in Kurpark. The place looks very pretty in the evenings, under the soft glow of its lamps. The large spa building, the Kurzentrum, is rather a blot on the landscape.

The best location to stay is in the pedestrian zone, which is relatively handy for most things including the slopes. A high proportion of hotels are a long walk from the lift station – but there is a shuttle-bus.

THE MOUNTAINS

The Schlossalm sector above Bad Hofgastein is linked to the Stubnerkogel area via the Angertal valley, forming the largest body of slopes in the valley.

The slopes Bad Hofgastein's main access lift is a short funicular that takes you up to a mid-station at Kitzstein, above which most of the slopes are found. Here, you have a choice between a cable-car or two-stage chair up to Schlossalm.

Snow reliability Snowmaking is fairly extensive up to 2050m/6,730ft. But the low altitude of the town means that snow-cover down to the bottom is unreliable.

Experts There are no real challenges on the local pistes but there is ample opportunity to go off-piste.

Intermediates Good intermediates will enjoy the local slopes, especially the long red run from Hohe Scharte back down to town.

Beginners If you stay in Bad Hofgastein, you'll have to catch a bus to the limited nursery area at Angertal.

Snowboarding The blue runs between Schlossalm and Angertal form the largest network of beginner runs in the area; however, you need to negotiate a few drag-lifts to ride them all.

Bad Gastein

109

Bad Hofgastein phone numbers
From elsewhere in Austria add the prefix 06432.
From abroad use the prefix +43 6432.

BAD HOFGASTEIN TOURIST OFFICE
Postcode A-5630
t 71100
f 711031
info@badhofgastein.co.at
www.badhofgastein.com

Cross-country Bad Hofgastein makes a fine base for cross-country when its lengthy valley-floor trails have snow.

Queues Both the funicular and the much lower capacity cable-car above it can generate big queues (30 minutes in the rush hour during peak season is not unusual). At such times, the chair is an obvious alternative to the cable-car and there's closed-circuit TV at the funicular base station which shows you the situation up at the cable-car.

Mountain restaurants The Schlossalm area boasts some of the best mountain huts in the valley (see Bad Gastein information).

Schools and guides We have received complimentary reports of the ski schools in the past, but haven't heard from recent visitors.

Facilities for children The Angertal school runs the village ski kindergarten, which can be very inconvenient for parents. Lack of many English-speaking children to play with may be another drawback.

STAYING THERE

How to go Bad Hofgastein is essentially a hotel resort. The hotels tend to be large and of good quality, and many have their own fine spa facilities. Some are within easy walking distance of the funicular, a few provide courtesy transport, and most of the rest are close to bus stops.

Hotels The Palace Gastein (6715-0) is a big 4-star with superb leisure facilities, including pool and thermal baths. The elegant Germania (6232-0) is similarly comfortable.

The high-quality Norica (8391-0) is atypically modern in design, but is well positioned in the pedestrian zone. The Alpina (8475-0) is another well located 4-star, five minutes from the slopes. The Astoria (6277-0) is well appointed but quite poorly positioned and doesn't supply courtesy transport.

The Kurpark (6301) has been recommended for its good food, service and central location.

Self-catering Accommodation can be organised through the tourist office.

Eating out There is a good range of restaurants, and many hotels offer good formal dining. The Moserkeller is an intimate restaurant, and Pension Maier one of the better informal places. The Pyrkerhöhe, on the slopes just above town, is worth an evening excursion, and Da Dino is a popular pizza and pasta place.

Après-ski It is very quiet by Austrian standards. Some reporters have been disappointed; others have loved the peacefulness. There are, however, a few animated places around. The Picolo ice bar in the centre of town is lively immediately after the lifts close. Evergreen has a friendly atmosphere. Visions is a spacious modern disco, while Match Box and C'est la Vie have loud music and are full of teenagers.

Most of Bad Hofgastein's clientele prefer something more sedate. Café Weitmoser is an historic little castle popular for its cakes at tea-time. The outdoor bar of the Osterreichischer Hof is a pleasant spot to catch the last of the sun. Another atmospheric tea-time rendezvous is the Tennishalle. Later, the West End bar is a cosy place for a quiet drink. The Glocknerkeller in Hotel Zum Toni and the Rondo bar in Hotel Kärnten have live music in a low-key ambience.

The Bad Gastein casino provides taxis to and from Bad Hofgastein.

Off the slopes The Kurzentrum is at the centre of things, and is arguably an even more impressive spa facility than that of Bad Gastein. It has a splendid thermal pool, and offers a range of therapies. Other off-slope amenities include artificial and natural ice skating, indoor tennis, squash and sleigh rides. There are lovely walks.

Dorfgastein 830m/2,720ft

Those who prefer not to stay in large, commercialised villages should consider Dorfgastein. Prices are lower, and the atmosphere is friendlier and more informal – a contrast to its rather cold setting, sheltered from the sun.

The extensive slopes are more suitable for early intermediates than the steeps above Bad Gastein. Runs are long and varied, amid lovely scenery. Unfortunately the low-altitude nursery slopes can be cold and icy. Bad Hofgastein's funicular is 15 minutes away by bus.

There are a few shops and après-ski places, a short walk or bus-ride from the slopes. Café St Ruperb is a nice village pizzeria. The Kirchenwirt (7251) and Römerhof (7777) are comfortable hotels, while Pension Skihausl (7516) is cheaper, does good food, and is next to the slopes.

There is an outdoor heated pool with sauna-solarium, a bowling alley and a ski kindergarten.

Dorfgastein phone numbers
From elsewhere in Austria add the prefix 06433.
From abroad use the prefix +43 6433.

DORFGASTEIN TOURIST OFFICE
Postcode A-5632
t 7277
f 763737
tourismus.dorf@aon.at
www.salzburg.com/tourismus/dorfgastein

Ellmau
800m/2,620ft

A quiet base from which to access the extensive Ski Welt area

WHAT IT COSTS

HOW IT RATES

The slopes

Snow	**
Extent	****
Experts	*
Intermediates	****
Beginners	****
Convenience	***
Queues	****
Restaurants	**

The rest

Scenery	***
Resort charm	***
Off-slope	***

Premier Collection

MOUNTAIN FACTS

Altitude	620m-1830m
	2,030ft-6,000ft
Lifts	93
Pistes	250km
	160 miles
Blue	43%
Red	48%
Black	9%
Snowmaking	135km
	84 miles

➕ Part of Ski Welt, Austria's largest linked ski and snowboard area

➕ Pretty, easy slopes

➕ Excellent nursery slopes (but snow reliability can be a problem)

➕ Massive recent investment in snowmaking has paid off

➕ Cheap by Austrian standards

➕ Quiet, charming family resort – more appealing than neighbouring Söll

➖ Poor natural snow record but increased snowmaking does compensate

➖ Village a bus-ride from slopes

➖ Mostly short runs and little for experts or good intermediates

➖ Lack of nightlife other than rep-organised events

➖ Ski Welt slopes can get crowded at weekends and in high season

Like nearby Söll, Ellmau gives access to the large Ski Welt circuit, with good slopes for early intermediates. The resort is a pleasant, quiet alternative to Söll, and offers more amenities than other neighbours such as Scheffau.

Although Ellmau's natural snow record is poor, continuing investment in snowmaking has made a big difference. The snow may not always be in tip-top condition, but at least there'll be some. The lifts are constantly being updated to make it possible to move around the mountain more quickly.

THE RESORT

Ellmau sits at the north-eastern corner of the Ski Welt. Although sizeable and becoming more commercialised each year, it remains quiet, with traditional chalet-style buildings, welcoming bars and shops, and a pretty church.

Ellmau has a compact centre, but its accommodation is scattered and the buses around the resort, necessary if you stay in the village, attract complaint for being infrequent. The position of your hotel is, therefore, quite important.

Make sure you get an Ellmau guest card entitling you to various discounts, including to the Kaiserbad leisure centre.

THE MOUNTAINS

The Ski Welt is the largest mountain circuit in Austria. It links Going, Scheffau, Söll, Itter, Hopgarten and

What's new

Snowmaking capacity in the Ski Welt has been hugely increased in recent years to cover 135km/84 miles of pistes (over half the pistes in the Ski Welt) and is the largest snowmaking facility anywhere in Austria.

For 2002/03 a second gondola – an eight-seater – will run from Scheffau to the summit of Brandstadl, replacing the existing chair-lift.

A high-speed six-person chair-lift replaces a T-bar running from Brixen's mid-station to the top station.

Brixen. Most runs are not difficult, but we receive complaints that it is slow to get about, due to the number of short connecting runs and the piste map – the resorts are trying to remedy this by installing new high-speed lifts each year. Westendorf is covered by the Ski Welt pass, though its local slopes are not linked. Kitzbühel, Waidring, Fieberbrunn and St Johann are in easy reach for day trips and covered by the Kitzbüheler Alpenskipass.

Slopes Ellmau is close to the best slopes in the area, above Scheffau. The funicular railway on the edge of the village takes you up to Hartkaiser, from where a fine long red (a favourite with reporters) leads down to Blaiken (Scheffau's lift station). A choice of gondolas (one new for 2002/03) take you up to Brandstadl, the start of three varied, long alternative runs back to Blaiken.

Immediately beyond Brandstadl, the slopes become rather bitty; an array of short runs and lifts link Brandstadl to Zinsberg. From Zinsberg, excellent, long, south-facing pistes lead down to Brixen. Then it's a short bus-ride to Westendorf's pleasant separate area. Part-way down to Brixen you can head towards Söll, and if you head up Hohe Salve you get access to a long, west-facing run to Hopfgarten.

Ellmau and Going share a pleasant little area of slopes on Astberg, slightly apart from the rest of the area, and well suited to the unadventurous and families. One piste leads to the

↑ The centre of pretty Ellmau is a 20-minute hike or a bus-ride from its funicular, the main way up the mountain.

ALBIN NIEDERSTRASSE

funicular for access to the rest of Ski Welt. The main Astberg chair is rather inconveniently positioned, midway between Ellmau and Going.

Snow reliability With a low average height, and important links that get a lot of sun, the snowmaking that the Ski Welt has installed is essential. And the Ellmau-Going sector now claims almost all its slopes are covered by snowmaking. This can, of course, only be used when it is cold enough and it cannot prevent slush and icy patches forming. This year reporters experienced slushy, spring-like conditions as early as late January. The north-facing Eiberg area above Scheffau holds its snow well.

Experts There's are steep plunges off the Hohe Salve summit, and a little mogul field between Brandstadl and Neualm, but the area isn't really suitable unless you seek out off-piste opportunities. The ski route from Brandstadl down to Scheffau is a highlight and you can go off-piste with a guide from Brandstadl to Söll.

Intermediates With good snow, the Ski Welt is a paradise for early intermediates and those who love easy cruising. There are lots of blue runs and many of the reds deserve a blue grading. It is a big area and you get a feeling of travelling around. The main challenge is when the snow isn't

LIFT PASSES

2002/03 prices in euros

Ski Welt Wilder Kaiser-Brixental
Covers all lifts in the Wilder Kaiser-Brixental area from Going to Westendorf, and the ski-bus.
Beginners Points tickets (100 points 24). Most beginner lifts cost from 3 to 10 points.
Main pass
1-day pass 30
6-day pass 148.50 (low season 126)
Children
Under 16: 6-day pass 89 (low season 75.50)
Under 6: free pass
Short-term passes
Single ascent on some lifts, passes starting from 11am, noon, 1pm and 2pm.
Alternative periods
5 in 7 days, 7 in 10 days, 10 in 14 days.
Alternative passes
Kitzbüheler Alpenskipass covers five large ski areas: Schneewinkel (St Johann), Ski Region Kitzbühel, Ski Welt Wilder Kaiser, Wildschönau and Alpbachtal (adult 6-day 170, children 93.50).

Phone numbers
From elsewhere in Austria add the prefix 05358.
From abroad use the prefix +43 5358.

ELLMAU TOURIST OFFICE

Postcode A-6352
t 2301
f 3443
ellmau@netway.at
www.ellmau.com

GOING TOURIST OFFICE

Postcode A-6353
t 2438
f 3501
going@netway.at
www.going.at

The best company to
improve your skiing & boarding skills with

- Great range of accommodation - chalets, lodges, hotels and apartments
- Special group deals - up to 1 in 5 travel free, free lift passes for group leaders on selected dates

Call our experts for advice or a brochure
0870 33 33 347
or visit www.neilson.com
Share our passion for the slopes

neilson

perfect – ice and slush can make even gentle slopes seem tricky. In general, the most difficult slopes are those from the mid-stations to the valleys. For timid intermediates the easy slopes of Astberg are on hand to Ellmau guests.

Beginners Ellmau has an array of good nursery slopes, now covered by snowmaking. The main ones are at the Going end, but there are some by the road to the funicular. The Astberg chair opens up a more snow-sure plateau at altitude. The Brandstadl-Hartkaiser area has a section of short, easy runs, and a nice long piste running the length of the funicular, which even near-beginners can manage.

Snowboarding Ellmau is a good place to try boarding as the local slopes are easy. For decent boarders it is more limited, but there is a terrain-park and quarter-pipe near Söll.

Cross-country When there is snow, there are long, quite challenging trails, but trails at altitude are lacking.

Queues Continued introduction of new lifts has greatly improved this once queue-prone area.

Mountain restaurants The smaller places are fairly consistent in providing good-value food in pleasant surroundings, but the larger restaurants should be avoided. The Rübezahl above Ellmau is our favourite in the whole Ski Welt and the hut at Neualm has also been recommended. The larger self-service restaurants are functional (the Jochstube at Eiberg is an exception) and suffer queues. Going is a good spot for a quiet lunch.

Schools and guides The three schools have good reputations – except that classes can be very large. We had a good report about the Top School last year: 'Both our six-year-old and our adult friend were very pleased with the service and the way they progressed.' As well as the main schools there are

mountaineering schools that organise tours in the Wilder Kaiser and the Kitzbühel mountains.

Facilities for children Ellmau is an attractive resort for families. Kindergarten facilities seem to be satisfactory and include fun ideas such as a mini train to the lifts. We have had no recent reports, however.

STAYING THERE

How to go Ellmau is essentially a hotel and pension resort, though there are apartments that can be booked locally.
Hotels Bär (2395) is an elegant but relaxed Relais & Châteaux chalet, but twice the price of any other hotel. 'Luxury without pretensions,' said a reporter who found the weekly gala dinner 'outstanding'. Hochfilzer (2501) is central, well equipped (with outdoor hot-tub) and popular with reporters (as is the simpler Pension Claudia, which it owns – use of hotel facilities allowed).
Self-catering There is a wide variety. The Landhof apartments (with pool and sauna) were highly praised by a reporter: 'An absolute treasure.'
Eating out The hotel Hochfilzer has a reputation for good food and the Café Bettina, midway between the funicular and the town, is good for afternoon coffee and cakes.
Après-ski The rep-organised events include bowling, sleigh rides, Tirolean folklore and inner-tubing, but there is little else. The Memory bar and Dorfstüberl are favourites, though both are very quiet.
Off the slopes The Kaiserbad leisure centre is good. There are many excursions available, including Innsbruck, Salzburg, Rattenburg and Vitipeno. St Johann in Tirol is a nice little town only a few miles away by bus. Valley walks are spoiled by the busy main road.

Going 775m/2,540ft

Going is a tiny, attractively rustic village, well placed for the limited but quiet slopes of the Astberg and for the vast area of nursery slopes between here and Ellmau. Prices are low, but it's not an ideal place for covering the whole of the Ski Welt on the cheap.

Going is ideal for families looking for a quiet time, particularly if they have a car for transport to Scheffau or St Johann when the Astberg's low ru have poor snow.

Ellmau

111

Powerful new lifts, excellent snow, varied slopes and villages

WHAT IT COSTS

HOW IT RATES

The slopes

Snow	★★★★★
Extent	★★
Experts	★★★
Intermediates	★★★
Beginners	★
Convenience	★★
Queues	★★★
Restaurants	★★

The rest

Scenery	★★★
Resort charm	★★★
Off-slope	★

➕ Tux valley includes one of the best glaciers in the world, with some great runs for intermediates and experts on guaranteed good snow

➕ Massive investment in new lifts has created new links to Mayrhofen and speeded up access to the glacier

➕ Some excellent off-piste opportunities

➕ Choice of quiet, delightfully unspoiled, traditional villages you can stay in

➕ Short transfers from Innsbruck

➖ Need to take 15-minute free bus-ride to get between Lanersbach and Hintertux

➖ Not for those who want a huge choice of shops and throbbing nightlife on their doorstep

➖ Glacier can be cold and bleak in midwinter and although you can get from top to bottom by gondola, some of the best slopes are served by T-bars or slow chairs

The attraction of staying in the Tux valley was transformed in 2001/02 by new links between the local slopes and those above neighbouring Mayrhofen and Finkenberg, forming a big, new, interlinked circuit. Add this to the guaranteed 365-days-a-year good snow of the Hintertux glacier (now served by powerful new gondolas) and the chance to stay in a small, pretty, traditional Austrian mountain village and you have a beguiling combination.

MOUNTAIN FACTS

for Ski and Glacier World Zillertal 3000

Altitude	630m-3250m
	2,070ft-10,66oft
Lifts	65
Pistes	235km
	146 miles
Blue	28%
Red	57%
Black	15%
Snowmaking	86km
	54 miles

The Tux valley has a variety of small villages to stay in. Hintertux itself is at the head of the valley and right by the glacier. Vorderlanersbach is the first village you come to as you enter the valley and Lanersbach the next (5km/3 miles from Hintertux and 15 minutes by bus). Both are small, traditional villages with attractive old buildings and small roads and paths, and their centres are bypassed by the main road so they remain peaceful and quiet.

Both have gondola links into the local slopes, which are part of an extensive circuit now that they are linked to the Penken slopes above neighbouring Mayrhofen – see separate chapter.

Free buses from both villages run regularly and take you up the valley to Hintertux and the glacier. On the way they pass through the two other Tux villages of Juns and Madseit. A free night-bus also runs between the villages until 2am.

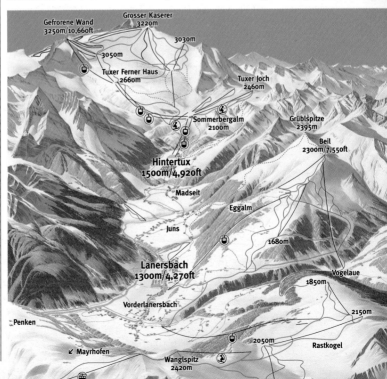

Tux has invested millions in its lift system in recent years. For 2001/02 the Eggalm/Rastkogel area above Lanersbach was linked with Mayrhofen's Penken slopes, via a new high-speed six-seater chair from Rastkogel with a new 150-person cable-car and a new piste to bring you back. This transforms the attraction of the Tux valley as a place to stay by opening up 143km/90 miles of lift-linked pistes.

The previous season (2000/01) saw the opening of powerful new gondolas on the Hintertux glacier, which whisk you from the base to the top of the glacier in under 20 minutes. These include the world's highest jumbo gondola, holding 24 people, and a new eight-person gondola from the base area.

For 2002/03 there will be a new indoor and outdoor après-ski venue at the bottom of the Hintertux lifts called the Hohenhaus-Tenne, which will have live music sometimes. The Almhit après bar opened by the hotel Neuhintertux last season.

There are some good rustic restaurants and bars and a few places along the valley with discos or live music. But nightlife tends to be quieter than in many bigger Austrian resorts (not a bad thing for many of us!).

The Tux valley is now part of what is called the Ski and Glacier World Zillertal 3000, which covers 232km/145 miles of slopes and 65 lifts. Two new lifts for 2001/02 linked for the first time the Eggalm and Rastkogel slopes above Lanersbach and Vorderlanersbach (reached by gondolas running from each village) with the Penken slopes above Finkenberg and Mayrhofen – forming a new circuit with 143km/90 miles of pistes. A new high-speed six-person chair takes you from Rastkogel to the top of the Penken slopes and a new 150-person cable-car brings you back.

Buses run all day between Lanersbach and Vorderlanersbach and the glacier slopes at Hintertux. The Hintertux area now has powerful new gondolas which take you all the way from the valley floor at 1500m/4,920ft to the top at 3250m/10,660ft in three stages and in under 20 minutes. The glacier is one of the best in the world, with varied terrain that attracts national ski teams for summer training.

In winter it provides guaranteed good snow even when lower resorts are suffering badly.

Lift passes of four days or more cover not only Ski and Glacier World Zillertal 3000 but also the whole Ziller valley: 153 lifts, 488km of pistes, the ski-buses and railway.

Hintertux 1500m/4,920ft

THE RESORT
Tiny Hintertux is bleakly set at the end of the Tux valley. It is little more than a small collection of hotels and guest houses; there is another, smaller group of hotels near the lifts, which lie a 15-minute walk away from the village, across a car park that fills with day-visitors' cars and coaches, especially when snow is poor in lower resorts.

THE MOUNTAINS
Hintertux's slopes are fairly extensive and, for a glacier, surprisingly challenging. On our last visit, when it was raining in lower resorts, we had a great time skiing powder.

Slopes A series of speedy new gondolas takes you up in three stages from the base to the top of the glacier (1750m/5,740ft vertical rise) in under 20 minutes. Two gondolas go from the

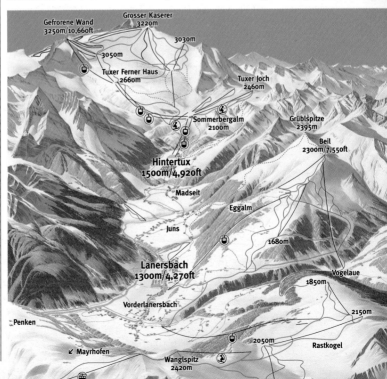

Gefrorene Wand
3250m/10,660ft

Grosser Kaserer
3220m

3030m

3050m

Tuxer Ferner Haus
2660m

Tuxer Joch
2460m

Sommerbergalm
2100m

Grüblspitze
2395m

Beil
2300m/7,550ft

Hintertux
1500m/4,920ft

Madseit

Eggalm

Juns

1680m

Lanersbach
1300m/4,270ft

Vogelaue

1850m

Vorderlanersbach

2150m

Penken

2050m

Rastkogel

↙ Mayrhofen

Wanglspitz
2420m

LIFT PASSES

2002/03 prices in euros

Ski and Glacier World Zillertal
Coverage depends on period – see notes.
Main pass
including glacier
1-day pass 34
6-day pass 161
Children
15 to 18: 6-day pass (including glacier) 129
6 to 14: 6-day pass (including glacier) 97
Under 6: free pass
Short-term passes
Passes available from 11am, 11.45am and 2pm.
Alternative periods
Ziller Valley Super Ski pass available for 4 days' skiing in 6, 5 days in 7, 6 days in 7 and 10 days in 14.
Notes Up to 3-day passes cover Hintertux glacier, Eggalm, Rastkogel and Penken areas; 4-day and over passes include all 153 Ziller valley lifts, 488km of piste, ski-bus and railway.

SCHOOLS/GUIDES

2002/03 prices in euros

Three schools in Tux:
Hintertux/Madseit, Happy Skiing Tux, **Luggi's** (prices are for Luggi's)

Classes 6 days
4hr: 6 days 116
Children's classes
Ages: 4 to 14
6 full days including lunch 153
Private lessons
1hr: 54 for 1 person, for each additional person 15

base to Sommerbergalm. From here two more gondolas, including a 24-person jumbo, go up to Tuxer Ferner Haus, beside the glacier. Then a short slope takes you down to another 24-person gondola, which whisks you up to Gefrorene Wand ('frozen face'). From Sommerbergalm, a fast quad chair serves the slopes below Tuxer Joch; from the top of this sector, an excellent secluded off-piste run goes down to the base station. Between the top of the glacier and Tuxer Ferner Haus there are further chairs and drag-lifts to play on and links across to another 1000m/3,300ft-vertical chain of lifts below Grosser Kaserer on the west. Behind Gefrorene Wand is the area's one sunny piste served by a triple chair. Descent to the valley involves a short ascent to Sommerbergalm on the way, now achieved by a six-seater chair-lift.
Snow reliability Snow does not come more reliable than this. Even off the glacier, the other slopes are high and face north, making for very reliable snow-cover. The runs from Tuxer Ferner Haus down to Sommerbergalm have snowmaking as well.
Experts There is more to amuse experts here than on any other glacier, with a couple of serious black runs at glacier level and steep slopes and ungroomed ski routes beneath. A lot of the off-piste is little used and one reporter this year said, 'We found untracked snow not far from the lifts two weeks after the last snowfall.'
Intermediates The area particularly suits good or aggressive intermediates. The long runs down from Gefrorene Wand and Kaserer are fun. And there is a pleasant, tree-lined ski route to the valley from Sommerbergalm and another from Tuxer Joch. Moderate intermediates will love the glacier.
Beginners The Hintertux glacier is not ideal for beginners.
Snowboarding There is Europe's highest World Cup half-pipe on the glacier (a popular hang-out throughout the summer), and a terrain-park. There are also some great off-piste opportunities. But boarders complain about the number of T-bars.
Cross-country See the Lanersbach information that follows.
Queues There used to be huge queues at Hintertux when snow was poor elsewhere. The splendid new lifts have largely solved this problem. But the main runs can get crowded, and then it

is best to head over to the quieter Keserer lifts and runs.
Mountain restaurants The mountain restaurants tend to get very crowded and the big self-service places lack charm. The 90-year-old Spannagelhaus is an exception and there are great views from Gletscherhütte, at the top.
Schools and guides There are three schools, which serve all the resorts in Tux, but we lack reports on them.
Facilities for children All three ski schools run children's classes for children aged 4 to 14 and lunch is provided.

STAYING THERE

How to go Most hotels are large and comfortable and have spa facilities, but there are also more modest pensions.
Hotels Close to the lifts are the 4-star Neuhintertux (8580) and Vierjahreszeiten (8525). We stayed in the Hintertuxerhof (85300) a short walk away and found it welcoming, with good food, sauna and steam room. Pensions Kössler (87490) and Willeiter (87492) are in the heart of the village.
Self-catering There are plenty of apartments.
Eating out Restaurants are mainly hotel-based. The Vierjahreszeiten cafe is pleasant and informal.
Après-ski There can be a lively après-ski scene at the bottom of the lifts as they shut, and a new venue is due to open this season. The Rindererhof has a popular tea dance, and there are a couple of local bars. The free night-bus gets you to and from the other villages until 2am, but Hintertux is not the place for keen clubbers.
Off the slopes The spa facilities are excellent but, in general, you're much better off in Mayrhofen if you don't want to use the slopes.

Vorderlanersbach/ Lanersbach 1300m/4,270ft

The attraction of staying in Lanersbach and neighbouring Vorderlanersbach has been transformed by the new link (for 2001/02) from the Rastkogel slopes above Vorderlanersbach directly into Mayrhofen's ski area.

THE RESORT

Lanersbach is an attractive, spacious, traditional village largely unspoiled by the busy road up to Hintertux that passes the main lift. Happily, the quiet centre near the pretty church is

Tux im Zillertal

1300 - 3250 m

Winter as far as the eye can see!

235 km of ski runs: • **37 km** • 135 km • 63 km

365 days of the year snowfun on the Hintertux Glacier

"The Glacier Tour" - a day's skiing of superlatives

rooms, Brochures, Information

Tourismusverband Tux, A-6293 Tux, Lanersbach 472, Tel. ++43/(0)5287/8506, Fax 8508

E-mail: info@tux.at, www.tux.at with search for available rooms

www.tux.at

The Hintertux glacier has great snow-sure slopes open 365 days a year →

TVB TUX / JB FANKHAUSER

CHILDCARE

All three ski schools run children's classes for children aged 4 to 14 where lunch is provided.

In Lanersbach, there is also a kindergarten for children aged 1 to 3 in the Tux Tourist Association building.

GETTING THERE

Air Salzburg, transfer 3½hr. Munich, transfer 3hr. Innsbruck, transfer 1½hr.

Rail Local line to Mayrhofen; regular buses from station.

ACTIVITIES

Indoor Bowling, tennis, squash, cave trekking, hotels with pools/saunas/ steam rooms/ solariums open to public, **Outdoor** Ice-skating rink, curling, 38km/24 miles of cleared paths, paragliding, tobogganing (2 runs of 5km/3 miles, 1 run of 3km/2 miles; all runs floodlit), snowshoe tours, ice climbing

Phone numbers
From elsewhere in Austria add the prefix 05287.
From abroad use the prefix +43 5287.

TUX TOURIST OFFICE

Postcode A-6293
t 8506
f 8508
info@tux.at
www.tux.at

bypassed by the road, yet within walking distance of the gondola up to Eggalm. The village is small and delightfully uncommercialised, but it has all you need in a resort. And prices are relatively low. Vorderlanersbach is even smaller, with a gondola up to the Rastkogel area.

THE MOUNTAINS

Slopes The slopes of Eggalm, accessed by the gondola from Lanersbach, have a high point at Beil, and a small network of pleasantly varied, mostly wooded pistes served by three other lifts and leading back to the village and across to Vorderlanersbach. From there you can take the Rastkogel gondola, which gives access to the new. high-speed, six-person chair-lift link with Mayrhofen's slopes. The area is also served by two old, slow chairs and two T-bars. There is no slope directly back to Vorderlanersbach (you take the gondola down), but there is a piste that leads to a chair-lift in the Eggalm sector.
Snow reliability Snow conditions are usually good, at least in early season; by Austrian standards, these are high slopes and there is some snowmaking on Eggalm, but the Vorderlanersbach sector, in particular, gets a lot of sun.
Experts There are no pistes to challenge experts, but there is a fine off-piste route starting a short walk from Beil and finishing at the village.
Intermediates The slopes suit intermediates best – especially now that they are linked in to Mayrhofen's Penken slopes.
Beginners Both areas have nursery slopes (as do Madseit and Juns) but there are few ideal progression slopes.
Snowboarding The Mayrhofen and Hintertux pipes and parks are easily accessed and floodlit boarding using the Hinterangerlift is popular.
Cross-country There are 14km/9 miles of cross-country trails, alongside the Tux creek, between Madseit and Vorderlanersbach, and a 6km/4 mile skating track in Juns/Madseit.
Queues We have no reports of any problems.
Mountain restaurants There are five marked on the map – usually quiet compared to those on the Penken.
Schools and guides There are three schools, which serve all the resorts in Tux, but we lack reports on them.
Facilities for children The non-ski nursery takes children aged from one

to three, and the schools take children from four years upwards.

STAYING THERE

How to go Lanersbach and Vorderlanersbach are essentially hotel-based resorts.
Hotels The Lanersbachherof (87256) is a good 4-star with pool, sauna, steam and hot-tub close to the lifts, but it is also on the main road. The cheaper 3-star Pinzger (87541) and Alpengruss (87293) are similarly situated. In Vorderlanersbach the 3-star Kirchlerhof (8560) is 'really friendly, with comfortable rooms and excellent food' says a reporter who visits each season.
Self-catering Quite a lot available.
Eating out Restaurants are mainly hotel-based.
Après-ski Nightlife is quiet by Austrian standards but there is a disco or two. We enjoyed the jolly Hühnerstall in Lanersbach (an old wooden building with traditional Austrian music) and the ancient wine bar in Vorderlanersbach.
Off the slopes Off-slope facilities are fairly good considering the size of the resorts. Some hotels have pools, hot-tubs and fitness rooms open to non-residents. There is a tennis centre in Vorderlanersbach which also has squash and bowling. Mayrhofen is a worthwhile excursion and Salzburg is just within range.

Innsbruck
575m/1,890ft

A cultured city base for a range of little ski resorts – and a big glacier

MOUNTAIN FACTS

Altitude	575m-3210m
	1,890ft-10,530ft
Lifts	63
Pistes	130km
	81 miles
Blue	35%
Red	42%
Black	23%
Snowmaking	34km
	21 miles

Premier Collection

What's new

The Mutters ski area will re-open for the 2002/03 season following construction of a new access gondola starting from a car park outside the village. Other new lifts will create an improved two-way link with Axamer Lizum's slopes.

Innsbruck is not a ski resort in the usual sense. It is an historic university city of 130,000 inhabitants, with a vibrant cultural life, set at a major Alpine crossroads, and a major tourist destination in summer. Its local slopes are of local interest. But the city has twice hosted the Olympic Winter Games, and it lies at the heart of a little group of resorts that share a lift pass and are accessible by efficient bus services. Among them, as it happens, is one of the three or four best glacier areas in the Alps – the Stubaier Gletscher. The area gets a boost this season with the re-opening of the slopes at Mutters, equipped with a new access gondola and improved links to Axamer Lizum.

The Inn valley is a broad, flat-bottomed trench hereabouts, but Innsbruck manages to fill it from side to side. It is a sizeable city, and as you would expect from its Olympic background it has an excellent range of winter sports facilities, as well as a captivating car-free medieval core. It has smart, modern, shopping areas, trendy bars and restaurants, museums (including, of course, one devoted to the Olympics), concert halls, theatres, a zoo and other attractions that you might seek out on a summer holiday, but normally wouldn't expect to find when going skiing.

Winter diversions off the slopes include 300km/185 miles of cross-country trails, some at valley level but others appreciably above it; curling and skating at the Olympic centre, including public ice-hockey sessions; several toboggan runs totalling 50km/30 miles, the longest (above

Birgitz) an impressive 10km/6 miles and 960m/3,150ft vertical; and rides on a four-man bob at Igls.

Not the least of the attractions of staying in such a place is that you don't pay ski resort prices for anything.

There are hotels, inns and guest-houses of every standard and style, with 3-star and 4-star hotels forming the nucleus. Among the more distinctive hotels are the grand 5-star Europa Tyrol (5931), the ancient 4-star Goldener Adler (571111) and the 3-star Weisses Kreuz (59479) in the central pedestrian zone, and the 4-star art nouveau Best Western Neue Post (59476).

As well as the traditional Austrian restaurants there's a wide choice of Italian ones, plus a smattering of more exotic alternatives from Mexican to Japanese.

There is an impressive 1400m/4,600ft vertical of slopes on the south-

LIFT PASSES

2002/03 prices in euros

Innsbruck Gletscher Skipass
Covers Seegrube–Nordkette, Patscherkofel (Igls), Axamer Lizum, Glungezer (Tulfes), Schlick 2000 (Fulpmes), Mutters, Stubaier Gletscher
6-day pass 145
Senior citizens
Over 60: 6-day pass 116
Children
Aged 7 to 15: 6-day pass 87
Super-Skipass
covers all the above plus one day in the Arlberg (St Anton) and one day in Kitzbühel
5 days out of 6 pass: 187.5 for adults
130 for children aged 7 to 15

Innsbruck & Igls phone numbers
Calling long-distance add the prefix 0512. From abroad use the prefix +43 512.

INNSBRUCK TOURIST OFFICE

Postcode A-6021
t 59850
f 598507
info@innsbruck.tvb.co.at
www.ski-innsbruck.at

IGLS TOURIST OFFICE

Postcode A-6080
t 377101
f 3771017
igls@tvb.co.at
www.tiscover.com/igls

↑ From the sunny top cable-car station at Seegrube there are grand views southwards across the Inn valley
INNSBRUCK TOURISMUS / MICHAEL GILHAUS

facing slopes of **Seegrube-Nordkette**. The focus of the slopes at Seegrube is reached by cable-car rising 1050m/3,450ft from Hungerburg on the outskirts of the city (with buses and a funicular up to the cable-car departure station). Although there are red runs to the valley, the snow is not reliable. You go up here expecting to ski the red runs of 370m/1,210ft vertical below Seegrube, served by a chair-lift. A further stage of the cable-car rises 350m/1,150ft vertical to access the Karinne ski route, which is said to be fearsomely steep (up to 70% gradient). You can ski it with a guide and collect not only a T-shirt but a certificate to prove you did it.

But for visitors, if not for residents, skiing usually means heading for the opposite side of the Inn trench, to east or west of the side valley that runs southwards towards the Brenner pass and Italy. The Brenner road opens up the possibility of excursions to resorts in the Dolomites, such as Selva.

The standard Innsbruck lift pass covers the lifts in all the resorts dealt with here, except Seefeld. The extraordinary Super-Skipass includes days in Kitzbühel to the east and St Anton to the west. Free ski-bus services run to and from all the lift-pass-covered areas, but only at the beginning and end of the day. A car makes life in general more convenient, especially if you are staying in one of the outlying villages rather than in downtown Innsbruck.

There are snowboard parks in the Seegrube and Axamer Lizum sectors, and at Schlick 2000 and the Stubaier Gletscher.

IGLS 900m/2,950ft
Igls seems almost a suburb of Innsbruck – the city trams run out to the village – but really it is a resort in its own right. Its famous downhill race course is an excellent piste.
The village of Igls is small and quiet, with not much in the way of diversions apart from the beautiful walks, the Olympic bob run and the tea shops. You can stay in Igls, and a couple of UK operators sell packages to its comfortable hotels. Most are small and concentrated in the centre of the village, a bit of a walk from the cable-car station. An exception is the family-run 5-star Sporthotel (377241), which occupies the prime site, centrally placed between the tram station and the cable-car station: 'Excellent facilities, good food and nice bar,' says a reporter.

The skiing on Patscherkofel revolves around the excellent, varied, long red run that formed the men's downhill course in 1976, when Franz Klammer took ski racing (and the Olympic gold medal) by storm. There is a blue-run variation on this run, as well as off-piste possibilities. A cable-car rises 1050m/3,450ft from the village (and you can take it down if the lower runs are poor or shut). At the top, a chair rises a further 275m/900ft to the summit offering wonderful views over Innsbruck. A fast quad and a couple of drags serve slopes below the cable-car station. There is a short beginner lift at village level, and another a short bus-ride up the hill. We have received mixed reports on the grooming of the trails, however.

In general the resort is very suitable for families, with good easy slopes at village level. Après-ski is quiet.

↑ Igls sits on a shelf about 350m/1,150ft vertical above Innsbruck, with the wooded slopes of Patscherkofel rising above it

Axamer Lizum phone numbers
Calling long-distance add the prefix 05234. From abroad use the prefix +43 5234.

AXAMER LIZUM TOURIST OFFICE

Postcode A-6094
t 681780
f 67158
axams@netway.at
www.tiscover.com/axams

Neustift phone numbers
Calling long-distance add the prefix 05226. From abroad use the prefix +43 5226.

NEUSTIFT TOURIST OFFICE

Postcode A-6167
t 2228
f 2529
tv.neustift@neustift.at
www.stubaital.at

← Götzens is one of several rustic villages around Innsbruck with comfortable accommodation

AXAMER LIZUM 1580m/5,180ft
The mountain outpost of the Inn-side village of Axams is a simple ski station and nothing more, but it does have some good slopes and reliable snow conditions – and, as a reporter says, 'You feel as if you are in a wilderness.'
Axamer Lizum could scarcely offer a sharper contrast to Igls. If offers much more varied slopes and a network of lifts, with the base station at a much higher altitude. The slopes here hosted all the Olympic Alpine events in 1976 except the men's downhill (which was at Igls), and this is the standard local venue for weekend sport – hence the huge car park which is the most prominent feature of the 'resort'.

The main slopes on Hoadl and Pleisen are blues and reds, almost entirely above the trees but otherwise nicely varied and there is scope to 'play in gullies and bumps, as well as true off-piste,' says our reporter. The vertical of the main east-facing slopes above the main lift station is 'only' 700m/2,300ft, but for good skiers at least there is the possibility (given good snow conditions) of a 1300m/4,250ft descent at the end of the day from Pleisen to the outskirts of Axams – an easy 6.5km/4 mile black.

On the opposite side of the base station, a chair-lift serves a fairly easy black slope. Beyond it are links to the re-opened slopes above Mutters.

There are two good nursery lifts, and two ski schools.

You can stay up here – there is a 4-star hotel at the lift base, the Lizumerhof (68244) – 'nice rooms and decent modern Austrian cuisine' says a reporter this year – and there are a couple of 3-stars, too. But there's little in the way of après-ski apart from a couple of bars – the Alm bar is the most atmospheric – and you have to eat in your hotel or go to Axams.

There is also accommodation not far away at lower altitude in Axams – including four 3-star hotels – and in other nearby villages such as Götzens (one 4-star hotel, two 3-star gasthofs) and Birgitz (two 3-star hotels).

STUBAIER GLETSCHER 1750m/5,740ft
The Stubaier Gletscher is one of the best glacier ski and snowboard areas in the world and you can visit here in summer as well as winter. The nearest place to stay is picturesque Neustift, 20km/12 miles away and served by regular buses.
The glacier is accessed by two alternative two-stage gondolas from the huge car park at Mutterberg. On the glacier a variety of chair- and drag-lifts allow fabulous high altitude cruising on blue and red runs, which normally have excellent snow on slopes between 3200m and 2300m (10,500ft and 7,550ft). A lovely 10km/6 mile ungroomed ski-route down via a deserted bowl takes you down to the valley – or if you start at the top, a descent of about 14km/9 miles and 1450m/4,760ft vertical is possible. There is also good off-piste on the glacier to be explored with a guide.

Continued improvements to the lift have virtually eliminated what used to be enormous queues.

Neustift is an attractive Tirolean village halfway along the Stubai valley, with the main road bypassing the village centre. It has a small area of local slopes but what you go for is the glacier. There are lots of 4- and 3-star hotels in the village – the Sonnhof (2224) and the Hoferwirt (2560) have been recommended by reporters. Most of the restaurants are hotel-based – reporters recommend Bellefonte's pizzas and the Hoferwirt.

If the bob-run is too scary and ice skating too tricky, there are always the countless toboggan runs →

Fulpmes phone numbers
Calling long-distance add the prefix 05225. From abroad use the prefix +43 5225.

FULPMES TOURIST OFFICE
Postcode A-6166
t 62235
f 63843
stubai@netway.at
www.tiscover.com/fulpmes

Mutters phone numbers
Calling long-distance add the prefix 0512. From abroad use the prefix +43 512.

MUTTERS TOURIST OFFICE
Postcode A-6162
t 548410
f 5484107
mutters@netway.at
www.tiscover.com/mutters

Tulfes phone numbers
Calling long-distance add the prefix 05223. From abroad use the prefix +43 5223.

TULFES TOURIST OFFICE
Postcode A-6060
t 78324
f 78808
info@tulfes.at
www.tiscover.com/tulfes

Seefeld phone numbers
Calling long-distance add the prefix 05212. From abroad use the prefix +43 5212.

SEEFELD TOURIST OFFICE
Postcode A-6100
t 2313
f 3355
info@seefeld.tirol.at
www.seefeld-tirol.com

FULPMES 935m/3,070ft
Fulpmes is a sizeable village between Innsbruck and Neustift, on the way to the Stubaier Gletscher, with a fair-sized ski area of its own called Schlick 2000.
A two-stage gondola leads to a series of chair- and drag-lifts serving a few mainly short blue and red runs on the Sennjoch. There are also a couple of tougher ungroomed ski-routes and a terrain-park.

MUTTERS 830m/2,720ft
Almost as close to Innsbruck as Igls, Mutters is a charming rustic village at the foot of long slopes of 900m/2,950m vertical. Its slopes were closed during the 2001/02 season but will re-open for the 2002/03 season with an improved link with Axamer Lizum.
Four new lifts are being built for the 2002/03 season, including a new access gondola from just outside the village. They will serve a couple of long red runs and one long blue right back to the valley as well as shorter runs near the top of the mountain. The Kalkkögel Express above Götzens will provide a link with the slopes of Axamer Lizum. There are also a couple of good long toboggan runs.
The half-dozen hotels in the village divide equally into 3-star and 4-star categories. There is a lively après-ski scene and great off-slope facilities including tennis courts, saunas, skating rinks and 40 curling lanes.

TULFES 920m/3,020ft
Tulfes gets rather overshadowed by the Olympic resorts of Igls and Axamer Lizum, but it has some worthwhile runs.
The runs are on the north-facing slopes of Glungezer. A chair-lift from a car park above the village serves red and blue runs of 600m/1,970ft vertical. This leads to a drag up to the tree line serving a red run of 500m/1,640ft vertical. And this in turn leads to two drags serving open red runs from the top height of 2305m/7,560ft – almost 1400m/4,600ft above the village.
Like Igls, the village sits on the shelf on the side of the Inn valley. There are a dozen hotels and gasthofs.

SEEFELD 1200m/3,940ft
Seefeld is a smart all-round winter holiday resort in a pretty setting, with highly recommended cross-country trails and off-slope activities, and a couple of small, separate areas of downhill slopes.

A classic postwar Tirolean tourist development, Seefeld is well designed in traditional Tirolean style, with a large, pedestrian-only centre. You can get there by train, if you wish, since it's on a main railway line.
Seefeld's slopes are divided into two main sectors – Gschwandtkopf and Rosshütte. Both are on the outskirts and reached from most hotels by a regular free shuttle-bus.
Gschwandtkopf is a rounded hill with 300m/1,000ft of intermediate vertical down two main slopes, while Rosshütte is more extensive and has a terrain-park and half-pipe. The top of Rosshütte can be reached by a funicular – 'very efficient' says a reader – and then a cable-car, and runs finish in adjacent Hermannstall. From Rosshütte two six-seater chairs go to the shoulder of Härmelekopf – an improvement on the old cable-car, allowing repeated runs as well as the long red run down.
Rosshütte has some seriously steep off-piste challenges for experts and will offer intermediates an interesting day out from Innsbruck – but the terrain is of no interest for a week's stay. The nursery slopes in the central village are broad and gentle, with extensive snowmaking facilities.
Seefeld's 200km/125 miles of excellent cross-country trails are some of the best in Europe and are one reason why Innsbruck has been able to hold the Winter Olympics twice and, more recently, the Nordic World Ski Championships.
Lots of people come here for the curling, skating and swimming rather than skiing. The upmarket nature of the resort is reflected in the hotels – there are six 5-stars and almost 30 4-stars. On our last visit we stayed at the 4-star Hiltpolt (2253), which was very comfortable with good food.

One of Austria's best – well worth the effort of learning a bit of German

WHAT IT COSTS

HOW IT RATES

The slopes

Snow	****
Extent	****
Experts	***
Intermediates	****
Beginners	**
Convenience	***
Queues	****
Restaurants	***

The rest

Scenery	***
Resort charm	****
Off-slope	***

➕ Charming old Tirolean village, expanded in sympathetic fashion

➕ High slopes with reliable snow

➕ Lots of good intermediate runs, extending over the Swiss border to duty-free Samnaun, plus plenty of off-piste terrain to amuse experts

➕ Countless fast lifts mean little time is wasted

➕ Very lively après-ski

➖ Not ideal for beginners or timid intermediates, for various reasons

➖ English less widely spoken than is usual in Austria

➖ Few seriously steep runs

➖ Very little wooded terrain to give shelter in bad weather

➖ EuroTrash-style après-ski – e.g. table-dancing in plush 4-star hotels – and a lot of heavy drinking

It's only in the last few years that UK tour operators have offered packages in Ischgl (which is dominated by German visitors) and it still has a very low profile in Britain. But it receives rave reviews from almost every reader who goes there, and deserves to be on most people's Austrian short-list.

Samnaun is tour-op-free, and likely to remain so. But for independent travellers it has attractions – it's a charming, relaxed village, has good home runs and for a party including some novices makes a better base than Ischgl.

What's new

For 2001/02 a fast eight-seater chair replaced a slow quad to the border at Idjoch. A new six-pack replaced two T-bars on Palinkopf and a quad chair was installed at Bodenalp. And Samnaun has installed a new six-pack up to Alp Trida Sattel, arrival point of the cable-car.

A new red run has been constructed from Pardatschgrat to the middle station. More snowmaking has been installed and the Idalp-Panorama and Höllboden restaurants have been renovated and expanded.

Plans for the 2002/03 season include a new chair-lift from Idalp to Pardatschgrat, a new ski route to Höllenkar from Greitspitz and more snowmaking. There will be a new covered car park at the Silvretta gondola.

The resort

Ischgl is a quite compact village tucked away in the long, narrow Paznaun valley, south of St Anton on the Swiss border (the skiing is shared with Swiss Samnaun). It's set where a stream (the Fimbabach) joins the river Trisanna, and part of the village is built on high ground between the converging rivers.

The narrow main street plus a couple of side-streets are traffic-free – the village is bypassed by the valley road up to Galtür – and at the west end of the pedestrian zone is the main access lift, the 24-person Silvrettabahn up to the main mid-mountain focus of Idalp. Two other gondolas – one to Idalp, the other to the higher point of Pardatschgrat – start close together on the eastern fringe of the village, beside

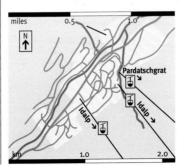

the Fimbabach. Because of the high ground in between, getting to these lifts from the middle of the village used to be hard work; but now an underground moving walkway (as in airports) connects them to the heart of the village.

The buildings are practically all in traditional chalet style, and the place has a neat, prosperous air. The wooded flanks of the valley rise steeply from the village, which as a result gets almost no sun in early season. There's a selection of lively bars, an excellent sports centre and a fair number of shops to stroll round. But drunken early-evening revellers can be intrusive.

Choice of location is much less important since the construction of the underground walkway, but the best spot, all things considered, is on or near the main street. Beware of accommodation across the bypass road, a long way from the lifts.

There is no need for vehicular transport in the resort, but there are frequent buses up the valley to Galtür (covered by the Silvretta ski pass), which is described at the end of this chapter, and a car makes trips to St Anton and Lech viable. It's a very long taxi-ride back from Samnaun, should you get stuck there.

123

The mountains

Ischgl is a fair-sized, relatively high, snow-sure area. Practically all the slopes are above the tree line, and bleak in bad weather, the main exception being the steep lower slopes above the village and a couple of short runs low down in the Fimbatal.

The slopes are shared with Samnaun in Switzerland; but the Ischgl lift company is in control, so the system has been coherently developed. Samnaun's duty-free status adds the spice of tobacco-shopping trips, but bear in mind that there are rules about importing stuff, and that if you have a backpack you may be 'interviewed'.

There are increasing numbers of ski routes on the piste map – some adding options, some (regrettably) replacing pistes. Only in German does the map explain that these routes are unpatrolled, and free of avalanche risk only near the widely spaced markers.

THE SLOPES
Cross-border cruising

The sunny **Idalp** plateau, reached by two of the village gondolas, is the hub of the slopes. It can be very crowded, especially at ski school meeting time and the end of the day. Pardatschgrat, reached by the third gondola, is about 300m/1,000ft higher. From here's an easy run down to Idalp – with the alternative of long, challenging runs towards Ischgl. Lifts radiate from Idalp, leading to a wide variety of mainly north-west- and west-facing runs.

A short piste brings you to the lifts serving the **Höllenkar** bowl, leading up to the area's south-western extremity and high-point at Palinkopf. There are further lifts beyond Höllenkar, on the west-facing flanks of the Fimbatal.

On the Swiss side the hub of activity is **Alp Trida**, surrounded by south- and east-facing runs with great views. From here a scenic red run goes down to Compatsch, from where there are buses to Ravaisch – for the cable-car back – and Samnaun-Dorf.

From Palinkopf there is a beautiful long run down an unspoiled valley to Samnaun-Dorf. It is not difficult, but is excessively sunny in parts and prone to closure because of avalanche risk. There is a long flat stretch at the end.

SNOW RELIABILITY
Very good

All the slopes, except the runs back to the resort, are above 2000m/6,560ft and many of those on the Ischgl side are north-west-facing. So snow conditions are generally reliable (which can lead to crowds when bus-loads of visitors arrive from lower resorts). There is snowmaking on various runs including several above Idalp, the two main descents to Ischgl and some key slopes on the Samnaun side.

FOR EXPERTS
Not much on-piste challenge

Ischgl can't compare with nearby St Anton for exciting slopes, and some of the runs marked black on the piste map would be red elsewhere. But there is plenty of beautiful off-piste to be found with a guide – and, because there are few experts around, it doesn't get tracked out quickly. The best areas to head for are Greitspitz and Palinkopf – the wooded lower slopes of the Fimbatal are delightful in a snowstorm. The best steep piste is 4, from Pardatschgrat towards Ischgl. You can do the top half of this repeatedly by catching the gondola at the mid-station. The variant 4a, into Velilltal, is now a ski-route.

FOR INTERMEDIATES
Something for everyone

Most of the slopes are wide, forgiving and ideal for intermediates.

At the tough end of the spectrum our favourite runs are those from Palinkopf down to Gampenalp and on along the valley to the secluded restaurant at Bodenalp.

There are also interesting and challenging black runs down the Hollspitz chair, and from both the top and bottom of the drag-lift from Idjoch

boarding *Between Idalp, the main station above the town, and Idjoch, a chair-ride further up, is a big half-pipe and an excellent terrain-park. The lifts are generally boarder-friendly; where there is a drag, there's often a chair option. The area is well suited to beginners and intermediates; experts will love Ischgl after fresh snow, even if the gradients are less impressive than in St Anton. The town rocks at night, with some very lively bars.*

MOUNTAIN FACTS

Altitude	1400m-2870m
	4,590ft-9,420ft
Lifts	42
Pistes	200km
	124 miles
Blue	25%
Red	60%
Black	15%
Snowmaking	52km
	32 miles
Recco detectors used	

up to Greitspitz. The reds from Pardatschgrat and Velillscharte down the beautiful valley to Velilltal and the red from Greitspitz into Switzerland are great for quiet, high-speed cruising.

For easier motorway cruising, there is lots of choice, including the Swiss side, where the runs from the border down to Alp Trida should prove ideal. The red runs that take you back to Idalp on the return journey are not difficult. But there are frequent moans about the red runs down to Ischgl itself; neither is easy, conditions can be tricky, and beer-lubricated crowds don't help. Quite a few people ride the gondolas down instead.

FOR BEGINNERS
Not ideal
Beginners go up the mountain to Idalp, where there are good, sunny, snow-sure nursery slopes and a short beginners' drag-lift. The blue runs on the east side of the bowl offer pleasant progression for fast learners. But away from this area there are few runs that are ideal for the near-beginner. You'd do better to learn elsewhere and come to Ischgl as an intermediate.

FOR CROSS-COUNTRY
Plenty in the valley
There is 48km/30 miles of cross-country track in the Paznaun valley between Ischgl, Galtür and Wirl. This tends to be pretty sunless, especially in early season, and is away from the main slopes, which makes meeting downhillers for lunch inconvenient.

QUEUES
An amazing transformation
Ischgl used to be renowned for its queues, but visitors these days are mightily impressed by the number of fast chairs on the mountain – as well as the three gondolas out of Ischgl and the world's biggest cable-car out of Samnaun. Queues can form both in the village (the Silvrettabahn is most queue-prone) and at various points up the mountain. Some may look serious, but most shift quickly.

MOUNTAIN RESTAURANTS
Much improved
Mountain restaurants tend to be very crowded but quite good quality, with over half now offering table-service. The Paznauner Taja, above Bodenalp, is an attractive, rustic chalet, but it gets very crowded. There is table-service upstairs and often a band playing on the terrace, or throbbing disco music. Down in Fimbatal is the Bodenalpe, a quieter, rustic restaurant (with table-service).

At Idalp there is a big self-service cafeteria, and a good table-service alternative (splendid views from the terrace). There's also a smaller,

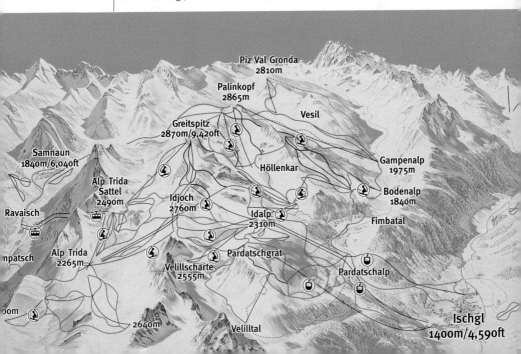

GETTING THERE

Air Innsbruck, transfer 1½hr. Zürich, transfer 3hr. Munich, transfer 3hr.

Rail Landeck (30km/19 miles); frequent buses from station.

AUSTRIA

126

SCHOOLS/GUIDES

2001/02 prices in euros

Ischgl-Silvretta
Classes 6 days
4hr: 10.30-12.30 and 1.30-3.30
5 full days: 145
Children's classes
Ages: from 6
6 full days including lunch: 145
Private lessons
Half- (2hr) or full-day (4hr) 105 for half-day; each additional person 15

CHILDCARE

The childcare facilities are all up the mountain at Idalp. There's a ski kindergarten for children aged 3 to 5; from age 5 they go into a slightly more demanding regime in an 'adventure garden'; lunch is included in both arrangements, which are open 6 days a week. Toilet-trained children can be left at a non-ski nursery; lunch is available.

crowded self-service nearby. The self-service up at Pardatschgrat tends to be quieter. The Schwarzwand pizzeria at the top of Höllenkar is again recommended by reporters. From Gampenalp you can be towed by snowmobile to the Heidelberghütte at the remote top of the Fimbatal.

The restaurants on the Swiss side at Alp Trida are pleasant. The Alp Bella (table- or self-service) has been recommended for a quiet time. Above the big Alp Trida self-service is the upmarket Marmotte, with table-service indoors and out (reservations needed).

Highly recommended by several reporters is the Schmuggler Alm in Samnaun – the first house you get to if you take the long red from Palinkopf: 'Table service, great food, good value – and they take euros.'

SCHOOLS AND GUIDES
Good despite language problems
The school meets up at Idalp and starts very late (10.30 to 12.30 and 1.30 to 3.30) – perhaps to allow people to get over their hangovers. We lack recent reports, but in the past we've had rave reports of both adult and children's classes. As well as normal lessons the school organises off-piste tours – this area is one of the best in the Alps for touring.

FACILITIES FOR CHILDREN
High-altitude options
The childcare facilities are all up at Idalp, but we have no first-hand reports of the service they provide.

Staying there

HOW TO GO
Few packages
Very few British tour operators offer Ischgl – they find it difficult to get firm allocations of affordable rooms.
Hotels There is a good selection from luxurious and expensive to basic B&Bs. A reporter found that many hotels don't take credit cards.
((((⑤ **Trofana Royal** (600) One of Austria's most luxurious hotels, with prices to match. Sumptuous spa facilities.
((((⑤ **Madlein** (5226) Convenient, modern family-run chalet. Pool, sauna, steam room. Nightclub and disco.
((((⑤ **Elisabeth** (5411) Right by the Pardatsch gondola with lively après-ski. Pool, sauna and steam room.
((((⑤ **Solaria** (5205) Near the Madlein and just as luxurious, but with a 'friendly family atmosphere'.
((((⑤ **Piz Tasna** (5277) Up hill behind church: 'Quiet location, friendly, lovely views over village, excellent food.'
(((④ **Sonne** (5302) Highly rated by reporters. In the centre of the village. Lively stube. Sauna, hot-tub, solarium.
((③ **Jägerhof** (5206) 'Jewel of a hotel,' said a reporter last year. Friendly, good food, large rooms. Sauna and steam.
((③ **Christine** (5346) Probably the best B&B in town. 'Huge rooms, nice views, good position near the lifts.'
((③ **Erna** (5555) Small, central B&B. Firmly recommended by a reporter who has holidayed in Ischgl 20 times.
(② **Dorfschmeide** (5769) Small, central B&B recommended by a reporter.
Self-catering Some attractive apartments are available.

ACTIVITIES

Indoor Silvretta Centre (bowling, billiards, swimming pool, sauna, steam baths, solarium), museum, library, gallery, tennis courts **Outdoor** Curling, skating, sleigh rides, hiking tours, 7km/4 miles floodlit toboggan run

Ischgl phone numbers
From elsewhere in Austria add the prefix 05444.
From abroad use the prefix +43 5444.

ISCHGL TOURIST OFFICE
Postcode A-6561
t 52660
f 5636
info@ischgl.com
www.ischgl.com

Galtür phone numbers
From elsewhere in Austria add the prefix 05443.
From abroad use the prefix +43 5443.

GALTUR TOURIST OFFICE
Postcode A-6563
t 8521
f 852176
galtuer@netway.at
www.galtuer.com

SAMNAUN TOURIST OFFICE
(Switzerland)
Note that the full international numbers are given.
Postcode CH-7563
t +41 (81) 868 5858
f +41 (81) 868 5652
info@samnaun.ch
www.samnaun.ch

EATING OUT
Plenty of choice
Our favourite places for dinner are the traditional Austrian restaurants and stubes, of which there's a wide choice. The Wippas stube in the Sonne is lively and serves good food – 'the best we tried for traditional Austrian fare,' says one reporter. For pizza try the Nona, the Schatzi (next to the Hotel Elisabeth) or the Trofana Alm, which is as much a bar as a restaurant, and for fondue the Kitzloch, with its galleries over the dance floor. The Grillalm, Salner and Tirol are also popular.

APRES-SKI
Very lively
Ischgl is one of the liveliest resorts in the Alps, from early afternoon on. Lots of people are still in ski boots late in the evening. After your last run head for Trofana Alm near the Silvrettabahn or the Schatzi bar of the hotel Elisabeth by the Pardatschgratbahn – indoor and outdoor bars and scantily clad dancing girls. Niki's Stadl across the road is a great place to sing along to live Austrian hits. The Kitzloch is said to have lost out a bit to these two places. The Sunn-Alm at the hotel Sonne gets crowded and has live music. The Kuhstahl under the Sporthotel Silvretta and Fire & Ice over the road are both lively all evening. Guxa and Allegra liven up after dinner and the Golden Eagle is 'good for live bands'. Two reporters recommend the new Coyote Ugly bar at the hotel Madlein. The place under the hotel Post has an ancient Roman theme. The Post also has a casino.

OFF THE SLOPES
No sun but a nice pool
The village gets little sun in the middle of winter, and the resort is best suited to those keen to hit the slopes. But there's no shortage of off-slope activities. There are 24km/15 miles of marked walks, a floodlit toboggan run and a splendid sports centre.

It's easy to get around the valley by bus, and there are restaurants that pedestrians can get to by gondolas.

STAYING DOWN THE VALLEY
Too far without a car
Ischgl is fairly isolated, but it is possible to stay in Landeck – an excellent base for visiting the surrounding resorts, including Serfaus, Nauders, Sölden and St Anton.

Galtür 1585m/5,200ft

Galtür has hit the headlines in recent years, but the village centre has been rebuilt and fortified since the 1999 avalanche disaster.

It is a charming, peaceful, traditional village clustered around a pretty little church, amid impressive mountain scenery. Quieter, sunnier and cheaper than Ischgl, it is a good base for a quiet family holiday. There are good 3-star and 4-star hotels – the Almhof (8253), the Flüchthorn (8202), the 'quiet and friendly' Alpenrose (8201) and the 'super' Ballunspitze (8214) have been recommended. The nightlife is quiet, but there are a couple of jolly bars. The Pyramid bar is recommended for its 'friendly' pub atmosphere.

Galtür's own slopes are not particularly challenging, but its black runs are ideal for intermediates and there are fine nursery slopes plus good 'graduation' pistes for improvers. The school has a high reputation.

Galtür is a better choice than Ischgl for cross-country skiers, with 60km/37 miles of loops.

If you intend to visit Ischgl a lot, bear in mind that while the bus service is reasonably frequent during the day, it finishes early in the evening.

Off-slope facilities are limited, but there's a natural ice rink and a sports centre with pool, tennis and squash.

Samnaun 1840m/6,040ft

Samnaun is a small, quiet community in a corner of Switzerland more easily reached from Austria – hence its duty-free status, which helps to ensure the highest visitor bed occupancy rate in the country.

There are four small components, roughly 1km/0.5 miles apart: Samnaun-Dorf, prettily set at the head of the valley – the main focus, with some swanky hotels and duty-free shops; Ravaisch, where the cable-car goes up; tiny Plan; and the hamlets of Laret and Compatsch, at the end of the main run down from the slopes, and location of the smart AlpenQuell spa-pool-fitness centre. We've stayed happily on the edge of Dorf in the Waldpark B&B, and have eaten well at La Pasta.

The smartly rustic Schmuggler Alm (see Mountain restaurants) is a natural port of call at the end of the run from Palinkopf (if you like rude DJs), and an attractive prospect for dinner, too.

Kitzbühel   760m/2,500ft

Wonderful old town and extensive slopes, but unreliable snow

HOW IT RATES

The slopes

Snow	**
Extent	****
Experts	***
Intermediates	****
Beginners	**
Convenience	**
Queues	**
Restaurants	****

The rest

Scenery	***
Resort charm	****
Off-slope	*****

Premier Collection

128

- ⊕ Large, attractive, varied slopes offering a sensation of travel both on- and off-piste
- ⊕ Beautiful medieval town centre
- ⊕ Vibrant nightlife
- ⊕ Plenty of off-slope amenities, both for the sporty and the not-so-sporty
- ⊕ A surprisingly large amount of cheap and cheerful accommodation
- ⊕ Jolly mountain restaurants

- ⊖ Unreliable snow especially on lower slopes (though increasing amount of snowmaking)
- ⊖ Surprisingly little expert terrain
- ⊖ Disjointed slopes, with quite a lot of bussing to get around them
- ⊖ Disappointing nursery area
- ⊖ Some crowded pistes

Kitzbühel is an impressive name to drop in the pub. Its Hahnenkamm race course is the most spectacular on the World Cup downhill circuit. But the race course is untypical of Kitzbühel and often its slopes are icy, slushy or just bare. We have visited Kitz countless times, and (like most of our reporters) rarely found decent snow on the lower slopes. Serious money has been invested in snowmaking (not least to prevent its famous race being cancelled, with all the resulting bad publicity). But Kitzbühel's low altitude means that its problems won't go away. Our advice is to book a holiday there at the last minute, when you know snow conditions are good and the forecast is for cold weather.

The resort has a beautiful, old, traffic-free centre complete with cobbled streets and lovely buildings. It has expensive, elegant hotels but there is also a huge amount of inexpensive hotel and guest-house accommodation, which attracts low-budget visitors, many of whom are young and like to party in its famous après-ski haunts.

What's new

Two new high-speed chair-lifts are due to be ready for 2002/03. Between Jochberg and Pass Thurn, the Bärenbadkogel II T-bar will be replaced by a six-pack. In Pass Thurn an eight-seater chair will replace the two Hartkaser T-bars below Zweitausender. They are also hoping to build a quad to replace the Resterhöhe T-bar in this area, but permission had not been given by the time we went to press.

At Kirchberg, the popular blue Fleck run into the valley (number 25) will have snowmaking all the way down.

In the longer term, there are plans to link the area with Westendorf in the Ski Welt via new lifts in the Aschau sector.

The resort

Set at a junction of broad, pretty valleys, Kitzbühel is a large, animated town, with separate areas of local slopes on each side. The beautiful walled medieval centre – with quaint church, cobbled streets and attractively painted buildings – is traffic-free and a compelling place to stay.

But the much-publicised old town is only a small part of Kitzbühel; the resort spreads widely, and busy roads surround the old town, reducing the charm factor somewhat. Visitors used to peaceful little Austrian villages are likely to be disappointed by its urban nature. But many visitors love the sophisticated, glitzy, towny ambience and swanky shops and cafes.

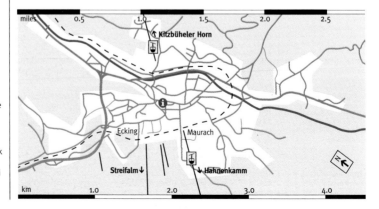

MOUNTAIN FACTS

Altitude 800m-2000m
2,620ft-6,560ft

Lifts	60
Pistes	160km
	100 miles
Blue	45%
Red	41%
Black	14%
Snowmaking	57km
	35 miles

Recco detectors used

LIFT PASSES

2002/03 prices in euros

Kitzbühel
Covers all lifts in Kitzbühel, Kirchberg, Jochberg, Pass Thurn, Bichlalm and Aschau, linking buses, and swimming pool.
Main pass
1-day pass 33
6-day pass 155
(low season 132)
Senior citizens
Over 60:
6-day pass 140
Over 80:
6-day pass 86
Children
Under 19:
6-day pass 124
Under 17:
6-day pass 86
Under 6: free pass
Short-term passes
Single ascent tickets for the major lifts; hourly refunds on day tickets; day tickets can be bought in half-hourly steps from 11am.
Notes 5% reduction for groups of over 15 people. The season pass is valid in Gstaad.
Alternative passes
Kitzbüheler Alpen-skipass covers five large ski areas – Schneewinkl (St Johann), Ski Region Kitzbühel, Ski Welt Wilder Kaiser, Bergbahnen Wildschönau and Alpbachtal (adult 6-day 170).

KITZBÜHEL TOURIST OFFICE

Don't be fooled: the snow lower down can be poor →

The bus service around town and to the outlying slopes has been highly praised by a regular visitor: 'More buses now, and extra ones at busy times.' But having a car is useful for visiting lots of other resorts covered by the Kitzbüheler Alpenskipass. It is also handy for visiting Salzburg and Innsbruck, though you can go by train, too (there are two stations in town).

The size of Kitz makes choice of location important. The old town is charming, and gives you most options. It's reasonably equidistant from the two main lift stations either side of town – both are within walking distance. However, the Hahnenkamm is very much the larger (and more snow-sure) of the two areas, and many visitors prefer to be close to its gondola. But the Hahnenkamm nursery slopes are often lacking in snow, and then novices are taken up the Horn.

The mountains

Snow and lift queues permitting, the mountain suits intermediates well. Although experts can find things to do, there are many better places for them. Kitz's total area is large, and includes access to sizeable Kirchberg.

THE SLOPES
Big but bitty

Kitzbühel's slopes are divided into four areas – three sizeable and one much smaller. Two of the major areas are connected by piste (almost) in one direction only.

The **Hahnenkamm** is by far the largest, and accessible from the town.

It is reached via a gondola or two chair-lifts, from the top of which a choice of steep and gentle runs lead down into Ehrenbachgraben; from there several chair-lifts fan out. One takes you to the gentle peak of Steinbergkogel, the high point of the sector. Beyond is the slightly lower peak of Pengelstein. On the far side of Pengelstein several long runs lead down to the west of the resort; shuttle-buses link their end-points at Aschau and Skirast with Obwiesen, Kirchberg and Kitz. Another lift from Ehrenbachgraben goes up to Ehrenbachhöhe, the focal point of the sector, linked by lifts and runs to Kirchberg and Klausen, on the road between Kitzbühel and Kirchberg.

Pengelstein is the start of the 'ski safari' route to the higher area of **Jochberg-Pass Thurn**. The piste from Pengelstein finishes at Trampelpfad, a short walk or taxi-ride from the Jochberg lifts. A parallel piste from Steinbergkogel ends at Hechenmoos – more than a walk from Jochberg, but you can get the shuttle-bus from here. Jochberg-Pass Thurn is well worth the excursion, with better snow and fewer crowds than the local slopes. Runs are short, but at last a few high-speed chairs are starting to replace T-bars, making the area more appealing. Pass Thurn is the terminus of the shuttle-bus, where it is worth ending the day to ensure a bus seat.

The very small **Bichlalm** area is of little interest except for getting away from the crowds, sampling the restaurants and working on your suntan. When conditions are good, the

top station (Stuckkogel) accesses an off-piste route to Fieberbrunn.

The **Kitzbüheler Horn** is equally sunny, with repercussions on snow-cover, but many slopes are above the mid-station at 1270m/4,170ft, accessed by a modern gondola starting close to the railway station, but some way from the centre. The second stage leads to the sunny Trattalm bowl, but the alternative cable-car takes you up to the summit of the Horn, from where a fine, solitary, east-facing piste leads down into the Raintal on the far side, with a chair-lift returning to the ridge. There are widely spread blue, red and black runs back towards town.

The piste map has been greatly improved by the addition of altitudes and mountain restaurants. And a reporter praised 'the people in bright jackets at the main lift stations, who offer advice on closures, directions etc'.

SNOW RELIABILITY
More snowmaking now

In a normal year, snow on the lower slopes can be thin or non-existent at times (though the snow at the top is often okay). The problem is that Kitzbühel's slopes have one of the lowest average heights in the Alps. The expansion of snowmaking in recent years has improved matters when it's cold enough to make snow – major runs right down to Kitzbühel, Kirchberg, Klausen and Jochberg are covered. But many slopes still remain unprotected. If snow is poor, head for Pass Thurn, which has the highest slopes and best snow in the area. An even better plan is to book at the last minute when snow-cover is known to be good. Otherwise, take a car for snow-searching excursions.

boarding *Kitzbühel was slow off the mark with boarding, keeping to its image of World Cup downhill venue/skier party town. However, things have changed, and now there is a half-pipe, terrain-park and boarder-cross course on the Kitzbüheler Horn, an area with few drag-lifts. Many lifts in the main area are drags, but all major lifts are gondolas and chair-lifts – the area suits beginners and intermediates well. The town is lively at night, with plenty of bars and clubs; the Londoner Pub is the main place with boarder appeal.*

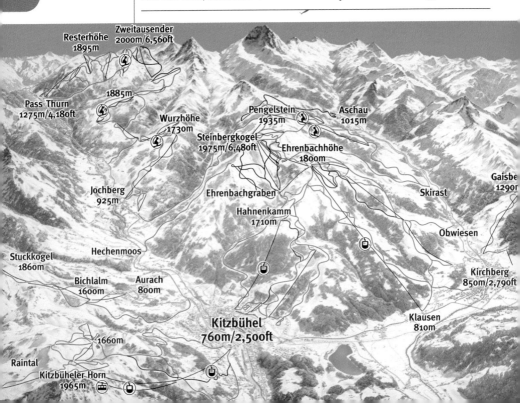

Kitzbühel's Hahnenkamm Downhill race, held in mid-January each year, is the toughest as well as one of the most famous on the World Cup circuit. On the race weekend the town is packed and there is a real carnival atmosphere, with bands, people in traditional costumes and huge (and loud) cowbells everywhere.

The race itself starts with a steep icy section before you hit the famous Mausfalle and Steilhang, where even Franz Klammer used to get worried. The course (now thankfully served by snow-guns) starts near the top of the new gondola and drops 860m/2,820ft to finish amid the noise and celebrations right on the edge of town. Ordinary mortals can now try most of the course after the race weekend, whenever the snow is good enough – it's an unpisted red ski route mostly. We tried it in 2001 and found it steep and tricky in parts going slowly – it must be terrifying at race speeds of 80mph or more. The course is normally closed from the start of the season until after the race.

SCHOOLS/GUIDES

2002/03 prices in euros

Hahnenkamm
Classes 6 days
4hr: 2hr am and pm
6 full days 125
Children's classes
Ages: up to 14
6 full days 140
Private lessons
On request.

Kitzbüheler Horn
Classes 6 days
4hr: 2hr am and pm
5 full days 120
Children's classes
6 full days 140
Private lessons
On request.

Total
Classes 6 days
4hr: 9.30-11.30 and 1pm-3pm
6 full days 130
Children's classes
Ages: 4 to 11
6 full days 130
Private lessons
On request

Red Devils
Classes 6 days
4hr: 2hr am and pm
6 full days 125
Children's classes
Ages: 4 to 11
6 full days 140
Private lessons
On request.

FOR EXPERTS
Plan to go off-piste
Steep pistes are concentrated in the ring of runs down into the bowl of Ehrenbachgraben, the most direct of which are challenging mogul fields. Nearby is the Streif red, the basis for the famous Hahnenkamm Downhill race – see the feature panel. When conditions allow, there is plenty of off-piste potential – some of it safely close to pistes, some requiring a guide.

FOR INTERMEDIATES
Lots of alternatives
The Hahnenkamm area is prime intermediate terrain. Good intermediates will want to do the World Cup downhill run, of course. And the long blue of 1000m/3,300ft vertical to Klausen from Ehrenbachhöhe is also satisfying. The east-facing Raintal run on the Horn is excellent for good intermediates to hone their skills on.

Most intermediates will want to head off on the safari route to Pass Thurn. The runs above Jochberg are particularly good for mixed abilities. Less adventurous types have some fine runs either side of Pengelstein, including the safari route and the Hieslegg piste above Aschau. The short, high runs at the top of the Pass Thurn area are ideal if you're more timid. There are also easy reds down to both Pass Thurn and Jochberg. Much of the Horn and Bichlalm is good cruising.

FOR BEGINNERS
Not ideal
The Hahnenkamm nursery slopes are no more than adequate, and prone to poor snow conditions. The Horn has a high, sunny, nursery-like section, and precocious learners will soon be cruising home from there on the long Hagstein piste. There are some easy runs to progress to if the snow is okay. But as a reporter said this year 'I would never send a beginner to Kitzbühel.'

FOR CROSS-COUNTRY
Plentiful but low
There are nearly 35km/22 miles of trails scattered around, but all are at valley level and prone to lack of snow.

QUEUES
Still some problems
Replacing the old Hahnenkamm cable-car with a speedy six-person gondola has vastly reduced morning queues. However, once up the mountain there are some bottlenecks at slow old chairs and drags. But we have had reports of queue-free weeks. Both the Horn and the Hahnenkamm can have overcrowded pistes. When lifts and pistes are busy here, head for Pass Thurn (which is often very quiet). We have received some complaints from reporters about the warning signs for avalanche danger and closed or icy pistes being in German only.

Kitzbühel

131

GETTING THERE

Air Salzburg, transfer 1¹/₂hr. Munich, transfer 2hr. Innsbruck, transfer 1¹/₂hr.
Rail Mainline station in resort. Postbus every 15 min from station.

ACTIVITIES

Indoor Aquarena Centre (2 pools, 2 slides, sauna, solarium, mud baths, aerated baths, underwater massage) – free entry with lift pass, indoor tennis hall, fitness centre, beauty centre, bridge, indoor riding school, local theatre, library, museum, jazz club, casino, 2-screen cinema.
Outdoor Ice rink (curling and skating), horse-riding, sleigh rides, toboggan run, ballooning, ski-bobs, flying school, wildlife park, hang-gliding, paragliding, 40km/25 miles of cleared walking paths (free guided tours), copper mine tours.

CHILDCARE

Most schools cater for small children, offering lunchtime supervision as well as lessons on the baby slopes – generally from age 3. There is no non-ski nursery, but babysitters and nannies can be hired.

MOUNTAIN RESTAURANTS
A highlight

'One of the reasons we keep going back,' says one of our Kitz regulars. 'This year we went to three different ones each day and still only got to less than half.' There are many restaurants, now thankfully marked on the piste map. Avoid the large self-service places and stick to the smaller huts. On the Horn the Hornköpfl-Hütte has good food and sunny terraces. Alpenhaus is good for a lively lunch, the Gipfelhaus is quieter with 'good views and food'. Gasthof Hagstein, an attractive farmhouse, serves up Austrian favourites. The Bichlalm in the next-door sector is also good if you want some peace. At Jochberg-Pass Thurn the Jägerwurzhütte and Trattenbachalm are recommended, and Panoramaalm has great views. We had a jolly time at Hangalm, where there was impromptu singing and dancing to an accordion player. The Steinbergkogel, Sonnbühel, Ochsalm, Seidalm, Fleckalm and Brandseit in the Hahnenkamm sector are good. The Kasereckhütte on the run from Pengelstein to Jochberg is 'brilliant'. The expensive Hochkitzbühel table-service restaurant at the top of the gondola has good food, but service has been criticised.

SCHOOLS AND GUIDES
Mixed reviews

There are now half-a-dozen competing schools. The original school, Rudi Sailer's famous Red Devils, got a scathing review from a reporter last year – when an instructor told a nervous woman to 'get down now', then left her after she fell. But someone this year thought they were 'very good'. In contrast to the 200-strong Red Devils, the other schools emphasise their small scale and personal nature. The Total school is the best established of these and includes video analysis. A reporter said: 'Never seen so many British instructors. Very good.' But a couple said, 'Our 13-year-old's instructor was so cautious that they had virtually no fun.'

FACILITIES FOR CHILDREN
Not an ideal choice

There is no non-ski nursery, but provided your children are able and willing to take classes, you can deposit them at any of the schools. The Total school has supervision until 5pm.

HOW TO GO
Mainly hotels and pensions

Kitz is essentially a hotel resort.
Chalets A few tour operators run chalet-hotels here.
Hotels There is an enormous choice, especially of 4-star and 3-star hotels.
((((5 **Tennerhof** (63181) Luxurious former farmhouse, with renowned restaurant. Beautiful panelled rooms.
((((5 **Schloss Lebenberg** (6901) Modernised 'castle' with smart pool, and free shuttle-bus to make up for secluded but inconvenient location. Free nursery for kids aged 3-plus.
((((4 **Weisses Rössl** (625410) Smartly traditional exclusive 5-star aparthotel.
((((4 **Goldener Greif** (64311) Historic inn, elegantly renovated; vaulted lobby-sitting area, panelled bar, casino.
((((4 **Jägerwirt** (6981) Modern chalet with 'helpful staff and wonderful food'. Not ideally placed.
((((4 **Schwarzer Adler** (6911) Traditional hotel, near centre, highly praised by reporter this year. 'Excellent food and splendid new fitness centre and spa.'
(((4 **Schweizerhof** (62735) Comfortable chalet right by Hahnenkamm gondola.
(((3 **Hahnenhof** (62582) Small and traditional, with rustic charm.
(((3 **Strasshofer** (62285) A favourite with a regular reporter – 'central, family-run, friendly, good food, good with children, quiet rooms at back'.
((2 **Mühlbergerhof** (62835) Small, friendly pension in good position.
Self-catering Many of the best (and best-positioned) are attached to hotels.

EATING OUT
Something for everyone

There is a wide range of restaurants to suit all pockets, including pizzerias and fast food outlets (even McDonald's). Some 4-star hotels have excellent restaurants; Zur Tenne and Maria Theresia have been recommended by reporters. But the Unterberger Stuben ('excellent but expensive' says a reporter) vies with Schwedenkapelle for the 'best in town' award. Good, cheaper places include the Huberbräu-Stüberl, Sportstüberl and Zinnkrug. Goldene Gams has both a traditional Austrian dining room and one serving modern Italian and French food. On Fridays and Saturdays you can dine at the top of the Hahnenkamm gondola.

Kitzbühel phone numbers
From elsewhere in Austria add the prefix 05356.
From abroad use the prefix +43 5356.

KITZBUHEL TOURIST OFFICE
Postcode A-6370
t 62155
f 62307
info@kitzbuehel.com
www.kitzbuehel.com

Kirchberg phone numbers
From elsewhere in Austria add the prefix 05357.
From abroad use the prefix +43 5357.

KIRCHBERG TOURIST OFFICE
Postcode A-6365
t 2309
f 3732
info@kirchberg.at
www.kirchberg.at

APRES-SKI
A main attraction

Nightlife is a great selling point of Kitz. There's something for all tastes, from throbbing bars full of teenagers to quiet little places, nice cafes and smart spots for fur-coat flaunting.

Immediately after the slopes close, the town is jolly without being much livelier than many other Tirolean resorts – try the Mockingstube, near the gondola, which often has live music. Cafes Praxmair, Kortschak, Langer and Rupprechter are among the most atmospheric tea time places for cakes and pastries. Stamperl is a very lively bar. Later the lively Big Ben British pub, American-style Highways bar and s'Lichtl (with thousands of lights hanging from the ceiling) get packed. Seppi's Pub is recommended for sport on TV, pizzas and the eccentric owner. Royal, Olympia and Take 5 are the main discos. The Londoner Pub is expensive as well as the loudest, most crowded, smokiest place in town; you often have to queue to be allowed in as other people leave.

Tour reps organise plenty of events, and there's a casino. A reporter says there's table dancing at the Go Go Bar Café Romantica 2km/1 mile out of town.

OFF THE SLOPES
Plenty to do

The Aquarena leisure centre is covered by the lift pass and is very impressive, with two pools, sauna, solarium and various health activities. There's a museum and concerts are organised. The railway makes excursions easy (eg to Salzburg and Innsbruck) and reps organise coach trips.

KITZBÜHEL TOURIST OFFICE

Kitzbühel's beautiful medieval centre is the nicest place to stay ↓

Kirchberg 850m/2,790ft

THE RESORT
Kirchberg is a large, spread out, lively village. If you stay in the village centre, it's a bus-ride to the lifts up to the main slopes. If you stay near the lifts, don't expect local nightlife.

THE MOUNTAIN
Slopes A gondola at Klausen on the road towards Kitzbühel takes you up into the main slopes that Kirchberg shares with Kitzbühel. The alternative route via three successive chair-lifts starts a bus-ride in the opposite direction. The separate small Gaisberg area is on the other side of the valley.
Snow reliability Only about 90m/300ft higher than neighbouring Kitzbühel, Kirchberg suffers from the same unreliable snow.
Experts Few challenging slopes.
Intermediates The main slopes it shares with Kitzbühel are ideal for intermediates when snow is good.
Beginners There's a beginner lift and area at the foot of the Gaisberg slopes.
Snowboarding Boarders might prefer Kitzbühel for the terrain-park on the Horn.
Cross-country There are plenty of trails – but at valley level so they can be affected by lack of snow. The area above Aschau is good and there is a night-time track on Lake Schwarz.
Queues As with Kitzbühel, poor snow conditions can cause overcrowding.
Mountain restaurants There are some good local huts.
Schools and guides There are three schools but we lack recent reports.
Facilities for children There are non-ski and ski kindergartens.

STAYING THERE
How to go There's a wide choice of chalet-style hotels and pensions.
Hotels The 4-star Klausen (2128) is close to the main gondola and has its own après-ski bar, the Sporthotel Tyrol (2787) is a bit out of the village centre with pool and spa facilities.
Self-catering There is some available.
Après-ski There's a good toboggan run on Gaisberg. Nightlife is very lively both in bars and in discos. Good bars include the traditionally Austrian Kupferstubn, the Boomerang, the Londoner (with frequent live music), Gismo and Fuchslokal.
Off the slopes Some hotels have swimming pools, saunas and so on.

Lech

1450m/4,760ft

Captivating blend of snow, extensive slopes and traditional style

WHAT IT COSTS

(((((6)

HOW IT RATES

The slopes

Snow	****
Extent	****
Experts	****
Intermediates	****
Beginners	****
Convenience	***
Queues	****
Restaurants	**

The rest

Scenery	***
Resort charm	****
Off-slope	***

What's new

Lech seems to be in consolidation mode – that is, not much is changing. The ski school has a more convenient location, near the Schlegelkopf chair-lift. Child safety devices have been fitted to all chair-lifts. The kids' Miniclub has had a makeover.

134

➕ Picturesque Alpine village

➕ Sunny slopes with excellent snow record and extensive snowmaking

➕ Fair-sized, largely intermediate piste network plus good and extensive off-piste terrain

➕ Easy access to the tougher slopes of St Anton and other Arlberg resorts

➕ Lively après-ski scene

➕ Some very smart hotels

➖ Surprising shortage of compelling mountain restaurants

➖ Local traffic intrudes on main street of Lech (and spoils Zürs entirely)

➖ Very few tough pistes, so the adventurous must go off-piste

➖ Blue runs back to the village are rather steep for nervous novices

➖ Generally expensive

➖ Still quite a few slow, old lifts

Lech and its higher, linked neighbour Zürs are the most fashionable resorts in Austria, each able to point to a string of rich and vaguely royal visitors. But, like all such 'exclusive' resorts, they aren't actually exclusive in any real sense. A holiday here is unlikely to be cheap, but it doesn't have to cost any more than in countless other international resorts in the Alps. We don't feel out of place here, and neither would you – unless it's because, like one unimpressed reporter this year, you encounter yobs pissing in the street. The days when we could describe Lech as 'a very chic resort' seem to have ended along with the cold war (one reporter this year notes a noisy Russian presence).

The real point about these resorts is that their combination of impressive snowfall and traditional Alpine atmosphere (in Lech, if not Zürs) is a rare and attractive thing. One of the few other Austrian resorts to offer it is St Anton, over the hill, covered by the same lift pass, and easily visited by bus.

One group of people who are likely to find a holiday here costly is adventurous skiers who lack the 'alpine experience' needed to tackle the ski routes that Lech offers instead of black pistes: you'll need an instructor to hold your hand.

The resort

Lech is an old farming village set in a high valley that spent long periods of winter cut off from the outside world until the Flexen pass road through Zürs was constructed at the end of the 19th century. (Even now, the road can be closed for days on end after an exceptional snowfall; a road tunnel is planned, but is not imminent.)

The village is attractive, with its upmarket hotels built in traditional chalet style, its gurgling river plus bridges, its adequately impressive scenery (notably the Omeshorn, looming over the valley to the south-west) and the high incidence of snow on the streets. But its appeal is dimmed slightly by traffic on the main street that forms its spine: although

LECH TOURIST OFFICE

← The village outdoor bars do brisk business from mid-afternoon – if the sun shines

MOUNTAIN FACTS

Altitude 1450m-2450m
4,760ft-8,040ft

Arlberg region
Lifts 83
Pistes 260km
162 miles
Blue 25%
Red 50%
Black 25%
Snowmaking 65km
40 miles
Recco detectors used

LIFT PASSES

2002/03 prices in euros

Arlberg Ski pass
Covers all St Anton, St Christoph, Lech, Zürs and Stuben lifts, and linking bus between Rauz and Zürs.
Main pass
1-day pass 37.5
6-day pass 174
(low season 157)
Senior citizens
Over 65 for men and 60 for women: 6-day pass 149
Children
Under 15: 6-day pass 104
Under 18: 6-day pass 149
Short-term passes
Single ascent tickets on some lifts throughout Arlberg. Half-day tickets (adults 28) from noon, afternoon 'taster' tickets (16) from 3pm. Day tickets have by-the-hour reimbursement.
Notes Main pass also covers Sonnenkopf (10 lifts) at Klösterle, 7km/4 miles west of Stuben. Discounts during wedel, firn and snow crystal weeks.

this street goes nowhere (and parking is controlled), it gets uncomfortably busy, especially at weekends.

The clientele is largely German and Austrian, with very few Brits. The fur coat count is one of the highest in the Alps, even if this is now countered by what one reporter calls 'the Russian mafia, with ski wear left over from the 1980s'.

The heart of the village is a short stretch of the main street beside the river; most of the main hotels are clustered here. Right on this street is the base station of the Rufikopf cable-car, departure point for exploration of the Zürs slopes. A short walk away, across the river, are the Schlegelkopf chair-lifts, leading up into Lech's main area of slopes. Chalets, apartments and pensions are dotted around the valley, and the village spreads along the main street for 2km/1.5 miles. Some of the cheaper accommodation is quite a walk from the lifts.

Not far from the centre is the cable-car up to the satellite resort of Oberlech – a small, traffic-free collection of 4-star hotels and chalets set on the mountainside above Lech; the cable-car works until 1am, allowing access to Lech's much livelier nightlife and shopping. If you stay there, luggage is delivered to your hotel via underground tunnels, leaving you unburdened for the short, snowy walk from the cable-car.

Zug is a hamlet, 3km/2 miles from Lech, with a lift into the Lech-Oberlech area. The small amount of accommodation is mostly bed and breakfast with one 4-star hotel. From Lech, Zug makes a good night out: you can take a horse-drawn sleigh for a fondue at the Rote Wand, Klösterle or Auerhahn, followed by a visit to the Rote Wand disco.

As well as Lech and Zürs, the Arlberg lift pass covers St Anton, St Christoph and Stuben, all reachable by car, by free but busy ski-bus, or by less crowded post-bus.

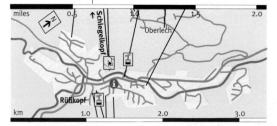

The mountains

Most of the slopes are treeless, the main exception being the lower runs below Oberlech.

The toughest runs here are classed as unpatrolled 'ski routes' (as at St Anton – read that chapter for more on this), or 'high-alpine touring runs', which are not protected against avalanche and should be skied only with a guide. We don't have much of a problem with the latter category – in other resorts, these off-piste runs would simply not appear on the piste map at all. But the ski route concept is bad news, reducing the resort's responsibility for runs that are a key part of the area, and that should be patrolled pistes. The only ways down to Zug, for example, are ski routes. And of the seven identified runs from the Kriegerhorn, six are ski routes.

The piste map attempts to cover the whole of the Arlberg region in one view, and as a result is unclear in places – particularly around Oberlech.

THE SLOPES
One-way traffic
The main slopes centre on **Oberlech**, 250m/820ft above Lech (just below the tree line), and can be reached from the village by chair-lifts as well as cable-car. The wide, open pistes above Oberlech are perfect for intermediates and there is also lots of off-piste potential for experts. Zuger Hochlicht, the high point of this sector, gives stunning views.

The **Rüfikopf** cable-car takes Lech residents to the west-facing slopes of Zürs. This mountainside, with its high point at **Trittkopf**, is a mix of quite challenging intermediate slopes and flat/uphill bits that would be a nightmare for boarders. On the other side of the village the east-facing mountainside is of a more uniform gradient. Chairs go up to **Seekopf** with intermediate runs back down. There's a chair up to **Muggengrat** (the highest point of the Zürs area) from below Zürsersee. This has a good blue run back under it and accesses the Muggengrat Täli – a lovely long red away from all the lifts back down to Zürs. But most people head for the Madloch chair. This chair – one of the most vulnerable to closure by wind – accesses the long ski route all the way back to Lech. You can peel off part-

AUSTRIA

 boarding *Lech's upper-crust image has not stood in the way of its snowboarding development, and it continues to improve its facilities. Chairs and cable-cars, with hardly any drags, and perfectly manicured pistes make the area ideal for beginner and intermediate boarders – lessons are with the local ski school. There's also a good terrain-park above the town at the Schlegelkopf, with jumps, a boarder-cross and a half-pipe. More confident boarders should hire a guide and track some powder. The town slips back to being an upmarket ski destination in the evenings – bars tend to be in 4-star hotels populated by 'beautiful people'.*

way down and head for Zug and the chair-lift up to the Kriegerhorn above Oberlech. There are no lifts back towards Zürs, so the circuit is clockwise-only.

SNOW RELIABILITY
One of Austria's best
Lech and Zürs both get a lot of snow, but Austrian weather station records show a big difference between them despite their proximity. Lech gets an average of almost 8m/25ft of snow between December and March, almost twice as much as St Anton and three times as much as Kitzbühel; but Zürs gets 50% more than Lech. The altitude is high by Austrian resort standards

and there is excellent snowmaking on Lech's sunny lower slopes.

This combination, together with excellent grooming, means that the Lech-Zürs area normally has good coverage from December until April. And the snow is frequently better here than on St Anton's predominantly south-facing slopes.

FOR EXPERTS
Off-piste is main attraction
There are only two black pistes on the map, and there is no denying that for the competent skier who prefers to stick to patrolled runs the area is very limited. There are the two types of off-piste route referred to above. The

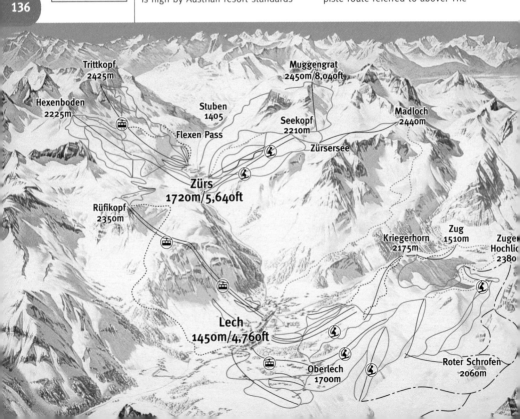

official recommendation is to visit these with a ski instructor or guide, though many ignore the advice. But experts will get a lot more out of the area if they do have a guide, as there is plenty of excellent off-piste other than the marked ski routes, much of it accessed by long traverses. Especially in fresh snow, it can be wonderful.

Many of the best runs start from the Steinmähder chair, which finishes just below Zuger Hochlicht. Some routes involve a short climb to access bowls of untracked powder. From the Kriegerhorn there are shorter off-piste runs down towards Lech and a very scenic long ski route down to Zug. Most runs, however, are south- or west-facing and can suffer from the sun.

At the end of the season, when the snow is deep and settled, the off-piste off the shoulder of the Wöstertäli from the top of the Rüfikopf cable-car down to Lech can be superb. There are also good runs from the top of the Trittkopf cable-car in the Zürs sector, including a tricky one above the Flexen Pass down to Stuben.

Experts will also enjoy cruising some of the steeper red runs and will want to visit St Anton during the week, where there are more challenging pistes as well as more off-piste.

Heli-lifts are available to a couple of remote spots, at least on weekdays.

FOR INTERMEDIATES
Flattering variety for all
The pistes in the Oberlech area are nearly all immaculately groomed blue runs, the upper ones above the trees, the lower ones in wide swathes cut through them. It is ideal territory for leisurely cruisers not wanting surprises. And even early intermediates will be able to take on the circuit to Zürs and back, the only significant red involved being the beautiful long (and not at all difficult) ski route back to Lech from the top of the Madloch chair in Zürs.

It's worth noting that the final blue-run descents to Lech (as opposed to Oberlech) are uncomfortably steep for nervous novices.

More adventurous intermediates should take the fast Steinmähder chair to just below Zuger Hochlicht and from there take the scenic red run all the way to Zug (the latter part on a 'ski route' rather than a piste). And if you feel ready to have a stab at some off-

The river is a central, soothing feature of the village ↓

Lech

137

SCHOOLS/GUIDES

2001/02 prices in euros

**Lech and Oberlech
Classes** 6 days
4hr: 10am-noon and 1pm-3pm
6 full days 150
Children's classes
Ages: 3½ to 13
6 full days 138
Private lessons
Full day only
183 for 1 day; each additional person 15

CHILDCARE

There are ski kindergartens in Lech, Zürs and Oberlech taking children from age 3, from 9am to 4pm.

piste, Lech is a good place to try it.

Zürs has many more interesting red runs, on both sides of the village. We particularly like the west-facing reds from Trittkopf and the usually quiet east-facing Muggengrat Täli, which starts in a steep bowl – you can take the plunge, or skirt it on a catwalk.

FOR BEGINNERS
Easy slopes in all areas
The main nursery slopes are in Oberlech, but there is also a nice isolated area in the village dedicated purely to beginners. There are good, easy runs to progress to, both above and below Oberlech.

FOR CROSS-COUNTRY
Picturesque valley trail
There are two cross-country trails in Lech. The longer one is 15km/9 miles; it begins in the centre of town and leads through the beautiful Zug valley, following the Lech river and ending up outside Zug. The other begins behind the church and goes to Stubenbach (another hamlet in the Lech area). In Zürs there is a 3km/2 mile track starting at Zürs and going to the Flexen Pass. This starts 1600m/5,250ft and climbs to 1800m/5,910ft.

QUEUES
No recent complaints
The region proudly boasts that it limits numbers on the slopes to 14,000 for a more enjoyable experience. There have been significant lift improvements in recent years, and recent reporters have not complained of any problems. But there are one or two remaining bottlenecks – the Schlegelkopf fast quad out of Lech gets very busy at times – and there are still lots of drag-lifts and slow chair-lifts, which means you spend a lot of time riding lifts. The crucial Madloch double chair at the top of the Zürs area must still generate peak-time queues on the one-way circuit to Lech.

MOUNTAIN RESTAURANTS
Seriously disappointing
There are surprisingly few cosy mountain huts in the area, and fewer still with table service. All part of a conspiracy, we guess, to steer big spenders towards eating in the villages, where there are some impressive gourmet options.

At least Oberlech is above valley level; there are several big sunny

terraces here, set prettily around the piste – though a reporter who recently spent a fortnight investigating the options here found no food of any merit. Quite often you'll find a live band playing outside one of the restaurants here. The Inga Stube is reported to have 'good food, rustic atmosphere, friendly staff and reasonable prices', which sounds close to perfection. The Alter Goldener Berg is a lovely old building, but the food and service are not reliable. The Mohnenfluh, at the top of the nursery lift, is said to do 'excellent' food.

The self-service Seekopf restaurant does decent food and has a good sun terrace – but you may have to queue to even get into the food serving area. Also popular is the self-service Palmenalpe above Zug, but it too gets very crowded. The Schröfli Alm, not marked on the piste map but just above the bottom of the Seekopf lift, is a pleasant chalet.

In view of the lack of options at altitude, we'll allow ourselves a couple of valley-level suggestions. Hus Nr 8, at the end of the route back from Zürs to Lech, is 300 years old and has good traditional food. In Zug, the hotel Rote Wand is popular, and the gasthof Auerhahn is roundly recommended by a reporter, not least for its 'exquisite' dumplings – yes, really.

SCHOOLS AND GUIDES
Excellent in parts
The ski schools of Lech, Oberlech and Zürs all have good reputations and the instructors speak good English. Group lessons are divided into no fewer than 10 ability levels. One past visitor enjoyed 'the best lessons I have ever had'. In peak periods, you should book both instructors and guides well in advance, however, as many are booked regularly every year by an exclusive clientele.

FACILITIES FOR CHILDREN
Oberlech's fine, but expensive
Oberlech does make an excellent choice for families who can afford it, particularly as it's so convenient for the slopes. The Sonnenburg and the Goldener Berg have in-house kindergartens. Reporters tell us the Oberlech school is great for children, with small classes, good English spoken and lunch offered.

Zürs 1720 m

Lech 1450 m

Stuben 1400 m

Know the best place for an argument?

The best skiing in the Alps. The best snow from open day in November until the closing day in May. The greatest variety in 440 km of pisted runs and snow left untouched just for you. The best ski guides to open the enormity of the Arlberg. Skischools and snowboard parks that mean fun for every age. Just 120 minutes from Zurich or Munich, you can practically commute. Lech - Zürs - Stuben am Arlberg - Austria at its best. Beyond argument.

Lech
ZÜRS
ARLBERG

Stuben

GETTING THERE

Air Zürich, transfer 2¼hr. Innsbruck, transfer 1¼hr.

Rail Langen (15km/9 miles); 9 buses daily from station, buses connect with international trains.

ACTIVITIES

Indoor Tennis, hotel swimming pools and saunas, squash, museum, art gallery, hotel spas
Outdoor 30km/19 miles of cleared walking paths, toboggan run (from Oberlech), artificial ice rink (skating, curling), sleigh rides, helicopter rides

Lech and Zürs phone numbers
From elsewhere in Austria add the prefix 05583.
From abroad use the prefix +43 5583.

LECH TOURIST OFFICE

Postcode A-6764
t 21610
f 3155
info@lech-zuers.at
www.lech-zuers.at

ZURS TOURIST OFFICE

Postcode A-6763
t 2245
f 2982
zuersinfo@lech-zuers.at
www.zuers.at

Stuben phone numbers
From elsewhere in Austria add the prefix 05582.
From abroad use the prefix +43 5582.

STUBEN TOURIST OFFICE

Postcode A-6762
t 3990
f 3994
info@stuben.at
www.stuben.com

Staying there

HOW TO GO
Surprising variety
There is quite a variety of accommodation from luxury hotels through to simple but spotless B&Bs.
Hotels There are three 5-star hotels, over 30 4-star and countless more modest places.
((((5 **Arlberg** (2134-0) Patronised by royalty and celebrities. Elegantly rustic chalet, centrally placed. Pool.
((((5 **Post** (2206-0) Lovely old Relais & Chateaux place on main street with pool, sauna. 'Perfect,' says a reporter.
((((4 **Krone** (2551) One of the oldest buildings in the village, in a prime spot by the river.
((((4 **Tannbergerhof** (2202-0) Splendidly atmospheric inn on main street, with outdoor bar and hugely popular disco (tea-time as well as later). Pool.
((((4 **Haldenhof** (2444-0) Friendly and well run, with antiques and a fine collection of prints and paintings.
((((4 **Burg Vital** (Oberlech) (2291-930) 'Excellent – no criticism,' said a reporter last year of this plush luxury hotel with pool, sauna and squash.
((((4 **Burg** (2291-0) Sister hotel of Burg Vital – same facilities and with famous outdoor umbrella bar by the cable-car.
((((4 **Sonnenburg** (Oberlech) (2147) Luxury on-piste chalet (popular for lunch). Good children's facilities. Pool.
((((4 **Monzabon** (2104) Well placed and 'characterful, with friendly staff,' says a reporter – but 'meals too grand'. Pool.
(((3 **Pension Angerhof** (2418) Beautiful ancient pension, with wood panels and quaint little windows.
(((3 **Pension Fernsicht** (2432) Pension with spa facilities.
Self-catering There is lots available to independent bookers.
Chalets There are a couple of catered chalets run by British tour operators.

EATING OUT
Not necessarily expensive
There are over 50 restaurants in Lech, nearly all of them in hotels. For reasonably priced meals try the Montana, which serves French cuisine and has an excellent wine cellar, the Krone, Ambrosius (above a shopping arcade), or the Post, which serves Austrian nouvelle-type food. The Madlochblick has a typically Austrian restaurant, very cosy with good solid

food. Hus Nr 8 is one of the best non-hotel restaurants (see Mountain restaurants) and does good fondue. Pizzeria Charly is popular for all kinds of Italian food. Bistro Casarole is a small casual place with a short menu of excellent, substantial grills. In Oberlech there is a good fondue at the Alte Goldener Berg, a tavern built in 1432. In Zug the Rote Wand is excellent for fondues and a good night out; it serves the best Kaiserschmarren (a delicious chopped pancake and fruit dessert) in the Arlberg. A reporter recommends Gasthaus Älpele near Zug – 3km/2 miles from the road, up the valley on the cross-country route – for its atmosphere and good food. Transport is provided in covered wagons attached to a snowcat.

APRES-SKI
Good but expensive
The umbrella bar of the Burg hotel at Oberlech is popular immediately after the slopes close, as is the champagne bar in Oberlech's Hotel Montana. Down in Lech itself the main focuses of afternoon action are the Hotel Krone's ice bar, which has a lovely setting by the river, and the outdoor bar of the Tannbergerhof. There's a tea dance disco inside the Tannbergerhof.

Later on, the Arlberg Hotel's Scotch Club disco (owned and run by former Olympic champion, Egon Zimmermann), and those in the hotels Almhof-Schneider and Krone liven up. The latter's Side Step specialises in 60s and 70s music. S'Pfefferkörndl is a good place for a drink, and you can get a steak or pizza there until late. The smart, modern Fux bar and restaurant has live music, pop art in the toilets and a huge wine list.

For a change of scene, the Rote Wand in Zug has a disco.

Taxi James is a shared minibus taxi, which charges a flat fare for any journey in Lech/Zürs – you phone and it picks you up within half an hour.

OFF THE SLOPES
At ease
Many visitors to Lech don't indulge in sports. The range of shopping isn't huge – it's a village, not a town – but the main street often presents a parade of fur-clad browsers. Strolz's plush emporium right in the centre is a good place to up the rate at which you're spending euros.

It's easy for pedestrians to get to

STUBEN-TOURISM

Stuben lies at the foot of the Arlberg pass to St Anton and the Flexen pass to Lech ↓

Oberlech or Zug to meet friends for lunch on the slopes – or for skiers and boarders to get back to the village. The village outdoor bars make ideal posing positions. There are various sporting activities and 30km/19 miles of walking paths – the walk along the river to Zug is especially beautiful.

Zürs 1720m/5,640ft

Ten minutes' drive towards St Anton from Lech, Zürs is almost on the Flexen Pass, with good snow virtually guaranteed. Austria's first recognisable ski lift was built here in 1937.

The village is even more upmarket than Lech, with no hotels of less than 3-star standing, and a dozen 4-star and 5-star hotels around which life revolves. But we find it a difficult place

to like. It has nothing resembling a centre (there are few shops) and the traffic doesn't so much intrude as ruin the place. Nightlife is quiet. There's a disco in the Edelweiss hotel (26620) and a piano bar in the Alpenhof (21910). Mathie's-Stüble and Kaminstüble are worth trying, as is Vernissage, at the Skiclub Alpenrose (22710), which is reported to be the best nightspot in town. Serious dining means the Zürserhof (25130) and the Lorünser (22540). All phone numbers given are for 4- or 5-star hotels.

Zürs has its own school, but many of the instructors are booked for the entire season by regular clients, and more than 80% of them are booked privately. The resort also has its own kindergarten.

Stuben 1405m/4,610ft

Stuben is linked by lifts and pistes to St Anton, but is on the Vorarlberg side of the Arlberg pass (St Anton is over in the Tirol). There are infrequent but timetabled buses between the village and Lech and Zürs, and more frequent ones from Rauz, reachable on skis.

Dating back to the 13th century, Stuben is a small, unspoiled village where personal service and quiet friendliness are the order of the day. Modern developments are kept to a minimum. The only concessions to the new era are a few unobtrusive hotels, a school, two or three bars, a couple of banks and a few little shops. The old church and traditional buildings, usually snow-covered, make Stuben a really charming Alpine village.

The Albona mountain above Stuben has north-facing slopes that hold powder well and some wonderful, deserted off-piste descents including beautifully long runs down to Langen (where you can catch the train) and back to St Anton. These are, however, 'high-alpine touring runs' and should be taken seriously. The slow village chair can be a cold ride. A quicker and warmer way to get to St Anton in the morning, if you have a car, is to drive up the road to Rauz. Stuben has sunny nursery slopes separate from the main slopes, but lack of progression runs make it unsuitable for beginners.

Evenings are quiet, but several places have a pleasant atmosphere. The charming old Post (7610) is a very comfortable 4-star renowned for its fine restaurant.

Lech

141

Mayrhofen 630m/2,070ft

Traditional British favourite with newly expanded area of slopes

WHAT IT COSTS

HOW IT RATES

The slopes

Snow	★★★
Extent	★★★
Experts	★
Intermediates	★★★
Beginners	★★
Convenience	★
Queues	★
Restaurants	★★★★

The rest

Scenery	★★★
Resort charm	★★★
Off-slope	★★★★

Premier Collection

What's new

Massive investment in lifts in recent years includes new high-capacity gondolas out of town and from Hippach and high-speed chairs on the mountain.

Last season, a new 150-person cable-car linked the Penken slopes with those of Rastkogel above Vorderlanersbach, previously a bus-ride away. This area links to the Eggalm area above Lanersbach. The link back is by a new high-speed six-pack. All this has meant a 40% increase in Mayrhofen's terrain to a total of 143km/90 miles.

Back in the original Mayrhofen area the old double chair up to Schafskopf was replaced by a high-speed six-pack for 2001/02. Another new six-pack was be built in this area, opening up a new run.

- ➕ New lifts for last season increased the local terrain by 40%
- ➕ Snow-sure by Tirol standards, plus the Hintertux glacier nearby
- ➕ Various nearby areas on the same lift pass, and reached by free bus
- ➕ Lively après-ski – though it's easily avoided if you prefer peace
- ➕ Excellent children's amenities
- ➕ Wide range of off-slope facilities

- ➖ Two widely separated areas of slopes and no runs back to the village itself from the main area
- ➖ Best beginner area on different mountain from the main one, so difficult to meet up with more advanced friends
- ➖ Slopes can be crowded
- ➖ Mainly short runs
- ➖ Little to challenge experts

Mayrhofen has long been a British favourite. Many visitors like it for its lively nightlife. But it's also an excellent family resort, with highly regarded ski schools and kindergartens and a fun pool with special children's area. The liveliest of the nightlife is confined to a few places, easily avoided by families.

Two new lifts for the 2001/02 season linked Mayrhofen's existing slopes with those of Lanersbach and Vorderlanersbach, increasing the local pistes by around 40% and giving some much needed longer runs – most of the runs in the original area are very short (typically 300m to 400m (1,000ft to 1,300ft) vertical). Intermediates who are willing to travel around on the free buses can have an enjoyably varied week visiting different ski areas on the Ziller valley lift pass, including the excellent glacier up at Hintertux. But if you plan to spend a lot of time at the glacier, consider staying in Lanersbach (see the Hintertux chapter).

Despite recent lift improvements, Mayrhofen itself is not a convenient resort – the main lift station is at one end of town and you have to catch the lift down as well as up, or end up a bus-ride from town.

The resort

Mayrhofen is a fairly large resort sitting in the flat-bottomed Zillertal. Most shops, bars and restaurants are on the one main, long, largely pedestrianised, street, with hotels and pensions spread over a wider area. As the village has grown, architecture has been kept traditional.

Despite its reputation for lively après-ski, Mayrhofen is not dominated by lager louts. They exist, but tend to gather in a few easily avoided bars. The central hotels are mainly slightly upmarket, and overall the resort feels pleasantly civilised (though we have had a few complaints about traffic).

The Penken lift station is towards one end of the main street, while the Ahorn cable-car is out in the suburbs, about 1km/0.5 miles from the centre.

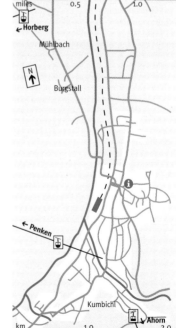

Not many of Mayrhofen's slopes are this gentle – most are challenging intermediate runs →

TVB MAYRHOFEN / A DÄHLING

MOUNTAIN FACTS

for Ski and Glacier World Zillertal 3000

Altitude	630m-3250m
	2,070ft-10,660ft
Lifts	65
Pistes	232km
	144 miles
Blue	28%
Red	57%
Black	15%
Snowmaking	86km
	54 miles

LIFT PASSES

2002/03 prices in euros

Ski and Glacier World Zillertal
Coverage depends on period – see notes.
Main pass
including glacier
1-day pass 34
6-day pass 161
Children
15 to 18: 6-day pass (including glacier) 129
6 to 14: 6-day pass (including glacier) 97
Under 6: free pass
Short-term passes
Passes available from 11am, 11.45am and 2pm.
Alternative periods
Ziller Valley Super Ski pass available for 4 days' skiing in 6, 5 days in 7, 6 days in 7 and 10 days in 14.
Notes Up to 3-day passes cover Penken, Eggalm, Rastkogel and Hintertux glacier areas; 4-day and over passes include all 153 Ziller valley lifts, 488km of piste, ski-bus and railway.

The free bus service can be crowded and there are different routes that you have to figure out. And it finishes early (5pm), so location is important. The original centre, around the market, tourist office and bus/railway stations, is now on the edge of things. The most convenient area is on the main street, close to the Penken gondola station.

The mountains

Of Mayrhofen's two areas of slopes Penken/Rastkogel/Eggalm is mainly suitable for intermediates, and Ahorn for beginners. Neither has much for experts. Free buses serve other resorts covered by the pass but get packed at peak times ('get the 8am bus and you'll be in Hintertux just as the lifts open,' recommends a reporter). When you buy a lift pass, make sure it covers the Hintertux glacier. Signposting of runs around the new link with Rastkogel is reportedly poor: 'Many made the same mistake as us (twice!) and ended up in Finkenberg as the lifts closed – with a huge queue for the hourly bus,' said one visitor.

THE SLOPES
Rather inconvenient

Lifts to the two main sectors are a longish walk or a bus-ride apart, and you often have to take them down as well as up. The largest area is **Penken**, accessed by the main jumbo gondola from one end of town. It is also accessible via the eight-person Hippach gondola, a bus-ride away, and by the gondola from Finkenberg. You cannot get back to Mayrhofen on snow – you either catch the main gondola down or, if cover is good, you can get back to both Finkenberg and Hippach on snow (the Finkenberg piste is a path, classified red, and there's an unpisted ski-route to Hippach). A new cable-car now links the Penken area with the **Rastkogel** and **Eggalm** areas, forming a linked area of 143km/90 miles of pistes – see the Hintertux chapter. Reporters love this new link but warn that 'it breaks down without good snow-cover' and that getting back involves 'either a stiff climb to catch the cable-car down or a long and, in parts, difficult red'.

The only trail from the mountains to Mayrhofen (the outskirts of it) is a black run from **Ahorn**.

Mayrhofen

143

boarding *Mayrhofen is not ideal for learning to snowboard – the nursery slopes are inconvenient and the lifts there are mainly drags. For intermediates, the Penken slopes are good and the lifts there are mainly gondolas and chairs. There is a terrain-park and a half-pipe on Penken. The British Championships used to be held here and now there is a new annual event called the Brit Games. More advanced riders will enjoy the Hintertux glacier, further up the valley – it's a boarder-friendly place (except for the drag-lifts), with Europe's highest World Cup half-pipe and some good off-piste possibilities. Budget prices and lively nightlife make Mayrhofen a popular boarder destination.*

SNOW RELIABILITY
Good by Austrian standards

Although the highest lift goes no higher than 2500m/8,200ft, the area is reasonably good for snow-cover because (apart from the unreliable valley runs) all of Mayrhofen's slopes are above 1580m/5,180ft. Snowmaking covers nearly all the main slopes in the Penken/Horberg/Gerent area. And there is one of the best glaciers in the Alps at Hintertux. As mentioned above reporters have had problems with poor snow on the run linking to Eggalm (the run was closed on our 2001 visit, too).

FOR EXPERTS
Not ideal

Mayrhofen itself doesn't have much for experts. But there are worthwhile challenges to be found (including off-piste areas, such as from the top of the slow chair up to the top of Rastkogel down to the bottom of the new cable-car). And reporters staying here and visiting the other resorts on the valley lift pass have been more than happy. The long unpisted trail to Hippach is the only challenging local slope, and is rarely in good order – as a report from a repeat visitor testifies: 'Snow conditions were the best I've known, yet some parts were extremely tricky due to poor snow-cover.'

FOR INTERMEDIATES
On the tough side

Most of Mayrhofen's slopes are on the steep side of the usual intermediate range and so great for confident or competent intermediates. And last season's expansion made the area much more interesting for avid piste-bashers. But most of the runs in the main Penken area are short. And there are few really gentle blue runs, making the area less than ideal for nervous intermediates or near beginners. Overcrowding of many runs can add to the intimidation factor.

If you're willing to travel, each of the main mountains covered by the Ziller valley pass is large and varied enough for an interesting day out.

FOR BEGINNERS
Overrated: big drawbacks

Despite its reputation for teaching, Mayrhofen is not ideal for beginners. The Ahorn nursery slopes are excellent – high, extensive and sunny – but it's a rather tiresome journey to and from them and intermediate mates will want to be on Penken most of the time. The overcrowded slopes and restaurants add to the hassle. The Penken nursery area is less satisfactory and there are very few easy blues to progress to from the nursery slopes.

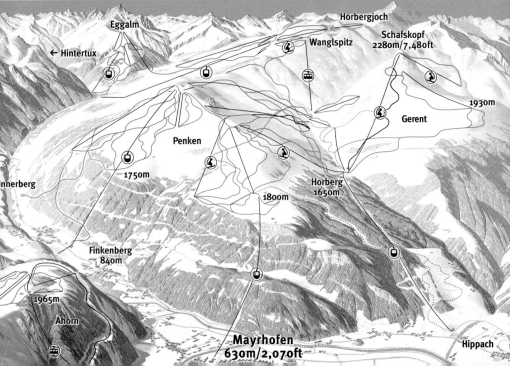

SCHOOLS/GUIDES

2001/02 prices in euros

Mayrhofen Red Profis
Classes 5 days
2½hr: 10am-12.30 or 1pm-3.30
6 half days 92
Children's classes
Ages: 4 to 14
6 full days including lunch 178
Private lessons
2½hr: 109 for 1 person, 123 for 2, 138 for 3

Mayrhofen Total
Classes 6 days
4hr: 10am-noon and 1pm-3pm
6 full days 118
Children's classes
Ages: 4 to 14
6 full days including lunch 178
Private lessons
Hourly and daily
43 for 1hr for 1 or 2 people

Mount Everest
Classes 6 days
4hr: 10am-noon and 1pm-3pm
6 full days 118
Children's classes
Ages: 5 to 14
6 full days including lunch 178
Private lessons
Hourly
40 for 1hr for 1 or 2 people

CHILDCARE

All three ski schools run children's classes for children aged 4 to 14 where lunch is provided. Two of them run ski kindergartens for children aged 1 to 4.

Wuppy's Kinderland non-skiing nursery at the fun pool complex takes children aged 3 months to 7 years, 9am to 5pm, Monday to Friday.

FOR CROSS-COUNTRY
Go to Lanersbach

There is a fine 20km/12 mile trail along the valley to Zell am Ziller, plus small loops close to the village. But snow here is not reliable. Vorderlanersbach has a much more snow-sure trail.

QUEUES
Still some problems

The Penken jumbo-gondola is very oversubscribed at peak times. A reporter this year tells of 'a queue halfway down the high street at 10am on my first day'. 'Get there before 9.10,' says another. 'And there are queues to get down at the end of the day, too. There are often lengthy queues for the Ahorn cable-car.

The slopes can also get very crowded, causing queues for some lifts. Buses to and from the more out-of-town gondolas are often crowded.

MOUNTAIN RESTAURANTS
Plenty of them

Most of Penken's many mountain restaurants are attractive and serve good-value food but can get crowded – Vroni's has been recommended, as has the Schneekar restaurant at the top of the Gerent section. To get away from the crowds try the restaurants on Eggalm. One reporter warns, 'A reasonable understanding of the language is essential as we found no translation anywhere – lots of tomatosuppen or take pot luck!'

SCHOOLS AND GUIDES
Excellent reputation

Mayrhofen's popularity is founded on its three schools and a high proportion of guests take lessons. We have received many positive reports over the years. But this year we heard of a complete beginner in a class of 15 with an instructor who spoke no English – 'we got by on sign language'.

FACILITIES FOR CHILDREN
Good but inconvenient

Mayrhofen has put childcare at the centre of its pitch, and the facilities are excellent. But you may prefer resorts where children don't have to be bussed around and ferried up and down the mountain. And we had a report this year of a 5-year-old girl being abandoned when her ski lesson lesson ended 15 minutes before her father arrived to pick her up, despite previous assurances of supervision.

Staying there

HOW TO GO
Plenty of mainstream packages

There is a wide choice of hotel holidays available from UK tour operators, but few catered chalets.
Hotels Most of the hotels packaged by UK tour operators are centrally located, a walk from the Penken gondola.
(((((5) **Elisabeth** (6767) The resort's only 5-star hotel, an opulent chalet in a fair position near the post office.
((((4) **Manni's** (633010) Well-placed, smartly done out; pool.
((((4) **Kramerwirt** (6700) Lovely Tirolean hotel simply oozing character. A visitor reports 'friendly and helpful staff, comfortable rooms, varied and interesting half-board menu'.
(((3) **Strass** (6705) Best placed of the 4-stars, very close to the Penken gondola. Lively bars, disco, fitness centre, solarium, pool, but rooms lack style.
(((3) **Rose** (62229) Well placed, near centre. Good food.
(((3) **Neue Post** (62131) Convenient family-run 4-star on the main street – 'good food and nice big rooms'.
(((3) **Waldheim** (62211) Smallish, cosy 3-star gasthof, not far from gondola.
(1) **Claudia** (62361), **Monika** (62178) Twin guest houses in a good position.
(1) **Kumbichl** (62371), **Kumbichlhof** (62458) Adjoining pensions, next to the Ahorn cable-car.

EATING OUT
Wide choice

Most visitors are on half-board, but there is a large choice of restaurants. Manni's is good for pizzas ('but expensive, especially for wine'). Kaiser Brundl has been recommended for its extensive menu and good food. Wirthaus zum Griena is a 'wonderful old wooden building offering traditional farmhouse cuisine'. A favourite with tour op reps is the Mount Everest in the Andrea hotel. The Singapore chinese and Rundrum have been recommended this year.

APRES-SKI
Lively but not rowdy

Nightlife is a great selling point. Mayrhofen has all the standard Tirolean-style entertainments, such as folk dancing, bier kellers and tea dances, along with bowling, sleigh rides, tobogganing, but also some seriously lively bars and discos.

GETTING THERE

Air Salzburg, transfer 3hr. Munich, transfer 2½hr. Innsbruck, transfer 1hr.

Rail Local line through to resort; regular buses from station.

ACTIVITIES

Indoor Bowling, adventure pool, 2 hotel pools open to the public, massage, sauna, squash, fitness centre, indoor tennis centre at Hotel Berghof (3 courts, coaching available), indoor riding-school, pool and billiards, cinema
Outdoor Ice-skating rink, curling, horse-riding, horse sleigh rides, 45km/28 miles of cleared paths, hang-gliding, paragliding, tobogganing (2 runs of 2.5km/1.5km), snowrafting

Phone numbers

From elsewhere in Austria add the prefix 05285.
From abroad use the prefix +43 5285.

MAYRHOFEN TOURIST OFFICE

Postcode A-6290
t 6760
f 676033
mayrhofen@zillertal.tirol.at
www.mayrhofen.com

FINKENBERG TOURIST OFFICE

Postcode A-6292
t 626730
f 62962
finkenberg@netway.at
www.tiscover.com/finkenberg

TVB MAYRHOFEN / A DÄHLING

Most shops, bars and restaurants are on ⸱ Mayrhofen's one long, largely car-free street
➔

At close of play, the Happy End umbrella bar, at the top of the Penken gondola, is lively, and the Ice bar, in the hotel Strass, gets packed out, as does Micky's. Some of the other bars in the Strass are rocking places later on – the Lobby bar has live music and the Sport's Arena club has a good atmosphere. Mo's American theme bar and Scotland Yard are also popular. The Schlussel disco can be 'wild'. Try Am Kamin (in the hotel Elisabeth) if you're after more Manhattan than Mayrhofen. The Neue Post bar and the Passage are good for a quiet drink.

OFF THE SLOPES
Good for all

The village travel agency arranges trips to Italy, and Innsbruck is easily reached by train. There are also good walks and sports amenities, including the swimming pool complex – with saunas, solariums and lots of other fun features. Pedestrians have no trouble getting up the mountain to meet friends for lunch.

Finkenberg 840m/2,760ft

Finkenberg is a much smaller, quieter village than Mayrhofen.

THE RESORT

Finkenberg is no more than a collection of traditional-style hotels, bars, cafes and private homes spread along the busy, steep main road between Mayrhofen and Lanersbach. Most hotels are within walking distance of the gondola, and many of the more distant ones run minibuses to the lift station.

THE MOUNTAIN

Finkenberg shares Mayrhofen's main Penken slopes.
Slopes A gondola gives good direct access to the Penken slopes.
Snow reliability The local slopes are not as well-endowed with snowmaking as Mayrhofen's.
Experts Not much challenge, though we did find a black run not marked on the piste map.
Intermediates The whole newly expanded area opens up from the top of the gondola.
Beginners There's a village nursery slope, but it's a sunless spot, and good conditions are far from certain.
Snowboarding No special facilities.
Cross-country Cross-country skiers have to get a bus up to Lanersbach.
Queues The gondola gives queue-free access to the Penken.
Mountain restaurants See the recommendations given for Mayrhofen.
Schools and guides There are two schools. The Finkenberg School has a particularly good reputation.
Facilities for children There's a non-ski nursery, and the ski nursery takes children from age four.

STAYING THERE

Hotels There are quite a few. Sporthotel Stock (6775) has great spa facilities and is owned by the family of former downhill champion Leonard Stock.
Eating out This is mostly hotel-based.
Après-ski The main après-ski spots are the Laterndl Pub and Finkennest, and there are rep-organised events such as tobogganing and bowling.
Off the slopes Curling, ice-skating, swimming and good local walks.

Montafon
650m-1430m (2,130ft-4,690ft)

Extensive slopes, well off the beaten package path

WHAT IT COSTS

The 40km/25 mile-long Montafon valley contains no less than eleven resorts and five main lift systems. Packages from the UK are few (accommodation on a serious scale is not easy to find), but for the independent traveller the valley is well worth a look – especially the Silvretta Nova area (linking Gaschurn and St Gallenkirch) and high, tiny, isolated Gargellen.

What's new

2001/02 saw the installation of a new six-pack and a fast quad on Silvretta Nova. The new lifts access several new runs. Improvements on Hochjoch include a new eight-person chair-lift and some new pistes at Seebliga. And there's a new six-pack in place of the old T-bar up to the top of Grüneck at Golm.

Other developments include new snowmaking on Schafberg – all the way down to Gargellen.

The Montafon is neglected by the UK travel trade. Its location in Vorarlberg, west of the Arlberg pass, makes it a bit remote from the standard Austrian charter airport of Salzburg – and the valley lacks the large hotels that big operators apparently need.

The valley runs south-east from the medieval city of Bludenz – parallel with the nearby Swiss border. The first sizeable community you come to is Vandans, linked to its Golm ski area by gondola. Next are Schruns, at the foot of Hochjoch, and Tschagguns, across the valley at the foot of Grabs. Further on are St Gallenkirch and Gaschurn, at opposite ends of the biggest area, Silvretta Nova. Up a side valley to the south of St Gallenkirch is Gargellen, close to the Swiss border – a tiny village, but not unknown in Britain.

The valley road goes on up to Partenen, where it climbs steeply to Bielerhöhe and the Silvrettasee dam, at the foot of glaciers and Piz Buin (of sunscreen fame) – the highest peak in the Vorarlberg. In summer you can drive over the pass to Galtür and

Ischgl. In winter Bielerhöhe is a great launch pad for ski-tours, and there are high, snow-sure cross-country trails totalling 20km/12 miles on and around the frozen lake. You get there by taking a cable-car from Partenen to Trominier, and then a mini-bus – free with the area lift pass.

There are more ordinary cross-country trails along the valley, and an 11km/7 mile woodland trail at Kristberg, above Silbertal – up a side valley to the east of Schruns. Trails total 100km/62 miles.

The shared valley lift pass covers the respectable post-bus service and the Bludenz-Schruns trains, as well as the 65 lifts – so exploration of the valley does not require a car.

The top heights hereabouts are no match for the nearby Arlberg resorts; but there is plenty of skiing above the mid-mountain lift stations at around 1500m/5,000ft, and most of the slopes are not excessively sunny, so snow reliability (aided by snowmaking on quite a big scale) is reasonable. Practically all of the pistes are

MONTAFON TOURIST OFFICE

Postcode A-6780
t 722530
f 74856
info@montafon.at
www.montafon.at

The tourist office is in Schruns, so from elsewhere in Austria add the prefix 05556, from abroad use the prefix +43 5556.

ALPENSZENE MONTAFON

Steep wooded lower slopes give way to gentler, open, higher slopes →

↑ Like so many
Austrian areas, the
Montafon has
countless bars on the
mountain that fill up
from mid-afternoon
ALPENSZENE MONTAFON

AUSTRIA

148

MOUNTAIN FACTS

Altitude	700m-2395m
	2,300ft-7,860ft
Lifts	65
Pistes	209km
	130 miles
Blue	54%
Red	32%
Black	14%
Snowmaking	62km
	39 miles
Recco detectors used	

Gargellen phone numbers
From elsewhere in
Austria add the prefix
05557.
From abroad use the
prefix +43 5557.

GARGELLEN TOURIST OFFICE

Postcode A-6787
t 6303
f 6690
tourismus@gargellen.to
www.gargellen.to

accurately classified blue or red, but there are plentiful off-piste opportunities (including 37km/23 miles of 'ski routes'). There are snowboard terrain-parks in most sectors and a half-pipe at Silvretta Nova.

There are 11 ski schools in the valley, operating in each of the different ski areas. And eight ski kindergartens take kids from age three.

Tobogganing is popular, and there are several runs on the different mountains – the Silvretta Nova's 6km/4 mile floodlit run down to St Gallenkirch being the most impressive.

GARGELLEN 1425m/4,675ft

Gargellen is a real backwater – a tiny village tucked up a side valley, with a small but varied piste network on Schafberg that is blissfully quiet.

The new eight-person gondola from the village up to the Schafberg slopes seems rather out of place in this tiny collection of hotels and guest houses, huddled in a steep-sided, narrow valley. The runs it takes you to are gentle, with not much to choose between the blues and reds; but there is lots of off-piste terrain. There are four unpatrolled ski-routes. A special feature is the day-tour around the Madrisa – a small-scale off-piste adventure taking you over to Klosters in Switzerland. It involves a 300m/1,000ft climb, but is otherwise easy.

The altitude of the village (the highest in the Montafon) and north-east facing slopes make for reasonable snow reliability. And there is now snowmaking on one of the several pistes to the valley, which include a couple of excellent away-from-the-lifts runs at the extremities of the area.

With care you can ski to the door of the hotel Madrisa (6331) among others. Behind the hotel is a rather steep nursery slope. There are three pleasant mountain restaurants, including two rustic huts at the tree line – the Obwaldhütte and the Kesslhütte. The former holds a weekly après-ski party after the lifts close, followed by a torchlit descent. (Slide shows and bridge are more typical evening entertainments.)

SCHRUNS 700m/2,300ft

Schruns is the most rounded resort in the valley – a towny little place, with the shops in its car-free centre catering for locals and for summer tourists.

A cable-car and gondola go up from points outside the village into the Hochjoch slopes. Above the trees is a fair-sized area of easy blue runs, with the occasional red alternative, served by slow chairs and drags and the fast new eight-seat Seebliga chair. There are restaurants at strategic points – the Wormser Hütte is a climbing refuge with 'stunning' views. Parents can leave their kids under supervision at the huge NTC Dreamland children's facility at the top of the cable-car, by the new skier services building. The blue run from Kreuzjoch back to Schruns is exceptional: about 12km/7.5 miles long and over 1600m/5,250ft vertical. Snow-guns cover the lower half of this, plus the Seebliga area.

Easily accessible across the valley are the limited slopes of Grabs, above the rather formless village of Tschagguns, and the more extensive area of Golm, where a gondola goes from Vandans up to a handful of chairs and drags serving easy slopes above

Piz Buin
3310m

Bielerhöhe

2275m/7.46oft

2150m

Schafberg

Grüneck
2085m

2010m

2100m

1720m

1850m

Gargellen
1425m/4,68oft

Hochegga
1600m

1520m

tenen

1480m

Silvretta
Nova

Golm
1000m

Gaschurn
000m/3,28oft

Gortipohl

St Gallenkirch
900m/2,95oft

Kreuzjoch
2395m/7,86oft

2300m

Grabs

Tschagguns

Vandan

1850m

Schruns
700m/2,3ooft

Hoch
Joch

1335m

Silbertal

Kristberg

Schruns phone numbers
From elsewhere in Austria add the prefix 05556.
From abroad use the prefix +43 5556.

SCHRUNS TOURIST OFFICE
Postcode A-6780
t 721660
f 72554
schruns.tourismus@vol.at
www.schruns.at

the trees, and offering a vertical descent of over 1400m/4,590ft. A new six-pack now goes to the top of the area. Snow-guns cover two major upper slopes, and the red run to the valley.

As you are reminded at every opportunity, Ernest Hemingway ensconced himself in Schruns in 1925/26, and his favourite drinking table in the hotel Taube (72384) is still there to be admired. The Löwen (7141) and the Alpenhof Messmer (726640) are elegant, well-equipped 4-stars with big pools, the former a hub of the après-ski scene.

GASCHURN / ST GALLENKIRCH
900m/2,950ft
Silvretta Nova is the biggest lift and piste network in the valley. As a result, German cars fill to overflowing the huge car parks at the valley lift stations. Gaschurn is an attractive place to stay.
The two main resorts here are quite different. Whereas St Gallenkirch is strung along the main road and spoiled by traffic, Gaschurn is a pleasant village, bypassed by the valley traffic, with the wood-shingled Posthotel Rössle (83330) in the centre.

The lift network covers two parallel ridges running north-south, with most of the runs on their east- and west-facing flanks. The slopes are accessed

Gaschurn phone numbers
From elsewhere in Austria add the prefix 05558.
From abroad use the prefix +43 5558.

GASCHURN TOURIST OFFICE
Postcode A-6793
t 8201
f 8138
info@gaschurn-partenen.com
www.gaschurn-partenen.com

from three points along the valley. A gondola from Gaschurn takes you up to the east ridge, while another gondola from St Gallenkirch goes up to Valisera on the west ridge. A chair-lift to Garfrescha gives access to the central valley from Gortipohl – on the road between the two resorts.

This is the most challenging area in the valley, with as many red as blue runs, and an occasional nominal black. Most of the slopes are above the tree line, typically offering 300m/1,000ft vertical. The new Rinderhütte six-pack has opened up new red pistes from the top of the area. There is lots of off-piste potential, including seriously challenging (and quite dangerous) slopes down into the central valley. The map shows four identified (but unexplained) 'ski routes'.

There are lots of mountain restaurants, many impressive in different ways. At the top of the east ridge is the state-of-the-art Nova Stoba, with seats for over 1,500 people in various rooms catering for different markets, including splendid panelled rooms with table-service. The big terrace bar gets seriously boisterous. At the top of the other ridge is the splendidly woody Valisera Hüsli.

There is snowmaking on one-third of the slopes, with cover down to the valley stations at Gortipohl and St Gallenkirch.

149

Chalet-style hotels on high, snow-sure slopes attract a loyal clientele

WHAT IT COSTS

HOW IT RATES

The slopes

Snow	*****
Extent	**
Experts	**
Intermediates	***
Beginners	****
Convenience	****
Queues	*****
Restaurants	**

The rest

Scenery	***
Resort charm	****
Off-slope	**

Premier Collection

- Glaciers apart, one of the Alps' most reliable resorts for snow – especially good for a late-season holiday
- Excellent area for beginners, timid intermediates and families
- Mainly queue- and crowd-free
- Traditional-style village with very little traffic
- Jolly tea-time après-ski
- Obergurgl and Hochgurgl slopes are now linked by gondola

- Limited area of slopes, with no tough pistes
- Exposed setting, with few sheltered slopes for bad weather
- Few off-slope leisure amenities except in hotels
- Disappointing mountain restaurants
- Village is surprisingly spread-out, in three disjointed parts
- For a small Austrian resort, rather expensive

A loyal band of visitors go back every year to Obergurgl or higher Hochgurgl, booking a year in advance in recognition of the limited supply of beds. They love the high, snow-sure, easy intermediate slopes, the end-of-the-valley seclusion and the civilised atmosphere in the reassuringly expensive hotels.

We're unconvinced. If we're going to a bleak, high, snow-sure resort where there is not much to do but ski or board, we'd rather go somewhere with rather more skiing or boarding to do. But, of course, most such places aren't in Austria – important to some – and their hotels might be less reassuringly expensive.

150

What's new

For 2001/02 a new eight-seater gondola was built from Untergurgl via Hochgurgl to a point high on the Wurmkogl slopes, making lowly Untergurgl a much more attractive bargain base.

A four-seater chair-lift has replaced the Übungs drag-lift in the Gaisberg sector.

A new six-pack, replacing the Steinmann and Sattel drag-lifts, is used extensively by ski schools.

The resort

Obergurgl is based on a traditional old village, set in a remote spot, the dead end of a long road up past Sölden. It is the highest parish in Austria and is usually under a blanket of snow from November until May. The surrounding slopes are bleak, with an array of avalanche barriers giving them a forbidding appearance.

Obergurgl has no through traffic and few day visitors. The village centre is mainly traffic-free, and entirely so at night. Village atmosphere is relaxed during the day, jolly immediately after the slopes close, but rather subdued later at night; there are some nightspots, but most people stay in their hotels. The resort is popular with British families and well-heeled groups looking for a relaxing winter break.

Despite its small size, this is a village of parts. At the northern entrance to the resort is a cluster of hotels near the main Festkogel gondola, which takes you to all the local slopes. This area is good for getting to the slopes and for ease of access by car, but it's a long walk or a shuttle-bus from the village centre and

the nursery slopes. The road then passes another group of hotels set on a little hill to the east, around the ice rink (beware steep, sometimes treacherous walks to and from other amenities). The village proper starts with an attractive little square with church, fountain, and the original village hotel (the Edelweiss und Gurgl). Just above are the Rosskar and Gaisberg chair-lifts to the local slopes. There is an underground car park in the centre of the village.

Hochgurgl, a bus-ride (or gondola-ride) away across the mountainside, is little more than a handful of hotels at the foot of its own slopes. It looks like

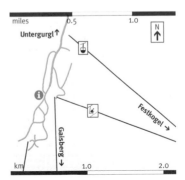

A village of parts: the real centre of Obergurgl is the distant bit, which is surprisingly separate from the high bit (in the middle of the picture) and the bit you get to first, in the foreground →

it might be a convenience resort dedicated to skiing from the door, but it isn't: from nearly all the hotels you have to negotiate roads and/or stairs to get to or from the snow. Hochgurgl is even quieter than Obergurgl at night.

In the valley below Hochgurgl (and now linked by gondola) is Untergurgl, also linked to Obergurgl by regular ski-buses. For a budget base, it is worth considering. For a day out, it's a short bus or car trip to Sölden (good, quite steep and extensive intermediate slopes), and a long car trip to Kühtai (a worthwhile high area near Innsbruck). Much closer is the tiny touring launch-pad of Vent.

The mountains

MOUNTAIN FACTS

Altitude	1795m-3080m
	5,890ft-10,100ft
Lifts	23
Pistes	110km
	68 miles
Blue	32%
Red	50%
Black	18%
Snowmaking	22km
	16 miles
Recco detectors used	

The slopes of Obergurgl and Hochgurgl are about 4km/2 miles apart but are now directly linked by gondola, as well as by road. Even so, the slopes are still surprisingly limited, and lacking interest or challenge for adventurous intermediates or experts. You don't get the sense of travel, as you do in bigger Alpine resorts.

Most of the slopes are very exposed – there are very few woodland runs to head to in poor conditions. Wind and white-outs can shut the lifts and, especially in early season, severe cold can curtail enthusiasm.

The lift pass is quite expensive for the relatively small area.

THE SLOPES
Limited cruising

Obergurgl is the smaller of the two linked areas. It is in two sections, well linked by piste in one direction, more loosely in the other. The gondola and the Rosskar fast quad chair from the village go to the higher Festkogl area. This is served by two drags and a chair up to 3035m/9,960ft (you can join the Rosskar lift at its mid-station too). From here you can head back to the gondola base or over to Gaisberg, with its high point at Hohe Mut, reached by a long, slow chair. On the lightly wooded lower part of this area, two new fast chair-lifts have replaced three drag-lifts. A double chair up from Obergurgl's village square provides the other link on to the Gaisberg slopes. There are two 'ski routes', one of them the only run from Hohe Mut. The piste map used to explain that these are unpatrolled, but no longer does so.

The Top Express gondola is the obvious way to travel to **Hochgurgl** during the day. But there is still the alternative of a regular and reliable free shuttle-bus to Untergurgl, for the gondola up to Hochgurgl.

The slopes of Hochgurgl consist of two high, gentle bowls, either side of the Schermerspitze, served by the continuing gondola and chair-lifts, and open mountainsides either side of the 'village' served by drag-lifts. From Wurmkogl there are spectacular views

challenging expeditions on the glaciers at the head of the valley.

FOR INTERMEDIATES
Good but limited

There is some perfect intermediate terrain here, made even better by the normally flattering snow conditions. The problem is, there's not much of it. Keen piste-bashers will quickly tire of travelling the same runs and be itching to catch the bus to Sölden, down the valley – unfortunately, there is no pass-sharing arrangement.

Hochgurgl has the bigger area of easy runs, and these make good cruising. For more challenging intermediate runs, head to the Vorderer Wurmkogellift, on the right as you look at the mountain. Less confident intermediates may find the woodland piste down from Hochgurgl to the bus stop at Untergurgl tricky.

The Obergurgl area has more red than blue runs but most offer no great challenge to a confident intermediate. There is some easy cruising around mid-mountain on the Festkogel. The blue run from the top of the Festkogel gondola down to the village, via the Gaisberg sector, is one of the longest cruises in the area. And there's another long enjoyable run down the length of the gondola, with a scenic off-piste variant in the adjoining valley.

In the Gaisberg area, there are very easy runs in front of the Nederhütte and back towards the village.

AUSTRIA

152

LIFT PASSES

2002/03 prices in euros

Obergurgl ski pass
Covers all lifts in Obergurgl and Hochgurgl, and local ski-bus.
Beginners Lift pass or points card.
Main pass
1-day pass 36
6-day pass 175
(low season 155)
Senior citizens
Over 60: 6-day pass 131
Children
Under 16: 6-day pass 107
Under 8: free pass
Short-term passes
Half-day (from 11am, noon, 1pm or 2pm).
Alternative periods
5 days' skiing in 7 and 11 days' skiing in 14 passes available.

of the Dolomites. A single run leads down through woods from Hochgurgl to Untergurgl.

SNOW RELIABILITY
Excellent

Obergurgl has high slopes and is arguably the most snow-sure of Europe's non-glacier resorts – even without its snowmaking, which is now impressively extensive. It has a longer season than most Austrian resorts.

FOR EXPERTS
Not generally recommendable

There are few challenges on-piste – most of blacks could easily be red, and where they deserve the grading it's only for short stretches (for example, at the very top of Wurmkogel). But the Hohe Mut ski route can offer challenging moguls, and there is a fair amount of enjoyable off-piste to be found with a guide – especially from Obergurgl – and the top school groups often go off-piste when conditions are right. This is a well-known area for ski touring, and we have reports of very

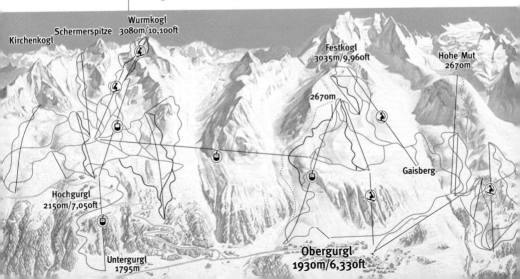

Kirchenkogl

Schermerspitze
Wurmkogl
3080m/10,100ft

Festkogel
3035m/9,960ft

Hohe Mut
2670m

2670m

Hochgurgl
2150m/7,050ft

Gaisberg

Obergurgl
1930m/6,330ft

Untergurgl
1795m

SCHOOLS/GUIDES

2002/03 prices in
euros

Classes (Obergurgl and Hochgurgl)
6 days
4hr: 10am-noon and
1.30pm-3.30pm
6 full days 150
Children's classes
Ages: from 5
6 full days including
lunch 150
Private lessons
Half and full day
167 for full day
106 for half day; each
additional person 8.

Hochgurgl
Classes 6 days
4hr: 10am-noon and
2pm-4pm
6 full days 150
Children's classes
Ages: from 5
6 full days 150
Private lessons
Hourly, half and full
day
55 for 1hr, for 1 or 2
people; each
additional person 15.
109 for half day, for 1
or 2 people; each
additional person 15

CHILDCARE

The ski schools at
Obergurgl and
Hochgurgl take
children over the age
of 5. Children can join
the ski kindergarten
from the age of 3.

The village
kindergarten in
Obergurgl also takes
children from the age
of 3.

The Alpina, Austria
and Hochfirst hotels
(among others) have
in-house
kindergartens.

FOR BEGINNERS
Fine for first-timers or improvers

The Mahdstuhl nursery drag-lift, inconveniently situated just outside Obergurgl, fell into disuse last year, and it's not clear when it will be replaced. Beginners who might have used it must now go up the Gaisberg chair to ski the gentle run back to the village, or to use the easy slopes served by the new Bruggenboden chair. This is not a bad arrangement, though it does seem a shame that you have to leave the village.

The Hochgurgl nursery slopes are an awkward walk from the hotels, but otherwise satisfactory.

Near beginners have plenty of easy blue runs to progress to in both sectors, though Hochgurgl perhaps has the edge in this respect. The quality of the snow makes learning here easier than in most lower Austrian resorts.

CROSS-COUNTRY
Limited but snow-sure

Three small loops, one each at Obergurgl, Untergurgl and Hochgurgl, give just 12km/7 miles of trail. All are relatively snow-sure and pleasantly situated. Lessons are available.

QUEUES
Few problems

The resort is small, is too remote to attract many day trippers, and does not encourage invasions when lower villages are struggling for snow. So major lift queues are rare – even at Christmas and New Year. You can expect high-season queues for the village lifts at the start of ski school, but these tend to clear quickly.

MOUNTAIN RESTAURANTS
Little choice

Compared with most Austrian resorts, mountain huts are neither numerous nor very special. At Gaisberg the Nederhütte is jolly, and David's Skihütte is friendly, cheerful and good value. The 'traditional and welcoming' Schönwieshütte, a 10-minute walk from the piste, has excellent views, as does the small hut at Hohe Mut. At Hochgurgl, Wurmkogelhütte is the only place for a proper meal – a big, but pleasantly woody and spacious, self-service. The tiny hut above it at Wurmkoglgipfel is in an exceptional position and does limited food. Many people return to one village or the other for lunch – one recent reporter 'much preferred' their hotel's sun terrace to 'shaded mountain huts'.

SCHOOLS AND GUIDES
Mainly good news

We've had nothing but good reports of the Obergurgl school in the last few years, with good English spoken and excellent lessons and organisation: 'highly efficient, very thorough testing of pupils before being put into a class', 'big effort to make school fun'. Class sizes are normally between 8 and 12 though we have received reports telling of 15 to a class at busy times.

FACILITIES FOR CHILDREN
Check out your hotel

Children's ski classes start at 5 years and children from age 3 can join Bobo's ski-kindergarten. There is also a non-skiing kindergarten, the Pingu Club for kids aged 3 and up. There's lunchtime supervision for ski school and kindergarten children alike. Many hotels offer childcare of one sort or another, and the Alpina has been particularly recommended.

Staying there

HOW TO GO
Plenty of good hotels

Most package accommodation is in hotels and pensions, but there are a number of comfortable apartments. Demand for rooms in Obergurgl exceeds supply, and for once it is true that you should book early to avoid disappointment.

Hotels Accommodation is of high quality: most hotels are 4-stars, and none is less than a 3-star. Couples at

Obergurgl

boarding *Obergurgl is a traditional ski destination, attracting an affluent and (dare we say it?) 'older' clientele. But the resort is actually pretty good for snowboarding. There's a terrain-park and quarter-pipe on the Festkogl in Obergurgl and a half-pipe on the Wurmkogl in Hochgurgl. Beginners will be pleased to find that much of the resort can be covered without having to ride drag-lifts. And there's also some off-piste potential for more advanced riders. Evenings tend to be a bit tame. .*

GETTING THERE

Air Innsbruck, transfer 2hr. Salzburg, transfer 3hr. Munich, transfer 4hr.

Rail Train to Ötz; regular buses from station, transfer 1½hr.

ACTIVITIES

Indoor Saunas, whirlpools, steam baths, massage, bowling, pool and billiards, squash, table tennis
Outdoor Natural skating rink (open in the evenings), snow-shoe outings

Phone numbers
From elsewhere in Austria add the prefix 05256.
From abroad use the prefix +43 5256.

TOURIST OFFICE

Postcode A-6456
t 6466
f 6353
info@obergurgl.com
www.obergurgl.com

the Alpina have rightly been surprised to be asked to share a table.

A cheaper option is to stay down the valley in Untergurgl, where the 4-star Jadghof is recommended. It's worth remembering that some hotels still don't accept credit cards.

(((4 **Edelweiss und Gurgl** (6223) The focal hotel – biggest, oldest, one of the most appealing; on the central square, near the main lifts. Pool.

(((4 **Alpina de Luxe** (600) Big, smart chalet with excellent children's facilities. Pool.

(((4 **Hochfirst** (63250) Recommended by recent reporter. Good spa facilities, comfortable, four or five minutes from gondola. Casino.

(((4 **Berggasthof Gamper** (6545) 'Excellent,' says a recent reporter – 'Good food, friendly staff.' Far end of town, past the square.

(((4 **Crystal** (6454) If you don't mind the ocean-liner appearance, it's one of the best near the Festkogl lift.

(((4 **Gotthard-Zeit** (6292) Spacious, comfortable, good food. Spa facilities. Small pool. Recommended.

(((3 **Fender** (6316) Good all-rounder with friendly staff; central.

(((3 **Wiesental** (6263) Comfortable, well situated, good value.

(((3 **Granat-Schlössl** (6363) Amusing pseudo-castle, surprisingly affordable.

(((2 **Alpenblume** (6278) Good B&B hotel, well-placed for Festkogl lift.

(((2 **Haus Gurgl** (6533) B&B near Festkogl lift; friendly, pizzeria, same owners as Edelweiss und Gurgl.

Hochgurgl has equally good hotels.

(((((5 **Hochgurgl** (6265) The only 5-star in the area. Luxurious, with pool.

(((4 **Angerer Alm** (6241) 'Excellent facilities and most welcoming staff,' says a recent reporter. Pool.

(((3 **Sporthotel Ideal** (6290) Well situated for access to the slopes. Pool.

(((3 **Laurin** (6227) Well equipped, traditional rooms, excellent food.

Self-catering The Lohmann is a high-standard large modern apartment block, well placed for the slopes, less so for the village centre below. The 3-star Pirchhütt has apartments close to the Festkogl gondola, and the Wiesental hotel has more central ones.

EATING OUT
Wide choice, limited range

Hotel dining rooms and à la carte restaurants dominate. The independent Pic Nic and Krumpn's Stadl are recommended. The Belmonte and the Romantika at the hotel Madeleine are popular pizzerias. Hotel Alpina has a particularly good reputation for its food – though a recent report says the Gotthard-Zeist and Hochfirst are 'just as good'. The restaurant at the Berggasthof Gamper is pleasantly cosy. The two restaurants in the Edelweiss und Gurgl are reportedly 'superb', food at the Josl 'excellent', but both food and service at the Jenewein were found disappointing. Nederhütte and David's Skihütte up the mountain are both open in the evenings. Remember, credit cards are not widely accepted.

APRES-SKI
Lively early, quiet later

Obergurgl is more animated in the evening than you might expect. The Nederhütte mountain restaurant has lively tea dancing – you have to ski home afterwards though. All of the bars at the base of the Rosskar and Gaisberg lifts are popular at close of play – the Umbrella Bar outside the Edelweiss hotel is particularly busy in good weather. The Hexenkuchl at the Jenewein is also popular.

Later on, the crowded Krumpn's Stadl barn is the liveliest place in town with live music on alternate nights – it's also recommended for its fondues. The Josl, Jenewein and Edelweiss und Gurgl hotels have atmospheric bars. The Bajazzo is a more sophisticated late-night haunt. The Edelweissbar and Austriakeller are discos (the latter appealing, when we visited, to an extraordinary age range – 6 to 60). There's now a casino at the Hochfirst.

Hochgurgl is very quiet at night except for Toni's Almhütte bar in the Olymp Sporthotel – one of three places with live music. There's also the African Bar disco.

OFF THE SLOPES
Very limited

There isn't much to do during the day, with few shops and limited public facilities. Innsbruck is over two hours away by post-bus. Sölden (20 minutes away) has a leisure centre and shopping facilities. Pedestrians can walk to restaurants in the Gaisberg area to meet friends for lunch and there are 11km/7 miles of hiking paths. Many of the larger hotels have leisure facilities, though these are generally closed to non-residents – the health suite at the Hochfirst has been recommended.

Obertauern

Small but varied area, with great snow record and lively après-ski scene

HOW IT RATES

The slopes

Snow	****
Extent	**
Experts	***
Intermediates	****
Beginners	*****
Convenience	****
Queues	****
Restaurants	***

The rest

Scenery	***
Resort charm	**
Off-slope	**

Last season a new high-speed quad chair-lift, the Zentralbahn, replaced the old drag-lift.

- ➕ Excellent snow record
- ➕ Well-linked, user-friendly circuit
- ➕ Slopes for all abilities
- ➕ Good modern lift system
- ➕ Good mountain restaurants
- ➕ Lively après-ski scene
- ➕ Short transfer from Salzburg

- ➖ Village lacks traditional charm
- ➖ Slopes have limited vertical and short runs
- ➖ Lifts and snow can suffer from exposure to high winds

If you like the après-ski jollity of Austria but have a hankering for the good snow of high French resorts, Obertauern could be just what you're looking for. The terrain is a bit limited by French standards, and the village is no Alpbach. But it's a lot prettier than Flaine – and if you've grown up on slush and ice in lower Austrian resorts, moving up 1000m/3,000ft or so will be a revelation.

THE RESORT

In the land of postcard resorts grown out of rustic villages, Obertauern is different – a mainly modern development at the top of the Tauern pass road. Built in (high-rise) chalet style, it's not unattractive – but it lacks a central focus of shops and bars.

THE MOUNTAINS

The slopes and lifts form a ring around the village. The Tauern pass road divides them into two unequal parts; that apart, the slopes are well linked to make a user-friendly circuit that can be travelled clockwise or anticlockwise in a couple of hours. Visitors used to big areas will soon start to feel they

have seen it all. Vertical range is limited, and runs are short – most major lifts are in the 200m to 400m (600ft to 1,300ft) vertical range. There's now a clearer new piste map but reporters complain that while pistes are numbered on the mountain, they are not on the map.

Slopes Most pistes are on the sunny slopes to the north of the road and village: a wide, many-faceted basin of mostly gentle runs, some combining steepish moguled pitches with long schusses. The slopes on the other side of the road – on Gamsleitenspitze, to the south-west – are generally quieter and have some of Obertauern's most difficult runs.

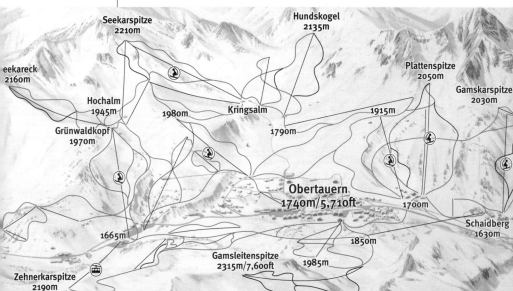

MOUNTAIN FACTS

Altitude	1630m-2315m
	5,350ft-7,600ft
Lifts	29
Pistes	120km
	75 miles
Blue	50%
Red	35%
Black	15%
Snowmaking	70km
	43 miles
Recco detectors used	

Phone numbers
From elsewhere in Austria add the prefix 06456.
From abroad use the prefix +43 6456.

TOURIST OFFICE

Postcode A-5562
t 7252
f 7515
info@ski-obertauern.com
www.obertauern.com

Snow reliability The resort has exceptional snow reliability because of its altitude. But lifts can be closed by wind (which may blow snow away too).
Experts There are genuinely steep black pistes from the Gamsleiten chair, but it is prone to closure. There is good off-piste throughout the area and reporters recommend joining an off-piste guided group.
Intermediates Most of Obertauern's circuit is of intermediate difficulty. Stay low for easier pistes, or try the tougher runs higher up. In the Hochalm area, the Seekareck and Panorama chairs take you to challenging, often mogully runs. The chair to Hundskogel leads to a red and a black. And over at the Plattenkar quad there are two splendid reds. Most of the lifts are chairs and you never have to take a drag unless you choose to.
Beginners Obertauern has very good nursery slopes, close to the village. After the first couple of lessons you can go up the mountain, because the Schaidberg chair leads to a drag-lift serving a high-altitude beginners' slope and there is an easy run to get you back to the village.
Snowboarding There is a terrain-park at Hochalm and drag-lifts are optional.
Cross-country There are 17km/11 miles of trails in the heart of the resort.
Queues When nearby resorts have poor snow, non-residents arrive by the bus-load. However, the lift system is modern and impressive and is continually being upgraded and our most recent reporters experienced no serious queues except for the Zehnerkar cable-car.
Mountain restaurants Mountain restaurants are plentiful and good, but crowded. The smaller huts are more atmospheric. The Edelweisshütte 'has to be savoured at least once in your

stay' for the afternoon sing-songs. The old Lürzer Alm at village level is good.
Schools and guides There are six schools. We have good reports of the Skischule Krallinger, despite large classes at peak times. A reporter this year especially recommends 'Bondi Bill' who works with them as 'excellent'.
Facilities for children Most of the schools take children.

STAYING THERE

How to go Two major British tour operators offer packages here.
Hotels Practically all accommodation is in hotels (mostly 3-star and 4-star) and guest houses. The following hotels have all been recommended: Petersbühel (72350); Steiner (7306) – 'lavish spa facilities, magnificent food'; Enzian (72070); Schütz (72040); Edelweiss (72450); Gamsleiten (7286); Alpina (73360).
Eating out The choices are mostly hotels and the busy après-ski bars at the foot of the north-side lifts. The Hochalm restaurant at the top of the Grünwaldkopf quad sometimes serves early-evening meals.
Après-ski Obertauern has a lively and varied après-ski scene. The Latsch'n Alm has a terrace, music and dancing and is good at tea time. Later, try the Lürzer Alm, which has farmyard-style decor and a disco. The Taverne has various bars, a pizzeria and disco. The Römerhof hotel bar has 'gorgeous girls working there' and Bar Havana and the Rossenhof nightclub are worth a look.
Off the slopes There's an excellent, large sports centre – with fitness room, tennis, squash and badminton, but no pool – but there's little else to do in the village in bad weather. However, Salzburg is an easy trip.
For lunch with friends, walkers can take the path to the Kringsalm hut.

Pitztal

1680m/5,510ft

One of Austria's best glacier areas – and one of its best-kept secrets

WHAT IT COSTS

HOW IT RATES

The slopes
Snow	*****
Extent	***
Experts	***
Intermediates	****
Beginners	***
Convenience	**
Queues	***
Restaurants	**

The rest
Scenery	****
Resort charm	***
Off-slope	***

What's new

For 2002/03 a run will be created from the glacier to the valley, giving a descent of an impressive 1700m/5,580ft vertical – and relieving any queues for the funicular at the end of the day. At HochZeiger, a new six-pack is being installed.

➕ Extensive and varied glacier area with worthwhile 700m/2,300ft vertical on guaranteed snow

➕ Fair amount of skiing in the valley as a whole

➕ Good-value accommodation

➖ Few hotels and guest-houses are convenient for the slopes

➖ Three separate slope areas, one at the bottom of the valley, two close together at the top

➖ Valley-head areas not ideal for beginners

You may not have heard of Pitztal, but most of Europe's ski racers have: its extensive glacier is a favourite spot for training in early and late season. In the main winter season, there are two other worthwhile ski areas to explore at less chilly altitudes – though all the areas are reasonably snow-sure.

THE RESORT
Pitztal is a long valley running roughly south from the Inn valley, just west of the similar but more familiar Oetztal – Sölden's glaciers are just over the ridge from Pitztal's.

Leaving aside the odd isolated drag-lift, there are three areas of slopes, only one of them attached to a recognisable resort village. This is Jerzens (1100m/3,610ft), set on an open mountainside close to the Inn valley, a short bus-ride from the base station of the HochZeiger slopes.

There are hamlets dotted all along the valley road. The main community is St Leonhard, which also embraces the top end of the valley, Innerpitztal, where the skiing of most interest is found. Right at the head of the valley is the major area, the Pitztal glacier, reached by an underground funicular (claimed to be the world's fastest) starting by a large car park at Mittelberg – a couple of hotels 1km/0.5 miles away from the small, recently developed village of Mandarfen. Here,

a six-seat gondola goes up into the third area, Rifflsee.

As you expect in Austria, all the development has been done in traditional chalet style, and even St Leonhard is nothing more than a quiet little village strung along the road.

THE MOUNTAINS
Like the glacier, the Rifflsee area is treeless, except that there are runs back to the valley station that pass areas of woodland. The lower HochZeiger area is partly forested, but again mainly open. Unusually, the glacier isn't open for summer skiing – it has too many crevasses. Lift passes are available for various combinations of areas, including the whole valley.
Slopes It takes only eight minutes for the funicular to whisk you up from the valley floor to the glacier. From there a 'pulse' gondola – the kind with rows of fixed cabins that stops and starts – goes up to the high point of Hinterer Brunnenkogel. From the top – Austria's highest cable-car or gondola station –

157

The glacier has a big, busy restaurant at the top of the funicular ➜

MOUNTAIN FACTS

Altitude	880m-3440m
	2,890ft-11,290ft
Lifts	19
Pistes	87km
	54 miles
Blue	41%
Red	39%
Black	20%
Snowmaking	20km
	12 miles
Recco detectors used	

Phone numbers
From elsewhere in
Austria add the prefix
05414.
From abroad use the
prefix +43 5414.

TOURIST OFFICE

Postcode A-6473
t 86999
f 8699988
info@pitztal.com
www.pitztal.com

TVB PITZTAL

There's plenty to
amuse experts and
intermediates at
Rifflsee ↓

there is a fabulous 360° view,
including a close-up of the Wildspitze.
There are red runs of almost 700m/
2,300ft vertical from here, and three
other main slopes, widely spread
across the glacier, served by drag-lifts.
A run to the valley is in preparation.

At Rifflsee the gondola delivers you
to a mid-mountain crest equipped with
a couple of drags and a beginner lift,
beyond which a fast quad serves
slopes of 600m/1,970ft vertical. A blue
piste and a red ski route go to the
valley.

HochZeiger has less of a high-
mountain feel. There are runs in the
trees served by a quaint single chair
and by the eight-seat gondola up to
the Zeigerrestaurant at mid-mountain.
The open upper slopes are served by a
fast quad supplemented by a double
chair and two drags.

Snow reliability Even the non-glacier
areas are fairly snow-sure: by Austrian
standards they are high. HochZeiger
has snow-guns on its lower slopes.
Experts There are black runs in all
areas, but they don't amount to much.
The glacier is predominantly rather
gentle in gradient, though there are
steeper pitches. The ski school guides
groups down to the valley station. The
high chair-lift at Rifflsee accesses large
amounts of worthwhile off-piste, and
there is gentler stuff at HochZeiger.
Intermediates All three areas are fine,
though the less confident are best
catered for at HochZeiger.

Beginners HochZeiger is the best place
to start – the most reassuring setting,
the least effort, the best slopes to
move on to from the nursery slopes.
But the other areas have beginner lifts.
Snowboarding There are terrain-parks
with half-pipes at all three areas.
Cross-country There are 70km/44 miles
of trails along the valley, plus a 6km/
4 mile trail up at Rifflsee and a 10km/
6 mile one at the lower end of the
glacier (2750m/9,020ft).
Queues We have a report of crowds on
one of the glacier drag-lifts. We would
also expect high-season queues for the
funicular down at the end of the day –
until the new piste to the valley opens.
Mountain restaurants There is a
restaurant with a huge terrace on the
glacier, at the top of the funicular –
'Good food,' says a reporter. Both the
lower areas offer a choice of smaller
places, but those at Rifflsee are said to
get rather crowded.
Schools and guides We lack recent
reports, but don't count on English-
speaking classes.
Facilities for children HochZeiger
seems the obvious spot: it has a very
impressive ski-kindergarten at mid-
mountain with four moving walkways,
plus a smaller setup at the base
station. The glacier also has a snow
garden area.

STAYING THERE
How to go Pitztal doesn't feature in UK
packages as far as we are aware.
Hotels There are dozens of 4-star, 3-
star and lesser hotels and guest-
houses spread along the valley, with
prices rising as you get nearer to the
glacier. We've stayed happily in the 3-
star Anger Alm (86308), close to the
funicular. A reporter says the Sturpen
at Neurur, 7km/4 miles down the
valley, is 'excellent – large rooms,
good food, low bar prices'.
Eating out There are plenty of hotel
restaurants, but little besides.
Après-ski The après-ski scene seemed
rather muted when we visited, and
neither we nor our lone recent reporter
found time to investigate the few
visible bars.
Off the slopes Pitztal wouldn't be high
on our list of places to send non-
skiers, but there are things to do –
snowshoe excursions, skating, walking.
At HochZeiger there's a 6km/4 mile
toboggan run served by the gondola in
the evenings. Trips to Innsbruck are
possible.

Wildspitze
3774m/12,38oft

Hinterer Brunnenkogel
3340m/10,96oft

Pitztaler Gletscher

3250m

2750m

2840m

Grubenkopf

2290m/7,51oft

Rifflsee

2290m

Mittelberg
1740m/5,71oft

Mandarfen

St Leonhard
1370m/4,49oft

2450m/8,04oft

HochZeiger

2000m

2390m

Jerzens
1100m/3,61oft

Arzl
88om/2,89oft

← Innsbruck

← Arlberg →

Saalbach-Hinterglemm

1000m/3,280ft

Attractive villages, lively nightlife and good intermediate circuit of runs

WHAT IT COSTS

HOW IT RATES

The slopes

Snow	★★★
Extent	★★★
Experts	★★
Intermediates	★★★★
Beginners	★★★
Convenience	★★★★
Queues	★★★
Restaurants	★★★★

The rest

Scenery	★★★
Resort charm	★★★★
Off-slope	★★

SAALBACH-HINTERGLEMM
TOURIST OFFICE

160

Saalbach's north-facing slopes will be served by a new gondola this season
↓

➕ Large, well-linked, intermediate circuit with open and tree-lined runs

➕ Saalbach is a big but pleasant, affluent village, lively at night

➕ Village main streets largely traffic-free

➕ Atmospheric mountain restaurants all over the mountain

➕ Sunny slopes

➕ Large snowmaking installation and excellent piste maintenance

➖ Large number of low, south-facing slopes that suffer from the sun

➖ Not much for experts

➖ Nursery slopes in Saalbach are not ideal – sunny, and crowded in parts

➖ Saalbach spreads along the valley and some rooms are far from central

➖ Hinterglemm sprawls along a long street with no real centre

➖ Can get rowdy at night

Like many Austrian resorts Saalbach-Hinterglemm has a pretty, traditional-style village and very lively nightlife, but unlike many it combines this with a very extensive circuit of slopes on both sides of a valley, and runs are linked by an efficient modern lift system. Its slopes resemble a French resort more than a traditional Austrian one – with the added advantage of excellent traditional mountain restaurants scattered here and there.

The main downside is the snow. Although it has impressive snowmaking, one side of the valley faces south and these slopes, especially the lower ones, deteriorate quickly in good weather.

Saalbach's après-ski is very lively – and can get rowdy – and is dominated by Scandinavian and German visitors. It rocks from 3pm until the early hours non-stop. There are also large parties of British schoolchildren around at times.

The resort

Saalbach and Hinterglemm, their centres 4km/2 miles apart, expanded along a narrow dead-end valley floor until, a few years ago, they adopted a single identity. Their slopes are spread across north- and south-facing mountainsides, with lifts and runs connecting the villages via both sides.

Saalbach is one of the most attractive winter villages in Austria. Wedged into the narrow valley, with pisted slopes coming right down to the traffic-free village centre, its traditional-style buildings are huddled together around a classic onion-domed church. Most buildings are modern reproductions – the main exceptions are the Post Inn and the church – and the result is pretty close to Austrian charm with French convenience.

Saalbach is a strange mixture. The attractive, largely traffic-free, main street is lined with expensive, upmarket hotels, restaurants and shops, festooned with fairy lights, but further out there are more cheap and

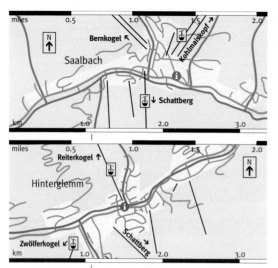

The mountains

The slopes form a 'circus' almost exclusively suitable for intermediates, much of it on lightly wooded slopes. Few runs are likely either to bore the aggressive intermediate or worry the timid one. There are sufficient open sections and changes of pitch and direction to give pistes variety, but not many genuinely black pistes.

THE SLOPES
User-friendly circuit

The complete circuit of the valley can only be travelled anticlockwise – going clockwise, at Vorderglemm there is no way up the slope on the opposite side of the valley. You can do a truncated clockwise circuit, crossing to the south side of the valley at Saalbach itself. The valley floor is very narrow, so there is very little walking necessary when changing sides. Where you finish at the end of the day is not important because of the excellent bus service, which runs every 20 minutes.

A good deal of the south-facing slopes is above 1400m/4,590ft, albeit with rather short runs. Five sectors can be identified – from west to east, **Hochalm**, **Reiterkogel**, **Bernkogel**, **Kohlmaiskopf** and **Wildenkarkogel**. The last connects via Seidl-Alm to Leogang – a small, high, open area, leading to a long, narrow, north-facing slope down to Leogang village, broadening towards the bottom. An eight-person gondola brings you most of the way back.

The connections across Saalbach-Hinterglemm's south-facing slopes work well: when traversing the whole hillside you need to descend to the valley floor only once, in whichever direction you go. At Saalbach a very short walk across the main street gets you from the Bernkogel piste to the Kohlmaiskopf lift and vice versa. Both these runs are well endowed with snowmaking to ensure the link normally remains open, and there is a choice of lifts going up, including a multi-cabin cable-way to Kohlmaiskopf.

The north-facing slopes are different in character – two distinct mountains, with long runs from both to the valley. Access from Saalbach should be vastly improved for 2002/3 by the eight-seat gondola planned to replace the old, queue-prone cable-car to **Schattberg**. The high, open, sunny slopes behind the peak are served by a fast quad.

What's new

For 2002/3 the old queue-prone cable-car from Saalbach to Schattberg Ost is due to be replaced by a new eight-seater gondola complete with mid-station.

This will bring the total number of gondolas serving the area up to seven. Together with eight high-speed chairs these form an impressive lift system that shifts crowds quickly.

cheerful pensions. The clientele are similarly mixed, with rich BMW and Mercedes drivers rubbing shoulders in the bars and clubs with teenagers (including British school kids) looking for a good time.

Hinterglemm is a more scattered, less appealing collection of hotels and holiday homes, with a small, virtually traffic-free zone in the centre. It offers a cheaper, though not inexpensive, alternative to Saalbach, with good access to the north-facing slopes.

The walk to lifts from Saalbach's central hotels is minimal. But Saalbach has seen a fair amount of expansion in recent years, and many of the cheaper hotels are in the least convenient part of the village. In Hinterglemm, position isn't so important. Most of the accommodation is near a lift.

Several resorts in Salzburg province are reachable by road – including Bad Hofgastein, Kaprun and Zell am See, the last a short bus-ride away.

MOUNTAIN FACTS

Altitude	930m-2095m
	3,050ft-6,870ft
Lifts	52
Pistes	200km
	124 miles
Blue	50%
Red	33%
Black	17%
Snowmaking	30km
	19 miles
Recco detectors used	

LIFT PASSES

2002/03 prices in euros

Saalbach-Hinterglemm-Leogang
Covers all the lifts in Saalbach, Hinterglemm and Leogang, and the ski-bus.

Main pass
1-day pass 33.50
6-day pass 154
(low season 143)

Children
Under 19: 6-day pass 140
Under 16: 6-day pass 79.50
Under 6: free pass

Short-term passes
Reduced price passes in the morning from 9am to 12.30, and in the afternoon after 2pm.

Notes Can pay extra 11 euros for free use of indoor pool in Hinterglemm. Sun ticket for pedestrians: 7-day pass 52.50 euros. Points cards for beginners.

Alternative pass
Salzburg Super Ski Card covers all lifts and pistes in Salzburgerland including Zell am See, Kaprun, Schladming and Bad Gastein.

From Schattberg, long runs go down to Saalbach village, Vorderglemm and Hinterglemm. From the latter, lifts go not only to Schattberg but also to the other north-facing mountain, **Zwölferkogel**, served by a two-stage eight-seater gondola. Drags serve open slopes on the sunny side of the peak, and a high-capacity gondola provides a link from the south-facing Hochalm.

SNOW RELIABILITY
A tale of two sides

Saalbach's slopes run along both the north- and south-facing sides of a valley. The south-facing slopes are in the majority and can suffer when the sun comes out. The north-facing slopes keep their snow better but can get icy. Good snowmaking facilities cover several main runs from top to bottom of the mountain on both sides of the valley. The long north-facing run down to Leogang often has the best snow in the area. The resorts also claim to be in a 'snow pocket'. Good piste maintenance helps to keep the slopes in the best possible condition, but an altitude range of 930m to 2100m (3,050ft to 6,890ft) is only a slight advance on Kitzbühel.

FOR EXPERTS
Little steep stuff

There are few challenging slopes. Off-piste guides are available, but snow conditions and forest tend to limit the potential. The north-facing slopes are steeper than those on the south-facing side of the valley. The long (4km/2.5 mile) run beneath the length of the new Schattberg gondola is the only truly black run – a fine fast bash first thing in the morning if it has been groomed. The other long black from Zwölferkogel is really a red with just a couple of short, steeper pitches. The World Cup downhill run from Zwölferkogel is interesting, as is the 5km/3 mile Schattberg West-Hinterglemm red (and its scenic 'ski route' variant).

FOR INTERMEDIATES
Paradise

This area is ideal for both the great British piste-basher, eager to clock up the miles, and the more leisurely cruiser. The south-facing pistes have mainly been cut through the pine forest at an angle, allowing movement across the area on easy runs.

For those looking for more of a challenge, the most direct routes down from Hochalm, Reiterkogel, Kohlmaiskopf and Hochwartalm are good fun. All the south-facing slopes are uniformly pleasant and, as a result, everyone tends to be fairly evenly distributed over them. Only the delightful blue from Bernkogel to Saalbach gets really crowded at times. The alternative long ski route is very pleasant, taking you through forest and meadows.

The north-facing area has some more challenging runs, and a section of relatively high, open slopes around Zwölferkogel, which often have good snow. None of the black runs is beyond an adventurous intermediate, while the long pretty cruise from Limbergalm to Vorderglemm gets you away from lifts for most of the time and is particularly quiet and pleasant first thing in the morning.

Our favourite intermediate run was the long cruise down on excellent north-facing snow to Leogang – over 1000m/3,300ft of vertical.

FOR BEGINNERS
Best for improvers

Saalbach's two nursery slopes are very well positioned for convenience, right next to the village centre. But they are both south-facing, and the upper one gets a lot of intermediate traffic taking a short-cut between the Kohlmaiskopf and Bernkogel areas. The lower one is very small, but the lift is free.

Alternatives are trips to the short, easy runs at Bernkogel and Schattberg. There is also a little slope at the foot of the Schattberg but the schools seem

boarding *Saalbach is great for boarding. Slopes are extensive, lifts are mainly chairs and gondolas (though there are some connecting drags), and there are pistes to appeal to beginners, intermediates and experts alike. For experienced boarders there's good off-piste terrain, a large half-pipe on the Bernkogel above Saalbach, another below Seidl-Alm and terrain-parks on the north-facing slopes just above Hinterglemm and below Kl. Asitz on the way to Leogang. There are also dedicated 'carving' zones for boarders and skiers. And the nightlife is some of the liveliest in Europe.*

loath to use it – so it's great for pottering about on your own at lunchtime. It's rather sunless and a little steeper than the other nursery areas, but perfectly usable.

Hinterglemm's spacious nursery area is separate from the main slopes. Being north-facing, it is much more reliable for snow later on in the season, but it consequently misses out on the sun in midwinter.

There are lots of easy blue runs to move on to, especially on the south-facing side of the valley.

FOR CROSS-COUNTRY
Go to Zell am See
Trails run beside the road along the valley floor from Saalbach to Vorderglemm and between Hinterglemm and the valley end at Lindlingalm. In mid-winter these trails get very little sun, and are not very exciting. The countryside beyond nearby Zell am See offers more scope.

QUEUES
Main bottleneck eliminated
The replacement of the Schattberg cable-car by a new gondola for 2002/3 will eliminate the only regular queues.

When all runs are in good shape there are few other problems, except small morning peak queues to leave Saalbach on the Bernkogel chair and the following drag to reach the sunniest slopes on the 'circuit'.

Saalbach-Hinterglemm does not get as overrun at weekends as many Austrian resorts – it's less accessible for the Munich hordes than the Ski Welt area and its neighbours.

MOUNTAIN RESTAURANTS
Excellent quality and quantity
The area is liberally scattered with around 40 attractive huts that serve good food. Many have pleasant rustic interiors and a lively ambience.

On the south-facing slopes, the Panorama on the Kohlmaiskopf slope, Waleggeralm on Hochalm and Turneralm close to Bründelkopf serve particularly good food. The little Bernkogelalm hut, overlooking Saalbach, has a great atmosphere. Reporters recommend the Reider Alm adjacent to the beginner slopes ('table-service and very prompt') and the Bärnalm near the top of the Bernkogel chair ('good food, good value'). The Wildenkarkogel Hütte has a big terrace

SCHOOLS/GUIDES

2002/03 prices in euros

Fürstauer
Classes 6 days
4hr: 10am-noon and 1pm-3pm
1 full day 50
6 full days 135
Children's classes
Ages: from 5
1 full day 50
6 full days 135
Private lessons
2hr and full-day
90 for 2hr, for 1 or 2 people; each additional person 8.
Snowboard classes
Half day 50
6 half days 137
Wolfgang Zink
Classes 6 days
4hr: 10am-noon and 1pm-3pm
1 full day 50
6 full days 135
Private lessons
2hr and full-day
90 for 2hr, for 1 to 2 people; each additional person 7.
Snowboard classes
3hr: 9am-noon or 1pm-4pm
3 half days 120

CHILDCARE

Some ski schools take children from about age 3 and can provide lunchtime care.

Several hotels have nurseries.

GETTING THERE

Air Salzburg, transfer 2hr. Munich, transfer 3½hr.

Rail Zell am See; hourly buses from station, transfer 40 min.

---

and possibly the loudest mountain-top music we've heard, with resident DJ from mid-morning.

On the north-facing slopes, the Bergstadl halfway down the red run from Schattberg West has stunning views and good food. Ellmaualm, at the bottom of the Zwölferkogel's upper slopes, is a quiet, sunny retreat with good food and 'palatial' toilets. The 12er Treff umbrella bar at the top of the Zwölferkogel gondola is good for lounging in the sun. The Simalalm at the base of the Limbergalm quad chair is 'great for the sun and the views'. The restaurant at the top of the Leogang gondola is recommended for its 'great waterwheel producing electricity feature and excellent use of stone water troughs to create one of the best toilets I have seen anywhere, let alone in the Alps. Atmospheric restaurant and good food too.'

SCHOOLS AND GUIDES
An excess of choice
We're all in favour of competition but visitors to Saalbach-Hinterglemm may feel that they are faced with rather too much of this good thing, with eight or nine schools to choose from. We have had good reports of Wolf, Zink and the 'excellent' Snowboard Academy.

FACILITIES FOR CHILDREN
Hinterglemm tries harder
Saalbach doesn't go out of its way to sell itself to families, although it does have a ski kindergarten. Hinterglemm has some good hotel-based nursery facilities – the one at the Theresia is reportedly excellent.

Staying there

HOW TO GO
Cheerful doesn't mean cheap
Chalets We are aware of a few 'club hotels' but Saalbach isn't really a chalet resort.
Hotels There are a large number of hotels in both villages, mainly 3-star and above. Be aware that some central hotels are affected by disco noise.
Saalbach
(((4 **Alpenhotel** (6666) Luxurious, with open-fire lounge, disco, small pool.
(((4 **Berger's Sporthotel** (6577) Liveliest of the top hotels, with a daily tea dance, and disco. Good pool.
(((4 **Kendler** (62250) Position second to none, right next to the Bernkogel chair. Classy, expensive, good food.

(((4 **Saalbacher Hof** (71110) Retains a friendly feel despite its large size.
(((3 **Haider** (6228) Best-positioned of the 3-stars, right next to the main lifts.
(((3 **Kristiana** (6253) Near enough to lifts but away from night-time noise. 'Excellent food.' Sauna, steam bath.
(((3 **König** (6384) Cheaper 3-star and more basic rooms.
Hinterglemm
(((4 **Theresia** (74140) Hinterglemm's top hotel, and one of the best for families. Out towards Saalbach, but nursery slopes nearby. Pool.
(((3 **Wolf** (63460) Small but well-equipped 4-star in the nursery-sharing scheme. 'Especially good' food, excellent position. Pool.
(((2 **Haus Ameshofer** (8119) Beside piste at Reiterkogel lift. 'Great value ski-in, ski-out B&B,' says a reporter.
Self-catering There's a big choice of apartments for independent travellers.

EATING OUT
Wide choice of hotel restaurants
Saalbach-Hinterglemm is essentially a half-board resort, with relatively few non-hotel restaurants. Peter's restaurant, at the top of Saalbach's main street, is atmospheric and serves excellent meat dishes cooked on hot stones. The Wallner Pizzeria on the main street is good value. The Auwirt hotel on the outskirts of Saalbach has a good à la carte restaurant.

APRES-SKI
It rocks from early on
Après-ski is very lively and can get very wild from mid-afternoon until the early hours. In Saalbach the rustic Hinterhagalm at the top of the main nursery slope is packed by 3.30. When it closes around 6pm, the crowds slide down to Bauer's Skialm and try to get into the already heaving old cow shed to continue drinking and dancing. The tiny Zum Turn (next door to the church and cemetery) is an atmospheric former medieval jail that also gets packed around 4pm with many who are still there at 11pm.

Later on, The Pub on the main road out of town is packed with young Brits enjoying the karaoke. The Neuhaus Taverne has live music and 'should be called the Saga Bar – full of 50+ medallion men and women'. Bobby's Bar is cheap, often full of British school kids, has bowling and serves Guinness. Bar No 8 attracts a young clientele and dancing on tables and

> More **snow**, more boards and more **attraction** -
> **Saalbach Hinterglemm** that's **action!**

Saalbach Hinterglemm

www.msm.at

... **such a** ski**circus!**

Reservations, bookings and information:
Touristoffice Saalbach Hinterglemm
A-5753 Saalbach Hinterglemm 550
Tel.:   0043/6541/6800-64
Fax: 0043/6541/6800-69
e-mail: contact@saalbach.com
w@p-Service: wap.saalbach.com

skicircus · carving · snowboard · après-ski · sun   **www.saalbach.com**

ACTIVITIES

Indoor Swimming pools, sauna, massage, solarium, bowling, billiards, tennis (Hinterglemm), squash
Outdoor Floodlit tobogganing, snow tubing, snowmobiling, sleigh rides, skating, ice hockey, ice climbing, curling, 35km/22 miles of cleared paths, paragliding

Phone numbers
From elsewhere in Austria add the prefix 06541.
From abroad use the prefix +43 6541.

SAALBACH TOURIST OFFICE

Postcode A-5753
t 680068
f 680069
contact@saalbach.com
www.saalbach.com

Leogang phone numbers
From elsewhere in Austria add the prefix 06583.
From abroad use the prefix +43 6583.

LEOGANG TOURIST OFFICE

Postcode A-5771
t 8234
f 7302
office@sale-touristik.at
www.salzburg.com/
leogang-tourismus

---

chairs. Kings Disco livens up after midnight. Classics Bar is recommended for its 'smart lapdancing room'. The Panther Bar has jungle decor, discreet music and well-heeled clientele. Zum Herrn'Karl, Hellis and Bergers are also popular. Arena disco has go-go dancers and is very popular. A reader recommends the Burgeralm as '3km up the toboggan track, marvellous atmosphere and reindeer steaks before a 1am descent'.

In Hinterglemm there are a number of ice bars which are crowded immediately after the lifts close, including the Gute Stube of Hotel Dorfschmiede in the centre of town with loud music blasting out and people spilling into the street. The Tanzkimmel is an open, glass-fronted bar with a dance floor, next door to the Londoner, which is the biggest attraction later on – live and disco music, smart, friendly. The Hexenhausl near the Zwölferkogel gondola gets packed and has an animated model of a witch revealing her undergarments. A similar fascination with moving models is demonstrated at the rustic Goasstall just above town by the piste down from Sportalm, where a model goat is equally revealing (and where real goats graze behind glass near the men's toilets). Bla Bla is small, modern and smart, with reasonable prices. The Alm Bar has good music and some dancing.

Tour operator reps organise tobogganing, sleigh rides and bowling.

OFF THE SLOPES
Surprisingly little to do
Saalbach is not very entertaining if you're not into winter sports. There are few shops other than supermarkets and ski shops. Walks tend to be restricted to the paths alongside the cold cross-country trails or along the Saalbach toboggan run to Spielberghs. But there are excursions to Kitzbühel and Salzburg.

Leogang 800m/2,620ft

A much less expensive alternative to Saalbach-Hinterglemm.

THE RESORT
Leogang is an attractive, although rather scattered, quiet, farming community-cum-mountain resort, better placed than Saalbach for those with cars wanting to visit other resorts. It's best to stay at Hütten, near the lift.

THE MOUNTAIN
The village is linked to the eastern end of the Saalbach-Hinterglemm ski circuit, rather out on a spur.
Slopes A gondola from Hütten takes you into the ski area. The local slopes tend to be delightfully quiet being off the main circuit.
Snow reliability The local slopes have some of the best snow in the region, being north- and east-facing, with snowmaking on the run home.
Experts Not much challenge here, except trying to get round the whole circuit and home again in a day.
Intermediates Great long red run cruise home from the top of the gondola. Plus the whole Saalbach-Hinterglemm circuit to explore.
Beginners Good nursery slopes by the village, and short runs to progress to.
Snowboarding The whole area is great for boarding and there's a half-pipe here, though Leogang nightlife is deadly dull compared with Saalbach.
Cross-country The best in the area. There are 25km/16 miles of trails, plus a panoramic high-altitude trail which links through to other resorts.
Queues No local problems.
Mountain restaurants A couple of good local huts.
Schools and guides Leogang Altenberger school has a high reputation – 'excellent service and lessons; highly recommended'.
Facilities for children There is a non-ski nursery, and children can start school at four years old.

STAYING THERE
Hotels The luxury Krallerhof (82460) has its own nursery lift, which can be used to get across to the main lift station. The 4-star Salzburgerhof (73100) is one of the best-placed hotels with sauna and steam, within a two-minute walk of the gondola.
Self-catering There are quiet apartments available.
Eating out Restaurants are hotel-based. The Krallerhof has the excellent food you would expect. The much cheaper Gasthof Hüttwirt has a high reputation for Austrian home cooking.
Après-ski The rustic old chalet Kralleralm is very much the focal tea-time and evening rendezvous.
Off the slopes Excursions to Salzburg are possible.

Schladming

745m/2,440ft

Pretty old town with extensive intermediate slopes

WHAT IT COSTS

HOW IT RATES

The slopes

Snow	★★★
Extent	★★★
Experts	★★
Intermediates	★★★★
Beginners	★★★★
Convenience	★★★
Queues	★★★★
Restaurants	★★★★

The rest

Scenery	★★★
Resort charm	★★★★
Off-slope	★★★★

➕ Extensive slopes on four interlinked mountains

➕ Excellent slopes for intermediates

➕ Extensive snowmaking operation and good piste maintenance

➕ Very sheltered slopes, among trees

➕ Lots of good mountain restaurants

➕ Charming town with friendly people and a life independent of tourism

➕ Ski Alliance Amadé lift pass covers wide range of nearby resorts

➖ Slopes lack variety – one mountain is much like the others

➖ Very little to entertain experts, on- or off-piste

➖ Most runs are north-facing, so can be cold and shady in early season

➖ Nursery slopes (at Rohrmoos) are inconvenient unless you stay beside them – and beginners are expected to pay for a full lift pass

Since its four previously separate mountains were linked by lifts and pistes, Schladming has been able to compete with major resorts that are better known internationally. A keen intermediate who wants to make the most of the links can get a real sense of travelling around on the snow. And as the list of plus-points suggests, we see many attractions in the place.

If you like your slopes to be reassuringly consistent, Schladming has a strong claim on your attention. If on the other hand you like the spice of variety and the thrill of a serious challenge, you might find it all rather tame.

167

The resort

TVB SCHLADMING

It's a big town but its traffic-free centre is near its tree-lined, snow-sure slopes ↓

The old town of Schladming has a long skiing tradition and has hosted World Cup races for many years. It sits at the foot of Planai, one of four mountains that are now linked by lifts and pistes to offer 115km/71 miles of runs. A gondola starting close to the centre goes most of the way up this home mountain. A mile to the east is the small, rustic village of Haus, where a cable-car and gondola go up to the highest of the four linked mountains, Hauser Kaibling. From the western suburbs of Schladming there are chair-lifts back towards Planai and on towards the next mountain to the west, Hochwurzen. The latter chain of lifts passes through Rohrmoos, a quiet, scattered village set on what is effectively a giant nursery slope.

The town (it is definitely not a village) has a charming, traffic-free main square, prettily lit at night, around which you'll find most of the shops, restaurants and bars (and some appealing hotels). The busy main road bypasses the town and is separated from it by a river. Much of the accommodation is close to the centre – just a few minutes' walk from the Planai gondola, but it can can be noisy into the early hours because of nearby bars. The modern sports centre and tennis halls are five minutes' walk from the centre. Rohrmoos makes an excellent base for beginners who aren't

LIFT PASSES

2002/03 prices in euros

Ski Alliance Amadé Ski Pass

The lift pass covers over 275 lifts in more than 30 ski resorts in this part of Austria: the Gastein valley and Grossarl; Salzburger Sportwelt (main areas: Flachau/ Wagrain/ St Johann and Zauchensee/ Kleinarl); Hochkönigs Winterreich (Maria Alm and neighbours). Buses, trains and road tolls between the resorts are covered by the pass.

Main pass
1-day pass 32.5 (low season 30)
6-day pass 156 (low-season 146)

Children
15-18: 6-day pass 144 (low season 136)
6-14: 6-day pass 78 (low season 73)
Under 6: free pass

Notes Morning and afternoon tickets are also available (as are tickets from 11am, 1pm and 2pm on). 1½-day and 2½-day tickets are possible.

looking for lively nightlife. Haus is preferable for those looking for more of a village atmosphere.

It can be quicker to get to a particular hill by car, taxi or bus rather than on skis or board – though we've had mixed reports about the efficiency of the bus services. Reporters were impressed with the free Internet access at the top of the Planai gondola: 'We sent emails instead of postcards,' said one.

The new Ski Alliance Amadé lift pass covers over 30 partially or wholly linked resorts in this part of Austria. Trips to Bad Gastein are feasible by rail but include at least one change. Drivers can also visit Wagrain/Flachau, Kleinarl and Maria Alm. Tour operators organise day trips to other resorts, too. Snow-sure Obertauern is not far away but is not included on the lift pass.

The mountains

Most pistes are on the wooded north-facing slopes above the main valley, with some going into the side valleys higher up, and there are some open slopes above the trees.

THE SLOPES
Four linked sectors – and more
Each of the linked sectors is quite a serious mountain with a variety of lifts and runs to play on. **Planai** and **Hauser Kaibling** are linked at altitude via the high, wooded bowl between them. In contrast, the links with **Hochwurzen** (where you can try night skiing or boarding; though it is not included on the lift pass) and the fourth linked mountain, **Reiteralm,** are at valley level. So although the links offer the ability to travel around, getting around the whole area can take time – and involves some uninteresting linking runs. Although from Schladming it's perfectly possible to get to Hauser Kaibling or Hochwurzen, if you want to spend time on Reiteralm it's more practical to get the bus, or a taxi, to the lift base at Pichl or Gleiming. The link between Planai and Hochwurzen involves riding a lift through a tunnel, whichever way you are travelling.

All the mountains have fairly similar terrain and views, with mainly red runs of much the same pitch down through heavily wooded north-facing slopes. Reporters continue to complain about the piste map and on-mountain signing being poor.

There are five or six other separate mountains. Galsterbergalm is above Pruggern, along the valley to the east, beyond Haus. Fageralm is above Forstau, up a side valley to the west. North of the main valley, Ramsau has its own low slopes and access to the Dachstein glacier. And near Gröbming is the small area of Stoderzinken.

SNOW RELIABILITY
Excellent in cold weather
Schladming's impressive snowmaking operation makes it a particularly good choice for early holidays; and the northerly orientation of the slopes and good maintenance help keep the slopes in better shape than in some neighbouring resorts. But it can be cold and some reporters have complained of poor grooming on the lower part of the mountains. They claim 100% snowmaking, and certainly the main runs to the valley have full cover. Be wary of the steep bottom part of the World Cup downhill run back to town – it can get extremely icy. The best natural snow is usually found on Reiteralm and Hochwurzen.

FOR EXPERTS
Strictly intermediate stuff
Schladming's status as a World Cup downhill venue doesn't make it macho. The steep black finish to the Men's Downhill course and the moderate mogul runs at the top of Planai and Hauser Kaibling are the only really challenging slopes. Hauser Kaibling's off-piste is good, although limited.

FOR INTERMEDIATES
Red runs rule
The area is ideal for intermediate cruising. The majority of runs are red but it's often difficult to distinguish them from many of the blues.

The open sections at the top of Planai and Hauser Kaibling have some more challenging slopes. And the two World Cup pistes, and the red that runs parallel to the Haus downhill course, are ideal for fast intermediates.

Hauser Kaibling has a lovely meandering blue running from top to bottom for the less confident intermediates, and Reiteralm has some gentle blues with good snow. Runs are well groomed, so intermediates will find the slopes generally flattering. Trips to other resorts covered by the lift pass are often organised by tour op reps (especially to Bad Gastein).

MOUNTAIN FACTS

Figures relate to the whole Sportregion Schladming-Ramsau/ Dachstein area

Altitude	745m-2015m
	2,440ft-6,610ft
Lifts	88
Pistes	167km
	104 miles
Blue	29%
Red	61%
Black	10%
Snowmaking	100%
Recco detectors used	

SCHOOLS/GUIDES

2001/02 prices in euros

Tritscher
Classes 5 days
4½hr: 2½hr am and
2hr pm
5 full days: 120
Children's classes
Ages: from 4
5 full days: 160
Private lessons
Half day: 80; full day: 150. Each additional person 15.

Snowboard School
Tritscher
Classes 5 days
5 full days: 120

CHILDCARE

At Rohrmoos the nursery takes children from 18 months.

Children in ski school can be looked after all day.

boarding *Schladming is popular with boarders. Most lifts on the spread-out mountains are gondolas or chairs, with some short drags around. There are two terrain-parks and half-pipes on the main linked area, with another park on the Galsterbergalm. The Blue Tomato snowboard shop also runs the specialist snowboard school. The area is ideal for beginners and intermediates, except when the lower slopes are icy, though there are few exciting challenges for expert boarders bar the off-piste tree runs. Nightlife can be quite lively.*

FOR BEGINNERS
Good slopes but poorly sited

Complete beginners generally start on the extensive but low-altitude Rohrmoos nursery area – fine if you are based there, a bus-ride away if you are not. Another novice area near the top of Planai is more convenient for most people and has better snow, but the runs are less gentle.

FOR CROSS-COUNTRY
Extensive network of trails

Given sufficient snow-cover, there are 300km/186 miles of trails in the region and the World Championships have been held at nearby Ramsau. There are local loops along the main valley floor and in the valleys between Planai and Hochwurzen. Further afield there are more snow-sure trails at Stoderzinken.

QUEUES
Avoid peak periods

The area (especially the Planai gondola first thing) can have queues at peak-season and weekends. The new gondola at Haus has relieved pressure there but the Reiteralm gondola is slow. Reporters recommend avoiding peak February dates and going to Fageralm on busy days.

MOUNTAIN RESTAURANTS
Plenty of nice places

There are plenty of attractive rustic restaurants in all sectors, though Planai probably has the edge. Onkel Willi's is popular for its live music, open fire, indoor nooks and crannies and large terrace, Mitterhausalm is good, and the Schladminger Hütte at the top of the Planai gondola has 'great food'. The Knapplhof at Hauser Kaibling is full of ski racing mementos and the Waldfriedalm at Hochwurzen is 'great value for huge pizzas'.

SCHOOLS AND GUIDES
Generally okay reports

We have generally had good reports. The Tritscher school has been praised by a reporter again this year (but another booked a private lesson and the instructor did not turn up). A reporter complains that the Blue Tomato snowboard school started him off on part of a red run.

FACILITIES FOR CHILDREN
Rohrmoos is the place

The extensive gentle slopes of Rohrmoos are ideal for building up youngsters' confidence. The nursery here takes children from 18 months.

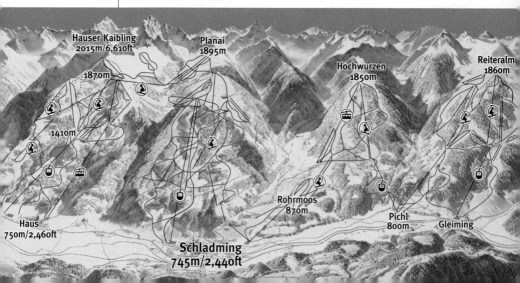

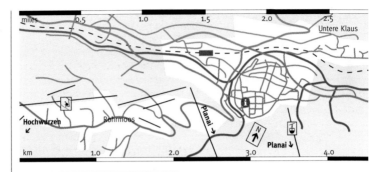

GETTING THERE

Air Salzburg, transfer 1½hr.

Rail Mainline station in resort.

ACTIVITIES

Indoor Swimming, sauna, bowling, indoor tennis court, squash, museum
Outdoor Ice skating, curling, night skiing, floodlit toboggan run (8km/5 miles), sleigh rides, 50km/30 miles of cleared paths in the Schladming and surrounding area, paragliding

Schladming phone numbers
From elsewhere in Austria add the prefix 03687.
From abroad use the prefix +43 3687.

SCHLADMING TOURIST OFFICE

Postcode A-8970
t 222680
f 24138
touristoffice@
schladming.com
www.schladming.com

Haus phone numbers
From elsewhere in Austria add the prefix 03686.
From abroad use the prefix +43 3686.

HAUS TOURIST OFFICE

Postcode A-8967
t 22340
f 22344
haus-ennstal@aon.at
www.haus.at

Staying there

HOW TO GO
Packages mean hotels

Packaged accommodation is in hotels and pensions, but there are plenty of apartments for independent travellers.
Hotels Most of the accommodation is in modestly priced pensions but there are also a few more upmarket hotels.
Sporthotel Royer (200) Big, smart and comfortable, a few minutes' walk from the main Planai lift. Pool.
Alte Post (22571) Characterful old inn with great position on the main square. Good food, but some rooms small and a reporter complains of her bed being an uncomfortable sofa-bed.
Zum Stadttor (24525) Similarly priced, although less charming and well placed. 'Comfortable with excellent food,' says a reporter.
Neue Post (22105) Large rooms, friendly, good food, central.
Schladmingerhof (23525) Bright, modern 'fairly basic' chalet in peaceful position, out in Untere Klaus.
Self-catering Haus Girik (22663) is close to the gondola.

EATING OUT
Some good places

We had a great meal at Fritzi's gasthaus (which has a good reputation). Other recommendations include the Kirchenwirt hotel ('excellent home cooking'), Giovanni's (for pizza), Gasthof Brunner ('good value') and Talbachschenke ('good grills and atmosphere'). Hotels Neue and Alte Post are 'good but expensive'.

APRES-SKI
Varied and quite lively

Some of the mountain restaurants are lively at the end of the afternoon, but reporters agree that down in the town there's a disappointing lack of tea time animation. Charly's Treff (with umbrella

bar) opposite the Planai gondola is the main exception (and has great photos of local hero Arnold Schwarzenegger inside). The Siglu also rocks from 3pm.

There is, however, no lack of options later on – many of the central bars open later and stay open until dawn. The local Schladminger beer is worth a try. Popular spots include the local brewpub Schwalbenbräu and Café Zauberkistl (translated as Magic Box), where the owner regularly performs conjuring tricks. The Beisl is a smart, beautiful bar attracting a varied age group. Hanglbar has wooden decor and middle-of-the-road music and occasional karaoke. Maria's Mexican is 'relaxing' with chilled music and margueritas. The Porta gets very crowded and has live music. The Gondl-Treff has a football theme and big-screen TV. The Sonderbar is a disco with three bars.

OFF THE SLOPES
Good for all but walkers

Non-skiers are fairly well catered for. Some mountain restaurants are easily reached on foot. The town shops and museum are worth a look. Train trips to Salzburg are easy (and recommended as worth a day off the slopes by several readers). Buses run to the old walled town of Radstadt. There's a public pool and ice rink.

Haus 750m/2,460ft

Haus is a real village with a life of its own and its own ski schools and kindergartens. The user-friendly nursery slopes are between the village and the gondola. There's a railway station, so excursions are easy, but off-slope activities and nightlife are very limited. Hotel prices are generally lower than in Schladming. Hotel Gürtl (2383) has been recommended for 'good food and ambience'.

Sölden   1380m/4,530ft

Extensive, snow-sure, intermediate slopes plus throbbing nightlife

WHAT IT COSTS

HOW IT RATES

The slopes
Snow	*****
Extent	***
Experts	***
Intermediates	****
Beginners	**
Convenience	**
Queues	***
Restaurants	***

The rest
Scenery	***
Resort charm	**
Off-slope	**

What's new

For 2001/02 the long Heidebahn chair up from Gaislachalm was replaced by a fast quad.

➕ Excellent snow reliability, with access to two glaciers

➕ Fairly extensive network of slopes suited to adventurous intermediates

➕ Impressive lift system, now linking with glacier slopes

➕ Very lively après-ski/nightlife

➖ Busy road through sprawling village

➖ Some central hotels are distant from the two main lifts

➖ Inconvenient beginners' slopes

➖ Drink-fuelled nightlife too rowdy for many visitors

➖ Limited off-slope activities

Sölden has recently invested massively in new lifts to link its home slopes, which suit adventurous intermediates best, with snow-sure runs on the Rettenbach and Tiefenbach glaciers – the latter, in particular, is a serious slope 2km/1 mile long – which may, in due course, be enough to establish this quite impressive resort on the international market at last.

THE RESORT
Despite its traditional Tirolean-style buildings and tree-filled valley, Sölden is no beauty: it is a large, traffic-filled place that sprawls along both sides of a river and main road (particularly crowded at weekends). The resort attracts a young, lively crowd – mostly Dutch and German – bent on partying.

Gondolas from opposite ends of town go up to Sölden's home slopes – the peak of Gaislachkogl and the lift junction of Giggijoch, 200m above the tiny satellite resort of Hochsölden. An efficient free shuttle-bus service runs between the lift stations, serving those based between the two.

THE MOUNTAINS
The two similar-sized sectors are linked by chair-lifts out of the Rettenbachtal that separates them. The Rettenbach and Tiefenbach glaciers – 15km/9 miles away by road, and until recently closed in winter – are now connected by a series of fast lifts from Rotkogl.
Slopes The Gaislachkogl runs are

almost entirely red or black, but there are several blue runs around Giggijoch. Both main sectors have red runs through trees to the village. The glacier slopes are blues and easy reds.
Snow reliability Most of the area is over 2100m/6,860ft – a good height for Austria – and north-east-facing, so the slopes are generally reliable for snow. With access to the glaciers, Sölden is now one of the best Alpine bets.
Experts None of the black pistes dotted around Sölden's map is particularly serious, but there are quite a few non-trivial reds. And off-piste is another story: there are extensive possibilities in both sectors – particularly from the Gaislachkogl to the mid-station. Guides are available. And at the top of the valley is one of the Alps' premier touring areas.
Intermediates Most of Sölden's main slopes are red runs ideal for keen intermediates, and there are some serious verticals to be racked up; try 11 then 7 from Rotkoglhütte to the village. There are several easy blacks, and the long, quiet piste down to Gaislachalm is ideal for high-speed cruising. Giggijoch offers gentler gradients, but gets extremely crowded.
Beginners The beginners' slopes are situated inconveniently – just above the village at Innerwald – and prone to poor snow. Near-beginners can use the blues at Giggijoch.
Snowboarding There are terrain-parks and half-pipes at Giggijoch and on the Rettenbach glacier.
Cross-country There are a couple of uninspiring cross-country loops by the

171

MOUNTAIN FACTS

Altitude 1380m-3250m
4,530ft-10,660ft
Lifts   34
Pistes   141km
                    88 miles
Blue   32%
Red   52%
Black   16%
Snowmaking   27km
                    17 miles
Recco detectors used

skiclub.co.uk
0845 45 807 80
skiers@skiclub.co.uk

Phone numbers
From elsewhere in
Austria add the prefix
05254.
From abroad use the
prefix +43 5254.

TOURIST OFFICE

Postcode A-6450
t 5100
f 510520
info@soelden.com
www.soelden.com

river, plus small areas at Zwieselstein
and Vent. The saving grace is altitude.
Queues Recent upgrades have done
away with most of the queues, though
one visitor reported late-afternoon
problems returning from the glaciers.
Mountain restaurants The restaurants
have improved in recent years, partly
because they have increased in
capacity. The self-service places around
Giggijoch get very crowded. Gampealm,
towards the end of piste 11, is an
atmospheric old hut. To escape the
crowds try the cluster of places around
Gaislachalm – or head down the
excellent red piste 7 to the calm, rustic
s'Pfandl at Ausserwald.
Schools and guides The only reports
we have of the three ski schools tell of
small class sizes.
Facilities for children Children aged
three and up can join the ski
kindergarten. There are special lift pass
deals for families.

STAYING THERE

How to go Sölden features in very few
UK packages.
Hotels Sölden has some good hotels.
The 5-star Central (22600) is the best
and one of the biggest in town. The 4-
star Regina (2301), by the Gaislachkogl
lift is heartily recommended by a
reporter. The Arno B&B (2488) on the
piste above the Giggijoch lift, and

Gasthof Grüner (2214) in Ausserwald
are also recommended. Self-catering
apartments at the Posthäusl (31380)
are of good quality.
Eating out The Tavola in the hotel
Rosengarten does good food of
various kinds, cheerfully served; they
don't take reservations. Other
recommendations include Café
Hubertus for everything from snacks to
full meals; Nudeltopf and Corso for
pizza; and s'Pfandl at Ausserwald on
the hillside for Tirolean stuff.
Après-ski Sölden's après-ski is famous.
It starts up the mountain, notably at
Giggijoch, and progresses via bars in
the main street – notably the
greenhouse-style Bla-Bla – to countless
places with live bands and throbbing
discos. It gets very loud and very
rowdy. Even our keenest après-ski
reporter was shocked on his last visit:
'Lots of drunks urinating and smashing
glasses in the street. There is table
dancing and striptease at Rodelhütte,
and Lawine has great theme nights if
you are into latex and leather.'
Somewhat tamer are the nightly
toboggan evenings, with drinking and
dancing before an exciting 6km/4 mile
floodlit run back to town from the
Gaislachalm mountain restaurant.
Off the slopes There's a new sports
centre, a swimming pool and an ice
rink. Trips to Innsbruck are possible.

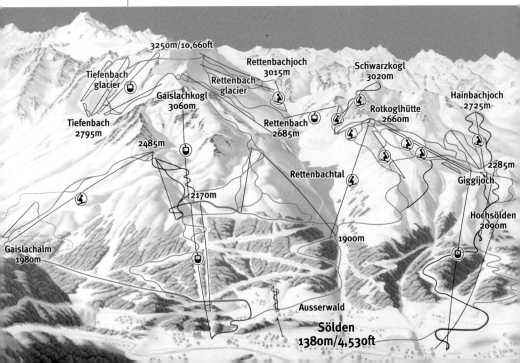

Söll

700m/2,300ft

Small, lively village with extensive Ski Welt slopes and lots of snowmaking

WHAT IT COSTS

HOW IT RATES

The slopes

Snow	**
Extent	****
Experts	*
Intermediates	****
Beginners	***
Convenience	**
Queues	***
Restaurants	**

The rest

Scenery	***
Resort charm	***
Off-slope	**

TiroI

Premier Collection

What's new

The snowmaking capacity in the Ski Welt has been hugely increased in recent years. It now covers 135km/84 miles of pistes (over half the pistes in the Ski Welt) and is the largest snowmaking facility anywhere in Austria.

For 2001/02 the off-piste itinerary on the south side of the Hohe Salve had snowmaking added and became an official black piste.

For 2002/03 a second gondola – an eight-seater – will run from Scheffau to the summit of Brandstadl, replacing the existing chair-lift.

A high-speed six-person chair-lift replaces a T-bar running from Brixen's mid-station to the top station.

SOLL TOURIST OFFICE

The pretty scenery and huge church add to Söll's charm ➜

- ➕ Part of Ski Welt, Austria's largest linked ski and snowboard area
- ➕ Local slopes are the highest and steepest in the Ski Welt and north-facing so keep their snow well
- ➕ Massive recent investment in snowmaking has paid off
- ➕ Plenty of cheap and cheerful pensions for those on a budget
- ➕ Pretty village with lively après-ski

- ➖ Poor natural snow record
- ➖ Long walk or infrequent bus-ride to the lifts
- ➖ Little for experts or good intermediates
- ➖ Ski Welt slopes can get crowded at weekends and in high season
- ➖ Local slopes are the most crowded in the Ski Welt
- ➖ Mostly short runs in local sector

Söll has long been popular with groups of British beginners and intermediates. Its pretty scenery, gentle slopes, small attractive traditional village, good-value accommodation and lively nightlife attract a mixture of young singles looking for a fun time and families looking for a quiet time. In the 1980s it gained notoriety as prime lager-lout territory; it still has some loud bars but has calmed down a lot. Many visitors find the village surprisingly small and are disappointed by the distance between it and the slopes (and by the bus service).

Until recently its main drawback has always been snow – or lack of it. Because of its low altitude and sunny slopes, pistes have often been slushy or bare, not just in Söll but also throughout the extensive Ski Welt circuit it is part of. But this problem has been tackled by a massive investment in snowmaking and half of the Ski Welt's 250km/155 miles of piste are now covered by snowmaking – more than in any other Austrian ski area. This ensures the region's main pistes and links stay open, though it can't prevent slush and ice developing.

When the snow is good Söll can be a great place for a holiday, cruising the attractive and undemanding pistes of Austria's largest linked area.

173

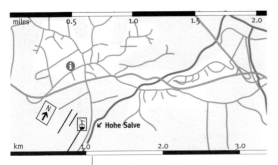

those who are prepared to walk to the slopes. The other side of town has the advantage that you can board the bus there before it gets too crowded. Be aware that some guest houses are literally miles from the centre and lifts, and that the ski-bus does not serve every nook and cranny of this sprawling community.

The mountains

The Ski Welt is the largest linked area in Austria, but that doesn't make it a Trois Vallées. It covers Hopfgarten, Brixen, Scheffau and Ellmau, but is basically a typically small, low, pastoral Austrian hill multiplied several times. One section is much like another, and most slopes best suit early to average intermediates. Runs are short and scenery attractive rather than stunning – although the panoramic views from the Hohe Salve are impressive.

Westendorf is separate, but covered by the area pass. The Kitzbüheler Alpenskipass also covers many other resorts easily reached by car including Kitzbühel, Schneewinkel (includes St Johann), Niederau and Alpbach – an impressive total of 260 lifts and 680km/420 miles of pistes.

THE SLOPES
Short run network
A gondola takes all but complete beginners up to the shelf of Hochsöll, where there are a couple of short lifts and connections in several directions.
These include an eight-person

MOUNTAIN FACTS

Altitude	620m-1830m
	2,030ft-6,000ft
Lifts	93
Pistes	250km
	160 miles
Blue	43%
Red	48%
Black	9%
Snowmaking	135km
	84 miles

AUSTRIA

174

The resort

Söll is a small, pretty, friendly village – much smaller than you might expect by its reputation; you can explore it in a few minutes and there aren't many shops. New buildings are traditional in design and there's a huge church near the centre which, according to a reporter, is well worth a visit at dusk as the graveyard is lit with candles. The pretty scenery adds to Söll's charm, and it benefits from being off the main road through the Tirol.

The slopes are a bus- or taxi-ride or a 15-minute walk from the centre, the other side of a busy road with a pedestrian tunnel underneath. You can leave your equipment at the bottom of the gondola for a small charge. The bus service has been criticised by most reporters as being too infrequent.

There is some accommodation out near the lifts but most is in or around the village centre – a free ski-bus-ride from the slopes. Being on the edge of town nearest the lifts is the best for

LIFT PASSES

2002/03 prices in euros

Ski Welt Wilder Kaiser-Brixental
Covers all lifts in the Wilder Kaiser-Brixental area from Going to Westendorf, and the ski-bus.
Beginners Points tickets (100 points 24). Most beginner lifts cost from 3 to 10 points.
Main pass
1-day pass 30
6-day pass 148.5 (low season 126)
Children
Under 16: 6-day pass 89 (low season 75.5)
Under 6: free pass
Short-term passes
Single ascent on some lifts, passes starting from 11am, noon, 1pm and 2pm.
Alternative periods
5 in 7 days, 7 in 10 days, 10 in 14 days.
Alternative passes
Söll pass available (6-day pass for adults 121.5, for children 73) covers 12 lifts, 34km/21 miles of piste. Kitzbüheler Alpenskipass covers five large ski areas – Schneewinkel (St Johann), Ski Region Kitzbühel, Ski Welt Wilder Kaiser, Wildschönau and Alpbachtal (adult 6-day 170, children 93.5).

boarding *Söll is a good place to try out boarding: slopes are gentle and there are plenty of gondolas and chairs. For decent boarders it's more limited – the slopes of the Ski Welt are tame. But there is a terrain-park and quarter-pipe near Hochsöll and lots of lively bars in the evening.*

gondola to the high point of Hohe Salve. From here there are stunning views and runs down to Kälbersalve, Rigi and Hopfgarten. Rigi can also be reached by chairs and runs without going to Hohe Salve – to which it is itself linked by chairs. Rigi is also the start of runs down to Itter. From Kälbersalve you can head down south-facing runs to Brixen or up to Zinsberg and Eiberg and towards Ellmau.

A quicker way to Ellmau without taking as many south-facing slopes is by taking a cable-car from Hochsöll.

The whole area is vast and will easily keep an early or average intermediate amused for a week.

We have had lots of criticism of the piste map by reporters: 'Direction of runs/lifts and the links not clear' and 'Piste map did not correspond with lift numbers – generally a very bad map.'

SNOW RELIABILITY
Artificial help saves the day
With a very low average height, and important links that get a lot of sun, the snowmaking that the Ski Welt has installed in recent seasons is essential. At 135km/84 miles and covering over half the area's pistes, it is Austria's biggest snowmaking installation. We were there one January before any major snowfalls, and snowmaking was keeping the links open well. It did not, however, prevent slush and icy patches forming – usually slush on south-facing slopes, ice on north-facing ones.

FOR EXPERTS
Not a lot
The two black runs from Hohe Salve towards Hochsöll and Kälbersalve and the black run alongside the Brixen gondola are the only challenging pistes. There are further blacks in Scheffau and Ellmau, but the main challenges are off-piste – from Brandstadl down to Söll, for example.

FOR INTERMEDIATES
Mainly easy runs
With good snow, the Ski Welt is a paradise for early intermediates and those who love easy cruising. There are lots of blue runs and many of the

reds in truth deserve a blue grading. It is a big area and you really get a feeling of travelling around – we skied it for two days on our last visit and felt we only scratched the surface. The main challenge you may find is when the snow isn't perfect – ice and slush can make even gentle slopes seem tricky. In general the most difficult slopes are those from the mid-stations to the valleys: the most direct of the runs between Brandstadl and Blaiken, the pistes down to Brixen and the red run from Hochsöll back to Söll, for example. Higher up, the red from Hohe Salve to Rigi is a good cruise.

FOR BEGINNERS
Excellent when snow is good
The big area of nursery slopes between the main road and the gondola station is ideal when snow is abundant – gentle, spacious, uncrowded and free from good skiers whizzing past. But it can get icy or slushy. In poor snow the Hochsöll area is used. Near-beginners and fast learners can get home to the bottom station when the narrow blue from Hochsöll is not too icy.

FOR CROSS-COUNTRY
Neighbouring villages are better
Söll has 35km/22 miles of local trails but they are less interesting than those between Hopfgarten and Kelchsau or the ones around and beyond Ellmau. Lack of snow-cover is a big problem.

QUEUES
Much improved
Continued introduction of new lifts has greatly improved this once queue-prone area. The new gondola at Scheffau-Blaiken should cut the weekend queues there. When snow is poor, the linking lifts to and from Zinsberg and Eiberg get crowded.

MOUNTAIN RESTAURANTS
Good, but crowded
There are quite a few jolly little chalets scattered about, but we have had a few complaints of insufficient seating and long queues. The atmospheric Stockalm (a converted cow shed), Kraftalm and Grundalm are all near

SCHOOLS/GUIDES

2002/03 prices in euros

Söll-Hochsöll
Classes 5 days
2hr or 4hr: 10am-noon and 1.30-3.30
5 full days: 115
Children's classes
Ages: 5 to 14
5 full days: 115
Private lessons
Hourly or full day (4hr)
43 for 1hr; each additional person 15

ProSöll
Classes 5 days
4hr: 10am-noon and 1.30-3.30
5 full days: 115
Children's classes
Ages: 5 to 14
(younger than 5 years on request)
5 full days: 115
Private lessons
Hourly or daily
40 for 1hr; each additional person 15

Austria
2001/02 prices in euros
Classes 6 days
4hr: 10am-noon and 1.30-3.30
5 full days: 95
Children's classes
Ages: 5 to 14
5 full days: 95
Private lessons
Hourly or daily
35 for 1hr; each additional person 11
137 daily; each additional person 22

CHILDCARE

The ski schools take children from age 5 in special snow-gardens on the nursery slopes from 9.45 to 4pm. Once they progress to Hochsöll, care has to be arranged with the instructor.

Next to the main ski kindergarten, the Söll-Hochsöll school operates a Mini Club for children aged 3 to 5 from 9.45 to 4pm.

Hochsöll. The Alpenrose, near the top of Hohe Salve, has a good sun terrace, generous portions and reasonable prices. Further afield, the Neualm, halfway down to Blaiken, is one of the best huts in the Ski Welt. The nearby Brantlalm has been recommended for lovely views. The Jochstubn at Eiberg is self-service but has a good atmosphere and excellent Tiroler Gröstl. The Filzalm above Brixen is a good place for a quick drink on the way back from the circuit. But our favourite is the Rübezahl above Ellmau – very rustic with wooden carvings, low doors, several rooms and good food.

SCHOOLS AND GUIDES
Three competing schools
The Austria school and the bigger Söll-Hochsöll school have fairly good reputations. But we have a report of an 'instructor with little patience'.

FACILITIES FOR CHILDREN
Fast becoming a family resort
Söll has fairly wide-ranging facilities – the Söll-Hochsöll ski kindergarten, a Mini Club, which looks after children aged three to five who don't want to spend all day on the slopes, and a special kids-only drag and slope on the opposite side of the village to the main lifts. Reports welcome.

Staying there 🔑

HOW TO GO
Mostly cheap, cheerful gasthofs
The major mainstream tour operators offer packages here.
Hotels There is a wide choice of simple gasthofs, pensions and B&Bs, and an adequate amount of better-quality hotel accommodation – mainly 3-star.
(((3 **Greil** (5289) The only 4-star – attractive, but out of the centre on the wrong side for the lifts and pool.
(((3 **Postwirt** (5081) Attractive, central old 3-star with own bar and stube.
(((3 **Bergland** (5484) Small 3-star, well placed between the village and lifts.
(((3 **Panorama** (5309) 3-star far from lifts but with own bus stop; wonderful views; pleasant rooms; good cakes.
(((3 **Tulpe** (5223) Next to the lifts.
((2 **Feldwebel** (5224) Central 2-star.
((2 **Schirast** (5544) Next to the lifts.
((2 **Garni-Tenne** (5387) B&B gasthof between centre and main road.
Chalets There are few catered chalets but a couple of big 'club hotels' run by British tour operators.

Self-catering The central Ferienhotel Schindlhaus has nice accommodation, though the best apartments in town are attached to the Bergland hotel.

EATING OUT
A fair choice
Some of the best restaurants are in hotels. The Greil and Postwirt are good, but the Schindlhaus is said to be the best. Giovanni does excellent pizzas, while other places worth a visit include the Dorfstub'n and the Venezia.

APRES-SKI
Still some very loud bars
Söll is not as raucous as it used to be, but it's still very lively and a lot of places have live music. The Salverstadl (Cow Shed) bar was recommended as 'the best with live music' by a reporter this year. Pub 15 is bit sleazy but lively. The Whisky Mühle is a large disco that can get a little rowdy, especially after other bars close. The Postkeller sometimes has a singalong. Buffalo's Western Saloon is popular. There's a floodlit piste and separate toboggan run – both from top to bottom of the gondola. And for a romantic evening you can hire the Gerhard Berger VIP gondola, complete with leather upholstery, curtains and a champagne bucket.

OFF THE SLOPES
Not bad for a small village
You could spend a happy day in the wonderfully equipped Panoramabad: taking a sauna, swimming, lounging about. The large baroque church would be the pride of many tourist towns. There are numerous coach excursions, including trips to Salzburg, Innsbruck and even Vipiteno over in Italy.

Hopfgarten 620m/2,030ft

Hopfgarten is an unspoiled, friendly and traditional resort tucked away from the busy Wörgl road.

THE RESORT
The village is a good size: small enough to be intimate, large enough to have plenty of off-slope amenities. Most hotels are within five minutes' walk of the chair-lift to Rigi.

THE MOUNTAIN
Hopfgarten offers queue-free access to Rigi and Hohe Salve – the high point of the Ski Welt.

GETTING THERE

Air Salzburg, transfer 2hr. Innsbruck, transfer 1¼hr.

Rail Wörgl (13km/8 miles) or Kufstein (15km/9 miles); bus to resort.

ACTIVITIES

Indoor Swimming, sauna, solarium, massage, bowling, squash
Outdoor Natural ice rink (skating, curling), sleigh rides, 3km/2 miles of floodlit ski and toboggan runs, snow shoeing, winter walking, paragliding, hang-gliding

Söll phone numbers From elsewhere in Austria add the prefix 05333. From abroad use the prefix +43 5333.

SOLL TOURIST OFFICE

Postcode A-6306
t 5216
f 6180
info@soell.com
www.soell.com

Hopfgarten phone numbers From elsewhere in Austria add the prefix 05335. From abroad use the prefix +43 5335.

HOPFGARTEN TOURIST OFFICE

Postcode A-6361
t 2322
f 2630
info@hopfgarten.tirol.at
www.tiscover.com/hopfgarten-brixental

Slopes When snow is good, the runs down to Hopfgarten and the nearby villages of Brixen and Itter are some of the best in the Ski Welt. But the fine, and relatively snow-sure, runs above Scheffau are irksomely distant.

For a change of scene, and perhaps less crowded pistes, take a bus to Westendorf (see separate chapter) or Kelchsau, both on the Ski Welt pass.
Snow reliability The resort's great weakness is the poor snow quality on the south-west-facing home slope.
Experts Experts should venture off-piste for excitement.
Intermediates The whole Ski Welt is great for intermediates.
Beginners There is a convenient beginners' slope in the village, but it is sunny as well as low, so lack of snow-cover is likely to mean paying for a lift pass to go up to the higher blue runs.
Snowboarding A terrain-park near Hochsöll can be accessed from the Hohe Salve above Hopfgarten.
Cross-country Hopfgarten is one of the best cross-country bases in the area. There are fine trails to Kelchsau (11km/7 miles) and Niederau (15km/9 miles), and the Itter-Bocking loop (15km/9 miles) starts nearby. Westendorf's trails are close.
Queues There's only a two-person chair out of the village, so queues can be a problem in the morning.
Mountain restaurants See Söll.
Schools and guides Partly because Hopfgarten seems to attract large numbers of Australians, English is widely spoken in the two schools.
Facilities for children Hopfgarten is a family resort, with a nursery and ski kindergarten.

↑ If you are lucky enough to get fresh snow, the Ski Welt's easy slopes are delightful
SKI WELT

STAYING THERE

How to go Cheap and cheerful gasthofs, pensions and little private B&Bs are the norm here.
Hotels The exceptions to the rule are the comfortable 4-star hotels Hopfgarten (3920) with pool, and Sporthotel Fuchs (2420), both well placed for the main lift.
Eating out Most of the restaurants are hotel-based, but there are exceptions, including a Chinese and a pizzeria.
Après-ski Après-ski is generally quiet, though a lively holiday can usually be ensured if you go with Aussie-dominated Contiki Travel.
Off the slopes Off-slope amenities include swimming, riding, bowling, skating, tobogganing and paragliding. The railway makes trips to Salzburg, Innsbruck and Kitzbühel possible.

Brixen 800m/2,620ft

It may not be pretty, but it has a queue-free, high-capacity gondola up to the main Ski Welt slopes.

THE RESORT

Brixen im Thale is a very scattered roadside village at the south-east edge of the Ski Welt, close to Westendorf. The main hotels are near the railway station, a bus-ride from the lifts.

THE MOUNTAIN

When snow is good, Brixen has some of the best slopes in the Ski Welt.
Slopes All three runs leading down under the gondola are fine runs in different ways: an unpisted route and a

Brixen phone numbers
From elsewhere in Austria add the prefix 05334.
From abroad use the prefix +43 5334.

BRIXEN TOURIST OFFICE
Postcode A-6364
t 8433
f 8332
brixen@skiwelt.at
www.brixenimthale.at

Scheffau phone numbers
From elsewhere in Austria add the prefix 05358.
From abroad use the prefix +43 5358.

SCHEFFAU TOURIST OFFICE
Postcode A-6351
t 7373
f 73737
info@scheffau.tirol.at
www.tiscover.com/scheffau

Itter phone numbers
From elsewhere in Austria add the prefix 05335.
From abroad use the prefix +43 5335.

ITTER TOURIST OFFICE
Postcode A-6300
t 2670
f 3028
tvb-itter@netway.at
www.tiscover.com/itter

black and a red with snowmaking. There's a small area of north-facing runs, including nursery slopes, on the other side of the village at Kandleralm.
Snow reliability A chain of snow-guns on the main south-facing piste helps to preserve the snow as long as possible.
Experts The black run alongside the Brixen gondola is one of the few challenging pistes in the area.
Intermediates Some challenging local slopes for intermediates to tackle.
Beginners The nursery slopes are secluded and shady, but meeting up with friends for lunch is a hassle – the area is a bus-ride from the village.
Snowboarding See Söll.
Cross-country Snow permitting, Brixen is one of the best cross-country bases in the Ski Welt and a 5km/3 mile loop up the mountain at Hochbrixen provides fine views and fairly reliable snow.
Queues New lifts have improved the once queue-prone area.
Mountain restaurants The Filzalm above Brixen has been recommended.
Schools and guides The ski school runs the usual group classes, and mini-groups for five to seven people.
Facilities for children Brixen is not as suitable as other Ski Welt resorts, but it has an all-day ski kindergarten.

STAYING THERE
How to go There are plenty of hotels and pensions.
Hotels The hotel Alpenhof (88320) and the Sporthotel (8191) are both 4-star hotels with pools.
Eating out Mainly hotel-based.
Après-ski Après-ski is quiet, but livelier Westendorf is a short taxi-ride.
Off the slopes Off-slope activities include tennis, hotel-based spa facilities and days out to Salzburg, Innsbruck and Kitzbühel.

Scheffau 745m/2,440ft

This is one of the most attractive of the Ski Welt villages.

THE RESORT
Scheffau is a rustic little place complete with pretty white church. It is spacious yet not sprawling and has a definite centre, a kilometre off the busy main road, which increases its charm at the cost of convenience. The Ski Welt lifts are at Blaiken, on the opposite side of the main road (where there are several hotels).

THE MOUNTAIN
Scheffau is well placed for the Ski Welt's best (and most central and snow-sure) section of pistes.
Slopes Two gondolas (including a new eight-seater for 2002/03) give rapid access directly to Brandstadl and the whole Ski Welt.
Snow reliability Nearby Eiberg is the place to go when snow is poor.
Experts The pistes above Blaiken are some of the longest and steepest in the Ski Welt.
Intermediates This is as good a base as any in the area.
Beginners The nursery slope is in the village and this location makes Scheffau a poor choice for mixed-ability parties – though even first-timers should make it up to Brandstadl by the end of the week.
Cross-country See Ellmau chapter.
Queues The new gondola should eliminate weekend queues at Blaiken.
Mountain restaurants See Ellmau.
Schools and guides The school is well regarded, but groups can be large.
Facilities for children Both the ski kindergarten and non-ski nursery have good reputations.

STAYING THERE
How to go Major operators offer packages here.
Hotels The 4-star Kaiser (8000) and 3-star Alpin (85560) are the best hotels and both have pool, sauna and steam room. The Wilder Kaiser (8118), Blaiken (8126) and Waldhof (8122) are good value gasthofs near the gondolas.
Eating out There aren't many village restaurants, and those staying in B&B places are advised to book tables.
Après-ski Après-ski is unlikely to draw Blaiken residents up the hill. The usual rep-organised events such as bowling and tobogganing are available.
Off the slopes Walking apart, there is little to do. Tour operators organise trips to Innsbruck and Salzburg.

Itter 700m/2,300ft

Itter is a tiny village halfway around the mountain between Söll and Hopfgarten, with nursery slopes close to hand and a gondola just outside the village into the Ski Welt, via Hochsöll.

There's a hotel and half a dozen gasthofs and B&Bs. The school has a rental shop, and when conditions are good this is a good beginners' resort.

St Anton   1305m/4,280ft

Non-stop on- and off-slope action and pretty village base

➕ Extensive, varied slopes for experts and adventurous intermediates, with more to explore in Lech-Zürs a bus-ride away

➕ Heavy snowfalls, backed up by a fair amount of snowmaking

➕ Very lively après-ski, from mid-afternoon onward

➕ Despite expansion, the resort retains some traditional charm – and the animated village centre is now train-free as well as (mainly) car-free

➕ Improved lift system has made Nasserein a viable base and reduced queuing problems, but ...

➖ Still some serious lift queues, at resort level and at mid-mountain

➖ Slopes far from ideal for beginners or timid intermediates

➖ Most of the tough stuff is off-piste – and the distinction between piste and off-piste is unhelpfully blurred

➖ Pistes can get very crowded – some of them dangerously so

➖ Main slopes get a lot of sun, quickly affecting the snow conditions

➖ Resort spreads widely, with some long treks to key lifts and bars

➖ Can get rowdy, with noisy drunks in the central streets in the early hours

St Anton is undeniably a big-league resort. For competent skiers and riders with an appetite for non-stop action and the stamina to keep up with it, we'd rate it even higher: it is one of the great resorts, with an après-ski scene that can be as taxing as the splendid bowls below the Valluga. The combination draws ski bums from around the world, as well as lots of regular holiday visitors.

But it won't suit everyone, as our ➖ points make clear. Many people who might be thinking of trying an Austrian change from Val-d'Isère, or of taking a step up from Kitzbühel, are liable be put off by this list, and rightly so. The St Anton formula works brilliantly for some people, but very badly for others.

The 2001 Alpine World Ski Championships have left a legacy that is worthwhile, but not quite the transformation that is advertised. The new leisure/conference centre looks as dreary as its name – Arlberg-well.com – sounds silly. Removal of the divisive railway line to the far side of the river has certainly simplified access to the lifts, but where the railway was there is now just a kind of gap. The improved lifts from village level to Gampen have eased the queues and given the suburb of Nasserein a huge boost, but further investment is still needed. The improvement that is most needed, though, is a new piste or two back to the village from Galzig, to relieve pressure on the spectacularly overcrowded Steissbachtal. There are off-piste routes that could be developed, given the will. If they can move the railway ....

179

The resort

St Anton is at the foot of the road up to the Arlberg pass, at the eastern end of a lift network that spreads across to St Christoph and across the pass to Stuben. The resort is a long, sprawling mixture of traditional and modern buildings crammed into a narrow valley. It used to be sandwiched between a busy road and the mainline railway – but the railway was moved before the start of the 2000/01 season, and where once there were tracks now

there is a little area of parkland.

Although it is crowded and commercialised, St Anton is full of character, its traffic-free main street lined by traditional-style buildings. It is an attractively bustling place, day and night. More than one reporter has observed that it has better-than-usual everyday shopping.

The main hub of the resort is around the base stations of the two-stage cable-car up via Galzig to Valluga Grat and the fast quad chair up to Gampen. The attractive, lively main

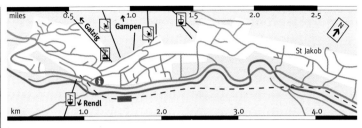

MOUNTAIN FACTS

Altitude 1305m-2650m
4,280ft-8,690ft

Arlberg region

Lifts	83
Pistes	260km
	162 miles
Blue	25%
Red	50%
Black	25%
Snowmaking	65km
	40 miles
Recco detectors used	

street and main hotels are only a short walk from these lifts, and for most purposes a location on or close to this main street is ideal.

The resort spreads down the valley, thinning out before broadening again to form the suburb of Nasserein. This backwater now has an eight-person gondola up to Gampen, and makes a quite appealing base for a quiet time. The nightlife action is a short bus-ride or 15-minute walk away.

Staying between central St Anton and Nasserein is also a more attractive proposition since construction of the Fang chair-lift, which gives access to the Nasserein gondola.

On the other side of the main road (a bearable walk from the centre, but there are also free buses) a gondola goes up to the Rendl area.

St Anton spreads up the hill to the west of the centre, towards the Arlberg pass – first to Oberdorf, then Gastig, 10 minutes' walk from the centre. Further up the hill are the suburbs of Dengert and Moos – a long way out, but quite close to the slopes.

Regular ski buses go to Stuben, Zürs

and Lech (all described in the Lech chapter) and the much less well-known but worthwhile Sonnenkopf area above Klösterle, all covered by the Arlberg lift pass. These buses can get crowded early and late in the day, and a recent reporter complained of 'a bit of a scramble' and lack of organisation collecting payment and storing skis. Van-style taxis can be economic if widely shared.

Serfaus, Nauders, Ischgl and Sölden are also feasible outings by car.

The mountains

St Anton, at 1305m/4,280ft, is well below the tree line, but the slopes are essentially open: only the descent from Rendl to the valley offers much shelter from bad weather.

St Anton vies with Val-d'Isère for the title of 'resort with most underclassified slopes'. There are plenty of red pistes that would be black in many other resorts, and plenty of blues that would be red.

Many of the most popular steep runs marked on the piste map are

classified as 'ski routes'. These have widely spaced markers, they may be groomed occasionally in part, but they are not patrolled and are protected from avalanches only 'in the immediate vicinity of the markers'.

Clearly you should not ski such runs alone, and the piste map recommends them only for people with 'alpine experience or with a ski instructor'. In theory this puts these routes out of bounds for many holidaymakers, but in practice many can't resist the temptation to tackle them without the services of an instructor. One reader sums up the problem with admirable clarity: 'It is entirely unreasonable to expect everyone to take guides on these routes, and it seems irresponsible to ignore the fact that people will go on them. The resort runs the risk of alienating those who want to move off red runs but are not quite ready to take on anything and everything. On some of the ski routes there were snow-guns. This doesn't fit with the idea that you're on your own.' Another reader points out that the routes vary from 'an easy red to a double-black-diamond nightmare'. On Rendl and on Galzig there are drag-lifts serving no pistes but only a single ski route. The situation is, to quote another reader, 'absurd'.

Until 1999, the piste map also showed several 'high-alpine touring runs' not marked on the ground at all, and not protected against avalanche. These no longer appear on the map, though runs of that kind are still shown over in Lech and Stuben. Read the Lech chapter for more on these.

The Arlberg region piste map is poor, attempting to fit too many different mountain aspects into a single view. It's at its worst over in Lech, but it's also unsatisfactory on Galzig. Fortunately the on-mountain maps and signs are clearer. Reporters have complained of poor and limited piste grooming. The local cable TV, showing the state of some of the pistes and queues, can be very useful.

THE SLOPES
Large linked area

St Anton's slopes fall into three main sectors, two of them linked but the third slightly detached.

The major sector is that beneath the local high-spot, the **Valluga**, accessed by cable-car via **Galzig**. The tiny top stage of the cable-car to the Valluga itself at 2810m/ 9,220ft is mainly for sightseeing – you can take skis or a board up only if you have a guide to lead you down the tricky off-piste route to Zürs. The slightly lower station of Valluga Grat gives access to St Anton's famous high, sunny bowls, and to the long, beautiful red/blue run to Rauz, at the western end of St Anton's own slopes. From here you can go on to explore the rather neglected slopes of Stuben, in Vorarlberg on the west side of the Arlberg pass.

All of these high runs can also be accessed by going west from Galzig to ride the Schindlergrat triple chair. Other runs from Galzig go south-west to St Christoph and east into the Steissbachtal. Most of the runs in this whole sector funnel into this 'Happy Valley', producing incredible congestion, especially late in the day.

Beyond this valley, with lift and piste links in both directions, is the **Gampen-Kapall** sector, reachable by chair-lift from central St Anton or gondola from Nasserein. From Gampen at mid-mountain, pistes lead back to St Anton and Nasserein. Or you can ride a six-pack on up to Kapall to ski the treeless upper mountain.

A handful of lifts serve the west-facing runs at the top of **Rendl**, with a single north-facing piste returning to the gondola bottom station.

SNOW RELIABILITY
Generally very good cover

If the weather is coming from the west or north-west (as it often is), the

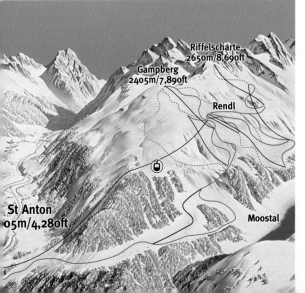

Riffelscharte
2650m/8,690ft

Gampberg
2405m/7,890ft

Rendl

St Anton
05m/4,28oft

Moostal

AUSTRIA

182

LIFT PASSES

2002/03 prices in euros

Arlberg Ski Pass
Covers all St Anton, St Christoph, Lech, Zürs and Stuben lifts, and linking bus between Rauz and Zürs.
Beginners Limited pass covering beginners' lifts.
Main pass
1-day pass 37.5
6-day pass 174
(low season 157)
Senior citizens
Over 65 for men and 60 for women: 6-day pass 149
Children
Under 15: 6-day pass 104
Under 18: 6-day pass 149
Short-term passes
Single ascent tickets on some lifts throughout Arlberg. Half-day tickets (adults 28) from noon, afternoon 'taster' tickets (16) from 3pm.
Notes Main pass also covers Sonnenkopf (10 lifts) at Klösterle, 7km/4 miles west of Stuben. Discounts during wedel, firn and snow crystal weeks.

Arlberg gets it first, and as a result St Anton and its neighbours get heavy falls of snow. They often have much better conditions than other resorts of a similar height, and we've had great fresh powder here as late as mid-April in recent years. But many of the slopes face south or south-east, causing icy or heavy conditions at times. It's vital to time the steeper runs off the Valluga to get decent conditions.

The lower runs are now well equipped with snowmaking, which generally ensures the home runs remain open (though possibly too hard to be enjoyable).

FOR EXPERTS
One of the world's great areas

St Anton vies with Chamonix, Val-d'Isère and a handful of other resorts for the affections of experts. It has some of the most consistently challenging and extensive slopes in the world. The jewel in the crown is the off-piste terrain in the bowls beneath the Valluga – see feature panel.

Lower down, there are challenging runs in many directions from both Galzig and Gampen-Kapall. These lower runs can be doubly tricky if the snow has been hit by the sun.

The several black pistes offer genuine challenges. These include the World Championship race courses – Kandahar from Kapall down to Gampen and the previously red Fang run from there down to the village. There are

countless opportunities for going off-piste. Guidance is very desirable.

The Rendl area across the road has plenty of open space beneath the top lifts and, with an accompanying guide, there is some delightful fun to be had off the back of this ridge.

One of our reporters particularly liked the Sonnenkopf area down-valley from Stuben for its excellent off-piste route to Langen.

On top of all this, bear in mind that many of the red runs on the piste map are long and challenging, too.

The ultimate challenge, perhaps, is to go with a guide off the back of the Valluga. The initial pitch is very, very steep (a fall is likely to be fatal). The run down to Zürs is very beautiful and, not surprisingly, usually deserted.

FOR INTERMEDIATES
Some real challenges

St Anton is well suited to good, adventurous intermediates. They will be able to try the Mattun run and the easier version of the Schindlerkar run from Valluga Grat (see feature panel). The run from Schindler Spitze to Rauz is very long (over 1000m/3,300ft vertical), varied and ideal for good (and fit) intermediates. Alternatively, turn off from this part way down and take the Steissbachtal to the lifts back to Galzig.

The Kapall-Gampen section is also interesting, with sporty bumps among trees on the lower half. Confident

boarding *Though steeped in skiing tradition, St Anton is moving with the times and improving facilities for boarders. Although we don't really recommend it to beginners, it is one of the best free-ride areas in the world, with lots of steep terrain and natural hits. There is a terrain-park and 100m/330ft half-pipe on Rendl. There are still a few T-bars around but fast chair-lifts are now the main ways around the mountains. Lessons are provided by the ski schools and the Snowboard Academy (part of the Arlberg school). A book could be written about the almost legendary nightlife.*

The off-piste runs in the huge bowl beneath the summit of the Valluga, reached by either the Schindlergrat chair or the Valluga I cable-car, are justifiably world-famous. In good snow, this whole area is an off-piste delight for experts.

Except immediately after a fresh snowfall, you can see tracks going all over the mountain – and some of the descents look terrifying. There are two main ski routes marked on the piste map – both long, steep descents that quickly get mogulled. The Schindlerkar is the first you come to and it divides into two – the Schindlerkar gully being the steeper option. For the second, wider and somewhat easier, Mattun run, you traverse further at the top. Both these feed down into the Steissbachtal gully where there are lifts back up to Galzig and Gampen. The Schweinströge – a high-alpine route no longer shown on the map – starts off in the same direction as the red run to Rauz, but you traverse the shoulder of the Schindler Spitze and down a narrow gully.

intermediates may enjoy the men's downhill run from the top to town (again over 1000m/3,300ft vertical).

Less adventurous intermediates will find St Anton less to their taste. There are few easy cruising pistes. The most obvious are the short blues on Galzig and the Steissbachtal (aka 'Happy Valley'). These are reasonably gentle but get uncomfortably crowded, particularly at peak times. The blue to St Christoph is generally quieter. The narrowish blues between Kapall and Gampen can have some challenging bumps. Intermediates looking for easy cruising will find the best by taking the bus to Lech.

In the Rendl area a variety of trails suitable for good and moderate intermediates criss-cross, including a lovely long tree-lined run (over 1000m/3,300ft vertical from the top) back to the valley gondola station. This is the best run in the whole area when visibility is poor, though it has some quite awkward sections.

St Anton

183

FOR BEGINNERS
Far from ideal
St Anton has better nursery slopes now, near the Fang lift. But there are no easy, uncrowded runs for beginners to progress to. A mixed party of experts, intermediates and novices would be better off staying in Lech or Zürs; those who want to explore St Anton can get on the bus to Rauz.

FOR CROSS-COUNTRY
Limited interest
St Anton is not a great cross-country resort, but trails total around 35km/22 miles and snow conditions are usually good. There are a couple of uninspiring trails near town, another at St Jakob 3km/2 miles away, and a pretty trail through trees along the Ferwalltal to the foot of the Albona area. There is also a tiny loop at St Christoph.

QUEUES
Improved, but still a problem
Queues are not the problem they once were, since the replacement of several lifts by fast chairs. But they can still be tiresome in peak season and at weekends. Recent reporters found long queues for the cable-car to Galzig and one hit 'massive' queues for the chair to Gampen, which attracts crowds when higher lifts are closed. At mid-mountain, the cable-car to Valluga Grat generates serious queues, as does the Zammermoos chair out of the Steissbachtal. There are US-style 'singles lines' at some lifts; but, despite taped exhortations in several languages, the chairs are rarely filled.

Perhaps more of a worry than the lift queues are the crowded trails. Clearly the worst is the Steissbachtal, which can be uncomfortably crowded even in January and a nightmare on a March weekend. One reader advocates skiing to Rauz or St Christoph and getting a bus rather than tangling with the Steissbachtal. This long-standing problem is not going to go away until the resort creates an alternative easy piste from Galzig to the village.

MOUNTAIN RESTAURANTS
Plenty of choice
We often seem to end up lunching in St Christoph, which doesn't really count, given that it is on a bus route. We always enjoy the atmospheric Hospiz Alm, not only for its slide down to the lavatories but also for its satisfying food; but some readers have met poor service, and it isn't cheap. The cheaper, cosy Almbar, just above it, and Traxl's ice bar at the Maiensee Hotel, have been recommended.

Many of the best restaurants not accessible by bus are just above St Anton. Readers recommend Sennhütte on the Galzig home run and Rodelalm on Gampen – 'A real hut with good food at low prices and a lovely fire.' Slightly lower still on Galzig, the Mooserwirt serves typical Austrian food at what seem high prices, but 'the portions are absolutely massive'; the Krazy Kanguruh does burgers, pizzas and snacks. The goulash soup at the Taps Bar next to Krazy Kanguruh has been recommended, and the Kaminstube gets beautiful sunsets.

Over on Rendl, the self-service Rendl restaurant is said to offer 'excellent food and value', with zero queuing even when busy. Bifangalm, near the end of the run to the valley, is 'friendly and atmospheric' and relatively uncrowded.

SCHOOLS AND GUIDES
Encouraging reports
The relatively new St Anton school has brought much-needed competition to the Arlberg school, which still generates conflicting reports. 'Complete beginner group much too big despite our complaints and we learned more from our friends,' said one reporter. But our most recent reporters were very happy: 'Children and parents were delighted ... kids were taught well'; 'Our guide was excellent.' We have skied with excellent off-piste guides, and reporters who have hired a guide to tackle the runs from the top of the Valluga have had a great day. We have also heard good reports of Piste to Powder, a guiding outfit run by British guide Graham Austick.

FACILITIES FOR CHILDREN
Getting better
St Anton might not seem an obvious resort for family holidays, but the resort works hard to accommodate families' needs: the youth centre attached to the Arlberg school is excellent, and the special slopes both for toddlers (at the bottom) and bigger children (up at Gampen) are well done. At Nasserein there is a moving walkway lift on the baby slope, and a reporter rates this an 'absolutely ideal' place to stay with young kids.

SCHOOLS/GUIDES
2002/03 prices in euros

Arlberg
Manager Richard Walter
Classes 6 days
4½hr: 2½hr am and 2hr pm, from 9.30
6 full days 190
Children's classes
Ages: 4 to 14
6 full days including lunch 190
Private lessons
Half or full day
202 for full day; each additional person 17

St Anton
Manager Franz Klimmer
Classes 6 days
4½hr: 9.30-noon and 1pm-3pm
6 full days 182
Children's classes
Ages: 5 to 14
6 full days 140
Private lessons
Half or full day
190 for full day; each additional person 16

Piste to Powder
Owner Graham Austick
Various levels of off-piste tuition and/or guiding around the Arlberg region
+43 664 174 6282
UK 01661 824318

CHILDCARE

The kindergarten at the Kinderwelt (2526) takes toilet-trained children aged 30 months to 14 years, from 10am to 4.30. Ski tuition with the Arlberg ski school in a special snow-garden is available for children aged 4.

GETTING THERE

Air Innsbruck, transfer 1½hr. Zürich, transfer 3hr.

Rail Mainline station in resort.

ACTIVITIES

Indoor Swimming pool (also hotel pools open to the public, with sauna and massage), tennis, squash, bowling, museum, cinema in Vallugasaal
Outdoor Swimming pool, 15km/9 miles of cleared walks, natural skating rink (skating, curling), sleigh rides, tobogganing, paragliding

Staying there

HOW TO GO
Austria's main chalet resort

There's a wide range of places to stay, from quality hotels to cheap and cheerful pensions and apartments.
Chalets In the land of the pension, St Anton also has many catered chalets offered by UK tour operators. They tend to be fairly expensive, though few are particularly luxurious and many are in the suburbs – chalets in the centre are virtually all apartment-based.
Hotels There is one 5-star hotel and lots of 4- and 3-stars and B&Bs.
(((((5) **Raffl's St Antoner Hof** (2910) Best in town, but its position on the bypass is less than ideal. Pool.
((((4) **Schwarzer Adler** (22440) Centuries-old inn on main street. Widely varying bedrooms.
((((4) **Alte Post** (2553) Atmospheric place on main street with lively après-ski bar. Endorsed by a reporter.
((((4) **Post** (2213) Comfortable if uninspiring 4-star at the centre of affairs, close to both lifts and nightlife.
((((4) **Sporthotel** (3111) Central position, varied bedrooms, good food. Pool.
(((3) **Grischuna** (2304) Welcoming family-run place in peaceful position up the hill west of the town; close to the slopes, five minutes to the cable-car.
(((3) **Goldenes Kreuz** (22110) A comfortable B&B hotel halfway to Nasserein, ideal for cruising home.
Self-catering There are plenty of apartments available but package deals are few and far between.

EATING OUT
Mostly informal

Plain, filling fare is the norm, with numerous places such as the Trödlerstube and Reselehof serving big portions of traditional Austrian food. The Fuhrmannstube is singled out for 'great value, with an excellent menu and cheery owner'. Possibly the best

food in town is to be had at the Museum where, as well as enjoying upmarket food and wine in elegant panelled rooms, you can learn about the history of the resort. Similarly ambitious in culinary terms but quite different in style is Ben.venuto, in the Arlberg-well.com building: stark.decor, eclectic.menu and excellent.cooking, as you might expect from an offshoot of the Arlberg Hospiz at St Christoph. Bobo's serves good, although expensive, Mexican. A reporter recommends Dixies for pizza, pasta, steaks and fish, though others prefer Scotty's or Pomodoro for pizza. In Nasserein, the Tenne is noted for game dishes and provides 'good, friendly service', while Alt St Anton is a cosy chalet doing a good range of excellent traditional dishes. The toboggan run above Nasserein is floodlit a couple of nights a week, and you can stop off at the Rodelalm for traditional food, beer and schnapps – booking is essential.

APRES-SKI
Throbbing till late

St Anton's bars rock from mid-afternoon until the early hours. Après-ski starts in a collection of bars on the slopes above the village. The Krazy Kanguruh is probably the most famous, but the Mooserwirt is now the 'in' place, filling up with revellers as soon as the lunch trade finishes. The owner has invested hugely in revamping the

People pack the Mooserwirt from early afternoon; later, suitably relaxed, they descend the slopes to the village →

Phone numbers
From elsewhere in Austria add the prefix 05446.
From abroad use the prefix +43 5446.

TOURIST OFFICE
Postcode A-6580
t 22690
f 253215
st.anton@netway.at
www.stantonamarlberg.com
www.tiscover.com/st.christoph

The long blue run down to Rauz is the link to Stuben and to the bus for Zürs ↓

place – not least in its beer delivery systems, which reputedly dispense more than any other bar in Austria. By 4pm tables inside and out are being danced on. All this is followed by a slide down the piste in the dark. The bars in town are in full swing by 4pm, too. Most are lively, with loud music; sophisticates looking for a quieter more relaxed time are less well provided for. The Underground bar has a great atmosphere and live music, but gets packed. Equally popular are the Hazienda and the Piccadilly ('great musicians late-on'). Recent reporters have recommended Scotty's (in Mark Warner's chalet-hotel Rosanna, with extended happy hour), Jacksy's, Pub 37, Bobo's, Alibi and Funky Chicken. In Nasserein, Tom Dooley's is 'relaxed and welcoming'. For late-night dancing, Kartouche and the Stanton in the centre of town are the key places.

OFF THE SLOPES
Some improvement
St Anton is a resort for keen skiers and riders, but it is not completely devoid of attractions for others – especially those who are attracted by the new fitness, swimming and skating facilities

of Arlberg-well.com. The village is lively during the day, with a fair selection of shops. Getting by bus to the other Arlberg resorts is easy. It's easy to visit Innsbruck by train. Many of the most attractive mountain huts are not readily accessible by lift for pedestrians – though some are reachable by a combination of taxi and walking.

STAYING DOWN THE VALLEY
Nice and quiet
Beyond Nasserein is the more complete village of St Jakob. It can be reached on snow, but is dependent on the free shuttle-bus in the morning.
Pettneu is a quiet village further down the valley, with slopes that most suit beginners. It's best for drivers.

St Christoph 1800m/5,910ft

A small, exclusive collection of hotels, restaurants and bars right by the Arlberg Pass, with drag-lifts for local slopes and a fast quad chair-lift to the heart of St Anton's slopes. Good for a serious lunch, it's expensive and deadly quiet to stay in. The most expensive hotel of all is the huge 5-star Arlberg-Hospiz.

St Johann in Tirol 650m/2,130ft

Relax on easy runs with plenty of pit stops and friendly locals

187

WHAT IT COSTS

HOW IT RATES

The slopes

Snow	**
Extent	**
Experts	*
Intermediates	***
Beginners	****
Convenience	***
Queues	***
Restaurants	****

The rest

Scenery	***
Resort charm	***
Off-slope	***

Premier Collection

What's new

For 2001/02 a new eight-seater gondola replaced the old single-person chair from Oberndorf, greatly improving access for day-trippers and taking pressure off the main village gondola.

In recent years a lot more snowmaking has been installed and it now covers almost half the slopes.

- ➕ Charming traffic-free centre
- ➕ Lots of mountain restaurants
- ➕ Plenty of off-slope activities
- ➕ Easy to visit neighbouring resorts
- ➕ Good ski and snowboard schools
- ➕ Few Brits by Tirol standards
- ➕ Ideal for beginners and intermediates
- ➕ Good snow record

- ➖ Very small area, with little to interest experts or keen piste-bashing intermediates
- ➖ Weekend crowds from Germany
- ➖ Can be especially crowded when nearby resorts with less reliable snow are suffering

This charming and friendly resort is an attractive place for beginners and leisurely part-timers who like to spend as much time having drinks and lunch as they do actually cruising the slopes. Keener and more proficient skiers and boarders will soon get bored unless they are prepared to visit surrounding resorts such as Kitzbühel and the Ski Welt (all covered under the Kitzbüheler Alpenskipass). There are a surprising number of lively bars in town, too.

THE RESORT

St Johann is a sizeable town with a life other than as a resort. The attractive traffic-free centre is wedged between a railway track, main roads and rivers and the five-minute walk from central hotels to the main lift includes a level crossing and walking beside a busy road. But the village gondola accesses the whole mountain.

Lifts at the hamlet of Eichenhof to the east are convenient for the slopes, but it's a trek along a busy road to the centre of town. A new gondola from Oberndorf, to the west, opened for the 2001/02 season.

Most accommodation is central, in or close to the traffic-free zone. But the hotels near the lifts are best for the slopes. Reporters emphasise the friendliness of the locals.

The local pass covers several other resorts. The Kitzbüheler Alpenskipass covers the whole region and Kitzbühel itself is only 10 minutes by car or train.

THE MOUNTAIN

St Johann's local slopes are on the north-facing side of the Kitzbüheler Horn – the 'back' side of Kitzbühel's 'second' and smallest mountain.

Slopes The main access lift from the village is a gondola, which transports you to the top of the slopes at Harschbichl with a mid-station at Angereralm. From the top, a choice of north-facing pistes lead back through the trees towards town. The slopes on the top half of the mountain are reds, while those below the gondola mid-station are wide blue runs. Two chair-lifts and the mid-station of the gondola

Kitzbüheler Horn 2000m

Harschbichl 1700m/5,580ft

Bergstation Penzing 1465m

Jodlalm 1500m

Oberndorf

Eichenhof

St Johann in Tirol 650m/2,130ft

SPECIALIST PACKAGES
TAILORMADE

SKI ON THE WILD SIDE

SKI WILD

www.skiwild.co.uk
tel:08707469668

MOUNTAIN FACTS

Altitude	670m-1700m
	2,200ft-5,580ft
Lifts	17
Pistes	60km
	37 miles
Blue	41%
Red	47%
Black	12%
Snowmaking	28km
	17 miles

Phone numbers
From elsewhere in
Austria add the prefix
05352.
From abroad use the
prefix +43 5352.

TOURIST OFFICE

Postcode A-6380
t 63335
f 65200
info@st.johann.tirol.at
www.st.johann.tirol.at

allow you to keep to the upper part of the mountain. There are more chairs and drags lower down. There is also a sunnier sector of west-facing pistes that can be accessed from the top or the mid-station and which lead down to the new gondola at Oberndorf.

Snow reliability St Johann gets more snow than neighbouring Kitzbühel and the Ski Welt, and this, together with its largely north-facing slopes, means that it often has better conditions. It also has substantial snowmaking. The Steinplatte above Waidring usually also has good snow and is a short bus ride away and covered by the local lift pass.

Experts There is nothing here to challenge an expert. The long black run on the piste map is really a moderate red – and the snow suffers from the strong afternoon sun.

Intermediates The slopes are varied. But keen piste-bashers will ski them all in a day and are likely to want to go on to explore nearby resorts. Decent intermediates have a fairly direct-running piste between Harschbichl and town and the black mentioned above. There are some easier red runs on the top part of the mountain, but the best (3a and 4b) are served by long drags or a slow, old chair. The Penzing piste is served by a high-speed quad chair. The less adventurous are better off getting off the village gondola at the mid-station and taking gentle pistes down from there.

Beginners The main nursery slopes are excellent. The slopes served by the first stage of the village gondola make good runs to progress to – though the last part just above the village is a bit steep for some. 'Superb. I could not have picked a better place to learn to ski,' said one reporter in 2001 who returned in 2002 and loved it again.

Snowboarding St Johann has a terrain-park, half-pipe and a carving course.

Cross-country Given good snow, St Johann is one of the best cross-country resorts in Austria. The wide variety of trails totals 75km/47 miles.

Queues Rare except at peak times.

Mountain restaurants With 14 restaurants spread over just 60km/37 miles of piste, St Johann must have the densest array of huts of any sizeable resort in Europe. Our favourite is the Angerer Alm, just above the gondola mid-station. It serves excellent local food and has the most amazing wine cellar. The Besgeigeralm is a lovely rustic restaurant on the Oberndorf side.

Schools and guides The St Johann and Eichenhof schools have a good reputation for their teaching and friendliness. One regular reporter said this year: 'The instructors I met were all very friendly. The one who took our group was 76 – a lovely man who got his message across despite a slight language barrier.'

Facilities for children The village nursery, geared to the needs of workers rather than visitors, offers exceptionally long hours. We have no recent reports of how this works in practice.

STAYING THERE

How to go British tour operators concentrate on hotels, but there are numerous apartments available.

Hotels All hotels are 3- or 4-star. The 4-stars are best placed for the slopes. There are dozens of B&B pensions. The 4-star Sporthotel Austria (62507) is near the lift, with pool, sauna and steam. The Post (62230) is a 13th-century inn on the main street. 'By far the nicest,' says a resort regular. Fischer (62332) is central and 'friendly, with good food'. Kaiserblick (62442) is a modest B&B in a quiet spot.

Self-catering The Alpenblick (expensive), Gratterer (mid-range) and Helfereich (very cheap) are some of the best-situated apartments.

Eating out The restaurants stick mostly to good old-fashioned Austrian cooking. The Huber-Bräu is a working brewery, which serves good food but closes early. The Bären specialises in Tirolean dishes, while the Lemberg serves international and Austrian fare. For a special meal, locals recommend the Ambiente. The Rialto does good pizza and the Hasianco Mexican and pizza.

Après-ski Ice bars and tea dancing greet you as you come off the slopes – Max's ice bar, at the bottom of the main piste, is a focal point. Jagglebach, on the main street, is popular day and night. Cafe Rainer hosts ski school presentations, Bunny's is lively and the Almbar is 'very small, great music and hosts, flowing schnapps and discarded underwear hanging from the ceiling'. Platzl is a comfortable late-night bar with excellent service. The Scala is the main disco. Tour reps organise sleigh rides, and tobogganing and the resort itself puts on an event most evenings.

Off the slopes A public pool, indoor tennis, artificial ice rink, curling and 40km/25 miles of cleared walks. Take the train to Salzburg or Innsbruck.

AUSTRIA

188

Westendorf 800m/2,620ft

Lively, friendly resort with own area of slopes and access to the Ski Welt

WHAT IT COSTS

HOW IT RATES

The slopes

Snow	**
Extent	*
Experts	*
Intermediates	**
Beginners	****
Convenience	***
Queues	****
Restaurants	***

The rest

Scenery	***
Resort charm	****
Off-slope	**

Premier Collection

What's new

Two T-bars at the top, up to Fleiding and Gampen were replaced by quad chairs for the 2001/02 season.

There are long-term plans to link Westendorf (and therefore the Ski Welt) with Aschau (and therefore Kitzbühel/Kirchberg) to form an enormous area.

MOUNTAIN FACTS

Altitude	800m-1890m
	2,620ft-6,200ft
Lifts	13
Pistes	45km
	28 miles
Blue	38%
Red	62%
Black	0%
Snowmaking	23km
	14 miles
Recco detectors used	

TVB WESTENDORF

New chair-lifts mean there's only one T-bar left on the upper mountain ➔

➕ Charming traditional Tirolean village

➕ Access to the extensive Ski Welt circuit via nearby Brixen

➕ Good local beginners' slopes

➕ Jolly if rather limited après-ski scene

➕ Fairly short transfers and day trips to Innsbruck

➖ Limited local slopes

➖ Lack of challenges for experts

➖ Poor natural snow record, though half of the pistes now benefit from snowmaking

Westendorf is on the Ski Welt lift pass (Austria's biggest lift-linked ski and snowboard area – see chapters on Söll and Ellmau). But the main circuit is a short bus-ride away. The resort has its own beginner and intermediate slopes and its prettiness and friendliness win many repeat visitors.

THE RESORT
Westendorf is a small Tirolean village with a charming main street and attractive onion-domed church (it was awarded 'Europe's most beautiful village' in the European Floral Competition a few years ago).

The centre is close to the village nursery slopes and a five-minute walk from the main gondola on the edge of the village.

THE MOUNTAINS
The local slopes are small, but you can get into the Ski Welt circuit easily via a bus to Brixen and then a gondola.
Slopes A two-stage gondola takes you to Talkaser, from where one main north-west-facing red run goes back to the resort (with blue options on the lower half). Short west- and east-facing pistes at the top run below the peaks of Choralpe, Fleiding and Gampen. A couple of red runs from Fleiding go down past the lifts to hamlets served by buses.
Snow reliability Westendorf's snow reliability is a bit better than some other Ski Welt resorts and half its pistes now have snowmaking.
Experts There are no real challenges and no black slopes.
Intermediates Nearly all the local terrain is intermediate and there is the whole of the Ski Welt to explore, which has mile after mile of great intermediate runs.
Beginners Extensive village nursery slopes are Westendorf's pride and joy. And there are a couple of easy blues

↑ The pretty local slopes are best for leisurely intermediates and beginners

TVB WESTENDORF

Phone numbers
From elsewhere in Austria add the prefix 05334.
From abroad use the prefix +43 5334.

TOURIST OFFICE

Postcode A-6363
t 6230
f 2390
westendorf@netway.at
www.westendorf.com

higher up that you can progress to.
Snowboarding There's a good terrain-park with a half-pipe.
Cross-country There are 30km/19 miles of local cross-country trails along the valley but snow-cover is erratic.
Queues Given good conditions, queues are rare, and far less of a problem than in the main Ski Welt area. If poor weather closes the upper lifts, queues can become long.
Mountain restaurants Alpenrosenhütte is woody and warm, with good food; Brechhornhaus is quiet; Gassnerhof is good but you have to catch a bus back to town.
Schools and guides The three ski schools have quite good reputations, though classes can be over-large. One reporter tells of her teenage son's 'excellent' private lesson with the Top school: 'He's been skiing since he was three, but this was a revelation.' Another praises the Westendorf school: 'Teachers very good, good value, great prize-giving in town hall.'
Facilities for children Westendorf sells itself as a family resort. Both the nursery and the ski kindergarten are open all day.

STAYING THERE
How to go Two of the major mainstream operators offer packages here.
Hotels There are central 4-star hotels – the Jakobwirt (6245) and the 'excellent' Schermer (6268) – and a dozen 3-star ones. The 3-star Post (6202) is 'good value, right in the centre, few facilities except rooms, dining room and bar'. Many reporters stay in more modest guest houses. Haus Wetti (6348) is popular and away from the church bells. Pension Ingeborg (6577) has been highly recommended and is next to the gondola.
Self-catering The Schermerhof apartments are of good quality.
Eating out Most of the best restaurants are in hotels – the Schermer, Mesnerwirt, Post and Jakobwirt are good. The Wasselhof and Klingler have also been recommended. Booking ahead is advisable. Get a taxi to Berggasthof Stimlach for a good evening out.
Après-ski Nightlife is lively but it's a small place with limited options. The One for the Road Bar and Liftstüberl, at the bottom of the gondola, are packed at the end of the day. The Moskito Bar has live music and theme nights but is said by a (42-year-old) reporter to be 'a bit of a dive'. The Village Pub, next to the hotel Post, is very popular and sells draught Guinness. The Cr@zy Pub is popular with locals, with music, pool, darts, table-football and a bowling alley.
Off the slopes There are excursions by rail or bus to Innsbruck, Salzburg and Kitzbühel. Walks and sleigh rides are very pretty.

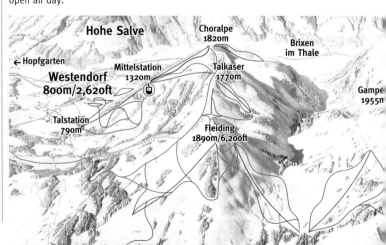

Wildschönau 830m/2,720ft

Niederau and neighbours – family resorts with friendly slopes

WHAT IT COSTS

HOW IT RATES

The slopes

Snow	**
Extent	*
Experts	*
Intermediates	**
Beginners	****
Convenience	***
Queues	****
Restaurants	**

The rest

Scenery	***
Resort charm	***
Off-slope	**

Premier Collection

What's new

For 2001/02 the old Hahnkopf and Kothkaser drag-lifts on Schatzberg were replaced by a new six-pack.

For 2002/03 more snowmaking will be installed.

Plans for a lift link between Schatzberg and Alpbach are still on the drawing board.

MOUNTAIN FACTS

Altitude	830m-1905m	
	1,720ft-6,250ft	
Lifts	26	
Pistes	51km	
	32 miles	
Blue	34%	
Red	50%	
Black	16%	
Snowmaking	12km	
	7.5 miles	

TVB WILDSCHONAU

Many people lunch in the villages, but you don't have to →

⊕ Attractive, traditional, family-friendly villages

⊕ Good nursery slopes at Niederau and Oberau

⊕ Jolly après-ski scene

⊖ Shuttle-buses or a drive between three separate ski areas

⊖ Limited slopes in separate areas

⊖ Poor snow reliability (but snowmaking is increasing)

Wildschönau is the dramatic-sounding brand name adopted by a group of attractive small resorts in the Tirol – Niederau, Oberau and Auffach. The slopes may be limited, but the resorts suit families looking for a friendly, unsophisticated but civilised atmosphere.

THE RESORTS

Niederau is the main resort; it's a spread-out little place, with a cluster of restaurants and shops around the gondola station forming the nearest thing to a focal point – but few hotels are more than five minutes' walk from a main lift. Auffach, 7km/4 miles away, is a smaller village but has the area's highest and most extensive slopes. On a low col between the two is Oberau – almost as big as Niederau and the valley's administrative and cultural centre. The villages are unspoiled, with traditional chalet-style buildings; roads are quiet, except on Saturdays; and the valley setting is lovely.

THE MOUNTAINS

Niederau's slopes are spread over a wooded mountainside that rises no higher than 1600m/5,250ft. The slopes at Auffach continue above the tree line.

Slopes The main lift from Niederau is an eight-person gondola to Markbachjoch. A few minutes' walk away is the alternative chair-lift, and above it a steep drag to the high point of Lanerköpfl. Beginner runs at the

bottom of the mountain are served by several short drag-lifts.

A reliable half-hourly bus (free) goes to Auffach. Its sunny, east-facing area, consisting almost entirely of red runs, goes up to Schatzberg, with a vertical of 1000m/3,300ft. The main lift up is a two-stage gondola. Drags and a six-pack serve the top runs.

The Kitzbüheler Alpen ski pass covers resorts in the Schneewinkel, Kitzbühel ski region, Ski Welt, and Alpbachtal as well.

Snow reliability The low altitude means that snow reliability is relatively poor – and if you can't use all the runs back to Niederau, the piste area there is tiny. Auffach is a better bet, with most of its runs above mid-mountain. Snowmaking has been increased in recent years and is now quite extensive. Grooming is good.

Experts The several black pistes are short and not severe, so are unlikely to hold the interest for long. There are off-piste routes to be found, though – the Gern route, from the top of Schatzberg down a deserted valley to the road a little way from Auffach, is

191

marked on the piste map.

Intermediates Niederau's ungroomed gully black runs are too awkward for most intermediates. The red runs generally merit their status, but don't add up to a lot. Auffach has more intermediate terrain, and the long main piste, from the top of Schatzberg to the village, is attractive.

Beginners There are excellent nursery slopes at the top and bottom of Niederau's main slopes, but the low ones don't get much sun in midwinter. Auffach has a slope just above the village. Oberau has its own nursery slopes, with a short black run above them. There are more beginner slopes along the hillside at Roggenboden. A real problem is the lack of really easy longer runs to progress to.

Snowboarding There's a half-pipe and a terrain-park on Schatzberg and a boarder-cross in Niederau.

Cross-country The 30km/19 miles of cross-country trails along the valley are good when snow is abundant.

Queues There are few queues in either of the main areas.

Mountain restaurants These are scarce but good, causing lunchtime queues as ski schools take a break. Many people lunch in the villages.

Schools and guides The ski schools have good reputations – a recent reporter raved about his beginner lessons. But classes can be large.

Facilities for children The kindergarten and nursery take kids from age two.

STAYING THERE

How to go There are a number of attractive hotels and guest houses in the three main villages – many with pools. Several major operators run packages to Niederau and Oberau.

Hotels In Niederau the 4-star Sonnschein (8353) is reportedly the best hotel. The Austria (8188) is another central recommendation. The hotel Vicky run by Thomson gets a rave review this year – 'friendly staff, excellent food, brilliant creche'. In Oberau is the oldest hotel in the valley – the 3-star Kellerwirt (8116), dating from 1200.

Eating out The choice is narrow. The restaurants at the hotels Alpenland and Wastl-Hof in Niederau have been recommended.

Après-ski Niederau has a nice balance of après-ski, neither too noisy for families nor too quiet for the young and lively. The Heustadl umbrella bar is popular at tea time. The Almbar and the Cave-Bar are popular later on. The Drift-Inn bar at Thomson's hotel Vicky is also recommended.

The other villages are quieter, once the tea-time jollity is over for the night.

Off the slopes There are excellent sleigh rides, horse-riding, organised walks and the Slow Train Wildschönau – on wheels not rails. Several hotel pools are open to the public and there's an outdoor ice rink. The best toboggan run is at Auffach. Shopping excursions to Innsbruck are possible.

Phone numbers
From elsewhere in Austria add the prefix 05339.
From abroad use the prefix +43 5339.

TOURIST OFFICE
Postcode A-6311
t 8255
f 2433
info@wildschoenau.
tirol.at
www.wildschoenau.
com

Joel
1970m

Schatzberg
1905m/6,250ft

Schönanger

Lanerköpfl
1600m/5,250ft

Markbachjoch
1500m

Thierbac
1175m

Auffach
875m/2,870ft

Roggenboden

Mühltal
780m

Oberau
935m/3,070ft

Niederau
830m/2,720ft

← Hopfgarten

exciting relaxing

Wildschönau Tyrol

The 50km of piste give skiers everything they are looking for, steep slopes and gentle family runs. The Wildschönau offers its guests a lift capacity that sets it aside from other resorts. With two gondolas, two chair lifts and 22 drag lifts there is no time lost by queuing and there are no overcrowded lifts.

The gentle Wildschönau hills are particularly suitable for families, but there are also plenty of opportunities for experienced skiers, e.g. the FIS runs for the giant slalom and Super G and some magnificent deep-snow slopes. There is also a measured section where skiers can test their top speed. Carvers and snowboarders are welcome on all pistes and the Schatzberg mountain offers an enormous fun park with a half pipe, high jump, fun-box, snake, quarter pipe and wave ride both for fun and competition.

WILDSCHÖNAU
aufregend antspannend Tirol

Zell am See

Charming lakeside town, varied slopes and glacier option at Kaprun

WHAT IT COSTS

HOW IT RATES

The slopes
Snow	**
Extent	**
Experts	**
Intermediates	***
Beginners	***
Convenience	**
Queues	**
Restaurants	***

The rest
Scenery	***
Resort charm	***
Off-slope	****

194

What's new

In Kaprun, a 24-person gondola has now replaced the funicular that suffered a tragic fire in autumn 2000 (and which will never be re-opened to the public as a mark of respect to the dead and bereaved). The first stage of the Gletscherjet opened for the 2001/02 season and the upper section taking you from near the Häusalm restaurant to the Alpincenter at the top of the defunct funicular is due to be finished in October 2002. The capacity of the new gondola is 50% greater than the funicular.

In Zell am See for 2001/02, a quad chair replaced a T-bar up to Schmittenhöhe from Hahnkopf/Kettingalm on the back of the mountain. And snowmaking now covers 70% of the lower slopes.

- ➕ Pretty, tree-lined slopes with great views down to the lake
- ➕ Lively, but not rowdy, nightlife
- ➕ Charming old town centre with beautiful lakeside setting
- ➕ Lots to do off the slopes
- ➕ Huge range of cross-country trails
- ➕ Kaprun glacier nearby
- ➕ Varied terrain including a couple of steep black runs

- ➖ Sunny, low slopes often have poor conditions despite snowmaking, which makes the area more limited
- ➖ Trek to lifts from much of the accommodation, and sometimes crowded buses
- ➖ Less suitable for beginners than most small Austrian resorts
- ➖ The Kaprun glacier gets lengthy queues when it is most needed

Zell am See is an unusual resort – not a rustic village like most of its small Austrian competitors, but a lakeside town with a charming old centre that seems more geared to summer than winter visitors. It's a pleasant place, but – despite a tunnel now acting as a bypass – the main street still has a lot of traffic.

Zell's slopes have a lot of variety and challenging terrain for a small area, but not enough to keep a keen intermediate or better happy for long, especially if, as some reporters have found, there's a lack of snow. Zell is very near the Kaprun glacier, but so are many low-altitude resorts, all of which run buses there if snow is in short supply. The result can be long queues.

Zell makes an attractive base for holidaymakers who enjoy travelling around. Having a car makes it easy to visit numerous other resorts – including Saalbach-Hinterglemm, Bad Gastein-Bad Hofgastein, Wagrain, Schladming and Obertauern.

The resort

Zell am See is a long-established, year-round resort town set between a large lake and a mountain. Its charming, traffic-free medieval centre is on a flat promontory, and the resort has grown up around this attractive core. A gondola at the edge of town goes up one arm of the horseshoe-shaped mountain, but Zell's cable-cars are 2km/a mile away. Access by another gondola at Schüttdorf is 3km/2 miles away. Most places to stay are a fair walk from the town gondola. Out by the cable-car station there is some accommodation, too.

Choice of location is tricky. The best bet is to either stay in the beautiful lakeside setting (which gets you on the shuttle-bus before it's too crowded); at the upper edge of the town centre (walking distance from the Zell gondola); or near the cable-car stations at the end of the valley.

Schüttdorf has easy access to the top of the mountain and some of the accommodation here is close to the

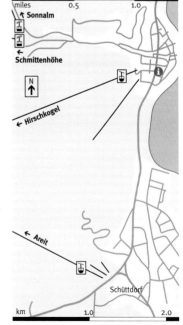

MOUNTAIN FACTS

For Zell and Kaprun

Altitude	755m-3030m
	2,480ft-9,940ft
Lifts	56
Pistes	130km
	81 miles
Blue	43%
Red	38%
Black	19%
Snowmaking	40km
	25 miles

Recco detectors used

gondola, but it is a characterless dormitory with little else going for it – much less appealing than Zell itself. Though closer to Kaprun, this is, perversely, a drawback unless you have a car. Trying to get on a glacier bus is tough, as they tend to be full when they leave Zell. Families wishing to use the Areitalm nursery and cross-country skiers stand to gain most from staying in Schüttdorf.

The mountains

Despite claims to the contrary, the extent of Zell's horseshoe of slopes is not large and the area is best suited to intermediates. The easiest runs are along the ridge, with steeper pistes heading down to the valley. Kaprun's snow-sure glacier slopes are only a few minutes by bus; Saalbach is easily reached by bus and Bad Hofgastein by train. At a push, Wagrain, Schladming and Obertauern are car trips.

THE SLOPES
Varied but limited
The town gondola (Zeller Bergbahn) takes you to Mittelstation. From there it's either an easy or a steep run to the valley cable-car station. Or you can take a chair up to Hirschkogel to meet the gondola up from Schüttdorf – you can ride this up further or take an alternative chair to Schmittenhöhe.

This is also where the main valley floor cable-car brings you. A gentle cruise and a single short drag-lift moves you to Sonnkogel. Here several routes lead down to Sonnalm mid-station – where another cable-car from the valley arrives. A black piste runs from here to the valley floor. At the end of the day you can take a gentle piste from the top (Schmittenhöhe) cable-car back to town or ride one of the lifts down.

SNOW RELIABILITY
Good snowmaking, but lots of sun
Zell am See's slopes get so much sun the snow can suffer as a result. Lots of slopes are now well covered by snow-guns, including the sunny home run to Schüttdorf and 70% of the lower slopes. But though reporters have seen 'lots of snowmaking in evidence', slush, ice and closed runs have still marred their holidays. The Kaprun glacier is snow-sure, but expect long queues there (and for buses to get there) when snow is short elsewhere.

FOR EXPERTS
Several blacks, but still limited
Zell has more steep slopes than most resorts this size, but can't entertain an expert for a week. When we were last there it was fabulous speeding down the immaculately groomed black runs 13 and 14 – they were deserted first thing in the morning. However, as a

LIFT PASSES

2002/03 prices in euros

Europa–Sportregion Kaprun–Zell am See
Covers all lifts in Zell and Kaprun, and buses between them.
Beginners Points card or limited pass.
Main pass
1-day pass 33.5
6-day pass 159
(low season 143)
Children
Under 15: 6 days: 80
Under 6: free pass
Short-term passes
Half-day pass for Zell only (from 11.30) 29.
Half-day pass for Maiskogel only (from 11.30) 17.
Alternative periods
5 in 7 days 152 and 10 in 14 days 242.
Notes 1-day pass valid at Zell am See or Kaprun only.
Alternative passes
Maiskogel only
1-day pass 21

SCHOOLS/GUIDES

2002/03 prices in euros

Zell am See
Classes 5 days
10am-noon, 1pm-3pm
5 full days: 135
Children's classes
Ages: from 3
5 full days including lunch: 187.5
Private lessons
Hourly: 50 for 1hr

CHILDCARE

The schools take children from age 4 and offer lunch-time care. The Areitbahn school runs a snow kindergarten from 9am to 4.30 for children from age 3.

The village nursery is Ursula Zink (56343), which takes children from age 3, from 9.30 to 3.30.

reporter points out, 'they are more like French reds'. Off-piste opportunities are limited.

FOR INTERMEDIATES
Bits and pieces for most grades
Good intermediates have a choice of fine, long runs, but this is not a place for mileage. All blacks are usually well groomed and within a brave intermediate's capability, and there's a lovely cruising run between Areit and Schüttdorf when conditions are good. Some Sonnkogel pistes are also suitable. The timid can cruise the ridge all day on quiet, attractive runs, or head past Mittelstation to Zell's cable-cars on an easy blue.

Kaprun's high, snow-sure glacier runs are also ideal for intermediates not looking for too great a challenge.

FOR BEGINNERS
Two low nursery areas
There are small nursery slopes at the cable-car area and at Schüttdorf, both covered by snow-guns. Near-beginners and fast learners have plenty of short, easy runs at Schmittenhöhe, Breiteck and Areit. Some are used by complete beginners when snow conditions are poor lower down, but it means buying a lift pass.

FOR CROSS-COUNTRY
Excellent if snow allows
The valley floor has extensive trails, including a superb area on the Kaprun golf course. At altitude there are just two short loops, one at the top of the Kaprun glacier, and the other at the top of the Zell gondola.

QUEUES
Not normally a problem
Zell am See doesn't have many problems except at peak times, when the Schmittenhöhe cable-cars are generally the worst hit. One reporter recommends getting to Schmittenhöhe via the Sonnalm cable-car as a quieter route.

When snow is poor there are few daytime queues at Zell – many people

are away queueing at Kaprun – but getting down by lift at the end of the day can involve delays.

MOUNTAIN RESTAURANTS
Plenty of little refuges
There are plenty of cosy, atmospheric huts. Among the best are Glocknerhaus, Kettingalm, Areitalm ('superb, freshly made strudel'), Pinzgauer and Brieteckalm. The Berghotel at Schmittenhöhe is good, but expensive. Its bar with loud music is lively (see Après-ski). The Panorama-Pfiff gets crowded, but 'has wonderful views and quite good food'.

SCHOOLS AND GUIDES
A wide choice
There is a choice of schools in both Zell am See and Kaprun. A reporter found boarding lessons from the main Zell school to be 'well organised', though classes were a bit large and English not always spoken fluently. There are also specialist cross-country centres at Schüttdorf and at Kaprun.

FACILITIES FOR CHILDREN
Schüttdorf's the place
We have no recent reports on the childcare provisions, but staying in Schüttdorf has the advantage of direct gondola access to the Areitalm snow-kindergarten, and the Ursula Zink nursery is at Zeller-Moos, just outside Schüttdorf. There's a children's adventure park on the mountain.

Staying there

HOW TO GO
Choose charm or convenience
Lots of hotels, pensions and apartments.
Hotels A broad range of hotels (more 4- than 3-stars) and guest houses.
((((4) **Salzburgerhof** (7650) Best in town – the only 5-star. It is nearer the lake than the gondola, but has courtesy bus and pool.
((((4) **Tirolerhof** (7720) Excellent 4-star in old town. Good pool, hot-tub and steam room. 'Food good, staff very friendly,' says a reporter this year.

boarding *Zell is well suited to boarders. There's a high proportion of chairs, gondolas and cable-cars and a terrain-park and half-pipe. You'll also find plenty of life in the evenings. The Kaprun glacier has a half-pipe and terrain-park, with powder in its wide, open bowl. But it also has a high proportion of drag-lifts – some beginners we heard from 'had to do a lot of walking'.*

Decent snow is assured on Kaprun's Kitzsteinhorn glacier →

TVB ZELL AM SEE

GETTING THERE

Air Salzburg, transfer 2hr. Munich, transfer 3hr.

Rail Station in resort.

ACTIVITIES

Indoor Swimming, sauna, solarium, fitness centre, spa, tennis, squash, bowling, museum, art gallery, cinema, library, massage, ice skating
Outdoor Riding, skating, curling, floodlit toboggan runs, plane flights, sleigh rides, shooting range, swimming (Kaprun), ice-sailing, ice-surfing, tubing

Zell phone numbers
From elsewhere in Austria add the prefix 06542.
From abroad use the prefix +43 6542.

ZELL AM ZEE TOURIST OFFICE

Postcode A-5700
t 770
f 72032
zell@gold.at
www.zellamsee.com

⟨⟨⟨⟨4 **Eichenhof** (47201) On outskirts of town, but popular and with a minibus service, great food and lake views.
⟨⟨⟨4 **Alpin** (7690) Modern 4-star chalet next to the Zell gondola.
⟨⟨⟨4 **Zum Hirschen** (7740) Comfortable 4-star, easy walk to gondola. Sauna, steam, splash pool, popular bar.
⟨⟨⟨4 **Schwebebahn** (724610) Attractive 4-star in secluded setting by cable-cars.
⟨⟨⟨4 **Metzgerwirt** (72520) 4-star close lake and centre. 'Very good, really wild decor, friendly,' says a 2002 visitor.
⟨2 **Hubertus** (72427) B&B near the Zell gondola.
⟨2 **Margarete** (72724) B&B by cable-cars.
Self-catering The budget Karger apartments (72858) are near the Zell gondola. Apartment Hofer (72430) is mid-range and close to the Ebenberg lift (linking to the gondola, but no boarders allowed). More comfortable are the 3-star Diana (72436) and Seilergasse (73300), both in the old centre, and the Mirabell (72665), which is close to the Zell gondola.

STAYING UP THE MOUNTAIN
Three options
As well as the Berghotel (72489) at the top of the Schmittenhöhe cable-car, the Breiteckalm (73419) and Sonnalm (73262) restaurants have rooms.

EATING OUT
Plenty of choice
Zell has more non-hotel places than is usual in a small Austrian resort. The Ampere is quiet and sophisticated; Giuseppe's is a popular Italian with excellent food; and Kupferkessel and Traubenstüberl both do wholesome regional dishes. There are Chinese restaurants in Zell and Schüttdorf. Car drivers can try the good value Finkawirt, across the lake at Prielau, or the excellent Erlhof.

APRES-SKI
Plenty for all tastes
Après-ski is lively and varied, with tea dances and high-calorie cafes, plus bars and discos aplenty. 'Even as a 55-year-old I had a great time pubbing,' says a reporter this year. When it's sunny, Schnapps Hans ice bar outside the Berghotel at Schmittenhöhe really buzzes, with 'great music, a crazy DJ and dancing on tables and on the bar. All ages loved it'. The Diele disco bar rocks; Crazy Daisy on the main road has two crowded bars and 'the group loved it' says one reporter. Classics (which used to be Evergreen) has a live band and 60s and 70s music. The Viva disco allows no under 18s; one reader proclaimed it 'excellent'. Or try the smart Hirschkeller, the cave-like Lebzelter Keller and the Sportstuberl with old ski photos on the walls.

OFF THE SLOPES
Lots of choices
There is plenty to do in this year-round resort. The train trip to Salzburg is a must, Kitzbühel is also well worth a visit and Innsbruck is within reach.
 You can often walk across the frozen lake to Thumersbach, plus there are good sports facilities, a motor museum, sleigh rides and flights.

Zell am See

197

Kaprun phone numbers
From elsewhere in Austria add the prefix 06547.
From abroad use the prefix +43 6547.

KAPRUN TOURIST OFFICE
Postcode A-5710
t 808021
f 8192
kapruninfo@kaprun.net
www.europa-sport-region.com

Kaprun 785m/2,580ft

THE RESORT
Kaprun is a spacious and quite lively village with lots of Tirolean charm. The main road to the glacier bypasses the village, leaving the centre pleasantly quiet compared with the road that runs through Zell am See.

THE MOUNTAIN
There is a small area of slopes on the outskirts of the village at Maiskogel, served by a cable-car and drag-lifts and best suited to early intermediates, and there is also a separate nursery area. But most people will want to spend most of their time on the slopes of the nearby Kitzsteinhorn glacier or on Zell am See's slopes. Both are an often crowded bus-ride away.

Slopes A 24-person gondola (Gletscherjet) has been built to replace the funicular which suffered a tragic fire in autumn 2000. The first-stage opened for the 2001/02 season and runs parallel with the existing eight-person gondola, ending in the same area. The second stage, which goes from there up to the Alpincenter and main slopes, is due to be completed for 2002/03. An alternative high-speed quad also goes from near the Gletscherjet mid-station to the Alpincenter. The main slopes are in a big bowl above the Alpincenter served by a cable-car, lots of T-bars and three chairs. The area above the top of the Alpincenter is open for summer skiing and riding and is particularly good for an early pre-Christmas or late post-Easter break.

Snow reliability Snow is nearly always good because of the glacier. And more snowmaking is being added for 2002/03.

Queues The powerful new gondola has a much higher capacity than the funicular it replaced, so queues at the bottom should be much relieved. But queues up on the mountain have always been bad at times when crowds are bussed in if snow is poor in lower resorts – and they may now be made worse by more people being carried up by the new gondola.

Mountain restaurants There are three decent mountain restaurants – the Gletschermühle and Krefelder Hütte near the Alpincenter and the Häusalm near the new gondola mid-station. All these get busy. There's also the Bella

Vista at the top of the mountain – good views but lacking in charm.
Experts There's little to challenge experts except for some good off-piste; the one slightly tough piste starts at the very top.
Intermediates Pistes are mainly gentle blues and reds and make for great easy cruising on usually good snow. From Alpincenter there is an entertaining red run down to the new gondola mid-station. This is our favourite run on the mountain, though it does get crowded. There's also a good unpisted ski route as an alternative.
Beginners There are a couple of nursery slopes in the village and there are gentle blues on the glacier to progress to.
Snowboarding There's a terrain-park on the glacier and some excellent natural half-pipes.
Cross-country The Kaprun golf course is superb, but at altitude there is just one short loop – at the top of the glacier.
Schools and guides There are several ski schools all offering the usual classes.
Facilities for children All of the schools offer children's classes and there's a kindergarten in the village.

STAYING THERE
How to go There are some catered chalets and chalet-hotels.
Hotels The Orgler (8205), Mitteregger (8207) and Tauernhof (8235) are among the best hotels.
Après-ski Nightlife is quiet, but the Baum bar is lively.
Eating out Good restaurants include the Dorfstadl, Hilberger's Beisl and Schlemmerstube.
Off the slopes Off-slope activities are good, and include a fine sports centre with outdoor rapids.

France overtook Austria as the most popular destination for British skiers and snowboarders some years ago, and it is by far the most popular country with our readers. It's not difficult to see why. France has the biggest lift-and-piste networks in the world; for those who like to cover as many miles in a day as possible, these are unrivalled. Most of these big areas are also at high altitude, ensuring high-quality snow for a long season. And French mountains offer a mixture of some of the toughest, wildest slopes in the Alps, and some of the longest, gentlest and most convenient beginner runs.

French resort villages can't be quite so uniformly recommended; but, equally, they don't all conform to the standard image of soulless, purpose-built service stations, thrown up without concern for appearance during the boom of the 1960s and 70s.

The French resorts we flock to are big names where prices are never going to seem low; but when the pound was down near 7 francs they seemed criminally high. When it went up to 10 francs, they were of no concern. As we go to press in July 2001, a pound buys you about 1.5 euros – a level at which most French resort prices still seem bearable, even if they have edged up with the arrival of the new currency.

Towards the front of the book there is a special chapter on driving to the French Alps – increasingly popular, especially with people going self-catering. The northern French Alps are easy to get to by car, and comfortable apartments are becoming more common as the French continue their retreat from the short-sighted ways of the 1960s.

199

Getting around the French Alps

Pick the right gateway – Geneva, Chambéry or Grenoble – and you can hardly go
wrong. The approach to Serre-Chevalier and Montgenèvre involves the
2058m/6,750ft Col du Lauteret; but the road is a major one and kept clear of
snow or reopened quickly after a fall. Crossing the French-Swiss border between
Chamonix and Verbier involves two closure-prone passes – the Montets and the
Forclaz. When necessary, one-way traffic runs beside the tracks through the rail
tunnel beneath the passes.

ANY STYLE OF RESORT YOU LIKE

The main drawback to France, hinted at in our introduction, is the monstrous architecture of some of the purpose-built resorts. But not all French resorts are hideous. Certainly, France has its fair share of Alpine eyesores, chief among them Les Menuires, central La Plagne, Flaine, Tignes, Isola 2000 and Les Arcs. The redeeming features of

places like these are the splendid quality of the slopes they serve, the reliability and quality of the snow, and the amazing slope-side convenience of most of the accommodation.

But the French have learnt the lesson that new development doesn't have to be tasteless to be convenient – look at Valmorel, Belle-Plagne and Les Coches, for example, and the newer parts of Isola 2000, Flaine or Les Menuires. Val-Thorens, always one of the more acceptable new resorts, is being extended sensitively, too.

If you prefer, there are genuinely old mountain villages to stay in, linked directly to the big lift networks. These are not usually as convenient for the slopes, but they give you a feel of being in France rather than a winter-holiday factory. Examples include Montchavin or Champagny for La Plagne, Vaujany for Alpe-d'Huez, St-Martin-de-Belleville for the Trois Vallées and Les Carroz, Morillon or Samoëns (now with a gondola to the slopes) for Flaine. There are also old villages with their own slopes that have developed as resorts while retaining some or all of their rustic ambience – such as Serre-Chevalier and La Clusaz. Megève deserves a special mention – an exceptionally charming little town combining rustic style with luxury and sophistication; shame about the traffic.

And France has Alpine centres with a long mountaineering and skiing history. Chief among these is Chamonix, which sits in the shadow of Mont Blanc, Europe's highest peak, and is the centre of the most radical off-piste terrain in the Alps. Chamonix is a big, bustling town, where skiing and boarding go on alongside tourism in general. At the opposite end of the vacation spectrum is tiny La Grave, at the foot of mountains that are almost as impressive – the highest within France – but with only a few simple hotels.

SNOWPIX.COM / CHRIS GILL

French purpose-built resorts are all about snow. This is the Combe de Thuit in Les Deux-Alpes, and it is surrounded by the stuff →

One of the most welcome developments on the French resort scene in recent years has been the availability of genuinely comfortable and stylish apartments, in contrast to the cramped and frankly primitive places that have dominated the market since the 1960s. Central to this shift has been a company called MGM, which has developed apartments (and some chalets) in 10 resorts, mostly with their own pool and spa as well as rooms of normal size.

This trend is reinforced by the involvement in French resorts of North American money and expertise, in the form of investment by the Canadian company Intrawest in the increasingly powerful Compagnie des Alpes. This enterprise now has a serious stake (in some cases a majority stake, and in one or two cases 100%) in the lift companies of Chamonix, Tignes, La Plagne, Les Arcs, Les Menuires, Méribel and Flaine – as well as Courmayeur in Italy and Saas-Fee and Verbier in Switzerland. Major developments such as the imminent cable-car link between La Plagne and Les Arcs start to make sense in this context. In the last few years the company has become active in land development in Les Arcs, Les Menuires, La Plagne and Flaine, and it's here that the Intrawest influence is most clear.

In particular Intrawest, developers of Whistler and other pace-setting resorts in North America, is in charge of a revolutionary development in (or rather just below) Les Arcs 2000. This new development – Arc 1950 – will offer accommodation of a quality and style rarely seen on a large scale in Alpine resorts. Intrawest seems to have got it right so far – the first phases have sold out within hours of being put on the market. We look forward to the arrival of the first apartments on the rental market, due for the 2003/04 season.

France has advantages in the gastronomic stakes. While many of its mountain restaurants serve fast food, most also do at least a *plat du jour* that is in a different league from what you'll find in Austria or the US. It is generally possible to find somewhere to get a half-decent lunch and to have it served at your table, rather than queuing repeatedly for every element of your meal. In the evening, most resorts have restaurants serving good, traditional, French food as well as regional specialities. And the wine is decent and affordable.

Many French resorts (though not all) have suffered from a lack of nightlife, but things have changed in recent years. In resorts dominated by apartments with few international visitors, there may still be very little going on after dinner, but places like Méribel are now distinctly lively in the evening. (It should also be said that nightlife isn't important to many British holidaymakers. Most of our reporting readers say they can't recommend nightspots because all they want to do after dinner is to fall into bed.)

France is unusual among European countries by using four grades of piste instead of the usual three – a system of which we heartily approve. The very easiest runs are classified green; except in Val-d'Isère, they are reliably gentle. Since it's relative novices who care most about choosing just the right sort of terrain to build confidence, this is a genuinely helpful system.

AVOID THE CROWDS
French school holidays always mean crowded slopes, so they are worth avoiding if you're not bound to go at half-term. The country is divided into three zones, with three fortnight holidays staggered over a four-week period – this season, 8 Feb to 8 Mar; from 15 Feb to 1 Mar two of the three zones are on holiday at the same time.

Alpe-d'Huez 1860m/6,100ft

An impressive all-rounder; just a pity that most slopes face south

WHAT IT COSTS

HOW IT RATES

The slopes

Snow	★★★★
Extent	★★★★
Experts	★★★★
Intermediates	★★★★
Beginners	★★★★★
Convenience	★★★★
Queues	★★★★
Restaurants	★★★★

The rest

Scenery	★★★★
Resort charm	★
Off-slope	★★★

What's new

For 2002/03 a new high-speed quad chair-lift is planned on the Sarenne glacier, opening up a new bowl with three new runs (two blues and a red). Extra snowmaking will be installed on the Lièvre Blanc run. You should be able to gamble in a new casino, and a new 3-star hotel with pool and steam room is due to open. For 2003/04 a big new gondola is planned from the top of the second stage of the Marmottes gondola to the Sarenne glacier – so you'll no longer have to queue for the cable-car.

For last season the Glacier double chair was replaced by a quad starting lower down on the glacier. The capacity of the first stage of the Marmottes gondola was increased. A new drag-lift and nursery slope opened at Alpette, at the top of the first stage of the Vaujany cable-car.

- ➕ Extensive, high, sunny slopes, split interestingly into various sectors
- ➕ Huge snowmaking installation to keep runs open despite the sun
- ➕ Vast, gentle, sunny nursery slopes right next to the resort
- ➕ Efficient, modern lift system, with few long waits
- ➕ Grand views of the peaks in the Ecrins national park
- ➕ Some good, surprisingly rustic mountain restaurants
- ➕ Short walks to and from the slopes
- ➕ More animated than most purpose-built resorts
- ➕ Pleasant alternative bases in outlying villages and satellites

- ➖ In late season the many south-facing runs can be icy early in the day and slushy in the afternoon
- ➖ Some main intermediate runs get badly overcrowded in high season
- ➖ Many of the tough runs are very high, and inaccessible or very tricky in bad weather
- ➖ Practically no woodland runs to retreat to in bad weather
- ➖ Run gradings tend to understate difficulty
- ➖ Messy, sprawling resort with a hotchpotch of architectural styles, no central focus and very little charm

There are few places to rival Alpe-d'Huez for extent and variety of terrain – in good conditions, it's one of our favourites. But, in late season at least, despite an ever-expanding snowmaking network, the 'island in the sun' suffers from the very thing it advertises: strong sun means that ice can make mornings miserably hard work, however alluring the prospect of slushy moguls in the afternoons.

The village has few fans, but if you don't like the sound of it you always have the alternative of staying in rustic Vaujany (with its mighty cable-car) or Villard-Reculas, or more modern Oz-en-Oisans and Auris.

203

The resort

Alpe-d'Huez is a large village spread across an open mountainside, high above the Romanche valley, east of Grenoble. It was one of the venues for the 1968 Grenoble Winter Olympics, and then grew quickly in a seemingly unplanned way. Its buildings come in all shapes, sizes and designs (including a futuristic church which hosts weekly organ concerts) – and many now look scruffy and in need of renovation. It is a large, amorphous resort; the nearest thing to a central focus is the main Avenue des Jeux in the middle, where you'll find the swimming pool, ice skating and some of the shops, bars and restaurants. The rest of the resort spreads out in a triangle, with lift stations at two of the apexes.

SNOWPIX.COM / CHRIS GILL

Crowds on the pistes are more of a problem than queues for the lifts ➔

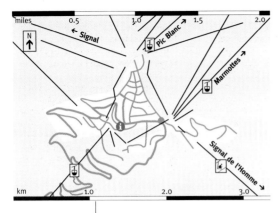

LIFT PASSES

2002/03 prices in euros

Grandes Rousses
Covers all lifts in Alpe-d'Huez, Auris, Oz, Vaujany and Villard-Reculas.
Beginners Daily lift passes for reduced areas. Beginner pass covers 11 lifts (10), Altitude 2000 covers 26 lifts (17.5).
Main pass
1-day pass 33
6-day pass 171.5
Senior citizens
Over 60: 6-day pass 121.5
Over 70: free pass
Children
Under 16: 6-day pass 121.5
Under 5: free pass
Notes Pass for 6 days or more includes one day's skiing at each of the Grande Galaxie resorts (Les Deux Alpes, Serre-Chevalier, Puy-St-Vincent and the Milky Way) and free entrance to the sports centre.
Alternative passes
Passes for Auris only (15 lifts), Oz-Vaujany only (20 lifts), Villard-Reculas only (8 lifts), and Altitude 2000 (26 lifts). Beginners passes for the outlying villages are available.

The bus service around the resort is free with the lift pass, and there's a handy, but slow, bucket lift (with a piste beneath it) running through the resort to the main lifts at the top.

A short distance from the main body of the resort (and linked by chair-lift) are the 'hamlets' – apartment blocks, mainly – of Les Bergers and L'Eclose. Les Bergers, at the eastern entrance to the resort is convenient for the slopes (with its own nursery area), but it's a trek from most of the other resort facilities. There are a couple of bar/restaurants and several shops near the slopes. L'Eclose, to the south of the main village, is the least convenient location and has even less to offer.

There is accommodation down the hill in Huez, linked by lift to the resort. Staying close to one of the gondolas is useful. Or else it's worth being near the village bucket-lift, though it is closed in the evenings.

Outings by road are feasible to other resorts covered on a week's lift pass, including Serre-Chevalier and Les Deux-Alpes. You can do a day-trip to Les Deux-Alpes by helicopter for a surprisingly modest fee.

The mountains

Alpe-d'Huez is a big-league resort, ranking alongside giants like Val-d'Isère or La Plagne for the extent and variety of its slopes. The piste grading is unreliable; although it occasionally overstates difficulty, it more often does the opposite.

THE SLOPES
Several well-linked areas
The slopes can be divided into four main sectors, with good connections between them.

The biggest sector is directly above the village, on the slopes of **Pic Blanc**. There is sport here for everyone, from excellent tough pitches at the top to vast, gentle beginner slopes at the bottom. The huge Grandes Rousses gondola, otherwise known as the DMC (a reference to its clever technology), goes up in two stages from the top of the village. Above it, a cable-car goes up to 3320m/10,890ft on Pic Blanc itself – the top of the Sarenne glacier – where the runs are genuinely black. A lower area of challenging runs at Clocher de Macle, previously accessed by a slow chair, is much more attractive now that it is served by the recently extended Marmottes gondola.

The Sarenne gorge separates the main resort area from **Signal de l'Homme**. A spectacular down-and-up fast chair-lift accesses this area from the Bergers part of the village. From the top you can take excellent north-facing slopes back down towards the gorge, or head south to Auris or west to the old hamlet of Chatelard. The return from here is now by a new double chair-lift, instead of the famously tricky drag-lift of old.

On the other side of town from Signal de l'Homme is the small **Signal** sector, reached by drag-lifts next to the main gondola or by a couple of chairs lower down. Runs go down the other side of the hill to the old village of Villard-Reculas. Happily, the Signal blue run is now floodlit three nights a week.

The **Vaujany-Oz** sector consists largely of north-west-facing slopes, accessible from Alpe-d'Huez via good red runs from either the mid-station or the top of the big gondola. At the heart of this sector is Alpette, the mid-station of the two-stage cable-car from Vaujany. From here a disastrously sunny red goes down to Oz, and a much more reliable blue goes north to the Vaujany home slopes around Montfrais. The links back to Alpe-d'Huez are made by the top cable-car from Alpette, or a gondola from Oz.

Since a piste was created from below Alpette to Enversin, just below Vaujany, an on-piste descent of 2200m/7,220ft has been possible – not the biggest vertical in the Alps, but not far short. The area does offer the longest piste in the Alps – the 16km/10 mile Sarenne on the back of the Pic Blanc (see the special feature box later in this chapter).

MOUNTAIN FACTS

Altitude 1120m-3320m
3,670ft-10,890ft

Lifts	87
Pistes	230km
	143 miles
Green	35%
Blue	27%
Red	25%
Black	13%
Snowmaking	53km
	33 miles
Recco detectors used	

SNOW RELIABILITY
Affected by the sun

Alpe-d'Huez is unique among major purpose-built resorts in the Alps in having mainly south- or south-west-facing slopes. The strong southern sun means that in late season, conditions may alternate between slush and ice on most of the area, with some of the lower runs being closed altogether. There are shady slopes above Vaujany and at Signal de l'Homme – and there is a small glacier area on the Pic Blanc, open in summer, but too small to pin all your hopes on in the winter. The orientation of the slopes is a real drawback of the area as a whole.

In more wintry circumstances the runs are relatively snow-sure, and the natural stuff is backed up by extensive snowmaking, covering the main runs above Alpe-d'Huez, Vaujany and Oz.

FOR EXPERTS
Plenty of blacks and off-piste

This is an excellent resort for experts, with long and challenging black runs (and reds that ought to be black) as well as serious off-piste options.

The slope beneath the Pic Blanc cable-car, usually an impressive mogul-field, is reached by a 300m/1,000ft tunnel from the back side of the mountain. The tunnel exit was altered a couple of years ago, supposedly creating a less awkward start to the actual slope; but it is still tricky. The slope itself is of ordinary black

steepness, but can be very hard in the mornings because it gets a lot of sun. The run splits up part-way down – a couple of variants take you to the Lac Blanc two-seater chair back up to the Pic Blanc cable-car.

The long Sarenne run on the back of the Pic Blanc is described in a special feature box. There are several off-piste variants. There are also other very long off-piste descents over the bigger glaciers to the north and east, with verticals of 1900m to 2200m (6,000ft to 7,000ft), for which guidance is essential. Some end up in Vaujany, others in Clavans (where you need a taxi back), others in more remote spots where you need a helicopter back.

There is good off-piste in several other sectors, too – notably from Signal towards Villard-Reculas and Huez – and from Signal de l'Homme in various directions; the slopes above Auris are a particular favourite of locals. And there's abundant off-piste on the lower half of the mountain that is excellent in good snow conditions, including lovely runs through scattered trees at the extreme northern edge of the area above Vaujany.

Some of the upper red pistes are tough enough to give experts a challenge. These include the Canyon and Balme runs accessed by the Lièvre Blanc chair-lift from the gondola mid-station – runs which are unprepared and south-facing (late in the day, perhaps best tackled on a board), and

steep enough to be classified black in many resorts. Above this, the Marmottes II gondola (which replaced the old Clocher chair in 2000/01) serves another series of steep black runs from Clocher de Macle including the beautiful, long, lonely Combe Charbonniere.

FOR INTERMEDIATES
Fine selection of runs
Good intermediates have a fine selection of runs all over the area. In good snow conditions the variety of runs is difficult to beat. Every section has some challenging red runs to test the adventurous intermediate. The most challenging are the Canyon and Balme runs, mentioned previously. There are lovely long runs down to Oz and to Vaujany. The off-piste among the trees above Vaujany, mentioned earlier, is a good place to start your off-piste career in good snow. The Villard-Reculas and Signal de l'Homme sectors also have long challenging reds. The Chamois red from the top of the gondola down to the mid-station is beautiful but quite narrow, and miserable when busy and icy. Fearless intermediates should enjoy most of the super-long black runs from Pic Blanc.

For less ambitious intermediates, there are usually blue alternatives. The main Couloir blue from the top of the big gondola is a lovely run, well served by snowmaking, but it does get scarily crowded at times.

There are some great cruising runs above Vaujany; but it's not easy for early intermediates to get over to the Vaujany sector from Alpe-d'Huez. The blue down to the mid-station of the Vaujany gondola is picturesque and well served by snowmaking.

Early intermediates will also enjoy the gentle slopes leading back to Alpe-d'Huez from the main mountain, and the Signal sector.

FOR BEGINNERS
Good facilities
The large network of green runs immediately above the village is as good a nursery area as you will find anywhere – its only flaw is that it carries a lot of through-traffic. A large area embracing half a dozen runs has been declared a low-speed zone protégée, but the restriction is not policed and so doesn't achieve much. Add to the quality of the slopes the convenience, availability of good lessons, a special lift pass covering 11 lifts, and usually reliable snow, and Alpe-d'Huez is difficult to beat. There are more good beginners' areas with gentle runs and generally good snow at the top of the Vaujany gondola and first cable-car, and small slopes in Oz and Auris.

FOR CROSS-COUNTRY
High-level and convenient
There are 50km/31 miles of trails, with three loops of varying degrees of difficulty, all at around 2000m/6,500ft and consequently relatively snow-sure. You need a cross-country pass to use the trails.

THE LONGEST PISTE IN THE ALPS – AND IT'S BLACK??

It's no surprise that most ski runs that are seriously steep are also seriously short. The really long runs in the Alps tend to be classified blue, or red at the most. The Parsenn runs above Klosters, for example – typically 12km to 15km (7 miles to 9 miles) long – are manageable in your first week. Even Chamonix's famously long Vallée Blanche off-piste run doesn't include steepness in its attractions.

So you could be forgiven for being sceptical about the 'black' Sarenne run from the top of the Pic Blanc to the Sarenne gorge that separates the resort from the Signal de l'Homme sector. Even though the vertical is an impressive 2000m/6,500ft, a run 16km/10 miles in length means an average gradient of only 11% – typical of a blue run. Macho-hype on the part of the lift company, presumably?

Not quite. The Sarenne is a run of two halves. The bottom half is virtually flat (boarders beware) but the top half is a genuine black if you take the direct route – a demanding and highly satisfying run (with stunning views) that any keen, competent skier will enjoy. The steep mogul-field near the top can now be avoided by taking a newly created easier option; and the whole run can now be tackled by an adventurous intermediate. The run gets a lot of sun, so pick your time with care – there's nothing worse than a sunny run with no sun.

↑ Alpe d'Huez
sprawls across the
mountainside and has
no central focus

AGENCE NUTS / OT ALPE-D'HUEZ

SCHOOLS/GUIDES

2002/03 prices in
euros

ESF
Classes 6 days
5½hr: 9.25-12.25 and
2.20-4.50
6 full days: 149
Children's classes
Ages: 4 to 16
6 full days: 135
Private lessons
(2000/01 prices)
Hourly. 31 for 1hr, for
1 or 2 people

2001/02 prices in
euros

International
Classes 6 days
2½hr am, 2hr pm
6 full days: 205.5
Children's classes
Ages: 2½ to 12
6 full days: 188.5
Private lessons
Hourly
30.5 for 1hr, for 1 or 2
people

QUEUES
Generally few problems
Even in French holiday periods, the
modern lift system ensures there are
few long hold-ups. Queues can build
up for the gondolas out of the village,
but the DMC shifts its queue
impressively quickly. And the capacity
of the Marmottes I was increased for
2001/02, shortening waiting times.
With the recently installed Lièvre Blanc
quad and the new Marmottes II
gondola, one of the old troublespots
has been eliminated. The downside is
that the Clocher de Macle area is no
longer so secluded.

The small Pic Blanc cable-car is still
queue-prone and is often closed by
bad weather. Although they may not
cause queues, there are lots of old
drag-lifts scattered around. The small
two-seater Lac Blanc chair-lift, back up
to the Pic Blanc cable-car from the
bottom of two of the black runs down
from the Tunnel, gets very congested –
though this can be avoided by taking
an alternative variant.

A greater problem than lift queues
over much of the area is that the main
pistes can be unbearably crowded.

MOUNTAIN RESTAURANTS
Some excellent rustic huts
Mountain restaurants are generally
good – even self-service places are
welcoming, and there are many more
rustic places with table-service than

you'd expect to find in French purpose-
built resorts. One of our favourites is
the cosy little Chalet du Lac Besson, on
one of the cross-country loops north of
the big gondola mid-station – the route
to it now has piste status (the
Boulevard des Lacs blue), but is no
easier to follow in practice.

The pretty Forêt de Maronne hotel at
Chatelard, below Signal de l'Homme, is
delightful and has a good choice of
traditional French cuisine. The Combe
Haute, at the foot of the Chalvet chair
in the gorge towards the end of the
Sarenne run, is welcoming but gets
very busy. The Hermine, at the base of
the Fontfroide lift, is recommended for
basic but good-value food. The terrace
of the Perce-Neige, just below the Oz-
Poutran gondola mid-station, attracts
crowds. The Plage des Neiges at the
top of the nursery slopes is one of the
best places available to beginners. The
Bergerie at Villard-Reculas has good
views and is highly recommended by
reporters. The Alpette and Super Signal
places are also worth a visit.
Chantebise 2100, at the DMC mid-
station, offers slick and cheerful table
service. The Cabane du Poutat, halfway
down from Plat de Marmottes, is
recommended for good food and
service. Back in the village, lunch on
the terrace at the Hotel Christina – by
the top of the bucket lifts – is a
pleasant option.

The restaurants in the Oz and
Vaujany sectors tend to be cheaper. At
Montfrais, the Airelles is a rustic hut,
built into the rock, with a roaring log
fire, atmospheric music and excellent,
good-value food.

SCHOOLS AND GUIDES
Contrasting views of the schools
We have a couple of reasonable
reports on the ESF, which has
apparently improved its act recently –
'Good spoken English and good level
of instruction.' However, class sizes are
seemingly on the big side and we have
witnessed classes of 12 students or

boarding *The resort suits experienced boarders well – the extent and variety
of the mountains mean that there's a lot of good free-riding to be
had. And, if there's good snow, the off-piste is vast and varied and well worth
checking out with a guide. There's also a good terrain-park and a half-pipe near
the main lift base as well as in Auris. Unfortunately for beginners, the main
nursery slopes are almost all accessed by drag-lifts, but these can be avoided once
a modicum of control has been achieved. Planète Surf is the main snowboard
shop and there are several cool bars to visit – the Freeride Café is recommended.*

CHILDCARE

The main schools run ski kindergartens.

At Les Bergers the ESF Club des Oursons (0476 803169), takes children from age 4 during ski school hours.

The Eterlous day care centre (0476 806785), in Les Bergers, has a private slope area and takes children aged 2 to 11 all day.

Les Crapouilloux day-care centre (0476 113923), next to the tourist information office, takes kids from 2 to 11.

The International school (0476 804277) runs the Baby-Club for children aged 3 to 4, and the Club des Marmottes for those aged 4 to 12.

The Club Med nursery takes children from 4, with or without lessons.

GETTING THERE

Air Lyon, transfer 3hr. Geneva, transfer 4hr. Grenoble, transfer 1½hr.

Rail Grenoble (63km/ 39 miles); daily buses from station.

more, although one recent visitor didn't think this was too damaging as the level of instruction was good.

We have had good reports in the past of Masterclass, an independent school run by private British instructor Stuart Adamson: 'We cannot praise him too highly.' Class sizes are limited to eight. Advance booking during high season is advised. The Bureau des Guides also has a good reputation.

FACILITIES FOR CHILDREN
Mixed reports
We've had rave reviews in the past of the International school's classes for children. Reports on the ESF, on the other hand, have been mixed. Les Crapouilloux day-care centre has been recommended, as has tour operator Crystal's child care operation by a reporter this season.

Staying there 🔑

HOW TO GO
Something of everything
Chalets There are not many classic chalets in Alpe-d'Huez, but there are quite a few chalet-hotels run by tour operators. Mark Warner has a new one for 2002/03 right next to the Tourist Office and the bucket lift to the slopes.
Hotels There are more hotels than is usual in a high French resort, and there's a clear downmarket bias, with more 1-stars than 2- or 3-stars, and only two 4-stars. There is a huge Club Med at Les Bergers.
((((4) **Royal Ours Blanc** (0476 803550) Central. Luxurious, with good food. Superb fitness centre. Free (but often oversubscribed) minibus to the lifts.
(((3) **Au Chamois d'Or** (0476 803132) Good facilities, modern rooms, one of the best restaurants in town and well placed for main gondola.
(((3) **Cimes** (0476 803431) South-facing rooms, excellent food; close to cross-resort lift and pistes.
(((3) **Grandes Rousses** (0476 803311) Comfortable but a bit dated and worn around the edges; close to lifts.
((2) **Mariandre** (0476 806603) Comfortable hotel with good food, recommended by readers. Some small rooms. Next to the bucket lift.
((2) **Gentianes** (0476 803576) Close to the Sarenne gondola in Les Bergers; a range of rooms, the best comfortable.
Self-catering There is an enormous choice of apartments available. The

Pierre et Vacances residence near the Marmottes gondola in Les Bergers offers a high standard of accommodation with good facilities. The Maison de l'Alpe close to the DMC has been recommended for its ideal location and good facilities.

EATING OUT
Good value
Alpe-d'Huez has dozens of restaurants, some of high quality; many offer good value by French resort standards. The Crémaillère, at the bottom end of town, is highly recommended by a frequent visitor. Au P'tit Creux gets a similarly positive review for excellent food, ambience and value. The 'outstanding' Génépi is a friendly old place with good cuisine. The Pomme de Pin is also very popular. The Fromagerie, Rabelais and Edelweiss are others worth a try. And the Origan and Pinocchio pizzerias serve good, wholesome Italian fare.

APRES-SKI
Getting better all the time
The resort gets more animated each year and there's now a wide range of bars on offer, some of which get fairly lively later on. One complaint is that they are widely dispersed, making pub crawls fairly time-consuming.

Of the British-run bars, the Roadhouse in Crystal's hotel Vallée Blanche and the Underground in Neilson's hotel Chamois are established favourites. O'Sharkey's and the Pacific (sister bar to the one in Val d'Isère) are also popular. Smithy's does good Tex-Mex food and can get pretty rowdy late on.

The little Avalanche bar is popular with locals and visitors alike, and often has live music. The P'tit Bar de l'Alpe takes some beating for atmosphere, and also has live music. The Sporting is a large but friendly French

↑ Tiny Oz-en-Oisans is quiet but has a few bars and restaurants
OT OZ-EN-OISANS

ACTIVITIES

Indoor Sports centre (tennis, gym, squash, aerobics, climbing wall), library, cinema, swimming pool, billiards, bridge
Outdoor Artificial skating rink (skating and curling), 30km/19 miles of cleared paths, outdoor swimming pool, hang-gliding, paragliding, all-terrain carts, quad-bikes

Phone numbers
From abroad use the prefix +33 and omit the initial 'o' of the phone number.

ALPE D'HUEZ TOURIST OFFICE

Postcode 38750
t 0476 114444
f 0476 806954
info@alpedhuez.com
www.alpedhuez.com

rendezvous with a live band. The Etalon and Free Ride cafes are also popular. And the Dutch-run Melting Pot does good tapas and is great for a relaxed drink, as is the Zoo.

The Stage One and Igloo discos liven up whenever the French are in town en masse.

OFF THE SLOPES
Good by purpose-built standards
There is a wide range of facilities, including an indoor pool, an open-air pool (boxer-style cozzies not allowed), Olympic-size ice rink and splendid sports centre. There's also an ice-driving school. Shops are numerous, but limited in range. The helicopter excursion to Les Deux-Alpes is amusing. It's a pity that the better mountain restaurants aren't easily accessible to pedestrians.

Vaujany 1250m/4,100ft

THE RESORT
Vaujany is a small village perched on the hillside opposite its own sector of the domain. Hydro-electric riches have financed huge continuing investment. There's a giant 160-person cable-car (that whisks you into the heart of the Alpe-d'Huez lift system), a two-stage gondola which takes you to Vaujany's

local slopes, a superb new sports centre and a new village centre by the lifts (with smart ski shop, cafe, deli and underground car park). There are some tasteful new self-catering developments up the mountainside. A mile or two up the valley (at the mid-station of the gondola) is the even smaller and more rustic hamlet of La Villette (just one tiny bar-restaurant). A regular visitor tells us that while still unspoiled and with friendly locals the village is becoming 'very English'.

THE MOUNTAINS
Although no slopes reach Vaujany itself, it is in practice a good base – its own slopes are not far away, and access to Alpe-d'Huez is speedy.
Slopes There are no village slopes, so even complete beginners have to ride the gondola to Montfrais, which has a mid-station at La Villette. There's a run back to La Villette, but you normally have to ride from there down to Vaujany. The alternative is a black piste, ending below the village at a lift.
Snow reliability A large snowmaking network and shady slopes help the area keep its snow-cover for longer.
Experts The huge cable-car offers quick queue-free access up towards Lac Blanc and the Pic Blanc cable-car up to the resort high-point and the main body of expert terrain. Local challenges include some off-piste runs through the trees and a couple of black runs, too.
Intermediates There's a nice variety of cruising runs in the local sector and the lack of crowds is a real bonus. A special lift pass covering 20 lifts in Oz and Vaujany is available.
Beginners There are some good nursery slopes at the top of both the gondola and the first stage of the cable-car and there are some nice cruisy blues to progress to. Complete beginners can buy a limited pass.
Snowboarding Although there are some good nursery slopes here, beginners will have difficulty negotiating the main drag-lift up towards Alpette. And there's no easy route across to the main Alpe d'Huez sector except by riding down lifts.
Cross-country The 20km/12 mile loop between Alpette and Alpe d'Huez is the most snow-sure circuit in the area.
Queues Vaujany gets some day visitors, but is generally a quiet spot. We've never seen the cable-car full.
Mountain restaurants The Airelles is probably the most atmospheric.

Phone numbers
From abroad use the prefix +33 and omit the initial 'o' of the phone number.

VAUJANY TOURIST OFFICE

Postcode 38114
t 0476 807237
f 0476 798249
vaujany@icor.fr
www.vaujany.com

AURIS TOURIST OFFICE

Postcode 38142
t 0476 801352
f 0476 802016
auris.en.oisans@
wanadoo.fr

OZ-EN-OISANS TOURIST OFFICE

Postcode 38114
t 0476 807801
f 0476 807904
info@oz-en-oisans.
com
www.oz-en-oisans.
com

VILLARD-RECULAS TOURIST OFFICE

Postcode 38114
t 0476 804569
f 0476 804569
info@villard-reculas.
com
www.villard-reculas.
com

Schools and guides Vaujany has its own ski school – reports have all been very positive ('no Gallic shoulder shrugs, friendly, well run').

Facilities for children There's a good day nursery by the lift station; book in advance because of limited places.

STAYING THERE

How to go There's a handful of simple hotels in Vaujany.

Chalets Ski Peak has comfortable, tastefully decorated catered chalets in Vaujany and La Villette. A minibus service for guests is available.

Hotels The Rissiou (0476 807100) is run by a British tour operator (Ski Peak) and is well situated for access to the cable-car. It has a popular bar, a pleasant dining room that serves good French cuisine (and wines), and has fairly basic bedrooms. The hotel Cîmes (0476 798650), over the road, is another option but is less rustic.

Self-catering New apartments have been built up the hill, including the spacious Oisans apartments available through Ski Peak.

Eating out There are a couple of restaurants in the village and the hotel restaurants are good.

Après-ski The bar at the Rissiou is popular and frequented by the locals. The Cîmes is useful for a change of bar scenery. And the Etendard, by the lift station, has a lively après-ski bar. There are two nightclubs.

Off the slopes As well as the excellent sports centre, there's an open-air ice rink, well-stocked sports shop, small supermarket, and a few chickens wandering the streets.

Oz-en-Oisans

1350m/4,430ft

The purpose-built ski station above the attractive old village of Oz-en-Oisans apparently now takes its parent's name. The village is now reasonably developed – with a ski school, three sports shops, nursery slopes, bars, four restaurants, a supermarket and a skating rink. There's also a large underground car park. Attractive new chalets and apartment blocks have been built in a sympathetic style, with much use of wood and stone and the hotel Hors Piste (0476 798662) has opened. Two gondolas whisk you out of the resort – one goes to Alpette above Vaujany and the other in two stages to the mid-station of the DMC

above Alpe d'Huez. To quote recent visitors, Oz is now 'taking off' and 'relatively lively'. But another complains that there is still no nightlife. The main run home is liberally endowed with snow-guns, but it needs to be.

Auris 1600m/5,250ft

Auris is a series of wood-clad, chalet-style apartment blocks with a few shops, bars and restaurants, pleasantly set close to the thickest woodland in the area. It's a fine family resort, with everything close to hand, including a nursery and a ski kindergarten. There's also a ski school. Beneath it is the original old village, complete with attractive, traditional buildings, a church and all but one of the resort's hotels. Staying here with a car you can drive up to the local lifts or make excursions to neighbouring resorts such as Serre-Chevalier.

Unsurprisingly, evenings are quiet, with a handful of bar-restaurants to choose from. The Beau Site (0476 800639), which looks like an apartment block, is the only hotel in the upper village. A couple of miles down the hill, the traditional Auberge de la Forêt (0476 800601) gives you a feel of 'real' rural France.

Access to the slopes of Alpe-d'Huez is no problem, but there are plenty of local slopes to explore, for which there is a special lift pass, covering 15 lifts and 45km/28 miles of piste. Most of the runs are intermediate, though Auris is also the best of the local hamlets for beginners.

Villard-Reculas

1500m/4,920ft

Villard is a secluded village, complete with an old church, set on a small shelf wedged between an expanse of open snowfields above and tree-filled hillsides below. Following the installation of a fast quad chair up to Signal (and the main Alpe d'Huez sector) a couple of years back, the village is becoming more popular as an access point and it is now beginning to find its feet as a 'resort'. Its 500 beds are mainly in self-catering apartments and chalets, though there is one 2-star hotel. There is a supermarket and a couple of bars and restaurants.

The local slopes have something for everyone, and there is an ESF here.

Purpose-built for holidays on the slopes, with exciting developments in store

WHAT IT COSTS

HOW IT RATES

The slopes

Snow	****
Extent	***
Experts	****
Intermediates	****
Beginners	****
Convenience	****
Queues	***
Restaurants	**

The rest

Scenery	***
Resort charm	*
Off-slope	*

What's new

For 2002/03 a third chair-lift (a quad) will take you from the top of the second chair up from Le Pré, allowing you to ski or board directly down to Arc 2000. And a new six-pack will replace an existing chair and two drags from Arc 1800 towards Col des Frettes.

For 2003/04 the long-awaited link between the Les Arcs and La Plagne slopes is planned to be in place – the world's biggest cable-car, a double-decker holding 200 people, will link Plan-Peisey to Montchavin in only four minutes. The result will be the world's third biggest linked ski area.

Also planned for 2003/04 is a new village called Arc 1950 – the first venture into the Alps by Canadian company Intrawest, who have built many attractive resorts in North America.

➕ Easy access to the slopes from most (but not all) of the apartments

➕ A wide range of runs to suit intermediates and experts

➕ Few serious queues

➕ Excellent woodland runs

➕ Option of staying in quiet, more traditional, lower villages

➕ Very easy rail access from UK

➕ Splendid views of Mont Blanc massif

➕ Glowing reports of friendly locals – unusual for French resorts

➖ Main village centres lack charm

➖ Few off-slope diversions

➖ Not the best resort for confidence-building green runs

➖ Still lot of slow old chairs and drags

➖ Very quiet in the evenings, and limited choice of bars/restaurants

➖ Some apartments are quite a walk from the nearest lifts

➖ Nearly all the accommodation is in apartments – there's a limited choice of alternatives

Les Arcs is a classic, purpose-built French resort, with all the usual advantages and drawbacks. If altitude and a short walk from front door to lift base are your priorities – and not village charm or animation – put it on the shortlist. A further attraction for some is that direct rail services to Bourg-St-Maurice connect with a funicular that takes you straight to Arc 1600 (though not to the other two Arcs).

The terrain isn't in quite the same league as the Three Valleys, La Plagne or Val-d'Isère/Tignes for sheer extent, but within its slightly smaller area it contains an impressive variety, including some of the longest descents in the Alps, plenty of steep stuff, and a very attractive area of woodland runs at one end of the area. For a keen mixed-ability group, it is a strong candidate.

211

The resort

Les Arcs is made up of three modern resort units, linked by road, high above the railway terminus town of Bourg-St-Maurice. The three villages are all purpose-built and apartment-dominated, and offer doorstep access to the snow with no traffic hazards, but they lack Alpine charm, off-slope activities and much evening animation. But reporters repeatedly comment on the friendliness of the locals.

Arc 1600 was the original Arc (it opened in December 1968). It has the advantage of a funicular railway up from Bourg-St-Maurice, giving easy access from Paris and the UK by train. Above the village, a trio of chair-lifts fan out over the lower half of the slopes, leading to links to the other Arcs. 1600 is set in the trees and has a friendly, small-scale atmosphere; and it enjoys good views along the valley and towards Mont Blanc. The central area is particularly good for families: uncrowded, compact, and set on even ground. But things are even quieter here at night than during the day.

Much the largest of the three 'villages' is Arc 1800. It has three sections, though the boundaries are indistinct. Charvet and Villards are small, scruffy shopping centres, mostly open-air but still managing to seem as claustrophobic as the indoor arcades of neighbouring La Plagne. Both are dominated by apartment blocks the size of ocean liners (getting to the shops or the lifts may involve a much longer walk inside your apartment building than outside it). More pleasant on the eye is Charmettoger, with smaller, wood-clad buildings nestling among trees. Arc 1800 is now also spreading up the hillside, with spacious new apartments in Le Chantel. The lifts depart from the Villards area – chair-lifts to mid-mountain, and the big Transarc gondola to Col de la Chal at the head of the Arc 2000 valley.

Arc 2000 is just a few hotels, apartment blocks and the Club Med, huddled together in a bleak spot, with little to commend it but immediate access to the highest, toughest skiing. There is only a handful of restaurants and shops – and it's a serious bus-ride

MOUNTAIN FACTS

Altitude 1200m-3225m
3,940ft-10,580ft
Lifts 60
Pistes 200km
124 miles
Green 9%
Blue 44%
Red 32%
Black 15%
Snowmaking 12km
7 miles
Recco detectors used

LIFT PASSES

2002/03 prices in
euros

**Massif Aiguille Grive–
Aiguille Rouge**
Covers all lifts in Les
Arcs and Peisey-
Nancroix, including
funicular from Bourg-
St-Maurice.
Beginners Five free
lifts; one in 1600 and
two each in 1800 and
2000.
Main pass
1-day pass 35.5
6-day pass 171
Senior citizens
Over 60: 6-day pass
129
Over 75: free pass
Children
Under 14: 6-day pass
129
Under 7: free pass
Short-term passes
Half-day afternoon
(adult 25). Half-day
(am or pm) passes for
each area (adult 18).
Single and return
tickets on most lifts
for walkers.
Notes All passes over
1 day cover La Plagne
and allow 1 day in La
Rosière-La Thuile and
Tignes-Val-d'Isère. 6-
day passes and over
allow one day each in
the 3V, Pralognan-la-
Vanoise and Les
Saisies. 5% reduction
on presentation of
previous season's
pass.
Alternative passes
(2001/02 prices)
1- and 2-day passes
(26.5 and 47.5
respectively) are
available; one covers
Arc 2000 and
Villaroger (21 lifts),
the other Arc 1600
and 1800 (38 lifts).

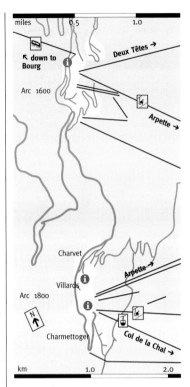

to Arc 1600. A smart new development
known as Arc 1950 is now being built
just below Arc 2000 by the Canadian
company Intrawest – the first
apartments are due to be ready for the
2003/04 season. This promises to be
by far the most attractive of the Arcs
villages. There are lifts all around
2000, including the Varet gondola up
towards the Aiguille Rouge.
At the southern end of the area,
linked by pistes but reachable by road
only by descending to the valley, is
Peisey-Vallandry. The key components
of this composite resort are Vallandry
and Plan-Peisey – recently developed
lift-base resorts above the old village
of Peisey, which has a bucket lift up to
Plan-Peisey. Vallandry is reportedly a

bit more lively than 'very quiet' Plan-
Peisey. Chair-lifts go up from both
bases to mid-mountain. The long-
awaited cable-car link with Montchavin
and La Plagne will be built here.
There are a couple of alternative
places to stay down in the valley at
the other, northern end of the ski area
– see the end of this chapter.

The mountains

Les Arcs' piste network is not huge.
But its terrain is notably varied; it has
plenty of runs suitable for experts as
well as beginners and intermediates,
and a good mixture of high, snow-sure
slopes and accessible low-level
woodland runs ideal for bad weather.

THE SLOPES
Well planned and varied
The slopes are very well laid out, and
moving around is quick and easy –
though direction-finding can be a
problem at times.
Arc 1600 and Arc 1800 share a west-
facing mountainside laced with runs
leading down to one or other village.
At the southern end is an area of
woodland runs – unusually extensive
for a high French area – down to Plan-
Peisey and Vallandry.
From various points on the ridge
above 1600 and 1800 you can head
down into the Arc 2000 bowl. On the
opposite side of this bowl, lifts take
you to the highest runs of the area,
from the Aiguille Rouge and the Grand
Col. As well as a variety of steep north-
west-facing runs back to Arc 2000, the
Aiguille Rouge is the start of a lovely
long run (over 2000m/6,500ft vertical
and 7km/4 miles long) right down to
the hamlet of Le Pré near Villaroger.
Arc 2000 has runs descending below
village level, to the lift-base, restaurant
and car park at Pré-St-Esprit, about
200m/650ft lower. You can reach Le
Pré from here, via a short drag-lift
(often closed, said one reporter).

boarding *Les Arcs calls itself 'the home of the snowboard'. Local boy Regis
Rolland played a big part in popularising the sport (not least with
his 'Apocalypse Snow' movies), and the resort is constantly developing its
boarding facilities. Some boarders are doubtless attracted by the budget self-
catering accommodation, but also by the great mix of terrain served mainly by
boarder-friendly lifts (though getting around can involve some long traverses on
near-flat catwalks). Arc 2000 and Vallandry have great smooth runs for
beginners and carvers, but some of the blues at 2000 are too flat for comfort.
There are a couple of specialist board schools and shops, a park and a half-pipe.*

SNOW RELIABILITY
Good – plenty of high runs
A high percentage of the runs are above 2000m/6,500ft and when necessary you can stay high by using lifts that start around that altitude. Most of the slopes face roughly west, which is not ideal. Those from the Col de la Chal and the long runs down to Le Pré are north-facing. There is limited snowmaking on some runs back to 1600, 1800 and Peisey-Vallandry. Grooming can be 'economical'.

FOR EXPERTS
Challenges on- and off-piste
Les Arcs has a lot to offer experts – at least when the high lifts are open (the Aiguille Rouge cable-car, in particular, is often shut in bad weather).

There are a number of truly black pistes above Arc 2000, and a couple in other areas. After a narrow shelf near the top (which can be awkward), the Aiguille Rouge-Le Pré run is superb, with remarkably varying terrain throughout its vertical drop of over 2000m/6,500ft. There is also a great deal of off-piste potential. There are steep pitches on the front face of the Aiguille Rouge, and secluded runs on the back side, towards Villaroger – the Combe de l'Anchette, for example. A short climb to the Grand Col from the chair-lift of the same name gives access to several routes, including a quite serious couloir and an easier option. The wooded slopes above 1600 are another attractive possibility – and there are open slopes all over the place.

FOR INTERMEDIATES
Plenty for all abilities
One strength of the area is that most main routes have easy and more difficult alternatives, making it good for mixed-ability groups. There are plenty of challenges, yet less confident intermediates are able to move around without getting too many nasty surprises. An exception is the solitary Comborcières black from Les Deux Têtes down to Pré-St-Esprit. This long mogul field justifies its rating and can be great fun for strong intermediates.

The woodland runs at either end of the domain, above Vallandry and Le Pré, and the bumpy Cachette red down to 1600, are also good for better intermediates. Those who enjoy speed will like the Vallandry area: its well groomed runs are remarkably uncrowded much of the time. Good intermediates can enjoy the Aiguille Rouge-Le Pré run (with red and blue detours available to avoid the toughest bits of the black piste).

The lower half of the mountainside is good for mixed-ability groups, with a choice of routes through the trees. The red runs down from Arpette and Col des Frettes towards 1800 are quite steep but usually well groomed.

Cautious intermediates have plenty of blue cruising terrain. Many of the runs around 2000 are rather bland and prone to overcrowding. The blues above 1800 are attractive but also crowded. A favourite blue of ours is Renard, high above Vallandry, usually with excellent snow.

Les Arcs

213

Aiguille Rouge
3225m/10,580ft

Grand Col
2835m

2670m

Col de la Chal
2600m

2300m

2180m

Col des Frettes

Arpette
2400m

Arc 2000
6,560ft

Plan-Peisey
1600m

Les Deux Têtes
2300m

Vallandry

Pré-St-Esprit
1825m

Arc 1800
5,910ft

Arc 1600
5,250ft

Le Pré
1200m

Bourg-St-Maurice

SCHOOLS/GUIDES

2001/02 prices in euros

ESF
Classes 6 days
3hr am or pm
6 half-days 108
Children's classes
Ages: 3 to 14
6 half-days: 108
Private lessons
Hourly
31 for 1hr, for 1 or 2 people

Other schools
Arc Aventures (ESI)
Virages
In Extremis
Tip-Top (based in Bourg-St-Maurice)

CHILDCARE

The ESF branches in all three stations take children from 3. The International school's Club Poussin in 1800 starts at 4.

At Arc 1600 the Garderie at the Hotel de la Cachette (0479 077050) runs three clubs for children from 4 months to 11 years, from 8.30 to 6pm, with ski lessons available.

At Arc 1800 various schemes running from 8.45 to 5.45 are offered by the Pommes de Pin (0479 041530). The Nurserie takes children aged 1 to 3, the Garderie those aged 3 to 6, and children aged 3 to 9 can have lessons through the two clubs based at the Garderie.

At Arc 2000 Les Marmottons (0479 076425) takes children aged 2 to 6 from 8.30 to 5.45, with lessons for those aged 3 to 6.

The Club Med (2000) has full childcare facilities – this is one of their 'family villages'.

FOR BEGINNERS
1800 best for complete novices

There are nursery slopes conveniently situated just above all three villages. The ones at Arc 1600 are rather steep, while those at 2000 get crowded with intermediate through-traffic at times. The sunny, spacious runs at 1800 are best. There is a lack of attractive, long, green runs to move on to. But Mont Blanc above 1600 is a beautiful, gentle blue, and you can take the gondola up to Col de la Chal and enjoy good snow on the easy runs towards 2000.

FOR CROSS-COUNTRY
Very boring locally

Short trails, mostly on roads, is all you can expect unless you travel down to the Nancroix valley's 40km/25 miles of pleasant trails.

QUEUES
Few problems now

Reporters have few complaints about queues except in one or two places. In sunny weather, Arc 2000 attracts the crowds and there may be non-trivial queues for either the gondola or the chair to Col de la Chal. In bad weather, it's the lifts serving the woodland slopes above Vallandry that cause the problem. There are sometimes lengthy waits for the Aiguille Rouge cable-car. 'Beware, a large proportion of the queue is hidden inside the cable-car building itself,' warned one reporter this year. A bigger problem than queues is the time taken riding slow old chair-lifts, some of them very long. At holiday times overcrowded pistes can be a problem, too.

MOUNTAIN RESTAURANTS
An adequate choice

Lunch isn't generally a highlight of the day unless you head for the hamlets at the extremes of the area. At the north end, the 500-year-old Belliou la Fumée

at Pré-St-Esprit is charmingly rustic. The Ferme and Aiguille Rouge down at Le Pré are both friendly, with good food. Chez Léa in Le Planay serves simple food in rustic surroundings. At the south end, a five-minute taxi-ride from Vallandry will bring you to the Ancolie, a delightful auberge with superb Savoyard food. Or take the bucket lift down to Peisey and head for the Ormelune, which does 'the best cheese fondue'.

The restaurants scattered here and there on the main slopes are mainly unremarkable. But the little Blanche Murée, just down from the Transarc mid-station, is consistently recommended – 'friendly service, fantastic food, reasonable prices' says one report this year. The Arpette is mainly notable for its wide range of dishes. The restaurant at Col de la Chal has fabulous views. And if you prefer skiing to eating the chain of Oxygene 3000 piste-side bars have been recommended for their popular, cheap and quick food – as has Pizza 2000 at Arc 2000 for 'excellent pizza'.

SCHOOL AND GUIDES
Ski évolutif recommended

The ESF here is renowned for being the first in Europe to teach ski évolutif, where you start by learning parallel turns on short skis, gradually moving on to longer skis. We have had reports of one beginner who astonished his experienced friends by 'doing perfect parallel turns on steep reds by the end of the week'. But we have reports this season of a couple being left behind at chair-lifts and limited English being spoken by some instructors. Private boarding lessons with the ESF have been 'very highly recommended'. The International school (Arc Aventures) has impressed reporters over the years: 'Good instruction with English well spoken.' We have had glowing reports of the Optimum ski courses, using British instructors, based in a catered chalet in Le Pré. There are mountain guides available.

FACILITIES FOR CHILDREN
Good reports

We have received good reports on the Pommes de Pin facilities in Arc 1800 – 'great care and attention', 'patient approach to teaching'. Comments on children's ski classes are favourable, too – 'nearly all instructors spoke English', 'classes went smoothly'.

GETTING THERE

Air Geneva, transfer 3½hr. Lyon, transfer 3½hr. Chambéry, transfer 2½hr.

Rail Bourg-St-Maurice; frequent buses and direct funicular to resort.

UK Representative

Erna Low Consultants
9 Reece Mews
London SW7 3HE
t 020 7584 2841
f 020 7589 9531
info@ernalow.co.uk
www.ernalow.co.uk

HOW TO GO

Apartments rule

Over three-quarters of the resort beds are in apartments. There is a Club Med 'village' at Arc 2000.

Chalets There are hardly any catered chalet holidays in Les Arcs but there are in the lower villages.

Hotels The choice of hotels in Les Arcs is gradually widening, particularly at the upper end of the market.

(((④ **Mercure Coralia** (1800) (0479 076500) Newish, and locally judged to be worth four stars rather than its actual three.

(((③ **Golf** (1800) (0479 414343) An expensive but good 3-star, with recently renovated rooms, sauna, gym, kindergarten and covered parking.

(((③ **Cachette** (1600) (0479 077050) Smartly renovated in the mid-1990s, with something of the style of an American resort hotel. But it can be 'dominated by kids' says one reporter.

((② **Aiguille Rouge** (2000) (0479 075707) Daily free ski guiding.

Self-catering The apartments are mostly tight on space, so paying extra

for under-occupancy is a sound investment. The recently built MGM Alpages du Chantel apartments (bookable through Erna Low), are exceptionally attractive, comfortable and spacious by French standards, with a pool, sauna and gym. Set high above Charvet, they are very convenient for skiing but very inconvenient for everything else. The Ruitor apartments, set among trees between Villards and Charmettoger, are reported to be 'excellent in all respects'. L'Aiguille Grive has been recommended for spacious apartments and excellent slope access. We look forward to seeing the spacious apartments and cute new village of Arc 1950 when it opens in December 2003.

EATING OUT

Reasonable choice in Arc 1800

In Arc 1600 and 2000 there are very few restaurants, none of them discussed here. 1800 has a choice of about 15 restaurants; an ad-based (so not comprehensive) guide is given away locally. The Petit Zinc restaurant in the Hôtel du Golf has haute cuisine and high prices; it has a Friday evening seafood buffet. The Gargantus is a

Les Arcs

215

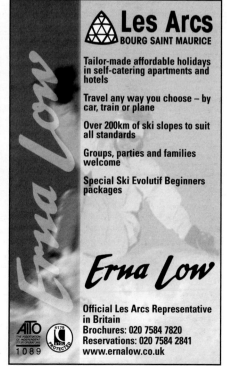

ACTIVITIES

Indoor Squash (3 courts 1800), saunas (1600, 1800), solaria, multi-gym (1800), cinemas, amusement arcades, music, concert halls, fencing (2000), bowling (1800)
Outdoor Natural skating rinks (1800 and 2000), floodlit skiing, speed skiing (2000), ski-jump, climbing wall (1800), organised snow-shoe outings, 10km/6 miles cleared paths (1800 and 1600), hang-gliding, horse-riding, sleigh rides, helicopter rides to Italy, ice grotto

Phone numbers
From abroad use the prefix +33 and omit the initial '0' of the phone number.

LES ARCS TOURIST OFFICE
Postcode 73706
t 0479 071257
f 0479 072490
lesarcs@lesarcs.com
www.lesarcs.com

BOURG-ST-MAURICE TOURIST OFFICE
Postcode 73703
t 0479 070492
f 0479 072490

PEISEY-VALLANDRY TOURIST OFFICE
Postcode 73210
t 0479 079428
f 0479 079534
info@peisey-vallandry.com
www.peisey-vallandry.com

good, informal place, although very cramped. Readers have been satisfied by 'enormous portions' at Equipage and 'good solid meals' at the Triangle Noir. Casa Mia is an excellent all-rounder with exceptionally friendly service. The Mountain Café does much more than the Tex-Mex it advertises, and copes well with big family parties. A popular outing is to drive halfway down the mountain to the welcoming and woody Bois de Lune at Montvenix, which has perhaps the best food in the area (booking advised – 0479 071792).

APRES-SKI
Arc 1800 is the place to be
1800 is the liveliest centre, though even so one reporter calls it 'very, very quiet'. The J.O. bar is open until the early hours and has a friendly atmosphere with live music. The friendly Red Hot Saloon has bar games and 'surprisingly good live music' some nights. The Fairway disco keeps rocking until 4am most mornings and the Apokalypse 'isn't terrible'. The cinemas at 1800 and 1600 have English-language films once or twice a week. In 1600 the bar opposite (and belonging to) the hotel Cachette has games machines, pool and live bands, and can be quite lively even in low season. The Red Rock in 2000 is 'good for youngsters but too crowded for grown-ups'.

OFF THE SLOPES
Very poor
Les Arcs is not the place for an off-the-slopes holiday. There is very little to do; it doesn't even have a swimming pool. You can go shopping in Bourg-St-Maurice (cheaper for buying ski equipment), preferably on Saturday for the market, and there are a few walks – nice ones up the Nancroix valley.

Bourg-St-Maurice
840m/2,760ft

Bourg-St-Maurice is a real French town, with cheaper hotels and restaurants and easy access to other resorts for day trips. The funicular goes straight to Arc 1600 in seven minutes. Hostellerie du Pt-St-Bernard has been reported to be a reasonable 2-star hotel – 'looks tatty but friendly with super food'.

Le Pré 1200m/3,940ft

Le Pré is a charming, quiet, rustic little hamlet with chair-lifts up towards Arc 2000. It has a couple of small bar-restaurants and a couple of British-run chalets, including a beautiful one that owners Martin and Deirdre Rowe renovated and run themselves. We can personally vouch for their good food, free-flowing wine, jolly bar and basic but adequate bedrooms; and the ski courses they run (Martin used to run the school in Andorra) have received rave reviews from reporters. But Le Pré is not at all suitable for beginners.

Peisey-Vallandry
1550m/5,090ft

Peisey-Vallandry is a cluster of five small villages. Peisey, linked by bucket lift to Plan-Peisey, dates back 1,000 years, and has a fine baroque church. The other, mostly old, buildings house a small selection of shops, bars and 'a good choice of restaurants'. Calèche serves traditional Savoyard food, as does Chez Felix (with superb views down the Isère valley). There are also pizza and other simpler places. The hotel Vanoise (0479 079219) in Plan-Peisey is recommended by readers for its position, food and 'extremely friendly and helpful staff'.

Avoriaz

The best base on the Portes du Soleil circuit for snow, but not for charm

(((((5)

HOW IT RATES

The slopes

Snow	***
Extent	*****
Experts	***
Intermediates	****
Beginners	****
Convenience	****
Queues	**
Restaurants	****

The rest

Scenery	***
Resort charm	**
Off-slope	*

Recent years have seen substantial investment in high-speed chairs (including some six-seaters) which have greatly reduced lift queue problems.

For 2001/02 a high-speed, six-seater chair replaced the double drag from Les Lindarets up to Avoriaz, cutting the queues at this bad bottleneck. A new piste built at the top joined the existing runs down to Les Lindarets.

'Free-ride areas' were introduced – these are ungroomed but avalanche controlled.

MOUNTAIN FACTS

for Portes du Soleil	
Altitude	975m-2350m
	3,200ft-7,710ft
Lifts	206
Pistes	650km
	400 miles
Green	13%
Blue	38%
Red	39%
Black	10%
Snowmaking	
	252 acres
Recco detectors used	

● Good position on the main Portes du Soleil circuit, giving access to very extensive, quite varied runs for all grades from novices to experts

● Generally has the best snow in the Portes du Soleil

● Accommodation right on the slopes

● Resort-level snow and ski-through, car-free village give Alpine ambience

● Good children's facilities

● Much of Portes du Soleil is low for a major French area, with the risk of poor snow or bare slopes low down

● Still a couple of lift bottlenecks and (especially in local Avoriaz area) some crowded pistes

● Non-traditional architecture, which some find ugly

● Little to do off the slopes

● Few hotels or chalets

For access to the impressive Portes du Soleil piste network, Avoriaz has clear attractions. In a low-altitude area where snow is not reliable, it has the best snow around – on relatively high, north-facing slopes of varying difficulty, including some of the most challenging terrain in the Portes du Soleil.

But there are drawbacks. First, the character of the village: we don't mind sleeping in purpose-built resorts to get instant access to high-altitude snow, but there is no really high-altitude terrain here. The Portes du Soleil has several attractive low-altitude villages, and we'd rather be based in one. Secondly, cost: Châtel and Morzine are cheap by French standards; Avoriaz is not. Queues can be a nuisance too, but they affect those exploring the Portes du Soleil from other bases as much as they affect those based in Avoriaz – more so, in fact.

The resort

Avoriaz is a purpose-built, traffic-free resort perched above a dramatic, sheer rock face. From the edge of town horse-drawn sleighs or snow-cats transport people and luggage from car parks to the accommodation – or you can borrow a sledge for a small deposit and transport your own! The problem of horse mess has been cut since they now wear 'nappies' and staff on snowmobiles scoop up what escapes! Cars are left in pay-for outdoor or underground parking – a reporter advises the latter to avoid a chaotic departure if it snows (it took him three hours). You can book space.

The village is set on quite a slope, but chair-lifts and elevators in buildings mean moving around is no problem except when paths are icy. Pistes, lifts and off-slope activities are close to virtually all accommodation.

The village is all angular, dark, wood-clad, high-rise buildings, mostly apartments. But it is compact and snow-covered and has a friendly Alpine feel despite the architecture.

The evenings are not especially

lively, but reporters have enjoyed the 'brilliant parade in half-term week, with a fire-eating display' in the past.

The main consideration when choosing accommodation in this steep village is whether you want to go out at night. By day you can get around by using chair-lifts, but at night it's a walk uphill – or nip in and out of apartment blocks using internal lifts.

Avoriaz is above the valley resort of Morzine, to which it is linked by gondola (but not by piste). It also has good links to Châtel in one direction and Champéry in the other. Car trips are possible to Flaine and Chamonix.

LIFT PASSES

2002/03 prices in euros

Portes du Soleil
Covers all lifts in all 12 resorts, and shuttle-buses.
Main pass
1-day pass 34
6-day pass 164
Senior citizens
Over 60: 6-day pass 131
Children
Under 16: 6-day pass 110
Under 5: free pass
Alternative passes
Day pass for Avoriaz lifts only: 27.5.
Beginner's day pass (limited area): 18.
Snowboarder day pass for terrain-park and a few other areas: 15.

The mountains

The slopes closest to Avoriaz are bleak and treeless, but snow-sure. They suit all grades from novice to expert and give quick access to the toughest runs in the Portes du Soleil. The whole circuit is easily done by intermediates of all abilities – and the booklet-style piste map makes for easy navigation. Reporters have praised the system of Discovery Routes around the Portes du Soleil – choose an alpine animal that suits your ability and follow the signs displaying it. The circuit breaks down at Châtel, where you need the frequent shuttle-bus. The slopes of Morzine and Les Gets, accessed from the far side of Morzine, are part of the Portes du Soleil but not on the core circuit. There is an electronic lift pass system, so you can keep your pass in your pocket.

THE SLOPES
Short runs and plenty of them
The village has lifts and pistes fanning out in all directions. Staying in Avoriaz assures the comfort of riding mostly chairs – some other parts of the Portes du Soleil (especially on the Swiss side) have a lot of drags. Facing the village are the slopes of **Arare-Hauts Forts** and, when snow conditions allow, there are long, steep runs down to Les Prodains.

The lifts off to the left go to the **Chavanette** sector on the Swiss border – a broad, undulating bowl. Beyond the border is the infamous Swiss Wall – a long, impressive mogul slope with a tricky start, but not the terror it is cracked up to be unless it's icy (it gets a lot of sun). Lots of people doing the circuit (or returning to Champéry) ride the chair down. At the bottom of the Wall is the open terrain of Planachaux, above Champéry, with links to the still bigger open area around Les Crosets and Champoussin. There are several ways to return, but the most amusing is the chair up the Wall, with a great view of people struggling down it.

Taking a lift up from Avoriaz (or traversing from some of the highest accommodation) to the ridge behind the village is the way to the **Lindarets-Brocheaux** valley, from where lifts and runs in the excellent Linga sector lead to Châtel. Getting back is a matter of retracing your steps, although there are several options from Lindarets.

Morgins is the resort opposite Avoriaz on the circuit, and the state of the snow may encourage you to travel anti-clockwise rather than clockwise, so as to avoid the low, south-facing slopes down from Bec de Corbeau.

SNOW RELIABILITY
High resort, low slopes
Although Avoriaz town is high, its slopes don't go much higher – and some parts of the Portes du Soleil circuit are much lower. Considering their altitude, the north-facing slopes below Hauts Forts hold snow well. In general, the snow in Avoriaz is usually much better than over the border on the south-facing Swiss slopes.

Piste maintenance is 'erratic and it is quite common for runs not to be groomed overnight,' says a reporter. Snow-guns have been introduced in some areas, including on some blacks, but we have had complaints of lack of snow-guns in the Lindarets area.

FOR EXPERTS
Several challenging runs
Tough terrain is scattered about. The challenging runs down from Hauts Forts to Prodains (including a World Cup downhill) are excellent. There is a tough red, and several long, truly black runs, one of which cuts through trees – useful in poor weather. Two chair-lifts serve the lower runs, which snow-guns help to keep open. The Swiss Wall at

Pointe de Mossettes
2275m

↓ Champéry

Chavanette   2215m   Hauts Forts
2465m/
8,090ft

↙ Châtel
Col du
Bassachaux
1920m

Avoriaz
1800m/5,900ft

Les Lindarets
1495m

Ardent

Les Prodains
1145m

Morzine
1000m/3,280ft

Chavanette will naturally be on your agenda, and Châtel is well worth a trip. The black runs off the Swiss side of Mossettes and Pointe de l'Au are worth trying. In the Hauts Forts and Mossettes areas last season they introduced 'free-ride areas', which are ungroomed but avalanche controlled – an excellent idea.

SCHOOLS/GUIDES

2002/03 prices in euros

ESF
Classes 6 days
5hr: 2½hr am and pm
6 full days: 137
Children's classes
Ages: 4 to 11
6 full days: 120
Private lessons
1hr, 1½hr or 2hr
30 for 1hr, for 1 or 2 people

L'Ecole de Glisse
Classes 6 days
2hr, am or pm
6 half-days: 92
Private lessons
2hr for 1 person 60;
2hr for 3 people 73

FOR INTERMEDIATES
Virtually the whole area
Although some sections lack variety, the Portes du Soleil is excellent for all grades of intermediates when snow is in good supply. Timid types not worried about pretty surroundings need not leave the Avoriaz sector; Arare and Chavanette are gentle, spacious and above the tree-line bowls. The Lindarets area is also easy, with pretty runs through the trees. Champoussin has a lot of easy runs, reached without too much difficulty via Les Crosets and Pointe de l'Au. Better intermediates have virtually the whole area at their disposal. The runs down to Pré-la-Joux and L'Essert on the way to Châtel, and those either side of Morgins, are particularly attractive – as are the long runs down to Grand-Paradis near Champéry when snow conditions allow. Brave intermediates may want to take on the Wall, but the chair to Pointe de Mossettes from Les Brocheaux is an easier route to Champéry.

FOR BEGINNERS
Convenient and good for snow
The nursery slopes seem small in relation to the size of the resort, but are adequate because so many visitors are intermediates. The slopes are sunny, yet good for snow, and link well to longer, easy runs. The main problem can be the crowded pistes.

FOR CROSS-COUNTRY
Varied, with some blacks
There are 45km/28 miles of trails, a third classified as black, mainly between Avoriaz and Super-Morzine, with other fine trails down to Lindarets and around Montriond. The only drawback is that several trails are not loops, but 'out and back' routes.

QUEUES
Main problems now gone
The queues for the lifts to Arare and Chavanette have been more or less eliminated by high-speed lifts. And the bottleneck at Les Lindarets to get back to Avoriaz has been eased by the new six-pack. There can still be long queues to get out of Les Lindarets towards Châtel though on the slow Chaux Fleurie chair-lift to Bassachaux. At weekends people pour into the resort and crowds on the pistes (especially around the village) can be worse than queues for the lifts, with care having to be taken to avoid collisions.

Avoriaz

219

boarding *Avoriaz has always encouraged snowboarding, opening France's first terrain-park in 1993. There's now an excellent 1.5km/1 mile terrain-park and half-pipe – served by three lifts – and a special pass for those whose only interest is riding them. There's a specialist snowboard school and a snowboard village for children aged 6 to 16. A micro terrain-park specially for children opened a couple of seasons ago. There's a Big Air competition on the plateau every Wednesday and Chalet Snowboard has a couple of chalets at Les Prodains. Only a few (mainly avoidable) drags are left after the lift upgrades. The blocks of self-catering accommodation may suit the budget boarder willing to be packed in with others. Nightlife revolves around a couple of bars.*

The slopes aren't usually this quiet – must be because it is getting dark! →

GETTING THERE

Air Geneva, transfer 2hr.

Rail Cluses (42km/26 miles) or Thonon (45km/28 miles); bus and cable-car to resort.

ACTIVITIES

Indoor Health centre 'Altiform' (sauna, gym, hot-tub), squash, Turkish baths, cinema, bowling
Outdoor Paragliding, hang-gliding, snow-shoe excursions, ice diving, floodlit tobogganing, dog-sleigh rides, walking paths, sleigh rides, skating, snow-scooter excursions, helicopter flights

CHILDCARE

Les P'tits Loups (0450 740038) takes children aged 3 months to 5, from 9am to 6pm; indoor and outdoor games, and so on. You have to book in advance.

The Village des Enfants (0450 740446) takes children aged 3 to 16, from 9am to 5.30.

The Club Med in Avoriaz is one of their 'family villages', with comprehensive childcare facilities.

Phone numbers
From abroad use the prefix +33 and omit the initial '0' of the phone number.

TOURIST OFFICE

Postcode 74110
t 0450 740211
f 0450 741825
info@avoriaz.com
www.avoriaz.com

MOUNTAIN RESTAURANTS
Good choice over the hill

The charming, rustic chalets in the hamlet of Les Lindarets are one of the great concentrations of mountain restaurants in the Alps. A particular Lindarets favourite of ours is the Crémaillière which has wonderful chanterelle mushrooms and great atmosphere. The Pomme de Pin is recommended for its warm welcome and friendly service. The rustic Grenuille du Marais near the top of the gondola up from Morzine has good value food, good views and atmosphere. The Abricotine, with table service, at Les Brocheaux and Chavanette at the top of the Swiss Wall have also been recommended. As has the Yéti, at the top of town: 'Has a terrace with a great view of a huge ski jump (which sees lots of action).'

SCHOOLS AND GUIDES
Try BASS

The ESF has a good reputation, but classes can be large. The British Alpine Ski School (BASS) has British instructors and has been highly recommended, especially for 'quite excellent children's lessons'. Emery is a specialist snowboard school.

FACILITIES FOR CHILDREN
'Annie Famose delivers'

The Village des Enfants, run by ex-downhill champ Annie Famose, is a key part of the family appeal of Avoriaz. Its facilities are excellent – a chalet full of activities and special slopes complete with Disney characters for children aged 3 to 16. There's a snowboard village too, with special terrain, jumps etc. Car-free Avoriaz must be one of the safest villages in the Alps, but there are still sleighs, skiers, and snowcats to watch out for.

Staying there

HOW TO GO
Self-catering dominates

Alternatives to apartments are few.
Chalets There are several available – comfortable and attractive but mainly designed for small family groups.
Hotels There is not much choice, but there is a Club Med 'village'.
《《3 **Dromonts** (0450 740811) The original Avoriaz construction in the resort centre, renovated for 2000/01.
《2 **Falaise** (0450 742600) At the top of the village; encourages families.

Self-catering Some of the better apartments are in the Falaise area by the resort entrance. Reporters have said that some apartments badly need refurbishing – a real problem hopefully being addressed, since the resort is giving owners incentives to do them up.

EATING OUT
Good; booking essential

There are more than 30 restaurants. The hotel Dromonts' Table du Marché has a celebrity chef and excellent French cuisine. The Igloo is also good. The Bistro is recommended as 'good food at good value'. The Ortolan is friendly and good value. You can buy meal vouchers for seven evening meals in a range of five good restaurants. 'Restricted menu but excellent value,' says a reporter.

APRES-SKI
Lively, but not much choice

A few bars have a good atmosphere, particularly in happy hour. The Choucas and The Place are lively and have bands, the Tavaillon (popular with Brits because tour op reps meet there) has a football theme and the Fantastique is worth a visit. Midnight Express club (free entry, expensive drinks) is popular.

OFF THE SLOPES
Not much at the resort

Those not interested in the slopes are better off in Morzine, which has more shops and sports facilities – though Avoriaz does have the Altiform Fitness Centre, with saunas and hot-tubs.

Chamonix 1035m/3,400ft

Views to die for and slopes that can kill: hire a guide to explore off-piste

WHAT IT COSTS

HOW IT RATES

The slopes
Snow	****
Extent	***
Experts	*****
Intermediates	**
Beginners	*
Convenience	*
Queues	**
Restaurants	**

The rest
Scenery	*****
Resort charm	****
Off-slope	*****

MOUNTAIN FACTS

Altitude	1035m-3840m
	3,400ft-12,600ft
Lifts	49
Pistes	152km
	94 miles
Green	21%
Blue	31%
Red	35%
Black	13%
Snowmaking	9km
	6 miles
Recco detectors used	

➕ A lot of very tough terrain, especially off-piste

➕ Amazing cable-car to the Aiguille du Midi, for the famous Vallée Blanche

➕ Stunning views of peaks and glaciers

➕ Lots of different resorts and areas covered on Mont Blanc lift pass

➕ Town steeped in Alpine traditions, with lots to do off the slopes

➕ Easy access by road, rail and air

➕ Excellent weekend destination

➖ Several separate mountains: mixed ability groups are likely to have to split up, and the bus service is far from perfect – we always take a car

➖ Pistes in each individual area are quite limited

➖ Runs down to the valley floor are often closed due to lack of snow

➖ Crowds, queues, lots of road traffic

➖ Bad weather can shut the best runs

Chamonix could not be more different from the archetypal high-altitude, purpose-built French resort. Unless you are based next to one mountain and stick to it, you have to drive or take a bus each day. There is all sorts of terrain, but it offers more to interest the expert than anyone else, and to make the most of the area you need a mountain guide rather than a piste map. Chamonix is neither convenient nor conventional.

But it is special. The Chamonix valley cuts deeply through Europe's highest mountains and glaciers. The views are stunning and the runs are everything really tough runs should be – not only steep, but high and long. If you like your snow and scenery on the wild side, give Chamonix a try. But be warned: there are those who try it and never go home – including lots of Brits.

The resort

Chamonix is a long-established tourist town that over the years has spread for miles along its valley in the shadow of Mont Blanc – the scale map below is one of the biggest in these pages.

On either side of the centre, just within walking distance of it, are lifts to two of the dozen slope areas in the valley – the famous cable-car to the Aiguille du Midi, and a gondola to Le Brévent. Also on the fringe of the centre is the nursery slope of Les

Planards. All the other lift bases involve drives or bus-rides – the nearest being the cable-car to La Flégère at the village of Les Praz.

Chamonix is a bustling town with scores of hotels and restaurants, visitors all year round and a lively Saturday market. The car-free centre of town is full of atmosphere, with cobbled streets and squares, beautiful old buildings and a fast-running river. Not everything is rosy: unsightly modern buildings have been built on to the periphery (especially near the

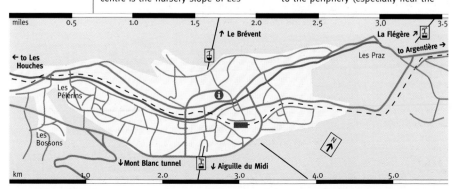

other resorts covered by the Mont Blanc pass, such as Megève and Les Contamines and Courmayeur in Italy.

The obvious place to stay is in Chamonix itself – it's central, has all the amenities you could want and some of the slopes are close at hand. For those who intend to spend most of their time in one particular area such as Argentière, Le Tour or Les Houches, staying nearby obviously makes sense. Whatever the choice, no location is convenient for everything.

The mountains

Once you get over the fact that the place is hopelessly disconnected, you come to appreciate the upside – that Chamonix has a good variety of slopes available, and that each of the different areas is worth exploring.

THE SLOPES
Very fragmented
If you really like getting about, the Mont Blanc lift pass covers 11 resorts, 25 mountains, over 200 lifts and almost 800km/500 miles of piste. Resorts covered include St-Gervais, Megève, Les Contamines and even Courmayeur in Italy.

The areas within the Chamonix valley – there are 11 in total – are either small, low, beginners' areas or are much higher up on the valley side, with cable-car or gondola access from the valley floor. If you are used to skiing from the door in more modern resorts, this may all seem very tedious.

The modern six-seater gondola for **Le Brévent** departs a short, steep walk from the centre of town, and the cable-car above takes you to the summit. At **La Flégère**, like Le Brévent, the runs are mainly between 1900m and 2450m (6,200ft and 8,000ft), and the stunning views of Mont Blanc are worth the price of the lift pass. The 50-person

↑ Les Grands Montets has endless off-piste options but very few pistes

SNOWPIX.COM / CHRIS GILL

Aiguille du Midi cable-car station), some of the lovely old buildings have been allowed to fall into disrepair, and at busy times traffic clogs the streets around the pedestrianised centre. Most of the day the town squares and pavement cafes are crowded with shoppers and sightseers sipping drinks and staring at the glaciers above. It all makes for a very agreeable ambience, though the resort is in danger of being dominated by Brits: one 2002 visitor said Chamonix is becoming 'over-English; in many bars and restaurants I did not hear any French being spoken'.

Chamonix's shops deal in everything from high-tech equipment to tacky souvenirs. But reporters often comment on the number and excellence of the former, and Chamonix remains essentially a town for mountain people rather than poseurs.

Strung out for 20km/12 miles along the Chamonix valley are several separate lift systems, some with attached villages, from Les Houches at one end to Argentière and Le Tour at the other. Regular buses link the lift stations and villages (there's an evening service too) but can get very crowded and aren't always reliable. Like many reporters, we rate a car as essential. A car also means you can get easily to

LIFT PASSES

2002/03 prices in euros

Cham'Ski pass
Covers all areas in the Chamonix Valley and the bus services between them, except Les Houches. Includes a day in Courmayeur.
Beginners Cham'Start 6-day pass covers all valley floor lifts, Cham'Baby 6-day pass covers the same for 4- to 11-year-olds. You can buy day extensions to higher lifts.
Main pass
1-day pass 40
6-day pass 171
Senior citizens
Over 60: 6-day pass 145.40
Children
12 to 15:
6-day pass 145.5
Under 12: 6-day pass 119.5
Under 4: free pass
Notes 6-day passes include two ascents on the Grands Montets cable-car. Additional ascents cost extra (2001/02 prices: 5 for 1 ascent, 73 for 20).
Alternative passes
Ski-pass Mont Blanc covers lifts in the 13 resorts of the Mont Blanc area (774km/480 miles of piste) and Courmayeur in Italy (6 days 205 for adults, 164 for children).

cable-car linking La Flégère and Le Brévent now make this side of the valley more user-friendly – though reporters have said it's subject to frequent closure in high winds.

There have been improvements to the system at **Les Grands Montets** above Argentière, including increased snowmaking and remodelled runs, but much of the best terrain is still accessed by a cable-car of relatively low capacity. This costs extra to ride and can be an expensive addition at 5 euros a trip in 2001/02 – though two free rides are included in a six-day pass. But it still attracts queues.

Le Tour has an area of predominantly easy pistes but is also the starting point for good off-piste runs, some of which end up over the border in Switzerland.

One of the valley-floor areas, Les Bossons, is open for floodlit skiing three nights a week. There is a valley piste map and an informative little Cham'Ski handbook, which includes all the local area piste maps with brief descriptions of each run and assessments of suitability for different abilities. But for navigation purposes the individual piste maps available at each area are best.

Most of our reporters have been more impressed than they expected with the piste grooming, but not with

the signposting of the runs ('virtually non-existent' said a reporter this year), or with 'antiquated chairs and drags'.

SNOW RELIABILITY
Good high up; poor low down

The top runs on the north-facing slopes above Argentière are almost guaranteed to have good snow, and the season normally lasts well into May. The risk of finding the top lift shut because of bad weather is more of a worry (and is the excuse for not including unlimited use of the lift on the main pass). The area above Le Tour has a snowy location and a good late-season record. The largely south-facing slopes of Brévent and Flégère suffer in warm weather, and runs to the resort are blacks and often closed. There's snowmaking on the busy Bochard piste and the run to the valley on Les Grands Montets, which means you can usually slide all the way down. Some of the small beginners' areas at valley level have snowmaking, too.

FOR EXPERTS
One of the great resorts

Les Grands Montets above Argentière is justifiably renowned for its extensive steep terrain. To get the best out of the area you really need to have a local guide. Without one you either stick to the relatively small number of

Chamonix

223

boarding *Chamonix is a place of pilgrimage for advanced boarders, but not the best place to learn. Head for Argentière and the Grands Montets for the hairiest action – the terrain-park and half-pipe host regular competitions. There's also a natural half-pipe/gully at Le Tour. Most of the areas are equipped mainly with cable-cars, gondolas and chairs, though there are quite a few difficult drags at Le Tour, which reporters say cause boarders problems. If you do the Vallée Blanche, be warned: the usual route is flat in places. If you're ready to tackle tougher off-piste, check out former British Champ Neil McNab's excellent Extreme Backcountry Camps (www.mcnab.co.uk). Staying in the town itself will certainly guarantee satisfactory nightlife.*

pistes or you put your life at risk. There is also lots of excellent off-piste reachable only by donning touring equipment and skinning or snow-shoeing up from the top of the lifts.

The Grands Montets cable-car takes you up to 3235m/10,610ft; if you've got the legs and lungs, climb the 121 steep metal steps to the observation platform and take in the stunning views. (But beware: it's 200 more steps down from the cable-car before you hit the snow.)

The ungroomed black pistes from here – Point de Vue and Pylones – are long and exhilarating. The Point de Vue sails right by some dramatic sections of glacier, with marvellous views of the crevasses. The off-piste routes from the top are numerous and often dangerous; the Pas de Chèvre route is serious stuff, eventually joining the Vallée Blanche run. There are many routes down the Argentière glacier.

The Bochard gondola serves a challenging red and a moderate black. Alternatively, head directly down the Combe de la Pendant bowl for 1000m vertical of wild, unpisted mountainside. The continuation down the valley side to Le Lavancher is equally challenging; it suffers frequently from lack of snow.

At Le Brévent there's more to test experts than the piste map suggests –

there are a number of variations on the runs down from the summit. 'Superb when open,' said one visitor. Some are steep and prone to ice, and the couloir routes are very steep and very narrow. The runs in the sunny Col de La Charlanon are uncrowded and include one marked red run and lots of excellent off-piste if the snow is good.

At La Flégère there are several good off-piste routes – in the Combe Lachenal, crossed by the linking cable-car, for example – and a pretty tough run back to the village when snow-cover permits. Le Tour boasts little tough terrain on-piste but there are good off-piste routes from the high points to the village and over the back towards Vallorcine or into Switzerland.

FOR INTERMEDIATES
It's worth trying it all
For less confident intermediates, the best areas are at the two extreme ends of the Chamonix valley. The Col de Balme area above Le Tour is good for easy cruising and usually free from crowds. And the slopes of the separate Prarion-Bellevue system above Les Houches (not included in the Cham'Ski pass for local political reasons) are mostly gentle tree-lined blue and red runs – good for building confidence.

More adventurous intermediates will

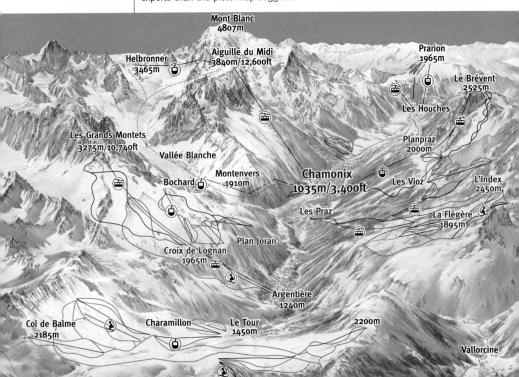

Stop to admire the
views before the ridge
walk to the start of
the Vallée Blanche →

OT CHAMONIX-MONT BLANC

ACTIVITIES

Indoor Sports
complex (sports hall,
gym, table tennis),
indoor and outdoor
skating and curling
rinks, ice hockey,
swimming pool with
giant water slide,
sauna, steam room,
six indoor tennis
courts, two squash
courts, fitness centre,
Alpine museum,
casino, three cinemas,
library, 10-pin
bowling, climbing wall
Outdoor Ski-jumping,
snow-shoe outings,
mountain biking,
hang-gliding,
paragliding, flying
excursions, heli-
skiing, ice skating

also want to try the other three main
areas, though they may find the
Grands Montets tough going (and
crowded). The bulk of the terrain at Le
Brévent and La Flégère provides a
sensible mix of blue and red runs; at
Le Brévent the slopes have been
redesigned to achieve this. If the snow
and weather are good, book a guide
and do the Vallée Blanche (see below).

A day trip to Courmayeur makes an
interesting change of scene, especially
when the weather's bad (it can be
sunny there when Chamonix's high lifts
are closed by blizzards or high winds).
This is practicable again now that the
Mont Blanc tunnel has reopened.

FOR BEGINNERS
Best to learn elsewhere

If there is snow low down, the nursery
lifts at La Vormaine, Les Chosalets, Les
Planards and Le Savoy are fine for
teaching first-timers; learners will not
be bothered by speed-merchants. The
Planards and Glacier du Mont Blanc
lifts both benefit from snowmaking.
But the slopes on the south side of the
valley can be dark and cold in winter.
And the separation of beginners'
slopes from the rest inhibits the
transition to real runs, and makes
lunchtime meetings of mixed groups
feasible. Better to learn elsewhere, and
come to Chamonix when you can
appreciate the tough terrain.

225

THE VALLÉE BLANCHE

*This is a trip you do for the stunning scenery rather than the challenge of the run,
which (although exceptionally long) is well within the capability of the average
intermediate so long as the snow is good. But a reporter warns that if snow is
sparse (as it was early last season) the run can turn tricky – there can be patches
of sheet ice, exposed stones and rocks and narrow snow bridges over gaping
crevasses. Be prepared for extreme cold at the top, for flat and uphill sections on
the way down, and for crowds of people – going early on a weekday gives you the
best chance of avoiding the crowds. Go in a guided group – dangerous crevasses
lurk to swallow those not in the know. The trip is popular so book up in advance
at the Maison de la Montagne or other ski school offices.*

*The amazing Aiguille du Midi cable-car takes you to 3840m/12,600ft. Across the
bridge from the arrival station on the Piton Nord is the Piton Central; the view of
Mont Blanc from the cafe a stair-climb higher should not be missed – and gives
you the opportunity to adjust to the dizzying altitude. A tunnel delivers you to the
infamous ridge-walk down to the start of the run. There is (usually) a fixed guide-
rope, and many parties rope up for this walk. You may still feel envious of those
strolling nonchalantly down in crampons; you may wish you'd stayed in bed.*

*After that the run seems a doddle; mostly effortless gliding down gentle slopes
with only the occasional steeper, choppy section to deal with. So stop often and
enjoy the surroundings fully. The views of the ice, the crevasses and seracs – and
the spectacular mountains beyond – are simply mind-blowing. There are variants
on the classic route, all more difficult and hazardous – the 'Vraie Vallée' and
'Envers du Plan' among them. Snow conditions may mean cutting short the full
24km/15 mile run down to Chamonix, in which case you catch a train from the
station at Montenvers. A short climb and gondola link the glacier to the station.*

SCHOOLS/GUIDES

2001/02 prices in euros

ESF
In both Chamonix and Argentière
Classes 6 days
5hr: am and pm
6 full days: 190
Children's classes
Ages: 4 to 12
6 days: 9.30-5pm, including supervised lunch: 225
Private lessons
1hr, 2hr, half- or full day
92 for 2hr, for 1 or 2 people; 102 for 3 or 4 people

CHILDCARE

The ESF runs classes for children aged 6 to 12. For children aged 4 to 6 there are lessons in a snow-garden. And children in either category can be looked after all day from 8.30 to 5pm.

The day-care centre at the Maison pour Tous (0450 533668) takes children aged 18 months to 6 years from 7.45 to noon and 2pm to 5.30.

The Panda Club takes children aged 10 months to 12 years.

The club at Argentière (0450 540476) has its own slopes, open to children aged 3 or more.

The smart way to a ski holiday

Alpine
Answers
020 8871 4656
ABTA D4050 ATOL 4791

www.alpineanswers.co.uk

FOR CROSS-COUNTRY
A decent network of trails

Most of the 42km/26 miles of prepared trails lie along the valley between Chamonix and Argentière. There are green, blue, red and black loop sections and the full tour from Chamonix to Argentière and back is 32km/20 miles. All these trails are fairly low; they're cold and shady in midwinter, and they fade fast in the spring sun.

QUEUES
Morning and afternoon problems

Getting down when the home runs are closed can be as bad as getting up the mountain in the morning. The Flégère cable-car is queue-prone (last a year a reporter waited 45 minutes and was told by a local that he had done rather well). A booking system comes into operation at the end of the day for getting down again. Another reporter also found queueing to get down on the Brévent gondola tedious.

In poor weather Les Houches is the most likely area to be open and the queues for the Bellevue cable-car can then be bad.

There are still long queues for the top cable-car on Les Grands Montets – often all day long. When they reach 30 minutes a booking system operates, so you can keep moving until it's your turn to ride.

MOUNTAIN RESTAURANTS
Surprisingly dull

The Panoramic at the top of Brévent enjoys amazing views over to Mont Blanc and the food's fine, but the place is dull. Altitude 2000 provides table-service at rip-off prices. The Bergerie at Planpraz – built in wood and stone – with self- and table-service does 'excellent salads and soups but service was very slow'. There's a self-service place at La Flégère with a large terrace and excellent views.

On the Grands Montets the Plan Joran serves good food and does table- and self-service. The restaurant at Lognan has been smartly renovated. The rustic Chalet-Refuge du Lognan, off the beaten track overlooking the Argentière glacier, has marvellous food and is very popular – book a table in advance. At Le Tour the Chalet de Charamillon is the place to head for.

The restaurants in the Prarion-Bellevue area at Les Houches are pleasant and good value.

SCHOOLS AND GUIDES
The place to try something new

The schools here are particularly strong in specialist fields – off-piste, glacier and couloir skiing, ski touring, snowboarding and cross-country. English-speaking instructors and mountain guides are plentiful and specialist Chamonix tour operators such as Collineige, Bigfoot and Ski Weekend can arrange them in advance for guests (and arrange special courses or tours).

At the Maison de la Montagne in Chamonix is the main ESF office and the HQ of the Compagnie des Guides, which has taken visitors to the mountains for 150 years. Competition is provided by a number of smaller, independent guiding and teaching outfits.

FACILITIES FOR CHILDREN
Better than they were

The Panda Club is used by quite a few British visitors and reports have been enthusiastic. The Argentière base can be inconvenient for meeting up with children for the afternoons. The Club Med nursery seems to go down well too. UK tour operator Esprit Ski has chalets here, with a nursery in the Sapinière chalet-hotel.

Beware of children being kept on the valley nursery slopes for the convenience of the school when they really should be getting some miles under their skis. And we have had reports of 12 to 14 in ESF classes.

Staying there

HOW TO GO
Any way you like

There is all sorts of accommodation, and lots of it.

Chalets Many are run by small operators that cater for this specialist market. Quality tends to be high and value for money good. Collineige has a large selection – all very comfortable. We've had good reports of Bigfoot's chalets and 'Mercedes mini-vans to run you to and from the slopes'. Cheaper places are offered by HuSki and big tour operators. Childcare specialist Esprit Ski has a couple of places, including the excellent Sapinière (formerly a highly rated 3-star hotel), which it has taken over this season) with stunning views of Mont Blanc and convenient for the Brévent gondola.

Hotels The place is full of hotels, many modestly priced, and the vast majority small, with fewer than 30 rooms. Hotel

GETTING THERE

Air Geneva, transfer 1¼hr. Lyon, transfer 3hr.

Rail Station in resort, on the St Gervais-Le Fayet/Vallorcine line.

Direct TGV link from Paris on Friday evenings and weekends.

bookings for a day or two are easy to arrange since Chamonix's peak season is summer. There's a Club Med 'village'.

《《《4 **Albert 1er** (0450 530509) Smart, traditional chalet-style hotel with 'truly excellent food' (Michelin stars, Gault-Millau rating). Visitors love the new indoor-outdoor swimming pool.

《《《4 **Auberge du Bois Prin** (0450 533351) A small modern chalet with a big reputation; great views; bit of a hike into town; closer to Le Brévent.

《《《4 **Mont-Blanc** (0450 530564) Central, luxurious.

《《《4 **Jeu de Paume** (Lavancher) (0450 540376) Alpine satellite of a chic Parisian hotel: a beautifully furnished modern chalet halfway to Argentière.

《《3 **Alpina** (0450 534777) Much the biggest in town: modernist-functional place just north of centre.

《《3 **Labrador** (Les Praz) (0450 559009) Scandinavian-style chalet close to the Flégère lift. Good restaurant.

《《3 **Vallée Blanche** (0450 530450) Smart, low-priced 3-star B&B hotel, handy for centre and Aiguille du Midi.

《2 **Richemond** (0450 530885) Traditional, comfortable, with good public areas. 'Excellent, very good value, superb food,' says a reporter.

《2 **Arve** (0450 530231) By the river, just off the main street; small newly decorated rooms. 'Good value and superb service run by Chamonix-born locals,' says a 2002 visitor.

《2 **Pointe Isabelle** (0450 531287) Not pretty, but central; friendly staff, good plain food, well-equipped bedrooms.

《1 **Faucigny** (0450 530117) Cottage-style; in centre.

Self-catering Many properties in UK package brochures are typically in convenient but cramped and charmless blocks in Chamonix Sud. The Balcons du Savoy (0450 553232) look much better, are well situated and have use of a swimming pool, a steam room and a solarium. The Splendid & Golf apartments in Les Praz (0450 559601) are charming and close to the Flégère cable-car. Erna Low has some luxury places available.

EATING OUT
Plenty of quality places
The good hotels all have good restaurants – the Eden at Les Praz and Bois Prin in Chamonix are first-rate – and there are many other good places to eat. The Sarpé is a lovely 'mountain' restaurant and The Impossible is rustic

Chamonix

227

Phone numbers
From abroad use the prefix +33 and omit the initial 'o' of the phone number.

**CHAMONIX
TOURIST OFFICE**
Postcode 74400
t 0450 530024
f 0450 535890
info@chamonix.com
www.chamonix.com

**ARGENTIERE
TOURIST OFFICE**
Postcode 74400
t 0450 540214
f 0450 540639
accueil@argentiere.com

**LES HOUCHES
TOURIST OFFICE**
Postcode 74310
t 0450 555062
f 0450 555316
info@leshouches.com
www.leshouches.com

OT CHAMONIX-MONT BLANC

The picturesque, car-free centre of Chamonix has a wide range of shops, bars and restaurants ↓

but smart and features good regional dishes. We like Atmosphere, by the river, and have had several good meals here (it now has a Michelin listing). Reporters have especially recommended the Panier des Quatre Saisons ('Excellent food at reasonable prices. Wonderful atmosphere'), the Crochon ('Good Savoyard fare, plus some varied and innovative dishes') and the Cabane restaurant next to the Labrador hotel in Les Praz. The Monchu is also good for Savoyard specialities. There are a number of ethnic restaurants – Mexican, Spanish, Japanese, Chinese etc – and lots of brasseries and cafes.

APRES-SKI
Lots of bars and music
Many of the bars around the pedestrianised centre of Chamonix get crowded for a couple of hours at sundown – none more so than the Choucas video bar. During the evening, The Pub, Wild Wallaby's, the Mill Street bar and the Bar du Moulin are busy. The Queen Vic is 'nice and dark and dingy with a snug, pool table, good music and Beamish on tap'. There's a lively variety of nightclubs and discos. The Choucas (again), and Dick's Tea bar are popular. The Cantina sometimes has live music and is open late. There are plenty of bars and brasseries for a quieter drink, too.

OFF THE SLOPES
An excellent choice
There's more off-slope activity here than in many resorts. Excursion possibilities include Annecy, Geneva, Courmayeur and Turin. The Alpine Museum is 'very interesting', the library has a good selection of English language books and there's a good sports centre and swimming pool.

Argentière 1240m/4,070ft

The old village is in a lovely setting towards the head of the valley – the Glacier d'Argentière pokes down towards it and the Aiguille du Midi and Mont Blanc still dominate the scene down the valley. There's a fair bit of modern development but it still has a rustic appeal. Le Tour, just beyond Argentière, is quiet and picturesque.

A number of the hotels are simple, inexpensive and handy for the village centre – less so for the slopes – but the Grands-Montets (0450 540666) is a large chalet-style building, right next to the piste and the Panda Club for children. The family-run Montana (0450 541499) is recommended for 'lovely rooms, excellent food'.

Restaurants and bars are informal and inexpensive. The Office is always packed with Brits. The Savoy bar is another British-dominated haunt.

Les Houches 1010m/3,310ft

Les Houches, 6km from Chamonix, is not on the valley pass, but is covered by the regional Mont Blanc pass. It's a pleasant village, sitting in the shade of the looming Mont Blanc massif – shady and cold in midwinter. There is an old core with a pretty church, but modern developments in chalet style have spread along the road up to Chamonix.

The area above Les Houches is served by a cable-car to Bellevue and a gondola to Prarion. Runs on the back of the mountain towards St-Gervais, and blue, red and black runs of 900m/3,000ft vertical down to Les Houches, make this the biggest single area of prepared runs in the Chamonix valley.

The almost entirely wooded slopes are popular when bad weather or the risk of avalanches closes other areas.

In good weather the slopes are quiet, and the views superb from the several attractive mountain restaurants. It is good for families, beginners and intermediates, with easy runs at the top of the mountain. Snow-cover on the lower slopes is not reliable, but there is a fair amount of snowmaking.

The village is quiet at night, but there are some pleasant bars and good restaurants. Reporters enjoyed staying in the hotel Bois (0450 545035), with its 'helpful staff and excellent restaurant' and 'a good local band in the bar on Saturday'. Buses run in and out of Chamonix all evening.

Châtel 1200m/3,940ft

A distinctively French base for touring the Portes du Soleil

WHAT IT COSTS

HOW IT RATES

The slopes

Snow	**
Extent	*****
Experts	***
Intermediates	****
Beginners	**
Convenience	**
Queues	***
Restaurants	***

The rest

Scenery	***
Resort charm	***
Off-slope	**

⊕ Very extensive, pretty, intermediate terrain – the Portes du Soleil

⊕ Wide range of cheap and cheerful, good-value accommodation

⊕ Easily reached – close to Geneva, and one of the shortest drives from the Channel

⊕ Pleasant, lively, French-dominated old village, still quite rustic in parts

⊕ Local slopes relatively queue-free

⊕ Good views

⊖ Both resort and top of skiing are low for a French resort, with resulting risk of poor snow – though extended snowmaking has helped

⊖ Bus or gondola ride to most snow-sure nursery slopes

⊖ Queues can be a problem in parts of the Portes du Soleil circuit, particularly at weekends

⊖ Village traffic can be congested at weekends and in peak season

Like neighbouring Morzine, Châtel offers a blend of attractions that is uncommon in France – an old village with plenty of facilities, cheap accommodation by French standards, and a large ski area on the doorstep. Châtel's original rustic charm has been largely eroded by expansion in recent years, but some of it remains, and the resort has one obvious advantage over smoother Morzine: it is part of the main Portes du Soleil circuit.

The circuit actually breaks down at Châtel, but this works in the village's favour. Whereas those doing the circuit from other resorts have the inconvenience of waiting for a bus mid-circuit, Châtel residents have the advantage of being able to time their bus-rides to avoid waits and queues. Those mainly interested in the local slopes should also consider Châtel. For confident intermediates, Châtel's Linga has few equals in the Portes du Soleil, while the nearby Torgon section has arguably the best views. The Chapelle d'Abondance slopes are pleasantly uncrowded at weekends. Châtel has become more beginner-friendly with nursery slopes at Super-Châtel and Pré-la-Joux, though these are a lift or bus-ride away.

229

What's new

For 2002/03 the triple Chaux des Rosées chair from Plaine Dranse will be replaced by a high-speed six-pack, which will cut queues here.

And a 1200m/3,940ft long cable was erected in the Pré-le-Joux area in summer 2002. You can be attached to the cable by a harness and flown down the cable 100m/330ft above the ground over the Plaine Dranse area at 80km/50 miles per hour! It is called the 'Fantasticable' and will be open in winter from 1 March when the weather is good.

For 2001/02 a new boarder-cross course and terrain-park were built in the Linga area and more snowmaking was installed here. For 2002/03 the Linga area will be floodlit and wired for sound effects for night skiing and boarding.

The resort

Châtel lies near the head of the wooded Dranse valley, at the north-eastern limit of the French-Swiss Portes du Soleil ski circuit.

It is a much expanded and now quite large but nonetheless attractive old village. New unpretentious chalet-style hotels and apartments rub shoulders with old farmhouses where cattle still live in winter.

Although there is a definite centre, the village sprawls along the road in from lake Geneva and the diverging roads out – up the hillside towards Morgins and along the valley towards the Linga and Pré-la-Joux lifts.

Lots of visitors take cars and the centre can get clogged with traffic – especially at weekends. Street parking is difficult but there is underground (pay-for) parking and day car parks at Linga and Pré-la-Joux (where the parking can

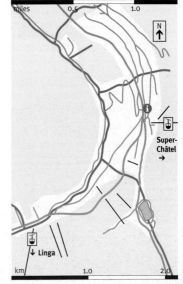

FRANCE

230

MOUNTAIN FACTS

for Portes du Soleil

Altitude	975m-2350m
	3,200ft-7,710ft
Lifts	206
Pistes	650km
	400 miles
Green	13%
Blue	38%
Red	39%
Black	10%
Snowmaking	
	252 acres
Recco detectors used	

LIFT PASSES

2002/03 prices in euros

Portes du Soleil
Covers all lifts in all 12 resorts, and shuttle-buses.
Main pass
1-day pass 34
6-day pass 164
Senior citizens
Over 60: 6-day pass 131
Children
Under 16: 6-day pass 110
Under 5: free pass
Short-term passes
Morning/afternoon passes for the Portes du Soleil (both 26), and for Châtel only (both 19).
Alternative periods
5 non-consecutive-days pass for Châtel only (adult 118).
Alternative passes
Châtel pass covers 54 lifts in Châtel, Linga, Super-Châtel, Torgon, Barbossine, and the link to Morgins (adult 6-day pass 123).

get very full in peak season). Other main French Portes du Soleil resorts are easy to reach by piste, but not by road.

A central position gives you the advantage of getting on the ski-bus to the outlying lifts before it gets very crowded and simplifies après-ski outings. But there is accommodation near the Linga lift if that's the priority.

A few kilometres down the valley is the rustic village of La Chapelle-d'Abondance (see end of chapter).

The mountains

The Portes du Soleil is classic intermediate terrain, and Châtel's local slopes are very much in character. Confident intermediates, in particular, will find lots to enjoy in the Linga and Plaine Dranse sectors. If you travel the Portes du Soleil circuit, the new booklet-style piste map makes for easy navigation. Reporters have also commented favourably on the recently introduced system of Discovery Routes guiding you around the Portes du Soleil – choose an alpine animal that suits your ability and follow the signs displaying it. An electronic lift pass means you can now keep your pass in your pocket.

THE SLOPES
The circuit breaks down here

Châtel sits between two sectors of the Portes du Soleil circuit – linked together by an 'excellent, practically continuous', free bus service. **Super-Châtel** is directly above the village – an area of easy, open and lightly wooded beginner slopes, accessed by a choice of gondola or two-stage chair. From here you can cross the Swiss border, either to quiet Torgon or clockwise around the Portes du Soleil to Morgins, Champoussin and Champéry, before going back into France above Avoriaz.

Linga is a bus-ride away. For intermediates and better, the area has some of the most interesting runs in the Portes du Soleil. The fastest way to Avoriaz is to stay on the bus at Linga and go to Pré-la-Joux. From here a high-speed quad goes to Plaine Dranse; then it's one more lift and run to Les Lindarets and the lifts to Avoriaz.

SNOW RELIABILITY
The main drawback

The main drawback of the Portes du Soleil is that it is low, so snow quality can suffer when it's warm. Châtel is at only 1200m/3,940ft and some runs home can be tricky or shut, especially

boarding *Avoriaz is the hardcore destination in the Portes du Soleil. But Châtel is not a bad place to learn or to go to as a budget option or as part of a mixed group of skiers and boarders. Most local lifts are gondolas or chairs and there's a terrain-park, a half-pipe and a boarder-cross course at Super-Châtel and a new terrain-park and a boarder-cross course at Linga for last season. The Linga area also has good, varied slopes and off-piste possibilities. There are a couple of lively bars.*

SCHOOLS/GUIDES

2002/03 prices in euros

ESF

Classes 6 days
2½hr am or pm
6 half-days: 100
Children's classes
Ages: 5 to 13
6 half-days: 96 am,
89 pm
Private lessons
1hr or 1½hr
30 for 1hr, for 1 or 2
people

International Classes

Special beginners: 5½
days. Sun afternoon
(2pm-5pm). Mon, Tue,
Thu and Fri mornings
(9am-noon): 115
Children's classes
Ages: from 8
6 afternoons: 118
Private lessons
1hr or 2hr
33 for 1hr, each
additional person 5

Stages Henri Gonon

Classes 5 days
3hr per day
5 days: 100 to 110
Children's classes
Ages: 7-16
3hr or 6hr per day
5 3hr days: 93 to 100.
Private lessons
1hr for 1 or 2 people:
33

Other schools include:
Francis Sports, Snow
Ride and Virages.

---

from Super-Châtel. But a lot of snowmaking has been installed at Super-Châtel and on runs down from Linga and to Pré-la-Joux. These last two are mainly north-facing and generally have the best local snow – a regular visitor tells us there is often good snow at Pré-la-Joux till May. But another told us of pistes to Morgins and Lindarets being closed in March.

FOR EXPERTS
Some challenges

The best steep runs – on and off-piste – are in the Linga and Pré-la-Joux area. Beneath the Linga gondola and chair, there's a pleasant mix of open and wooded ground which follows the fall line fairly directly. And there's a mogul field between Cornebois and Plaine Dranse which has been described as 'steeper and narrower than the infamous Swiss Wall in Avoriaz'. An unpisted trail from Super-Châtel towards the village is also fun. And there are two blacks from the top of the Morclan chair at Super-Châtel, including a long run down to Barbossine which is quite narrow and tricky at the top. There's also a great off-piste route from Tête du Linga down the valley of La Leiche – hire a guide. Two pistes from the Rochassons ridge are steep and kept well groomed. And the Hauts Forts sector beyond Avoriaz is challenging.

FOR INTERMEDIATES
Some of the best runs in the area

When conditions are right the Portes du Soleil is an intermediate's paradise. Good intermediates need not go far from Châtel; Linga and Plaine Dranse

---

have some of the best red runs on the circuit. The moderately skilled can do the circuit without problem, and will particularly enjoy runs around Les Lindarets and Morgins. Even timid types can do the circuit, provided they take one or two short-cuts and ride chairs down trickier bits. The chair from Les Lindarets to Pointe de Mossettes leads to a red run into the Swiss area, which is a lot easier than the 'Swiss Wall' from Chavanette and also speeds up a journey round the circuit.

Leaving aside attempts to complete the circuit in both directions, there are rewarding out-and-back expeditions to be made clockwise to the wide open snowfields above Champoussin, beyond Morgins, and anticlockwise to the Hauts-Forts runs above Avoriaz.

FOR BEGINNERS
Three possible options

There are good beginners' areas at Pré-la-Joux (a bus-ride away) and at Super-Châtel (a gondola ride). And there are nursery slopes at village level if there is snow there. A recent reporter praises the Super-Châtel slopes and lifts which 'allow the beginner to progress' but criticises their access: 'Maybe a bus, then an uphill walk to the crowded gondola.' The Pré-la-Joux slopes are easier to reach but 'have less variety of slopes and quite a steep drag-lift'.

FOR CROSS-COUNTRY
Pretty, if low, trails

There are plenty of pretty trails along the river and through the woods on the lower slopes of Linga, but snow-cover can be a problem.

Châtel

231

CHILDCARE

The ESF's ski kindergarten is for children from age 4.

Le Village des Marmottons takes children from 2 to 10, from 8.30 to 5.30, with ski lessons for those aged 3 up.

Henri Gonon takes children over 6.

The Ski and Surf International School and Snow Ride takes children from 8.

Francis Sports caters for 3 to 5 year olds at the Pitchounes.

QUEUES
Bottlenecks being eased

Queues to get to Avoriaz have been eased by the high-speed quad at Pré-la-Joux installed a couple of seasons ago. But there are still a couple of bottlenecks, which tend to be worse at weekends (although we do have reports of little queuing even during half-term and New Year). The worst is at Les Lindarets, where there is often a lengthy wait for the Chaux Fleurie chair-lift to the Col du Bassachaux on the way back to Châtel. But the queue the other way up to Avoriaz has been eased by the new six-pack introduced for 2001/02 – see Avoriaz chapter. You can face queues to get down from Super-Châtel if the slope back is shut by poor snow. Reporters have also found lengthy queues at the Tour de Don and Chermeu drag-lifts at certain times of day, causing difficulties for skiers rushing back to Super-Châtel to pick up children from ski school.

MOUNTAIN RESTAURANTS
Some quite good local huts

Atmospheric chalets can be found, notably at Plaine Dranse (the Bois Prin, Chez Crépy, Tân o Marmottes and Chez

Denis have been recommended). In the Linga area the Ferme des Pistes gets the thumbs up. The Perdrix Blanche at Pré-la-Joux scarcely counts as a mountain restaurant, but is an attractive (if expensive) spot for lunch. It does get crowded as there's nowhere else. At Super Châtel the Portes du Soleil at the foot of the Coqs drags is much better than the big place at the top of the gondola. The Escale Blanche is worth a visit.

SCHOOLS AND GUIDES
Plenty of choice

There are now six ski and snowboard schools in Châtel. The International school has been recommended by a reporter and the ESF came in for praise with comments such as 'very helpful and customer-focused instructors', and 'skiing progressed by leaps and bounds'.

FACILITIES FOR CHILDREN
Increasingly sympathetic

The Marmottons nursery (now with their own snowmaking machine) has good facilities, including toboggans, painting, music and videos, and children are reportedly happy there. Francis Sports ski school has its own nursery area with a drag lift and chalet at Linga: 'Very organised, convenient and reasonably priced.' The ESF has had a rave report this year: 'I was very impressed. Our five-year-old grandson had four instructors who all spoke sufficient English and his skiing progressed by leaps and bounds. They also seemed very caring for the kids in their charge.'

Staying there

HOW TO GO
A wide choice, including chalets

Although this is emphatically a French resort, packages from Britain are no problem to track down.

Chalets A fair number of UK operators have places here, including some Châtel specialists.

Hotels Practically all of the hotels are 2-stars, mostly friendly chalets, wooden or at least partly wood-clad. None of the 3-stars is particularly well placed. Cornettes in La Chapelle (see end of chapter) is an interesting alternative.

((3 **Macchi** (0450 732412) Modern chalet, most central of the 3-stars.

((3 **Fleur de Neige** (0450 732010) Welcoming chalet on edge of centre;

GETTING THERE

Air Geneva, transfer 1½hr.

Rail Thonon les Bains (42km/26 miles).

ACTIVITIES

Indoor Swimming pool, bowling, cinema, library

Outdoor Skating rink, horse-drawn carriage rides, helicopter rides, dog-sledding, snow-shoe excursions, farm visits, toboggan run, floodlit skiing at Linga

Phone numbers
From abroad use the prefix +33 and omit the initial 'o' of the phone number.

CHATEL TOURIST OFFICE

Postcode 74390
t 0450 732244
f 0450 732287
touristoffice@
chatel.com
www.chatel.com

LA CHAPELLE D'ABONDANCE TOURIST OFFICE

Postcode 74360
t 0450 735141
f 0450 735604
ot@lachapelle
dabondance.com
www.lachapelle
dabondance.com

Grive Gourmande restaurant does about the best food in town.
(((3) **Lion d'Or** (0450 813440) In centre, 'basic rooms, good atmosphere'.
((2) **Belalp** (0450 732439) Very comfortable, with excellent food.
(1) **Kandahar** (0450 733060) One for peace-lovers: a Logis by the river, a walkable distance from the centre.
(1) **Rhododendrons** (0450 732404) 'Great service, friendly, comfortable, clean.'

Self-catering Many of the better places are available through Châtel and self-drive specialists. The Gelinotte (out of town but near the Linga lifts and children's village) and the Erines (central and close to the Super-Châtel gondola) look good. The Flèche d'Or apartments are not well positioned for lifts or shops. The Aveniers is right by the Linga gondola. A couple of reporters have mentioned that Châtel's supermarkets are small and over-crowded – it may be worth shopping on the way if you're driving. There is also a large supermarket if you drive out in the direction of Chapelle d'Abondance.

EATING OUT
Fair selection
There is an adequate number and range of restaurants. Cornettes in La Chapelle-d'Abondance is one of our favourites – amazingly good-value menus with excellent food (but 'disappointing' desserts, comments one reporter). The Vieux Four, in an old farm building, has a reputation for the best steaks in Châtel. The Fleur de Neige hotel has a good restaurant and the Fiacre is also popular. The Perrier serves Savoyard specialities. The Ripaille, almost opposite the Linga gondola, was highly recommended by a past reporter, especially for its fish.

APRES-SKI
All down to bars
Châtel is getting livelier, especially at weekends. The Tunnel bar is very popular with the British and has a DJ or live music every night. The Isba has apparently slightly fallen from grace since its supremo moved on to run the very popular English pub-style Avalanche. La Godille – close to the Super-Châtel gondola and crowded at tea-time – has a more French feel. The bar in the hotel Soldanelles is also pretty lively. The bowling alley, The Vieille Grange, also has a good bar.

The Jean'Club disco at the Super-Châtel bubble is crowded at weekends, and there's also the Lagon Bleu in the same area. A reporter has recommended the Saf disco in Morgins.

OFF THE SLOPES
Better to stay in Morzine
Those with a car have some entertaining excursions available: Geneva, Thonon and Evian. Otherwise there is little to do but take some pleasant walks along the river, or visit the cheese factory and the two cinemas. The tourist office organises daily events for non-slope-users. But those not using the slopes would find more to do in Morzine. The Portes du Soleil as a whole is less than ideal for those not using the slopes who like to meet their more active friends for lunch: skiers and boarders are likely to be above at some distant resort at lunchtime.

La Chapelle-d'Abondance
1010m/3,310ft
This unspoiled, rustic farming community, complete with old church and friendly locals, is 5km/3 miles along a beautiful valley from Châtel. 'A car and a bit of French is virtually essential,' says a reporter. It's had its own quiet little north-facing area of easy wooded runs for some years, but has more recently been put on the Portes du Soleil map by a gondola and three chair-lifts that now link it to Torgon in Switzerland and, from there, Super-Châtel. This section is only a spur of the Portes du Soleil circuit. But, taken together with Chapelle's own little area, it is worth exploring – good at weekends when Châtel gets crowded and 'excellent for beginners'.

Nightlife is virtually non-existent – just a few quiet bars, a cinema and torchlit descents.

The hotel Cornettes (0450 735024) is an amazing 2-star with 2-star rooms but 4-star facilities, including an indoor pool, sauna, steam room, hot-tubs, excellent restaurant (see Eating out) and atmospheric bar. Look out for showcases with puppets and dolls and eccentric touches, such as ancient doors that unexpectedly open automatically. It has been run by the Trincaz family since 1894. The Alpage and the Chabi are other hotel options. The Airelles apartments have received a favourable report.

La Clusaz-Le Grand-Bornand 1100m/3,610ft

Very attractive, distinctly French all-rounders; all they lack is altitude

WHAT IT COSTS

HOW IT RATES

The slopes
Snow	**
Extent	***
Experts	***
Intermediates	****
Beginners	****
Convenience	***
Queues	***
Restaurants	****

The rest
Scenery	****
Resort charm	****
Off-slope	***

234

➕ Mountain villages in a scenic setting, retaining traditional character

➕ Extensive, interesting slopes – pistes best for beginners and intermediates

➕ Very French atmosphere

➕ Very short transfer from Geneva, and easy to reach by car from UK

➕ Attractive mountain restaurants

➕ Good cross-country trails

➕ Slopes at La Clusaz and Le Grand-Bornand linked by shuttle-bus

➖ Snow conditions unreliable because of low altitude (by French standards)

➖ Not many challenging pistes for experts – though there are good off-piste runs

➖ Crowded at weekends

Few other major French resorts are based around what are still, essentially, genuine mountain villages that exude rustic charm and Gallic atmosphere. Combine that with over 200km/125 miles of largely intermediate slopes, above and below the tree line, spread over five linked sectors in La Clusaz and the separate Le Grand-Bornand area, and there's a good basis for an enjoyable, relaxed week.

The area's one big problem is its height, or lack of it. Snowmaking has been installed in recent years and is continually increased, but it's still on a modest scale, and of course makes no difference in mild weather. So pre-booking a holiday here remains, as in other low resorts, a slightly risky business.

What's new

The terrain-park and hiking paths were improved for 2001/02.

In Le Grand-Bornand, the Lachat chair – to the resort high point – was upgraded to a new six-pack. This now accesses the new red Piste 2000 which runs from the top of Lachat, around the back of the mountain and down to the Maroly area above Chinaillon.

Snowmaking has been extended and will be further increased for next season. 2002/03 will also see the opening of Espace Grand-Bo – a new resort centre incorporating cinema, conference hall and day nursery.

The resort

La Clusaz was once frequented almost entirely by the French. But it has developed into a major international resort – summer and winter. As one of the most accessible resorts from Geneva and Annecy, it's good for short transfers, but it does get crowded, and there can be weekend traffic jams.

The village is built beside a fast-flowing stream at the junction of a number of narrow wooded valleys, and has had to grow in a rather rambling and sprawling way, with roads running in a confusing mixture of directions. But, unlike so many French resorts, La Clusaz has retained the charm of a genuine mountain village. (It's the kind of place that is as attractive in summer as under a blanket of snow in winter.)

In the centre is a large old church, and other original old stone and wood buildings; and, for the most part, the new buildings have been built in chalet style and blend in well. Les Etages is a much smaller centre of accommodation above the main town, where two of the mountain sectors meet.

La Clusaz has a friendly feel to it.

The villagers welcome visitors every Monday evening in the main square with vin chaud and a variety of local cheeses. There's a weekly market, tempting food shops and a wide choice of typically French bars.

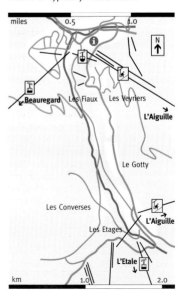

MOUNTAIN FACTS

La Clusaz

Altitude	1100m-2500m
	3,610ft-8,200ft
Lifts	55
Pistes	132km
	82 miles
Green	29%
Blue	32%
Red	29%
Black	10%
Snowmaking 50 acres	
Recco detectors used	

Le Grand-Bornand

Altitude	1000m-2100m
	3,280ft-6,890ft
Lifts	39
Pistes	82km
	51 miles
Green	33%
Blue	30%
Red	30%
Black	7%
Snowmaking 114 acres	

For much of the season La Clusaz is a quiet and peaceful place for a holiday. But in peak season and at weekends the place gets packed out with French and Swiss families.

Le Grand-Bornand, also covered by the Aravis lift pass, is an even more charming village, with even more sense that it remains a mountain community. This is partly because most of the development as a winter sports resort has gone on up the road at the satellite village of Le Chinaillon, which has been developed in chalet style. Le Grand-Bornand has quite extensive slopes and is well worth exploring for a day or two, or considering as an alternative, quieter base.

Le Grand-Bornand and La Clusaz are linked by a free buses doing the 10-minute journey every 30 minutes during the day – these become more erratic in peak-time traffic.

If you are taking a car, you might also consider basing yourself at **St-Jean-de-Sixt** – a small hamlet midway between La Clusaz and Le Grand-Bornand, with a small slope nearby, mainly used for sledging.

The mountains

Like the village, the slopes at **La Clusaz** are rather spread out – which makes them all the more interesting (and scenic). There are five main areas, each connecting with at least one other. At **Le Grand-Bornand** the slopes spread out along the mountainside and can be accessed from either the village or Le Chinaillon up the road.

The Aravis pass, covering the lifts of both resorts, costs very little more than the La Clusaz pass, but appreciably more than the one for Le Grand-Bornand.

THE SLOPES
Pretty and varied

Several points in **La Clusaz** have lifts giving access to the predominantly west- and north-west facing slopes of **L'Aiguille**. Links between this sector and the slightly higher and shadier slopes of **La Balme** area have improved massively in recent years: a long red and a black piste have replaced the off-piste route from L'Aiguille towards La Balme, and a gondola now returns you to Cote 2000 on L'Aiguille – cutting out the need to take a long, flat run back to La Clusaz. La Balme is a splendid, varied area with good lifts (a high-capacity gondola from the bottom linking to a quad chair up to the top); from the top there are wonderful views towards Mont Blanc.

Going the other way from L'Aiguille leads you to **L'Etale** via another choice of easy runs and the Transval cable-car, which shuttles people between two areas. From the bottom of L'Etale, you can head back along another path to the village and the cable-car up to the fourth sector of **Beauregard** which, as the name implies, has splendid views and catches a lot of sunshine.

From the top of Beauregard you can link via another easy piste and a two-way chair-lift with the fifth area of **Manigod**. From here you can move on to L'Etale.

The main village at **Le Grand-Bornand** has two gondolas on the outskirts up to a gentle open area of easy runs (including nursery slopes) lying between 1400m and 1500m (4,600ft and 4,900ft). Chairs fan out above this point, one going up to the high point of **Le Lachat,** where there are serious red and black runs. Other lifts and runs go across the

boarding *Snowboarding is popular in La Clusaz, and although there are still a lot of drag-lifts, most are avoidable. There are some good nursery slopes, served by chair-lifts, and great cruising runs to progress to. La Balme is a great natural playground for good free-riders. There's a terrain-park and a half-pipe on Aiguille and another in Le Grand-Bornand. During the week the resorts are fairly quiet, but La Clusaz livens up at the weekend.*

LIFT PASSES

2001/02 prices in euros

Aravis pass
Covers La Clusaz and Le Grand-Bornand
Main pass
6 days 139 (119 low season)
Senior citizens
Over 60: 6 days 115
Over 75: free pass
Children
Under 15: 6 days 105
Under 5: free pass

La Clusaz pass
All lifts in La Clusaz.
Main pass
1-day pass 24.5
6-day pass 128
(low season 108)
Senior citizens
Over 60: 6-days 105
Over 75: free pass
Children
Under 15: 6-days 94
Under 5: free pass

Le Grand-Bornand pass
All lifts in Le Grand-Bornand.
Main pass
1-day pass 22.5
6-day pass 109.5
(low season 98.5)
Senior citizens
Over 60: 6 days 103.5
(low season 93)
Over 75: free pass
Children
Under 16: 6 days 90.5
Under 5: free pass

mountainside to the slopes above **Le Chinaillon**. Here there is a broad, open mountainside with a row of chairs and drags serving blue and red slopes, and links to the rest of the domain – a wide area of blue and red runs.

SNOW RELIABILITY
Variable because of low altitude
Most of the runs are west- or north-west facing and tend to keep their snow fairly well, even though most of the area is below 2000m/6,500ft. The best snow is usually on the north-west-facing slopes at La Balme, where a lift takes you up to 2500m/8,200ft. La Clusaz itself is at only 1100m/3,610ft and, in late season, the home runs can be dependent on snowmaking – of which there is now virtually blanket coverage. However, the long paths linking La Balme and l'Etale to the village are devoid of snow-guns and

can suffer from lack of snow. The main lifts to Beauregard and Crêt du Merle will carry people down as well as up. You can also ride the gondolas down to Le Grand-Bornand and the runs above Chinaillon have extensive snowmaking facilities.

FOR EXPERTS
Plenty to do, especially off-piste
The La Clusaz piste map doesn't seem to have a lot to offer experts, but most of the sectors present off-piste variants to the pistes, and there are more serious adventures to undertake – all the more attractive for being ignored by most visitors.

The best terrain is at La Balme, where there are several fairly challenging pistes above mid-mountain. The black Vraille run, which leads to the speed skiing slope, is seriously steep. On the opposite side

La Tête des Annes
1870m
Col des Annes
Le Maroly
Le Lachat
2100m/6,890ft
Lac des Confins
Les Chenons
1275m
Le Bouchet
Le Chinaillon
1300m
La Clusaz
1100m/3,610ft
Le Grand-Bornand
950m/3,120ft
St-Jean-de-Sixt
960m/3,150ft

of the sector, the entirely off-piste Combe de Bellachat can be reached.

The Noire run down the face of Beauregard can be tricky in poor snow and is often closed. The Tetras on L'Etale and the Mur Edgar bumps run below Crêt du Loup on L'Aiguille have been reclassified as blacks, and rightly so. L'Aiguille has a good off-piste run down the neglected Combe de Borderan, and the piste map now shows the long new Lapiaz black run down the Combe de Fernuy – a continuation of the awkward black down from Cote 2000 to the parallel running Fernuy red.

In Le Grand-Bornand the steepest runs, including the black Noire du Lachat, go from the top of Le Lachat.

FOR INTERMEDIATES
Good if snow is good

Most intermediates will love La Clusaz if the snow conditions are good. Early intermediates will delight in the gentle slopes at the top of Beauregard and over on La Croix-Fry at Manigod, where there's a network of gentle tree-lined runs. And they'll be able to travel all over the area on the gentle, green linking pistes, where poling or walking is more likely to be a problem than

any fears about steepness.

L'Etale and L'Aiguille have more challenging but wide blue runs.

More adventurous intermediates will prefer the steeper red slopes and good snow of La Balme and the long red down Combe du Fernuy from L'Aiguille.

Le Grand-Bornand is full of good cruising blue and red intermediate runs stretching in both directions above Le Chinaillon – well worth a visit for a day or two if you are staying in La Clusaz.

FOR BEGINNERS
Splendid beginner slopes

There is a nursery slope at village level at La Clusaz, and a couple of others just above it, but the best nursery slopes are up the mountain at the top of the Beauregard cable-car and at Crêt du Merle. The Beauregard area has lovely gentle blue runs to progress to, including one long run around the mountain right back to the village. There are also some beginner slopes at Le Grand-Bornand and St-Jean-de-Sixt.

FOR CROSS-COUNTRY
Excellent

The region has much better cross-country facilities than many resorts, with around 60km/37 miles of loops of

La Clusaz

237

La Balme
2500m/8,200ft
L'Aiguille
2400m
L'Etale
2000m
Cote 2000
Col des Aravis
Lac des Confins
Crêt du Loup
1870m
Les Chenons
1275m
Le Bouchet
Crêt du Merle
1525m
Les Etages
Merdassier
1500m
Beauregard
1690m
La Clusaz
1100m/3,610ft
La Croix-Fry
1480m
St-Jean-de-Sixt
960m/3,150ft
Manigod

GETTING THERE

Air Geneva, transfer 1½hr. Lyon, transfer 2½hr.

ACTIVITIES

Indoor Various hotels have saunas, massage, hot-tub, weights rooms, aerobics, sun beds and swimming pools
Outdoor Ice skating, paragliding, micro-light flights, snow-shoe excursions, ice carts, winter walks, horse-drawn carriage rides, quad-bikes, swimming pool

SCHOOLS/GUIDES

2001/02 prices in euros
ESF
Classes 6 days
4hr: 9.30-11.30, 2.45-4.45
5 full days: 131
Children's classes
Ages: 5 to 12
5 full days: 119
Private lessons
Hourly
30 for 1 to 3 people;
42 for 4 or 5 people
Sno Academie
Classes
3½hr a day
5 days: 116
Private Lessons
1 or 2 people:
2hr 58
3 or 4 people:
2hr 72

CHILDCARE

The ESF runs a ski kindergarten for children aged 5 to 12.

The two all-day kindergartens in La Clusaz operate 8.30 to 6pm. The Club des Mouflets (0450 326957) takes non-skiing children from 8 months to 4½ years. The Champions' Club (0450 326950) takes children 3½ to 6.

Le Grand-Bornand kindergarten takes children from 3 months.

varying difficulty. In La Clusaz, one good area is near the Lac des Confins, reached by bus. There's also a lovely sunny area at the top of the Beauregard cable-car. At Le Grand-Bornand there are extensive trails in the Vallée du Bouchet and towards Le Chinaillon. And there are further trails at St-Jean-de-Sixt.

QUEUES
Not a problem

Lift queues aren't a problem, except on peak weekends or if the lower slopes are shut because of snow shortage. The chair-lifts up the front face of L'Aiguille are the main weekend black spots; they are avoidable.

MOUNTAIN RESTAURANTS
High standard

Mountain restaurants are one of the area's strong points. There are lots of them and, for the most part, they are rustic and charming, and serve good, reasonably priced – often Savoyard – food. We have had excellent reports on the Télémark above the chair lift to L'Etale and the Chenons at the bottom of La Balme. There are several other good restaurants higher up in the Aiguille sector, of which the Bercail is said to be the best. Chez Arthur at Crêt du Merle has a calm little table-service restaurant tucked away behind the crowded self-service. The restaurant at Beauregard by the cross-country trail is sunny and peaceful, with good views. The Relais de L'Aiguille at Crêt du Loup is also popular. In Le Grand Bornand, the Névé at Le Rosay and the Terres Rouges are recommended. The Vieille Ferme at Merdassier (see Eating out) is also open at lunchtime.

SCHOOLS AND GUIDES
Mixed reports

There are tales of large classes and poor instruction in ESF group lessons, but we've heard from some satisfied customers too – especially those who took private lessons. According to reports, the smaller Sno Academie – with smaller class sizes – is much more reliable.

FACILITIES FOR CHILDREN
Good – in theory

We have had mixed reports about the kindergarten in La Clusaz and none about those in Le Grand-Bornand. Generally, however, the resorts are places where families can feel at home.

Staying there

HOW TO GO
Decreasing choice of packages

There's a fair choice of packages to La Clusaz, mostly from smaller operators, some of whom go to Le Grand-Bornand too. The drive from the Channel and the transfer from Geneva airport are both among the shortest you'll find.
Chalets There are some chalets, including some charmingly rustic ones.
Hotels Small, friendly 2-star family hotels are the mainstay of the area; luxury is not an option here.
③ **Carlina** (0450 024348) A reporter says it's the best; central with pool and grounds.
③ **Beauregard** (0450 326800) Comfortable; on the fringe of the village. Pool. 'Fantastic for families, excellent food,' says a recent reporter.
③ **Alp'Hôtel** (0450 024006) Comfortable modern chalet close to the centre, with one of the better restaurants. Pool.
③ **Alpen Roc** (0450 025896) Big but stylish, central and comfortable, although one reporter said his room was 'very cramped'. Pool.
③ **Saytels** (0450 022016) Only 3-star in Le Grand-Bornand. Close to church.
③ **Cimes** (0450 270038) 3-star in Le Chinaillon.
② **Aravis** (0450 026031) Traditional place with 'dated' rooms but 'great' food, in la Clusaz centre, close to lifts.
② **Alpage de Tante Pauline** (0450 026328) Dinky chalet at foot of L'Etale slopes (bus stop outside).
Self-catering There's quite a good choice, including self-catering chalets as well as apartments. Some are out of town and best for those with a car.

EATING OUT
Good choice

There's a wide choice of restaurants, some a short drive away, including the Vieux Chalet, which is one of our favourites – good food and service in a splendid, creaky old chalet. It has a nice sunny terrace for a lunchtime blowout too. The St Joseph at the Alp'Hotel is regarded as the best restaurant in La Clusaz. Ecuelle is the place to go for Savoyard specialities. The Cordee and the Outa are simple places giving great value for money. At the other end of the price scale is the more formal Symphonie restaurant in the hotel Beauregard – highly

There's more to Le
Chinaillon than this
rustic hamlet ➔

BASILE / JC PIRONON

Phone numbers
From abroad use the
prefix +33 and omit
the initial 'o' of the
phone number.

TOURIST OFFICES

La Clusaz

Postcode 74220
t 0450 326500
f 0450 326501
infos@laclusaz.com
www.laclusaz.com

Le Grand-Bornand

Postcode 74450
t 0450 027800
f 0450 027801
infos@legrandbornand.
com
www.legrandbornand.
com

St-Jean-de-Sixt

Postcode 74450
t 0450 022412
f 0450 027878
infos@saintjeandesixt.
com
www.saintjeandesixt.
com

Vallées des Aravis

Postcode 74450
t 0450 027874
f 0450 023851
infos@aravis.com
www.aravis.com

recommended by a recent reporter.
   We're told some of the best food in
the area is at the Ferme du Lormay in
La Vallée du Bouchet, about 5km/3
miles on from Le Grand-Bornand. But
another reporter rates the Vieille Ferme
at Merdassier his favourite place in the
Alps – an old farm building with
'serious food, classy staff, perfect
atmosphere'. The Foly, overlooking the
Lac des Confins, is a firm favourite
with both tourists and locals alike.

APRES-SKI
La Clusaz getting livelier
These resorts have always seemed to
us typically quiet French family places,
with the difference that La Clusaz is
definitely the the place to stay for a
livelier time – especially at the
weekend. The Caves du Paccaly, in the
centre of La Clusaz, is a newish place
with woody decor and live music. The
Pressoir is a focal bar, popular for
sports videos. Pub le Salto is run by a

British couple and has Sky TV and
draught Guinness. The Bali bar is a
more French central recommendation.
The Ecluse disco has apparently lost its
glass dance floor with a floodlit stream
running beneath it. Club 18 rocks,
often with live bands.

OFF THE SLOPES
Some diversions
The villages are pleasant. It's easy for
pedestrians to get around the valley by
bus and to get up to several mountain
restaurants for lunch. There are good
walks along the valleys, and a day trip
to the beautiful lakeside town of
Annecy is possible.

STAYING UP THE MOUNTAIN
Cheap and panoramic
The Relais de l'Aiguille at Crêt du Loup
has five adequate bedrooms that are
about the cheapest in the resort. And
there are no fewer than three places to
stay at the top of Beauregard.

La Clusaz

239

Selected chalets in La Clusaz   ADVERTISEMENT

Les Contamines 1160m/3,800ft

A hidden gem: a charming, unspoiled French village with reliable snow

WHAT IT COSTS

HOW IT RATES

The slopes
Snow	****
Extent	**
Experts	**
Intermediates	***
Beginners	***
Convenience	**
Queues	***
Restaurants	****

The rest
Scenery	***
Resort charm	****
Off-slope	**

MOUNTAIN FACTS

Altitude	1160m-2485m
	3,810ft-8,150ft
Lifts	26
Pistes	120km
	75 miles
Green	16%
Blue	23%
Red	40%
Black	21%
Snowmaking	3km
	2 miles
Recco detectors used	

OT LES CONTAMINES

The charming old village is a delightful contrast to French purpose-built resorts ↓

240

- ➕ Traditional, unspoiled French village
- ➕ Fair-sized intermediate area
- ➕ Good snow record for its height
- ➕ Lift pass covers several nearby resorts, easily reachable by road

- ➖ Limited scope for experts, and not ideal for beginners
- ➖ Quiet nightlife
- ➖ Lifts a bus-ride from main village
- ➖ Can be some lengthy queues

Only a few miles from the fur coats of Megève and the ice-axes of Chamonix, Les Contamines is a charming contrast to both, with pretty wooden chalets, impressive old churches, a weekly market in the village square and prices more typical of rural France than of international resorts. Its position at the shoulder of Mont Blanc gives it an enviable snow record. What more could you want?

THE RESORT

The core of the village is compact, but the resort as a whole spreads widely, with chalets scattered here and there over a 3km/2 mile stretch of the valley, and the main access lift is 1km/half a mile from the centre. You can stay by the lift at Le Lay or in the charming village centre, a shuttle-bus ride from the lifts. A car is useful, but the main Mont Blanc lift pass option covers the local buses, as well as the lifts of Chamonix and Megève (among others).

THE MOUNTAINS

Most of the slopes are above the tree line and there are some magnificent views, though the runs down from Signal are bordered by trees (as is the run from La Ruelle down to Belleville). They amount to a respectable 120km/75 miles of pistes.

Slopes From Le Lay a two-stage gondola climbs up to the slopes at Signal. Another gondola leads to the Etape mid-station from a car park a little further up the valley. Above these, a sizeable network of open, largely north-east-facing pistes fans out, with lifts approaching 2500m/8,200ft in two places. You can drop over the ridge at Col du Joly to south-west-facing runs down to La Ruelle, with a single red run going on down to Belleville. From Belleville, a 16-person gondola has replaced the old chair-lift back up to La Ruelle. A high-speed chair takes you the rest of the way back up to Col du Joly.

Snow reliability Many of the shady runs on the Contamines side are above 1700m/5,575ft, and the resort has a justifiable reputation for good snow conditions, said to be the result of proximity to Mont Blanc. There's snowmaking on the home runs from Signal down to the gondola bases.

Experts The steep western section has black runs, which are enjoyable but not terribly challenging for experts. The main attraction is the substantial and varied off-piste terrain – taking a guide is advisable. You can also visit the other resorts on the Mont Blanc lift pass – notably Chamonix.

Intermediates Virtually all the runs are ideal for intermediates, with a good blend of blues and reds. Some of the best run from the gondola's top station to its mid-station and others are served by the Roselette and Buche Croisee lifts. Given good snow, the south-facing runs down to La Ruelle are a delight. And the black runs are enjoyable for good intermediates.

Beginners In good snow, the village nursery area is adequate for beginners. There are other areas at the mid-

What's new

A 16-person gondola on the back side of the mountain, from Belleville to La Ruelle replaced the old chair-lift a couple of seasons ago.

There has for a long time been talk of linking the slopes with those of Megève but no definite plan or timetable is in place yet.

Phone numbers
From abroad use the prefix +33 and omit the initial 'o' of the phone number.

TOURIST OFFICE

Postcode 74170
t 0450 470158
f 0450 470954
info@lescontamines.com
www.lescontamines.com

station and the top of the gondola. The piste map shows no long greens to progress to but a reporter tells of a 'very gentle run from Col du Joly back to Le Signal' that is not on the map.

Snowboarding There is a boarder-cross and half-pipe on the Tierces slope, accessed by the fast Tierces chair-lift.

Cross-country There are trails of varying difficulty totalling 29km/18 miles. One loop is floodlit twice a week.

Queues There can be peak-period queues in the morning, especially if people are bussed in from other resorts with less snow. A bottleneck can occur where the two gondolas meet for the second stage up to Signal. But we've had a report of minimal queues even at weekends.

Mountain restaurants There are quite a few lovely rustic mountain restaurants – not all of which are marked on the piste map. The Ferme de la Ruelle is a jolly barn and Col du Joly has great views. Best of all are two cosy chalets – Roselette and Bûche Croisée.

Schools and guides We have had mixed reports in the past on the ESF – some parents thought their children's classes too strict and overcrowded. However, our most recent reports are positive. 'The best tuition I've ever experienced,' said one reporter this year. Excursions are offered, including a guided trip to the famous Vallée Blanche. The new International school opened a couple of seasons ago, and there are also two guiding companies.

Facilities for children The new all-day village nursery, next to the central Loyers nursery slopes, takes children from one to seven years. Children can join ski school from age three.

STAYING THERE

How to go A couple of operators run catered chalets here, and there are a dozen modest hotels.

Hotels The 3-star Chemenaz (0450 470244) at Le Lay is praised by two reporters this year 'comfortable and best food in the village'.

Eating out There are restaurants and crêperies in town for eating out. Recommendations include the Husky, Auberge du Barattet and the Op Traken – and the Savoisien and the Auberge du Chalezan for Savoie specialities.

Après-ski Après-ski is quiet, but there are several bars, some with live jazz on later, others that get a reasonable crowd at tea time. The Saxo near the gondola has been recommended. There's also a disco for those looking for late-night entertainment. Weekly events are organised, such as music and free vin chaud by the village fountain for a 6pm welcome on Saturdays and torchlit descents.

Off the slopes There are good walks, a toboggan run and a natural ice rink, but St-Gervais, Megève and Chamonix have more to offer.

Les Contamines

241

Les Contamines-Montjoie 116om/3,81oft

Courchevel 1300m-1850m/4,270ft-6,070ft

Gourmet skiing and boarding – and it doesn't have to cost a fortune

➕ Extensive, varied local terrain to suit everyone from beginners to experts – plus the rest of the Three Valleys

➕ Great easy runs for near-beginners

➕ Lots of slope-side accommodation

➕ Impressive, continuously updated lift system, particularly above 1850

➕ Excellent piste maintenance, and widespread use of snowmaking

➕ Wooded setting is pretty, and useful in bad weather

➕ Choice of four very different villages – only 1850 is notably expensive

➕ Some great restaurants, and good après-ski by French standards

➖ Some pistes get unpleasantly crowded (but they can be avoided)

➖ Rather soulless villages with intrusive traffic in places – central 1850, especially, is surprisingly drab

➖ 1850 has some of the most expensive hotels, bars and mountain restaurants in the Alps

➖ Losing a little of its French feel as more and more British visitors discover its attractions

➖ Little to do away from the slopes, especially during the day – no public swimming pool, in particular

Courchevel 1850 – the highest of the five components of this big resort – is the favourite Alpine hangout of the Paris jet set, who fly directly in to the mini-airport in the middle of the slopes. Its top hotels and restaurants are among the best in the Alps, and the most expensive. But don't be put off: a holiday here doesn't have to cost a fortune (especially in the lower villages), the atmosphere is not particularly exclusive, and the slopes are excellent. Courchevel is the most extensive and varied sector of the whole Three Valleys, with everything from long gentle greens to steep couloirs. Many visitors never leave the Courchevel sector; but there is good access to the rest of the Three Valleys, too.

Le Praz is an overgrown, but still pleasant village, **1550** is quieter and good for families, **1650** has more of a village atmosphere than it seems from the road through, and the posh bits of **1850** are stylishly woody. But overall the resort is no beauty. Well, nothing's perfect. Courchevel's long list of merits is enough to attract more and more Brits, but it remains much more French than Méribel, over the hill, as well as having better snow.

The resort

Courchevel is made up of four varied villages, generally known by numbers supposed to represent their altitudes (in fact, as we revealed a few years back, they exaggerate the altitudes appreciably). A road winds up the hill, running from Le Praz (1300) past 1550 and through 1650 to 1850. From the skiing point of view, things work a bit differently: runs go down from 1850 to 1550 and 1300, but the slopes of 1650 form a distinct sector.

1850 (lift base altitude 1750m/ 5,740ft) is the largest village, and the focal point of the area, with most of the smart nightlife and shops. Two gondolas go over its lower slopes

towards the links with Méribel and the rest of the Three Valleys. It's conspicuously upmarket, with some very smooth hotels on the slopes just above the village centre, and among the trees of the Jardin Alpin a suburb is served by its own gondola. There's also a spreading area of smart private chalets. But the centre of the village is a bit of a messy sprawl, and the approach by road is, frankly, shabby.

While some readers 'couldn't afford a second week', others say, 'It's not as upmarket as it's made out to be.' You can pay through the nose to eat, drink and stay, but more affordable places are not impossible to find.

The main road cuts through **1650** but there's also an attractive old village

The summit of La
Vizelle is at the heart
of the Courchevel
slopes ➜

OT COURCHEVEL / J KELAGOPIAN

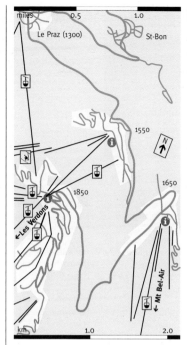

MOUNTAIN FACTS

For the Three Valleys

Altitude	1300m-3230m
	4,270ft-10,600ft
Lifts	200
Pistes	600km
	370 miles
Green	17%
Blue	34%
Red	37%
Black	12%
Snowmaking	90km
	56 miles
Recco detectors used	

centre, lively bars and quietly situated
chalets. Its local slopes (whose main
access is an escalator-served gondola)
are relatively peaceful. 1650 isn't the
most convenient base for exploration of
the Three Valleys, but a day trip to Val-
Thorens is well within reach, and 1650
is 'a pleasant start and end to the day'.

1550 is a quiet dormitory, a gondola
ride from 1850. It has the advantage of
having essentially the same position as
1850, with cheaper accommodation
and restaurants. But it's a long trip to
1850 by road if you want to go there in
the evening. Some accommodation is a
fair distance from the gondola.

Le Praz (or 1300) remains
essentially a traditional village set
amid woodland, despite expansion and
'improvements' triggered by the 1992
Olympics – the Olympic ski jump is a
conspicuous relic. It's quiet, 'excellent
for children', with gondolas going up
over the forest to 1850 and towards
Col de la Loze, for Méribel. Near-
beginners face rides down as well as
up: the pistes back to the village are
red and black, and at this altitude
snow conditions are often poor.

Free buses run between the villages,
and within them a car is of no great
value. Champagny is an easy road
outing, for access to the extensive
slopes of La Plagne.

The mountains

243

Although there are plenty of trees
around the villages, most of the slopes
are essentially open, with the
conspicuous exception of the runs
down to 1550 and Le Praz, which is
great for experts when the weather
closes in. Piste maintenance is superb,
and daily maps are available showing
which runs have been groomed
overnight (normal in America but very
rare in Europe). Snowmaking is
abundant but the runs to Le Praz are
still prone to closure in warm weather.
The main complaint we've had is that
some slopes get busier than expected
(but these can be avoided). Many
reporters recommend buying only a
Courchevel pass ('I was still finding
new runs after two weeks') and buying
daily extensions when you want to try
the rest of the Three Valleys.

THE SLOPES
Huge variety to suit everyone
A network of lifts and pistes spreads out
from **1850**, which is very much the focal
point of the area. The main axis is the
Verdons gondola, leading to a second
gondola to **La Vizelle** and a nearly
parallel cable-car up to **La Saulire**. Both
the high points give access to a wide
range of intermediate and advanced

FRANCE

244

LIFT PASSES

2002/03 prices in
euros

Three Valleys
Covers all lifts in
Courchevel, La Tania,
Méribel, Val-Thorens,
Les Menuires and St-
Martin-de-Belleville.
Beginners 11 free lifts
in the Courchevel
valley.
Main pass
1-day pass 39
6-day pass 193
Senior citizens
Over 59: 6-day pass
154
Over 71: free pass
Children
Under 13: 6-day pass
145
Under 5: free pass
Family pass
Available for 2 adults
plus 2 children under
18: 6-day pass 620
Short-term passes
Half-day (from 12.30)
for Courchevel valley
(adult 24) and the
Three Valleys (adult
29).
Notes 6-day pass and
over valid for one day
each in Tignes-Val-
d'Isère, La Plagne-Les
Arcs, Pralognan-la-
Vanoise and Les
Saisies. Reductions
for families.
Alternative passes
Vallée de Courchevel
pass covers 67 lifts
and 150km/93 miles
of piste around
Courchevel and La
Tania. Adult 6-day
157. One-day
extension for Three
Valleys, 18. Family 6-
day pass 510.

terrain (including a number of couloirs),
Méribel and all points to Val-Thorens.
You can also get over to 1650 from here.

To the right looking up from 1850
the **Chenus** gondola goes towards a
second departure point for Méribel, the
Col de la Loze. Easy and intermediate
runs go back to 1850, with more
difficult runs in the woods above **La
Tania** (covered in a separate chapter)
and **Le Praz**.

To the left of the Verdons gondola
is the Jardin Alpin gondola, which
leads to some great beginner terrain,
and serves the higher hotels and runs
until 8pm. It also gives access to 1650
via the valley of Prameruel.

1650 offers a good mix of beginner
and intermediate slopes away from the
crowds, and is an ideal area for
confidence-building. Getting to and
from Méribel and the rest of the Three
Valleys involves slightly more effort
than from the rest of Courchevel, but if
you run late on the way back you can
always catch the bus from 1850.

SNOW RELIABILITY
Very good
The combination of Courchevel's
orientation (its slopes are north- or
north-east-facing), its height, an
abundance of snowmaking and
excellent piste maintenance usually
guarantees good snow down to at
least the 1850 and 1650 villages. On
countless visits we have found that the
snow is usually much better than in
neighbouring Méribel, where the slopes
get the afternoon sun.

FOR EXPERTS
Some black gems
There is plenty to interest experts, even
without the rest of the Three Valleys.

The most obvious expert runs are
the couloirs you can see on the right
near the top of the Saulire cable-car.
These used to be black pistes (some of

the steepest in Europe). But last
season's piste map reclassified the
Téléphérique (seriously narrow) and
Emile Alais as itinéraires. The Grand
Couloir is the widest and easiest way
down, and remains an official piste –
but you have to traverse further along
the narrow bumpy, precipitous access
ridge to reach it.

There is a lot of steep terrain, on-
and off-piste, on the shady slopes of
La Vizelle, both towards Verdons and
towards the link with 1650. Some of
the reds on La Vizelle verge on black
steepness and the black M piste is
surprisingly little used. If you love
moguls, don't miss the top of the
black Suisses. Chanrossa, which comes
towards 1850 from the top of 1650, is
quite difficult – the off-piste just next
to it is tougher. For a change of scene
and a test of stamina, a couple of long
(700m/2,300ft vertical), genuinely
steep blacks cut through the trees
down to Le Praz.

There is plenty of off-piste terrain to
try with a guide and a bit of climbing –
high, north-facing slopes right at the
top of the 1650 sector, for example
(the Vallée des Avals is a great run).
Also ask about the mysterious Hidden
Valley in 1650, and the huge bowl
accessed from the Creux Noir chair.

FOR INTERMEDIATES
Paradise for all levels
The Three Valleys is the greatest
intermediate playground in the world,
but all grades of intermediates will
love Courchevel's local slopes too.

Above 1650 novices have the
wonderful long runs of Pyramides and
Grandes Bosses. Gentle blues such as
Biollay in 1850 are fine, gentle slopes,
leading to the two easy home runs on
either side of the Jardin Alpin.

Those of average ability can handle
most red runs without difficulty. Our
favourite is the long, sweeping Combe

de la Saulire from top to bottom of the cable-car – but you have to time it right. Very pleasant first thing, when it's well groomed and free of crowds, it's a different story when it's icy or at the end of the day – cut up snow and very crowded. Creux, behind La Vizelle, is another splendid, long red that gets bumpy and unpleasantly crowded. Marmottes from the top of Vizelle is quieter and more challenging.

The Chenus sector has excellent blues and reds down towards 1850 and 1550, and through the trees towards La Tania – long, rolling cruises 'guaranteed to put a smile on your face'. Over at 1650, the reds on Mt Bel Air and Signal are excellent, if short, and usually quiet (or at least they were before construction for last season of the new six-pack to the top of Signal).

FOR BEGINNERS
Great graduation runs

There are excellent nursery slopes above both 1650 and 1850. At the former, lessons are likely to begin on the short drags close to the village, but quick learners will soon be able to go up the gondola. The best nursery area at 1850 is at Pralong, above the village, near the airstrip. A green path links this area with chairs to 1650, so adventurous novices can soon move further afield. The Bellecôte green run down into 1850 is an excellent, long, gentle slope – but does get crowded. It is served by the Jardin Alpin gondola, and a drag which is one of 11 free beginner lifts in Courchevel. 1550 and Le Praz have small nursery areas, but most people go up to 1850 for its more reliable snow.

FOR CROSS-COUNTRY
Long wooded trails

Courchevel has a total of 66km/41 miles of trails, the most in the Three Valleys. Le Praz is the most suitable village, with trails through the woods towards 1550, 1850 and Méribel. Given enough snow, there are also loops around the village.

QUEUES
There are always alternatives

Even at New Year and Easter, when 1850 in particular positively teems with people, queues are minimal, thanks to the excellence of the lift system. The Chenus, Verdons and Jardin Alpin gondolas have all had their capacity increased over the past few years, improving these old bottlenecks. However, as one reader points out, 'there can be a build-up at 1850 for the gondolas'. At such times 'it's best to avoid skiing back to 1850'. For example, try using the Plantrey chair, below 1850, or the Coqs chair, above it, to get over to the Col de la Loze, Le Praz and La Tania. The Biollay chair is very popular with the ski school (which gets priority) and can also be worth avoiding. Queues for the huge Saulire cable-car have been all but eliminated by the upgrading of the parallel Vizelle gondola.

MOUNTAIN RESTAURANTS
Good but can be very expensive

Mountain restaurants are plentiful and pleasant, but it is sensible to check the prices; for table-service restaurants reservations may be needed.

There are three expensive places on the fringes of Courchevel 1850 that just about count as mountain restaurants (you can ski away from them after your indulgent lunch). Most expensive is the big Chalet de Pierres, on the Verdons piste – a comfortable, smooth place in traditional style, doing excellent food (including superb cakes). Only a little way behind this for price comes the Cap Horn, near the airstrip, which makes a recent report of insanitary loos rather surprising. The Bergerie on the Bellecôte piste seems to attract a particularly fashionable crowd.

For a good-value lunch above 1850 try the busy Altibar, with a fine terrace, good food and both self-service and table-service sections. The Verdons is well placed for piste-watching and La Soucoupe is an atmospheric self-service place, now with table-service upstairs too. The Panoramic at the top of Saulire re-opened last season after being gutted by fire the previous winter. It seems as popular as before – 'very good value' and 'friendly', although one February visitor found the service very slow. Behind the main lift station at 1850 the Telemark terrace is a great suntrap, with good pizzas.

If we're paying the bill, our favourite Courchevel restaurant is Mont Bel-Air, at the top of the gondola above 1650 – good food, friendly and efficient table-service, and a splendid tiered terrace, although some visitors last season found it 'expensive'.

---

boarding *For an upmarket resort, Courchevel goes out of its way to attract boarders. There's a terrain-park and a half-pipe just below 1850 and the Verdons terrain-park (all for skiers as well as boarders) just above 1850. Except above 1650, it's easy to get around the Three Valleys using chairs and gondolas. The big snowboard hangout is 'Prends ta luge et tire toi', a combined shop/bar/Internet cafe in the centre of 1850.*

SCHOOLS AND GUIDES
Size is everything
Courchevel's branches of the ESF add up to the largest ski school in Europe, with a total of almost 500 instructors. This year, as in earlier years, we've received only negative reports about the 1850 branch. Happily, alternatives exist – though the tourist office staff may be 'quite sniffy and evasive' when asked about them.

Ski Academy, an independent group of French instructors, was 'superb, and that's from my daughter'. Ski Supreme in 1850 is owned and staffed by British instructors and we continue to get good reports. New Generation is a school that started as Le Ski School in 1650, linked to the tour operator of the same name – but has now branched out into 1850 and Méribel too. It consists of highly qualified young British instructors committed to giving clients enjoyment as well as technique. We are still receiving rave reviews about them, for adults and children alike: 'Young and highly motivated. Adapt teaching to the clients' needs, not ski school dogma', 'We learned more in the week than we had over many years previously', 'We cannot praise the

CHILDCARE
There are kindergartens in 1850 (0479 080847) and 1650 (0479 083369) which take children from age 18 months, until 5pm. The ESF branches in all main parts of the resort have ski kindergartens.

instructor enough, he made the lessons fun and gave my husband the confidence and knowledge he required to get him up and going.'

The Bureau des Guides runs all-day off-piste excursions.

FACILITIES FOR CHILDREN
Lots of chalet-based options
There is a ski kindergarten in 1850 – but a reporter this year found it overstretched, with 19 children in a class of five to seven year olds.

Several tour operators run their own nurseries using British nannies – an alternative that many families have found attractive.

Courchevel

247

Staying there

GETTING THERE

Air Geneva, transfer 3½hr. Lyon, transfer 3½hr. Chambéry, transfer 2½hr. Direct flights to Courchevel altiport from London at weekends only (contact tourist office for details). Also scheduled flights from Geneva to Courchevel.

Rail Moûtiers (24km/15 miles); transfer by bus or taxi.

HOW TO GO
Value chalets and apartments
Huge numbers of British tour operators go to Courchevel, with a wide choice of accommodation.

Chalets There are plenty of chalets available from dozens of UK tour operators. As usual in a French resort with a stock of ageing hotel buildings, there are also some chalet-hotels run by UK tour operators. The majority of our reporters stay in chalets.

In 1850 there are several operators offering notably comfortable chalets, and a few that are genuinely luxurious. FlexiSki has two cosily woody chalets off the Bellecôte piste. Scott Dunn has several upscale places. Lotus Supertravel has a number of luxurious 'superchalets' with upmarket food and wines and free massages – we have greatly enjoyed staying in the splendid Chalet Founets a couple of times.

Mark Warner has two chalet-hotels in 1850; the Dahu is convenient and is reported to serve 'excellent food'.

In 1650 Le Ski is long-established as the leading UK operator, and now has

11 good-value chalets; its flagship chalet Rikiki is all en-suite and set on the piste. Ski Olympic has two chalets and a central chalet-hotel, Les Avals, recommended by a reader this year.

Esprit Ski and Simply Ski have a major childcare operation built around their several chalets down in Le Praz.

The big-league operators are in Courchevel, too. Neilson has a couple of chalets. Thomson's refurbished flagship St Louis chalet-hotel is in a great position just across from the Bellecôte piste. Crystal has a chalet-hotel with pool (New Solarium) in the pretty Jardin Alpin. Inghams has a wide range of chalets.

Hotels There are nearly 50 hotels in Courchevel, mostly at 1850 – including more 4-stars than anywhere else in France except Paris.

(((((5) **Bellecôte** (1850) (0479 081019) Our favourite among the more swanky places – it offers some Alpine atmosphere as well as sheer luxury.

(((((5) **Mélezin** (1850) (0479 080133) Superbly stylish and luxurious – and in an ideal position beside the bottom of the Bellecôte home slope.

(((((5) **Carlina** (1850) (0479 080030) Luxury piste-side pad, next to Mélezin.

ACTIVITIES

Indoor Artificial skating rink, climbing wall, bridge, chess, squash, swimming and saunas (hotels), gymnasium, health and fitness centres (swimming pools, sauna, steam-room, hot-tub, water therapy, weight-training, massage), bowling, exhibitions (galleries in 1850 and 1650), cinema, games rooms, billiards, language courses

Outdoor Hang-gliding, paragliding, flying lessons, parachuting, floodlit skiing, ski jumping, snow-shoe excursions, dog-sledding, snowmobile rides, 35km/22 miles cleared paths, toboggan run, curling, ice-climbing, flight excursions

((((⑤ **Byblos des Neiges** (1850) (0479 009800) Next to first stop on Jardin Alpin gondola; spacious public rooms, good pool, sauna, steam complex.

(((④ **Grandes Alpes** (1850) (0479 080335) On piste next to main lifts.

(((④ **Rond Point** (1850) (0479 080433) Family atmosphere, central position.

((③ **Croisette** (1850) (0479 080900) Next to main lifts; recently refurbished. It contains the popular Le Jump bar.

((③ **Courcheneige** (1850) (0479 080259) Pleasantly informal chalet in a quiet position on the piste above the resort, and with a popular lunchtime terrace.

((③ **Ducs de Savoie** (1850) (0479 080300) Pleasant, wood-built; well placed for skiing to the door, but only ten minutes' walk from centre.

((③ **Sivoliere** (1850) (0479 080833) No beauty, but comfortable (though small lounge), pleasantly set among pines.

((③ **Golf** (1650) (0479 009292) Rather impersonal 3-star, in a superb position on the piste next to the gondola.

((③ **Ancolies** (1550) (0479 082766) 'A real find,' said a US visitor impressed by the friendly staff and excellent food.

(② **Edelweiss** (1650) (0479 082658) 'Slightly run down', but good value and position we're told.

(② **Peupliers** (1300) (0479 084147) Well placed and cheap by local standards.

Self-catering There's a large selection of apartments, though high-season dates can sell out early. Some UK tour operators have places in the smart and central Forum complex in 1850 (some of these are offered as catered chalets, too). As with all French apartments, check room dimensions and book a place advertised for more people than there are in your party.

EATING OUT
Pick your price

There are a lot of good, very expensive French restaurants in Courchevel. Among the best, and priciest, are the Chabichou (though a reporter calls it 'overrated') and the Bateau Ivre in 1850 – both with two Michelin stars. Recommendations for Savoyard food include the cosy Saulire (booking essential), the 'wonderful' Fromagerie, the Arbé for 'good fondues at a reasonable price' and the Telemark. Booking is also advisable for dinner at the small, friendly Plancher des Vaches. The Chapelle grilled a 'fabulous and filling meal of lamb' on an open fire for one reader's party. For a fire to sit around while you wait for your pizza or other Italian speciality, try the Via Ferrata. If you crave a burger late at night (it opens at 11pm) one reader recommends the Vache Qui Ski. Also mentioned by readers are the Cloche ('good atmosphere'), the Mazot ('very traditional') and the Cendrée ('a wonderful Italian'). Still in 1850, the Potinière does good, cheap pizzas, steaks and pasta. The Locomotive has an American feel, with railway-theme decor and a varied menu, and the hotel Tovets has 'reasonable prices and delicious food'.

In 1550, the Oeil du Boeuf is good for grills. The Cortona does good-value pizza. In 1650 the Eterlou, Montagne

Courchevel

249

Courchevel 1650 has wide, gentle slopes immediately above the village →

FRANCE

Some parts of 1850
look positively
irresistible – other
parts look less so ↗

OT COURCHEVEL / J KELAGOPIAN

Phone numbers
From abroad use the
prefix +33 and omit
the initial 'o' of the
phone number.

TOURIST OFFICE

Postcode 73122
t 0479 080029
f 0479 081563
pro@courchevel.com
www.courchevel.com

250

and the Petit Savoyard do good
traditional Savoyard food and cheaper
pizza and pasta. In Le Praz, Bistrot du
Praz is expensive but excellent. The
Ya-ca is small and 'very French'.

APRES-SKI
1850 has most variety
If you want lots of nightlife, it's got to
be 1850. But it doesn't have the same
loud Brit-oriented scene as Méribel,
observes one reporter. There are some
exclusive nightclubs, such as the
Grange and the Caves, with top Paris
cabaret acts and sky-high prices. The

popular Kalico has DJs and cocktails
and gets packed. The Bergerie does
themed evenings – food, music,
entertainment – but prices there are
high.

The Jump at the foot of the main
slope is the place to be as the lifts
close but it does get packed. One
reader comments that there is 'no real
large meeting place for après-ski'. The
Saulire (aka Jacques) and the cheap and
cheerful Potinière are also popular.

Cinemas in 1850, 1650 and La Tania
show English-speaking films.

In 1650 the Bubble is the hub, has
satellite TV and Internet access. With
cheap bar prices, happy hour, strong
Mutzig beer and frequent live music it
has a largely British clientele. Signal,
on the main street, is another favourite
après-ski venue. Rocky's (in Ski
Olympic's chalet-hotel Avals) is popular
with young Brits and has satellite TV
and loud music. Au Plouc is a tiny
French bar. The Space pub has pool,
games and live music.

In 1550 the Chanrossa bar is British-
dominated, with occasional live music,
the Taverne also has English owners.

OFF THE SLOPES
1850 isn't bad
The Forum sports centre in 1850
includes a climbing wall in the
shopping centre – good for spectating
too. There are a fair number of shops
in 1850 and excellent markets at most
levels. There's a fun ice-driving circuit
and an ice-climbing structure. A
pedestrian lift pass for the gondolas
and buses in Courchevel and Méribel
makes it easy for non-slope users to
get around the area and meet
companions for lunch on the slopes.
And you can take joyrides from the
altiport and try to spot friends on the
slopes below.

Les Deux-Alpes 1650m/5,410ft

It's a long way up to the glacier and a narrow way down

251

WHAT IT COSTS

HOW IT RATES

The slopes

Snow	****
Extent	***
Experts	****
Intermediates	**
Beginners	***
Convenience	***
Queues	**
Restaurants	**

The rest

Scenery	****
Resort charm	**
Off-slope	**

➕ High, snow-sure slopes, including an extensive glacier area

➕ Varied high-mountain terrain, from motorway cruising to seriously steep blacks and off-piste slopes

➕ Efficient, modern lift system

➕ Excellent, sunny nursery slopes

➕ Stunning views of the Ecrins peaks

➕ Lively, varied nightlife

➕ Wide choice of hotels

➖ Piste network modest by French mega-resort standards – we're sceptical about the claimed 200km/125 miles – and it's badly congested in places

➖ Only one easy run back to the resort; others are red or black, with snow often ruined by sun

➖ Virtually no woodland runs

➖ Spread-out, traffic-choked resort

➖ Few appealing mountain restaurants

We have a love–hate relationship with Les Deux-Alpes. We quite like the buzz of the town – arriving here is a bit like driving into Las Vegas from the Nevada desert – and we understand the appeal of its vibrant nightlife. We love the high-Alpine feel of its main mountain, and the good snow to be found on the north-facing runs in the middle of the mountain. But we're very unimpressed by the extent of those slopes, and we hate the piste congestion that results when most of the town's 35,000 visitors are crammed on to them. Crowding apart, keen intermediates spoiled by high-mileage French mega-resorts (and not up to the excellent off-piste) will simply find the usable area of slopes rather small.

What's new

An eight-seater chair has replaced the old Jandri 3 gondola running from mid-mountain to the glacier. This has helped reduce lift queues on the second stage of the Jandri Express.

The resort

Les Deux-Alpes is a narrow village sitting on a high, remote col. Access is from the Grenoble-Briançon road to the north or by gondola from Venosc. The village is a long, sprawling collection of hotels, apartments, bars and shops, most lining the busy main street and the parallel street that completes the one-way traffic system. Although there is no centre as such, lifts are spread fairly evenly along the village and a couple of focal points are evident. And the resort has a lively ambience.

The village has grown haphazardly over the years, and there is a wide range of building styles, from old chalets through 1960s blocks to more sympathetic recent developments. Locals point out that it looks better as you leave than as you arrive, because all the buildings have their balconies facing the southern end of the resort.

The village sprawls along the road at the foot of the slopes and there's a wide range of building styles ➔

MOUNTAIN FACTS

Altitude 1300m-3570m
4,270ft-11,710ft
Lifts   58
Pistes   200km
                  125 miles
Green   24%
Blue   39%
Red   24%
Black   13%
Snowmaking 59 acres
Recco detectors used

LIFT PASSES

Super ski pass
Covers all lifts in Les
Deux-Alpes, entry to
swimming pool and
skating rink.
Beginners 4 free lifts
Main pass
1-day pass 32
6-day pass 153
(low season 137.5)
Senior citizens
Over 60: 6-day pass
114.5 (low season
103.5)
Over 75: free pass
Children
Under 13: 6-day pass
114.5 (low season
103.5)
Under 5: free pass
Short-term passes
Half-day passes
available. 25.5 from
midday.
Notes 6-day pass
includes one day's
skiing in Alpe-d'Huez,
Serre-Chevalier, Puy-
St-Vincent and the
Milky Way.
Alternative passes
2 limited area passes:
'Ski sympa' covers 21
lifts, 'Grand ski'
covers 32 lifts.
La Grave: a
supplement for this
with a two-day or
longer pass.

Alpe de Venosc, at the southern end
of town, has many of the nightspots
and hotels, the most character, the
fewest cars, the best shops and the
Diable gondola up to the tough terrain
around Tête Moute. More generally
useful is the Jandri Express from the
middle of the resort, where there is a
popular outdoor ice rink and good
good restaurants and bars. The village
straggles north from here, becoming
less convenient the further you go.

The free shuttle-bus service saves
on some very long walks from one end
of town to the other.

The six-day pass covers a day in
each of several resorts including Alpe-
d'Huez and Serre-Chevalier. All are
easily reached by car. Helicopter trips
to Alpe-d'Huez are good value and a
recent reporter describes it as a 'must'.
More economical is the shuttle-bus
service on Wednesdays.

The mountains

For a big resort, Les Deux-Alpes has a
disappointingly small piste area,
despite recent improvements. Although
extremely long and tall (it rises almost
2000m/6,560ft), the main sector is also
very narrow, with just a few runs on
the upper part of the mountain, served
by a few long, efficient lifts. The piste-
grading is rather inconsistent and
some runs are graded differently on
the map and on the mountain.

THE SLOPES
Long, narrow and fragmented
The western **Pied Moutet** side of Les
Deux-Alpes is relatively little-used,
although recent improvements in the
lift and snowmaking systems have
made the area more popular. It is
served by lifts from various parts of
town but reaches only 2100m/6,890ft.
As well as the short runs back to town
which get the morning sun, there's an
attractive, longer north-facing red run
down through the trees to the small
village of Bons. The only other tree-
lined run in Les Deux-Alpes goes down
to another low village, Mont-de-Lans.

On the eastern side of the resort,
the broad, steep slope immediately
above it offers a series of relatively
short, challenging runs, down to the
nursery slopes ranged at the bottom.
Most of these runs are classified as
black, and rightly so: they aren't
groomed and are usually moguled,
and often icy when not softened by the

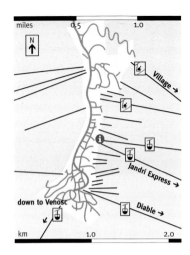

afternoon sun. As a result, many
visitors are forced to take the gondolas
or the long winding green back down.

The ridge of **Les Crêtes** above the
village has lifts and gentle runs along
it, and behind it lies the deep, steep
Combe de Thuit. Lifts span the combe
to the main mid-mountain station at
2600m/8,530ft, at the foot of the
slopes on **La Toura**. The middle section
of the mountain, above and below this
point, is made up primarily of blue
cruising runs and is very narrow. At
one point, there is essentially just a
single run down the mountain. There is
also the alternative of taking the
roundabout (ie partly flat) blue Gours
run to the bottom of the combe, where
a chair-lift takes you up to Les Crêtes.
This pleasant run passes the base of
the Fée chair, serving an isolated (and
neglected) black run.

The top **Glacier du Mont de Lans**
section, served by drag-lifts and the
warmer underground funicular, has
some fine, very easy runs which afford
great views and are ideal for beginners
and the less adventurous. You can go
from the top here all the way down to
Mont-de-Lans – a descent of
2268m/7,440ft vertical which, as far as
we know, is the world's biggest on-
piste vertical. A walk (or snowcat tow)
in the opposite direction takes you
over to the splendid La Grave area for
advanced skiers with a guide (a
supplement is charged for the lifts).

SNOW RELIABILITY
Excellent on higher slopes
The snow on the higher slopes is
normally very good, even in a poor
winter – one of the main reasons for

Les Deux-Alpes' popularity. Above 2200m/7,220ft most of the runs are north-facing, and the top glacier section guarantees good snow. You should worry more about bad weather shutting the lifts, or extremely low temperatures at the top, than about snow shortage. But the runs just above the village face west, so they get a lot of afternoon sun and can be icy at the beginning and end of the day. Snowmaking on some of the lower slopes helps keep them usable.

FOR EXPERTS
Off-piste is the main attraction
With good snow and weather conditions, the area offers wonderful off-piste sport. There are several good off-piste runs within the lift network, including a number of variations from underneath the top stage of the Jandri Express down to the Thuit chair-lift. The best-known ones are marked on the piste map. The Fée chair built a few years ago opened up new off-piste possibilities into the Combe de Thuit. There are also more serious routes that end well outside the lift network, with verticals of over 2000m/6,560ft. One reporter recommends the 'renowned' descent to St-Christophe (hire a guide, who will arrange transport back).

A Free Respect festival is held each year with free advice on off-piste safety and free-ride competitions.

The Super Diable chair-lift, from the top of the Diable gondola, serves the steepest black run around. The brave can also try off-piste variations here.

If the conditions are right, an outing across the glacier to the largely off-piste slopes of La Grave is a must.

FOR INTERMEDIATES
Limited cruising
Les Deux-Alpes can disappoint keen intermediates. A lot of the runs are either rather tough – some of the blues could be reds – or boringly bland. The steep runs just above the resort put off many. As one of our reporters (who classes himself as an 'advanced' skier) said, 'I myself fell from top to bottom. I was lucky. A girl in a different group broke her back. You cannot afford to be complacent here.'

The runs higher up generally have good snow, and there is some great fast cruising, especially on the mainly north-facing pistes served by the chair-lifts off to the sides. You can often pick gentle or steeper terrain in these bowls as you wish, but avid piste-bashers will explore all there is to offer in a couple of days. Many visitors take the opportunity of excursions to Alpe-d'Huez and Serre-Chevalier.

Les Deux-Alpes

253

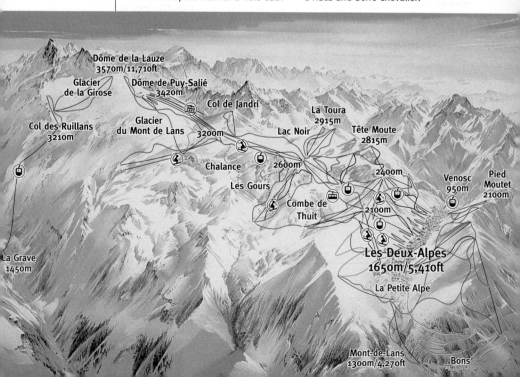

SCHOOLS/GUIDES

2001/02 prices in euros

ESF
Classes 6 days
2¼hr am or pm
6 mornings: 120
Children's classes
Ages: 6 to 12
6 mornings: 100
Private lessons
2hr over lunch or full day Sunday: 30 for 1hr, for 1 to 3 people

International St-Christophe
Classes 6 days
2¼hr am or pm
6 mornings: 113
Children's classes
Ages: 6 to 12
6 mornings: 88.5
Private lessons
1hr over lunchtime
25 for 1hr, for 1 to 4 people

European Ski School
Classes 5 or 6 days
3hr am, 6 mornings (beginners only): 137
5 mornings: 122
Children's classes
Ages: 6 to 10
3hr for 5 days: 137
Under 6
2hr for 5 days: 129
Private lessons
38 for 1hr, for 1 or 2 people

Primitive School – snowboard
Classes 6 days
2hr or 3hr am or pm
6 days: 175 for 2hr, 230 for 3hr
Children's classes
From 9.15 to 5pm
Ages: 12 to 15
Private lessons
40 for 1hr for 1 person; 55 for 2 people

ACTIVITIES

Indoor 2 sports centres; Club Forme (squash, swimming pool, sauna, hot-tub), Tanking Centre (flotation chambers, physiotherapy, pressotherapy, sauna, hot-tub, Turkish baths)
Outdoor Ice skating, swimming pool, ice driving lessons, ice gliders (dodgems), snow-shoe excursions

boarding

Les Deux-Alpes has been catering for snowboarders for years, and has built up an excellent reputation. There's a specialist Primitive school and lots of boarder-friendly facilities. There's a terrain-park with a boarder-cross, a half-pipe, music and a barbecue higher up the mountain in the Toura sector, where most of the lifts are chairs. This is relocated up to the glacier in the summer (access is by T-bar or funicular), which is where the Mondial du Snowboard competition is hosted each year. There's even a kids' park and the ESF offers freestyle classes, using trampolines and a huge air-bag to practise on. But for beginner and timid intermediate boarders the narrow, flat crowded areas in mid-mountain and the routes down to the village are intimidating. There's some great off-piste in the local area for free-riders and the link to La Grave offers some of the best off-piste terrain in the world for advanced riders – a guide is recommended. With cheap and plentiful accommodation, and noisy, lively nightlife in the bars and discos, it's a good place for experienced riders.

Less confident intermediates will love the quality of the snow and the gentleness of most of the runs on the upper mountain. Their problem might lie in finding the pistes too crowded, especially if snow is poor in other resorts and people are bussed in. At the end of the day, you can ride the Jandri Express down or take the long winding green back to town.

FOR BEGINNERS
Good slopes
The nursery slopes beside the village are spacious and gentle. The run along the ridge above them is excellent, too. The glacier also has a fine array of very easy slopes – but bear in mind that bad weather can close the lifts.

FOR CROSS-COUNTRY
Needs very low-altitude snow
There are three small, widely dispersed areas. La Petite Alpe, near the entrance to the village, has a couple of snow-sure but very short trails. Given good snow, Venosc, reached by a gondola down, has the only worthwhile picturesque ones. Total trail distance is 20km/12 miles. You can ski the Mont de Lans glacier with a qualified guide.

QUEUES
Can be a problem
Les Deux-Alpes has a great deal of hardware to keep queues minimal. But the village is large, and queues at the mid-morning peak can be 'diabolically' long for the Jandri Express and Diable gondolas. The Jandri queue moves quickly and the new eight-seater chair from the mid-station to the glacier has reduced the bottleneck for the second stage. Problems can also occur when people are bussed in when snow is in

short supply elsewhere. The top lifts are prone to closure if it's windy, putting pressure on the lower lifts. High winds caused one visitor to get stuck on a chair-lift for 10 minutes. 'Others in our chalet reported being stuck on a stationary lift for 45 minutes.' Another visitor reported queues for the gondolas back to the village when large numbers of people declined to tackle the tricky blacks or the crowded green run back down. The narrow mid-section of the mountain, particularly the Grand Nord blue run, is a real bottleneck late in the day.

MOUNTAIN RESTAURANTS
On the up
There are mountain restaurants at all the major lift junctions, but they are generally pretty poor. The Pastorale, at the top of the Diable gondola, was for years the only recommendable place. But a few years ago the choice was doubled by the construction of the splendid Chalet de la Toura, in the middle of the domain at about 2600m/8,530ft, with a big terrace, a welcoming woody interior and efficient table-service. The pizzas are highly rated by one reporter. The Panoramic has been recommended.

SCHOOLS AND GUIDES
One of the better ESFs
The ski schools have a fairly good reputation for their teaching and English, although class sizes can be large. There are several specialist courses available, as well as off-piste tours and trips to other resorts. We have had very good reports this year of the Primitive snowboard school – for both advanced (off-piste and in the half-pipe) and intermediate riders.

CHILDCARE

The ESF (0476 792121) and International St-Christophe (0476 790421) run kindergartens on more-or-less identical terms – taking children aged 3 to 6 until 5pm.

The Crèche du Village offers an excellent service for babies from 6 months to 2 years, from 8.30 to 5.30.

The Garderie du Bonhomme de Neige is for children aged 2 to 6 years from 9am to 5.30.

A list of babysitters is available from the tourist office.

GETTING THERE

Air Lyon, transfer 3¹⁄₂hr. Grenoble, transfer 2hr. Chambéry, transfer 3hr. Geneva, transfer 4¹⁄₂hr.

Rail Grenoble (70km/43 miles); 4 daily buses from station.

Phone numbers
From abroad use the prefix +33 and omit the initial 'o' of the phone number.

TOURIST OFFICE

Postcode 38860
t 0476 792200
f 0476 790138
les2alp@les2alpes.com
www.les2alpes.com

FACILITIES FOR CHILDREN
Fine for babies
Babies from six months to two years old can safely be entrusted to the village nursery. The kindergarten takes kids from two to six years, and there are chalet-based alternatives run by UK tour operators. There are also four free T-bars for children at the village level.

Staying there

HOW TO GO
Wide range of packages
Les Deux-Alpes has something for most tastes, including that rarity in high-altitude French resorts, reasonably priced hotels.

Chalets There are a number of catered chalet packages available from UK tour operators, but some use apartments.
Hotels There are over 30 hotels, of which the majority are 2-star or below. There's a Club Med 'village' here, too.

(((3))) **Bérangère** (0476 792411) Smartest in town (but dreary exterior) with an excellent restaurant and pool; on-piste, at less convenient north end of resort.

((2)) **Mariande** (0476 805060) Highly recommended, especially for its 'excellent' five-course dinners. At Venosc end of resort.

((2)) **Chalet Mounier** (0476 805690) Smartly modernised. Good reputation for its food, and well placed for the Diable bubble and nightlife.

((2)) **Souleil'or** (0476 792469) Looks like a lift station, but pleasant and comfortable, and well placed for the Jandri Express gondola. The rooms and food are reportedly 'fantastic'.

((2)) **Brunerie** (0476 792223) 'Basic and cheerful', large 2-star with plenty of parking and quite well positioned.
Self-catering Many of the apartments are stuck out at the north end of the resort – well worth avoiding.

EATING OUT
Plenty of choice
The hotel Bérangère has an excellent restaurant and the Chalet Mounier has a high reputation. The Petite Marmite has good food and atmosphere at reasonable prices. Bel'Auberge does classic French and is 'quite superb' – booking is advised. The Patate, the Dahu and Crêpes à Gogo are also recommended. Visitors on a budget can get a relatively cheap meal at either the Vetrata or the Spaghetteria and a moderately priced English breakfast at Smokey Joe's Tex-Mex.

APRES-SKI
Unsophisticated fun
Les Deux-Alpes is one of the liveliest of the French resorts, with plenty of bars, several of which stay open until the early hours. The Rodéo has a mechanical bucking bronco which attracts great numbers of rowdy après-skiers. Mike's and the Windsor are other noisy British enclaves. Corrigans, Smokey Joe's, the Secret Bar and the Baron are recommended. Bar Brésilien has 'great music and tremendous atmosphere'. The Avalanche is the most popular of the discos and the Opera is recommended by locals. There are quieter places too – the 'cosy' Bleuets is recommended.

The resort has contrived a couple of ways of dining at altitude – you can snowmobile to the glacier and back, eating on the way, or at full moon you can ski or board back to town after dinner (accompanied by ski patrollers).

OFF THE SLOPES
Not recommended
Les Deux-Alpes is not a particularly good choice for people not hitting the slopes. The pretty valley village of Venosc is worth a visit by gondola, and you can take a scenic helicopter flight to Alpe-d'Huez. There is a good pool and lots of scenic walks. Several mountain restaurants are accessible to pedestrians. Snowcat tours across the glacier provide wonderful views.

STAYING DOWN THE VALLEY
Worth considering
Close to the foot of the final ascent to Les Deux-Alpes are two near-ideal places for anyone thinking of travelling around to Alpe-d'Huez, La Grave and Serre-Chevalier, both Logis de France – the cheerful Cassini (0476 800410) at Le Freney, and the even more appealing Panoramique (0476 800625), at Mizoën.

Functional family favourite, with appealing alternative bases for the rest of us

WHAT IT COSTS

HOW IT RATES

The slopes

Snow	★★★★
Extent	★★★★
Experts	★★★★
Intermediates	★★★★★
Beginners	★★★★★
Convenience	★★★★★
Queues	★★★★
Restaurants	★★

The rest

Scenery	★★★★
Resort charm	★
Off-slope	★

What's new

A new eight-seat gondola linking the village of Samoëns directly to Samoëns 1600 at mid-mountain, originally planned for 2001/02, will be opened for the 2002/03 season.

A new high-speed quad from Morillon 1100 opened last season to serve the Bergin run. The Pro-Jam Park snowboarding park has been further improved and car parking has been expanded.

For 2002/03 a new bowling alley will open in the village.

Flaine is now owned by Compagnie des Alpes, itself part-owned by Intrawest (a Canadian company that owns Whistler and other resorts with attractive villages). There are long-term plans to expand the resort's bed base and perhaps to build a funicular link from Magland, down in the valley, to bring in day visitors.

➕ Big, varied area, with off-piste challenges for experts as well as extensive intermediate terrain

➕ Huge recent investment in new lifts

➕ Reliable snow in the main bowl

➕ Compact, convenient, mainly car-free village, right on the slopes

➕ Excellent facilities for children

➕ Alternative of staying in traditional villages elsewhere in ski area

➕ Scenic setting, and glorious views

➕ Very close to Geneva airport

➖ Bleak 1960s Bauhaus buildings are not to everyone's taste, although architecturally 'listed'

➖ Main Flaine bowl has only a few short runs below the tree line, so bad weather can be a problem

➖ Links to outer sectors of the area are prone to closure by high winds

➖ No proper hotels in Flaine itself – only club-hotels and apartments

➖ Not much nightlife

➖ Little to do off the slopes

So long as you don't care about the uncompromising architecture or narrow range of nightlife, Flaine has a lot going for it. It has slopes that intermediates will love, and lots of them – the area deservedly calls itself the Grand Massif and is said to be the third biggest area of linked slopes in France. It also caters well for beginners, with free access to nursery slope lifts – and the ski school has improved in recent years too. There is also challenging terrain for experts – particularly for those prepared to take guidance and go off-piste. Many visitors, especially those with children, love it.

The hotels have now all become club hotels run by tour operators such as Club Med and Crystal. The only alternative is to rent an apartment. But we increasingly receive reports from satisfied guests who choose to stay in the more traditional outlying villages such as Samoëns, Morillon and Les Carroz. The only problems are that these lower villages may suffer poor snow conditions and that links with the high Flaine bowl may be cut off in bad weather.

The resort

We have to say we fall in the group that does not find Flaine's Bauhaus architecture attractive. The concrete massifs that form the core of the resort were conceived in the sixties as 'an example of the application of the principle of shadow and light'. They look particularly shocking from the approach road – a mass of blocks nestling at the bottom of the impressive snowy bowl. From the slopes they are less obtrusive, blending into the rocky grey hillside. For us, the outdoor sculptures by Picasso, Vasarely and Dubuffet do little to improve Flaine's austere ambience.

In common with other French Alpine purpose-built resorts, Flaine has improved its looks in recent years. The relatively new development of Hameau-de-Flaine is built in a much more attractive chalet style – but is inconveniently situated 1km/0.5 miles from the slopes and main village.

In Flaine proper, everything is close by: supermarket, sports rental shops, ski schools, main lifts out etc. The resort itself is also easy to get to – only 70km/43 miles from Geneva, and about 90 minutes from the airport.

There are two parts to the main resort. The club hotels, and some apartments, are set in the lower part, Forum. The focus of this area is a snow-covered square with buildings on

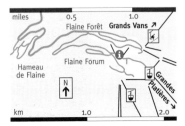

MOUNTAIN FACTS

Covers Grand Massif
ski area

Altitude	700m-2480m
	2,300ft-8,140ft
Lifts	75
Pistes	265km
	165 miles
Green	12%
Blue	41%
Red	38%
Black	9%
Snowmaking	25%
Recco detectors used	

LIFT PASSES

2001/02 prices in
euros

Grand Massif
Covers all the lifts in
Flaine, Les Carroz,
Morillon, Samoëns
and Sixt.
Beginners Four free
lifts. Ski pass for
beginners covers
three more lifts (13
per day for adults, 9
for children aged 5-11,
10 for 12-15-year-
olds).
Main pass
1-day pass 30
6-day pass 151
Senior citizens
Over 60: 6-day pass
127
Over 75: free pass
Children
Under 12: 6-day pass
110
Under 5: free pass
Notes Discount on all
ski-passes for 12-15-
year-olds: 6-day 119.
Alternative passes
Flaine area only (1-
day pass 26 for
adults, 21 for
children)
Short-term passes
A half-day Flaine area
only from 11.30 costs
24 for adults, 19 for
children aged 12-15,
and 17 for those aged
5-11.

FLAINE TOURIST OFFICE

Hameau-de-Flaine is
radically different
from central Flaine in
style ➜

three sides, the open fourth side
blending with the slopes. Flaine Forêt,
up the hillside and linked by lift, has
its own bars and shops and most of
the apartment accommodation.

There are children all over the
place; they are catered for with play
areas, and the resort is supposed to
be traffic-free. This has become rather
lax, in fact, and there is a fair amount
of traffic; but the central Forum itself,
leading to the pistes, is pretty safe. A
regular bus service linking Hameau to
the main village is said to be
'excellent'. A car is of no value around
the resort, but does open up the
possibility of visiting Chamonix (or
even Courmayeur via the reopened
Mont Blanc tunnel).

The mountains

With its 265km/165 miles of pistes, the
Grand Massif claims to be the third
largest resort in France (behind the
Three Valleys and Espace Killy – the
Franco-Swiss Portes du Soleil doesn't
count). Certainly it is a genuinely
impressive area, with plenty of scope
for any level of skier or boarder,
provided you can get to all of it – the
greater part of the domain lies outside
the main Flaine bowl and there are
some fairly low altitude slopes.

THE SLOPES
A big white playground
The day begins for most people at the
Grandes Platières jumbo gondola,
which speeds you in a single stage up
the north face of the Flaine bowl to the
high-point of the Grand Massif, and a
magnificent view of Mont Blanc.

Most of the runs are reds (though
there are some blues curling away to
the right as you look down the
mountain, and one direct black). There
are essentially four or five main ways

down the barren, treeless, rolling
terrain back to Flaine, or to chairs in
the middle of the wilderness going
back to the summit.

On the far right, the easy 14km/9
mile, picturesque Cascades blue run
(one of the longest in the Alps) leads
away from the lift system behind the
Tête Pelouse and down to the
outskirts of Sixt at 770m/2,530ft
(giving a vertical drop of over
1700m/5,580ft). There is no lift back
but there is a regular shuttle-bus
service to the lifts at Samoëns or
Morillon. Sixt has its own little west-
facing area offering red and black
slopes of 700m/2,300ft vertical – and
is now reachable from the bottom of
the Cascades run by drag-lift.

On the other side of the Tête
Pelouse, a broad cat-walk leads to the
experts-only **Gers** bowl. At the bottom,
a flat trail links with the Cascades run
or there's a drag back to the ridge.

Back at Platières, an alternative is
to head left down the long red
Méphisto (many of the runs in this
area have diabolic names – Lucifer,
Belzebuth etc) to the **Aujon** area. This
opens up another sector of the bowl,
again mostly red runs but with some
blues further down. The lower slopes
here are used as slalom courses. This
sector is also reachable by gondola or
drag-lifts from below the resort.

The eight-seater Grands Vans chair,
reached from Forum by means of a
slow bucket lift (aka télébenne), gives
access to the extensive slopes of
Samoëns, Morillon and Les Carroz. You
come first to the wide Vernant bowl
equipped with three fast chair-lifts, one
starting from a car park on the road up
to Flaine. Beyond here the lie of the
land is complicated, and the piste map
does not represent it clearly. In good
snow there is a choice of blues and
reds winding down to **Les Carroz** or

Flaine

257

skiclub.co.uk
0845 45 807 80
skiers@skiclub.co.uk

boarding *Flaine suits boarders quite well – there's lots of varied terrain and plenty of off-piste with interesting nooks and crannies, including woods outside the main bowl. The key lifts are all now chairs or gondolas – with few unavoidable drag-lifts. There's a big terrain-park (called the Pro-JAM Park – standing for Jib and Air Maniacs) just below Les Grands Vans. The ESF runs a special 'Mini surf park' for kids, a great idea for a family-oriented resort like this. Black Side is the local specialist shop, in the central Forum.*

FRANCE

258

Morillon, the latter with a halfway point at 1100m/3,610ft. While there is a choice of blue, red and black runs on the top section above **Samoëns 1600**, the runs below here to Vercland are challenging blacks and reds.

Arrival back in Flaine can cause a problem: some reporters have said that it's difficult to get between the top of the resort and Forum. The trick is to loop round away from the buildings and approach from under the gondola – or catch the bucket down.

We have had past reports of lifts breaking down too often and being too easily closed because of high winds, cutting off links with the lower villages. Piste signing and grooming have, however, been praised.

SNOW RELIABILITY
Usually keeps its whiteness
The main part of Flaine's slopes lie on the wide north- and north-west-facing flank of the Grandes Platières. Its direction, along with a decent height, means that it keeps the snow it receives. There is snowmaking on the greater part of the Aujon sector and on the nursery slopes. The runs towards Samoëns 1600 and Morillon 1100 are north-facing too, and some lower parts have snowmaking, but below here can be tricky or impossible. The Les Carroz runs are west-facing and can suffer from strong afternoon sun, but a couple of runs have snowmaking.

FOR EXPERTS
Great fun with guidance
Flaine's family-friendly reputation tends to obscure the fact that it has some seriously challenging terrain. But much of it is off-piste and, although some of it looks like it can safely be explored without guidance, this impression is mistaken. The Flaine bowl is riddled with rock crevasses and potholes, and should be treated with the same caution that you would use on a glacier. There have been some tragic cases of off-piste skiers coming across

nasty surprises, including a British skier falling to his death only yards from the piste.

All the black pistes on the map deserve their grading. The Diamant Noir, down the line of the main gondola, is a challenging 850m/2,790ft descent, tricky because of moguls, narrowness and other people rather than because of great steepness; the first pitch is the steepest, with spectators applauding from the overhead chair-lift.

To the left of the Diamant Noir as you look down are several short but steep off-piste routes through the crags of the Grandes Platières.

The Lindars Nord chair serves a shorter slope that often has the best snow in the area, and some seriously steep gradients if you look for them.

The Gers drag-lift, outside the main bowl beyond Tête Pelouse, serves great expert-only terrain. The piste going down the right of the drag is a proper black, but by departing from it you can find slopes of up to 45°. To the left of the drag is the impressive main Gers bowl – a great horseshoe of about 550m/1,800ft vertical, powder or moguls top to bottom, all off-piste. You can choose your gradient, from steep to very steep. As you look down the bowl, you see more adventurous ways into the bowl from the Grands Vans and Tête de Veret lifts.

There are further serious pistes on the top lifts above Samoëns 1600.

Touring is a possibility behind the Grandes Platières, and there are some scenic off-piste routes from which you can be retrieved by helicopter – such as the Combe des Foges, next to Gers.

FOR INTERMEDIATES
Something for everyone
Flaine is ideal for confident intermediates, with a great variety of pistes (and usually the bonus of good snow conditions, at least above Flaine itself). The diabolically named reds that dominate the Flaine bowl are not really

UK Representative
Erna Low Consultants
9 Reece Mews
London SW7 3HE
t 020 7584 2841
f 020 7589 9531
info@ernalow.co.uk
www.ernalow.co.uk

SCHOOLS/GUIDES

2001/02 prices in euros

**International
Classes** 6 days
3hr per day
6 days 109
Children's classes
Ages: 6 to 12
6 days 86
Private lessons
1hr, 2hr or full day
30 for 1hr, for 1 or 2 people

ESF
2001/02 prices
Classes 6 days for
3hr per day
6 days: 105
Children's classes
Ages: 5 to 12
6 days 80
Private lessons
26 for 1hr, for 1 or 2 people

Flaine Super Ski
Advanced skiers only
0450 908288

Independent instructors
Hired by the day, hour or week;
contact Guy Pezet
0450 478454

as hellish as their names imply – they tend to gain their status from short steep sections rather than overall difficulty, and they're great for improving technique. There are gentler cruises from the top of the mountain – Cristal, taking you to the Perdrix chair, or Serpentine, all the way home. The blues at Aujon are excellent for confidence-building, but the drag serving them is not.

The connections with the slopes outside the main bowl are classified blue but at least one blue-run reporter has found them tricky. Once outside the bowl, all intermediates will enjoy the long tree-lined runs down to Les Carroz, as long as the snow is good. The Morillon slopes are also excellent intermediate terrain.

FOR BEGINNERS
Very good
There are excellent nursery slopes right by the village, served by free lifts which make a pass unnecessary until you are ready to go higher up the mountain. There are no long green runs to progress to in the Flaine bowl – there is one above Morillon – but there are one or two gentle blues (see 'For intermediates').

CROSS-COUNTRY
Very fragmented
The Grand Massif claims 64km/40 miles of cross-country tracks but only about 10km/6 miles of that is around Flaine itself. The majority is on the valley floor and dependent on low snow. There are extensive tracks between Morillon and Les Carroz, with some tough uphill sections. Samoëns 1600 has its own tracks and makes the best base for cross-country enthusiasts.

QUEUES
Few real problems
The massive recent investment in new lifts has eliminated the main trouble-spots. When the resort is full, the Grandes Platières gondola is prone to queues at the start of the day, but they move quickly.

A recent reporter warns that if you leave the Flaine bowl it's worth allowing plenty of time for the Vernant chair on the way back as this can be a bottleneck. Other queues are usually small, although some of the lifts are still somewhat antiquated, and the area does suffer a weekend influx because of its proximity to Geneva.

Queues can also be bad when the lifts out of the Flaine bowl are shut

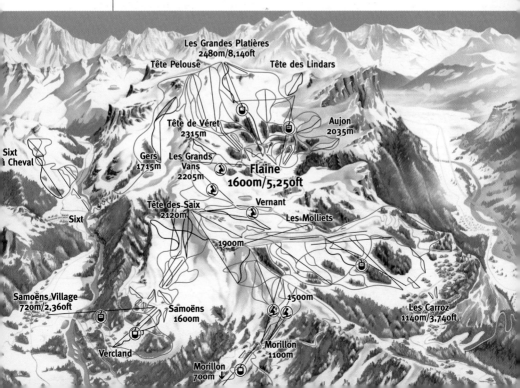

GETTING THERE

Air Geneva, transfer 1½hr.

Rail Cluses (30km/19 miles); regular bus service.

ACTIVITIES

Indoor Top Form centre (swimming pool complex with sauna, solarium, gymnasium, massage), bowling, arts and crafts gallery, cinema, auditorium, concerts, indoor climbing wall, cultural centre with library (some books in English)
Outdoor Natural ice rink, snow-shoe excursions, hang-gliding, paragliding para-skiing, helicopter rides, snow scooters, high mountain outings, ice-driving car circuit

CHILDCARE

Both schools operate ski kindergartens. The ESF (0450 908100) and the SEI (0450 908441) both take children aged 3 to 12, until 5pm. Club Med Flaine (0450 908166) has a nursery for babies aged from 4 months. There is also an independent nursery, the Petits Loups (0450 908782) for children aged from 6 months to 4 years.

due to high winds or when the weather is warm and the lower resorts have poor snow.

MOUNTAIN RESTAURANTS
Back to base, or quit the bowl
In the Flaine bowl, there are few restaurants above the resort's upper outskirts. The Blanchot, at the bottom of the Serpentine run, is popular and rustic, with basic food, but it can get very crowded.

At Forum level, across the piste from the gondola, is a pair of chalets containing the welcoming Michet, with very good Savoyard food and table service, and the self-service Eloge – friendly but with a very limited menu. Up at Forêt level, Chalet Bissac has a good atmosphere, traditional decor and excellent plain food. The nearby Cascade is self-service, with a good terrace. Epicéa near the end of the Faust piste has a rustic atmosphere, terrace and rave reviews.

Outside the Flaine bowl, we loved the remote Chalet du Lac de Gers (book in advance and ring for a snowcat to tow you up from part way down the Cascades run) – simple food but splendid isolation and views of the frozen lake. Reporters recommend the Igloo above Morillon and the Oreade at the top of the gondola from Les Carroz.

SCHOOLS AND GUIDES
Getting better
The few reports we've had in recent years on the ESF have been mixed. But recent reporters have praised the International school ('Good English spoken ... and good fun ideas') and the small specialist Super Ski school ('small class sizes, good instruction'). The ESF children's private lessons in Samoëns were described as 'excellent'. A recent reporter criticised Nouvelle Dimension in Les Carroz: 'Nobody spoke English and the teacher had no patience with the English beginner.'

FACILITIES FOR CHILDREN
Parents' paradise?
Flaine prides itself on being a family resort, and the number of English-speaking children around is a bonus.

Club Med Flaine has good childcare facilities (open to residents only). The Petits Loups nursery takes children from 6 months to 4 years. Some other accommodation units have kids' clubs of their own.

Staying there

HOW TO GO
Plenty of apartments
Accommodation is overwhelmingly in self-catering apartments.

Chalets There are few catered chalet options, but they include a couple of attractively traditional Scandinavian-style huts in Hameau. Crystal now run the Hotel Totem as a club-hotel.
Hotels There's the 2-star Hotel Aujon (0492 126212) and there's a Club Med. Those apart, for a conventional hotel you have to go for one of the lower, more traditional villages.
Self-catering The best apartments are out at Hameau. In Flaine Forêt, the recently renovated Forêt and Grand Massif apartment buildings are attractively woody inside and there are hotel facilities such as a restaurant, bar and kindergarten.

EATING OUT
Not many stars
The Perdrix Noire in Forêt is a good bet – smart, busy but friendly. Its bar is also popular. The Michet (see 'Mountain restaurants') is open in the evening. Chez la Jeanne is apparently the best pizza restaurant. Chez Daniel offers a good range of Savoyard specialities, and has also been recommended for lunchtime crêpes and galettes. The Cîmes Rock is 'excellent, but it's best to go early because it gets very crowded' (see below).

APRES-SKI
Signs of life
Recent reports suggest that the après-ski scene is picking up. The resort is no longer limited to family groups, and some bars show signs of life.

The White Grouse pub is boisterous: extreme sports videos compete with rock music and punters trying to get pints in before the end of happy hour. Later, the more French Cîmes Rock is liveliest, with bands or karaoke. The 'seedy' Diamant Noir pool hall is open late.

OFF THE SLOPES
Curse of the purpose-built
As with most purpose-built resorts, there are few walks, and no town to explore. Not recommended for people who don't want to hit the slopes. But there is a great ice-driving circuit where you can take a spin (literally) in your

Phone numbers
From abroad use the
prefix +33 and omit
the initial 'o' of the
phone number.

**FLAINE TOURIST
OFFICE**
Postcode 74300
t 0450 908001
f 0450 908626
flaine@laposte.fr
www.flaine.com

**LES CARROZ
TOURIST OFFICE**
Postcode 74300
t 0450 900004
f 0450 900700
info@lescarroz.com
www.carroz.com

**SAMOENS
TOURIST OFFICE**
Postcode 74340
t 0450 344028
f 0450 349582
info@samoens.com
www.samoens.com

**MORILLON
TOURIST OFFICE**
Postcode 74440
t 0450 901576
f 0450 901147
info@ot-morillon.fr
www.ot-morillon.fr

own car or, more sensibly, have a lesson in theirs (as we did). Snowmobile tours and the weekly torchlight descent are popular, and there's a cinema, gymnasium and swimming pool.

Les Carroz 1140m/3,740ft

This is a spacious, sunny, traditional, family resort where life revolves around the village square with its pavement cafes and interesting little shops. It has a lived-in feel of a real French village, with more animation than Flaine – 'a delight' says a recent visitor, who recommends the 3-star hotel Arbaron (0450 900267) for food, service and views. Also highly recommended is the 2-star Bois de la Char (0450 900618): 'It is perfectly situated beside the piste. The food was good, the staff friendly and it was excellent value for money.'

The gondola and chair-lift go straight into the Grand Massif area, but there's a steep 300m/1,000ft walk up from the centre – the nursery drag is a help or you can catch the free ski-bus (every 20 minutes).

Apartments make up a high percentage of the beds available.

The ski school's torchlit descent is apparently 'not to be missed' – it starts off with fireworks and ends with vin chaud and live jazz in the square.

Samoëns 720m/2,360ft

This is the only resort in France to be listed as a 'Monument Historique'. Medieval fountains, rustic old buildings, an ancient church – it's all there, although one recent reporter feels that it doesn't add up to a more charming village than Les Contamines, say. Despite the village's recent growth on the outskirts, the traditional-style bars and restaurants still give you a feel for 'real' rural France. A reporter recommends the Pizzeria Louisiana for its wood oven pizzas and 'highly alcoholic' ice creams. Another praises Chalet Fleurie (0450 901011) – 'five courses for 90 francs given 24 hours' notice' – and Chardon Bleu (0450 907466), both a car-ride away in Verchaix.

A new gondola straight from the village to the slopes – originally planned to be built for last season – should be open for the 2002/03 season, cutting out the need to take a bus to and from the lift. The local terrain is generally challenging and on the whole best suited to confident skiers – though there is a good beginners' area at Samoëns 1600.

Morillon 700m/2,300ft

Not quite in the Samoëns league, but still a pretty rustic village, Morillon makes an excellent base, with an efficient gondola from the upper fringes of the village to the mid-mountain mini-resort of Morillon 1100 (Les Esserts) – also reachable by road. Up here there is a large and 'delightful' ski kindergarten plus good slopes for adult beginners and brand new apartments right on the piste – it's 'dead as a dodo in the evenings', though, says a reporter.

La Grave
1450m/4,760ft

A superb mountain for good skiers and free-riders

262

WHAT IT COSTS

HOW IT RATES

The slopes

Snow	★★★
Extent	★★
Experts	★★★★★
Intermediates	★
Beginners	★
Convenience	★★★
Queues	★★★★
Restaurants	★★

The rest

Scenery	★★★★
Resort charm	★★★
Off-slope	★

What's new

La Grave does not change much, and that is half the charm of the place.

- ✚ Legendary off-piste mountain
- ✚ Crowd-free – apart from real peak times such as Easter weekend
- ✚ Usually good snow conditions, with powder higher up
- ✚ Link to Les Deux-Alpes
- ✚ Easy access to other nearby resorts

- ➖ Rather drab, charmless village
- ➖ Poor weather spells regular lift closures – on average, two days per week
- ➖ Suitable for experts only, despite some easy slopes at altitude
- ➖ Nothing to do off the slopes

La Grave enjoys legendary status among experts. It's a quiet old village with around 500 visitor beds and just one serious lift – a small stop-start gondola serving a high, wild and predominantly off-piste mountainside. The result: an exciting, usually crowd-free area. Strictly, you ought to have a guide, but in good weather hundreds of people risk it and go it alone. When the weather shuts the lift, you can head for Alpe-d'Huez, Les Deux-Alpes or Serre-Chevalier.

THE RESORT

La Grave is an unspoiled mountaineering village set on a steep hillside facing the impressive glaciers of majestic La Meije. It's rather drab, and the busy road through to Briançon doesn't help. But it still has a rustic feel, and prices in the handful of small hotels, food shops and bars are low by resort standards.

The village is small and most accommodation is convenient for the central lift station.

Storms close the slopes on average two days a week – so a car is useful for access to other resorts nearby.

THE MOUNTAIN

A slow two-stage 'pulse' gondola (with an extra station at a pylon halfway up the lower stage) ascends into the slopes and finishes at 3200m/10,500ft. Above that, a short walk and a drag-lift

give access to a second drag serving twin blue runs on a glacier slope of about 350m/1,150ft vertical – from here you can ski to Les Deux-Alpes. But the reason that people come here is to explore the legendary slopes back towards La Grave. These slopes offer no defined, patrolled, avalanche-protected pistes – but there are two marked itinéraires (with several variations now indicated on the 'piste' map) of 1400m/4,590ft vertical down to the pylon lift station at 1800m/5,910ft, or all the way down to the valley – a vertical of 2150m/7,050ft.

Slopes The Chancel route is mostly of red-run gradient; the Vallons de la Meije is more challenging but not too steep. People do take these routes without a guide or avalanche protection equipment, but we couldn't possibly recommend it.

There are many more demanding

The village is no beauty, however splendid its setting →

MOUNTAIN FACTS

Altitude 1450m-3550m
4,760ft-11,650ft
Lifts   4
Pistes   5km
                     3 miles
Green/Blue   100%
The 'difficulty' figure
relates to on-piste;
practically all the
skiing – at least 90%
– is off-piste
Snowmaking   None
Recco detectors used

Phone numbers
From abroad use the
prefix +33 and omit
the initial 'o' of the
phone number.

TOURIST OFFICE

Postcode 05320
t 0476 799005
f 0476 799165
ot.la.meije@wanadoo.fr
www.la.meije.com

runs away from the itinéraires,
including couloirs that range from the
straightforward to the seriously
hazardous, and long descents from the
glacier to the valley road below the
village, with return by taxi, bus, or
strategically parked car. The dangers
are considerable, and guidance is
essential. You can also descend
southwards to St-Christoph, returning
by bus and the lifts of Les Deux-Alpes.
Snow reliability The chances of powder
snow on the high, north-facing slopes
are good, but there are essentially no
pistes to fall back on if conditions are
tricky. The biggest worry is poor
weather keeping the mountain closed
for several days at a time.
Experts La Grave's uncrowded off-piste
slopes have earned it cult status
among hard-core skiers. Only experts
should contemplate a stay here – and
then only if prepared to deal with bad
weather by sitting tight or struggling
over the Col du Lautaret to the woods
of Serre-Chevalier.
Intermediates The itinéraires get
tracked into a piste-like state, and
adventurous intermediates could tackle
the Chancel. But the three blue runs at
the top of the gondola won't keep
anyone occupied for long. The valley
stations of Villar d'Arène and Lautaret,
around 3km/2 miles and 8km/5 miles
to the east respectively, and Chazelet,
3km/2 miles to the north-west, offer

very limited slopes with a handful of
intermediate and beginner runs.
Beginners Novices tricked into coming
here can go up the valley to the
beginner slopes at Le Chazelet.
Snowboarding There are no special
facilities for boarders, but advanced
free-riders will be in their element on
the open off-piste powder.
Cross-country There is a total of
30km/19 miles of loops in the area.
Queues Normally, there are short
queues only at weekends – at the
bottom station first thing, and at the
mid-station later. If snow conditions
back to the valley are poor, queues
can build up for the gondola down
from the mid and lower stations.
Mountain restaurants Surprisingly,
there are three decent mountain
restaurants; the best is the refuge on
the Chancel itinéraire.
Schools and guides There are a dozen
or so guides in the village, offering a
wide range of services through their
bureau.
Facilities for children Babysitting can
be arranged through the tourist office.

STAYING THERE

How to go There are several simple
hotels.
Hotels The Edelweiss (0476 799093) is
a comfortable, friendly 2-star with a
cosy bar and restaurant.
Self-catering Self-catering
accommodation is bookable through
the tourist office.
Eating out Most people eat in their
hotels, though there are alternatives.
Après-ski The standard tea-time après-
ski gathering place is the central
Glaciers bar, known to habitués as
chez Marcel. O'Neill's Irish pub and the
Vieux Guide are crowded later. The
Candy bar is now called the Vallons.
Off the slopes Anyone not using the
slopes will find La Grave much too
small and quiet.

La Grave

263

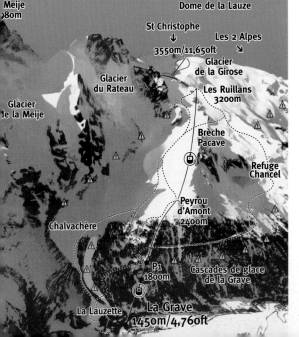

Meije
?80m

Dome de la Lauze

St Christophe
↓
3550m/11,650ft

Les 2 Alpes
↘

Glacier
de la Girose

Glacier
du Rateau

Les Ruillans
3200m

Glacier
le la Meije

Brèche
Pacave

Refuge
Chancel

Peyrou
d'Amont
2400m

Chalvachère

P1
1800m

Cascades de glace
de la Grave

La Lauzette

La Grave
1450m/4,760ft

Maurienne valley

Everything from cute old villages to 1960s monstrosities

WHAT IT COSTS

What's new

New snowmaking was installed in all three main ski areas for 2001/02 and more is planned for 2002/03.

Go to the southern extremity of the Val-Thorens pistes or set off ski-touring northwards from La Grave, and you come to the same place: the Maurienne valley – a great curving trench cut by a river appropriately called the Arc. This backwater has over 20 winter resorts, ranging from pleasant old valley villages to convenience resorts purpose-built in the 1960s. What they have in common are piste and lift networks that are rather limited in size, prices that are low by French resort standards and participation in a special five-day pass deal that allows you to visit a different resort each day. The three resorts covered below are the pick of the crop; the others are in our directory at the back of the book.

Many of these resorts are close enough to be linked – and in the 1970s grand plans were formulated to link Valfréjus with Valmeinier and Valloire to the west, and with Bardonecchia in Italy. But the linking lifts were never built.

A visit can also take in Europe's highest resort and some of its best snow: the valley non-village of Orelle has a big gondola up to the Val-Thorens lift network.

VALLOIRE 1430m/4,690ft
Valloire is the best known of the Maurienne resorts internationally, and it offers the most extensive slopes, shared with the twin stations of Valmeinier 1500 and 1800. The village has a rustic French feel to it and retains a life as a farming community.

THE RESORT

The resort is quite a drive up from the valley. Despite considerable development, it has retained a feeling of 'real' France, complete with impressive old church, crêperies, fromageries, reasonable prices, villagey atmosphere – including a street market – and friendly locals.

THE MOUNTAIN

The 150km/93 miles of piste are spread over three similar-sized sectors, two above Valloire and the third above the separate resort of Valmeinier.
Slopes The sectors accessible from Valloire are Sétaz – shady slopes, part open and part wooded, served by gondola to Thimel at mid-mountain – and Crey du Quart – broad, open, west-facing slopes reachable from the village by chair-lift or gondola, or from Sétaz by chair-lift. Black, blue and green runs from Crey du Quart provide links to the two parts of Valmeinier (1500 and 1800) and so to the open west-facing slopes beyond. Each of these sectors has top heights in the range 2400m to 2600m (7,870ft to 8,530ft) and verticals of around 1000m/3,300ft. The slopes are almost

entirely of intermediate difficulty; Les Karellis (a 45-minute drive) is better for more taxing runs (and for better snow and scenery). One reporter complains about piste map inaccuracies.
Snow reliability Reliable snow-cover is not a strong point. Despite snow-guns on many of the lower slopes, ensuring that most of the area is reliably accessible, some important links – notably the runs down to Valmeinier 1500 from Crey du Quart – can suffer terribly from poor snow. One reporter found these closed in mid-February. The largely north-facing tree runs in the Sétaz area hold their snow well. Grooming is reportedly good.
Experts Sétaz has several black runs, but they don't represent a challenge for experts – the mogul field down to Valmeinier 1500 is steeper.
Intermediates There are plenty of intermediate options in all three sectors. The Crey du Quart section is particularly good for an easy day.
Beginners There are limited village nursery areas but better slopes up the mountain on Sétaz and Crey du Quart.
Snowboarding There's a terrain-park with a half-pipe and a boarder-cross course on the Valloire slopes and the extent of the terrain means that there is a fair bit of good free-riding to do. Novices beware: the return from Valmeinier includes some drag-lifts.
Cross-country There are 25km/16 miles of cross-country trails.
Queues There are few bottlenecks given good snow, but they do occur when lower slopes become patchy.

MOUNTAIN FACTS

Valloire/Valmeinier

Altitude	1430m-2595m
	4,690ft-8,515ft
Lifts	33
Pistes	150km
	93 miles
Green	25%
Blue	27%
Red	37%
Black	11%
Snowmaking	10km
	6 miles
Recco detectors used	

Valfréjus

Altitude	1550m-2735m
	5,085ft-8,975ft
Lifts	12
Pistes	52km
	32 miles
Green	20%
Blue	50%
Red	10%
Black	20%
Snowmaking	1 km
	0.5 miles
Recco detectors used	

Val-Cenis

Altitude	1400m-2800m
	4,595ft-9,185ft
Lifts	22
Pistes	80km
	50 miles
Green	21%
Blue	23%
Red	42%
Black	14%
Snowmaking	10km
	6 miles
Recco detectors used	

Mountain restaurants Mountain restaurants are in short supply but of good quality. Descending to the village for lunch may be the best option.

Schools and guides The two schools are the ESF and the International.

Facilities for children The Aiglons nursery takes children from six months to six years.

STAYING THERE

How to go There's a fair choice of hotel and apartment accommodation, and there's a Club Med.

Hotels The 3-star Grand (0479 590095) and 2-star Christiania (0479 590057) are recommended, both well placed.

Eating out Most of the restaurants are pizza and fondue joints. The Gastilleur has the best French cuisine in town.

Après-ski Après-ski is fairly quiet but picks up at the weekend. The Irish pub gets 'packed, with great atmosphere'.

Off the slopes There's an ice rink, a cinema, some walking paths and paragliding.

VALFREJUS 1550m/5,090ft

Valfréjus is a small and unusual modern resort – built in the woods, with most of the slopes higher up above the tree line.

THE RESORT

The resort is a compact and quite pleasant affair, built on a narrow, shady shelf, with woods all around. There are several apartment blocks grouped around the main lift station, and chalets scattered here and there on the hillside.

THE MOUNTAIN

There are runs of all grades back through the trees towards the village,

but the focus of the slopes is Plateau d'Arrondaz, at 2200m/7,215ft, reached by gondola or chair-lift.

Slopes Above Plateau d'Arrondaz are steep, open slopes – genuine bumpy blacks, with excellent snow – on Punta Bagna (2735m/8,975ft), served by the second stage of the gondola, and gentler blue runs from Col d'Arrondaz. From both the top and the col there are also sunny intermediate runs to Le Pas du Roc on the back side of the hill, with chair-lifts back to both high points or the option of the glorious long away-from-the-lifts blue Jeu run (with off-piste variations and some narrow paths along the way) to the village – almost 1200m/3,400ft vertical.

Snow reliability Snow-cover in the main open area is pretty reliable, but snowmaking on the lower runs to the village is urgently required.

Experts There is good off-piste sport above the main plateau and heli-skiing over the border in Italy is available.

Intermediates Within the small area, there is something for everyone. Near-beginners might welcome more easy blues, but it would be a good place for a confident intermediate to get in some serious practice on good snow.

Beginners There are nursery slopes at mid-mountain and village levels.

Snowboarding There's a natural terrain-park and some good off-piste potential. Beginners can get around without having to negotiate any drags.

Cross-country Just a small 2km/1 mile loop up at Plateau d'Arondaz.

Queues A recent visitor reported no real problems, though the Pas du Roc chairs are very slow.

Mountain restaurants The 'basic' Punta Bagna, at the top of the gondola, has superb views, and the

Bergerie at the mid-station has table-service inside and out.

Schools and guides Lessons are offered by the ESF and the International school.

Facilities for children One nursery takes babies aged from three months to three years. Two nurseries take children aged three to six years.

STAYING THERE

How to go There are two hotels and 10 tourist residences in the resort.

Hotels The 3-star Valfréjus (0492 126212) is central and has a pleasant restaurant. The 2-star Grand Vallon (0479 050807) has superb views.

Eating out Restaurants in the village include a pizzeria and a crêperie.

Après-ski Après-ski is limited – the Snow Club, the Bois Brûlé and the Javana are the liveliest bars.

Off the slopes Activities are limited. There are marked walks and a natural skating rink and paragliding facilities.

VAL-CENIS 1400m/4,595ft

Val-Cenis is a marketing concept rather than a place. It comprises two pleasant villages in the Haute Maurienne, the high and remote part of the valley.

THE RESORT

Lanslebourg is a long, linear place, spreading along the Route Nationale 6 (a dead end in winter, when the road over the Col du Mont-Cenis becomes a piste). It's pleasant enough, but no great beauty. A bus-ride up the valley, Lanslevillard is more captivating – off the road, randomly arranged, rustic, and split into three.

THE MOUNTAIN

There are lifts up into the north-facing slopes from a number of points along the valley, including Lanslebourg and three points in Lanslevillard. The main one, a gondola, starts between the two villages, on the fringes of Lanslevillard. The lift pass also covers the 35km/22 miles of slopes in Termignon-la-Vanoise (10 minutes by bus) and allows a free day in one of the other Maurienne resorts.

Slopes Above mid-mountain is a good range of open runs to suit every ability, served by chairs and drags. Below mid-mountain all the runs are prettily wooded – there is usually an easy blue or green alternative to the various red runs back down as well.

Snow reliability Most of the runs are north-facing and there is snowmaking on the protected tree runs back to each of the base stations.

Experts There is ample off-piste but little else to challenge experts. From the top station there is a good, mogulled black down the shady front face and a sunny isolated black over the back to the Col.

Intermediates There are intermediate runs all over the mountain allowing for some top-to-bottom cruises of up to 1400m/4,595ft vertical. A visit to Termignon's mainly easy slopes is highly recommended by 'impressed' reporters, but beware 'savage drags'.

Beginners There are easy runs by the base stations and winding through the forest – including a splendid green following the hairpin road from the Col.

Snowboarding Beginners should stay in Lanslevillard to avoid some long access drags. There is a terrain-park.

Cross-country There are 6km/4 miles of free trails locally and a further 80km/50 miles of trails higher up at Bessans, further up the valley.

Queues This year's reporters confirm that queues are rare – 'mainly at the gondola in the afternoon' – and tend to move quite quickly.

Mountain restaurants A reporter recommends both the rustic Fema at mid-mountain and Mélèzes (table-service) at the gondola base.

Schools and guides A recent reporter comments that the instructors spoke very little English, but that the class sizes were small.

Facilities for children The two village nurseries take kids from six months. The tour operator Snowcoach has its own facilities for looking after non-skiing children.

STAYING THERE

How to go There are modest hotels in both villages.

Hotels The best is the 3-star Alpazur (0479 059369). The food and the outside hot-tub are also recommended.

Eating out There is a reasonable range of modest eating-out alternatives with a dozen restaurants in each village.

Après-ski Après-ski is quiet but there are a couple of discos open till late. The Napoleon and the Blue Ice bars received recommendations this year.

Off the slopes There is not a lot for non-skiers. There's a new leisure centre in Lanslevillard, with a pool, and an artificial ice rink. And there are various walking paths to explore.

Phone numbers
From abroad use the prefix +33 and omit the initial '0' of the phone number.

TOURIST OFFICES

Valloire
Postcode 73450
t 0479 590396
f 0479 590966
infos@valloire.net
www.valloire.net

Valmeinier
Postcode 73450
t 0479 595369
f 0479 592005
info@valmeinier.com
www.valmeinier.com

Valfréjus
Postcode 73500
t 0479 053383
f 0479 051367
info@valfrejus.com
www.valfrejus.com

Val-Cenis
Postcode 73480
t 0479 052366
f 0479 058217
info@valcenis.com
www.valcenis.com

Megève
1100m/3,61oft

One of the traditional old winter holiday towns

HOW IT RATES

The slopes

Snow	**
Extent	*****
Experts	**
Intermediates	****
Beginners	***
Convenience	**
Queues	****
Restaurants	*****

The rest

Scenery	***
Resort charm	****
Off-slope	****

What's new

For 2002/03 a major extension of the slopes of Le Jaillet will create a link with the village of La Giettaz, west of Megève on the road to La Clusaz.

This appears to be the first stage in a grand plan to create a vast 600km/375 mile piste network linking Megève with half a dozen other resorts.

There will be at least one new gondola in the Princesse area, we guess replacing the existing one. A new magic carpet lift has been installed at the Princesse ski kindergarten.

The Liberty ski pass, valid for 7 days, allows you to choose which days you will ski – when you pass through the first control you are debited a day.

MEGEVE TOURIST OFFICE

It's a cute little town – even if you can't count on this amount of snow ➔

- ➕ Extensive slopes, with miles of easy pistes, ideal for intermediates
- ➕ Scenic setting, with splendid views
- ➕ Charming old village centre, with very swanky shopping
- ➕ Some lovely luxury hotels
- ➕ Gourmet mountain lunches in attractive surroundings
- ➕ Excellent cross-country trails
- ➕ Different lift pass options cover other worthwhile resorts nearby
- ➕ Great for weekends – cooperative hotels, short drive from Geneva
- ➕ If it snows, deserted mountains
- ➕ Plenty to do off the slopes

- ➖ With most of the slopes below 2000m/6,56oft there's a risk of poor snow, especially on runs to the village – although the grassy terrain does not need a thick covering and snowmaking has improved a lot
- ➖ Three separate mountains, two linked by lift but not by piste and the third not linked at all
- ➖ Not many challenging pistes – the few blacks are not extreme – but good off-piste potential
- ➖ Traffic jams and fumes at weekends and peak season

Megève is the essence of rustic chic. It has a medieval heart, but it was, in a way, the original purpose-built French ski resort – conceived in the 1920s as a French alternative to Switzerland's St Moritz. And although Courchevel took over as France's most fashionable winter sports resort ages ago, Megève's sumptuous hotels and chalets still attract plenty of 'beautiful people' with fur coats and fat wallets. Happily, you don't need either to enjoy it.

The risk of poor snow still makes us nervous about booking way ahead; but it is certainly true that a few inches of snow is enough to give skiable cover on the grassy slopes. And the list of plus-points above is as long as they come.

The resort

Megève is in a lovely sunny setting and has a beautifully preserved traditional medieval centre, which is pedestrianised and comes complete with open-air ice rink, horse-drawn sleighs, cobbled streets and a fine church. Lots of smart food, clothing, jewellery, and antique and gift shops add to the chic atmosphere.

The main Albertville-Chamonix road bypasses the centre, and there are expensive underground car parks. But the resort's clientele arrives mainly by car and the resulting traffic jams and fumes are a major problem, though a recent reporter detects improvement. It's worst at weekends, but can be serious every afternoon in high season.

The clientele are mainly well-heeled French couples and families, who come here as much for an all-round winter holiday and for the people-watching potential as for the slopes themselves.

LIFT PASSES

2001/02 prices in euros

Evasion Mont Blanc
Covers all lifts on Rochebrune, Mont d'Arbois, St-Gervais, Le Bettex, St-Nicolas, Le Jaillet, Combloux, Les Contamines and Bellevue.
Beginners Pay by the ride.
Main pass
1-day pass 30
6-day pass 145
Senior citizens
Over 60: 6-day pass 131
Children
Under 15: 6-day pass 116
Under 5: free pass
Short-term passes
Half-day pass available in the afternoon.
Alternative passes
Mont Blanc pass covers all lifts in the resorts of the Mont Blanc area (700km/435 miles of piste and 190 lifts) plus Courmayeur in Italy 6 days out of 6 (6 days 200 for adults and 160 for children). Jaco pass valid for Le Jaillet, Christomet and Combloux.

AGENCE NUTS / ST-GERVAIS TOURIST OFFICE

St-Gervais is a cheaper and less fashion-conscious base sharing the Megève slopes ↓

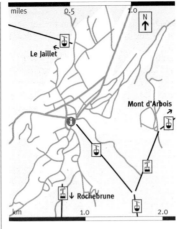

The nightlife is, as you'd expect, smart rather than lively.

A gondola within walking distance of central Megève gives direct access to one of the three mountains, Rochebrune. This sector can also be reached directly by a small cable-car from the southern edge of town. The main lifts for the bigger Mont d'Arbois sector start from an elevated suburb of the resort – though there is also a link from Rochebrune. The third sector, Le Jaillet, starts some way out on the north-west fringes of the town.

Staying close to one of the main lifts makes a lot of sense. Some accommodation is a long walk from the lifts, and the free bus services are not super-convenient.

There is a variety of different lift passes available, the widest-ranging covering Les Contamines, Les Houches and Chamonix. A car is handy for visiting other resorts included on the various passes.

The mountains

The three different mountains provide predominantly easy intermediate cruising, much of it prettily set in the woods. But there are tough runs to be found, and large areas of off-piste that are neglected by most visitors. The wooded slopes make it a great resort to head for in poor weather. Reporters claim that piste grading is inconsistent and that less advanced skiers should not be too complacent.

THE SLOPES
Pretty but low

Two of the three areas of slopes are linked by a cross-valley lift, though not by piste. The third is separate (but about to be extended to the village of La Giettaz).

The biggest, highest and most varied sector is **Mont d'Arbois**, accessible not only from the town but also by a gondola from La Princesse, way out to the north-east of town. It offers some wooded slopes but is mainly open, especially higher up.

Most of the slopes face more-or-less west, but there are north-east-facing slopes to Le Bettex and on down to St-Gervais. A two-stage gondola returns you to the top, with a mid-station at Le Bettex. You can work your way over to Mont Joux and up to the small Mont Joly area – Megève's highest slopes. And from there you can descend to the backwater village of St-Nicolas-de-Véroce; chair-lifts bring you back to Mont Joux. Directly behind Mont Joly, further up the same valley as St-Nicolas-de-Véroce, is the substantial resort of Les Contamines. You can get to it off-piste.

From the Mont d'Arbois lift base, the Rocharbois cable-car goes across the valley to **Rochebrune**. Alpette is the starting point for Megève's historic downhill course. A network of gentle, wooded, north-east-facing slopes, served by drags and chair-lifts, lead across to the high-point of Côte 2000.

The third area, and much the quietest, is **Le Jaillet**, accessed by gondola from just outside the north-west edge of town. From the top of the gondola are predominantly easy, east-facing pistes. The high point is Christomet, served by a long chair-lift. In the other directions, a series of long, tree-lined runs and lifts serves the area above Combloux.

MOUNTAIN FACTS

Altitude	850m-2355m
	2,790ft-7,730ft
Lifts	79
Pistes	300km
	186 miles
Green	17%
Blue	30%
Red	40%
Black	13%
Snowmaking	160 acres
Recco detectors used	

SNOW RELIABILITY
The area's main weakness
The problem is that the slopes are low, with very few runs above 2000m/6,560ft, and partly sunny – the Megève side of Mont d'Arbois gets the afternoon sun. So in a poor snow year, or in a warm spell, snow-cover and quality on the lower slopes can suffer badly – in which case you may need to ride the lifts back down.

Fortunately, the grassy slopes don't need much depth of snow, and the resort has made great strides in tackling this weakness, expanding its snowmaking network to 252 snow-guns at the last count. Some runs are now entirely covered, including the long red Olympique run at Rochebrune. There is also a high standard of piste grooming.

FOR EXPERTS
Off-piste is the main attraction
The Mont Joly and Mont Joux sections offer the steepest slopes. The top chair here serves a genuinely black run, and the slightly lower Epaule chair has some steep runs back down and also accesses some good off-piste runs, as well as pistes, down to St-Nicolas.

The steep area beneath the second stage of the Princesse gondola can be a play area of powder runs among the trees. Côte 2000 has a small section of steep runs, including some off-piste.

The black run under the Christomet

chair is no longer on the map and, given decent snow, could be a good spot to practise off-piste technique.

FOR INTERMEDIATES
Superb if the snow is good
Good intermediates will enjoy the Mont d'Arbois area best. The black runs below the Princesse gondola are perfectly manageable. The runs served by the Grand Vorasset drag and the most direct route between Mont d'Arbois and Le Bettex are also interesting. Similarly challenging are the steepest of the Jaillet sector pistes.

It's a great area for the less confident. A number of comfortable runs lead down to Le Bettex and La Princesse from Mont d'Arbois, while nearby Mont Joux accesses long, problem-free runs to St-Nicolas. Alpette and Côte 2000 are also suitable.

Even the timid can get a great deal of mileage in. All main valley-level lifts have easy routes down to them (although the Milloz piste to the Princesse mid-station is a little steep). There are some particularly good, long, gentle cruises between Mont Joux and Megève via Mont d'Arbois. But in all sectors, you'll find easy, blue runs.

FOR BEGINNERS
Good choice of nursery areas
There are beginner slopes scattered here and there at valley level, and more snow-sure ones at altitude on

Megève

269

SCHOOLS/GUIDES

2001/02 prices in
euros

ESF
Classes 2½hr 5
mornings 110; 2½hr
6 afternoons 89
Children's classes
Ages: 5 to 12
5 mornings 98
6 afternoons 80
Private lessons
Hourly or daily
33 for 1hr, for 1 or 2
people.
All-day classes are
available.

International
Classes 5 mornings
2hr 10am-12 noon 80
Children's classes
Ages: 4 to 12
6 mornings 120
Private lessons
Hourly or daily
1 to 5 people: 1 hr 41

CHILDCARE

There are three
kindergartens dotted
around the sprawling
resort, all offering
skiing. Age limits and
hours vary. Caboche
(0450 589765) at the
Caboche gondola
station: ages 3 to 10,
until 5pm. Meg'Loisirs
(0450 587784) is a
comprehensive
nursery: ages 3 to 6,
until 6pm. Princesse
(0450 930086), out at
the Princesse
gondola: ages 2½ to
6, until 6pm.

each of the main mountains. There are
also plenty of very easy longer green
runs to progress to.

FOR CROSS-COUNTRY
An excellent area
There are 75km/47 miles of varied
trails spread throughout the area.
Some are at altitude (1300m–1550m/
4,270ft–5,090ft), making lunchtime
meetings with Alpine skiers or walkers
simple.

QUEUES
Few weekday problems
Megève is relatively queue-free during
the week, except at peak holiday time.
But school holidays and sunny Sunday
crowds can mean some delays. The
Lanchettes drag between Côte 2000
and the rest of the Rochebrune slopes
gets busy – as does the gondola
linking the two mountains. Crowded
pistes at Mont Joux and Mont d'Arbois
can also be a problem. Go out in
falling snow and you'll have the
mountain to yourself. The hands-free
pass system 'works like a dream'.

MOUNTAIN RESTAURANTS
The long lunch lives
Megève is one of the great gourmet
lunch destinations. Many of the 30
restaurants have table-service and
many of the terraces have magnificent
views. Not surprisingly, they can be
expensive. Booking ahead is advisable.
   The Mont d'Arbois area is
particularly well endowed. There are
two suave places still owned by the
Rothschilds, original promoters of
Megève, both popular with poseurs
with small dogs and fur coats – the
Club House and the Idéal Sports. The
Igloo, with wonderful views of Mont
Blanc, has both self-service and table-
service sections – recent reports of the
self-service section are disappointing.
   Above St-Nicolas are several little
chalets offering great charm and good
food at modest prices as well as
glorious views.
   At the base of the Mont Joux lift,

Chez Marie du Rosay is recommended.
On the back side of the hill, at Les
Communailles, the Alpage was a key
factor in one reader's decision to go
back to Megève.
   At the foot of the Côte 2000 slopes
is a former farm, popular for its
atmosphere, friendly service and good
quality; Radaz, up the slope a little,
enjoys better views and is similarly
cosy, but the service can be slack.
   Alpette, atop the Rochebrune ridge,
offers excellent all-round views
outside, a comfortable lounge inside.

SCHOOLS AND GUIDES
Adventurous
The two schools offer expeditions to
the Vallée Blanche and heli-skiing (in
Italy) as well as conventional teaching.
The International school appears to be
more popular with readers than its
rival, the ESF. A recent reporter found
the ESF children's classes to be
inefficient, with impatient instructors.
We understand that British instructor
Simon Brown is setting up an
independent school this season.

FACILITIES FOR CHILDREN
Language problems
A comfortable low-altitude resort like
Megève attracts lots of families who
can afford day care. The facilities seem
impressive – the kindergartens offer a
wide range of activities as an
alternative to the slopes. Lack of
English-speaking staff (and
companions) could be a drawback.

boarding *Boarding doesn't really fit with Megève's traditional, rather staid,
upmarket image. But there is a terrain-park and a half-pipe on
Mont Joux – and free-riders will find lots of untracked off-piste powder for a few
days after new snowfalls. It's a good place to try boarding for the first time, with
plenty of fairly wide, gentle runs and a lot of chair-lifts and gondolas; though
there are a fair number of drag-lifts, they are generally avoidable. Nightlife tends
to be rather sophisticated, but there are a few noisy bars as well.*

Staying there

HOW TO GO
Few packages

Relatively few British tour operators go to Megève, but there is an impressive range of accommodation.

Chalets A few UK tour operators offer catered chalets. For a cheap and very cheerful base, you won't do better than Stanford's Sylvana – a creaky, unpretentious old hotel, reachable on skis, now run along chalet lines. Superb food when we visited, a couple of years back. Stanford now offers another similar property, the Rond Point, in the centre.

Hotels Megève offers a range of exceptionally stylish and welcoming hotels. There are simpler places, too.

⟨⟨⟨⟨ Mont Blanc (0450 212002) Megève's traditional leading hotel – elegant and fashionable. Right in the centre, and close to the main gondola.

⟨⟨⟨⟨ Chalet du Mont d'Arbois (0450 212503) Prettily decorated, former Rothschild family home, now a Relais & Châteaux hotel in a secluded position above town, near the Mont d'Arbois gondola.

⟨⟨⟨⟨ Fer à Cheval (0450 213039) French rustic-chic at its best, with a warmly welcoming wood-and-stone interior and excellent food. Close to the centre.

⟨⟨⟨ Coin du Feu (0450 210494) 'Very well managed' chalet midway between Rochebrune and Chamois lifts.

GETTING THERE

Air Geneva, transfer 1hr. Lyon, transfer 2½hr.

Rail Sallanches (13km/8 miles); regular buses from station.

⟨⟨⟨ Grange d'Arly (0450 587788) Wrong side of the road, but still quite close to the centre; a beautifully furnished chalet.

⟨⟨⟨ Ferme Hôtel Duvillard (0450 211462) Smartly restored farmhouse, perfectly positioned for the slopes, at the foot of the Mont d'Arbois gondola.

⟨⟨ Gai Soleil (0450 210070) Comfortable family-run place – five minutes' walk from the centre of town and the main gondola.

⟨⟨ Mourets (0450 210476) Entirely inconvenient location but repeatedly recommended by readers: 'basic but spacious accommodation with good food and wonderful views'; 'very friendly'; 'excellent hosts'.

⟨⟨ Sévigné (0450 212309) Ten minutes from the centre, but 'really delightful – very, very quaint, excellent Savoyard cuisine'.

Self-catering There are some very comfortable and well positioned apartments available – not cheap.

EATING OUT
Very French

Megève naturally has lots of high-quality, expensive restaurants – many of which are recommended in the top restaurant guides. The restaurants in all the best hotels – eg the Fermes de Marie, Chalet du Mont d'Arbois and Mont Blanc – are excellent but extremely expensive. The Cintra, also expensive and fashionable, is 'great for fresh seafood'. The Flocons de Sel, although quite expensive, is highly recommended for its quality and

Megève

271

Selected chalets and club hotels in Megève

service. Michel Gaudin is one of the best in town – with very good value set menus. The Taverne du Mont d'Arbois is a lovely woody chalet at the foot of the Mont d'Arbois lifts.

Some reporters wish for more variety of cuisine. The Phnom-Penh is one of the few possibilities. Mama Mia is a popular Italian restaurant, though recent reports are mixed. The Pallas is recommended for burgers and pizzas.

APRES-SKI
Bit of a gamble?
The only recent reporter who has taken an interest in such things – and who was there in high season – reckons there is a shortage of lively après-ski bars. The Chamois has been recommended. The Puck is an atmospheric locals' bar, while Harry's Bar is an informal British rendezvous, popular for its wide range of beers, a weekly live band, karaoke and satellite TV. The casino, opened a few seasons ago, has more slot machines than blackjack tables. The Club de Jazz (aka the 5 Rues) is something of an institution – a very popular, if rather expensive, jazz club-cum-cocktail bar, that gets some big-name musicians.

OFF THE SLOPES
Lots to do
There is something for most tastes, with an excellent sports centre, an outdoor ice rink, plenty of outdoor activities and a weekly market. Trips to Annecy and Chamonix are possible. And St-Gervais is worth visiting for a spa treatment. Walks are excellent, with 50km/30 miles of marked paths, many at altitude. There is a special map of the paths, classified for difficulty. Meeting friends on the slopes for lunch is easy.

STAYING UP THE MOUNTAIN
Several possibilities
As well as mid-mountain Le Bettex (see St-Gervais), there are hotels further up on the slopes, near the summit of Mont d'Arbois. One is the 3-star Igloo (0450 930584), another the 2-star Chez la Tante (0450 213130).

St-Gervais 850m/2,790ft
St-Gervais is a handsome 19th-century spa town set in a narrow river gorge, halfway between Megève and Chamonix, at the entrance to the side-valley leading up to St-Nicolas and Les

Contamines. It has direct access to the Mont d'Arbois slopes via a 20-person gondola from just outside the town.

It's a pleasant place to explore, with interesting food shops and cosy bars. Among its diversions are thermal baths and an Olympic skating rink. Prices are noticeably lower than over the hill in Megève. Two hotels convenient for the gondola are the Hostellerie du Nerey (0450 934521), a pleasantly traditional 2-star, and the 3-star Carlina (0450 934110), best in town.

At the gondola mid-station is Le Bettex, a small collection of hotels, private chalets and new apartments, conveniently situated for the runs but with little evening animation.

You can go up, on the opposite side of St-Gervais, on a rack-and-pinion railway which in 1904 was intended to go all the way to the top of Mont Blanc but didn't quite make it that far – it actually takes you to the slopes of Les Houches (see Chamonix chapter). Given enough snow, you can descend to St-Gervais off-piste.

Its position makes St-Gervais a good base for touring the different resorts covered by the Mont Blanc regional lift pass, especially if you have the use of a car.

Other resorts

Praz-sur-Arly and Notre-Dame-de-Bellecombe are much cheaper options for independent car travellers – they are not part of the Megève lift network (yet). Praz (1035m/3,400ft) is a small, quiet place, but has hotels, restaurants, bars, sports club, ski school and ski kindergarten. It has fair-sized slopes of its own, with short, mainly easy runs served by a rather slow old lift system. Most runs face roughly north, and a recent visitor found good snow here when many runs in Megève were closed. Notre-Dame (1130m/3,710ft) is further along the road past Praz, a pleasant village with mainly apartment accommodation, simple hotels, and several bars and restaurants. It has its own varied, pretty area.

St-Nicolas-de-Véroce is part of the Megève lift network, and has a handful of simple small hotels.

One reporter spent a very rewarding few days based at the hotel Terminus (0450 936800) in Le Fayet, below St-Gervais, travelling to a different resort each day by coach.

ACTIVITIES
Indoor 'Palais des Sports' (climbing wall, swimming pool, sauna, solarium, skating, gym), judo, classical and contemporary dance classes, music lessons, bridge, tennis, bowling, archery, language classes, museum, library, cinemas, pottery, casino, concert and play hall, body-building hall, curling, tennis
Outdoor 50km/ 30 miles of cleared paths, snow-shoe excursions, skating rink, riding, sleigh rides, plane and helicopter trips, paragliding, hot-air ballooning, horse-riding, rock-climbing, ice driving, mountaineering

Phone numbers
From abroad use the prefix +33 and omit the initial '0' of the phone number.

MEGEVE TOURIST OFFICE
Postcode 74120
t 0450 212728
f 0450 930309
megeve@megeve.com
www.megeve.com

ST-GERVAIS TOURIST OFFICE
Postcode 74170
t 0450 477608
f 0450 477569
welcome@st-gervais.net
www.st-gervais.net

Les Menuires
1850m/6,070ft

The bargain base for the Trois Vallées – but you pay a price in visual terms

WHAT IT COSTS

HOW IT RATES

The slopes

Snow	★★★★
Extent	★★★★★
Experts	★★★★
Intermediates	★★★★★
Beginners	★★★
Convenience	★★★★★
Queues	★★★★
Restaurants	★★★

The rest

Scenery	★★★
Resort charm	★
Off-slope	★

- ➕ Probably the cheapest place to stay in the famously extensive Three Valleys area – biggest in the world
- ➕ Some great local slopes
- ➕ Extensive artificial snowmaking
- ➕ Lots of slope-side accommodation
- ➕ Development of outlying parts of the village in traditional chalet style is starting to pay off

- ➖ Possibly the ugliest resort in the Alps, but gradually improving
- ➖ Main intermediate and beginner slopes get a lot of sun
- ➖ No woodland slopes
- ➖ Nursery slopes are crowded as well as overexposed to the sun

Les Menuires is trying hard to lose its reputation as the carbuncle of the Alps (see the What's new section for developments). But, whatever you may think of its appearance, it is certainly the bargain base for the Trois Vallées, with the bonus of immediate access to the excellent, challenging slopes on La Masse, rarely used by visitors from the other valleys.

What's new

The Tortollet chair, providing access from some outlying accommodation to the main lifts, is due to be replaced with a faster quad.

The two comfortable fast chairs from the centre, new last season, give faster access to Mont de la Chambre and the links with Méribel and Val Thorens.

A dedicated nursery slope area was created for last season – an overdue improvement.

There are plans to extend snowmaking to the top of Mont de la Chambre.

The programme of building more traditional chalets, away from the ugly centre, continues. Restaurants and shops are also appearing in these satellite areas – Les Bruyères in particular is now self-contained.

The resort

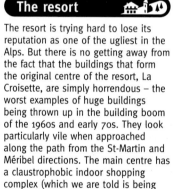

The resort is trying hard to lose its reputation as one of the ugliest in the Alps. But there is no getting away from the fact that the buildings that form the original centre of the resort, La Croisette, are simply horrendous – the worst examples of huge buildings being thrown up in the building boom of the 1960s and early 70s. They look particularly vile when approached along the path from the St-Martin and Méribel directions. The main centre has a claustrophobic indoor shopping complex (which we are told is being given a facelift). Newer outposts such as Reberty and Les Bruyères are much less offensive – all new building is now

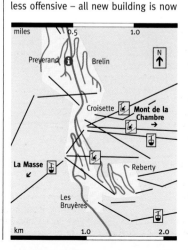

in traditional Savoyard (stone and wood) style and there are some luxury developments. The new outposts have their own shops and bars – Les Bruyères, in particular, is now a more-or-less self-contained resort.

Three Valleys lift passes for six days or more also give you a day in Val-d'Isère/Tignes, La Plagne or Les Arcs, but such outings take a bit of effort.

The mountains

Les Menuires has two main attractions: La Masse, a challenging and neglected mountain; and the swift links to the rest of the Trois Vallées.

THE SLOPES
A good base for the Trois Vallées

Les Menuires and St-Martin-de-Belleville share a local area with 160km/100 miles of runs and 42 lifts. The west-facing slopes have the vast bulk of the runs. The two fast six-packs take you up from La Croisette to **Mont de la Chambre**, from where you can head back south to Val-Thorens or east over the ridge to the Méribel slopes. Chairs and drags serve the local slopes, and you can head north to the old village of St-Martin.

The north-east-facing slopes of **La Masse** usually have excellent snow on the top half and are served by a two-stage high-capacity gondola.

boarding *Les Menuires gets a fair number of boarding visitors – not surprising since it gives relatively economical access to such a huge area of terrain. There is plenty here for every style of rider. Lots of chairs and gondolas in the massive lift system make for comfortable travel, but be warned – there are some flattish sections of piste to negotiate in places. And we'd certainly recommend beginners to go somewhere with more secluded nursery slopes and better snow. There's a terrain-park with a half-pipe just above the main village.*

SNOW RELIABILITY
Cover guaranteed but not quality
La Masse's height and orientation ensure good snow for a long season. The opposite, west-facing slopes are supplied with abundant artificial snow (the resort boasts 323 snow-guns). But although cover there is guaranteed – so long as the weather is cold enough to make snow – the snow lower down is often icy or slushy.

MOUNTAIN FACTS

for the Three Valleys

Altitude	1300m-3230m
	4,270ft-10,600ft
Lifts	200
Pistes	600km
	370 miles
Green	17%
Blue	34%
Red	37%
Black	12%
Snowmaking	90km
	56 miles
Recco detectors used	

LIFT PASSES

2002/03 prices in euros

Three Valleys
See Méribel chapter.
Alternative passes
Vallée des Belleville pass covers 74 lifts and 300km/186 miles of piste in Val-Thorens, Les Menuires and St-Martin (adult 6-day 180). Les Menuires and St-Martin pass covers 42 lifts and 160km/100 miles of piste (adult 6-day 151).

GETTING THERE

Air Geneva, transfer 3½hr. Lyon, transfer 3½hr. Chambéry, transfer 2½hr.

Rail Moûtiers (27km/17 miles); regular buses from station.

FOR EXPERTS
Hidden treasures
La Masse has some of the steepest and quietest pistes in the Trois Vallées – most people doing the 'circuit' skip it. Long reds and a black come down beneath the top stage of the gondola. Other steep blacks, usually mogulled, are the Dame Blanche and Lac Noir.

From the top there are also some marvellously scenic off-piste runs, some sporadically marked as itinéraires, others requiring guidance. The wide, sweeping, but not too steep, Vallon du Lou goes towards Val-Thorens. Others go in the opposite direction to various villages from which you need transport back, but the Les

Yvoses run takes you back to the lifts.
There's easy access to the rest of the Trois Vallées: within an hour of your door are the steepest slopes of Méribel or Val-Thorens. Courchevel doesn't take much longer.

FOR INTERMEDIATES
600km/370 miles of pistes
With good snow, you may find little reason for leaving the local slopes, which are virtually all blue and red. But because most slopes face west, the snow is often better elsewhere in the Trois Vallées. This is paradise for intermediates who like to travel. You can approach Méribel from five different peaks on the ridge. Even a second- or third-timer should have no problem cruising from valley to valley. In poor snow conditions the attractions of Val-Thorens become evident, and there's blue as well as red-run access.

FOR BEGINNERS
Try elsewhere
There are wide and gentle slopes and a special lift pass for beginners. But the place is not ideal: beginners can't escape from the resort's dreary

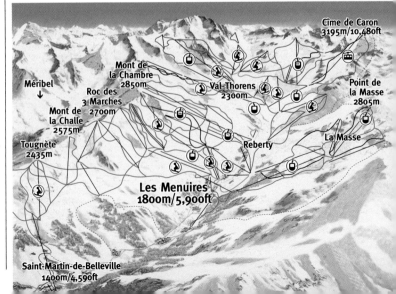

ACTIVITIES

Indoor Library, cinema, fitness centres, sauna
Outdoor Two outdoor heated swimming pools, microlight flights, hang-gliding, guided walks, snow-scooters, artificial skating rink, snow-shoe excursions, paragliding, guided tours, tubing

SCHOOLS/GUIDES

2002/03 prices in euros
ESF
Classes 6 half days: adult: from 95
Children's classes Ages: up to 12
6 half days: from 86
Private lessons Hourly 33 for 1 or 2 people

CHILDCARE

The ESF-run Village des Schtroumpfs (0479 006379) takes children aged 3 months to 12 years. It has a nursery for babies, a Baby Club for toddlers and a leisure centre for older children, with activities and ski lessons for children aged 2½ or more.

At Reberty-les-Bruyères, the Village des Marmottons (0479 006950) offers similar facilities, but no nursery.

Phone numbers
From abroad use the prefix +33 and omit the initial '0' of the phone number.

TOURIST OFFICE

Postcode 73440
t 0479 007300
f 0479 007506
lesmenuires@
lesmenuires.com
www.lesmenuires.com

---

buildings, and the snow quality on the nursery slopes is a worry. There is now a slope for the exclusive use of beginners, which is a big step in the right direction. But the blue slopes you progress to can get extremely crowded.

FOR CROSS-COUNTRY
Valley hike
There are 28km/17 miles of prepared trails along the valley floor towards St-Martin and Val-Thorens.

QUEUES
Big bottleneck goes
The new fast six-packs up from La Croisette seem to have largely solved the problem of queues throughout the day to get to the Mont de la Chambre. However, queues in Val Thorens seem to be growing as it becomes more easily accessible from Les Menuires. The other new problem is in getting skiers from some expanding sectors of the resort on to the slopes first thing.

MOUNTAIN RESTAURANTS
A surprisingly atmospheric place
In this area many people seem to prefer to head down to the villages for lunch. If you share the tendency and want a serious lunch, seek out the Bouitte, in nearby St-Marcel. It's reachable off-piste, and they'll drive you to the lifts after lunch. Just above Les Menuires, on the left of the main piste down to La Croisette, is one of the nicest stops in the Trois Vallées, the Etoile – a rustic old hut with smart terrace and good food served by waiters in berets and traditional dress. At higher altitude there is 'excellent food and below average prices' on the large terrace at the Alpage, on the 4 Vents piste.

SCHOOLS AND GUIDES
Lack of competition
Reports vary but one thing is for sure – the ESF has the monopoly here. One reader declined lessons when the school would not guarantee tuition in English. (He had also spotted classes of up to 23 children.) But another found it 'excellent', with 'well-organised, friendly instructors'.

FACILITIES FOR CHILDREN
All-embracing
This is very much a family resort, and the childcare arrangements seem well organised. The new separate nursery slope is a welcome development.

Staying there

HOW TO GO
Budget packages
Some big UK tour operators have a fair selection of hotels and apartments, and some specialist chalet operators now have a presence in Reberty. There is a Club Med above Reberty.
Hotels None of the hotels is above 3-star grading.
⊞③ **Ours Blanc** (0479 006166) Best in town: a wood-clad, chalet-style 3-star on the slopes above Reberty 1850.
⊞③ **Latitudes** (0479 007510) 3-star on the lower fringe of Les Bruyères.
⊞② **Menuire** (0479 006033) Neat, well-equipped place on the southern fringe of the resort; but we have had some negative reports.
Self-catering The older apartments are cheap and small. But the newer ones are more attractive, spacious and luxurious. The Montagnettes and Alpages, both in Reberty, are among the best, the latter being an MGM development with a pool.

EATING OUT
Good authentic French cuisine
Though some restaurants lack atmosphere, there's no shortage of good food, including Savoyard specialities. Alternatives include Italian and Tex-Mex. The Trattoria, with its 'rustic French' ambience, is highly recommended. The set menus at the Snow are 'reasonably priced' and the tartiflette is 'particularly good'. The Géant de Marmite is getting a name for its 'excellent food, good prices and pleasant atmosphere', and it caters for children.

APRES-SKI
Improving but still very limited
There isn't a huge après-ski scene. The Sphere Bar is popular with the young British crowd. A reader preferred the 'lighter, French' ambience of the Bar du Lou. The Taverne bar in Les Bruyères is 'lively and welcoming' and has theme nights. The Liberty and Passeport discos pick up later on.

OFF THE SLOPES
Forget it
Les Menuires is a resort for keen piste-bashers wanting to explore the world's most extensive slopes, though there are some pretty walks.

The best-looking base for the wonderful Three Valleys

WHAT IT COSTS

(((((6)

HOW IT RATES

The slopes
Snow	★★★★
Extent	★★★★★
Experts	★★★★
Intermediates	★★★★★
Beginners	★★★
Convenience	★★★
Queues	★★★★
Restaurants	★★★★

The rest
Scenery	★★★
Resort charm	★★★
Off-slope	★★★

➕ In the centre of the biggest linked piste network in the world – ideal for intermediates who love covering the miles, but plenty for experts, too

➕ Modern, constantly improved lift system means little queueing and rapid access to all slopes

➕ Good piste grooming and snowmaking

➕ Village purpose-built in pleasing chalet-style architecture

➖ Not the best snow in the Three Valleys, and pistes can get crowded

➖ Main village spread out, straggling along a long, winding road, with much of the accommodation well away from the slopes

➖ Expensive

➖ Méribel-Mottaret and Méribel Village satellites are rather lifeless

➖ Not the place to go for real French atmosphere – too many Brits

For keen piste-bashers who dislike tacky purpose-built resorts, Méribel is difficult to beat. It is slap in the middle of the Three Valleys – the biggest lift network in the world. With 200 lifts and 600km/370 miles of pistes, and endless off-piste possibilities, the area can keep anyone amused for a fortnight. The orientation of Méribel's local slopes means its snow is often not as good as in Courchevel and Val-Thorens. But its Mont du Vallon area keeps its snow well and access to every part of the Three Valleys is quick and easy.

Méribel is built entirely in tasteful chalet-style, with wood cladding everywhere. The centre is very pleasant, with raised walkways by the shops above the one-way road, and is fairly animated in the evening – though one reader last March found that the village had a 'deserted feeling after 7pm'. The village has grown rapidly in recent years, at least partly because of its popularity on the British market. Chalets (many of them luxurious) have been built further and further from the pistes and many tour operators run mini-buses to and from the slopes. English is more commonly heard than French on the slopes and in the bars (many of which are British-run). It remains decidedly up-market and it's not cheap. But regular visitors love it and regret their occasional expeditions elsewhere. And we still have a soft spot for it (one of us learned to ski here).

Rond Point, at the top of the village, is one of the pivots of life in Méribel ↓

The Plan des Mains chair – a bottleneck on the way from Val-Thorens to Mottaret – will be replaced for 2002/03 by a fast six-seat chair.

The Martre blue piste down into Mottaret from Plattières is being remodelled to make it more friendly.

More snow-guns are being installed at Altiport and down to Méribel Village.

The resort

Méribel occupies the central valley of the Three Valleys system and consists of two main resort villages.

The original resort of Méribel-les-Allues (now simply known as Méribel) is built on a single steepish west-facing hillside with the home piste running down beside it to the main lift stations at the valley bottom. All the buildings are wood-clad, low-rise and chalet style, making this one of the most tastefully designed of French purpose-built resorts. A road winds up from the village centre to the Rond Point des Pistes, and goes on through woods to the outpost of the Altiport (an airport with snow-covered runway for little planes with skis).

The resort was founded by a Brit, Peter Lindsay, in 1938, and has retained a strong British presence ever since. It has grown enormously over recent years, and although some accommodation is right on the piste, much of the newer building is more than a walk away – check your location carefully if you don't like having to rely on buses (or tour operator mini-buses). One clear exception is Belvédère, an upmarket enclave built on the opposite side of the home piste (there's a tunnel for road access). There are collections of shops and restaurants at a couple of points on the road through the resort – Altitude 1600 and Plateau de Morel. The hotels and apartments of Altiport enjoy splendid isolation in the woods, and are convenient for some of the slopes.

The satellite village of Méribel-Mottaret was developed in the early 1970s. The original development was beside the piste on the east-facing slope, but in recent years the resort has spread up the opposite hillside and further up the valley. Both sides

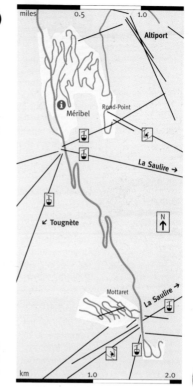

are served by lifts for pedestrians – but the gondola up to the original village stops at 7.30 and it's a long, tiring walk up. Mottaret looks modern, despite wood-cladding on its apartment blocks. Even so, it's more attractive than many other resorts built for slope-side convenience. It has many fewer shops and bars and much less après-ski than Méribel, but reporters have found it makes a pleasant change, and enjoyed the convenience.

Local buses are free (though some readers complain they are inadequate), and many UK tour operators run their own minibus services to and from the lifts. A car is mainly of use for outings to other resorts. Lift passes for six days or more give you a day in Val-d'Isère-Tignes (an hour and a half away by car), La Plagne or Les Arcs (an hour or so away).

There are some alternative bases lower down the mountain (and the price scale), described at the end of this chapter. These include Méribel-Village – an old village set on the road from Méribel to La Tania and Courchevel, now being developed, with a chair-lift up to Altiport.

Méribel

277

LIFT PASSES

2002/03 prices in euros

Three Valleys
Covers all lifts in Courchevel, La Tania, Méribel, Val-Thorens, Les Menuires and St-Martin-de-Belleville.
Beginners Two free lifts in Méribel-Mottaret and two in Méribel; reduced price lift pass with beginners' lessons.
Main pass
1-day pass 39
6-day pass 193
Senior citizen
Over 59: 6-day pass 154
Over 71: free pass
Children
Under 13: 6-day pass 145
Under 5: free pass
Family pass
Available for 2 adults plus 2 children under 18: 6-day pass 620
Short-term passes
Half-day passes (from 12.30) available for Vallée de Méribel (adult 24), Méribel Alpina (adult 20.5) and Three Valleys (adult 29).
Notes 6-day pass and over valid for one day each in Tignes-Val-d'Isère, La Plagne-Les Arcs, Pralognan-la-Vanoise and Les Saisies.
Alternative passes
Vallée de Méribel pass covers 150km/93 miles of runs in Méribel and Méribel-Mottaret (adult 6-day 157).
One-day Three Valleys extension 18).

The mountains

It's keen piste-bashers who will get the best out of what Méribel has to offer. There's endless cruising to be had, as well as challenging terrain. The lift system is generally very efficient and is planned to cut out walks and climbs. Piste grading is not always reliable, however – reporters found 'some blues more difficult than some reds'.

To appreciate the merits of the whole Three Valleys region you'll need to read the chapters on Courchevel, Les Menuires and Val-Thorens, too.

THE SLOPES
Highly efficient lift system
The Méribel valley runs north-south. On the eastern side, gondolas leave both Méribel and Mottaret for **La Saulire**. From here you can head back down towards either village or down the other side of the ridge towards Courchevel.

From Méribel a gondola rises to **Tougnète**, on the western side of the valley, from where you can get down to Les Menuires or St-Martin-de-Belleville. You can also head for Mottaret from here. From there, a fast chair then a drag take you to another entry point for the Les Menuires runs.

The Mottaret area has seen rapid mechanisation over the last decade. The **Plattières** gondola rises up the valley to the south, ending at yet another entry point to the Les Menuires area. To the east of this is the big stand-up gondola to the top of **Mont du Vallon**. There are wonderful views from the top. A fast quad from near this area goes south up to **Mont de la Chambre**, giving direct access to Val-Thorens.

SNOW RELIABILITY
Not the best in the Three Valleys
Méribel's slopes aren't the highest in the Three Valleys, and they mainly face east or west, getting the full force of the morning or afternoon sun. So snow conditions are often better elsewhere. And grooming seems to be rather better in neighbouring Courchevel.

The lower runs now have substantial snowmaking and lack of snow is rarely a problem, but ice or slush at the end of the day can be. The west-facing La Saulire side gets the afternoon sun, and conditions deteriorate here first – but then you

can always go over to Courchevel. The north-west-facing slopes above Altiport generally have decent snow.

At the southern end of the valley, towards Les Menuires and Val-Thorens, a lot of runs are north-facing and keep their snow well, as do the runs on Mont du Vallon.

FOR EXPERTS
Exciting choices
The size of the Three Valleys means experts are well catered for. In the Méribel valley, head for Mont du Vallon. The long, steep, Combe du Vallon run here is classified red; it's a wonderful, long, fast cruise when groomed, but presents plenty of challenge when mogulled. And there's a beautiful itinéraire (not marked on the piste map) in the next valley to the main pistes, leading back to the bottom of the gondola.

The slopes down from the top of the Val-Thorens sector were all off-piste when we old hands first visited Méribel. Since the new lifts were installed up here, there are two pistes back from Val-Thorens, but still plenty of opportunity for getting off-piste in the wide open bowls.

A good mogul run is down the side of the double Roc de Tougne drag-lift which leads up to Mont de la Challe. And there is a steep black run all the way down the Tougnète gondola back to Méribel. Apart from a shallow section near the mid-station, it's unrelenting most of the way.

At the north end of the valley the Face run was built for the women's downhill in the 1992 Olympics. Served by a fast quad, it's a splendid cruise when freshly groomed, and you can terrify yourself just by imagining what it must be like to go straight down.

Nothing on the Saulire side is as steep or as demanding as on the other side of the valley. The Mauduit red run

MOUNTAIN FACTS

For the Three Valleys

Altitude	1300m-3230m
	4,270ft-10,600ft
Lifts	200
Pistes	600km
	370 miles
Green	17%
Blue	34%
Red	37%
Black	12%
Snowmaking	90km
	56 miles
Recco detectors used	

boarding *Méribel is increasingly boarder-oriented. The terrain locally and further afield has lots to offer, you rarely have to take a drag-lift, and there's one terrain-park with half-pipe, two quarter-pipes and a boarder-cross below the second stage of the Plattières gondola; the Moon Park near the Arpasson drag above the Tougnète gondola mid-station has a quarter-pipe and trick course. The resort hosts a number of big-air and boarder-cross competitions. Specialist shops include Board Brains, Exodus and Quiksilver, and you're bound to feel at home in at least one of the lively bars.*

is quite challenging, though – it used to be black.

Throughout the area there are good off-piste opportunities. The ESF runs excellent-value guided groups.

FOR INTERMEDIATES
Paradise found

Méribel and the rest of the Three Valleys is a paradise for intermediates; there are few other resorts where a keen piste-basher can cover so many miles so easily. Virtually every slope in the region has a good intermediate run down it, and to describe them would take a book in itself.

For less adventurous intermediates, the run from the second station of the Plattières gondola back to Mottaret is ideal, and used a lot by the ski school. It is a gentle, north-facing, cruising run and is generally in good condition.

Even early intermediates should find the runs over into the other valleys well within their capabilities, opening up further vast amounts of intermediate runs. Go to Courchevel or

Val-Thorens for the better snow.

Virtually all the pistes on both sides of the Méribel valley will suit more advanced intermediates. Most of the reds are on the difficult side.

FOR BEGINNERS
Not ideal

Méribel isn't ideal for beginners. The resort lacks good nursery slopes set apart from the main areas. There is a small one at Rond-Point, mainly used by the children's ski school.

The best area for beginners is at Altiport, accessible direct from the village at Altitude 1600 by the Morel chair-lift. Alternatively, take the free bus which runs regularly from Chaudanne in the centre via Morel and Rond-Point to Altiport. There is a gentle out-of-the-way area here that can be treated as a nursery slope. And you can progress to one of the best and most attractively situated green pistes we know, the Blanchot – long, gentle, wide and tree-lined, with little through-traffic.

Méribel

279

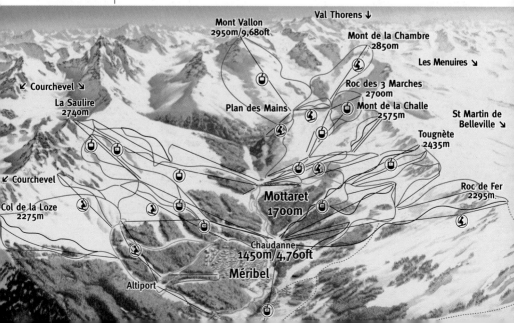

SCHOOLS/GUIDES

2002/03 prices in euros

ESF
in Méribel and Méribel-Mottaret
Classes Adults
6 full days: 201
Children's classes
Ages: 5 to 13
6 full days: 161
Private lessons
2hr for 2 people 89
International section
In Méribel and Méribel-Mottaret
Classes Adults
6 sessions of 2½hr:
130
Children's classes
Ages: 5 to 13
6 sessions of 2½hr:
110

New Generation
2002/03 prices in sterling
Classes 10hr £89
Freeride clinic
7½hr £85
Check Up clinic
4hr £50
Private lessons
2hr £75 for 1 or 2 people, £15 per additional person

Magic in Motion
2002/03 prices in euros
Classes Adults 12hr
145
Children's classes
Ages: 4 to 5, 10hr
175; 6 to 17: 4 mornings and 2 whole days 360
Private lessons
2hr 105 for 1 or 2 people, 18 per additional person

FOR CROSS-COUNTRY
Scenic routes
The main area is in the woods near Altiport. There is about 17km/11 miles of prepared track here, a pleasant introduction to those who want to try cross-country for the first time. There's also a loop around Lake Tueda, in the nature reserve at Mottaret, and for the more experienced an 8km/5 mile itinéraire from Altiport to Courchevel.

QUEUES
Easily avoided, normally
Huge lift investment over the years has paid off in making the area virtually queue-free most of the time, despite the huge numbers of people. The last big bottleneck – the Plan des Mains chair used by everyone returning from Val-Thorens – should be sorted out by the new six-pack due for this season. This and the lifts from the centre of Val-Thorens can get very busy when Méribel-based skiers are spending their days there in search of better snow. Generally, however, the excellent lift network means that if you do find a queue, there is usually an alternative quieter route you can take. The Plattières gondola at Mottaret can get crowded at ski school time, when the schools get priority – take the alternative Combes fast chair.

MOUNTAIN RESTAURANTS
Lots of choice, but not cheap
There is lots of choice, but most places get very crowded. You might want to take lunch early or late. The self-service Pierres Plates, at the top of the Saulire gondolas, has magnificent views, but the food and atmosphere are nothing special. Chardonnet, at the mid-station of the Mottaret gondola, has table-service and excellent food, but is expensive. The large terrace at Rhododendrons, at the top of the Altiport drag, remains a popular spot –

its varied menu encouraged one reader to eat there several times during his holiday. Rond Point, just below the mid-point of the Rhodos gondola, offers tasty paninis at lunch time as well as delicious rostis in the restaurant for those with a little more time. The Altiport hotel has a great outdoor buffet in good weather and the 'best tarts in town' but, again, is expensive. The cosy Crêtes, below the top of the Tougnète gondola, continues to provide 'good food and service'. The Sitelle, above the first section of the Plattières gondola, has decent self-service food and magnificent views towards Mont du Vallon.

SCHOOLS AND GUIDES
No shortage of instructors
The main schools all have English-speaking instructors.

The ESF is by far the biggest, with over 300 instructors. It has a special international section with instructors speaking good English. Recent reports have been mixed, but we've heard tales of instructors behaving more like guides, and abilities being too mixed within a class. One reporter had problems with his Internet booking, and another also found fault with ESF's administrative procedures.

The ESF offers useful alternatives to standard classes, such as off-piste groups, heli-skiing on the French/Italian border and 'Ski Discovery' tours of the Three Valleys.

Magic in Motion, the second largest school, also offers heli-skiing, couloir and extreme sessions in addition to skiing and boarding lessons. They keep classes small, no more than 7, and generally get good reports. You need to book ahead for busy weeks.

New Generation, a British school new to Méribel last season, seems set to extend the good reputation it has

CHILDCARE

The ESF runs P'tits Loups kindergartens at both Méribel and Méribel-Mottaret, with snow-gardens (lifts, inflatable characters etc) for children aged 3 to 5. Open 9am to 5pm.

Les Saturnins in the Olympic Centre building in Méribel takes children aged 18 months to 3 years, offering indoor games and handicrafts, sledging and other outdoor activities.

GETTING THERE

Air Geneva, transfer 3½hr. Lyon, transfer 3½hr. Chambéry, transfer 2½hr.

Rail Moûtiers (18km/11 miles); regular buses to Méribel.

built up in Courchevel. One reader says, 'I cannot recommend them highly enough, they were patient and kept groups small.'

Snow Systems is another new operator but one beginner found their boarding lessons 'very poor', consisting of 'pushing a nervous beginner down the hill before they were ready, and shouting at them'.

FACILITIES FOR CHILDREN
Tour operators rule
We guess readers needing childcare plug into the facilities of chalet operators who run their own nurseries – we rarely get reports on the resort facilities. We have heard, though, that Les Saturnins in the Olympic Centre caters well for toddlers.

Staying there

HOW TO GO
Huge choice but few bargains
Package holidays are easy to find, both with big UK tour operators and smaller Méribel specialists. There are three Club Med 'villages', all in CM's top comfort category, none with the usual children's club facilities; two occupy very attractive hotel buildings in the Belvédère area.

Chalets Méribel has more chalets dedicated to the British market than any other resort, and over 50 operators offering them. What really distinguishes Méribel is the range of luxurious chalets, many with minibuses on hand to compensate for their inconvenient locations. Méribel specialist Meriski has an extensive portfolio of luxury chalets, some among our own favourites. Lotus Supertravel's smaller range includes a couple of luxy places. Scott Dunn has four chalets. Neilson's half-dozen chalets include three that are all en-suite. If money is no object, try one of The Ski Company's four luxury chalets (two of which share an outdoor pool and hot-tub) or Descent International's Brames (which you have to take over as one group of up to 20, at a cost of around £30,000 a week).

Of the few chalet-hotels, Mark Warner's Bellevue is handy for the Morel lift and is 'adults only' outside school holidays. They also have the Tarentaise, right on the piste at Mottaret. Ski Olympic has the Parc Alpin at Méribel 1600.

Hotels Méribel has some excellent hotels, but they're not cheap.

《《《④ **Grand Coeur** (0479 086003) Our favourite almost-affordable hotel in Méribel. Just above the village centre. Welcoming, mature building with plush lounge. Magnificent food. Huge hot-tub, sauna, etc.

《《④ **Altiport** (0479 005232) Modern and luxurious hotel, isolated at the foot of the Altiport lifts. Convenient for Courchevel, not for Val-Thorens.

《《④ **Mont Vallon** (0479 004400) The best hotel at Mottaret; good food, and excellently situated for the Three Valleys' pistes. Pool, sauna, hot-tub, squash, fitness room, etc.

《③ **Adray Télébar** (0479 086026) Welcoming piste-side chalet with pretty, rustic rooms, good food and popular sun terrace.

《② **Roc** (0479 086416) A good-value B&B hotel, in the centre, with a bar-restaurant and crêperie below.

Self-catering There is a huge number of apartments and chalets to let in both Méribel and Mottaret. Make sure that the place you book is conveniently situated and has enough space.

EATING OUT
Fair choice
There is a reasonable selection of restaurants, from ambitious French cuisine to relatively cheap pizza and pasta. For the best food in town, in plush surroundings, there are top hotels – Grand Coeur ('so pleased, we ate there several times'), Allodis and Kouisena in L'Eterlou. Other readers' recommendations include: Chez Kiki – 'the best steaks we have tasted in a long time and an apple tart to die for'; the Taverne – 'nice relaxed atmosphere'; the Tremplin – 'good for families, friendly service, reasonably priced'; and the Cactus Café – 'good food, makes children welcome'.

Alternatives include the Galette, the Fromagerie, the Refuge, the Cava, the Plantin (on the road out towards La

Tania) and Cro Magnon up the hill in Morel – all popular for raclette and fondue. The Marée Blanche specialises in seafood and the Blanchot, just below Altiport, offers the choice of two dining areas, one dedicated to dishes of the region. In Méribel Village, the Lodge du Village is said to be 'friendly', with 'a good range of Italian food'. Another reader recommends the Crocodile in the Hameau at Mottaret. Scott's does good American-style food, and there's even a Pizza Express.

At Les Allues, the Tsaretta will provide a free taxi service to transport you to enjoy the imaginative creations of the Australian chef. The Chaumière offers 'good value inclusive menus in pleasant, rustic surroundings'.

APRES-SKI
Méribel rocks – loudly

Méribel's après-ski revolves around British-run places. Dick's Tea Bar is now well established but is remote from the slopes. At close of play it's the piste-side Rond Point that's packed – happy hour starts around 4pm – and has live music and toffee vodka. The sun terrace of Jack's, near the main lift stations, remains very popular.

The ring of bars around the main square do good business at tea time. The Taverne (run by the same company that owns Dick's Tea Bar) gets packed. Just across the square is The Pub, with videos, pool and sometimes a band. Here too you will find a couple of alternatives to the loud pubs complained about in the past. The Poste (not to be confused with 'la poste' – the post office next door) 'serves the best vin chaud'. The Dawido is comfortable and has a pool table, and the Refuge (a little further down the road towards the lifts) is that rare thing in Méribel: a place where you'll be understood if you use your French.

There is late dancing at Scott's (next to The Pub) and, of course, there's Dick's Tea Bar (free entry and sub-disco drinks prices until 11.30). One reader was put off by the queues at The Pub, and having paid to get in to Dick's found it a 'bit of a dive'. The weekly session in Pizza Express (above Dick's and under the same ownership) by a very convincing Beatles tribute band continued to be hugely popular last season. El Poncho's serves Mexican dishes and Desperados (beer mixed with tequila).

Méribel

283

ACTIVITIES

Indoor Parc Olympique Méribel (skating rink, swimming pool), Forme Méribel (spa, sauna, gym, bowling, billiards, climbing wall), library, bridge, fitness centres, hot-tub, two cinemas, concert hall

Outdoor Flying lessons and excursions, snow-mobiles, snow-shoe excursions, para-gliding, 20km/12 miles of cleared paths, dog sledding, hot air balloon

Phone numbers
From abroad use the prefix +33 and omit the initial '0' of the phone number.

TOURIST OFFICE

Postcode 73551
t 0479 086001
f 0479 005961
info@meribel.net
www.meribel.net

In Mottaret the bars at the foot of the pistes get packed at tea time – Rastro and DownTown are the most popular, though reporters say that Zig Zag has lower prices. Later on the Rastro disco gets going.

Both villages have a cinema.

OFF THE SLOPES
Flight of fancy

Méribel is not really a resort for people who want to languish in the village, but it is not unattractive. There's a good public swimming pool and an Olympic ice rink. You can also take joyrides in the little planes that operate from the altiport.

The pedestrian's lift pass covers all the gondolas, cable-cars and buses in the Méribel and Courchevel valleys, and makes it very easy for pedestrians to meet friends for lunch. There are pleasant, marked walks in the Altiport area and a signposted trail through some of the hamlets down to Les Allues (return from there or Le Raffort in the Olympic gondola).

STAYING DOWN THE VALLEY
Quieter, cheaper choices

For the 1992 Olympics the competitors were accommodated in **Brides-les-Bains** (600m/1,970ft), an old spa town way down in the valley, and a new gondola was built linking it to Méribel. It is very cheap compared with the higher resorts, and worth considering if the budget is tight. It has some simple hotels, adequate shops and 'plenty of good-value restaurants and friendly bars used by locals', says our one reporter this year. Ski Weekends now runs its own chalet-hotel here, the Verseau. There is a casino, but evenings are distinctly quiet. The long gondola ride to and from Méribel (about 25 minutes) is tedious and can be cold, but there are also buses to Méribel and Courchevel, and in good conditions you can ski off-piste to one or other of the mid-stations at the end of the day. Given a car, Brides makes a good base for visiting other resorts.

Some UK tour operators have places in the old village of **Les Allues**, down the road from the resort and close to a mid-station on the gondola up from Brides-les-Bains. There are a couple of bars and a good-value, well renovated hotel – the Croix Jean-Claude (0479 086105). Rooms are small, though, and a reporter says the service is poor.

The new development of **Méribel-Village** (1400m/4,590ft) is linked by chair-lift to the Altiport area with a blue run back. There are some luxury chalets and apartments here but little else apart from one bar and restaurant, but if nightlife is not a priority it's a pleasant place to stay for an uncrowded way in to the lift system. Having a car is advisable to reach nearby La Tania or Méribel proper – the bus service is 'appalling'.

SNOWPIX.COM / CHRIS GILL

Mottaret now spreads up the west-facing slope as well as the original east-facing slope →

The snowiest part of the Franco-Italian Milky Way circuit

WHAT IT COSTS

HOW IT RATES

The slopes

Snow	****
Extent	****
Experts	**
Intermediates	****
Beginners	*****
Convenience	****
Queues	****
Restaurants	**

The rest

Scenery	***
Resort charm	***
Off-slope	*

- ➕ Good snow record, and local slopes largely north-facing – often the best snow in the Milky Way area
- ➕ Plenty of intermediate cruising and good, convenient nursery slopes
- ➕ Few queues on weekdays, unless people are being bussed in from other resorts with poor snow
- ➕ A lot of accommodation close to the slopes, and some right on them
- ➕ Great potential for car drivers to explore other nearby resorts

- ➖ Poor base for exploring the Italian Milky Way resorts if you don't have a car
- ➖ Slow lifts and short runs can be irritating
- ➖ Busy road lined by tatty bars reduces village charm and family appeal – crossing can be tricky
- ➖ Little to challenge experts on-piste

Montgenèvre is set at one end of the big Milky Way network, reaching over into Italy. It's a time-consuming trek to Sestriere and Sauze d'Oulx at the far end (you may have to ride lifts down as well as up). But it's much quicker by car, which also facilitates day trips to other French resorts such as Serre-Chevalier. And you'll probably find the best snow for miles on the local slopes shared with Clavière (in Italy, but only a mile down the road).

The village is quite pleasant once you get away from the main road. Sadly, you can't avoid the road altogether if you want to make use of the bigger area of slopes on the south side of the pass. But most visitors seem to come to terms with it, and don't find that it spoils their enjoyment.

285

What's new

For 2002/03 another 5km/3 miles of snowmaking will be installed (adding 50% to the existing amount) and a new boarder-cross course and a terrain-park will be built.

A new 2-star hotel, Alpis Cottia, will open.

The resort

Montgenèvre is a narrow roadside village set on a high pass only a mile from the Italian border. It is one of the resorts where the euro has really simplified things – no longer do you need to bother about lira when you cross the border. At first glance the resort appears a rather inhospitable place – a collection of tatty-looking bars and restaurants lining the side of the sometimes windswept and often busy main road over the col. But the

The main slopes are this side of the main road – Italy is one mile to the right ➔

LIFT PASSES

2001/02 prices in euros

Montgenèvre
Covers Montgenèvre lifts only.
Beginners One free drag-lift. Points cards available.
Skiing by the hour is available (3-, 4- or 5-hr 'à la carte' passes).
Main pass
1-day pass 21
6-day pass 104
Senior citizens
Over 60: 6-day pass 83
Over 75: free pass
Children
Under 12: 6-day pass 83
Under 8: free pass
Short-term passes
Single ascent for foot passengers of Le Chalvet or Chalmettes (adult 5).
Notes 6-day pass and over allows free days at Alpe-d'Huez, Les Deux-Alpes, Puy-St-Vincent and Serre-Chevalier. Reductions for families. Extensions by the day to main pass for the Voie Lactée (adult 12).
Alternative passes
Montgenèvre-Monts de la Lune (Clavière) (adults 23 per day, children 18 per day). Voie Lactée (Milky Way) covers Montgenèvre, Clavière, Cesana, Sansicario, Sauze d'Oulx, Sestriere – 400km/250 miles (6 day pass: adults 129, under 13 or over 60 118.50).

cheap and cheerful cafes and bars add an animated atmosphere sometimes missing from French resorts. And tucked away off the main road is a quite pleasant old village, complete with quaint church and friendly natives. The place gets a lot of snow, which adds to the charm factor.

The slopes are convenient, despite the road; most of the accommodation is less than five minutes from a lift. The main ones are gondolas from opposite ends of the village. On the village side of the road are the south-facing slopes of Le Chalvet. The more extensive north-facing slopes of Les Anges and Le Querelay are across the main road, with nursery slopes at the bottom. Both sectors have piste links with Clavière, gateway to the other Italian resorts of the Milky Way – eg Sansicario, Sestriere and Sauze d'Oulx.

There are hotels, chalets and apartments available, all of which are cheap and cheerful places. Don't expect to find much luxury here. Location is becoming more important as the village expands – some of the newer accommodation is uphill, away from the slopes – though there is a free shuttle-bus.

The best way to get to other resorts is to travel by car. Serre-Chevalier and Puy-St-Vincent, with lift pass sharing arrangements, are easily reached by car, and well worth an outing each. Different lift pass options cater for most requirements.

The mountains

Montgenèvre's local slopes are best suited to leisurely intermediates, with lots of easy cruising on blues and greens, both above and in the woods.

Run gradings on the local area and Milky Way piste maps have differed in the past, which can be confusing – however, none of the blacks are much more than a tough red. We have have had a complaint that the local piste map 'looked like a place mat setting'.

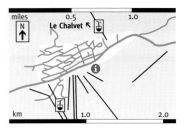

There is floodlit skiing and boarding one evening a week during the French school holidays.

THE SLOPES
Nicely varied
The major north-facing Les Anges sector offers easy intermediate slopes above the mid-mountain gondola station, with more of a mix of runs lower down. It has a high-altitude link via Collet Vert (reached by a quad chair) to the slopes above Clavière, in Italy (covered on the Monts de la Lune lift pass). The main complaint about the Clavière area is the number of long, awkward drag-lifts (tricky for boarders and we have reports of skiing 'kids dropping like flies'). But this whole area around the border is attractively broken up by rocky outcrops and woods and the scenery is quite spectacular. The runs of the sunny Chalvet sector are mainly on open slopes above its mid-mountain gondola station. When conditions permit, a long blue run from Col de l'Alpet in this sector goes down to Clavière, for access to Italy.

SNOW RELIABILITY
Excellent locally
Montgenèvre has a generally excellent snow record, receiving dumps from westerly storms funnelling up the valley. The high north-facing slopes naturally keep their snow better than the south-facing area but both have snowmaking on the main village-bound pistes.

boarding There's plenty to attract boarders to Montgenèvre. There are good local beginner slopes and long runs on varied terrain for intermediates. The only real drawback is that many of the lifts in the area are drags, and you will have to use them to get around – getting over to Sestriere and back involves lots (and some flat sections to skate along as well). A new terrain-park and a boarder-cross course are due for 2002/03, and there are some excellent off-piste areas for more advanced boarders. Snow Box is the local specialist shop.

The north-facing slopes of the Les Anges sector keep their snow well →

MOUNTAIN FACTS

Altitude	1850m-2680m
	6,070ft-8,790ft
Lifts	39
Pistes	100km
	62 miles
Green	15%
Blue	27%
Red	39%
Black	19%
Snowmaking	15km
	9 miles
Recco detectors used	

The following figures relate to the whole Milky Way area

Altitude	1390m-2825m
	4,560ft-9,270ft
Lifts	92
Pistes	400km
	250 miles
Blue	12%
Red	67%
Black	21%
Snowmaking	80km
	50 miles

FOR EXPERTS
Limited, except for off-piste

There are very few challenging pistes in the Montgenèvre-Clavière-Cesana sectors. Many of the runs are overclassified on the map. There is, however, ample opportunity for off-piste excursions, and heli-skiing on the Italian side when conditions are right (122 euros).

The remote north-east-facing bowl beyond the Col de l'Alpet on the Chalvet side is superb in good snow and has black and red pistes, too. The open section between La Montanina and Sagna Longa on the Italian side is another good powder area. Those with a car should visit Sestriere for the most challenging runs.

FOR INTERMEDIATES
Plenty of cruising terrain

The overclassified blacks are just right for adventurous intermediates, though none holds the interest for very long. The pleasantly narrow tree-lined runs to Clavière from Pian del Sole, the steepest of the routes down in the Chalvet sector and the runs off the back of Col de l'Alpet are all fine in small doses.

Average intermediates will enjoy the red runs, though most are short. On the major sector, both the runs from Collet Vert – one into Italy and one back into France – can be great fun.

Getting to Cesana via the lovely sweeping run starting at the top of the Serra Granet double-drag, and heading home from Pian del Sole, is easier than the gradings suggest, and can be tackled by less adventurous intermediates, who also have a wealth of cruising terrain high up at the top of the Les Anges sector. These are served by several upper lifts, but you have the option of continuing right down to town. These long, gentle runs are wonderfully flattering cruises.

Further afield, the run down to Clavière from the top of the Gimont drags, on the Italian side, is a beautifully gentle cruise.

287

SCHOOLS/GUIDES

2001/02 prices in euros

ESF
Classes 6 half days mornings or afternoons
1 half day: 18
6 half days: 84.5
Children's classes
Ages: Up to 12
1 half day: 18
6 half days: 83
Private lessons
Hourly or daily
29 for 1hr; for 2 or 3 people 33

CHILDCARE

The Halte Garderie takes children aged 6 months to 6 years, from 9am to 5pm. Meals you provide can be administered.

The ESF's kindergarten takes children aged 3 to 5.

FOR BEGINNERS
Good for novices and improvers
There is a fine selection of convenient nursery slopes with reliable snow at the foot of the north-facing area. Progression to longer runs could not be easier, with a very easy blue starting at Les Anges, leading on to a green and finishing at the roadside 600m/1,970ft below.

FOR CROSS-COUNTRY
Having a car widens horizons
Montgenèvre is the best of the Milky Way resorts for cross-country enthusiasts, but it's useful to have a car. The two local trails, totalling 25km/16 miles, offer quite a bit of variety, but a further 75km/47 miles of track starts in Les Alberts, 8km/5 miles away in the Clarée valley.

QUEUES
No problems most of the time
The slopes are wonderfully uncrowded during weekdays, provided surrounding resorts have snow. Some lifts become crowded at weekends and when nearby Bardonecchia is lacking snow. And queues for the two gondolas out of the village can occur first thing.

Links with Italy have improved but many of the lifts are still old and slow.

MOUNTAIN RESTAURANTS
Head for Italy
Restaurants are in very short supply locally. Most people travel back to the village for lunch. The Ca del Sol cafe-bar does a good pizza. There are several nice spots in Italy and the Gran Bouc in Clavière has been recommended.

SCHOOLS AND GUIDES
Encouraging reports
Our latest reports on the ESF are good ('great instructor, good with kids').

MONTGENÈVRE
mountain without frontier

Heliski outing from Montgenèvre.
Enjoy the best of free riding thanks to helicopters that let you on the over 3000 m italian summits.

Pearl in the Southern Alps, Montgenèvre can be proud for two reasons: optimal snowing-up and amazing sunlight for the skiers greatest pleasure.

First ski resort in France, Montgenèvre had been, in 1907, the stage of the 1st international ski competition. In the 30ies, the Parisian «jet-set» used to come there in winter.
Located on the border between France and Italy, it is today one of the jewels in the international area of the Milky Way, one of the vastest in Europe, chosen to host the Winter Olympic Games in 2006.

TOURIST OFFICE
1 : +33 492 251 252
www.montgenevre.com

Montgenèvre
1860 m   2700 m

GETTING THERE

Air Turin, transfer 2hr. Grenoble, transfer 3hr. Lyon, transfer 4½hr.

Rail Briançon (15km/9 miles) or Oulx (20km/12 miles); 5 or 6 buses per day to/from Briançon and 4 to/from Oulx.

ACTIVITIES

Indoor Library, cinema
Outdoor Natural skating rink, paragliding, snow-scooters, sledge runs

Phone numbers
From abroad use the prefix +33 and omit the initial '0' of the phone number.

TOURIST OFFICE

Postcode 05100
t 0492 215252
f 0492 219245
office.tourisme.mont
genevre@wanadoo.fr
www.montgenevre.com

FACILITIES FOR CHILDREN
Pity about the traffic
The intrusive main road apart, Montgenèvre would seem a fine family resort. Reports on the school's children's classes have been complimentary of both class size and spoken English.

Staying there

HOW TO GO
Limited choice
UK tour operators concentrate on cheap and cheerful catered chalets, though some apartments are also available and a few operators also package hotels.

Hotels There are a handful of simple places offering good value.
(2) **Valérie** (0492 219002) Central rustic old 3-star.
(2) **Napoléon** (0492 219204) 3-star on the roadside.
(1) **Alpet** (0492 219006) Basic 2-star near the centre.
(1) **Chalet des Sports** (0492 219017) Among the cheapest rooms in the Alps.
(1) **Boom** (0492 219835) Cheap and cheerful place with tiny rooms.

Self-catering Résidences La Ferme d'Augustin (0492 030457) are simple, ski-to-the-door apartments on the fringes of the main north-facing slopes, five minutes' walk (across the piste) from town.

EATING OUT
Cheap and cheerful
There are a dozen places to choose from. The Ca del Sol and the Cesar have been recommended by reporters. The Estable and Transalpin serve good-value traditional fare. Chez Pierrot and the Jamy have an authentic French feel. The 3-star Napoléon is the only hotel with a restaurant open to non-residents – a pizzeria. A trip to Clavière is worthwhile – reporters have testified to the excellence of the restaurants.

APRES-SKI
Mainly bars, but fun
The range is limited. The Graal is a friendly, unsophisticated place; the Ca del Sol bar is a cosy place with an open fire. Pub Chaberton is also recommended. The little Blue Light disco is popular. The Refuge, the Crepouse and the Jamy are the focal cafe-bars at tea-time.

OFF THE SLOPES
Very limited
There is a weekly market and you can walk the cross-country routes, but the main diversion is a bus-trip to the beautiful old town of Briançon.

STAYING IN OTHER RESORTS
Only for the dedicated
Cesana and Clavière are small villages with few facilities. Cesana is a 15-minute walk from its lifts. Clavière's nursery slope is small and steep but usually uncrowded and snow-reliable – and we have glowing reports of its ski school ('lovely instructors, brilliant with the kids, very good with adults, but big classes'). Clavière is popular with school groups and après-ski is quiet. Both resorts are best for dedicated intermediates keen to make the most of the Milky Way slopes without much après-ski.

Montgenèvre

289

SNOWPIX.COM / CHRIS GILL

← Cruising the pistes over the Franco-Italian border is fun – and now you don't need lire

Morzine 1000m/3,280ft

A lively, year-round resort linked by lift to the Portes du Soleil

WHAT IT COSTS

HOW IT RATES

The slopes
Snow	**
Extent	*****
Experts	***
Intermediates	****
Beginners	***
Convenience	**
Queues	***
Restaurants	***

The rest
Scenery	***
Resort charm	***
Off-slope	***

What's new

For 2001/02 a big new beginner-only area was created at the top of the Le Pléney gondola. A border-cross course was built nearby. A high-speed quad chair-lift replaced two drag-lifts from Grand Pré towards Chamossière. And the ESF built a big new chalet facility for children aged 3 upwards.

A lot is planned for 2002/03, for the Les Gets area. A fast six-pack is due to replace the two Nauchets drag-lifts in the Les Chavannes-Le Ranfolly sector. A new high-speed quad is planned for the La Rosta slopes. The Mont Chéry gondola will be renovated and new six-seater bubbles installed. And it is intended to build a new car park at Les Perrières on the outskirts of Les Gets, with a drive-in lift pass office and fast six-pack to take day visitors in to the slopes.

➕ Part of the vast Portes du Soleil lift network

➕ Larger local piste area than other Portes du Soleil resorts

➕ Good nightlife by French standards

➕ Quite attractive old town – a stark contrast to Avoriaz

➕ One of the easiest drives from the Channel (a car is very useful here)

➕ Few queues locally (but see minus points)

➖ Takes a while to get to Avoriaz and main Portes du Soleil circuit

➖ Bus-ride or long walk to lifts from much of the accommodation

➖ Low altitude means there is an enduring risk of poor snow, though increased snowmaking has helped

➖ Low altitude or inconvenient nursery slopes

➖ Not a great resort for experts

➖ Weekend crowds

Morzine is a long-established French resort, popular for its easy road access, traditional atmosphere and gentle tree-filled slopes, where children do not get lost and bad weather rarely causes problems. For keen piste-bashers wanting to travel the Portes du Soleil circuit, the main drawback to staying in central Morzine is having to take a bus and cable-car or several lifts to get to Avoriaz and the main circuit. Morzine's local slopes can suffer from poor snow.

Such problems can be avoided by taking a car or using a tour operator who will drive you around. The little-used Ardent gondola, a short drive from Morzine, gives access to a clockwise circuit via Châtel, missing out often crowded Avoriaz. If local snow is poor, you can visit nearby Flaine by car, which is better than Avoriaz at coping with crowds looking for snow.

The resort

Morzine is a traditional mountain town sprawling amorphously on both sides of a river gorge. In winter, under a blanket of snow, its chalet-style buildings look charming, and in spring the village quickly takes on a spruce appearance.

The old centre is next to the river and shops, restaurants and bars line the road up to the Le Pléney lifts, where more amenities are clustered. Accommodation is widely scattered, and a good multi-route bus service links all parts of the town to outlying lifts, including those for Avoriaz.

As the extensive network of bus routes implies, Morzine is a town where getting from A to B can be tricky. It is well worth making sure that your accommodation is near the lifts that you expect to be using, which for most visitors means the gondola and cable-car to Le Pléney, the gondola to Super-Morzine or the cable-car to Avoriaz.

Morzine is a family resort, and village ambience tends to be fairly subdued. Our view that the resort suits car drivers is widely shared. Roads are busy, but parking problems have been somewhat relieved by new car parks built recently near Le Pléney.

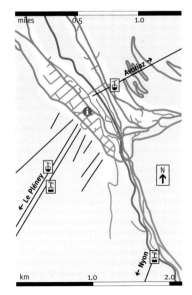

Gentle, pretty wooded slopes is what Morzine and Les Gets (pictured) are all about →

OT MORZINE

MOUNTAIN FACTS

for Portes du Soleil

Altitude	975m-2350m
	3,200ft-7,710ft
Lifts	206
Pistes	650km
	400 miles
Green	13%
Blue	38%
Red	39%
Black	10%
Snowmaking	
	252 acres
Recco detectors used	

LIFT PASSES

2002/03 prices in euros

Portes du Soleil
Covers all lifts in all 12 resorts, and shuttle-buses.
Main pass
1-day pass 34
6-day pass 164
Senior citizens
Over 60: 6-day pass 131
Children
Under 16: 6-day pass 110
Under 5: free pass
Short-term passes
Half-day pass for Portes de Soleil (adult 26).
Also (2001/02 prices) for Super-Morzine-Avoriaz (adult 21.5) and Morzine-Gets (adult 18).
Notes Discounts for groups of 13 or more and holders of the Carte Neige.
Alternative passes
2001/02 prices
Morzine-Les Gets pass covers 85 lifts (adult 6-day 118, child 88).

The mountains

The local slopes suit intermediates well, with excellent areas for beginners and near-beginners too: 'More variety than expected,' said one recent visitor. The Portes du Soleil now has an electronic lift pass system, so you can keep your pass in your pocket. Reporters have commented favourably on the recently launched system of Discovery Routes around the Portes du Soleil – choose an alpine animal that suits your ability and follow the signs displaying it around the circuit.

THE SLOPES
No need to go far afield
Morzine is not an ideal base for the Portes du Soleil circuit (described in the Avoriaz, Châtel and Champéry chapters). But it has an extensive local area shared with Les Gets.

A cable-car and parallel gondola rise from the edge of central Morzine to **Le Pléney**, where numerous routes return to the valley, including a run down to Les Fys – a quiet junction of chairs which access **Nyon** and, in the opposite direction, the ridge separating Morzine from the **Les Gets** slopes. Nyon can also be accessed by cable-car, situated

a bus-ride from Morzine, and is connected to the slopes of Les Gets higher up the valley that separates the two, with a lift up from Le Grand Pré to Le Ranfolly. The Nyon sector has two peaks – Pointe de Nyon and Chamossière – accessible from Nyon and Le Grand Pré respectively.

From Le Ranfolly you can descend directly to Morzine without using a lift. To get to Morzine from the slopes above Les Gets you go first to the mid-mountain lift junction of Les Chavannes, then to the Folliets chair which takes you up to Le Pléney.

Beyond Les Gets is another small but worthwhile sector, on Mont Chéry. The short walk or 'petit train' shuttle through the village from the base of Chavannes takes about five minutes.

One means of access to the main Portes du Soleil circuit (on the opposite side of the valley from Le Pléney) is via a gondola from near the centre of town – another handy 'petit train' shuttle service runs between this and the Le Pléney lifts. The gondola takes you up to **Super-Morzine**, and a series of pistes and lifts lead to Avoriaz. A recent reporter found this route 'not worth the trouble', preferring the alternatives. These are a bus-ride

boarding *Avoriaz is the hard-core boarding HQ of the Portes du Soleil, with excellent terrain-park and half-pipe – and a special pass for those whose only interest is riding them. CSb Mountain Holidays (formerly Chalet Snowboard) has Morzine chalets, and former British Champ Becci Malthouse teaches with the British Alpine Ski & Snowboard school. With interesting, tree-lined runs and few drags, the local Morzine slopes are good for beginners and intermediates and there's also a boarder-cross area. There are a few lively bars.*

or short drive to either Les Prodains (from where you can get a cable-car to Avoriaz or a chair-lift into the **Hauts Forts** slopes above it) or to Ardent, where the recently renovated gondola accesses Les Lindarets for lifts towards Châtel, Avoriaz or Champéry. The tree-lined slopes in this area are good in poor visibility and the area at the top of the gondola is a good one for mixed ability groups to meet up. Car trips to Flaine and Chamonix are also feasible.

SNOW RELIABILITY
Poor
Morzine has a very low average height, and when snow disappears from the valley, the local slopes become very small and unconnected. There is some snowmaking, most noticeably on runs linking Nyon and Le Pléney, and on the reds and blues back to town. Les Gets recently benefited from extended snowmaking – but more is needed.

FOR EXPERTS
Limited on-piste
The run down from Pointe de Nyon is challenging, but for piste challenges the cable-car at Les Prodains is the place to head for, taking you up to Avoriaz. The Hauts Forts black runs, including the World Cup downhill

course, are excellent. The above-the-tree-line slopes of Chamossière offer some of the best off-piste possibilities, and Mont Chéry is also well worth exploring. We've also had reports of great off-piste off the back of Col du Fornet down towards the Vallée de la Manche (but you'd need a guide).

FOR INTERMEDIATES
Something for everyone
Good intermediates will enjoy the challenging reds and blacks down from the Chamossière and Pointe de Nyon high points. Mont Chéry at Les Gets has some fine steepish runs.

Those of average ability have a great choice, though most runs are rather short. Le Ranfolly accesses a series of good cruisers on the Les Gets side of the ridge, and a nice piste back to Le Grand Pré. Le Pléney has a compact network of pistes that are ideal for groups with mixed abilities: mainly moderate intermediate runs, but with some easier alternatives for the more timid, and a single challenging route for the aggressive. Nyon's slopes are rather bitty for those not up to at least the Chamossière runs.

Less experienced intermediates have lots of options on Le Pléney, including a snow-gun-covered cruise from the

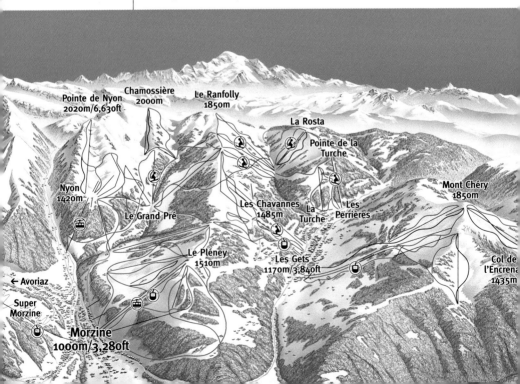

top to the main lift station. Heading from Le Ranfolly to Le Grand Pré is also a nice run. And the slopes down to Les Gets from Le Pléney are easy when conditions allow (they face south).

The new high-speed chairs planned for 2002/03 will make Le Ranfolly and La Rosta sectors more attractive.

And, of course, there is the whole of the Portes du Soleil circuit to explore by going up the opposite side of the valley to Avoriaz or Les Lindarets.

FOR BEGINNERS
Good for novices and improvers
The wide village nursery slopes are convenient, and benefit from snow-guns. Some of the best progression runs are over at Nyon. However, adventurous novices also have the option of easy pistes around Le Pléney. Near-beginners can get over to Les Gets via Le Pléney, and return via Le Ranfolly.

FOR CROSS-COUNTRY
Good variety
There is a wide variety of cross-country trails, not all at valley level. The best section is in the pretty Vallée de la Manche beside the Nyon mountain up to the Lac de Mines d'Or where there is a good restaurant. The Pléney-Chavannes loop is pleasant and relatively snow-reliable.

QUEUES
Few problems when snow is good
Queues are not usually a problem in the local area but we had a report of 'horrendous queues and frequent lift breakdown in the Les Gets area' this year – doubtless why they are planning several fast new lifts. The Nyon cable-car and Belvédère chair-lift (Le Pléney) are weekend bottlenecks. Queues to and from Avoriaz are much improved in recent times, but are still bad when snow is in short supply.

MOUNTAIN RESTAURANTS
Within reach of some good huts
The nice little place at the foot of the d'Atray chair is perhaps the best local hut. On the Avoriaz side, Les Lindarets, Les Marmottes and Plaine Dranse are not too far and have some good restaurants. Pommes de Pin at the top of the télécabine d'Ardent is friendly with reasonably priced food. The Restaurant des Crêtes de Zore above Super-Morzine is good.

SCHOOLS AND GUIDES
British ski school here
The British Alpine Ski & Snowboard School, featuring BASI-qualified instructors, is based in Morzine and Les Gets and we have good reports on the lessons. Reports on the ESF are generally good except for some complaints about class sizes. One reporter visiting during half-term week this year had a tale of '22 people in my son's class with one instructor and some sort of helper'.

FACILITIES FOR CHILDREN
Lots of possibilities
The facilities of the Outa nursery are quite impressive, but we've received reports of poor spoken English and low staff ratios. A new ESF childcare centre, Club Piou-Piou, opened last season, but we have no reports. The Dérêches Farm offers days learning about animals, snow-shoeing and tobogganing. A reporter's three and five year olds were both happy with the ESF, making 'rapid progress with friendly, attentive instructors'. But see above for a warning about class sizes. Esprit Ski's facilities are good, with in-chalet nurseries, an afternoon Snow Club for children attending morning ski school and their own teaching scheme. Ski Famille and Ski Hillwood are other family specialists, based in Les Gets.

SCHOOLS/GUIDES
2001/02 prices in euros

ESF
Classes 6 days
5hr: 9.30-noon and 2.30-5pm; 2½hr: am or pm
6 half-days: 107
Private lessons
Hourly
30 for 1 or 2 people
Children's classes
Ages: 7 to 12
6 full days including lunch: 290

CHILDCARE
The Halte Garderie l'Outa (0450 792600) takes children aged 2 months to 5 years, from 8.30 to 6pm. From age 3 they can have one-hour introductory lessons. The Piou-Piou takes children aged 3 to 12, with ESF instruction and lunch provided (half or full days).

Staying there

GETTING THERE

Air Geneva, transfer 1½hr. Lyon, transfer 3½hr.

Rail Cluses or Thonon (30km/19 miles); regular bus connections to resort.

HOW TO GO
Good-value hotels and chalets

The tour operator market concentrates on hotels and chalets.

Chalets There's a wide choice, with something to suit all tastes. Position varies enormously: you can be in the centre of town or right on the edge of the slopes; many are on the outskirts, however, without either convenience. Ski Activity had a luxurious new chalet built for last season near the Nyon cable-car and Ski Morzine tell us that they are converting a disused 4-storey nunnery into a 'superlative' catered chalet and drive their clients to/from the Ardent gondola each day.

Hotels The handful of 3-star hotels includes some quite smooth ones. But the core of the resort is its dozens of 2-stars and 1-stars. If there is a resort with more hotels in the Logis de France group, we have yet to find it. (((((4)))) **Dahu** (0450 759292) Upmarket 3-star; elegant public areas and good restaurant and pool. Some distance from all lifts and public buses except the Ardent route, but private shuttle. (((((4)))) **Airelles** (0450 747121) Central 3-star close to Pléney lifts and Prodains and Nyon bus routes. Good pool. (((((4)))) **Champs Fleuris** (0450 791444) Comfy 3-star next to Pléney lifts. Pool. (((((3)))) **Tremplin** (0450 791231) Also next to the lifts; 'friendly staff, good food'. (((((3)))) **Bergerie** (0450 791369) Rustic, old-fashioned chalet with a few rooms

and many more studios, in centre. Friendly staff. Pool and gym. (((2))) **Côtes** (0450 790996) Simple, upwardly-mobile 2-star, with more studios than rooms. Pool compensates for poor position on the edge of town. (((2))) **Equipe** (0450 791143) One of the best 2-stars; next to the Pléney lift.

Self-catering The Télémark apartments are high quality, and close to the Super-Morzine gondola. We're told those by the Prodains cable-car are excellent.

EATING OUT
A fine choice

Morzine is scarcely a gourmet's resort, but it has a wide choice of good restaurants. The expensive Chamade has high-quality French cuisine, Café Chaud is popular and atmospheric, and does good fondue, The Airelles has a fine restaurant (Jardins d'Ulysse), known for its hot buffets, and the Dahu also has good food. The Etale is an excellent, atmospheric pizza joint, bedecked in hundreds of different

---

Selected chalets in Morzine and Les Gets

ACTIVITIES

Indoor Skating, bowling, cinemas, massage, table tennis, fitness track **Outdoor** Horse-riding, sleigh rides, snow-shoe classes, artificial climbing wall, tennis, paragliding

Phone numbers
From abroad use the prefix +33 and omit the initial '0' of the phone number.

MORZINE TOURIST OFFICE

Postcode 74110
t 0450 747272
f 0450 790348
touristoffice@morzine-avoriaz.com
www.morzine.com

football scarves, also serving local specialities – booking is advisable. Reporters also recommend Clin d'Oeil, the Don Camillo, the Gavottes, the Grange and the Combe á Zore.

APRES-SKI
One of the livelier French resorts

Every evening on the Le Pléney slopes last season, the tourist office organised some family fun such as tobogganing, torchlight descents, ski races, firework displays, washed down with free vin chaud.

Nightlife is good by French standards. Le Dixie gets animated, with Eurosport, MTV, a great little cellar bar and some live music. At the Crépuscule, near the Le Pléney lifts, dancing on the tables in ski boots to deafening music seems compulsory at après time. Just below, the Cavern is popular with resort staff; the Buddha, with cosy Asian decor, is great for a quieter drink. The tiny Sherpa, on the outskirts of town, is also worth a try. L'Opéra, The Paradis du Laury's and La Caverne (a ten-pin bowling alley-cum-disco-cum-pool-hall-cum-bar) are the late night haunts. Taxis to outlying accommodation are said to be difficult

to come by in the small hours. There are two cinemas.

OFF THE SLOPES
Quite good; excursions possible

There is an excellent ice rink, which stages ice hockey matches and skating galas. Some hotels have pools, which non-residents can pay to use. Buses run to Thonon for shopping, and car owners can drive to Geneva, Annecy or Montreux. There are lots of very pretty walks, and other activities include horse-drawn sleigh rides, horse-riding, paragliding and a cheese factory visit.

Les Gets 1170m/3,840ft

Decent children's facilities, French ambience, convenience, nice village (partly car-free), restaurants, fine nursery slopes and reasonable prices make Les Gets a good choice for families and many others. Several reporters said that it feels tucked away and rather secret. But it's a major trek to get into the main Portes du Soleil circuit on snow.

Morzine

295

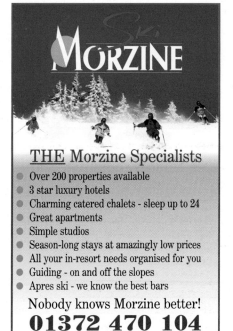

THE RESORT

Les Gets is a little old village of mainly traditional chalet buildings, 6km/4 miles from Morzine. Although the village has a scattered appearance, most facilities are conveniently close to the main lift station. It is on a through road, but traffic does not intrude too much. It is fairly quiet in the evenings except at weekends when the atmosphere becomes more chic.

The local pass covers all Les Gets, Nyon and Le Pléney lifts, saves a fair bit on a Portes du Soleil pass, and is worth considering by less experienced skiers and riders if the snow is good.

THE MOUNTAINS

Les Gets is not an ideal base for the Portes du Soleil, but its local slopes have far more pistes than any of the resorts on the circuit.

Slopes As well as the local slopes that are linked to Morzine (see earlier in chapter), Les Gets has runs on Mont Chéry, accessed by gondola and parallel chair. The front slopes face south-east – bad news at this altitude; but the other two flanks are shadier.

Snow reliability Despite having a slightly higher elevation than Morzine, snow conditions can again be erratic. A lot more snow-guns were installed recently, improving cover to the resort.

Experts Black runs from the Chéry Nord chair are steep and challenging in parts.

Intermediates High-mileage piste-bashers will enjoy cruising the Portes du Soleil circuit, and the local slopes are not bad for the less adventurous.

Beginners The village nursery slopes are convenient, but there are better, more snow-sure ones up at Chavannes. Progression is simple, with a very easy run between Chavannes and the resort and a pleasant green from La Rosta.

Snowboarding The local Les Gets and Morzine slopes are good for beginners and intermediates. Experts will enjoy the excellent terrain-park in Avoriaz.

Cross-country Morzine is better, with excellent trails. But Les Gets has 46km/29 miles of good varied loops on Mont Chéry and Les Chavannes.

Queues Provided there's good snow, not much of a problem, though weekend crowds are a drawback.

Mountain restaurants See Morzine.

Schools and guides We've had mixed reports of the ESF, with tales of 'instructors shouting at our four-year-olds in French' but also of children enjoying 'a great instructor'. Beginners

should, if conditions are poor, try to have lessons at Chavannes.

Facilities for children There is a non-ski nursery for children aged three months to three years, and two ski kindergartens. Ski Espace's 'Ile des Enfants' is reputedly the better of the two. ESF's Club Fantaski has been criticised for inattentive supervision. Tour operators Ski Famille and Ski Hillwood have been recommended.

STAYING THERE

How to go Many visitors stay in private chalets, quite a few of which are on the British market in catered form. Most are pleasant, comfy, no-frills places.

Hotels All the hotels are 3-star and below, mostly cheap and cheerful old 2-stars. The 3-star Crychar (0450 758050), 100m/330ft from central Les Gets at the foot of the slopes, is one of the best. The 2-star Alpen Sports (0450 758055) is a friendly, family run hotel – 'excellent food and good value for money' says a reporter. We've also had good reports of the the Nagano (0450 797146) and the Marmotte (0450 758033) – both 3-star.

Self-catering The tourist office has a long list of apartments.

Eating out Les Gets has a wide variety of places to eat – including Le Boomerang, with an Australian flavour. Most hotels have good restaurants. The Tyrol and the Schuss are good for pizza. The rustic Vieux Chêne for Savoyard specialities; the Flambeau and Tourbillon are also recommended.

Après-ski Après-ski is quiet, especially on weekdays. The Pub Irlandaise and Prings, an English-owned pub, get very crowded, and Bar les Copeaux has been recommended. The Igloo and Havana Noche are popular discos.

Off the slopes There's a well-equipped fitness centre with a pool, and an artificial ice rink. Outings to Geneva, Lausanne and Montreux are possible.

A huge variety of villages spread across a vast playground

WHAT IT COSTS

HOW IT RATES

The slopes

Snow	****
Extent	****
Experts	***
Intermediates	*****
Beginners	****
Convenience	*****
Queues	***
Restaurants	**

The rest

Scenery	****
Resort charm	*
Off-slope	*

What's new

For 2002/03, getting to Roche de Mio (and so to the glacier) will be made much faster by two new high-speed six-packs. One will start from Plagne Bellecôte and go up to the top of the ridge which leads to Champagny. The other starts a little below the ridge and takes you on up to Roche de Mio.

A couple of years ago the Grande Rochette gondola from Plagne-Centre was replaced by a new one with triple the capacity.

For 2003/04, the long-awaited link to Les Arcs is due to open – the world's biggest cable-car, a double-decker holding 200 people, will link Montchavin to Plan-Peisey in only four minutes. The result will be the world's third biggest linked ski area. At the same time, the Roche di Mio gondola will be renovated and its capacity increased by almost half and there will be a lot more snowmaking.

➕ Extensive intermediate slopes, plus plentiful off-piste terrain

➕ Good nursery slopes

➕ High and fairly snow-sure – and with some wonderful views

➕ Purpose-built resort units are convenient for the slopes, and some are not unpleasant

➕ Attractive, traditional-style villages lower down share the slopes

➕ Wooded runs of lower resorts are useful in poor weather

➕ Good cross-country trails

➖ Pistes in the main bowl don't have much to offer experts

➖ Pistes can get very crowded in places

➖ Lower villages can suffer from poor snow – Champagny especially

➖ Unattractive architecture in some of the higher resort units

➖ Not many green runs for nervous beginners to go on to – though some blues are very easy

➖ Nightlife very limited

With 220km/137 miles of slopes and 86% of these being blue or red, the area is an intermediate's paradise. And with much-needed lift improvements happening at last, the resort is going up in our estimation. It has a reputation for plug-ugly, soulless, purpose-built villages and some of them justify that view. But there are ten different villages to choose from – and as well as delightful old mountain villages at the foot of the slopes, there are some attractive purpose-built centres too. While the slopes aren't steep enough for on-piste expert fun, those who are prepared to hire a guide can have a splendid time off-piste with some long descents which are often deserted and untracked compared with the classic off-piste runs of more macho resorts like Val d'Isère.

The resort

La Plagne consists of no fewer than ten separate 'villages'; six are purpose-built at altitude in the main bowl, on or above the tree line and linked by road, lifts and pistes; the other four are scattered around outside the bowl.

Each is self-contained with its own shops, bars, restaurants, schools and lift pass offices. Even the core resorts vary a lot in character. The first to be built, in the 1960s, was Plagne-Centre – still the focal point for shops and après-ski. Typical of its time, it has ugly blocks and dreary indoor 'malls' that house a reasonable selection of shops, bars and restaurants. Some new developments just above Plagne-Centre are more pleasing to the eye.

Lifts radiate from Centre to all sides of the bowl, the major one being the big new twin-cable gondola to Grande Rochette. Another is a cable-car up to the even more obtrusive 'village' of Aime-la-Plagne – a group of monolithic blocks that attract derisory comments from most reporters.

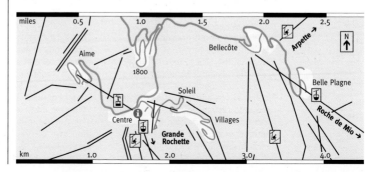

The mountains are pretty but some of the high, purpose-built centres like Aime-la-Plagne aren't ➔

LIFT PASSES

2002/03 prices in euros

La Plagne
Covers all lifts in La Plagne and Champagny-en-Vanoise.
Beginners Free baby-lift in each centre.
Main pass
1-day pass 36
6-day pass 171
(low season 128)
Senior citizens
Over 60: 6-day pass 146
Over 72: free pass
Children
Under 14: 6-day pass 128
Under 5: free pass
Short-term passes
Half-day pass (26.5).
Single ascent on inter-area links.
Notes Standard 6-day pass and over allows one day each in Les Arcs, Tignes-Val-d'Isère, the Three Valleys, Pralognan-la-Vanoise and Les Saisies.
5% discount on presentation of a La Plagne pass in your name from the last two seasons.
Family discounts are also available.
Alternative passes
Village area passes available for Montchavin-Les Coches, Plagne Montalbert, or Champagny.
Limited 'Discovery' passes in each area.

Below these two, and a bit of a backwater, is Plagne 1800, where the buildings are small-scale and chalet style, and many are indeed individual chalets that find their way on to the UK package market. Access to the main bowl from here is by lifts to Aime-la-Plagne and reporters comment on a drag-lift which links with no other lifts.

A little way above Plagne-Centre is the newest development, Plagne-Soleil, still small as yet, but with attractive new chalets. This area is officially attached to Plagne-Villages, which is a rather strung-out but attractive collection of small-scale apartments and chalets in traditional style, handy for the slopes but for nothing else.

The two other core resort units are a bus-ride away, on the other side of a low hill. The large apartment buildings of Plagne-Bellecôte form a wall at the foot of the slopes down to it. Some way above it is Belle-Plagne – as its name suggests, easy on the eye, with a Disneyesque neo-Savoyard look, and complete with entirely underground parking. Reporters have complained of exhaustion when moving between the different levels in Belle Plagne (the bars and other facilities are mainly in the lower part), but have also praised the efforts that have been made to make it feel like a village. The two new chairs for 2002/03 (see What's new) will mean Bellecôte will now have good links to both the snow-sure glacier area and to two of the lower resorts in the valleys outside the bowl – the old village of Montchavin and its recently developed neighbour Les Coches at the northern extremity of the area, and Champagny at the southern extremity. At the western extremity is the modern Montalbert development. For a description of these lower villages, see the end of this chapter.

A free bus system between the core villages within the bowl runs until after midnight. But you may have to change in Plagne Centre.

Day trips to Les Arcs are easy, trips to Val-d'Isère, Tignes or the Three Valleys more time-consuming – all are covered for a day with a six-day pass.

The mountains

The majority of the slopes in the main bowl are above the tree line, though there are trees scattered around most of the resort centres. The slopes outside the bowl are open at the top but descend into woodland. The gondola up to the exposed glacier slopes on Bellecôte, to the west of the main bowl, is prone to closure by high winds or poor weather and the top drags are normally shut in winter. We have had a glowing report of the Salomon Station in Plagne Centre where you can test any Salomon equipment under the guidance of hosts/instructors for 60 euros a day.

THE SLOPES
Multi-centred; can be confusing
La Plagne boasts 220km/137 miles of pistes over a wide area that can be broken down into seven distinct but interlinked sectors. From Plagne-Centre you can take a lift up to **Le Biolley**, from where you can head back to Centre, to Aime-la-Plagne or down gentle runs to **Montalbert**, from where you ride several successive lifts back up. But the main lift out of Plagne-Centre leads up to **La Grande Rochette**. From here there are good sweeping runs back down and an easier one over to Plagne-Bellecôte, or you can drop over the back into the predominantly south-facing **Champagny** sector (from which a lift arrives back

MOUNTAIN FACTS

Altitude 1250m-3250m
4,100ft-10,66oft

Lifts	109
Pistes	220km
	137 miles
Green	9%
Blue	58%
Red	28%
Black	5%

Snowmaking 50 acres
Recco detectors used

up at Les Vardons and another brings you out much further east). From the Champagny sector there are great views over to Courchevel.

From Plagne-Bellecôte and Belle Plagne, an old gondola heads up to **Roche de Mio**. For 2002/03 two new fast chairs will get you there too (see What's New). From there runs spread out in all directions – towards La Plagne, Champagny or **Montchavin/Les Coches**. Montchavin/Les Coches can also be reached by taking a chair from Plagne-Bellecôte to Arpette. From Roche de Mio you can also take a gondola down then up to the **Bellecôte glacier**. The drag-lifts at the top serve summer skiing and are normally shut in winter – but if open they offer excellent snow and stunning views.

In good snow there is an easy off-piste run from the foot of Bellecôte to Les Bauches, and the Montchavin slopes. Otherwise, you have to return to Roche de Mio.

The special 'evasion' map identifies five circuits of varying difficulty.

Several reporters have indicated that run grading is inconsistent; some runs are more difficult than their grading suggests, others are easier.

SNOW RELIABILITY
Generally good except low down

Most of La Plagne's runs are snow-sure, being at altitudes between 2000m and 2700m (6,56oft and 8,86oft) on the largely north-facing open slopes above the purpose-built centres. But during the exceptionally poor conditions of early 2002 several reporters commented on poor piste grooming, rocks and bare patches and the need for more snowmaking on the runs into the villages – especially the busy runs into Plagne-Bellecôte. 40km/25 miles of extra snowmaking is planned over the next few seasons.

Runs down to the valley resorts can cause more problems, and you may have to take the lifts at times. This is particularly true of Champagny, where the two home runs are both south-facing. The runs down to Les Coches and Montchavin are north-facing and have snowmaking – these, and a few runs around Montalbert and Plagne-Bellecôte, are the main ones with snowmaking at the moment.

FOR EXPERTS
A few good blacks and off-piste

There are two great black runs from Bellecôte to the chair-lift up to the gondola mid-station at Col de la Chiaupe – both beautiful long runs with a vertical of some 1000m/3,300ft that take you away from the lift system. But these are often closed due to too much or too little snow.

The long Emile Allais down from above Aime-la-Plagne through the forest is classified black only at its final stage. With a couple of drag-lifts taking you back up, it is little used, although north-facing and very enjoyable in good snow. The shorter Coqs and Morbleu runs in the same sector are seriously steep.

The long, sweeping Mont de la Guerre red, with a 1250m/4,100ft vertical from Les Verdons to Champagny, is also a beautiful run in good snow (a rare event).

There are other good long reds to cruise around on. But experts will get the best out of La Plagne if they hire a guide and explore the vast off-piste potential – which takes longer to get tracked out than in more 'macho' resorts. There are popular off-piste variants on the aforementioned black runs from Bellecôte down to Les Bauches (a drop of over 1400m/4,60oft). You can also head down off-

FRANCE

300

piste to Peisey-Nancroix and take the lifts up to the Les Arcs slopes. Another beautiful and out-of-the-way off-piste run from Bellecôte is over the Col du Nant glacier to Champagny-le-Haut (it starts with a long climb to the top of the glacier if the summer skiing drag-lifts aren't working).

In fresh snow, you can find great powder in the woods above Montchavin and Montalbert.

FOR INTERMEDIATES
Great variety

Virtually the whole of La Plagne's area is a paradise for intermediates, with blue and red runs wherever you look. Your main choice will be whether to settle for one area for the day and explore it thoroughly, or just cruise

around the pistes that form the main arteries of the network.

For early intermediates there are plenty of gentle blue motorway pistes in the main La Plagne bowl, and a long, interesting run from Roche de Mio back to Belle Plagne, Les Inversins (involving a tunnel). The blue runs either side of Arpette, on the Montchavin side of the main bowl, are glorious cruises. In poor weather the best place to be is in the trees on the gentle runs leading down to Montalbert. The easiest way over to Champagny is from the Roche de Mio area rather than from Grande Rochette.

Better intermediates have lots of delightful long red runs to try. Roche de Mio to Les Bauches is a drop of 900m/2,95oft (the first half 'Le Clapet'

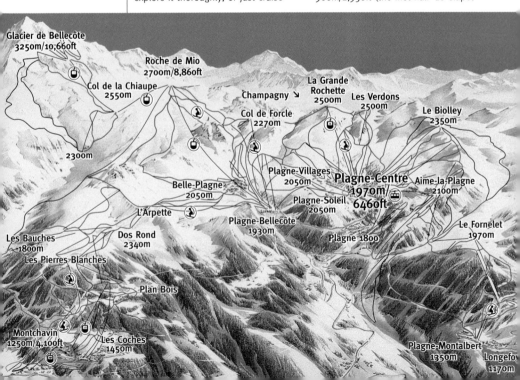

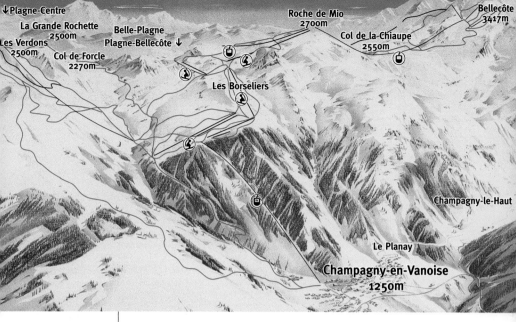

↓Plagne-Centre

La Grande Rochette
2500m

Les Verdons
2500m

Col de Forcle
2270m

Belle-Plagne
Plagne-Bellecôte ↓

Les Borseliers

Roche de Mio
2700m

Col de la Chiaupe
2550m

Bellecôte
3417m

Champagny-le-Haut

Le Planay

Champagny-en-Vanoise
1250m

is a fabulous varied run with lots of off-piste diversions possible; the second half is marked as a black but isn't that steep). There are challenging red mogul pitches down from the glacier to the Col de la Chiaupe mid-station. And the main La Plagne bowl has enjoyable reds in all sectors.

The Champagny sector has a couple of tough reds – Kamikaze and Hara-Kiri – leading from Grande Rochette. And the long blue cruise Bozelet has one surprisingly steep section. The Mont de la Guerre red to Champagny (1250m/4,100ft vertical) is a satisfying run for adventurous intermediates.

FOR BEGINNERS
Excellent facilities for the novice
La Plagne is a good place to learn, with generally good snow and above average facilities for beginners, especially children. Each of the main centres has nursery slopes on its doorstep. There's a free drag-lift in each resort as well. There are no long green runs to progress to, but no shortage of easy blues. The Plan Bois

area above Les Coches has good gentle slopes. Several reporters commented that the runs back into Plagne 1800 were difficult for novices.

CROSS-COUNTRY
Open and wooded trails
There are 90km/56 miles of prepared and marked cross-country pistes scattered around. The most beautiful of these are the 30km/19 miles of winding track set out in the sunny valley around Champagny-le-Haut. The north-facing areas have more wooded trails that link the various centres.

QUEUES
Main problems being sorted
La Plagne used to have some big bottlenecks. But the new Grande Rochette gondola from Plagne-Centre has solved the problem there and the two new six-packs for 2002/03 (see What's New) will take the pressure off the old Roche de Mio gondola and the Arpette chair from Plagne-Bellecôte towards Montchavin. Two six-packs in the Champagny sector have greatly

boarding La Plagne offers some pretty good terrain for all levels of rider – there's a good mix of long, easy runs and high, open slopes with some fantastic off-piste variations that should be done with a guide. Whether on- or off-piste, be prepared for some flat areas, though. There are terrain-parks at Plagne-Bellecôte, Belle-Plagne and above Montchavin-Les Coches. The broad, gentle pistes are ideal for beginners and carvers (crowds permitting). Most lifts are gondolas or chairs, though there are still some difficult-to-avoid drag-lifts.

CHILDCARE

There are ESF ski kindergartens in all the high resort units, generally taking children from age 3. The ESF also runs all-day nurseries in most of the villages, mostly taking children aged 2 to 6 (18 months to 3 years in Belle Plagne). In Centre, independent nursery Marie Christine does much the same.

In Montchavin and Les Coches very young skiers go to the Nursery Club, the ESF taking over at age 4.

improved things on that side.

But there are still several lifts that can generate queues that you can't avoid, once you've descended to them – at Les Bauches for example. And the gondola to the glacier is queue-prone when snow is poor lower down.

Crowds on the pistes have been as much of a problem as lift queues, particularly above Bellecôte in the afternoon (and this is likely to get worse as more lifts are improved).

MOUNTAIN RESTAURANTS
An improving choice

Mountain restaurants are numerous, varied and crowded only in peak periods, as many people prefer to descend to one of the resorts – particularly Champagny or Montchavin/Les Coches – at the end of the morning. Recommendations by readers include the Crystal des Neiges, Carroley, Plan Bois, Plan Soleil and Preizes on the Montchavin/Les Coches slopes. Two great rustic restaurants in which to hole up in poor weather for a

long lunch of Savoyard dishes are the Sauget, above Montchavin, and Au Bon Vieux Temps, just below Aime-la-Plagne. Reservations may be required at either. Chalet des Colosses above Plagne Bellecôte and Chalets des Inversens at Roche de Mio ('fabulous views, good food') have been highly recommended. We love Roc des Blanchets at the top of the Champagny gondola – friendly staff, both table-and self-service, beautiful views over to Courchevel from the terrace and good basic cooking. The little Breton cafe at the bottom of the Quillis lift at the start of the Levasset piste has been recommended. The Forperet, above Montalbert, is also popular.

SCHOOLS AND GUIDES
Better alternatives to ESF

Each centre has its own ESF school, offering classes for all abilities. Groups can be much too large (a visitor reports seeing classes of up to 20 students) and instructors speak English of varying standard. But reports about

---

Selected chalets in La Plagne

SKI BEAT *Chalet specialists*   T **01243 780 405**   **www.skibeat.co.uk**

Ski Beat specialises in quality catered chalet holidays to La Plagne, Les Arcs, La Tania and Val d'Isère.

A 'Select Service' is provided in chalet Beryl (pictured) as well as other chalets in each resort.

Ski Beat has a good selection of chalets which sleep 6-20 guests. The chalets are spacious with comfortable living rooms and most bedrooms are en-suite. Ski Beat offers superb food, ski hosting and a childcare service.

Travel options include flights at civilised times, daytime and overnight trains and self-drive.

On-line availability and booking service.

CHALET BERYL →

SCHOOLS/GUIDES

2002/03 prices in euros

ESF
Schools in all centres. Prices vary; Belle-Plagne's are given here.
Classes 6 days 2½hr, 3hr, 5hr, 6hr, depending on centre, day and season
6 full days: 185 (275 during French February school holidays)
Children's classes
Ages: Up to 13 or 16 depending on village
6 full days: 166 (225 during French February school holidays)
Private lessons
1hr, 1½hr, 2hr
31 for 1hr

EL Pro
In Belle-Plagne
Classes 6 days 3hr am or pm
6 half days: 175
Children's classes
Ages: Up to 14
6 full days: 185

Oxygène
In Plagne-Centre
Classes 6 days am or pm
5 mornings: 171
Children's classes
Ages: 3 to 12
5 mornings: 171
Private lessons
Hourly, 35 for 1hr

GETTING THERE

Air Geneva, transfer 3½hr. Lyon, transfer 3½hr. Chambéry, transfer 2½hr.

Rail Aime (18km/11 miles) and Bourg-St-Maurice (35km/22 miles) (Eurostar service to Bourg-St-Maurice and Aime available); frequent buses from station.

private lessons are generally positive. However, the consensus seems to be that the alternatives are preferable. The Oxygène school in Plagne-Centre has impressed reporters. And this year we have had yet another glowing report on the El Pro school in Belle-Plagne ('good English, asked us what we wanted to do, strong focus on technique and safety'). We have had good reports on Evolution 2 (based in Montchavin) – 'Wonderful,' says the parent of one junior pupil. Antenne Handicap offers private lessons for skiers with any kind of disability.

FACILITIES FOR CHILDREN
Good choice
Children are well catered for with facilities in each of the villages. The nursery at Belle-Plagne is 'excellent, with good English spoken'. However, one reporter complained that her daughter was the only English speaker in her ESF class. The Club Med at Aime-la-Plagne is one of their 'family' villages. Several UK chalet operators run childcare services.

Staying there

HOW TO GO
Plenty of packages
For a resort that is very apartment-dominated, there is a surprising number of attractive chalets available through British tour operators. There are few hotels, but there are some attractive, simple 2-stars in the lower villages. There are two Club Meds. Accommodation in the outlying satellite resorts is described at the end of the chapter. A reporter suggests checking the resort website for special promotional deals.
Chalets There's a large number available – the majority are fairly simple, small, and located in 1800.
Hotels There are very few, all of 2-star or 3-star grading.
Ⓒ **Balcons** (0479 557676) New 3-star at Belle-Plagne. Pool.
Ⓒ **Eldorador** (0479 091209) Adequate hotel in Belle-Plagne – 'Single rooms tiny, food good but service chaotic,' says a 2002 visitor.
Ⓒ **Terra Nova** (0479 557900) Big, new, 120-room 3-star in Plagne-Centre.
Self-catering La Plagne is the ultimate apartment resort, but communal facilities are generally poor. Fortunately, many tour operators have allocations in the above-average Pierre

et Vacances apartments in Belle-Plagne and the relatively spacious MGM apartments in Aime-la-Plagne. Two new 4-star residences – in Aime-La-Plagne and Plagne-Villages have also improved the general standard.

EATING OUT
Nothing fancy
Throughout the resort there is a good range of casual restaurants including pizzerias and traditional Savoyard places serving raclettes and fondue.
Reader recommendations in Plagne-Centre include the Métairie ('the most enjoyable we've encountered in the Alps') and the Bec Fin ('nice atmosphere, best tomato soup in Europe, but food quality variable').
In Plagne-Villages, the Chevrette is good for pizzas and steaks. In Plagne 1800, the Loup Garrou, next to the chair-lift and the Mama Mia pizzeria have been praised. Au Bon Vieux Temps (see Mountain restaurants) at Aime-la-Plagne is open in the evening.
In Plagne-Bellecôte, the Ferme and Chalet des Colosses are recommended for Savoyard specialities. The Matafan in Belle-Plagne is popular for Savoyard dishes (at lunch as well as dinner). The Cloche, Pappagone pizzeria and Maître Kanter have also been recommended.

APRES-SKI
Bars, bars, bars
Though fairly quiet during low season, La Plagne has a wide range of après-ski, catering particularly for the younger crowd. In Belle-Plagne, Mat's and the Cheyenne are the main bars. The Maître Kanter has been recommended. The King Café (with a massive TV) and the Luna are the liveliest bars in Plagne-Centre, and sometimes have live music. Plagne 1800 is fairly quiet at night – the Mine (complete with old train and mining artifacts) is the best place. The Lincoln Pub in Plagne-Soleil is recommended. Plagne-Bellecôte is very limited at night, with only one real bar – Showtime. Aime-la-Plagne is also quiet. Neal's (Plagne-Centre), the Jet 73 (Plagne-Bellecôte) and the Saloon (Belle-Plagne) are the main discos.

OFF THE SLOPES
OK for the active
As well as the sports and fitness facilities, winter walks along marked trails are pleasant. It's also easy to get up the mountain on the gondolas,

← Champagny: a charming mountain village with a powerful gondola into the slopes

OT LA PLAGNE / PHILIPPE GAL

Les Coches (1450m/4,760ft) is only a walk away, and shares the same slopes. It is a sympathetically designed modern mini-resort that reporters have liked for its 'small, quiet and friendly' feel and its traffic-free centre. It has its own school and kindergarten. The Last One pub is good for après-ski, with a big screen TV and regular live bands. Poze and Taverne du Monchu are recommended for eating out.

Montalbert (1350m/4,430ft) is a traditional but much expanded village with quicker access into the main area – though it's a long way from here across to the Bellecôte glacier. The local slopes are easy and wooded – a useful insurance against bad visibility. The Aigle Rouge (0479 555105) is a simple hotel.

Champagny-en-Vanoise (1250m/ 4,100ft) is a charming village in a pretty, wooded setting, with its modern expansion done sensitively. Champagny is better placed than any of the other outlying villages for access into the main bowl – and well placed for an outing by taxi or car to Courchevel (or the beautiful Vanoise national park with its 500km/310 miles of marked walking paths). Given good snow, there are lovely runs home from above Plagne-Centre but their southerly orientation means you may have to get a gondola instead. There are several hotels, of which the two best are both in the Logis de France consortium. The Glières (0479 550552) is a rustic old hotel with varied rooms, a friendly welcome and good food. The Ancolie (0479 550500) is smarter, with modern facilities, and the Palais Seigneur des Dodes are more spacious than most local apartments. The village is quiet in the evenings.

ACTIVITIES

Indoor Sauna and solarium in most centres, skating (Bellecôte and Aime-la-Plagne), squash (1800), fitness centres (Belle-Plagne, 1800, Centre, Bellecôte), cinemas, bowling
Outdoor Heated swimming pool (Bellecôte), bob-sleigh (La Roche), 30km/19 miles marked walks, paragliding, skidoos, climbing, skating, hang-gliding, snow-shoe excursions, dog sleigh tours

which both have restaurants at the top. The Olympic bob-sleigh run is a popular evening activity (see feature box). Excursions are limited.

STAYING IN THE LOWER RESORTS
A good plan

Montchavin (1250m/4,100ft) is a relatively unspoiled old farming community where wooden barns and sheds are much in evidence. Restaurant terraces set in orchards at the foot of the slopes add to the scene. There are adequate shops, a kindergarten and a school. Reaching the La Plagne slopes involves a series of lifts; but the local slopes have quite a bit to offer – the local lift pass covers 30km/19 miles of mostly easy, pretty, sheltered runs, well endowed with snowmaking, with nursery slopes at village level and up at Plan Bois. Those who do venture further afield can return from Roche de Mio in one lovely long swoop (partly black). The more usual way home involves some of the trickiest blue runs we have encountered. Après-ski is quiet, but the village doesn't lack atmosphere and has a couple of nice little bars and a cinema. The Bellecôte hotel (0479 078330) is conveniently placed for the slopes.

UK Representative

Erna Low Consultants
9 Reece Mews
London SW7 3HE
t 020 7584 2841
f 020 7589 9531
info@ernalow.co.uk
www.ernalow.co.uk

Phone numbers

From abroad use the prefix +33 and omit the initial 'o' of the phone number.

TOURIST OFFICE

Postcode 73211
t 0479 097979
f 0479 097010
bienvenue@
la-plagne.com
www.la-plagne.com

TRY THE OLYMPIC BOB-SLEIGH RUN

If the thrills of a day on the slopes aren't enough, you can round it off by having a go on the 1992 Winter Olympics bob-sleigh run. The floodlit 1.5km/1 mile run drops 125m/400ft and has 19 bends. You can go in a proper four-man 'taxi-bob' (78 euros in 2001/02 – certain nights of the week only) or in a special padded driverless bob raft (32 euros). Most people find the bob raft's 80kph/50mph quite thrilling enough.

With the taxi-bob, you are one of three passengers wedged in behind the driver. You reach a maximum speed of 110kph/68mph and the pressure in turns can be as high as 3g – be sure your physical state is up to it. You must be over 18. Additional insurance is available (yours may not be valid).

Portes du Soleil

Low altitude cross-border cruising

The Portes du Soleil vies with the Trois Vallées for the title of World's Largest Ski Area, but its slopes are very different from those of Méribel, Courchevel, Val-Thorens and neighbours. The Portes du Soleil's slopes are spread out over a large area and most of them are part of an extensive circuit straddling the French-Swiss border; you can travel the circuit in either direction, with a short bus-ride needed only at Châtel. There are smaller areas to explore slightly off the main circuit. The runs are great for keen intermediates who like to travel long distances and through different resorts. There are few of the tightly packed networks of runs that encourage you to stay put in one area – though there are exceptions in one or two places. The area also has some nice rustic mountain restaurants, serving good food in pleasant, sunny settings.

The lifts throughout the area have been improved in recent years with several new high-speed chair-lifts eliminating some bad bottlenecks. But the slopes are low by French standards, with top heights in the range 2000m to 2300m (6,600ft to 7,500ft) and good snow is far from assured (though snowmaking has been expanded in recent years). When the snow is good you can have a great time racing all over the circuit (as we did in fresh powder on our last visit). But the slopes can get very crowded, especially at weekends and in the Avoriaz area.

Purpose-built Avoriaz has the most snow-sure slopes and is especially

good for families, with a big snow-garden right in the heart of the car-free village. And it is good for snowboarders, with a 1.5km/1 mile terrain-park. But its local slopes do get crowded, especially at weekends when crowds pour in from nearby Geneva. The other French resort on the main circuit is Châtel. Given good snow, it has some of the best runs in the area. It is an old and quite characterful village, but it's a busy, traffic-jammed place. It has some good beginner areas both at resort level and up the mountain. Morzine is close to Avoriaz. It is linked by lift but there's no piste all the way back to town. It's a summer as well as a winter resort – a pleasant, bustling little town with good shops and restaurants, busy traffic and long walks to the lifts from much of the accommodation. The local slopes are extensive, and linked to those of the slightly higher, quieter, traditional village of Les Gets. But they are low and good snow is certainly not assured. You can use Morzine as a base to ski the main Portes du Soleil circuit, but it's not ideal. Les Gets is even further off the main circuit.

On the Swiss side Champéry is a classic charming, attractive Swiss village – but again just off the main circuit. You have to take a cable-car down from the main slopes as well as up to them or, if there is enough snow, a bus from a piste which ends out of town. Champéry used to be very popular with British tour operators but now few go there.

Champoussin and Les Crosets are purpose-built mini-resorts set on the very extensive open slopes between Champéry and Morgins, with fairly direct links over to Avoriaz. Morgins, in contrast to Champéry, has excellent village slopes – but they are low and very sunny, and although its more serious local runs are enjoyable and prettily wooded, they are also limited in extent.

On a spur off the main circuit are the resorts of La Chapelle d'Abondance (which has one of our favourite hotel-restaurants) in France and Torgon in Switzerland (which has splendid views over Lake Geneva). This area can be reached from above the Super-Châtel area and is usually quiet even when the rest of the circuit is packed.

SNOWPIX.COM / CHRIS GILL

Lightly wooded slopes above Les Gets ↓

Puy-St-Vincent · 1400m-1600m/4,590ft-5,250ft

Underrated little modern resort with some serious slopes

307

WHAT IT COSTS

((3))

HOW IT RATES

The slopes

Snow	★★★
Extent	★★
Experts	★★★
Intermediates	★★★
Beginners	★★★
Convenience	★★★★★
Queues	★★★★
Restaurants	★★★

The rest

Scenery	★★★
Resort charm	★★
Off-slope	★

What's new

For 2002/03 we're told the repeatedly delayed new blue run – the Tournoux, on the left of the area – will be open. Last season saw increased snowmaking and a new tourist residence at 1600.

Future developments include a new lift between 1400 and 1600, more snowmaking and more new pistes.

MOUNTAIN FACTS

Altitude	1250m-2700m
	4,100ft-8,860ft
Lifts	16
Pistes	67km
	42 miles
Green	16%
Blue	37%
Red	41%
Black	6%
Snowmaking	10km
	6 miles
Recco detectors used	

SNOWPIX.COM / CHRIS GILL

The main monolith at the foot of the lifts is unusual – boldly styled and largely finished in white →

➕ Mostly convenient purpose-built resort that isn't too hideous

➕ Good variety of slopes with challenges for all abilities

➕ Reasonable snow reliability

➕ Low prices by resort standards

➕ Friendly locals

➕ Some great cross-country routes

➖ Slopes very limited in extent by Alpine standards

➖ Some accommodation is inconveniently located

➖ Upper village has only apartment-based accommodation

➖ Limited après-ski

➖ Not a lot to do off the slopes

Puy-St-Vincent's ski area may be limited, but we like it a lot – more, to be honest, than we expected before we went. It offers a decent vertical and a lot of variety, including a bit of steep stuff. Provided you pick your spot with care, it makes an attractive choice for a family not hungry for piste miles.

THE RESORT

Puy-St-Vincent proper is an old mountain village, not far south-west of Briançon. The modern resort of PSV is a two-part affair – the minor part, Station 1400, is just along the mountainside at 1400m/4,590ft; the major part, Station 1600, is a few hairpins (or a chair-lift ride) further up (yes, at 1600m/5,250ft), and there are buildings in various styles scattered around the mountainside. Compact it may be, but 1600 is not perfectly laid out; beware walks to the lifts. We and our reporters have found PSV friendly ('even the lift operators') and well run.

THE MOUNTAINS

Within its small area, PSV packs in a lot of variety, with runs from green to black that justify their gradings.

Slopes There are gentle slopes between the two villages, but most of the runs are above 1600. A fast quad goes up to the tree line at around 2000m/6,560ft. Entertaining red runs go back down, and a green takes a less direct route. The main higher lift is a long chair to 2700m/8,860ft, serving excellent open slopes of red and genuine black steepness. The shorter Rocher Noir drag serves another steep slope, but also accesses splendid cruising runs that curl around the eastern edge of the area. These runs are also accessed by a fast quad chair from just below 1600. The six-day Galaxie pass covers a series of major resorts beyond Briançon. More to the point for most visitors, it also covers a

day's skiing above the valley hamlet of Pelvoux, 10 minutes' drive away. This area has blue, red and black runs, often used for race training, and a vertical of over 1000m/3,300ft served by a chair and a drag.

Snow reliability The slopes face north-east and are reasonably reliable for snow. Snowmaking has increased and now covers one run down to 1400 and several above 1600.

Experts The black runs are short but genuinely black, and there are off-piste routes to be tackled with guidance. There are itinéraires outside the piste

Phone numbers
From abroad use the prefix +33 and omit the initial 'o' of the phone number.

TOURIST OFFICE

Postcode 05290
t 0492 233580
f 0492 234523
courrier@puysaint
vincent.net
www.puysaintvincent.
com

network, including one to the valley.

Intermediates Size apart, it's a good area for those who like a challenge – but there aren't many very easy runs.

Beginners Beginners should be happy on either of the nursery slopes, and on the long green from 2000m/6,56oft.

Snowboarding There is a floodlit terrain-park with half-pipe at 1600, but boarders are not allowed on the Rocher Noir drag-lift.

Cross-country There are 40km/25 miles of cross-country trails, including some splendid routes between 1400m and 1700m (4,590ft and 5,575ft), ranging from green to black difficulty.

Queues Queues are rare – a recent reporter was surprised to find none on Easter Monday.

Mountain restaurants There is a modern but pleasantly woody restaurant at mid-mountain, but in good weather the sunny terraces down at 1600 are the natural choice.

Schools and guides You have a choice of French and International ski schools, and a British tour operator, Snowbizz, has its own school, which a reader

recommends; it provides free guiding in the afternoons, as well as 'good instruction' in small groups.

Facilities for children There are nurseries taking children from 18 months in both villages, and both schools run ski kindergartens.

STAYING THERE

How to go A number of UK operators now offer accommodation here.

Hotels There are four cheap hotels in 1400, but none in 1600.

Self-catering 1600 consists entirely of apartments, and there are more in 1400. The cheaper apartments may be rather cramped.

Eating out The bar-restaurants in each village are the main dining options.

Après-ski Après-ski amounts to a few bar-restaurants in each village.

Off the slopes There are 25km/16 miles of walking and snow-shoe trails. Paragliding, dog-sled rides, floodlit tobogganing and outdoor ice skating (weather permitting) are available. And there is a cinema showing English-speaking films.

Risoul

Villagey modern resort in an attractive setting – and a big shared area

HOW IT RATES

The slopes

Snow	★★★
Extent	★★★
Experts	★★
Intermediates	★★★★
Beginners	★★★★
Convenience	★★★★
Queues	★★★★
Restaurants	★★★

The rest

Scenery	★★★
Resort charm	★★
Off-slope	★

What's new

The first eight-seater chair in the southern French Alps was built for 2001/02, from the village to the middle of the slopes on Peyrefolle. The base station of the Clos du Vallon chair is to be moved higher up.

Snowmaking in Vars has been extended to the top of the Olympiquel and the Combe Froide area.

- ➕ One of the more attractive and convenient purpose-built resorts
- ➕ Scenic slopes linked with Vars add up to a fair-sized area
- ➕ High resort with reasonable snow reliability
- ➕ Good resort for beginners, early intermediates and families
- ➕ Plenty of good-value places to eat

- ➖ Not many modern lifts – lots of long drag-lifts
- ➖ Not too much to challenge expert skiers and boarders
- ➖ Limited après-ski
- ➖ Little to do off the slopes

Slowly but surely the international market is waking up to the merits of the southern French Alps. Were they nearer Geneva, Risoul and its linked neighbour Vars would be as well known as Les Arcs and Flaine. The village of Risoul is a lot more attractive than either.

THE RESORT

Risoul, purpose-built in the late 1970s, is a quiet, apartment-based resort, popular with families. Set among the trees, with excellent views over the Ecrins national park, it is made up of wood-clad buildings – mostly bulky, but with some concessions to traditional style. It has a busy little main street that, surprisingly, is very far from traffic-free. But the village meets the mountain in classic style with an array of sunny restaurant terraces facing the slopes. Several reporters have commented on the friendliness of the natives. The village does not offer a very impressive array of resort amenities. Airport transfers (usually from Turin) are not short.

THE MOUNTAINS

Together with neighbouring Vars, the area amounts to one of the biggest domains in the southern French Alps – the combined area is marketed as the Forêt Blanche.

Slopes The slopes, mainly north-facing, spread over several minor peaks and bowls, and connect with the sunnier slopes of neighbouring Vars via the Pointe de Razis and the lower Col des Saluces. Plans to install a new fast quad from Valbelle up to the Pic de Chabrières above Vars, the area's highest point – providing a third access link between the two – have been put on hold. The upper slopes are open, but those leading back into Risoul are attractively wooded, and

309

OT RISOUL

The lightly wooded lower slopes form an attractive setting for the village ➜

MOUNTAIN FACTS

These figures relate to the entire Forêt Blanche ski area

Altitude	1660m-2750m
	5,445ft-9,020ft
Lifts	57
Pistes	180km
	112 miles
Green	18%
Blue	37%
Red	35%
Black	10%
Snowmaking	29km
	18 miles

Recco detectors used

good for bad-weather days. Recent improvements in the lift system, including the introduction of some fast chairs, mean that the link can now be made in both directions without having to ride any drag-lifts. Nevertheless, reporters still complain that the system as a whole has too many 'long and steep' drag-lifts. Piste grooming is reportedly poor.

Snow reliability Risoul's slopes are all above 1850m/6,070ft and mostly north-facing, so despite its southerly position snow reliability is reasonably good. Snowmaking is fairly extensive and is being extended. Visitors recommend going over to the east-facing Vars slopes for the morning sun, and returning to Risoul in the afternoon.

Experts The pistes in general do not offer much to interest experts. However, Risoul's main top stations access a couple of steepish descents. And there are some good off-piste opportunities if you have a guide.

Intermediates The whole area is best suited to intermediates, with some good reds and blues in both sectors. Almost all Risoul's runs return to the village, making it difficult to get lost in even the worst conditions. So intermediate children can be let off the leash without much worry.

Beginners Risoul's local area boasts some good, convenient, nursery slopes with a free lift, and a lot of easy longer pistes to move on to.

Snowboarding There is a lot of good free-riding to be done throughout the whole area, although beginners might find the large proportion of drag-lifts a problem. There is a good terrain-park

with a half-pipe near the village base, and there are weekly competitions.

Cross-country There are 45km/28 miles of cross-country trails in the whole domain, of which 20km/12 miles are in Risoul itself. A trail through the Peyrol forest links the two resorts together.

Queues Outside French school holidays, Risoul has impressively quiet slopes. Queues to get out of the village in the morning should be eased by the new eight-seat chair.

Mountain restaurants The mountain restaurants have increased in quantity and quality – the newish Tetras is a stylish chalet and the Refuge de Valbelle is recommended; but most people return to the village terraces.

Schools and guides We have had mainly positive reports on the ESF and Internationale schools, but our most recent reporter describes his private ESF instruction as 'most indifferent'.

Facilities for children Risoul is very much a family resort. It provides an all-day nursery for children over six months. Both ski schools operate ski kindergartens, slightly above the village, reached by a child-friendly lift. One parent reckons many other drags have a dangerous 'whiplash' effect.

STAYING THERE

How to go Most visitors stay in self-catering apartments, but there are a few hotels and more chalets are becoming available from UK operators.

Hotels The Chardon Bleu (0492 460727) is handy for the slopes. You can also stay overnight at the Tetras mountain refuge (0492 460983) at 2000m.

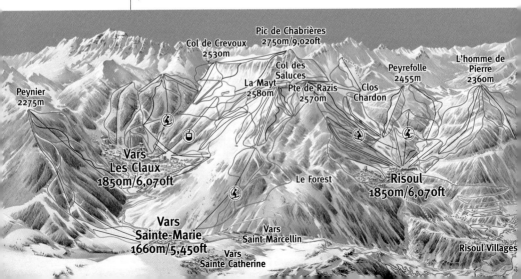

Self-catering The Constellation Forêt Blanche apartments are adequate but cramped.

Eating out There's plenty of choice for eating out, from pizza to good French food, and it's mostly good value – the Ecureuil and the Snowboard cafe, at the foot of the slopes, have been highly recommended by reporters. More expensive is the Assiette Gourmande.

Après-ski Après-ski is limited to a cinema and a few fairly quiet bars. The best are the Licorne, the Cimbro, the Chérine and Ecureuil. The Yeti is the liveliest and full of Scandinavians.

Off the slopes There is little to do; excursions to Briançon are possible.

Vars 1850m/6,070ft

THE RESORT
Vars includes several small, old villages on or near the road running southwards towards the 2110m/6,920ft Col de Vars. But for winter visitors it mainly consists of purpose-built Vars-les-Claux, higher up the road. The resort has convenience and reasonable prices in common with Risoul, but is bigger and has far more in the way of amenities. There are a lot of block-like apartments, but Les Claux is not a complete eyesore, thanks mainly to surrounding woodland. There are two centres: the original, geographical one – where the main gondola starts and which has most of the accommodation and shopping – and Point Show, a collection of bars, restaurants and shops, 10 minutes' walk away at another main lift station.

THE MOUNTAINS
There are slopes on both sides of the village, linked by pistes and by chair-lift at the lower end of Les Claux. Lifts also run up from both sides of Ste-Marie, lower down the mountain.
Slopes The wooded, west-facing Peynier area is the smaller sector, and reaches only 2275m/7,465ft – though there are good long descents down to Les Claux and Ste-Marie. The main slopes are in an east-facing bowl beneath the Pic de Chabrières, with direct links to the Risoul slopes at the top and at the Col des Saluces. There's a speed-skiing course at the top (you can have a go on it, via the ski school). Beneath it are easy runs, open at the top but descending into trees, with red runs either side.

Snow reliability The main slopes get the morning sun, and are centred at around 2000m/6,560ft, so snow reliability is not as good as in Risoul, but snowmaking is widespread.

Experts There is little of challenge for experts, though the Crête de Chabrières top section accesses some off-piste, an unpisted route and a tricky couloir at Col de Crevoux. The Olympic red run from the top of La Mayt down to Ste-Marie is a respectable 920m/3,020ft vertical.

Intermediates Most of the area is fine for intermediates, with a good mixture of comfortable reds and easy blues, particularly in the main bowl.

Beginners There is a nursery area close to central Vars, with lots of 'graduation' runs throughout the area. Quick learners will be able to get over to Risoul by the end of the week.

Snowboarding There's a terrain-park just above Les Claux.

Cross-country There are 25km/16 miles of trails in Vars itself. Some start at the edge of town, but those above Ste-Marie are more extensive.

Queues Queues are rare outside the French holidays, and even then Vars is not overrun as some family resorts are.

Mountain restaurants There are several in both sectors, but a lot of people head back to the villages for lunch.

Schools and guides Lack of English-speaking has been a problem.

Facilities for children The ski school runs a nursery for children from two years old. There is also a ski kindergarten. A list of babysitters can be obtained from the tourist office.

STAYING THERE
How to go There are a few small hotels, but Les Claux is dominated by apartment accommodation.

Hotels The Caribou (0492 465043) is the smartest of the hotels and has a pool. The Ecureuil (0492 465072) is an attractive, modern chalet (no restaurant). There are more hotels in the lower villages, including Ste-Marie.

Eating out The range of restaurants is impressive, with good-value pizzerias, crêperies and fondue places. Chez Plumot does proper French cuisine.

Après-ski Après-ski is animated at tea-time, less so after dinner – except at weekends when the discos warm up.

Off the slopes The amenities are rather disappointing, given the size of Vars – there are 35km/22 miles of walking paths and an ice rink, but that's it.

Phone numbers
From abroad use the prefix +33 and omit the initial 'o' of the phone number.

RISOUL TOURIST OFFICE
Postcode 05600
t 0492 460260
f 0492 460123
o.t.risoul@wanadoo.fr
www.risoul.com

VARS TOURIST OFFICE
Postcode 05560
t 0492 465131
f 0492 465654
vars.ot@pacwan.fr
www.vars-ski.com

La Rosière 1850m/6,070ft

Pop over to Italy from the sunniest slopes in the Tarentaise

WHAT IT COSTS

HOW IT RATES

The slopes
Snow	★★★
Extent	★★★
Experts	★★
Intermediates	★★★
Beginners	★★★★★
Convenience	★★★
Queues	★★★
Restaurants	★

The rest
Scenery	★★★
Resort charm	★★★
Off-slope	★

What's new

For 2002/03, new MGM apartments will be open in the centre of the resort. For 2001/02 a free drag-lift and a new green piste were opened. The official resort website, new for 2001/02, includes an online accommodation booking service.

MOUNTAIN FACTS

Covers combined La Rosière and La Thuile area
Altitude	1175m-2640m
	3,855ft-8,660ft
Lifts	36
Pistes	140km
	87 miles
Green	12%
Blue	36%
Red	35%
Black	17%
Snowmaking	22km
	14 miles
Recco detectors used	

312

- ➕ Attractive purpose-built resort
- ➕ Fair-sized area of slopes linked with La Thuile in Italy
- ➕ Sunny home slopes
- ➕ Heli-skiing over the border in Italy
- ➕ Good nursery slopes

- ➖ Links to Italy prone to closure because of high winds
- ➖ Snow affected by sun in late season
- ➖ Few on-piste challenges for experts
- ➖ Limited après-ski
- ➖ Few off-slope diversions

Like Montgenèvre a long way to the south, La Rosière enjoys a position on the watershed with Italy that brings the twin attractions of big dumps of snow and access to cheap Chianti. The former is crucial: given the very unusual sunny orientation of the slopes, average snowfalls wouldn't do the trick. The Chianti is less significant, because La Thuile lacks attractive restaurants.

THE RESORT
La Rosière has been built in attractive, traditional chalet style beside the road that zigzags its way up from Bourg-St-Maurice to the Petit-St-Bernard pass to Italy (closed in winter). It's a quiet place with a few shops and friendly locals; but don't expect lively nightlife. The most convenient accommodation is in the main village near the lifts, or just below, in Le Gollet or Vieux Village. There is also accommodation by the other main lift, in Les Eucherts.

THE MOUNTAINS
The link with Italy means La Rosière has a big area of slopes. Its sunny home slopes are south-facing and offer great views over the valley to Les Arcs and La Plagne.
Slopes The chair and drag out of the village take you into the heart of the slopes, from where a series of drags and chairs, spread across the mountain, takes you up to Col de la Traversette. From there, you can get over the ridge and to the lifts which link with Italy at Belvedere.
Snow reliability Snow reliability is surprisingly good despite its south-facing direction (it had much more snow than the Italian side when we were there this January); most of the slopes are between 1850m and 2400m (6,070ft and 7,875ft). Most of the area's snowmaking is in Italy. The link with Italy's slopes is prone to closure because of high winds or heavy snow.
Experts Other than excellent heli-skiing from just over the Italian border (including a very long run which ends up near Ste-Foy, just down the road

from La Rosière) and guided off-piste, there is little excitement for experts. The steepest terrain is on the lowest slopes, down the Marcassin run to Le Vaz and down the Ecudets and Eterlou runs to Les Ecudets.
Intermediates La Rosière would be nothing special on its own, but there's lots to explore if you take into account its links to La Thuile. Apart from the runs mentioned above, the bottom half of La Rosière's slopes are mainly gentle, open, blue and green runs, ideal for early intermediates to brush up their technique. The top half of the mountain, however, below Le Roc Noir and Col de la Traversette, boasts steeper and more interesting red runs.
The red over the ridge from Col de la Traversette has good snow and views, but is narrow along its top section. Weaker intermediates can avoid it by taking a chair down.
Beginners There are good nursery slopes and short lifts near the village and near Les Eucherts.
Snowboarding There is a terrain-park and a half-pipe.
Cross-country 12km of trails are set around the tree line near the altiport.
Queues Queues are not usually a problem – apart from early in the day on the chair out of the village – but it is much busier here than over in Italy.
Mountain restaurants There are two mountain restaurants, both with big, sunny terraces. A reporter recommends the self-service Plan du Repos for its 'friendly staff, huge pasta portions and lovely salads', but found the table-service at the Traversette was 'understaffed and unable to cope with

↑ You get a clear picture of La Rosière's open slopes from the top of Les Arcs; looming on the left is Mont Blanc

SNOWPIX.COM / CHRIS GILL

Phone numbers
From abroad use the prefix +33 and omit the initial 'o' of the phone number.

TOURIST OFFICE

Postcode 73700
t 0479 068051
f 0479 068320
info@larosiere.net
www.larosiere.net

lunch time crowds'. There are a couple of bars near the top, which are fine for picnics. Many people prefer to take lunch back in the village, which is perfectly convenient. Two of our reporters recommend the Relais du Petit St Bernard at the base of the pistes: 'Good value, wide menu choice,' comments one. Another recommends the P'tit Relais: 'Self-service and lots of choice.'

Schools and guides There are two schools. Past reporters have praised the Evolution 2 school for its 'good teaching, sympathetic instructors and small groups', but reports of the ESF school have been less favourable: 'large groups' and 'insufficient supervision of small children'.

Facilities for children The Village des Enfants has a snow garden, and British tour operator Esprit runs a nursery.

STAYING THERE

How to go A number of British tour operators now offer packages here.

Hotels There are a few 2-star hotels in the village, and more in the valley.

Chalets Of the chalets available we have had reports of Chalethotel Roc Noir ('well placed', 'good food') and of Ferme d'Elisa ('lovely accommodation but a 150m hike up to the lifts').

Self-catering You can book through UK tour operators or the resort's central booking service.

Eating out The Chalet, the Terrasse du Yéti and the Ancolie have all been recommended.

Après-ski Après-ski is limited to a couple of bars in town.

Off the slopes There are scenic flights and walks and a cinema. The ski schools offer paragliding and organise various non-skiing expeditions on foot.

La Rosière

313

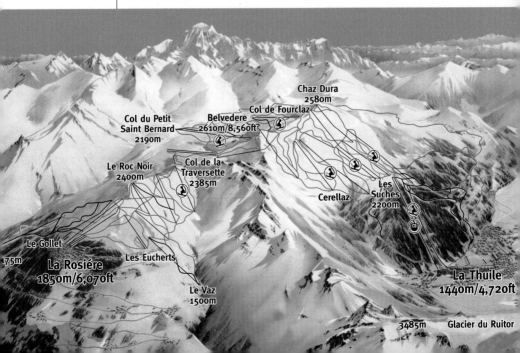

Chaz Dura 2580m
Col de Fourclaz
Col du Petit Saint Bernard 2190m
Belvedere 2610m/8,560ft
Le Roc Noir 2400m
Col de la Traversette 2385m
Cerellaz
Les Suches 2200m
Le Gollet
75m
Les Eucherts
La Rosière 1850m/6,070ft
Le Vaz 1500m
La Thuile 1440m/4,720ft
3485m   Glacier du Ruitor

Serre-Chevalier 1350m-1500m/4,430ft-4,920ft

One of the few big French resorts based on a string of old mountain villages

WHAT IT COSTS

(((③)))

HOW IT RATES

The slopes
Snow	★★★★
Extent	★★★★
Experts	★★★
Intermediates	★★★★
Beginners	★★★★
Convenience	★★★
Queues	★★★
Restaurants	★★★

The rest
Scenery	★★★★
Resort charm	★★★
Off-slope	★★

What's new

For 2002/03 a new blue piste, Les Myrtilles, will open in Chantemerle. Snowmaking has been increased again this season, improving the link between Chantemerle and Villeneuve and the main Aya piste down to Le Monêtier. An ice cave exhibiting ice sculptures will open at the top of the Bachas chair-lift in Le Monêtier.

For 2001/02 a fast six-seater chair replaced the parallel Prorel drag-lifts, linking the Chantemerle section to the Briançon slopes.

Other developments included a new British ski school (EurekaSKI), a new terrain-park with a super-pipe at Alpage, above Villeneuve, and a new children's snow park at Bachas.

A new Club Med in Villeneuve also opened.

⊕ Big, varied mountain, with something for everyone

⊕ Interesting mixture of wooded runs (ideal for blizzards) and open bowls (with acres of off-piste)

⊕ One of the few big French areas based on old villages with character

⊕ Good-value and atmospheric old hotels, restaurants and chalets

⊕ Lift pass covers days elsewhere

⊕ Spectacular drive from Grenoble

⊖ A lot of indiscriminate new buildings, which look awful from the slopes

⊖ Still lots of slow, old lifts, including many drags – some of them vicious

⊖ Serious queues in French holidays

⊖ Busy road runs through the resort villages, with traffic jams at times

⊖ Limited nightlife

⊖ Inadequate piste map

⊖ Few off-slope diversions

Serre-Chevalier is a big-league resort, but isn't as well known outside France as many of its rivals to the north and west. Maybe that's because it doesn't lend itself to marketing hype – the slopes are not super-high, the lifts are not super-efficient, the hotels are far from super-smooth. But we like it a lot: it's one of the few French resorts where you can find the ambience you might look for on a summer holiday – a sort of Provence in the snow, with lots of small, family-run hotels and restaurants housed in old stone buildings (but with ugly modern buildings tagged on to the traditional old villages).

The slopes are likeable, too. Although there are runs on only one side of the long valley, they are split into different segments, so you get a real sensation of travel. In good snow conditions there are excellent off-piste opportunities to keep experts happy, as well as intermediates. What really sets the area apart from the French norm are the woodland runs, making Serre-Chevalier one of the best places to be when snow is falling – though there are plenty of open runs, too.

The resort

The resort is made up of a string of 13 villages set on a valley floor running roughly north-west to south-east, below the north-east-facing slopes of the mountain range that gives the resort its name. From the north-west – coming over the Col du Lautaret from Grenoble – the three main villages are Le Monêtier (or Serre-Che 1500), Villeneuve (1400) and Chantemerle (1350), spread over a distance of 5km/3 miles. Finally, at the extreme south-eastern end of the mountain, is Briançon (1200) – not a village but a town (the highest in France). Nine smaller villages can be identified, and some give their names to the communes: Villeneuve is in the commune of La Salle les Alpes, for example. Confusing.

Serre-Chevalier is not a smart resort, in any sense. Although each of its parts is based on a simple old village, there is a lot of modern development, which ranges from brash to brutal, and even the older parts are roughly rustic

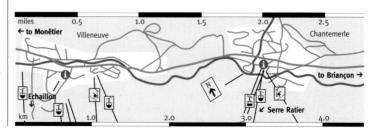

↑ The resort is made up of 13 villages spread along the valley floor beneath the mountain range that gives it its name

AGENCE ZOOM

MOUNTAIN FACTS

Altitude	1350m-2780m
	4,430ft-9,120ft
Lifts	77
Pistes	250km
	155 miles
Green	19%
Blue	19%
Red	49%
Black	13%
Snowmaking	40km
	24 miles
Recco detectors used	

rather than chocolate-box pretty. (A ban on corrugated iron roofs would help.) Because the resort is so spread out, cars and buses are difficult to escape. But when blanketed by snow the older villages and hamlets do have an unpretentious charm, and we find the place as a whole easy to like.

There are no luxury hotels or swanky restaurants; on the other hand, there are more hotels in the Logis de France 'club' here than in any other ski resort. This is a family resort, which fills up (even more than most others) with French children in the February high season. You have been warned.

The heart of the resort is **Villeneuve**, which has two gondolas and a fast quad chair going up to widely separated points at mid-mountain. The central area of new development near the lifts is brutal and charmless. But not far away is the peaceful and traditional hamlet of Le Bez, which has a third gondola, and across the main road and river is the old stone village of Villeneuve with its quiet main street lined by cosy bars, hotels and restaurants.

Not far down the valley **Chantemerle** gives access to opposite ends of the mid-mountain plateau of Serre Ratier via a gondola and a cable-car, both with second stages above. Chantemerle has some tasteless modern buildings in the centre and along the main road. The old sector is a couple of minutes' walk from the lifts, with a lovely church and most of the restaurants, bars and small hotels.

At the top of the valley, **Le Monêtier** has one main access lift - a fast quad chair to mid-mountain, reached from the village by bus or a long and steepish

walk, tricky when ice is around. Le Monêtier is the smallest, quietest and most unspoiled of the main villages, with a bit of a Provençal feel to its narrow streets and little squares, and new building which is mostly in sympathetic style. Sadly, the through-road to Grenoble, which skirts the other villages, bisects Le Monêtier; pedestrians stroll about bravely, hoping the cars will avoid them.

Briançon has a gondola from right in the town to mid-mountain and on almost to the top. The area around the lift station has a wide selection of modern shops, bars, hotels and restaurants, but no character. In contrast, the lovely 17th-century upper quarter is a delight, complete with impressive fortifications, narrow cobbled streets and traditional restaurants, auberges and patisseries. Great views from the top, too.

Regular and reliable ski-buses (covered on the free guest card) link all the villages and lift bases along the valley - but they finish quite early, and taxis aren't cheap. A hands-free lift pass system is also in operation.

A six-day area pass covers a day in each of Les Deux-Alpes, Alpe-d'Huez, Puy-St-Vincent and the Milky Way (several reporters have enjoyed a day out to Montgenèvre, at the French end of that area). All of these outings are possible by public transport, but are much more attractive to those with a car. If driving, you are likely to approach over the high Col du Lautaret, which is occasionally closed because of avalanche danger.

Turin airport is closer but there are more cheap flights to Lyon airport.

LIFT PASSES

2002/03 prices in euros

Grand Serre-Chevalier
Covers all lifts in Briançon, Chantemerle, Villeneuve and Le Monêtier.
Main pass
1-day pass 30.5
6-day pass 152.5
Senior citizens
Over 65: 6-day pass 108.5
Over 75: free pass
Children
Under 12: 6-day pass 108.5
Under 6: free pass
Notes Passes of 6 days or more give one day in each of Les Deux-Alpes, Alpe-d'Huez, Puy-St-Vincent and Voie Lactée (Milky Way). Reductions for families.
Alternative passes
Passes covering individual areas of Serre-Chevalier.
Adult 6-day pass: Briançon, 96, Le Monêtier 115.5, Chantemerle/Villeneuve 130.5
Morning and afternoon passes.
Night-skiing pass.
Beginner's pass.
Non-skier's pass.

The mountains

Trees cover almost two-thirds of the mountain, providing some of France's best bad-weather terrain. The Serre-Chevalier massif is not particularly dramatic, but from the peaks and some other points there are fine views of the Ecrins massif, the highest within France (ie not shared with Italy).

The trail map is supposed to have been improved, but it remains infuriatingly unclear and imprecise in places. Readers have found navigation is made even more challenging by 'particularly poor' signposting and the tendency of runs to 'change colour halfway down'. On our last visit, we found that the signposting at altitude is not up to the job when a storm socks in; take great care.

Piste classification is inclined to exaggerate difficulty – many reds, in particular, could be classified blue.

THE SLOPES
Interestingly varied and pretty
Serre-Chevalier's 250km/155 miles of pistes are spread across four main sectors above the four main villages. The sector above Villeneuve is the most extensive, reaching back a good way into the mountains and spreading over four or five identifiable bowls. The main mid-station is Fréjus. This sector is reliably linked to the slightly smaller Chantemerle sector at quite a low level – well below the tree line. The link from here to Briançon is over a high, exposed col and is via a newish six-pack. The link between Villeneuve and Le Monêtier is liable to closure by high winds or avalanche danger.

SNOW RELIABILITY
Good – especially upper slopes
Most slopes face north or north-east and so hold snow well, especially high up (there are lots of lifts starting above 2000m/6,600ft). The weather pattern is different from that of the northern Alps and even that of Les Deux-Alpes or Alpe-d'Huez, only a few miles to the west. It can get good snow when there is a shortage elsewhere, and vice versa. There is snowmaking on long runs down to each village, which was doubled for last season and has been improved further for 2002/03.

FOR EXPERTS
Deep, not notably steep
There is plenty to amuse experts – except those wanting extreme steeps.

The broad black runs down to Villeneuve and Chantemerle are only just black in steepness, but they are fine runs with their gradient sustained over an impressive vertical of around 800m/2,600ft. One or the other may be closed for days on end for racing or training. The rather neglected Tabuc run, sweeping around the mountain away from the lifts to Le Monêtier, has a couple of genuinely steep pitches but is mainly a cruise; it makes a fine end to the day. For moguls, look higher up the mountain to the steeper slopes served by the two top lifts above Le Monêtier and the three above Villeneuve. The runs beside these lifts – on and off-piste – form a great playground in good snow. The more roundabout Isolée black is a readers' favourite – 'scenic and challenging'.

There are also plenty of more serious off-piste expeditions to be done. Highlights include: Tête de Grand Pré to Villeneuve (a climb from

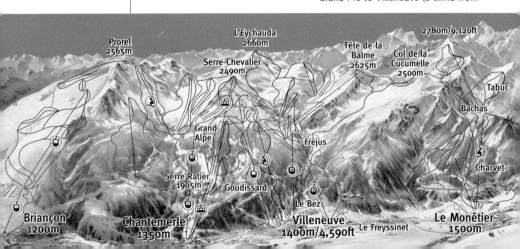

SCHOOLS/GUIDES

2001/02 prices in euros

ESF In all centres
Classes 6 days, 5hr: 3hr am and 2hr pm
6 full days: 170
Children's classes
Ages: up to 12
6 full days: 166
Private lessons
Hourly: 29

Ecole de Ski Buissonnière
Classes am or pm
6 mornings: 92
Children's classes
Ages: up to 12
6 mornings: 90
Private lessons
Hourly: 29

Génération Snow
6 mornings: 110
1½hr: 42

Montagne Adventure
Off-piste, ski-touring

Compagnie des Guides de l'Oisans
Off-piste, ski tours, ice-climbing, snow-shoes

Montagne à la carte
Off-piste, ski-touring, heli-skiing, climbing, snow-shoes

EurekaSKI
Prices in sterling
Main base in Le Monêtier but works in all centres
Classes 7 days
2hr: 9.15-11.15, 11.30-1.30, 2-4
3 2hr sessions: £63
Children's classes
Ages: 5 to early teens
5 2hr sessions: £92
Expert Ski Clinics
2½hr: £35
Private lessons
Hourly: £35 for 1; each additional person £7.50

Cucumelle); off the back of L'Eychauda to Puy-St-André (isolated, beautiful, taxi-ride home); L'Yret to Le Monêtier via Vallon de la Montagnolle; Tabuc (steep at the start, very beautiful) – and the Mecca of La Grave is nearby (see separate chapter).

FOR INTERMEDIATES
Ski wherever you like

Serre-Chevalier's slopes ideally suit intermediates, who can buzz around without worrying about nasty surprises on the way. On the trail map red runs far outnumber blues – but most reds are at the easy end of the scale and the grooming is usually good, so even nervous intermediates shouldn't have problems with them.

There's plenty for more adventurous intermediates, though. Many runs are wide enough for a fast pace. Cucumelle in the Villeneuve sector is a favourite – a beautiful long red away from the lifts, with a challenging initial section. The red runs off the little-used Aiguillette chair in the Chantemerle sector are worth seeking out – quiet, enjoyable fast cruises.

If the reds are starting to seem a bit tame, there is plenty more to progress to. Unless ice towards the bottom is a problem, the (often well-groomed) blacks on the lower mountain should be first on the agenda, and the bumpier ones higher up can be tackled if snow is good.

FOR BEGINNERS
All three areas OK

All three main villages have nursery areas (at Chantemerle it's small, and you generally go up to Serre Ratier or Grand Alpe – both rated as good by a recent beginner reporter) and there are some easy high runs to progress to. Villeneuve has excellent green runs above Fréjus. Both sectors have green paths down from mid mountain. But they are narrow, and not enjoyable when the runs become rutted and others are speeding along. Le Monêtier's easy runs are at resort level, next to excellent nursery slopes, and beginners have recommended it for 'better snow and fewer people'.

FOR CROSS-COUNTRY
Excellent if the snow is good

There are 45km/28 miles of tracks along the valley floor, mainly following the gurgling river between Le Monêtier and Villeneuve and going on up towards the Col du Lautaret.

QUEUES
Avoid French school holidays

More than most resorts, Serre-Chevalier seems to fill up with French families in the February holidays, producing serious queues all over the place. The Aiguillette chair in the Chantemerle sector is a good place to escape to.

At other times a range of big lifts means there are few problems getting

Serre-Chevalier

317

boarding *Serre-Che is a snowboarding hot-spot, popular mainly with advanced boarders because of the off-piste powder and because the resort has invested in loads of fun features. There's big air in Briançon, boarder-cross in Villeneuve and Chantemerle and a half-pipe in Villeneuve, all with sound-systems. The diverse pistes with open and tree-lined runs also suit intermediates, though there are annoying flat sections between some lifts and several tracks the less confident might find tricky. The main lifts are chairs and gondolas but there are a lot of difficult-to-avoid and violent drag-lifts. Evenings are fairly quiet but there's at least one lively bar in each centre.*

GETTING THERE

Air Turin, transfer 2½hr. Grenoble, transfer 2½hr. Lyon, transfer 3½hr.

Rail Briançon (6km/4 miles); regular buses from station.

---

out of the valley. But old, slow lifts still cause queues at altitude. The Prorel double drag from Chantemerle towards Briançon has been replaced by a six-pack, eliminating the crush there.

MOUNTAIN RESTAURANTS
Not a highlight

Mountain restaurants are quite well distributed, but the few good ones are mostly concentrated in the central sectors. If lunch is an important part of your day, plan it carefully; if it's a very important part, go elsewhere.

For a serious lunch, we head for Pi Maï in the hamlet of Fréjus, a little way below the Fréjus lift station. Its table-service meals are not cheap, but the food is good and the spacious, rustic restaurant with log fire is a fine place to retreat to on a bad day. Also in the Villeneuve sector is Echaillon, a lofty building with table-service food that we and some others have enjoyed; finding it is a bit of a challenge.

At Serre Ratier, above Chantemerle, is a popular and noisy self-service. Higher up, the big Grand Alpe offers good views but last season a reporter suffered 'the worst croque monsieur I've ever had (including UK)'.

In the Briançon sector, the little chalet just down from the top of Prorel has great views and is reasonably priced.

Above Le Monêtier the choice is between the unremarkable self-service Bachas at mid-mountain and the cosy Peyra Juana much lower down, where we and readers alike have enjoyed excellent service, food and value.

SCHOOLS AND GUIDES
New British school

We have received a number of reports on the Ecole de Ski Buissonnière over the years – most of them full of praise. For example: 'We thoroughly enjoyed a two-hour introductory snowboarding class. Instructors speak good English and classes are small.' We've also had an enthusiastic report on an ESF class in Le Monêtier that was 'almost like a private lesson'. But this year a near beginner complained of 'appalling treatment' of two English clients in a group with eight French: 'By Wednesday I was reduced to tears and we left our class halfway down a blue run.'

EurekaSKI, a British ski school run by BASI instructors, started up last season. Classes range from beginner to free-ride masterclass, there are expert ski clinics (eg bumps, steeps, off-piste, carving) and the maximum group size is six. There's a satisfaction guarantee: if you feel you don't benefit from your first session your money will be refunded. For contact details see the advertisement on the left.

FACILITIES FOR CHILDREN
Facilities at each village

We have had no very recent reports, but the Ecole de Ski Buissonnière (see above) has been praised in the past, as has Les Schtroumpfs in Villeneuve.

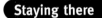
Staying there

HOW TO GO
A good choice of packages

There's a wide choice of packages from UK tour operators, offering all kinds of accommodation.

Chalets Several operators offer chalets in the different parts of the resort. Handmade's chalet Pyrene and chalet hotel Rif Blanc have both been approved by readers (and you can book into the latter for a couple of nights locally if there's room – UK number 01285 642555).

Hotels One of the features of this string of little villages is the range of

CHILDCARE

Each of the main villages has its own non-ski nursery that takes children all day (9am to 5pm). At Villeneuve, Les Schtroumpfs (0492 247095) caters for kids from age 6 months; meals not provided. At Chantemerle, Les Poussins (0492 240343) takes them from age 8 months; meals provided. At Le Monêtier, Garderie de Pré-Chabert (0492 244575) takes them from age 18 months (6 months out of school holiday times); meals not provided.

ACTIVITIES

Indoor Swimming pool, sauna, fitness centres, cinemas, bridge
Outdoor At Chantemerle: skating rink, paragliding, cleared paths, snow-shoe walks, snowmobiling. At Villeneuve: ice-driving circuit, skating rink, horse-riding, sleigh rides, cleared paths, paragliding, snow-shoe walks, snowmobiling. At Le Monêtier: skating rink, cleared paths, hang-gliding, hot springs, snow-shoe walks, ski-joring.

Phone numbers
From abroad use the prefix +33 and omit the initial 'o' of the phone number.

TOURIST OFFICE

Postcode 05240
t 0492 249898
f 0492 249884
contact@ot-serrechevalier.fr
www.serre-chevalier.
com

attractive family-run hotels – many of them part of the Logis de France. There's also a Club Med in Villeneuve. In Monêtier:
③ **Choucas** (0492 244273) Smart, wood-clad rooms, and 'excellent, seven-course dinners in stone-vaulted restaurant – but mediocre breakfast and erratic service'.
② **Europe** (0492 244003) Simple but well run Logis in heart of old village, with pleasant bar and decent food.
② **Alliey** (0492 244002) Our favourite place to eat (see Eating out).
In Villeneuve:
② **Lièvre Blanc** (0492 247405) Former coaching inn, with a large, busy stone-vaulted bar. British-owned, with its own guide and rental shop.
② **Christiania** (0492 247633) Traditional hotel on main road, crammed with ornaments.
② **Vieille Ferme** (0492 247644) Stylish conversion on the edge of the village.
② **Cimotel** (0492 247822) Modern and charmless, with good-sized rooms and 'excellent' food.
① **Chatelas** (0492 247474) Prettily decorated simple chalet by river.
In Chantemerle:
② **Plein Sud** (0492 241701) Modern; pool and sauna.
② **Boule de Neige** (0492 240016) Comfortable, friendly, in the old centre.
① **Ricelle** (0492 240019) Charming, but across the valley from the slopes in Villard-Laté. Good food.
Self-catering There are plenty of modern apartment blocks in Villeneuve, Briançon and Chantemerle. Few have charm.

EATING OUT
Unpretentious and traditional

In Le Monêtier, there are several good hotel-based options. Our favourite is the panelled restaurant of the Alliey, which offers excellent food at astoundingly moderate prices and an impressive wine list. The Auberge du Choucas considers itself the best in town and is certainly the most expensive. The Europe has reliable French cooking at reasonable prices, and the Boîte à Fromages does a 'magnificent' fondue.

In the old part of Villeneuve, the Pastorale is a crowded, cramped vault with a warm welcome, an open-fire grill and good-value menu. The Marotte, a tiny stone building with classic French cuisine, has been highly praised. The Noctambule and the Refuge specialise in fondue and raclette. And there are

good crêperies – try the Petit Duc, or the Manouille. Over in Le Bez, the Bidule is said to have 'first-class food and service, at good value', while the Siyou in La Salle is good for 'local specialities at very reasonable prices'.

In Chantemerle, the Couch'où is good value for fondue and raclette, and has a pizzeria upstairs. The candlelit Crystal is the smartest, most expensive place in town. The Kandahar is a charming pizzeria and the rustic Ricelle offers amazing value.

APRES-SKI
Quiet streets and few bars

Nightlife seems to revolve around bars, scattered through the various villages.

In Le Monêtier the Alpen has a happy hour, free nibbles and welcoming staff. The British-run Rif Blanc bar now rivals the Pub in popularity. If you want to forget you're in a ski resort (and see French smoking laws at their least effective), hit the Cibouit.

In Villeneuve the bar of the Lièvre Blanc is popular with Brits; the Iceberg is a pub-style bar frequented by teenagers. The Frog is cramped, but has 'good atmosphere'. In Chantemerle the Yeti and the Underground beneath it are focal. The Kitzbühel has a good atmosphere, particularly when sporting events are shown, and is 'not too full of fellow Brits'. After everything else has closed, a karaoke bar with 'an erratic door policy' may still let you in.

OFF THE SLOPES
Try the hot baths

Serre-Chevalier doesn't hold many attractions for non-slope-users, and it's certainly not for avid shoppers, but the old town of Briançon is well worth a visit. Visitors have enjoyed walking in the valley on 'well-prepared trails', and the indoor-outdoor thermal bath in Le Monêtier makes a great place to watch the sun go down. The swimming pool in the hotel Sporting in Villeneuve is open to non-residents. And each of the main villages has its own cinema.

STAYING UP THE MOUNTAIN
Worth considering

Chalet hotel Serre Ratier (0492 241581), at the mid-station of the Chantemerle cable-car, does full board at reasonable rates. A more seductive possibility is to stay at Pi Maï (0492 248363) in Fréjus, above Villeneuve (see Mountain restaurants).

Ste-Foy-Tarentaise   1550m/5,090ft

Secret off-piste haven for those in the know

320

WHAT IT COSTS

HOW IT RATES

The slopes

Snow	★★★
Extent	★
Experts	★★★★
Intermediates	★★★
Beginners	★★
Convenience	★★★
Queues	★★★★★
Restaurants	★

The rest

Scenery	★★★
Resort charm	★★★
Off-slope	★

MOUNTAIN FACTS

Altitude	1550m-2620m
	5,090ft-8,600ft
Lifts	5
Pistes	25km
	16 miles
Green	8%
Blue	15%
Red	54%
Black	23%
Snowmaking	None

What's new

Development in keeping with the stone and wood character of Ste-Foy is in evidence at the ski station. More new chalets, apartments and shops are being built over the next two seasons, and the tourist office is to start a central reservations system from 2002/03. Improvements to a couple of runs are planned for 2002/03, and new lifts are on the cards in the long run.

- ✚ No crowds
- ✚ Lots of excellent off-piste and untracked powder
- ✚ Cheap lift pass and good value lodging
- ✚ Tarentaise mega-resorts nearby for a change of scene

- ⦵ Tiny mountain hamlet offers few off-slope diversions
- ⦵ Very limited piste network for high-mileage piste-bashers
- ⦵ Few off-slope diversions
- ⦵ Limited après-ski

This small area in the Tarentaise has been developed only since 1990. The millions who flock to the nearby mega-resorts of Val-d'Isère and Les Arcs never give it a thought. But those in the know are well rewarded. It's an uncrowded gem with some wonderful off-piste slopes for experts and intermediates.

THE RESORT

There isn't much of one; that's part of the charm of this place – it's ideal for getting away from the crowds. The ski station of Ste-Foy, also known as Bonconseil, is a tiny hamlet set 4km off the main road between Val-d'Isère and Bourg-St-Maurice: turn off at La Thuile, just after the village of Ste-Foy. A largish complex at the station houses the tourist and ticket office, a cafe/bar, a small grocery shop and a ski shop (Zigzags, which readers have criticised in the past for shocking service).

If you don't have a car it's most convenient to stay at the ski station, as free buses to and from Ste-Foy village run only every hour or so (the trip takes 20 minutes). Buses now visit nearby villages too, such as La Masure.

THE MOUNTAIN

Off-piste guides from Val regularly impress clients by bringing them to Ste-Foy's deserted slopes, accessed by three quad chairs, rising one above the other to the Col de l'Aiguille. Impressive as the off-piste can be, you may want to spread your wings from the tiny resort during a week's stay, particularly if the snow is unkind. Luckily Val d'Isère, Tignes, Les Arcs (via Villaroger) and La Rosière are all within easy reach (with a car). You're entitled to a free day in La Rosière, and almost half-price tariffs in all the rest, on presentation of a current Ste-Foy six-day pass – which at 89 euros last season was around half the price of neighbouring Val d'Isère. A day pass was a bargain 17 euros.

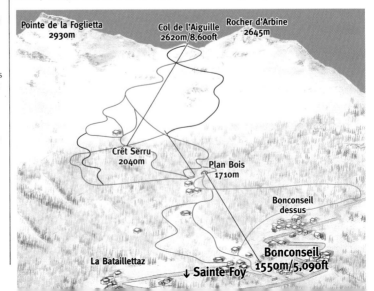

Pointe de la Foglietta 2930m · Col de l'Aiguille 2620m/8,600ft · Rocher d'Arbine 2645m · Crêt Serru 2040m · Plan Bois 1710m · Bonconseil dessus · La Bataillettaz · ↓ Sainte-Foy · Bonconseil 1550m/5,090ft

Phone numbers
From abroad use the prefix +33 and omit the initial 'o' of the phone number.

TOURIST OFFICE

Postcode 73640
t 0479 069519
f 0479 069509
stefoy@wanadoo.fr
www.saintefoy.net

Slopes The top lift accesses almost 600m of vertical above the tree line and superb, long off-piste routes on the back of the mountain. The two lower chairs serve pleasant green, blue and red runs through trees and back to the base station. Don't come here for quality grooming or modern lifts, but one reporter didn't care: 'Most of my ski career I've been in Verbier, Zermatt and Vail. Skiing in Ste-Foy is better.'

Snow reliability The slopes face north or west. Snow reliability is good on the former but can suffer on the latter, especially as there is no snowmaking. But lack of crowds means you can still make fresh tracks days after a storm.

Experts Experts can pass happy times on and off the sides of Ste-Foy's black and red runs, but it's the more serious off-piste you come for, for which you need a guide. There are wonderful runs from the top of the lifts down through deserted old villages to the road between Ste-Foy and Val-d'Isère and a splendid route off to the left which starts with a hike and takes you through trees and over a stream down to the tiny village of Le Crot. The ESF runs group off-piste trips, and arranges transport back to the station. There are three refuges in the area if you fancy an overnight adventure.

Intermediates Intermediates can enjoy 1000m/3,280ft vertical of uncrowded reds – ideal for confidence building and sharpening technique. The higher slopes are the more difficult – the red L'Aiguille is a superb test for confident intermediates, who should also try the off-piste (with a guide). Anyone who doesn't fancy experimenting with off-piste will tire of the limited runs in a day or two and be champing at the bit to get to Val d'Isère or Les Arcs.

Beginners Not the best place, but there is a small nursery drag at the base. After that you can progress to a green run off the first chair – a pleasant, gentle track through trees – and a gentle blue off the second.

Snowboarding Great free-riding terrain and a terrain park near Crêt-Serru.

Cross-country No prepared trails, but ask the tourist office about marked itinerary routes such as Planay dessus.

Queues You have more chance of winning the lottery than finding a lift queue at Ste-Foy.

Mountain restaurants There are two rustic restaurants at the top of the first chair, Chez Léon, which a reporter recommends, and the Brevettes. The

Ruelle, at the bottom of the first chair, is a good, rustic bar-restaurant, and the Maison à Colonnes, also at the base, gets good write-ups: 'Friendly, interesting menu, nice atmosphere.' There's also the Pitchouli for drinks and snacks in the main base building.

Schools and guides We've had good reports of ski school, especially for children (from age four). There's a good chance classes will not be large.

Facilities for children There is a nursery, Les P'tits Trappeurs, which takes children from age three to eight.

STAYING THERE

How to go Ste-Foy is hardly on the UK market, so most people organise their own trip. Ste-Foy village is only about 20 minutes from the Eurostar terminal at Bourg St Maurice.

Hotels Auberge sur la Montagne (0479 069583), just above the turn-off at La Thuile, sleeps 20, has excellent food and atmosphere and is run by an English couple. Yellow Stone Chalet (0479 069606) is a Gîte de France at the ski station, run by an American and highly recommended by a recent reporter: 'Beautifully appointed, modern with good food.' Hotel Monal (0479 069007), in Ste-Foy village, is a basic auberge.

Chalets Chalet Number One (UK number: 01572 717259), in the village of La Masure, is run by British snowboarder Lloyd Rogers, serving good food in comfortable, rustic surroundings. Skiers are welcome. too!

Self-catering There are quite a few apartments and chalets to rent in the area, including the new ones being built near the lifts – the tourist office has a brochure and is running a central reservation system from 2002/03. And one of our assistant editors has a new chalet to rent – see www.ste-foy-chalet.co.uk.

Eating out Book the excellent Chez Mérie, in the village of Le Miroir, well in advance (for lunch, too). In La Thuile book the Auberge sur la Montagne. In Ste-Foy village, the Grange at the Monal does 'good food' and a reporter enjoyed the Ruelle at the ski station, which opens by arrangement in the evenings, as does Chez Léon.

Après-ski Pretty quiet. There may be a short-lived après-ski scene in one of the bars at the ski station, and the bar of the Monal can get busy.

Off the slopes Not a lot – parapenting, dog-sledding and snow-shoeing.

St-Martin-de-Belleville 1400m/4,590ft

Explore the Three Valleys from a traditional old village

WHAT IT COSTS

HOW IT RATES

The slopes

Snow	★★★
Extent	★★★★★
Experts	★★★★
Intermediates	★★★★★
Beginners	★★★
Convenience	★★★
Queues	★★★★
Restaurants	★★★★

The rest

Scenery	★★★
Resort charm	★★★★
Off-slope	★

What's new

A gondola is to replace the chair out of the village for the 2002/03 season. The drag-lift on the slope up from the church will be moved to the side of the slope and made less vicious.

➕ Attractively developed traditional village with pretty church

➕ Easy access to the whole of the extensive Three Valleys network

➕ Long easy intermediate runs on rolling local slopes

➕ Extensive snowmaking keeps local runs open in poor conditions, but ...

➖ Snow at resort level suffers from altitude, and sun in the afternoon

➖ No green runs for beginners to progress to

➖ The climb up from the lower part of the village can be taxing

➖ Limited après-ski

➖ Few off-slope diversions

St-Martin is a lived-in, unspoiled village, with old church (prettily lit at night), small square and wood and stone buildings, a few miles down the valley from Les Menuires. As a quiet, inexpensive, attractive base for exploration of the Three Valleys, it's unbeatable. All our reporters who stayed there have loved it.

THE RESORT

In 1950 St-Martin didn't even have running water or electricity. Later, while new resorts were developed nearby, St-Martin was a bit of a backwater, though it remained the administrative centre for the Belleville valley (which includes the resorts of Val-Thorens and Les Menuires). But in the 1980s chair-lifts were built, linking it to the slopes of Méribel and Les Menuires. The old village has been developed, of course, but the architecture of the new buildings fits in well with the old, and you can walk around it in a few minutes. The main feature of the centre remains the lovely old 16th-century church – prettily floodlit at night. There are some good local shops and few 'touristy' ones.

THE MOUNTAINS

The whole of the Three Valleys can be easily explored from here.
Slopes Two chair-lifts – the upper one a fast quad – take you to a ridge from which you can access Méribel on one side and Les Menuires on the other.
Snow reliability Natural snow reliability is not the best in the Three Valleys – the local slopes face west and get the full force of the afternoon sun, and the village is relatively low. But there is now snowmaking from top to bottom of the main run to the village, and reporters agree that it is impressively effective at keeping the run open.
Experts Locally there are large areas of gentle and often deserted off-piste. And access to La Masse for steep north-facing slopes is just one run away from the top of the local lifts.
Intermediates The local slopes are pleasant blues and reds, mainly of interest to intermediates – including one of our favourite runs in the Three Valleys: the long, rolling, wide Jerusalem red. The Verdet blue from the top of the Méribel lifts is a wonderful easy cruise with great views and is usually very quiet. The whole of the Three Valleys is, of course, an intermediate's paradise.
Beginners St-Martin is not ideal – there's a nursery slope but no easy green runs to progress to.
Snowboarding There is some great

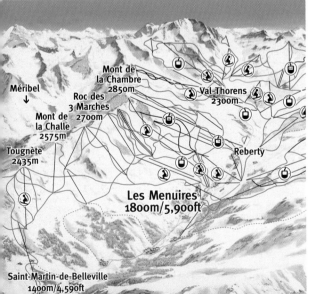

Méribel ↓

Mont de la Chambre 2850m

Roc des 3 Marches 2700m

Mont de la Challe 2575m

Tougnète 2435m

Val-Thorens 2300m

Reberty

Les Menuires 1800m/5,900ft

Saint-Martin-de-Belleville 1400m/4,590ft

MOUNTAIN FACTS

For the Three Valleys

Altitude	1300m-3230m
	4,270ft-10,600ft
Lifts	200
Pistes	600km
	370 miles
Green	17%
Blue	34%
Red	37%
Black	12%
Snowmakers	90km
	56 miles
Recco detectors used	

OT ST-MARTIN-DE-BELLEVILLE / PIERRE EXANDIER

The contrast with Les Menuires, further up the valley, is a sharp one ↓

local off-piste free-riding available.

Cross-country There are 28km/18 miles of trails in the Belleville valley.

Queues Queues are not usually much of a problem – the local lifts can easily cope with the morning rush and any increase in demand should be absorbed by the new gondola from the village to mid-mountain, planned to be opened for this season. This will eventually be extended to Roc de Fer, as an alternative to the existing fast chair to Tougnete.

Mountain restaurants There are three atmospheric old mountain restaurants on the main run down to the village. Chardon Bleu and Corbeleys near the mid-mountain lift junction are good for lunch, and Loe, lower down, is popular as the lifts close. At village level a favourite is Brewski's (on the left, halfway down the local village slope with the drag-lift – watch for the signs) which does good-value pub grub (pies are a speciality) and has sunny terraces with views down the valley – it attracts customers from all over the Three Valleys. For a real blow-out, the Bouitte in St-Marcel (an off-piste run away) is one of the best restaurants in the Three Valleys and features in the Gault-Millau gourmet guidebook – it's a traditional, welcoming, rustic French auberge with linen on the tables and

with charming service. It's not cheap.

Schools and guides The ski school is said to have instructors with good English, but not all past reporters have encountered them. We lack recent reports.

Facilities for children We've had good reports of the nursery, the Village des Ecureuils, which is housed in a new purpose-built building and takes children from two and a half years old.

STAYING THERE

How to go For such a small village there's a good variety of accommodation.

Hotels The Alp Hôtel (0479 089282), at the foot of the slope by the main lift and close to the nursery, is deservedly popular. Our regular reporter stands by last year's verdict – 'Good food and wine list, comfortable rooms.' But we hear that it may now belong to a German tour operator. The Saint Martin (0479 008800) is right on the slope, and the Edelweiss (0479 089667) is in the village itself. All are 3-stars. But the best value accommodation is the B&B offered at Brewski's (0479 006234), again right on the slope with well furnished en suite rooms of various sizes. This also gives you the chance to try some of the excellent local restaurants.

St-Martin-de-Belleville

323

01285 642 555
www.handmade-holidays.co.uk
AITO ATOL PROTECTED 4479

Phone numbers
From abroad use the prefix +33 and omit the initial 'o' of the phone number.

TOURIST OFFICE
Postcode 73440
t 0479 089309
f 0479 089171
lesmenuires@les
menuires.com
www.st-martin-belle
ville.com

Chalets The number of chalet beds in the resort is on the increase, with major UK operators starting to take an interest. Chalets de St Martin has traditionally been the main British chalet operator in town – it has operated here ever since the first lift was built. Ski Total now runs some of its chalets, but it still operates chalet Rousette, with cooking by professional chefs and a variety of quality wines to match the food (the owner is a wine merchant).

Self-catering Chalets de St Martin has a variety of self-catered chalets and apartments to rent, and plenty of others are available.

Eating out For such a small village there is a good variety of restaurants on hand. One reader found the Montagnard's rustic decor 'slightly contrived' but says the service was 'friendly' and the 'good helpings' of Savoyard food 'reasonably priced'. The Voute is good value too and is recommended for its salads and pizzas. Brewski's does 'good pub grub and specialises in unusual pies (even lamb curry pie)'. The Grenier, in the hotel St Martin, has impressed – 'Smart but not cheap.' The Etoile de Neige is a smart,

traditional French restaurant but a recent reporter thought that it was a bit over-priced when compared to the Bouitte, just down the road in St-Marcel, which is deemed to be the best restaurant in the valley – see Mountain restaurants. A bit further, at Les Granges, is the rustic Chez Bidou – popular with locals and 'highly recommended for a Savoyard evening' by a reporter this year.

Après-ski Après-ski centres around two bars. The Pourquoi Pas? piano bar is delightfully cosy, with a roaring log fire and comfortable easy chairs and sofas. Brewski's has a pool table, activities such as karaoke, sumo wrestling or live bands most nights and photos of old pop stars – such as Frank Zappa, Cream, the Beatles, Tina Turner and the Sex Pistols – on the walls. One of the fun-loving Kiwi owners may do his Elvis impersonation if you buy him enough drinks.

Off the slopes If you don't use the slopes, there are better places to base yourself. There are pleasant walks and a sports hall, but not much else. There is talk of building a swimming pool, but it won't happen overnight.

FRANCE

324

Les Chalets de St. Martin

La Tania
1350m/4,430ft

Small, family-friendly base for exploring the Three Valleys

What's new

For 2002/03 the snowmaking will be further extended to allow more visitors to ski back to their accommodation.

➕ Part of the Three Valleys – the world's biggest linked ski area

➕ Quick access to the slopes of Courchevel and Méribel

➕ Long, rolling, intermediate runs through woods back to the village

➕ Greatly improved snowmaking

➕ Attractively developed, small, traffic-free village

➖ Small development without much choice of après-ski – and no pharmacy or cashpoint

➖ Main nursery slope is part of the blue run to the village, and gets a lot of through-traffic

➖ Runs home are too steep for those progressing from the nursery slopes

➖ Some accommodation is a long walk from the centre and the main lifts

La Tania does not try to compete with its more upmarket neighbours, Courchevel and Méribel. It has carved out its own niche as a good-value, small, quiet, family-friendly base from which to hit the snow-sure slopes of Courchevel and to explore the whole of the Three Valleys. It is prettily set in the trees, and the wood-clad buildings make it one of the more attractive French purpose-built resorts (development started in the early 1990s, by which time lessons had been learned from the resorts that were developed in the 1960s and 70s, with their tiny apartments and uncompromisingly functional architecture). As a budget base for the Three Valleys, it has a lot to be said for it.

THE RESORT
La Tania is set just off the minor road linking Le Praz (Courchevel 1300) to Méribel. It has grown into a quiet, attractive, car-free collection of mainly ski-in, ski-out chalets and apartments set among the trees, most with good views. There are few shops other than food and sports shops and not much choice of bars and restaurants. You can walk around the place in a couple of minutes.

A gondola leads up into the slopes, and there are two wonderful sweeping intermediate runs down. The nursery slope is on your doorstep, and visitors say that La Tania is 'very child friendly'. The steepness of the runs back to the village is its key weakness.

Hourly buses go to Courchevel in the daytime, but for those with a car Méribel is probably a bigger draw – 1850, Courchevel's main shopping and nightlife focus, is appreciably further.

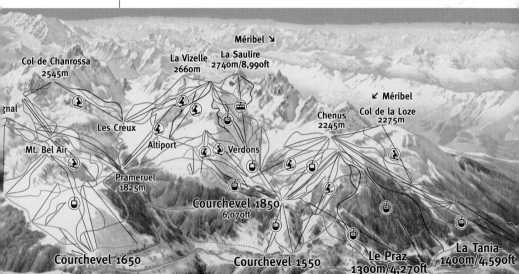

FRANCE

326

MOUNTAIN FACTS

For the Three Valleys

Altitude	1300m-3230m
	4,270ft-10,600ft
Lifts	200
Pistes	600km
	370 miles
Green	17%
Blue	34%
Red	37%
Black	12%
Snowmaking	90km
	56 miles
Recco detectors used	

THE MOUNTAINS

As well as good, though limited, local slopes, the whole of the Three Valleys can be explored easily from here, with just two lifts needed to get to either the Courchevel or the Méribel slopes.

Slopes The gondola out of the village goes to Praz-Juget. From here a drag-lift takes you to Chenus and the slopes above Courchevel 1850 and a high-speed quad goes to the link with Méribel via Col de la Loze. An alternative way to the slopes above 1850 is to take two successive drag-lifts from the village to Loze. From all these points, varied, interesting intermediate runs take you back into the La Tania sector.

Snow reliability Good snow-cover down to Bouc Blanc is usual all season. Below that the snow is less assured. Snowmaking now covers the whole of the blue run back to the village; some reporters found this very satisfactory, but others still found the need to ride the gondola at times.

Experts There are no particular challenges directly above La Tania, but there's the whole of the Three Valleys

to explore and some tough runs and good off-piste are close by in the Courchevel sector.

Intermediates There are two lovely, long, undulating intermediate runs back to La Tania – though on the higher slopes you have a choice of three or four pistes. Both Lanches and Dou des Lanches are excellent challenging reds. The blue way down is not the easiest of blues. The quick access to the rest of the Three Valleys' 600km/370 miles of well-groomed pistes makes the area an adventurous intermediate's paradise.

Beginners There is a good beginner area and lift right in the village and beginner children, in particular, are well catered for. But there are no very easy, long, local slopes to progress to; the intermediate runs back to the village are quite challenging. Think about Courchevel 1650 instead.

Snowboarding There is no local terrain-park or half-pipe, but you can get to Courchevel's easily. There's a cheap place to stay that might appeal to boarders on a budget (see Staying there, right) and one lively local bar.

Cross-country There are trails at altitude with links to Méribel and Courchevel.
Queues A queue can build up for the village gondola but it is quick-moving, and one of the attractions of La Tania in general is the lack of crowds. Elsewhere in the Three Valleys there are few remaining bottlenecks.
Mountain restaurants Bouc Blanc, near the top of the gondola out of La Tania, has friendly table-service, good food and a big terrace. Roc Tania, higher up at Col de la Loze is tiny, but very pretty inside – good for a scenic coffee stop; one reader found the food good at lunch time, another was disappointed with food and service. Check out the Courchevel and Méribel places, too.

Schools and guides Magic in Motion was 'absolutely wonderful' for the five children in a recent reporter's group.
Facilities for children We have had excellent reports of tour operator Le Ski's nursery here. The local kindergarten takes children from the age of three.

STAYING THERE
How to go Around 30 British tour operators go here.
Hotels The Montana (0479 088008) is a slope-side 3-star next to the gondola with a sauna and fitness club. It was said by a reporter to be 'very good value, with friendly, English-speaking staff and excellent food'. The Mountain Centre (www.themountaincentre.com or

---

Phone numbers
From abroad use the
prefix +33 and omit
the initial 'o' of the
phone number.

TOURIST OFFICE
Postcode 73125
t 0479 084040
f 0479 084571
info@latania.com
www.latania.com

FRANCE

328

OT LA TANIA / JM GOUEDARD

Children are well
catered for, with the
gentlest of nursery
slopes ↓

01273 897525 in the UK) opened last
season and has 'cheap backpacker-
style accommodation' from £17 a night
B&B, with dinner costing £6 and
bedding and a towel a few pence
more. Just our kind of place.
Chalets Several tour operators have
splendid newish ski-in, ski-out chalets
with fine views, though reporters have
complained of 'poor soundproofing' in
some. The choice gets wider every
year.
Self-catering There are lots of
apartments – and most are more
spacious and better equipped than
usual in France. The Saboia and the
Christiania have been recommended.
There is a deli and a bakery, as well as
a small supermarket.
Eating out The Ferme de la Tania and
the Farçon get generally good reviews

for their Savoyard fare. Pub Le Ski
Lodge has 'damn good chilli burgers'.
The Chanterelles is 'highly
recommended' for crêpes and pizzas
and the Taîga does 'very good pizzas
and is friendly and quite cheap'.
Après-ski Pub Le Ski Lodge is the focal
après-ski place, with Murphy's on
draught and frequent live bands and
theme nights – the Shibboleth band, a
long-standing regular feature, is a
'must see'. The hotel Montana bar and
the Taîga (a bar-pizzeria) are quieter.
But if you want a lively varied nightlife,
you need to go elsewhere – La Tania is
too small.
Off the slopes Unless you have a car,
La Tania will be deadly dull for anyone
not intending to hit the slopes.
Surprisingly, there is a cinema with two
English showings a week.

Good snow, varied high-mountain terrain and ... er, that's about it

WHAT IT COSTS

HOW IT RATES

The slopes
Snow	*****
Extent	*****
Experts	*****
Intermediates	*****
Beginners	**
Convenience	****
Queues	****
Restaurants	***

The rest
Scenery	***
Resort charm	**
Off-slope	*

What's new

In 2001/02, a new slope to the base of the Chaudannes chair at Le Lavachet was created, giving direct access from the western slopes.

For 2002/03 the slow Tommeuses chair-lifts – a major bottleneck on the way back from Val – will at last be replaced, by a fast eight-seater.

A smart new hotel is being built, expected to merit 4 stars.

OT TIGNES / DANIEL ROUSSELOT

The monstrous blocks of Le Bec Rouge are an inescapable feature of Tignes-le-Lac, from either side of the Tignes bowl →

➕ Good snow guaranteed for a long season – about the best Alpine bet

➕ One of the best areas in the world for lift-served off-piste runs

➕ Huge amount of terrain for all abilities, with swift access to Val-d'Isère's Bellevarde area

➕ Lots of accommodation close to the slopes (though there is also quite a bit that involves some walking)

➕ Attempts to make the resort villages more welcoming are paying off

➖ Resort buildings spoil the views from the slopes

➖ Bleak, treeless setting – hardly any woodland runs, and many slopes liable to closure during and after storms

➖ Still lots of long, slow chair-lifts

➖ Near-beginners looking for long green runs have to buy an area pass and go to the Val-d'Isère slopes

➖ Limited après-ski

The appeal of Tignes is simple: good snow, spread over a wide area of varied terrain, shared with Val-d'Isère. Together the two resorts form the enormous Espace Killy – a Mecca for experts, and ideal for adventurous intermediates.

We prefer to stay in Val, which is a more human place. But in many ways Tignes makes the better base: appreciably higher, more convenient, surrounded by intermediate terrain, with quick access to the Grande Motte glacier. And the case for Tignes gets stronger as results flow from the resort's campaign to reinvent itself in a more cuddly form. Cars have been largely pushed underground, new buildings are being designed in traditional styles and some old ones are getting a facelift. It all helps to combat the impression that you've landed on the Moon.

Tignes built some impressive lifts in the 1990s, but enjoyment of the expansive western side of the Tignes bowl – and some other areas of the Espace Killy, too – is limited by the time you spend riding slow chair-lifts. Upgrades are overdue.

But you keep coming back to the snow. On several occasions – last Easter was just one – we have been mighty glad to be heading for Tignes rather than some lower resort with a cosier village and slicker lift system.

The resort

Tignes was created before the French discovered the benefits of making purpose-built resorts look acceptable. Later than most of its contemporaries, a few years back it woke up to the demand for traditional Alpine ambience. Traffic is now discouraged (and in places routed underground), and the villages are certainly more pleasant as a result, even if their 'traffic-free' status is pretty nominal.

The original and main village – Tignes-le-Lac – is still the hub of the resort. Some of the smaller buildings in the central part, Le Rosset, are being successfully revamped in chalet style. But the place as a whole is dreary, and the blocks overlooking the lake from the quarter called Le Bec-Rouge will be monstrous until the day

329

MOUNTAIN FACTS

For entire Espace Killy area

Altitude	1550m-3455m
	5,090ft-11,340ft
Lifts	97
Pistes	300km
	186 miles
Green	15%
Blue	46%
Red	28%
Black	11%
Snowmaking	24km
	15 miles

Recco detectors used

LIFT PASSES

2002/03 prices in euros

L'Espace Killy
Covers all lifts in Tignes and Val-d'Isère.
Beginners Free lifts on all main nursery slopes; special beginners' half-day pass.
Main pass
1-day pass 36.5
6-day pass 172.5
Senior citizens
Over 60: 6-day pass 147
Over 75: free pass
Children
Under 13: 6-day pass 129.5
Under 5: free pass
Short-term passes
Half-day pass from 12.30 (adult 26).
Alternative periods
14 non-consecutive days pass available.
Notes 6-day pass and over valid for one day each in the Three Valleys, Pralognan-la-Vanoise, Les Saisies and Valmorel. On 3- to 15-day passes, pass reimbursed if all lifts are shut due to bad weather. Discount on new passes on presentation of previous season's pass. Extra discount for senior citizens aged 70 to 74.
Alternative passes
Super Tignes ski pass covers the lifts on the Tignes side of the Espace Killy only (adult 6-day 146).

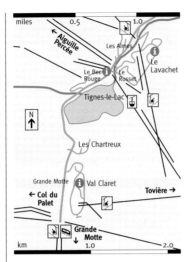

they are demolished. It's at the point where these two sub-resorts meet that the lifts are concentrated – two slow old chair-lifts up the western slopes and a powerful gondola towards Tovière and Val-d'Isère. Some attractive new buildings are being added on the fringes, in a suburb known as Les Almes. A nursery slope separates Le Rosset from the slightly more inviting suburb of Le Lavachet, below which there are now good fast lifts up both sides of the valley.

Val-Claret (2km/1 mile up the valley, beyond the lake) was mainly developed after Le Rosset, and is a bit more stylish. The main part of the village, Centre, is an uncompromisingly modern-style development on a shelf above the valley floor; a couple of lifts go up the eastern slopes from here. Down on the valley floor there are major lifts up to the Grande Motte glacier, as well as lifts accessing the sides of the bowl and the slopes of Val-d'Isère. Beside the road along the valley to the lifts is a ribbon of more recent development in traditional style. The two levels of Val-Claret are connected by a couple of indoor elevators with associated stairs as well as hazardous paths.

Below the high valley of the main resort villages are two smaller settlements. Tignes-les-Boisses, quietly set in the trees beside the road up to the main Tignes villages, consists of a barracks and a couple of simple hotels. Lower Tignes-les-Brévières is a renovated old village at the lowest point of the slopes – a favourite lunch spot, and a friendly place to stay.

Location isn't crucial, as a regular and very efficient free bus service connects all the villages until midnight – though in the daytime the route runs along the bottom of Val-Claret, leaving residents of Val-Claret Centre with some hiking.

A six-day pass covers a day in some other resorts, including Les Arcs or La Plagne and the Three Valleys, all most easily reached with the aid of a car. Preserve your pass and you'll get a loyalty discount off next year's.

The mountains

The area's great weakness is that it can become unusable in bad weather. There are no woodland runs except immediately above Tignes-les-Boisses and Tignes-les-Brévières, heavy snow produces widespread avalanche risk and wind closes the higher chairs.

THE SLOPES
High, snow-sure and varied
Tignes' biggest asset is the **Grande Motte** – and the runs from, as well as on, the glacier. The underground funicular from Val-Claret whizzes you up to over 3000m/9,850ft in seven minutes. There are blue, red and black runs to play on up here, as well as beautiful long runs back to the resort.

The main lifts towards Val-d'Isère are efficient: a high-capacity gondola from Le Lac to **Tovière**, and a fast 'bubble' chair from Val-Claret to **Col de Fresse**. You can head back to Tignes from either: the return from Tovière to Tignes-le-Lac is via a steep black run (not so difficult now the moguls are regularly smoothed out), but there is an easier run to Val-Claret.

Going up the opposite side of the valley takes you to a quieter area where a series of drags and chair-lifts serve predominantly east-facing slopes split into two main sectors, linked in both directions – **Col du Palet** and **L'Aiguille Percée**. From the latter, you can descend to Tignes-les-Brévières, on blue, red or black runs. (We're please to note that our campaign to get the Chardons run classified as red rather than blue has at last been successful.) There's an efficient gondola back.

The Col des Ves chair-lift, at the south end of the Col du Palet sector, is not normally opened until high season and several recent reporters have commented that some lifts started later in the day than advertised.

SNOW RELIABILITY
Difficult to beat

Tignes has all-year-round runs (barring brief closures in spring or autumn) on its Grande Motte glacier. And the resort height of 2100m/6,890ft generally means good snow-cover right back to base for most of the long winter season – November to May. The west-facing runs down from Col de Fresse and Tovière suffer from the afternoon sun, although they now have serious snowmaking. There are snow-guns on some other low slopes, too.

FOR EXPERTS
An excellent choice

It is the off-piste possibilities that make Tignes such a draw for experts. Go with one of the off-piste groups that the schools organise, and in good snow you'll have a great time.

One of the big adventures is to head for Champagny (linked to the La Plagne area) or Peisey-Nancroix (linked to the Les Arcs area) – very beautiful runs, and not too difficult. Your guide will organise return transport.

Another favourite of ours is the Tour de Pramecou, from the Grande Motte glacier. After some walking and beautiful isolated runs, you end up on a steep, smooth north-facing slope that takes you back to Val-Claret. There are other descents across the glacier to the Leisse chair-lift.

The whole western side of the bowl has lots of off-piste possibilities. The terrain served by the Col des Ves chair is often excellent. To the left (looking up) there are wonderfully secluded, scenic and challenging descents. On the right, lower down, is a less heavily used and gentler area, ideal for off-piste initiation. To the north, there are excellent variants on the Sache run to Les Brévières (see below).

The schools and guides offer the bizarre French form of heli-skiing: mountaintop drops are forbidden, but from Tovière you can ski down towards the Lac du Chevril to be retrieved by chopper. Or you can be dropped over the border in Italy.

The only serious challenge within the piste network is the long black run from Tovière to Tignes-le-Lac, with steep, usually heavily mogulled

Snow

01285 642 555
www.handmade-holidays.co.uk
AITO ATOL PROTECTED 4479

boarding *This is a big area, with a big boarder reputation. Snow-sure (if a bit flat) boarding on the glacier gives way to steep tree-hopping above the lowest part, Tignes-les-Brévières. In between, the lift system relies more on chairs and gondolas than drags, and long, wide pistes to blast down, with acres of powder between them to play in. The glacier is a good place for near-beginners to practise. And there are a couple of specialist snowboard schools/shops. You can buy a specific pass for the terrain-park and half-pipe. Hiring a guide and exploring the off-piste is recommended for good free-riders.*

FRANCE

332

OT TIGNES / DANIEL ROUSSELOT

This pedestrian-friendly area of Tignes-le-Lac was dominated by traffic until they pushed it underground a couple of years back ↓

sections – though no longer so difficult at the bottom, according to this year's reporters. Parts of this run get a lot of afternoon sun. Our favourite black run is the Sache, from Aiguille Percée down a secluded valley to Tignes-les-Brévières, which can become very heavily mogulled at the bottom.

A reporter recommends the black 'Silene' piste: 'big moguls – very challenging and enjoyable'.

FOR INTERMEDIATES
One of the best
For the keen intermediate piste-basher the Espace Killy is one of the top three or four areas in France, or the world.

Tignes' local slopes are ideal intermediate terrain. The red and blue runs on the Grande Motte glacier nearly always have superb snow. The glacier run from the top of the cable-car is a gentle blue. The Leisse run down to the chair-lift is now classified black and can get very mogulled but has good snow. The long red run all the way back to town is a delightful long cruise – though often crowded.

From Tovière, the blue 'H' run to Val-Claret is an enjoyable cruise and generally well groomed. But again, it can get very crowded.

There is lots to do on the other side of the valley. We particularly like the uncrowded Ves red run reached by the low-capacity Col des Ves chair – the highest point of Tignes' non-glacier runs at 2840m/9,320ft. After an initial mogul field (sometimes quite challenging) the run becomes an interesting undulating and curvy cruise, usually with good snow and a few moguls. The runs down from Aiguille Percée to Tignes-les-Boisses and Tignes-les-Brévières are also scenic and enjoyable. There are red and blue options as well as the beautiful Sache black run – adventurous intermediates shouldn't miss it. The runs down from Aiguille Percée to Le Lac are gentle, wide blues, and they were particularly popular with one of our reporter families this year. The Bleuets blue from the top of the Aiguille Rouge chair is a more challenging alternative.

FOR BEGINNERS
Good nursery slopes, but ...
The nursery slopes of Tignes-le-Lac and Le Lavachet (which meet at the top) are excellent – convenient, snow-sure, gentle, free of through-traffic and served by a slow chair and a drag. The ones at Val-Claret are less appealing:

MAISON DE TIGNES le lac

an unpleasantly steep slope within the village served by a drag, and a less convenient slope served by the fast Bollin chair. All of these lifts are free.

There are no easy longer runs in Tignes – for long green runs you have to go over to the Val-d'Isère sector. You need an Espace Killy pass to use them, and to get back to Tignes you have a choice between the blue run from Col de Fresse (which has a tricky start) or riding the gondola down from Tovière. And in poor weather, the high Tignes valley is an intimidatingly bleak place – enough to make any wavering beginner retreat to a bar with a book.

FOR CROSS-COUNTRY
Interesting variety
The Espace Killy has 40km/25 miles of cross-country trails. There are tracks on the frozen Lac de Tignes, along the valley between Val-Claret and Tignes-le-Lac, at Les Boisses and Les Brévières and up the mountain on the Grande Motte.

QUEUES
Very few
The queues here depend on snow conditions. If snow low down is poor, the Grande Motte funicular generates queues; the fast chairs in parallel with it are often quicker, despite the longer ride time. These lifts jointly shift a lot of people, with the result that the run down to Val-Claret can be seriously unpleasant. The worst queues now are for the cable-car on the glacier – half-hour waits are common.

Of course, if higher lifts are closed by heavy snow or high winds, the lifts on the lower slopes have big queues.

The famous afternoon queues for the slow Tommeuses chairs bringing Tignes residents back from the Val slopes to Tovière should now be a fond memory, as a fast eight-seat replacement is promised for 2002/03. This will also relieve pressure on the Borsat fast quad to Col de Fresse, the easiest way back to Val-Claret.

MOUNTAIN RESTAURANTS
An improvement at last
The restaurants built for last season at the top of the Chaudannes chair – the Alpage for self-service and Lo Soli for table-service – are a huge improvement on the western side of the bowl. Their adjacent terraces share a superb view of the Grande Motte, and Lo Soli provides 'superb service'. The Palet –

at the Col du Palet mid-mountain lift junction – was considered by one reporter to offer 'reasonably priced adequate food', but he also warns of 'slow-moving queues'. There is also an expensive and crowded old hut, now being upgraded and rebuilt – the Savouna – just above Tignes-le-Lac.

The opposite side of the bowl has the atmospheric chalet at the top of Tovière ('very good portions') and the modern but pleasantly woody Chalet du Bollin – just a few metres above Val-Claret. Both offer table and self-service.

The big restaurant at the top of the Grande Motte funicular has great panoramic views from its huge terrace, but it is traversed every few minutes by the next funicular-full of people.

There are lots of easily accessible places for lunch in the resorts. One ski-to-the-door favourite of ours is the ground-floor restaurant of the hotel Montana, on the left as you descend from the Aiguille Percée. The Place is reported to be 'a genuine delight with good food and real family hospitality' and a new bar in Val-Claret, the Fish Tank, is described as 'very good value'. In Les Brévières, a short walk round the corner into the village brings you to places much cheaper than the two by the piste.

SCHOOLS AND GUIDES
Enormous choice
There are half a dozen schools, plus various independent instructors. Reporters advise that pre-booking is 'essential' at busy times like Easter. The ESF and Evolution 2 are the main schools, with sections in each resort

Tignes

333

GETTING THERE

Air Geneva, transfer 3½hr. Lyon, transfer 3½hr. Chambéry, transfer 2½hr.

Rail Bourg-St-Maurice (30km/19 miles); regular buses or taxi from station.

CHILDCARE

The hotel Diva in Val-Claret (0479 067000) has a nursery taking children from age 18 months.

The Marmottons kindergarten in Le Lac (0479 065167) takes children from 2 to 8, with skiing with Evolution 2 instructors for those aged 3½ or more.

centre. Evolution 2 has received good reports, with class sizes of eight and standards of English good – the chaos on registration days is also mentioned. The ESF also receives praise apart from the class sizes – sometimes as large as 14, says a reporter this year. A reporter praises the Ski Company's teaching.

FACILITIES FOR CHILDREN
Mixed reports

In the past, we have had good reports on the Marmottons kindergartens, and on the 'experienced minders' of the Evolution 2 school in Le Lac. A reporter on the ESF considered the classes for five-year-olds too large.

Staying there

HOW TO GO
Unremarkable range of options

Although all three main styles of accommodation are available through tour operators, there isn't a lot of choice in any category, especially for those who like their creature comforts.
Chalets The choice of catered chalets is limited by comparison with other major French resorts – notably Val-d'Isère – and there are few out-of-the-ordinary ones. Ski Olympic's Chalet Rosset has been recommended by a reporter as an exception: 'Superb, with a lovely lounge with views, but a bit of an uphill plod at the end of the day.' Their Chardon is also rated 'excellent'. Neilson have a handful of places. Crystal's hotel-style Curling, plumb in the centre of Val-Claret, has neat public areas and spacious bedrooms.
Hotels The few hotels are small and concentrated in Le Lac. There are Club Meds at Val-Claret and Les Brévières.
((③ Campanules (0479 063436) Smartly rustic chalet (since its makeover) in upper Le Lac, with well equipped rooms and a good

ACTIVITIES

Indoor 'Vitatignes' in Le Lac (balneotherapy centre with spa baths, sauna etc), 'Espace Forme' in Le Lac, 'Les Bains du Montana' in Le Lac, Fitness Club in Val-Claret (body-building, aerobics, squash, golf practice and simulation, sauna, hammam, Californian baths, hot-tub, swimming pool, massage), cinemas, covered tennis court, bowling, climbing wall **Outdoor** Natural skating-rink, hang-gliding, paragliding, helicopter rides, snow-mobiles, husky dog-sleigh rides, diving beneath ice on lake, heli-skiing, 'La Banquise' for children (ice skating, snow sliding, solarium, snow activities, climbing activities, ski-joring)

Phone numbers
From abroad use the prefix +33 and omit the initial '0' of the phone number.

TOURIST OFFICE

Postcode 73321
t 0479 400440
f 0479 400315
information@tignes.net
www.tignes.net

restaurant, run by the friendly Reymond brothers.

(((3) **Village Montana** (0479 400144) New, stylishly woody complex on the east-facing slopes above Le Lac, with suites and apartments as well as rooms. Outdoor pool, and spa treatments available. One reporter enthuses about the food but felt the accommodation was fairly 'ordinary'.

(2) **Arbina** (0479 063478) Well-run place close to the lifts in Le Lac, with lunchtime terrace, crowded après-ski bar and one of the best restaurants.

(2) **Neige et Soleil** (0479 063294) Excellent family-run place in Le Lac – central, clean, cosy, comfortable, with good food.

(2) **Marais** (0479 064006) Prettily furnished, simple little hotel in Tignes-les-Boisses.

Self-catering In upper Val-Claret, close to the Tovière chair, the Maeva 'Residence Le Borsat' apartments are about the best – not too cramped, reasonably well equipped and with a communal lounge. The Chalet Club in Val-Claret is a collection of simple studios, but has the benefit of free indoor pool, sauna and in-house restaurant and bar. The supermarket at Tignes-le-Lac is reported to be 'comprehensive but very expensive'.

EATING OUT
Good places scattered about
Each of the main centres has a range of restaurants, although the options in Le Lavachet are rather limited. Reservations are recommended for many restaurants. Finding anywhere with some atmosphere is difficult in Le Lac, though the food in some of the better hotels is good. We and readers have been impressed by the hotels Arbina and Campanules – 'a meal of the highest quality, excellent service and attention to detail' – and reporters recommend enthusiastically the small, friendly, atmospheric Clin d'Oeil.

In Val-Claret the Bouf'Mich is a favourite ('terrific food, reasonable prices, helpful service, pretty interior'). The Cavern is recommended: 'Superb, and there's entertainment – have to book.' Pizza 2000 is recommended for 'reasonable prices, helpful staff, especially with large parties'. There is some debate over whether the pizzas are better here or at the Pignatta. The Ski d'Or is a swanky Relais & Châteaux hotel. Terrasses du Claret is recommended for large groups.

The Cordée in Les Boisses is said to offer unpretentious surroundings, great traditional French food, modest prices.

APRES-SKI
Early to bed
Tignes is rather quiet at night, though there is no shortage of bars, some doing food as well. Val-Claret has some early-evening atmosphere and happy hours are popular – the 'pub-like' Crowded House under Crystal's chalet hotel Curling gets most mentions, followed by the Wobbly Rabbit. Other recommendations include the Fish Tank, a new bar above the ski school meeting area – 'excellent audio visual system and satellite TV'.

Le Lac is a natural focus for immediate après-ski drinks, but don't expect anything too riotous. The bar of the hotel Arbina is our kind of spot – adequately cosy, spacious enough to absorb some groups, friendly service.

The most animated bar in Le Lavachet is Harri's – 'very good', 'good atmosphere and ambience', 'always lively' are this year's verdicts. The satellite TV here is popular. The Alpaka Lodge is recommended as 'relaxed, great for conversation and cocktails'.

Caves du Lac, Café de la Poste and Jack's are popular late haunts.

OFF THE SLOPES
Forget it
Despite the range of alternative activities, Tignes is a resort for those who want to use the slopes, where anyone who doesn't is liable to feel like a fish out of water.

STAYING DOWN THE VALLEY
Only for visiting other resorts
See the Val-d'Isère chapter; the same considerations apply broadly here. But bear in mind that there are rooms to be had in simple hotels in Tignes-les-Boisses and Tignes-les-Brévières.

Tignes

335

Les Trois Vallées

The biggest lift-linked ski area in the world

01285 642 555
www.handmade-holidays.co.uk
AITO   ATOL PROTECTED 4479

Despite competing claims, notably from the Portes du Soleil, in practical terms the Trois Vallées cannot be beaten for sheer quantity of lift-served terrain. There is nowhere like it for a keen skier or boarder who wants to cover as much mileage as possible while rarely taking the same run repeatedly. It has a lot to offer everyone, from beginner to expert. And its resorts offer a wide range of alternatives – not only the quite widely known attractions of the four mega-resorts (Courchevel, Méribel, Les Menuires and Val-Thorens) but also the increasingly appreciated low-key appeal of the smaller villages that have grown up more recently – St-Martin-de-Belleville and La Tania. Every keen skier and boarder will find at least one of the six compelling.

The runs of the Trois Vallées and their resorts are dealt with in six chapters. The four major resorts are Courchevel, Méribel, Les Menuires and Val-Thorens, but St-Martin-de-Belleville, a small village along the mountainside from Les Menuires, and La Tania, a relatively new development on the slopes between Courchevel and

Méribel, also get their own chapters.
    None of the resorts is cheap. **Les Menuires** is the cheapest but it is also the ugliest (though new developments around the original one are now being built in a more acceptable style). The slopes around the village get too much sun for comfort, but across the valley are some of the best (and quietest)

challenging pistes in the Trois Vallées on its north-facing La Masse. Down the valley from Les Menuires is **St-Martin-de-Belleville**, a charming traditional village which has been expanded in a sympathetic style. It has good-value accommodation and improving lift links into the rest of the area.

Up rather than down the Belleville valley from Les Menuires, at 2300m/7,550ft **Val-Thorens** is the highest resort in the Alps, and at 3230m/10,560ft the top of its slopes is the high point of the Trois Vallées. The snow in this area is almost always good, and it includes two glaciers where good snow is guaranteed. But the setting is bleak and the lifts are vulnerable to closure in bad weather. The purpose-built resort is very convenient. Visually it is not comparable to Les Menuires, thanks to the smaller-scale design and more thorough use of wood cladding, but it still isn't to everyone's taste.

Méribel is a two-part resort. The higher component, **Méribel-Mottaret**, is the best placed of all the resorts for getting to any part of the Trois Vallées system in the shortest possible time. It's now quite a spread-out place, with some of the accommodation a long way up the hillsides – great for access to the slopes, less so for access to nightlife. **Méribel** itself is 200m lower and has long been a British favourite, especially for chalet holidays. It is the most attractive of the main Trois Vallées resorts, built in chalet style beside a long winding road up the hillside. Parts of the resort are very convenient for the slopes and the village centre; parts are very far from either. The growing hamlet of **Méribel-Village** has its own chair-lift into the system but is very isolated and quiet. A gondola leads up to Méribel from the old spa town of **Brides-Les-Bains** which has cheap accommodation but no piste back to it.

Courchevel has four parts. 1850 is the most fashionable resort in France, and can be the most expensive resort in the Alps (though it doesn't have to cost a fortune to stay there). The less expensive parts are Le Praz (aka 1300), 1550 and 1650. They don't have the same choice of nightlife and restaurants, and only 1550 enjoys the same central location in the lift system. Many people rate the slopes around Courchevel the best in the Trois Vallées, with runs to suit all standards. The snow tends to be better than in neighbouring Méribel, because many of the slopes are north-facing. And the piste grooming is the best in the Trois Vallées, if not the best in Europe.

La Tania was built for the 1992 Olympics, just off the small road linking Le Praz to Méribel. It has now grown into a quiet, attractive, car-free collection of chalets and chalet-style apartments set among the trees and is popular with families. It has a good nursery slope and lovely long intermediate runs, but there are no very easy runs back to it.

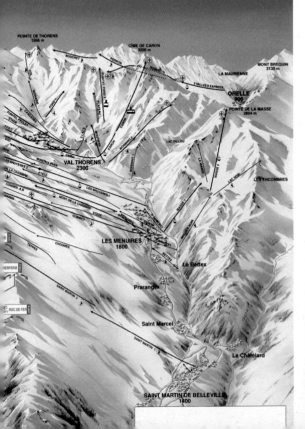

One of our favourites, with powerful attractions for all keen skiers and riders

WHAT IT COSTS

(6)

HOW IT RATES

The slopes

Snow	★★★★★
Extent	★★★★★
Experts	★★★★★
Intermediates	★★★★★
Beginners	★★★
Convenience	★★★
Queues	★★★★
Restaurants	★★

The rest

Scenery	★★★
Resort charm	★★★
Off-slope	★★

➕

- ➕ Huge area linked with Tignes, with lots of runs for all abilities
- ➕ One of the great resorts for lift-served off-piste runs
- ➕ High altitude of most slopes means snow is more or less guaranteed
- ➕ Wide choice of schools, especially for off-piste lessons and guiding
- ➕ For a high resort, the town is attractive, very lively at night, and offers a good range of restaurants
- ➕ Wide range of package holidays and accommodation
- ➕ Piste grooming and staff attitudes have improved noticeably

➖

- ➖ Piste grading understates the difficulty of many runs – though moguls on greens now uncommon
- ➖ You're quite likely to need the bus at the start or end of the day
- ➖ Most lifts and slopes are liable to close when the weather is bad
- ➖ Runs to valley level often tricky
- ➖ Nursery slopes not ideal
- ➖ High-season crowds on some runs
- ➖ Still some lifts in need of upgrading
- ➖ Main off-piste slopes get tracked out very quickly
- ➖ Seems at times more British than French – especially in low season
- ➖ Few good mountain restaurants

MOUNTAIN FACTS

For entire Espace Killy area

Altitude	1550m-3455m
	5,090ft-11,340ft
Lifts	97
Pistes	300km
	185 miles
Green	15%
Blue	46%
Red	28%
Black	11%
Snowmaking	24km
	15 miles
Recco detectors used	

Val-d'Isère is one of the world's best resorts for experts – attracted by the extent of lift-served off-piste – and for confident, mileage-hungry intermediates. But you don't have to be particularly adventurous to enjoy the resort, and the village ambience has improved greatly in recent years.

The list of drawbacks above looks long, but they are mainly petty complaints, whereas the plus-points are mainly things that weigh heavily in the balance, both for us and for the many enthusiastic reporters we hear from. The last of the plus-points – the clear recent improvements in piste grooming and lift staff attitudes – is as welcome as it is surprising. If the lift company would make a serious attempt to grade its runs sensibly, Val would make more friends than it does at present among nervous intermediates who panic on mogul fields.

Despite the lack of compelling mountain restaurants – normally a key requirement of your editors – this is, in the end, simply one of our favourite resorts in the world.

The resort

Val-d'Isère spreads along a remote valley, which is a dead end in winter. The road in from Bourg-St-Maurice brings you dramatically through a rocky defile to the satellite mini-resort of La Daille – a convenient but hideous slope-side apartment complex and the base of lifts into the major Bellevarde sector of the slopes. The outskirts of Val proper are dreary, but as you approach the centre the legacy of the 1992 Olympics becomes more evident: new wood- and stone-cladding, culminating in the tasteful pedestrian-only Val Village complex. The few remnants of the original old village are tucked away behind this.

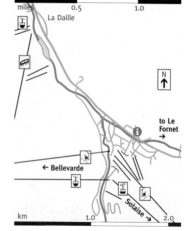

What's new

Many first-time visitors find the resort much 'prettier' than they expect a big-name high resort to be, and returning visitors generally find things improving.

Turn right at the centre and you drive under the nursery slopes to Val's big lifts up to Bellevarde and Solaise; there is now a lot of development here, most of it beyond the lifts. Continue up the main valley instead, and you come to Le Fornet – an old village and the third major lift station.

There is a lot of traffic around, but the resort is working to get cars under control to make the centre more pedestrian-friendly.

The location of your accommodation isn't crucial. Free shuttle-buses run along the main street linking the main lift stations. It is one of the most efficient bus services we've come across; even in peak periods, you never have to wait more than a few minutes. But in the evening frequency plummets and dedicated après-skiers will want to be within walking distance of the centre. The development up the side valley beyond the main lift station is mainly attractive; some places are a pleasant stroll from the centre, but the farthest-flung are a long slog – unless you're happy to pay for taxis, you need a car or a tour operator that provides transport. La Daille and Le Fornet have their (quite different) attractions for those less concerned about nightlife.

A car is of no great value around the resort, but simplifies outings to other resorts. A six-day lift pass gives a day in Les Arcs or La Plagne, plus the Trois Vallées. Other resorts nearby are Ste-Foy and La Rosière.

The mountains

Although there are wooded slopes above the village on all sectors, in practice most of the runs here are on open slopes above the tree line.

This year's reporters thought that piste grooming had improved 'much better than we'd expected', 'almost up to Courchevel standard in some places'. We continue to get complaints about the poor signing, particularly at piste junctions – and of the piste grading ('a joke' and 'dodgy' are two remarks made by reporters this year). The local radio carries good weather reports in English as well as French.

THE SLOPES
Vast and varied

Val-d'Isère's slopes divide into three main sectors. **Bellevarde** is the mountain that is home to Val-d'Isère's famous downhill course – the OK piste, which opens each season's World Cup Alpine circus in early December. You can reach Bellevarde by funicular from La Daille; up to now this has been the favoured route, and even people based in central Val have taken the bus to La Daille at the start of the day. But for the coming season a powerful new gondola will replace the old cable-car from the edge of the Val nursery slope. From the top you can get back down to the main lifts, play on a variety of drags and chairs at altitude or take a choice of lifts to the Tignes slopes.

Solaise is the other mountain accessible directly from Val-d'Isère. The Solaise Express fast quad chair-lift takes you a few metres higher than the

LIFT PASSES

2002/03 prices in euros

L'Espace Killy
Covers all lifts in Tignes and Val-d'Isère.

Beginners 7 free beginners' lifts on main nursery slopes.

Main pass
1-day pass 36.5
6-day pass 172.5

Senior citizens
Over 60: 6-day pass 147
Over 75: free pass

Children
Under 13: 6-day pass 129.5
Under 5: free pass

Short-term passes
Half-day pass from 12.30 (adult 26).

Alternative periods
14 non-consecutive days pass available.

Notes 6-day pass and over valid for one day each in the Three Valleys, Pralognan-la-Vanoise and Les Saisies. On 3- to 15-day passes, pass reimbursed if all lifts are shut due to bad weather. Discount on new passes on presentation of your lift pass for any one of the previous three seasons. Extra discount for senior citizens aged 70 to 74.

boarding *Val-d'Isère is good for boarders, though Tignes is a more popular boarder destination. Most of the main lifts are cable-cars, chair-lifts and gondolas, with very few drag-lifts. But there are a few flat areas where you'll need to scoot or walk. Experts will revel in the off-piste. There's a terrain-park with a half-pipe on Bellevarde, under the Mont Blanc chair-lift, and another at La Daille. There are several specialist snowboard shops and schools. The village nursery area is ideal for trying boarding for the first time and Le Fornet is good to progress to. Val's nightlife – with its huge selection of bars – is difficult to beat.*

parallel cable-car. Once up, a short drag takes you over a plateau and down to a variety of chairs that serve this very sunny area of predominantly gentle pistes.

From near the top of this area you can catch a chair over to the third main area, above and below the **Col de l'Iseran**, which can also be reached by cable-car from Le Fornet in the valley. The chair-lift ride is spectacular or scary, depending on your head for heights: it climbs over a steep ridge and then drops suddenly down the other side. There is an alternative way over: a short and steep drag-lift takes you to a narrow tunnel through the ridge, leading to an awkward black run which is often closed. The runs at Col de l'Iseran are predominantly easy, with spectacular views and access to the region's most beautiful off-piste terrain. The defunct Cascade chair-lift has been replaced by a fast quad giving access to the runs on the Pissaillas glacier beyond the col.

SNOW RELIABILITY
Difficult to beat
In years when lower resorts have suffered, Val-d'Isère has rarely been short of snow. Its height means you can almost always get back to the village, especially because of the snowmaking facilities on the lower slopes of all the main routes home. But even more important is that in each sector there are lots of lifts and runs above mid-mountain, between about 2300m and 2900m (7,500ft and 9,500ft). Many of the slopes face roughly north. And there is access to glaciers at Pissaillas or over in Tignes, although both take a while to get to.

FOR EXPERTS
One of the world's best
Val-d'Isère is one of the top resorts in the world for experts. The main attraction is the huge range of beautiful off-piste possibilities – see feature panel. There may be better resorts for really steep pistes – there are certainly lots in North America – but there is plenty to amuse the expert here, despite the small number of blacks on the piste map. Many of the red and blue runs are steep enough to get mogulled.

On Bellevarde the famous Face run is the main attraction – often mogulled from top to bottom, but not worryingly steep. Epaule is the sector's other black run – where the moguls are hit

3300m/10,830ft

Glacier de Pissaillas

Col Pers

2950m

Col de l'Iseran
2765m

2900m

Tignes

Col de
Fresse
2770m

Tour Charvet

Le Manchet
1940m

2325m

Bellevarde
2705m

Solaise
2560m

Le Châtelard

Le Fornet
1930m

Le Laisinant

Val d'Isère
1850m/6,070ft

La Daille
1785m

by long exposure to sun and can be slushy or rock-hard too often for our liking. There are several challenging ways down from Solaise to the village: all steep, though none fearsomely so. This has traditionally been classic bumps territory, but one of our regular reporters ruefully notes that the resort's new enthusiasm for grooming has extended even to these slopes: 'Solaise bumps the size of small cars are nothing now but a fond memory.'

FOR INTERMEDIATES
Quantity and quality
Val-d'Isère has even more to offer intermediates than experts. There's enough here to keep you interested for several visits – though there are complaints about crowded high-season pistes, and the less experienced should be aware that many runs are under-classified. This remains a regular reporter complaint.

In the Solaise sector is a network of gentle blue runs ideal for building confidence. And there are a couple of beautiful runs from here through the woods to Le Laisinant, from where you catch the bus – these are ideal for bad weather, though prone to closure in times of avalanche danger.

Most of the runs in the Col de l'Iseran sector are even easier – ideal for early and hesitant intermediates. Those marked blue at the top of the glacier could really be classified green.

Bellevarde has a huge variety of runs ideally suited to intermediates of all levels. From Bellevarde itself there is a choice of green, blue and red runs of varying pitch. And the wide runs from Tovière normally give you the choice of groomed piste or moguls.

A snag for early intermediates is that runs back to the valley can be challenging. The easiest way is to head down to La Daille, where there is a green run – but it should be classified

blue (in some resorts it would be red), and it gets very crowded and mogulled at the end of the day. None of the runs from Bellevarde and Solaise back to Val itself is really easy. The blue Santons run from Bellevarde takes you through a long, narrow gun barrel which often has people standing around plucking up courage, making things even trickier. On Solaise there isn't much to choose between the blue and red ways down – and they're both narrow in places. At the top, there's no option other than the red run in full view of the lifts. Many early intermediates sensibly choose to ride the lifts down – take the chair for a spectacular view.

FOR BEGINNERS
OK if you know where to go
The nursery slope right by the centre of town is 95 per cent perfect; it's just a pity that the top is unpleasantly steep. The lifts serving it are free.

Once off the nursery slopes, you have to know where to find easy runs; many of the greens should be blue, or even red. One local instructor admits: 'We have to have green runs on the map, even if we don't have so many green slopes – otherwise beginners wouldn't come to Val-d'Isère.'

A good place for your first real runs off the nursery slopes is the Madeleine green run on Solaise – now served by a fast six-pack. The Col de l'Iseran runs are also gentle and wide, and not overcrowded. There is good progression terrain on Bellevarde, too, but no genuinely easy way back to the valley.

FOR CROSS-COUNTRY
Limited
There are a couple of loops towards La Daille and another out past Le Laisinant. More picturesque is the one going from Le Châtelard (on the road

Off Piste Ski School
Val d'Isère

Alpine Experience
is a band of half-a-dozen guides (Scottish, Canadian, French, Italian) who specialise in leading or teaching small off-piste groups.

winter/spring:
t 00 33 479 062881
summer/autumn:
t 01483 425840
info@alpineexperience.com
www.alpineexperience.com

Few resorts can rival the extent of lift-served off-piste skiing in Val-d'Isère and Tignes; there are countless classic runs waiting to be discovered. To give you a feel for what's available, we've asked TJ Baird of Alpine Experience, one of Val-d'Isère's leading guiding companies, to describe some of the best routes.

Don't be tempted to undertake any of these routes without guidance. Many of the more popular runs are skied into an almost piste-like state soon after a fresh snowfall, but the risks of all off-piste skiing remain – avalanches, cliffs, crevasses on glaciers. A guide will steer you away from these dangers, and will be able to get you off that piste-like main run to find fresh snow, if any remains – particularly if you are equipped with touring kit and are prepared to hike a bit.

For this feature, we've asked TJ to focus on runs around Val-d'Isère and to leave Tignes aside, so he's had to leave out some of his favourites – Lognan, the Tour de Pramecou. Maybe next year, TJ.

Part of the delight of off-piste skiing is the splendid views and the feeling of being alone with your group in high, unspoiled and untamed mountains. I have tried to capture this feeling by giving each run a rating for High Mountain Ambience (HMA). Here are some of my favourites.

*The **Pays Désert**, 3200m-2780m (10,500ft-9,120ft), on the Pissaillas glacier, sits above Le Fornet, the small village at the head of the valley. It is reached by traversing away from the pistes at the top of the lift system, above cliffs. Open vistas on easy slopes that are isolated from the pistes by cliffs make this a first choice for intermediate off-piste skiers. The terrain is varied enough to make this run interesting but not too challenging. There are no crevasses on that side of the glacier but the Pays Désert T-bar must be working or you'll be walking out. For intermediate skiers. HMA 7/10*

*For a small-scale tour, you can't beat the **Tour du Charvet**, 2700m-1950m (8,860ft-6,400ft), which starts from the top of the Grand Pre chair-lift on the back of Bellevarde. With no walking involved, it appeals to a lot of skiers and presents you with all you could hope for: a fabulous panorama, solitude and a variety of wildlife from chamois to alpine hare and perdrix blanche (ptarmigan). Beginning with gentle meadows it has steepish pitches between rock ledges in the middle (37 degrees) and winds around the Charvet to bring you out at the bottom of the Manchet chair-lift in the Solaise sector. For accomplished skiers. HMA 9/10*

*A similar itinerary to the Tour du Charvet, **Col Pers**, 2950m-1900m (9,680ft-6,230ft), starts from the Pissaillas glacier. A short but sometimes tricky traverse brings you to a small pass. Once over this you are miles from civilisation. A long, gentle valley overlooked by 3200m/10,500ft peaks leads you to the Isère valley floor, with the Italian frontier draped with glaciers to your right. The exit is via the Gorge de Malpasset, which must have a good snow-cover to permit passage back to the resort along the closed Route Nationale road. Again wildlife abounds, with even a herd of bouquetin overlooking your trail. For accomplished skiers. HMA 9/10*

***Cugnai**, 2960m-1950m (9,710ft-6,400ft), is a wide, secluded bowl at the far end of the Solaise sector, with direct access via the Cugnai chair-lift. Skiing over to the far side presents a magnificent, 'gun-barrel' view from the top of a steep slope (37 degrees) underneath a sheer black rock wall. The slope narrows down into a gully to the valley floor, bringing you to the Manchet chair-lift. It's important not to do this run too late in the day – the valley floor is overlooked by massive south-facing slopes, which can slide. HMA 8/10*

*Moving up the scale, the **Banane**, 2650m-1880m (8,690ft-6,170ft), is easily accessible from the Face de Bellevarde piste but it is not easy to find the entrance and avoid the Clochton couloirs. It's a long and impressive run (37–40 degrees) with spectacular views across the Manchet valley. The danger is always highest at the entrance because of large snowdrifts. For advanced skiers. HMA 9/10*

*Capping all of these is the **Couloir des Pisteurs**, 2860m-2490m (9,380ft-8,170ft), which requires a 20-minute climb from the Tour du Charvet. The view from the top is simply stunning. A very narrow steep chute (44 degrees) bounded by rock faces brings you out on to a wide open slope above Le Grand Pré, right opposite Bellevarde. A must for intrepid expert skiers. HMA 11/10*

Val-d'Isère

343

SCHOOLS/GUIDES

Prices in euros

ESF
2001/02 prices
Classes 6 days
5½hr: 3hr am, 2½hr
pm. 6 full days: 187
Children's classes
Ages: from 4
6 full days: 182
Private lessons
1hr, mornings,
afternoons, or whole
days. 33 for 1hr

Snow Fun
2001/02 prices
Classes 6 days
3hr am and 2½hr pm
5 mornings: 92
Children's classes
Ages: up to 13
6 full days: 167
Private lessons
Hourly or daily
31 for 1hr

Top Ski
2001/02 prices
Specialises in slalom,
mogul and off-piste
courses for small
groups (max 6)
Classes 4 days
4hr: 9am-1pm; 2hr:
2pm-4pm
4 days: 168
Private lessons
am, pm or full day:
72 for 2hr, 107 for 3hr

Alpine Experience
2002/03 prices
Specialises in off-
piste guiding and
teaching for small
groups (max 6)
Guiding groups
7 days a week
am only (8.45-1pm):
1 day 46, 5 days 220,
private guide am 245,
full day 312
Classes
pm only (1.55-4.15)
1 afternoon 29
private 90

Other major schools
Evolution 2

Other minor schools
Altimanya
Mountain Masters
Oxygène
Stages Val Gliss
Tétra Hors-Piste

past the main cable-car station) to the
Manchet chair. But keen cross-country
enthusiasts should go elsewhere.

QUEUES
Few problems
Queues to get out of the resort have
been kept in check by new lifts – first
the funicular at La Daille, then fast
chair-lifts as alternatives to the two
main cable-cars, and now the
replacement of the Bellevarde cable-car
by a big new gondola.

For some years the quickest way to
Tignes has been to take the fast quad
to Col de Fresse, but replacement of
the slow and crowded Tommeuses
chairs should make travel via Tovière a
realistic proposition once again.
Coming back from Val-Claret at the end
of the day is now much quicker thanks
to a fast, dual-loading, six-person
chair-lift direct to Col de Fresse, with a
run down to Bellevarde. Make sure you
get into the correct queue: half the
chairs stop part-way up the hill,
serving runs back into Val-Claret.

The number of slow chair-lifts
scattered about the area, particularly in
Tignes, is a common complaint.
Crowded pistes is another.

At the end of the day, there's
usually a wait for the chair back from
Col de l'Iseran to Solaise (though you
can always descend to Le Fornet
instead). A reporter regularly found a
queue for the slow Lac chair that links
the bottom of the Madeleine up to the
Tête Solaise.

If you plan a return visit, keep your
lift pass – those with a week's pass
bought in the last three years are
entitled to a 'loyal customer' reduction.

MOUNTAIN RESTAURANTS
Getting better – slowly
The mountain restaurants mainly
consist of big self-service places with
vast terraces at the top of major lifts.

The Fruitière at the top of La Daille
gondola, a table-service place kitted
out with stuff rescued from a dairy in
the valley, continues to get good
reports: 'Excellent, the best we have
been to,' says one. The Folie Douce is
a functional but popular self-service
place at the same spot. Other
recommendations: the Trifollet, about
halfway down the OK run – 'fast
service, good pizzas and an
entertaining view of the slopes' – 'very
good for egg and chips' – 'soak up the
sun on the balcony or curl up in front
of the log fire'; Marmottes, in the
middle of the Bellevarde bowl – big
sunny terrace, self-service – 'a good
coffee stop'; the Signal at the top of
the Le Fornet cable-car – 'excellent
service and value, huge portions' says
one reporter, but 'mediocre food at the
self-service section', says another; the
'small and friendly' Bar de L'Ouillette,
at the base of the Madeleine chair-lift –
'good selection of snack meals'; the
Datcha, at the bottom of the Cugnai lift
– 'excellent salads, if expensive'; and
the Tanière, set between the two chairs
going up Face de Bellevarde – 'food
well priced and service friendly,
popular with lifties and pisteurs'.

There are restaurants on the lower
slopes at La Daille that are reachable
on snow and by pedestrians. Tufs is 'a
busy, friendly place that does rather a
good pizza', and the Toit du Monde
(formerly the Crêch'ouna), just above it
offers 'excellent service'.

Of course there are lots of places
actually in the resort villages. When at
Col de l'Iseran, one possible plan for
lunch on a wintry day is to descend to
the rustic Arolay at Le Fornet – 'The
food was good and the staff were
charming,' says a reporter this year.
Lunch over in Tignes-les-Brévières is a
popular option for those on a high-
mileage mission.

New
Flagship Store
Launches into 2003

PRECISION

BIGGER AND BETTER THAN EVER BEFORE

Our new 600m² flagship store in the town centre offers a totally different resort-shopping experience......

- Even bigger choice of skis, boots and boards
- Daily on-snow equipment testing
- For the first time, technical and casual clothing the 'Precision' way
- Val d'Isère's biggest and best equipment rental department
- New specialist bootfitting centre like you've never seen before

And so you can relax and enjoy the whole 'Precision Experience', we've opened our brand new in-shop café/bar....breakfast before hitting the hill, something different for lunch, great après-ski and snacks, coffee (or something stronger) while the rest of the family get kitted out.

Added to all of this, we have even more professionally trained, knowledgeable and friendly ENGLISH SPEAKING staff and extra special services. No wonder we've been voted 'European Ski Shop of the Year' yet again.

We're not just 'any old ski shop' – we're THE ski shop in Val d'Isère!

www.precision-ski.com

SCHOOLS AND GUIDES
A very wide choice

There is a huge choice of schools and private instructors to choose from. Practically all of the schools run off-piste guided groups at various levels of competence – an excellent way to get off-piste safely without the cost of hiring a guide as an individual, and one of the real attractions of Val for experts. Outside the ESF, practically all the instructors and guides speak good English, and many are native English-speakers.

There are two major rivals to the ESF. We've heard from lots of satisfied Snow Fun pupils: 'excellent' was the general verdict among this year's reporters. Reporters are also full of praise for Evolution 2: 'really good, with very encouraging instructors', 'excellent teachers'.

There are several smaller outfits that specialise in leading and teaching small groups, usually off-piste. In peak periods it's best to book in advance. Mountain Masters is a small group of British and French instructors and guides. Recent reports say Top Ski (18 guides, mostly French) is 'highly recommended' and 'efficient'; Alpine Experience (half-dozen guides, Canadian, French, Italian, British) provide 'excellent off-piste lessons'. We have also had good reports on Ski Prestige. We've had great days ourselves with both Alpine Experience and Top Ski.

This year the big news in the schools business is the launch of a new school, The Development Centre, based in a huge new Precision Ski shop in the heart of the village – a

group of forward-thinking British instructors offering intensive clinics for all levels of skier.

Heli-trips can be arranged – you are dropped over the border in Italy because heli-drops are banned in France.

FACILITIES FOR CHILDREN
Good tour op possibilities

Many people prefer to use the facilities of UK tour operators such as Mark Warner or Ski Beat. But there's a 'children's village' for 3- to 13-year-olds, with supervised indoor and outdoor activities on the village nursery slopes. It's open daily from 8.30 to 6.30. A past reporter was 'very pleased' with the childcare there: 'The staff speak English, and are very organised, in particular about the children's safety.'

We have personal experience of the indifference of the ESF's handling of children, reinforced by a more recent report from the father of two children who were placed in classes of French pupils and subsequently 'abandoned in mid-class' by their instructors.

CHILDCARE

Le Village des Enfants (0479 400981), in the centre of town, takes children from 3 to 13, from 8.30 to 6.30.

The Petit Poucet (0479 061397) in the Residence les Hameaux de Val takes children from age 3, from 9am to 5.30.

Both provide indoor and outdoor activities and delivery to and collection from ski school.

Snowfun's Club Nounours takes children aged 3 to 6 for lessons of 1½hr, 2hr or 3hr. Older children can be left in classes all day.

The ESF runs a ski nursery for age 4 up, with rope tows and a heated chalet.

The tourist office has a list of babysitters.

GETTING THERE

Air Geneva, transfer 4hr. Lyon, transfer 4hr. Chambéry, transfer 3hr.

Rail Bourg-St-Maurice (31km/19 miles); regular buses from station.

Staying there

HOW TO GO
Lots of choice

More British tour operators go to Val-d'Isère than to any other resort. The choice of chalets and chalet-hotels is vast. There is a Club Med 'village'.

Chalets There is everything from budget chalets – some away from the centre, at Le Châtelard, Le Laisinant and Le Fornet – to the most luxurious you could demand. The resort has a fair number of chalet operators who don't go anywhere else, including YSE and Val d'Isère Properties. Both of these offer some luxury places, as do Scott Dunn Ski, Finlays, Lotus Supertravel and The Ski Company Limited, which has a group of luxury chalets on the edge of the village with fabulous views up the Manchet valley – with a new property being built there for this season. Le Ski has four splendid all-en-suite chalets on the edge of town, not far from YSE's lovely old Mountain Lodges. Ski Beat has a smart five-unit chalet at La Daille.

There are lots of chalet hotels. Mark Warner has four, including the family-friendly, 'very good-value' Cygnaski, the nightlife hot spot Moris – 'basic rooms but ideal location and helpful staff' – and the Val d'Isère, which enjoys free use of the adjoining village swimming pool – 'Excellent location, spacious rooms but a touch tired.'

Hotels There are about 40 to choose from, mostly 2- and 3-star, but for such a big international resort surprisingly few are notably attractive.

((((4) **Christiania** (0479 060825) Recently renovated big chalet, probably best in town. Chic, with friendly staff. Sauna.

((((4) **Latitudes** (0479 061888) Modern, stylish. Piano bar, nightclub. Leisure centre: sauna, steam room, whirlpool, massage.

((((4) **Blizzard** (0479 060207) Renovated for Olympics. Indoor-outdoor pool. Convenient. A non-resident praises the food very highly.

(((3) **Grand Paradis** (0479 061173) Excellent position. Good food.

(((3) **Savoyarde** (0479 060155) Rustic decor. Leisure centre. Good food. Rooms a bit small.

(((3) **Kandahar** (0479 060239) Smart, newish building above Taverne d'Alsace on main street.

Val-d'Isère

347

ACTIVITIES

Indoor Swimming pool, sports hall (basketball, volleyball, table tennis, badminton, trampoline and gymnastics), library, bridge, health centres in the hotels Christiania, Brussels and Le Val d'Isère (sauna, hammam, hot-tub, body building, massages, solarium etc), cinema **Outdoor** Natural skating rink, hang-gliding, quad-bikes, all-terrain karts, ice driving, snow-mobiles, paragliding, snow-shoe outings, heli-skiing, microlight trips, ice-climbing, dog-sledding, walking

((($ **Mercure** (0479 061293) Highly recommended by one of our most reliable reporters: 'It doesn't look much from the outside, but the food and the wine list are excellent.'
((($ **Sorbiers** (0479 062377) Modern but cosy B&B hotel, not far out. 'Clean, comfortable, good-sized rooms.'
((($ **Samovar** (0479 061351) In La Daille. Traditional, with good food.
Self-catering There are thousands of properties to choose from. UK operators offer lots of them, but they tend to get booked up early. Local agency Val-d'Isère Agence has a good brochure. The local supermarkets are said to be well stocked to meet the needs of self-caterers.

EATING OUT
Plenty of good, affordable places
Restaurant standards are generally high. The 70-odd restaurants include Italian, Alsatian, Tex-Mex, even Japanese ones, but most offer good French dishes. A very helpful Guide des

Tables is freely distributed. High-season visitors have found that it is essential to book ahead – especially on Wednesday when UK chalet staff get the night off.

There are plenty of pleasant mid-priced places. The 'bustling and busy' Perdrix Blanche is popular, offering 'brilliant' fish dishes in particular. Or head for the Taverne d'Alsace, another old favourite – 'Big and busy, but good fare.' Tufs, a little way up the slopes at La Daille, is recommended, and will provide transport for groups. The Toit du Monde nearby (formerly the Crêch'ouna) offers Tibetan cuisine and is praised for 'making a real effort to be a bit different'. Family-run Chez Paolo, next to the bus stop for Le Fornet, is praised for its 'excellent pizzas and pastas'.

But our favourite – and that of many reporters – for a special night out is the Chalet du Crêt, off the road on the northern edge of downtown Val. Set in a 300-year-old stone farmhouse, beautifully renovated by the Franco-British couple who run it, this place serves a fixed-price menu starting with a magnificent hors-d'oeuvres spread. Not cheap, but highly satisfying.

Those on tight budgets should try Chez Nano (next to Dick's Tea Bar) – 'Fantastic pizza and profiteroles.' The Melting Pot also gets good reviews for its unusual menu, which includes Thai dishes and 'a good selection of veggie options'. The Corniche is recommended for being 'traditional French, very enjoyable'; the Pub for being 'very

---

Selected chalets in Val d'Isère

Phone numbers
From abroad use the prefix +33 and omit the initial 'o' of the phone number.

TOURIST OFFICE

Postcode 73155
t 0479 060660
f 0479 060456
info@valdisere.com
www.valdisere.com

French and well worth seeking out'; and Casa Scara for 'good food though the service was slow'. The leading equipment retailers Precision Ski are opening an innovative all-day cafe-bar-restaurant within their new flagship store in the middle of the resort.

APRES-SKI
Very lively
Nightlife is surprisingly energetic, given that most people have spent a hard day on the slopes. There are lots of bars, many with happy hours followed by music and dancing later on.

The Folie Douce, at the top of the La Daille gondola, has become an Austrian-style tea-time rave, with music and dancing; normally you can ride the gondola down, but it can be closed by the weather, so be prepared to ski down. At La Daille the bar at the Samovar hotel is 'a good spot for a beer after skiing'. In downtown Val, Café Face (very lively, excellent) and the Moris pub (in the Mark Warner chalet) fill up as the slopes close, and Bar Jacques (also mentioned for its food) and the Perdrix Blanche bar are popular with locals. The Aventure, next to Killy Sports, has household decor,

including a fridge, a bath and a bed – it serves good food in a separate eating area. Victor's bar is popular before it turns into a restaurant later on – black-and-white decor and stainless steel toilets. The basement Taverne d'Alsace is quiet and relaxing. The famous Dick's Tea Bar received mixed reports this year, but the 'ayes' have it: 'So good we were boring and went there all the time,' says one.

For those who like a quieter time, there are hotel bars, piano bars and cocktail lounges.

OFF THE SLOPES
Not much
Val is primarily a resort for those keen to get on to the slopes – though one non-skier this year was 'very satisfied' with the facilities. The swimming pool has been renovated, but the other sports facilities are not particularly impressive. Two reporters this year commented on the range of shops, which is better than in most high French resorts. Lunchtime meetings present problems: the easily accessible mountain restaurants are few, and your friends may prefer lunching miles away in places like Les Brévières.

Val-d'Isère

Wherever you're based in Val there's a Snowfun shop close at hand, redesigned for 2003 to take the hassle out of renting your kit. We've widened our equipment ranges to offer you even more choice, while still offering the same quality, value-for-money and informed advice skiers and boarders have relied on for years.

- Iseran 2000
- Portillo
- Grand Cocor
- Solaise
- Rond Point des Pistes

Check us out when you visit Val d'Isère

www.snowfun.fr

Valmorel

1400m/4,595ft

Pretty, purpose-built resort with fair-sized area of slopes

350

WHAT IT COSTS

HOW IT RATES

The slopes
Snow	★★★
Extent	★★★
Experts	★★
Intermediates	★★★★
Beginners	★★★★★
Convenience	★★★★★
Queues	★★★★
Restaurants	★★

The rest
Scenery	★★★
Resort charm	★★★★
Off-slope	★★

What's new

For 2001/02, a new fast six-pack was added. Le Marquis chair is on the far side of St François Longchamp 1650. New accommodation called Valériane with 73 new apartments is situated 5 minutes' walk from the centre of Valmorel, next to the Altispace chair-lift. And 35 new snow cannons were installed.

⊕ Fairly extensive slopes provide something for everyone

⊕ The most sympathetically designed French purpose-built resort

⊕ Largely slope-side accommodation

⊕ Beginners and children particularly well catered for

⊕ One of the most accessible of the Tarentaise resorts

⊕ Relatively cheap package holidays

⊖ Few challenging pistes

⊖ Fairly low in altitude, so good snow not guaranteed

⊖ Little variety in accommodation or in restaurants and bars

⊖ A few fast chairs have improved the lift system, but there are still a lot of slow lifts

Built from scratch in the mid-1970s, Valmorel was intended to look and feel like a mountain village: a traffic-free main street with low-rise hamlets grouped around it and along the lower slopes, and traditional Savoie stone and wood materials throughout. The end result is an attractive, friendly sort of place.

The slopes are extensive by most standards – though Valmorel can't rival its huge neighbours, the Trois Vallées or Val-d'Isère/Tignes. But with good snow conditions and the whole system open, there's enough here to keep everyone except real experts happy. As the snow conditions deteriorate, the variety of available runs reduces rapidly. Unashamedly aimed at the middle ground (intermediates, families and mixed-ability groups), Valmorel has considerable appeal because it has been so well put together.

The resort

Valmorel, a short drive from Moûtiers and the mega-resorts of the Trois Vallées and La Plagne, is the main resort in 'Le Grand Domaine' – a ski area that links the Tarentaise with the Maurienne, by way of the Col de la Madeleine.

Bourg-Morel is the heart of the resort – a traffic-free street where you'll find most of the shops, the restaurants, visitor information – just about everything – in a 200m stretch. It's pleasant and usually lively, with a distinctly family feel. And the slopes are right at hand, with the main pistes back to the resort and the chair-lift out meeting at the end of the street. Nearby is an information board

showing lift and piste status and what's on locally.

Scattered here and there on the hillside, but not very far from the centre, are the six 'hameaux' with most of the accommodation. Most is self-catering and of a reasonably high standard.

Valmorel is a traffic-free resort, with drop-off points for the accommodation. At the bottom end of Bourg-Morel is the base station of the Télébourg, a cross-village lift providing access to the 'Hameau-du-Mottet'.

Walking between the other hameaux and Bourg-Morel doesn't take long – but some of the pathways can be icy. Hameau-du-Mottet is convenient – it is at the top of the Télébourg, with good access to the main lifts and from the return runs. Hameau-du-Crève-Coeur was highly recommended by a reporter: 'Convenient for slopes (especially the beginner area) and with own supermarket and boulangerie.'

A car is of no use in the resort but very handy for trips to other resorts. All the mega-ski areas of the Tarentaise are within reasonable

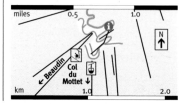

driving distance – the Trois Vallées, La Plagne, Les Arcs and even Val-d'Isère/Tignes. An off-piste tour through a number of these resorts starts from the Col du Mottet above Valmorel.

The mountains

MOUNTAIN FACTS

Altitude	1260m-2550m
	4,130ft-8,370 ft
Lifts	56
Pistes	153km
	95 miles
Green	33%
Blue	39%
Red	19%
Black	9%
Snowmaking	9km
	6 miles
Recco detectors used	

Beginners and intermediates will take to Valmorel. Those looking for more of a challenge will find it more limited. Variety is provided by sectors of quite distinctive character, and the system is big enough to provide interesting, if hardly epic, exploratory trips to its farthest boundaries. There are still a few long, awkward drag-lifts where you can become airborne at the start, but most can be avoided. Piste grooming is said to be better in Valmorel than in neighbouring Longchamp.

THE SLOPES
A big system in miniature
The 56 lifts and 153km/95 miles of piste are spread out in an interesting arrangement over a number of minor valleys and ridges either side of the Col de la Madeleine, with Valmorel at the eastern extremity of the system and runs coming down into the village on three sides.

The most heavily used route out of the village is via the high-speed Altispace covered quad, which takes you over the main pistes down to the resort. From the top, a network of lifts and pistes takes you over to the **Col de la Madeleine** and beyond that to Lauzière (the highest point of the ski area) or the slopes of **St-François** and **Longchamp** at the far western end of the area.

The Pierrafort gondola for the **Mottet** sector and the Crève-Coeur chair for the **Gollet** area take off from Hameau-du-Mottet at the top end of the village. Both have their own runs back towards the village, or you can work your way over to the Beaudin and Madeleine sectors. There's an easy link in the other direction.

Adjacent to the village there are nursery areas with good easy runs.

SNOW RELIABILITY
Sort of average
With a top station of 2550m/8,370ft and many of the runs below 2000m/6,560ft, good snow conditions are not guaranteed. Low runs are often closed, and even Lauzière, which has the system's high point but faces south, can suffer during sunny spells. Mottet is north-facing and usually has the best snow.

boarding Valmorel is a good place to try boarding for the first time – there's a separate beginners' slope and gentle runs to progress to served by chairs and gondolas. There's a basic terrain-park ('poorly kept' says a reporter), a gentle boarder cross-type course and half-pipe and decent intermediate runs – but inexperienced boarders will find some of the many drag lifts tricky. The main attraction for advanced boarders is the off-piste, though it's no longer as deserted as it used to be. Nightlife is far from throbbing in this family-oriented resort.

Valmorel

OT ST-FRANCOIS-LONGCHAMP

Don't worry: this monstrosity is St-François-Longchamp, not Valmorel →

LIFT PASSES

2002/03 prices in euros

Le Grand Domaine
Covers all lifts in Valmorel and St-François-Longchamp.
Beginners Limited area lift pass covers beginner lifts and runs.
Main pass
1-day pass 30
6-day pass 155
(low season 141)
Senior citizens
Over 60: 6-day pass 132
Children
8-13: 6-day pass 132
5-7: 101
Under 5: free pass
Short-term passes
Half-day from 12.30 (23)
Alternative passes
Valmorel Domaine covers 37 lifts in Valmorel only (6 days 147 for adults in high season, 125 for children aged 8-13, 96 for ages 5-7).

Snowmaking covers the nursery slopes and runs under the Altispace chair and the Pierrafort gondola down to village level.

FOR EXPERTS
Quiet off-piste: hire a guide

There are a few challenging pistes, but it is the off-piste that is attractive. Because the resort does not attract experts, off-piste powder can lie untracked for days after a snowfall, though more people are discovering this every year – so get there quickly to see the best of it. Gollet is usually a good place for moguls – plenty of them, but not too big and not too hard. We've done a great off-piste run from here with a guide, which started with a long traverse from the top of the drag-lift and ended right down in the village of Les Avanchers, way below Valmorel, passing through forests and over streams on the way. The off-piste between Gollet and Mottet has lots of couloirs and jumps to attempt.

There are steep black runs below the top section of the Mottet chair and some interesting off-piste variants. The Riondet drag-lift to the north of here is now usually closed because of avalanche danger – but we hiked up with a guide to some fine off-piste towards the Madeleine sector.

The Lauzière chair can seem a bit of a trek, but once there you'll probably find the area underused and a lot of

fun, provided it hasn't suffered too much sun. There are three marked runs and plenty of acreage in which to pick your own route – there are some steep pitches and often some big bumps. You can also explore a lovely deserted north-facing off-piste run here if you hire a guide – we found long stretches of great powder over a week after the last snowfall.

Touring is a popular activity in the region, and trips such as the Nine-Valley safari can be organised.

FOR INTERMEDIATES
Plenty to keep you busy

Pretty much the whole area except the steepest black runs is ideal for intermediates. A lot of people seem to mill around Beaudin and the Arenouillaz drag and Biollène chair – the adjacent runs are quite friendly. The runs into the Celliers valley are a little more challenging and advanced intermediates will enjoy the red and the black served by the Madeleine chair and the Grande Combe quad.

For a day out, the slopes down to St-François-Longchamp are within easy striking distance, and form a big area of mainly broad, flattering runs.

Valmorel is also a fine place for intermediates to get their first taste of off-piste on the gentle, open fields beside pistes.

The main thoroughfare back to the village – from Beaudin along the line of the snow-guns – is classified blue

then red, and the red stretch can be quite daunting at the end of the day. The snow tends to pile up in surprisingly large heaps, as do tired beginners. After much use even the blue Les Traverses is not easy.

The red route from the top of Mottet is outstandingly boring on the upper half – more push-and-walk than anything else – but the views are some compensation, and the lower half is much better.

The runs back to the village served by the Pierrafort gondola are classified blue but are long, interesting and in parts tricky. The adjacent Gollet slopes also provide plenty of scope for good intermediates to amuse themselves.

FOR BEGINNERS
An excellent choice
Valmorel suits beginners – there are dedicated learning areas ('still the best we've seen, 10/10' according to one reporter) right by the village for both adults (at Bois de la Croix) and children (in the snow garden of the children's club), and lots of expertise among the instructors.

The terrain does not allow extensive nursery areas in the valley, so progress from novice to beginner usually sees the children heading for the top of the Pierrafort gondola and adults for the Beaudin sector. The lifts up to these areas can also be ridden down back into the village.

If the snow-cover is complete, there is a very pleasant green run through the trees down to Combelouvière.

FOR CROSS-COUNTRY
Inconvenient and not extensive
Valmorel is not for aficionados – more for those giving it a try. Trails adding up to 23km/14 miles, at a number of locations in the valley (and so likely to have a limited season only), can be reached by special bus.

QUEUES
Much improved in recent years
Two main bottlenecks have been addressed by the Altispace and Grande Combe chairs, so getting on to the slopes in the morning and over to the St-François and Lauzière side now presents fewer problems. But there can still be 10-minute waits. The Frêne drags can't cope when everyone is returning to Valmorel. Lauzière, on the other hand, can be positively lonely, says a reporter.

MOUNTAIN RESTAURANTS
Fair to middling
There are half a dozen or so mountain restaurants in the area, none of them either appalling or wonderful. The Altipiano at the top of the gondola has been recommended for good food and value for money and a sunny, peaceful terrace. Prariond, lower down, is livelier but more expensive, with good food and loud music. The Arbet at the top of Lanchettes is reasonable value. The Banquise 2000 has been suggested as a good stopping point after a visit to the views and more challenging runs off Lauzière. Grolla at Combelouvière has 'good service and view'.

SCHOOLS AND GUIDES
Good, especially for first-timers
We've had some good reports about the school over the years. Instructors generally speak good English and are enthusiastic and imaginative. Teaching for first-timers is a speciality of the resort, and likely to produce good results. A reporter told us of a visitor who had never skied before: 'He had one private lesson with the ESF, which he said was fine, and then managed to ski with his friends quite satisfactorily.'

FACILITIES FOR CHILDREN
Comprehensive, but book early
Saperlipopette is a comprehensive childcare facility, though past reports have varied from children loving it to being bored or distraught. We have no very recent reports. Children aged between four and eight taking ski lessons at the ski-school can also have lunch at Saperlipopette, being brought from or taken to their lesson by the staff. Advance booking is essential except for very quiet times.

Valmorel

353

GETTING THERE

Air Geneva, transfer 3¹⁄₂hr. Lyon, transfer 3¹⁄₂hr. Chambéry, transfer 2¹⁄₂hr.

Rail Moûtiers (18km/11 miles); regular buses from station.

ACTIVITIES

Indoor Cinema
Outdoor Microlight flights, ice-climbing, snow-shoe outings, 12km/7 miles of prepared walks, paragliding, horse-drawn carriage rides

Phone numbers

From abroad use the prefix +33 and omit the initial '0' of the phone number.

TOURIST OFFICE

Postcode 73260
t 0479 098555
f 0479 098529
info@valmorel.com
www.valmorel.com

Staying there

HOW TO GO
Take a package for value
Self-catering packages are the norm. Beginners may prefer staying at the Bois de la Croix end of the village to avoid having to walk with ski gear.
Chalets There are some run by UK tour operators, but they tend to be catered apartments.
Hotels There are only three hotels.
(((3) **Planchamp** (0479 099700) Best in town, family run, with a good French restaurant. Right on the piste.
(((3) **Fôret** (0479 098777) Across the piste from the Planchamp. 'Good food, very good value, large rooms for France,' says a reporter.
((2) **Bourg** (0479 098666) Simple place in the middle of Bourg-Morel.
Self-catering Most people do cater for themselves. Some 8,500 apartment beds are distributed throughout the six hamlets and they are generally well equipped. While it's great having a view over the piste, the downside of certain locations in Mottet and Planchamp is the proximity of some very noisy snow-guns: the soundproofing is not quite good enough for light sleepers. The new Athamante et Valeriane apartments have been praised by resort regulars as being a step up from other places.

EATING OUT
Good enough but rarely thrilling
You can check out the menus of most of Valmorel's restaurants in 15 minutes of wandering up and down the main street. A pattern soon emerges – pizza, pasta, fondues and a smattering of Savoie fare. Couscous and galettes are also available. Not a huge variety but enough, and you're likely to get decent food and fair value. Many of the places need to be booked for any chance of a seat at a reasonable time.

The restaurant of the hotel Planchamp is relatively upmarket with prices to match. The Petit Savoyarde is a mid-range place recommended by reporters. The Ski Roc is 'excellent but expensive and popular with the local ski club'. The Marmite in the hotel Bourg has been recommended but 'isn't cheap'. The Grenier in Mottet offers a bit of everything, is in a slightly different location and is highly recommended by a reporter who 'ate there every night but one' (and

regretted their night off). Locals also recommend the Grange, the Perce-Neige, the Cordee and Tex-Mex at Jimbololo. A pizza or fondue in the popular Pizzeria Chez Albert or Pizzeria du Bourg or a takeaway (they deliver) from the Casa Pizz' are good value.

APRES-SKI
Unexciting
Immediate après-ski is centred on the outdoor cafes at the end of Bourg-Morel and Le Grenier. Both are lively spots. The after-dark activities are, like everything else, concentrated around that main street. Café de la Gare has live music but can be full of ESF staff and 'cliquey'. Casbah is popular with Brits while the Perce-Neige frequently gets packed and boisterous. Cocktails can be enjoyed in more polished surroundings at the Shaker in hotel Fôret. Jeans is the resort's one disco.

You may catch an occasional musical event at the village hall, or a street parade (there's a Mardi Gras with medieval costumes and fireworks). A two-screen cinema and a wine-tasting evening are other possibilities.

OFF THE SLOPES
Pleasant but boring
It's a very pretty little place, friendly and traffic-free. But it's not a great place to hang around if you're not using the slopes – unless you are happy spending time in cafes. There are some cleared walks around the village and at the top of all the main lifts and there's a pretty baroque church in Les Avanchers. Several mid-mountain restaurants are accessible to pedestrians, and it's also quite practical for friends using the slopes to return to the village for a lunchtime meet.

Snow-shoe treks and dog-sleigh trips can be organised – you can even learn to 'mush' the dogs.

STAYING DOWN THE VALLEY
Less than appealing
We have stayed at the Edelweiss down at Les Avanchers, which had decent French food, a rustic atmosphere and an eccentric patron. But there is little else there. A regular reporter stays at Combelouvière, and finds it 'has almost as much ski convenience as Valmorel, with a pleasanter run home at the end of the day'. However, it's quiet in the evenings.

Val-Thorens

2300m/7,550ft

Europe's highest resort, with guaranteed good snow

WHAT IT COSTS

HOW IT RATES

The slopes

Snow	★★★★★
Extent	★★★★★
Experts	★★★★
Intermediates	★★★★★
Beginners	★★★★
Convenience	★★★★★
Queues	★★★
Restaurants	★★★★

The rest

Scenery	★★★
Resort charm	★★
Off-slope	★★

What's new

Amazingly, a third big Funitel gondola is to be installed for 2002/03, replacing the Bouquetin chair towards Méribel – not only cutting queues but also reducing the chance of closure by strong winds.

This follows last year's construction of the Grand Fond Funitel towards the fourth valley, the Maurienne. A new blue run is now being created from the top of this lift. The nearby Plateau drags will be replaced by a chair.

The Sports Centre is to be renovated and will do massage etc.

Other improvements last season included new lifts over in the Maurienne valley taking the Three Valleys system to a new high-point of 3230m/10,600ft, and a 120-metre/400ft-long moving carpet on the beginner piste.

BASILE / MARK BUSCAIL

That's why you come here: the snow →

- ⊕ Extensive local slopes to suit all abilities, and good access to the rest of the vast Three Valleys
- ⊕ The highest resort in the Alps and one of the most snow-sure, with north-facing slopes guaranteeing good snow for a long season
- ⊕ Convenient, gentle nursery slopes
- ⊕ Not as much of an eyesore as most high, purpose-built resorts
- ⊕ Compact village with direct slope access from most accommodation

- ⊖ Can be bleak in bad weather – not a tree in sight
- ⊖ Parts of the village are much less attractive to walk through in the evening than to ski past in the day
- ⊖ Not much to do off the slopes
- ⊖ Some very crowded piste intersections
- ⊖ Still some queues – especially for the Cîme de Caron cable-car.

For the enthusiast looking for the best snow in the Alps, it's difficult to beat Val-Thorens – especially given that it's also one of the least unpleasant purpose-built resorts. But we still prefer a cosier base elsewhere in the Three Valleys. That way, if a storm socks in, we can play in the woods around Méribel or Courchevel; if the sun is scorching, we have the option of setting off for Val-Thorens. The formula doesn't work the other way round.

The resort

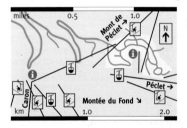

Val-Thorens is built high above the tree line on a sunny, west-facing mountainside at the head of the Belleville valley, surrounded by peaks, slopes and lifts. The village streets are supposedly traffic-free. Practically all visitors' cars are banished to car parks, except on Saturday. But workers' cars still generate a fair amount of traffic, and weekends can be mayhem with people entering and leaving the resort. One reporter recommends you leave 2½ hours to get to Moûtiers on a Saturday. Many parts of the resort are designed with their 'fronts' facing the slopes, and their relatively dreary backs facing the streets. There are quite extensive shopping arcades, a fair choice of bars and restaurants, and a good sports centre.

It is a classic purpose-built resort – compact, with lots of convenient slope-side accommodation. It's quite a complicated little village; but since it's quite compact, it doesn't matter much where you stay. At its heart is the snowy Place de Caron, where pedestrians mix with skiers and boarders. Many of the shops and restaurants are clustered here, along with the best hotels, and the sports

centre is nearby. The village is basically divided in two by a little slope (with a drag-lift) that leads down to the main slope running the length of the village. The upper half of the village is centred on the Place de Péclet. A road runs across the hillside from here to the new chalet-style Balcons development. The lower half of the village is more diffuse, with the Rue du Soleil winding down from the dreary bus station to the big Temples du Soleil apartments.

Seen from the slopes, it is not as hideous as many of its rivals. The buildings are mainly medium-rise and wood-clad; some are distinctly stylish.

The mountains

Take account of the height, the extent of its local slopes and the easy access to the rest of the Three Valleys, and the attraction of Val-Thorens becomes clear. The main disadvantage is the lack of trees. Heavy snowfalls or high wind can shut practically all the lifts and slopes, and even if they don't close, poor visibility can be a problem.

THE SLOPES
High and snow-sure
The resort has a wide piste going right down the front of it, leading down to a number of different lifts. The big **Péclet** gondola, with 25-person cabins, rises 700m/2,300ft to the Péclet glacier, with three red runs down. One links across

to a wide area of intermediate runs served by lifts to cols either side of the **Pointe de Thorens**. You can descend into the 'fourth valley', the Maurienne, from one of these – the **Col de la Montée du Fond,** now accessible by the new Grand Fond jumbo gondola. A chair brings you back and also serves red and blue slopes of 660m/2,170ft vertical. In the Maurienne valley two new chairs opened last season, going up to 3230m/10,600ft on the virgin flanks of **Pointe du Bouchet** and serving some excellent new pistes. This is now the highest lift-served point in the Three Valleys, surpassing the **Cîme de Caron**. The cable-car to this summit can be reached by skiing across from mid-mountain, or by coming up on the gondola which starts below the village. From the top there is the choice of red and black pistes down the front or a black into the Maurienne.

Two further chairs from the lowest

MOUNTAIN FACTS

For the Three Valleys

Altitude	1300m-3230m
	4,270ft-10,600ft
Lifts	200
Pistes	600km
	370 miles
Green	17%
Blue	34%
Red	37%
Black	12%
Snowmaking	100km
	56 miles
Recco detectors used	

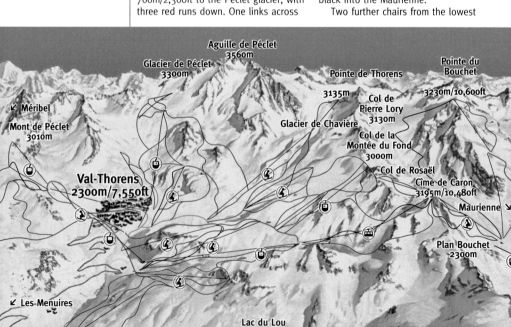

Aguille de Péclet
3560m
Glacier de Péclet
3300m
Pointe du Bouchet
Pointe de Thorens
3135m
Col de Pierre Lory
3130m
Méribel
Glacier de Chavière
3230m/10,600ft
Mont de Péclet
3010m
Col de la Montée du Fond
3000m
Col de Rosaël
Val-Thorens
2300m/7,550ft
Cîme de Caron
3195m/10,480ft
Maurienne
Plan Bouchet
2300m
Les Menuires
Lac du Lou

The newest, highest
bits of Val-Thorens
are built in traditional
chalet style ➔

BASILE / MARK BUSCAIL

LIFT PASSES

2002/03 prices in
euros

Three Valleys
Covers all lifts in
Courchevel, La Tania,
Méribel, Val-Thorens,
Les Menuires and St-
Martin-de-Belleville.
Beginners 4 free lifts
in Val-Thorens.
Main pass
1-day pass 39
6-day pass 193
6-day low-season
pass 115
Senior citizens
Over 60: 6-day pass
146
Over 70: 6-day pass
91
Over 75: free pass
Children
Under 17: 6-day pass
137
Under 10: 118
Under 5: free pass
Short-term passes
Half-day passes (from
12.30) available for
Val-Thorens lifts
(adult 23) and the
Three Valleys (adult
29).
Notes 6-day pass and
over valid for one day
each in Tignes-Val-
d'Isère, La Plagne-Les
Arcs, Pralognan-la-
Vanoise and Les
Saisies. Reductions
for families.
Alternative passes
Vallée des Belleville
pass covers 74 lifts,
300km/186 miles
piste here and in Les
Menuires: 6-day 180.
Local pass covers 32
lifts, 140km/87 miles
of piste: 6-day 146.

part of the domain, Biosmint and Plan
de l'Eau, serve an underused area of
intermediate runs.

Chair-lifts heading north from the
resort serve sunny slopes above the
village and also lead to the Méribel
valley. Les Menuires can also be
reached via these lifts; the alternative
Boulevard Cumin along the valley floor
is nearly flat, and can be hard work.

SNOW RELIABILITY
Difficult to beat

Few resorts can rival Val-Thorens for
reliably good snow-cover, thanks to its
altitude and generally north-facing
slopes. Snowmaking now covers 20%
of the pistes, including the crowded
south- and west-facing runs on the way
back from the Méribel valley. Reporters
this year have noted that grooming is
good but is not done often enough.

FOR EXPERTS
Lots to do off-piste

Val-Thorens' local pistes are primarily
intermediate terrain. The runs down
from the Cîme de Caron cable-car are
challenging, but not seriously steep.
Over in the Maurienne valley the new,
very long black Pierre Lory run may
now present the biggest challenge in
the area, particularly if you stray from
the piste near the start. We haven't
skied it yet, but a reader describes it
as a 'truly magnificent' run, mellowing
into a schuss after that steep start. The

fast Cascades chair serves a good
steep run – now restored to the piste
map as a black – that quickly gets
mogulled. The sunny Marielle run is
one of the easiest blacks we've come
across.

The long Lac du Lou itinéraire –
marked on some maps but not others
– goes from the Cîme de Caron to the
Plan de l'Eau chair. There is also a
great deal of unmarked off-piste terrain
to explore with a guide, particularly on
the north-facing slopes reached from
the Col, Grand Fond, Deux Lacs and
Boismint lifts. It is rocky terrain with
serious hazards. You can also climb up
from the top of the Péclet lifts and
take a long off-piste run towards
Méribel – a guide and high level of
fitness are essential.

FOR INTERMEDIATES
Unbeatable quality and quantity

The scope for intermediates throughout
the Three Valleys is enormous. It will
take a keen intermediate only 90
minutes or so to get to Courchevel at
the far end, if not distracted by the
endless runs on the way.

The local slopes in Val-Thorens are
some of the best intermediate terrain
in the region. Most of the pistes are
easy reds and blues, made even more
enjoyable by the excellent snow.

The snow on the red Col run is
always some of the best around. The
blue Moraine below it is gentle and

boarding *The best resort-level snow in Europe appeals to boarders as well as
skiers – and pulls in considerable numbers. There are pistes to suit
all abilities, and the good snow is great for beginners and carvers. There's plenty
of off-piste choice for free-riders, though if you want trees you'll have to travel.
The lifts are now mainly chairs and gondolas, though one or two drags remain.
The terrain-park towards the bottom of the Caron sector, served by a fast chair,
has a half-pipe and a sound system, and hosts weekly competitions. Nightlife
centres around bars and discos – because of all the young people in the resort
(especially Scandinavians and Dutch), they are usually noisy and entertaining.*

SCHOOLS/GUIDES

2002/03 prices in euros

ESF
Classes 6 days
3hr am or 2½hr pm
6 mornings 123
Children's classes
Ages: 4 to 12
6 mornings: 110
Private lessons
Hourly from 33 for 1 or 2 people

Ski Cool
2002/03 prices
Classes 6 days
3hr, am or pm
6 mornings: 112
Children's classes
6 days for 3 hours: 99
Private lessons
Hourly or daily
67 for 2hr, for 1 or 2 people

OTHER SCHOOLS
Prosneige
International

CHILDCARE

The ESF can provide all-day care and offers classes for children from age 3. It also runs two Mini Club nurseries, at the top and bottom of the resort, taking children from age 3 months to 4 years.

popular with the schools. The runs on the top half of the mountain are steeper than those back into the resort. The Grand Fond gondola serves a good variety of red runs. The Pluviometre from the Trois Vallées chair is a glorious varied red, away from the lifts. Adventurous intermediates shouldn't miss the Combe du Caron runs. The black run is not intimidating – it's very wide and usually has good snow.

FOR BEGINNERS
Good late-season choice
The slopes at the foot of the resort are very gentle and provide convenient, snow-sure nursery slopes, now with moving walkway lifts. There are no long green runs to progress to, but the blues immediately above the village are easy. The resort's height and bleakness make it cold in midwinter, and intimidating in bad weather.

FOR CROSS-COUNTRY
Try elsewhere
Val-Thorens is a poor base for cross-country, with only 4km/2.5 miles of local trails.

QUEUES
Persistent at the Cîme de Caron
Recent reports suggest that the longest queues are for the largest lifts, notably the Cîme de Caron cable car, the Grand Fond and the Funitel Péclet. The queues move fairly quickly, but this year as in earlier years we hear that visits to the Cîme de Caron really need to be timed to miss the crowds.

The Plein Sud six-pack chair-lift does a good job of getting the crowds out of the village towards Méribel and Courchevel in the afternoon, and will now deliver you to Val-Thorens' third jumbo gondola, replacing the Bouquetin chair. The Côte Brune chair, on the Mottaret side, is a bottleneck for returning Val-Thorens residents.

When snow is in short supply elsewhere the pressure on the Val-Thorens lifts can increase markedly.

MOUNTAIN RESTAURANTS
Lots of choice
For a high, modern resort, the choice of restaurants is good. We like the Chalet de Génépi, on the run down from the Moraine chair – great views, an open fire and a wide range of good dishes. The Bar de la Marine, on the Dalles piste, does excellent food, but

service can be stretched. The Moutière, near the top of the chair of the same name, is one of the more reasonably priced of the huts (which are generally expensive). The Plan Bouchet refuge in the Maurienne valley is very popular and welcoming, but bar service can be slow. You can stay the night there, too. Chalet Plein Sud, below the chair of the same name on the east side of the resort, has excellent views but a 'rather limited menu'. The big Chalet de Thorens has been praised for its food and reasonable prices. Lots of people lunch in the village. The Panini self-service is 'very big but friendly'.

SCHOOLS AND GUIDES
A mixed bag
Like so many branches of the ESF, this one is incompetently run (to judge by past reports – we lack new ones this year). The ESF have a Trois Vallées group for those who want to cover a lot of ground while receiving lessons – available by the day or the week, and can include off-piste. In contrast, a reporter last year found Pros Neige classes 'really excellent – my wife's skiing changed dramatically'. Ski Cool class sizes are guaranteed not to exceed 10. They also have off-piste courses. There are several specialist guiding outfits.

FACILITIES FOR CHILDREN
Coolly efficient
Previous reports of the ESF nursery were conflicting but a reader this year found the facilities convenient and the service efficient. In spite of the fact that the staff were 'not particularly warm or friendly' by the end of the week all the children were 'comfortable' on skis.

Staying there

HOW TO GO
Surprisingly high level of comfort
Accommodation is of a higher standard than in many purpose-built resorts.
Chalets These are catered apartments, and many are quite comfortable.
Hotels There are plenty of hotels, and there's a Club Med, too.
(((((5) **Fitz Roy** (0479 000478) The sole 4-star is a swanky but charming Relais & Châteaux place with lovely rooms. Pool. Well placed.
((((4) **Val Thorens** (0479 000433) Welcoming and comfortable; next door to Fitz Roy.

GETTING THERE

Air Geneva, transfer 3½hr. Lyon, transfer 3½hr. Chambéry, transfer 2½hr.

Rail Moûtiers (37km/23 miles); regular buses from station.

ACTIVITIES

Indoor Sports centre (tennis, squash, climbing wall, roller skating, golf simulator, swimming pool, saunas, massage, hot-tub, volleyball, weight training, table tennis, fitness, badminton, football), games rooms, music recitals, cinema, beauty centre.

Outdoor Paragliding, snowmobiles, snow-shoe excursions, walks, toboggan run.

Phone numbers
From abroad use the prefix +33 and omit the initial 'o' of the phone number.

TOURIST OFFICE

Postcode 73440
t 0479 000808
f 0479 000004
valtho@valthorens.com
www.valthorens.com

《③ **Sherpa** (0479 000070) Highly recommended for atmosphere and food. Less-than-ideal position at the top of the resort.

《③ **Val Chaviere** (0479 000033) Friendly, convenient, 'good food and plenty of it'.

《③ **Bel Horizon** (0479 000477) Friendly, family-run 3-star, popular with reporters – 'cuisine wonderful'.

Self-catering The options include apartments of a higher standard than usual in France. The Résidences Village Montana is said to be 'outstanding'.

EATING OUT
Surprisingly wide range

Val-Thorens has something for most tastes and pockets. The Fitz Roy and the Val Thorens hotels do classic French food. For something more regional, the best bets are the 'excellent' Vieux Chalet and the Chaumière. The Scapin is cosily done out in wood and stone, with 'good' food. Other readers' recommendations include the Montana ('good food and service'), El Gringo's ('great for Tex-Mex food' and 'very popular so get there early'), Auberge des Balcons ('wonderful raclette'). The Galoubet has been recommended for local specialities, especially raclettes and pierrades. The Blanchot is an unusually stylish wine bar with a simple but varied carte and of course an excellent range of wines. Several pizzerias are recommended, including the Grange, in the Temples du Soleil.

↑ A setting like this is fine when the sun is shining – less so when a storm socks in and most of the lifts and runs are closed
BASILE / MARK BUSCAIL

APRES-SKI
Livelier than you'd imagine

Val-Thorens is surprisingly lively at night. The Red Fox up at Balcons is crowded at close of play, with karaoke. At the opposite extreme the Sherlock in the Temples du Soleil is 'always lively'. The Frog and Roast Beef at the top of the village is a cheerful British ghetto with a live band at tea-time and half-price beer while it plays. It claims to be the highest pub in Europe. The Monde, Friends and the Viking pub are all lively bars on the same block. The Underground nightclub in Place de Péclet has an extended happy hour but 'descends into europop' when its disco gets going. Bloopers is another popular bar-disco. The Malaysia cellar bar is recommended for good live bands, and gets very crowded after 11pm. Quieter bars include the 'very pleasant' O'Connells, the cosy Rhum Box (aka Mitch's) and the St Pierre.

OFF THE SLOPES
Forget it

There's a good sports centre, but the small pool can get crowded. You can get to some mountain restaurants by lift, and the 360° panorama from the top of the Cîme de Caron cable-car is not to be missed. But it is not a good bet for a holiday off the slopes.

Val-Thorens

359

The French Pyrenees

Decent skiing and boarding at half the price of the Alps

It took us a long time to get round to visiting the resorts of the French Pyrenees – mainly because we had the idea that they were second-rate compared with the Alps. Well, it is certainly true that they can't compete in terms of size of ski area with the mega-resorts of the Trois Vallées and La Plagne. But don't dismiss them: they have considerable attractions, including price – hotels cost half as much as in the Alps, and meals and drinks are cheap.

We went with several preconceived ideas, not least that the Pyrenees are hills compared with the mountains of the Alps. Not true: the Pyrenees are serious mountains, and have dramatic picturesque scenery too. They are also attractively French. Unlike the big plastic mega resorts, many Pyrenean bases have a rustic, rural Gallic charm.

The biggest ski area is shared by **Barèges** and **La Mongie**. Between them they have 100km/62 miles of runs and 45 lifts. The runs are best suited to intermediates, with good tree-lined runs above Barèges and open bowl skiing above La Mongie. The best bet for an expert is to try off-piste with a guide – one beautiful run away from all the lifts starts with a scramble through a hole in the rocks. There are atmospheric mountain huts scattered around the slopes. And when we were there, locals dressed in traditional costume were having a fun race near one of the nicest of them.

Barèges is a spa village set in a narrow, steep-sided valley, which gets little sun in midwinter. It's also the second oldest ski resort in France and the pioneer of skiing in the Pyrenees. Accommodation is mainly in basic 1-star and 2-star hotels. One reporter stayed in nearby Luz in the Chimes hotel, describing the food as 'divine'. The rather drab buildings and one main street of Barèges grow on you, though there's little to do in the evenings other than visit the thermal spa and a restaurant. La Mongie, on the other hand, is a modern, purpose-built resort reminiscent of the Alps.

Cauterets is another spa town but a complete contrast to Barèges. It is much bigger (18,000 beds compared with 3,500) and set in a wide, sunny valley. It is a popular summer destination, and even in March we were able to sit at a pavement cafe with a drink after dinner. It wasn't until 1964 that skiing started here, when the cable-car to the slopes 850m/2,790ft above the town was built – you have to ride down as well as up. There are only 30km/19 miles of slopes (mainly intermediate), set in a semi-circular bowl that can be cold and windy.

But Cauterets' jewel is its cross-country, set a long drive or bus-ride from town at Pont d'Espagne and served by a gondola. It is the start of the Pyrenees National Park and the old smugglers' route over the mountains between France and Spain. The 36km/22 miles of snow-sure cross-country tracks run up this beautiful deserted valley, beside a rushing stream and a stunning waterfall.

Font-Romeu has about 45km/28 miles of pistes and 29 lifts, serving mainly easy and intermediate pistes (15 of its 40 pistes are green) and is popular with families. The slopes get a lot of sun and the snow can suffer as a result. But it has 460 snow-guns – the biggest snowmaking set-up in the Pyrenees – and so cover is assured so long as it is cold enough at night to make snow. Weekend crowds arrive from nearby Perpignan and over the border from Spain and both lifts and pistes can get crowded. It also boasts 90km of cross-country skiing. The village is a bus-ride from the slopes and hotels are mainly 2- and 3-star.

The other major Pyrenean resort is **St-Lary-Soulan**, a traditional village with houses built of stone, with a cable-car at the edge going up to the slopes, of which there are 80km/50 miles, mainly suiting intermediates. It has a terrain-park and half-pipe. There's a satellite called **St-Lary-Espiaube**, which is purpose-built and right at the heart of the slopes.

All the areas welcome snowboarders – but Cauterets provides the most facilities and is the Pyrenees' leading boarding resort.

Phone numbers
From abroad use the prefix +33 and omit the initial '0' of the phone number.

TOURIST OFFICES

Barèges
t 0562 921600
www.bareges.com

La Mongie
t 0562 919415
www.bagneresdebigorre
-lamongie.com

Cauterets
t 0562 925027
www.cauterets.com

Font-Romeu
t 0468 306830
www.font-romeu.fr

St-Lary-Soulan
t 0562 395081
www.saintlary.com

Italy's popularity as a winter sports destination started because it was cheap compared with its Alpine competitors. It is no longer quite such a bargain so it now has to compete in terms of the quality of the holidays offered. And it is trying hard to do so. It has some enduring attractions such as its food and wine, the jolly atmosphere and the splendid scenery – especially in the Dolomites. And many resorts now have powerful, modern lift systems and huge snowmaking systems.

In general, Italians don't take their skiing or boarding too seriously. A late start, long lunch and early finish is the norm – leaving the slopes delightfully quiet for the rest of us. And many resorts become busy only at weekends. This pattern is especially noticeable at the chic resorts such as Cortina, Courmayeur and Madonna and resorts which have not yet found international fame such as the Monterosa region. In some areas, such as the Sella Ronda circuit in the Dolomites, there's a much greater German influence and things aren't quite so relaxed. But almost everywhere mountain restaurants are welcoming places, encouraging leisurely lunching. Pasta – even in the most modest establishment – is delicious. And eating and drinking on the mountain is still cheaper than in other Alpine resorts, whatever the euro is doing to harmonise prices.

One thing that Italian resorts do have to contend with is erratic snowfalls. While the snow in the northern Alps tends to come from the west, Italy's tends to come from storms arriving from the south. So it can have great conditions when other countries are suffering; or vice versa. Last season was a terrible one for most Italian resorts, but

DOLOMITI SUPERSKI LIFT PASS

The Dolomiti Superski lift pass is one of the wonders of the world, covering 45 resorts and 460 lifts. We describe the most important resorts in our chapters on Cortina d'Ampezzo, Madonna di Campiglio and Selva, but there are countless others worth a visit and we can only touch on a few here.

The Superski region, which straddles the provinces of Veneto, Trentino and Alto Adige/Südtirol (predominantly German-speaking, hence the alternative names), is broken down into 12 areas, each embracing a number of resorts.

One of the most interesting areas is in the north-east corner of the region, the Val Pusteria/Pustertal, which leads off eastwards towards the Slovenian border from the Brenner motorway. The main town is Brunico/Bruneck; we have fond memories of one of our first weeks on skis, spent near here on Plan de Corones/Kronplatz – an extraordinary dome-shaped mountain with easy, open slopes around its bare summit, and more testing stuff lower down. Brunico now has lift access to the mountain by gondola from an outlying suburb, and what looks like an exciting black run through the woods to the base.

Just to the east is the area know as the Alta Val Pusteria/Hochpustertal. There are three small towns dotted along the valley. Westernmost is Villabassa/Niederdorf, chiefly of interest to cross-country skiers. At the watershed of the gently sloping valley, where it starts to descend towards Slovenia, is Dobbiaco/Toblach, with some short slopes on its fringes and very scenic cross-country trails. And further east is San Candido/Innichen, with a long chair-lift serving intermediate slopes.

Up an elevated side valley from here (again with scenic cross-country trails) is the main resort of this area, the village of Sesto/Sexten. This has nursery slopes all around it, and two major lifts. From close to the village a cable-car gives access to a variety of open intermediate slopes on Gallo Cedrone/Hahnspiel, with a long red of 1100m/3,610ft vertical to the base of a gondola up from the Val Pusteria.

WINTER SUN

The enjoyment hotline: **0039/0471/999 999** The enjoyment click:

the previous season had been a bumper one. Italian resorts have extensive snowmaking and our observation is that they tend to use it more effectively than other Alpine countries. We have skied in Courmayeur and in the Dolomites when little natural snow had fallen and in each case there was excellent cruising on man-made snow.

DRIVING IN THE ITALIAN ALPS

There are four main geographical groupings of Italian resorts, widely separated. Getting to some of these resorts is a very long haul, and moving from one area to another can involve very long drives.

The handful of resorts to the west of Turin – Bardonecchia, Sauze d'Oulx, Sestriere and neighbours in the Milky Way region – are easily reached from France via the Fréjus tunnel from Modane, or via the good road over the pass that the resort of Montgenèvre sits on.

Further north, and about equidistant from Milan and Turin, are the resorts of the Aosta valley – Courmayeur, Cervinia, La Thuile and the Monterosa are the best known among them. Now that the Mont Blanc road tunnel from Chamonix in France has reopened, Courmayeur is again the easiest of all Italian resorts to reach from Britain. The Aosta valley can also be reached from Switzerland via the Grand St Bernard tunnel. The approach is high and may require chains. The road down the Aosta valley is a major thoroughfare, but the roads up to some of the other resorts are quite long, winding and (in the case of Cervinia) high.

To the east is a string of scattered resorts, most close to the Swiss border, many in isolated and remote valleys involving long drives up

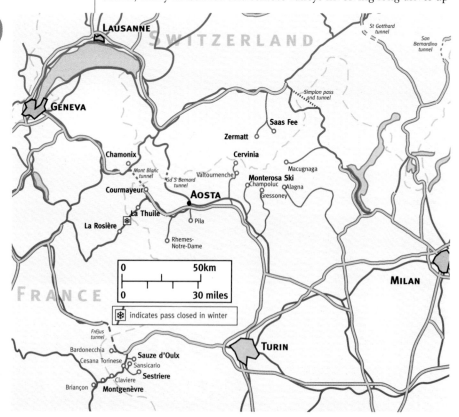

from the nearest Italian cities, or high-altitude drives from Switzerland. The links between Switzerland and Italy are more clearly shown on our larger-scale Switzerland map at the beginning of that section. The major routes are the St Gotthard tunnel between Göschenen (near Andermatt) and Airolo – the main route between Basel and Milan – and the San Bernardino tunnel reached via Chur.

Finally, further east still are the resorts of the Dolomites. Getting there from Austria is easy, over the Brenner motorway pass from Innsbruck. But getting there from Britain is a very long drive indeed – allow at least a day and a half. We wouldn't lightly drive there and back except as part of a longer tour. It's also worth bearing in mind that once you arrive in the Dolomites, getting around the intricate network of valleys linked by narrow, winding roads can be a slow business – not helped by impatient Italian driving.

Introduction

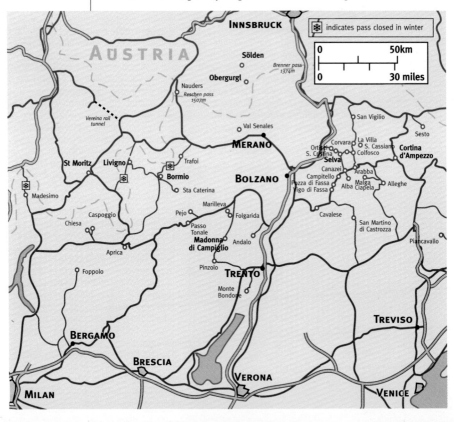

Bormio

1225m/4,020ft

A tall, narrow mountain above a very unusual, historic resort town

WHAT IT COSTS

HOW IT RATES

The slopes

Snow	★★★
Extent	★★
Experts	★
Intermediates	★★★
Beginners	★★
Convenience	★★★
Queues	★★★
Restaurants	★★★★

The rest

Scenery	★★★
Resort charm	★★★★
Off-slope	★★★★

What's new

A new fast quad is supposed to have replaced the Isabella double chair from Bormio 2000 for 2001/02, helping to reduce the queues for the second stage of the cable-car.

Bormio has been chosen to host the Alpine skiing World Championships in 2005, 20 years after it first staged them.

➕ Good mix of high, open pistes and woodland runs adding up to some good long runs

➕ Worthwhile neighbouring resorts

➕ Attractive medieval town centre – quite unlike any other winter resort

➕ Good mountain restaurants

➖ Slopes all of medium steepness

➖ Rather confined main mountain, with second area some way distant

➖ Still many slow old lifts

➖ Long airport transfers

➖ Crowds and queues on Sundays

➖ Central hotels inconvenient

If you like ancient Italian towns and don't mind a lack of Alpine resort atmosphere, you'll find the centre of Bormio very appealing – though you're unlikely to be staying right in the centre. Given the limited slopes of Bormio's own mountain, plan on taking the free bus out to the Valdidentro area and perhaps make longer outings, to Santa Caterina at least.

THE RESORT

Bormio is in a remote spot, close to the Swiss and Austrian borders – though road improvements have cut the airport transfer to three hours. The 17th-century town centre is splendid, with narrow cobbled streets and grand stone facades. It has been a spa since Roman times. It's very colourful during the evening promenade.

The town centre is a 15-minute walk from the cable-car and gondola stations across the river to the south. There are reliable free shuttle-buses, but many people walk. Closer to the lifts is a characterless suburban sprawl mainly made up of hotels built for skiers. Several major hotels are on Via Milano, leading out of town, which is neither convenient nor atmospheric.

THE MOUNTAINS

There's a nice mix of high, snow-sure pistes and lower wooded slopes. The main slopes are tall (vertical drop 1800m/5,900ft) and narrow. Most pistes face north-west and head to town.

Both the piste map and the piste marking need substantial improvement. Reporters have complained about the abundance of slow old lifts, and the resort policy of opening certain lift links only at weekends and busy times.

The Valdidentro area, a short bus-ride out of Bormio, shouldn't be overlooked. The open and woodland runs are very pleasant and usually empty (and have great views). Day trips to Santa Caterina (20 minutes by bus) and Livigno (90 minutes) are covered by the Alta Valtellina lift pass. A six-day pass includes a day in St Moritz (3 hours).

Slopes The two-stage Cima Bianca cable-car goes from bottom to top of the slopes via the mid-mountain mini-resort of Bormio 2000. An alternative gondola goes to Ciuk.

Snow reliability Runs above Bormio 2000 are usually snow-sure, and there is snowmaking on the lower slopes, though these were bare when we visited in late March. The Valdidentro area is more reliable, and the high, shaded, north-facing slopes of Santa Caterina usually have good snow.

Experts There are a couple of short black runs in the main area, but the main interest lies in off-piste routes from Cima Bianca to both east and west of the piste area.

Cima Bianca
3010m/9,88oft

2550m

2200m

Valdidentro

Val di Sotto

Bormio 2000

Oga
1535m

Le Motte
1430m

Ciuk
1620m

Bormio
1225m/4,020ft

366

↑ The town enjoys a fine setting

MOUNTAIN FACTS

Figures relate to the Bormio, Valdidentro and Santa Caterina areas only

Altitude	1225m-3010m
	4,020ft-9,880ft
Lifts	36
Pistes	120km
	75 miles
Blue	36%
Red	48%
Black	16%
Snowmaking	47km
	29 miles
Recco detectors used	

Phone numbers

From abroad use the prefix +39 (and do **not** omit the initial 'o' of the phone number).

TOURIST OFFICE

Postcode 23032
t 0342 903300
f 0342 904696
aptbormio@provincia.
so.it
www.valtellinaonline.it

Intermediates The men's downhill course starts with a steep plunge, but otherwise is just a tough red, ideal for strong intermediates. Stella Alpina, down to 2000, is also fairly steep. Many runs are less tough – ideal for most intermediates. The longest is a superb top-to-bottom cruise. The outlying mountains are also suitable for early intermediates.

Beginners The nursery slopes at Bormio 2000 offer good snow, but there are no very flattering longer pistes to move on to. Novices are better off at nearby Santa Caterina.

Snowboarding The slopes are too steep for novices, and there's little to attract experienced boarders either.

Cross-country There are some trails either side of Bormio, towards Piatta and beneath Le Motte and Valdidentro, but cross-country skiers are better off at snow-sure Santa Caterina.

Queues Both sections of the cable-car suffer delays in the morning peak period and on Sundays. The fast quad from Bormio 2000 built for last season should help to relieve the pressure here. When the lower slopes are incomplete, queues form to ride down. Otherwise there are few problems outside carnival week.

Mountain restaurants The mountain restaurants are generally good. Even the efficient self-service at Bormio 2000 has a good choice of dishes. At La Rocca, above Ciuk, there is a welcoming chalet and a smart, modern place with table- or self-service. Cedrone, at Bormio 2000, has a good terrace and a play area for children. The very welcoming table-service Baita de Mario, at Ciuk, is a great place for a long lunch. The new San Colombano in Valdidentro is recommended.

Schools and guides We have received good reports of both the Alta Valtellina and Nazionale schools.

Facilities for children The Bormio 2000 school has a roped-off snow garden at mid-mountain with a moving carpet lift.

STAYING THERE

How to go There are plenty of apartments, but hotels dominate the package market.

Hotels Most of Bormio's 40-plus hotels are 2- and 3-star places. The 4-star Palace (0342 903131) is the most luxurious in town. The Posta (0342 904753) is in the centre of the old town – rooms range from adequate to very good. The Baita dei Pinti (0342 904346) is the best placed of the top hotels – on the river, between the lifts and centre. The Ambassador (0342 904625) is close to the gondola.

Self-catering The modern Cristallo apartments have been recommended.

Eating out There's a wide selection of restaurants. The atmospheric Taulà does excellent modern food with great service. The Kuerc and the Vecchia Combo are also popular. There are excellent pizzerias, including the Jap.

Après-ski The après-ski scene starts on the mountain at La Rocca, and there are popular bars around the bottom lift stations. The Clem Pub, Gordy's, Cafe Mozart and the Aurora piano bar are popular spots. Shangri-La is a friendly bar. The King's Club is said to be the best disco.

Off the slopes Diversions include thermal baths – apparently now including reopened Roman baths – riding and walks in the Stelvio National Park. There is also an excellent sports centre, ice rink and 'superb' swimming pool. St Moritz and duty-free Livigno are popular excursions.

Staying up the mountain The modern Girasole, at Bormio 2000, is simple but well run by an Anglo-Italian couple, with lots of events.

Cervinia   2050m/6,730ft

Mile after mile of high-altitude, snow-sure cruising and link to Switzerland

368

WHAT IT COSTS

HOW IT RATES

The slopes
Snow	*****
Extent	***
Experts	*
Intermediates	****
Beginners	*****
Convenience	***
Queues	***
Restaurants	***

The rest
Scenery	****
Resort charm	**
Off-slope	*

What's new

Last season, the terrain-park was moved from the low Cieloalto area to Plan Maison. New snowmaking was put in here and on a blue run above it. A new speed-skiing slope was opened to the public on Saturdays. And a new Club Med village opened.

MOUNTAIN FACTS

Altitude 1525m-3480m
5,000ft-11,420ft
Lifts	30
Pistes	200km
	125 miles
Blue	28%
Red	60%
Black	12%
Snowmaking	17km
	11 miles

Recco detectors used

CERVINIA TOURIST OFFICE

Cervinia is not all as pretty as this →

➕ Extensive mountain with miles of long, consistently gentle runs – ideal for early intermediates and anyone wary of steep slopes or bumps

➕ High, sunny and snow-sure slopes amid impressive scenery

➕ Link with Zermatt in Switzerland provides even more spectacular views and good lunches

➖ Very little to interest good or aggressive intermediates and above

➖ Almost entirely treeless, with little to do in bad weather

➖ Lifts prone to closure by wind, particularly early in the season

➖ Link with Zermatt isn't quite as valuable as you might expect

➖ Village spoils some of the views

➖ Steep uphill walk to main lifts, followed by lots of steps in station

➖ Few off-slope amenities

If there is a better resort for those who like gentle, late-season cruising on mile after mile of easy, snow-sure, well-groomed, sunny slopes we have yet to find it. And all this at the foot of southern side of the Matterhorn (Monte Cervino), with the easiest of Zermatt's slopes just over the Swiss border and linked by lift and piste. But Breuil Cervinia (as the resort now styles itself) will not suit everyone. It can be cold and bleak in early season and the top lifts and link with Switzerland can close. The more adventurous will soon get bored by the easy slopes and find that Zermatt's most interesting challenges are out of range for a relaxing day trip. And the resort itself is a bit of an eyesore. Oh ... and the hole-in-the ground mountain loos tend to go down badly with our readers.

The resort

Cervinia is at the head of a long valley leading off the Aosta valley on the Italian side of the Matterhorn. The old climbing village developed into a winter resort in a rather haphazard way, and it has no consistent style of architecture. It's an uncomfortable hotchpotch, neither pleasing to the eye nor as offensive as the worst of the French purpose-built resorts. The centre is pleasant, compact and traffic-free. But ugly surrounding apartment blocks and hotels make the whole place feel less friendly and welcoming.

A lot of people stay near the village centre, at the foot of the nursery slopes. You can take a series of drags from here to the slopes. But the main gondola and cable-car to Plan Maison at mid-mountain start an awkward uphill walk away, above the village. To avoid the walk to these lifts, choose a

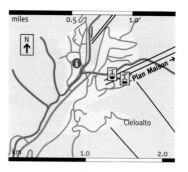

LIFT PASSES

2001/02 prices in euros

Breuil-Cervinia
Covers all lifts on the Italian side of the border including Valtournenche.
Beginners 'First bends' passes available.
Main pass
1-day pass 29
6-day pass 152
(low season 122)
Senior citizens
Over 65: 6-day pass 115
Children
Under 12: 6-day pass 115
Under 8: free pass with one adult paying pass
Short-term passes
Half-day from noon for Cervinia. Single and return tickets on some lifts.
Notes Daily extension for Zermatt lifts at Klein Matterhorn and Schwarzsee (20) or for all areas (26).
Alternative passes
The International Matterhorn pass includes Zermatt's Klein Matterhorn and Schwarzsee lifts: 6-day pass 178. The International Zermatt pass covers all of Zermatt: 6-day pass 191. Limited area passes for Carosello/Cretaz (seven lifts).

hotel with its own shuttle-bus. There is more accommodation further out at the Cieloalto complex and on the road up to it – but some of these buildings are among the worst eyesores.

As well as the usual souvenir shops there are some smart clothes shops and jewellers. At peak periods, the resort fills up with day trippers and weekenders from Milan and Turin who bring cars and mobile phones, making parts of the village traffic- and fume-ridden at times, and the hills alive with the sound of ringing tones.

There are surprisingly few off-slope amenities, such as kindergartens, marked walks and spa facilities.

The slopes link to Valtournenche further down the valley (covered by the lift pass) and Zermatt over in Switzerland (covered by a daily supplement, or a more expensive weekly pass). More about this later in the chapter.

Day trips by car are possible to Courmayeur, La Thuile and the Monterosa Ski resorts of Champoluc and Gressoney (all covered by the Aosta valley lift pass).

The mountains

Cervinia's main slopes are on a high, large, open and sunny west-facing bowl. It has Italy's highest pistes and some of its longest (13km from Plateau Rosa to Valtournenche – with only a short drag-lift part-way). Nearly all the runs are accessible to intermediates. The weather is more of a problem than steepness. If it's bad, the top lifts often close because of high winds. And even the lower slopes may be unusable because of poor visibility. There are few woodland pistes.

THE SLOPES
Very easy
Cervinia has the biggest, highest, most snow-sure area of easy, well groomed pistes we've come across – though

we're very sceptical of the recent hike in the claimed total to 200km. The high proportion of red runs on the piste map is misleading: most of them would be classified blue elsewhere. The slopes just above the village are floodlit some evenings.

The main lifts take you to the mid-mountain base of **Plan Maison**. From there a further gondola then a giant cable-car go up to **Plateau Rosa** and a link with Zermatt. Three successive fast quads (all with windshields) from Plan Maison go up to a slightly lower point on the border, and another link with Zermatt.

From the top you can ski back on some of Cervinia's easiest slopes to Plan Maison or down to the village. If instead you turn right at Plateau Rosa you take the splendid wide Ventina run. You can use the cable-car to do the top part repeatedly, or go all the way down to Cervinia (8km/5 miles and over 1400m/4,600ft vertical). Or you can branch off left down towards **Valtournenche**. The slopes here are served by a number of slow old lifts above the initial gondola from Valtournenche to Salette. You can't get back to Plan Maison from this sector except by riding down the gondola.

There is also the small, little-used **Cieloalto** area, served by three lifts to the south of the cable-car at the bottom of the Ventina run. This has some of Cervinia's steeper pistes and

Cervinia

369

boarding *Cervinia has great slopes for learning to snowboard – gentle, wide and usually with good snow. And the main lifts around the area are chairs, gondolas and cable-cars, but beware, there are a lot of drag-lifts (especially difficult to negotiate in high winds) and some long flat bits as well. There's not much to interest better boarders – just as there's not much to interest better skiers. The terrain-park, border-cross course and half-pipe are now at Plan Maison. There's an even better one over the Swiss border on Zermatt's Klein Matterhorn slopes (but beware of long T-bars to get back if the Klein Matterhorn cable-car is closed). Nightlife is fairly limited.*

SCHOOLS/GUIDES

2001/02 prices in euros

Cervino
Classes 6 days
2hr 45min 10am-12.45
5 days 108.5
Children's classes
Ages: 5 to 7
Private lessons
Hourly
28.5 for 1 person; 31 for 2 people

can be very useful in bad weather as it has the only trees in the area.

Several reporters have criticised the fact that old lift stations and pylons have been left on the slopes as eyesores after the lifts have been scrapped. The piste map is another cause for complaint.

SNOW RELIABILITY
Superb

The mountain is one of the highest in Europe and, despite getting a lot of afternoon sun, can usually be relied on to have good snow conditions. Lift closures due to wind are a bigger worry. Several reporters have complained about the biting winds and one claimed that every lift stopped due to high winds at some point in his holiday.

The village nursery slopes, the bottom half of the Ventina run and the runs under the top chair-lifts down to Plan Maison have snowmaking. But the run below the top of the gondola to lower-lying Valtournenche doesn't – and has been closed on our last two visits.

FOR EXPERTS
Forget it

This is not a resort for experts (though heli-drops with guides can be arranged). There are several black runs scattered here and there, but most of them would be classified red

elsewhere. Many reporters head over to Zermatt for more challenging slopes but don't necessarily find them – more about this in the margin on the right.

FOR INTERMEDIATES
Miles of long, flattering runs

Virtually the whole area can be covered comfortably by average intermediates. And if you like wide, easy, motorway pistes, you'll love Cervinia: it has more long, flattering runs than any other resort. The easiest slopes are on the left as you look at the mountain. From top to bottom here there are gentle blue runs and almost equally gentle reds in the beautiful scenery at the foot of the south face of the Matterhorn.

The area on the right as you look at the mountain is best for adventurous intermediates. The Ventina run is a particularly good fast cruise. The long run down to Valtournenche is easy for most of its length. Good intermediates will be capable of the black runs.

FOR BEGINNERS
Pretty much ideal

Complete beginners will start on the good village nursery slope, and should graduate quickly to the fine flat area around Plan Maison and its gentle blue runs. Fast learners will be going all the way from the top to the bottom of the mountain by the end of the week.

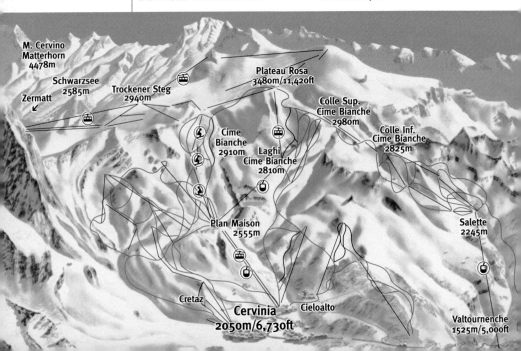

M. Cervino
Matterhorn
4478m

Schwarzsee
2585m

Zermatt

Trockener Steg
2940m

Plateau Rosa
3480m/11,420ft

Colle Sup.
Cime Bianche
2980m

Colle Inf.
Cime Bianche
2825m

Cime
Bianche
2910m

Laghi
Cime Bianche
2810m

Plan Maison
2555m

Salette
2245m

Cretaz

Cervinia
2050m/6,730ft

Cieloalto

Valtournenche
1525m/5,000ft

THE ZERMATT CONNECTION

If the weather is good, you're bound to be tempted to go over to Zermatt. And quite right – the restaurants are simply the best, and it's only from the Swiss side that you get the classic view of the Matterhorn. But there are snags.

For a start, the two lift companies can't even convey clearly where you can cross over. Testa Grigia on one side of the joint map becomes Plateau Rosa on the other; Theodulpass becomes nameless. Pathetic.

Then there's the runs. You come first of all to even gentler glacier motorways than on the Cervinia side. There are more challenging pistes once you get down to Schwarzsee. But there is no way to get to Zermatt's classic terrain on Stockhorn and Rothorn without making the long descent to the village, and bussing, walking or taking a taxi the length of the village to other lifts.

You could do this, but you couldn't do it enjoyably – partly because you have to set off back early on account of the lift links back to the border. Recent reporters tell of long afternoon queues for the Trockener Steg-Klein Matterhorn cable-car. And if this link is closed by high winds – as is often the case – there may be horrendous queues in grim conditions for the alternative route via two long, slow and very exposed T-bars.

You can get a taste of Zermatt from Cervinia, but you're unlikely to get your fill.

FOR CROSS-COUNTRY
Hardly any
There are a couple of short trails, but this is not a cross-country resort.

QUEUES
Can still be problems
Although much improved recently, there are still some antiquated lifts, and the system still has drawbacks. The two main access lifts to Plan Maison can get crowded (twenty minute queues at peak times) and the alternative series of drags and chairs need upgrading. The series of slow lifts back up from Valtournenche are another source of complaint. There can also be queues for many lower lifts when upper lifts are shut due to high wind.

MOUNTAIN RESTAURANTS
Disappointing for Italy
The mountain restaurants are not as appealing as you might expect in an Italian resort (and the toilet facilities can be primitive hole-in-the-ground affairs), so some reporters prefer to head over to Zermatt's wonderful huts for lunch.

However, the Châlet Etoile, beneath the Rocce Nere chair-lift at Plan Maison, is highly praised by reporters – 'The best mountain restaurant I've been to,' says one – and it has a 'first-class toilet'. Booking in advance is recommended. The Rocce Nere is also recommended. The British-run Igloo, at the top of the Bardoney chair just off the Ventina piste, serves huge burgers and has 'a UK-style toilet'. Baita Cretaz, near the bottom of the Cretaz pistes, is good value, but disappointed a recent visitor. The Bontadini at the top of the Fornet chair has been praised this year.

The restaurants are cheaper and less crowded on the Valtournenche side. The Motta, at the top of the drag-lift of the same name, does excellent food including goulaschsuppe that is 'out of this world'.

SCHOOLS AND GUIDES
Getting better
Cervinia has two main schools, Cervino and Breuil. Reports on both are fairly positive. This year we have also had good reports on the private lessons: 'Excellent value and level of tuition very good with good standard of English spoken and pleasant instructors.'

FACILITIES FOR CHILDREN
Could be better
The Cervino ski school runs a ski kindergarten. And there's a babysitting and kindergarten area at Plan Maison. The slopes, with their long gentle runs, should suit families.

Staying there

HOW TO GO
Plenty of hotel packages
Most of the big tour operators come here, providing between them a wide selection of hotels, though other types of accommodation are rather thin on the ground. A Club Med opened last season.
Hotels There are almost 50 hotels, mostly 2- or 3-stars, but there are a few 4-stars.
Hermitage (0166 948998) Small, luxurious Relais et Château just out of the village on the road up to Cieloalto. Great views, pool, free bus to lifts.

Up by the Matterhorn the snow is usually cold and powdery ↓

CHILDCARE

The ski school runs a snow garden with mini-lift at the foot of the Cretaz slopes and one mini-lift in Plan Maison. Care arrangements 10am to 1pm.

GETTING THERE

Air Turin, transfer 2½hr. Geneva, transfer 2½hr.

Rail Châtillon (27km/17 miles); regular buses from station.

ACTIVITIES

Indoor Hotels with swimming pools and saunas, fitness centre, bowling
Outdoor Natural skating rink (until March), paragliding, hang-gliding, mountaineering, skidoos, heli-skiing, quad, cross country

Phone numbers
From abroad use the prefix +39 (and do **not** omit the initial 'o' of the phone number).

TOURIST OFFICE

Postcode 11021
t 0166 949136
f 0166 949731
breuil-cervinia@ montecervino.it
www.montecervino.it

((((4) **Punta Maquignaz** (0166 949145) Captivating chalet-style 4-star, in centre near Cretaz lifts.
(((3) **Sporthotel Sertorelli** (0166 949797) Excellent food, sauna and hot-tub. Ten minutes from lifts.
(((3) **Europa** (0166 948660) Friendly and family run; near Cretaz lifts. Pool.
(2) **Astoria** (0166 949062) Right by main lift station. Family run and simple. 'Comfortable but that's all,' says a reporter.
(2) **Marmore** (0166 949057) Friendly, family run, with 'quite good food'; on main street – an easy walk to the lifts.
Self-catering There are many apartments in the resort, but few are available through British tour ops.

EATING OUT
Plenty to choose from
Cervinia's 50 or so restaurants allow plenty of choice. The Chamois and Matterhorn are excellent, but quite expensive. The Grotta belies its name with good food. Casse Croute serves probably the biggest, and best, pizzas. The Copa Pan has a lively atmosphere and is again recommended by several reporters. The Bricole, the Rustico and the Nicchia have also been praised, and the Maison de Saussure does 'very good local specialities'. An evening out at the Baita Cretaz mountain hut makes a change.

APRES-SKI
Disappoints many Brits
Plenty of Brits come here looking for action but find there isn't much to do except tour the mostly fairly ordinary bars. The Copa Pan (see Eating out) is lively, good value and serves generous measures. The Dragon Bar is popular with Brits and Scandinavians and has satellite TV and videos. Lino's (by the ice rink), the Yeti, Labatt and Café des Guides (with mementos of the owner's Himalayan mountaineering trips) are all recommended by reporters. The discos liven up at weekends – the Garage is reputedly the best. There are tour-rep-organised events such as snow-mobiling on the old bob-sled run, quiz nights, bowling and fondue nights.

OFF THE SLOPES
Little attraction
There is little to do for those who don't plan to hit the slopes. The pleasant town of Aosta is reached easily enough, but it's a four-hour round trip. Village amenities include

hotel pools, a fitness centre and a natural ice rink. The walks are disappointing. The mountain restaurants that are reachable by gondola or cable-car are not special.

STAYING UP THE MOUNTAIN
To beat the queues
Up at Plan Maison, the major lift junction 500m/1,640ft vertical above the resort, Lo Stambecco (0166 949053) is a 50-room 3-star hotel ideally placed for early nights and early starts. Less radically, the Cime Bianche (0166 949046) is a rustic 3-star chalet on the upper fringes of the resort (in the area known as La Vieille).

STAYING DOWN THE VALLEY
Great home run
Valtournenche, 9km/5.5 miles down the road, is cheaper than Cervinia, has a genuine Italian atmosphere and a fair selection of simple hotels, of which the 3-star Bijou (0166 92109) is the best.

A new gondola that opened a few years ago has cut the weekend waits to get out of town. But the slow lifts above it mean it takes quite a time to reach the top. The exceptionally long run back down, however, is a nice way to end the day – when it is all open (the bottom section is often closed due to lack of snow). The main street through the village is very busy with cars going to and from Cervinia.

Cortina d'Ampezzo   1225m/4,020ft

The scenery will take your breath away even if the slopes don't

373

WHAT IT COSTS

HOW IT RATES

The slopes

Snow	★★★
Extent	★★★
Experts	★★
Intermediates	★★★
Beginners	★★★★★
Convenience	★
Queues	★★★
Restaurants	★★★★

The rest

Scenery	★★★★★
Resort charm	★★★★
Off-slope	★★★★★

What's new

For 2001/02 two new ski itineraries were invented – there are supposed to be signs on the slopes and maps available at the ski pass office. 'Skitour Olympia' takes you on the 1956 Olympic courses where you can try the downhill, GS and slalom courses and the Bobsled run – and sample some of the 'Olympic dishes' served in the mountain huts. For the less adventurous, 'Skitour Romantic Views' covers the Lagazuoi-Cinque Torri area.

A new terrain-park was built in the Cinque Torri area.

There is a new miniclub for children age 3-12 and a new 5-star hotel, Cristallo, with health spa and beauty centre.

CORTINA TURISMO

Waking up to a view like this is worth the cost of the holiday alone →

➕ Magnificent Dolomite scenery – perhaps the most dramatic of any winter resort

➕ Marvellous nursery slopes and good long cruising runs, ideal for nervous intermediates

➕ Access to the vast area covered by the Dolomiti Superski pass

➕ Attractive, although rather towny, resort, with lots of upmarket shops

➕ Good off-slope facilities

➕ Remarkably uncrowded slopes

➖ Several separate areas of slopes, which are inconveniently spread around all sides of the resort and linked by buses

➖ Erratic snow record

➖ Expensive by Italian standards

➖ Gets very crowded during Italian holidays

➖ Very little to entertain experts

➖ Mobile phones and fur coats may drive you nuts

Nowhere is more picturesque than chic Cortina, the most upmarket of Italian resorts. Dramatic pink-tinged cliffs and peaks rise vertically from the top of the slopes, giving picture-postcard views from wherever you are.

Cortina's slopes are fine for its regular upmarket visitors from Rome and Milan, many of whom have second homes here and enjoy the strolling, shopping, people-watching and lunching as much as the odd leisurely excursion on to the slopes. For beginners and leisurely intermediates, the splendid nursery slopes and long, easy, well-groomed runs are ideal. For keen piste-bashers, Cortina's fragmented areas can be frustrating, especially if snow is scarce and the area is fragmented even more; but the access to the Sella Ronda and other Dolomiti Superski resorts, though time-consuming, is some compensation – having a car is best for exploring. For experts, there are few tough runs, and the best of those are liable to poor snow conditions and closure because they face south.

LIFT PASSES

2002/03 prices in euros

Dolomiti Superski
Covers 460 lifts and 1200km/745 miles of piste in the Dolomites, including all Cortina areas.
Main pass
1-day pass 35
6-day pass 175
(low season 154)
Senior citizens
Over 60: 6-day pass 149 (low season 131)
Children
Under 16: 6-day pass 123 (low season 105)

Alternative pass
Cortina d'Ampezzo
Covers all lifts in Cortina, San Vito di Cadore, Auronzo and Misurina, and ski-buses.
Main pass
1-day pass 31
6-day pass 154
(low season 135)
Children
Under 16: 6-day pass 108
Under 8: free pass

ITALY

374

The resort

In winter, more people come to Cortina for the clear mountain air, the stunning views, the shopping, the cafes and to pose and be seen than for the winter sports – 70% of all Italian visitors don't bother taking to the slopes. Cortina attracts the rich and famous from the big Italian cities. Fur coats and glitzy jewellery are everywhere.

The resort itself is a widely spread town rather than a village, with exclusive chalets scattered around the woods and the roads leading off into the countryside. The centre is the traffic-free Corso Italia, full of chic designer clothes, jewellery and antique shops, art galleries and furriers – finding a ski shop can seem tricky. The cobbles and picturesque church bell tower add to the Italian atmosphere. In early evening, the street is a hive of activity, with everyone parading up and down in their finery, window-shopping, people-watching and finalising their clubbing arrangements on mobile phones. Seeing anyone dressed for the slopes at 5pm is a rarity. But all this glamour doesn't mean Cortina has to be expensive.

Unlike the rest of the Dolomites, Cortina is pure Italy. It has none of the Germanic traditions of Selva and the Sud Tirol, and doesn't attract many German visitors.

Surrounding the centre is a horrendous one-way system, often traffic-clogged and stinking of fumes – a nasty contrast to the stunning scenery everywhere else you look. The lifts to the two main areas of slopes are a fair way from the centre, and at opposite sides of town. Other lifts are a lengthy bus-ride away. There's a wide range of hotels in the centre and scattered in the outskirts. To get the most out of the town, staying centrally is the best bet – though you could plump for one of the main cable-cars and base yourself near that. The local bus service is good (though it could do with being more frequent). A car can be useful, especially for getting to the outlying areas – and certainly helps to make the most of other areas on the Dolomiti Superski pass. San Cassiano is not far to the west, with links from there to Corvara and the other Sella Ronda resorts.

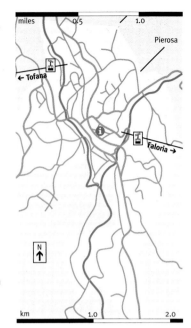

miles 0.5 1.0
Pierosa
← Tofana
Faloria →
N ↑
km 1.0 2.0

The mountains

Cortina first leapt to fame as host of the 1956 Winter Olympics. At the time, it was very modern; now its facilities feel dated. There is a good mixture of slopes above and below the tree line.

THE SLOPES
Inconveniently fragmented

All Cortina's smallish separate areas are a fair trek from the town centre. The largest is **Socrepes**, accessed by chair- and drag-lifts a bus-ride away. It links with **Tofana**, Cortina's highest area, also reached by two-stage cable-car from near the Olympic ice rink.

On the opposite side of the valley is the tiny **Mietres** area. Another cable-car from the east side of town leads to the **Faloria** area, from where you can head down to the chairs that lead up into the limited but dramatic runs beneath the **Cristallo** peak.

Other areas are reachable by road. The cable-car from Passo Falzarego up to Lagazuoi accesses a beautiful red run to Armenterola, which takes you away from all lifts and signs of civilisation to the stunning scenery of the Hidden Valley. On the way to Passo Falzarego is the tiny but spectacular Cinque Torri area. Its excellent, north-facing slopes are now accessed by a high-speed quad.

Reporters praise the excellent

boarding *Despite its upmarket chic, Cortina is a good resort for learning to board. The Socrepes nursery slopes are wide, gentle and served by a fast chair-lift. And progress on to the resort's other easy slopes is simple because you can get around in all areas using just chairs and cable-cars – though there are drags, they can be avoided. There are terrain-parks at Faloria and Cinque Torri, but there's little off-piste to interest experienced boarders.*

MOUNTAIN FACTS

Altitude 1225m-2930m
4,020ft-9,610ft
Lifts	51
Pistes	140km
	87 miles
Blue	33%
Red	62%
Black	5%
Snowmaking	133km
	83 miles

Recco detectors used

grooming and quiet slopes with few queues, but complain about the piste map not showing some runs, poor piste marking, World Cup races disrupting January skiing, and having to take some cable-cars down as well as up if snow is poor or you want to avoid poling. Many of the red runs on the map seem to have been reclassified blue in the last few years.

SNOW RELIABILITY
Lots of artificial help
The snowfall record is erratic – it can be good here when it's poor on the north side of the Alps (and vice versa). But the resort has invested heavily in snowmaking and over 90% of the pistes are now covered, so cover should generally be good if it is cold enough to make snow. But last time we visited, the link between Tofana and Socrepes was closed because of lack of snow on a key south-facing slope – which made the areas even more fragmented.

FOR EXPERTS
Limited
The run down from the second stage of the Tofana cable-car at Ra Valles is deservedly graded black; it goes through a gap in the rocks, and a steep, narrow, south-facing section

gives wonderful views of Cortina, deep down in the valley. It's often tricky because of poor snow conditions.

Cortina's other steep run goes from the top of the Cristallo area at Forcella Staunies. A chair-lift takes you to a steep, south-facing couloir which is often shut due to avalanche danger or poor snow.

Other than these two runs (both shut on our last visit) there's little to keep experts happy for a week.

Heli-skiing is available.

FOR INTERMEDIATES
Fragmented and not extensive
To get the most out of Cortina you must like cruising in beautiful scenery and not mind repeating runs.

The runs at the top of Tofana are short but normally have the best snow. The highest are at over 2800m/9,190ft and mainly face north. But be warned: the only way back down is by the tricky black run described above or by cable-car. The reds from the linked Pomedes area are longer and offer good cruising.

Faloria has a string of fairly short north-facing runs – we loved the Vitelli red run, around the back away from all signs of lifts. And the Cristallo area has a long blue (formerly red), served by a fast quad.

SCHOOLS/GUIDES

2001/02 prices in euros

Cortina
Classes 6 days
2½hr: 9.30-noon; 2hr: noon-2pm
6 2½hr days: 175
Private lessons
Hourly
36 for 1hr; each additional person 12

Azzurra Cortina
Classes 6 days
3½hr: 9.15-1pm;
6½hr: 9.15-4pm
6 3½hr days: 410
Private lessons
Hourly
41 for 1hr; each additional person 13.5

It is well worth making the trip to Cinque Torri for wonderful, deserted fast cruising on usually excellent north-facing snow. The Hidden Valley run from Lagazuoi at the top of the Passo Falzerego cable-car to Armenterola is a must – a very easy red and one of the most beautiful runs we've come across. It offers isolation amid sheer pink-tinged Dolomite peaks and frozen waterfalls. Make time to stop at the atmospheric Scotoni rifugio near the end, then it's a long pole, skate or walk to the welcome sight of a horse-drawn sled (with ropes attached) which tows the weary to Armenterola. Shared taxis take you back to Passo Falzerego (if you've time, try the slopes of Alta Badia, accessed from Armenterola).

FOR BEGINNERS
Wonderful nursery slopes
The Socrepes area has some of the biggest nursery slopes and best

progression runs we have seen. Some of the blue forest paths can be icy and intimidating. But you'll find ideal gentle terrain on the main pistes.

FOR CROSS-COUNTRY
One of the best
Cortina has around 75km/47 miles of trails, mainly in the woods towards Dobbiaco. There are also trails below the Cristallo area.

QUEUES
No problem
Most Cortina holidaymakers rise late, lunch lengthily and leave the slopes early – if they get on them at all. That means few lift queues and generally uncrowded pistes – a different world to the crowded Sella Ronda circuit. 'Lack of queues was one of the highlights of our holiday,' said one reporter.

MOUNTAIN RESTAURANTS
Good, but get in early
Lunch is a major event for many Cortina visitors. At weekends you often need to book or turn up very early to be sure of a table. Many restaurants can be reached by road or lift, and pedestrians arrive as early as 10am to sunbathe, admire the views and idle the time away on their mobile phones.

Although prices are high in the swishest establishments, we've found plenty of reasonably priced places, serving generally excellent food. In the Socrepes area, the Col Taron is highly recommended and the Piè de Tofana, Rifugio Pomedes and El Faral are also good. The Socrepes sector also has several hotels along the road at its edge – including the best restaurant in the resort, the Michelin-starred Tivoli.

At Cristallo the Rio Gere at the base of the quad chair and Son Forca, with fabulous views at the top of it (and owned by Alberto Tomba's former trainer), are both worth a visit.

The restaurants at Cinque Torri, the Scoiattoli ('magnificent home-made pastas') and the Rifugio Averau, offer fantastic views as well as good food, and, unusually, are non-smoking. Rifugio Lagazuoi, a hike up from the top of the Passo Falzerego cable-car, also has great views and no smoking.

CORTINA TURISMO

← You'll be relieved to know that trying out the Olympic ski jump is not a compulsory part of the new 'Skitour Olympia' on offer

ACTIVITIES

Indoor Swimming pool, saunas, health spa, museums, art gallery, cinema, indoor tennis court, public library
Outdoor Rides on Olympic bob run, snowrafting down Olympic ski jump, crazy sledge for moonlit excursions, snow-shoe tours, all at Adrenalin centre; Olympic ice-stadium (2 rinks), curling, ice hockey, sleigh rides, horse-riding school, 6km/4 miles of walking paths, toboggan run, heli-skiing

CHILDCARE

There is non-skiing childcare, and schools offer all-day classes for children.

GETTING THERE

Air Venice, transfer 2½hr (free transfer available for hotel guests; advance booking required).

Rail Calalzo (35km/22 miles) or Dobbiaco (32km/20 miles); frequent buses from station.

Phone numbers
From abroad use the prefix +39 (and do **not** omit the initial '0' of the phone number).

TOURIST OFFICE

Postcode 32043
t 0436 866252
f 0436 867448
cortina@dolomiti.org
www.cortina.dolomiti.org

SCHOOLS AND GUIDES
Mixed reports

Of the four ski schools, we've had mixed reports of the Cortina school over the years – though we lack recent reports. The Gruppo Guide Alpine offers off-piste and touring.

FACILITIES FOR CHILDREN
Better than average

By Italian standards childcare facilities are outstanding, with a choice of all-day care arrangements for children of practically any age. This is one resort where Mamma gets a break. Given the small number of British visitors, you can't count on good spoken English. And the fragmented area can make travelling around with children difficult.

Staying there

HOW TO GO
Now with more packages

Hotels dominate the market but there are some catered chalets.
Hotels There's a big choice, from 5-star luxury to 1-star and 2-star pensions.
(((((5) **Miramonti** (0436 4201) Spectacularly grand hotel, 2km/1 mile south of town. Pool.
((((4) **Poste** (0436 4271) Reliable 4-star, at the heart of the town.
((((4) **Ancora** (0436 3261) Elegant public rooms. On the traffic-free Corso Italia.
((((4) **Parc Victoria** (0436 3246) Rustic 4-star with small rooms but good food, at the Faloria end of the town centre.
((((4) **Faloria** (0436 2959) Newish, near ski jump, splendid pool, good food.
(((3) **Olimpia** (0436 3256) Comfortable B&B hotel in centre, near Faloria lift.
(((3) **Menardi** (0436 2400) Welcoming roadside inn, a long walk from centre and lifts.
(((3) **Villa Resy** (0436 3303) Small and welcoming, just outside centre, with British owner.
(((3) **Montana** (0436 862126) 'Excellent B&B. Amazing value and central location,' says a 2002 reporter.
Self-catering There are some chalets and apartments – usually out of town – available for independent travellers.

EATING OUT
Huge choice

There's an enormous selection, both in town and a little way out, doing mainly Italian food. The very smart and expensive El Toulà is in a beautiful old barn, just on the edge of town. Many of the best restaurants are further out

– such as the Michelin-starred Tivoli, Meloncino, Leone e Anna, Rio Gere and Baita Fraina. Reasonably priced central restaurants include the Cinque Torri and the Passetto for pizza and pasta. A recent reporter who went in February high-season commented on 'excellent, good value pizzerias and not at all overcrowded in bars and restaurants'.

APRES-SKI
Lively in high season

Cortina is a lively social whirl in high season, with lots of well-heeled Italians staying up very late. Don't go on the early evening walkabout if fur coats and mobile phones annoy you.

Bar Lovat is one of several popular, high-calorie tea-time spots. There are many good wine bars: Enoteca has 700 different wines and good cheese and meats; Osteria has good wines and local ham; and Villa Sandi, Brio di Vino and Febar have all been recommended. The liveliest bar is the Clipper, with a bob-sleigh by the door, and lots of designer beers. Discos liven up after 11pm.

OFF THE SLOPES
A classic resort

Along with St Moritz, Cortina rates as one of the leading resorts if you're happier off the slopes. The setting is stunning, the town attractive, the shopping extensive, the mountain restaurants easily accessible by road (a car is handy). And there's plenty more to do, including swimming, ice skating and dog-sledding. You can have a run (with driver!) down the Olympic bob-sleigh run. There's horse jumping and polo on the snow occasionally. There are several museums and art galleries.

Trips to Venice are easily and inexpensively organised.

Cortina d'Ampezzo

377

Courmayeur 1225m/4,020ft

Seductive village and stunning scenery on the sunny side of Mont Blanc

WHAT IT COSTS

HOW IT RATES

The slopes

Snow	★★★★
Extent	★★
Experts	★★★
Intermediates	★★★★
Beginners	★★
Convenience	★
Queues	★★★★
Restaurants	★★★★

The rest

Scenery	★★★★
Resort charm	★★★★
Off-slope	★★★

SNOWPIX.COM / CHRIS GILL

Some of the 27 mountain huts have even more stunning views than this ↓

➕ Charming, traditional village, with car-free centre and stylish shops

➕ Stunning views of Mont Blanc massif

➕ Pleasant range of intermediate runs

➕ Day trips to Chamonix (including doing the Vallée Blanche run) possible

➕ Good base for heli-skiing

➕ Comprehensive snowmaking

➕ Good mountain restaurants

➕ Lively, but not rowdy, après-ski

➖ Lack of nursery slopes and easy runs for beginners to progress to

➖ No tough pistes

➖ Relatively small area, with mainly short runs; high-mileage piste bashers will get bored in a week

➖ Slopes very crowded on Sundays

➖ Tiresome walk and cable-car journey between village and slopes

Courmayeur is very popular, especially at weekends, with the smart Italian set from Milan and Turin. It's easy to see why: it's very easy to get to and certainly the most captivating of the Val d'Aosta resorts.

The scenery, the charm of the village, the stylish bars and restaurants and the nightlife are big draws. The main slopes are fine but nothing special given their limited range of difficulty, inconvenient location across the valley from the village and their limited size; a keen piste-basher will cover Courmayeur in a day. But the Mont Blanc tunnel has reopened, making the option of a quick trip to Chamonix feasible again.

The resort could make a jolly week for those who want to party as much as hit the slopes. It also appeals to those with quite different ambitions, who want to explore the spectacular Mont Blanc massif with the aid of a guide and other local peaks with the aid of a helicopter.

The resort

Courmayeur is a traditional old Italian mountaineering village that, despite the nearby Mont Blanc tunnel road and modern hotels, has retained much of its old-world feel.

The village has a charming traffic-free centre of attractive shops, cobbled streets and well-preserved buildings. An Alpine museum and a statue of a long-dead mountain rescue hero add to the historical feel.

The centre has a great atmosphere, focused around the Via Roma. As the lifts close, people pile into the many bars, some of which are very civilised. Others wander in and out of the many small shops, which include a salami specialist and a good bookshop. At weekends people-watching is part of the evening scene, when the fur coats of the Milanese and Torinese take over.

The village is quite large and its huge cable-car is right on the southern edge of town, a fair distance from much of the accommodation. There is

What's new

The Mont Blanc tunnel reopened in March 2002 after the tragic fire of 1999. This makes day trips to Chamonix and access from Geneva airport quick and easy once again.

2001/02 saw a new 'snow park' for children in the Dolonne area, and a new Congress centre.

The annual Momentum City Ski Championships are now run here. Teams of four compete, with prizes for all standards – great fun and free champagne! This season's dates are 30 Jan to 2 Feb 2003. To enter, call Momentum Ski on 020 7371 9111.

MOUNTAIN FACTS

Altitude	1210m-2755m
	3,970ft-9,040ft
Lifts	23
Pistes	100km
	62 miles
Blue	20%
Red	70%
Black	10%
Snowmaking	18km
	11 miles
Recco detectors used	

---

no shuttle-bus alternative to walking, but you can leave skis, boards and boots in lockers at the top – highly recommended by reporters. There is another short walk from the top to the other lifts before you can get going.

Having accommodation close to the village cable-car is handy. Parking at the cable-car is very limited, but drivers can go to Entrèves, a few kilometres away, where there is a large car park at the Val Veny cable-car. Buses, infrequent but timetabled, link Courmayeur with La Palud, just beyond Entrèves, for the Punta Helbronner-Vallée Blanche cable-car.

The mountains

The pistes suit intermediates, but are surprisingly limited for such a well-known, large resort. They are varied in character, if not gradient. Piste marking could be improved.

THE SLOPES
Small but interestingly varied

The slopes are separate from the village: you have to ride a cable-car to them and either take it down or take a bus from Dolonne at the end of the day. The cable-car arrives at the bottom of the slopes at Plan Checrouit (where you can store your equipment).

There are two distinct sections, both almost entirely intermediate. The north-east-facing **Checrouit** area accessed by the Checrouit gondola catches morning sun, and has open, above-the-tree-line pistes. The 25-person, infrequently running Youla cable-car goes to the top of Courmayeur's pistes. There is a further tiny cable-car to Cresta d'Arp. This serves only long off-piste runs but it is no longer compulsory to have a guide with you to go up it.

Most people follow the sun over to the north-west-facing slopes towards **Val Veny** in the afternoon. These are interesting, varied and tree lined, with great views of Mont Blanc and its glaciers. Connections between the two areas are good, with many alternative routes. The Val Veny slopes are also accessible by cable-car from Entrèves, a few miles outside Courmayeur.

A little way beyond Entrèves is La Palud, where a cable-car goes up in three stages to Punta Helbronner, at the shoulder of **Mont Blanc**. There are no pistes from the top, but you can do the famous Vallée Blanche run to Chamonix from here without the

---

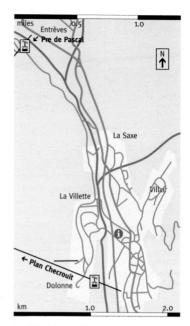

horrific ridge walk on the Chamonix side – you catch a bus or a taxi back from Chamonix through the Mont Blanc tunnel. Or you can tackle the tougher off-piste runs on the Italian side of Mont Blanc. None of these glacier runs should be done without a guide.

La Thuile and Pila are an easy drive to the south, and Cervinia is reachable.

SNOW RELIABILITY
Good for most of the season

Courmayeur's slopes are not high – mostly between 1700m and 2250m (5,600ft and 7,400ft). Those above Val Veny face north or north-west, so keep their snow well, but the Plan Checrouit side is rather too sunny for comfort in late season. There is snowmaking on most main runs, so good coverage in early- and mid-season is virtually assured – we were there in the January 2002 snow drought and enjoyed decent skiing entirely on man-made snow.

FOR EXPERTS
Off-piste is the only challenge

Courmayeur has few challenging pistes. The only black – the Competizione, on the Val Veny side – is not hard, and few moguls form elsewhere. But if you're lucky enough to find fresh powder – as we have been several times – you can have fantastic fun among the trees.

Classic off-piste runs go from Cresta d'Arp, at the top of the lift network, in three directions – a clockwise loop via

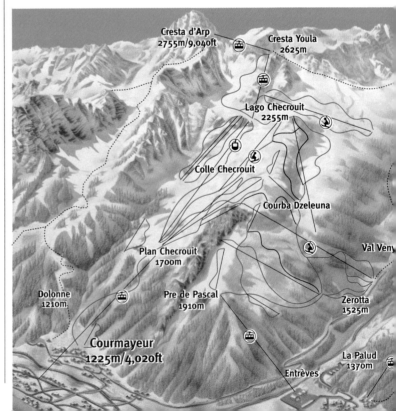

boarding *Courmayeur's pistes suit intermediates, and most areas are easily accessible by novices as the main lifts are cable-cars, chairs and gondolas – but it's all a bit steep for beginners. The biggest draws for the more experienced are the off-piste routes to be done with a guide. Like a lot of Italian resorts, Courmayeur has no terrain-park or half-pipe; but it still attracts quite a few boarders, and you shouldn't find yourself in too much of a minority. Nightlife is lively in a stylish way, and there's plenty of diversity in the bars.*

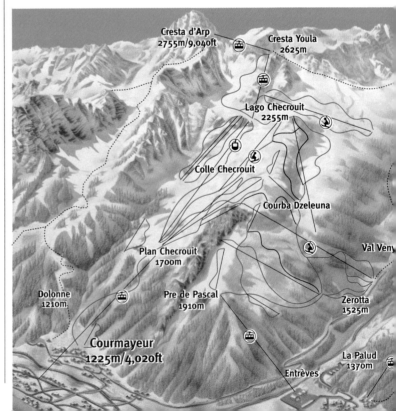

LIFT PASSES

2002/03 prices in euros

Courmayeur Mont Blanc
Covers all lifts in Val Veny and Checrouit, and the lifts on Mont Blanc up to Punta Helbronner.
Beginners Two free nursery lifts at Plan Checrouit and top of Val Veny cable-car (which can be paid for by the ride).
Main pass
1-day pass 31
6-day pass 169
(low season 152)
Short-term passes
Single ascent on some lifts and half-day pass (afternoon) available.
Children
Under 12: 6-day pass 126.5
Under 8: 42 with accompanying adult buying the same type of pass.
Notes Passes of two or more days are valid on the Mt Blanc lift. Passes of three or more days cover all lifts in the Aosta Valley (including La Thuile, Monterosa Ski, Cervinia, Pila). Mont Blanc and Snow Safari formula passes are valid for the whole Mont Blanc ski area (including Chamonix and Argentière) and in Verbier.

Arp Vieille to Val Veny, with close-up views of the Miage glacier; east down a deserted valley to Dolonne or Pré St Didier; or south through the Youla gorge to La Thuile.

On Mont Blanc, the Vallée Blanche is not a challenge (though there are more difficult variations), but the Toula glacier route on the Italian side from Punta Helbronner to Pavillon most certainly is, often to the point of being dangerous. There are also heli-drops available, including a wonderful 20km/12 mile run from the Ruitor glacier down into France – you catch the lifts back up from La Rosière and ski or board down to La Thuile (a taxi-ride from Courmayeur). And you can do a day trip to Chamonix through the Mont Blanc tunnel.

FOR INTERMEDIATES
Ideal gradient but limited extent

The whole area is suitable for most intermediates, but it is small. The avid piste-basher will find it very limited.

The open Checrouit section is pretty much go-anywhere territory, where you can choose your own route and make it as easy or difficult as you like. The blue runs here are about Courmayeur's gentlest. In Val Veny, the reds running the length of the Bertolini chair are more challenging and very enjoyable. They link in with the pretty, wooded slopes heading down to Zerotta.

The Zerotta chair dominates Val Veny, with lots of alternatives from the top – good for mixed abilities since runs of varying difficulty meet up at several places on the way down.

SCHOOLS/GUIDES

2001/02 prices in
euros

**Monte Bianco
Classes** 5 days
3hr: 10am-1pm 130

Children's classes
Ages: from 4
6 full days incl lunch
and childcare: 175.5
Private lessons
Hourly
27 to 39 for 1 person;
each additional
person 5

CHILDCARE

The Kinderheim at
Plan Checrouit (0165
842477) takes
children from the age
of 6 months, from
9.30 to 4pm. Children
taking lessons can be
deposited at the ski
school in Courmayeur
at 9am, and they will
be looked after for
the whole day (lesson
am, play pm). There
is a new 'snow park'
for children at
Dolonne. The
Kinderheim at the
Sports Centre takes
children from the age
of 6 months.

The Vallée Blanche, although off-piste, is easy enough for adventurous, fit intermediates to try. So is the local heli-skiing, which costs from £70 a drop including a guide; you are picked up on the piste so there's no wasted time.

FOR BEGINNERS
Consistently too steep
Courmayeur is not well suited to beginners. There are several nursery slopes, none ideal. The area at Plan Checrouit gets crowded, and there are few easy runs for the near-beginner to progress to. The small area served by the short Tzaly drag, just above the Entrèves cable-car top station, is the most suitable beginner terrain, and it tends to have good snow.

FOR CROSS-COUNTRY
Beautiful trails
There are 35km/22 miles of trails scattered around Courmayeur. The best are the four covering 20km/12 miles at Val Ferret, served by bus. Dolonne has a couple of short trails.

QUEUES
Sunday crowds pour in
The Checrouit and Val Veny cable-cars suffer queues only on Sundays, and even these can be beaten with an early start. Patience is needed when waiting for the infrequent Youla cable-car – 'Not sure it's worth waiting more than 15 minutes for the one steep red,' said a reporter. Overcrowded slopes on Sundays, particularly down to Zerotta, can also be a problem.

MOUNTAIN RESTAURANTS
Lots – some of them good
The area is lavishly endowed with 27 establishments ranging from rustic on-piste huts to larger self-service places. Most huts do table-service of delicious pizza and pasta and it is best to book.

But there are also snack bars selling more basic fare and relying on views and sun to fill their terraces.

Several restaurants are excellent. Maison Vieille, at the top of the chair of the same name and run by the charming mountain man Giacomo, is our favourite – a welcoming rustic place with superb home-made pastas. Chiecco, next to the drag-lift with the same name at Plan Checrouit, has good food, friendly service and good views of struggling beginners. The pick of the Plan Checrouit places is the Christiania – book a table downstairs, where you can savour the food (including excellent pizzas) in peace.

On the other side of the mountain in Val Veny is another clutch of places worth noting – the Zerotta, at the foot of the eponymous chair has a sunny terrace and good food; the nearby Petit Mont Blanc, the atmospheric Monte Bianco climbing refuge and the jolly Grolla are also recommended. One of the better snack bars is Courba Dzeleuna, with incredible views and delicious home-made myrtle grappa (beware of the alcohol-soaked berries left in the bottom of your glass if you want to hit the slopes again), just below the top of Dzeleuna chair.

SCHOOLS AND GUIDES
Good reports
'We had the best instructor for ages – possibly ever,' said a reporter about the Monte Bianco ski school. There is a thriving guides' association ready to help you explore the area's off-piste; it has produced a helpful booklet showing the main possibilities.

FACILITIES FOR CHILDREN
Good care by Italian standards
Childcare facilities are well ahead of the Italian norm, but Courmayeur is far from an ideal resort for a young family.

Courmayeur

381

GETTING THERE

Air Turin, transfer 2hr.

Rail Pré-St-Didier (5km/3 miles); regular buses from station.

ACTIVITIES

Indoor Swimming pool and sauna at Pré-St-Didier (5km/3 miles), Alpine museum, cinema, library. Sports centre with climbing, skating rink, curling, fitness centre, indoor golf, squash, tennis, basketball, volley ball, sauna and Turkish bath

Outdoor Walking paths in Val Ferret, paragliding, snow-biking, dog-sledding

Phone numbers
From abroad use the prefix +39 (and do **not** omit the initial '0' of the phone number).

TOURIST OFFICE

Postcode 11013
t 0165 842060
f 0165 842072
apt.montebianco@
psw.it
www.courmayeur.net

Staying there

HOW TO GO
Plenty of hotels
Courmayeur's long-standing popularity ensures a wide range of packages (including some excellent weekend deals), mainly in hotels. Tour op Interski has cheap hotels out of town and buses people in. One or two UK operators have catered chalets.
Hotels There are nearly 50 hotels, spanning the star ratings.

((((4) **Gallia Gran Baita** (0165 844040) Luxury place with antique furnishings, panoramic views and 'superb food'. Pool. Shuttle-bus to cable-car.

(((4) **Pavillon** (0165 846120) Comfortable 4-star near cable-car, with a pool. Friendly staff.

(((3) **Auberge de la Maison** (0165 869811) Small atmospheric 3-star in Entrèves under same ownership as Maison de Filippo (see Eating Out).

(((3) **Bouton d'Or** (0165 846729) Small, friendly B&B near main square.

(((3) **Berthod** (0165 842835) Friendly, family-run hotel near centre.

(((3) **Grange** (0165 869733) Rustic, stone-and-wood farmhouse in Entrèves.

(((3) **Triolet** (0165 846822) 'Excellent location 100m/300ft from lift. Comfy, well furnished.'

((2) **Edelweiss** (0165 841590) Friendly, cosy, good-value; close to the centre.

((2) **Lo Scoiattolo** (0165 846721) Good rooms, good food, shame it's at the opposite end of town to the cable-car.

Self-catering There is quite a lot available to independent bookers.

EATING OUT
Jolly Italian evenings
There is a great choice, both in downtown Courmayeur and within taxi-range; there's a handy promotional booklet describing many of them (in English as well as Italian). The touristy but very jolly Maison de Filippo in Entrèves is famous for its fixed-price, 36-dish feast. We've been impressed by the traditional Italian cuisine of both Pierre Alexis and Cadran Solaire. The Terrazza ('excellent pasta and very friendly, jolly service') is a rising star and has just been renovated. The Tunnel pizzeria and Mont-Frety ('good value', 'its antipasti a must') have been recommended by reporters. Restaurants tend to be busy, so book well in advance.

APRES-SKI
Stylish bar-hopping
Courmayeur has a lively evening scene, centred on stylish bars with comfy sofas or armchairs to collapse in. Our favourites are the Roma (reporters have been very taken with the free canapés), the back room of the Caffe della Posta and the Bar delle Guide. The Cadran Solaire is where the big money from Milan and Turin hangs out. The American Bar has good music and an excellent selection of wines. The Red Lion is worth a visit if you're missing English pubs, though a recent reporter found it 'sadly empty'. Ziggy's is an Internet cafe popular with local teenagers. Poppys has been recommended for dancing. There are two good night clubs in Entrèves – Jimmys and the Maquis.

OFF THE SLOPES
Much improved for sporty types
If you're not interested in hitting the snow you'll find the village pleasant. You can go by cable-car up to Punta Helbronner, by bus to Aosta, or up the main cable-car to Plan Checrouit to meet friends for lunch. The huge sports centre is good (indoor tennis, climbing wall, ice skating, squash, golf practice, gym, sauna, steam, but no pool).

STAYING UP THE MOUNTAIN
Why would you want to?
Visiting Courmayeur and not staying in the charming village seems perverse – if you're that keen to get on the slopes in the morning, this is probably the wrong resort. But at Plan Checrouit, the 1-star Christiania (0165 843572 – see Mountain restaurants) has simple rooms and the 3-star Baita (0165 843570) is smarter; you need to book way in advance.

Livigno 1815m/5,950ft

Lowish prices and highish altitude – a tempting combination

WHAT IT COSTS

HOW IT RATES

The slopes

Snow	****
Extent	**
Experts	**
Intermediates	***
Beginners	****
Convenience	**
Queues	****
Restaurants	***

The rest

Scenery	***
Resort charm	***
Off-slope	**

➕ High altitude plus snowmaking ensures a long season and a good chance of snow to resort level

➕ Large choice of beginners' slopes

➕ Modern and improving lift system

➕ Cheap by the standards of high resorts, with the bonus of duty-free shopping – a great place to treat yourself to new equipment

➕ Cosmopolitan, friendly village with some Alpine atmosphere

➕ Long, snow-sure cross-country trails

➖ No difficult pistes

➖ Long airport transfer – around 5hr

➖ Slopes split into two quite widely separated areas

➖ Village is very long and straggling, and a bit rough round the edges

➖ Few off-slope amenities

➖ Bleak, windy setting – often resulting in upper lifts being shut

➖ Not many really comfortable hotels bookable through UK tour operators

➖ Nightlife can disappoint

Livigno offers the unusual combination of a fair-sized mountain, high altitude and fairly low prices. Despite its vaunted duty-free status, hotels, bars and restaurants are not much cheaper than in other Italian resorts, but shopping is – there are countless camera and clothes shops. As a relatively snow-sure alternative to the Pyrenees or to the smallest, cheapest resorts in Austria, Livigno seems attractive. But don't overlook the long list of drawbacks.

What's new

A six-pack from Valfin on the Mottolino slopes to the top of Monte Della Neve opened up a couple of easy black runs a couple of years ago. For 2001/02 a new fast quad chair was installed for access to the Mottolino lifts from valley level, as an alternative to the existing gondola.

MOUNTAIN FACTS

Altitude	1815m-2800m
	5,950ft-9,190ft
Lifts	32
Pistes	115km
	71 miles
Blue	35%
Red	48%
Black	17%
Snowmaking	70km
	43 miles
Recco detectors used	

The resort

Livigno is an amalgam of three villages in a wide, remote valley near the Swiss border – basically a string of hotels, bars, specialist shops and supermarkets lining a single long street. The buildings are small in scale and mainly traditional in style, giving the village a pleasant atmosphere. The

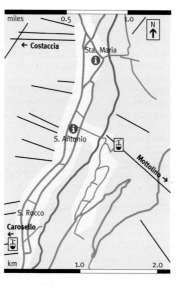

original hamlet of San Antonio is the nearest thing Livigno has to a centre, and the best all-round location. Here, the main street and those at right angles linking it to the busy bypass road are nominally traffic-free. The road that skirts the 'traffic-free' area is constantly busy, and becomes intrusive in the hamlets of Santa Maria, 1km/0.5 miles to the north, and San Rocco, a bit further away to the south (and uphill).

Lifts along the length of the village access the western slopes of the valley. The main lift to the eastern slopes is directly across the flat valley floor from the centre.

The bus services, on three colour-coded routes, are free and fairly frequent, but can get overcrowded at peak times and stop early in the evening. Minibus taxis are an affordable alternative for groups.

The lift pass covers Bormio and Santa Caterina, an easy drive or free bus-ride if the high pass is open, and a six-day pass entitles you to a discount rate on a one-day pass in St Moritz, reached via a road tunnel – a 'fantastic' day out, says a reader this year.

The airport transfer from Bergamo is long – five hours with a snack stop.

LIFT PASSES

2002/03 prices in euros

Alta Valtellina
Covers all lifts in Livigno, Bormio (40km/25 miles away), Valdidentro (30km/19 miles away) and Santa Caterina (50km/31 miles away).

Main pass
1-day pass 29.5
6-day pass 148
(low season 126)

Senior citizens
Over 60: 6-day pass 103

Children
Under 13: 6-day pass 103
Free pass under 8

Short-term passes
Morning and afternoon passes for Livigno only 22.

Notes Day pass price is for Livigno lifts only. 6-day pass and over entitles you to a one-day pass at a discounted rate in St Moritz and Engadine.

Alternative passes
Livigno-only pass for up to two days (adult 2-day 43).

The mountain

The mainly open slopes, on either side of the valley, are more extensive than in many other budget destinations.

THE SLOPES
Improved links

There are three sectors, all of them suitable for moderate and leisurely intermediates, and two of them are reasonably well linked.

A two-seater chair from the nursery slopes at the north end of the village take you up to **Costaccia**, where a long fast quad chair-lift goes along the ridge towards the **Carosello** sector. The blue linking run back from Carosello to the top of Costaccia is flat in places and may involve energetic poling if the snow conditions and the wind are against you. Carosello is more usually accessed by the optimistically named Carosello 3000 gondola at San Rocco, which goes up, in two stages, to 2750m/9,020ft. Most runs return

towards the village, but there are a couple on the back of the mountain, on the west-facing slopes of Val Federia – served by a double drag-lift.

The ridge of **Mottolino** is reached by an efficient gondola from Teola, a tiresome walk or a short bus-ride across the valley from San Antonio. From the top, you can descend to fast quads on either side of the ridge or, if you must, take a slow antique chair up the ridge to Monte della Neve. There is now the alternative of a fast quad starting a little way along the valley, and linking with a six-pack to Monte della Neve.

Signposting is patchy and the piste map isn't always entirely accurate.

SNOW RELIABILITY
Very good, despite no glacier

Livigno's slopes are high (you can spend most of your time around 2500m/8,000ft), and with snow-guns on the lower slopes of Mottolino and Costaccia, the season is long.

boarding *Livigno attracts a fair number of boarders and young people generally. There's a half-pipe and a good, if underused, terrain-park/boarder-cross in the Mottolino area. And there are some good long, high runs for free-riders and carvers, as well as ample off-piste opportunities for intermediate riders. Most of the resort can be accessed by cable-cars and chairs. However, the excellent beginner slopes are mainly served by drags.*

SCHOOLS/GUIDES

2001/02 prices in euros

Livigno Inverno/Estate
Classes 6 days
2hr: 9am-11am or 11am-1pm
6 2hr days: 73
Children's classes
Ages: from 3
6 2hr lessons and 2hr nursery
Private lessons
Hourly
27 for 1hr; each additional person 6

Azzurra Livigno
Classes 6 days
2½hr: 10am-12.30pm
6 2½hr days: 97
Private lessons
Hourly
28 for 1hr

OTHER SCHOOLS

Livigno Italy
Livigno Soc Coop
Top Club Mottolino

FOR EXPERTS
Not recommended
The piste map shows a few black runs but these are not particularly steep. Even the all-black terrain served by the six-pack on Monte della Neve is really no more than stiff red in gradient. There is off-piste to be done, but guidance would be needed.

FOR INTERMEDIATES
Flattering slopes
Good intermediates will be able to tackle all of the blacks without worry. The woodland black run down from Carosello past Tea da Borch is narrow in places and can get mogulled and icy at the end of the day. The runs on the back of Carosello down to Federia are challenging, and bumpy. Moderate intermediates have virtually the whole area at their disposal. The long run beneath the Mottolino gondola is one of the best. Leisurely types have several long cruises available in all sectors. The run beneath the Valandrea-Vetta fast chair, at the top of the Costaccia sector, is a splendid slope for confidence-building – 1.5km/1 mile long, dropping only 260m/850ft.

FOR BEGINNERS
Excellent but scattered slopes
A vast array of nursery slopes along the sunny lower flanks of Costaccia, and other slopes around the valley, make Livigno excellent for novices – although some of the slopes at the

northern end are on the steep side. There are lots of longer runs suitable for fast learners and near-beginners.

CROSS-COUNTRY
Good snow, bleak setting
Long snow-sure trails (40km/25 miles in total) follow the valley floor, making Livigno a good choice, though the scenery is bleak. There is a specialist cross-country school, and the resort organises major cross-country races.

QUEUES
Few problems these days
Despite recent reports of queues for the Costaccia chair at midday and short delays for the Carosello gondola in peak season, lift queues are not generally a problem. Investment in fast new chairs at Carosello and Mottolino has rid the area of long queues. A bigger problem is that strong winds often close the upper lifts, causing overcrowding lower down. The red run under the Mottolino gondola is prone to congestion.

MOUNTAIN RESTAURANTS
More than adequate
On Mottolino, the recently renovated refuge at the top of the gondola is impressive, with smart self- and table-service sections, a solarium and a nursery, but 'immense' lunch-time queues. The rustic restaurants at Passo d'Eira and Trepalle are a good option for a quiet stop. And there are some

Livigno

385

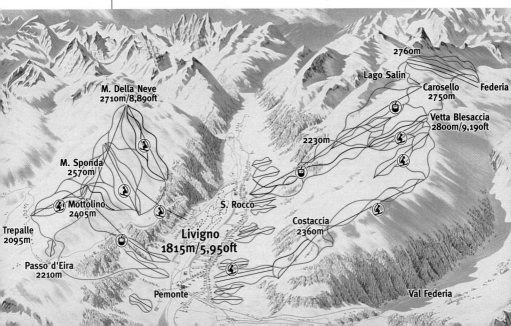

GETTING THERE

Air Bergamo, transfer 5hr.

Rail Tirano (48km/30 miles), Zernez (Switzerland, 28km/17 miles); regular buses from station, weekends only.

CHILDCARE

The Livigno school runs the Alì Babà kindergarten for children aged 3 and over. Lessons and lunches available. The staff speak English.

ACTIVITIES

Indoor Sauna, gym, body-building, games room, bowling, cinema
Outdoor Cleared paths, skating rink, snowmobiles, horse-drawn sleigh rides, horse-riding, paragliding, mountaineering

Phone numbers
From abroad use the prefix +39 (and do **not** omit the initial '0' of the phone number).

TOURIST OFFICE

Postcode 23030
t 0342 996379
f 0342 996881
info@aptlivigno.it
www.aptlivigno.it

more charming places lower down. The welcoming Tea del Vidal is at the base of the same sector. Costaccia's Tea del Plan is pleasantly rustic and sunny, with good food and a great atmosphere. The self-service place at the top of Carosello is acceptable and Tea da Borch, in the trees lower down, serves great food in a Tirolean-style atmosphere, though the run down can be tricky. Lunch in the valley at the hotel Sporting (near the Carosello gondola station) is popular. The terrace at the hotel Möta, at the base of the Costaccia lifts, is also recommended.

SCHOOLS AND GUIDES
Watch out for short classes
There are several schools. English is widely spoken, and recent reports are complimentary. A common complaint is that most of the schools only offer short (two-hour) classes. Another complaint is that beginners spend too long on the nursery slopes before progressing up the mountain. It also seems to be the case that the schools on the Costaccia-Carosello side avoid the Mottolino sector altogether.

FACILITIES FOR CHILDREN
Limited
The schools run children's classes, and the Livigno school's Alì-Babà nursery offers all-day care.

Staying there

HOW TO GO
Lots of hotels, some apartments
Livigno has an enormous range of hotels and a number of apartments. There are some attractively priced catered chalets from UK operators.
Hotels Most of the hotels are small 2- and 3-star places, with a couple of 4-stars out of the centre.
Intermonti (0342 972100) Modern 4-star with all mod cons (including a pool); some way from the centre, on the Mottolino side of the valley.
Bivio (0342 996137) The only hotel in central Livigno with a pool.
Steinbock (0342 970520) Nice little place, far from major lifts but a short walk from some nursery slopes.
Loredana (0342 996330) Modern chalet on the Mottolino side. 'Very good – too much food.'
Larice (0342 996184) Stylish little 3-star B&B well placed for Costaccia lifts and slopes.

Montanina (0342 996060) Good central 2-star.
Camana Veglia (0342 996310) Charming old wooden chalet. Popular restaurant, well placed in Santa Maria.
Self-catering All the big tour operators that come here have apartment options. Most are cheap and cheerful.

EATING OUT
Value for money
Livigno has lots of traditional, unpretentious restaurants, many hotel-based. Hotel Concordia has some of the best cooking in town. Mario's has one of the largest menus, serving seafood, fondue and steaks in addition to the ubiquitous pizza and pasta. Bait dal Ghet and the Bivio restaurant are popular with the locals, and the Rusticana does wholesome, cheap food. Pesce d'Oro is good for seafood and Italian cuisine. The Bellavista, Ambassador, Mirage, Grolla and the Garden are also recommended.

APRES-SKI
Lively, but disappoints some
It's not that there isn't action in Livigno, but simply that the scene is quieter than some people expect in a duty-free resort. Also, the best places are scattered about, so the village lacks evening buzz. At tea time many people return to their hotels for a quiet drink. But Tea del Vidal, at the bottom of Mottolino, gets lively, as does the Stalet bar at the base of the Carosello gondola. The Caffè della Posta umbrella bar, near the centre, is also popular. We hear Europe's highest brewery is in production at the Echo. Nightlife gets going only after 10pm. Galli's pub, in San Antonio, is 'a full-on party pub', popular with Brits. The Kuhstall under the Bivio hotel is an excellent cellar bar with live music, as is the Helvetia, over the road. The San Rocco end is quietest, but Daphne's and Marco's are popular. The stylish Art bar is also recommended. Kokodi and Cielo are the main discos.

OFF THE SLOPES
Look lively, or go shopping
Livigno offers a small range of outdoor alternatives to skiing and boarding – horse-riding among them. Walks are uninspiring and there is no sports centre or public swimming pool. However, the duty-free shopping more than makes up for this. Trips to Bormio and St Moritz are popular.

Madonna di Campiglio 1520m/4,990ft

Extensive, easy slopes amid stunning scenery

387

WHAT IT COSTS

HOW IT RATES

The slopes

Snow	★★★
Extent	★★★
Experts	★★
Intermediates	★★★★
Beginners	★★★★
Convenience	★★
Queues	★★★
Restaurants	★★★

The rest

Scenery	★★★★
Resort charm	★★★
Off-slope	★★★

What's new

The most exciting news we have is that one or two ski schools may provide nursery care next winter. Don't count on it.

➕ Pleasant traditional-style town with car-free centre

➕ Fairly extensive network of slopes, best for beginners and intermediates

➕ Excellent mountain restaurants

➖ Spread-out resort and infrequent shuttle-bus service

➖ Quiet après-ski

Like Cortina, Madonna is a pleasant Dolomite town with an affluent, almost exclusively Italian, clientele – though the scenery isn't in quite the same league. Folgarida and Marilleva, with which Madonna shares its slopes, are quite different, attracting a lot of British groups, including schools.

THE RESORT

Madonna is a spread-out, modern, but traditional-style town with a pedestrian-only centre, set in a prettily wooded valley beneath the impressive Brenta Dolomites. There is more development 1km/0.5 miles south, and a frozen lake between the two.

Madonna attracts an affluent, young, Italian clientele. It has almost as many 4-star hotels as 3-stars, and lots of smart shops. Many visitors stay around the village in the day, and promenading is an early evening ritual.

There are several mountain access lifts, and they are quite widely spread; it's worth staying near one of them. The main nursery slopes are some way out at Campo Carlo Magno. The free ski-bus runs to a timetable, but is not frequent. Some hotels run mini-buses.

THE MOUNTAINS

There are three areas of linked slopes around Madonna: Pancugolo to the west, Pradalago to the north, and Passo Grostè (the highest area) to the east. Pradalago is also linked by lift and piste to Monte Vigo, where the slopes of Folgarida and Marilleva also meet. There are long-term plans for a link between Pancugolo and the separate little resort of Pinzolo.

Slopes The terrain is mainly intermediate, both above and below the tree line. Reporters recommend skiing the Marilleva and Folgarida slopes in the afternoon to avoid crowded ski school classes.

Snow reliability Although many of the runs are sunny, they are at a fair altitude, and there has been hefty investment in snowmaking. As a result, snow reliability is reasonable.

Experts Experts should plan on heading off-piste. But the 3-Tre race course and the Spinale Direttissima are steep. Pista Nera, above Folgarida, can be a challenging mogul field.

Intermediates Pancugolo, Madonna's racing mountain, is ideal: early or timid intermediates will love the area and have no difficulty exploring most of the network, though the connection to Folgarida is a bit trickier. Grostè and Pradalago have long, easy runs, though the former can get crowded.

Beginners It's a good resort for beginners, if you don't mind using the bus service out to the excellent nursery slopes at Campo Carlo Magno.

Snowboarding There's a terrain-park and a half-pipe at Grostè. The resort was on the FIS World Snowboard Championship circuit last season.

Cross-country There are 30km/19 miles of pretty trails through the woods.

Queues The links with Marilleva are the main black spot – there can be hour-long waits for the chair back. The new magic carpet link from Grostè to Pradalago is a bottleneck at midday. One reporter tells of pushy queues for

MADONNA TOURIST OFFICE

The setting is prettily wooded, but without the spectacular peaks found further east in the Dolomites →

MOUNTAIN FACTS

Altitude	1550m-2505m
	1,085ft-8,220ft
Lifts	50
Pistes	150km
	93 miles
Blue	44%
Red	40%
Black	16%
Snowmaking	72km
	45 miles
Recco detectors used	

Phone numbers

From abroad use the prefix +39 (and do **not** omit the initial '0' of the phone number).

TOURIST OFFICE

Postcode 38084
t 0465 442000
f 0465 440404
info@campiglio.net
www.campiglio.net

the Pradalago chair at the start of ski school classes.

Mountain restaurants This year's reporters are less impressed than past ones. The Rifugio Graffer is recommended for its 'freshly cooked burgers'. The hotel Alaska, beside run 2 at Folgarida, was described as 'fantastic, great value'.

Schools and guides There are several ski schools; not surprisingly, some instructors don't speak English. A reporter last season had several complaints about the Nazionale – but was impressed by the helmets child pupils were given (for keeps).

Facilities for children Only now is Madonna making plans for a nursery.

STAYING THERE

How to go There is a wide choice of hotels, and some self-catering is sold by tour operators.

Hotels The 4-star Spinale (0465 441116) is convenient. The central 3-star Milano (0465 441210) is also recommended. At Campo Carlo Magno

the Zeledria (0465 441010) is 'a good 4-star with friendly staff'.

Eating out There are around 20 restaurants to choose from. Belvedere, the Roi and Stube Diana have all been recommended. Some of the mountain huts are also open in the evening.

Après-ski Après-ski is quiet. Franz-Joseph Stube, Bar Suisse and Cantina del Suisse are recommended – and the Alpes is perhaps the smartest club.

Off the slopes Window-shopping, skating and walking are popular.

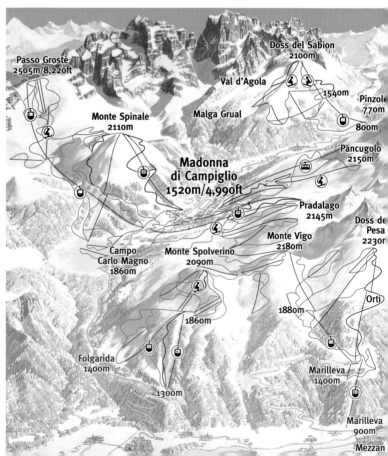

Passo Grostè 2505m/8,220ft

Doss del Sabion 2100m

Val d'Agola

1540m

Pinzolo 770m

800m

Monte Spinale 2110m

Malga Grual

Pancugolo 2150m

Madonna di Campiglio 1520m/4,990ft

Pradalago 2145m

Doss de Pesa 2230m

Monte Vigo 2180m

Campo Carlo Magno 1860m

Monte Spolverino 2090m

1880m

Orti

1860m

Folgarida 1400m

Marilleva 1400m

1300m

Marilleva 900m

Mezzan

Monterosa Ski 1640m/5,380ft

Europe's best kept secret – an undiscovered gem

WHAT IT COSTS

HOW IT RATES

The slopes

Snow	***
Extent	****
Experts	***
Intermediates	****
Beginners	**
Convenience	****
Queues	****
Restaurants	**

The rest

Scenery	****
Resort charm	***
Off-slope	*

MOUNTAIN FACTS

Altitude 1200m-3550m
3,940ft-11,650ft

Lifts	37
Pistes	180km
	125 miles
Blue	29%
Red	63%
Black	8%
Snowmaking	70km
	44 miles

Recco detectors used

- ➕ Fairly extensive network of pistes
- ➕ Fabulous intermediate and advanced off-piste, including heli-skiing
- ➕ Beautiful scenery
- ➕ Good snow reliability and grooming
- ➕ Quiet, pretty, unspoiled villages
- ➖ Fragmented slopes
- ➖ Links to and from Alagna currently off-piste only
- ➖ Few off-slope diversions
- ➖ Limited après-ski

Monterosa Ski is Italy's little-known and less extensive answer to France's Trois Vallées and has a good lift system which is set for further big development over the next few years. Yet it is hardly heard of on the international market. It is popular with Italians at weekends, when they drive up for the day from Milan and Turin. But during the week it is deserted. The pistes are mostly intermediate and they offer the same feeling of travelling around as the Trois Vallées does, amid impressive scenery. And the off-piste is fabulous (and usually deserted). It is the only major ski area we have come across in Europe where there is no real well-developed resort to stay in. The villages that access the slopes have avoided commercialisation and still retain a friendly, small-scale, local ambience. Our advice is to get there soon before all this changes.

THE RESORTS

The main resorts are Champoluc in the western valley, Gressoney, in the central valley, and Alagna to the east. While Champoluc and Alagna have a very Italian ambience, Gressoney shows more Swiss-German influence, even having some signs in German.

Champoluc is towards the end of a long, winding road up from the Aosta valley motorway. It is strung out along the road for quite a distance but retains a certain quiet charm and very Italian feel. The first part you come to is the attractive old village centre with the church and a fast-running river.

Small shops and hotels line the road between here and the gondola, several minutes' walk away. You can store boots and board there overnight. More accommodation is on the road to Frachey, where there is a chair-lift into the slopes.

Gressoney La Trinité is a quiet, neat little village, with cobbled streets, wooden buildings and an old church. It

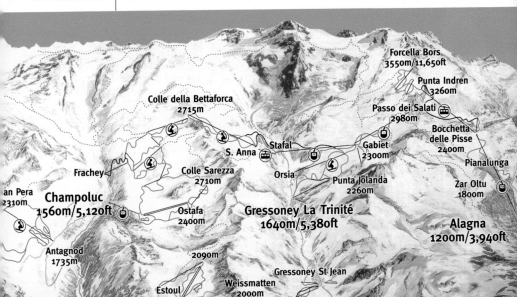

Snow

01285 642 555
www.handmade-holidays.co.uk
AITO   ATOL PROTECTED 4479

What's new

The plan is to link Alagna properly by lifts and piste to Gressoney – but not before 2003/04. A couple of years ago, the ancient cable-car out of Alagna was replaced by a new gondola to Pianalunga, followed by a new chair-lift, which takes you to the top cable-car (still tiny and ancient) up to Punta Indren.

The next stage is to build a lift connection from Pianalunga to Passo dei Salati and make the off-piste route from Passo dei Salati to Pianalunga an official piste.

Each year, more snowmaking is added and they now claim an impressive 70km.

SNOWPIX.COM / CHRIS GILL

That's it, folks: the famous Monte Rosa that the area is named after ↓

is about 800m/0.5 miles from the chair-lift into the slopes, where there are a few convenient hotels. It is a bus-ride from the outpost of Stafal at the head of the valley, which is the link between the Gressoney and Champoluc slopes and has a few rather soulless blocks. Gressoney St Jean, a bigger village, is 5km/3 miles down the valley and has its own separate slopes. Local buses are covered by the lift pass.

The main resort in the east valley is Alagna, a strange place with some large, deserted and dilapidated buildings as well as smaller charming wooden buildings and church.

Trips to Cervinia, La Thuile and Courmayeur (covered by the Aosta Valley pass) are possible by car.

THE MOUNTAINS

The slopes of Monterosa Ski are relatively extensive, and very scenic. The pistes are almost all intermediate (and well groomed), and the lifts are mainly chairs and gondolas, with few drag-lifts. The terrain is undulating and fragmented; runs are attractively varied and long, but many lifts serve only one or two pistes. The piste map is poor: 'Woefully inadequate,' said a reporter.

Slopes A gondola from Champoluc followed by a couple of slow chairs takes you up to the steep, narrow, bumpy link with the rest of the slopes. Taking the bus to the Frachey chair is a quicker way into the main cruising runs and the link via Colle Bettaforca with Stafal in the Gressoney valley.

At Stafal a cable-car followed by a high-speed chair take you back to the Champoluc slopes and a two-stage 12-person gondola opposite takes you up to Passo dei Salati. From there runs lead back down to Stafal and to Gressoney La Trinité and Orsia, both served by more chair-lifts. Or you can

head down towards Alagna on an easy, popular off-piste run (due to become a piste in the next couple of years).

From Alagna a gondola (new for 2000/01) goes to Pianalunga at mid-mountain, where a new two-person chair-lift carries you up to a tiny, ancient cable-car, which accesses the high slopes around Punta Indren. There are a couple of drag-lifts and short pistes up here but the only ways back to Gressoney are off-piste. On the Alagna side there is lots of off-piste and an ungroomed black run that leads to an old bucket lift that you jump into while it is still moving (it takes you back to the cable-car).

Gressoney St Jean and Antagnod, near Champoluc, have their own small areas of slopes.

Snow reliability Generally good, thanks to extensive snowmaking, high altitude and good grooming – though like most of Italy, the area was very short of snow for the early part of last season.

Experts The attraction is the off-piste, with great runs from the high-points of the lift system in all three valleys and some excellent heli-drops. A mountain guide is essential for getting the best out of the area. We had a fabulous day with Claudio from Gressoney (all the younger guides speak good English), skiing down to Alagna and exploring the deserted bowls above Gressoney, where snow can lie untracked for days. Alagna is a cult area for expert off-piste. There is an epic run down to the Champoluc valley from the top of the Cervinia-Zermatt area.

There are a few black pistes but none of them really deserve their grading. And many of the reds would be blue in other resorts.

Intermediates For those who like to travel on easy, undemanding pistes, the area is great, with long cruising runs from the ridges down into the valleys. There isn't much on-piste challenge for more demanding intermediates, but those willing to take a guide and explore some of the gentler off-piste will have a great time. If you stick to the pistes, a weekend rather than a full week might be worth trying: 'It's great for a short break,' said a recent reporter.

Beginners The high nursery slopes at the top of the gondola at Champoluc are better than the lower ones at Gressoney. But Gressoney has better easy runs to progress to than Champoluc (where it is best to go to

Phone numbers
From abroad use the prefix +39 (and do **not** omit the initial 'o' of the phone number).

TOURIST OFFICE

Postcode 11020
t 0125 303111
f 0125 303145
kikesly@tin.it
www.monterosa-ski.com

the Frachey chair or to Antagnod.
Snowboarding There is no park or half-pipe but great off-piste free-riding.
Cross-country There are long trails around St Jean, and shorter ones up the valley; Brusson, in the Champoluc valley, has the best trails in the area.
Queues Only at weekends, when the hordes from Turin and Milan arrive, are there any queues. The worst bottleneck is the tiny top cable-car on the Alagna side, where waits of over an hour are possible. Pistes can get crowded at weekends, too, but the off-piste is still delightfully quiet.
Mountain restaurants The mountain restaurants are good and cheap. The

Chamois at Punta Jolanda, Bedemie on the way to Gressoney from Gabiet, Del Ponte above Gabiet, Vieux Crest and Belvedere, above Champoluc, and the Guglielmina, Lys and Gabiet refuges are recommended.
Schools and guides We have had decent reports on the ski schools and excellent ones on the Gressoney and Alagna mountain guides.
Facilities for children There is a special kids' ski school and snow park at Antagnod near Champoluc and a mini-club at Gressoney St Jean.

STAYING THERE
How to go More tour operators are discovering the area. We've had good reports of Monterosa specialists Ski 2.
Hotels At Champoluc the Castor (0125 307117) in the old centre is 'an absolute gem' and is managed by a British guy. At the amazing hotel California (0125 307977 – the owners speak no English) every room is dedicated to a pop star or group (eg the Byrds, Bob Dylan, Joan Baez, the Doors) and their music plays whenever you turn on the light. It's quite a way out of the centre. The Breithorn (0125 08734), two minutes from the gondola, opened for 2001/02 and is a luxury 4-star with health centre converted from a 100-year-old building.
At Gressoney La Trinité reporters recommend the Jolanda Sport (0125 366140) and Dufour (0125 366139); in Alagna, the Monterosa (0163 923209) and Cristallo (0163 91285).
Eating out Both Gressoney and Champoluc have a few stand-alone restaurants, but most are in hotels.
Après-ski Après-ski is quiet. At weekends, the disco beneath hotel California in Champoluc gets going. The bar of the hotel Castor is cosy.
Off the slopes There is little to amuse those who don't head for the slopes.

Monterosa Ski

391

Sauze d'Oulx

1510m/4,950ft

'Suzy does it' still, but with more dignity than in the past

WHAT IT COSTS

HOW IT RATES

The slopes

Snow	**
Extent	*****
Experts	**
Intermediates	****
Beginners	**
Convenience	**
Queues	***
Restaurants	***

The rest

Scenery	***
Resort charm	**
Off-slope	*

What's new

Turin has been chosen to host the 2006 Olympic Winter Games; most of the Alpine events will be held at Sansicario and Sestriere, and freestyle competitions at Sauze d'Oulx.

Snowmaking has been improved in the Sportinia area.

The Tuassieres drag-lift is to be rebuilt for 2002/03.

MOUNTAIN FACTS

Figures relate to the whole Milky Way area

Altitude	1390m-2825m
	4,560ft-9,270ft
Lifts	92
Pistes	400km
	250 miles
Blue	12%
Red	67%
Black	21%
Snowmaking	80km
	50 miles

- ➕ Extensive and uncrowded slopes, great intermediate cruising
- ➕ Linked into Milky Way network
- ➕ Mix of open and tree-lined runs is good for all weather conditions
- ➕ Entertaining nightlife
- ➕ Some scope for off-piste adventures
- ➕ One of the cheapest major resorts there is – and more attractive than its reputation suggests

- ➖ Still lots of ancient lifts, making progress around the slopes slow
- ➖ Erratic snow record – and still far from comprehensive snowmaking
- ➖ Crowds at weekends
- ➖ Brashness and Britishness of resort will not suit everyone
- ➖ Very few challenging pistes
- ➖ Mornings-only classes, and the best nursery slopes are at mid-mountain
- ➖ Steep walks around the village, and an inadequate shuttle-bus service

If you're looking for a cheap holiday in a resort with extensive slopes, put Sauze on your shortlist. In the 1980s it became known as prime lager-lout territory; but it always was a resort of two halves – young Brits on a budget alongside mature second-home owners from Turin – and these days the two halves seem to be much more in balance, especially at weekends. It still has lively bars and shops festooned in English signs, but sober Brits like you and us need not stay away. When we visit, we like it more than we expect to – as do many reporters.

We are slightly haunted, though, by the memory of the bare slopes of our first visit, in the mid-1980s. Thin cover three seasons ago brought it all back: Sauze is a resort that needs comprehensive snowmaking, and doesn't yet have it.

The resort

Sauze d'Oulx sits on a sloping mountain shelf facing north-west across the Valle di Susa, with impressive views of the towering mountains forming the border with France. Most of the resort is modern and undistinguished, made up of block-like hotels relieved by the occasional chalet, spreading down the steep hillside from the foot of the slopes. Despite the shift in clientele described above, the centre is still lively at night; the late-closing bars are usually quite full, and the handful of discos do brisk business – at the weekend, at least.

Sauze also has an attractive old core, with narrow, twisting streets and houses roofed with huge stone slabs. There is a central car-free zone, but traffic roams freely through most of the village, which can be congested morning and evening. The roads can become icy and treacherous at night – with few pavements.

Out of the bustle of the centre, where most of the bars and nightclubs

are located, there are quiet, wooded residential areas full of secluded apartment blocks. A number of good restaurants are also tucked out of the way of the front line. Chair-lifts go from the top of the village and from two points on its fringes. There's also a chair from nearby Jouvenceaux.

Most of the hotels are reasonably central, but the Clotes lift is at the top of the village, up a short but steep hill, and the Sportinia chair is an irritatingly long walk beyond that. Buses (not covered by the lift pass) are infrequent and can't cope with high-season crowds. The service around lunch-time is particularly poor, and signposting of stops is unclear.

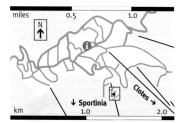

The mountains

Sauze's mountains provide excellent intermediate terrain. The piste grading fluctuates from year to year, if you believe the resort's map – and we're never sure we've caught up with the latest changes from blue to red and red to blue. But most reporters agree that many runs graded red or even black should really be graded blue; challenges are few and far between. (The same might be said of the whole extensive Milky Way area, of which Sauze is one extreme.)

THE SLOPES
Big and varied enough for most

Sauze's local slopes are spread across a broad wooded bowl above the resort, ranging from west- to north-facing. The main lifts are chairs, from the top of the village up to **Clotes** and from the western fringes to **Sportinia** – a sunny mid-mountain clearing in the woods, with a ring of restaurants and hotels (see Staying up the mountain) and a small nursery area.

The high point of the system is **Monte Fraiteve**. From here you can travel west on splendid broad, long runs to **Sansicario** – and on to chair-lifts near **Cesana Torinese** that link with **Clavière** and then **Montgenèvre**, in France, the far end of the Milky Way (both are reached more quickly by car).

You normally get to **Sestriere** from the lower point of Col Basset, on the shoulder of M Fraiteve. The alternative of descending the sunny slope from M Fraiteve itself has been reinstated after a few years of closure; but snow here is not reliable, which we're told is why the old lift from Sestriere up this slope was removed some years ago. You can make the link via the gondola but this is prone to closure in bad weather.

As in so many Italian resorts, piste marking, direction signing and piste map design are not taken particularly seriously.

The slopes of Montgenèvre and Sestriere are dealt with in separate chapters. If you have a car, you can go beyond Montgenèvre to Briançon, Serre-Chevalier and Bardonecchia.

SNOW RELIABILITY
Can be poor, affecting the links

The area is notorious for erratic snowfalls, occasionally suffering acute droughts. Another problem is that many of the slopes get a lot of afternoon sun. At these modest altitudes, late-season conditions are far from reliable. Reporters have found icy, bare slopes at vital link points earlier in the season, too – particularly from M Fraiteve. There's snowmaking on a couple of slopes, notably the key home run from P Rocca via Clotes to the village.

FOR EXPERTS
Head off-piste

Very few of the pistes are challenging. The best slopes are at virtually opposite ends of Sauze's local area – a high, north-facing run from the shoulder of M Fraiteve, and the sunny slopes below M Moncrons.

The main interest is in going off-piste. There are plenty of minor opportunities within the piste network, but the highlights are long, top-to-bottom descents of up to 1300m/4,270ft vertical from M Fraiteve, ending (snow permitting) at villages dotted along the valleys. The best known of these runs (which used to be marked on the piste map but is no longer) is the Rio Nero, down to the road near Oulx. When snow low down is poor, some of these runs can be cut short at Jouvenceaux or Sansicario.

SAUZE D'OULX TOURIST OFFICE

The village slopes down from the bottom of the home run from Clotes →

boarding *Sauze has good snowboarding slopes – it's got local tree-lined slopes (with space in the trees, too), high, undulating, open terrain, and links to other resorts in the Milky Way. But although it has a fair number of chair-lifts, there are also lots of drags – a serious drawback for novice riders. There's no park or pipe, but the amount and variety of terrain make up for this. Sauze's mainly young visitors ensure lively, entertaining nightlife.*

FOR INTERMEDIATES
Splendid cruising terrain
The whole area is ideal for confident intermediates who want to clock up the kilometres. For the less confident, the piste map doesn't help because it picks out only the very easiest runs in blue – there are many others they could manage. The Belvedere and Moncrons sectors at the east of the area are served only by drags but offer some wonderful, uncrowded high cruising, some of it above the tree line.

The long runs down to Sansicario and down to Jouvenceaux are splendid, confidence-boosting intermediate terrain. Getting back to Sauze involves tackling some of the steepest terrain in the area – the black run from M Fraiteve to the Col Basset lifts at Malafosse. This presents a problem for many intermediates and is a serious shortcoming in the circuit. The run down to Sestriere gets a lot of sun but is worth it for the somewhat more challenging intermediate terrain on the opposite side of the valley. If

conditions are too poor, you can always ride the gondola down.

At the higher levels, where the slopes are above the tree line, the terrain often allows a choice of route. Lower down are pretty runs through the woods, where the main complication can be route-finding. The mountainside is broken up by gullies, and pistes that appear to be quite close together but may in fact have no easy connections between them.

FOR BEGINNERS
There are better choices
Sauze is not ideal for beginners: its village-level slopes are a bit on the steep side and the main nursery area is up the mountain, at Sportinia. Equally importantly, the mornings-only classes don't suit everyone.

FOR CROSS-COUNTRY
Severely limited, even with snow
There is very little cross-country skiing, and it isn't reliable for snow.

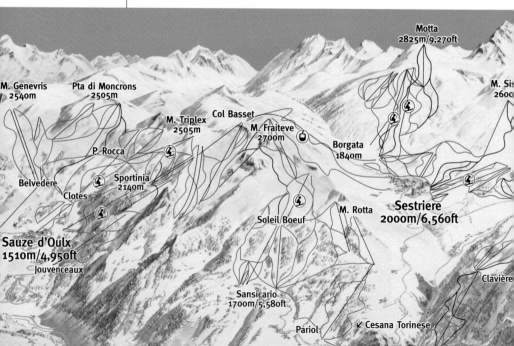

CHILDCARE

The village kindergarten, Little Dumbo, has English and Italian staff and takes children up to 6 years, from 9am to 5pm. You have to provide lunch, but it can be heated up.

GETTING THERE

Air Turin, transfer 2hr.

Rail Oulx (5km/3 miles); frequent buses.

SCHOOLS/GUIDES

2001/02 prices in euros

**Sauze Sportinia
Classes** 6 days
3hr: 10am-1pm
6 3hr days: 113
Children's classes
Ages: from 6
6 3hr days: 113
Private lessons
Hourly
29 for 1hr

**Sauze d'Oulx
Classes** 6 days
3hr: 10am-1pm
6 3hr days: 113
Children's classes
Ages: from 6
6 3hr days: 113
Private lessons
Hourly
29 for 1hr

Sauze Project
Offers instruction in Italian only.

QUEUES
Slow lifts the biggest problem

There can be 10-minute waits at Sportinia when school classes are setting off or immediately after lunch; otherwise the system has few bottlenecks. But, despite the recent introduction of three fast quads, most of the lifts are ancient and terribly slow. The chair-lift from the village to Clotes is an extreme case: a museum-piece which requires you to carry your skis in your lap and hit the ground running at the top. This lift is simply inadequate. Breakdowns of elderly lifts may also be a nuisance. And a February visitor reports that several lifts were opened only at weekends, when the Italian crowds arrive.

MOUNTAIN RESTAURANTS
Some pleasant possibilities

Restaurants are numerous and generally pleasant, though few are particularly special and a reader last year complained about lack of variety on the menus. One place that's certainly worth picking out is the hotel Capricorno, at Clotes – one of the most civilised and appealing lunch spots in the Alps. It is not cheap, though. There are more modest mid-mountain restaurants across the mountainside, with the main concentration at Sportinia, though a recent reporter preferred to go elsewhere to avoid the crowds. The Capannina self-service is popular and the food at Cicci's has been recommended. The Ciao Pais, at the top of the Clotes chair-lift, the Chalet Pian della Rocca and the Chalet Clot Bourget have also pleased visitors. The Marmotta on Triplex is one reader's tip for 'drinks and service with a smile'.

SCHOOLS AND GUIDES
Lessons variable, large classes

Our only recent reporter pronounces his companions' lessons satisfactory, but past reports have been mixed. Classes are only half a day, but last three hours.

FACILITIES FOR CHILDREN
Tour operator alternatives

Although there is a resort kindergarten, you might want to look at the nursery facilities offered by some of the major UK tour operators in the chalets and chalet-hotels that they run here – Crystal and Neilson, for example.

Staying there

HOW TO GO
Packaged hotels dominate

All the major mainstream operators offer hotel packages here, but there are also a few chalets.
Hotels Simple 2-star and 3-star hotels form the core of the holiday accommodation, with a couple of 4-stars and some more basic places.
⟨⟨⟨3⟩ **Torre** (0122 850020) Cylindrical 4-star landmark 200m/650ft below the centre. Excellent rooms, 'good food', 'plenty of choice'; mini-buses to lifts.
⟨2⟩ **Hermitage** (0122 850385) Neat chalet-style hotel in about the best spot for the slopes – beside the home piste from Clotes.
⟨2⟩ **Gran Baita** (0122 850183) Comfortable place in quiet, central backstreet, with excellent food and good rooms, some with sunset views.
⟨2⟩ **Biancaneve** (0122 850160) Pleasant, with smallish rooms. Near the centre.
⟨2⟩ **Amis** (0122 858488) Down in Jouvenceaux, but near bus stop; simple hotel run by Anglo-Italian couple.
Self-catering Apartments and chalets available, some through UK operators.

Sauze d'Oulx

395

ACTIVITIES

Indoor Bowling, cinema, sauna, massage
Outdoor Artificial skating rink, torchlit descents, heli-skiing, ice-climbing, snow-shoeing

Phone numbers
From abroad use the prefix +39 (and do **not** omit the initial '0' of the phone number).

SAUZE TOURIST OFFICE

Postcode 10050
t 0122 858009
f 0122 850700
sauze@montagnedoc.it
www.montagnedoc.it

CESANA TORINESE (SANSICARIO) TOURIST OFFICE

Postcode 10054
t 0122 89202
f 0122 89202

EATING OUT

Caters for all tastes and pockets

Typical Italian banquets of five or six courses can be had in the upmarket Godfather (formerly the Don Vincenzo) and Cantun restaurants. The Falco does a particularly good three-course 'skiers' menu'. In the old town, the Borgo and the Griglia are popular pizzerias. The Lampione is the place to go for 'pub grub' – good-value Chinese, Mexican and Indian food. Sugo's spaghetteria provides delicious, filling and economic fare. The Pecore Nere also gets good reviews. Reservations are generally recommended.

APRES-SKI

Suzy does it with more dignity

Once favoured almost solely by large groups of youngsters, some of whom were very rowdy, the number and atmosphere of Sauze's bars now impress reporters young and old.

The Assietta terrace is popular for catching the last rays of the sun at the end of the day. The excellent New Scotch bar is also recommended. As is the Lampione, in the old town.

After dinner, more places warm up. One of the best is the smart, atmospheric cocktail bar Moncrons, which holds regular quiz nights. We also like the late-night Village Café, which is popular with Italians and workers; you can eat here too. The Cotton Club provides good service, directors' chairs, video screen and draught cider. The Rock Café has as many Italian clients as Brits. Miravallino is a 'very Italian' café bar. Paddy McGinty's is especially popular with resort staff and has a lively atmosphere. Gran Trün has live music and reminded us of a Majorcan barbecue venue, with bottles on the wall and white stucco decor. The 'very cosy' Derby is nice for a quiet drink in a relaxed setting. Of the discos, the Bandito is a walk away, and popular with Italians. Schuss runs theme nights and drink promotions – entrance is normally free.

Tour reps organise activities, including torchlit descents, bowling and 'broomball' on the ice rink.

OFF THE SLOPES

Go elsewhere

Sauze is not a particularly rewarding place in which to while away the days if you don't want to hit the slopes. Shopping is limited, there are no gondolas or cable-cars for pedestrians and there are few off-slope activities. Turin or Briançon are worth a visit.

STAYING UP THE MOUNTAIN

'You pays your money ... '

In most resorts, staying up the mountain is an amusing thing to do and is often economical – but usually you pay the price of accepting simple accommodation. Here, the reverse applies. The 4-star Capricorno (0122 850273), up at Clotes, is one of the most comfortable hotels in Sauze, certainly the most attractive and by a wide margin the most expensive. It's a charming little chalet beside the piste, with a smart restaurant and terrace (a very popular spot for a good lunch) and only eight bedrooms.

Not quite in the same league are the places up at Sportinia. Thomson runs a couple of them now – one as a chalet-hotel. Reporters who stayed here enjoyed the isolation and easy access to the slopes – but access to the village depends on expensive skidoo taxis.

Sansicario 1700m/5,580ft

If any resort is ideally placed for exploration of the whole Milky Way, it is Sansicario. It is a modern, purpose-built, self-contained but rather soulless little resort, mainly consisting of apartments linked by monorail to the small shopping precinct. The 45-room Rio Envers (0122 811333) is a reasonably comfortable, expensive hotel. Visitors recommend the Chalmettes for its views and food at lunch-time, and the Enoteca in the evening for fondue and grappa. The place will doubtless get a boost from the 2006 Olympics – the downhill and super G races will be held here.

Selva/Sella Ronda

Endless intermediate slopes amid spectacular Dolomite scenery

WHAT IT COSTS

HOW IT RATES

The slopes

Snow	****
Extent	*****
Experts	***
Intermediates	*****
Beginners	****
Convenience	***
Queues	***
Restaurants	****

The rest

Scenery	*****
Resort charm	***
Off-slope	***

What's new

For 2002/03, we understand, a new gondola is planned to replace the endless series of drag-lifts from Colfosco towards Dantercëpies – the slowest part of the counterclockwise Sella Ronda circuit.

The lifts and runs on either side of Ortisei are now linked (or nearly so) by a series of moving walkways and escalators, so that skiers can move more easily between the Seceda and Alpe di Siusi areas.

➕ Vast network of connected slopes – suits intermediates particularly well

➕ Stunning, unique Dolomite scenery

➕ Superb snowmaking and grooming

➕ Jolly mountain huts with good food

➕ Many new lifts have cut out all but a few bad bottlenecks on the famous Sella Ronda circuit

➕ Good nursery slopes

➕ Excellent value

➖ Small proportion of tough runs

➖ Lifts and slopes can be crowded, especially on Sella Ronda circuit

➖ High proportion of short runs, not so many long ones

➖ Selva is not a particularly attractive village, nor especially convenient

➖ Erratic snow record; slopes vulnerable to warm weather

This is an area unlike any other. The Sella Ronda is an amazing circular network of lifts and pistes taking you around the spectacular Gruppo Sella – a mighty limestone massif with villages scattered around it, the biggest of them being Selva (or Selva Val Gardena / Wolkenstein, to give the resort its Sunday name and alternative German form). As well as this impressive main circuit, there are major lift systems leading off it at four main points. In overall scale, the network rivals the famed Trois Vallées in France. And the Superski lift pass covers dozens of other resorts reachable by road. So there's plenty to keep you busy.

The scenery is fabulous – almost a match for nearby Cortina. But the Dolomite landscape that provides the visual drama also dictates the nature of the slopes. Sheer limestone cliffs rise out of gentle pastureland; you spend your time on the latter, gazing at the former. There is scarcely a black run to be seen, and runs of more than 500m/1,600ft vertical are rare – whereas runs of under 300m/1,000ft vertical are not.

Although we hinge this chapter on Selva, you certainly shouldn't overlook the several alternative bases around the circuit. For experts, in particular, Arabba has clear attractions. It's here that the classic Dolomite landscape gives way to a more familiar kind of terrain, with longer, steeper slopes. For nervous intermediates, on the other hand, the obvious alternative to Selva is Corvara.

397

When other resorts ask why they don't get ***** for scenery, we send them this picture; Sasso Lungo (or Langkofel) towers above the slopes around Selva →

The resort

MOUNTAIN FACTS

Figures are for the
linked lift network of
Val Gardena, Alta
Badia and Arabba

Altitude 1235m-2520m	
	4,050ft-8,270ft
Lifts	163
Pistes	355km
	220 miles
Blue	40%
Red	50%
Black	10%
Snowmaking	240km
	150 miles
Recco detectors used	

LIFT PASSES

2002/03 prices in
euros

Dolomiti Superski
Covers 460 lifts and
1200km/745 miles of
piste in the
Dolomites, including
all Sella Ronda
resorts.
Main pass
1-day pass 35
6-day pass 175
(low season 154)
Senior citizens
Over 60: 6-day pass
149 (low season 131)
Children
Under 16: 6-day pass
123 (low season 105)

Alternative pass
Val Gardena pass
covers all lifts in
Selva Gardena,
S Cristina, Ortisei and
Alpe di Siusi.

Selva is a long roadside village, almost merged with the next village of Santa Cristina. It suffers from traffic but has traditional-style architecture and an attractive church. The area is famed for wood carvings – you'll see them all over.

The village enjoys a lovely setting under the impressive pink-tinged walls of Sassolungo and the Gruppo Sella – a fortress-like massif about 6km/ 4 miles across that lies at the hub of the Sella Ronda circuit (see the feature box later in the chapter). Despite its World Cup fame (as Val Gardena, the name of the valley) and animated atmosphere, Selva is neither upmarket nor brash. It's a good-value, civilised family resort – and is undoubtedly the biggest and liveliest of the places to stay right on the Sella Ronda circuit.

For many years the area was under Austrian rule, and reporters admire the Tirolean charm of the resort. German is the main language, not Italian, and most visitors are German, too. Selva is also known as Wolkenstein and the Gardena valley as Gröden. The local dialect is Ladino, which has resisted being absorbed into German or Italian.

Ortisei is the administrative centre of Val Gardena – pretty, and more of a complete community – but it is not so convenient for the Sella Ronda slopes. For a brief description of the other villages on or near the circuit, see the end of this chapter.

From Selva, gondolas rise in two directions. One goes east from the top of the nursery slopes towards Colfosco and Corvara and the clockwise Sella Ronda route. The other takes you south from the village to Ciampinoi and the anti-clockwise route. The most convenient position is near one of these gondolas. There is a regular bus service throughout the valley until early evening – free to ski pass holders, almost free for others – but reporters say this can get very oversubscribed and one complains about the lack of buses to Corvara and Plan de Gralba. Some prefer to share cheap taxis. Others suggest a beer or two before heading for home, to avoid the rush.

The Dolomiti Superski pass covers not only the Sella Ronda resorts but dozens of others. It's an easy road trip to Cortina – worth it for the fabulous scenery alone. But many other drives in this area are very tortuous and slow – it's often quicker on skis.

The mountain

The slopes cover a vast area, all amid stunning scenery and practically all ideally suited to intermediates who don't mind shortish runs. There are different piste maps for different areas, and a common complaint is that they are inadequate. In addition to special maps for the Sella Ronda circuit, there is now one setting out a circuit of the slopes around Selva, S Cristina and Ortisei. Piste marking and signing also come in for criticism.

THE SLOPES
High mileage piste excursions
A gondola and parallel-running chair go up from Selva to **Ciampinoi**, from where several pistes, including the famous World Cup Downhill run, spread out across the mountain and lead back down to Selva, **Santa Cristina** and **Plan de Gralba**. From Plan de Gralba, you can head off towards **Passo Sella**, **Canazei** and the rest of the Sella Ronda.

Across the valley from the Ciampinoi gondola is a chair that links with the Dantercëpies gondola. This accesses the Sella Ronda in the opposite direction or you can return to Selva on the Ladies Downhill course. From the top you head down to **Colfosco**, then

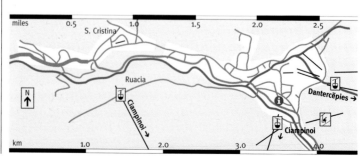

lifts link with **Corvara**, and you go on to **Arabba** and the rest of the Sella Ronda circuit.

At Passo Pordoi between Canazei and Arabba is the one breach in the defences of the Gruppo Sella: a cable-car goes up to Sass Pordoi at 2950m/9,680ft, giving access to off-piste routes – and spectacular views.

There are several linked areas that are not directly on the Sella Ronda circuit that are worth exploring. The biggest is the **Alta Badia** area to the west of Corvara, from which you can get down to **San Cassiano** and **La Villa**.

Local to Selva is the **Seceda** area, accessed by a gondola, a bus-ride from town and on the outskirts of Santa Cristina. You can head back down to the bottom or go on to **Ortisei**. And from Ortisei a cable-car goes up the other side of the valley to **Alpe di Siusi** – a gentle elevated area of quiet, easy runs, cross-country tracks and walks.

The Marmolada glacier near Arabba is open most of the winter and is now included on the main lift pass. One

reader recommends it 'for the spectacular views rather than for the typically boring glacier slopes'.

SNOW RELIABILITY
Excellent when it's cold

The slopes are not high – there are few above 2200m/7,220ft and most are between 1500m and 2000m (5,000ft and 6,500ft). And natural snowfalls are erratic. But we have experienced excellent pistes here in times of severe natural snow shortage – the area has invested heavily in snowmaking and now has one of the largest capacities in Europe. Most areas have snow-guns on the main runs to the resorts, and almost all Selva's local pistes are well endowed. World-class piste grooming adds to the effect. Last season a December visitor described the snowmaking as 'a revelation – quite superb', and later visitors called it 'wonderful' and 'stunning'.

Problems arise only in poor snow years when temperatures are too high to make snow.

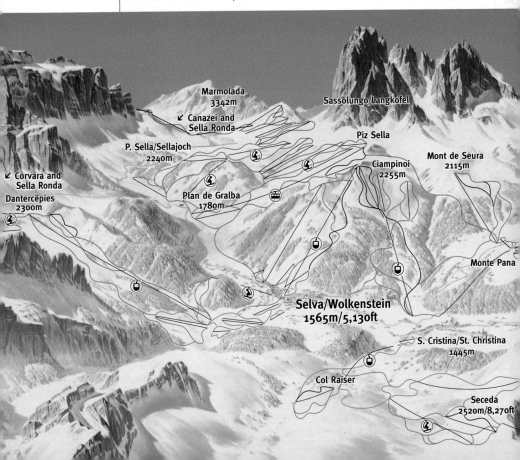

FOR EXPERTS
A few good runs
In general, experts may find the region too tame, especially if they're looking for lots of steep challenges or moguls.

Arabba has the best steep slopes (and snow). North-facing blacks and reds from Porta Vescovo back to Arabba are served by an efficient high-capacity gondola and are great fun. The black run down to La Villa is worth a visit, too. The Val Gardena World Cup piste, the 'Saslonch', is one of several steepish runs between Ciampinoi and both Selva and Santa Cristina. Unlike many World Cup pistes it is kept in racing condition for Italian team practices, but it is open to the public much of the time. It's especially good in January, when it's not too crowded. The unpisted trail down to Santa Cristina, accessed from the Florian chair on Alpe di Siusi, is not difficult, but pleasantly lonely.

Off-piste is limited because of the sheer-drop nature of the mountain tops in the Dolomites, but for the daring – and with a guide – there is excitement to be found. The itinerary from Sass Pordoi back to the cable-car station is not too difficult; the much longer route to Colfosco ends in a spectacular narrow descent through the Val de Mesdi.

FOR INTERMEDIATES
A huge network of ideal runs
The Sella Ronda region is famed for easy slopes. For early or timid intermediates, the runs from Dantercëpies to Colfosco and Corvara, and over the valley from there in the Alta Badia, are superb for cruising and confidence-boosting. They're easy to reach from Selva, but returning from Dantercëpies may be a little daunting. Riding the gondola down is an option.

Nearer to Selva, the runs in the Plan de Gralba area are gentle. The Alpe di Siusi runs above Ortisei are ideal for confidence-building – very gentle, quiet, amid superb scenery. On the rather neglected Seceda sector there is a splendid easy blue back to S Cristina.

Average intermediates have a very large network of suitable pistes, though there are few long runs. One notable one is the beautiful red swoop down the far side of the Seceda massif from Cucasattel to Ortisei. The Plan de Gralba area, the runs on either side of the Florian chair on Alpe di Siusi, and the main pistes to San Cassiano and La Villa in the Alta Badia area are other recommended cruises. Don't neglect the Edelweiss valley, off the Sella Ronda circuit at Colfosco – 'a little gem'.

Several reporters also enjoyed the area above Canazei, below the Belvedere: 'Well served with efficient lifts, and good snow. The red to Lupo Bianco is an especially beautiful run through the trees.'

The runs back down to the valley direct from Ciampinoi are a bit more challenging, as are the descents from Dantercëpies to Selva. And, of course, most intermediates will want to do the Sella Ronda circuit at least once during a week – see feature panel. The spectacular Hidden Valley is also worth a visit. It's reached via a cable-car at Lagazuoi, which you get to via a bus or shared taxi from Armentarola. See the Cortina chapter for details.

FOR BEGINNERS
Great slopes, but ...
Near-beginners have numerous runs, and the village nursery slopes are excellent – spacious, convenient, and kept in good condition. There are splendid gentle runs to progress to. Visiting beginners have thoroughly recommended the area in the past. However, we have varying reports about the school – see Schools and guides section.

FOR CROSS-COUNTRY
Beautiful trails
There are over 90km/56 miles of trails, all enjoying wonderful scenery. The 12km/7 mile trail up the Vallunga-Langental valley is particularly attractive, with neck-craning views all around. The largest section of trails (40km/25 miles) has the advantage of being at altitude, running between Monte Pana and Seiseralm, and across Alpe di Siusi.

boarding *Snowboarding is not particularly big in the area. The main lifts out of Selva are all gondolas or chairs and you can do the Sella Ronda clockwise using only one drag – the anti-clockwise route has more. Either way, there are some frustratingly flat sections where you have to scoot or walk. There are enough lively bars to have a good time in the evenings.*

QUEUES
Still a few problems

New lifts have vastly improved the area, and bottlenecks are no longer as common. But we still get complaints about parts of the Sella Ronda circuit. One bottleneck going clockwise is the Corvara gondola. The chair-lifts from Arabba in both directions have been a problem, as have the long, cold drag-lifts from Colfosco to Selva. For some visitors the character of the queues is an extra problem – 'Lots of pushing and shoving at Selva, and the scrum at Corvara was awful,' says one.

You may find the crowds on the Sella Ronda pistes worse than the queues for lifts. In peak periods Arabba has some of the worst crowds, on the red run from Porta Vescovo.

MOUNTAIN RESTAURANTS
One of the area's highlights

There are lots of huts all over the area, and virtually all of them are lively, with helpful staff, good food, plenty of character and modest prices.

In Val Gardena the Panorama is a small, cosy, rustic suntrap at the foot of the Dantercëpies drag. On the way down to Plan de Gralba from Ciampinoi, the Vallongia Rolandhütte is tucked away on a corner of the piste. In the Plan de Gralba area the top station of the cable-car does excellent pizza; the Comici is atmospheric, with a big terrace. Piz Seteur is recommended late in the day (see Après-ski).

The trio of little huts in the Colfosco area – Forcelles, Edelweiss and Pradat – are all very pleasant.

THE SELLA RONDA

The Sella Ronda is one of the world's classic intermediate circuits. The journey around the Sella massif is easily managed in a day by even an early intermediate. The slopes you descend are almost all easy, and take you through Selva, Colfosco, Corvara, Arabba and Canazei. You can do the circuit in either direction by following very clear coloured signs. We prefer the clockwise route; it is slightly quicker, avoids a tedious series of drag-lifts above Colfosco (though these should by now have been replaced by a gondola) and offers more interesting slopes. But why not do both? There are two free maps of the circuit available; for map-literate people, the better bet is the proper topographical one with contour lines.

The runs total around 23km/14 miles and the lifts around 14km/9 miles. The lifts take a total of about two hours (plus any queuing). We've done it in just three and a half hours plus some diversions and hut stops; five or six hours is a realistic time during busy periods, when there are crowds both on the pistes and on the lifts. If possible, choose low season or a Saturday, and set out early.

Not everyone likes it. 'It's a bit of a slog,' said one reporter. Others have found the circuit 'boring', and 'a bit of a rat race' but agree that 'it is a good way to get to other areas'. If you set out early, you can make more of the day by taking some diversions from the circuit. Among the most entertaining segments are the long runs down from Ciampinoi to Santa Cristina and Selva, from Dantercëpies to Selva, from the top of the Boe gondola back down to Corvara and from the top of the Arabba gondola. Take in all those in a day doing the circuit and you'll have had a good day.

Intermediates could take time out to explore the off-the-circuit Alta Badia area from Corvara. Groups of different abilities can do the circuit and arrange to meet along the way. There are plenty of welcoming rifugios at which to take a break.

SCHOOLS/GUIDES

Selva Gardena
Classes for adults and children
6 days
14 hr in total: 116
Private lessons
Hourly
31 for 1hr for 1 person

Ortisei
Classes 6 days
28 hr: 153
Children's classes
Age: from 3
5 1½ days: 78
Age: from 8
5 whole days: 196
Private lessons
Hourly
31 for 1hr for 1 person

S Cristina
Classes 6 3½hr days: 127
Children's classes
Ages: from 3
6 days: 180
Private lessons
Hourly
31 for 1hr for 1 person

ACTIVITIES

Indoor Swimming, sauna, solarium, bowling alley, squash, artificial skating rink, ice hockey, museum, concerts, cinema, billiards, tennis, climbing wall, fitness centre
Outdoor Sleigh rides, torch-light descents, snow-shoeing, toboggan runs, paragliding, horse-riding, extensive cleared paths around Selva Gardena and above S Cristina and Ortisei

CHILDCARE

The ski schools run a kindergarten for children aged 1 to 4, with skiing available for the older children. Those attending proper ski school classes can be looked after all day.

At Alta Badia the Piz Sorega above San Cassiano gets very crowded. Pride of place must go to Trappers' Home – a Wild West cabin with totem pole, teepee, country music and a Harley Davidson in the basement. Cherz above Passo di Campolongo has great views of Marmolada.

Around Arabba, Bec de Roces and Col de Burz are both suntraps. The rifugio at the top of the Porta Vescovo lifts has been recommended as 'modern, clean, bright, efficient and with excellent food'. Capanna Bill, on the long run down to Malga Ciapela, has stunning views of Marmolada.

In the Seceda sector there are countless options. The cosy Sangon 'has bags of atmosphere', though a recent reporter pronounces Baita Gamsblut her favourite – 'super rustic hut with a good menu and a warm, friendly atmosphere'. The Seceda does 'wonderful food, served by waitresses in miniskirts or leather shorts', which brightened our reporter's day.

On Alpe di Siusi the rustic Sanon refuge gets a good review, particularly since 'the barman came out to serenade us with his accordion'. And the Williams hut at the top of the Florian chair has 'superb views'.

Above Canazei there are at least six huts scattered around the Belvedere bowl. Baita Belvedere is 'a good place for lunch, with excellent service'. Lower down, Lupo Bianco is a notable rendezvous point and suntrap. As well as restaurants, there are lots of little snow bars for a quick grappa.

SCHOOLS AND GUIDES
Mixed views
The Selva school is capable of good instruction, provided you get into a suitable group. A recent visitor found that the level of tuition was good 'but groups tended to alter on a daily basis, dependent on numbers'. The emphasis seemed to be on economic grouping rather than learners' needs. Another visitor calls the ski school at Pecol, above Canazei, 'excellent'.

FACILITIES FOR CHILDREN
Good by Italian standards
There are comprehensive childcare arrangements, but German and Italian are the main languages here and English is not routinely spoken. That said, in the past we have had reports of very enjoyable lessons and of children longing to return.

Staying there

HOW TO GO
A reasonable choice
Selva and its neighbours now feature in quite a few tour operator brochures.
Chalets There is a fair choice of catered chalets, and some of the properties are good quality, with en suite bathrooms.
Hotels There are a dozen 4-stars, over 30 3-stars and numerous lesser hotels. Few of the best are well positioned.
(((3 **Gran Baita** (0471 795210) Large, luxurious sporthotel, with lots of mod cons including indoor pool. A few minutes' walk from centre and lifts.
(((3 **Aaritz** (0471 795011) Best-placed 4-star, opposite the Ciampinoi gondola, and with an open fire.
((2 **Astor** (0471 795207) Family-run chalet in centre, below nursery slopes. Good value.
((2 **Continental** (0471 795411) 3-star situated right on the nursery slopes.
((2 **Linder** (0471 795242) 'Friendly, family-run with good food' but no credit cards taken.
((2 **Olympia** (0471 795145) Well positioned 3-star.
((2 **Pralong** (0471 795370) An uphill walk from the centre, but 'one of the best hotels we've visited', says a recent reporter.
((2 **Solaia** (0471 795104) 3-star chalet, superbly positioned for lifts and slopes.
Self-catering There are plenty of apartments to choose from. We have had excellent reports of the Villa Gardena (0471 794602) and Isabell (0471 794562) apartments over the years.

EATING OUT
Plenty of good-value choices
Selva offers the best of both Austrian and Italian food at prices to suit all pockets. The higher-quality restaurants are mainly hotel-based. The Antares and Laurin have especially good menus. The Bellavista is recommended for good pasta and Doug and Dagi's Costabella for Tirolean specialities and 'large measures of spirits'. Rino's has 'excellent pizza'.

APRES-SKI
Above average for a family resort
Nightlife is lively and informal, though the village is so scattered there is little on-street atmosphere. La Stua is an

GETTING THERE

Air Verona, transfer 3hr; Bolzano, transfer 45min; Innsbruck, transfer 3hr.

Rail Chiusa (27km/17 miles), Bressanone (35km/22 miles), Bolzano (40km/25 miles); frequent buses from station.

Phone numbers
From abroad use the prefix +39 (and do **not** omit the initial '0' of the phone number).

SELVA TOURIST OFFICE

Postcode 39048
t 0471 795122
f 0471 794245
selva@valgardena.it
www.valgardena.it

ORTISEI TOURIST OFFICE

Postcode 39046
t 0471 796328
f 0471 796749
ortisei@valgardena.it
www.valgardena.it

CORVARA TOURIST OFFICE

Postcode 39033
t 0471 836176
f 0471 836540
altabadia@dolomiti superski.com
www.dolomitisuperski .com/altabadia

COLFOSCO TOURIST OFFICE

Postcode 39030
t 0471 836145
f 0471 836744
altabadia@DolomitiSu perski.com
www.dolomitisuperski .com/altabadia

SAN CASSIANO TOURIST OFFICE

Postcode 39030
t 0471 849422
f 0471 849249
altabadia@DolomitiSu perski.com
www.dolomitisuperski .com/altabadia

après-ski bar on the Sella Ronda route, with live music on some nights. For an early drink we are told that the Piz Seteur bar, above Plan de Gralba, is worth a little detour from the route – 'fun, loud and a bit raunchy' (pick the right day and you'll find scantily clad girls dancing on the bar). For a civilised early drink try the good value ski-school bar at the base of the Dantercëpies piste. Or the Costabella – cosy, serving good gluhwein. Café Mozart on the main street is 'a great place for coffee and cakes' as well as a good selection of lunch-time snacks.

Ardent après-skiers should visit the Posta Zirm in Corvara. 'The ski-boot tea dance was excellent,' recommends one reporter. Tour operators often organise transport back to other resorts.

For thigh-slapping in Selva later on, the Laurinkeller has good atmosphere though it's 'quite expensive', while the popular Luislkeller is described by a recent visitor as 'a very weird place' with loud music and barmaids in Tirolean garb.

The Bula has 'a DJ and great music, as well as the bar and restaurant' and could do with a dance floor, too. The disco of the hotel Stella next door has a 'good crowd and is well used by Brits'.

OFF THE SLOPES
Good variety
There's a sports centre, lovely walks and sleigh rides on Alpe di Siusi; and snow-shoeing around Chertz is reputed to be good. There is a bus to the charming town of Ortisei. It is well worth a visit for its large hot-spring swimming pool, shops, restaurants and lovely old buildings.

Pedestrians can reach numerous good restaurants, nicely scattered around the mountains, by gondola or cable-car. Car drivers have Bolzano and Innsbruck within reach and tour operators do trips to Cortina.

Ortisei 1235m/4,050ft

Ortisei is a market town with a life of its own, and its local slopes aren't on the main Sella Ronda circuit. It's full of lovely buildings, pretty churches and pleasant shops. The lift to the south-facing slopes is very central, and the north-facing Alpe di Siusi lifts are only slightly further out. The nursery area, school and kindergarten are at the foot of these slopes, but there's a fair range of family accommodation on the piste side of the road. The fine public indoor pool and ice rink are also here.

There are hotels and self-catering to suit all tastes and pockets and many good restaurants, mainly specialising in local dishes. Après-ski is quite jolly, and many bars keep going till late.

Corvara 1570m/5,150ft

Corvara is the most animated Sella Ronda village east of Selva, with plenty of hotels, restaurants, bars and sports facilities.

It's well positioned, with village lifts heading off to reasonably equidistant Selva, Arabba and San Cassiano. The main shops and some hotels cluster around a small piazza, but the rest of the place sprawls along the valley floor.

Colfosco 1645m/5,400ft

Colfosco is a smaller, quieter version of Corvara, 2km/1 mile away. It has a fairly compact centre with a sprawl of large hotels along the road towards Selva. It's connected to Corvara by a horizontal-running chair-lift. In the opposite direction, a series of drag-lifts head off to the Passo Gardena and on to Selva.

Several large hotels between them provide plenty of services.

San Cassiano 1530m/5,020ft

San Cassiano is a pretty little village, set in an attractive, tree-filled valley. It's a quiet, slightly upmarket resort, full of well-heeled Italian families and comfortable hotels. The local slopes, the Alta Badia, though sizeable and fully linked, are something of a spur of the main Sella Ronda. Adventurers who want to do the circuit will find it a tiresome business.

The best hotel in town is the 4-star Rosa Alpina (0471 849500). The tea

Phone numbers
From abroad use the
prefix +39 (and do
not omit the initial 'o'
of the phone
number).

**LA VILLA
TOURIST OFFICE**

Postcode 39030
t 0471 847037
f 0471 847277
altabadia@DolomitiSu
perski.com
www.dolomitisuperski
.com/altabadia

**CANAZEI
TOURIST OFFICE**

Postcode 38032
t 0462 601113
f 0462 602502
infocanazei@fassa.
com
www.fassa.com

**CAMPITELLO
TOURIST OFFICE**

Postcode 38031
t 0462 750500
f 0462 750219
infocampitello@fassa.
com
www.fassa.com

**ARABBA
TOURIST OFFICE**

Postcode 32020
t 0436 780019
f 0436 780019
arabba@rolmail.net
www.arabba.org

dance in Corvara's Posta Zirm is a must if you want something lively. Stop there at the end of the day, taxi home afterwards. Later nightlife is very limited: the Rosa Alpina has dancing and there's a bowling alley. Walking in the pretty scenery is the main off-slope activity; swimming is the other. There is no nursery or ski kindergarten.

La Villa 1435m/4,710ft

La Villa is similar to neighbouring San Cassiano in most respects – small, quiet, pretty, unspoiled – but it is slightly closer to Corvara, making it rather better placed for the main Sella Ronda circuit. There is a home piste that features on the World Cup circuit, and village amenities include a pool, and bowling and skating on a frozen lake.

Canazei 1440m/4,720ft

Canazei is a sizeable, bustling, pretty, roadside village of narrow streets, rustic old buildings, traditional style hotels and nice little shops, set in the Sella Ronda's most heavily wooded section of mountains. There's plenty going on generally – and it has been recommended by many reporters.

A 12-person gondola is the only mountain access point, but it shifts the queues (which can be long) quickly.

A single piste back to the village is linked to runs returning from both Selva and Arabba, but it is often closed. The local Belvedere slopes are uniformly easy with mountain restaurants scattered here and there. The village nursery slope is good but inconveniently located and is unlikely to be used after day one. The Bellavista at the top of the gondola has a lovely sun terrace and is recommended for 'excellent food and wine'.

Lack of spoken English in the school can be a problem. Children have an all-day nursery and ski kindergarten. But again the lack of spoken English could pose problems.

There are no really luxurious hotels, but the grand 3-star Dolomiti (0462 601106) in the middle of town is one of the original resort hotels. The chalet-style Diana (0462 601477) is charming and five minutes from the village centre. The 4-star Astoria (0462 601302) has a pool and minibus transfers to and from the gondola.

There are numerous restaurants. The Stala, Melester and Te Cevana are all worth a try. And après-ski is really animated. La Stua dei Ladins serves good local wines. The Husky and Roxy bars are worth a visit.

Off-slope entertainment consists of beautiful walks and shopping. There's also a pool, sauna, Turkish baths and skating in neighbouring Alba.

Campitello 1445m/4,740ft

Campitello is a pleasant, unremarkable village, smaller and quieter than next-door Canazei and still unspoiled.

It's remarkably quiet during the day, having no slopes to the village. A cable-car takes you up into the Sella Ronda circuit. If you don't wish to return by lift, take the piste to Canazei and catch a bus.

A reader this year recommends the 4-star hotel Sorognes: 'Superb food and accommodation, helpful staff, excellent facilities.' Campitello is quite lively – we've had trouble getting near the bar of the throbbing Da Giulio in the early evening, and a recent reporter suggests that it's even busier later on. There's an ice rink, with weekly hockey matches. There are no children's facilities.

Arabba 1600m/5,250ft

Arabba is a small, traditional, still uncommercialised village. But the lifts into the Sella Ronda in both directions make it very convenient. The high, north-facing slopes have the best natural snow and steepest pistes in the Dolomites. For accommodation reporters recommend the large, 3-star Portavescovo (0436 79139): 'An excellent hotel, wonderful food, nicely furnished rooms and a well-equipped fitness centre.' It has the only pool in town. Apartment-conversion chalets and self-catering accommodation are available.

Venues for eating out are limited. 7 Sass and Ru De Mont are cheap and cheerful pizzerias. The après-ski is also limited – but it is cheap. The atmospheric Rifugio Plan Boe is good for a last drink on the pistes before heading back to the village. Bar Peter and hotel bars are the focal points. The Delmonego family's bar-caravan, at the bottom of the piste, is the tea-time rendezvous.

Sestriere 2000m/6,560ft

Modern resort with access to the Milky Way

What's new

Turin has been chosen to host the 2006 Olympic Winter Games; Sestriere will host many of the Alpine events.

Baby 1, 2 and Jolly chairs, from the village, have been renewed.

MOUNTAIN FACTS

Figures relate to the whole Milky Way area

Altitude	1390m-2825m
	4,560ft-9,270ft
Lifts	92
Pistes	400km
	250 miles
Blue	12%
Red	67%
Black	21%
Snowmaking	80km
	47 miles
Recco detectors used	

PISTE MAP

Sestriere is covered on the Sauze d'Oulx map a few pages back.

➕ Part of the extensive Franco-Italian Milky Way area

➕ Snow reliability is usually good, with extensive snowmaking back-up

➕ Local slopes suitable for most levels, with some tougher runs than most neighbouring resorts

➖ Much of the purpose-built village is scruffy, though likely to improve for the 2006 Winter Olympics

➖ Situated at one extreme of the Milky Way area – so inconvenient for exploration of the whole network

➖ Weekend and peak-period queues

➖ Little après-ski during the week

Sestriere was built for snow – high, with north-west-facing slopes – and it has very extensive snowmaking, too. So even if you are let down by the notoriously erratic snowfalls in this corner of Italy, you should be fairly safe here – certainly safer than in Sauze d'Oulx, over the hill.

THE RESORT
Sestriere was the Alps' first purpose-built resort. It sits on a broad, sunny and windy col at 2000m/6,560ft. Neither the site nor the village, with its large apartment blocks, looks very hospitable, though the buildings have benefited from recent investment, and they'll doubtless get more in the run-up to the Olympics. There are some interesting buildings, but much of the village still seems rather scruffy.

This is not the most convenient of purpose-built resorts, but location is not crucial. Borgata is less convenient for nightlife and the shops and a recent report suggests that buses to and from Sestriere are infrequent.

THE MOUNTAINS
Sestriere is at one extreme of the big Franco-Italian Milky Way area. The local

slopes have two main sectors: Sises, directly in front of the village, and more varied Motta, above Borgata – to the north-east and 225m/740ft higher.
Slopes There are mainly drag- and chair-lifts on the local north-west-facing slopes. Access to Sansicario and the rest of the Milky Way is via gondola from Borgata to Col Basset, at the top of the Sauze d'Oulx area, and a drag-lift back up to Monte Fraiteve. Snow permitting, the return to Sestriere is via a long red from the top of the gondola at Col Basset – or the recently restored red run down from Monte Fraiteve. But it more often depends on riding the gondola down. Signposting and the piste map are poor.
Snow reliability With most of the local slopes facing north-west and ranging from 1840m to 2820m (6,040ft to 9,250ft), and an extensive snowmaking

Phone numbers
From abroad use the prefix +39 (and do **not** omit the initial 'o' of the phone number).

TOURIST OFFICE

Postcode 10058
t 0122 755444
f 0122 755171
sestriere@montagne doc.it
www.sestriere.it
www.vialattea.it

SESTRIERE TOURIST OFFICE

Sestriere has good snowmaking – but in this part of the world you need it ↓

network covering most of the Sises sector and half of Motta, snow-cover is usually reliable for most of the season. The notoriously erratic snowfalls in the Milky Way often leave the rest of the area seriously short of snow while the extensive snowmaking in Sestriere provides fairly reliable cover. The sunny runs down from Sauze suffer from poor snow and do not benefit from any artificial back-up.

Experts There is a fair amount to amuse experts – steep pistes served by the drags at the top of both sectors, and off-piste slopes in several directions from here and Monte Fraiteve.

Intermediates Both sectors also offer plenty for confident intermediates, who can explore practically all of the Milky Way areas, conditions permitting.

Beginners The terrain is good for beginners, with several nursery areas and the gentlest of easy runs down to Borgata. However, one reporter points out that there is a lack of easy intermediate runs to progress to.

Snowboarding There is a terrain-park next to the Cit Roc chair on Sises.

Cross-country There are two loops covering a total of 10km/6 miles.

Queues The lifts are mainly modern though there are still some inadequate old ones. But queues for the main lifts occur at the weekends and holidays. The lifts from Borgata to Sestriere can be a bottleneck at the end of the day.

Queues occur when poor weather closes the gondola link to Sauze. Reporters here, as in Sauze, complain that some lifts may be kept closed during the week, either to save money or conserve snow for the weekends.

Mountain restaurants The local ones could only be described as 'fair' – the one at Sises is best – but there are better ones further afield.

Schools and guides Lack of spoken English can be a problem.

Facilities for children There are no special facilities for children.

STAYING THERE

How to go Most accommodation is in apartments.

Hotels There are a dozen hotels, mostly of 3-star or 4-star status. Just out of the village (but not far from a lift) is the luxurious Principi di Piemonte (0122 7941). The Savoy Edelweiss (0122 77040) is a central, attractive 3-star. The distinctive round towers in the centre are the Club Med quarters.

Eating out There are plenty of options. Try Lu Peirol for home-made ravioli and atmosphere. Tre Rubineti has been highly recommended for 'outstanding Italian cooking' and an enormous wine list. Last Tango and the Baita are also well regarded.

Après-ski Après-ski is quiet during the week but becomes lively at weekends: the Black Sun pub-cum-disco and the Tabatà club are great fun, and the Prestige and Palace are two of the many little bars that liven up. The Pinky is one of the best of the bars that double as eateries, with lots of low sofas in the classic Italian casual-chic style.

Off the slopes There's quite a bit to do, but it isn't a very attractive place, despite some smart shops.

La Thuile
1450m/4,760ft

Little-known resort with extensive, easy slopes and link with France

What's new

For 2002/03 the old triple chair from the Petit St Bernard Pass to Belvedere will be replaced by a new high-speed quad, speeding up the link to France.

MOUNTAIN FACTS

Covers combined La Rosière and La Thuile area
Altitude	1175m-2640m
	3,855ft-8,660ft
Lifts	36
Pistes	140km
	87 miles
Green	12%
Blue	36%
Red	35%
Black	17%
Snowmaking	22km
	14 miles
Recco detectors used	

GETTING THERE

Air Geneva, transfer 2½hr; Turin, transfer 2½hr; Milan, transfer 3½ hr.

Rail Pré-St-Didier (10km/6 miles); regular buses to resort.

- ⊕ Fair-sized area with good lift system linked to La Rosière in France
- ⊕ Free of crowds and queues
- ⊕ Excellent beginner and easy intermediate slopes
- ⊕ Some very handy accommodation

- ⊖ Most of the seriously tough pistes are low down, and most of the low, woodland runs are tough
- ⊖ Mountain restaurants are generally disappointing
- ⊖ Not the place for lively après-ski

La Thuile deserves to be better known internationally. The slopes best suit beginners and intermediates not seeking challenges, but are not devoid of interest for experts, particularly if the snow conditions are good.

When you venture over the border to La Rosière, you'll notice that Italian grooming is better than French, and Italian piste classification often overstates difficulty. Moving from gentle red runs to bumpy blues may be a shock.

The resort

La Thuile is a resort of parts. At the foot of the lifts is the modern Planibel complex, with places to stay, a leisure centre, bars, shops and restaurants – like a typical French purpose-built resort, but with a distinctly Italian atmosphere (and on a much smaller scale). But many people find this rather soulless and prefer to stay in the old town across the river (served by a regular free bus service). La Thuile was a mining town that largely fell into disrepair until the slopes were developed. Much of the old town has been restored and new buildings (and a huge underground car park) tastefully added. There are reasonable restaurants and bars but not many entertaining shops.

The slopes link with La Rosière, over the border in France. Courmayeur is easily reached by car, and Cervinia is about an hour away. A car isn't a great help around the resort, especially if staying in the Planibel complex.

The mountains

La Thuile has quite extensive slopes, with the great attraction that they are normally very uncrowded. Many runs are marked red, but deserve no more than a blue rating. The lift system is excellent in general: a fast chair or gondola takes you up the mountain, and there are high-speed chairs to the top. The new Petit St Bernard quad will speed up getting to the Belvedere area and over into France.

THE SLOPES
Big and gentle

The lifts out of the village take you to **Les Suches**, with shady black runs going back down directly to the village through the trees, and reds taking a more roundabout route. From here chairs and drags take you to **Chaz Dura** for access to a variety of gentle bowls facing east. You can go off westwards from here to the Petit St Bernard road. From both sides there are lifts back to the ridge, the high-point of Belvedere being the launch pad for excursions via the Col de la Traversette to La Rosière in France. What is not clear from the map is that the French slopes are largely south-facing. They also tend to be steeper than those in La Thuile.

SNOW RELIABILITY
Good

Most of La Thuile's slopes are north- or east-facing and above 2000m/6,560ft, so the snow generally keeps well. There's also a decent amount of snowmaking. You can check the conditions at Les Suches via a camera and screens in the resort.

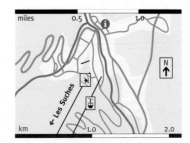

407

LIFT PASSES

2001/02 prices in euros

Dominio Internazionale
Covers all lifts in La Rosière and La Thuile.
Beginners One baby-lift in village. Points tickets (50 points 40).
Main pass
1-day pass 29
6-day pass 147 (low season 132)
Senior citizens
Over 65: 6-day pass 114 (low season 102)
Children
Under 12: 6-day pass 114 (low season 102)
Under 6: free pass with every purchase of an adult pass of the same length
Short-term passes
Half-day pass (adult 20).
Alternative passes
Valle d'Aosta pass covers La Thuile, Courmayeur, Gressoney, Champoluc, Alagna, Cervinia, Valtournenche and Pila (adult 6-day 161).

boarding *These are great slopes for learning to board. You can confine yourself to riding chair-lifts and the gondola, and most of the slopes are very easy with good snow. For more experienced boarders there are some great tree runs, and the link with France offers some good off-piste possibilities. Though there are no specific facilities for boarders, there is a lot of good free-riding to be had, as well as some good long carving runs. The nightlife is pretty quiet during the week.*

FOR EXPERTS
Rather limited

The only steep pistes are those down through the trees from Les Suches back to the resort. The steepest of these, the Diretta and Tre, are serious stuff. The best of the rest is the area above the Petit St Bernard road, where there is some genuinely black terrain and plenty of off-piste – the new high-speed quad will mean you can do quick circuits in this area. You'll find many red runs overclassified.

Heli-lifts are available. One of the best, to the Ruitor glacier, has a 20km/12 mile run into France ending near Ste-Foy, a short taxi ride from La Rosière and the lifts back to La Thuile.

FOR INTERMEDIATES
Something different

La Thuile has some good intermediate runs, and its link with La Rosière adds adventure. But timid intermediates may

be best off staying on home ground: the start of the route back from La Rosière is a short but fairly tricky red, and most of La Rosière – particularly the top half of the mountain – is quite challenging. The blue Choucas run is the easiest route down to La Rosière.

The bowls above Les Suches have many gentle blue and red runs, ideal for cruising and practising. There are also long reds through the trees back to the resort. The red runs on the other side of the top ridge, down towards the Petit St Bernard road, offer a greater challenge.

FOR BEGINNERS
Good, but take the gondola down

There are nursery slopes at village level and up at Les Suches. There's a good gentle green run above Les Suches, and some shallow blues, but nothing is segregated from the main

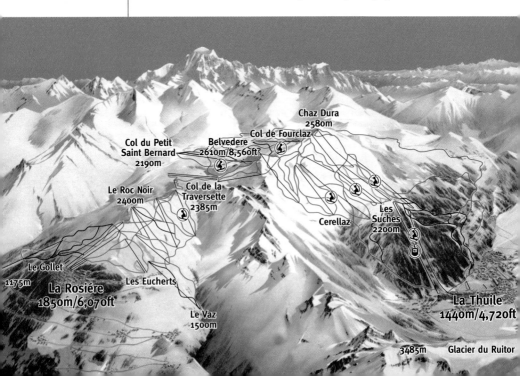

Chaz Dura 258om
Col de Fourclaz
Col du Petit Saint Bernard 2190m
Belvedere 2610m/8,560ft
Le Roc Noir 2400m
Col de la Traversette 2385m
Cerellaz
Les Suches 2200m
Le Gollet
Les Eucherts
1175m
La Rosiére 1850m/6,070ft
Le Vaz 1500m
La Thuile 1440m/4,720ft
3485m Glacier du Ruitor

↑ The old village is across a river from the slopes

LA THUILE TOURIST OFFICE

SCHOOLS/GUIDES

2001/02 prices in euros

La Thuile
Classes
6 2hr days: 105
Private lessons
1hr: 30 for 1 person

CHILDCARE

There is a free non-skiing kindergarten for children from 4 to 12 years and a reporter tells of an 'excellent' nursery near the edge of town run by the Commune which takes babies of 3 months to 3 years – 'the best nursery we have used in Europe'.

The tourist office has a list of childminders.

ACTIVITIES

Indoor Two swimming pools, amusement arcade, gymnasium, solarium, sauna, squash, library
Outdoor heli-skiing, children's snowpark, winter walks.

Phone numbers
From abroad use the prefix +39 (and do **not** omit the initial 'o' of the phone number).

TOURIST OFFICE

Postcode 11016
t 0165 884179
f 0165 885196
lathuile@lathuile.net
www.lathuile.net

slopes. Promenade is 'a very easy blue and good for beginners', but is served by drag-lifts. But the runs down to the resort are red and black – so taking the gondola back down is the only sensible option.

FOR CROSS-COUNTRY
Varied choice
La Thuile has four loops of varying difficulty on the valley floor, adding up to 20km/12 miles of track.

QUEUES
Very rare
The resort has a very effective lift system for the number of visitors, and all our reporters comment that they never had to queue. A recent reporter says: 'We didn't queue once all week, and were often the only people on the lift.'

MOUNTAIN RESTAURANTS
Disappointing
There are still no signs of improvement in the mountain restaurants. Only in the Riondet (on Chaz Dura) has a reporter found 'genuinely good food and hospitality'.

SCHOOLS AND GUIDES
Good instruction
Reporters say the ski school normally has reasonably sized classes and fair instruction, though a group was spotted being walked down the side of a blue run. Interski clients were overheard as 'happy'.

FACILITIES FOR CHILDREN
OK when they're older
There's an 'excellent' nursery (see left), a Miniclub, and children over the age of five can join adult ski classes. One reporter used a registered childminder to look after his daughter.

Staying there

HOW TO GO
Some choice of packages
The number of tour operators going to La Thuile is increasing.
Hotels The choice is between the swanky, characterless 4-star Planibel, a few 3-stars and some simpler places.
⦅⦅⦅4 Planibel (0165 884541) All mod cons, including a pool and underground parking. Right at the base of the lifts.
⦅⦅⦅3 Eden (0165 885050) Comfortable modern hotel in traditional wood and stone style. Very close to lifts.
⦅⦅2 Chalet Alpina (0165 884187) Simple place with the atmosphere of a catered chalet, across the river from the lifts.
Self-catering The Planibel apartments are spacious, right by the lifts and great value. Some have been refurbished recently – others are said to be 'showing signs of wear'.

EATING OUT
Limited, but consistently good
Reader recommendations include: La Fordze (French/Italian dishes), Brasserie du Bathieu ('huge portions but lots of cigarette smoke'), Lo Créton and La Grotta (pizza and pasta), and the Eden (an 'excellent' buffet table).

APRES-SKI
Early to bed
Après-ski and nightlife are limited. The Cage aux Folles is popular from 4pm till late. The Bricole is the busiest and liveliest bar. The Fantasia disco warms up well after midnight.

OFF THE SLOPES
Limited options
The Planibel complex has a good pool (bathing caps compulsory), but there are few attractive walks or shops. Excursions to Courmayeur can be organised. Pedestrians can ride up the gondola for lunch.

La Thuile

409

Switzerland is home to some of our favourite resorts. For sheer charm and spectacular scenery, the essentially traffic-free villages of Wengen, Mürren, Saas-Fee and Zermatt take some beating. Many resorts have impressive slopes too – including some of the biggest, highest and toughest runs in the Alps, as well as a lot of reassuring intermediate terrain. For fast, efficient, queue-free lift networks, Swiss resorts rarely match French standards – but the real bottlenecks are gradually disappearing. And there are compensations – the world's best mountain restaurants, for example.

People always seem to associate Switzerland with high prices. Barring some catastrophic accident to the Swiss franc, prices are never going to be low, but usually they are not greatly different from prices in major French resorts; and what you get for your money is first class.

While France is the home of the purpose-built resort, Switzerland is the home of the mountain village that has transformed itself from traditional farming community into year-round holiday resort. Many of Switzerland's most famous mountain resorts are as popular in the summer as in the winter, or more so. This creates places with a much more lived-in feel to them, and a much more stable local community. Many villages are still dominated by a handful of families who were lucky or shrewd enough to get involved in the early development of the area.

This has its downside as well as advantages. The ruling families are able to stifle competition and prevent newcomers from taking a slice of their action. Alternative ski schools, competing with the traditional school and pushing up standards, are much less common

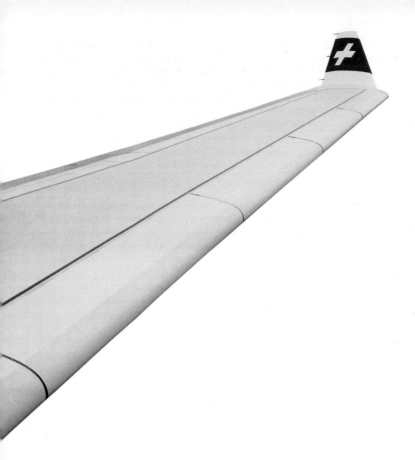

Comfort, care, dedication. We've put it all in our airline.

Special meals: 18
Qualiflyer members: 3.5 million
First Class bed: 203 cm
Maîtres de cabine: 850+
Destinations: 126
Plastic wine glasses: none

Welcome to civilised aviation.

Direct from London Heathrow, London City, Manchester, Birmingham, Guernsey, Jersey and Dublin to the slopes.

For travel information and booking call SWISS on 0845 601 0956, contact your travel agent or visit swiss.com

SWISS

Swiss
International
Air Lines

than in other Alpine countries, for example.

Switzerland means high living as well as high prices, and the swanky grand hotels of St Moritz, Gstaad, Zermatt and Davos are beyond the dreams of most ordinary holidaymakers. And even in more modest resorts, nothing is cheap. But the quality of the service you get for your money is generally high. Swiss hotels are some of the best in the world. The trains run like clockwork to the advertised

timetable (and often they run to the top of the mountain, doubling as ski-lifts). The food is almost universally of good quality and much less stodgy than in neighbouring Austria. In Switzerland you get what you pay for: even the cheapest wine, for example, is not cheap; but it is reliable – duff bottles are very rare.

Perhaps surprisingly for such a long-established, traditional, rather staid skiing country, Switzerland has gone out of its way to attract

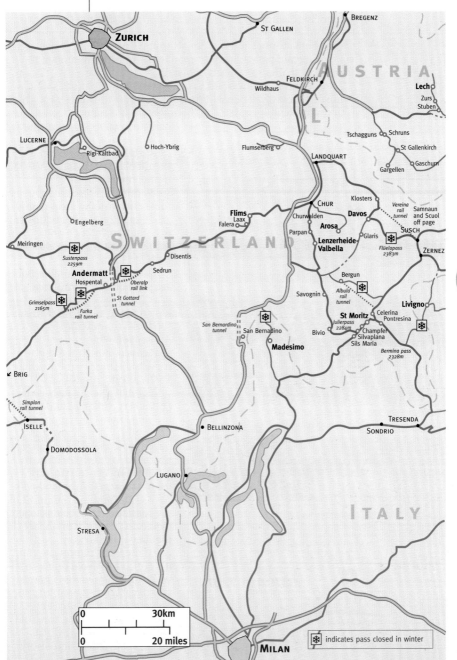

Introduction

413

snowboarders by developing the facilities they look for. Even such apparently upright resorts as Davos cater for boarders thoroughly.

GETTING AROUND THE SWISS ALPS

Access to practically all Swiss resorts is fairly straightforward when approaching from the north – just pick your motorway. Many of the high passes that are perfectly sensible ways to get around the country in summer are closed in winter, which can be inconvenient if you are moving around from one area to another. There are car-carrying trains linking the Valais (Crans-Montana, Zermatt etc) to Andermatt via the Furka tunnel and Andermatt to the Grisons (Flims, Davos etc) via the Oberalp pass – closed to road traffic in winter but open to trains except after very heavy snowfalls.

St Moritz is more awkward to get to than other resorts, as well as being further away. The main road route is over the Julier pass. This is normally kept open, but at 2285m/7,500ft it is naturally prone to heavy snowfalls that can shut it for a time. The fallback is the car-carrying rail tunnel under the Albula pass. A major new rail tunnel opened in November 1999, offering an alternative route. The Vereina tunnel runs for 19km/12 miles from Klosters to a point near Susch and Zernez, down the Inn valley from St Moritz.

These car-carrying rail services are painless unless you travel at peak times, when there may be long queues – particularly for the Furka tunnel from Andermatt, which offers residents of Zürich the shortest route to Zermatt and the other Valais resorts. Another rail tunnel that's very handy is the Lötschberg, linking Kandersteg in the Bernese Oberland with Brig in the Valais. Apart from helicopters, there's no quicker way from Wengen to Zermatt.

There is a car-carrying rail tunnel linking Switzerland with Italy – the Simplon. But most of the routes to Italy are kept open by means of road tunnels. See the Italy introduction.

To use Swiss motorways (and it's difficult to avoid doing so if you're driving serious distances) you have to buy a permit to stick on your windscreen (costing SF40 in 2001/02). They are sold at the border, and are for all practical purposes compulsory.

Adelboden
1355m/4,450ft

Chocolate-box village with fragmented but extensive slopes, linked to Lenk

WHAT IT COSTS

 (3)

HOW IT RATES

The slopes

Snow	**
Extent	***
Experts	**
Intermediates	***
Beginners	****
Convenience	***
Queues	***
Restaurants	**

The rest

Scenery	***
Resort charm	****
Off-slope	****

What's new

2001/02 saw the installation of a new fast quad on Tschenten and a 20% capacity increase on the Geils-Laveygrat three-seater chair.

Other developments include a hands-free lift pass system, a new toboggan run on Tschenten and improvements to the parking system.

ADELBODEN TOURIST OFFICE

All the buildings are small in scale, and traditional in style ↓

➕ Traditional chocolate-box-pretty mountain village

➕ Extensive slopes to suit all abilities, linked to Lenk

➕ Several other worthwhile resorts within day-trip range

➕ Good off-slope facilities

➖ Fragmented slopes – two sectors are a bus-ride away

➖ Low top heights mean unreliable snow cover

➖ Few challenges unless you look off-piste

Adelboden is unjustly neglected by the international market: for intermediates who find relaxing, pretty surroundings more important than convenience for the slopes it has a lot of appeal. The slopes are extensive, and investment in lifts over recent years has meant great improvements.

THE RESORT

Adelboden fits the traditional image of a Swiss mountain village: old chalets with overhanging roofs line the quiet main street (cars are discouraged), and 3000m/9,840ft peaks make an impressive backdrop. Adelboden is in the Bernese Oberland, to the west of the much better-known Jungfrau resorts (Wengen etc). These resorts are within day-trip range, as is Gstaad to the west.

The village is compact, and there are efficient buses to the outlying areas (covered on the lift pass); the ideal location for most people is close to the main street.

THE MOUNTAINS

Adelboden's slopes are split into five sectors (no longer six) – two of them unlinked and a bus-ride from the village. The rest of the sectors are linked, by piste if not by lift, and the ski area stretches across to the village of Lenk, with its own local slopes a bus-ride across the valley from the main body of slopes shared with Adelboden. The Swiss ski school has started running American-style free mountain tours on Sundays.

Slopes Lifts near the main street access three of the sectors. Schwandfeldspitz (aka Tschenten), just above the village, is reached by a cable-car/gondola hybrid. The main gondola to nearby Höchsthorn and then on to more remote Geils-Sillerenbühl starts down below the village at Oey (where there is a car park), but a connecting mini-gondola starts from close to the main street. This is much the biggest sector, with long, gentle runs (and some short, sharp ones) from 2200m down to 1350m (7,215ft down to 4,430ft) – back to the village and over to Lenk.

Engstligenalp, a flat-bottomed high-altitude bowl is reached by a cable-car 4km/2.5 miles south of the resort; Elsigenalp is more remote, but more extensive.

Snow reliability Most pistes are below 2000m/6,560ft and snowmaking is limited – so snow reliability is not a strong point, despite mostly north-facing slopes above 1500m/4,920ft.

Experts There are some genuine black pistes at Geils, and a less genuine one on Höchsthorn. Off-piste possibilities are good and remain untracked for much longer than in other, more macho resorts: the Laveygrat and Chummi chairs in the Geils bowl access routes down to both Adelboden and Lenk (though there are protected forest

2290m
Elsigenalp
2355m/7,730ft
Engstligenalp
Luegli 2140m
Metschstand 2105m
Leite 2000
Elsigbach 1250m
Fleckli Unter Birg
Höchsthorn 1905m
Geils 1710m
Hahnenmoos 1960m
Stoss 1645m
Adelboden 1355m/4,450ft
Oey
Boden
Sillerenbühl 1975m
Laveygrat 2200m
Stand 2020m
Lenk 1070m/3,510ft
1135m
Tschenten 1950m
1540m
1645m

SWITZERLAND

416

MOUNTAIN FACTS

Altitude 1070m-2355m
3,510ft-7,730ft
Lifts 56
Pistes 170km
106 miles
Blue 40%
Red 50%
Black 10%
Snowmaking 20km
12 miles
Recco detectors used

Phone numbers
From elsewhere in
Switzerland add the
prefix 033.
From abroad use the
prefix +41 33.

TOURIST OFFICE

Postcode CH-3715
t 673 8080
f 673 8092
info@adelboden.ch
www.adelboden.ch

areas to avoid). Engstligenalp has off-
piste potential too – and is a launching
point for tours around the Wildstrubel.
Intermediates All five areas deserve
exploration by intermediates. At Geils
there is a lot of ground to be covered
– and trips across to Lenk's gentle
Betelberg area (covered by the lift
pass) are possible.
Beginners There are good nursery
slopes in the village and at the foot of
nearby sectors. At Geils there are
glorious long, easy runs to progress to.
Snowboarding There's a good terrain-
park and a half-pipe at Hahnenmoos,
and a natural playground at
Engstligenalp. Two specialist schools
offer lessons. Beginners may find the
high proportion of drag-lifts off-putting.
Cross-country There are extensive trails
along the valley towards Engstligenalp
with its high altitude, snow-sure circuit.
There's also a short loop at Geils.
Queues The main gondola isn't entirely
free of queues. And the old
Hahnenmoos gondola is a bottleneck,
overdue for replacement. If snow low
down is poor, the Engstligenalp cable-
car becomes oversubscribed.
Mountain restaurants There are
pleasant mountain restaurants with
terraces in the Geils sector. Aebi is

particularly charming. A reporter
recommends the Metschstand: 'Sunny,
small, simple, but good.'
Schools and guides Past reports on
the Adelboden ski school have been
mixed – 'caring, good English', but 'mix
of abilities within group'.
Facilities for children The kindergarten
takes children from three to six years
and there's a playroom and child-
minding service up at Hahnenmoos.
Several hotels have childcare facilities.

STAYING THERE

How to go The choice of how to go is
wide. Several UK operators go there,
and there are locally bookable chalets
and apartments and some 30 pensions
and hotels (mainly 3- and 4-star).
Hotels The 4-star Park Hotel Bellevue
(673 8000) is expensive, but we have
received good reports of its food and
spa facilities. The central 3-star Adler
Sporthotel (673 4141) is pretty and
recommended. The little Bären (673
2151) is a simple but captivating
wooden chalet.
Eating out Possibilities are varied, and
include a couple of mountain
restaurants. Guests on a half-board
arrangement can 'dine around' at
affiliated hotels twice a week.
Après-ski The après-ski is traditional,
based on bars and tea rooms – the
Iglu and Time Out are recommended.
Off the slopes There is a fair bit to do.
There are hotel pools open to the
public, indoor and outdoor curling and
skating rinks, several toboggan runs,
and hiking paths. Some mountain
restaurants are easily reached on foot.

ADELBODEN TOURIST OFFICE

← This is one of those Swiss resorts where you
can still have a traditional winter holiday

Andermatt

An old-fashioned resort with some great off-piste and a good snow record

WHAT IT COSTS

HOW IT RATES

The slopes

Snow	****
Extent	*
Experts	****
Intermediates	**
Beginners	*
Convenience	***
Queues	**
Restaurants	*

The rest

Scenery	***
Resort charm	****
Off-slope	**

What's new

For 2002/03 new snow-guns will be installed on the lower and middle slopes of the Gemsstock, and a swimming pool and ice rink complex is planned for 2003/04.

⊕ Attractive, traditional village

⊕ Excellent snow record

⊕ Great off-piste terrain

⊖ Three separate areas of slopes are all fairly limited if you stay on-piste

⊖ Unsuitable for beginners

⊖ Limited off-slope diversions and après-ski

⊖ Cable-car queues at peak times

Little old Andermatt was rather left behind in the mega-resort boom of the 1960s and 70s. But its attractions have not faded for those who like their mountains tall, steep and covered in deep powder.

THE RESORT

Andermatt is quite busy in summer and gets weekend winter business, but at other times seems deserted apart from groups of soldiers – there are barracks here. The town is quietly attractive, with wooden houses lining the dog-leg main street that runs between railway and cable-car stations, and some imposing churches. A recent visitor described the village as 'homely ... somewhere you would go to visit an aunty rather than for a holiday'. The railway is the only link in winter with the Grisons to the east and the Valais to the west – trains carry cars. Most people arrive by train, and links are easy from Zürich. The town is fairly small and location is not much of an issue – though there are no buses.

THE MOUNTAINS

Andermatt's skiing is split over three unlinked mountains. The slopes are almost entirely above the trees, and the individual areas are all limited in extent. You buy a pass covering the three mountains and trains between them. The Gotthard-Oberalp lift pass also covers the nearby resorts of Sedrun and Disentis – reached by train over the Oberalp pass.

Slopes A two-stage cable-car from the edge of the village serves magnificent, varied slopes on the open, steep and usually empty slopes of Gemsstock. Across town is the gentler Nätschen/ Gütsch area. And a bus- or train-ride along the valley is Winterhorn (above Hospental). There is also an isolated nursery slope further along at Realp.

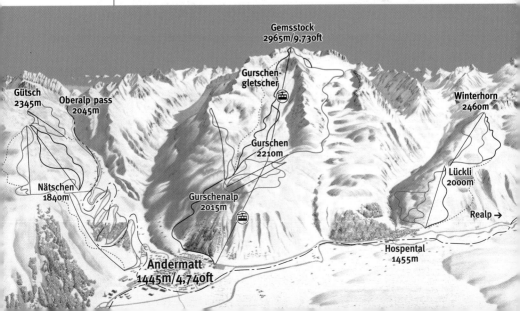

↑ Andermatt gets lots of snow and is an attractive, old village

ANDERMATT TOURIST OFFICE

MOUNTAIN FACTS

Altitude	1445m-2965m
	4,740ft-9,725ft
Lifts	13
Pistes	56km
	35miles
Blue	29%
Red	42%
Black	29%
Snowmaking	None
Recco detectors used	

Phone numbers
From elsewhere in Switzerland add the prefix 041.
From abroad use the prefix +41 41.

TOURIST OFFICE

Postcode CH-6490
t 887 1454
f 887 0185
info@andermatt.ch
www.andermatt.ch

Snow reliability The area has a justified reputation for reliable snow. Piste grooming is generally good.

Experts It is most definitely a resort for experts. The top Gemsstock cable-car serves two main slopes: the north-facing bowl beneath it is a glorious, long black slope (about 800m/2,625ft vertical), usually with excellent snow, down which there are countless off-piste routes and one marked run, which branches into two. One side is the Bernhard Russi run, named after Andermatt's Olympian, and never groomed. The Sonnenpiste is a fine open red run curling around the back of the mountain to the mid-station, also flanked by off-piste opportunities. From mid-mountain to the village there is a black run, not too steep but heavily mogulled. There are guides for off-piste adventure, and a trip off the back of Gemsstock is recommended, which can bring you out back at the village, or near the welcoming St Gotthard hotel and restaurant in Hospental. Nätschen and Winterhorn both have black pistes and off-piste.

Intermediates Intermediates needn't be put off Gemsstock: the Sonnenpiste can be tackled (especially as there are immaculately groomed sections of the piste 'created especially for carvers'), and there is a pleasant red run at mid-mountain. The latter is served by a steep T-bar, however, which one reporter found extremely daunting. Winterhorn's modest lift system offers pistes to suit all abilities down the 1000m/3,280ft vertical, while Nätschen's south and west-facing mountain is perfect for confidence-building.

Beginners The lower half of Nätschen has a good, long, easy run. But this is not a good resort for beginners.

Snowboarding There are facilities (park and pipe) on Nätschen and Gemsstock.

Cross-country There is a 20km/12 mile loop along the valley towards Realp.

Queues The Gemsstock cable-car can generate morning queues in the village and at mid-mountain when conditions are attractive. It takes a while to get going after heavy snow, and may close because of it.

Mountain restaurants The few mountain restaurants are basic and there's a friendly bar in a tent at the Gemsstock mid-station. Reporters suggest a trip down to Andermatt ('try traditional dishes at the Sternen') from Gemsstock for lunch. The St Gotthard at Hospental is also recommended for its sunny terrace and large portions.

Schools and guides The good work of the Swiss ski school is overshadowed by the excellent Alpine Adventures Mountain Reality, an off-piste guiding outfit run by Alex Clapasson.

Facilities for children There are no special facilities; but there are slopes they can handle at Nätschen and the Swiss school takes children's classes.

STAYING THERE

How to go Andermatt's accommodation is in cosy 2- and 3-star hotels.

Hotels Gasthaus Sternen (887 1130), in the centre, is an attractive old chalet with a lively restaurant and bar. The 3-star Sonne (887 1226), between the centre and the lift, is welcoming and comfortable. The neighbouring 2-star Bergidyll (887 1455) is a British favourite. Alpenhotel Schlüssel (888 7088) is newish, with spacious rooms.

Eating out Of a handful of restaurants and bars, the Kronen hotel's restaurant has been highly recommended.

Après-ski Après-ski revolves around cosy local bars. Later on, try the Piccadilly pub and the bars at the hotel Monopol ('great cocktails, stays open late') and the hotel Schweizerhof.

Off the slopes There's a toboggan run at Nätschen. The churches and the museum of local history, housed in an old wooden building, are worth a visit.

Classic all-round winter resort, where walkers are as welcome as skiers

WHAT IT COSTS

HOW IT RATES

The slopes
Snow	★★★
Extent	★★
Experts	★
Intermediates	★★★
Beginners	★★★★
Convenience	★★★
Queues	★★★★
Restaurants	★★★★

The rest
Scenery	★★★
Resort charm	★★
Off-slope	★★★★

What's new

There are plans to replace the Plattenhorn T-bar (an important link from Tschuggen to Hörnli) with a quad chair – but no firm date has been set for this yet.

MOUNTAIN FACTS

Altitude	1800m-2655m
	5,910ft-8,710ft
Lifts	14
Pistes	70km
	43 miles
Blue	38%
Red	57%
Black	5%
Snowmaking	9km
	6 miles
Recco detectors used	

➕ Classic winter sports resort ambience

➕ Some of the best cross-country loops in the Alps

➕ Few queues

➕ Relatively good snow reliability

➕ Plenty to do off the slopes

➕ Several other worthwhile resorts within day-trip range

➖ Spread-out village means some inconveniently situated accommodation

➖ Limited slopes for mileage-hungry intermediates

➖ Few challenges for experts

➖ Some very dreary buildings in main village

The classic image of a winter sports resort is perhaps an isolated, snow-covered Swiss village, surrounded by big, beautiful mountains, with skating on a frozen lake, horse-drawn sleighs jingling along snowy streets and people in fur coats strolling on mountain paths. Arosa is exactly that. It's just a pity that many of its comfortable hotels date from a time when pitched roofs were out of fashion.

THE RESORT
High and remote, Arosa is in a sheltered basin at the head of a beautiful wooded valley, in contrast to the open slopes. It's a long, winding drive or splendid rail journey from Chur (both take under an hour). Obersee, at the centre, is not a pretty sight due to its block-like buildings, though its lakeside setting adds charm. The rest of Arosa is scattered, with a hill separating Obersee from the older, prettier Inner-Arosa. Arosa is quiet; its relaxed ambience attracts an unpretentiously wealthy clientele of families and older people, with very few Brits.

The village is a spread-out place and some accommodation is a long walk from the lifts, but where you stay is not very important as there is an excellent free shuttle-bus. Inner-Arosa has the advantage of lifts into both sectors of the slopes.

You can get to Davos-Klosters, Flims and Lenzerheide by road.

THE MOUNTAINS
Arosa's slopes are situated in a wide open bowl, with all the runs returning eventually to the village at the bottom.
Slopes The area is modest and lacking in challenges, with slopes spread widely over two main sectors. The Weisshorn sector faces mainly south and south-east. Tschuggen, halfway to the Weisshorn peak, is the major lift junction, reachable from both Obersee and Inner-Arosa. An inconveniently sited gondola below Inner-Arosa is the main access to the east and north-east-facing slopes of the second

419

AROSA TOURIST OFFICE

Most of the slopes are well above the tree line ➔

Phone numbers
From elsewhere in Switzerland add the prefix 081. From abroad use the prefix +41 81.

TOURIST OFFICE
Postcode CH-7050
t 378 7020
f 378 7021
arosa@arosa.ch
www.arosa.ch

sector, Hörnli. Drags and chair-lifts allow you to travel either way between the two sectors. One reporter commented on the abundance of walking paths crossing pistes, and points out the need for caution at these intersections.

Snow reliability Arosa has relatively good snow reliability. The best south-facing pistes are above 2000m/6,560ft, and the shadier Hörnli slopes hold their snow well. Grooming is good.

Experts Arosa isn't the resort for a keen expert. The two black runs don't deserve their grading, but you can ski off-piste to and from Lenzerheide – with a guide. And there are several off-piste 'free ride' routes on the map.

Intermediates This is a good area for intermediates who want to take it easy and aren't looking for high mileage or much challenge. The home run from the Carmenna middle-station to Obersee (the last section through woodland) is 'a delight'.

Beginners The Tschuggen nursery slopes are excellent and usually have good snow, but they get a lot of through traffic. Inner-Arosa has a quieter but more limited area usually reserved for children.

Snowboarding There is a park and a half-pipe and a specialist school.

Cross-country Though it lacks the sheer length of trails of many resorts, Arosa (with 27km/17 miles) has some of the best and most varied cross-country loops in the Alps.

Queues Arosa does not suffer from serious queues. There can be waits for the Weisshorn cable-car, though recent reporters have had no problems.

Mountain restaurants The mountain restaurants can get crowded in peak season. Carmennahütte is the best, while Tschuggenhütte is a rustic little refuge with a nice sun terrace. Alpenblick does 'very good food' and Hörnli is a 'welcoming hut in a dramatic position' at the top of the gondola. Weisshorn, Sattelhütte and Brüggerstuba are also recommended.

Schools and guides Swiss and ABC are the main schools. There's a lot of demand for private lessons from the affluent Arosa guests.

Facilities for children Arosa seems a good choice for families. Several hotels have kindergartens and the two schools offer children's classes.

STAYING THERE

How to go Arosa is a hotel resort, with a high proportion of 3- and 4-stars.

Hotels The 4-star Waldhotel National (378 5555) with 'really special food' and direct access to the slopes is recommended. As is the 4-star Sporthotel Valsana (377 0275).

Eating out Most restaurants are hotel-based, some with a very high reputation. The Kachelofa-Stübli at the Waldhotel National is excellent.

Après-ski Après-ski is quite lively. The Carmenna hotel by the ice rink has a popular piano bar. Later the popular bar of the Eden hotel has live music.

Off the slopes There are plenty of alternatives. You can get a pedestrian's lift pass, and many mountain restaurants are reachable via 60km/37 miles of cleared, marked walks. Sleigh rides in the mountains are beautiful, and there's a popular outdoor ice rink.

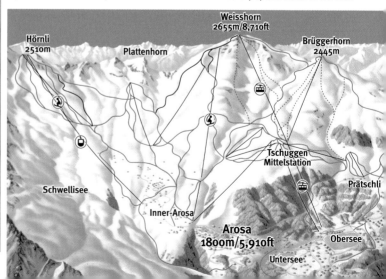

Champéry

1050m/3,440ft

Picture-postcard village, with access to the Portes du Soleil

421

WHAT IT COSTS

(((3)))

HOW IT RATES

The slopes

Snow	**
Extent	*****
Experts	***
Intermediates	****
Beginners	**
Convenience	*
Queues	****
Restaurants	***

The rest

Scenery	****
Resort charm	****
Off-slope	***

What's new

For 2002/03 two fast six-packs are planned to replace the old double chairs from Grand Paradis and at Planachaux – but final permission to build them had not been given when we went to press.

There are also plans to replace six old lifts in the Morgins-Champoussin area by another two fast six-packs and to create a new piste in the Foilleuse sector. But not until 2003/04 or later.

- ➕ Charmingly rustic mountain village
- ➕ Cable-car takes you into the very extensive Portes du Soleil slopes
- ➕ Quiet, relaxed – yet plenty to do off the slopes

- ➖ Local slopes suffer from the sun
- ➖ No runs back to the village – and sometimes none back to the valley
- ➖ Not good for beginners
- ➖ Not many tough slopes nearby

With good transport links and sports facilities, Champéry is great for anyone looking for a quiet time in a lovely place, especially if they have a car – but not if they're beginners. Not bad access to the Portes du Soleil: Avoriaz is fairly easy to get to – and there may be fresh powder there when Champéry is suffering.

THE RESORT

Set beneath the dramatic Dents du Midi, Champéry is a village of old wooden chalets. Friendly and relaxed, it would be ideal for families if it wasn't separated from its slopes by a steep, fragmented mountainside.

Down a steepish hill, away from the main street, are the cable-car, sports centre and railway station.

THE MOUNTAINS

The local slopes are as friendly and relaxing as the village.

Slopes Champéry's sunny slopes are part of the extensive Portes du Soleil circuit. The village cable-car or a chair-lift from Grand Paradis, a short bus-ride from Champéry, go to the Planachaux bowl. If snow conditions permit there are a couple of pistes back to Grand Paradis. There are no pistes back to Champéry, though on rare occasions conditions allow off-piste trips. Explore the Portes du Soleil by heading west towards Avoriaz or north-east to Champoussin, Morgins and Châtel. For more on the Portes du Soleil, see the

Avoriaz, Châtel and Morzine chapters.

Snow reliability The snow on the north-facing French side of the area is usually better than on the sunnier Swiss side to the south. The area would benefit from more snowmaking.

Experts Few local challenges and badly placed for most of the tough Portes du Soleil runs. The Swiss Wall, on the Champéry side of Chavanette, is intimidatingly long and steep, but not that terrifying. There's scope for off-piste at Chavanette and on the broad slopes of Les Crosets and Champoussin.

Intermediates Confident intermediates have the whole Portes du Soleil at their disposal. Locally, the runs home to Grand Paradis are good when the snow conditions allow and Les Crosets is a junction of several fine runs. Also worth trying are the slightly tougher pistes down from Mossettes and Pointe de l'Au, Champoussin's leisurely cruising, and runs to Morgins – delightful tree-lined meanders.

Beginners Go elsewhere if you can. The Planachaux runs, where lessons are held, are steepish.

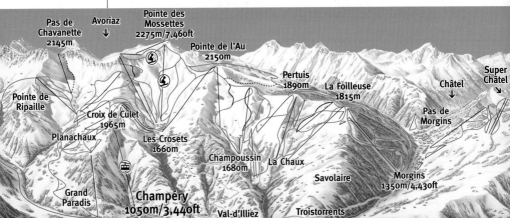

MOUNTAIN FACTS

for Portes du Soleil

Altitude	975m-2350m
	3,200ft-7,710ft
Lifts	206
Pistes	650km
	400 miles
Green	13%
Blue	38%
Red	39%
Black	10%
Snowmaking	
	252 acres
Recco detectors used	

Phone numbers
From elsewhere in
Switzerland add the
prefix 024.
From abroad use the
prefix +41 24.

**CHAMPERY
TOURIST OFFICE**

Postcode CH-1874
t 479 2020
f 479 2021
champery-ch@portes
dusoleil.com
www.champery.ch

**LES CROSETS
TOURIST OFFICE**

Postcode CH-1873
t 479 1400
f 479 1404
lescrosetstourisme@
bluewin.ch
www.valdilliez.com

**CHAMPOUSSIN
TOURIST OFFICE**

Postcode CH-1873
t 477 2727
f 479 1404
champoussintourisme
@bluewin.ch
www.valdilliez.com

**MORGINS
TOURIST OFFICE**

Postcode CH-1875
t 477 2361
f 477 3708
touristoffice@morgins.
ch
www.morgins.ch

Snowboarding Not ideal for beginners, and access to the Portes du Soleil circuit is by drag-lifts. There are a couple of terrain-parks and half-pipes nearby, and the daddy of all terrain-parks is in Avoriaz – well worth a look.
Cross-country Advertised, but very unreliable snow.
Queues Few local problems. If snow is good, avoid end-of-the-day queues for the cable-car down by taking the Grand Paradis run to the valley floor and getting the free bus back to town.
Mountain restaurants Chez Coquoz at Planachaux and Chez Gaby above Champoussin are recommended. The tiny Lapisa on the way to Grand Paradis is delightfully rustic (they make cheese and smoke their own meats on-site).
Schools and guides The few reports that we've had are free of criticism.
Facilities for children The tourist office has a list of childminders. The Swiss ski school takes three- to seven-year-olds.

STAYING THERE

How to go Limited packages available. Easy access for independent travellers.
Chalets Tour op Piste Artiste has some.
Hotels Wide choice from 3-star down. Prices low compared with smarter Swiss resorts. The Champéry (479 1071) is the best – a comfy chalet on the main street. Beau Séjour (479 1701) is at the southern end. The National (479 1130) has 'friendly staff, lovely breakfast'. The luxurious-looking De La Paix accepts only whole hotel (16 beds) bookings (UK: 01248 726037).
Self-catering Some apartments are available to independent travellers.
Eating out A fair choice. Two of the best for local specialities are just outside the village: Cantines des Rives is a beautiful traditional chalet; the Grand Paradis is excellent if you don't mind stuffed animals on the wall. Locally, try the the Farinet or the Hotel du Nord. Mitchell's bar has a good

restaurant and the Café du Centre serves Asian food. Two evenings a week, the slopes are floodlit and the restaurant at the top of the cable-car opens.
Après-ski Mitchell's has big sofas, a fireplace and a great atmosphere. Below the 'rather seedy' Pub, the Crevasse disco is one of the liveliest places. The underground Mines d'Or has 'ridiculously high' drink prices. The Café du Centre has its own micro brewery. Try the Bar des Guides or the Farinet's spacious cellar nightclub.
Off the slopes Walks, particularly along to Val d'Illiez, are pleasant, and the narrow-gauge railway allows excursions to Montreux, Lausanne and Sion. There's a decent sports centre.

Les Crosets 1660m/5,450ft

A good base for a quiet time and slopes on the doorstep. Good snow and a prime position on the Portes du Soleil with beautiful views of the Dents du Midi. Not much here, but the Télécabine (479 1421) is homely, with great food in a rustic dining room.

Champoussin 1680m/5,510ft

A good family choice – no through traffic, near the slopes, no noisy late-night revellers and the comfortable Royal Alpage Club hotel (pool, gym, disco, two restaurants – 476 8300).

Morgins 1350m/4,430ft

A fairly scattered, but attractive, quiet resort (though with some nightlife). It suits those with a car, who can get to the higher slopes and bars of Châtel – though this can make the town busy with traffic. We had a report this year of 'very icy' walks to the lifts. The Bellevue (477 8171) and Pension de Morgins (477 1143) are well thought of. Ski Morgins has catered chalets.

Sun-soaked slopes with stunning long-distance views and big town base

WHAT IT COSTS

HOW IT RATES

The slopes

Snow	**
Extent	***
Experts	**
Intermediates	****
Beginners	***
Convenience	**
Queues	***
Restaurants	***

The rest

Scenery	****
Resort charm	**
Off-slope	****

➕ Large, varied piste area

➕ Splendid wooded setting with magnificent panoramic views

➕ Fair number of woodland slopes – good in bad weather

➕ Modern, well-designed lift system, with few queues

➕ Golf course provides excellent, gentle nursery slopes

➕ Excellent cross-country trail

➕ Very sunny slopes, but ...

➖ Snow badly affected by sun except in early season

➖ Large town (rather than village) composed partly of big chalet-style blocks but mainly of dreary cubic blocks – and therefore entirely without Alpine atmosphere

➖ Bus- or car-rides to lifts from much of the accommodation

➖ Few challenges except off-piste

When conditions are right – clear skies above fresh, deep snow – Crans-Montana takes some beating. The mountains you bounce down with the midday sun full on your face are charmingly scenic, the slopes broken up by rock outcrops and forest. The mountains you gaze at – Zermatt's Matterhorn just discernible among them – are mind-blowing. When conditions are right, mountain-lovers may forgive Crans-Montana anything – in particular, its inconvenient, linear layout and the plain, towny style of its twin resort centres.

Sadly, conditions are more often wrong. Except in the depths of winter, the strong midday sun bakes the pistes. For someone booking months ahead, this is enough to keep Crans-Montana off the shortlist. For those who can time a visit according to the weather – and are more interested in impressive distant views than cosy immediate surroundings – the resort is worth serious consideration.

423

What's new

The Nationale and Barmaz lifts have been upgraded and now have loading carpets.

Screens at the cable car stations provide information on weather and piste conditions.

The casino at Ycoor, Montana, is now open and intended for year-round operation.

The resort

Crans-Montana celebrated 100 years as a resort in 1993, but is far from being a picturesque Swiss chocolate-box village. Set on a broad shelf facing south to the great mountains across the Rhône valley, it is really two villages, their centres a mile apart and their fringes now merging. Strung along a busy road, the resort's many hotels, villas, apartments and smart shops are mainly dull blocks with little traditional Alpine character.

Fortunately, the resort's many trees help to screen the buildings, and they make some areas positively attractive. And its wonderful setting means you get a lot of sun as well as superb views over the Valais. There are several lakes and two golf courses, one home to the Swiss Open.

The resort is reached by good roads, and by a fast funicular railway up from Sierre to Montana. It depends heavily on summer conference business, which sets the tone even in winter. Hotels tend to be comfortable

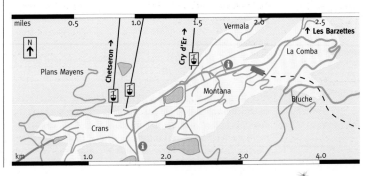

MOUNTAIN FACTS

Altitude 1500m-3000m
4,920ft-9,840ft
Lifts 35
Pistes 160km
100 miles
Blue 38%
Red 50%
Black 12%
Snowmaking 17km
11 miles
Recco detectors used

LIFT PASSES

2001/02 prices in
Swiss francs

Crans-Montana-Aminona
Covers all lifts in
Crans-Montana and
Aminona and the ski-bus.
Beginners Points card
Main pass
1-day pass 54
6-day pass 253
Senior citizens
Over 65 (men), 62
(women) 6-day pass
215
Children
Under 19: 6-day pass
215
Under 15: 6-day pass
152
Under 6: free pass
Short-term passes
Half day from 11
(adult 45) or 12.30
(adult 36).
Alternative periods
6 non-consecutive
days (adult 292).

and fairly formal, village facilities varied but daytime-oriented, and visitors middle-aged and dignified. In the evenings there's little Alpine-village atmosphere.

Gondolas go up to the main slopes from both villages. Crans is the more upmarket, with expensive jewellery shops, a casino, and a high fur-coat count. It is well situated for the pretty golf course area, which has baby lifts for complete beginners, a cross-country trail and lovely walks. Montana has somewhat cheaper restaurants and bars.

Crans-Montana is quite sprawling. A free shuttle-bus links the villages and satellite lift stations during the day but can get very crowded – one reporter recommends taking a car. The main Crans and Montana gondola stations are above the main road and a tiring walk away. Many people store their equipment at lift stations overnight.

Anzère is nearby to the west, though the slopes aren't linked. You can make expeditions to Zermatt, Saas-Fee and Verbier by road or rail.

There are other gondola base stations and places to stay further east: at Violettes in Les Barzettes (the lift from here connects directly to the top glacier lift and is the fastest way to the top) and at Aminona.

The mountains

Although it has achieved some prominence in ski-racing, Crans-Montana has slopes that suit intermediates well, with few challenges and no nasty surprises. Beginners are well catered for.

THE SLOPES
Interestingly fragmented

Crans-Montana's 160km/100 miles of piste are spread over three well-linked areas, all equally suitable for intermediates of varying abilities and persuasions. The upper runs are wide and good but many of those down to the valley are narrow woodland paths.

Cry d'Er is the largest sector – an open bowl descending into patchy forest, directly above Montana. Cry d'Er itself is the meeting point of many lifts and the starting point of the cable-car up to the sector high point of Bella-Lui. Cry d'Er is served directly by two gondolas – a newish eight-person one from just above Crans, and another from just above central Montana, which has a useful mid-station where beginners can get off and access high-altitude nursery slopes. A third gondola goes from the west side of Crans to Chetseron, with a drag above going on to Cry d'Er.

The next sector, reached by another powerful gondola directly from Les Barzettes (labelled 'Violettes' on the resort piste map), is focused on Les Violettes, starting point of the jumbo gondola up to the Plaine Morte glacier. There are three linking routes from Cry d'Er to the **Violettes-Plaine Morte** sector. The highest, starting at Bella-Lui (or, strictly, at Col du Pochet, a short run and drag beyond) used to be off-piste but is now an official red run. Bella-Lui is also the start of the Men's

SCHOOLS/GUIDES

2000/01 prices in Swiss francs

Swiss
Classes 6 days
3hr: 9.30-12.30
6 days: 170
Children's classes
Ages: from 3
9.30-12.30 or 9.30-4pm
Half day 45
1 day with meal 80
Private lessons
Hourly
60 for 1hr

Ski & Sky
Private lessons
Hourly
60 for 1hr

Stoked Snowboard
Classes Half day 50

Downhill course (Piste Nationale) that goes past Cry d'Er to Les Barzettes.

The third, **Petit Bonvin**, sector is served by a gondola up from Aminona at the eastern end of the area. This is linked to Les Violettes by red and blue runs passing the drag and chair-lift at La Toula.

A piste on Cry d'Er is floodlit on Friday evenings for three hours.

Reporters complain of confusion caused by poor signing.

SNOW RELIABILITY
The resort's main drawback
Crans-Montana's slopes go up to glacier level at 3000m/9,840ft, but this is misleading; the runs on the Plaine Morte glacier are very limited and, excellent though it is, the solitary run down from there does not make this a snow-sure area as a whole. Few of the other slopes are above 2250m/7,380ft, and practically all get a lot of direct sun. Late in the season, at least, this makes for slush in the afternoons, rock-hard ice in the mornings, and a tendency for snow to disappear. There is now snowmaking on the main runs down from both Violettes and Cry d'Er

to Montana, from Cry d'Er to Crans and the bottom part of the run from Chetseron. We applaud these efforts; but it is a losing battle. We have never experienced good snow on the runs down to the valley.

FOR EXPERTS
Lacks challenging pistes
There are few steep pistes and the only decent moguls are on the short slopes at La Toula. There's plenty of off-piste in all sectors, but particularly beneath Chetseron and La Tza; guides are usually easy to book. The off-piste tour from Plaine Morte to Aminona is recommended.

The Piste Nationale course is far from daunting taken at 'normal' speed, but has some enormous jumps just above Les Marolires. The direct run from La Tza to Plumachit is fairly challenging in places, especially when icy.

FOR INTERMEDIATES
Lots of attractive, flattering runs
Crans-Montana is very well suited to intermediates. Pistes are mostly wide, and many of the red runs don't justify

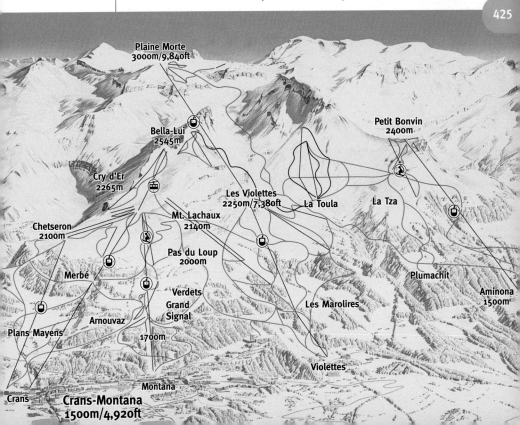

Plaine Morte 3000m/9,840ft
Bella-Lui 2545m
Petit Bonvin 2400m
Cry d'Er 2265m
Les Violettes 2250m/7,380ft
La Toula
La Tza
Chetseron 2100m
Mt. Lachaux 2140m
Pas du Loup 2000m
Merbé
Plumachit
Aminona 1500m
Verdets
Grand Signal
Les Marolires
Plans Mayens
Arnouvaz
1700m
Violettes
Montana
Crans
Crans-Montana
1500m/4,920ft

CHILDCARE

The Montana ski
school runs a
kindergarten with
skiing available up at
Signal and the Crans
school on the golf
course for children
aged 3 to 6, from
9.30 to 4.30.

There are several
other kindergartens.
In Montana, Fleurs
des Champs takes
children aged 3
months to 7 years;
and Zig-Zag takes
children from 2 to 6
years.

the grading. They tend to be uniform in difficulty from top to bottom, with few nasty surprises for the nervous. Avid piste-bashers enjoy the length of many runs, plus the fast lifts and good links that allow a lot of varied mileage.

The 11km/7 mile run from Plaine Morte to Les Barzettes starts with top-of-the-world views and powder snow, and finishes among pretty woods. But many people love the top half so much ('my favourite run in Europe') they do it repeatedly, curtailing their descent halfway down at either the Barmaz or Cabane de Bois chair-lifts to Les Violettes, for quicker access to the top gondola. Because of the gondola's high capacity the run can get crowded.

The short runs from Bella-Lui to just below Cry d'Er have some of the best snow and quietest slopes in the area, and provide fine views of awesome Montagne de Raul. The Piste Nationale is a good test of technique, with plenty of bumps but also lots of room. The quietest area, and good for groups of varying intermediate standards, is the Petit Bonvin sector.

FOR BEGINNERS
Plenty to offer the first-timer
There are three excellent nursery areas, with slopes of varying difficulty. Complete beginners have very gentle slopes on the golf course next to Crans. Cry d'Er has an area of relatively long, easy runs, with up-the-mountain views and atmosphere as well as better snow. But the runs aren't just for beginners, and you do need a full lift pass. The Verdets-Grand Signal run is steeper, and the drag-lift can get terribly icy. Near-beginners can try the little run up at Plaine Morte.

FOR CROSS-COUNTRY
Excellent high-level trails
There are 40km/25 miles of cross-country trails altogether. There are some pretty, easy trails (skating-style as well as classic) on and around the golf course. But what makes Crans-Montana particularly good for cross-country is its high-level route, in and out of woods, across the whole mountainside from Plans Mayens to beyond Aminona. 10km/6 miles of trails at Plaine Morte are open when the lower trails are closed.

QUEUES
Few problems
The resort's big investment in new gondolas – notably the jumbo 'Funitel' gondola from Les Violettes to the Plaine Morte glacier slopes and the lift out of Crans – has greatly alleviated any queue problems, though bottlenecks can occur at the Nationale drag-lifts. Reporters say you rarely wait longer than five minutes – except occasionally if snow lower down is in poor condition. More of a problem can be bottlenecks on some pistes, including the top glacier run. The resort does not get weekend crowds.

← One of the chair-lifts back to Violettes from the end of the glacier run – and the ever-present view over the Rhône valley

GETTING THERE

Air Sion, transfer
30min. Geneva,
transfer 3hr.

Rail Sierre (15km/9
miles), Sion (22km/14
miles); regular buses
to resort.

ACTIVITIES

Indoor Hotel
swimming pools,
tennis, bowling,
bridge, chess, golf
simulator, squash,
snow-shoe walking,
concerts, cinemas,
casino, curling, ice
skating, galleries
Outdoor Toboggan
run, ski-bob, horse-
riding, ice skating,
paragliding, balloon
flights

Phone numbers
From elsewhere in
Switzerland add the
prefix 027.
From abroad use the
prefix +41 27.

TOURIST OFFICE

Postcode CH-3962
t 485 0404
f 485 0460
info@crans-montana.ch
www.crans-montana.ch

MOUNTAIN RESTAURANTS
A good choice
There are 20 mountain restaurants,
many offering table-service. The Merbé,
at the Crans-Cry d'Er gondola mid-
station, is one of the most attractive,
with good food in a pleasant setting
just above the tree line. Advance
bookings are recommended because it
does get busy. Bella-Lui's terrace (with
service) offers good views. The
Chetseron eatery has fine views.

Petit Bonvin, at the top of the
Aminona sector, has self-service and
table-service sections, with superb
views. There is not much choice in the
Violettes sector, but we had a good
meal on the table-service terrace of the
main restaurant. And the small self-
service Cabane des Violettes, 50m/
165ft below, gets rave reviews for food
and views (be there early for a seat).

SCHOOLS AND GUIDES
Good reports
Both local branches of the Swiss
school have attracted mainly
favourable comments over the years.

FACILITIES FOR CHILDREN
Adequate, but few reports
The resort facilities for children seem
to be adequate, especially in Montana,
but we have no recent reports.

Staying there

HOW TO GO
Much more choice on your own
There is a wide choice of hotels and
apartments, and some are available
through UK tour operators.
Hotels This conference resort has over
50 mainly large, comfy, expensive
hotels. Most have three or more stars
though there are more modest places.
《《《⑤ **Crans-Ambassador** (485 4848)
Health spa, with some rooms a bit
shabby for its 5-star rating. Excellent
treatments such as plant baths, mud
packs. Just above Montana gondola.
《《《⑤ **Pas de l'Ours** (485 9333) Our
favourite. Chic, attractive, wood and
stone Relais & Chateaux place with
nine individually designed suites.
《《《④ **Aïda Castel** (485 4111) Beautifully
furnished in chic rustic style. Between
the two resort centres. Outdoor pool.
《《③ **Forêt** (480 2131) Highly
recommended. Almost at Les Barzettes,
with minibus to lifts. Pool, good views.
《《③ **Curling** (481 1242) Comfortable,
near centre of Montana.

《《③ **Robinson** (481 1353) B&B only;
well placed near the National, in Crans.
Self-catering There are many
apartments available.

EATING OUT
Plenty of alternatives
There is a good variety of restaurants
from French to Lebanese. The best is
the Bistrot in the Pas de l'Ours hotel.
Almost all the cheaper places are in
Montana. The Dent-Blanche is
recommended for fondues. We had a
good, simple Italian meal at the
Padrino in Crans. The Nouvelle
Rotisserie is reputed to be excellent.
The Gréni is a welcoming restaurant on
the western fringe of Montana. The
Cervin up at Vermala is unusually
rustic. A restaurant guide is given away
locally, but it is not comprehensive.

APRES-SKI
Can be ritzy, but otherwise quiet
Crans-Montana visitors tend to prefer
quiet meals and drinks to raucous
nightlife. Amadeus 2006 and Chez
Nanette are tents on Cry d'Er serving
close-of-play vin chaud. The George &
Dragon in Crans is one of the liveliest,
most crowded bars with 'the cheapest
beer in town'. Reporters recommend
Bar 1900, the Grange and Indiana Café.
The outdoor ice rink in Montana is
'fun'. The cinema has films in English.
Bridge is played in the hotels Royal
and Aïda.

OFF THE SLOPES
Excellent, but little charm
There are plenty of off-slope activities
including lovely walks. Swimming is
available in several hotels.

Sierre is easily reached for
shopping, and the larger Sion is only a
few minutes further. Montreux is within
reach. Mountain restaurants are mainly
at gondola and cable-car stations, so
accessible to pedestrians.

Davos 1550m/5,090ft

A big, grey town surrounded by a glorious Alpine playground

WHAT IT COSTS

((((5)

HOW IT RATES

The slopes

Snow	****
Extent	*****
Experts	****
Intermediates	*****
Beginners	**
Convenience	**
Queues	**
Restaurants	***

The rest

Scenery	****
Resort charm	**
Off-slope	*****

➕ Very extensive slopes

➕ Some superb, long and mostly easy pistes away from the lifts

➕ Lots of accessible off-piste terrain, with several marked itineraries

➕ Good cross-country trails

➕ Plenty to do off the slopes – from sports to shopping

➕ Some cute mountain restaurants

➕ Klosters is an attractively villagey alternative base

➕ Funicular out of Davos Dorf is at last being upgraded

➖ Dreary block-style buildings of Davos spoil the views

➖ Davos is a huge, city-like place, plagued by traffic and lacking Alpine atmosphere and après-ski animation

➖ The slopes are spread over five or six essentially separate areas

➖ Preponderance of T-bars is a problem for some visitors

➖ Klosters-Davos trains no longer covered by the lift pass

➖ Only pistes back to Davos are blacks finishing on the outskirts

Davos was one of the original mega-resorts, with slopes on a scale that few resorts can better, even today. But it's a difficult resort to like. It's easy to put up with slopes spread over separate mountains and relatively ancient, queue-prone lifts if that's the price of staying in a captivating Alpine village. But Davos is far from that.

Whether you forgive the flaws probably depends on how highly you value three plus-points: the distinctive, super-long intermediate runs of the Parsenn area; being able to visit a different sector every day; and the considerable off-piste potential. We value all three, and we always look forward to visiting.

You don't have to stay in Davos to enjoy its slopes: Klosters offers a much more captivating alternative. Despite royal connections, it is not particularly exclusive. But it is less well placed than Davos for exploring all the mountains.

What's new

The long-awaited upgrading of the ancient Parsennbahn railway is due for 2002/03, with a bigger, faster train shifting people from Dorf to the mid-station at 3 to 4 times the rate of the old train.

The Schatzalp/Strela lift system is no longer included in the area lift pass and the link to Weissfluhjoch is closed.

Free local transport is no longer included in the lift pass, but comes with the Guest Card, issued free by accommodation providers. But this is a local deal, covering only the resort you are staying in (and giving a modest discount on train fares between Davos and Klosters). Negotiations are under way to get train travel between Davos and Klosters covered by the lift pass again.

The resort

Davos is set in a high, broad, flat-bottomed valley, with its lifts and slopes either side. Arguably it was the very first place in the Alps to develop its slopes. The railway up the Parsenn was one of the first built for skiers (in 1931), and the first drag-lift was built on the Bolgen nursery slopes in 1934. But Davos was already a health resort; many of its luxury hotels were built as sanatoriums.

Sadly, that's just what they look like. There are still several specialist clinics and it is for these, along with its conferences and sporting facilities, that Davos has become well known. It is also a popular destination for athletes wanting to train at high altitude.

It has two main centres, Dorf and Platz, about 2km/1 mile apart. Although transport is good, with buses around the town as well as the railway linking Dorf and Platz to Klosters and other villages, location is important. Easiest access to the slopes is from Dorf to the main Parsenn area, via the funicular railway; Platz is better placed for the Strela and Jakobshorn areas (with a cable-car and chair to the latter), the big sports facilities, the smarter shopping and evening action.

Davos shares its slopes with the famously royal resort of Klosters, down the valley – an attractive village with good links into the Parsenn area and its own separate sector, the sunny Madrisa. Sadly, a lunatic local dispute means that for now any use of the train between Klosters and Davos has to be paid for separately – see What's new. Klosters is described in more detail at the end of this chapter.

Trips are possible by car or rail to St Moritz (the Vereina rail tunnel offers access to the Engadine area without having to negotiate the snowy Flüelapass) and Arosa, and by car to Flims-Laax and Lenzerheide.

LIFT PASSES

2002/03 prices in
Swiss francs

Top Card
Covers all Davos and
Klosters, the railway
in the whole region
and buses between
the resorts.
Beginners Single and
return tickets on main
lifts in each area.
Main pass
1-day pass 61
6-day pass 279
Children
Under 18: 6-day pass
187
Under 13: 6-day pass
93
Under 6 (with adult):
free pass
Notes
A confusing array of
passes are available
for individual areas
(Parsenn, Gotschna,
Schatzalp,
Jakobshorn,
Rinerhorn, Gotschna
and Madrisa) and
combined areas, from
a half day to 17 days.
Several reporters
have complained that
not all passes are
available at each base
station.

The mountains

The slopes here have something for
everyone, though experts and nervous
intermediates need to choose their
territory with care.

THE SLOPES
Vast and varied
You could hit a different mountain
around Davos every day for a week.
The out-of-town areas tend to be
neglected by most visitors – and so are
much quieter than the ones directly
accessible from the town.

The Parsennbahn funicular from
Davos Dorf takes you to the major lift
junction of Weissfluhjoch, at one end
of the **Parsenn**. The only run back to
the valley is a black to the outskirts of
Dorf. At the other end of the wide,
open Parsenn bowl is Gotschnagrat,
reached by cable-car from Klosters.
There are excellent intermediate runs
down to Klosters, and to other villages
(see feature panel). From Davos Platz,
a funicular goes up to Schatzalp, at the
base of the **Strela** area. This limited lift
system is no longer covered by the
area lift pass, and seems doomed.

Across the valley, **Jakobshorn** is
reached by cable-car or chair-lift from
Davos Platz; this is the main
snowboarders' hill. There is also a
small floodlit slope area here.
Rinerhorn and **Pischa** are reached by
bus or (in the case of Rinerhorn) train.

Beyond the main part of Klosters, a
gondola goes up from Klosters Dorf to

the sunny, scenic **Madrisa** area.

There are still too many T-bars for
the comfort of some reporters –
Rinerhorn, Pischa and Madrisa consist
of little else.

SNOW RELIABILITY
Good, but not the best
Davos is high by Swiss standards. Its
mountains go respectably high, too –
though not to glacial heights. Not
many of the slopes face directly south,
but not many face directly north either.
Snow reliability is generally good
higher up but can be poor lower down
– you may have to take the lifts down
after using the Parsenn slopes. Snow-
guns cover a couple of the upper runs
on the Parsenn and Jakobshorn and
the home runs from the Parsenn to
Davos Dorf and Klosters.

FOR EXPERTS
Plenty to do, on- and off-piste
A glance at the piste map may give the
misleading impression that this is an
intermediate's resort – there aren't
many black runs. But there are some
excellent runs among them – the
Meierhofer Tälli run to Wolfgang is a
favourite. There are also half a dozen
off-piste itineraries (marked on the
map and on the ground, but not
prepared or patrolled). These are a key
feature, adding up to a lot of expert
terrain that can be tackled without
expensive guidance. Some are on the
open upper slopes, some in the woods
lower down, some from the peaks right
to the valley. Two of the steepest runs
go from Gotschnagrat directly towards
Klosters – around the infamous
Gotschnawang slope. The Wang run is
a seriously steep ski route (and rarely
open, in our experience). Drostobel is
less scary, though the overall gradient
is little different.

There is also excellent 'proper' off-
piste terrain for which guidance is

Davos

429

boarding *The nursery slopes are not ideal and it is intermediate and advanced boarders who will get the most out of Davos's vast terrain and off-piste potential. The established boarder mountain is the Jakobshorn, with its half-pipe, terrain-park, boarder-cross course and funky Jatz Bar nearby. The Rinerhorn and Pischa each have a terrain-park. Be warned: the long runs down the Schifer gondola have lengthy flattish bits. There are several cheap and cheerful hotels specially for boarders, including the 180-bed Bolgenhof hotel near the Jakobshorn, the Snowboardhotel Bolgenschanze and the Snowboarder's Palace.*

SWITZERLAND

430

needed, and some short tours. Arosa can be reached much more quickly on snow than by road or rail, but requires a return by rail via Chur. From Madrisa you can make tours to Gargellen in Austria's Montafontal. This means an exhausting one-hour walk on skins on the way back. A reader also recommends the descent from Madrisa to St Antönien, north of Küblis, not least for 'spectacular views', returning by bus and train.

FOR INTERMEDIATES
A splendid variety of runs

For intermediates of any temperament, this is a great area. There are good cruising runs on all five mountains, so you would never get bored in a week. This variety of different slopes taken together with the wonderful long runs to the valleys makes it a compelling area with a unique character.

The epic runs to Klosters and other places (described in the feature panel) pose few difficulties for a confident intermediate or even an ambitious near-beginner (one of your editors did the run to Klosters on his third day on skis, and we have heard from reporters

who did the run to Küblis on their second holiday). And there are one or two other notable away-from-the-lifts runs to the valley. In particular, you can travel from the top of Madrisa back to Klosters Dorf via the beautiful Schlappin valley (it's an easy black – classified red until the mid-1990s).

Pischa is a relatively gentle area – in absolute terms, it could all be classified blue – whereas the Jakobshorn has some genuine challenges. Rinerhorn comes somewhere between the two.

FOR BEGINNERS
Platz is the more convenient

The Bolgen nursery slope is adequately spacious and gentle, and a bearable walk from the centre of Platz. But Dorf-based beginners face more of a trek out to Bünda – unless staying out at the hotel of the same name.

There is no shortage of easy runs to progress to, spread around all the sectors. The Parsenn sector probably has the edge, with long, early intermediate runs in the main Parsenn bowl, as well as in the valleys down from Weissfluhjoch.

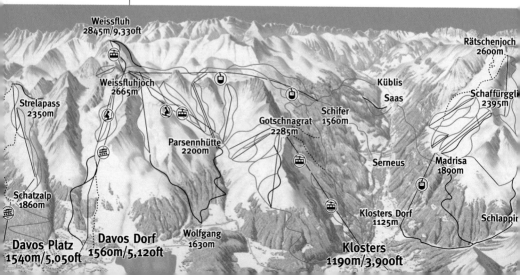

CHILDCARE

The Bobo-Club
(formerly Pinocchio
nursery) at Bünda
takes children aged
between 4 and 7 from
10am to noon and
from 2pm to 4pm,
and offers a 'playful
approach to snow
and skiing'. Lunch
supervision is
possible.

The day nursery
Kinderhotel Muchetta
at Wiesen takes
children from 3 years.
There is also a day
nursery for babies
from 6 months.

New last season, the
Madrisa Kids' Land
offers ski school and
childcare for children
between the ages of
2 and 6. There are
also free facilities for
parents with babies,
and a children's
restaurant, open from
noon to 2pm.

The runs from Weissfluhjoch that head north, on the back of the mountain, make this area special for many visitors. The pistes that go down to Schifer and then to Küblis, Saas and Serneus, and the one that curls around the mountain to Klosters, are classified red but are not normally difficult – though the latter parts can be challenging if they are not groomed. What marks them out is their sheer length (10-12km/6-7 miles) and the sensation of travel they offer – plus the welcoming huts in the woods towards the end.

Since construction of the long Schiferbahn gondola you can descend the 1100m/ 3,610ft vertical to Schifer as often as you like. For those based in Davos, going on down to Klosters and getting the train home (as we old timers did at the end of the day in the 1970s) is now an expensive option, because the lift pass doesn't cover the trains. This is part of a wrangle between the train company and the lift companies, which we hear also accounts for closure of the runs to Küblis, Saas and Serneus at times when snow was not conspicuously lacking. This wrangle needs to be sorted, and soon.

FOR CROSS-COUNTRY
Long, scenic valley trails

Davos has a total of 75km/47 miles of trails running in both directions along the main valley and reaching well up into Sertigtal, Dischmatal and Flüelatal. There is a cross-country ski centre and special ski school on the outskirts of town.

QUEUES
May be eased this year

Some of the longest queues in the Alps will be eased this season, if replacement of the first stage of the Parsennbahn goes ahead. Bigger, faster trains should shift the crowds out of Davos Dorf at almost four times the rate of the old train. It remains to be seen whether the existing lifts from the mid-station — a six-pack and the

existing railway — can cope; you may just end up in a queue with a different view. Queues elsewhere are not usually a problem — though one high-season visitor found a 45-minute morning queue for the Madrisa gondola.

MOUNTAIN RESTAURANTS
Stay low down

The main high-altitude restaurants are dreary self-service affairs. The main exception is the highest of all – Bruhin's at Weissflügipfel is a great place for a hang-the-cost blow-out on a snowy day, with table-service of excellent rustic as well as gourmet dishes, and some knockout desserts.

There are other compelling places lower down in the Parsenn sector. A reader describes 'lunching on big portions of chicken and noodles' at the

Davos

431

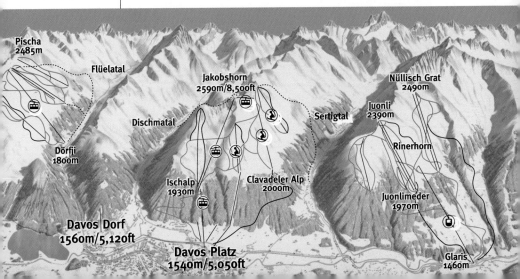

SCHOOLS/GUIDES

2001/02 prices in
Swiss francs

Classes
4hr: 2hr am and pm
5 full days: 240
Children's classes
Ages: 4 to 16
5 full days: 240
Private lessons
Half day 190
Full day 310

GETTING THERE

Air Zürich, transfer
2hr by car, 3hr by rail
or bus.

Rail Stations in Davos
Dorf and Platz. 20
minutes from Davos
to Klosters.

bar outside the mid-station of the Parsennbahn as 'heaven'. The old favourites, the rustic 'schwendis' in the woods on the way down to the Klosters valley from the Parsenn, still attract crowds, though a long-standing visitor detects declining standards. Singled out this year is the 'excellent' Berghaus Schwendi at Schifer with oriental dishes 'freshly cooked in front of our eyes'. These are fun places to end up as darkness falls – Klosters Schwendi, at least, sells wax torches to illuminate your final descent.

On Jakobshorn the Jatzhütte near the boarders' terrain-park is wild – with changing scenery such as mock palm trees, parrots and pirates.

Both restaurants on the Madrisa slopes have been pronounced 'disappointing' in terms of food choice and quality. The Erika at Schlappin below Madrisa is noted for cheese fondue at lunchtime.

At Pischa, the Mäderbeiz at Flüelameder is a friendly and spacious woody hut, cheering on a cold day. On the Rinerhorn, the Hubelhütte was preferred by one reporter to the main restaurant at the top of the gondola.

SCHOOLS AND GUIDES
Don't count on English
A reporter this year says that 'nearly all instructors spoke English and were skilled and friendly – both my kids had a terrific time'. There is an alternative ski school called New Trend and Top Secret is the competing snowboard school.

FACILITIES FOR CHILDREN
Not ideal
Davos is a rather spread-out place in which to handle a family – and indeed the school's nursery is in a rather isolated spot, at Dorf's Bünda nursery slope. A recent reporter tells us the nursery is 'well organised, but even good instructors forget at times that your child doesn't speak German'.

Staying there

HOW TO GO
Hotels dominate the packages
Although most beds are in apartments, hotels dominate the UK market.
Hotels A dozen 4-star places and about 30 3-stars form the core of the Davos hotel trade, though there are a couple of 5-stars and quite a few cheaper places, including B&Bs. You can book any hotel by calling 415 2121.
(((5 **Flüela** (410 1717) The more atmospheric of the two 5-star hotels, in central Dorf, and quite well placed to beat the Parsenn queues. Pool.
(((4 **Golfhotel Waldhuus** (416 8131) As convenient for langlaufers as for golfers. Quiet, modern, tasteful. Pool.
(((4 **Davoserhof** (414 9020) Best in town. Small, old, beautifully furnished, with excellent food; well placed in Platz.
(((4 **Sunstar Park** (413 1414) At far end of Davos platz. Pool, sauna, games room. Recommended for 'excellent' food.
(((3 **Parsenn** (416 3232) Right opposite the Parsenn railway in Dorf. An attractive chalet marred by the big McDonald's on the ground floor.
(((3 **Berghotel Schatzalp** (415 5151) On the tree line 300m/1,000ft above Platz; reached by funicular (free to guests).
((2 **Alte Post** (414 9020) Traditional and cosy; in central Platz. Popular with boarders.
((2 **Hubli's Landhaus** (417 1010) 5km/3 miles out at Laret, towards Klosters. Quiet country inn with sophisticated, expensive food.
(1 **Snowboarder's Palace** (414 9020) Close to Schatzalp lift, offers good-value dormitory accommodation.

ACTIVITIES

Indoor Artificial skating rink, fitness centre, tennis, squash, swimming, sauna, cinema, museums, galleries, libraries, massage, badminton, golf-driving range
Outdoor Over 80km/ 50 miles of cleared paths (mostly at valley level), snow-shoe trekking, full-moon skiing, toboggan run, snow volleyball, natural skating rink, curling, horse-riding, mule-trekking, sleigh rides, hang-gliding, paragliding

Phone numbers
From elsewhere in Switzerland add the prefix 081.
From abroad use the prefix +41 81.

DAVOS TOURIST OFFICE

Postcode CH-7270
t 415 2121
f 415 2100
info@davos.ch
www.davos.ch

KLOSTERS TOURIST OFFICE

Postcode CH-7250
t 410 2020
f 410 2010
info@klosters.ch
www.klosters.ch

EATING OUT
Wide choice, mostly in hotels

In a town this size, you need to know where to go – if you just walk around hoping to spot a suitable place to eat, you may starve. For a start, get the tourist office's Gastroführer booklet. Most of the more ambitious restaurants are in hotels. There is a choice of two good Chinese restaurants – the lavish Zauberberg in the Europe and the Zum Goldenen Drachen in the Bahnhof Terminus. Good-value places include the jolly Al Ponte (pizza and steak both approved), La Carretta (good for home-made pasta) and the small and cosy Gentiana (with an upstairs stübli). For local specialities try Heidi's und Haui's Bündnerstübli. An evening excursion for dinner out of town is popular. Schatzalp (reached by a funicular), the Schneider and Landhaus in Frauenkirch have also been recommended.

APRES-SKI
Lots on offer, but quiet clientele

There are plenty of bars, discos and nightclubs, and a large casino in hotel Europe. But we're not sure how some of them make a living – Davos guests tend to want the quiet life. At tea-time, mega-calories are consumed at the Weber, and Scala has a popular outside terrace. The liveliest place in town is the rustic little Chämi bar (popular with locals); it has 'the best atmosphere later in the evening', according to one recent reporter. The smart Ex Bar attracts a mixed age group. Nightclubs tend to be sophisticated, expensive and lacking atmosphere during the week. The most popular are the Cabanna and the Cava Grischa (both in the hotel Europe), the Rotliechtli, Millennium! and Bar Senn.

Bolgenschanze and Bolgen are popular boarder hang-outs.

OFF THE SLOPES
Great apart from the buildings

Provided you're not fussy about building style, Davos can be unreservedly recommended for off-slope fun. The towny resort has shops and other diversions, and transport along the valley and up on to the slopes is good – though the best of the mountain restaurants are well out of range for pedestrians. The sports facilities are excellent; the natural ice rink is said to be Europe's biggest, and is supplemented by artificial rinks,

both indoor and outdoor. Spectator events include speed skating as well as hockey. And there are lots of walks up on the slopes as well as around the lake and along the valleys.

Klosters 1190m/3,900ft

In a word association game, Klosters might trigger 'Prince of Wales'. The enlarged cable-car to Gotschna – and the Parsenn – is named after him.

Don't be put off. We don't know why HRH likes to ski in Klosters particularly, but it is certainly not because the place is the exclusive territory of royalty. Most of the really smart socialising goes on behind closed doors, in private chalets.

THE RESORT

Klosters is a comfortable, quiet village with a much more appealing Alpine flavour than Davos. Klosters Platz is the main focus – a collection of upmarket, traditional-style hotels around the railway station, at the foot of the steep, wooded slopes of Gotschna. The Davos road traffic is a problem; a bypass is being built.

The village spreads along the valley road for quite a way before fading into the countryside; there's then a second concentration of building in the even quieter village of Klosters Dorf.

THE MOUNTAIN

Slopes A cable-car takes you to the Gotschnagrat end of the Parsenn area and a gondola from Klosters Dorf takes you up to the scenic Madrisa area.
Snow reliability It's usually reliable higher up but can be poor lower down – you may have to take the lifts down after using the Parsenn slopes.
Experts The off-piste possibilities are the main appeal for experts.

...p in the ...e one of the ...s of the runs ...to Klosters →

434

Intermediates There are excellent cruising runs in all five ski areas shared with Davos.

Beginners There are some nursery lifts at valley level, but the wide sunny slopes of Madrisa are more appealing.

Snowboarding Boarders are better off staying in Davos since Jakobshorn is the established boarder mountain.

Cross-country There are 35km/22 miles of trails and a Nordic ski school offers lessons. Further trails are easily accessible at Davos.

Queues Queues for the Gotschna cable-car have been reduced by a doubling of its capacity, but can still be a problem at weekends – a reporter tells of hour-long morning queues.

Mountain restaurants There are a number of atmospheric huts in the woods above the village.

Schools and guides There is a choice of three ski and snowboard schools.

Facilities for children The ski schools offer classes for children from the age of four and the Madrisa Kids' club takes children aged two to six.

STAYING THERE

How to go There is a wide choice of packages offered by UK tour operators.

Hotels There are some particularly attractive hotels – all bookable on the central reservations phone number, 410 2020. The central Chesa Grischuna (422 2222) is still a firm favourite, combining traditional atmosphere with modern comfort – and a lively après-ski bar. The 3-star Cresta (422 2525) remains popular. The very cosy old Wynegg (422 1340) is popular with British visitors. The Bündnerhof (422 1450), next door, is the recommended choice for the 'budget conscious'.

Eating out Good restaurants abound, but a reporter comments that there is a shortage of the cheap and cheerful variety. Top of the range is the Walserhof. Al Berto's serves the best pizza in town and the rösti at the Alpina is recommended. The Chesa Selfranga is 20 minutes' walk from the centre of town, but is noted for fondue, both cheese and Chinoise.

Après-ski In the village, the Chesa Grischuna is a focus from tea-time onwards, with its live music, bowling and restaurant. A reporter enjoyed the live music 'being played at a volume which allowed you to converse'. The newly rebuilt hotel Vereina is recommended for its piano bar.

Gaudy's at the foot of the slopes is a popular pit stop after skiing, as is the lively bar at the four-star Alpina and the warmly panelled Wynegg.

The Casa Antica is a small disco that livens up on Saturday night. The Kir Royal, under the hotel Silvretta Park, is bigger and more brash.

Off the slopes Klosters is an attractive base for walking and cross-country skiing. There is a sport and leisure centre, and some hotels have pools. An excursion by train to the spa at Scuol Tarasp is recommended by one reporter, another suggests a local trip to the spa in the hotel Bad Serneus.

Flims 1100m/3,610ft

A splendid, spacious area that should be better known outside Switzerland

WHAT IT COSTS

HOW IT RATES

The slopes

Snow	★★★
Extent	★★★★
Experts	★★★
Intermediates	★★★★★
Beginners	★★★★
Convenience	★★★
Queues	★★★
Restaurants	★★★

The rest

Scenery	★★★
Resort charm	★★★
Off-slope	★★★

➕ Extensive, varied slopes suitable for all but experts, shared with Laax

➕ Impressive lift system

➕ Virtually queue-free on weekdays

➕ Fair number of slopes above 2000m/6,500ft, partly offsetting effects of their sunny south-east orientation

➕ Lots of wooded runs for bad-weather days

➕ Just 90 minutes from Zürich airport

➖ Though well intentioned, the unique piste grading system is confusing

➖ Sunny orientation can cause icy or slushy pistes and shut lower runs

➖ Village very spread out, which detracts from its charm, and means long walks or bus-rides to lifts from much of the accommodation

➖ Very subdued in the evenings

➖ Weekend crowds

Flims has an impressive 220km/137 miles of mainly intermediate pistes. The resort is very popular with weekenders and has some high-capacity lifts which help it cope. It can be very quiet during the week, and is virtually unknown outside the Swiss and German markets. Some scatologically minded English-speakers may be put off by the local dialect – all the peaks are called crap, a top après-ski venue is the Crap Bar – but they're making a mistake.

The place has always had some real, more important drawbacks but, amazingly, the major one has been created by the lift company: a unique and bizarre piste classification system. This Slope System™ means that formerly black and red runs have become green (to signify 'Allround Slope' – apparently for carving), red now means 'Freestyle Slope', off-piste areas are shaded yellow. American-style black diamonds have appeared next to runs of all shades. Blue means beginner pistes, but blue off-piste areas also seem to be marked. Orange means a link or home run – no clue as to difficulty. This is all mad, bad and dangerous. Until it's dropped, only those who can tackle any slope should think of going here.

435

What's new

The children's Dreamland is being further developed for 2002/03.

The youth/boarding oriented Riders Palace Hotel (Edition II) – the 'first high tech hotel in the Alps' – has opened in Laax.

The resort

Flims is made up of two parts 1km/0.5 miles apart on a sunny, wooded mountain terrace. Dorf sprawls along a busy road lined with shops, hotels, restaurants, bars and the main lift station. Waldhaus is a more sedate huddle of hotels quietly set in the trees. Both parts look traditional, with wooden chalet-style buildings.

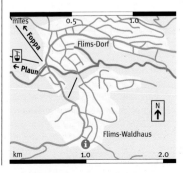

The slopes spread across the mainly south-east-facing mountain to another lift base-station at Murschetg (1.5km/1 mile from Waldhaus), an outpost of Laax. From here there's an efficient jumbo gondola and a less efficient cable-car – this is the easiest entry point for those with cars. There's also a high-speed quad at Falera, 5km/3 miles from Waldhaus.

New Technology Centres, now at all three lift bases, offer a package of ski clothing and equipment rental by the day – turn up in city clothes and get all you need from SF115, including lift pass and a shower after you finish.

It may seem best to stay near the lifts in Dorf, but in practice the better hotels in Waldhaus (and remote bits of Dorf) are well worth considering – they run efficient courtesy buses to and from the slopes. These satisfy most guests, especially as there's not much to tempt you into town after dinner.

AIN FACTS

∂ 1100m-3020m
3,610ft-9,910ft
╵   29
Pistes   220km
              137 miles
Blue   29%
Red   45%
Black   26%
(% refers to old map
and conventional
colour gradings – see
right for new system)
Snowmaking   13km
              8 miles
Recco detectors used

LIFT PASSES

2001/02 prices in
Swiss francs
Alpine Arena
Covers all lifts and
buses between Flims,
Laax and Falera.
Main pass
1-day pass 59
6-day pass 301
Senior citizens
Over 65 (men) or 62
(women): 6-day pass
241
Children
Under 17: 6-day pass
251
Under 13: 6-day pass
151
Under 6: free pass
Short-term passes
Half day from 12.15
(adult 48).
Alternative passes
One day Pipe & Park
pass for Crap Sogn
Gion 35.
Beginner passes for
limited lifts in Flims,
Laax (both 35) and
Falera (30).
Notes Free Alpine
Arena Clubcards can
get you discounts on
passes – register on
the Internet at
www.alpenarena.ch/
clubcard/eng/register.
htm or in resort. You
need a Clubcard to
claim senior citizen or
teenager (Jackdaw)lift
pass discounts. You
get extra points on
the Clubcard, which
can be exchanged for
further discounts
when you spend
money in the Alpine
Arena.

The mountains 🏔️

Flims has extensive, varied slopes: some long runs and some high, exposed peaks (which can be very windswept), including a small glacier. Because of its sunny aspect, lower runs can deteriorate quickly, making it difficult to get back to Flims on snow (there is some snowmaking). In poor visibility there are plenty of tree-lined runs. Trips are possible to Lenzerheide, Davos-Klosters and Arosa.

Flims now grades its slopes according to its own innovative Slope System™: yellow for 'backcountry' (or off-piste), red for 'freestyle', blue for 'beginner', green for 'allround', orange for 'dorfpiste' (home run). Difficult slopes are indicated by black diamonds – two for difficult and three for very difficult. So, for instance, the formerly black Sattel run from the Vorab glacier is marked green with two black diamonds. We regard this system as confusing and dangerous. In our map, we have continued to use the conventional grading of the resort's previous piste map.

The new map does, however, show the time it takes to ride each lift – an excellent idea that makes meeting others on time very easy.

THE SLOPES
Impressive and well planned

There are essentially four sectors, each good for all grades but expert. Slopes are well planned, and getting around is easy but can mean a lot of traversing.

The gondola from Flims has two mid-stations, the first at Plaun, where you change cabins or catch a fast six-person chair to **Crap Sogn Gion** at the heart of the Laax slopes. From here you can go towards Murschetg, Laax or Falera or catch a cable-car up to **Crap Masegn**. This is the biggest area.

If, instead, you continue in the

gondola there's another mid-station at Scansinas before the top at Nagens – alighting at either will allow you to get over to **La Siala**, from where there's a run to the high **Vorab glacier**.

There is also a link via a two-way, two-stage gondola (which can be closed by wind) between the Vorab glacier and Crap Masegn. And there's a slope linking Crap Masegn with Plaun.

The **Cassons** sector above Flims Dorf is the smallest, particularly when runs to the village are incomplete. It is reached via two chairs and a cable-car and linked to Nagens and Grauberg.

SNOW RELIABILITY
Good higher up

The upper runs are generally snow-sure. But due to the sunny aspect, the runs back to Flims itself can suffer. There is snowmaking on three main runs from Crap Sogn Gion, including the splendid black race course run right down to Murschetg. There is also snowmaking from Segnes-Hütte to Flims and on the bottom part of the run to Alp Ruschein.

FOR EXPERTS
Bits and pieces

There is a fair amount to challenge, but it's rather scattered about, with the added frustration that some of it is on short sections of otherwise easy pistes. The toughest run is the steep, unpisted Cassons run to the bottom of its cable car, reached by a steep climb from the top of the cable-car. Other off-piste trips from this summit might look tempting, but we'd recommend hiring a guide (they get three black diamonds on the new piste map). Throughout the area the off-piste is generally between pistes (and is now marked in yellow on the piste map).

One of the great pleasures of the area is the men's World Cup Downhill course (formerly a black run, now marked green on the piste map) from

boarding *Flims/Laax is a snowboard hot spot. Crap Sogn Gion is a popular meeting point, with plenty of loud music from the outdoor Rock Bar and the No-Name Café, which overlook two of four half-pipes on the mountain – their walls can be built to an amazing 6.7m/22ft with the worldbeating Pipe Monster. A Pipe & Park day pass is available if that's all you're into, but the slopes are well suited to all levels of rider. As the slopes close, the Crap Bar at Murschetg is popular. The Arena in Flims is good for live gigs. The Riders Palaces in Murschetg and Mountain Hostel up the mountain at Crap Sogn Gion have great value accommodation. Flims/Laax also hosts lots of international snowboarding events.*

Crap Sogn Gion to Murschetg. It's so long (1000m/3,300ft vertical) and pretty that doing it repeatedly using the Murschetg cable-car doesn't get boring. And the Sattel piste from Vorab – see For Intermediates – is long and beautiful. The Nagens-Startgels run is short but steep.

FOR INTERMEDIATES
Paradise for all
In general this is a superb area for all intermediates. When conditions allow, the area just above Flims is splendid for easy cruising. But a real highlight for early intermediates is a trip to the Vorab glacier and back on easy intermediate runs. On the way back you can take the cable-car down from Grauberg to Startgels to avoid steeper slopes.

For more adventurous intermediates there's a wonderful descent of over 1700m/5,580ft vertical if you start at La Siala and go all the way down to Flims. One of the two unpisted runs from Cassons is a lovely trip along the shoulder of the mountain into a valley and on to Startgels – but check snow conditions first and be warned, there's a hike to get to it. The run from Crap Sogn Gion to Larnags via Curnius is also great fun.

Good intermediates will enjoy the superb, long and beautiful Sattel run from the glacier to Ruschein at the extreme west of the area. It starts with a challenging mogul field but develops into a fast cruise.

The Crap Sogn Gion to Plaun routes are interesting, being quite steep and sheltered – and are some of the few runs not to face the sun directly.

Less confident intermediates should note that some easy runs have short steep sections. The links from Nagens towards Flims can be intimidating.

FOR BEGINNERS
Plenty of options
There's a good nursery area in Dorf, and alternatives at Startgels and Nagens if snow is poor. The Foppa and Naraus areas have good confidence-building runs to move on to. Getting the bus to the lovely easy runs above Falera is another option for those just off the nursery slopes. There are plenty of lessons in English.

FOR CROSS-COUNTRY
One of the best
An excellent choice. There are 70km/43 miles of beautiful, well marked, mainly forest trails. Loops range from 3km to 20km (2 miles to 12 miles). Another fine 60km/37-mile network starts near Laax. The ski school, centred at Waldhaus, has a good reputation and organises group classes. 3km/2 miles of trail are floodlit. The only drawback is the possibility of poor snow.

QUEUES
Some delays
There is generally little queuing during the week, but we have had a report of long waits for the Cassons, Crap Sogn Gion and Crap Masegn cable-cars. At weekends, with coach loads of day

Flims

437

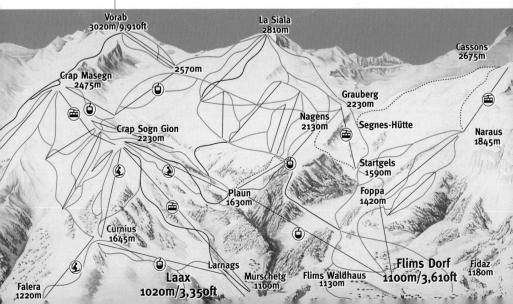

Vorab
3020m/9,910ft

La Siala
2810m

Cassons
2675m

Crap Masegn
2475m

2570m

Grauberg
2230m

Crap Sogn Gion
2230m

Nagens
2130m

Segnes-Hütte

Naraus
1845m

Startgels
1590m

Plaun
1630m

Foppa
1420m

Curnius
1645m

Larnags

Flims Dorf
1100m/3,610ft

Fidaz
1180m

Murschetg
1100m

Flims Waldhaus
1130m

Falera
1220m

Laax
1020m/3,350ft

SCHOOLS/GUIDES

2001/02 prices in
Swiss francs

Swiss
Classes 5 days
3hr
5 full days: 260
Children's classes
Ages: up to 12
5 full days: 340 with
lunch
Private lessons
Full day 320

CHILDCARE

The ski school runs
ski kindergartens
(Dreamlands) taking
children from age 4 –
in Flims, Laax and
Falera from 9.30 to
11.30 and 1.30 to
3.30.

Several hotels claim
special facilities for
children – the Park
Hotel Waldhaus has
its own nursery.

GETTING THERE

Air Zürich, transfer
1½hr.

Rail Chur (22km/14
miles); regular buses
to resort.

visitors arriving at Murschetg, the lifts
there get crowded. But delays out of
Flims in the morning are rare. The chair
towards La Siala can generate queues,
as can the slow two-person Alp
Ruschein chair and some T-bars. Lifts
closing because of wind (especially up
to Cassons) has been a common
complaint among reporters.

MOUNTAIN RESTAURANTS
Good, wide selection

Mountain restaurants are numerous
and generally good. The large
cafeterias at Curnius, Sogn Gion and
Vorab are clean, efficient and serve
good wholesome food. Nagens has a
place with great views, a sun terrace
and live music, but the nicest refuges
are lower down, such as The Spaligna
below Foppa and the Startgels Hütte
above Foppa. We had a great lunch
(with electronic ordering) in the rustic
Tegia by the Murschetg gondola mid-
station at Larnags. The Runcahöhe,
where the Stretg piste flattens out and
crosses the path down from Startgels,
is another good cosy cabin. For a more
expensive menu the restaurant at Crap
Masegn is highly recommended.

SCHOOLS AND GUIDES
Plenty of English instruction

The school has a good reputation and
standards of English are reported to be
good too. They offer Early Bird specials
on empty pistes followed by breakfast
– a great North American concept not
generally available in Europe.

FACILITIES FOR CHILDREN
Good Dreamland centres

Children aged three and over (skiers or
not) can be looked after at one of
three Dreamland centres in Dorf,
Murschetg and Falera. The facilities
have recently been extended. For
children under three the resort can
recommend qualified nannies.

Staying there

HOW TO GO
Few tour operators

Only a handful of UK tour operators
feature Flims.
Hotels The majority are either 3-star or
simple B&B places. Of six top hotels,
five are in Waldhaus.
((((5 **Park** (928 4848) Enormous and
very comfortable, but rather institutional,
5-star in wooded grounds at Waldhaus.
Efficient courtesy bus. Pool.
(((4 **Adula** (928 2828) Big 4-star in
Waldhaus, highly recommended by
recent reporters. Good pool. 'Superb
food and service,' says reporter.
(((4 **Sunstar Surselva** (911 1121) Part
of the reliable Sunstar chain but run in
a rather more institutionalised way
than most. Quiet situation in Waldhaus
with excellent new spa facilities.
(((3 **Grischuna** (911 1139) Pretty little
3-star just outside Dorf, close to lifts.
(((3 **Cresta** (911 3535) Rave review:
'Helpful staff, fabulous spa facilities
and food, unpretentious family hotel.'
(((3 **Curtgin** (911 3566) Attractive, quiet
place on edge of town, quite near lifts.
(((3 **Albana Sporthotel** (911 2333)
Modern 3-star beside lifts, with focal
après-ski bar.
(((3 **Waldeck** (911 1228) Neat 3-star in
Waldhaus, with pleasant restaurant.
Self-catering The tourist office has a
long list of available apartments, which
you can view and book on the website.

EATING OUT
Varied options

Most Flims restaurants are in hotels.
The National, by the bus station, has
good fish dishes. The Meiler hotel
restaurant also has a good reputation.
For something a bit different, go up to
the Spaligna mountain restaurant and
use the toboggan run to get home.
Little China is a good Chinese, and the
Alpina Garni (Waldhaus) is very good
value, does good pizzas and is 'busy
and fun', says a recent reporter.

APRES-SKI
Not a strong point

Flims is very quiet après-ski. The
Spaligna trip mentioned under Eating
Out is the highlight of the week. The
Iglou bar at the base of the Flims
gondola is packed when the slopes
close, as is the Stenna-Bar, opposite,
which has a tea dance. Just across the
road the Albana Pub is popular with a

Laax has retained a lot of its original character →

ACTIVITIES

Indoor Large public swimming pool and over 20 hotel pools (many open to the public), saunas, 4 indoor tennis courts, covered hall with ice skating and 4 curling rinks, fitness centres (including Prau La Selva), table tennis, whirlpool, solarium
Outdoor 60km of cleared paths, riding, natural skating rinks, curling, sleigh rides, toboggan runs, ski-bob, paragliding, hot-air ballooning, hang-gliding, go-karting, snow-shoeing, helicopter flights and night skiing

Phone numbers
From elsewhere in Switzerland add the prefix 081.
From abroad use the prefix +41 81.

FLIMS TOURIST OFFICE

Postcode CH-7017
t 920 9200
f 920 9201
tourismus@alpen arena.ch
www.alpenarena.ch

LAAX TOURIST OFFICE

Postcode CH-7031
t 921 8181
f 921 8182
tourismus@alpen arena.ch
www.alpenarena.ch

FALERA TOURIST OFFICE

Postcode CH-7153
t 921 3030
f 921 4830
tourismus@alpen arena.ch
www.alpenarena.ch

young crowd. Later, the focal spot is also in Dorf, at the hotel Bellevue's Caverna, an atmospheric old wine vault. The Angel is a late-night club. The Park hotel is the centre of limited action in Waldhaus, having an old cellar with entertainer, and the Chadafo bar with dancing to live music. At Murschetg, the Crap Bar is lively when the slopes close and Casa Veglia has live bands and dancing.

OFF THE SLOPES
Lots to do
There are plenty of things to do. The enormous sports centre has a huge range of activities, including shooting – and 'guest cards' from hotels and the tourist office provide a discount. There are extensive (60km/37 miles) marked walks, some through the ski areas. Historic Chur is a short bus-ride away, and there are other excursions to be done. The Glacier Express train from Chur to Andermatt takes you through some wonderful scenery.

STAYING UP THE MOUNTAIN
Hostel St John
The Crap Sogn Gion Mountain Hostel, 1100m/3,610ft above Murschetg in the centre of the slopes, has budget 4-bedded rooms as well as single and double. You can also stay above Flims in the more traditional Berghaus Nagens.

Laax 1020m/3,350ft

Laax is a quiet, spacious old farming community which has retained a lot of its original character. Most of its modern development has taken place

a short bus-ride away at Murschetg, a modern, functional complex at the base of the lifts. The oldest house in Laax dates from 1615, and the setting is pleasant enough, but the old village is no more than routinely charming.
Laax has its own school and ski kindergarten.
The Laaxerhof (920 8200) and Signina (927 9000) are Murschetg 4-stars. The 4-star Arena Alva (927 2727) is a more attractive building in the old village, with transport to the lifts. The charming, central old Posta Veglia (921 4466) has a lively stubli and piano bar. A good central B&B is the Cathomen (921 4545). The two Riders Palaces (927 9000) offer dorm accommodation at a bargain price at the base station.
Restaurants and bars are mostly hotel-based. The Laaxer Bündnerstuben in the Posta Veglia is best for a meal in traditional surroundings. The limited nightlife centres around the Bistro Bar in the Capricorn hotel, live music in the Vallarosa Bar or Laaxerhof, and, again, the Posta Veglia. At Murschetg the Crap Bar gets packed when the lifts close – popular with snowboarders.

Falera 1220m/4,000ft

Along the road from Flims, beyond Laax, lies the tiny village of Falera, a quiet traffic-free place, with two old churches. Sitting on a sunny plateau, it has good views over three valleys. Two successive fast quad chairs take you to the heart of the slopes.
Accommodation is mostly in apartments, but the Siala (927 2222) is a large 3-star hotel with pool. Its Spielkeller is the only real nightspot.

Flims

439

Grindelwald 1035m/3,400ft

Traditional mountain town in spectacular scenery at the foot of the Eiger

WHAT IT COSTS

HOW IT RATES

The slopes
Snow	**
Extent	***
Experts	**
Intermediates	*****
Beginners	***
Convenience	**
Queues	**
Restaurants	***

The rest
Scenery	*****
Resort charm	****
Off-slope	****

➕ Dramatically set in magnificent scenery directly beneath the towering north face of the Eiger

➕ Lots of long, gentle runs, ideal for intermediates, with links to Wengen

➕ Pleasant old village with long mountaineering history, though the tourist trade now sets the tone

➕ Fair amount to do off the slopes, including splendid walks and recently expanded toboggan runs

➖ Village gets very little midwinter sun

➖ Few challenging pistes for experts

➖ Inconvenient for visiting Mürren

➖ Snow-cover unreliable

➖ Major area accessed by a slow gondola, queue-prone especially at weekends, and by very slow and infrequent trains – life revolves around timetables

For stunning views from your hotel window and from the pistes, there are few places to rival Grindelwald, and two of them are just over the hill. The village is nowhere near as special as Wengen or Mürren, but staying here does give you direct access to Grindelwald's own First area. But you can spend hours queueing for, waiting for or sitting in the gondola or trains up into the Kleine Scheidegg area shared with Wengen. (The gondola ride takes over half an hour.) Grindelwald regulars accept all this as part of the scene, and some elderly skiers even find it adds to the holiday by enforcing a slow pace.

What's new

A new high-speed quad chair will replace the old Schilt T-bar at the top of the First area for 2002/03.

The sports centre has added a sauna and steam room to its pool and other facilities.

There is a new Intersport rental network which covers the whole Jungfrau region and allows you to change rental equipment easily. See Wengen chapter for details.

The resort

Grindelwald is set either side of a road along a narrow valley. Buildings are mainly traditional chalet-style. Towering mountains rise steeply from the valley floor, and the resort and main slopes get very little sun in January.

Grindelwald can feel very jolly at times, such as during the ice-carving festival in January, when huge ice-sculptures are on display along the main street. The village is livelier at night than the other Jungfrau resorts of Wengen and Mürren. There's live music in several bars and hotels, but it isn't a place for bopping until dawn.

The main lifts into the slopes shared with Wengen are at Grund, right at the

bottom of the sloping village. Near the opposite end of the village, a gondola goes to the separate First area. Trains run between the centre and Grund, and buses link the lift stations – but these get congested at times and reporters say they are too infrequent.

The most convenient place to stay for the slopes is at Grund. But this is out of the centre and rather charmless. There's a wide range of hotels in the heart of the village, handy enough for everything else, including the First area, at the foot of which are nursery slopes, ski school and kindergarten.

Trips to other resorts are not very easy, but you can drive to Adelboden. Getting to the tougher, higher slopes of Mürren is a lengthy business unless you go to Lauterbrunnen by car.

The mountains

The major area of slopes is shared with Wengen and offers a mix of wooded slopes and open slopes higher up. The smaller First area is mainly open, though there are wooded runs to the village. The Aletsch glacier which can be seen from the Jungfraujoch station (see feature panel later in this chapter) has been declared a UNESCO World Nature Heritage Site.

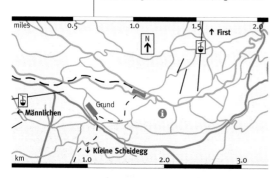

MOUNTAIN FACTS

Altitude	945m-2970m
	3,100ft-9,740ft
Lifts	44
Pistes	213km
	133 miles
Blue	30%
Red	50%
Black	20%
Snowmaking	34km
	21 miles
Recco detectors used	

LIFT PASSES

2002/03 prices in
Swiss francs

**Jungfrau Top Ski
Region**
Covers all 44 lifts and
213km/133 miles of
pistes in Wengen,
Mürren and
Grindelwald, trains
between them and
Grindelwald ski-bus.
Beginners Points
card: adult 100 points
(50), lifts cost 7 to 13
points.
Main pass
1-day pass 55
6-day pass 282
Senior citizens
Over 62: 6-day pass
254
Children
16 to 19: 6-day 226
Under 16: 6-day pass
141 Under 5
accompanied by an
adult free.
Short-term passes
Single ascent tickets
for most lifts. Half-day
pass for Kleine
Scheidegg-
Männlichen-First
(adult 42) and
Mürren-Schilthorn
(adult 42).
Alternative periods
3 days in 7 pass
available (170).
Notes
Day pass price is for
Kleine Scheidegg-
Männlichen-First area
only (160km/100
miles) of pistes, 30
lifts, as Jungfrau Top
Ski Region pass is
only available for 2
days or over.
Alternative passes
Non-skiers pass: adult
6-day pass 212.

boarding *There is a terrain-park and a half-pipe at Oberjoch and a super-pipe at Schrekfeld on First. Intermediates will enjoy the area most – the beginners' slopes can be bare, while experts will hanker for Mürren's steep, off-piste slopes. Nightlife caters mainly for the affluent, middle-aged visitor.*

THE SLOPES
Broad and mainly gentle
From Grund, near the western end of town, you can get to **Männlichen** by an appallingly slow two-stage gondola or to **Kleine Scheidegg** by an even slower cog railway. The slopes of the separate south-facing First area are reached by a long, slow three-stage gondola starting a bus-ride east of the centre. From all over the slopes there are superb views, not only of the Eiger but also of the Wetterhorn and other peaks. Piste marking is poor, and one reporter complains that from First it is difficult to determine which run you are on and therefore easy to end up at the wrong point in the valley, a bus-ride from where you want to be.

SNOW RELIABILITY
Poor
Grindelwald's low altitude (the slopes go down to below 1000m/3,300ft and few are above 2000m/6,500ft) and the lack of much snowmaking mean this is not a resort to book far in advance. And it's not the place for a late-season holiday. First is sunny, and so even less snow-sure than the main area.

FOR EXPERTS
Very limited
The area is quite limited for experts. The black run on First beneath the gondola back to town is quite tough, especially when the snow has suffered from too much sun – late in the season, the run is one of the first to

close. See also the Wengen chapter.
Heli-trips with mountain guides are organised if there are enough takers.

FOR INTERMEDIATES
Ideal intermediate terrain
In good snow, First makes a splendid intermediate playground, though the general lack of trees makes the area less friendly than the larger Kleine Scheidegg–Männlichen area. The runs to the valley are great fun. Nearly all the runs from Kleine Scheidegg are long blues or gentle reds. On the Männlichen there's a choice of gentle runs down to the mid-station of the gondola up from Grund. In good snow, you can get right down to the bottom on easy red runs – 'barely deserving the grade', says a reporter (and one of these runs used to be marked black).
For tougher pistes, head for the top of the Lauberhorn lift and the runs to Kleine Scheidegg, or to Wixi (following the start of the downhill course). You could also try the north-facing run from Eigergletscher to Salzegg, which often has the best snow late in the season.

FOR BEGINNERS
In good snow, wonderful
The nursery slope is friendly and scenic, just above the village, but in late season it can suffer from the sun and low altitude. There are splendid

For close-up views of dramatic peaks, it's difficult to beat Grindelwald ↓

Grindelwald

441

THE JOURNEY TO THE TOP OF EUROPE

From Kleine Scheidegg you can take a train through the heart of the Eiger to the highest railway station in Europe – Jungfraujoch at 3454m/11,332ft.

The journey itself is a bit tedious – you're in a tunnel most of the time. You stop part way up to look out of a viewing gallery carved into the sheer north face of the Eiger, with magnificent views down the valley and over to Männlichen. At the top is a big restaurant complex. There's a fascinating 'ice palace' carved in the glacier with beautiful ice sculptures and slippery walkways, an outdoor 'plateau' to wander around and a panoramic viewing tower called the Sphinx, from which you have fabulous views of the Aletsch glacier (a UNESCO World Heritage Site).

The return trip costs SF48 if you have a Jungfrau lift pass for three days or more, but SF99.50 if you don't. At almost 3500m the air is thin, and we met people having breathing and balance problems.

CHILDCARE

The ski school takes children from age 3, and they can be looked after at lunchtime in the Children's Club kindergarten at the Bodmi nursery slopes. This takes children from age 3, from 9.30 to 4pm. It apparently ceases to function if snow shortage closes the nursery slopes.

The Sunshine nursery on First takes children from 1 month from 8.30-5pm.

longer runs served by the railway to Kleine Scheidegg, notably the easy scenic blue Mettlen-Grund run, right from the top to the bottom.

FOR CROSS-COUNTRY
Good but shady
There are over 25km/16 miles of prepared tracks. Almost all of this is on the valley floor at around 1000m, so it's very shady in midwinter and may have poor snow later in the season.

QUEUES
Can be dreadful at peak times
The queues for the gondola and train at Grund can be very bad in high season, especially when weekend visitors pour in. One Christmas week

reporter experienced half-hour waits for the Männlichen gondola and long waits for the gondola back down from First, as all the lower runs were closed. Queues for the Oberjoch chair on First should be eased by the new Schilt quad.

MOUNTAIN RESTAURANTS
Wide choice
See the Wengen chapter for restaurants around Kleine Scheidegg and down towards Wengen. Brandegg, on the railway, is recommended for its 'wonderful' apple fritters and sunny terrace. Berghaus Bort does very good rösti, but the 'best rösti anywhere' is at the Jägerstubli, 500m/1,650ft up the road from the Aspen, off the Rennstrecke piste.

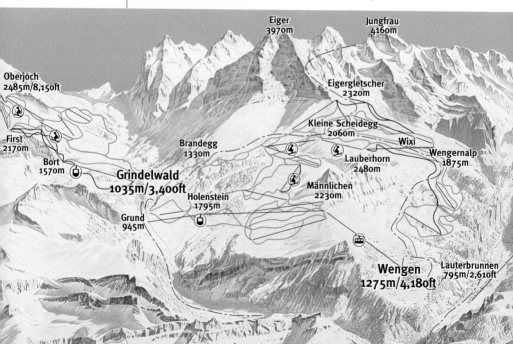

Eiger 3970m
Jungfrau 4160m
Oberjoch 2485m/8,150ft
Eigergletscher 2320m
First 2170m
Kleine Scheidegg 2060m
Wixi
Brandegg 1330m
Bort 1570m
Lauberhorn 248om
Wengernalp 1875m
Grindelwald 1035m/3,400ft
Holenstein 1795m
Männlichen 2230m
Grund 945m
Wengen 1275m/4,180ft
Lauterbrunnen 795m/2,610ft

SCHOOLS/GUIDES

2002/03 prices in
Swiss francs
Swiss
Classes 5 days
5 full days: 255
Children's classes
Ages: 3 to 14
5 full days: 255
Private lessons
2hr or 5hr
180 for 2hr

GETTING THERE

Air Zürich, transfer
3hr. Bern, transfer
1½hr.
Rail Station in resort.

ACTIVITIES

Indoor Sports centre
(swimming pool,
sauna, steam, table
tennis, fitness room,
games room), indoor
skating rink, curling,
bowling, cinema
Outdoor 80km of
cleared paths, train
rides to Jungfraujoch,
tobogganing, snow-
shoe excursions,
cross-country skiing,
sleigh rides,
paragliding, heli-
skiing and boarding,
open-air ice skating,
snowrafting, glacier
tours, husky rides.

Phone numbers
From elsewhere in
Switzerland add the
prefix 033.
From abroad use the
prefix +41 33.

TOURIST OFFICE

Postcode CH-3818
t 854 1212
f 854 1210
touristcenter@
grindelwald.ch
www.grindelwald.ch

SCHOOLS AND GUIDES
One of the better Swiss schools
One report declares the Swiss school
'very good'; spoken English is normally
excellent. It now has some competition
in the form of private lessons from the
Buri Sport school.

FACILITIES FOR CHILDREN
Good reputation
A past reporter who put four children
through the Grindelwald mill praised
caring and effective instructors, and
another rates them 'brilliant'. The First
mountain restaurant runs a day
nursery, which is a neat idea.

Staying there

HOW TO GO
Limited range of packages
The hotels UK tour operators offer are
mainly at the upper end of the market,
but traditional little B&B pensions and
self-catering apartments are widely
available to independent bookers.
Hotels One 5-star, a dozen 4-stars, and
a good range of more modest places is
available.
((((5) **Regina** (854 8600) The one 5-
star. Big and imposing; right next to
the railway station. Nightly music in
the bar. Pool.
((((4) **Belvedere** (854 5454) Family-run,
recently renovated, close to the station
and with a 'wonderful' pool.
((((4) **Schweizerhof** (853 2202)
Beautifully decorated 4-star chalet at
west end of the centre, close to the
station. Pool.
((((4) **Bodmi** (853 1220) Little chalet
right on the village nursery slopes.
(((3) **Hirschen** (854 8484) Family-run 3-
star in central position at foot of
nursery slopes. Good food. Security
can be a problem – one reporter had
skis stolen from the ski room.
(((3) **Fiescherblick** (854 5353)
Hospitable chalet on the eastern fringe
of the village, five minutes from the
First gondola.
(((3) **Derby** (854 5461) Popular, modern
3-star next to station, with 'first-class'
service, good food and great views.
((2) **Tschuggen** (853 1781) Modest
chalet in a central position below the
nursery slopes.
(1) **Hotel Wetterhorn** (853 1218) Cosy,
simple chalet way beyond the village,
with great views of the glacier.
Self-catering One reporter has
recommended the apartments of the
hotel Hirschen (854 8484) for comfort

and space. Another said an apartment
in the hotel Eiger (854 3131) was
'excellent, great value'.

EATING OUT
Hotel based
There's a wide choice of good hotel
restaurants, but cheaper pizzeria-style
places are in short supply. The Latino
does home-made Italian cooking.
Among the more attractively traditional
places are: the Swiss Chalet in the
Eiger; Schmitte in the Schweizerhof;
Challi-Stübli in the Kreuz; and the Alte
Post. The Fiescherblick's Swiss Bistro
is repeatedly recommended – 'brilliant
but expensive'. The Kirchbühl and
Oberland are good for vegetarians, the
Bahnhof in the Derby for fondue and
raclette. Hotel Spinne has many
options: Italian, Mexican, Chinese and
the candlelit Rôtisserie for a special
romantic meal. There's even a
Japanese restaurant, the Samurai.

APRES-SKI
Relaxed
Nightlife is not the special subject of
our Grindelwald reporters, but we can
say that there are at least three discos
and a handful of bars that aim to keep
going late. There's also a cinema, plus
ice hockey and curling matches to
watch. There's an excellent sports
centre with pool. Tobogganing and
tubing are organised on First, and
some evenings a 'Sledge Express' train
takes people up to Brandegg/ Alpiglen
for fondues and tobogganing.

OFF THE SLOPES
Plenty to do, easy to get around
There are many cleared paths with
magnificent views, especially around
the First area – and there's a special
(though expensive) pedestrian bus/lift
pass. A trip to Jungfraujoch is
spectacular (see opposite), and
excursions by train are easy to
Interlaken and possible to Bern.
Tobogganing has undergone a bit of a
renaissance, with runs up 15km on
First (Europe's longest) and 70km of
runs in total. Helicopter flights from
Männlichen are recommended.

STAYING UP THE MOUNTAIN
Several possibilities
See the Wengen chapter for details of
rooms at Kleine Scheidegg. The
Berghaus Bort (853 1762), at the
gondola station in the middle of the
First area, is an attractive alternative.

Grindelwald

443

Surprisingly unpretentious 'exclusive' resort, with extensive, pretty slopes

WHAT IT COSTS

HOW IT RATES

The slopes

Snow	*
Extent	****
Experts	**
Intermediates	***
Beginners	***
Convenience	*
Queues	***
Restaurants	***

The rest

Scenery	***
Resort charm	****
Off-slope	****

What's new

The Diablerets glacier lifts were upgraded two seasons ago.

The Grand Hotel Bellevue is being totally renovated in time for the 2002/03 season.

444

GSTAAD TOURIST OFFICE

There is no shortage of terraces from which to admire the pleasant (rather than spectacular) views ↓

- ➕ Traditional village, traffic-free in centre, without the towny feel of other fashionable Swiss resorts
- ➕ Lift pass covers large area of slopes
- ➕ Good long runs for intermediates
- ➕ Lively après-ski scene
- ➕ Wide range of off-slope diversions, including swanky shops

- ➖ Fragmented slopes, none convenient for central hotels – so you are always using buses and trains
- ➖ Unreliable snow-cover, except on the limited (and distant) Diablerets glacier slopes
- ➖ No budget accommodation
- ➖ Few challenges for experts

Gstaad is renowned as a jet-set resort, but for 'ordinary' holidaymakers, too, it has attractions – especially for those with a relaxed outlook, who can happily spend time on trains looking at the landscape without feeling it's precious piste time wasted. It's just a pity most of the slopes are below 2100m/6,900ft.

THE RESORT

Gstaad is a traditional, year-round resort in a spacious, sunny setting surrounded by a horseshoe of wooded mountains. The main street, lined with hotels, smart shops and cafes, has a pleasant and relaxed feel now that it's traffic-free. The Montreux-Oberland-Bernois (MOB) railway station is only yards away, and accesses the numerous surrounding villages. These are smaller (and cheaper), and with their own lifts form good alternative bases to Gstaad itself. Three areas of slopes are accessed via lifts scattered around the fringes of Gstaad and served by a regular shuttle-bus service.

THE MOUNTAINS

There are four main areas of slopes, covered by a single, very unclear and confusing map. Most of the slopes are below the tree line, with just the top sections reaching above that.

Slopes Wasserngrat (to the east of the

village) and Wispile (to the south) are both small areas with one or two main lifts and runs alongside them. Eggli (to the west) is more complex, and leads via the valley of Chalberhöni to the crags of Videmanette, also accessible by gondola from the rustic village of Rougemont, just over the border into French-speaking Switzerland.

The largest sector is accessed from the lift stations at Saanenmöser and Schönried. The slopes here have for years been linked with those above St Stephan, over the mountain, and more recently have been linked to those above Zweisimmen. Saanenmöser and Schönried are no more inconvenient than Gstaad's local lift stations, given a train timetable. Schönried also has a separate sunny area of slopes on the opposite side of the valley.

The Glacier des Diablerets is also covered by the main area pass but is 15km/9 miles away to the south, with lifts at Reusch and Col du Pillon. There

There is a seriously challenging descent to Rougemont from La Videmanette beneath the gondola, but the usual way down is this lovely valley, away from all the lifts →

SNOWPIX.COM / CHRIS GILL

MOUNTAIN FACTS

Altitude	950m-3000m
	3,120ft-9,840ft
Lifts	66
Pistes	250km
	155 miles
Blue	48%
Red	36%
Black	16%
Snowmaking	12km
	7 miles

Phone numbers
From elsewhere in Switzerland add the prefix 033.
From abroad use the prefix +41 33.

TOURIST OFFICE

Postcode CH-3780
t 748 8181
f 748 8183
gst@gstaad.ch
www.gstaad.ch

are excellent runs below glacier level, but the glacier itself is limited.

Slightly further afield, past Rougemont, but included on the map and connected by rail, are Château d'Oex and Les Moulins – both with their own small ski areas, and included on the main pass.

Snow reliability A lack of altitude means that snow-cover can be unreliable except on the glacier, but most of the slopes are roughly north-facing. A handful of valley runs now have snow-guns.

Experts Few runs challenge experts. Black runs rarely exceed red difficulty, and some should be blue. There are off-piste possibilities – steep ones on the wooded flanks of Wispile and Eggli. Heli-skiing is available.

Intermediates Given good snow, this is a superb area for intermediates, with long, easy descents in the major area to the villages scattered around its edges – that to St Stephan being rather more challenging than most. The run to Rougemont from the top of the Eggli sector is lovely, with no lifts in view. The adventurous should take a trip to the Diablerets glacier for the splendid shady red run down the lift-free Combe d'Audon – an Alpine classic.

Beginners The nursery slopes at the bottom of Wispile are adequate, and there are plenty of runs to progress to.

Snowboarding There's a terrain-park at Eggli, a half-pipe at Zweisimmen and a boarder-cross course at Horneggli.

Cross-country The 60km/37 miles of trails are very pretty, and there are some epic journeys to be done given the stamina. Most loops are low down and can suffer from poor snow; but there are higher loops, notably at the special langlauf centre at Sparenmoos.

Queues Time lost on buses or trains is more of a problem than queues, except at peak times and weekends.

Mountain restaurants Mountain restaurants are plentiful, and most are attractive, although expensive.

Schools and guides English is more widely spoken by the ski school than in many other Brit-free zones. It has a good reputation, too.

Facilities for children There is a ski kindergarten at Schönried, but there are no facilities for non-skiing children.

STAYING THERE

How to go Gstaad is certainly exclusive, with over three-quarters of its accommodation in private chalets and apartments. The remainder of the beds are in 3-star hotels and above.

Hotels The 5-star Palace (748 5000) is extravagantly swish, in secluded grounds. The Bernerhof (748 8844) and the Christiania (744 5121) are recommended 4-stars. The Olden (744 3444) is a charming, central, chalet-style building.

Self-catering There is a wide choice of self-catering accommodation locally.

Eating out Restaurants are mainly hotel-based, and expensive. The Bagatelle in the Grand Chalet and the Chesery are recommended for gourmet meals. The rustic Chlösterli – a massive 350-seat establishment a short drive out – is a popular place to eat and dance. Hotel Rössli is reasonably priced and the locals' bar in the central hotel Olden offers filling, value-for-money meals.

Après-ski In season nightlife is lively both at tea-time and later on.

Off the slopes Gstaad's activities are wide-ranging. The tennis centre and swimming pool complex are impressive. There are toboggan runs, ice skating and 50km/30 miles of pretty cleared walks. Getting around is easy, and excursions by rail to Montreux and Interlaken or even further afield are possible.

Gstaad

445

Mürren
1650m/5,410ft

Stupendous views, an epic run, and a chocolate-box village

446

- ⊕ Tiny, charming, traditional 'traffic-free' village, with snowy paths and chocolate-box chalets
- ⊕ Stupendous scenery, best enjoyed on the challenging run from the panoramic Schilthorn
- ⊕ Good sports centre
- ⊕ Good snow high up, even when the rest of the region is suffering

- ⊖ Extent of local pistes very limited no matter what your level of expertise
- ⊖ Lower slopes can be in poor condition
- ⊖ Quiet, limited nightlife
- ⊖ Like all other Swiss 'traffic-free' villages, Mürren is gradually admitting more service vehicles

Mürren is one of our favourite resorts – for a short visit, at least. There may be other Swiss mountain villages that are equally pretty, but none of them enjoys views like those from Mürren across the deep valley to the rock faces and glaciers of the Eiger, Mönch and Jungfrau: simply breathtaking. And then there's the Schilthorn run, which draws us back like a magnet – 1300m vertical that combines varied terrain and glorious views like no other run we know.

Our visits are normally one-day affairs; holidaymakers, we concede, are likely to want to explore the extensive intermediate slopes of Wengen and Grindelwald, across the valley. And you have to accept that getting there takes time.

It was in Mürren that the British more or less invented modern skiing. Sir Arnold Lunn organised the first ever slalom race here in 1922. Some 12 years earlier his father, Sir Henry, had persuaded the locals to open the railway in winter so that he could bring the first winter package tour here. Sir Arnold's son Peter, who first skied here in November 1916, now skis here with his children and grandchildren. Mürren's that kind of place.

The resort

Mürren is set on a shelf high above the Lauterbrunnen valley floor, across from Wengen, and can be reached only by cable-car from Stechelberg (via Gimmelwald) or funicular and then railway from Lauterbrunnen. Once you get there you can't fail to be struck by Mürren's tranquillity and beauty. The tiny village is made up of paths and narrow lanes weaving between tiny wooden chalets and a handful of bigger hotel buildings. The roofs and paths are normally snow-covered.

Two further stages of the cable-car take you up to the high slopes of Birg and the Schilthorn, nearby lifts go to the main lower slopes, and a recently modernised funicular halfway along the village accesses the other slopes.

Although in our summary above we protest against the gradual 'traffic' increase, Mürren still isn't plagued by electric carts and taxis as most other traditional 'traffic-free' resorts now are. It's not the place to go for lively

nightlife, shopping or showing off your latest gear to admiring hordes. It is the place to go if you want tranquillity and stunning views.

The village is so small that location is not a concern. Nothing is more than a few minutes' walk.

The mountain

Mürren's slopes aren't extensive (53km/33 miles in total). But it has something for everyone, including one of our favourite runs, and a vertical of some 1300m/4,270ft. And those happy to take the time to cross the valley to Wengen–Grindelwald will find plenty of options. These resorts are covered by the Jungfrau lift pass.

THE SLOPES
Small but interesting

There are three connected areas around the village, reaching no higher than 2145m/7,040ft. The biggest is **Schiltgrat**, served by a fast quad chair behind the cable-car station. You can

MOUNTAIN FACTS

Altitude 945m-2970m
3,100ft-9,740ft
Lifts   44
Pistes   213km
                133 miles
Blue   30%
Red   50%
Black   20%
Snowmaking   34km
                21 miles
Recco detectors used

SCHOOLS/GUIDES

2001/02 prices in
Swiss francs

Swiss
Classes 6 days
2hr am
6 half days 135
Children's classes
Ages: 5 and over
2hr am
6 half days: 135
Private lessons
2hr or full day
110 for 2hr; 270 for a
full day.

also get there from the top of the modernised funicular that goes from the middle of the village to the nursery slope at **Allmendhubel** – from where a run and the new chair take you to the slightly higher **Maulerhubel**. Runs go down from here to the Winteregg stop on the railway, too. These lower slopes take you up to around 2000m/6,600ft.

Much more interesting are the higher slopes reached by cable-car. The first stage takes you to Birg and the **Engetal** area, where an old T-bar serves short, steep, shady slopes. Two chair-lifts below the Engetal serve some snow-sure intermediate slopes. But plans for a third chair, back up to Birg, have been shelved. To get back to the Birg cable-car station and avoid the tricky black run down to the village, you face an annoying walk up from these chairs to the old T-bar.

The final stage of the cable-car takes you up to the summit of the **Schilthorn** and the Piz Gloria revolving restaurant, made famous by the James Bond film *On Her Majesty's Secret Service*. In good snow you can go all the way from here to Lauterbrunnen – a distance of almost 16km/10 miles. The Inferno race (see box) takes place over this course, conditions permitting. Below Winteregg it's all boring paths.

The Jungfrau piste map doesn't deal with Mürren's slopes at all well. The one used in the Mürren brochures (on which our own is based) is better.

SNOW RELIABILITY
Good on the upper slopes

The Jungfrau region does not have a good snow record – but Mürren always has the best snow in the area. When Wengen-Grindelwald (and Mürren's lower slopes) have problems, the Schilthorn and Engetal often have packed powder snow because of their height and orientation – north-east to east. Piste grooming has improved in recent years.

FOR EXPERTS
One wonderful piste

The run from the top of the Schilthorn starts with a steep but not terrifying slope, in the past generally mogulled but now often groomed. It flattens into a schuss to Engetal, below Birg. Then there's a wonderful, wide run with stunning views over the valley to the Eiger, Mönch and Jungfrau. Since the chair-lifts were built here you can play on these upper runs for as long as you like. Below the lifts you hit the Kanonenrohr (gun barrel). This is a very narrow shelf with solid rock on

Mürren

447

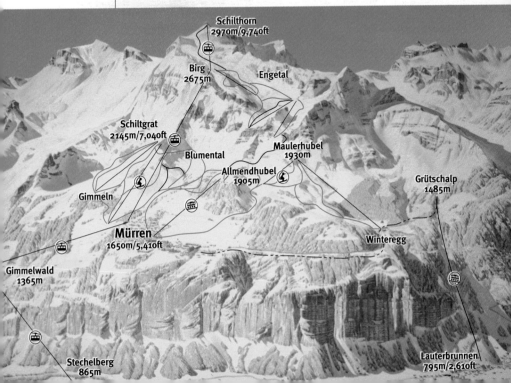

LIFT PASSES

2002/03 prices in Swiss francs

Jungfrau Top Ski Region
Covers all 44 lifts and 213km/133 miles of pistes in Wengen, Mürren and Grindelwald, trains between them and Grindelwald ski-bus.

Beginners Points card: adult 100 points (50), lifts cost 7 to 13 points.

Main pass
1-day pass 55
6-day pass 282

Senior citizens
Over 62: 6-day pass 254

Children
16 to 19: 6-day 226
Under 16: 6-day pass 141 Under 5 accompanied by an adult free.

Short-term passes
Single ascent tickets for most lifts. Half-day pass for Kleine Scheidegg-Männlichen-First (adult 42) and Mürren-Schilthorn (adult 42).

Alternative periods
3 days in 7 pass available (170).

Notes
Day pass price is for Kleine Scheidegg-Männlichen-First area only (160km/100 miles) of pistes, 30 lifts, as Jungfrau Top Ski Region pass is only available for 2 days or over.

Alternative passes
1- and 2-day passes available for First-Kleine and Scheidegg-Männlichen (adult 2-day 102), Mürren-Schilthorn (adult 2-day 100). Non-skiers pass: adult 6-day pass 212.

boarding *Like other Swiss resorts, Mürren has a traditional image, but it is trying to move with the times and offer a more snowboard-friendly attitude. This may be at odds with the resort's usual clientele, but they build a half-pipe and terrain-park every season, and the major lifts are cable-cars and chair-lifts. The terrain above Mürren is suitable mainly for good free-riders – it's steep, with a lot of off-piste routes. Intermediates will find the area tough and limited, but nearby Wengen is ideal and is much better for beginners. At night, Mürren is quiet, with not much scope for raving.*

one side and a steep drop on the other – protected by nets. After an open slope and scrappy zig-zag path, you arrive at the 'hog's back' and can descend towards the village on either side of Allmendhubel.

From Schiltgrat a short, serious mogul run – the Kandahar – descends towards the village, but experts are more likely to be interested in the off-piste runs into the Blumental – both from here (the north-facing Blumenlucke run) and from Birg (the sunnier Tschingelchrachen) – or the adventurous runs from the Schilthorn.

FOR INTERMEDIATES
Limited, but Wengen nearby
Keen piste-bashers will want to make a few trips to the long cruising runs of Wengen-Grindelwald. The best easy cruising run in Mürren is the north-facing blue down to Winteregg. The reds on the other low slopes can get mogulled, and snow conditions can be poor. The area below the Engetal normally has good snow, and you can choose your gradient.

FOR BEGINNERS
Not ideal, but adequate
The nursery slopes at Allmendhubel, at the top of the funicular, are on the steep side. And there are not many

easy runs to graduate to – though the blue down the Winteregg chair is easy, and the Schilt-Apollo blue served by the long Gimmeln drag and the less tiring Schiltgrat chair are ideal.

FOR CROSS-COUNTRY
Forget it
There is one small loop above the village in the Blumental, and more extensive loops down at Lauterbrunnen or Stechelberg. But snow is unreliable at valley height.

QUEUES
Generally not a problem
Mürren doesn't get as crowded as Wengen and Grindelwald, except on sunny Sundays. There can be queues for the cable-cars – usually when snow shortages bring in people from lower resorts. The top stage has only one cabin. The new Allmendhubel funicular goes at twice the speed of the old one.

MOUNTAIN RESTAURANTS
Disappointing at altitude
Piz Gloria revolves once an hour, displaying a fabulous 360° panorama of peaks and lakes, but don't expect particularly good food, or a small bill. By the Engetal chair-lifts, the Schilthorn Hutte is small and rustic.

The views across the Lauterbrunnen valley from Wengen to Mürren are quite amazing →

CHILDCARE

The ski school takes children from age 5.

There is non-skiing childcare in the sports centre for children up to 5 years old for SFR50 per day.

GETTING THERE

Air Zürich, transfer 3½hr. Bern, transfer 1½hr.

Rail Lauterbrunnen; transfer by mountain railway and tram.

ACTIVITIES

Indoor 'Alpine Sports Centre Mürren' swimming pool, whirlpool and children's pool, library, children's playroom, gymnasium, squash, sauna, solarium, steam bath, massage, fitness room **Outdoor** Artificial skating rink (curling, skating), toboggan run to Gimmelwald, 15km/9 miles cleared paths

Phone numbers From elsewhere in Switzerland add the prefix 033. From abroad use the prefix +41 33.

TOURIST OFFICE

Postcode CH-3825
t 856 8686
f 856 8696
info@muerren.ch
www.wengen-muerren.ch

Lower down, the Suppenalp in the Blumental is rustic and quietly set, does 'excellent food' but gets no sun in January. Sonnenburg is sunnier. Gimmelen is a self-service place with a large terrace, famous for its apple cake. Winteregg does something similar, as well as 'the best burger east of the Rockies'. Both have little playgrounds to amuse kids.

SCHOOLS AND GUIDES
Small, not perfectly formed
Reporters speak of good progress for beginners, but also of one English speaker who had a rather lonely week in a group with six Germans.

FACILITIES FOR CHILDREN
Adequate
There is a baby slope with a rope tow. And there is a children's club at the sports centre. The ski school takes children from five years.

Staying there

HOW TO GO
Mainly hotels, packaged or not
A handful of operators offer packages to Mürren.
Hotels There are fewer than a dozen hotels, ranging widely in style.
(((④ **Palace** (855 2424) Victorian pile near station – recently renovated.
(((④ **Eiger** (856 5454) Plain-looking 'chalet' blocks next to railway station, widely recommended; good blend of efficiency and charm; good food; pool.
(((③ **Alpenruh** (856 8800) Attractively renovated chalet next to the cable-car.
(((③ **Edelweiss** (855 1312) Block-like but friendly; good food and facilities.
(((③ **Jungfrau** (855 4545) Perfectly placed for families, in front of the baby slope and close to the funicular.
(② **Alpenblick** (855 1327) Simple, small, modern chalet near station.

Self-catering There are plenty of chalets and apartments in the village for independent travellers to rent.

EATING OUT
Mainly in hotels
The main alternative to hotels is the rustic Stägerstübli – a bar as well as restaurant. The locals eat in the little diner at the back. The food at the Eiger hotel is good, and the Bellevue and Alpenruh get good reports.

APRES-SKI
Not devoid of life
The Eiger Bar (in the Eiger guest house, not the hotel) is the Brits' meeting place. The tiny Stägerstübli is cosy, and the place to meet locals. Other activities are hotel-based. The Palace's Balloon bar is an attempt at a trendy cocktail bar; it also has a weekend disco, the Inferno. The Bliemli Chäller disco in the Blumental caters for kids, the nightly Tachi disco in the Eiger for a more mixed crowd.

OFF THE SLOPES
Tranquillity but not much else
There isn't a lot to amuse people who don't want to hit the slopes. But there is a very good sports centre, with an outdoor ice rink. Excursions by car or train to Interlaken and to Bern are easy. It's no problem for friends to return to the village for lunch. The only problem with meeting at the top of the cable-car instead is the expense.

STAYING DOWN THE VALLEY
A cheaper option
Lauterbrunnen is a good budget place to stay. It has a resort atmosphere and access to and from both Wengen and Mürren until late. We've often stayed at the Schützen (855 3026) and Oberland (855 1241) for a night or two at a time and they are fine.

THE INFERNO RACE

Every January 1,800 amateurs compete in the spectacular Inferno race. Conditions permitting, and they usually don't, the race goes from the top of the Schilthorn right down to Lauterbrunnen – a vertical drop of 2175m/7,140ft and a distance of almost 16km/10 miles, incorporating a short climb at Maulerhubel. The racers start in pairs at 30-second intervals and the fastest finish the course in around 15 minutes, but anything under half an hour is very respectable.

The race was started by Sir Arnold Lunn in 1928 when he and his friends climbed to the top of the Schilthorn, spent the night in a mountain hut and then raced down in the morning. For many years the race was organised by the British-run Kandahar Club, and there is still a strong British presence among the competitors.

Saas-Fee 1800m/5,910ft

Beautiful, car-free village with slopes on top of the world

What's new

A family offer will be extended to the 2002/03 season – children aged up to 16 ski for free if two adults buy a 6-day pass or a 5-days-in-7 pass. An Internet access area next to the Alpin Express and called Cyber Lion will be open daily from 9am to 11pm.

450

➕ Spectacular setting amid peaks and glaciers – slopes open year-round

➕ Traditional, 'traffic-free' village

➕ Good percentage of high-altitude, snow-sure slopes

➕ Powerful lift access to highest slopes for year-round skiing

➕ Good off-slope facilities – even a mountain specially for walking and tobogganing

➖ Disappointingly small area of slopes, with mainly easy runs

➖ Glacier stops off-piste exploration

➖ Much of the area is in shadow in midwinter – cold and dark

➖ Bad weather can shut the slopes

➖ Long village can mean quite a bit of walking to and from the slopes

➖ Some visitors suffer altitude problems at top of mountain

Saas-Fee is one of our favourite places. It oozes Swiss charm, and the setting is stunning – spectacular glaciers and 4000m peaks surround the place. And good snow is guaranteed, even late in the season: the altitude you spend most of your time at – between 2500m and 3500m (8,200ft and 11,500ft) – is unrivalled in the Alps.

But we tend to drop in for a couple of days at a time, so the limited extent of the slopes never becomes a problem; for a week's holiday, it would. Top to bottom there is an impressive 1800m/5,900ft vertical – but there aren't many alternative ways down. Keen, mileage-hungry intermediates should look elsewhere, as should experts (except those prepared to go touring). For the rest, it's a question of priorities and expectations. Over to you.

The resort

Like nearby Zermatt, Saas-Fee is a high-altitude mountain village centred on narrow streets lined by attractive old chalets and free of cars (there are car parks at the resort entrance) but not free of electric milk floats posing as taxis. On most other counts, Saas-Fee and its more exalted neighbour are a long way apart in style.

There are some very smart hotels (plus many more modest ones) and plenty of good eating and drinking places. But there's little of the glamour and greed that, for some, spoil Zermatt – and even the electric taxis here are driven at a more considerate pace. Saas-Fee still feels like a village, with its cow sheds more obviously still containing cows. The village may be chilly in January, but when the spring sun is beating down, Saas-Fee is a quite beautiful place in which to just stroll around and relax, admiring the impressive view.

Depending on where you're staying and which way you want to go up the mountain, you may do more marching than strolling. It's a long walk from one

end of the spread-out village to the other, though your hotel may run a courtesy bus to and from the lifts. Three major lifts start from the southern end of the village, at the foot of the slopes, and lots of the hotels and apartments are 1km or more away. The modern Alpin Express starts below the centre, though, quite near the entrance to the resort.

The village centre has the school and guides' office, the church and a

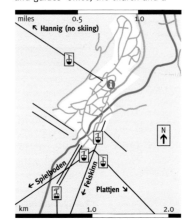

MOUNTAIN FACTS

Altitude 1800m-3600m
5,910ft-11,820ft

Lifts	32
Pistes	125km
	75 miles
Blue	25%
Red	50%
Black	25%
Snowmaking	12km
	7 miles
Recco detectors used	

LIFT PASSES

2002/03 prices in
Swiss francs

Saas-Fee area
Covers all lifts in
Saas-Fee only.
Beginners Village
area pass covers 5
beginners' lifts. 1-day
22, 6 days 90
Main pass
1-day pass 60
6-day pass 290
Children
Under 16: 6-day pass
174
Under 6: free pass
Short-term passes
Single and return
tickets on most main
lifts. Half-day pass
from noon (adult 47).
Notes Discount for
groups of 20 or more.
Alternative passes
Separate passes for
each of the other ski
areas in the Saastal
(Saas-Grund, Saas-
Almagell, Saas-Balen).
Pass for all four
villages in the Saastal
also available, and
includes ski-bus
between them. 6-day
pass, 314.

few more shops than elsewhere, but
doesn't add up to much. On a sunny
day, though, the restaurant terraces
fronting the nursery slopes at the far
end of the village are a magnet, with
breathtaking views up to the ring of
4000m/13,000ft peaks – you can see
why the village is called 'The Pearl of
the Alps'.

Staying near a main lift makes most
sense. If you do end up at the wrong
(north) end of the village – and most
budget accommodation is there – ease
the pain by storing kit near the lifts.

The slopes of Saas-Almagell and
Saas-Grund are not far away, and you
can buy a lift pass that covers all these
resorts and buses between them. Day
trips to Zermatt, Grächen and Crans-
Montana are also realistic options for
those itching for a change.

The mountain

The area is a strange mixture of
powerful new lifts (a two-stage 30-
person gondola followed by an
underground funicular which take you
up 1700m/5,580ft vertical) and a lot of
old-fashioned t-bars (there's only one
chair-lift). Many visitors complain about
this, and about fragmented layout of
the slopes: 'the drag-lifts can be
exhausting – especially the one that
takes over 15 minutes'. But the reason
for these complaints is also Saas-Fee's
strong point – its snow-sure glacier
slopes. The glacier can move downhill
by 100m/330ft a year and drag-lift
pylons can be moved to cope, but
chair-lifts are not practicable.

The upper slopes are largely gentle,
while the lower mountain, below the
glacier, is steeper and rockier.

Saas-Fee is one of the leading
resorts for mountaineering and ski-
touring. Several nearby peaks can be
climbed, and the extended Haute
Route from Chamonix ends here.

The top of the funicular at 3500m/
11,500ft means some suffer faintness
there because of the thin air.

Saas-Fee

451

THE SLOPES
A glacier runs through it

The main **Felskinn** area can be reached
in three ways. The efficient 30-person
Alpin Express jumbo gondola takes you
to Felskinn, starting across the river
from the main village. It has a mid-
station at Maste 4 (where you have to
change cabins).

The Felskinn cable-car, starting a
short drag-lift away from the foot of
the main pistes and nursery slopes at
the southern end of the village, also
takes you to Felskinn.

From Felskinn, the Metro Alpin (an
underground funicular) hurtles to the
thin air at Mittelallalin. From below
here the top two drag-lifts access the
high point of 3600m/11,820ft.

Also from the south end of the
village, a gondola leaves for
Spielboden. This is met by a cable-car
which takes you up to **Längfluh**.

Between Felskinn and Längfluh is an
off-limits glacier area. A very long drag-
lift from Längfluh takes you to a point

boarding *Saas-Fee encourages boarding in a big way. In summer, in
particular, its glacier slopes are dominated by boarders. Facilities
include a half-pipe, a fun-park and a boarder-cross. The nearby Maste 4 snow-
bar is the place for a break. While the gentle glacier slopes are ideal for learning,
only main access lifts are boarder-friendly (gondolas, cable-cars and a funicular);
nearly all the rest are drags. There are a couple of specialist schools. Expert free-
riders may be frustrated by the limits imposed on off-piste riding by the glacier.
But nightlife doesn't disappoint – the Popcorn board shop and bar is popular.*

where you can get down to the Felskinn area. These two sectors are served mainly by drag-lifts, and you can get down to the village from both.

Another gondola from the south end of the village goes up to Saas-Fee's smallest area, **Plattjen**.

SNOW RELIABILITY
Good at the highest altitudes
Most of Saas-Fee's slopes face north and many are above 2500m/8,200ft, making this one of the most reliable resorts for snow in the Alps. The glacier is open most of the year. Visitors tell us that the substantial recent investment in snow-guns still doesn't completely ensure good coverage on the rocky lower slopes, though piste grooming is 'excellent'. Conversely, after heavy snowfalls you may find yourself limited to the nursery area for a while.

FOR EXPERTS
Not a lot to keep your interest
There is not much steep stuff, except on the bottom half of the mountain where the snow tends not to be as good. The highest drag-lift on the left near Felskinn serves two short, steep blacks and one easy one. The slopes

around the top of Längfluh often provide good powder and there are usually moguls above Spielboden. The blacks and trees on Plattjen are worth exploring. The glacier puts limits on the local off-piste even with a guide – crevasse danger is extreme. But there are extensive touring possibilities, especially late in the season.

FOR INTERMEDIATES
Great for gentle cruising
Saas-Fee is ideal for early intermediates and those not looking for much of a challenge. For long cruises, head for Mittelallalin. The top of the mountain, down as far as Längfluh in one direction, and as far as Maste 4 in the other, is ideal, with usually excellent snow. Gradients range from gentle blues to slightly steeper reds which can build up smallish bumps.

'Beautiful, wide blue and red cruising runs accessed by the drag between Maste 4 and Felskinn,' is typical of reporters' comments.

The 1800m/5,900ft vertical descent from Mittelallalin (via Felskinn or Längfluh) to the village is a great test of stamina – or, if you choose, an enjoyable long cruise with plenty of view stops. The lower runs have

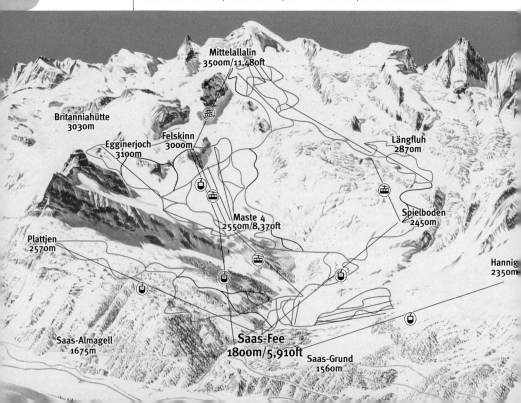

Mittelallalin
3500m/11,480ft

Britanniahütte
3030m

Felskinn
3000m

Egginerjoch
3100m

Längfluh
2870m

Maste 4
2550m/8,370ft

Spielboden
2450m

Plattjen
2570m

Hannig
2350m

Saas-Almagell
1675m

Saas-Fee
1800m/5,910ft

Saas-Grund
1560m

There is something beautifully Swiss about the idea of a revolving restaurant – and all three pivoting pubs in the Alps are in Switzerland. 'Customers not getting a share of the views? Can't have that. Only one thing for it: spin the whole restaurant about once an hour.' Actually, they spin only the bit of floor with the tables on it; the stairs stay put (along with the windows – watch your gloves).

Two years after Saas-Fee built the Alps' highest funicular railway in 1984, it crowned that with the world's highest revolving restaurant – a good 500m/1,650ft higher than the famous original on Mürren's Schilthorn. We don't rate the views from Mittelallalin so highly. But it's an amusing novelty that most visitors enjoy. To reserve a table next to the windows phone 957 1771. And the third spinning speisesaal? At Leysin.

SCHOOLS/GUIDES

2002/03 prices in
Swiss francs

Swiss
Classes 5 days
3hr (10am-1pm) 46
5 days (15hr) 172
Children's classes
5-day ski courses
including lunch, from
age 3
Private lessons
Hourly or daily
58 for 1hr for 1 or 2
people

SNOWPIX.COM / CHRIS GILL

These crevasses in
the glacier severely
limit Saas Fee's off-
piste potential, and
mean you ride drag-
lifts rather than chairs
➔

steepish, tricky sections and can have poor snow, especially if it isn't cold enough to make snow – timid intermediates might prefer to take a lift down from mid-mountain.

Plattjen has a variety of runs, all of them fine for ambitious intermediates and often underused.

FOR BEGINNERS
Usually a nice place to start
There's a good, large, out-of-the-way nursery area at the edge of the village. Those ready to progress can head for the gentle blues on Felskinn just above Maste 4 – it's best to return by the Alpin Express. There are also gentle blues at the top of the mountain, from where you can head down to Längfluh. Again, use the lifts to return to base.

A useful beginners' pass covers all the short lifts at the village edge, for those not ready to go higher.

FOR CROSS-COUNTRY
Good local trail and lots nearby
There is one short (8km) pleasant trail at the edge of the village. It snakes up through the woods, providing about 150m of climb and nice views. There are more options in the valley.

QUEUES
Only problems at peak times
Lift improvements seem to have done their job and queues are now rare except at peak times. Most reports this year say there were no problems except at the 10am morning peak when ski school starts. But things can be different at busy times of the year. One Easter visitor this year found 'it could take 75 minutes to reach the upper slopes and then queues for all the drag-lifts were very long'.

MOUNTAIN RESTAURANTS
Fair choice, but not like Zermatt
The restaurants at the main lift stations are functional. The best places are slightly off the beaten track: the Berghaus Plattjen (just down from Plattjen) and the Gletschergrotte, halfway down from Spielboden (watch for the path from the piste). Both have good food in old huts. If you're up for a trek, the Britanniahütte is a real mountain refuge, with atmosphere and views. The restaurant at the top of Plattjen has 'friendly service and the best rösti in the resort'. At Spielboden there's 'good food', a terrace and views of tricky slopes. At Längfluh the large terrace has spectacular views of huge crevasses, and Popcorn Plaza nearby is popular. Maste 4 has 'cheap and very good' pizza. Back in the village, the sunny, piste-side terrace of the Waldesruh Hotel serves 'wonderful' rösti and the terrace of the Belmont is a popular sunbathing spot.

CHILDCARE

The Bären-Klub (Bears Club) kindergarten takes children for full days or half days. From age 3, they can go here in the morning and to ski school in the afternoon. Full junior ski school starts at age 4. Lunchtime care and meals can be provided with all programmes.

There's also a children's day centre for kids aged 2 to 6 in Saas Grund.

GETTING THERE

Air Sion, transfer 1hr. Geneva, transfer 3½hr. Zürich, transfer 4hr. Milan, transfer 3hr.

Rail Brig (38km/24 miles); regular buses from station.

ACTIVITIES

Indoor Bielen leisure centre (swimming, hot-tub, steam bath, whirlpool, solarium, sauna, massage, tennis, gym), cinema, museum, concerts, badminton

Outdoor 30km/19miles cleared paths, natural skating rink (skating, curling, ice hockey), toboggan run, paragliding

Phone numbers
From elsewhere in Switzerland add the prefix 027.
From abroad use the prefix +41 27.

TOURIST OFFICE

Postcode CH-3906
t 958 1858
f 958 1860
to@saas-fee.ch
www.saas-fee.ch

SCHOOLS AND GUIDES
No choice

For skiing, it's the Swiss school or nothing. This year we have had a report of an instructor who was 'very critical and gave little constructive advice'. And a beginner was 'not at all impressed; the instructor left weaker members of the group in a restaurant to make their own way down by lift while he skied down to the village with the bolder members of the group'. On the other hand, we heard from another beginner who had 'excellent tuition'.

FACILITIES FOR CHILDREN
Good reports

The school takes children from four years old, and most of the reports we have had have been positive – 'most classes quite small and English spoken', 'their instructor was strict but they had a fabulous time'. But classes of as many as 15 were spotted. One solution for younger ones is to stay at a hotel with an in-house kindergarten.

Staying there

HOW TO GO
Check the location

Quite a few UK tour operators sell holidays to Saas-Fee. But there are surprisingly few chalet holidays.

Hotels There are over 50.

((((⑤ **Fletschhorn** (957 2131) Elegant chalet in woods, with original art and individual rooms, a trek from the village and lifts, but fabulous food.

(((④ **Walliserhof** (958 1900) Excellent 4-star. Superb, friendly welcome and service, delicious dinners, champagne breakfast. Spa.

(((④ **Schweizerhof** (957 5159) Stylish, in quiet position above the centre. 'Fantastic food, friendly staff, excellent kindergarten, wonderful service.' Pool.

((③ **Beau-Site** (958 1560) 'First-rate' but quiet 4-star in central, but not convenient, position. Good food. Pool.

((③ **Saaserhof** (957 3551) Modernised old chalet in good position, over river from nursery slopes. Sauna, whirlpool.

((③ **Alphubel** (957 1112) At the wrong end of town, praised by reporters for its own 'brilliant nursery'.

((③ **Waldesruh** (957 2232) Strongly recommended by a reporter: 'Best situation for the Alpin Express.'

((③ **Hohnegg** (957 2268) Small rustic alternative to the Fletschhorn, in a similarly remote spot.

(② **Belmont** (958 1640) The most appealing of the hotels looking directly on to the nursery slopes.

Self-catering Most apartments featured by UK operators are at the north end of the village, remote from the slopes, but they are generally spacious and well equipped. Independent travellers can choose better situated apartments.

EATING OUT
Good variety – but book a table

One reporter this year emphasised that you need to reserve a table in advance as restaurants get very busy. Gastronomes will want to head for the highly acclaimed Fletschhorn – expensive but excellent. Our favourite is the less formal Bodmen along a path into the woods. It has great food (from rösti to fillet steak) and rustic ambience. We had a delicious Thai meal in one of the Walliserhof's several restaurants. Boccalino is cheap and does pizzas – book or get there early. Alp-Hitta specialises in rustic food and surroundings. The hotel Dom's restaurant specialises in endless varieties of rösti. Arvu-Stuba, Zur Mühle, Gorge, Feeloch, Skihütte and Ferme have all been recommended.

APRES-SKI
Excellent and varied

Late afternoon, Nesti's ski-bar, Zur Mühle and the little snow-bars such as Black Bull, near the lifts, are all pretty lively, especially if the sun's shining. Later on, Nesti's and the Underground keep going till 1am. Popcorn is packed and praised for 'lively atmosphere, brilliant music and catering for all ages'. The Art Club is smarter and more sophisticated, with live music. The Metro Bar is like being in a 19th-century mine shaft; Why Not pub is popular; The Metropol has the Crazy Night disco and a couple of other bars.

OFF THE SLOPES
A mountain for pedestrians

The whole of the Hannig mountain is dedicated to walking, tobogganing and paragliding – skiers and boarders are banned. In the village, the splendid Bielen leisure centre boasts a 25m/80ft pool, indoor tennis courts and a lounging area with sunlamps. There's also the interesting Saas museum and the Bakery Museum, where children can make bread. Don't miss the largest ice pavilion in the world, carved out of the glacier at Mittelallalin and including a wedding chapel.

St Moritz 1770m/5,810ft

Luxury living – on and off the flatteringly easy slopes

WHAT IT COSTS

(6)

HOW IT RATES

The slopes

Snow	****
Extent	*****
Experts	****
Intermediates	****
Beginners	**
Convenience	**
Queues	**
Restaurants	****

The rest

Scenery	****
Resort charm	*
Off-slope	*****

What's new

The Alpine World Ski Championships are to be held in St Moritz from 1 to 16 February 2003 and the event has prompted improvements to road access, lift updating, more snowmaking and refurbishment of all the 5-star hotels.

For 2002/03 a new, faster 100-person cable-car from Corviglia to Piz Nair will replace the old queue-prone 40-person one.

A high-speed six-pack will replace the FIS and Pitschen T-bars on Corviglia.

For 2001/02 there were two new high-speed quads on Corviglia.

And on Fridays, 9km of floodlit slopes opened at Corvatsch with a 'great party atmosphere' till 2am.

SWISS-IMAGE.CH

The scenery is spectacular and the town doesn't look as bad when it's covered in snow (this is the prettiest part though)
→

- ➕ Beautiful panoramic scenery
- ➕ Off-slope activities second to none – including the Cresta Run, horse-racing and lots of varied festivals
- ➕ Extensive, mainly intermediate slopes
- ➕ Fairly snow-sure, thanks to altitude and extensive snowmaking
- ➕ Good après-ski, for all tastes
- ➕ Good mountain restaurants, some with magnificent views
- ➕ Painless rail access via Zürich

- ➖ Some hideous block buildings
- ➖ A sizeable town, with little traditional Alpine character
- ➖ No proper nursery slopes at resort level – except at Celerina
- ➖ Several unlinked mountains, with a bus, train or car needed to most
- ➖ Runs on two main mountains all fairly easy and much the same
- ➖ Expensive

St Moritz is Switzerland's most famous 'exclusive' winter resort: glitzy, expensive, fashionable and, above all, the place to be seen – it's the place for an all-round winter holiday with an unrivalled array of different diversions, including such wacky pursuits as polo, golf and cricket on snow, and gourmet and music festivals. The slopes on the two main mountains are almost uniformly easy intermediate – we don't rate St Moritz highly for complete beginners, and experts must be prepared to venture off-piste. But for cross-country, it is superb.

The town of St Moritz doesn't have the chocolate-box image of a Swiss mountain resort, all wooden huts and cows with bells round their necks. Many buildings resemble council flats (extremely neat and clean ones – it is Switzerland, after all).

But you may find, as some readers have, that St Moritz's spectacular setting, beside the lowest in a long chain of lakes at the foot of the 4000m/13,000ft Piz Bernina, blinds you to the town's aesthetic faults. This is one of those areas where our progress on the mountain is regularly interrupted by the need to stand and gaze. It may not have quite the drama of the Jungfrau massif, or the Matterhorn, or the Dolomites, but its wide and glorious mountain landscapes are equally special. And the langlauf, walking and other activities on the frozen lake give it a real 'winter wonderland' feel.

The resort

St Moritz has two distinct parts. Dorf is the fashionable main part, on a steep hillside above the lake. It has two main streets lined with boutiques selling Rolex watches, Cartier jewellery and Hermes scarves, a few side lanes and a small main square. A funicular takes you from Dorf to the main slopes of Corviglia, also reached by gondola from down the road at Celerina, and by cable-car from Dorf's other half, the spa resort of St Moritz Bad, spread around one end of the lake.

Everything in Bad is less prestigious. Many of the modern buildings are uncompromisingly

455

Come and go
top class with
Alps4U.com
or Tel:
0845 069 9900

LIFT PASSES

2002/03 prices in
Swiss francs

Upper Engadine
Covers all lifts in St
Moritz, Celerina,
Surlej, Sils Maria,
Maloja, Lagalb,
Diavolezza,
Pontresina, Punt
Muragl, Samedan,
Müsella and Zuoz,
and the swimming
pools in St Moritz and
Pontresina.
Main pass
1-day pass 66
6-day pass 314
Children/teenagers
Age 16-20: 6-day pass
283
Under 16: 6-day pass
157
Under 6: free pass
Short-term passes
Half-day pass from
11.45 (adult 55).
Notes Prices are for
high season. Mid-
season adult 6-day
pass 294; low season
261. Child reductions
too. Deposit of SF5
gets you a hands-free
pass. Six-day pass
gives one day's skiing
in Livigno.
Alternative passes
Half-day and day
passes for individual
areas within the
Upper Engadine.

skiclub.co.uk
0845 45 807 80
skiers@skiclub.co.uk

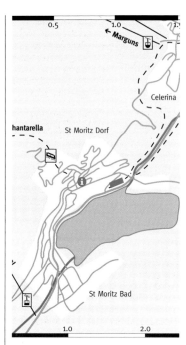

rectangular and spoil otherwise superb
views. In winter the lake is used for
eccentric activities including horse and
greyhound racing, show jumping, polo,
'ice golf' and even cricket. It also
makes a superb setting for walking
and cross-country skiing.

Other downhill slopes, at Corvatsch,
are reached via lifts at Surlej and Sils
Maria. Cross-country skiing is the main
activity around the outlying villages of
Samedan and Pontresina.

The town's clientele is typified by
the results of a Cresta Run race we
saw on one of our visits. In the top 29
were three Lords, one Count, one
Archduke and a Baronet.

For high society and a better choice
of bars and restaurants, stay in Dorf.
Bad has the advantage that you can
get back to it from Corvatsch and
Corviglia. Celerina is another option.

The mountains

Like the resort, most of the slopes are
made for posing. There are lots of long,
wide, well-groomed runs, with varied
terrain. There's an occasional black
run, but few are seriously steep. But
there is tough off-piste, and it doesn't
get tracked out as it does in more
macho resorts. Beginners' slopes are
few and far between. Trips to other
resorts such as Klosters, Davos (both
around 90 minutes by train or car) and
Livigno (an hour by car) are possible.

THE SLOPES
Big but broken up
The several distinct areas add up to a
substantial 350km/217 miles of pistes.
The main slopes, shown on our maps,
are nearby Corviglia-Marguns and
Corvatsch-Furtschellas, a bus-ride away
(you can get back to Bad on snow).
But some of the more distant slopes
are well worth an outing. It helps to
have a car, although the free bus
service is reported to be fairly efficient.

From St Moritz Dorf a two-stage
monorail goes up to **Corviglia**, a fair-
sized area with slopes facing east and
south. The peak of Piz Nair, reached
from here by a new cable-car, splits
the area – sunny runs towards the main
valley, and less sunny ones to the
north. From Corviglia you can head
down (snow permitting) to Dorf and
Bad, and via the lower lift junction of
Marguns to Celerina.

From Surlej, a few miles from St
Moritz, a two-stage cable-car takes you
to the north-facing slopes of **Corvatsch**.
From the mid-station at Murtèl you
have a choice of reds to Margun-Vegl
and Alp Margun. From the latter you
can work your way to **Furtschellas**, also
reached by cable-car from Sils Maria.

Diavolezza (2980m/9,780ft) and
Lagalb (2960m/9,710ft), the main
additional areas, are on opposite sides

boarding *Despite the high prices and its glitzy image, the terrain in St
Moritz is boarder-friendly and there's a special boarders' booklet
with recommended 'secret spots', 'natural freestyle' and beginner areas. On
Corviglia there is a half-pipe above the Signal area and there are two terrain-
parks in the Corvatsch/Furtschellas area (though a reporter this year 'thought the
pipe poor and didn't see any prepared terrain-park on Corvatsch'). The Corvatsch
area has links that rely on drags – otherwise, most lifts are chairs, gondolas,
cable-cars and trains. The extent of well-groomed cruising runs should appeal to
any hard-booter, and there are several specialist snowboard shops. At night, there
are a few places you don't have to wear a dinner jacket to get in.*

SWITZERLAND

456

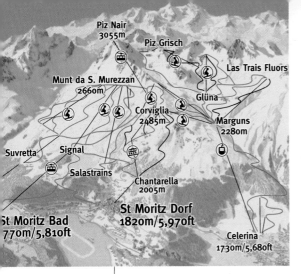

Piz Nair 3055m
Piz Grisch
Las Trais Fluors
Munt da S. Murezzan 2666m
Glüna
Corviglia 2485m
Marguns 2280m
Suvretta
Signal
Salastrains
Chantarella 2005m
St Moritz Bad 770m/5,81oft
St Moritz Dorf 1820m/5,97oft
Celerina 1730m/5,68oft

of the road to the Bernina pass to Italy, less than half an hour away by bus. **Diavolezza** has excellent north-facing pistes of 900m/2,950ft vertical, down under its big 125-person cable-car, and a very popular and spectacular off-piste route off the back, across a glacier and down a valley beneath Piz Bernina to Morteratsch. **Lagalb** is a smaller area with quite challenging slopes, with an 80-person cable-car serving the west-facing front slope of 850m/2,790ft vertical.

SNOW RELIABILITY
Reasonable
This corner of the Alps has a rather dry climate, but the altitude means that any precipitation is likely to be snowy. There is snowmaking in every sector: several easy slopes around Corviglia

are covered, as is an excellent 800m vertical run on Corvatsch (Murtèl to Surlej), much of Diavolezza and part of Lagalb. A regular reporter says that 'every season conditions have been better on Corviglia than on Corvatsch, despite its more southerly orientation.'

FOR EXPERTS
Dispersed challenges
If you're looking for challenges, you're liable to find St Moritz disappointing on-piste. Red runs (many of which should really be classified blue) far outnumber the black, and mogul fields are few and far between. The few serious black runs are scattered about in different sectors.

The blacks at Lagalb and Diavolezza are the most challenging pistes. The direct Minor run down the Lagalb cable-car has 850m/2,800ft vertical of non-stop moguls.

There are plenty of opportunities to venture a little way off-piste in search of challenges – there is an excellent north-facing slope immediately above the Marguns lift junction, for example. Experts often head for the tough off-piste runs on Piz Nair or the Corvatsch summit. More serious expeditions can be undertaken – such as down the splendid Roseg valley from Corvatsch. The off-piste potential is all the better for being relatively little exploited.

FOR INTERMEDIATES
Good but flattering
St Moritz is great for intermediates. Most pistes on Corviglia and Corvatsch are very well-groomed, easyish reds

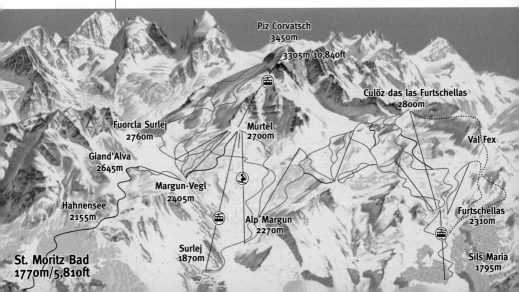

Piz Corvatsch 3450m
3305m/10,84oft
Culöz das las Furtschellas 2800m
Fuorcla Surlej 2760m
Murtèl 2700m
Val Fex
Giand'Alva 2645m
Margun-Vegl 2405m
Alp Margun 2270m
Hahnensee 2155m
Furtschellas 2310m
Surlej 1870m
Sils Maria 1795m
St. Moritz Bad 1770m/5,81oft

MOUNTAIN FACTS

Altitude 1730m-3300m
5,680ft-10,830ft

Lifts	56
Pistes	350km
	217 miles
Blue	16%
Red	71%
Black	13%
Snowmaking	70km
	43 miles

Recco detectors used

SCHOOLS/GUIDES

2001/02 prices in
Swiss francs

St Moritz
Classes 6 days
4hr 10am-noon and
1.30-3.30
1 half day 45
6 full days 250
Children's classes
Ages: from 4
6 full days 250
Private lessons
Half-day (2hr) or full-
day (5hr)
180 for half-day

Suvretta
Small groups of 4 to
6 people
Classes 6 days
2hr, 3hr, 4hr or full
day (5hr)
6 full days 270

that could well have been classified blue. Ideal cruising terrain. As one reporter said this year, 'as ideal as can be imagined for intermediates'.

One of the finest runs for adventurous intermediates is Hahnensee, from the northern limit of the Corvatsch lift system at Giand'Alva down to St Moritz Bad – a black-classified run that is of red difficulty for most of its 6km/4 mile length and 900m/2,950ft vertical drop. It's a five-minute walk from the end of the run to the cable-car up to Corviglia. (But note that a reporter found this run 'closed during our visits in each of the last three years'.)

Diavolezza is mostly intermediate. There is an easy open slope at the top, served by a fast quad, and a splendid long intermediate run back down under the lift. The popular off-piste run to Morteratsch requires a bit of energy and nerve. After a gentle climb, you cross the glacier on a narrow ledge, with crevasses waiting to gobble you up on the right. When we last did it, there were ice-picks and shovels at intervals along the path, put there by the enterprising proprietors of the beautifully laid out, welcoming ice bar which greets you at the end of the 30-minute slog. After that, it's downhill through the glacier, with splendid views. Lagalb has more challenging pistes.

FOR BEGINNERS
Not much to offer

St Moritz is not ideal for beginners. It sits in a deep, steep-sided valley, with very little space for nursery slopes at the lower levels. Beginners start up at Salastrains or Corviglia, or slightly out of town, at Suvretta. Celerina has good, broad nursery slopes at village level. Progression from the nursery slopes to intermediate runs is rather awkward – these always include a difficult section.

FOR CROSS-COUNTRY
Excellent; go to Pontresina

The Engadine is one of the premier regions in the Alps for cross-country, with 150km/90 miles of trails, including floodlit loops, amid splendid scenery and with pretty reliable snow. The famous Engadine Ski Marathon is held here every March – over 12,000 racers take part. Pontresina makes a great base, with lots of other activities.

QUEUES
Not much of a problem

St Moritz has invested heavily in new lifts lately. Once you get up the mountain, Corviglia has high-speed chairs everywhere. But the area as a whole has a lot of cable-cars – both for getting up the mountain from the resort and for access to peaks from mid-mountain. Queues can result, though reporters have had good experiences lately – the enlarged cable-car from Surlej to Murtèl is a big improvement, as will be the new one to Piz Nair. The top Corvatsch cable-car will probably generate the biggest queues this coming season. Happy reporters comment that St Moritz's visitors are often late risers, and that lunch can signal the end of skiing – leaving the slopes pretty clear at the start and end of the day. 'Peak period is 11am to 12.30pm, and congestion can be a problem above Marguns on Corviglia and on the run down from Murtèl on Corvatsch,' says a reporter.

MOUNTAIN RESTAURANTS
Some special places

Mountain restaurants are plentiful, and include some of the most glamourous in Europe. Prices can be high, and reservations are advisable. But there are plenty of cheaper places too.

On Corviglia, the gourmet highlight is the Marmite; but it is outrageously

THE CRESTA RUN

No trip to St Moritz is really complete without a visit to the Cresta Run. It's the last bastion of Britishness (until recently, payment had to be made in sterling) and male chauvinism (women have been banned since 1929 – unless you can secure an invitation from a club member for the last day of their season).

Any adult male can pay around £200 for five rides on the famous run (helmet and lunch at the Kulm hotel included). Watch out for the Shuttlecock corner – that's where most people come off, and the ambulances ply for trade. You lie on a toboggan (aptly called a 'skeleton') and hurtle head-first down a sheet ice gully from St Moritz to Celerina. David Gower, Sandy Gall and many others are addicts. Fancy giving it a go?

CHILDCARE

The St Moritz ski school operates a pick-up service for children. St Moritz and Suvretta schools provide all-day care.

Children aged 3 or more can be looked after in the Schweizerhof hotel nursery, open from 9am to 5.30.

GETTING THERE

Air Zürich, transfer 3hr (or fly into small Upper Engadine airport 5km away).

Rail Mainline station in resort.

ACTIVITIES

Indoor Curling, swimming, sauna, solarium, golf driving range, tennis, squash, museum, health spa, cinema (with English films), aerobics, beauty farm, health centre, casino, Rotary International club
Outdoor Ice skating, sleigh rides, ski jumping, toboggan run, hang-gliding, golf on frozen lake, Cresta run, 180km/112 miles cleared paths, greyhound racing, horse-riding and racing, polo tournaments, cricket tournaments, ski-bob run, paragliding, skydiving, kite-sailing on frozen lake, ice-skating, curling

expensive. And it is housed in the Corviglia lift station, known locally as the highest post office in Switzerland because of its bright yellow paint. Much better for charm is the Paradiso, with glorious panoramic views from the terrace, the inviting terrace of the Chamanna and the Lej de la Pesch behind Piz Nair. A reader recommends Mathis for 'first-class food and wine'.

On the Corvatsch side, we've heard good reports about the self-service place at the top and the sunny Sternbar, with live music, at the bottom of Rabguisa. Fuorcla Surlej is delightfully secluded, as is Hahnensee, on the lift-free run of the same name down to Bad – a splendid place to pause in the sun on the way home. On stormy days, most captivating is the rustic Alpetta, near Alp Margun (table-service inside).

The hotel-restaurant up at Muottas Muragl, between Celerina and Pontresina, is well worth a visit. It has truly spectacular views overlooking the valley, as well as good food.

Morteratsch restaurant (at the end of the off-piste run from Diavolezza) is splendid – sunny, by the cross-country area and tiny railway station, and with excellent, good-value food.

SCHOOLS AND GUIDES
Internal competition

As well as the St Moritz and Suvretta schools, there is The Wave snowboarding school and The St Moritz Experience, for heli-trips. A free 'ski safari' is offered on Thursdays, something we've only seen in North America before. Some hotels have their own instructors for private lessons.

FACILITIES FOR CHILDREN
Choose a hotel with a nursery

Children wanting lessons have a choice of schools, but others must be deposited at a hotel nursery. Club Med has its usual good facilities.

Staying there

HOW TO GO
Several packaged options

Packages are available, but many people make their own arrangements. There is a Club Med – its all-inclusive deal cuts the impact of high prices. The tourist office can provide a list of apartments.
Hotels Over half the hotels are 4-stars and 5-stars – the highest concentration of high-quality hotels in Switzerland.

We don't like any of the famous 5-stars or their jacket-and-tie policies. If made to choose we'd prefer the glossy, secluded Carlton or even more secluded Suvretta House to the staid Kulm or Gothic Badrutt's Palace.
((((**Crystal** (836 2626) Big 4-star in Dorf, as close to the Corviglia lift as any. Recently renovated and now part of the 'Small Luxury Hotels' group.
((((**Schweizerhof** (837 0707) 'Relaxed' 4-star in central Dorf, five minutes from the Corviglia lift, with 'excellent food and very helpful staff'.
((((**Albana** (836 6161) 4-star in Dorf, with walls adorned with big game trophies bagged by proprietor's family.
(((**Monopol** (837 0404) Good value (for St Moritz) 4-star in centre of Dorf. Excellent buffet breakfasts. Pool, sauna.
(((**Nolda** (833 0575) One of the few chalet-style buildings, close to the cable-car in St Moritz Bad.
((**Bellaval** (833 3245) A two-star between the station and the lake.

EATING OUT
Mostly chic and expensive

It's easy to spend £50 a head eating out in St Moritz – without wine – but you can eat more cheaply. We liked the excellent Italian food at the down-to-earth Cascade in Dorf and the three restaurants in the Chesa Veglia. A reporter this year had a 'week of gourmet eating. The two top restaurants, Jöhri's Talvo at Champfèr and Bumann's

SWITZERLAND

Phone numbers
From elsewhere in Switzerland add the prefix 081.
From abroad use the prefix +41 81.

ST MORITZ TOURIST OFFICE
Postcode CH-7500
t 837 3333
f 837 3377
information@stmoritz.ch
www.stmoritz.ch

CELERINA TOURIST OFFICE
Postcode CH-7505
t 830 0011
f 830 0019
info@celerina.ch
www.celerina.ch

PONTRESINA TOURIST OFFICE
Postcode CH-7504
t 838 8300
f 838 8310
info@pontresina.com
www.pontresina.com

Chesa Pirani in La Punt both approach the top restaurants in London or Paris for quality and price – we spent SF200 a head in each. We also liked the rustic Landhotel Meierei, in a bay of the lake opposite Bad.'

Try an evening up at Muottas Muragl for the spectacular views, splendid sunset and unpretentious dinner.

APRES-SKI
Caters for all ages
There's a big variety of après-skiing age groups here. The fur coat count is high – people come to St Moritz to be seen.

At tea-time, head for Hanselmann's 'fabulous tea and strudels'. We've also heard good things about Café Hauser.

The pub-style Bobby's Bar (with Internet access), and the Prince (with a 'disco/lounge') attract a young crowd, as does the loud music of the Stübli, one of three bars in the Schweizerhof: the others are the Muli, with a country and western theme and live music, and the chic Piano Bar. The Cresta, at the Steffani, is popular with the British, while the Cava below it is louder, livelier and younger. It is also amusing to put on a jacket and tie and explore bars in Badrutt's Palace and the Kulm.

The two most popular discos are Vivai (expensive) at the Steffani, and King's at Badrutt's Palace (even more expensive; jackets and ties required). And if they don't part you with enough cash, try the Casino.

OFF THE SLOPES
Excellent variety of pastimes
Even if you lack the bravado for the Cresta Run, there is lots to do. In midwinter the snow-covered lake provides a playground for bizarre events (see earlier in chapter) but in March the lake starts to thaw. There's an annual 'gourmet festival', with chefs from all over the world.

Some hotels run special activities, such as a curling week. Other options are hang-gliding, indoor tennis and trips to Italy (Milan is four hours by car). There's a public pool in Bad. St Moritz gets a lot of sun – 322 sunny days a year, they claim – so lounging on sunny terraces is popular.

STAYING UP THE MOUNTAIN
Excellent possibilities
Next door to each other at Salastrains are two chalet-style hotels, the 3-star Salastrains (833 3867), with 60 comfy beds, and the slightly simpler and much smaller Zauberhütte (833 3355). Great views, and no queues.

Celerina 1730m/5,680ft
At the bottom end of the Cresta Run, Celerina is unpretentious and villagey, if quiet, with good access to Corviglia. It is sizeable, with a lot of second homes, many owned by Italians (the upper part is known as Piccolo Milano). There are some appealing small hotels (reporters suggest Chesa Rosatsch 837 0101) and a couple of bigger 4-stars.

Pontresina 1805m/5,920ft
Pontresina is small and sedate and an excellent base for the extensive cross-country skiing on its doorstep.

It's a sheltered, sunny village with one main street, spoiled by the usual sanatorium-style architecture. Pontresina's own hill, Languard, has a single long piste.

Much is made of Pontresina being cheaper to stay in than St Moritz, but cheaper doesn't mean cheap. But there is a Club Med here (offering its usual all-inclusive deal). Dining is mostly hotel-based and nightlife is quiet.

Verbier
1500m/4,920ft

Paradise for nightlife-loving powder hounds with cash

➕ Extensive, challenging slopes with a lot of off-piste potential and some good bump runs

➕ Lively, varied nightlife

➕ Sunny, panoramic setting, and upper slopes offer real high-mountain feel plus great views

➕ Wide range of chalet holidays

➕ Hardly any drag-lifts in Verbier (though still lots in linked resorts)

➕ Fewer queues than there used to be

➕ Good advanced-level lessons

➕ Much improved piste grooming in recent seasons

➖ Overcrowded pistes in certain areas

➖ Sunny lower slopes will always be a problem, even with snowmaking

➖ Still some serious queues, particularly on 4 Valleys links

➖ Piste map and direction signposting still hopelessly inadequate

➖ Busy traffic (and fumes) in centre

➖ Some long walks/rides to lifts

➖ Easily accessed off-piste slopes get tracked out very quickly

➖ The 4 Valleys network is no rival for the Three Valleys in France

➖ Pretty expensive

What's new

For 2002/03 the jumbo Funitel gondola from Les Ruinettes to Les Attelas will have an extra 25% capacity.

The two-stage gondola from Le Châble to Verbier and on to Les Ruinettes, has already been upgraded – though the capacity remains modest.

Verbier's first six-pack will replace the Saxon chair and Nord drag on the back of the Savoleyres ridge.

There is new snowmaking capacity in La Chaux and the lower part of La Tzoumaz.

There is no doubt that Verbier is trying hard to retain its international visitors, improving over the last few years its grooming, snowmaking, ski school and lifts – most notably with the overdue replacement of the Tortin gondola. But major grouses remain. Some are down to the organisation of the resort – the kind of piste signposting shown later in the chapter would be comical if it were not infuriating – but others are down to the lie of the land.

For experts prepared to hire a guide in order to explore off-piste, Verbier is one of the big names. With its 4 Valleys lift network and a claimed 400km of pistes, Verbier also seems at first sight to rank alongside the French mega-resorts such as Courchevel or La Plagne for piste skiers. But it doesn't; the 4 Valleys is an inconveniently sprawling affair, while Verbier's local pistes are surprisingly confined. Of course, piste skiers can have a satisfying holiday here – but you can do that in scores of modest resorts from Alpbach to Zell am See. Whether they can match Verbier's famously vibrant nightlife is another question.

461

The resort

Verbier is an amorphous sprawl of chalet-style buildings, without too much concrete in evidence, and with an impressive setting on a wide, sunny balcony facing spectacular peaks. It's a fashionable, but informal, very lively place that teems with a youngish, cosmopolitan clientele. But it's no longer exclusive. The resort attracts a range of British holidaymakers, and there are plenty of Scandinavians, too.

Most of the smart shops and hotels (but not chalets) are set around the Place Centrale and along the sloping streets stretching down the hill in one direction and up it in the other to the main lift station at Medran 500m/ 1,600ft away. Much of the nightlife is here, too, though bars are rather scattered. These central areas get unpleasantly packed with cars at busy times, especially weekends.

More chalets and apartments are built each year – which means building sites spoil the views in places – with

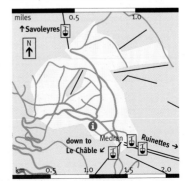

462

LIFT PASSES

2001/02 prices in Swiss francs

4 Valleys/Mont-Fort
Covers all lifts and ski-buses in Verbier, Mont-Fort, Bruson, La Tzoumaz, Nendaz, Veysonnaz and Thyon.
Beginners Station pass covers five beginner lifts.
Main pass
1-day pass 58
6-day pass 303
Senior citizens
Over 65: 6-day pass 212
Children
Under 6: free pass
Under 16: 6-day pass 212
Under 20: 258
Short-term passes
Half-day pass from 11am (adult 53) or 12.30 (adult 48).
Notes Reductions for families and groups.
Alternative passes
Limited passes for Savoleyres-La Tzoumaz, Bruson, and Verbier only.

newer properties inconveniently situated along the road to the lift base for the secondary Savoleyres area, about 1.5km/1 mile from Medran.

Staying at the top of the resort, close to the Medran lift station, is convenient for the slopes and sufficiently distant from nightlife to avoid late evening noise. If nightlife is not a priority, staying somewhere near the upper (north-east) fringes of the village may mean that you can almost ski to your door – and there is a piste linking the upper nursery slopes to the one in the middle of the village.

But in practice most people just get used to using the free buses, which run efficiently on several routes until 7pm. Some areas have quite an infrequent service. We are told that from 7pm to 8.30 there is a special taxi service that will drop you at any of the usual bus stops within the resort for five francs per person.

Verbier is at one end of a long, strung-out series of interconnected slopes, optimistically branded the 4 Valleys and linking Verbier to the resorts of Nendaz (described at the end of this chapter), Thyon and Veysonnaz. Other small areas reached by bus are covered by the lift pass, including Bruson – also reached by riding a gondola down to Le Châble and taking a bus from there. Chamonix and Champéry are within reach by car. But a car can be a bit of a nuisance in Verbier itself. Parking is tightly controlled; your chalet or hotel may not have enough, which means a hike from the free parking at the sports centre or paying for garage space.

boarding As with its skiing, Verbier is one of Europe's best off-piste and extreme boarding resorts for those able and willing to pay for a guide or to join a group. The main area is served by gondolas, cable-cars and chairs, with no drag-lifts at all. There are two terrain-parks (the Swatch-sponsored boarder-cross course at La Chaux and another one at La Tournelle) and a half-pipe at Col des Gentianes. Less experienced boarders should try Savoleyres, though there are a few drag-lifts. To see some real experts in action, hang around the resort in late March, when the world's best congregate here for the Red Bull Xtreme contest, on the cliff-like north face of the Bec des Rosses. There is a specialist snowboard school and a couple of specialist snowboard shops. And then there's the nightlife, which gets pretty wild at times.

MOUNTAIN FACTS

Altitude 1500m-3330m
4,920ft-10,930ft
Lifts	100
Pistes	410km
	255 miles
Blue	32%
Red	42%
Black	26%
Snowmaking	50km
	31 miles
Recco detectors used	

The mountains

Essentially this is high-mountain terrain. There are wooded slopes directly above the village, but the runs here are either bumpy itinéraires or winding paths. There is more sheltered skiing in other sectors – particularly above Veysonnaz.

THE SLOPES
Very spread out

Savoleyres is the smaller area, mainly suited to intermediates and reached by a gondola from the north-west end of town. This area is underrated and generally underused. It has open, sunny slopes on the front side, and long, pleasantly wooded, shadier runs on the back. When conditions are good you can get back to Verbier on south-facing slopes, but in sunny weather these deteriorate quickly.

You can take a catwalk across from Savoleyres to the foot of Verbier's main slopes. These are served by lifts from Medran, at the opposite end of town. Two gondolas, recently upgraded, rise to **Les Ruinettes** and then on to **Les Attelas**. From Les Attelas a small cable-car goes up to Mont Gelé, for steep off-piste runs only. Heading down instead, you can go back westwards to Les Ruinettes, south to La Chaux or north to Lac des Vaux. From here chairs go back to Les

Attelas and on to Chassoure, the top of a wide, steep and shady off-piste mogul field leading down to **Tortin**, with a gondola back.

La Chaux is served by two slow chair-lifts and is the departure point of a jumbo cable-car up to Col des Gentianes and the glacier area. A second, much smaller cable-car then goes up to **Mont-Fort,** the high point of the 4 Valleys. From the glacier is another off-piste route down to Tortin, a north-facing run of almost 1300m/4,300ft vertical. A cable-car returns to Col des Gentianes.

Tortin is the gateway to the rest of the 4 Valleys. From there you head down to **Siviez**, where one chair goes off into the long, thin **Nendaz** sector and another heads for the **Thyon** and **Veysonnaz** sectors, reached by a couple of lifts and a lot of catwalk skiing. Both these sectors suit intermediates best.

Allow plenty of time to get to and from these remote corners – you don't want to be stranded in the wrong valley. It's an expensive taxi-ride.

SNOW RELIABILITY
Improved snowmaking

The slopes of the Mont-Fort glacier always have good snow. The runs to Tortin are normally snow-sure too. But nearly all of this is steep, and much of it is formally off-piste. Most of Verbier's main local slopes face south

Verbier

463

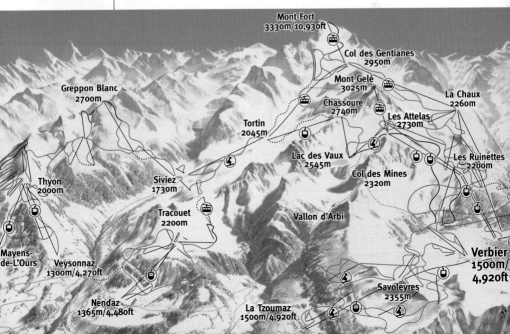

Mont-Fort
3330m/10,930ft

Col des Gentianes
2950m

Mont Gelé
3025m

Greppon Blanc
2700m

Chassoure
2740m

La Chaux
2226m

Les Attelas
2730m

Tortin
2045m

Lac des Vaux
2545m

Les Ruinettes
2200m

Thyon
2000m

Siviez
1730m

Col des Mines
2320m

Tracouet
2200m

Vallon d'Arbi

Mayens-
de-L'Ours

Veysonnaz
1300m/4,270ft

Savoleyres
2355m

Verbier
1500m/
4,920ft

Nendaz
1365m/4,480ft

La Tzoumaz
1500m/4,920ft

or west and are below 2500m/8,200ft – so they can be in poor condition at times. Snowmaking on the lower slopes has improved a lot in recent years and there are further additions this season. The north-facing slopes of Savoleyres and Lac des Vaux are normally much better.

FOR EXPERTS
The main attraction

Verbier has some superb tough slopes, many of them off-piste and needing a guide. The very extreme couloirs between Mont Gelé and Les Attelas and below the Attelas gondola are some of the toughest. There are safer, more satisfying off-piste routes from Mont Gelé to Tortin and La Chaux.

There are hardly any conventional black pistes – most of the runs that should have this designation are now defined as itinéraires, which in theory means they are not patrolled. We have been told this isn't so, but it would be foolish to go down these runs alone. The blacks that do exist are mostly indistinguishable from nearby reds.

The front face of Mont-Fort is a conspicuous exception: a wonderful tough mogul field, all of black steepness (and these days all classified black) but with a choice of gradient from seriously steep to intimidatingly steep. Occasionally you can get from Mont-Fort all the way to Le Châble off-

piste. You can also head off-piste down to Siviez via one of two spectacular couloirs off the back of Mont-Fort. The North Face of Mont-Fort is one of the hottest of expert runs.

The two itinéraires to Tortin are both excellent in their different ways. The one from Chaussoure is just one steep slope, normally a huge mogul field. The north-facing itinéraire from Gentianes is longer, less steep, but feels much more of an adventure. Those willing to walk up a steep slope near the start (known as the Highway to Heaven) are rewarded by usually good powder in a quiet valley parallel to the main run. Les Attelas is the start of shorter runs towards the village.

A couple of long, but easy, off-piste routes go from Lac des Vaux via Col des Mines. One is a popular route back to Verbier, down a long open slope to Carrefour at the top of the village, the other a very beautiful run through Vallon d'Arbi to La Tzoumaz. They are not always open: a piste-basher needs to form a ledge across a steep slope to the Col – without that, the traverse is scary.

The World Cup run at Veysonnaz is a steepish, often icy, red, ideal for really speeding down. There is also an entertaining off-piste run from Greppon Blanc at the top of the Siviez–Thyon sector down to Leteygeon. There are 'memorable' heli-trips.

FINDING YOUR WAY AROUND THE SLOPES OF VERBIER

It isn't easy. The main area is complicated, and difficult to represent on a single map. A couple of years back the lift company, Téléverbier, dropped its hopeless map and produced a booklet of maps dealing separately with each sector. This, too, was hopeless. Now we seem to be back with one hopeless map.

Direction signposting on the mountain is equally frustrating. There are two problems. One is a strange faith in the kind of 'motorway' signs shown here. We and most of our readers find these impossible to relate to the real choices of route. The second is that although the signs religiously use piste numbers there are no such numbers on the piste map. So how do you connect the two?

Navigation is further complicated by confusion over where it is prudent to go. For years now, runs that once were black pistes have been defined as 'itinéraires à ski' (eg both runs down to Tortin) or 'itinéraires de haute-montagne' (eg the Col des Mines run home from Lac des Vaux). We've long campaigned for these runs to be restored to piste status, but at least their non-piste status needs to be clear.

With patience, you can work out that neither is patrolled, and possibly deduce that 'itinéraires de haute-montagne' are 'not protected against mountain dangers' (ie avalanches) and should be tackled only in the company of an experienced mountaineer or a guide. But it is far from clear.

No other resort finds all this so difficult to resolve. All it takes is a modest budget, some awareness of visitors' needs and half a brain. Which does Téléverbier lack?

FOR INTERMEDIATES
Go to Savoleyres

Many mileage-hungry intermediates find Verbier disappointing. The intermediate slopes in the main area are concentrated between Les Attelas and the village, above and below Les Ruinettes, plus the little bowl at Lac des Vaux and the sunny slopes served by the chairs at La Chaux. This is all excellent and varied intermediate territory, but there isn't much of it – to put it in perspective, this whole area is no bigger than the slopes of tiny Alpbach – and it is used by the bulk of the visitors staying in one of Switzerland's largest resorts. So it is often very crowded, especially the otherwise wonderful sweeping red from Les Attelas to Les Ruinettes served by the big gondola. Even early intermediates should taste the perfect snow on the glacier (provided you don't mind T-bars). The red run from Col des Gentianes to La Chaux is not too difficult, but its high-mountain feel can be unnerving and it's no disgrace to ride the cable-car down instead.

Intermediates should make much more use of the Savoleyres area. This has good intermediate pistes, usually better snow and far fewer people (especially on Sundays). It is also a good hill for mixed abilities, with variations of many runs to suit most levels of intermediate.

The area as a whole presents some difficulties for early intermediates, as editorial daughter Laura can confirm. There is excellent easy blue-run skiing at La Chaux, but there is no easy way back to Les Ruinettes from there. From Savoleyres there is an easy way across to Medran but there may be no easy way down to that link from the top of Savoleyres. In both cases, we had to take quite challenging red runs. Laura managed it, but in a properly run resort the difficulties would have been foreseen and sorted out.

FOR BEGINNERS
Progression is the problem

There are sunny nursery slopes close to the middle of the village and at Les Esserts, at the top of it. These are fine provided they have snow (they have a lot of snowmaking, which helps). The problem is what you do after the nursery slopes. There are easy blues on the back side of Savoleyres, and at La Chaux, but they are not easy to get back from (see above).

FOR CROSS-COUNTRY
Surprisingly little on offer

Verbier is limited for cross-country. There's a 4km/2.5 mile circuit in Verbier, 4km/2.5 miles at Les Ruinettes-La Chaux and 30km/19 miles down at Le Châble/Val de Bagnes.

QUEUES
Not the problem they were

It's clear that Verbier's queue problems have been greatly eased by recent investment. The jumbo gondola to Les Attelas has virtually eliminated queues at Les Ruinettes, but it has increased the overcrowding on the pistes back down. The mega-queues at Tortin for Chassoure are a thing of the past, thanks to the new eight-seater gondola. The new fast chair at Lac des Vaux has greatly eased the bottleneck there. But the cable-car from Tortin to Col des Gentianes can produce queues, and the Mont-Fort cable-car above it can still generate very long ones.

Some queues at the main village lift station at Medran persist when day visitors fill one of the gondolas by boarding down in the valley at Le Châble. The recent upgrade of this gondola has helped, though even with a 60% boost, capacity is still modest.

There are continuing reports of queues for outdated double chairs and for inadequate drag-lifts in the outlying 4 Valleys resorts – and at La Chaux when crowds descend from the glacier. Overall, though, recent reporters find the lift system much improved.

SCHOOLS/GUIDES

2001/02 prices in Swiss francs

Swiss Ski School
Classes 6 days
2½hr: 9.15-11.45
5 half days: 155
Children's classes
Ages: 3 to 12
5 half days: 142
Private lessons
Hourly, half or full day
135 for 2hr for 1 or 2 people

OTHER SCHOOLS

Fantastique
Adrénaline
Altitude

CHILDCARE

The ski school's Kids Club kindergarten (775 6333), on the slope at Les Moulins, has its own drag-lift and takes children from aged 3 from 8.30 to 5pm.

The Schtroumpfs non-ski kindergarten (771 6585), close to the middle of the resort, takes children of any age up to 4 years (older ones by arrangement), from 8.30 to 5.30.

MOUNTAIN RESTAURANTS
Disappointing in main area

There are not enough huts, which means queues and overcrowding in high season. Savoleyres is the best area. The hotel by the Tzoumaz chair takes some beating for value and lack of crowds. Also worth trying are Chez Simon ('simple and cheap'), Au Mayen (beneath the Combe 1 chair – 'good service, sunny terrace') and the rustic Marmotte ('wicked, excellent rösti'). Le Sonalon, on the fringe of the village, is 'excellent, with great views', but reached off-piste.

In the main area, the rustic Chez Dany at Clambin, on the off-piste run down from the Chaux area, is about the best, and gets packed despite being a bit tricky to get to at times. Carrefour is popular and well situated at the top of the village, above the golf course. The restaurants at Les Ruinettes – table-service upstairs – have big terraces with splendid views. The Olympique at Les Attelas is a good table-service restaurant.

Everyone loves the Cabane Mont Fort – a proper mountain refuge off the run to La Chaux from Col des Gentianes; cosy on a bad day, and great views on a good one, but very busy – get there early.

SCHOOLS AND GUIDES
Good reports

Verbier is an excellent place for advanced skiers, in particular, to get lessons. Several reporters have been complimentary about the off-piste lessons with the Swiss ski school. More than 20 guides are available for heli-trips, which include trips to Zermatt and the Aosta valley. The Vallée Blanche at Chamonix and a trip to Zinal are cheaper excursions. Verbier is also quite big on snowboard and telemark lessons. The consensus is that the Swiss school's standards have improved generally, partly thanks to the retirement of some old-timers. Of the others, the Adrénaline international school gets rave reviews, particularly for its private lessons.

FACILITIES FOR CHILDREN
Wide range of options

The Swiss school's facilities in the resort are good, and the resort attracts quite a lot of families. The playground up at La Chaux has also received favourable reports. Space on the bus back is limited, and priority is given to school groups. The possibility of leaving very young babies at the Schtroumpfs nursery is valuable. British families can travel with family-oriented chalet operators – Esprit Ski and Mark Warner both have nurseries, and Simply Ski has a nanny service you can arrange in advance.

There are considerable reductions on the lift pass price for families on production of your passports.

Staying there

HOW TO GO
Plenty of options

Verbier is the chalet-party capital of the Alps. Given the size of the place there are surprisingly few apartments and pensions available, though those on a budget have inexpensive B&B options in Le Châble. Hotels are expensive in relation to their grading. Given a sleeping bag you can bed down at the sports centre for about £10 a night – and that includes the use of the pool.

Chalets There are chalets available for most tastes. Small ones, of the kind that you might take over for a family or small group of friends, are particularly common. There are also large chalets good for groups, places handy for the slopes, and others slap bang in the centre of Verbier's lively nightlife. There are a few luxury options on the UK package market. Flexiski has one property – the deeply comfortable chalet Bouvreuil. Ski Verbier's 10 properties include some impressively luxurious chalets and apartments. This season it is adding a dinky little chalet that sleeps just two people – but you have to do your own cooking. The Ski Company's chalet Goodwood is superb, and central. Last season Descent introduced a swish 12-bed place with hotel-style service.

Hotels There are five 4-star hotels, a dozen 3-star and a handful of simpler places. Opening in December 2002 is Verbier Lodge, newly built in timber.
(((((5) **Chalet d'Adrien** (771 6300) The new best-in-town? A beautifully furnished low-rise chalet, with top-notch cooking to match. Close to the Savoleyres lift.
((((4) **Rosalp** (771 6323) The great attraction is the food in Roland Pierroz's Michelin-starred restaurant, which is the best you'll find in a Swiss resort. Good position midway between centre and lifts.

GETTING THERE

Air Geneva, transfer 2hr.

Rail Le Châble (7km); regular buses to resort or gondola.

SNOWPIX / CHRIS GILL

The run down from Attelas to Ruinettes is a fine intermediate slope, but can get much more crowded than this ↘

(((⟨4⟩ **Montpelier** (771 6131) Very comfortable 4-star, but out of town (a courtesy bus is provided).

(((⟨4⟩ **Vanessa** (775 2800) Central 4-star with spacious apartments as well as rooms; 'great food,' says a reporter.

(((⟨3⟩ **Rotonde** (771 6525) Much cheaper, well positioned 3-star between centre and lifts; some budget rooms.

(((⟨3⟩ **Chamois** (771 6402) 3-star close to Medran lifts.

(((⟨3⟩ **Poste** (771 6681) Well placed 3-star midway between centre and lifts; still the only hotel pool. Some rooms rather small.

(((⟨3⟩ **de Verbier** (771 6688) Central 3-star, popular with tour operators and their clientele; renowned for good food; atmospheric and traditional, with helpful owners and staff.

(⟨2⟩ **Farinet** (771 6626) Central 3-star hotel, now British-owned, with a focal après-ski bar on its elevated terrace.

Self-catering Apartments bookable through tour operators are rare. Self-caterers usually book direct. The comfortable Richemont and Troika apartments are close to the nursery slopes, a trek from the main lifts. The similar standard Blizzard is midway between Place Centrale and lifts.

EATING OUT
Very big choice

There is a very wide range of restaurants. Hotel Rosalp is clearly the best (and most expensive) in town, and among the best in Switzerland, with an awesome wine cellar to match its excellent Michelin-starred food – splash out on the seven-course Menu Gastronomique if you can afford it. The Pinte bistro in the hotel basement is a less expensive option – worth trying.

The Grotte à Max does a vast variety of rösti plus unusual meats such as ostrich and kangaroo. The popular King's bar developed a restaurant a couple of years back, and

Verbier

467

its innovative food ('not a fondue in sight') quickly gained favour. An equally refreshing newcomer is the stylish Millénium, above the Toro Negro steak-house.

The Farinet restaurant is atmospheric and has good food at affordable prices. For Swiss specialities, try the Relais des Neiges, the Robinson, the Caveau ('romantic ambience' says a reporter), Au Vieux-Verbier by the Medran lifts or Esserts by the nursery slopes. The Fer à Cheval is a very popular and lively place for pizza and other simple dishes. Arguably the best-value Italian food in town is at Al Capone's out near the Savoleyres gondola. The Hacienda Café is another inexpensive place. Harold's is Verbier's burger joint.

You can be ferried by snowmobile up to Chez Dany or the Marmotte for an evening meal, followed by a torchlit descent.

APRES-SKI
Throbbing but expensive

It starts with a 4pm visit to the Offshore Café at Medran, for people-watching, milk shakes and cakes. The nearby Big Ben pub is 'great and lively on a sunny afternoon'. Au Mignon at the bottom of the golf course has become popular since it was given a large sun deck.

Then if you're young, loud and British it's on to the Pub Mont-Fort – there's a widescreen TV for live sporting events. The Nelson is popular with locals. The Farinet is particularly good in spring, its live band playing to the audience on a huge, sunny terrace – there's now a conservatory-type cover over it when it's cold. Au Fer à Cheval is a fun place full of locals and regular Verbier-ites.

After dinner the Pub Mont-Fort is again popular with Brits and locals alike (the shots bar in the cellar is

worth a visit). Crok No Name has good live bands or a DJ and is entertaining for its cosmopolitan crowd. Murphy's Irish pub in the Garbo hotel is popular, with a good resident DJ. The much-loved King's is a quiet candlelit cellar bar with 60s decor – 'hip crowd, good music'. Bar New Club is a sophisticated piano bar, with comfortable seating and a more discerning clientele. Jacky's is a classy piano bar frequented by big spenders on their way to the Farm Club – an outrageously expensive nightclub which inexplicably is very popular, especially with balding geriatrics with much younger girls in tow (tables are difficult to book). It's packed with rich Swiss paying SF220 for bottles of spirits on Fridays and Saturdays and has more Brits on Tuesdays (chalet girls' day off on Wednesdays!).

More within the pocket of most Brits is the noisy, glitzy Marshal's Club, which sometimes has live music. Taratata is a friendly club that seems to be growing in popularity. Scotch is the cheapest disco in town and popular with teenagers and snowboarders. Big Ben is another cheaper, young place.

The nursery slope at Les Esserts is floodlit for tubing etc on Saturday and Sunday evenings.

OFF THE SLOPES
No great attraction

Verbier has an excellent sports centre and some nice walks, but otherwise very little to offer if you don't want to hit the slopes. Montreux is an enjoyable train excursion from Le Châble, and Martigny is worth a visit for the Roman arena and museums. Various mountain restaurants are accessible to pedestrians. Both toboggan runs – on the shady side of Savoleyres and from Les Ruinettes – are an impressive 10km long.

ACTIVITIES

Indoor Sports centre (swimming, skating, curling, squash, sauna, solarium, steam bath, hot-tub), cinema, ice hockey, indoor golf
Outdoor Ski-bob, 25km cleared walking paths, paragliding, hang-gliding, mountaineering, sledging

STAYING IN OTHER RESORTS
A lot going for them

There are advantages to staying in the other resorts of the 4 Valleys. For a start, you can avoid the worst of the morning queues if you set off early, spend the day in the Verbier area and wave to the crowds on your way home.

Secondly, they are substantially cheaper for both accommodation and incidentals. What you lose is the Verbier ambience and its range of restaurants, bars and nightlife.

Nendaz is a sizeable and quite rounded resort, described below.

Veysonnaz and Thyon are both small resorts, with mainly apartment accommodation. Veysonnaz is by far the more attractive – an old village complete with church. It has adequate bars, cafes and restaurants, a disco, sports centre with swimming pool, and school and guides. Thyon is a functional, ugly, purpose-built place.

Le Châble is a village a gondola-ride below Verbier. As changing gondola cars is not necessary for moving on to Les Ruinettes and Les Attelas, access to the slopes can be just as quick (or even quicker) from the queue-free valley. Le Châble is particularly convenient for those travelling by train, and for drivers who want to visit other resorts.

Nendaz 1365m/4,480ft

Nendaz is a big resort with over 17,000 beds and handily placed for exploring all of the 4 Valleys. It deserves more attention, especially if you want a cheaper base from which to use Verbier's slopes – but avoid the Sloanes and other Brits it attracts. Airport transfers are quick.

THE RESORT
Nendaz itself is a large place on a shelf above and with great views of the Rhône valley. Most of the resort is modern but built in traditional chalet-style and the original old village of Haute-Nendaz is still there, with its narrow streets, old houses and barns, and baroque chapel dating from 1499.

THE MOUNTAIN
Nendaz has a central and convenient location in the 4 Valleys and allows you to avoid some of the worst queues.

Slopes There's a 12-person gondola straight to the top of the local north-facing slopes at Tracouet. Here there are good, snow-sure nursery slopes plus blue and red intermediate runs back to town through the trees.

Intermediate and better skiers and boarders can head off down the back of Tracouet to a cable-car which takes you to Plan de Fou at 2430m/7,970ft. From there you can go down to Siviez and the links to Tortin, Mont Fort and the local Verbier slopes in one direction and Thyon and Veysonnaz in the other.

Snow reliability Nendaz sits on a north-facing shelf so its local slopes don't get the sun that affects Verbier.

Experts Access to the tough stuff is a bit slower from here than from Verbier.

Intermediates Nendaz makes an excellent base for 4 Valleys exploration. Coming back to Nendaz you have to use an unpisted ski route but intermediates can take the Plan de Fou cable-car down instead. Or you can take a shuttle-bus between Nendaz and Siviez.

Beginners There are good nursery slopes at Tracouet.

Snowboarding There is also a snowboard terrain-park.

Cross-country There are 17km/11 miles of cross-country tracks.

Queues There may be queues at Siviez at the end of the day.

Mountain restaurants The most compelling are in the Verbier area.

Schools and guides A reporter tells us that families seemed pleased with the school.

Facilities for children The school has a nursery area at Tracouet.

STAYING THERE
How to go The resort is virtually unheard of on the British market.

Hotels There are a few friendly and traditional hotels. Reporters recommend the Sourire – 'simple, but good food'.

Self-catering There is no shortage of apartments bookable locally or through Interhome.

Eating out There are several good restaurants; readers recommend the hotel Sourire and the nearby Mont Rouge restaurant.

Après-ski There are plenty of bars and four discos; a 17-year-old reporter recommends the Cactus Cantina and the Bodega as the liveliest spots.

Off the slopes Nendaz has 70km/43 miles of winter walks, an open-air rink, a fitness centre and squash courts.

Verbier

469

Phone numbers
From elsewhere in Switzerland add the prefix 027.
From abroad use the prefix +41 27.

VERBIER TOURIST OFFICE
Postcode CH-1936
t 775 3888
f 775 3889
info@verbier.ch
www.verbier.ch

NENDAZ TOURIST OFFICE
Postcode CH-1997
t 289 5589
f 289 5583
info@nendaz.ch
www.nendaz.ch

Villars 1300m/4,270ft

Traditional old resort with a much-needed but far-flung glacier

WHAT IT COSTS

HOW IT RATES

The slopes

Snow	**
Extent	***
Experts	**
Intermediates	***
Beginners	****
Convenience	***
Queues	***
Restaurants	***

The rest

Scenery	***
Resort charm	****
Off-slope	****

470

➕ Pleasant, relaxing year-round resort

➕ Fairly extensive intermediate slopes linked to Les Diablerets

➕ Good nursery slopes

➕ Quite close to Geneva airport

➕ Good range of off-slope diversions

➖ Unreliable snow-cover

➖ Overcrowded mountain restaurants

➖ Getting up the mountain means a slow, often crowded train journey or a bus-ride from the town centre to the gondola

With its mountain railway and gentle low-altitude slopes, Villars is the kind of place that has been overshadowed by modern mega-resorts. But for a relaxing and varied family holiday the attractions are clear – and the link with Les Diablerets and its high glacier, now known as Glacier 3000, adds to the appeal.

THE RESORT

Villars sits on a sunny shelf, looking across the Rhône valley to the Portes du Soleil. A busy high street lined with a variety of shops gives it the air of a pleasant small town; all around are chalet-style buildings, with just a few block-like hotels. You can travel to the centre of Villars on a picturesque cog train which goes up to the slopes. It leaves from Bex in the valley, which is served by direct trains from Geneva airport (as is Aigle, a bus-ride from

Villars). A gondola at one end of town is the main lift; stay nearby if you can, since shuttle-buses get crowded at peak times. You can also stay in Gryon.

The Glacier-Alpes Vaudoises pass covers Villars, the linked slopes of Les Diablerets and Glacier 3000, plus Leysin and Les Mosses, both of which are easy jaunts by rail or road. Other resorts (eg Champéry and Verbier) are within driving distance. See the end of the chapter for more on Les Diablerets, Leysin and Les Mosses.

MOUNTAIN FACTS

Includes Glacier 3000 and Les Diablerets

Altitude	1115m-3000m 3,660ft-9,840ft
Lifts	45
Pistes	125km 78 miles
Blue	40%
Red	50%
Black	10%
Snowmaking	4km 2.5 miles
Recco detectors used	

What's new

For 2001/02 a speedy new six-seater chair was installed between La Rasse and Chaux Ronde, accessing a new 3km/2 mile red run to La Rasse, with a 600m/1,970ft vertical drop.

The next couple of seasons will see new snowmaking on lower slopes between Villars and Gryon, and on the slopes down to the villages.

THE MOUNTAINS

There's a good mix of open and wooded slopes throughout the area.

Slopes The train goes up to the col of Bretaye, which has intermediate slopes on either side, with a maximum vertical of 300m/1,000ft back to the col and much longer runs back to the village. To the east, open slopes (often spoilt by sun) go to La Rasse and the link to the otherwise separate Les Chaux sector. The gondola from town takes you to Roc d'Orsay, from where you can head for Bretaye or back to Villars. From Bretaye you can head for the slow two-way chair-lift which is the connection to Les Diablerets and Glacier 3000. The piste map and piste marking are both poor. Reporters have been scathing: For sheer lack of information and poor detail it is in a class of its own,' said one. 'A conspiracy to encourage you to hire a local guide,' said another.

Snow reliability Low altitude and sunny orientation mean snow reliability is not good, especially back to the village – they badly need the extra snowmaking planned. If local snow is poor, head for Glacier 3000 (see Les Diablerets overleaf) – though it is a long trek.

Experts The main interest for experts is off-piste. There is plenty to enjoy from Chaux Ronde, for example.

Intermediates The local slopes and Les Diablerets offer a good variety and add up to a fair amount of terrain. The lengthy trip to Glacier 3000 for the splendid red run down the Combe d'Audon is worth it if you're adventurous (see Les Diablerets overleaf).

Beginners Beginners will enjoy the village nursery slopes and riding the train to Bretaye. There are gentle runs here, too, but it's also very crowded.

Snowboarding There's a terrain-park at Les Chaux and Villars is home to a big end-of-season snowboarders' party (visit www.snowbombing.com).

Cross-country The trails up the valley past La Rasse are long and pretty, and there are more in the depression beyond Bretaye (44km/27 miles in all).

Queues Queues appear for the lifts at Bretaye mainly at weekends and peak periods. A recent visitor reported some overcrowding on the buses and train.

Mountain restaurants They are often oversubscribed, especially at Bretaye. The Golf Club is expensive but good, as is the Col de Soud ('best rösti ever'); Lac des Chavonnes (open at peak periods) is worth the walk.

Schools and guides The Villars ski school – aka Ecole Moderne (using the ski évolutif method) – and the Swiss ski school get good reports. A reporter this year gave the Swiss School '10 out of 10'. Riderschool is a specialist snowboard outfit. The Bureau des Guides organises heli-trips.

Facilities for children Both ski schools run children's classes. There is also a non-ski nursery for children up to six and a Club Med with good facilities.

STAYING THERE

How to go Several tour operators offer packages here. We had a glowing report on the Club Med here in 2002 ('brilliant for families').

Hotels The Golf (496 3838) is popular ('great, family tries hard'). The Eurotel Victoria (495 3131) lacks style but is near the gondola. The Bristol (496 3636) is not, but offers 'comfort, good food and service'. All are 4-star.

Eating out Many restaurants are hotel-based. Apart from these, the Sporting is recommended for pizza and the Vieux-Villars for local specialities.

Après-ski Charlie's, the Central, the Sporting and the Mini-Pub are popular bars. The bowling can be a laugh; El Gringo, Live and Fox are the discos.

Off the slopes Tennis courts, walks, swimming, skating and curling; or trips on the train – to Lausanne for instance.

Phone numbers
From elsewhere in
Switzerland add the
prefix 024.
From abroad use the
prefix +41 24.

**VILLARS
TOURIST OFFICE**
Postcode CH-1884
t 495 3232
f 495 2794
information@villars.ch
www.villars.ch

**LES DIABLERETS
TOURIST OFFICE**
Postcode CH-1865
t 492 3358
f 495 2348
info@diablerets.ch
www.diablerets.ch

**LEYSIN
TOURIST OFFICE**
Postcode CH-1854
t 494 2244
f 494 1616
tourisme@leysin.ch
www.leysin.ch

**LES MOSSES
TOURIST OFFICE**
Postcode CH-1862
t 491 1466
f 491 1024
otm@lesmosses.ch
www.lesmosses.ch

LES DIABLERETS 1150m/3,770ft
**Unspoiled but spread-out village
towered over by the Diablerets massif,
with two areas of local slopes, plus
Glacier 3000 and link to Villars.**
The village has two 4-stars: Hôtel des
Diablerets (492 0909) and Eurotel-
Victoria (492 3721), the latter modern,
the former in chalet style and centrally
situated. Both have pool and sauna.
Mon Abri (492 3481) is a rustic chalet
with a bar (Bar'B) and disco (B'Bar).

A high-speed quad on the outskirts
of town, followed by a slow two-person
chair, leads up to the red runs of the
Meilleret area and the link to Villars. A
gondola in the centre of town takes
you to Isenau, a mix of blues and reds
served by drag-lifts.

From Isenau there's a red run down
to Col du Pillon and the cable-car to
and from the glacier. You can also
reach the glacier cable-cars by bus from
town. On Glacier 3000, you'll find blue
runs at over 3000m/10,000ft, stunning
views and the long, red Combe
d'Audon – a wonderful, usually quiet,
run away from all the lifts with sheer
cliffs rising up on both sides,
descending over 1000m/3,300ft to
Oldenalp. The towering Quille du Diable
rock on the glacier is supposedly the
haunt of ghosts and witches.

The splendid new Botta 3000
restaurant with stunning views at the
top of the glacier is recommended for
lunch (especially the table-service
Restaurant des Glaciers with 'views to
die for'). Or try the rustic Vioz (for
lunch or dinner) at the bottom of
Meilleret. The Locanda Livia (Italian
and Chinese) and the Potinière (local
fare) are both recommended. Barwise,
try those at the Mon Abri, or more
centrally, MTB and Pote Saloon disco.

There's a 7km/4 mile evening
toboggan run down from Les Mazots
(head torches supplied). There's also
an ice rink and skate park.

LEYSIN 1300m/4,260ft
**Another spread-out village, climbing
up a wooded hillside. Cheese is still
made locally – you may hear the cows
going off for milking in the morning.**
The lifts are to the east of the village.
The 4-star Classic (493 0606) and the
Bel Air (494 1339) are the most
convenient hotels. The happily named
Hiking Sheep (494 3535) and the
Chalet Emina (494 1261) are not far.

The slopes are a pretty mix of
mainly reds and blues. A gondola

takes you up to La Berneuse at
2050m/6,720ft. From here you head
down to the two-stage Chaux de Mont
chair, which takes you to the resort's
highest point of 2205m/7,230ft.
There's a choice of black or red back
down, both easily sun-damaged. On
the lower half of the slope is a terrain-
park, home to some major snowboard
competitions. Snowboarders like Leysin
because there are very few drag-lifts.
Itineraries from the top of Chaux de
Mont provide Leysin's best options for
experts, along with a heli-operation.

From the bottom of Chaux de Mont
it's easy to go to the other side of the
resort, using a series of chairs and
fairly short, mainly blue, runs in and
out of trees, with rockfaces towering
above. Instead of the gondola, you can
take a chair from the valley to Tête
d'Aï (1910m/6,270ft). There are nursery
slopes at village level.

The revolving Kuklos restaurant at
La Berneuse has stunning views over
the mountains and Lake Geneva; Les
Fers has great food, an outdoor bar
and deckchairs to slump in.

After hours Leysin has a swimming
pool and an excellent seven-slope
tubing park. This is next to a teepee
restaurant, where wood-smoked
salmon is the speciality. Try the Leysin,
Chez Giuliano and the Caleche for
fondue – they serve several types –
and the Top pub for a few drinks.

LES MOSSES 1450m/4,760ft
**The resort of Les Mosses-La Lécherette
packs 60km/40 miles of downhill
pistes and 35km/20 miles of cross-
country trails into a small area.**
There's also a terrain-park, a few
chalet-style hotel-restaurants, shops
and a rather fine church. Of the hotels,
the Relais Alpin (491 1631) is a family-
owned 3-star, while the Fontaines (491
1212) boasts a bar and dancing. Les
Mosses is easily reached from Villars,
Leysin and Les Diablerets and recent
Villars visitors have recommended it
for its quiet slopes and great views.
However, there are only drag-lifts to
access the mainly red and blue runs,
though a chair is planned to Pic
Chaussy (2355m/7,720ft – the current
highest point is 1870m/6,130ft). Lunch
is mostly at valley level – try Buvette
de l'Arsat or the self-service Drosera.

Les Mosses prides itself on the
number of activities on offer – such as
ice-diving, a natural ice rink and an
international dog-sled racing course.

Wengen
1275m/4,180ft

Charming village, stunning views and extensive intermediate terrain

WHAT IT COSTS

HOW IT RATES

The slopes

Snow	**
Extent	***
Experts	**
Intermediates	****
Beginners	***
Convenience	***
Queues	***
Restaurants	****

The rest

Scenery	*****
Resort charm	*****
Off-slope	****

What's new

There is a new Intersport rental network which covers the whole Jungfrau region. Rent equipment from one of 11 outlets, then you can swap it for another model at a different outlet if you decide you fancy a change during the day and don't want to go back to the branch you hired it from.

A new restaurant, Café Allemand, opened in December 2001 next to the Allmend station (midway between Wengen and Wengernalp). It replaces Café Oberland, which was lower down and destroyed by an avalanche in 1999.

➕ Some of the most spectacular scenery in the Alps

➕ Traditional, 'traffic-free' Alpine village, reached only by cog railway

➕ Lots of long, gentle runs, ideal for intermediates, leading down to Grindelwald

➕ Rebuilt cable-car now an attractive alternative to trains up to the slopes

➕ Nursery slopes in heart of village

➕ Calm, unhurried atmosphere

➖ Limited terrain for experts

➖ Despite some snowmaking, snow conditions are unreliable – especially on the sunny home run and village nursery slope

➖ Trains to slopes from here and from Grindelwald are slow and infrequent – you have to plan your movements with the aid of timetables

➖ Getting to Grindelwald's First area can take hours

➖ Subdued in the evening, with little variety of nightlife

Given the charm of the village, the friendliness of the locals and the drama of the scenery, it's easy to see why many people – including numbers of middle-aged British people who have been going for decades – love Wengen. But non-devotees should think carefully about the lack of challenge, the unreliable snow and the dependence on cog railways before signing up.

The last of these drawbacks is slightly less serious than it was. The Männlichen cable-car station, destroyed in the devastating avalanches of 1999, was rebuilt in the heart of the village, where it is not only less vulnerable to avalanche but also much more convenient. Of course, the cable-car is now more popular, and gets queues. So those willing to gear their holiday activities to timetables – or to accept half-hour waits for trains – will still mainly rely on the railway. Others will probably conclude that life is too short, and go elsewhere with more reliable snow.

The resort

Wengen is set on a shelf high above the Lauterbrunnen valley, opposite Mürren, and reached only by a cog railway, which carries on up the mountain as the main lift. Wengen was a farming community long before skiing arrived; it is still tiny, but it is dominated by sizeable hotels, mostly of Victorian origin. So it is not exactly pretty, but it is charming and relaxed, and almost traffic-free. The only traffic is electric hotel taxi-trucks, which gather at the station to pick up guests, and a few ordinary petrol-engined taxis. (Why, we wonder?)

The short main street is the hub of the village. Lined with chalet-style shops and hotels, it also has the ice rink and village nursery slopes right next to it. The nursery slopes double as the venue for floodlit ski-jumping and parallel slalom races.

The views across the valley are stunning. They get even better higher up, when the famous trio of peaks comes fully into view – the Mönch (Monk) protecting the Jungfrau (Maiden) from the Eiger (Ogre).

The main way up the mountain is the regular, usually punctual trains from the southern end of the street to Kleine Scheidegg, where the slopes of Wengen meet those of Grindelwald. The cable-car is a much quicker way to the Grindelwald slopes, and now starts conveniently close to the main street.

Wengen is small, so location isn't as crucial as in many other resorts. The main street is ideally placed for the station. There are hotels on the home piste, convenient for the slopes. Those who don't fancy a steepish morning climb should avoid places down the hill below the station.

You can get to Mürren by taking the train down to Lauterbrunnen, and a funicular and connecting train up the other side. The Jungfrau lift pass covers all of this. Outings further afield aren't really worth the effort.

473

LIFT PASSES

Jungfrau Top Ski Region
Covers all 44 lifts and 213km/133 miles of pistes in Wengen, Mürren and Grindelwald, trains between them and Grindelwald ski-bus.
Beginners Points card: adult 100 points (50), lifts cost 7 to 13 points.
Main pass
1-day pass 55
6-day pass 282
Senior citizens
Over 62: 6-day pass 254
Children
16 to 19: 6-day 226
Under 16: 6-day pass 141 Under 5 accompanied by an adult free.
Short-term passes
Single ascent tickets for most lifts. Half-day pass for Kleine Scheidegg-Männlichen-First (adult 42) and Mürren-Schilthorn (adult 42).
Alternative periods
3 days in 7 pass available (170).
Notes
Day pass price is for Kleine Scheidegg-Männlichen-First area only (160km/100 miles) of pistes, 30 lifts, as Jungfrau Top Ski Region pass is only available for 2 days or over.
Alternative passes
1- and 2-day passes available for First-Kleine and Scheidegg-Männlichen (adult 2-day 102), and Mürren-Schilthorn (adult 2-day 100).
Non-skiers pass: adult 6-day pass 212.

The mountains

Although it is famous for the fearsome Lauberhorn Downhill course – the longest and one of the toughest on the World Cup circuit – Wengen's slopes are best suited to early intermediates. Most of the Downhill course is now open to the public. But the steepest section (the Hundschopf jump) can be avoided by an alternative red route for those who don't fancy it.

Most of Wengen's runs are gentle blues and reds, ideal for cruising.

THE SLOPES
Picturesque playground

Most of the slopes are on the Grindelwald side of the mountain. From the railway station at Kleine Scheidegg you can head straight down to Grindelwald or work your way across the mountain with the help of a couple of lifts to the top of the Männlichen. This area is served by drag- and chair-lifts, and can be reached directly from Wengen by the improved cable-car.

There are a few runs back down towards Wengen from the top of the **Lauberhorn**, but below Kleine Scheidegg there's really only one.

SNOW RELIABILITY
Why not use the guns?

Most slopes are below 2000m/6,500ft, and at Grindelwald they go down to less than 1000m/3,300ft. Very few slopes face north and Wengen's snowmaking facilities are not up to protecting them. The real shame is that the snowmaking that exists isn't always used when it's needed. As a reporter said this year, 'At least three machines were parked up and decorating the landscape at Kleine Scheidegg and never moved all week while the field below Wengernalp was 500 yards of sheet ice.'

While we've found wonderful snow a couple of times in late March, we've also struggled to find decent snow to ski on in January.

FOR EXPERTS
Few challenges

Wengen is quite limited for experts. The only genuine black runs in the area take you from Eigergletscher towards Wixi and include Oh God (which used to be off-piste but has now been reclassified as a 'free-ride

piste'). For most of its length, the Lauberhorn Downhill course is merely of intermediate red run gradient.

There are some decent off-piste runs such as White Hare from under the north face of the Eiger and more adventurous runs from the Jungfraujoch late in the season. For more challenges it's well worth going to nearby Mürren, an hour away by train and funicular. Heli-trips with mountain guides are organised if there are enough takers.

FOR INTERMEDIATES
Wonderful if the snow is good

Wengen and Grindelwald share superb intermediate slopes. Nearly all are long blue or gentle red runs – see Grindelwald chapter. The run back to Wengen is a relaxing end to the day, as long as it's not too crowded.

For tougher pistes, head for the top of the Lauberhorn lift and then the runs to Kleine Scheidegg, or to Wixi (following the start of the Downhill course). You could also try the north-facing run from Eigergletscher to Salzegg, which often has the best snow late in the season.

FOR BEGINNERS
Not ideal

There's a nursery slope in the centre of the village – it's convenient and gentle, but the snow is unreliable. A small part of it is now served by a moving carpet lift, ideal for children. There's a beginners' area at Wengernalp, but to get back to Wengen you either have to climb up to the train or tackle the run down, which can be tricky. There are plenty of good, long, gentle slopes to progress to.

FOR CROSS-COUNTRY
There is none

There's no cross-country skiing in Wengen itself. There are tracks down in the Lauterbrunnen valley, but the snow there is unreliable.

QUEUES
Improving, but a long way to go

The Männlichen cable-car has helped cut the queues for the trains but both can still suffer from horrific bottlenecks in peak periods, as well as daily scrambles to board the trains that the school uses. Weekend invasions can increase the crowds on the Grindelwald side, especially. Queues up the mountain have been alleviated a lot

boarding *Wengen is not a bad place for gentle boarding – the nursery area is not ideal, but beginners have plenty of slopes to progress to, with lots of long blue and red runs served by the train and chair-lifts. Getting from Kleine Scheidegg to Männlichen means an unavoidable drag-lift though. There's a terrain-park by the Bumps t-bar, below Wengernalp. But for the steepest slopes and best free-riding, experts will want to head for Mürren.*

MOUNTAIN FACTS

Altitude	945m-2970m
	3,100ft-9,740ft
Lifts	44
Pistes	213km
	133 miles
Blue	30%
Red	50%
Black	20%
Snowmaking	34km
	21 miles
Recco detectors used	

in the last few years by the installation of fast quad chairs on the Grindelwald side – though plenty of slow old lifts remain.

MOUNTAIN RESTAURANTS
Plenty of variety
A popular but expensive place for lunch is Wengernalp, where the rösti is excellent and the views of the Jungfrau are superb. The highest restaurant is at Eigergletscher. If you get there early on a sunny day, you can grab a table on the narrow outside balcony and enjoy magnificent views of the glacier. The station buffet at Kleine Scheidegg gets repeated rave reviews, so it's not surprising that it also gets packed – the take-away rösti and sausage are a popular option. The Grindelwaldblick is a worthwhile trudge uphill from Kleine Scheidegg, with great food and views of the Eiger.

There's a new restaurant with wonderful views from the terrace at Allmend (the train stops there on the way up to Wengernalp). In the village,

the Gruebi cafe, a short walk from the cable-car station, is highly recommended. For restaurants down towards Grindelwald, see the Grindelwald chapter.

SCHOOLS AND GUIDES
Healthy competition
A reporter says, 'The Swiss school is definitely trying harder than a few years ago.' The lessons and the standard of English are usually good. The independent Privat school has been recommended for private lessons.

Snowboarders are well served. And guides are available for heli-trips and powder excursions.

FACILITIES FOR CHILDREN
Apparently satisfactory
Our reports on children's facilities are from observers rather than participants, but are all favourable. It is an attractive village for families, with the baby slope in the centre.

The train gives easy access to higher slopes.

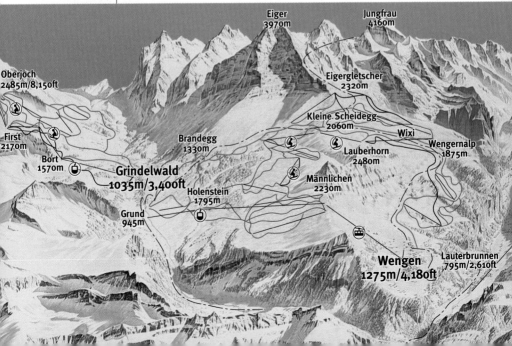

SCHOOLS/GUIDES

2001/02 prices in Swiss francs

Swiss
Classes 6 days
3hr: am
6 half days: 225
Children's classes
Ages: 4 to 12
6 half days: 225
Private lessons
2hr, 3hr or 5hr
138 for 2hr

CHILDCARE

The kindergarten on the first floor of the Sport Pavilion takes children from 18 months from 8.30 to 5pm, Sunday to Friday. Children can be taken to and from lessons with the ski school, which starts at age 4.

Sunshine nursery takes children from 1 month upwards. Children can be collected from and returned to your hotel or apartment.

A couple of 4-star hotels have their own kindergartens.

Staying there

HOW TO GO
Wide range of hotels

Most accommodation is in hotels. There is only a handful of catered chalets (and no especially luxurious ones). Self-catering apartments are few, too. There is a Club Med.
Hotels There are about two dozen hotels, mostly 4-star and 3-star, with a handful of simpler places.
(((4 **Beausite Park** (856 5161) Reputedly the best in town. Good pool. But poorly situated at top of nurser slopes – a schlep up from the main street.
(((4 **Wengener Hof** (856 6969) No prizes for style or convenience, but recommended for peace, helpful staff

and spacious, spotless rooms with good views.
(((4 **Sunstar** (856 5200) Modern hotel on main street right opposite cable-car. Comfortable rooms (though one reporter thought them 'small and dismally decorated' this year); lounge has a log fire. Live music some nights. Pool with views. Food good. Friendly.
(((4 **Regina** (856 5858) Quite central. Smart, traditional atmosphere. 'Best food in Wengen.' Carousel nightclub.
(((4 **Silberhorn** (856 5131) Comfortable, modern 4-star in central position opposite station, with a choice of restaurants.

THE BRITISH IN WENGEN

There's a very strong British presence at Wengen. Many Brits have been returning to the same rooms in the same hotels in the same week, year after year, and treat the resort as a sort of second home. There is an English church with weekly services, and a British-run club, the DHO (Downhill Only) – so named when the first Brits persuaded the locals to keep the summer railway running up the mountain in winter so they would no longer have to climb up in order to ski down again. That greatly amused the locals, who until then had regarded skiing in winter as a necessity rather than a pastime to be done for fun. The DHO is still going strong and organises regular events throughout the season.

GETTING THERE

Air Zürich, transfer 3½hr. Bern, transfer 1½hr.

Rail Station in resort.

ACTIVITIES

Indoor Swimming pool (in Beausite Park and Sunstar hotels), sauna, solarium, whirlpool, massage (in hotels), cinema (with English films), billiards
Outdoor Skating, curling, 50km cleared paths, toboggan runs, paragliding, glacier flights, sledging excursions, hang-gliding

Phone numbers
From elsewhere in Switzerland add the prefix 033.
From abroad use the prefix +41 33.

TOURIST OFFICE

Postcode CH-3823
t 855 1414
f 855 3060
info@wengen.ch
www.wengen-muerren.ch

Caprice (856 0606) Small, smartly furnished chalet-style hotel across the tracks from the Regina. Kindergarten. 'Comfortable and friendly' according to a reporter.

Belvédère (856 6868) Some way out, but we have good reports of buffet-style meals ('good for families'), spacious rooms and grand art nouveau public rooms.

Alpenrose (855 3216) Long-standing British favourite; eight minutes' climb to the station. Small, simple rooms, but good views; 'first-class' food; friendly staff.

Eiger (856 0505) Very conveniently sited, right next to the station. Focal après-ski bar. Rebuilt with comfy modern rooms.

Falken (856 5121) Further up the hill. Another British favourite, known affectionately as 'Fawlty Towers'.
Self-catering The hotel Bernerhof's decent Résidence apartments (855 2721) are well positioned just off the main street, and hotel facilities are available to guests.

EATING OUT
Lots of choice

Most restaurants in the village are in the hotels. They offer good food and service, and are open to non-residents. The Eiger has a traditional restaurant and a stube with Swiss and French cuisine. The Bernerhof has good-value traditional dishes. The little hotel Hirschen has good steaks. There's no shortage of fondues in the village. Several bars do casual food, including good-value pizza at Sina. Cafe Gruebi has been recommended for 'the most wonderful cakes'. You could eat at Wengernalp's excellent restaurant – but you have to get back on skis or on a toboggan.

APRES-SKI
It depends on what you want

People's reactions to the après-ski scene in Wengen vary widely, according to their expectations and appetites. If you're used to raving in Kitzbühel or Les Deux-Alpes, you'll rate Wengen dead, especially for young people. If you've heard it's dead, you may be pleasantly surprised to find that there is a handful of bars that do good business both early and late in the evening. But it is only a handful of small places. The Schnee-Bar, at the Bumps section of the home run, is a popular final run stop-off. And the

stube at the Eiger and the tiny, 'always welcoming' Eiger Bar are popular at the end of the day. The traditional Tanne and the funky Chili Peppers are almost opposite on the main street, and generally lively. Sina's, a little way out by Club Med, usually has live music. The Caprice bar is recommended. There are discos and live music in some hotels. The cinema often shows English-language films.

OFF THE SLOPES
Good for a relaxing time

Wengen is a superb resort for those who want a completely relaxing holiday, with its unbeatable scenery and pedestrian-friendly trains and cable-car (there's a special, though expensive, pass for pedestrians). There are some lovely walks, ice skating and a curling club. Several hotels have health spas. Excursions to Interlaken and Bern are possible by train, as is the trip up to the Jungfraujoch (see the Grindelwald chapter). Helicopter flights from Männlichen are recommended.

STAYING UP THE MOUNTAIN
Great views

You can stay at two points up the mountain reached by the railway: the expensive Jungfrau (855 1622) at Wengernalp and at Kleine Scheidegg, where there's a choice of rooms in the big Scheidegg-Hotels (855 1212) or dormitory space above the Grindelwaldblick restaurant and the station buffet. The big restaurant at Männlichen also has rooms.

STAYING DOWN THE VALLEY
The budget option

Staying in a 3-star hotel like the Schützen (855 3026) or Oberland (855 1241) in Lauterbrunnen will cost about half as much as similar accommodation in Wengen. The train from Wengen runs until 11.30pm and is included in your lift pass. Staying in Lauterbrunnen also improves your chances of getting a seat on the train to Kleine Scheidegg rather than joining the scramble at Wengen – though of course it also means a longer journey time. Lauterbrunnen is also much better placed for Mürren.

You can save even more by staying in Interlaken. Choose a hotel near Interlaken Ost station, from which you can catch a train to Lauterbrunnen (22 minutes) or Grindelwald (36 minutes). Driving can take longer at weekends.

Wengen

477

Magical in many respects – both on and off the slopes

WHAT IT COSTS

((((5))))

HOW IT RATES

The slopes

Snow	****
Extent	****
Experts	*****
Intermediates	****
Beginners	*
Convenience	*
Queues	***
Restaurants	*****

The rest

Scenery	*****
Resort charm	*****
Off-slope	****

➕ Wonderful, high and extensive slopes and three varied areas

➕ Spectacular high-mountain scenery, dominated by the Matterhorn

➕ Charming, if rather sprawling, old mountain village, largely traffic-free

➕ Reliable snow at altitude

➕ New, highly-rated ski school

➕ World's best mountain restaurants

➕ Extensive helicopter operation

➕ Nightlife to suit most tastes

➕ Smart shops

➕ Linked to Cervinia in Italy

➖ Getting to main lift stations may involve a long walk, a crowded (but free) bus or an expensive taxi-ride

➖ Beginners should go elsewhere

➖ One-way link only between the other two areas and the Klein Matterhorn

➖ Getting up the mountain and around the different areas can be slow

➖ Some lift queues at peak periods, but new lift for 2002/03 should help worst problems

➖ Annoying electric taxis detract from the otherwise relaxed, car-free village ambience

You must try Zermatt before you die. Few places can match its combination of excellent advanced and intermediate slopes, reliable snow, magnificent scenery, Alpine charm and mountain restaurants with superb food and stunning views.

Many people complain that the car-free village is spoiled by intrusive electric carts and taxis; some complain about the time it takes to get to the top of the mountain; others say that the atmosphere is of Swiss efficiency and international tourism rather than mountain-village friendliness. But friendliness and service have improved and there's a magical feel to both the village and the mountains.

Zermatt's flaws are minor compared to its attractions, which come close to matching perfectly our notion of the ideal winter resort. It's one of our favourites.

What's new

A new Matterhorn Express 8-seater gondola is due to open for the 2002/03 season and replace the old Zermatt-Furi gondola and Furi-Schwarzsee cable-car. It will go from Zermatt via Furi to Schwarzsee in just 10-minutes. Carrying 3000 people per hour it will have 50% more capacity than the old gondola and 10 times the capacity of the old cable-car. It should solve queueing problems at both village level and at Furi. But it may cause congestion on the pistes at Schwarzsee.

The resort

Zermatt started life as a traditional mountain village, developed as a mountaineering centre in the 19th century, then became a winter resort too. Summer is still as important as winter here.

Be warned: Zermatt is big business and most restaurants and hotels are owned by a handful of families. Many of the workers are brought in from outside Switzerland – but that is probably one of the reasons many reporters have remarked on the increased friendliness and improved service in recent years.

The village sprawls along either side of a river, mountains rising steeply on each side. It is a mixture of chocolate-box chalets and modern buildings, most in traditional style. You arrive by rail or taxi from Täsch, where cars have to be left, for a fee. They can be left for free at more distant Visp, from where you can also get a train. The main street runs past the station, lined with luxury hotels and shops.

Zermatt doesn't have the relaxed, quaint feel of other car-free resorts, such as Wengen and Saas-Fee. That's partly because the electric vehicles are more intrusive and aggressive, and partly because the clientele is more overtly part of the jet set, with large contingents from the US and Japan.

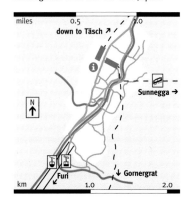

MOUNTAIN FACTS

Altitude	1620m-3820m
	5,310ft-12,530ft
Lifts	71
Pistes	250km
	155 miles
Blue	22%
Red	50%
Black	28%
Snowmaking	43km
	27 miles
Recco detectors used	

For a resort with such good and extensive slopes, there's a remarkably high age profile. Most visitors seem to be over 40, and there's little of the youthful atmosphere you get in rival resorts with comparable slopes, such as Val-d'Isère, St Anton and Chamonix. The main street, with the station square near one end, is the focal point of village life. The cog railway to the Gornergrat area leaves from opposite the main station, and the underground funicular to the Sunnegga area is a few minutes' walk away. From here the gondola to the Klein Matterhorn area (and the link to Cervinia) is a 15-minute trek, a bus-ride or an expensive taxi-ride. ('The best daily SF20 investment of the trip,' said a reader.)

The school and guides office, the tourist office and many hotels, shops, restaurants, bars and nightspots are on or near the main street. Another main street runs along the river. To each side are narrow streets and paths; many are hilly and treacherous when icy.

Bill Baker in Julen Sport is one of the best boot fitters in the world – pay him a visit if your boots are giving you problems.

Choosing where to stay is very important in Zermatt. The solar-powered shuttle-buses are crowded, but at least they are now large, free to lift-pass holders and more frequent than they used to be. Walking from one end of the village to the furthest lifts can take 15 to 20 minutes and can be unpleasant because of treacherous icy paths.

The best spot for most people is near the Gornergrat and Sunnegga railways, near the end of the main street. Some accommodation is up the steep hill across the river from the centre in Winkelmatten. This is less isolated than it appears say reporters – you can ski back to it from all areas and the bus to town is reliable.

Getting up to the village from Täsch is no problem. The trains run on time and have automatically descending ramps that allow you to wheel luggage trolleys on and off. You are met at the other end by electric and horse-drawn taxis and hotel shuttles.

The mountains

There are slopes to suit all abilities except absolute beginners, for whom we don't recommend the resort. For intermediates and experts Zermatt has few rivals, with marvellously groomed cruising trails, some of the best moguls around, long, beautiful scenic runs out of view of the lift system, exciting heli-trips and off-piste possibilities, as well as the opportunity to get down into Italy for the day and lunch on pasta and chianti. The hands-free, electronic lift pass system means you never have to get it out of your pocket.

THE SLOPES
Beautiful and varied
Zermatt consists of three separate areas, two of which are now well linked. The **Sunnegga-Blauherd-Rothorn** area is reached by the

Zermatt

479

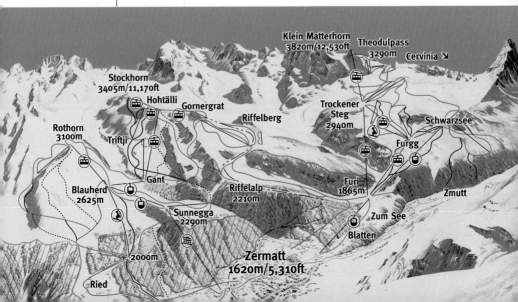

Zermatt by cog railway trains which leave every 24 minutes and take 30 or 40 minutes to get to the top – arrive at the station early to get a seat on the right-hand side and enjoy the fabulous views. It can be an uncomfortable journey if you have to stand.

From Gornergrat, there's a piste, followed by a short walk, to Furi to link up with the third and highest area, **Klein Matterhorn–Trockener Steg-Schwarzsee**. But you can't do the journey in the opposite direction: once on the Klein Matterhorn, moving to a different mountain means heading down and getting from one end of the village to the other to catch a lift up. The Klein Matterhorn gives access to Cervinia – you need to buy an 'international pass' or pay a daily supplement to your Zermatt lift pass and the high lifts are sometimes shut because of high winds.

There are pistes back to the village from all three areas – though some of them can be closed or tricky due to poor snow conditions at times.

SNOW RELIABILITY
Good high up, poor lower down

Zermatt has rocky terrain and a relatively dry climate. But it also has some of the highest slopes in Europe, and quite a lot of snowmaking.

All three areas go up to over 3000m/10,000ft, and the Klein Matterhorn cable-car is the highest in Europe, ending at over 3800m/12,500ft and serving a summer glacier. There are loads of runs above 2500m/8,200ft, many of which are north-facing, so guaranteeing decent snow except in freak years such as last season.

Snowmaking machines serve some of the pistes on all three areas, from around 3000m to under 2000m (10,000ft down to 6,500ft). The runs back to the village can still be patchy,

underground funicular starting about five minutes' walk from the station. This shifts large numbers rapidly but can lead to queues for the subsequent gondola – you can take a run down to a high-speed quad alternative.

From the top of this area you can make your way – via south-facing slopes served by snowmaking – to Gant in the valley between Sunnegga and the second main area, **Gornergrat–Hohtälli–Stockhorn**. A 125-person cable-car opened a few seasons ago linking Gant to Hohtälli in just seven minutes – a vast improvement on the two gruelling steep T-bars that were the only links before. A gondola makes the link back from Gant to Sunnegga. Gornergrat can be reached direct from

boarding *Boarders in soft boots have one big advantage over skiers in Zermatt – they have much more comfortable walks to and from the lift stations! Even so, there aren't many around. The slopes are best for experienced free-riders, because tough piste and off-piste action is what Zermatt is really about. There are acres of underused powder to ride, plus a world-class terrain-park and half-pipe near Riffelberg (with a new igloo and trendy tepee bar for 2002/03). There is another park and pipe on Klein Matterhorn and a park, boarder-cross course and quarter-pipe at Blauherd – so all three mountains are well-served. The main lifts are boarder-friendly: train, funicular, gondolas and cable-cars, but there are T-bars too. The resort is not ideal for learning, just as it isn't ideal for first-time skiers. Evenings have something for all.*

LIFT PASSES

2002/03 prices in
Swiss francs

Area Pass
Covers all lifts on the
Swiss side of the
border.
Main pass
1-day pass 64
6-day pass 320
Senior citizens
Over 65 (male), 63
(female): 6-day pass
272
Children
Under 16: 6-day pass
160
Under 9: free pass
Short-term passes
Single ascent tickets
for most lifts.
Notes Daily
supplement available
to cover all lifts in
Cervinia and
Valtournenche (38).
Alternative passes
Passes for any period
available for each
area of Zermatt
(Gornergrat-
Stockhorn, Sunnegga-
Rothorn, Trockener
Steg-Klein
Matterhorn-
Schwarzsee), and
combinations of
areas. Pass available
for Zermatt, Cervinia
and Valtournenche (1-
day 72; 6-day 366).

but we've had noticeably better reports on piste maintenance recently. But we still get a trickle of complaints about poor signposting.

FOR EXPERTS
Good – with superb heli-trips
If you've never been, Zermatt has to be on your shortlist. If you have been, we're pretty sure you'll want to return.

If you love long, fluffy mogul pitches, the slopes at Triftji, below Stockhorn, are the stuff of dreams. From the top of the Stockhorn cable-car there's a run down to the T-bar that serves another two steep 2km/1 mile runs – one each side of the lift. The whole mountainside here is one vast mogul field – steep, but not extremely so. Being north-facing and lying between 3400m and 2700m (11,150ft and 8,860ft), the snow is usually the best around, which makes the huge moguls so forgiving that even we can enjoy them. The snag in early season is that this whole area is unlikely to open until well into January, and possibly later.

You can continue down from here to Gant and catch the gondola up to Blauherd. On that mountain there are a couple of wonderful off-piste 'downhill routes' from Rothorn, which have spectacular views down towards the village and over to the Matterhorn.

On the Klein Matterhorn, the best area for experts is Schwarzsee, from where there are several steep north-facing gullies through the woods. Access to these runs will be much improved by the new Matterhorn Express gondola for 2002/03.

There are marvellous off-piste possibilities from the top lifts in each sector, but they aren't immediately obvious to those without local knowledge. They are also dangerous because of rocky and glacial terrain.

We don't recommend anyone going off-piste without a guide. You can join daily ski touring groups but there aren't standard off-piste groups as there are in resorts such as Val-d'Isère and Méribel. Unless you join The Ski School Zermatt off-piste free-ride classes, you have to hire a guide privately for a full day, and that's expensive unless you have a fair-sized group. The Ski Club of Great Britain usually hires a guide for off-piste

We once met a man who had been coming here for 20 years simply because of the mountain restaurants. The choice is enormous (the tourist information says 38, but it seems more). Most have table-service, nearly all of those we (and reporters) have tried serve excellent food and many are in spectacular settings. It is impossible to list here all those worth a visit – so don't limit yourself to those we mention. It is best to book – and check prices are within your budget when you do!

The restaurants at Fluhalp (live music and 'great glühwein and chocolate mit rum') and Grünsee have beautiful isolated situations and good food. The large terrace at Sunnegga has decent food and great views. Up at Rothorn, the restaurant has excellent food – we had wonderful lamb – and views. Down at Findeln are several attractive, busy, rustic restaurants, including Findlerhof (aka Franz & Heidy's), Chez Vrony ('this year's must'), Paradies and Enzian ('less busy than others'). And the restaurant at Tuftern sells good Heida white wine from the highest vineyard in Europe – just down the valley at 1200m/3,940ft.

At Furi, the Restaurant Furi, Aroleid above it and Simi's on the road below all have large sun terraces and good food. The hotel at Schwarzsee is right at the foot of the Matterhorn, with staggering views and endless variations of rösti. Round the back from here Stafelalp is simple but charmingly situated. Up above Trockener Steg Gandegghütte has stunning views of the glacier and 'good polenta'. On the way back to the village below Furi, Zum See is a charming old hut serving the best mountain food in Zermatt (which means it is world-class: we had delicious beef, lamb and raspberry tart here). Blatten is good too.

The Kulmhotel, at 3100m/10,170ft at Gornergrat, has both self-service and table-service restaurants with amazing views of lift-free mountains and glaciers.

Wherever you go, don't miss the local alcoholic coffee – in its many varieties!

skiing once a week – we joined that group a couple of years ago and had a great day.

Zermatt is the Alps' biggest heli-trip centre; the helipad resembles a bus station at times, with choppers taking off every few minutes. There are only three main drop-off points, so this can mean encountering one or two other groups on the mountain, even though there are multiple ways down. From all three points there are routes that don't require great expertise. The epic is from Monte Rosa, at over 4000m/13,000ft, down through wonderful glacier scenery to Furi. If there isn't much snow you may need the help of a rope that's fixed at the almost vertical, icy end of the glacier to get down.

FOR INTERMEDIATES
Mile after mile of beautiful runs
Zermatt is ideal for adventurous intermediates. Many of the blue and red runs tend to be at the difficult end of their grading. There are very beautiful reds down lift-free valleys from both Gornergrat and Hohtälli to Gant – we love these first thing in the morning, before anyone else is on them. A variant to Riffelalp ends up on a narrow wooded path with a sheer cliff and magnificent views to the right.

On Sunnegga, the 5km/3 mile Kumme run, from Rothorn to the bottom of the Patrullarve chair, also gets away from the lift system and has an interesting mix of straight-running and mogul pitches. On Klein

Matterhorn, the reds served by the Hörnli and Garten drags and the fast four-person chair from Furgg are all long and gloriously set at the foot of the Matterhorn.

For less adventurous intermediates, the blues on Sunnegga and above Riffelberg on Gornergrat and the runs between Klein Matterhorn and Trockener Steg are best. Of these, the Riffelberg area often has the best combination of good snow and easy cruising, and is popular with the school. Sunnegga gets a lot of sun, but the snowmaking means that the problem is more often a foot or more of heavy snow near the bottom than bare patches.

On the Klein Matterhorn, most of the runs, though marked red on the piste map, are very flat and represent the easiest slopes Zermatt has to offer, as well as the best snow. The problem here is the possibility of bad weather because of the height – high winds, extreme cold and poor visibility can make life very unpleasant. To get to Cervinia, you set off from Testa Grigia with a choice of two routes – even an early intermediate should find the easier 10km/6 mile route (on the left as you look at the Cervinia piste map) down to the village manageable. The red Ventina run is a delightful cruise for better intermediates.

Beware of the run from Furgg to Furi at the end of the day, when it can be tricky and very crowded (the only reason it is graded black that we can see, because it isn't very steep).

Horse-drawn sleigh rides are even more expensive than the annoying electric taxis →

SCHOOLS/GUIDES

2001/02 prices in Swiss francs

Swiss
Classes 5 days
6hr: 3hr am and pm
5 full days 280
Children's classes
Ages: 4-6 and 6-12
5 full days including lunch 330 to 370
Private lessons
1hr, 2hr or full-day
Full day 330 for 1 or 2 people; each additional person 20

The Ski School
Classes 5hr: 9.30-noon and 1-3.30
5 full days 395
Children's classes 5 full days including lunch 390
Private lessons
half or full-day
Full day 310; or 360 for VIP pick-up from hotel and video filming; each additional person 40

CHILDCARE

There are nurseries in two upmarket hotels. The one in the Nicoletta (966 0777) takes children aged 2 to 8, from 9am to 5pm. The Kinderclub Pumuckel at the Ginabelle (966 5000) takes children from 30 months, from 9am to 5pm, and ski lesson are available on the spot. The Kinderparadies (967 7252) takes children from 3 months from 9am to 5pm. The Snowflakes kindergarten at Trockener Steg takes children from age 4 by the hour (967 7020). Private babysitters are available, too.

Ski school lessons start at age 4.

FOR BEGINNERS
Learn elsewhere

Zermatt is to be avoided by beginners. The easiest slopes are outlined above. And there's no decent nursery slope area. Unless you have a compelling reason to start in Zermatt, don't.

FOR EVERYONE
A spectacular cable-car ride

The Klein Matterhorn cable-car is an experience not to miss if the weather is good. The views down to the glacier and its crevasses, as the car swings steeply into its hole blasted out of the mountain at the top, are stupendous. When you arrive, you walk through a long tunnel, to emerge on top of the world for the highest piste in Europe – walk slowly, the air is thin here and some people have altitude problems. The ice grotto cut into the glacier here is well worth a visit, with 'incredible ice carvings'. The top drag-lifts are open in the summer only.

FOR CROSS-COUNTRY
Fairly limited

There's a 4km/2.5 mile loop at Furi, 3km/2 miles near the bottom of the gondola to Furi, and 12 to 15km/7 to 9 miles down at Täsch (don't count on there being snow). There are also some 'ski walking trails' – best tackled as part of an organised group.

QUEUES
Main problem being solved

Zermatt has improved its lift system hugely in recent years, eliminating major bottlenecks. The major complaint we've had in the last few years has been the scramble for the gondola from town to Furi, followed by lengthy queues at Furi. These problems should both be solved by the new Matterhorn Express gondola due to open in November 2002 from Zermatt, via mid-stations at Furi and at 2300m/7,540ft to Schwarzsee. But it remains to be seen whether this leads to congestion on the Schwarzsee slopes and the lifts out of Furgg towards the Klein Matterhorn. The run down from Furgg is overcrowded at the end of the day – as are the buses back to town from the end of the piste home.

The other problem is the Gornergrat train – you may find there's only standing room (which can be tiring and uncomfortable – 'better to wait for the next one,' says a reporter).

To avoid the crowds, start early.

One thing we love about Zermatt is that the lifts start at 8am. Get out early and you can enjoy deserted slopes for at least two hours, followed by a late breakfast!

SCHOOLS AND GUIDES
Welcome competition at last

The main Swiss school has a poor reputation: 'Awful – in three days, the instructor taught our early intermediate no technique, spoke no English and used the follow-me method the whole time,' said a reporter.

There's a separate Stoked snowboard school, which we have good reports of. This has now combined with The Ski School Zermatt, which started in 2000/01 and is made up of talented young instructors, some of whom are British and all of whom speak good English. A reporter who took a private instructor highly recommends them and another was impressed by group lessons (with a British instructor). Their programme includes off-piste free-ride classes and freestyle classes (tricks in the terrain-park) as well as standard lessons.

FACILITIES FOR CHILDREN
Good hotel nurseries

The Nicoletta and Ginabelle hotels have obvious attractions for families who can afford them (though their nurseries are open to others). There's also a Snowflakes kindergarten for children aged at least 4 run by Stoked/The Ski School at Trockener Steg which can be used by the hour (SF15 for one hour). Despite our fat file of reports on Zermatt, we have no first-hand reports on them.

Staying there

HOW TO GO
A wide choice, packaged or not

Chalets Several operators have places here, many of the most comfortable contained in large apartment blocks. The Ski Company will have three luxury chalets here for 2002/03 – a penthouse for six and two brand-new chalets for ten being built next to each other and with jacuzzi, steam and fitness facilities.
Hotels There are over 100 hotels, mostly comfortable and traditional-style 3-stars and 4-stars, but taking in the whole range.
((((5 **Mont Cervin** (966 8888) Biggest in town. Elegantly traditional. Good pool.
((((5 **Zermatterhof** (966 6600)

GETTING THERE

Air Geneva, rail transfer 4hr. Zürich, rail transfer 5hr. Sion, transfer 1½hr.

Rail Station in resort.

SWITZERLAND

484

ACTIVITIES

Indoor Sauna, tennis, hotel swimming pools (some open to public), salt water pool, keep-fit centre, squash, billiards, curling, bowling, gallery, excellent Alpine museum, cinema, indoor golf **Outdoor** Skating, curling, sleigh rides, 30km cleared paths, helicopter flights, paragliding, cycling, ice-diving

Traditional 'grand hotel' style with piano bar and pool.

((((⑤ **Riffelalp Resort** (966 0555) Up the mountain, recent smart extension, pool and spa, own evening trains.

((((④ **Alex** (966 7070) Close to station. Good facilities, including a pool. Reporters love it. 'First class,' said one.

((((④ **Ambassador** (966 2611) Peaceful position near Gornergrat station. Large pool; sauna.

((((④ **Monte Rosa** (966 0333) Well-modernised original Zermatt hotel, near southern end of village – full of climbing pictures and mementos.

((((④ **Ginabelle** (966 5000) Smart pair of chalets not far from Sunnegga lift; great for families – on-the-spot ski nursery as well as day care.

((((④ **Nicoletta** (966 0777) Modern chalet quite close to centre, with nursery.

((((④ **Sonne** (966 2066) Traditionally decorated, in quiet setting away from main street; 'Roman Bath' complex.

((③ **Julen** (966 7600) Charming, modern-rustic chalet over the river, with Matterhorn views from some rooms.

((③ **Butterfly** (966 4166) 'Small, friendly, close to and as well furnished as the Alex, but much better food,' says a recent reporter.

(② **Atlanta** (966 3535) No frills, but good food; close to centre, with Matterhorn views from some rooms.

(② **Alpina** (967 1050) Modest but very friendly, and close to centre.

Self-catering There is a lot of apartment accommodation, but not much finds its way to the UK package market,. We have enjoyed staying in the hotel Ambassador apartments, with free use of all facilities such as pool and sauna. The tourist office web site has apartment details.

STAYING UP THE MOUNTAIN
Comfortable seclusion
There are several hotels at altitude, of which the pick is the Riffelalp Resort at the first stop on the Gornergrat railway (see Hotels above) – but you might find its limited evening train service a bit restricting. At the top of the railway, at 3100m/10,170ft, is the Kulmhotel Gornergrat – a rather austere building with basic accommodation.

STAYING DOWN THE VALLEY
Attractive for drivers
In Täsch, where visitors must leave their cars, there are five 3-star hotels, costing less than half the price of the

equivalent in Zermatt. The Täscherhof (967 1818) is next to the station; the City (967 3606) close by. It's a 13-minute ride from Zermatt, with trains every 20 minutes for most of the day; the last train down is 11.10. You can also get taxis to the edge of Zermatt.

EATING OUT
Huge choice at all price levels
There are over 100 restaurants to choose from, ranging from top-quality haute cuisine, through traditional Swiss food, Chinese, Japanese and Thai to egg and chips and even a McDonald's.

Mood's is a new restaurant in the premises that used to house the excellent 'Enzo, Vrony'. The Mazot is highly rated and highly priced. All the top hotels have classy restaurants open to non-residents. At the other end of the scale, Café du Pont has good-value pasta and rösti.

The Schwyzer Stübli has local specialities and usually live Swiss music and dancing. The Bahnhof Buffet has been rebuilt and serves reasonable food in a dining room built like a panoramic railway carriage.

Rua Thai is in the basement of the hotel Abana Real has been recommended by one visitor for excellent food and beautiful decor.

Da Mario, Casa Rustica, Baku (see Après-ski) and the Spaghetti Factory (in the hotel Post complex) have all been recommended by readers.

APRES-SKI
Lively and varied
A good mix of sophisticated and informal fun, though it helps if you have deep pockets. On the way back from the Klein Matterhorn there are lots of restaurants below Furi for a last drink and sunbathe – and delicious fruit tarts at Zum See. Recent visitors rave about the new Baku, on the way back to Winkelmatten. It's got a

↑ The third photo of the Matterhorn in this chapter: wherever you go it's always in sight (Zermatt in the foreground this time)

ZERMATT TOURIST OFFICE / TONI MOHR

Phone numbers
From elsewhere in Switzerland add the prefix 027.
From abroad use the prefix +41 27.

TOURIST OFFICE

Postcode CH-3920
t 966 8100
f 966 8101
zermatt@wallis.ch
www.zermatt.ch

wigwam outside so you can't miss it: 'The staff are friendly, some of the food is exceptional and there is a great atmosphere.' On the way back from Sunnegga, Othmar's Hutte is popular and the Olympia Stübli often has live music. Near the church at Winkelmatten, the Sonnenblick is 'a great place to watch the sun set'.

In town the Papperla is one of the few popular early places (it's crowded after dinner, too). Elsie's bar is atmospheric and gets packed with an older crowd both early and late. The North Wall is frequented by seasonal workers and Murphy's Irish pub is the place if you're interested in 'loud music and beer'. Promenading the main street checking out expensive shoes and watches is popular.

Later on, the remarkable hotel Post complex has something for everyone, from a quiet, comfortable bar (David's Boathouse) to a lively disco (Broken); Pink Elephant has live music (jazz, Irish etc) and a selection of restaurants.

Grampi's has dancing and is worth a visit. Z'Alt Hischi and the Little Bar are good for a quiet drink. The Hexenbar is cosy too. The hotel Alex draws a mature clientele for eating, drinking and dancing, with 'middle-of-the-road

music and candlelit tables,' says a recent reporter.

The Vernissage is our favourite bar in town for a quiet evening drink. It is an unusual and stylish modern place, with the projection room for the cinema built into the upstairs bar and displays of art elsewhere. Mood's has a cocktail bar downstairs and restaurant above.

If all this is not enough, you should be able to gamble your spare money away in a new casino due to open in December 2002.

OFF THE SLOPES
Considerable attractions
Zermatt is an easy place to spend time (and money). If lunch up the mountain appeals, this is a great resort for pedestrians – it is easy to get around on the lifts and there are some nice walks. The Ice Grotto at Klein Matterhorn is worth the trip and the Alpine museum in town is recommended – as is a helicopter trip around the Matterhorn. There is an 'excellent' cinema, and a reader tells us the free village guided tour is 'well worth doing'. You can also try ice-diving (wetsuit provided) at Trockener Steg.

It was snow that first took the British to America in large numbers, during the Alpine snow droughts of the late 1980s. The super-high Rockies had the reputation of getting limitless quantities of super-light snow. The reputation went slightly beyond the reality, but in practice it didn't matter; there were lots of other aspects to American resorts that kept their new customers satisfied.

In general, people are captivated by the American experience and by the contrasts with European resorts. Nearly everyone is struck by the high standards of service and courtesy you receive, by the relatively deserted pistes, by the immaculate piste grooming and by the top-quality accommodation. Depending on the resort, you may also be struck by the cute Wild West ambience and the superb quality of the snow – and for those who like it deep and steep there is the benefit in many resorts of large areas of expert terrain that can be tackled without costly guides.

But don't fall into the trap of lumping all US resorts together – they differ enormously. That's one reason why we have organised our American chapters in five regional sections – California, Colorado, Utah, Rest of the West and New England. US skiing does have some distinct disadvantages, too. Read on.

The snow remains an attraction. Most American resorts receive serious amounts of snow (average snowfall is typically in the region of 6m to 12m (20ft to 40ft) in a season). And most resorts have serious snowmaking facilities too. What's more, they use them well – they lay down a base of artificial snow early in the season, rather than patching up shortages later on in the European fashion.

There are wide differences in quantity and quality of snowfall, both between individual resorts and between regions – we discuss some of these in our regional introductions.

Piste grooming is taken very seriously – most American resorts set standards that the best Alpine resorts are only now attempting to match. Every morning you can expect to step out on to perfect 'corduroy' pistes. But this doesn't mean that there aren't moguls – far from it. It's just that you get moguls where the resort says you can expect moguls, not everywhere. Some resorts have now taken to grooming half the width of some runs and leaving the other half mogulled.

The slopes of most American resorts are blissfully free of crowds – a key advantage that becomes more important every year as the pistes of Courchevel, St Anton and Verbier become ever more congested. If you want to let those new carving skis run, take them to the States. And, because they are mostly below the tree-line, the slopes offer good visibility in bad weather.

The good organisation of American resorts doesn't stop at grooming. Many

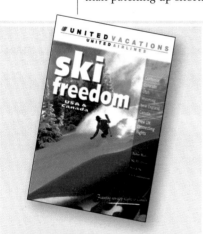

offer free guided tours of the area. Lift queues are short, partly because they are highly disciplined, and spare seats on chair-lifts are religiously filled, with the aid of cheerful, conscientious attendants. Piste maps and tissues are freely available at the bottom of most lifts. Mountain 'hosts' are on hand to advise you about the best possible routes to take. School standards are uniformly high, with the added advantage that English is the native language. Practically all the reports we get from readers are rave reviews, and complaints are virtually unknown – in sharp contrast to Europe. And facilities for children are impressive too – our reporters are universally glowing in their praise about children's ski school classes.

Many Europeans have the idea that American resorts don't have off-piste terrain, but this seriously misrepresents the position. It's true that resorts practically always have a boundary, and that venturing beyond into the 'back-country' may be discouraged or forbidden (though in some resorts it's just limited to certain gates). But within the area there is often very challenging terrain that is very much like off-piste terrain in an Alpine resort – with the important advantage that it is patrolled and avalanche-controlled. Far from being a weakness of American resorts, we rate their expert terrain as one of their great attractions.

There are drawbacks to the US as well, though. One is that many resorts (including big names) have slopes that are very modest in extent compared with major Alpine areas. But many US resorts are very close to each other – so if you are prepared to travel a bit, you won't get bored. A more serious problem is that the day is ridiculously short. The lifts often shut at 3pm or 3.30. That may explain another drawback for those who like a good lunch on the mountain – the

dearth of decent mountain restaurants. Monster self-service cafeterias doing fast food are the norm – so that people can spend as much time on the slopes and as little time eating as possible. Small atmospheric restaurants with table-service and decent food are rare – but growing in number as resorts try to attract more European guests.

It's also true that in many resorts the terrain is slightly monotonous. You don't get the spectacular mountain scenery and the distinctive high-mountain runs of the Alps. Most trails have clearly been cut through the forest; whereas in the Alps the artificial nature of the runs is rarely obvious when they are blanketed by snow, in the Rockies it is inescapable.

The grading of pistes (or trails, to use the local term) is different from that in Europe. Red runs don't exist. The colours used are combined with shapes. Green circles correspond fairly closely to greens in Europe (that is, in France, where they are mainly found). American blue squares largely correspond to blues in Europe, but also include tougher intermediate runs that would be red in the Alps; these are sometimes labelled as double-blue squares, although in some resorts a hybrid blue-black grading is used instead. Black diamond runs correspond to steeper European reds and easier European blacks. But then there are multiple diamonds. Double-diamond runs are seriously steep – often steeper than the steepest pistes in the Alps and including high, open bowls. A few resorts have started to class their very steepest runs as triple-diamonds.

US resort towns vary widely in style and convenience. But two important things that they all have in common are good-value, spacious accommodation and good, reasonably priced restaurants. There are old restored mining towns such as Telluride, Crested Butte and Aspen, genuine cowboy towns such as Jackson Hole, purpose-built monstrosities such as Snowbird, and even skyscraping gambling dens such as Heavenly. There is an increasing number of cute car-free, slope-side villages such as Keystone's River Run, Copper Mountain's revamped base and the fledgling village at Squaw Valley.

In the end, your reaction to skiing and snowboarding in America may depend mainly on your reaction to America. If repeated cheerful exhortations to have a nice day wind you up – or if you like to be left in silence on chair-lifts – perhaps you'd better stick to the Alps.

What about the cost? It's never going to be cheap, but the basic cost of getting there is lower than you might think – you can get room-plus-hire-car February packages to California for under £500, eating out is not expensive and it's not difficult to find rooms with kitchenettes where you can economise by doing some of your own catering. But lift passes, tuition and childcare are very expensive by European standards. You can often save, especially on lift passes, by buying in advance through tour operators – look out for these deals. As we go to press, the US$ has fallen below parity with the euro, so there is at least a possibility that your pound will go further in the States this season than in the recent past.

California? It means surfing, beaches, wine, Hollywood, Disneyland and San Francisco cable-cars. But it also has the highest mountains in continental USA and some of America's biggest winter resorts, usually reliable for snow from November to May (one sometimes remains open until the Independence Day holiday, the 4th of July). What's more, winter holidays in California are less expensive than you might expect.

Holidays here are relatively cheap because winter is low season for much of the accommodation and for scheduled flights from Britain into Los Angeles and San Francisco. There is huge capacity available for the massive summer tourist trade, and hotel owners and airlines are happy to offer cut-price deals to keep a contribution coming in towards their overheads.

California's mountains get a lot of snow. In several recent seasons, Californian resorts have recorded the deepest snow-cover in North America. A common allegation is that the snow that falls in California is wet 'Sierra Cement'. Our fat file of reports from visitors has some complaints about that – especially late in the season – but most people have found the snow just fine. So have we: in March 2002 we enjoyed two of the best days of the season skiing powder in the trees of Heavenly and Mammoth.

You might want to start getting to grips with Californian skiing by reading the Lake Tahoe chapter, covering half a dozen resorts dotted around the mountains that ring this spectacular lake. You could visit them all from a single base using a car, and most using buses and boats.

The resorts you might think of spending most time in are Heavenly, Squaw Valley and Mammoth (a long drive south of Tahoe) – all impressive

mountains, with something for all abilities of skier or boarder. In the past our main reservation has been the character of the resorts themselves; they don't have the traditional mountain-town ambience that we look for in the States. That's partly because this is California, where walking is regarded as an eccentric way to get around. In compensation, Heavenly, at least, offers uniquely big-time entertainment in its casinos. And the scenery, particularly around Lake Tahoe, is simply stunning.

But things are changing, with several new 'pedestrian villages' being developed. At Heavenly a new gondola goes from the centre of South Lake Tahoe right into the heart of the slopes – and work on the new car-free 'village' at the gondola base has now started. It won't transform the town, but it will surely help. The first stage of the new village at Squaw Valley was open at the base of the slopes for the 2001/02 season, and much more will be finished this season, making this a viable base. A couple of smaller Lake Tahoe resorts – Kirkwood and Northstar – have developed small, attractive slope-side villages. Mammoth has new slope-side accommodation, and work has started on construction of a pedestrian 'village' that will eventually be linked to the slopes by gondola and piste.

489

Many California resorts offer terrain that's a great compromise between the dense forests of Colorado and the open slopes of high Alpine resorts; this is Mammoth ➜

Knockout views over Lake Tahoe, and a unique nightlife scene

WHAT IT COSTS

HOW IT RATES

The slopes

Snow	****
Extent	***
Experts	***
Intermediates	****
Beginners	****
Convenience	*
Queues	****
Restaurants	*

The rest

Scenery	****
Resort charm	*
Off-slope	**

➕ Spectacular setting, with amazing views of Lake Tahoe and Nevada

➕ Fair-sized mountain which offers a sensation of travelling around – common in the Alps, not in the US

➕ Large areas of widely spaced trees, largely on intermediate slopes – fabulous in fresh powder

➕ Some serious challenges for experts

➕ Numerous other worthwhile resorts within an hour's drive

➕ A unique nightlife scene

➕ Good snow record plus impressive snowmaking facilities

➕ Gondola from downtown South Lake Tahoe and pedestrian 'village' under construction are real improvements

➖ South Lake Tahoe, where you stay, is a bizarre and messy combination of high-rise casino-hotels and shabby low-rise motels, shops and restaurants that spreads for miles along a busy highway

➖ The new resort 'village' isn't going to transform the whole place

➖ No trail back to South Lake Tahoe, so it's a gondola ride or bus-ride home if you're based there

➖ Very little traditional après-ski activity – though the new 'village' should help put that right

➖ If natural snow is in short supply, most of the challenging terrain is likely to be closed

A resort called Heavenly invites an obvious question: just how close to heaven does it take you? Physically, close enough: with a top height of 3060m/10,040ft and vertical of 1065m/3,500ft, it's the highest and biggest of the resorts clustered around scenic Lake Tahoe (look at the next chapter for more about that). Metaphorically, it's not quite so close. In particular, anyone who (like us) is drawn to Heavenly partly by its exceptionally scenic setting is likely to be dismayed by the appearance and atmosphere of the town of South Lake Tahoe.

The official line is that the place is being transformed into something like a European ski resort by the new gondola from downtown up to the mountain and by the construction of a pedestrian 'village' around its base. We don't buy that. The 'village' will be somewhere for skiers to spend time and money painlessly at the end of the day. But the general feel of SLT won't be much affected.

Packages here are not quite as cheap as they were, which may explain why the flow of readers' reports seems to be dwindling. Do report if you go this season.

What's new

490

The first phase of a 34-acre pedestrian 'village' around the base of the Heavenly gondola, with shops, accommodation, restaurants, ice rink and multi-screen cinema, will open for the 2002/03 season.

Two new gladed runs opened for 2001/02 in the upper Nevada area off Skyline Trail.

MOUNTAIN FACTS

Altitude	1995m-3060m
	6,540ft-10,040ft
Lifts	29
Pistes	4,800 acres
Green	20%
Blue	45%
Black	35%
Snowmaking	
	500 acres
Recco detectors used	

The resort

Heavenly is on California's border with Nevada, at the south end of Lake Tahoe. There are over a dozen resorts dotted around the lake; some of the others are described in the Lake Tahoe chapter that follows this one.

Heavenly's base-town – South Lake Tahoe – is primarily a summer resort. In this respect it is unusual, but not unique. What really sets it apart is that its economy is driven by gambling. The Stateline area at its centre is dominated by a handful of monstrous hotel-casinos located just inches on the Nevada side of the line. These brash but comfortable hotels offer

good-value accommodation (subsidised by the gambling), swanky restaurants and big-name entertainers, as well as roulette wheels, craps and endless card games – though they basically exist to allow gambling-starved Americans to feed bucketloads of quarters into slot machines.

The casinos are a conspicuous part of the amazing lake views from the lower slopes (though not from above mid-mountain). They look like a classic American downtown area, which you'd expect to be full of shops and bars. But they are actually just a cluster of high-rise blocks; what's more, the central area is bisected by the seriously busy US Highway 50. The rest

HEAVENLY SKI RESORT /
SHERRY MCMANUS

The new gondola goes up directly from downtown South Lake Tahoe, close to the casinos. Pity there is no run back to the base ↓

of the town spreads for miles along this pedestrian-hostile road – dozens of low-rise hotels and motels (some quite smart, but many rather shabby), stores, wedding chapels and so on. The general effect is less dire than it might be, thanks to the camouflage of the tall trees that blanket the area.

The new 'village' being built on the California side of the stateline will be a great improvement, providing an après-ski focus that the resort currently lacks. It will doubtless be attractively designed in the modern American mountain style, and if you can afford it this will be the obvious place to stay – right next to the base of the new gondola into the heart of the skiing.

Some of the casino-hotels are also within 5 minutes' walk of the gondola, making these an attractive choice even for those not keen on the gambling and entertainment, but others are enough of a hike away to justify using the shuttle buses. And much of the cheaper accommodation is literally miles away. If that's where you're staying, you may prefer to access the mountain from the original lift base, California Lodge, up a heavily wooded slope a mile out of South Lake Tahoe.

Like the town, the slopes spread across the border into Nevada – and there are two other lift bases, which can easily be reached by road, around the mountain in Nevada. There are 'excellent' free shuttle-bus services to the three out-of-town bases. A car is still handy to explore the other resorts around Lake Tahoe and to get to many of the best bars and restaurants away from the casinos.

An amusing way to visit Squaw Valley is to go by boat. It costs $87 including lift pass and ground transport. The outward trip can now be done by fast launch; leaving at 7.15, this gets you on to the cable-car by 8.45. The return is more leisurely – an après-ski party with live band 'doing decent cover versions' aboard the stern-wheeler Tahoe Queen. For an extra $20 you can get a 'decent three-course dinner', seated apart from the increasingly 'emotional' throng.

The mountain

Most of Heavenly's slopes suit intermediates down to the ground, but there are also good beginner slopes at the California base, and some splendid easy runs to progress to. Experts can find genuine challenges on the Nevada side – as well as lots of fun in acre upon acre of widely spaced trees. As always in America, this off-piste terrain is avalanche controlled. But it's 'patrolled' only by hollering; since collision with a tree may render you insensible, don't ski the trees alone.

THE SLOPES
Interestingly complex
Heavenly's mountain is quite complicated, and getting from A to B requires more careful navigation than is usual on American mountains. Quite a few of the links between different sectors involve flat tracks.

There is a fairly clear division between the California side of the mountain (the slopes directly above South Lake Tahoe) and the Nevada side (above Stagecoach Lodge and Boulder Lodge). The new gondola takes you (almost) to the fast Tamarack six-seater chair, which gives access to either side. Near the Nevada border you can see beautiful views over Lake Tahoe in one direction and the arid Nevada 'desert' in the other.

On the California side there are four main sectors: blue runs from the

Heavenly

491

LIFT PASSES

2001/02 prices in
dollars

Heavenly
Covers all lifts on
Heavenly mountain.
Beginners 3-day learn
to ski packages
include lift pass and
rental (adult 233).
Main pass
1-day pass 57
6-day pass 306
Senior citizens
Over 65: 6-day pass
144
Children
13 to 18: 6-day pass
246
Under 13: 6-day pass
144
Under 5: free pass
Short-term passes
Half-day passes
available from 12.30
to 4pm (adult 42)
Notes Passes of three
days or more allow
one non-skiing day;
6-day pass valid for 7
days, with one non-
skiing day.

Tamarack chair; black and blue runs
from the fast Sky quad, supplemented
by two slow chairs; everything from
black to green runs from the slow
Waterfall and Powderhorn chairs; and
the lower slopes served by the
Tramway and fast Gunbarrel chair –
unrelenting steep black runs down the
front face, often heavily mogulled, with
the alternative of the narrow, blue
Roundabout trail snaking its way down
the mountain. Right at the California
Lodge base is a great beginner area.
From here uplift is by a mid-sized
cable-car and the recently upgraded
Gunbarrel fast quad.

On the Nevada side there are three
main bowls. The central one, above
East Peak Lodge, is an excellent
intermediate area served by two fast
quad chairs, with a downhill extension
of the bowl served by the Galaxy chair.
On one side of this central bowl is the
steeper, open terrain of Milky Way
Bowl, leading to the seriously steep
Mott and Killebrew canyons, served by
the Mott Canyon chair. On the other
side is the North Bowl, with lifts up
from Nevada's two base lodges.

There are no really easy runs on the
Nevada side, apart from limited nursery
slopes at the base.

SNOW RELIABILITY
No worries

Heavenly was one of the first resorts to
invest heavily in snowmaking, which
proved its value when a severe snow
drought hit in the late 80s and early
90s. The system now covers around
70% of the trails and ensures that
most sections are open most of the
time. In recent years Californian resorts
have consistently recorded some of the
deepest snow cover of any North
American resorts – and Heavenly is
now able to claim a five-year average
of an impressive 360in. Both of our
most recent visits have been blessed
by excellent conditions.

FOR EXPERTS
Some specific challenges

There are genuine challenges for the
more advanced. The runs under the
California base lifts – including The
Face and Gunbarrel (often used for
mogul competitions) – are of proper
black steepness, and very challenging
when the snow is hard. Ellie's, at the
top of the mountain, may offer
continuous moguls too.

The really steep stuff is on the
Nevada side. Milky Way Bowl provides
a gentle single-diamond introduction to

SCHOOLS/GUIDES

2001/02 prices in dollars

Perfect Turn
Clinics 3 days
1¾hr from 10am,
12.30 or 2.30
Children's clinics
Ages: 4 to 13
per 5hr day including
pass, rental and lunch
119
Private clinics
1hr, 2hr, 4hr and 6hr
140 for 2hr

CHILDCARE

Heavenly's state-of-the-art Day Care Center opens at 8.30 to care for children between the ages of 2 months and 4 years. Book ahead.

Children between 4 and 13 can enrol in the Perfect Kids programme. It offers skiing from age 4 and a snowboarding option from 8 upwards. It is an all-inclusive day of supervision, lessons, lunch, lift access, equipment and snacks. The programme is based at California Lodge (which includes an indoor play area) or at Boulder Lodge. There are also 'Tag-along' private lessons where a parent can observe their child's progress.

---

the emphatically double-diamond terrain beyond it. The seriously steep Mott and Killebrew canyons have roped gateways. The less expert are steered to lower gates. The Mott Canyon chair is slow, but you may welcome the rest it affords.

All over the mountain there is excellent off-piste skiing among widely spaced trees – tremendous fun when the conditions are right. Some wooded slopes are identified on the trail map, but you are not confined to those. The trail map gives a good indication of the density of trees in different areas, and the grading of nearby trails gives a good idea of steepness.

FOR INTERMEDIATES
Lots to do
Heavenly is excellent for intermediates, who are made to feel welcome and secure by excellent piste grooming and signposting. The California side offers a progression from the relaxed cruising of the long Ridge Run, starting right at the top of the mountain, to more challenging blues dropping off the ridge towards the Sky Deck restaurant. The confident intermediate may want to spend more time on the Nevada side, where there is more variety of terrain, some longer runs down to the lift bases and more space to indulge in some fast carving.

FOR BEGINNERS
An excellent place to learn
The California side is more suited to beginners, with gentle green runs served by the Pioneer drag-lift and the Powderbowl chair-lift at the top of the cable-car. There are good nursery slopes at base lodge level.

FOR CROSS-COUNTRY
A separate world
The Spooner Lake Cross Country Area located close to Tahoe is an extensive meadow area of over 100km/60 miles in 21 prepared trails. There are ample facilities for both instruction and

rental. Organised moonlit tours are a popular alternative to the noise and bright lights of the casinos.

QUEUES
Some at weekends
Lift lines are generally not a problem, except during some weekends and public holidays when the entire Tahoe area is swamped with weekenders and day-trippers. Thanks to the new gondola, the key lifts moving people out from the base lodges are now under less pressure on busy days.

MOUNTAIN RESTAURANTS
Even refuelling is problematic
The on-mountain catering is inadequate, at least in bad weather. The only recommendable restaurant is the table-service Monument Peak at the top of the tram from California Lodge – simple food but a calm atmosphere and the famous lake view (reservations necessary). But last time we were there it was closed for a private function. The next-door cafeteria was bursting at the seams, so we had the privilege of sitting on the outdoor Sky Deck eating a burger being rapidly cooled by the blizzard. We were not pleased. In Nevada, East Peak Lodge has a terrace and barbie, but it too gets hideously overcrowded when the weather drives people indoors.

SCHOOLS AND GUIDES
Good system
The Perfect Turn ski and ride programmes build on your strengths rather than focusing on your weaknesses and are highly regarded.

FACILITIES FOR CHILDREN
Comprehensive
The Perfect Kids learning centre in the California Base Lodge was expanded by 30% for 2001/02. It attracted particular praise from one reporter: 'This was an excellent facility – very convenient and very professionally run. I would thoroughly recommend it.'

---

boarding *Lake Tahoe is quickly becoming known as the snowboarding hub of North America and, as you would expect, boarders are very well catered for at Heavenly. There are good terrain-parks and half-pipes on both the California and Nevada sides. The off-piste in trees and double-black-diamond bowls make a great playground for good free-riders. Beginners and intermediates will enjoy great cruising runs and the easy-to-ride chair-lifts. There are a couple of specialist board shops in South Lake Tahoe, but quite an absence of lively boarder-friendly bars.*

The wedding industry in South Lake Tahoe is almost as big as the ski industry →

HEAVENLY SKI RESORT / SHERRY MCMANUS

GETTING THERE

Air San Francisco, transfer 3½hr. Reno, transfer 75 min. South Lake Tahoe, transfer 15 min.

Phone numbers

The state line runs through Heavenly, so two different area codes are used. For this chapter only, therefore, the area code is included with the number.

From distant parts of the US, add the prefix 1. From abroad, add the prefix +1.

ACTIVITIES

Indoor 6 casinos, 6 cinemas, cheap factory shops, ice skating, bowling, gyms, spas, Western museum
Outdoor Boat cruises, snowmobiling, horse-drawn sleigh rides, horse riding, ice skating, hot springs, ghost town tours

TOURIST OFFICE

Postcode NV 89449
t 775 586 7000
f 775 588 5517
info@skiheavenly.com
www.skiheavenly.com

Staying there

HOW TO GO
Hotel or motel?

Accommodation in the South Lake Tahoe area is abundant and ranges from the glossy casinos to small, rather ramshackle motels. Hotel and motel rooms are easy to find midweek, but can be sold out at busy weekends.

Chalets UK tour operators run some good catered chalets, including some lakeside ones.

Hotels Of the main casino hotels, Harrah's (775 558 6611) and Harveys (775 558 2411) are the closest to the gondola. Rooms booked on the spot are expensive; packages are good value.

((((4 **Embassy Suites** (530 544 5400) Luxury suites in a modern, traditional-style building ideally placed between the casinos and the new gondola.
((2 **Station House Inn** (530 542 1101) 'Very good, and well located, near the gondola.'
((2 **Tahoe Chalet Inn** (530 544 3311) Clean, friendly, near casinos. Back rooms (away from highway) preferable.
((2 **Timber Cove Lodge** (530 541 6722) Bland but well run, with lake views from some rooms.

Self-catering Plenty of choice. Some are available from tour operators. We've had a rave report about The Ridge Tahoe condos near Stagecoach Lodge: 'Luxury accommodation. The bathroom was big enough for waltzing.' There's an indoor-outdoor pool, hot-tub and a private gondola to whisk you to the slopes.

EATING OUT
Good value

The casino hotels offer fantastic value in their buffet-style all-you-can-eat dining. They have some more ambitious 'gourmet' restaurants too – some high enough up their tower blocks to give superb lake views (try Harrah's 18th floor). The sprawling resort area offers a great choice of international dining, from cosy little pizza houses to large, traditional American diners, Mexican tequila-and-tacos joints, and English and Irish pubs. Visitors' suggestions include Fresh Ketch at Tahoe Keys Marina for 'wonderful fresh fish and harbour views – though don't expect snazzy presentation'. The Riva Grill is also recommended.

APRES-SKI
Extraordinary

The casinos on the Nevada side of the stateline aren't simply opportunities to throw money away on roulette or slot machines: top-name entertainers, pop and jazz stars, circus acts and Broadway revues are also to be found in them – designed to give gamblers another reason to stay. You can dance and dine your way across the lake aboard an authentic paddle steamer.

OFF THE SLOPES
Luck be a lady

If gambling is your weakness, you're in luck. Or then again, perhaps not. If you want to get away from the bright lights, try a boat trip on Lake Tahoe, snowmobiling a short drive from South Lake Tahoe, or a hot-air balloon ride.

Pedestrians can use the cable-car or the gondola to share the lake views.

Lake Tahoe 1890m/6,200ft

A resort a day for a week or even a fortnight – and splendid lake views

WHAT IT COSTS

What's new

First Ascent, phase one of the new base village at Squaw Valley, opened for the 2001/02 season. It includes shops, restaurants and underground parking. Over the next few years, the size of the village will quadruple.

Spectacularly set high in the Sierra Nevada 320km/200 miles east of San Francisco, Lake Tahoe is ringed by skiable mountains containing 14 downhill and 7 cross-country centres – the highest concentration of winter sports resorts in the US. One or two of the resorts may have the extent and variety of slopes to keep you amused for a week, but the real appeal of this area is that from a single base you can easily visit several resorts, spending a day or two at each.

Two resorts stand out from the herd, at least in terms of size. Heavenly (covered in detail in the previous chapter) is the biggest in the area, and has at the foot of its slopes much the biggest development – the bizarre gambling-based town of South Lake Tahoe. It makes an obvious base for visiting a range of resorts both south and north of the lake. Squaw Valley, the biggest north-shore resort, comes a close second to Heavenly in terms of area, but doesn't yet have much choice of accommodation.

In this chapter are brief descriptions of Squaw and four other resorts – all appreciably smaller than Heavenly and Squaw, but all offering a worthwhile 2,000 to 2,500 acres of terrain. At the end of the chapter are very brief pointers on a couple of other resorts worth visiting. Most of the resorts mainly attract weekend visitors from the cities of California's coastal area. Peak weekends apart, the slopes are uncrowded, and queues are rare.

Most of the minor resorts are not fully formed 'destination' resorts of the kind that you find in Colorado or the Alps. Increasing numbers have some

accommodation, but few other facilities. A few have no nearby accommodation at all; but there are lots of B&Bs and motels scattered around the lake, and a couple of quite pleasant small towns. The obvious alternative to staying in South Lake Tahoe is the small tourist town of Tahoe City, on the lake a short drive from Squaw Valley, Alpine Meadows and Northstar. It has a range of touristy shops and some good restaurants and bars. Our regular Tahoe reporter suggests Incline Village at the north-east corner of the lake (handy for Diamond Peak and Mount Rose) for its 'country charm and ambience, and friendly people'. It comes a close second to Tahoe City for choice of bars and restaurants.

The area has a generally impressive snowfall record, particularly in recent years. Last season was a bit erratic, with dodgy conditions in February, but when we visited in mid-March we enjoyed superb conditions. There is also a lot of snowmaking. When we visited a few years ago the snow-guns at Heavenly were invisible – entirely buried by real snow.

495

SNOWPIX.COM / CHRIS GILL

Squaw has great terrain for experts and adventurous intermediates →

MOUNTAIN FACTS

Alpine Meadows

Altitude 2085m-2630m

6,840ft-8,640ft
Lifts	12
Pistes	2,000 acres
Green	25%
Blue	40%
Black	35%
Snowmaking	
	220 acres
Recco detectors used	

Kirkwood

Altitude 2375m-2985m
7,800ft-9,800ft
Lifts	12
Pistes	2,300 acres
Green	15%
Blue	50%
Black	35%
Snowmaking 55 acres	
Recco detectors used	

Northstar-at-Tahoe

Altitude 1930m-2625m
6,330ft-8,610ft
Lifts	15
Pistes	2,420 acres
Green	25%
Blue	50%
Black	25%
Snowmaking	
	220 acres

Sierra-at-Tahoe

Altitude 2025m-2700m
6,640ft-8,850ft
Lifts	9
Pistes	2,000 acres
Green	25%
Blue	50%
Black	25%

Squaw Valley

Altitude 1890m-2760m
6,200ft-9,050ft
Lifts	30
Pistes	4,000 acres
Green	25%
Blue	45%
Black	30%
Snowmaking	
	360 acres
Recco detectors used	

SIERRA-AT-TAHOE

Sierra is only a half-hour drive south-west of South Lake Tahoe, off Highway 50. It's a wooded area with a vertical of 675m/2,210ft, and nothing at the base but a day lodge and a car park.
Sierra claims an average of 480in of snow a year – almost a match for better-known Kirkwood. The slopes are spread over two flanks of Huckleberry Mountain, above the base lodge, and West Bowl, off to one side. Both sectors include a fast quad chair among their lifts. The front of the main area and West Bowl both offer good intermediate cruising plus some genuine single-diamond blacks. The back of the main hill has easier slopes.

There are five gates in the area boundary accessing backcountry terrain, and half-day tours guided by ski patrollers. There are terrain parks for skiers and boarders, and a 'super' half-pipe with huge 17-foot walls The trees provide shelter, so it's a good place to be in bad weather. But bear in mind that the road from SLT passes over the 2250m/7,380 ft Echo Summit, which may require chains. In addition to the day lodge at the base, there's a restaurant at the top of the hill.

KIRKWOOD

Kirkwood is renowned for its powder, and has a lot to offer experts and confident intermediates. It is only a little way south of Sierra, but is twice as far away from South Lake Tahoe. The small base village includes a growing range of condos.
Kirkwood is reached from SLT over the 2360m/ 7,740ft Luther Pass and the 2615m/ 8,575ft Carson Pass. There is a daily shuttle bus from SLT, arriving at Kirkwood at 9.30 – reservations needed; the round trip costs only $5.

Kirkwood claims an annual average snowfall of over 500 inches, which puts it right in the first rank alongside Utah's Alta and Snowbird.

The resort sits at the centre of a semicircle of slopes – lightly wooded at the top, more densely at the bottom. The lift system consists almost entirely of slow chair-lifts radiating from the main base area. One goes up to the top of the main bowl above the base, as does the resort's one fast quad. These two long lifts also give access to bowls to left and right of the main one. All three bowls have single black slopes at the top, and the main one has a row of seriously steep

double diamond chutes. All of these blacks merge with blue runs lower down, served by their own shorter chairs. The two outer bowls also have green runs; the right-hand one is the main beginner area, with the separate Timber Creek day lodge and children's centre at the base.

Over the back of the left-hand bowl is a lightly wooded mountainside of blue/black gradient served by two more chairs, one of them the very long (and slow) Sunrise. This gives access to a range of adventurous ways back to the front of the mountain – mostly double diamonds but including one splendid easy single diamond.

What all this adds up to is that this is an excellent resort for experts and adventurous intermediates, and fine for beginners, but rather limited for less confident intermediates not happy to tackle blacks. For them, the Sunrise lift is much the best bet. Deep snow is part of the attraction, but many of the blacks get groomed.

A small 'village' with ski-in, ski-out apartment accommodation is taking shape at the base. There are several bars and restaurants. A recreation centre with outdoor heated pool, spa and sun deck was opened for 2001/02. There is a new ice rink on the edge of the village plaza.

SQUAW VALLEY

The major resort at the north end of the lake, with 4,000 acres of open and lightly wooded bowls on six linked peaks. It's about an hour's drive from South Lake Tahoe. The small base village is undergoing major development by Intrawest.

There are daily shuttle buses to Squaw from South Lake Tahoe, and you can go by boat (see Heavenly chapter).

The possibilities for experts here are phenomenal, with lots of steep slopes, chutes and big mogul fields – many extreme skiing and boarding movies are made here. But it is also good for intermediates, with lovely long groomed runs including a top-to-bottom three-mile cruise. And there's a superb beginner area at altitude.

Until now, Squaw has had very little accommodation at the base. The main options were Squaw Valley Lodge and the self-contained, luxurious conference-oriented Resort at Squaw Creek, linked into one end of the lift network by its own chair-lift.

But a new resort village is being developed by Intrawest, owners of Whistler and several other pace-setting resorts. Last season, from the mountain the village looked like one huge building site – although some buildings were complete (in the familiar style of Intrawest).

The peaks and high bowls of the area are treeless, but much of the terrain is lightly wooded – a very attractive compromise between the usual US wooded terrain and the open Alpine style of terrain. The average snowfall is 450 inches – slightly less than at Alpine Meadows and Kirkwood.

Squaw is unusual in having no trails marked on its piste map. Instead it has lifts classified green, blue and black. Like all such wacky ideas, it doesn't actually work as well as a conventional system for the user – by which we mean the newcomer to the resort. In some sectors, those who are adventurous but not truly expert could find themselves in real difficulty.

There are two impressively powerful lifts out of the village – North America's first twin-cable jumbo Funitel gondola (as in Verbier and Val-Thorens) and a big cable-car (called, unusually for the US, the Cable Car). Both rise 600m/2,000ft to the twin mid-mountain stations of Gold Coast and High Camp. Above these two points (linked by a pulse gondola) is a gentle area of snow-sure beginner slopes, served by several slow chairs.

The peak beyond Gold Coast and High Camp is Emigrant, with fast chairs of limited vertical on both flanks serving great blue cruises and gentle off-piste – an excellent intermediate area. Beyond this is Granite Chief, with a slow triple chair serving a very varied valley with some seriously steep stuff but also easy black slopes. You can get into some of this from the top of Emigrant, too. From the top of the Granite Chief chair people hike up to the steepest slopes on the peak.

From High Camp or the lower peak of Broken Arrow you can descend into a steep-sided valley from which the Silverado chair is the return. For access there is a system of gates – all but two 'For Experts Only'. There are signs saying that falls in this area can result in long slides and serious injury. What they mean is death; we wouldn't go into the expert slopes without a guide to keep us away from the cliffs.

The high point of the whole Squaw area is Squaw Peak, served by a slow double chair, the Siberia fast quad and the Headwall six-pack, which lifts you 460m/1,500ft – a modest figure, but one of the biggest verticals on the upper mountain. The high slopes either side of Siberia are broad, not too steep, open off-piste slopes of the kind you so often find in the Alps. The Headwall lift mainly serves the front of the mountain which offers a range of steepness from black to very black.

There are two peaks accessed from the village. The fast quad to KT22 gives a quick 550m/1,800ft vertical. Down the front, there are countless steep routes, for which guidance would be prudent at first.

Snow King, at the extreme of the area and reached by the slow Red Dog chair, shouldn't be neglected. Not only are there some excellent cruises – particularly the one down to the Resort at Squaw Creek. But also there is lots of advanced/expert terrain to explore.

You can eat at either of the mid-mountain areas. Avoid Gold Coast's Food Court – a dreary place serving rubbish fast food slowly.

Squaw is a big snowboarding centre and at night a terrain-park and half-pipe are floodlit, along with a run (for skiers too) down from mid-mountain.

Squaw's cable-car runs in the evenings to serve the floodlit slopes and the dining facilities at High Camp.

Phone numbers
From distant parts of the US, add the prefix 1. From abroad, add the prefix +1.

In this chapter area codes are included in the numbers given.

TOURIST OFFICE

Alpine Meadows

Postcode CA 96145
t 530 583 4232
f 530 583 0963
info@skialpine.com
www.skialpine.com

Kirkwood

Postcode CA 95646
t 877 547 5966
f 209 258 8899
kwd-info@
ski-kirkwood.com
www.kirkwood.com

Northstar-at-Tahoe

Postcode CA 96160
t 530 562 1010
f 530 562 2215
northstar@
boothcreek.com
www.skinorthstar.com

Sierra-at-Tahoe

Postcode CA 95735
t 530 659 7453
sierra@boothcreek.com
www.sierratahoe.com

Squaw Valley

Postcode CA 96146
t 530 583 6926
f 530 581 7106
squaw@squaw.com
www.squaw.com

This is an incredible mid-mountain complex, with several restaurants and bars, outdoor pool, ice skating, tennis and bungee jumping.

ALPINE MEADOWS

Squaw's next-door neighbour has similar, lightly wooded terrain, with runs of all classifications and an impressive snow record, but a modest total vertical of 550m/1,800ft. There's nothing but a day lodge at the base.
The base is surrounded by excellent beginner slopes with a variety of slow lifts. The major mountain access lift is a six-pack – the resort's only fast chair – to the top of the broad bowl under Ward Peak; it accesses a wide range of black runs (single and double diamond) at the top of the bowl, some of them involving long traverses, but there are also blue runs down to the generally blue terrain lower down the bowl, served by lower chairs. There is also a double chair – Alpine Bowl – on the upper slopes.

Separated from Ward Peak by a low saddle is Scott Peak; a double chair goes up over the steep black slopes on the front, and on the back pleasant blue runs are served by a triple. A second triple serves part of the open slopes on the back of Ward Peak, with steeper areas accessed by the Alpine Bowl chair on the front of the hill.

With an top-notch average snowfall of 495 inches, Alpine Meadows is known for its long season and excellent spring snow; conditions can still be good in July in some years.

As well as self-service and table-service options at the base, there is a little Chalet at the base of the Scott Chair – self-service, but woody and welcoming. There's a terrain-park and half-pipe just above the base.

NORTHSTAR AT TAHOE

Northstar, a few miles from Squaw, is a classic US-style mountain with runs cut through dense forest – mainly blue and single diamond black. With a gondola and four fast chairs, the lift system is slicker than at other minor resorts in the area. It has a tiny car-free 'village' at the base, and is locally regarded as a friendly, well-run resort – a good bet for families.
The whole area is very sheltered and good for bad-weather days. It enjoys long views in various directions.

A short gondola goes up to a mid-mountain lodge at Big Springs, only 160m/525ft above the village. From this point two fast chairs and one slow one radiate to serve a broad bowl with some short steep pitches at the top, with easier blue runs lower down and around the ridges at either extremity – the latter giving excellent runs to the village of almost 700m/2,300ft vertical.

On the back-side of the mountain is a second, steeper bowl with a central fast quad chair rising 575m/1,885ft; on either side of it are three or four runs that are at the easy end of the black spectrum (especially when groomed).

For 2000/01 a new fast chair-lift opened up another four black runs with a modest vertical of 390m/1,280ft in a smaller bowl beneath a subsidiary peak called Lookout Mountain, reached by a short tope tow. This is what you see if you approach Northstar by driving south from Truckee; the runs look seriously steep, and the two close to the chair are. The two outer runs are less so (and were groomed when we visited) but are still genuine blacks.

You can eat on the hill. The grand-sounding Summit Grille is a self-service affair in a small woody chalet, with a sun terrace. The several options at Big Springs include a Tex-Mex restaurant.

The small 'village' at the base is a pleasant car-free affair consisting of two stages of development in unrelated styles – one angular and wooden, the other more traditional. Both have apartments and hotel-style rooms (though no recognisable hotel) over shops, a couple of restaurants and a couple of bars. The gondola station is at one end of the village, a short walk from the highly organised drop-off zone and the premium ($15 a day) parking lot – free parking is a bit further away, served by buses. There is also an area of small condo units a little way down the access road.

OTHER RESORTS

There are eight other resorts you might visit in the Tahoe region – most are marked on our map. Much the most impressive on paper is Sugarbowl (460m/1,500ft vertical, lifts include four fast quads). But a regular visitor to the region also recommends Diamond Peak (vertical 560m/1,840ft, six chairs) for its 'breathtaking views and fab restaurant' and the relatively high Mount Rose (440m/1,440ft vertical, seven lifts including a six-pack) for its 'great snow always and carving runs' – and both for quiet slopes.

Mammoth Mountain 2425m/7,950ft

A big, sprawling mountain above a car-oriented, sprawling resort

WHAT IT COSTS

HOW IT RATES

The slopes

Snow	****
Extent	***
Experts	****
Intermediates	****
Beginners	****
Convenience	**
Queues	****
Restaurants	*

The rest

Scenery	***
Resort charm	**
Off-slope	*

What's new

Mid Chalet, the main on-mountain lodge, was reborn as McCoy Station for 2002.

In December 2002 the first restaurants and shops in the new Village at Mammoth are planned to open, along with a new 15-person gondola linking it to Canyon Lodge lift base

A Super-Duper half-pipe with 7m/22ft walls is being built.

Canyon Lodge is the main base for most skiers, even without the new gondola ↓

➕ One of North America's biggest ski hills, with something for everyone

➕ Good mix of open Alpine-style bowls and classic American wooded slopes

➕ Combination of location and altitude means a good snowfall record

➕ Uncrowded slopes during the week

➕ Good views, including more Alpine drama than usual in the US

➕ Excellent daytime bus service

➖ Mammoth Lakes is a rather straggling place with no focus, where it helps to have a car

➖ Most accommodation is miles from the slopes – though development is taking place at the lift bases

➖ Weekend crowds from Los Angeles

➖ Trail map and signing still poor

➖ Wind can close high lifts, and upper runs can be icy and windblown

Mammoth may not be giant in Alpine terms – from end to end, it is less than one-third of the size of Val-d'Isère/Tignes, in area more like one-sixth – but it is among the biggest resorts in the US, and big enough to amuse many people for a week. As we confirmed last season, it can be a superb mountain for anyone who is happy off-piste. The main thing it lacks is a real village at the base.

Enter Intrawest, owner of Whistler and now of various key plots of land (and the majority of development rights) here. Intrawest is investing heavily, planning to create 10,000 more guest beds over the next decade. It opened the first stage of a new slope-side development, Juniper Springs, a couple of years ago, and the first (quite limited) phase of a new pedestrian 'village' on the edge of the town of Mammoth Lakes is due to open in December 2002. As we go to press at the end of July, we hear that the new gondola linking this development to the mountain will also be opening for Christmas.

The resort

The mountain is set above Mammoth Lakes, a small year-round resort town that spreads over a wide area of woodland. The place is entirely geared to driving, with no discernible centre – hotels, restaurants and little shopping centres are scattered along the four-lane highway called Main Street and Old Mammoth Road which crosses it.

The buildings are generally timber-clad in traditional style – even McDonald's has been tastefully designed – and are set among trees, so although it may be short on resort ambience, the place has a pleasant enough appearance – particularly when under snow.

The town meets the mountain at two lift bases, both a mile or two from most of the hotels and condos. The major base is Canyon Lodge, with a big day lodge and four chair-lifts; there are hotels, condos and individual homes in the area below the lodge. Not far from here, Intrawest is building its new pedestrian 'village', which will now be linked to the slopes above Canyon Lodge by a gondola and (we're pleased to hear) a trail. The minor base, with a single six-pack lift, is Little Eagle – also known as Juniper Springs, which strictly is the name of the recently built condos at the base.

A road runs along the north fringe of the mountain past an anonymous chair-lift base to two major base areas: The Mill Cafe, with two fast chairs, and Main Lodge, a mini-resort with three

MOUNTAIN FACTS

Altitude 2425m-3370m
7,950ft-11,050ft
Lifts 30
Pistes 3,500 acres
Green 30%
Blue 40%
Black 30%
Snowmaking
450 acres
Recco detectors used

LIFT PASSES

2001/02 prices in
dollars

Mammoth Mountain
Covers all lifts at
Mammoth.
Beginners 69 a day
learn-to-ski packages
include pass, lessons
and rental.
Main pass
1-day pass 56
6-day pass 293
Senior citizens
Over 65: 6-day pass
145
Over 80: free pass
Children
13-18: 6-day pass 218
Under 13: 6-day pass
145
Under 6: free pass
Short-term passes
Scenic Mammoth
Gondola ride (adult
16); afternoon pass
(adult 45)
Notes Main pass also
covers the eight lifts
at June Mountain.
Passes of over 2 days
allow for one non-
skiing day – 5-day
pass is valid for 6
days, with one non-
skiing day, and
passes over five days
allow for 2 non-skiing
days.

fast access lifts and a big day lodge.
You can stay here, in the Mammoth
Mountain Inn; but who wants to be
four miles from practically all of the
resort's restaurants?

Shuttle-buses run efficiently on
several colour-coded routes serving the
lift bases, but they are limited after
5.30 and a car is useful.

The Mammoth lift pass also covers
June, a small mountain half an hour's
drive north, chiefly attractive for its
astonishingly people-free slopes.

The drive up from Los Angeles,
along a good road, takes six hours;
but there is lots of interest on the way.
You pass through the Santa Monica
mountains close to Beverly Hills, then
the San Gabriel mountains and Mojave
Desert (with the world's biggest jet-
plane parking lot) before reaching the
Sierra Nevada range, of which
Mammoth is part. There are plans to
extend Mammoth Lakes' small airport
to take jet flights.

The mountain

The 30 lifts access an impressive area
suitable for all abilities. The highest
runs are almost all steep bowls and
chutes for experts. In general, the lower
down you go, the easier the terrain.

Finding your way around is not easy
at first. Many of the chair-lifts now have
names, rather than numbers, but the
trail map still shows trails by means of
isolated symbols, not continuous lines,
so it's difficult to see where a run
starts and finishes. The signposting of
runs on the mountain leaves a lot to
be desired, too. On the lower part of
the mountain this doesn't matter a lot:
head downhill, and you'll come to a
lift. But higher up there are real
dangers, especially in poor visibility.

The map uses a six-point trail
difficulty scale, with intermediate
green/blue and blue/black categories;
rather pointless when the signposting
means you may end up on entirely the
wrong trail anyway.

THE SLOPES
Interesting variety

From **Main Lodge** the two-stage
Panorama gondola goes via McCoy
Station right to the top. The views are
great, with Nevada to the north-east
and the jagged Minarets to the west.
From the top, there are essentially
three ways down. The first, on which
there are countless variations, is down
the front of the mountain, which
ranges from steep to very steep – or
vertical if the wind has created a
cornice, as it often does. The second is
off the back, down to **Outpost 14**,
whence chairs 14 or 13 bring you back
to lower points on the ridge. The third
is to follow the ridge, which eventually
brings you down to the Main Lodge
area. This route brings you past an
easy area served by chair 12, and a
very easy area served by the Discovery
fast quad.

McCoy Station can also be reached
using the Stump Alley fast chair from
The Mill Cafe, on the road up from
town. The fast Gold Rush quad from
here takes you into the more heavily
wooded eastern half of the area. This
has long, gentle runs served by lifts up
from **Canyon Lodge** and **Little Eagle**
and seriously steep stuff as well as
some intermediate terrain on the
subsidiary peak known as Lincoln (un-
named on the resort map) served by
lifts 25 and 22.

SNOW RELIABILITY
A long season

Mammoth has an impressive snow
record – an annual average of 380
inches, which puts it in the second
rank, ahead of major Colorado resorts
and about on a par with Jackson Hole
(but a long way behind Alta and
Snowbird). Mammoth is appreciably
higher than other Californian resorts,
and it has an ever-expanding array of
snow-guns, so it enjoys a long season
– staying open as late as 4 July in
many years. But the upper mountain
can get icy and windswept.

boarding *Mammoth initially set out to attract boarders to its sister
mountain June, where there's a good terrain-park and half-pipe.
But Mammoth itself now has three impressive 'Unbound' terrain parks and half-
pipes for different abilities – and this season gets an astonishing Super-Duper
pipe with 6.7m/22ft walls. The rest of Mammoth's slopes are ideal for all
abilities, with some excellent free-riding in the high bowls and perfect beginner
and intermediate runs below. There's only one tiny drag-lift . There are some
good bars in town, lively at weekends.*

FOR EXPERTS
Some very challenging terrain

The steep bowls that run the width of the mountain top provide wonderful opportunities for experts. There are one or two single-diamond slopes, but most are emphatically double-diamond runs requiring a lot of bottle. The snow up here can suffer from high winds and it can be difficult to find your way – marking is virtually non-existent.

There is lots of challenging terrain lower down, too; Chair 5, Chair 22 and Broadway are often open in bad weather when the top is firmly shut, and their more sheltered slopes may in any case have the best snow. (The top of Chair 22 is higher than the very top of Heavenly, remember.) There are plenty of good slopes over the back towards Outpost 14, too.

Many of the steep trails are short (typically under 400m/1,300ft vertical), but we've had some great powder days here (with guidance).

FOR INTERMEDIATES
Lots of great cruising

Mammoth's piste maintenance is generally good, and many slopes that might become intimidatingly mogulled are kept easily skiable. And there is plenty for all levels of intermediate.

Some of the mountain's longest runs, served by chairs 9 and 25, are ideal for good intermediates. And a couple of lovely, fairly steep, tree-lined pistes run from the top of the Goldrush chair down to The Mill Cafe.

The tree-lined runs above Juniper Springs Lodge are flattering, and there are several easy cruises.

A reporter recommends the quiet little Santiago bowl at the western extremity of the slopes down to Outpost 14 : 'The whole group enjoyed runs like Arriba, Surprise and Oops.'

The less adventurous have some good, wide runs through trees in the triangle between Main Lodge, The Mill Cafe and Mid Chalet.

June mountain is great for a leisurely day out. Most of its runs are overclassified. Blues are easy cruisers, single blacks groomed and double blacks advanced rather than expert.

FOR BEGINNERS
Good instruction

'Excellent for beginners,' says one visitor. 'Good nursery slopes and lots of marvellous improving slopes.' Excellent instruction, fine piste grooming and snow quality usually make progress speedy.

FOR CROSS-COUNTRY
Very popular

Two specialist centres, Tamarack and Sierra Meadows (ungroomed), provide lessons and tours. There are 70km/43 miles of trails in all, including some through the pretty Lakes Basin area, and lots of scenic ungroomed tracks.

QUEUES
Weekend invasions

During the week the lifts and slopes are usually very quiet, with no queues. But even the efficient lift system can struggle when 15,000 visitors arrive from LA on fine weekends. That's the time to try June Mountain – it is remarkably uncrowded. Mind you, as one reporter put it: 'The weekend rush is like a quiet day in the Alps.'

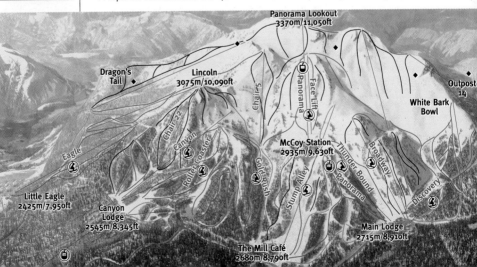

Panorama Lookout
3370m/11,050ft

Dragon's Tail

Lincoln
3075m/10,090ft

Chair 5

Panorama

Face Lift

Panorama

Outpost 14

White Bark Bowl

Chair 22

Canyon

Roller Coaster

Eagle

Goldrush

McCoy Station
2935m/9,630ft

Thunder Bound

Broadway

Panorama

Stump Alley

Discovery

Little Eagle
2425m/7,950ft

Canyon Lodge
2545m/8,345ft

Main Lodge
2715m/8,910ft

The Mill Café
2680m/8,790ft

GETTING THERE

Air Los Angeles, transfer 5hr. Reno, transfer 3hr. Mammoth Lakes, transfer 20 minutes.

ACTIVITIES

Indoor Mammoth museum, art galleries, theatre, mini golf

Outdoor Snowmobiling, ski touring, bob-sleigh, dog-sledding, ice climbing, mountain biking, ice skating, tobogganing, sleigh rides, hot air balloon rides, snow-shoe tour

CHILDCARE

Children's classes are handled by the Woollywood Ski and Snowboard School in the Panorama gondola building, which 'interfaces' with Small World Child Care (934 0646) based at the nearby Mammoth Mountain Inn. Small World Child Care takes children from newborn to age 12, from 8am to 5pm.

Phone numbers From distant parts of the US, add the prefix 1 760. From abroad, add the prefix +1 760.

TOURIST OFFICE

Postcode CA 93546
t 934 0745
f 934 0616
woolly@mammoth-mtn.com
www.mammoth mountain.com

MOUNTAIN RESTAURANTS
Better than the American norm

The only real mountain restaurants are at the gondola mid-station now called McCoy Station. This has been stylishly revamped and away from weekends, at least, the self-service restaurant offers 'a good choice' of roasts, Italian, Asian and other dishes – but does get 'very busy'. The Parallax table-service restaurant next door does satisfying food and offers a calm atmosphere and a splendid view. The other on-mountain possibility in good weather is the outdoor BBQ at Outpost 14.

Most people eat at the bases. Talons at Little Eagle is reported to be the best bet. The revamped Canyon Lodge offers Mexican, Italian, Asian and more. The Yodler at Main Lodge is relatively quiet and has 'pleasant staff, mammoth portions'.

SCHOOLS AND GUIDES
Excellent reports

A reporter rated his three-hour advanced class 'excellent'. We also have reports of beginners making 'excellent progress', though our most recent reporter complains of 'no continuity' of instructors (a familiar problem in the US) and time-wasting daily reassessments. There are some special 'camps' for experts, and for seniors and women.

FACILITIES FOR CHILDREN
Family favourite

Mammoth is keen to attract families. The children's Woollywood school, now based in the new Panorama gondola station, works closely with the nearby Small World childcare centre. We've had glowing reports; one reporter noted the 'family feel of the resort'.

Staying there

HOW TO GO
Good value packages

A good choice of hotels (none very luxurious or expensive) and condos. The condos tend to be out of town, near the lifts or on the road to them. **Mammoth Mountain Inn** (934 2581) Way out of town at Main Lodge. Handy for the gondola, but dreary. **Quality Inn** (934 5114) Good main street hotel with a big hot-tub. **Alpenhof Lodge** (934 6330) Comfortable and friendly, in central location. Shuttle-bus stop and plenty of restaurants nearby.

Austria Hof (934 2764) Ski-out location near Canyon Lodge, recommended by a reporter despite modest-sized rooms. **Sierra Nevada Rodeway Inn** (934 2515) Central, good value, 'great spa'. **Self-catering** The Juniper Springs Lodge is near lifts and town. Close to the Canyon Lodge base-station, the 1849 Condominiums are spacious and well equipped. The Mammoth Ski and Racquet Club, a 10-minute walk from the same lifts, is very comfortable.

EATING OUT
Outstanding choice

There are over 50 restaurants, scattered over a wide area, catering for most tastes and pockets. Make sure you pick up the Mammoth Menus guide, and make reservations at the places you fancy. This year we have had a spectacular report from a couple who dined in 14 different restaurants. The pick of their findings: Slocums Grill – very good meal in wood-panelled room; Angel's – popular good-value diner; Matterhorn – excellent Swiss-style food, good service; Ocean Harvest – delicious scallops; Nevados – best in town, excellent modern cooking; Cervino's – faultless, good-value Italian meal, exceptionally welcoming staff; Charthouse – excellent seafood, varied meat dishes; Alpenrose – intimate chalet-style place, good food. We've had excellent dinners at Skadi and Whiskey Creek, too.

APRES-SKI
Lively at weekends

The liveliest immediate après-ski spot is the Yodler, at the Main Lodge base – a chalet transported from Switzerland (so they say). Later on, things revolve around a handful of bars, which come to life at weekends. The Clocktower cellar is reported to be 'best in town – lively, friendly, good music, great choice of beers'. Whiskey Creek is the liveliest (and stays open latest); it has live bands at weekends and Wild Wednesday discos. Slocums is popular with locals and 'ideal for an after-dinner drink'. Grumpy's is a typically American sports bar (big screen TVs).

OFF THE SLOPES
Mainly sightseeing

The main diversion is sightseeing by car (preferably 4WD). The town of Bishop, 40 minutes' drive south, makes an amusing day out.

Colorado was the first US state to market its resorts internationally and is still the most popular American destination for UK visitors. And justifiably so: it has the most alluring combination of attractive resorts, slopes to suit all abilities and excellent, reliable snow – dry enough to justify its 'champagne powder' label. It also has direct flights from London to Denver.

Colorado has amazingly dry snow. Even when the snow melts and refreezes, the moisture seems to be magically whisked away, leaving it in soft powdery condition. The snow is good even in times of unusual snow shortage; in December a few years ago, when very little snow had fallen so far that season, we had a great week cruising on magical man-made snow in Breckenridge and Keystone.

Colorado resorts vary enormously, both in the extent and variety of slopes and in the character of the villages. If you want cute, restored buildings from the mining boom days of the late 1800s, try the dinky old towns of Telluride or Crested Butte (but beware: both these have separate, modern mountain villages too) or the much bigger Aspen (which also has its modern outpost at Snowmass).

Some resorts have easy access to others nearby (eg Breckenridge, Keystone and Copper Mountain). Others, such as Steamboat, Crested Butte and Telluride are rather isolated.

The two biggest Colorado resorts of Vail and Aspen both have substantial amounts of terrain suitable for every ability. And both have been developing their exciting ungroomed terrain in recent years – Vail has opened up Blue Sky Basin, while Aspen has extended its steep bowls at Aspen Highlands.

Colorado is a good area to do a road trip around. As well as linking several of the resorts we give full chapters to, there are entertaining smaller resorts to pop into for a day. These include: snow-sure Loveland, which you can see from the main I70 highway that leads to Breckenridge, Keystone, Copper Mountain and Vail; Monarch, which has snowcat as well as lift-served slopes and is near Crested Butte; and Durango (used to be called Purgatory) and Silverton, both quite near Telluride. Silverton was formerly heli-ski country but for the 2001/02 season its super-steep, ungroomed runs were served by a lift for the first time; you need an avalanche transceiver, a probe and a shovel.

503

Aspen/Snowmass 2420m/7,950ft

Don't be put off by its ritzy image – it's America's best resort

WHAT IT COSTS

HOW IT RATES

The slopes

Snow	*****
Extent	****
Experts	*****
Intermediates	*****
Beginners	*****
Convenience	**
Queues	****
Restaurants	****

The rest

Scenery	***
Resort charm	****
Off-slope	****

MOUNTAIN FACTS

Altitude	2400m-3815m
	7,870ft-12,510ft
Lifts	37
Pistes	4,803 acres
Green	10%
Blue	48%
Black	42%
Snowmaking	
	608 acres
Recco detectors used	

504

- ➕ Endless slopes to suit all abilities, with a vertical drop at Snowmass of 1340m/4,410ft – biggest in the US
- ➕ Notably uncrowded slopes, even by American standards
- ➕ Attractive, characterful, old mining town, with lots of smart shops
- ➕ Lively, varied nightlife and a great range of restaurants in the town
- ➕ Some of the best mountain restaurants in the States
- ➕ Large amounts of slope-side accommodation at Snowmass

- ➖ Four mountains are widely separated (though there's efficient, free transport between them)
- ➖ Some accommodation in Aspen town is a long walk or a bus-ride from the local lifts
- ➖ Expensive

Aspen is our favourite American resort. We reached that view four editions back, and subsequent visits by both editors have simply confirmed it. And readers who have reported on it all love it too. You have to catch (efficient and free) buses to different areas and it is expensive, but those are the only serious drawbacks. The extent and variety of slopes are unparalleled in the USA. The town is authentic modernised Wild West. The restaurants are tremendous. If you're thinking America, put Aspen at the top of your shortlist.

Worried by the film-star image? Forget it. Yes, the resort has many rich and famous guests, with their private jets parked at the local airport, and for connoisseurs of cosmetic surgery it can be a fascinating place. But most celebs are keen to keep a low profile and, like all other 'glamorous' ski resorts, Aspen is actually filled by ordinary holidaymakers.

The resort

In 1892 Aspen was a booming silver-mining town, source of one-sixth of the USA's silver, with 12,000 inhabitants, six newspapers, an opera house and a red-light district. But Aspen's fortunes took a nose-dive when the silver price plummeted in 1893, and by the 1930s the population had shrunk to 700 or so. Handsome Victorian buildings – such as the Wheeler Opera House and the Hotel Jerome – had fallen into disrepair. Development of the skiing started on a small scale in the late 1930s. The first lift (then the world's longest chair-lift) was opened shortly after the Second World War, and Aspen hasn't looked back since. Now, the historic centre – with a typical American grid of streets – has been beautifully renovated to form the core of the most fashionable ski town in the Rockies. There's a huge variety of shops, bars, restaurants and galleries –

some amazingly upmarket. Spreading out from this centre, you'll find a mixture of developments, ranging from the homes of the super-rich to the mobile homes for the workers. Though the town is busy with traffic, pedestrians seem to have priority in much of the central area.

Twelve miles away is Snowmass, with its own mountain and modern

What's new

For 2002/03 the amount of steep, ungroomed but avalanche controlled and patrolled terrain in Highland Bowl at the top of Aspen Highlands (one of our favourite areas) will be increased by almost 50%. And a free snowcat service will allegedly run to save the hike to the start of the Bowl. Facilities are to be improved at the Family Zone at Snowmass with interactive kids' trails. The Trenchtown terrain-park at Snowmass will double in size, running from top-to-bottom of the Coney Glade lift. For the second year the ESPN Winter X Games will be held on Buttermilk Mountain from 30 Jan to 2 Feb and will be free to the public.

2001/02 was the first season that snowboarding was allowed on Aspen Mountain, after 54 years of being a skiers-only mountain. Last season also saw a new top-to-bottom terrain-park (one of the world's biggest) on Buttermilk, built for the ESPN Winter X Games. For 2002/03 this Crazy T'rain Park will have a new run and a sound system near the super-pipe.

The new base area at Aspen Highlands opened for 2001/02, with a new bar and restaurant, and Ritz Carlton Club lodging.

ASPEN SKIING COMPANY /
KAREN KEENET

Aspen Mountain is right on the edge of the historic old mining town →

Aspen offers special experiences for small numbers of skiers or riders.

Fresh Tracks *The first eight skiers to sign up each day get to ride the gondola up Aspen Mountain at 8am the next morning, and to get first tracks on perfect corduroy or fresh powder. Free!*

Off-piste Tours *Backcountry guides lead expert skiers and riders around the famous expert terrain of Snowmass (eg Hanging Valley) on Wednesdays and Highlands (eg Steeplechase and Highland Bowl) on Fridays. 10am–3pm, $105.*

Powder Tours *Spend the day exploring the backcountry beyond Aspen Mountain, with a 10-passenger heated snowcat as your personal lift. Away from the lifts and other people, your two guides search out untracked snow – there's 1,500 acres to choose from. You're likely to squeeze in about 10 runs in all. At midday, you break for lunch at an old mountain cabin. Full day, $275 (in 2001/02).*

accommodation right on the slopes – and set for a big expansion over the next few years. Aspen Highlands now has limited accommodation, too.

Aspen town is the liveliest place to stay, and near the gondola is the most convenient location. Buses for the other areas also leave from nearby. Snowmass offers ski-out convenience at 95% of its properties, and buses from Aspen run until 1am or later.

The mountains

Aspen has lots for every ability; you just have to pick the right mountain. All of them have regular free guided tours, given by excellent amateur ambassadors, and other guest services on the slopes such as free sunscreen, drinks and biscuits. The ratio of acres to visitor beds is high, and the slopes are usually blissfully uncrowded.

THE SLOPES
Widely dispersed

There are four mountains, only one accessible directly from Aspen town. Each is big enough to keep you amused for a full day or more, but Snowmass is in a league of its own – almost five miles across, with over 60% of Aspen's total skiable acreage and the biggest vertical in the US.

Getting around between the areas by free bus is easy, and for $5 you can have your equipment ferried from one mountain to another overnight.

The Silver Queen gondola takes you from the edge of town to the top of **Aspen Mountain** in 14 minutes. A series of chairs serves the different ridges – Gentleman's Ridge along the eastern edge, the Bell in the centre, and Ruthie's to the west – with gulches in between. In general, there are long cruising blue runs along the valley floors and short steep blacks down

505

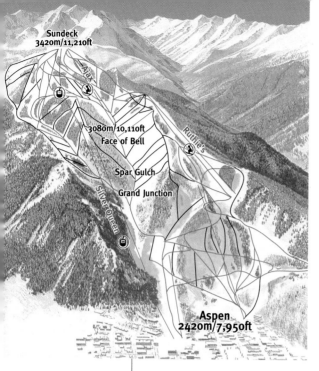

Sundeck
3420m/11,210ft

Ajax

3080m/10,110ft
Face of Bell

Ruthie's

Spar Gulch

Grand Junction

Silver Queen

Aspen
2420m/7,950ft

from the ridges. There are no greens.
Snowmass is a separate resort some
12 miles west of Aspen town, opened
in 1967. Chair-lifts fan out from the
purpose-built village at the base
towards four linked sectors – Elk
Camp, High Alpine, Big Burn and Sam's
Knob. You can also access the
mountain via the Two Creeks lift base,
which is much nearer to Aspen town,
and has free slope-side parking. There
are free shuttle-buses between here

and Aspen town, as there are between
all four mountains. Many of the
Snowmass runs are wide, sweeping
cruisers. But it also has some of the
toughest terrain.

Buttermilk is the least challenging
mountain. The runs fan out from the
top in three directions. The West
Buttermilk and Main Buttermilk areas
are almost all gentle; Tiehack, to the
east, is a bit more demanding – ideal
for an intermediate keen to progress.

Aspen Highlands was bought by the
Aspen Skiing Company 10 years ago
and has since seen radical
transformation, with a network of slow
lifts replaced by three fast quad chairs.
Broadly, the mountain consists of a
single ridge, with easy and
intermediate slopes along the ridge
itself and steep black runs on the
flanks – very steep ones at the top.
And beyond the lift network is the
Highland Bowl, where gates give
access to a splendid open bowl of
entirely double-black gradient (with
almost 50% more terrain due to open
here for 2002/03). The views from the
upper part of Highlands are the best
that Aspen has to offer – the famous
Maroon Bells that appear on countless
postcards. A new base lodge with
underground parking and a Ritz-Carlton
aparthotel is now finished.

SNOW RELIABILITY
Rarely a problem
Aspen's mountains get an annual
average of 300 inches of snow – not in
the front rank, but not far behind. In
addition, all areas have substantial
snowmaking. Immaculate grooming
adds to the quality of the pistes.

FOR EXPERTS
Buttermilk is the only soft stuff
There's plenty to choose from – all the
mountains except Buttermilk offer lots
of challenges. Consider joining a
guided group as an introduction to the
best of Snowmass or Highlands. Aspen
Mountain has a formidable array of
double-black-diamond runs. From the
top of the gondola, Walsh's, Hyrup's
and Kristi are double-diamonds on a
lightly wooded slope that link up with
Gentleman's Ridge and Jackpot to form
the longest black run on the mountain.
A series of steep glades drop down
from Gentleman's Ridge. The central
Bell ridge has less extreme single-
diamonds on both its flanks. On the
opposite side of Spar Gulch is another

West Summit
3015m/9,900ft

ASPEN HIGHLANDS

Cliffhouse
2965m/9,720ft

BUTTERMILK

West
Buttermilk
2655m/
8,710ft

Summit

Tiehack
2450m/
8,040ft

Main
Buttermilk
2400m/7,890ft

LIFT PASSES

2002/03 prices in dollars

Four Mountain Pass
Covers Aspen Mountain, Aspen Highlands, Buttermilk and Snowmass, and shuttle-bus between the areas.
Beginners Included in price of beginners' lessons; 327 for 3-day learn-to-ski or snowboard lessons and rental.
Main pass
1-day pass 68
6-day pass 384
Senior citizens
Over 65: 6-day pass 366
Over 70: season pass 149 (2001/02 price).
Children
Under 17: 6-day pass 306
Under 12: 246
Under 7: free pass

Advance purchase
Big savings can be made if you buy lift passes for 4 days or more well in advance or through certain tour operators.

Book by 1 December and you will get a 20% saving, 7 days in advance saves 10% off adult passes.

row of proper double-blacks collectively called the Dumps, because waste was dumped here in the silver-mining days.

At Snowmass, our favourite area is around the Hanging Valley Wall and Glades – beautiful scenery and wonderful tree-covered slopes, and steep enough everywhere to satisfy the keenest – well worth the short hike. The other seriously steep area is the Cirque. The Cirque drag-lift takes you well above the tree-line to Aspen's top altitude of almost 3815m/12,51oft. The Headwall is open and not terrifyingly steep, but there are also narrow, often rocky, chutes – Gowdy's is one of the steepest in the whole area. All these runs funnel into a pretty, lightly wooded valley.

At Highlands there are challenging runs from top to bottom of the mountain. Highland Bowl, beyond the top lift, is superb in the right conditions: a big open bowl with pitches from a serious 38° to a terrifying 48° – facts you can check in the very informative Highlands Extreme Skiing Guide leaflet. There are allegedly free snowcat rides from Lodge Meadow to the first access gate of Highland Bowl but on our visits these have often not been operating frequently, in which case it's a 20-minute hike. Almost 50% more terrain is due to open here for 2002/03. Within the lift system, the Steeplechase area consists of a number of parallel natural avalanche chutes, and their elevation means the snow stays light

and dry. The Olympic Bowl area on the opposite flank of the mountain has great views of the Maroon Bells peaks and some serious moguls. The Thunderbowl chair from the base serves a nice varied area that's often underused.

FOR INTERMEDIATES
Grooming to die for
Snowmass is the best mountain for intermediates and the Big Burn is definitely the first place to head for. The huge lightly wooded area is a

SCHOOLS/GUIDES

2002/03 prices in dollars

Aspen Skiing Company
Snowmass and Buttermilk for all abilities; Aspen Mountain and Aspen Highlands for intermediate and advanced only
Mountain Explorers
4 days
5hr: 10am-3pm;
4 full days: 349
Private lessons
460 for full day
317 for half day
(up to 5 people)
Other options
Beginner's Magic
1 full day: 115
Extra days: 90 a day
Small group lessons
Approx four skiers
105 for full day
89 for each extra day
Off-piste tours
Full day 105
Children's classes
Ages: 3-6 (incl lunch)
One day 94
5 days 470
Ages: 7-12 (incl lunch)
One day 73
5 days 340
Ages: 13-17
One day 68
5 days 320

cruising paradise. The runs merge into each other, though there's a satisfying variety of terrain and some trees to add interest – and the tempting Powerline Glades for the adventurous. The easiest intermediate slopes are reached from the Elk Camp lift. There's a choice of runs from the top, through spruce trees, and long runs all the way down to Two Creeks. Long Shot is a glorious, ungroomed, three-mile run, lost in the forest, and well worth the short hike up to get to the start. In the centre of the area, the two chair-lifts below High Alpine serve yet more intermediate slopes – a little trickier and more varied. The Sam's Knob sector offers slightly more advanced challenges, including some regularly groomed single-black runs. Finally, Green Cabin, at the top of the High Alpine lift, is a magical intermediate run cruising from top to bottom of the mountain, with spectacular views.

Most intermediate runs on Highlands are concentrated above the mid-mountain Merry-Go-Round restaurant, many (including the very popular Scarlet's Run) served by the Cloud Nine fast quad chair. But there are good slopes higher up and lower down – don't miss the vast, neglected expanses of Golden Horn, on the eastern limit of the area.

Aspen Mountain has its fair share of intermediate slopes, but they tend to be tougher than on the other mountains. Copper Bowl and Spar Gulch, running between the ridges, are great cruises early in the morning but can get crowded later. Upper Aspen Mountain, at the top of the gondola, has a dense network of well-groomed blues. The unusual Ruthie's chair – a fast double, apparently installed to rekindle the romance that quads have destroyed – serves more cruising runs and the popular Snow Bowl, a wide, open area with moguls on the left but groomed on the right and centre.

The Main Buttermilk runs offer good, easy slopes to practise on. And

good intermediates should be able to handle the relatively easy black runs in the Tiehack area.

FOR BEGINNERS
Can be a great place to learn
Buttermilk is a great mountain for beginners. West Buttermilk has beautifully groomed, gentle runs. The easiest slopes of all, though, are at the base of the Main Buttermilk sector – on Panda Hill. The easiest beginner slope at Snowmass is the wide Assay Hill, at the bottom of the Elk Camp area. Right next to Snowmass Village Mall is the Fanny Hill fast quad and beginners' run. Further up, from Sam's Knob, there are long, gentle cruises.

Despite its macho image, Highlands boasts the highest concentration of green runs in Aspen.

FOR CROSS-COUNTRY
Backcountry bonanza
There are 80km/50 miles of groomed trails between Aspen and Snowmass in the Roaring Fork valley – the most extensive maintained cross-country system in the US. And the Ashcroft Ski Touring Centre maintains around 30km/20 miles of trails around Ashcroft, a mining ghost-town. Take the opportunity of eating at the Pine Creek Cookhouse: excellent food and accessible by ski, board or sledge only. In addition, there are limitless miles of ungroomed trails. Aspen is at one end of the famous Tenth Mountain Division Trail, heading 370km/230 miles north-east almost to Vail, with 13 huts for overnight stops.

QUEUES
Few problems
There are rarely major queues on any of the mountains. At Aspen Mountain, the gondola can have delays at peak times, but you have alternative lifts to the top. Snowmass has so many alternative lifts and runs that you can normally avoid any problems. But some long, slow chairs can be cold in

boarding *There is great snowboarding for every ability. The ban on snowboarding on Aspen Mountain was lifted from 1 April 2001. It bowed to pressure after becoming one of just five major areas in the world open to skiers only. All four mountains are served almost entirely by chairs or gondolas and there are lots of special boarder facilities. Buttermilk has a two-mile long terrain-park with a beginner and intermediate area, 30 rails and 25 jumps, a boarder-cross course and a 400ft-long super-pipe. Snowmass has three terrain-parks and a half-pipe. Some bars can be quite entertaining at night.*

CHILDCARE

The childcare possibilities are too numerous to list in detail.

There's a children's 'learning center' at Buttermilk with a special children's shuttle-bus from Aspen. The Powder Pandas classes there take children aged 3 to 6. At Snowmass, the Big Burn Bears ski kindergarten takes children from age 3½, and children aged 8 weeks to 3½ have the Snow Cubs playschool. The Nighthawks programme looks after children aged 3 to 10 from 4pm to 11pm.

There are several all-day non-skiing nurseries.

GETTING THERE

Air Aspen, transfer ½hr. Eagle, transfer 1½hr. Denver, transfer 4hr.

Rail Glenwood Springs (63km/40 miles).

mid-winter, and the home slope gets very crowded. Aspen Highlands is almost always queue-free, even at peak times. The two lifts out of Main Buttermilk sometimes get congested.

MOUNTAIN RESTAURANTS
Good by American standards

On Aspen Mountain the new Sundeck at the top has quite a stylish self-service section with a good range of food. Sadly the swanky lunch club that shares the new building is strictly for members. The mid-mountain restaurant Bonnies has a two-tier deck.

At Snowmass, Gordon's High Alpine is an elegant restaurant serving excellent food. The best views are from Sam's Knob, where there is a self-service and an impressive Italian table-service restaurant, Finestra.

At Highlands the Cloud Nine 'Alpine bistro' is the nearest thing you will find in the States to an Alpine chalet with Alpine views and excellent food – thanks to an Austrian chef. The Merry-Go-Round has the biggest terrace in the valley.

On Buttermilk the mountaintop Cliffhouse is known for its 'Mongolian Barbecue' stir-fry bar and great views.

SCHOOLS AND GUIDES
Simply the best?

There's a wide variety of specialised instruction – mountain exploration groups, off-piste tours, adrenaline sessions, women's groups, and so on. Every 2002 reporter raves about the small group lessons ('they say average of three people, but we did five days and my wife had one-to-one the whole time and I did for four days'); 'the best class ever'; 'wonderful instruction'). The Wizard Ski Deck is an indoor ski and snowboard simulator used in combination with some classes or available for a private lesson.

FACILITIES FOR CHILDREN
Choice of nurseries

There is no shortage of advertised childcare arrangements. We have no recent first-hand reports, but reporters' observations were that, as usual in the US, all the kids were having the time of their lives. And past reports have always been first class. Young children based in Aspen town are taken from the gondola building each morning around 9am by the Max the Moose bus to Buttermilk's very impressive Fort Frog – a wooden frontier-style fort, with lookout towers, flags, old wagons, a jail, a saloon and a native American teepee village – and delivered back at 4pm. Snowmass has its own facilities. The Kids' Trail Map is a great way to get them used to finding their way around using maps.

Staying there

HOW TO GO
Accommodation for all pockets

There's a mixture of hotels, inns, B&Bs, lodges and condos.

Chalets Several UK tour operators have chalets here – some very luxurious.

Hotels There are places for all budgets.
((((5 **St Regis** (920 3300) Opulent city-type hotel, near gondola. Fitness centre, outdoor pool, hot-tubs, sauna.
((((5 **Little Nell** (920 4600) Stylish, modern hotel right by the gondola with popular bar. Fireplaces in every room, outdoor pool, hot-tub, sauna.
((((5 **Jerome** (920 1000) Step back a century: Victorian authenticity combined with modern-day luxury. Several blocks from the gondola.
((((4 **Sardy House** (920 2525) Elegantly furnished, intimate little hotel 10 minutes from the gondola. Small outdoor pool, hot-tub.
((((4 **Lenado** (925 6246) Smart modern B&B place with open-fire lounge, individually designed rooms.

Aspen

509

The Ajax Tavern and the bar of the Little Nell at the bottom of the gondola are popular for 4pm après-ski →

ACTIVITIES

Indoor The Aspen Club and Spa (racquetball, swimming, free weights, aerobics classes, sauna, steam, hot-tubs), skating, museum

Outdoor Ballooning, paragliding, snowcat tours, snow-shoe tours, sleigh rides, dog sledding, snow tubing, snowmobiles, tours of mines, ice skating

Phone numbers
From distant parts of the US, add the prefix 1 970.
From abroad, add the prefix +1 970.

TOURIST OFFICE

Postcode CO 81612
t 925 1220
f 920 0771
intlres@skiaspen.com
www.aspensnowmass.com

(((④ **Silvertree** (923 3520) Large slope-side hotel at Snowmass. Pools.
(((③ **Innsbruck Inn** (925 2980) Tirolean-style hotel, 10 minutes from lifts. Consistently liked by reporters.
(((③ **Stonebridge Inn** (923 2420) Good-value hotel close to Snowmass slopes; nice restaurant, pool, hot-tub.
(((③ **Hotel Aspen** (925 3441) Best 'moderate' place in town; 10 minutes from the gondola; comfortable rooms, pool, hot-tubs.
Self-catering The standards here are high, even in US terms. Many of the smarter developments have their own free shuttle-buses. The Gant is luxurious and close to the gondola. Chateau Roaring Fork and Eau Claire, four blocks from the gondola, are spacious and well-furnished. The Tamarack, Terrace House and Top of the Village have all been highly recommended by reporters. A reader says the two small supermarkets are 'exceptionally well stocked'.

EATING OUT
Dining dilemma
You can dine in whatever style you like in Aspen town. As you'd expect, there are excellent upmarket places, but also plenty of cheaper options.

Piñons serves innovative American food in South-Western surroundings. Syzygy is a suave upstairs place with live jazz from 10pm. Conundrum (modern American food, expensive) and Pacific (seafood) are top-notch. Poppie's Bistro Cafe is famous for its breads and desserts. L'Hostaria, The Mother Lode and Campo de Fiori are good Italians. Cache Cache does good-value Provençal. Ute City is in the upmarket surroundings of an old bank and good for local game.

Cheaper recommendations include: Bentley's (main courses $8 upwards), Boogie's (a 50s-style diner, great for families), Main Street Bakery, O'Leary's, Mezzaluna, Red Onion, Hickory House and the Skier's Chalet steak house. At Snowmass, the choice is adequate. You can also take snowcat rides for dinner at Cloud Nine on Aspen Highlands some nights and to the Lynn Brit Cabin (with live bluegrass music) at Snowmass.

APRES-SKI
Party time (later)
As the lifts shut, a few bars at the bases do reasonable business. At Snowmass, the slope-side Cirque Cafe

has live bands most days. At Highlands the Commonwealth Pub gets packed. In Aspen the Ajax Tavern is popular. The bar at the Little Nell is a great place for observing the rich and famous, fur coats and face-lifts.

Many of the restaurants are also bars – Ajax, Jimmy's (spectacular stock of tequila), Mezzaluna, O'Leary's, Red Onion, and Ute City, for example. The J-bar of the Jerome hotel still has a traditional feel. Shooters is a splendid country-and-western dive with pool and line-dancing. For pool in more suave circumstances, there's Aspen Billiards adjoining the fashionable Cigar Bar, with its comfortable sofas (and smoking permitted!). The Double Diamond has live bands most nights (from 11pm). Popcorn Wagon is the place for munchies after the bars close at 2am. You can get a week's membership of the famous members-only Caribou club.

OFF THE SLOPES
Silver service
Aspen has lots to offer, especially if you've got a high credit card limit. There are literally dozens of galleries, as well as the predictable clothes and jewellery shops. Just wandering around town is pleasant. It's a shame that all the best mountain restaurants are awkward for pedestrians to get to. Most hotels have excellent spa facilities. There's tubing at Snowmass.

Beaver Creek

2470m/8,100ft

Smoother than Vail and even pricier, but in many respects more attractive

WHAT IT COSTS

(((((6)

HOW IT RATES

The slopes
Snow	*****
Extent	***
Experts	****
Intermediates	****
Beginners	*****
Convenience	****
Queues	*****
Restaurants	**

The rest
Scenery	***
Resort charm	***
Off-slope	***

MOUNTAIN FACTS

Altitude	2255m-3490m
	7,400ft-11,440ft
Lifts	13
Pistes	1,625 acres
Green	34%
Blue	39%
Black	27%
Snowmaking	
	605 acres

- ➕ Blissfully quiet slopes, in sharp contrast to nearby Vail
- ➕ Mountain has it all, from superb novice runs through fast cruisers to long, daunting mogul fields
- ➕ Compact, largely traffic-free village centre (though with spacious suburbs beyond it)
- ➕ Some very convenient lodgings

- ➖ Rather urban feel to the village core – far from the Wild West atmosphere Europeans might look for
- ➖ Very expensive
- ➖ Disappointing mountain restaurants – the best ones are exclusive members-only affairs

In contrast to its better-known neighbour, Vail, Beaver Creek is a haven of peace – both on and off the slopes. It gets rather overshadowed by big sister, but we wouldn't dream of making a trip to Vail without spending a day or two in Beaver, and there's a lot to be said for doing it the other way round – if you can live with the prices in this most exclusive of Colorado resorts.

THE RESORT

Beaver Creek, ten miles to the west of Vail, was developed by Vail Resorts in the 1980s. It is unashamedly exclusive, with a choice of top-quality hotels and condos right by the slopes. It centres on a large pedestrian square featuring escalators to the slopes, exclusive shops, exquisite bronze statues and an open-air ice rink. Lifts go up to the slopes from three points around the village, so choice of location isn't of great importance.

The lift system spreads across the mountains through Bachelor Gulch to Arrowhead, which has luxury condos at the base of the mountain. Most of the nightlife, bars and restaurants are in Beaver Creek and the choice is much more limited than in Vail, a 25-minute bus-ride away. There's a free resort shuttle-bus and a taxi service.

THE MOUNTAINS

Beaver Creek, Bachelor Gulch and Arrowhead offer a small-scale version of the linked lift networks of the Alps. Free mountain tours are held four days a week. British guests may get the opportunity to ski the area with Martin Bell, Britain's best-ever downhiller and now UK ski ambassador for Vail Resorts (he lives in Vail in the winter).
Slopes The slopes immediately above Beaver Creek (where the men's downhill and super-G were held in the 1999 World Championships) divide into two sectors, each accessed by a fast quad chair. The major sector is centred

on Spruce Saddle, with lifts above it reaching 3490m/11,440ft. The other is lower and smaller, but forms the link with Bachelor Gulch and Arrowhead. Up the valley a little, and between these two sectors, is Grouse Mountain.

Resorts within a two-hour drive include Breckenridge and Keystone (owned by Vail Resorts and covered by multi-day lift passes), Aspen, Steamboat and Copper Mountain.
Snow reliability As well as an exceptional natural snow record, Beaver Creek has extensive snowmaking facilities, normally needed only in early season. The Grouse Mountain slopes can suffer from thin snow cover (some locals call it Gravel Mountain). Grooming is excellent.
Experts There is quite a bit of intimidatingly steep double-diamond terrain. In the Birds of Prey and Grouse Mountain areas most runs are long, steep and mogulled from top to bottom. The Larkspur Bowl area has three short steep mogul runs.
Intermediates There are marvellous long, quiet, cruising blues almost everywhere you look, including top to bottom runs with a vertical of 1000m/3,300ft from the top of the Birds of Prey chair. The Larkspur and Strawberry Park chairs serve further cruising runs – and lead to yet more ideal terrain served by the Bachelor Gulch and Arrowhead fast chairs.
Beginners There are excellent nursery slopes at resort level and at altitude. And there are plenty of easy longer

511

Snow

01285 642 555
www.handmade-holidays.co.uk
AITO ATOL PROTECTED 4479

LIFT PASSES

See Vail chapter.

Central reservations phone number

1 800 427 8308
(toll free from within the US).

Phone numbers
From distant parts of the US, add the prefix 1 970.
From abroad, add the prefix +1 970.

TOURIST OFFICE

Postcode CO 81658
t 845 5745
bcinfo@vailresorts.com
www.beavercreek.com

runs to progress to, including runs from top to bottom of the mountains.
Snowboarding Good riders will love the excellent gladed runs, perfect carving slopes and two well-equipped terrain parks, one with a super-pipe. The resort is great for beginners, too.
Cross-country There's a splendid, mountain-top network of tracks at McCoy Park (over 32km/20 miles), reached via the Strawberry Park lift.
Queues The slopes are delightfully deserted and virtually queue-free, even at peak times – it is amazing that more skiers don't come here from Vail.
Mountain restaurants There's not much choice. Spruce Saddle at mid-mountain is the main place – a food court in a spectacular log and glass building, where 'greeters' in Old West costumes radio around to find you a table. Redtail Camp does decent barbecues. Rendezvous Bar and Grill at the foot of the main slope is very civilised, with good food. The Broken Arrow at Arrowhead is recommended.
Schools and guides The school has an excellent reputation.
Facilities for children The facilities for young children look excellent, and we've had good reports on the children's school. There are splendid children's areas with adventure trails and themed play areas.

STAYING THERE

How to go There's a reasonable choice of packages.
Hotels There are lots of upmarket places. The luxury Inn at Beaver Creek

(845 7800) has ski-in/ski-out convenience and a pool. And the Hyatt Regency (949 1234) has impeccable service, a lively bar and a major spa.
Self-catering There's a wide choice of condos available. However, one reporter complained that grocery shopping is very limited – a drive to Avon to stock up is advised.
Eating out The SaddleRidge is a luxurious wooden building packed with photos and Wild West artefacts. The Mirabelle, at the bottom of the access road, is also rather special. The sleigh ride to Beano's Cabin makes a good evening out – like Allie's and Zach's, a beautiful log cabin that is a members-only club at lunchtime but open for dinner. Toscanini's, the Golden Eagle (American), Dusty Boot, and Blue Moose (pizzas) are all recommended.
Après-ski Rendezvous at the base of the lifts and the Coyote Cafe in the centre are the recommendations from the handful of bars. Head to Vail for a lively time.
Off the slopes Smart boutiques and art galleries, an impressive ice rink, and some great shows and concerts at the 500-seat Vilar Center. Hot-air balloon rides are popular. There are three seriously indulgent spas.
Staying up the mountain Trappers Cabin is a luxurious private enclave up the mountain, which a group can rent (for a small fortune) by the night.
Staying along the valley Avon, a mile away at the foot of the approach road, has budget motels. The Minturn Inn in Minturn is a stylish B&B (827 9647).

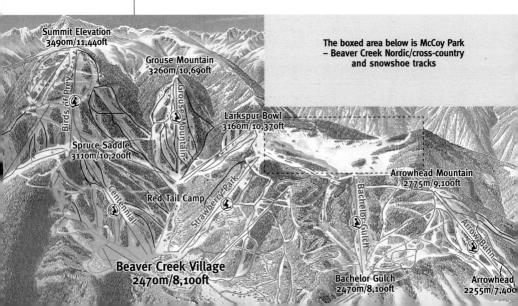

Summit Elevation
3490m/11,440ft

Grouse Mountain
3260m/10,690ft

The boxed area below is McCoy Park – Beaver Creek Nordic/cross-country and snowshoe tracks

Birds of Prey

Grouse Mountain

Larkspur Bowl
3160m/10,370ft

Spruce Saddle
3110m/10,200ft

Arrowhead Mountain
2775m/9,100ft

Centennial

Strawberry Park

Red Tail Camp

Bachelor Gulch

Arrow Bahn

Beaver Creek Village
2470m/8,100ft

Bachelor Gulch
2470m/8,100ft

Arrowhead
2255m/7,400

Breckenridge 2925m/9,600ft

Popular introduction to Colorado, with new linked mountain for 2002/03

What's new

For 2002/03 there will be a lift on Peak 7 for the first time: a six-pack serving new intermediate runs (increasing the resort's intermediate terrain by 30%).

And a new high-speed quad will start above Beaver Run on Peak 9 and run to Peak 8, with a mid-station for boarding higher up.

Peak 8 will have a third terrain-park and half-pipe aimed at park and pipe novices.

VAIL RESORTS, INC / BOB WINSETT

They groom all night to produce miles of fresh corduroy ↓

➕ Four varied local mountains, with something for all abilities

➕ Good snow record and lots of artificial help

➕ Shared lift pass with nearby Keystone and Arapahoe Basin and not-so-nearby Vail and Beaver Creek

➕ Efficient lifts mean few queues

➕ Lively bars, restaurants and nightlife by US standards

➕ Based on restored Victorian mining town, with many new buildings in attractive 19th-century style

➕ One of the nearest major resorts to Denver, so relatively short transfer

➖ Few long runs

➖ Best advanced slopes can be windy

➖ At this extreme altitude there is an appreciable risk of sickness for visitors coming straight from lower altitudes (although the lift-accessed terrain does not go super-high, at 2925m/9,600ft the village is one of the highest you will encounter)

➖ The 19th-century style gets a bit overblown in places, and there are some out-of-place modern buildings that detract from its charm

➖ Main Street is just that – always busy with traffic

Breckenridge is very popular with first-time visitors to Colorado. It's easy to see why: it is one of the closest resorts to Denver Airport, has slopes for all abilities, usually excellent dry snow, good facilities for families, relatively lively nightlife and good-value slope-side accommodation. Add to that a new lift opening up another linked mountain for the 2002/03 season and the image of a restored Wild West mining town and you have a very compelling package.

It is true that the slopes do not cover a huge area and most runs are short and that the town is rather spoiled by out-of-style buildings in parts and a rather Disneyesque feel to other parts. But it has skiing and boarding for all abilities, and there are lots of other areas to try on day trips, some covered by a shared lift pass (Vail, Beaver Creek, Keystone and Arapahoe Basin), some not (such as Copper Mountain) – much more than you could cover in a week or 10 days. But take heed of the altitude warnings; drink plenty of water and stay well hydrated.

The resort

Breckenridge was founded in 1859 and became a booming gold-mining town. The old clapboard buildings have been well renovated and form the bottom part of Main Street. New shopping malls and buildings have been added in similar style – though they are obvious modern additions.

The town centre is lively in the evening, with over 100 restaurants and bars. Christmas lights and decorations remain throughout the season, giving the town an air of non-stop winter festivity. This is enhanced by a number of real winter festivals such as Ullr Fest – a carnival honouring the Norse God of Winter – and Ice Sculpture championships, which leave sculptures for weeks afterwards.

Hotels and condominiums are spread over a wide, wooded area and are linked by regular free shuttle-buses (less frequent in the evening). If you stay in a condo and don't have a car, shopping at the local supermarket can be hard work – it is not in the centre

513

LIFT PASSES

2002/03 prices in dollars

The Colorado Ticket
Covers all Vail, Beaver Creek, Breckenridge and Keystone resorts, plus Arapahoe Basin.
Main pass
1-day pass 63
6-day pass 270
Senior citizens
Over 65: 6-day pass 220
Over 70: season pass 99
Children
Under 13: 6-day pass 150
Under 5: free pass
Short-term passes
Half-day pass from noon available.
Notes
The Colorado ticket is available only to international visitors who pre-book through a UK tour operator. It is not available at the ticket window in the resort. Prices quoted are regular season rates.

of town. Although there is a lot of slope-side accommodation – Breckenridge boasts more slope-side lodging than any other Colorado resort – there is also a fair amount away from Main Street and the lift base-stations.

The mountains

There are four separate peaks, linked by lift and piste. Boringly, they are named Peaks 7, 8, 9 and 10 – going from right to left as you look at the mountain. Though there's something for all abilities, the keen piste-basher will want to explore other resorts too. Breckenridge and Keystone were bought in 1996 by the owners of Vail and Beaver Creek (around an hour away); a multi-day lift ticket covers these four resorts and Arapahoe Basin, also nearby. Copper Mountain is not covered by the same ticket. All six of these resorts are linked by regular buses (free except for the trips to Vail or Beaver Creek). Steamboat and Winter Park are both less than two hours' drive away.

THE SLOPES
Small but fragmented
Two high-speed chair-lifts go from the top end of town up to **Peak 9**, one accessing mainly green runs on the lower half of the hill, the other mainly blues higher up. From there you can get to **Peak 10**, which has a large number of blue and black runs served by one high-speed quad.

The **Peak 8** area – tough stuff at the top, easier lower down – will be able to be reached by the new high-speed quad from Peak 9, which will have a mid-station for loading further up the mountain. The base lifts of Peak 8 at the Bergenhof can also be reached by the town shuttle-bus or the Snowflake lift from the edge of town. From the top of the Rocky Mountain Express on Peak 8, you can access the new runs

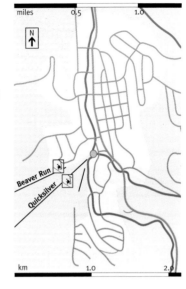

and six-pack on **Peak 7**. Taking a T-bar up from Peak 8 gets you to the resorts' best ski-anywhere bowls.

For the end of the day three trails lead back to town from Peak 8. A regular free shuttle runs around the resort to the Peak 9 and Peak 8 lifts. The grooming is excellent and the signposting very clear.

There are free mountain tours at 9.30 daily. And some weeks British guests can ski one day with Martin Bell, Britain's best-ever downhiller and now Vail Resorts' UK ski ambassador.

SNOW RELIABILITY
Excellent
With the village at almost 3000m (the highest of the main North American resorts), the slopes going up to almost 4000m/13,125ft and a lot of east and north-east-facing slopes, Breckenridge boasts an excellent natural snow record. That is supplemented by substantial snowmaking (used mainly pre-Christmas to form a good base).

boarding *Breckenridge is pretty much ideal for all boarders and hosts several major US snowboarding events. Beginners have ideal nursery slopes and easy greens to progress to, and intermediates have great cruising runs, all served by chairs. For good boarders there's one of the best terrain-parks in the US on Peak 8, with a series of great jumps, obstacles and an enormous championship half-pipe, which one reporter described as 'massive, steep, well kept and awesome'. There are also intermediate and beginner parks and pipes on Peak 8. The powder bowls at the top of Peaks 7 and 8 make for great riding – unfortunately accessed only by an awkward T-bar, which does not. Nearby Arapahoe Basin is another area for hardcore boarding in steep bowls and chutes.*

MOUNTAIN FACTS

Altitude 2925m-3960m

9,600ft-12,140ft
Lifts	26
Pistes	2,208 acres
Green	13%
Blue	32%
Black	55%
Snowmaking	
	516 acres
Recco detectors used	

CHILDCARE

There are children's
ski school/day-care
facilities at the bases
of Peak 8 and Peak 9.
There's a complex
array of options for
all-day care from 8.30
to 4.30 for children
from aged 2 months.
Prior reservation for
day care is essential
(453 3528).

FOR EXPERTS

Quite a few short but tough runs

A remarkable 55% of Breckenridge's
runs are classified as 'most difficult'
(single-black-diamond) or 'expert'
(double-black-diamond) terrain. That's
a higher proportion than the famous
'macho' resorts, such as Jackson Hole,
Taos and Snowbird. But remember that
Breckenridge is not a big area by
European standards, so most experts
there for a week or more will want to
spend some of their time exploring the
other nearby resorts.

The key to reaching Breckenridge's
best steep slopes is taking the T-bar at
the top of Peak 8. You can then
traverse or hike up to great steep runs
on Peak 7 with good snow on north-
east-facing slopes or to the steepest
slopes in Imperial Bowl and Lake
Chutes. Without hiking you can reach
good open terrain on Peak 8 in
Horseshoe and Contest bowls, where
the snow normally remains good.

We particularly liked the back bowls
of Peak 8. This is basically terrain
among a thin covering of trees and
bushes accessed from the T-bar or Lift
6 (which starts just below the top of
Lift 4). Lots of runs, such as Lobo,
Hombre, Amen and Adios, are marked
on the trail map. But in practice you
can easily skip between them and
invent your own way down. It's
picturesque and not too steep. Steep
black mogul fields lead down under
Chair 4 to the junction with Peak 9.

Peak 9 itself has nothing to offer
experts except very steep blacks from
the top down under Chair E (so steep
that we have never seen them
retaining good snow).

Peak 10 offers much more interest.
Off to the right of the chair as you
come down the mountain, at the edge
of the area, is a network of interlinking
black mogul runs by the side of the
downhill course – consistently steep
and bumpy. To the left of the chair is a
lovely, lightly wooded off-piste area
called The Burn.

Breckenridge

515

Peak 8
3965m/13,000ft

3865m/
12,680ft

Imperial
Bowl

Peak 7
Bowl

3700m/12,140ft

Horseshoe
Bowl

North
Bowl

Art's
Bowl

Peak 10
3540m/11,610ft

Peak 9
3495m/11,460ft

Contest
Bowl

Cucumber
Bowl

Vista Haus

Falcon

Mercury

Beaver Run

Peak 8 SuperConnect

Colorado

Rocky Mountain

Independence

Bergenhof
Lodge

Quicksilver

Beaver Run
Resort

Breckenridge
2925m/9,600ft

COLORADO

516

SCHOOLS/GUIDES

2001/02 prices in dollars

Breckenridge Classes
5hr: 9.45-12.15 and 1.30-4pm; 2½hr: am or pm
1 full day 65
Children's classes
Ages: 3 to 12
1 full day 80 (including lunch)
Private lessons
1hr, 1½hr, 3hr or 6hr – prices are per instructor regardless of 1 to 6 persons.
1hr 120; 1½hr 160; 3hr 290; 6hr 450.

GETTING THERE

Air Denver, transfer 2½hr.
BA has direct flights from London to Denver.

FOR INTERMEDIATES
Nice cruising, limited extent

Breckenridge has some good blue cruising runs for all intermediates. The development of Peak 7 for 2002/03 will increase the intermediate terrain by 30 per cent. But dedicated piste-bashers are still likely to find the runs short and limited in extent and will want to visit the other nearby resorts – see 'The Mountains' earlier in chapter.

Peak 9 has the easiest slopes. It is nearly all gentle, wide, blue runs at the top and almost flat, wide, green runs at the bottom. And the ski patrol enforces slow-speed skiing in narrow and crowded areas. Peak 10 has a couple of more challenging runs classified blue-black, such as Crystal and Centennial, which make for good fast cruising. Peak 8 has a choice of blues on trails cut close together in the trees. Peak 7 promises more of the same. More adventurous intermediates will also like to try some of the high bowl runs (see For experts).

FOR BEGINNERS
Excellent

The bottom of Peak 9 has a big, virtually flat area and some good gentle nursery slopes. There's then a good choice of green runs to move on to. Beginners can try Peak 8 too, with another selection of green runs and a choice of trails back to town. Reporters praise the good-value beginner package which includes lessons, equipment rental and lift pass.

FOR CROSS-COUNTRY
Specialist centre in woods

Breckenridge's Nordic Center is prettily set in the woods between the town and Peak 8 (served by the shuttle-bus). It has 38km/24 miles of trails.

QUEUES
Not normally a problem

Breckenridge's eight high-speed chair-lifts make light work of peak-time crowds. We've never come across serious queues, and neither have our reporters, except at exceptional times, such as President's Day weekend and on powder days – when the T-bar at Peak 8 can get crowded.

MOUNTAIN RESTAURANTS
Varied but nothing special

Breckenridge is making an effort to improve on the standard US cafeterias.

Ten Mile Station, situated between Peaks 9 and 10, is the newest and best, with a heated outdoor deck as well as indoors. Border Burritos is in the Bergenhof at the base of Peak 8.

ACTIVITIES

Indoor Sports clubs, swimming, sauna, massage, hot-tubs, cinema, theatre, art gallery, library, indoor miniature golf course, ice skating, good leisure centre (pool, tubs, gym, climbing wall) on the outskirts of town – accessible by bus
Outdoor Horse- and dog-sleigh rides, fishing, snow-mobiles, toboggans, scooters, mountain biking, snow-shoeing, ice skating, hot-air balloon rides

Phone numbers
From distant parts of the US, add the prefix 1 970.
From abroad, add the prefix +1 970.

TOURIST OFFICE

Postcode CO 80424
t 453 5000
f 453 3202
international@vail resorts.com
www.breckenridge.com

Spencer's at Beaver Run does an all-you-can-eat breakfast and lunch menu. Vista Haus, at the top of Peak 8, has a couple of restaurants.

SCHOOLS AND GUIDES
Excellent reports
Our reporters are unanimous in their praise for the school: classes of five to eight, doing what the class, not the instructor, wanted. Special clinics include bumps, telemark and powder.

FACILITIES FOR CHILDREN
Excellent facilities
Every report on the children's school and nursery is full of plaudits. Typical comments: 'excellent, combining serious coaching with lots of fun', 'our boys loved it', 'so much more positive than ski schools in Europe'.

Staying there

HOW TO GO
Lots of choice
A lot of tour operators feature Breckenridge and it's easy to arrange your own holiday there too. There are frequent bus transfers from Denver Airport but for a group of four for a week it can be cheaper to hire a car.
Chalets Several tour operators have very comfortable chalets. We were very impressed by a stay at Whispering Pines (sold through Ski All America) – and a 2002 reporter said, 'Very comfortable, excellent food and obliging, well-trained staff.' Ski Independence's two traditional chalets look good – and we have been impressed by their efficiency on various trips we've taken with them.
Hotels There's a good choice of style and price range.
(((4 **Great Divide** (453 4500) Used to be the Hilton but is now owned by Vail Resorts. Prime location, vast rooms and recently renovated. Pool, tubs.
(((4 **Lodge at Breckenridge** (453 9300) Stylish luxury spa resort set out of town among 32 acres, with great views. Private shuttle-bus. Pool, tubs.
(((4 **Little Mountain Lodge** (453 1969) Luxury B&B near ice rink.
(((3 **Beaver Run** (453 6000) Huge, resort complex with 520 spacious rooms. Great location, by one of the main lifts up Peak 9. Pool, hot-tubs.
(((3 **Williams House** (453 2975) Beautifully restored, charmingly furnished four-room B&B on Main St.
(((3 **Village** (547 5725) Central 3-star. Recommended by several reporters.

Self-catering There is a huge choice of condominiums, many set conveniently off the aptly named Four O'Clock run. There are lots of houses to rent, too – excellent for big groups.

EATING OUT
Over 100 restaurants
There's a very wide range of eating places, with pretty much everything you'd expect, from typical American food to 'fine-dining'. Pick up a copy of Breckenridge Dining Guide which lists a full menu of most places.
The Brewery is famous for its enormous portions of appetisers such as Buffalo Wings – as well as its splendid brewed-on-the-spot beers. We particularly liked the Avalanche beer.
Poirier's Cajun Café and the sophisticated food at both Café Alpine and Pierre's Riverwalk Café have been recommended. Sushi Breck and Mi Casa (Mexican) have had good reviews. The Hearthstone is said to do 'lovely food in good surroundings'. And Michael's Italian is recommended for 'good food, extensive menu, large portions and reasonable prices'.

APRES-SKI
The best in the area
The Breckenridge Brewery, Shamus O'Toole's, Tiffany's, the Liquid Lounge and Sherpa & Yetti's are popular. The Gold Pan saloon dates from gold rush days, and is reputedly the oldest bar west of the Mississippi. Cecelia's has good cocktails. The Underworld is a trendy disco bar. Mount Java is a relaxed cafe-cum-bookshop with Internet access.

OFF THE SLOPES
Pleasant enough
Breckenridge is a pleasant place to wander around with plenty of souvenir and gift shops. Silverthorne (about 30 minutes away and connected by a free bus service) has excellent bargain factory outlet stores such as Levi, Gap and Ralph Lauren. It is easy to get around and visit other resorts.

STAYING DOWN THE VALLEY
Good for exploring the area
Staying in Frisco makes sense for those touring around or on a tight budget. It's a small town with decent bars and restaurants. There are cheap motels, a couple of small hotels and some B&Bs; Hotel Frisco (668 5009) has been recommended.

Copper Mountain

2960m/9,700ft

Great terrain for all ability levels above a born-again resort

518

WHAT IT COSTS

HOW IT RATES

The slopes

Snow	*****
Extent	**
Experts	****
Intermediates	****
Beginners	****
Convenience	****
Queues	****
Restaurants	*

The rest

Scenery	***
Resort charm	**
Off-slope	*

What's new

For 2002/03, West Lake Market, a seven-building complex centred around West Lake and next to the New Village at Copper, is due to be completed. It will offer a Russian-themed vodka bar, an Irish pub, restaurants and shops.

➕ Convenient purpose-built resort undergoing exciting renaissance

➕ Fair-sized mountain, with good runs for all abilities

➕ Excellent snow reliability

➕ Efficient lift system – few queues

➕ Several other good resorts nearby

➖ One fast-food mountain restaurant

➖ Limited vertical on black-diamond bowls at the top

➖ Village still rather limited when compared with established resorts

➖ Can be long lift queues at weekends

➖ Risk of altitude sickness for visitors coming straight from sea level

Copper's slopes are some of Colorado's best, and now there's a fine new village to match the quality of the slopes. As a result, Copper now makes a much more attractive destination. But watch out for that altitude sickness; Copper's village and the top of its slopes are even higher than at Breckenridge.

THE RESORT

Copper Mountain was originally built rather like the French resorts of the 1960s – high on convenience, low on charm. Because of that it never took off on the international market. But it has always had one of Colorado's best ski areas. And the resort has now been transformed by its new owners, Intrawest. 2000/01 saw the opening of 'The New Village at Copper' – four new impressive wood-and-stone-clad buildings with shops, restaurants and car-free walkways and squares, forming the heart of the resort. The New Village is at the foot of the main intermediate area, with two fast quads up to the heart of the slopes.

There is also an East Village – with recently built accommodation and base lodge and easy access to the resort's expert and intermediate terrain. A regular free shuttle-bus runs between the two main bases and the family skiing and beginners' area at Union Creek.

Keystone, Breckenridge and Arapahoe Basin are all nearby, and Vail, Steamboat and Winter Park are within an hour or two's drive.

MOUNTAIN FACTS

Altitude	2925m-3765m
	9,170ft-12,300ft
Lifts	23
Pistes	2,450 acres
Green	21%
Blue	25%
Black	54%
Snowmaking	
	400 acres
Recco detectors used	

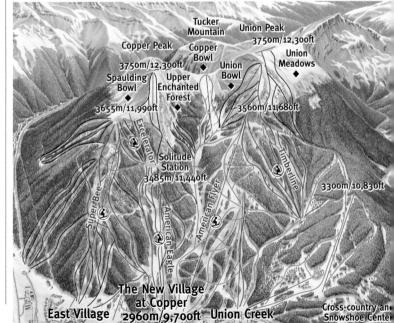

Phone numbers
From distant parts of
the US, add the prefix
1 970.
From abroad, add the
prefix +1 970.

Central reservations
Call 968 2882.

Toll-free number
(from within the US)
1 888 263 5302.

TOURIST OFFICE

Postcode CO 80443
t 968 2882
f 968 3156
copper-marketing@
coppercolorado.com
www.coppercolorado.
com

THE MOUNTAIN

The area is quite sizeable by American standards, and has great runs for all ability levels. Mountain tours with a Copper guide are available daily.
Slopes As you look up at the mountain, the easiest runs are on the right-hand side and the forested terrain gradually gets steeper and more challenging the further left you go. Above the forest, a series of steeper open bowls is served by two chairs and a drag on the front and two further chairs on the back side. There is also a free snowcat service to cut out some hiking. And you can access the back-country through a gate and get a resort bus back.
Snow reliability Height and an extensive snowmaking operation give Copper an early opening date each season and excellent snow reliability.
Experts There is a lot of good expert terrain, especially in the steep and wild Copper Bowl on the back side of the mountain and the bump runs through the trees below Spaulding Bowl.
Intermediates Good intermediates will find long steep runs in the section on the left of the mountain as you look at it. The slightly less proficient can enjoy gentler runs on the middle section of the mountain, and early intermediates have gentle cruisers below the Union Peak area on the right.
Beginners The nursery slopes are excellent, and there are plenty of very easy green runs to graduate to.
Snowboarding There are great slopes for all abilities and there's also a terrain-park and two half-pipes.
Cross-country There are 25km/15 miles of trails through the White River forest.

Queues Weekend day visitors pour in from Denver and we have reports of '20-minute queues' then. But mid-week queues are rare because of the efficient lift system.
Mountain restaurants Grim. The main place is a fast-food court at Solitude Station. The alternatives are outdoors – a soup shack and a burger bar.
Schools and guides The school offers a wide variety of courses and has a fine reputation, especially for children.
Facilities for children The Belly Button childcare facility, in The New Village at Copper, takes children from two months old and ski school (in the Schoolhouse at Union Creek) starts from age three.

STAYING THERE

How to go A number of tour operators offer packages to Copper.
Hotels There are no identifiable hotels, but some of the condo buildings are hotel-like in style and look splendidly luxurious, with outdoor hot-tubs, etc.
Eating out Blue Moose pizza is new in the main village. Endo's and JJ's Rocky Mountain Tavern are also popular. Evening sleigh rides take people out to Western-style dinners in tents.
Après-ski In the past – because the resort mainly catered for day trippers – après-ski was lively at lift closing time, but quiet later on. But now there's a bit more life. Endo's Adrenaline cafe in the main village, and JJ's Rocky Mountain Tavern (formerly Molly B's) in the East village, are popular venues.
Off the slopes Facilities include a fine sports club, with a huge pool and indoor tennis, and an ice rink. There's also a multi-screen cinema nearby.

Copper Mountain

519

COPPER MOUNTAIN RESORT

Heavily wooded
slopes, and some
worthwhile views ➔

Crested Butte 2860m/9,380ft

A Jekyll and Hyde resort: one short lift takes you from greens to extremes

WHAT IT COSTS

((((((6))

HOW IT RATES

The slopes

Snow	****
Extent	**
Experts	****
Intermediates	***
Beginners	****
Convenience	***
Queues	*****
Restaurants	*

The rest

Scenery	***
Resort charm	****
Off-slope	**

➕ Lots of 'extreme' and expert terrain

➕ Excellent for beginners and for near-beginners, with long easy runs

➕ Charming, tiny, restored Victorian mining town with good restaurants

➕ Convenient 'village' at lift base

➕ Excellent school

➕ Attractive scenery, for Colorado

➖ Limited for confident intermediate piste-bashers

➖ Old town is 10 minutes from resort village by shuttle-bus

➖ Out on a limb, away from mainstream Colorado resorts

➖ Only one satisfactory mountain restaurant

Among experts who are at home on steep, unprepared runs – and 'extremists' who like their mountains as steep as possible – Crested Butte enjoys cult status. Meanwhile, the commercial success of the place depends on beginners and timid intermediates, who love the long, gentle slopes of the main area. These two groups can safely include Crested Butte on their shortlists. But keen, mileage-hungry intermediates will find there isn't enough suitable terrain.

What's new

The Crested Butte Marriot Resort hotel at the foot of the slopes is now a Club Med.

520

MOUNTAIN FACTS

Altitude	2775m-3620m
	9,100ft-11,880ft
Lifts	14
Pistes	1,058 acres
Green	14%
Blue	32%
Black	54%
Snowmaking	
	300 acres
Recco detectors used	

The mountain that gives the resort its name – the crested butte (pronounced 'beaut') ➔

THE RESORT

Crested Butte is a small resort in a remote corner of Colorado. It takes its name from the local mountain – an isolated peak (a butte, pronounced 'beaut') with a distinctive shape. It started life as a coal-mining town in the late 1800s and is now one of the most attractive resorts in the Rockies – a few narrow streets with beautifully restored wooden buildings and sidewalks and a tiny town jail – straight out of a Western movie.

The town is a couple of miles from the mountain, linked by a regular free shuttle-bus. But at the foot of it is the resort 'village' of Mount Crested Butte – modern and characterless, with a cluster of bars and restaurants at the foot of the slopes, a couple of big hotels and a sprawling area of houses and condos. There is some accommodation in the town, but most is at the resort village. You can stroll to the lifts from some of it; but from many condos you need the bus.

THE MOUNTAIN

It's a small area, but it packs in an astonishing mixture of perfect beginner slopes, easy cruising runs and expert terrain. There are free daily mountain tours for intermediates or better.

Slopes Two fast quad chairs leave the base. The Silver Queen takes experts to black runs and links with lifts to the steepest runs. The Keystone lift takes you to the easiest runs. Intermediates

can access cruising blue runs from either of these two lifts.

Snow reliability The resort apparently benefits from snowstorms from several directions, and has a substantial snowmaking installation.

Experts For those who like steep, ungroomed terrain, Crested Butte is idyllic – the 448 acres of the Extreme Limits at the top of the mountain offer seriously steep but prettily wooded

Phone numbers
From distant parts of
the US, add the prefix
1 970.
From abroad, add the
prefix +1 970.

TOURIST OFFICE

Postcode CO 81225
t 349 2286
f 349 2250
info@cbmr.com
www.crestedbutte
resort.com

and safe terrain. But the area needs a
lot of snow-cover – it is not unusual
for it to be closed until late January.
Guided tours of the North Face are
available. Though there are also some
'ordinary' black runs, these are few.

Irwin Lodge, a few miles away, runs
a snowcat skiing and riding operation
on its secluded slopes (see later).
Intermediates Good intermediates are
likely to find the area limited. For early
intermediates, there are lots of wide,
fairly gentle, well-groomed and
normally uncrowded cruising runs.
Beginners There are excellent nursery
slopes near the village and lots of
good long runs to progress to.
Snowboarding There's lots of extreme
terrain and a terrain-park for good
riders. Beginners have a large section
of long, wide green runs to the base.
Cross-country There are 30km/20
miles of cross-country trails near the
old town and backcountry tours are
available in Elk Mountain and the
Gunnison National Forest.
Queues Virtually non-existent.
Mountain restaurants Most people go
back to the base for lunch. The
restaurant at the base of the Paradise
lift is fairly civilised, though, with
Bubba's table-service restaurant as
well as a cafeteria and barbecue.
Schools and guides The school has
an excellent reputation.
Facilities for children Parents praise
the teaching and separate kids' area.

STAYING THERE

How to go Most tour operators with
serious US programmes include
Crested Butte. Right at the foot of the
slopes is a Club Med.

Hotels There's a wide range. In the
resort village, the Sheraton Crested
Butte Resort (349 2333) is one of the
smartest options, with a pool and
outdoor hot-tub and great views. The
Nordic Inn B&B (349 5542) is a short
walk from the lifts: 'Full of character,
charming hosts', outdoor hot-tub and
large rooms (we have stayed there and
loved its ambience). On the outskirts of
the old town, the 'Scandinavian-style'
Inn at Crested Butte (349 1225) is a
non-smoking hotel with an outdoor
hot-tub. Elk Mountain Lodge B&B (349
7533) is a renovated miners' hotel.
Self-catering There are thousands of
apartments available in the village.
Eating out Top of the pile is Soupçon,
a tiny place in an old log cabin just off
the main street in the old town,
serving refined French food. The
Bosquet runs it close, and Bacchanale
is a good Italian. The Idle Spur micro-
brewery is popular. In the resort village,
the WoodStone Grille is recommended.
Bubba's (reached by sleigh) and
Twister (4.30pm chair-lift) on the
mountain open three nights a week.
Après-ski Kochevar's, in the old town,
is an amusing Wild West saloon. The
Wooden Nickel and the Powerhouse
are recommended. At the resort village,
Rafters and Casey's are popular.
Off the slopes Activities are limited,
though there are some galleries, a
theatre and a cinema.
Staying up the mountain Irwin Lodge
(349 2773) is a great wooden barn in a
remote backcountry area, reached in
winter only by snowcat or snowmobile.
It has an outdoor hot-tub, great views
and simple rooms above a huge
communal sitting room with open fire.

Crested Butte

521

For those who want a peaceful, quiet, pampered time

WHAT IT COSTS

HOW IT RATES

The slopes

Snow	★★★★★
Extent	★★
Experts	★★★
Intermediates	★★★★
Beginners	★★★★
Convenience	★★
Queues	★★★★
Restaurants	★★★

The rest

Scenery	★★★
Resort charm	★★
Off-slope	★★

What's new

For 2002/03, Keystone will continue to expand its terrain-park.

For 2001/02 two new hotel-condominium buildings opened in River Run, including the ski-in, ski-out Lone Eagle next to the gondola.

Everyone staying at a resort-owned property receives a free mountain passport with over $200-worth of free activities (such as tubing, ice skating, yoga classes and wine tastings). And guests booking through selected tour operators will get 25% off at certain restaurants and activities.

522

➕ Good mountain for everyone but the double-diamond diehard; extensive, immaculately groomed intermediate slopes are a particular strength

➕ Huge night-skiing operation – almost half the runs are floodlit and open until 8pm

➕ Lots of other nearby resorts, and a shared lift pass with Breckenridge, Vail, Beaver Creek and A-Basin

➕ Efficient lift system – few queues

➕ Luxurious condominiums

➕ Very impressive childcare facilities

➖ Very quiet in the evenings

➖ Very high – altitude sickness can be a problem for some visitors

➖ Night-skiing can be bitterly cold

➖ Much of the accommodation is a bus-ride to and from lifts

➖ Resort lacks village atmosphere except in the newish River Run development

➖ Poor shops for self-catering

➖ Limited choice of restaurants by usual US resort standards

Keystone's slopes are impressive from many points of view. If there was a proper village at the foot of them, it would be easily recommendable. But there isn't. Luxurious condos are scattered over a wide area – perfect for a quiet relaxing time for those who enjoy self-catering. And there are some excellent restaurants for the odd dinner out (one up the mountain and others scattered around the resort). The nearest thing to a 'village' is the new car-free River Run development near the gondola. This is attractive, compact and convenient for the slopes but you can check out its handful of bars, restaurants and shops in a five-minute stroll. If you want something livelier or more interesting, base yourself elsewhere and visit Keystone's slopes for a day (or an evening).

The resort

Keystone is a sprawling resort of condominiums spread over wooded countryside at the foot of Keystone Mountain, beside Snake River and the highway to Loveland Pass. It has no clear centre and is divided into seven 'neighborhoods', with regular free buses weaving roundabout routes between them. Some consist of little more than groups of condos, while others have shops, restaurants and bars (though no supermarkets or liquor stores – they are on the main highway).

River Run, at the base of the main gondola, is the nearest thing to a conventional ski resort village. It is a recently built, attractively designed, car-free development with several condo buildings, a small main street, a square and a handful of restaurants, bars and shops. A second lift base area half a mile to the west, Mountain House, is much less of a village but is also convenient. Another mile west is Keystone Village, set around a lake – a huge natural ice rink in winter. These and some other 'neighborhoods' are shown on our resort plan; Ski Tip (with famous Lodge) is off to the east.

The mountains

By US standards Keystone offers extensive intermediate slopes and some challenging steeper stuff. The resort is owned by Vail Resorts, who also own Vail, Beaver Creek and Breckenridge nearby. Lift tickets between the four resorts are interchangeable, and there is bus transport between them. Copper Mountain is nearby and Arapahoe

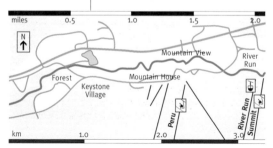

MOUNTAIN FACTS

Altitude 2835m-3720m
          9,300ft-12,200ft

Lifts	22
Pistes	1,861 acres
Green	13%
Blue	36%
Black	51%
Snowmaking	
	859 acres

LIFT PASSES

2002/03 prices in
dollars

The Colorado Ticket
Covers all Vail, Beaver
Creek, Breckenridge
and Keystone resorts,
plus Arapahoe Basin.
Main pass
1-day pass 63
6-day pass 270
Senior citizens
Over 65: 6-day pass
220
Over 70: season pass
99
Children
Under 13: 6-day pass
150
Under 5: free pass
Short-term passes
Half-day pass from
noon available.
Notes
The Colorado ticket is
available only to
international visitors
who pre-book through
a UK tour operator. It
is not available at the
ticket window in
resort. Prices quoted
above are regular
season rates.

Basin (or A-Basin as it is known
locally) a few minutes by road, but
both are separately owned. Your lift
ticket covers a trip to A-Basin, but not
to Copper. In contrast to Keystone's
superb modern lifts, A-Basin is still
served by a series of slow old chairs.

THE SLOPES
A keen intermediate's dream

Three tree-lined, interlinked mountains
form Keystone's local slopes. The only
one directly accessible from the resort
is **Keystone Mountain**, to which lifts
depart from Mountain House or River
Run. The front face of the mountain
has Keystone's biggest network of lifts
and runs by far, mainly of easy and
intermediate gradient. From the top
you can drop over the back down to
Keystone Gulch, where there are lifts
back up to Keystone Mountain and on
to the next hill, **North Peak**. Or you can
ride the Outpost gondola directly to
the top of North Peak. From North
Peak you can get back to the bases of
both Keystone Mountain and the third
peak, known as **The Outback**. This area
is served by another high-speed quad.

On certain weeks British guests can
ski Keystone with Martin Bell, Britain's
best-ever downhiller and now Vail
Resorts' UK ski ambassador.

SNOW RELIABILITY
Not a natural strength

Keystone's annual snowfall is low by
Colorado standards – a mere 230
inches, whereas many other resorts get
300 inches or more. But shortage of
snow is rarely a problem, not least
because Keystone has one of the
world's biggest snowmaking systems
as back-up.

One of the main reasons for the
snowmaking is to help form an early-
season base. Keystone traditionally
vies with Killington to be the first

major US resort to open its runs for
the season – normally in October.

And it sounds like A-Basin is trying
to outdo them both. It's planning to
introduce snowmaking for 2002/03 so
that it can open earlier in the season.
But it doesn't need it most of the time
– it has the highest lift-served terrain
in the US, at almost 4000m/13,000ft,
and the base-station is at an
impressive 3285m/10,780ft. The slopes
are normally open well into June.

FOR EXPERTS
Some steeps, no super-steeps

Keystone has a reputation for great
groomers, but it also has a lot of
steeper ungroomed terrain (though
none of it gets a double-diamond
grading). Windows is a 60-acre area of
experts-only glade runs on Keystone

boarding *Until six years ago, snowboarding was banned at Keystone. Then
they invested $2.5 million in facilities – these include the 20-acre
Jackwhacker terrain-park and adjoining Area 51 half-pipe, on the front side of
Keystone Mountain – floodlit to make the biggest night-snowboarding operation
in the US (you can actually ride from 8.30am to 8pm – if you've got superhuman
stamina and are mad enough, that is). And they continue to expand the terrain-
park. Keystone as a whole is ideal for beginners and intermediates, with mainly
chair-lifts and gondolas, good beginner areas (there are a couple of easily
avoidable drag-lifts here) and superb cruising runs. Experienced riders will love
The Outback and the bowls and chutes of nearby A-Basin, a favourite area with
hardcore boarders. Evenings are quiet.*

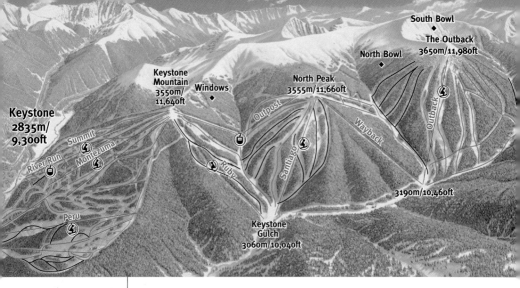

Keystone
2835m/
9,300ft

Keystone
Mountain
3550m/
11,640ft

Windows

North Peak
3555m/11,660ft

North Bowl

South Bowl

The Outback
3650m/11,980ft

Outpost

Wayback

Outback

Summit

Montezuma

River Run

Ruby

Santiago

3190m/10,460ft

Peru

Keystone
Gulch
3060m/10,040ft

SCHOOLS/GUIDES

2001/02 prices in
dollars

Keystone
Classes 7 days
2½hr: 10.30-1pm or
1.30-4pm; 2hr
evening: 4.30-6.30
half day 45
Children's classes
Ages: 3 to 14
Full day including
lunch, equipment
rental and ski-pass:
92
Private lessons
1½hr, 2hr, half or full
day
125 for 1½hr

Mountain's back side, opened in 1998.
The trail map identifies around 10, but
on the ground they are not clearly
defined. All three mountains have
some good mogul runs, such as
Ambush and Geronimo, and there are
splendid glade runs on both North
Peak and The Outback. Traversing from
the top of the lift on The Outback
takes you to open and glade runs in
the North Bowl and the South Bowls,
which are basically ski-anywhere areas.

Arapahoe Basin, down the road, is a
good place for those looking for more
of a challenge. The East Wall here has
some splendid steep chutes. And the
opposite side of the bowl is riddled
with steep bump runs – although none
of the runs is particularly long.

Copper Mountain, Breckenridge, Vail
and Beaver Creek have some good
challenging terrain, for those prepared
to travel around.

FOR INTERMEDIATES
A cruiser's paradise
Keystone is ideal for intermediates.
The front face of Keystone Mountain
itself is a network of beautifully
groomed blue and green runs through
the trees. Enthusiastic piste-bashers
will love it.

The Outback and North Peak also
have easy cruising blues, and The
Outback has some of the steepest blue
runs, including a couple of blue-blacks
through the trees that are pretty much
off-piste and unmarked.

On top of that, Vail, Beaver Creek
and Copper Mountain all have great
intermediate terrain.

FOR BEGINNERS
Nice gentle greens
There are good nursery slopes (floodlit
in the evening) at the top and bottom
of Keystone Mountain, which also has
some excellent long green runs to
progress to – one of them,
Schoolmarm, goes right from top to
bottom of the mountain. There's
another long green on North Peak,
accessible by gondola.

FOR CROSS-COUNTRY
Extensive facilities
The special Cross-Country and Touring
Centre between Keystone and A-Basin
is served by a shuttle-bus. There are
16km/10 miles of groomed trails. And
50km/31 miles of unprepared trails
take you through spectacular scenery
in the Montezuma area, with great
views of the Continental Divide. Some
trails lead to old mining ghost-towns.
The Cross-Country and Touring Centre
runs guided tours, including a Full
Moon evening tour.

QUEUES
Not a problem
Keystone has an efficient, modern lift
system, and, except at the morning
peak, there are few queuing problems.
Last time we tried the night skiing the
River Run gondola stopped running
and the parallel high-speed chair made
for a mind-numbingly cold ride. The
trails are usually beautifully quiet,
except for Mozart, the only blue run
down from Keystone Mountain to
North Peak and The Outback.

GETTING THERE

Air Denver, transfer 2hr.

CHILDCARE

The Children's Center at the base of the mountain caters for children aged 2 months to 12 years and is open from 8am to 9pm. They can also provide evening babysitting in your own room. From age 3, children can join in the Snowplay programmes.

The school's Mini Minor's Camp takes children aged 3 to 4, the Minor's Camp those from 5 to 12.

MOUNTAIN RESTAURANTS
A resort of extremes

There are two mountain restaurant complexes. Summit House at the top of Keystone Mountain has a food court, a pizza place and a bar, all inclined to get over-crowded – 'Eat at the base,' says a reporter. The Outpost Lodge at the top of North Peak is beautifully designed in wood, with high ceilings, picture windows and a big terrace. Its Timber Ridge food court is strictly for refuelling, but the table-service Alpenglow Stube is something else. It has a luxury atmosphere rarely found in mountain restaurants, even in Europe (they even store your boots and give you slippers) – but it is, of course, expensive. There's a simple cabin and outdoor grill at Keystone Gulch, at the foot of North Peak.

SCHOOLS AND GUIDES
Advanced classes a bargain

As well as the normal lessons, there are bumps, race, women-only and various other advanced classes. There are also special courses run by Olympic medallists Phil and Steve Mahre, designed for experienced adult skiers. Reporters have been very impressed by the school's advanced classes, partly because they found themselves in tiny groups or even receiving one-to-one instruction for the price of a group lesson.

FACILITIES FOR CHILDREN
Excellent

Childcare facilities are excellent, with programmes tailored to specific age groups, and nursery care going on into the evening. Children have their own teaching areas, with 'magic carpet' lifts. Ske-cology classes are designed to teach children about the environment and the resort's ecology while learning to ski.

Staying there

HOW TO GO
As you please

It's easy to fix your own lodgings, and regular shuttles operate from Denver airport, but packages can offer very attractive prices. There are hotels but most accommodation is in condominiums.

Hotels There isn't a great choice but they're all of a high standard.

(((4 **Chateaux d'Mont** (800 239 1639) Luxury condo-hotel near the lifts; only 15 suites, with private hot-tubs and other luxuries.

(((4 **Keystone Lodge** (496 3715) Large, recently renovated hotel in Keystone Village. All rooms have mountain views. Pool and fitness centre.

(((3 **Inn at Keystone** (496 4825) Modern, comfortable, resort-owned hotel. Hot-tubs with great views. Liked by reporters who stayed there.

(((3 **Ski Tip Lodge** (496 4950) Former stagecoach halt and home of Keystone's founder, Max Dercum, who restored and extended it and used

Keystone

525

GOURMET NIGHT SKIING

Keystone has the biggest floodlighting operation in the US, covering Keystone Mountain top to bottom. When the light begins to fade, the floodlights come on and you can continue skiing or riding up to 8pm. A gondola, high-speed quad and drag-lift serve 17 green and blue runs (longest top-to-bottom trail over three miles long) and a 20-acre terrain-park. Cruising through falling snow illuminated by the bright lights can be delightful. On a clear night, though, it can be bitterly cold.

You can combine the action with dinner on the mountain. The Alpenglow Stube, at the top of North Peak (reached by gondola), stays open until 8.15 to serve haute cuisine with a Colorado flavour for pedestrians, skiers and snowboarders. Slippers are provided. A cheaper option is next door's Der Fondue Chessel which features fondue, raclette and 'Bavarian' music and dancing.

ACTIVITIES

Indoor Swimming, hot-tubs, tennis
Outdoor Floodlit ice skating, sleigh and stagecoach rides, snowmobiling, horse-riding, tubing, night skiing, snow-shoeing, winter fly fishing, star gazing workshops, weekly firework display, torch-light descents, dog-sledding, evening gondola trips

Central reservations phone number
1 800 427 8308
(toll free from within the US).

Phone numbers
From distant parts of the US, add the prefix 1 970.
From abroad, add the prefix +1 970.

TOURIST OFFICE

Postcode CO 80424
t 496 6772
f 453 3202
international@vail resorts.com
www.keystoneresort.com

---

broken ski tips found on the slopes as door handles – hence the name. Atmospheric old rooms, bar and lounge with log fires. 'Superb food and attentive service,' reports one visitor.

Self-catering All the condominiums we've seen or heard about are large and luxurious – and we've stayed in some fabulous ones with nice touches, such as log fires and two-storey floor-to-ceiling windows. Most condos have use of a pool and hot-tub. Except for their position, we particularly liked the Lakeside condos (near the lake!). The equally comfortable and well-positioned Frostfire condos have fewer amenities, but each unit has an en-suite whirlpool bath. Cinnamon Ridge at Mountain View, Slopeside at Mountain House and Flying Dutchman in the Forest 'neighborhood' are other recommended places. There are lots of condos at the River Run development.

EATING OUT
Not the widest choice
You can have your evening meal up the mountain. The Summit House, at the top of the gondola on Keystone Mountain, remains busy at the end of the normal day because of the floodlit sessions at night. There's live country and western entertainment and simple food – hamburgers, ribs and so on. The Outpost, on North Peak, is a hive of dining activity including Der Fondue Chessel (live music and dancing) and the Alpenglow Stube (see Mountain restaurants on previous page).

There are some good upmarket places at valley level too. We've eaten well at the Ski Tip Lodge by the cross-country track – a charming former stagecoach halt. The Keystone Ranch, well outside the resort, serves six-course dinners in a building based on a 19th-century homestead. The Garden Room of Keystone Lodge overlooks the lake and reports are favourable: 'Small menu but good food.'

River Run and Keystone Village each offer half a dozen options, including steak houses and pizza places. But there isn't the range of mid-market restaurants that makes eating out such a pleasure in many American resorts – and it's in the nature of the place that the restaurants are scattered here and there in different parts of the resort. Paisano's is an 'excellent' Italian at River Run, where there are also two taverns. The cosy Snake River Saloon in the Mountain View neighbourhood is

recommended for grills. The Bighorn Steakhouse in Keystone Lodge is well worth avoiding – a dreary room and, when we went, lousy service.

There are also dinner sleigh rides to rustic homesteads where cowboys sing country and western while you eat.

APRES-SKI
Pretty quiet in the evenings
Immediately after coming off the slopes, it can be quite lively. The Summit House at the top of the gondola has live music and caters for people using the slopes at night as well as après-skiers. As well as skiing and boarding you can go tubing and snow-biking, or skating on part of the enormous lake. The Kickapoo Tavern at River Run has a sunny deck and eight Colorado microbrews on tap. The Last Lift Bar at Mountain House has good live music. Some of the eateries double as bars with live music. The Snake River Saloon has a happy hour, 5–7pm, and is highly recommended by a reporter: 'Brilliant restaurant and lively bar – including a fire-eating barman.' Ida Belle has ragtime music and a miners' tavern decor.

However, places empty out quite early and Keystone isn't really the place for late-night revellers.

The Inxpot is a laid-back coffee house, cum bar, cum bookstore, with comfy armchairs and a great selection of books. Other popular hangouts with the locals are The Goat (the 'liveliest place in town') and Out of Bounds.

OFF THE SLOPES
OK if you want a peaceful time
It is easy for pedestrians to get to both mountain restaurant complexes by gondola. It's also easy to visit Breckenridge and Vail.

There are plenty of other activities, including skating on the frozen lake (the largest outdoor maintained rink in the US) and indoor tennis.

STAYING DOWN THE VALLEY
Possible, good for exploring
A few years ago a couple of reporters stayed in Silverthorne. The Alpen Hutte (468 6336) was friendly and had its own private bus transfer. Frisco is a good centre for visiting other nearby resorts – reporters recommend the Alpine Inn with indoor pool and hot-tub (668 3122), Best Western Lake Dillon (668 5094) and the 19th-century Frisco Lodge (668 0195).

Steamboat 2100m/6,900ft

Where they invented the term Champagne Powder™

HOW IT RATES

The slopes

Snow	★★★★
Extent	★★★
Experts	★★★
Intermediates	★★★★
Beginners	★★★★★
Convenience	★★★
Queues	★★★★
Restaurants	★★★

The rest

Scenery	★★★
Resort charm	★★
Off-slope	★★

What's new

Last season a new Bashor terrain-park opened with the 183m/600ft-long Mavericks Superpipe. For 2002/03 a music system will be added.

Steamboat's terrain has expanded a lot in recent years – first into Morningside Park and then into the Pioneer Ridge area. Another lift and another 500 acres of terrain are longer-term plans.

➕ Excellent beginner and early intermediate runs

➕ Famed for its gladed powder terrain

➕ Good snow record combined with modest altitude – sickness problems are very unlikely

➕ Good (but not cheap) mountain restaurants – open evenings too

➕ Plenty of slope-side lodging

➕ Excellent childcare facilities

➕ Town of Steamboat Springs has some Western character – though it's less of a wild cowboy town than the hype leads you to expect

➖ Old town is a couple of miles from the slopes, and the resort as a whole sprawls over a large area

➖ Modern resort 'village' at the foot of the slopes is rather a mess, with some big eyesore buildings

➖ Not enough tough blue/easy black runs to amuse keen intermediates for a week

➖ Not a huge amount of double-black terrain – some of it a hike away

Steamboat's brochures routinely feature horse-riding, Stetson-wearing, lasso-wielding cowboys. But after several visits, we've still not seen any on the slopes or in the town. There are working cowboys around, but as Steamboat the ski resort has grown it has rather swamped Steamboat Springs the cattle town – without itself developing much of a village atmosphere.

Steamboat's mountain may not be a match in extent and challenge for some Colorado neighbours – experts and keen piste-bashers going for a week or more might do well to plan a two-centre holiday. But Steamboat is one of the best resorts for powder fun among the trees.

The resort

Steamboat is rather isolated with no other mainstream resorts nearby – a long drive or short flight from Denver. The resort village itself is a 10-minute bus-ride from the old town of Steamboat Springs. Near the gondola station there are a few shop- and restaurant-lined multi-level squares.

Some of the accommodation is up the sides of the piste, but the resort also sprawls across the valley.

The old town can be a bit of a disappointment after the hype of the brochures. It may be a working cattle town – it's certainly a great place to buy a Stetson (at the famous FM Light & Son). But the Wild West isn't much in evidence except when the Cowboy

SNOWPIX.COM / CHRIS GILL

Steamboat's slope-side village is spread out over a big area ➔

527

COLORADO

528

MOUNTAIN FACTS

Altitude 2100m-3220m
6,900ft-10,570ft
Lifts 20
Pistes 2,939 acres
Green 13%
Blue 56%
Black 31%
Snowmaking
438 acres

LIFT PASSES

2001/02 prices in dollars
Steamboat
Covers all lifts at Steamboat only.
Beginners One free lift at base (Preview); day pass for lower mountain lifts (adult 40).
Main pass
1-day pass 61
6-day pass 324
(low season 270)
Senior citizens
Over 65: 6-day pass 222
Over 70: 114
Children
Teen 13 to 18: 6-day pass 294
Under 13: 216 – but can be free, see Notes below
Under 5: free pass
Short-term passes
Afternoon passes from 12.15 (adult 49). Single ascent on Silver Bullet Gondola for non-skiers only (adult 17).
Alternative periods
3-day pass is valid for 4 days with one non-skiing day. Passes of 4 days and over allow two non-skiing days, so 4 days' skiing in 6, 6 in 8.
Notes Children up to 12 ski free when parent/grandparent buys full lift pass and stays for 5 days or more (one child per adult). Discounts for groups.

Downhill brings cowhands into town from the Denver Rodeo to compete in a fun race, lassoing and saddling competition (on 21 January in 2003).

The main (and almost only) street in the old town is very wide, with multiple lanes of traffic each way – it was built that way to allow cattle to be driven through town. It is lined with bars, hotels and shops, built at various times over the last 120 years, in a wide mixture of styles, from old wooden buildings to modern concrete plazas.

The town got its name in the mid-1800s, when trappers going along by the Yampa river heard a chugging they thought was a steamboat. It turned out to be the bubbling of a hot spring.

Our preference is to stay on the slopes and make occasional excursions to Steamboat Springs. The free shuttle-buses are very efficient.

The mountain

Located in the Routt National Forest, Steamboat's slopes are prettily set among trees, with extensive views over rolling hills and the wide Yampa valley below. On our last late-season visit we glimpsed a black bear and her cubs ambling across a piste.

It claims to be one of Colorado's biggest areas. But even if the long-term expansion goes ahead, it still won't rival places such as Aspen and Vail.

With an Early Bird pass ($11 including breakfast) you can ride the gondola at 8.15, and get fresh tracks when the slopes open at 8.30, before having a buffet breakfast at Thunderhead when the crowds arrive.

There are various complimentary guiding deals. Mountain hosts do tours of blue and black runs daily at 10.30. Olympic medallist Billy Kidd takes groups down the mountain most days at 1pm. Nelson Carmichael, bronze medallist at the 1992 Albertville

Olympics, runs a free mogul clinic on some Sundays at 1pm. There are nature ski tours three times a week. And five days a week at 9am local guides lead groups of over-50s on a 'mellow cruise' of groomed runs. There are also snow-shoeing tours 6 days a week at 1pm.

Holiday visitors generally overlook Steamboat Springs' little local hill, Howelsen. As well as a row of ski jumps, it has a modest area of pistes, floodlit most evenings.

If you have a car, Vail, Beaver Creek, Copper Mountain, Keystone, Breckenridge and Winter Park are all less than a two-hour drive.

THE SLOPES
Five different flanks
The slopes divide naturally into five sectors, and most have runs to suit all abilities. The gondola from the village rises to **Thunderhead**. From here you can choose the runs back to the village. Or you can go down to the left to catch a chair up to **Storm Peak** or to the new **Pioneer Ridge** area. From Storm Peak you can drop over the back into the **Morningside Park** area. If you turn right from Thunderhead you can catch a long, slow chair up to **Sunshine Peak** which also accesses Morningside Park. Get hold of a daily grooming report to keep up to date with conditions.

SNOW RELIABILITY
Good despite 'low' altitude
Steamboat is relatively low by Colorado standards; it goes from 2100m to 3220m (6,900ft to 10,570ft). So its highest slopes are below the height of the base of Arapahoe Basin. Despite this it has an excellent snow record, with an annual average of 334 inches – more than most of the higher resorts. This is where they invented the term Champagne Powder™. There is also snowmaking from top to bottom of the mountain.

boarding *Steamboat is ideal for first-time boarders – there's a special learning area, ideal gentle slopes to progress to and you can get all over the mountain using chair-lifts and the gondola. The snowboard school even offers another lesson free if you can't ride from the top of the beginners' area after the first. For experienced riders, the Bashor terrain-park includes the Mavericks super-pipe which is claimed to be the longest in North America (though a reporter says the terrain-park was not built by last New Year but the pipe was). And riding the glades in fresh powder is unbeatable. There's also a choice of specialist snowboard shops, and benches and tools at the top of lifts.*

FOR EXPERTS
Powder glades are the highlight

The main attraction of Steamboat for experts is the challenging 'off-piste' terrain in the forest glades. The trees are fantastic with fresh powder though, sadly, conditions have never been perfect on our visits.

A great area is on Sunshine Peak below the Sundown Express. You simply take off through the aspens and choose a route where the trees are spaced as you like them – wide or narrow. Of the marked black runs in this area, the two to the left of the lifts as you go up – Closet and Shadows – are only loosely pistes: the trees have just been thinned out a bit. On the right of the lift as you go up are some clearer marked black runs (sometimes half-groomed, half with bumps).

Morningside Park and Pioneer Ridge also have excellent gladed terrain, without any scary gradients.

The scary gradients are reached via the lift back from Morningside – three numbered chutes are easily accessed, and a short hike gets you to the tree skiing of Christmas Tree Bowl. But the steep runs are short and apart from the glades there isn't much for experts.

Most other marked blacks are easy for good intermediates and make great fast runs if they've been groomed. For bumps, try the series of runs off Four Points – including Nelson's, named after local hero Nelson Carmichael.

Steamboat Powder Cats (aka Blue Sky West) run snowcat skiing tours over 15 square miles of backcountry.

FOR INTERMEDIATES
Some long cruises

Much of the mountain is ideal intermediate territory, with long cruising blue runs such as Buddy's Run, Rainbow and Ego on Storm Peak and High Noon and One O'Clock on Sunshine Peak. Some black runs, such as West Side and Lower Valley View, also make good, challenging intermediate runs when the bumps have been groomed out of them.

Morningside Park is a great area for easy black as well as blue slopes. And don't ignore Thunderhead – there are lots of good runs that are easy to miss if you always head straight to the top. The runs on Sunshine (yes ... the sunniest side of the mountain) at the far right-hand side of the area are very gentle. Tomahawk and Quickdraw are marked blue but are perfectly possible for those who normally stick to green. Locals call this area 'Wally World'.

For keen intermediates the area is

Steamboat

529

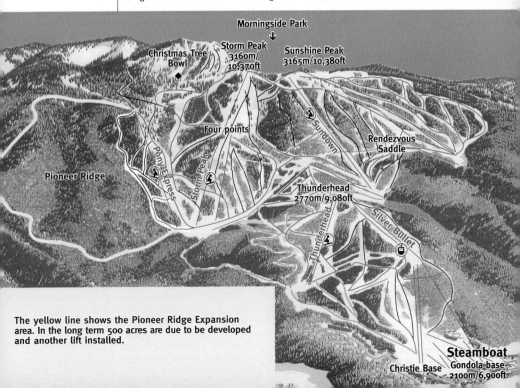

The yellow line shows the Pioneer Ridge Expansion area. In the long term 500 acres are due to be developed and another lift installed.

Morningside Park

Christmas Tree Bowl

Storm Peak
3160m/
10,370ft

Sunshine Peak
3165m/10,380ft

Four points

Sundown

Rendezvous
Saddle

Pony Express

Storm Peak

Pioneer Ridge

Thunderhead
2770m/9,080ft

Thunderhead

Silver Bullet

Steamboat

Christie Base   Gondola base
2100m/6,900ft

SCHOOLS/GUIDES

2001/02 prices in dollars

Steamboat
Classes 3 days
Adult 3 full days: 204
Children's classes
Ages: 6 to 15
5 5hr days including lunch: 360
Private lessons
1hr, 2hr, 3hr or full-day
125 for 1hr

CHILDCARE

The Kids' Vacation Center is run by the resort in the lower gondola station. The Kiddie Coral nursery takes children aged 6 months to 6 years, for half or full days. Those aged 2 can opt for the Buckaroos programme with a one-hour private lesson (ski rental not included). Older children go on to the Mavericks, Sundance and Jackalopes group classes.

The ski school has all-day Desperados and Teen Challenge programmes for children up to 17.

The Adventure Club at Night offers evening childcare in the Vacation Center for ages 4 to 12, from 6pm to 10pm Tuesday to Friday. Reservations necessary.

The Steamboat Grand has childcare facilities.

GETTING THERE

Air Yampa Valley regional airport, transfer ¼hr. Denver, transfer 3½hr.

limited – not really enough to keep you interested for a week unless you enjoy repeating the same runs.

FOR BEGINNERS
Excellent learning terrain

There's a big, gentle nursery area at the base of the mountain served by several lifts. You progress from this to the Christie chairs to a variety of gentle green runs such as Yoo Hoo and Giggle Gulch. A green run winds all the way down from Thunderhead, but there is rather a shortage of 'proper' green runs up the mountain for those not ready for the psychological leap to the easy blues on Sunshine.

FOR CROSS-COUNTRY
Plenty out of town

There's no cross-country in Steamboat itself but a free shuttle service takes you to the Touring Center, where there are 30km/20 miles of groomed tracks and lessons available. There are also Forest Service trails around Rabbit Ears Pass – many quite challenging, apparently.

QUEUES
A morning rush

Queues can form for the gondola at the start of the day; but they are well organised and move quickly ('10 minutes maximum at peak season,' says a reporter) and you can avoid them with the Early Bird pass mentioned above. Fast quad chairs have cut out the worst bottlenecks up the mountain, though the slow Sunshine lift serving the easiest top-of-the-mountain runs can be crowded. Useful information boards indicate waiting times for the main lifts.

MOUNTAIN RESTAURANTS
Good by US standards

There are two main restaurant complexes on the mountain, both of which include excellent table-service restaurants. At Thunderhead there's a choice of the big BK Corral self-service food court, a barbecue on the sun deck, or table-service in the Stoker bar or more elegant Hazie's restaurant. At Rendezvous Saddle there's a slightly smaller alternative, which has a two-floor self-service section including a pizza bar, another sun deck and barbecue and Ragnar's table-service Scandinavian restaurant. You can book for Ragnar's and Hazie's. There's also a snack bar and sun deck at Four Points.

SCHOOLS AND GUIDES
Lots of variety

The programme includes special workshops such as bumps and 'extreme challenge' steep and deep clinics. Reports on the school are very positive: 'A fantastic tree skiing lesson.' There's a First Tracks option at 8am for $35 for 90 minutes – great on a powder day.

FACILITIES FOR CHILDREN
Kids Go Free

Steamboat has a Kids Go Free scheme – free lift pass for one child of up to age 12 per parent or grandparent buying a pass for at least five days. The school has a variety of courses for different abilities and age groups. Reporters' comments include 'Louis (aged four) pleaded with us to up his half day to a full day,' and 'the camaraderie between instructors and pupils is great'. There's a special kids-only Rough Rider Basin area with fun terrain and a Wild West theme, including teepees, a mine shaft and a log cabin. Childcare arrangements are exceptional, including evening entertainment or excursions from 6pm.

Staying there

Our preference is to stay on the slopes and make occasional excursions to Steamboat Springs. The free shuttle-buses are very efficient.

HOW TO GO
Plenty of packages

A fair number of UK tour operators have Steamboat in their programme. There's accommodation for all tastes.
Chalets There are some catered chalets run by UK tour operators.
Hotels The smarter hotels out at the resort have less character than some of the in-town options.
(((4 **Steamboat Grand** (871 5500) 330-room resort-owned condo-hotel near lifts, with pool, hot-tubs, child care.
(((4 **Best Western Ptarmigan Inn** (879 1730) Ideally situated just above the gondola station and right on the piste, with an outdoor pool and hot-tub, a sauna and good après-ski bar.
(((4 **Sheraton** (879 2220) Big, comfortable, ugly, impersonal hotel near gondola, with pool and hot-tub.
(((3 **Harbor** (879 1522) The oldest hotel in the old town. Rooms vary in size and style; sauna, steam room and two hot-tubs.

ACTIVITIES

Indoor Ice skating, hot-tubs, swimming pools, tennis, gym, weights room, climbing wall, museum

Outdoor Ice driving school, dog-sledding, snowmobiling, ballooning, hot springs, dinner sleigh rides, horse-riding, skating, ice and rock climbing, fly-fishing, snowcat skiing, snow-shoeing, cross-country skiing, tubing

Phone numbers
From distant parts of the US, add the prefix 1 970.
From abroad, add the prefix +1 970.

Central reservations phone number
1 800 922 2722 (toll free from within the US).

TOURIST OFFICE

Postcode CO 80487
t 879 6111
f 879 7844
info@steamboat.com
www.steamboat.com

STEAMBOAT / CYNTHIA HUNTER
Steamboat's powder in the trees is its main attraction for good skiers and boarders ↓

② **Bristol** (879 3083) Traditional little hotel on main street of old town, with 'small but fairly priced' rooms.
② **Alpiner Lodge** (879 1430) Bavarian style economy place in old town.
② **Rabbit Ears Motel** (879 1150) Recommended by reporter: 'Excellent. Family run, comfortable rooms.'
Self-catering There are countless apartment developments, many with good pool/tub facilities and own shuttle-buses. Recommendations include Bear Claw condos at the top of the nursery slope; Timber Run, a short shuttle-ride from the centre with multiple hot-tubs; The Lodge at Steamboat, close to the gondola station; Thunderhead Lodge & Condominiums; and the aptly named Ski Inn. Storm Meadows condos at Christie Base are 'wonderful'. All condos are on a free bus route that runs every 20 minutes at peak times.

EATING OUT
Huge variety
There are over 70 bars and restaurants. Pick up a dining guide booklet to check out the menus.

Steamboat specialises in mountain-top dining, in three restaurants accessed via the gondola to Thunderhead. Five nights a week the Western BBQ does an all-you-can-eat buffet, with country and western music and dancing. Or you can have a gourmet treat at Hazie's, where the menu goes somewhat upmarket from lunchtime. Four nights a week you can take a sleigh hauled by a snowcat to Ragnar's at Rendezvous Saddle for a Scandinavian meal with live music.

In the resort, the Slopeside Grill has a good selection of pizza and pasta dishes and doubles as a bar, with live music some nights. The Steamboat Grand has Chaps, a popular cowboy-style bar and grill, and The Cabin, which 'does seriously good food'.

In downtown Steamboat Springs try the Apogee for fine French-style food, or the cheaper Harwig's Grill on the same premises. The Montana is a good upmarket Mexican. The Steamboat Yacht Club on the river bank has fine seafood and views of ski-jumping. Antares is deservedly popular for its excellent international cuisine. The Steamboat Brewery has a wide-ranging menu and its own beers. For more traditional American fare try the Old West Steakhouse or the Ore House at the Pine Grove. Cantina has been recommended for Tex-Mex, Cugino's for Italian and the Boomerang for good-value 'cook your own' steaks. Cottonwood Grill offers Pacific Rim Cuisine. For a real budget buy, head for the Double Z, popular with locals.

APRES-SKI
Fairly lively
Restaurants apart, the old town is quiet in the evening. The Old Town Pub has live music at weekends. The Tap House is 'a must for Brits missing their soccer', with 30 TVs as well as the best draft beer choice in town.

The base lodge area is livelier. Popular places at close of play are the Slopeside Grill and the Inferno, in the gondola square, both with live music and a happy hour. The mountain hosts regularly serve up free hot apple cider and hot chocolate at the base of the gondola in the afternoons. The Inferno is the place for dancing to loud live music – and on Sundays it has a very popular 'Disco Inferno' night. Dos Amigos and the Tugboat Tavern are popular bars for drinks by the pitcher. The Ptarmigan Inn offers a rather more sophisticated atmosphere. The Stoker Comedy Club up at Thunderhead has live stand-up acts from 7 until 10pm.

Evening activities include watching floodlit ski-jumping in the old town and tubing on the floodlit nursery slope at the main ski area.

OFF THE SLOPES
Lots to do
Getting up to Thunderhead restaurant complex is easy for pedestrians. Visiting town is, too. And you can go and relax in outdoor Strawberry Park Hot Springs six miles from town. The snowmobiling terrain around Rabbit Ears Pass looks great to our untutored eye. The ice rink is Olympic size.

Telluride 2660m/8,750ft

Massive expansion of slopes has made this cute old town worth considering

What's new

Last season three new high-speed chairlifts opened up Prospect Bowl and another 733 acres of terrain – a 70% increase – and over 20 new runs, creating an entirely different feel to the resort. Yet another upscale restaurant, the Blue Point and its swanky Noir Bar, has joined Telluride's fray of restaurants that are surprisingly excellent for such a tiny, faraway town. In the Mountain Village, Station Recreation opened with evening tobogganing, snowbiking and tubing on floodlit slopes.

532

➕ Charming restored Victorian gold- and silver-mining town with a real Wild West atmosphere

➕ Slopes for all abilities

➕ Dramatic, craggy mountain scenery – unusual for Colorado

➖ Isolated location

➖ Despite expansion still a small area

➖ Mountain Village is still a little quiet but vastly improved on a few years ago

➖ Limited mountain restaurants

We love the old town of Telluride – it has lots of character, lovely old buildings, good restaurants and shops and dramatic views of the San Juan mountains. The addition of Prospect Bowl last season has nearly doubled the extent of the slopes. But it is still a small area – only one western US resort in this book has a significantly smaller area of slopes. Keen piste-bashers should rent a car and combine it with another destination for a one-week or 10-day holiday.

THE RESORT

Telluride is an isolated resort in south-west Colorado. The town first boomed when gold was found – and Butch Cassidy robbed his first bank here. Some say its name is a version of 'To hell you ride', but it's more probably due to the presence of tellurium in the rock. The town's old wooden buildings and sidewalks have been well-restored and it has more Wild West charm than any other resort. Shops and restaurants have gone decidedly up-market since its 'hippy' days of a few years ago. But Telluride is still friendly and small-scale. On the slopes, the Mountain Village is a development of lavish modern condos and hotels. A gondola links the town and Village and runs until midnight.

THE MOUNTAINS

There is something for everyone here. **Slopes** Two chair-lifts and a gondola serve the steep wooded slopes above the town, and give access to the bowl beyond which leads down to Mountain Village. This has steep slopes at the top, intermediate terrain in the middle and ideal, wide and gentle beginner slopes beyond the village down to Big Billie's and under the Sunshine Express lift. The new Gold Hill lift serves some of the steepest, trickiest slopes in Colorado. The newly opened terrain in Prospect Bowl is mainly intermediate, with dozens of rolling pitches that meander and weave their way through thickets of trees. A very relaxing and pretty area.

Palmyra Peak 4060m/13,320ft
Gold Hill
3735m/12,250ft
3650m/11,980ft
Giuseppe's
3600m/11,810ft
Gold Hill 1/4
Palmyra 5
Prospect Bowl #2
Outer Park
3280m/10,760ft
3315m/10,880ft
Station St Sophia 3210m/10,540ft
Sunshine 10
Gorrono Ranch
Station Telluride
Station Mountain Village 2910m/9,540ft
2910m/9,540ft
Coonskin Base 2660m/8,730ft
Big Billie's 2790m/9,160ft
Telluride

MOUNTAIN FACTS

Altitude 2660m-3625m
        8,730ft-12,250ft
Lifts   16
Pistes   1,700 acres
Green   25%
Blue   36%
Black   39%
Snowmaking
          204 acres
Recco detectors used

Phone numbers
From distant parts of the US, add the prefix 1 970.
From abroad, add the prefix +1 970.

Central reservations
Call 728 7507.

Toll-free number (from within the US) 1 888 827 8050.

TOURIST OFFICE

Postcode CO 81435
t 728 3041
f 728 6475
skitelluride@telski.com
www.telski.com

Snow reliability With an average of 309 inches of snow a year and a fair amount of snowmaking, snow reliability is average for Colorado, but there have been some slow starts to recent seasons.
Experts The double-black bump runs directly above the town are what has given the area its expert reputation and there are steep gladed runs from all along the ridge between Giuseppe's and Gold Hill – no longer a hike away thanks to the new Gold Hill lift. Gold Hill has some truly challenging terrain from wide open steeps to narrow chutes and gnarly wooded trails. There are heli- and snowcat operations.
Intermediates There are ideal blue cruising runs with awesome views right from the top down to Mountain Village (including the aptly-named See Forever). The new terrain in the Prospect Bowl area is largely easy cruising and the main easy way back down the front to town is the winding Telluride Trail. Even with the new expansion keen piste-bashers could get bored after a couple of days.
Beginners There are ideal runs in the Meadows below Mountain Village, and splendid long greens and blues served by the Sunshine Express chair.
Snowboarding The 8-acre terrain-park (with half-pipe) next to Gorrono Ranch, is the largest in the south-west.
Cross-country The scenic beauty of the area makes it splendid for cross-country – the Telluride Nordic Centre runs over 35km/22 miles of trails.
Queues These are rarely a problem – there are no weekend crowds, and the lift system is increasingly impressive.
Mountain restaurants Gorrono Ranch is the main on-mountain restaurant, with a big terrace, live music and a BBQ. At the top of the Prospect Bowl lift, you can get sandwiches. Giuseppe's is tiny but good for spaghetti and meatballs, pizzas and stunning views.
Schools and guides As well as the usual, the ski school offers an all day

clinic and Four-Max Clinics limited to, you guessed it, four clients only. Bump clinics are a speciality.
Facilities for children The Adventure Club provides indoor and outdoor play before and after children's lessons. The new Mountain Village Activity Center has a nursery for toddlers.

STAYING THERE

Telluride is tricky to get to from the UK, involving two or three flights or a long 335 mile drive from Denver.
How to go Packages fly into nearby Montrose or the tiny Telluride airport (prone to closure by the weather).
Hotels Hotel Columbia is luxurious – overstuffed pillows and uniquely decorated rooms. It's closely followed by the plush yet friendly Camel's Garden Hotel and Spa at the base of the gondola. The New Sheridan is one of the town's oldest hotels. The big Wyndham Peaks Resort in the Mountain Village is enormous but has a spectacular lounge area and impressive spa facilities.
Self-catering There are plenty of condos. The Inn At Lost Creek in Mountain Village is the most lavish of the self-catering options.
Eating out The Cosmopolitan in the Hotel Columbia is renowned as the best in town. Other sophisticated options include the Marmotte and Harmon's (in the old station). Allred's at the top of the gondola is a private club for lunch but offers gourmet dining in the evenings.
Après-ski There's a lively bar-based après-ski scene. Leimgruber's is popular in the early evening. The New Sheridan has a lovely old bar. The Swede Finn and the Last Dollar have been recommended by locals. The Fly Me to the Moon Saloon has live music and stays open late. There's a new swanky candle lit lounge called the Noir Bar attached to the Blue Point Restaurant. There are often concerts at the historic Sheridan Opera House. The Nugget Theatre shows latest cinema releases. Station Recreation at the Mountain Village has floodlit tubing, sledding and snowbiking.
Off the slopes There's quite a lot to do around town if you are not skiing or boarding, such as dog sledding, horse riding, snow-shoeing, ice skating and glider rides. The Golden Door Spa in the Wyndham Peaks Resort was voted one of the top 10 spas in the world by Conde Nast Traveller readers.

Telluride

533

Vail

Luxury living, high prices and the US's biggest single ski area

WHAT IT COSTS

(((((6)

HOW IT RATES

The slopes

Snow	*****
Extent	****
Experts	****
Intermediates	*****
Beginners	****
Convenience	***
Queues	**
Restaurants	**

The rest

Scenery	***
Resort charm	***
Off-slope	***

MOUNTAIN FACTS

Altitude	2475m-3525m
	8,120ft-11,570ft
Lifts	33
Pistes	5,289 acres
Green	18%
Blue	29%
Black	53%
Snowmaking	
	380 acres
Recco detectors used	

01285 642 555
www.handmade-holidays.co.uk
AITO   ATOL PROTECTED 4479

534

➕ Biggest area in the US – great for confident intermediates

➕ The Back Bowls are big areas of treeless terrain – unusual in the US

➕ Fabulous area of ungroomed, wooded slopes recently opened at Blue Sky Basin

➕ Largely traffic-free resort village, with great bus service

➖ Slopes can be crowded by American standards, with some lift queues even in low season

➖ The famous Back Bowls may be closed in early season – and can suffer from the sun

➖ Inadequate mountain restaurants

➖ Tirolean-style Vail Village doesn't impress many Europeans

➖ Expensive

Blue Sky Basin, an area of shady, wooded, largely ungroomed slopes, has transformed Vail's attraction for good skiers and riders. Not only does it bring a much-needed bit of spice to the resort, but it gets you away from the crowds that are Vail's most serious drawback.

Vail's slopes are now undeniably compelling, especially when you take account of nearby sister-resort Beaver Creek (see separate chapter). What continues to push Vail down our American shortlist is its style and atmosphere – a curious mixture of pseudo-Tirol and anonymous suburbs. The resort works well, largely thanks to the efficient buses. But if you hope to be captivated, Vail can't compete with the distinctive Rockies resorts based on old mining or cowboy towns. If we're going that far West, we like it to be a bit Wild.

The resort

Standing in the centre of Vail Village, surrounded by chalets and bierkellers, you could be forgiven for thinking you were in the Tirol – which is what Vail's founder, Pete Seibert, intended back in the 1950s. But Vail Village is now just part of an enormous resort, mostly built in anonymous modern style, stretching for miles beside the I-70 freeway – the main route westwards through the Rockies from Denver.

The vast village benefits from a free and efficient bus service, which makes choice of location less than crucial. But there's no denying that the most convenient – and expensive – places to stay are in mock-Tirolean Vail Village, near the Vista Bahn fast chair, or in functional Lionshead, near the gondola. There is a lot of accommodation further out – the cheapest tends to be across the I-70.

Beaver Creek, ten miles away, is covered by the lift pass and is easily reached by bus (see separate chapter). Other resorts within a two-hour drive include Breckenridge and Keystone (both owned by Vail Resorts and covered by the lift pass), Aspen, Steamboat and Copper Mountain.

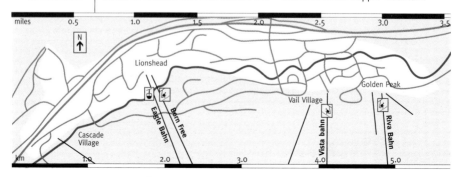

The best powder is usually in Blue Sky Basin and on the front of the mountain rather than in the Back Bowls ➔

VAIL RESORTS, INC

What's new

In December 2002 Vail will celebrate its 40th birthday. The ski area opened on 15 December 1962 with a gondola and two chair-lifts. It now has major plans for Vail Village and Lionshead. Work probably won't start until Spring 2003 and will include revamping the base of the Vista Bahn with escalators, heated walkways and a new underground lift-pass sales, equipment hire and ski school office.

On a longer-term basis at Lionshead, some existing buildings will be demolished and new accommodation including a 100-room luxury 5-star hotel is planned.

For 2001/02, grooming capacity was increased by 15%, Blue Sky Basin had tree stumps and rocks removed, and snowmaking was improved.

Several hotels were renovated and redeveloped and Vail Resorts bought the Marriot, the largest hotel in Vail (349 rooms).

The mountains

Vail has the biggest area of slopes in the US, with immaculately groomed trails and ungroomed terrain in open bowls and among the trees. There are runs to suit every taste. The main criticism is that some of the runs (especially blacks) are overclassified.

THE SLOPES
Something for everyone
The slopes above **Vail** can be accessed via three main lifts. From right next to Vail Village, the Vista Bahn fast chair goes up to the major mid-mountain focal point, Mid-Vail; from Lionshead, the Eagle Bahn gondola goes up to the Eagle's Nest complex; and from the Golden Peak base area just to the east of Vail Village, the Riva Bahn fast chair goes up towards the Two Elk area.

The front face of the mountain is largely north-facing, with well-groomed trails cut through the trees. At altitude the mountainside divides into three bowls – Mid-Vail in the centre, with Game Creek to the south-west and Northeast Bowl to the, er, north-east. Lifts reach the ridge at three points, all giving access to the **Back Bowls** (mostly ungroomed and treeless) and through them to the **Blue Sky Basin** area (mostly ungroomed and wooded).

The slopes have yellow-jacketed patrollers who stop people speeding recklessly. There's a 'new technology center' where you can test the latest equipment. British guests may get the chance of skiing with Martin Bell, Britain's best-ever downhiller and now UK ski ambassador for Vail Resorts (he lives in Vail in the winter).

SNOW RELIABILITY
Excellent, except in the Bowls
As well as an exceptional natural snow record, Vail and Beaver Creek both have extensive snowmaking facilities, normally needed only in early season. Although snow in the Back Bowls is often poor because of its largely south-facing aspect, Blue Sky Basin is largely north-facing and sheltered from sun by trees – so the snow quality can be expected to be excellent, with powder lasting for days after the latest fall.

FOR EXPERTS
Transformed by Blue Sky Basin
Vail's Back Bowls are vast areas, served by three chair-lifts and a couple of short drag-lifts. You can go virtually anywhere you like in the half-dozen identifiable bowls, trying the gradient

Vail

535

BLUE SKY BASIN

This is the one of biggest new developments in any Colorado ski area for years – and the prospect of it caused outrage among environmental groups, some of whom burnt down the Two Elk mountain restaurant, the ski patrol HQ and some lift stations in protest. The first 520 acres of it, served by two high-speed quads, opened in January 2000. The following season saw the addition of Pete's Express (named after Vail's founder Pete Seibert), another fast quad, accessing a further 125 acres of gentler terrain – making up 645 acres in total.

We skied the Basin two months after opening and loved it. There are some easy blue runs that are frequently groomed but most of the area is left ungroomed and the runs among the trees – some widely spaced, some very tight – are delightful for strong skiers and boarders. Few of the runs are very steep, but because you are basically finding your own way much of the time, there is a great feeling of adventure. The snow is usually much better than in the Back Bowls because of the shelter given by the trees and the generally north-facing aspect.

Two Elk Lodge
3420m/11,220ft

Summit
3430m/11,250ft

Wildwood
3345m/10,980ft

Northeast Bowl

Game Creek Bowl

Northwoods

Mountaintop

Wildwood

Game Creek

Mid-Vail
3095m/10,150ft

Avanti

Eagle's Nest
3155m/10,350ft

Riva Bahn

Vista Bahn

Pride

Born Free

Eagle Bahn

Golden Peak

Vail Village
2500m/8,200ft

Lionshead
2475m/8,120ft

Cascade
Village

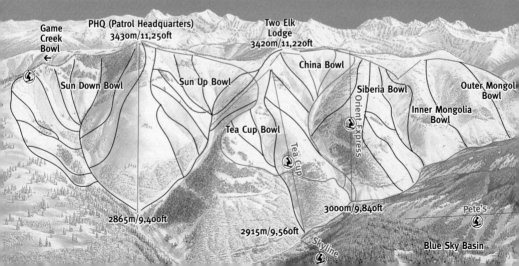

Game
Creek
Bowl
←

PHQ (Patrol Headquarters)
3430m/11,250ft

Two Elk
Lodge
3420m/11,220ft

Sun Down Bowl

Sun Up Bowl

China Bowl

Siberia Bowl

Outer Mongolia
Bowl

Orient Express

Inner Mongolia
Bowl

Tea Cup Bowl

Tea Cup

2865m/9,400ft

3000m/9,840ft

Pete's

2915m/9,560ft

Skyline

Blue Sky Basin

LIFT PASSES

2002/03 prices in dollars

The Colorado Ticket
Covers all Vail, Beaver Creek, Breckenridge and Keystone resorts, plus Arapahoe Basin.
Main pass
1-day pass 63
6-day pass 270
Senior citizens
Over 65: 6-day pass 220
Over 70: season pass 99
Children
Under 13: 6-day pass 150
Under 5: free pass
Short-term passes
Half-day pass from noon available.
Notes
The Colorado ticket is available only to international visitors who pre-book through a UK tour operator. It is not available at the ticket window in the resort. Prices quoted are regular season rates.

boarding *Vail has been wooing boarders with excellent facilities and a positive attitude for years. With beautifully groomed, gentle slopes and lots of high-speed chairs, this is a great area for beginners, and there's plenty for experts too, including some wonderful gladed runs and an excellent terrain-park and super-pipe on Golden Peak. There are specialist board shops and good instruction and a Burton test centre at the top of Vail mountain. The lively bars and nightlife are another draw.*

and terrain of your choice. There are interesting lightly wooded areas as well as the open slopes that dominate the area. 87 per cent of the runs in the Back Bowls are classified black but are not particularly steep, and they have disappointed some of our more confident reporters.

Blue Sky Basin has some great adventure runs in the trees – see feature panel.

On the front face there are some genuinely steep double-black-diamond runs which usually have great snow; they are often mogulled but sometimes groomed to make wonderful fast cruising. The Highline lift on the extreme east of the area serves three. And Prima Cornice, served by the Northwoods Express, is one of the steepest runs on the front side.

If the snow is good, try the backcountry Minturn Mile – you leave the ski area through a gate in the Game Creek area for a European-style off-piste run starting with a powder bowl and finishing on a path by a river – ending up in the atmospheric Saloon (see Après-ski).

FOR INTERMEDIATES
Ideal territory

The majority of Vail's front face is great intermediate territory, with easy cruising runs. Above Lionshead, especially, there are excellent long, relatively quiet blues – Born Free and Simba both go from top to bottom. Game Creek Bowl, nearby, is excellent, too. Avanti, underneath the chair of the same name, is a nice cruiser.

As well as tackling some of the easier front-face blacks, intermediates will find plenty of interest in the Back Bowls. Some runs are groomed. Several of the runs are classified blue, including Silk Road, which loops around the eastern edge of the domain, with wonderful views. Some of the unpisted slopes make the ideal introduction to powder. Confident intermediates will also enjoy Blue Sky Basin – choose the clearly marked blue runs to start with.

FOR BEGINNERS
Good but can be crowded

There are excellent nursery slopes at resort level and at altitude and easy longer runs to progress to. But they can be rather crowded.

Vail

537

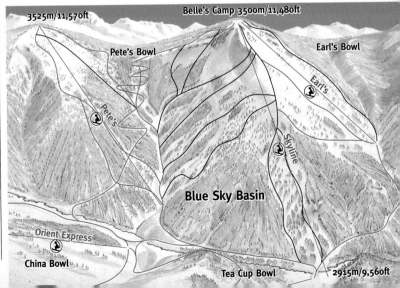

3525m/11,570ft
Belle's Camp 3500m/11,480ft
Pete's Bowl
Earl's Bowl
Earl's
Pete's
Skyline
Blue Sky Basin
Orient Express
China Bowl
Tea Cup Bowl
2915m/9,560ft

Americans like Vail's Back Bowls because they are unusual in having hardly any trees, But they are nothing special by Alpine standards →

COLORADO

538

SCHOOLS/GUIDES

2001/02 prices in dollars

Classes 7 days
Full day: 9.45-3.30
Half day: 3hr: am or pm
1 full day: 90
Children's classes
Ages: 3 to 14
Full day: including lift pass and lunch
1 full-day: 94
Private lessons
1-hour, 2-hour, half and full day
1hr: 130, for 1 to 6 people
Half day: 360 (am) or 330 (pm), for 1 to 6 people.
Full day: 485

CHILDCARE

School lessons are based at Children's Ski Centers located at Golden Peak and Lionshead. There are separate programmes to suit children of different ages and ability – Mini-Mice for children aged three, Mogul Mice and Superstars for those aged four to six.

Small World Play School, located at Golden Peak, provides day care for children aged two months to six years, from 8am to 4.30. Reservations essential – call 479 3285.

SKE-Cology classes let kids learn about mountain wildlife while skiing/snowboarding.

Kids aged 7-14 can take part in such events as race days and bump and bash sessions through the terrain-parks.

FOR CROSS-COUNTRY
Some of the best
Vail's cross-country areas are at the foot of Golden Peak and at the Nordic Center on the golf course.

QUEUES
Can be bad
Vail has some of the longest lift queues we've hit in the US, especially at weekends because of the influx from Denver. Most queues move quickly. But at Mid-Vail waits of 15 minutes are common and we have reports of 45-minute waits. The Northwoods Express lift can also be very busy because the alternative Highline lift is so slow.

MOUNTAIN RESTAURANTS
Surprisingly poor (though pricey)
As other major American resorts are gradually improving their mountain restaurants, Vail's are slipping further behind: demand is increasing to the point where the major self-service restaurants can be unpleasantly crowded from 11am to 2pm. They are also expensive (especially Two Elk, where a reporter said 'a hot dog, fries and coke cost £10'). There's table-service (with limited menu) at Eagle's Nest – book ahead.

SCHOOLS AND GUIDES
Among the best in the world
The Vail-Beaver Creek school has an excellent reputation. All the reports we've had of it have again been glowing. Class sizes are usually small – as few as four is not uncommon. Having tried three different instructors, we can vouch for the high standard. There are specialist half-day workshops in, for example, bumps and powder and adventure tours of Blue Sky Basin. You can sign up on the mountain.

FACILITIES FOR CHILDREN
Excellent
The comprehensive arrangements for young children look excellent, and we've had good reports on the children's school. There are splendid children's areas with adventure trails and themed play areas.

Staying there 🔑

HOW TO GO
Package or independent
There's a big choice of packages to Vail. It's easy to organise your own visit, with regular airport shuttles.
Chalets Vail offers a wide choice of catered chalets in the US, via a range of UK tour operators. Many chalets are out of the centre at East Vail or West Vail or across the busy freeway.
Hotels Vail has a fair choice of hotels, though most tend to be expensive. The Vail Village Inn and Chateau Vail are currently closed for renovation.
(((((5) **Vail Cascade** One of the best in town. A resort within a resort – lots of facilities and a chair-lift right outside.
(((((5) **Sonnenalp Bavaria Haus** Very smart and central. Large spa and splendid piano bar-lounge.
(((((5) **Lodge at Vail** Owned by Vail Resorts, right by the Vista Bahn in Vail Village. Some standard rooms small. Huge buffet breakfast. Outdoor pool.
((((4) **Evergreen Lodge** Cheaper (for Vail!) option. Between village and Lionshead. Outdoor pool. Sports bar.
Self-catering For those who want lots of in-house amenities, the Racquet Club at East Vail is superb. The Mountain Haus has high-quality condos in the centre of town. There are plenty of cheaper options, and several tour operators have allocations conveniently close to the Lionshead gondola.

GETTING THERE

Air Eagle, transfer 1hr.
Denver, transfer 2½hr.

ACTIVITIES

Indoor Athletic clubs and spas, massage, museum, cinema, theatre, tennis courts, artificial skating rink, library, galleries
Outdoor Hot-air ballooning, skating, ice hockey, sleigh rides, fishing, mountaineering, snowmobiles, snow-shoe excursions, snowcat tours, dog-sledding, paragliding, tubing hill, ski biking, thrill sledding, laser tag

Phone numbers
From distant parts of the US, add the prefix 1 970.
From abroad, add the prefix +1 970.

Central reservations phone number
Call 1 800 270 4870 (toll-free from within the US).

TOURIST OFFICE

Postcode CO 81658
t 496 9090
international@vail
resorts.com
www.vail.com

EATING OUT
Endless choice

Whatever kind of food you want, Vail has it – but most of it is not cheap. 'All restaurants require a fat wallet' and 'high standards but at New York prices' are typical comments from reporters. Booking in advance is essential.

Recommended fine-dining options include the Wildflower, in the Lodge, Ludwig's, in the Sonnenalp Bavaria Haus, and the Tour.

For a budget option we liked the Hubcap Brewery in Vail Village, with local ales and filling American food.

Recommendations from readers include May Palace (Chinese) in West Vail, Sapphire (seafood), Blu's (good value), Montauk (seafood) at Lionshead, the Bistro at the Racquet Club, Amigos, Russell's, Bottega and Vendetta's.

APRES-SKI
Fairly lively

Gravity at Lionshead is convenient for the end of the day and has live music. Garfinkel's has a DJ and happy hour. The Red Lion in the village centre is popular, with big-screen TVs and huge portions of food. The George tries to be an English-style pub. The Ore House serves 'mean margaritas and very hot chicken wings'.

The Swiss Chalet attempts to recreate European 'gemütlichkeit'; King's Club is the place to go for high-calorie cakes, and becomes a piano bar later; and Los Amigos and the Hubcap Brewery are other lively places at four o'clock.

You can have a good night out at Adventure Ridge at the top of the Eagle Bahn gondola. As well as bars and restaurants, there's ice skating, tubing, snowmobiling, snow-shoeing and snowbiking – though a reporter reckons the tubing hill is boring and badly run compared with Keystone's.

Later on, Club Chelsea is a popular disco. 8150 is also good, with a suspended floor that moves with the dancing; the Bully Ranch at the Sonnenalp is famous for its 'mudslide'

drinks; The Bridge (formerly Nick's) is a snowboard hangout; Vendetta's does good pizza and beer. A new nightclub called The Sanctuary has opened.

Out of town in Minturn, the Saloon is worth a trip – genuine old-west style with photos of famous skier patrons on the wall.

OFF THE SLOPES
A lot to do

Getting around on the free bus is easy, and there are lots of activities to try. Balloon rides are popular. The factory outlets at Silverthorne are a must for shopaholics who can't resist a bargain.

STAYING UP THE MOUNTAIN
Great if you can afford it

Game Creek chalet above Vail (like Trappers Cabin at Beaver Creek) is a luxurious private enclave up the mountain, which a group can rent by the night (for a small fortune). You ski in at the end of the day to a champagne welcome, soak in an outdoor hot-tub and enjoy a gourmet dinner. The cabin-keeper then leaves, returning in the morning to prepare your breakfast.

STAYING ALONG THE VALLEY
Cheaper but quiet

Staying out of central Vail is certainly cheaper but not so lively. If you rent a car, staying out of town and visiting nearby resorts makes for an interesting holiday. East Vail and West Vail both have reasonably priced lodging.

Vail

539

Winter Park

Good value, great terrain, huge snowfalls, unpretentious town

WHAT IT COSTS

(((((5)))))

HOW IT RATES

The slopes

Snow	★★★★★
Extent	★★★
Experts	★★★★
Intermediates	★★★★
Beginners	★★★★★
Convenience	★★★
Queues	★★★★
Restaurants	★★★

The rest

Scenery	★★★
Resort charm	★★
Off-slope	★

➕ The best snowfall record of all Colorado's major resorts

➕ Superb beginner terrain and lots of groomed cruises

➕ Lots for experts, including great tree skiing and countless challenging mogul slopes

➕ Quiet on weekdays, and impressive lift system copes with weekends

➕ Leading resort for teaching people with disabilities to ski and ride

➕ Great snow and expert terrain at Berthoud Pass, accessed by snowcat

➕ Good views by US standards

➕ Largely free of inflated prices and ski-resort glitz, but ...

➖ Also largely lacking the the range of restaurants and shops you expect in a big international resort

➖ Town is a bus-ride from the slopes, and strung-out along the main road

➖ New 'village' at the lift base is very limited, and dead in the evening

➖ Trails tend to be either easy cruises or stiff mogul fields

➖ One or two slow lifts in key spots

➖ The nearest big resort to Denver, so can get crowded at weekends – mainly a problem on runs close to the base, and in rental shops

When we first visited Winter Park – developed for the recreation of the citizens of nearby Denver, and still owned by the city – we were surprised by that we found: a mountain of world class. Now there seems to be the prospect of a world-class resort at the base, too: dynamic Intrawest (developers of famously wonderful Whistler) have signed a 30-year agreement to operate and develop the whole resort. The resort's future looks bright.

For the present, if value for money and snow are more important to you than glamour or variety of shops and restaurants, the place should be high up on your Colorado shortlist. Some of our reporters rate it their favourite Colorado resort, partly because it makes such a refreshing change from the norm.

What's new

For 2002/03 Winter Park has revised and expanded its terrain parks and half pipe.

There is a new deli (the Boxcar) for skiers and riders at the West Portal base station.

Intrawest's agreement to operate and develop the resort comes too late to affect this season, but will doubtless lead to major developments in the future.

The resort

Winter Park started life around the turn of the century as a railway town, when Rio Grande railway workers climbed the slopes to ski down. One of the resort's mountains, Mary Jane, is named after a legendary 'lady of pleasure' who is said to have received the land as payment for her favours.

The railway still plays an important part in Winter Park's existence, with a station right at the foot of the slopes where trains deposit day trippers from Denver every Saturday and Sunday.

Most accommodation is down in town, but in the last couple of years, stylish accommodation has been developed at or near the foot of the slopes, most recently a car-free mini-resort known variously as The Village or Winter Park Resort. But most accommodation is a shuttle-bus-ride away in spacious condos scattered around either side of the road through downtown Winter Park – US highway 40, which continues to the nearby town of Fraser. There are also motels, bars and restaurants along the road, and at night Winter Park resembles an established ski resort town – but in the daytime it's clear that the place doesn't amount to much. Reporters complain there's no real 'town centre'. Confusingly, an area between the mountain and the town is known as Old Town. The locals are friendly and helpful – typical small-town America.

Shuttle-buses run regularly between the town and the lift base, and the hotels and condos also provide shuttle services. But a car does simplify day trips to Denver or to other resorts – within a two-hour drive are Steamboat, Breckenridge, Copper Mountain, Keystone and Vail.

540

MOUNTAIN FACTS

Altitude 2740m-3675m
9,000ft-12,060ft

Lifts	22
Pistes	2,886 acres
Green	9%
Blue	34%
Black	57%
Snowmaking	
	294 acres

LIFT PASSES

2002/03 prices in US dollars

Winter Park Resort
Covers all lifts in Winter Park.
Main pass
1-day pass 56
6-day pass 246
(low season 216)
Senior citizens
Over 61: 6-day pass 204 (low season 192)
Over 70: free pass
Children
Under 14: 6-day pass 108 (low season 90)
Under 6: free pass
Short-term passes
Half-day passes up to 12.45 37
from noon 37
Alternative periods
Passes of 2 days and over allow one non-skiing day, eg 6-day pass valid for 7 days with one day off..
Notes Special rates for disabled skiers. Reduction for all skiing before 3 Dec and after 31 Mar.

WINTER PARK RESORT

There are easier ways into Vasquez Cirque than this, thank goodness ↓

Winter Park has a mountain that's big by US standards, and an excellent mix of terrain that suits all abilities.

THE SLOPES
Interestingly divided
There are five distinct, but well-linked, sectors. From the main base, a fast quad takes you to the peak of the original **Winter Park** mountain. From there, you can descend in all directions. Runs lead back towards the main base and over to the **Vasquez Ridge** area on the far right, served by the Pioneer fast quad.

From Winter Park mountain you descend to the base of **Mary Jane** mountain, where four chairs up the front face serve tough runs; other chairs serve easier terrain on the flanks. From the top you can head up to **Parsenn Bowl** via the slow double Timberline chair, which has intermediate terrain above and in the trees. This chair is exposed at the top, and can be closed for long periods in bad weather. From here, conditions permitting, you can now get a tow by snowmobile (the 'Ridge Ride') for $5 (or hike for up to half an hour) to access the advanced and extreme slopes of **Vasquez Cirque**. A long ski-out takes you to the bottom of Vasquez Ridge and the Pioneer lift.

SNOW RELIABILITY
Among Colorado's best
'Copious amounts of beautiful, dry powder,' enthuses a reporter. Winter Park's position, close to the watershed of the Continental Divide, gives it an average yearly snowfall of over 350 inches – the highest of any major Colorado resort. As a back-up,

snowmaking covers a high proportion of the runs on Winter Park mountain.

FOR EXPERTS
Some hair-raising challenges
Mary Jane has some of the steepest mogul fields, chutes and hair-raising challenges in the US ('mogul city USA', in the words of one reporter). The fearsome runs of Mary Jane's back side are accessed by a control gate off a long black run called Derailer. Hole in the Wall, Awe Chute, Baldy's Chute and Jeff's Chute are all steep, narrow and bordered by rocks. More manageable are the wider mogul fields such as Derailer, Long Haul and Brakeman. There are some good challenges on Winter Park Mountain. Parsenn Bowl offers superb blue/black gladed runs (though you have to take two slow chairs to ski them) and tougher tree skiing on the back side.

When it's open, Vasquez Cirque has excellent ungroomed expert terrain with extensive views. You don't get much vertical before you hit the forest, though. The Improvement Center does a three-hour Cirque Adventure Tour.

FOR INTERMEDIATES
Choose your challenge
From pretty much wherever you are on Winter Park mountain and Vasquez Ridge you can choose a run to suit your ability. Most are well groomed every night, giving you perfect early morning cruising on the famous Colorado 'corduroy' pistes.

For bumps try Mary Jane's front side, where 'the blue/blacks are particularly enjoyable'. Parsenn Bowl has grand views and some gentle cruising pistes as well as more challenging ungroomed terrain. It's an intermediate paradise and an ideal place to try your hand off-piste.

Winter Park

541

SCHOOLS/GUIDES

2002/03 prices in dollars

Intermediate and advanced classes
6 days
2½hr: from 9.30 or 12.45
6 2½hr days 240

Beginner classes
6 days
2½hr from 9.30 or 12.45
6 2½hr days 162

Children's classes
Ages: 3 to 13
6 full days including pass and lunch 540

Private lessons
1½hr, 3hr or 6hr
115 for 1½hr, for 1 or 2 people

National Sports Center for the Disabled
Special programme for disabled skiers and snowboarders

Private lessons
3hr or 6hr, with pass and special equipment
40 for 3hr; 80 for 6hr

CHILDCARE

The ski school runs special classes for children aged 3 to 13 and provides lunch. The Children's Center has a popular non-skiing programme for children aged 2 months to 5 years. You can rent out bleepers to keep in touch. Book early to ensure a place. The Children's Center is open 8am to 4pm. Lessons are 10am to 3pm.

WINTER PARK RESORT

Winter Park's new Zephyr Mountain Lodge condos are pretty convenient for the slopes →

boarding *This season's improvements should make things even better for Winter Park riders. The Cheshire Cat terrain park has been replaced by the impressive-sounding TBD jib park on upper Winter Park mountain. The half-pipe, now moved to just above Snoasis mid-mountain restaurant and expanded to 150m/500ft, is excellent for both experts and novices. There is some great advanced and extreme boarding terrain. Winter Park is also an ideal beginner and intermediate boarder area, with excellent terrain for first steps on a board, and a good school. The bars get crowded and lively at weekends – and boarders tend to hang out at Slade's Underground downtown.*

FOR BEGINNERS
The best we've seen
Discovery Park is a 25-acre dedicated area for beginners, reached by a high-speed quad and served by two more chairs. As well as a nursery area and longer green runs, it has an adventure trail through trees and a special terrain park. Once out of the Park, there are easy runs back to base.

FOR CROSS-COUNTRY
Lots of it
There are several different areas, all with generally excellent snow, totalling over 200km/125 miles of groomed trails, as well as backcountry tours.

QUEUES
Rarely a problem
During the week the mountain is generally quiet, though there may be a crowd waiting for the opening of the Zephyr Express from the main base and there can be queues on the slow double Timberline chair. At weekends the Denver crowds arrive – even then the network of more than 20 lifts (including eight fast quads) makes light work of the crowds.

MOUNTAIN RESTAURANTS
Some good facilities
The highlight is the Lodge at Sunspot, at the top of Winter Park mountain –

'The nicest I've found in the States,' says one reader. This wood and glass building has a welcoming bar with a roaring log fire, a table-service restaurant and very good self-service food. Avoid 11.30 to 1.30 if you want a table. Lunch Rock Cafe at the top of Mary Jane does quick snacks and has a deli counter, and there is a self-service at Snoasis, by the beginner area. Otherwise, it's down to the bases. The Club Car at the base of Mary Jane offers 'a good atmosphere and more varied menu' than the American fast-food norm.

SCHOOLS AND GUIDES
A good reputation
Recent visitors confirm that the school is well run and effective. As well as standard classes there are ideas such as Family Private, for different abilities together; themed lessons such as Mogul Mania; and Quick Tips, a 'quick fix' based on video analysis (only $5).

FACILITIES FOR CHILDREN
Some of the best
The Children's Center at Winter Park base area houses day-care facilities and is the meeting point for children's classes, which have their own areas, including 'magic carpet' lifts. 'Very positive feelings, echoed by others,' says our most recent reporter.

NATIONAL SPORTS CENTER FOR THE DISABLED

If you are able-bodied, the most striking and humbling thing you'll notice as you ride your first chair-lift is the number of people with disabilities hurtling down the mountain faster than many of us could ever hope to. There are blind skiers, skiers with one leg, people with paralysis – whatever their problem, they've cracked it.

That's because Winter Park is home to the US National Sports Center for the Disabled (NSCD) – the world's leading centre for teaching skiing and snowboarding to people with disabilities. As well as full-time instructors, there are 1,000 trained volunteers who help in the programme. More than 40 disabilities are specially catered for. If you are disabled and want to learn to ski or snowboard, there's no better place to go. It's important to book ahead so that a suitable instructor is available. The NSCD can help with travel and accommodation arrangements:

NSCD, PO Box 36, Winter Park, CO 80482, USA. Tel: 726 1540.

Winter Park

543

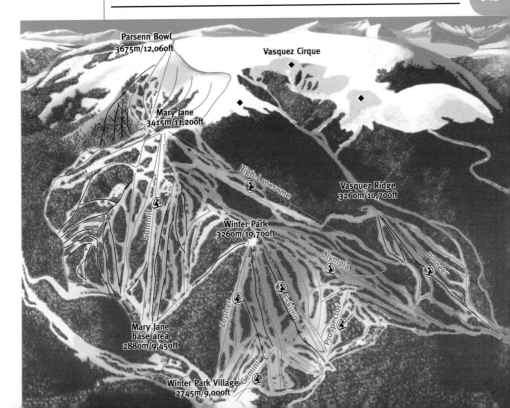

Parsenn Bowl
3675m/12,06oft

Vasquez Cirque

Mary Jane
3415m/11,200ft

High Lonesome

Vasquez Ridge
3260m/10,700ft

Winter Park
3260m/10,700ft

Olympia

Pioneer

Summit

Zephyr

Eskimo

Prospector

Gemini

Mary Jane
base area
288om/9,45oft

Winter Park Village
2745m/9,oooft

Staying there

GETTING THERE

Air Denver, transfer 1½hr.

Rail Leaves Denver Sat and Sun at 7.15am and returns at 4.15pm. Journey time 2hr.

ACTIVITIES

Indoor Cinema, swimming pool, roller skating, amusement arcade, health club, comedy club, aerobics, racquetball **Outdoor** Dog-sledding, sight-seeing flights, snow-shoe, sleigh rides, 'tubing', ice skating, snowmobiling, snowbiking, snowcat tours, ice fishing, hot springs

HOW TO GO
Fair choice

Several UK operators offer Winter Park. **Chalets** Several operators offer them. **Hotels** There are a couple of outstanding hotel/condo complexes. ((((4) **Iron Horse Resort** Slope-side, comfortable, condo-style. ((((4) **Vintage** Near resort entrance; good facilities but some poor past reports of it. (((3) **Winter Park Mountain Lodge** Across the valley from the lifts; micro-brewery above the bar; lacking character but 'friendly, with large rooms, nice pool, good food'. **Self-catering** There are a lot of comfortable condos, including the new slope-side Zephyr Mountain Lodge.

EATING OUT
A fair choice

The range of options is gradually improving, but still isn't a match for that in more established 'destination' resorts. Reporters are keen on the long-established Deno's – seafood, steaks etc. Try the Crooked Creek Saloon at Fraser for atmosphere and typical American food. Smokin' Moe's (for sports TV and grills), New Hong Kong (for 'tasty' Chinese) and the Divide Grill (for pasta, seafood and grills) are all in the Cooper Creek

Square area. For Tex-Mex readers recommend the 'pleasant and lively' Shed or Carlos and Maria's, for pizza/pasta the 'dark but rustic' Hernandos, with open fires. Gasthaus Eichler does German food, at slightly higher prices. One reader reckons Wildcreek now best in town. The Lodge at Sunspot, up the mountain, is open some nights, with a 'fantastic' five-course fine-dining option on Saturday. They put gondola eggs on the chair-lift to get you up there in comfort.

APRES-SKI
If you know where to go ...

Look out for the Black Diamond Nightlife Tour Map, which also gets you two-for-one drink deals. At close of play, there's action at the Kickapoo Tavern and Derailer Bar at the main lift base and the Club Car at the base of Mary Jane. Later on, try The Slope (in Old Town) for live music and dancing or Adolph's, just across the road. The Shed can be lively. The Crooked Creek is popular with locals. Randi's Irish Saloon is 'a pleasant and lively bar'.

OFF THE SLOPES
Mainly the great outdoors

Most diversions involve getting about on snow in different ways. If you like shopping, you'll rapidly exhaust the local possibilities and want to visit Silverthorne's factory outlet stores (90 minutes away on Interstate 70).

Phone numbers
From distant parts of the US, add the prefix 1 970.
From abroad, add the prefix +1 970.

Central reservations
Call 726 5587.
Toll-free number (from within the US) 1 800 979 0332.

TOURIST OFFICE
Postcode CO 80482
t 726 5514
f 726 1572
wpinfo@mail.skiwinter park.com
www.winterparkresort.com

DON'T PASS ON BERTHOUD PASS

The drive to Winter Park from Denver – unusually for an American resort – involves a winding climb. It takes you to the summit of Berthoud Pass (3450m), on the Continental Divide, where the average snowfall is somewhere between 400 and 500 inches a year. This puts Berthoud in the Jackson Hole/Alta league. Last time we visited, the two chair-lifts at the pass were in operation, supplemented by a beaten-up bus to bring you back up to the pass from much lower points on highway 40. Sadly, they're now out of action.

In a period of intense price competition between Colorado resorts, the economics of Berthoud didn't work. This is no surprise – when we skied it, we reckoned there were only a few dozen people on the hill, each paying about $30 for the day.

But a snowcat/touring operation has started up, so the excellent terrain here is still accessible, and even less crowded. Like the lifts, the snowcat is supplemented by a bus. There are runs to suit every ability, but in practice this is a mountain for good skiers and riders – the slopes down to the road below the pass are steep, and some are very steep.

A day's snowcat skiing including meals and demo powder skis costs $185 – or a group of 12 can book the whole cat for $1,700, or $142 a person. A full-day guided hiking tour costs $100 per person, with a minimum of two.

For more information go to www.berthoudpass.com.

Utah

Salt Lake City and the resorts just to the east of it got a bit of a boost to their international profile last season, hosting the 2002 Winter Olympics in February. Now it's back to business as usual, relying on one major ingredient to bring in the customers: The Greatest Snow on Earth.

DEER VALLEY RESORT

Utah's Deer Valley is generally recognised as the leader in skier pampering – though this visitor, strangely, is having to unload his own skis ↘

Until recently Utah's extravagant climatic claim featured on every local car number plate. The state now seems to be targeting broader markets with its number plates, but the claim stands. It's open to debate: the Colorado resorts say that their famous powder is drier, and have figures to prove it. What they can't dispute is that some Utah resorts do get huge dumps – up to twice the amount, over the season, that falls on some big-name Colorado resorts. In any case, by Alpine standards the snow here is wonderful stuff. If you like the steep and deep, you should at some point make the pilgrimage to Utah.

There are differences in snowfall, though. The biggest dumps have traditionally been reserved for Snowbird and Alta (an average of 500 inches a year), close together in Little Cottonwood Canyon. The snow record of these small resorts has made them the powder capitals of the world. And

as of last season their slopes are linked, with a shared lift pass for the first time.

Park City, the main 'destination' resort of the area, and upmarket Deer Valley next door hosted the lion's share of the Olympic events. These resorts and The Canyons nearby are only a few miles, as the crow flies, from Alta and Snowbird, but they get 'only' 300 to 350 inches (still more than most Colorado resorts). But it was unknown Snowbasin (400 inches) that got the prestige downhill and super-G Olympic events. Separate chapters follow on these six resorts.

But there are other Utah resorts that are well worth visiting too. If you enjoy seeing different resorts you can construct a compelling holiday by staying in Park City (by far the liveliest resort) or Salt Lake City (with a big city rather than a ski resort ambience) and driving to a different resort each day. The roads are generally good.

545

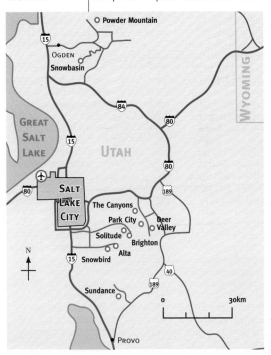

In recent years, the snow record of Alta and Snowbird has been matched by that of **Brighton** (2670m/8,760ft, vertical 530m/1,750ft, seven lifts, 64 runs, 850 acres), at the head of next-door Big Cottonwood Canyon. What's more the snow here gets tracked out less quickly because the resort attracts far fewer visitors. There are a lot of trails packed into quite a small area. Two of the three major lifts – including the area's one fast quad – serve mostly easy-intermediate slopes, but the Great Western slow quad goes over a more testing slope that represents the resort's full vertical of 530m, and the separate Mount Millicent area has some good steep slopes, both in and out of bounds. There are several accommodation options, including a slope-side lodge, cabins and chalets.

Just down the canyon from Brighton, **Solitude** (2435m/7,990ft, vertical 625m/2,050ft, seven lifts, 63 runs, 1,600 acres) gets nearly as much snow – an average of 450 inches) and covers a much bigger area, even without counting the excellent out-of-bounds terrain that you can get to from the top lift. Basically, the slopes here get steeper as you go up the mountain – except that the area's one fast quad, Eagle, serves a slightly separate ridge that is almost entirely blue in gradient, and starts slightly down the valley from the main base. We haven't yet had a chance to explore the entirely black 400 acres of Honeycomb Canyon, reached from the top lift. There is one

↑ Typical Utah terrain at The Canyons – virtually a suburb of Park City, with the potential to become America's biggest resort

HUGHES MARTIN / THE CANYONS

hotel – the 46-room Inn at Solitude (536 5700) – a few small condo developments and some houses.

The other Utah resort that gets a bit of international attention – not least because it's owned by Robert Redford – is **Sundance** (1860m/6,100ft, 655m/2,150ft vertical, four lifts, 41 runs, 450 acres). It gets 'only' 320 inches of snow a year – but this is comfortably more than most resorts in Colorado. It's a small, narrow mountain but the vertical is respectable, the setting beneath Mt Timpanogos is spectacular and there is terrain to suit all abilities. The lower mountain is easy-intermediate, served by a quad chair, the upper part steeper: one triple chair serves purely black slopes, the other blue and black trails. Bearclaw's Cabin, at the top of it, is a small, basic restaurant with spectacular views. There are 24km/15 miles of cross-country trails, of varying difficulty, in a separate area just beyond the downhill slopes. There are beautifully furnished 'cottages' to rent, and grander chalets. A reporter commends the 'emphasis on renewable resources' and craft workshops.

You can ski from Park City to Snowbird via Solitude, Brighton and Snowbird on the Utah Interconnect guided tour – see Park City chapter.

Phone numbers
From distant parts of the US, add the prefix 1 801.
From abroad, add the prefix +1 801.

TOURIST OFFICES

Brighton
www.skibrighton.com
Solitude
www.skisolitude.com
Sundance
www.sundanceresort.com

Cult powder resort, now sharing one of America's biggest areas

WHAT IT COSTS

HOW IT RATES

The slopes

Snow	*****
Extent	***
Experts	*****
Intermediates	***
Beginners	***
Convenience	****
Queues	***
Restaurants	**

The rest

Scenery	****
Resort charm	**
Off-slope	*

What's new

For 2001/02, Alta emerged from its time-warp and installed its first fast quad in place of the slow triple Sugarloaf chair.

From the top of this lift you can now ski down into Snowbird's Mineral Basin to access the whole of Snowbird's terrain as well as Alta's on a joint area lift pass. A new quad the other side brings you back. The terrain available has been more than doubled to 4,700 acres, making it the biggest lift-linked area in Utah and one of the biggest in the US. The resorts are keeping separate ownership and operation, and Alta still refuses to allow snowboarding.

The Point Supreme lift has inherited the old Sugarloaf chairs to become a triple.

ALTA / SUNSPOT

Powder is what Alta is all about ➔

➕ Phenomenal snow and steep terrain means cult status among experts

➕ New link to Snowbird making one of the largest ski areas in the US

➕ Very cheap local lift pass

➕ Ski-almost-to-the-door convenience

➕ Easy to get to other Utah resorts (so long as access road open)

➖ 'Resort' is a scattering of lodges – not much après-ski atmosphere and few off-slope diversions

➖ No snowboarding allowed

➖ Old-fashioned lift network

➖ Limited groomed runs for intermediates, though the new link with Snowbird doubles the terrain

Alta is famous for remarkable amounts of powder snow arriving with great regularity, for one of the cheapest lift passes around and for a stubborn refusal to develop or modernise, or do any deals with slick Snowbird a few yards down the canyon. But things seem to be changing: the Sunnyside fast triple chair, installed four years ago specially for beginners, has now been followed by the resort's first fast quad specially to connect Alta to Snowbird. How long, we wonder, before Alta really joins the modern world, and admits snowboarders to its hallowed slopes?

THE RESORT

Alta sits at the craggy head of Little Cottonwood Canyon, 2km/1 mile beyond Snowbird and less than an hour's drive from downtown Salt Lake City. The peaceful location was once the scene of a bustling and bawdy mining town. The 'new' Alta is a strung-out handful of lodges and parking areas, and nothing more; life revolves around the two separate lift base areas – Albion and Wildcat – linked by a bi-directional rope tow along the flat valley floor.

All in all, there are about a dozen places to stay – simple hotels and apartments.

THE MOUNTAINS

Alta's slopes are still served by mainly slow double and triple chairs. Check out the Snowbird chapter for information about the slopes there.

Slopes The dominant feature of Alta's terrain is the steep end of a ridge that separates the area's two basins. To the left, above Albion Base, the slopes stretch away over easy green terrain towards the black runs of Point Supreme and Devil's Castle; to the right is a more concentrated bowl with blue runs down the middle and blacks either side. These two sectors are linked at altitude, and by a flat rope tow along the valley floor.

Snow reliability The quantity and quality of snow that falls here, and the

northerly orientation of the slopes, put Alta among the world's best.

Experts Even without a link with Snowbird, Alta had cult status among local experts, who flocked to the high ridges after a fresh snowfall. There are dozens of steep slopes and chutes throughout the area. The new link makes the shared area the world's best for powderhounds.

547

MOUNTAIN FACTS

For Alta and Snowbird combined area

Altitude 2410m-3355m
7,760ft-11,000ft
Lifts 26
Pistes 4700 acres
Green 25%
Blue 37%
Black 38%
Snowmaking
150 acres
Recco detectors used

For Alta only

Altitude 2600m-3245m
8,530ft-10,646ft
Lifts 13
Pistes 2200 acres
Green 25%
Blue 40%
Black 35%
Snowmaking 50 acres
Recco detectors used

Phone numbers
From distant parts of the US, add the prefix 1 801.
From abroad, add the prefix +1 801.

TOURIST OFFICE

Postcode UT 84092
t 359 1078
f 799 2340
info@alta.com
www.alta.com

Intermediates Adventurous intermediates who are happy to try ungroomed slopes and learn to love powder should like Alta, too. There are good blue bowls in both Alta and Snowbird and not-so-tough blacks to progress too. But if it is miles of perfectly groomed piste you are after there are plenty of better resorts.
Beginners Timid intermediates and beginners will be happy on the Albion side, where the lower runs are broad, gentle and well groomed.
Snowboarding Boarding is banned.
Cross-country There's little provision for cross-country skiing; but the surrounding backcountry offers adventures for those with guidance.
Queues Bottlenecks are not unknown at Alta – the snow record, easy access from Salt Lake City and the slow chair-lifts see to that – especially in spring and on sunny weekends. The slopes remain uncrowded though.
Mountain restaurants There's a mountain restaurant in each sector of the slopes – Alf's on the Albion side is recommended and Collins Grill on the Wildcat side has table-service – and several places in the valley are open for lunch.
Schools and guides The famous Alf Engen ski school naturally specialises in powder lessons – though all the

regular classes and clinics are also available. The ski school organises children's lessons.
Facilities for children Day care for those over 3 months old is available at the Children's Center at Albion Base.

STAYING THERE

How to go None of the hotels is luxurious in US terms. Most get booked up well in advance by repeat visitors. Unusually for America, most lodges (as they're called) operate half-board deals with dinner included. One reporter recommends staying more cheaply down in Sandy or South Jordan, within 24km/15 miles of Alta.
Hotels The Alta Lodge (742 3500) is one of Alta's oldest, and feels rather like an over-crowded chalet-hotel in the Alps. Rustler Lodge (742 2200) is more luxurious, with a big outdoor pool, but impersonal. The comfortable, modern Goldminer's Daughter (742 2300) and the basic Peruvian Lodge (742 3000) are cheaper.
Eating out Eating in is the routine.
Après-ski This rarely goes beyond a few drinks and possibly a sports film in the lodges. The Goldminer's Daughter has the main après-ski bar.
Off the slopes There are few options other than a sightseeing trip to Salt Lake City.

UTAH

548

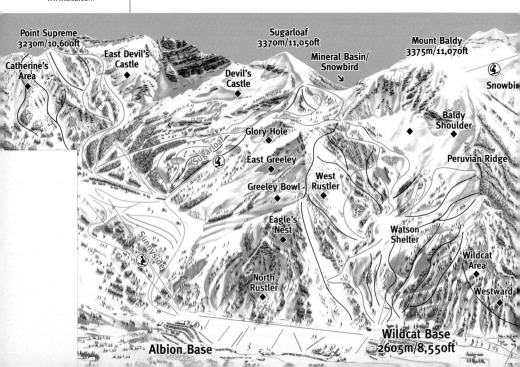

The Canyons
2075m/6,800ft

Potentially the biggest mountain in the US, and already impressive

WHAT IT COSTS

(((((6)

HOW IT RATES

The slopes

Snow	****
Extent	***
Experts	***
Intermediates	***
Beginners	***
Convenience	****
Queues	****
Restaurants	***

The rest

Scenery	***
Resort charm	**
Off-slope	**

MOUNTAIN FACTS

Altitude	2075m-3045m
	6,800ft-9,990ft
Lifts	16
Pistes	3,500 acres
Green	14%
Blue	44%
Black	42%
Snowmaking	
	160 acres
Recco detectors used	

THE CANYONS

It's a broad area – sixth biggest in the US, with the potential to get much bigger ↓

➕ Extensive area of slopes for all abilities – potentially the biggest area in the US

➕ Modern lift system with few queues

➕ Convenient new purpose-built resort village taking shape at the base

➕ Park City is nearby – an entertaining alternative base with its own slopes

➕ Easy access to other Utah resort

➕ Excellent snow in general, but ...

➖ Snow on the many south-facing slopes often not up to the usual Utah standards

➖ Because the area is a series of canyons (valleys) many runs are short and the area is a bit disjointed

➖ Resort village offers limited après-ski and dining possibilities, and few off-slope diversions

The resort formerly known as Park West and later as Wolf Mountain is now approaching its sixth season as The Canyons, the new kid on the Park City block. The American Skiing Company's ambitious plans to make the slopes the most extensive in the US are gradually being implemented: the area has already more than doubled in size and briefly ranked in the American top five biggest areas until the linking of Alta and Snowbird pushed it down to joint sixth – amazing, considering its low international profile. The lift system is virtually new; the snow, if not out of the top Utah drawer, is by other standards great; a new slope-side resort village is up and running. What are you waiting for?

THE RESORT
When we visited in March 1999 there wasn't a resort – just a muddy car park and building site. A year later the car-free village was really taking shape and there is now a basic selection of shops, bars and restaurants at the main station. Although there is some convenient accommodation at the resort village, staying in Park City will suit many people better at present – regular shuttle-buses run to the resort.

THE MOUNTAINS
The Canyons gets its name from the valleys between the various mountains (now eight of them) that make up the ski area.

Slopes Red Pine Lodge, at the heart of the slopes, is reached by an eight-person gondola from the village base. From here you can move in either direction across a series of ridges – and the valleys between them. These ridges range from Dreamscape to the south (closest to Park City) to Murdock Peak to the north. Runs come off both sides of each ridge, meaning that they generally face north or south (see Snow reliability section). Most runs finish in the valley floors with some long, relatively flat run-outs. Five of the major lifts are fast quads, all put in – along with the gondola – since 1997. Complimentary mountain tours are offered twice daily.

549

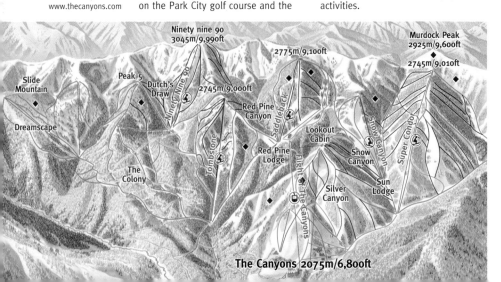

What's new

For 2002/03 there will be increased capacity on the gondola out of the village.

There will also be more snowmaking, glade thinning and trail enhancement.

For 2001/02 an additional chair-lift was installed, opening up new runs close to the existing Dreamscape area.

A new terrain-park was built near the Red Hawk quad lift at the base area.

The kids' nursery area at Red Pine Lodge has two new lifts, one a magic carpet.

Central reservations phone number
Call 1 800 472 6309 (toll-free from within the US).

Phone numbers
From distant parts of the US, add the prefix 1 435.
From abroad, add the prefix +1 435.

TOURIST OFFICE

Postcode UT 84098
t 649 5400
f 649 7374
info@thecanyons.com
www.thecanyons.com

Snow reliability Snow reliability is not the best in Utah. The Canyons gets as much snow on average as next-door Park City (350in) and more than Deer Valley. But although the north-facing slopes are normally in good condition, the south-facing ones suffer in sunny late-season conditions.

Experts There is steep terrain all over the mountain. We particularly liked the north-facing runs off Ninety-Nine-90, with steep double-black-diamond runs plunging down through the trees to a pretty but almost flat run-out trail. Go south at the top of the lift and (when the gate is open) you can legally enter the backcountry – with the right kit and guidance, of course. There is also lots of double-diamond terrain on Murdock Peak.

Intermediates There are groomed blue runs for intermediates on all the main sectors except Ninety-Nine-90. Some are quite short, but you can switch from valley to valley for added interest. A reporter recommends the runs off the Super Condor fast chair.

Beginners There's a new area just for beginners behind Red Pine Lodge. But the run you progress to gets very crowded with through-traffic.

Snowboarding It's a great area to snowboard in, with lots of natural hits, five natural half-pipes and a great terrain-park and half-pipe. Canis Lupis (aka James Bond trail) is a mile-long, tight, winding natural gully with high banked walls and numerous obstacles – like riding a bob-sleigh course. For beginners and intermediates there's easy cruising served by chair-lifts.

Cross-country There are prepared trails on the Park City golf course and the Homestead Resort course. There is also lots of scope for backcountry trips.

Queues We've heard of no problems.

Mountain restaurants The central Red Pine Lodge, a large, attractive log-and-glass building with a busy self-service cafeteria and a table-service restaurant, is recommended. The Lookout Cabin has wonderful views, and we've had excellent table-service food there. Sun Lodge, with sun decks, is another option, though a recent reporter found it 'noisy'.

Schools and guides The ski school uses the American Skiing Company's Perfect Turn formula, which focuses on an individual's strengths and builds on them (rather than correcting faults).

Facilities for children There's day care for children from 18 months.

STAYING THERE

How to go Accommodation at the resort village is still fairly limited, but you do have the choice of hotel rooms or self-catering.

Hotels The luxurious Grand Summit is right at the base of the gondola.

Self-catering The new Sundial Lodge condos are part of the resort village.

Eating out The Cabin restaurant, in the Grand Summit hotel, serves eclectic American cuisine. And there are many more options in Park City.

Après-ski The Grand Summit contains several bars, and there are many more in Park City.

Off the slopes There's a fair bit going on in Park City – shops, galleries etc – and Salt Lake City has some good concerts, shopping and sights. Balloon rides and snowmobiling are popular activities.

Deer Valley

2195m/7,200ft

The ultimate upmarket ski resort

551

WHAT IT COSTS

$(((((6)$

HOW IT RATES

The slopes

Snow	****
Extent	**
Experts	***
Intermediates	****
Beginners	****
Convenience	****
Queues	****
Restaurants	****

The rest

Scenery	***
Resort charm	***
Off-slope	**

➕ Highly convenient, upmarket resort with superb skier services

➕ Immaculate piste grooming, good snow record and lots of snow-guns

➕ Good tree skiing

➕ No queues

➕ Slopes of Park City and The Canyons very close, and access to Salt Lake City and other Utah resorts is easy

➖ No snowboarding allowed

➖ Relatively expensive

➖ Deer Valley itself is quiet at night – though Park City is right next door

Deer Valley prides itself on pampering its guests, with free valet ski storage, gourmet dining, immaculately groomed slopes, limited numbers of skiers on the mountain, no snowboarding. But there's more to it than that – it has some excellent slopes, with interesting terrain for all abilities. All of which has recently won the resort top slot in a US ski magazine's North American rankings. It hosted the freestyle and slalom competitions in the 2002 Olympics.

What's new

For 2001/02, a much-needed new day lodge and restaurant opened at Empire Canyon. The Quincy triple chair was replaced by a fast quad. And a new snowmaking reservoir was built and new guns added.

2002/03 will see the Ruby chair-lift replaced by a fast quad. And the resort is to host the 2003 Freestyle World Ski Championships.

MOUNTAIN FACTS

Altitude 2000m-2920m
6,570ft-9,570ft

Lifts	19
Pistes	1,750 acres
Green	15%
Blue	50%
Black	35%
Snowmaking	
	500 acres
Recco detectors used	

DEER VALLEY RESORT

Although Deer Valley prides itself on its grooming, it has good bump, bowl and tree skiing too ➔

THE RESORT
Just a mile from the end of Park City's Main Street, Deer Valley is unashamedly upmarket and famed for the care and attention lavished on both slopes and guests. Valets will unload your equipment before you park your car – it's very obviously aimed at people who are used to being pampered and can pay for it.

The lodgings – luxurious private chalets and swanky hotels – are scattered around the fringes of the slopes, with more concentrated clusters on the valley floor near the main lift base and at Silver Lake Lodge (mid-mountain but accessible by road). There is no village as such. For any real animation you need to head for Park City, and many visitors prefer to stay there. There are free buses between the two resorts.

THE MOUNTAINS
The slopes are varied and interesting. Deer Valley's reputation for immaculate grooming is justified, but there is also a lot of exciting tree skiing (great when snow is falling) – and some steep mogul runs too.

Slopes Two fast quads take you up to Bald Eagle Mountain, just beyond which is the mid-mountain focus of Silver Lake Lodge. You can ski from here to the isolated Little Baldy Peak, served by a gondola and a quad chair-lift, with mainly easy blue and green

runs to serve property being developed there. But the main skiing is on three linked mountains above Silver Lake Lodge. From left to right these are Bald Mountain, Flagstaff Mountain and Empire Canyon. Empire is serviced by a fast quad – the top of which is just a few metres from the runs of the Park City ski area and could easily be linked. Empire also has a family area.

Phone numbers
From distant parts of the US, add the prefix 1 435.
From abroad, add the prefix +1 435.

Central reservations phone number
Call 645 6528.

TOURIST OFFICE
Postcode UT 84060
t 649 1000
f 645 6939
patti@deervalley.com
www.deervalley.com

UTAH

Snow reliability As you'd expect in Utah, snow reliability is excellent, and there's plenty of snowmaking too.

Experts Despite its image of pampered luxury there is excellent expert terrain on all three main mountains, including fabulous glade skiing as well as bumps, defined chutes and open bowl slopes. And because the place doesn't attract many hotshots the snow doesn't get skied out quickly.

Intermediates There are lots of immaculately groomed blue runs all over the mountains.

Beginners There are nursery slopes at Silver Lake Lodge as well as the base, and gentle green runs to progress to on all the mountains.

Snowboarding Boarding is banned.

Cross-country There are prepared trails on the Park City golf course and the Homestead Resort course, just out of town. There is also lots of scope for backcountry trips.

Queues Waiting in lift lines is not something that Deer Valley wants its guests to experience, so it limits the number of lift tickets sold.

Mountain restaurants There are attractive wood-and-glass self-service places run by the resort at both Silver Lake Lodge and the base lodge, with free valet ski storage. The food is fine (though expensive). The grill restaurant at the new Empire Canyon Lodge should relieve overcrowding at Silver

Lake. For a bit of a treat, we can recommend the table-service restaurants at the Stein Eriksen Lodge or the Goldener Hirsch. Stein's buffet is also highly recommended.

Schools and guides The ski school is doubtless excellent.

Facilities for children Deer Valley's Children's Center gives parents complimentary pagers.

STAYING THERE

How to go A car is useful for visiting the other nearby Utah resorts, though Deer Valley, Park City and The Canyons are all linked by regular shuttle-buses.

Hotels Stein Eriksen Lodge and the Goldener Hirsch at Silver Lake Village are two of the plushest hotels in any ski resort.

Self-catering There are many luxury apartments and houses to rent.

Après-ski The Lounge of the Snow Park Lodge at the base area is the main après-ski venue, with live music. There are lively bars and restaurants around Main Street, in Park City.

Eating out Of the gourmet restaurants, the Mariposa is the best. The Seafood Buffet and McHenry's grill are also recommended. Park City has a number of good restaurants.

Off the slopes Park City has lots of shops, galleries etc. Salt Lake City has concerts, sights and shopping. Balloon rides and snowmobiling are popular.

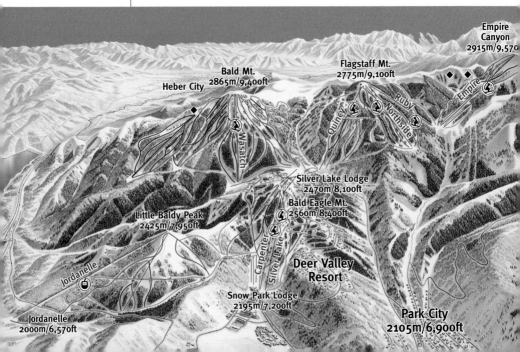

Park City
2105m/6,900ft

An entertaining base for excursions into Utah's famously deep powder

WHAT IT COSTS

HOW IT RATES

The slopes

Snow	****
Extent	***
Experts	****
Intermediates	****
Beginners	****
Convenience	***
Queues	****
Restaurants	**

The rest

Scenery	***
Resort charm	***
Off-slope	***

What's new

For 2001/02 a bridge was built linking the slopes directly to the base of the Town Lift, next to Main Street.

➕ Increasingly touristy Wild West-style main street, convenient for slopes

➕ Lots of bars and restaurants make nonsense of Utah's Mormon image

➕ Well maintained slopes, good snow record, and lots of snowmaking

➕ Good lift system including four fast six-packs

➕ Good base for visiting other major Utah resorts – Deer Valley and The Canyons are effectively suburbs and other resorts less than an hour away

➖ Rest of town doesn't have same charm as main street – lots of recent building has created an enormous sprawl (and building continues)

➖ The blue and black runs tend to be rather short – most lifts give a vertical of around 400m/1,300ft

➖ Although the snowfall record is impressive by normal standards, it comes nowhere near that of Alta and Snowbird, a few miles away

➖ Lack of spectacular scenery

Park City has clear attractions, particularly if you ignore its sprawling suburbs and stay near the centre to make the most of the lively bars and restaurants in its beautifully restored and developed main street. But the place really comes into its own as a base for touring other resorts as well.

Deer Valley is separated from Park City's slopes by a fence between the tops of two lifts, and by separate ownership with quite different objectives. All that is required to link them is to remove the fence – a small step that is unlikely to be taken, given Deer Valley's exclusive nature. To European eyes, all very strange.

The Canyons is only a little further away, on the outskirts of town, and reached by free buses. And then there are the famously powdery resorts of Snowbird and Alta, less than an hour away by car or bus. Even the Olympic downhill slopes of Snowbasin are within easy reach if you have a car.

Park City
2105m/6,900ft

The resort

MOUNTAIN FACTS

Altitude	2100m-3050m
	6,900ft-10,000ft
Lifts	14
Pistes	3,300 acres
Green	18%
Blue	44%
Black	38%
Snowmaking	
	475 acres
Recco detectors used	

Park City is in Utah's Wasatch Mountains, about 45 minutes by road from Salt Lake City. It was born with the discovery of silver in 1872. By the turn of the century it boasted a population of 10,000, a red-light district, a Chinese quarter and 27 saloons. Careful restoration has left the town with a splendid historic centre-piece in Main Street.

The old wooden sidewalks and clapboard buildings are now filled with a colourful selection of art galleries, shops, boutiques, bars and restaurants – though it is getting rather touristy, with some tacky shops selling T-shirts and souvenirs. New buildings have been tastefully designed to blend in smoothly. But away from the centre

the resort lacks charm, sprawls over a wide area and is still expanding.

The Town Lift is a triple chair up to the slopes from Lower Main Street, but the main lift base is Resort Center, on the fringes, with modern buildings and its own bars, restaurants and lodgings.

Deer Valley and The Canyons are almost suburbs of Park City, but all three retain quite separate identities. They are linked by free shuttle-buses, which also go around town and run until late. A trolley-bus runs along Main Street. A car is useful for visiting other ski areas on the good roads.

If you're not hiring a car, pick a location that's handy for Main Street and the Town chair or the free bus.

The mountain

Mostly the area consists of blue and black trails cut through the trees on the flanks of rounded mountain ridges, with easier runs running along the ridges and the gullies between. The bite in the system is in the lightly wooded bowls and ridges at the top of the resort's slopes.

THE SLOPES
Bowls above the woods

A fast six-seat chair-lift whisks you up from Resort Center, and another beyond that up to Summit House, the main mountain restaurant.

Most of the easy and intermediate runs lie between the Summit House and the base area, and spread along the sides of a series of interconnecting ridges. Virtually all the steep terrain is above Summit House in a series of ungroomed bowls, and accessed by the new McConkey's six-pack and the old Jupiter double chair.

There are a few old wooden mine buildings scattered around the slopes, which add extra atmosphere; there are free daily tours. Twice a week tours of the black-diamond slopes are offered.

A long floodlit run is available until 9pm, together with a floodlit half-pipe.

SNOW RELIABILITY
Not quite the Greatest on Earth

Utah is famous for the quality and quantity of its snow. Park City's record doesn't match those of Alta and Snowbird, but an annual average of 350 inches is still impressive, and ahead of most Colorado figures. And there's snowmaking on about 15% of the terrain.

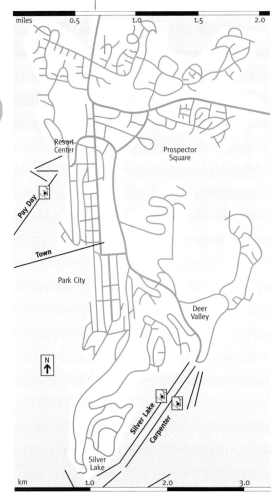

boarding *The Olympic boarding events have banished from memory the time when boarding was banned here, and provided a legacy in the form of the 105m/350ft long Pay Day Super Pipe. There are two terrain-parks and half-pipes – one floodlit at night. The resort has wonderful free-ride terrain, its higher lifts giving access to some great powder bowls. Beginners have their own excellent area, good easy cruising and a lift system which is entirely chair-lifts. Intermediates have to put up with fairly short cruising runs.*

LIFT PASSES

2001/02 prices in dollars

Park City
Covers all lifts in Park City Mountain Resort, with free ski-bus.
Main pass
1-day pass 63
6-day pass 318
Senior citizens
Over 70: free pass
Over 65: 1-day 34
Children
Under 12: 6-day pass 144
Under 6: free
Short-term passes
Half-day passes from 1pm to 4pm (adult 48). Twilight skiing pass 1pm-9pm (56). Night pass 4pm-9pm 26.
Notes All multi-day passes are good for one week, allowing for days off. Reductions for groups but not for students.
Alternative passes
Multi-area passport is available through UK tour operators.

FOR EXPERTS
Lots of variety

There is a lot of excellent advanced and expert terrain at the top of the lift system. It is now all marked as double-diamond on the trail map but there are many runs that deserve only a single-diamond rating – so don't be put off. We particularly like the prettily wooded McConkey's Bowl, served by a six-pack and offering a range of open pitches and gladed terrain. The old Jupiter lift accesses the highest bowls, which include some serious terrain – with narrow couloirs, cliffs and cornices – as well as easier wide-open slopes. The Jupiter bowl runs are under the chair, but there is a lot more terrain accessible by traversing and hiking – turn left for West Face, Pioneer Ridge and Puma Bowl, right for Scotts Bowl and the vast expanse of Pinecone Ridge, stretching literally for miles down the side of Thaynes Canyon.

Lower down, the side of Summit House ridge, serviced by the Thaynes and Motherlode chairs, has some little-used black runs, plus a few satisfying trails in the trees. There's a zone of steep runs towards town from further round the ridge. And don't miss Blueslip Bowl near Summit House – so

called because in the past, when it was out of bounds, ski company employees caught skiing it were fired, and were given their notice on a blue slip.

Good skiers (no snowboarders, due to some long flat run-outs and hikes) should not miss the Utah Interconnect – see feature panel. For bigger budgets, Park City Powder Guides offers heli-skiing on 20,000 acres of private backcountry land.

FOR INTERMEDIATES
Many better places

There are blue runs served by all the main lifts, apart from Jupiter. The areas around the King Con high-speed quad and Silverlode high-speed six-pack have a dense network of great (but fairly short) cruising runs. There are also more difficult trails close by, for those looking for a challenge.

But the keen intermediate piste-basher who might be happy at Vail or Snowmass won't be so happy here. There are few long, fast cruising runs – most trails are around 1km to 2km/one mile, and many have long, flat run-outs. The Pioneer and McConkey's chair-lifts are off the main drag and serve some very pleasant, often quiet runs. One reporter complains of too

Park City

555

The old part of the town is right at the foot of the slopes – but the newer parts sprawl for miles out of this shot →

CHILDCARE

The ski school's Mountain School takes children aged from 3 to 6, from 8.30 or 9.30 to 4.30, mixing skiing instruction with other indoor and outdoor activities. $115 per day or $330 for three days. There are several different nurseries in the town.

GETTING THERE

Air Salt Lake City, transfer ½hr.

SCHOOLS/GUIDES

2001/02 prices in dollars

Park City
Classes 5 days
3hr: 9.30-12.30 or
1pm-4pm 325
Children's classes
Ages: 5 to 12
Full day 105 (incl lunch)
Private lessons
1hr, 2hr, half- or full-day
100 for 1hr; 495 for full day; additional cost for more than one person

---

many ungroomed mogul runs, 'leaving a choice of ultra-easy cruising or bump-running, with little in between'.

Intermediates will certainly want to visit The Canyons and Deer Valley for a day or two (see separate chapters).

FOR BEGINNERS
A good chance for fast progress
Novices get started on short lifts and a dedicated beginners' area near the base lodge. The beginners' classes graduate up the hill quite quickly, and there's a good, very gentle and wide 'easiest way down' – the three-and a half-mile Home Run – clearly marked all the way from Summit House. It's easy enough for most beginners to manage after only a few lessons. The Town chair can be ridden down.

FOR CROSS-COUNTRY
Some trails; lots of backcountry
There are prepared trails on both the Park City golf course, next to the downhill area, and the Homestead Resort course, just out of town. There is lots of scope for backcountry trips.

QUEUES
Peak period problems only
Lift queues aren't normally a problem with all the high-speed six-seat chairs in the area. But it can get pretty crowded (on some trails as well as the lifts) on busy weekends.

MOUNTAIN RESTAURANTS
Standard self-service stuff
The Mid-Mountain Lodge is a 19th-century mine building which was heaved up the mountain to its present location near the bottom of Pioneer chair. The food is standard self-service fare but most reporters prefer it to the alternatives. The Summit House is cafe-style – serving chilli, pizza, soup etc. The Snow Hut is a smaller log building and usually has an outdoor grill. The Skiosk is an on-mountain yurt (a tent) serving snacks, halfway down the Bonanza chair-lift. There's quite a choice of restaurants back at the base area including the food court at the new Legacy Lodge.

SCHOOLS AND GUIDES
Thorough, full of enthusiasm
The school offers performance workshops (Moguls and Beyond, Dealing with the Diamonds) and Power Clinics (for strong intermediates) as well as beginner and private lessons.

FACILITIES FOR CHILDREN
Well organised; ideal terrain
There are a number of licensed carers who operate either at their own premises or at visitors' lodgings. The ski school takes children from the age of three. Book in advance.

Staying there

HOW TO GO
Packaged independence
Park City is the busiest and most atmospheric of the Utah resorts, and a good base for visiting the others.
Hotels There's a wide variety, from typical chains to individual little B&Bs.
(((4 **Silver King** (649 5500) Deluxe hotel/condo complex at base of the slopes, with indoor-outdoor pool.
(((4 **Radisson Inn Park City** (649 5000) Excellent rooms and indoor-outdoor pool, but poorly placed for nightlife (out of town on main road).
(((4 **Yarrow** (649 7000) Recently renovated with big welcoming lobby, outdoor pool and hot-tub. Free shuttle.
(((4 **Washington School Inn** (649 3800) 'Absolutely excellent' historic inn in a great location near Main Street, with free wine and snacks creating a thriving après-ski social scene.
(((3 **Best Western Landmark Inn** (649 7300) Way out of town near The Canyons and factory outlet mall. Swimming pool. 'Good place to stay with car to visit other resorts.'
(((3 **Old Miners' Lodge** (645 8068) 100-year-old building next to Town lift, restored and furnished with antiques.
((2 **Chateau Apres Lodge** (649 9372) Close to the slopes: comfortable, faded, cheap.
((2 **1904 Imperial Inn** (649 1904) Quaint B&B at the top of Main Street.
Self-catering There's a big range available. The Townlift studios near Main Street and Park Avenue condos are both modern and comfortable and the latter have outdoor pool and hot-tubs. Silver Cliff Village is adjacent to the slopes and has spacious units and access to the facilities of the Silver King Hotel. Blue Church Lodge is a well-converted 19th-century Mormon church with luxury condos and rooms.

EATING OUT
Book in advance
There are over 100 restaurants but they all get busy, so book in advance. Zoom is the old Union Pacific train depot, now a trendy restaurant owned by

This is what makes resorts like this so good for experts: the ski patrol making seriously steep Puma Bowl safe by setting off avalanches ➔

SNOWPIX.COM / CHRIS GILL

ACTIVITIES

Indoor Park City Racquet Club (4 indoor tennis courts, 2 racquetball courts, heated pool, hot-tub, sauna, gym, aerobics, basketball), Silver Mountain Spa (racquetball courts, weights room, swimming pool, aerobics, spa, massage and physical therapy, whirlpool, sauna), art galleries, concerts, theatre, martial arts studio, bowling
Outdoor Snowmobiles, ballooning, sleigh rides, ski jumping, ice skating, bob-sleigh and luge track, snow tubing, sports and recreation opportunities for disabled children and adults

Phone numbers
From distant parts of the US, add the prefix 1 435.
From abroad, add the prefix +1 435.

TOURIST OFFICE

Postcode UT 84060
t 649 8111
f 647 5374
info@pcski.com
www.parkcitymountain.com

Robert Redford. The Riverhorse is in a beautiful, high-ceilinged first-floor room with live music. Chimayo has great south-west cuisine. The Juniper at the Snowed Inn has won awards. Chez Betty is small and has perhaps the best food in town – expensive though. Cheaper places include the US Prime Steakhouse ('best steak ever'), the Grub Steak Restaurant at Prospector Square, Cisero's and Grappa (Italian), Jambalaya (Cajun), Wasatch Brew Pub (good value and an interesting range of beers) and Baja Cantina (Mexican).

APRES-SKI
Better than you might think
Although there are still some arcane liquor laws in Utah, provided you're over-21 and can prove it the laws are never a serious barrier to getting a drink. At the bars and clubs that are more dedicated to drinking (ie don't feature food but do serve spirits) membership of some kind is required. This may involve handing over $5 or more – one member can introduce numerous 'guests' – or else there'll be some old guy at the bar already organised to 'sponsor' you (sign you in) for the price of a beer. But a recent reporter points out that the system can be very expensive if you visit different resorts most days and just want a quick beer before hitting the road.

As the slopes close, the Pig Pen in the new lodge is the place to head for at the Resort Center – but you can of course make directly for Main Street. The Wasatch Brew Pub makes its own ale. The Claimjumper, JB Mulligans and the scruffy Alamo are lively places and there's usually live music and dancing

at weekends. Harry O's and Cisero's nightclub are good too.

OFF THE SLOPES
Should be interesting
There's a factory outlet mall near The Canyons. Scenic balloon flights and excursions to Nevada for gambling are both popular. Snowmobiling is big. In January there's Robert Redford's Sundance Film Festival.

There are lots of shops and galleries and the museum and old jail house are worth a visit. Salt Lake City has some good concerts and shopping and a few points of interest, many connected with its Mormon heritage. The Capitol Building is open until 8pm and gives 'an interesting perspective on the State' and good views of the city.

You might like to learn to ski-jump or try the Olympic bob track at the Winter Sports Park down the road.

Park City

557

THE UTAH INTERCONNECT

Good skiers should not miss this excellent guided backcountry tour that runs four days a week from Park City to Snowbird. (Three days a week it runs from Snowbird, but only as far as Solitude.) When we did it we got fresh tracks in knee-deep powder practically all day. After a warm-up run to weed out weak skiers, you head up to the top of the Jupiter chair, go through a 'closed' gate in the area boundary and ski down a deserted, prettily wooded valley to Solitude. After taking the lifts to the top of Solitude we did a short traverse, then down more virgin powder towards Brighton. After more powder runs and lunch back in Solitude, it was up the lifts and a 30-minute hike up the Highway to Heaven to north-facing, tree-lined slopes and a great little gully down into Alta. How much of Alta and Snowbird you get to ski depends on how much time is left.

The price ($150) includes two guides – one leading, another at the rear – lunch, lift tickets for all five resorts you pass through and transport home.

Snowbasin
1950m/6,390ft

An excellent mountain, worth including in a tour of Utah's finest

HOW IT RATES

The slopes

Snow	*****
Extent	***
Experts	****
Intermediates	****
Beginners	**
Convenience	*
Queues	*****
Restaurants	**

The rest

Scenery	****
Resort charm	**
Off-slope	*

What's new

For 2001/02 the resort constructed not only a grand base lodge but also two impressive mountain restaurants.

SNOWPIX.COM / CHRIS GILL

Lightly wooded slopes in the main ↓

558

- ➕ Fair-sized ski area
- ➕ Impressive new lift system
- ➕ Excellent snow record

- ➖ No resort village as yet
- ➖ The nearest accommodation is down in nearby Ogden or Huntsville
- ➖ Bit of a trek from Park City etc

The four Olympic downhill events (men's and women's downhills, plus the downhill elements of the combined) and the two super giant slaloms which were held here in February 2002 have put Snowbasin firmly on the map. It's a great hill, and it gets great snow (usually). All it needs is a great village – and the ski world waits to see what owner Earl Holding (also owner of Sun Valley, Idaho) has got in mind. For now, it makes a great day out from Park City.

THE RESORT

There is no resort, in the European sense of a village with accommodation. But big investment in hotels and other accommodation is expected over the next few years. For now you have to stay elsewhere – Ogden is the closest big town. It's also possible to stay nearer the mountain in (or close to) the backwater town of Huntsville. But we'd recommend staying in another Utah resort and making a day trip to Snowbasin in a rental car. A reporter made the 100km/60-mile trip from Park City in less than an hour. It is 65km/40 miles from Salt Lake City.

THE MOUNTAINS

Snowbasin's slopes cover a lot of pleasantly varied terrain and are served by nine lifts including a fast quad chair and two gondolas, all three installed in 1998. And there are other attractions. Not the least is the amazing view over the ridge at the top of the Strawberry Express gondola across the Great Salt Lake and surrounding plain. Another is the excursion to cutely named Powder Mountain, a few miles away across the other side of the Huntsville basin. This has (as you might hope) a reputation for powder and has an extensive snowcat skiing operation.

Slopes A new base lodge in the plush style of those at Sun Valley was built for the 2002 Olympics. From this main base, the Middle Bowl gondola goes up to the area's central core, which has lots of different slopes and gullies presenting different challenges. The John Paul fast quad chair goes up to the right from the base and serves great black slopes, on- and off-piste, with just one blue alternative way down. Above it, a small cable-car goes up to Allen's Peak and the dramatic start of the Olympic men's downhill course. The Strawberry gondola serves good blue runs at the opposite end of the ski area.

Snow reliability At 400 inches the average snowfall is in the usual Utah class. And there's lots of snowmaking.

Experts This is a great mountain for experts. All the lifts serve worthwhile terrain – even Strawberry has some severe chutes reached by hiking from the top, but most of the steep stuff is at the other end of the area. The cable-car serves a short black slope that was

MOUNTAIN FACTS

Altitude 1785m-2850m
      5,860ft-9,350ft
Lifts   9
Pistes   3,200 acres
Green   13%
Blue   49%
Black   38%
Snowmaking
          580 acres
Recco detectors used

Phone numbers

From distant parts of
the US, add the prefix
1 435.
From abroad, add the
prefix +1 435.

Accommodation phone number

For accommodation
information call the
Ogden Chamber of
Commerce on
627 8228

TOURIST OFFICE

Postcode UT 84317
t 399 1135
f 399 1138
info@snowbasin.com
www.snowbasin.com

mogulled when we were there but was glass-smooth when it served as the start of the Olympic downhill race course. The course, designed by Bernhard Russi – who else? – drops 883m/2,897ft and is already claimed to be a modern classic. The parts of it that were open when we visited were certainly impressive. Between the race course and the area boundary is a splendid area of off-piste wooded glades and gullies, served by the fast John Paul chair. This is where most experts will want to spend their time. Less extreme challenges are to be found on the countless blacks in the middle of the mountain, served by the gondola and several slow chairs.

Intermediates It's also a good mountain for intermediates. The Strawberry gondola accesses mainly long open blue runs but also leads to a lightly wooded steeper slope at the extremity of the area. Middle Bowl is great terrain for the adventurous, with a complex network of blue and black runs on lightly wooded slopes.

Beginners A place like this can't seriously be recommended for beginners other than lucky locals, but there is a nursery slope, and there are a few green runs to progress to.

Snowboarding Although there are no specific facilities for boarders, there is some excellent free-ride terrain.

Cross-country Nordic Valley is nearby.
Queues Queues are unlikely.
Mountain restaurants There are two brand-new mountain restaurants, both self-service only but otherwise pleasant. Needles Lodge has a sun terrace with windshields.
Schools and guides The school has special women's clinics as well as the normal offerings.
Facilities for children The new services building at the main base includes a day care centre.

STAYING THERE

Hotels Ogden has various standard-issue hotels and motels. Huntsville has a small hotel, a couple of small B&Bs and Utah's oldest tavern (opened in 1879), the Shooting Star – a splendid scruffy relic of times past. On the walls are not only stuffed moose and elk but a stuffed St Bernard dog – apparently a beast of record-breaking enormity.
Eating out The Shooting Star, in Huntsville, is famous for its huge Starburgers, which come with sausage, as well as multiple burger patties, etc.
Après-ski There are a couple of bars and eating places at the new base lodge. Otherwise it's back into town for evening entertainment.
Off the slopes Visits to Ogden, Park City or Salt Lake City are the options – you'll probably stay in one of them!

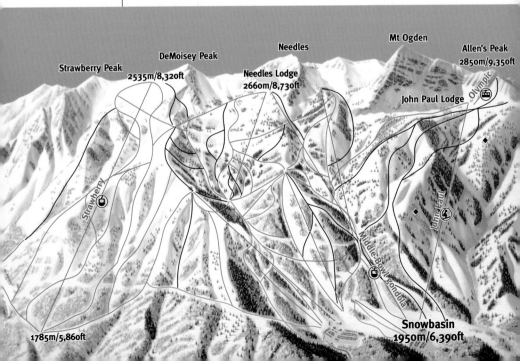

One of the best spots for powderhounds, now with access to Alta's acres

WHAT IT COSTS

(((((6)))))

HOW IT RATES

The slopes

Snow	*****
Extent	***
Experts	*****
Intermediates	***
Beginners	**
Convenience	*****
Queues	**
Restaurants	*

The rest

Scenery	***
Resort charm	*
Off-slope	*

What's new

A second fast quad in Mineral Basin – up to Sugarloaf saddle – linked Snowbird to Alta for 2001/02. A joint lift pass is now available to skiers (but not boarders, as Alta still bans them).

Snowmaking has been improved.

MOUNTAIN FACTS

For Snowbird and Alta combined area

Altitude	2410m-3355m
	7,760ft-11,000ft
Lifts	26
Pistes	4,700 acres
Green	25%
Blue	37%
Black	38%
Snowmaking	
	150 acres
Recco detectors used	

Snowbird only

Altitude	2410m-3355m
	7,760ft-11,000ft
Lifts	11
Pistes	2,500 acres
Green	27%
Blue	38%
Black	35%
Snowmaking	
	100 acres
Recco detectors used	

560

➕ Quantity and quality of powder snow unrivalled except by next-door Alta

➕ New link to Alta makes one of the largest ski areas in the US

➕ Fabulous ungroomed slopes, with steep and not-so-steep options

➕ Luxurious accommodation with excellent facilities

➕ Slopes-at-the-door convenience

➕ Easy to get to other Utah resorts (so long as access road open)

➖ Limited groomed runs for intermediates, though the new link with Alta doubles the terrain

➖ Tiny, claustrophobic resort 'village'

➖ Uncompromising modern architecture

➖ Frequent queues for main cable-car

➖ Avalanche risk can close the road as well as the slopes and keep you indoors

➖ Very quiet at night

There can be few places where nature has combined the steep with the deep better than at Snowbird and neighbouring Alta, and even fewer places where there are also lifts to give you access. At long last the two resorts have agreed to a shared lift pass – and lifts and trails to link the two have been created. The combined area is one of the top powder-pig paradises in the world (with an average snowfall of 500 inches a year) and one of the US's biggest lift-linked ski areas. So it is a shame that Snowbird's concrete, purpose-built 'base village' is so lacking in charm and animation. If you are planning on a week's stay, you may prefer the more traditional (but equally quiet) Alta next door. Snowboarders are banned from Alta's slopes so cannot take advantage of the joint lift pass.

The resort

Snowbird lies 40km/25 miles south-east of Salt Lake City in the Wasatch mountains, up Little Cottonwood Canyon – just before Alta. The setting is rugged and rather Alpine – and both the resort and (particularly) the approach road are prone to avalanches and closure: visitors are sometimes confined indoors for safety. The resort buildings are mainly block-like and dull – but they provide high-quality lodging and are convenient for the slopes (as well as strong enough to withstand avalanches).

The resort area and the slopes are spread along the road on the south side of the narrow canyon. The focal Snowbird Center (lift base/shops/restaurants) is towards the eastern, up-canyon end; much of the rest consists of car-parking areas.

All the lodgings and restaurants are within walking distance of each other. The Tram station is central and the Gad lifts can be reached on snow. There are shuttle-bus services linking the lodgings, the lifts and the car parks, and a regular service up to Alta.

The mountain

Snowbird's new link with Alta (see separate Alta chapter) forms one of the largest ski areas in the US. The resorts haven't quite got the hang of these things yet, so the two trail maps don't mesh well (they use different names for one of the linking lifts).

THE SLOPES
Looming above the resort
The north-facing slopes rear up from the edge of the resort. Five access lifts are ranged along the valley floor, the main one being the 125-person cable-car (the Aerial Tram) to Hidden Peak. The toughest terrain is on the flanks of the ridge beneath the line of the Tram. To the west, in Gad Valley, there are runs ranging from very tough to nice and easy – and six chair-lifts. Mineral Basin, on the back of Hidden Peak, added 500 acres of terrain for all abilities in 1999/2000. A second fast quad there forms the link with Alta.

The First Tracks deal gets you up the mountain at 8am. Numbers limited: book ahead ($20). Free daily mountain tours are also available.

LIFT PASSES

2001/02 prices in dollars

Snowbird
Covers lifts and Aerial Tram in Snowbird.
Beginners Chickadee chair pass (10 per day).
Main pass
1-day pass 56
6-day pass 258
Senior citizens
Over 65:
1-day pass 43
Children
Under 12: free (chair-lifts only, up to 2 children per adult; upgrade to Tram is 15)
Short-term passes
Half-day (am or pm) pass available (adult 48)
Alternative passes
Joint Snowboard-Alta pass prices (68 per day)

Day- and half-day passes for Snowbird chair-lifts only (47 per day for adults, 35 for seniors, free for two children under 12 with an adult)

SCHOOLS/GUIDES

2001/02 prices in dollars

Snowbird
Classes 5 days
Half- (pm only) or full-day. 5 full days: 335
Children's classes
Ages: 3 to 15
5 full days including lunch: 395
Private lessons
1hr, 3hr or 6hr
90 for 1hr, for 1 or 2 people, 125 for 3-6 people

CHILDCARE

The Camp Snowbird day camp, in the Cliff Lodge, takes children from 3 to 12, from 8.30 to 4.30. The nursery takes infants from 6 weeks to 3 years.

The Chickadees ski classes start at age 3. Evening babysitting is available.

boarding *Unfortunately for snowboarders, the joint Alta-Snowbird pass is not available for them as Alta still bans boards. But ask any Utah boarder where the best place to ride is and you'll get the same answer, 'the Bird's the word'. Competent free-riders will have a wild time in Snowbird's legendary powder and there is a terrain-park and half-pipe. However, Snowbird's attractions would be wasted on beginners. And the nightlife's deadly dull.*

SNOW RELIABILITY
Exceptional
With Little Cottonwood Canyon's huge snowfalls, north-facing slopes and all runs above 2365m/7,760ft, snow reliability is very good. Snowbird and Alta typically average 500 inches of snowfall a year – twice as much as some Colorado resorts and around 50% more than the nearby Park City area. Snowmaking helps to ensure excellent cover in busy areas.

FOR EXPERTS
Steep and deep – superb
Snowbird was created for experts, with a lot of tough terrain. The trail map is liberally sprinkled with double-black-diamonds, and some of the gullies off the Cirque ridge – Silver Fox and Great Scott, for example, are exceptionally steep and frequently neck-deep in powder. Lower down lurk the bump runs, including Mach Schnell – a great run straight down the fall line through trees. There is some wonderful ski-anywhere terrain in the bowl beneath the high Little Cloud chair, and the Gad 2 lift opens up some attractive tree runs. Mineral Basin has added more expert terrain but can get skied out fairly quickly. Backcountry tours

are available, and Wasatch Powderbird Guides offer heli-skiing and boarding.

FOR INTERMEDIATES
Quality, not quantity
The winding Chip's Run on the east side of the Cirque ridge provides the only comfortable route down from the top for intermediates. For adventurous intermediates wanting to try powder skiing, the bowl below the Little Cloud lift is a must – you'll rarely find better powder than this. There are some challenging runs through the trees off the Gad 2 lift. There are also some nice long cruises in Mineral Basin and from the new link with Alta. But if you want miles of perfectly groomed piste, there are plenty of better resorts.

FOR BEGINNERS
Better than you'd expect
Beginners have the Chickadee lift right down in the resort – and then there's a small network of trails to progress to.

FOR CROSS-COUNTRY
Go elsewhere
There are no prepared cross-country trails at Snowbird. All-terrain skiers can hike into the backcountry, but for loops you need to go elsewhere.

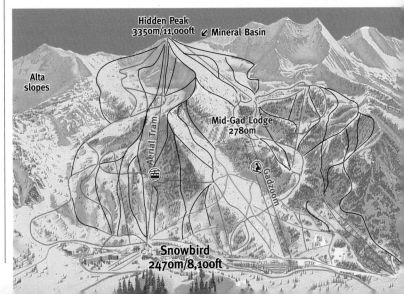

Hidden Peak
3350m/11,000ft ↙ Mineral Basin

Alta slopes

Aerial Tram

Mid-Gad Lodge 2780m

Gadzoom

Snowbird
2470m/8,100ft

↑ Mineral Basin – a very worthwhile recent addition to the area

SNOWBIRD / ED BLANKMAN

GETTING THERE

Air Salt Lake City, transfer ½hr.

ACTIVITIES

Indoor Snowbird Canyon Racquet Club (tennis, racquetball, squash, climbing wall, aerobics, weight training, fitness room), hot-tubs, The Cliff Spa (fitness room, aerobics, beauty centre, sauna, steam room, solarium), conference centre, art gallery **Outdoor** Swimming pools, hot-tubs, ice skating, tubing, snow-shoeing

Central reservations phone number
Call 1 800 640 2002 (toll-free from within the US).

Phone numbers
From distant parts of the US, add the prefix 1 801.
From abroad, add the prefix +1 801.

TOURIST OFFICE

Postcode
UT 84092-9000
t 742 2222
f 933 2298
info@snowbird.com
www.snowbird.com

QUEUES
Avoid the Tram
For much of the season queues of up to 40 minutes for the Tram are common. The Gadzoom fast quad and the slow and exposed Little Cloud chair – sadly, also rather queue-prone – above it are the only alternative if high winds close it down.

MOUNTAIN RESTAURANT
Note the use of the singular
It's the Mid Gad Lodge self-service cafeteria – or 'fuel stop', to use the resort's own description – or else it's back to base. In either case you'll encounter lunchtime crowds unless you eat early or late.

SCHOOLS AND GUIDES
Something for everyone
The ski school offers a progressive range of lessons and speciality clinics – such as women-only clinics, over-50s lessons, bumps and diamonds lessons, and experts-only programmes ('A life-altering experience,' said one reporter).

FACILITIES FOR CHILDREN
All ages well cared-for
The 'kids ski free' programme allows two children (12 and under) to ski for free ($15 a day extra for use of the Tram) with each adult buying an all-day lift ticket. The childcare facilities at the Cliff Lodge look comprehensive.

Staying there

HOW TO GO
Package or independent
Salt Lake City airport is close, and well set up to handle independent travellers. There are several companies offering frequent transfers. If you plan to visit several other resorts, you'll want to hire a car, and it's worth

considering Salt Lake City as a base – not least because avalanche danger can close Little Cottonwood Canyon after heavy snowfalls, in which case you won't be able to tour around.

A few UK tour operators feature accommodation in Snowbird. Some UK holidaymakers combine a stay in Snowbird with a stay in Park City.
Hotels There are several lodges, and smaller condominium blocks.
(((4 **Cliff Lodge** The main place: a huge luxury hotel and restaurant complex just up the nursery slopes from the Snowbird Center. There's a rooftop pool and hot-tub, sauna, steam room and gym. Prices here are understandably high, but if you can bear to share a four-bed 'dorm' room they're great value, considering the facilities you can use.

EATING OUT
A reasonable choice
Generally, eating out revolves around Cliff Lodge and Snowbird Center – both house a number of restaurants. It's advisable for at least one member of a party to pay a few dollars to join the Club at Snowbird (guests at the Cliff Lodge are automatically registered) as most of the better restaurants are classed as private clubs. The Aerie and the Wildflower are quite upmarket venues, the Mexican Keyhole Junction and the Forklift are easier on the pocket and better for families.

APRES-SKI
Very quiet weekdays
Après-ski in Snowbird tends to be a bit muted, especially during the week. The Tram Club under the Tram itself was rocking with live music as the slopes closed when we were there. The Keyhole Cantina also has a good atmosphere at end-of-play. A sunset swim and a few cocktails at the rooftop pool in Cliff Lodge is relaxing. It's quite feasible to head into Salt Lake City for the occasional night out.

OFF THE SLOPES
Head down-canyon
People not using the slopes will be bored at Snowbird once they've tried the Cliff Spa and its treatments. You could head towards the city – the Racquet Club down the valley is owned by Snowbird and has superb tennis facilities, and there are some attractions downtown, particularly around Temple Square.

The Rest of the West

This section covers a varied group of isolated resorts in different parts of the great Rocky Mountain chain that stretches the length of the United States from Montana and Idaho down through Wyoming and Colorado to New Mexico. Each has its own unique character – and each is well worth knowing about.

Sun Valley, Idaho, was America's first purpose-built resort, developed in the 1930s by the president of the Union Pacific Railway. It quickly became popular with the Hollywood jet set and has managed to retain its stylish image and ambience over the years. It hasn't become a big international destination because of its rather isolated location, limited hotel accommodation and poor reputation for snow – although this has largely been rectified by the huge snowmaking installation. But if you want to indulge yourself a little and be pampered, bear it in mind – it has one of our favourite luxury hotels.

If you don't mind a bit of a cross-state drive, you might combine a visit to Sun Valley with a visit to the famously snowy resorts of Utah or to Jackson Hole in Wyoming – another resort with an impressive snow record. Jackson is the nearest there is to a resort with a genuine Wild West cowboy atmosphere (though with an increasingly up-market twist to it with new luxury hotels and galleries). The old town is lined with wooden sidewalks and there are lively saloons, where modern-day working cowboys drink, play pool and dance to country music. The mountain is a 15-minute drive away and offers some of America's most extreme terrain, with steeps, jumps and bumps to suit all – a sharp contrast to the tame,

immaculately groomed runs typical of many US resorts. It does have easier runs, but that's not why most people go there.

A little way north of both Sun Valley and Jackson, just inside Montana, is Big Sky, not to be confused with Big Mountain at the far northern end of the state, or indeed Big White, over the Canadian border in British Columbia. Big Sky has one of the biggest verticals in America (1280m/4,200ft) thanks to its Lone Peak cable-car, going way above the tree line to 3400m/11,170ft. Its extensive slopes have something for everyone, from extreme steeps at the top to countless gentle cruises at the bottom. But there's not much to do here except ski and board.

Taos, New Mexico, is the most southerly major resort in America, and because of its isolation is relatively unknown on the international market. There's a tiny resort development at the foot of the slopes, which are set high above the traditional adobe town of Taos, 18 miles away in the arid valley. The area was developed in the 1950s by a European and is still family-run, with a friendly feel to it. It is one of the few resorts still to ban snowboarders from its slopes, which have many very challenging runs, including some major mogul fields and terrain you have to hike to.

563

TOURIST OFFICE

Taos
www.skitaos.org

JACKSON HOLE /
BOB WOODALL / FPI

In many ways the Best of the West, Jackson Hole now offers lift access to large amounts of backcountry terrain, reached through gates like this ➔

Big Sky

2285m/7,500ft

Vast, empty slopes for all abilities, with a fledgling village at the base

WHAT IT COSTS

HOW IT RATES

The slopes

Snow	****
Extent	***
Experts	*****
Intermediates	****
Beginners	****
Convenience	****
Queues	*****
Restaurants	*

The rest

Scenery	***
Resort charm	**
Off-slope	**

MOUNTAIN FACTS

Altitude	2125m-3405m
	6,970ft-11,170ft
Lifts	17
Pistes	3,600 acres
Green	17%
Blue	25%
Black	58%
Snowmaking	
	350 acres
Recco detectors used	

564

➕ Extensive ski area with runs for all abilities, including great expert runs

➕ Excellent snow reliability

➕ Big vertical by US standards

➕ Few queues, empty slopes

➖ Only a small resort village as yet, quiet in the evenings

➖ Some slow, old chair-lifts

➖ Only one fast-food mountain eatery

➖ Long journey from the UK

Big Sky is renowned for its powder, steeps and big vertical, and has lots of blissfully empty gentler slopes. At present, there's not much more than three hotels (including a luxury 5-star), with a few shops, restaurants and condos around them. Nightlife is limited, to say the least. If that's what you like, go soon – the owners have big expansion plans to put Big Sky in the first division. But it's a long journey from the UK right now – at least three flights last season.

THE RESORT

Big Sky, now over 25 years old, has started to attract a few international visitors who have heard of its huge snowfalls and fabulous, deserted slopes. And as well as locals who live to ski, it is also attracting affluent guests from around the US.

The resort is set amid the wide open spaces of Montana, one hour's drive from airport town Bozeman. And as it's built on private land, it doesn't have to quibble with the US Forest Service for permission to grow. At the foot of the slopes is Mountain Village –

with three hotels, some slope-side condominiums and a few shops and restaurants. Despite free buses, condos scattered around more distant locations hold little appeal.

Bridger Bowl is 90 minutes' drive away, and makes a worthwhile outing, especially after a fresh snowfall – when its broad, steep, lightly wooded slopes offer wonderful powder descents.

THE MOUNTAINS

The slopes cover a big area spread over two linked mountains, with long runs for all abilities. Lone Mountain,

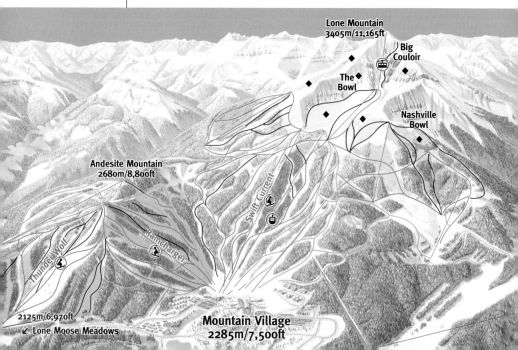

Lone Mountain
3405m/11,165ft

Big Couloir

The Bowl

Nashville Bowl

Andesite Mountain
2680m/8,800ft

Swift Current

Ramcharger

Thunder Wolf

2125m/6,970ft
Lone Moose Meadows

Mountain Village
2285m/7,500ft

It sure is a big mountain for such a little village ➔

BIG SKY RESORT

What's new

For 2002/03, more gladed runs will be opened on Andesite Mountain. Eight new trails will also be cut into the north side of Lone Mountain, ready for 2003/04 once a new lift is installed in summer 2003. This will add 600 acres of skiing to the resort.

Penthouse units in the Summit Hotel and the new 80-room Mountain Inn hotel in the Mountain Village were finished for 2001/02.

The resort's $400 million, 10-year expansion plan is for more accommodation and over 100 shops and restaurants in a much expanded pedestrian village, six new high-speed lifts and 1,800 acres of additional terrain.

Central reservations phone number
Call 1 800 548 4486 (toll-free from within the US).

Phone numbers
From distant parts of the US, add the prefix 1 406.
From abroad, add the prefix +1 406.

TOURIST OFFICE

Postcode MT 59716
t 995 5000
f 995 5001
info@bigskyresort.com
www.bigskyresort.com

with steep open upper slopes and trees lower down, has fabulous 360 degree views from the top and 1280m/ 4,200ft vertical. Andesite mountain is a much more modest wooded hill of 400m/1,300ft vertical. Although there are three fast quads, most of the chair-lifts are old triples and doubles. There are daily free mountain tours.

Slopes Eight chairs and a gondola serve the wooded lower half of Lone Mountain. The Lone Peak chair accesses slopes at the bottom of the main bowl and leads to the Lone Peak Tram – a tiny 15-person cable-car to the top, which serves great experts-only terrain all around the top bowl.

Snow reliability Snowfall averages 400+ inches, which puts Big Sky ahead of most Colorado resorts and alongside Jackson Hole. Grooming is good, too.

Experts The terrain accessed from the Tram is great, and includes the Big Couloir (which the ski patrol often limits to two people at a time) and numerous long narrow chutes called by the locals the A to Zs. Castro's Shoulder is the steepest route at 50°. There are good black slopes lower down, around the tree line.

Intermediates There is lots of cruising terrain – the shady runs on Andesite from the Ramcharger chair are splendid, but practically all the lower lifts serve worthwhile blue runs.

Beginners Good nursery area at the base and long greens to progress to.

Snowboarding There is a good terrain-park and a half-pipe on Andesite and a natural half-pipe on Lone Mountain.

Cross-country There are 65km/40 miles of trails at Lone Mountain Ranch. There are also trails at West Yellowstone.

Queues The tiny tram attracts queues of experts on powder days. Other than

that, queues are unheard of unless high winds close the upper lifts. And the runs are deserted: there are 3,600 skiable acres and on an average day they sell 2,000 lift tickets; do the sums.

Mountain restaurants The Dug-Out, on Andesite does fast food and BBQs. Or you can head back to base to eat.

School and guides The ski school receives excellent reviews. A reporter described his children's lessons as a '100% success'.

Facilities for children Handprints nursery in the slope-side Snowcrest lodge takes children from age six months ('It was perfection – four to an adult,' says a reporter). Children under 10 years ski for free.

STAYING THERE

Hotels The new slope-side Summit with spa baths in the rooms and sculptures in the foyer is 'hugely impressive and up-market' says a recent visitor. Huntley Lodge has also been highly recommended. Mountain Inn was new for 2001/02 and is less expensive, as is Buck's T4 Lodge, seven miles away.

Self-catering The Stillwater condos are much the cheapest and have been recommended by reporters, along with Arrowhead, Beaverhead and Big Horn.

Eating out Huntley and Moonlight Lodges have smart restaurants, The Peaks (in the Summit) and Dante's Inferno are popular. Shuttle-buses and courtesy cars run to far-flung places.

Après-ski Chet's bar has live music, pool and poker games. The Carabinier lounge in the Summit, Roosters and Black Bear are also popular.

Off the slopes The main things to do are snowmobiling, horse-riding, sleigh rides, visiting Yellowstone national park and shopping in Bozeman.

Big Sky

565

Jackson Hole   1925m/6,310ft

Wild West cowboy town near exciting slopes and expanding resort village

➕ Big, steep mountain, with some real expert-only terrain and one of the US's biggest verticals: 1260m/4,140ft

➕ Jackson town has an entertaining Wild West ambience

➕ Unspoiled, remote location with impressive scenery and wildlife

➕ Excellent snow record

➕ Even more snow (and empty slopes) 90 minutes away at Grand Targhee – with snowcat- and lift-served slopes

➕ Cheap lodgings (winter is off-peak)

➕ Plenty to do off the slopes

➕ Airport is only minutes from town

➖ Intermediates lacking the confidence to tackle ungroomed black runs will find the area very limited

➖ Inadequate mountain restaurants

➖ The cable-car serving the top runs still generates long queues

➖ Low altitude, and slopes face roughly south-east, so snow can deteriorate quickly (and good snow is needed on steep slopes like these)

➖ Town is 15 minutes from the slopes, though the slope-side village has lodgings (and is growing quickly)

➖ Getting there from the UK involves two or three flights

566

For those who like the idea of steep slopes smothered in deep powder or plastered with big bumps, Jackson Hole is Mecca. Like many American mountains, Jackson has double-diamond steeps that you can't find in Europe except by going off-piste with a guide. What marks it out from the rest is the sheer quantity of terrain that is classified black, and the scale of the mountain.

Utah devotees will tell you that the snow here isn't as light as at Alta/Snowbird; but it's light enough, and falls in quantities somewhere between those found in Colorado and those famously found in Alta – the average annual total is around 400in, but in recent seasons it has often been around or above the 500in mark.

With its wooden sidewalks, country-music saloons and pool halls, tiny Jackson is a determinedly Western town – great fun, if you like that kind of thing. We do.

The resort

Teton Village at the foot of the slopes is growing rapidly ↓

The town of Jackson sits at the south-eastern edge of Jackson Hole – a high, flat valley surrounded by mountain ranges, in north-west Wyoming. This is real 'cowboy' territory, and the town strives to maintain its Wild West flavour, with traditional-style wooden buildings and sidewalks, and a couple of 'cowboy' saloons. Jackson gets many more visitors in summer than winter (thanks to the nearby national parks), and has lots of clothing and souvenir shops as well as upmarket galleries appealing to second-home owners. But in winter it's basically a ski town with a Western feel.

The slopes, a 15-minute drive north-east, rise abruptly from the flat valley floor. At the base is Teton Village – going through a phase of rapid expansion and described by two 2002 reporters as a 'building site' – with purpose-built lodgings, shops and restaurants in a pleasantly woody setting, some neo-Alpine but increasingly in local style. The public bus service to the mountain ($2 single) has had mixed reports recently. Get a timetable and buy a book of tickets in advance, as it doesn't give change.

What's new

For 2001/02, there was a new super-pipe and terrain-park at the base of Apres Vous mountain.

In Grand Targhee, a new high-speed quad added 500 acres of what was previously snowcat skiing to the lift-served slopes. But there is still a separate 1000 acres of great terrain for snowcat-only skiing and boarding.

New for 2002/3 in Teton Village will be the 80-unit Teton Mountain Lodge condominiums with indoor and outdoor pools and hot-tubs, spa, and ski rental and servicing. Also in Teton Village, a luxurious Four Seasons Resort Hotel should be finished by June 2003.

For 2001/02 the Snake River Lodge and Spa underwent an 18 million dollar refurbishment and now boasts three saunas, two steamrooms, four hot-tubs and plenty of beauty treatments in its Avanyu Spa and Health Club.

The mountains

Jackson Hole has long been recognised as one of the world's most compelling resorts for advanced and expert skiers. With recent improvements to the lifts and the new buildings at Teton Village, the resort may seem less of a cult destination for hard-core experts and more of a conventional resort, with something for everyone. Don't be fooled: the beginner slopes are fine, but intermediates wanting to build up confidence should look elsewhere. Most American mountains have green run options from the top of most lifts – but in Jackson only the two lowest lifts offer this. You should also keep an eye out for moose on the slopes – and be wary because they can be aggressive.

THE SLOPES
One big mountain, one small one
Trail gradings are accurate at Jackson: our own small map doesn't distinguish black from double-black-diamond runs, but the distinction matters once you are there – 'expert only' tends to mean just that. Some of the double-black runs are simply steep; but there are also cliffs, bumps, jumps and couloirs, including the infamous Corbet's.

One big mountain makes Jackson Hole famous – **Rendezvous**. The summit, accessed by a mid-sized cable-car (the Tram), provides a 1260m/ 4,130ft vertical drop – exceptional for the US. Conditions and thighs permitting, you can go from top to almost bottom on black slopes. From the top of the Tram you can now

access the backcountry of Cody Bowl. It can be incredibly cold and windy at the top of the Tram even when it's warm and calm below. The wind is an advantage in one way because it blows the snow and gives you fresh tracks.

To the right looking up is **Apres Vous** mountain, with half the vertical and mostly much gentler runs, accessed by the short Teewinot and the longer Apres Vous fast quads.

Between these two peaks is a broad mountainside split by gullies, accessed by the Bridger gondola. This gives speedy access to the Thunder and Sublette quad chairs serving some of the steepest terrain on Rendezvous.

To get your bearings, take the Rendezvous Trail from the top of the Tram. This turns into South Pass traverse and goes all the way past the main lifts to the far end of the area on Apres Vous. There are complimentary tours of the mountains, starting from the Host building at 9.30.

Snow King is a separate area right next to Jackson town. Locals use it in their lunch-hour and in the evening (it's partly floodlit).

Grand Targhee, famous for its powder snow, is just 90 minutes' drive from Jackson Hole – buses run daily.

SNOW RELIABILITY
Steep lower slopes can suffer
The claimed average of 402 inches of 'mostly dry powder' snow is much more than most Colorado resorts claim – and for a core three-month season conditions are likely to be reasonable. But the base elevation is relatively low for the Rockies, and the slopes are

Rendezvous Mountain
3185m/10,450ft

Headwall

Casper Bowl

Apres Vous Mountain
2585m/8,480ft

Sublette

Thunder

Bridger

Tram

Apres Vous

Teewinot

Teton Village
1925m/6,310ft

LIFT PASSES

2002/03 prices in dollars

Jackson Hole
Covers all 11 lifts
Main pass
1-day pass 61
6-day pass 330
6-day low season pass 240

Senior citizens
Over 65: 6-day pass 165
Children
15 to 21: 6-day pass 248
Under 15: 6-day pass 165
Under 5: free pass
Short-term passes
Afternoon pass from 12.30
Notes Prices may be cheaper when booked in advance through UK tour operators. Beginners can ride Teewinot and Eagle's Rest chairs for $10 per day.

quite sunny – they basically face south-east. If you're unlucky, you may find the steep lower slopes like the Hobacks in poor shape, or even shut. We've asked the locals and they seem to think that conditions are likely to be ideal roughly half the time in an average week. Snowmaking covers runs from the gondola and on Apres Vous.

FOR EXPERTS
Best for the brave
For the good skier or boarder who wants challenges without the expense of hiring a guide to go off-piste, Jackson is one of the world's best resorts – maybe even the best.

Rendezvous mountain offers virtually nothing but black and very black slopes. The routes down the main Rendezvous Bowl are not particularly fearsome; but some of the alternatives are. Go down the East Ridge at least once to stare over the edge of the notorious Corbet's Couloir. The Tram passes right above it, giving a great view of people leaping off the lip. It's the jump-in that's special; the word is that the slope you land on is a mere 50° to the horizontal.

Below Rendezvous Bowl, the wooded flanks of Cheyenne Bowl offer serious challenges, at the extreme end of the single-black-diamond spectrum. If instead you take the ridge run that skirts this bowl to the right, you get to the Hobacks – a huge area of open and lightly wooded slopes, gentler than those higher up, but still black.

Corbet's aside, most of the seriously steep slopes are more easily reached from the slightly lower quad chairs. From Sublette, you have direct access to the short but seriously steep Alta chutes, and to the less severe Laramie Bowl beside them. Or you can track over to Tensleep Bowl – pausing to inspect Corbet's from below – and on to the less extreme (and less chute-like) Expert Chutes, and the single black Cirque and Headwall areas). Casper Bowl – accessed through gates

only – is recommended for untracked powder. Thunder chair serves further steep, narrow, north-facing chutes.

Again, the lower part of the mountain here offers lightly wooded single-black slopes.

The gondola serves terrain not without interest for experts. In particular, Moran Woods is a splendid under-utilised area. And even Apres Vous itself has an area of serious single blacks in Saratoga bowl.

The gates into the backcountry access over 3,000 acres of amazing terrain and you should hire a guide to take you there. There are some heli-ski and heli-board operations.

FOR INTERMEDIATES
Exciting for some
There are great cruising runs on the front face of Apres Vous, and top-to-bottom quite gentle blues from the gondola. But they don't add up to a great deal of mileage, and you shouldn't consider Jackson unless you want to tackle the blacks. It's then important to get guidance on steepness and snow conditions. The steepest single blacks are steep; intimidating when mogulled and fearsome when hard. The daily grooming map is worth consulting.

FOR BEGINNERS
Fine, up to a point
There are a few broad, gentle runs: fine for getting started. The progression to the blue Werner run off the Apres Vous chair is gradual enough – but what then? Most of the blues are traverses and the exceptions will not help build a novice's confidence.

FOR CROSS-COUNTRY
Lots of possibilities
There are three centres, offering varied trails. The Spring Creek Nordic Center has some good beginner terrain and moonlight tours. The Nordic Center at Teton has 17km/10 miles of trails and organises trips into the National Parks.

boarding *Jackson Hole is a cult resort for expert snowboarders, just as it is for expert skiers. The steeps, cliffs and chutes make for a lot of high-adrenalin thrills for competent free-riders. There's a terrain-park and a half-pipe, and Dick's Ditch is a natural pipe. It's not a bad resort for novices either, with the beginner slopes served by a high-speed quad. Intermediates not wishing to venture off the groomed runs will find the resort limited. There are some good snowboard shops, including the Hole-in-the-Wall at Teton Village. The nightlife in the bars around the town square is reasonably lively.*

Staying there

HOW TO GO
In town or by the mountain
Teton Village is convenient. But stay in Jackson for cowboy atmosphere.

Hotels Because winter is low season, prices are low.

((((5) **Amangani Resort** (734 7333) Hedonistic (expensive) luxury in isolated position way above the valley.

(((4) **Alpenhof** (733 3242) Our favourite (and our readers') in Teton Village. Tirolean-style, with rooms of varying standard and price. Extended and refurbished for last season. Good food. Pool, sauna, hot-tub.

(((4) **Wort** (733 2190) Comfortable, right in the centre of town, above the lively Silver Dollar Bar. Hot-tub.

(((4) **Rusty Parrot Lodge** (733 2000) A stylish place in town, with a rustic feel and handcrafted furniture. Hot-tub.

(((4) **Snake River Lodge & Spa** (733 3657) At Teton Village. Smartly welcoming as well as comfortable and convenient, with fine new spa facilities.

(((4) **Spring Creek Ranch** (733 8833) Exclusive retreat between town and slopes; cross-country on-hand. Hot-tub.

(((4) **Huff House Inn** (733 4164) Charming old inn – the best of Jackson's many luxury B&B places.

(((4) **Painted Porch** (733 1981) Gorgeous B&B full of antiques.

(((3) **Lodge at Jackson Hole** (733 2992) Western-style place on fringe of Jackson town. Comfortable mini-suite rooms, and free breakfast/après-ski munchies. Pool, sauna, hot-tubs.

(((3) **Parkway Inn** (733 3143) Friendly, family-run, central in Jackson town; big rooms, antique furniture, lap pool, hot tubs. Recommended by a reporter.

((2) **Hostel x** (733 3415) Basic, good value ($51 a night), at Teton Village. Recommended by a reporter.

((2) **Trapper Inn** (733 2648) Friendly, good value, a block or two from Town Square. Hot-tubs.

Self-catering There is lots of choice at Teton Village, within and around Jackson and at more isolated locations.

SCHOOLS/GUIDES
2001/02 prices in dollars

Jackson Hole
Classes Full day 65
Half day 60
Mountain Masters (for advanced skiers: max 4 per group)
Full day 85
Children's classes
Ages: 3 to 6 (inc lunch and lift ticket):
Full day 80
Half day 55
Ages: 12 to 17 (inc lunch and lift ticket):
Full day 99
Private lessons
1-5 people
Early tram (8.30),
Full day (7 hr) 435
Half day (4 hr) 330
All day from 9am 415
Backcountry guiding
1-5 people
Full day 435
Half day am 330
Half day pm 245

CHILDCARE
The Kids' Ranch (739 2691) in the Cody House at Teton Village takes children aged 2 months to 6 years, from 8.30 to 4.30, with indoor and outdoor games and one-to-one ski lessons from age 3. Kids use the Fort Wyoming snow-garden, with 'magic carpet' lift.

QUEUES
Always queues for the Tram
The Bridger gondola has relieved some of the pressure on the 30-year-old Tram. But the Tram is still the quickest way up Rendezvous, still the only way to the very top and still not able to keep up with demand; there may be queues all day (10 to 15 minutes if you're lucky). You can access nearly all the mountain except Rendezvous Bowl from the Sublette chair.

MOUNTAIN RESTAURANTS
Head back to base
There's only one real restaurant on the mountain – at the base of the Casper chair-lift; it does a good range of self-service food, but gets very crowded. There are simple snack-bars at four other points on the mountain. At the base, Nick Wilson's in the Clocktower, the Alpenhof restaurant and the Mangy Moose are favourites.

SCHOOLS AND GUIDES
Learn to tackle the steeps
As well as the usual lessons, there are also special types – steep and deep, women-only, for example – on certain dates. You can book Early Tram lessons and be first on the slopes. Backcountry guides can be hired.

FACILITIES FOR CHILDREN
Just fine
The area may not seem to be one ideally suited to children, but in fact there are enough easy runs and the 'Kids' Ranch' care facilities are good.

Jackson Hole

569

GETTING THERE

Air Jackson, transfer ½hr.

ACTIVITIES

Indoor Art galleries, ice skating, cinemas, swimming, theatre, concerts, wildlife art museum

Outdoor Snowmobiles, mountaineering, horse riding, snow-shoe hikes, snowcat tours, floodlit skiing, heli-skiing, sleigh rides, dog-sledding, walks, wildlife safaris and tours of Yellowstone National Park, Grand Teton National Park.

Phone numbers

From distant parts of the US, add the prefix 1 307.
From abroad, add the prefix +1 307.

JACKSON HOLE TOURIST OFFICE

Postcode WY 83001
t 733 7182
f 733 1286
info@jacksonhole.com
www.jacksonhole.com

GRAND TARGHEE TOURIST OFFICE

Postcode WY 83422
t 353 2300
f 353 8619
info@grandtarghee.com
www.grandtarghee.com

EATING OUT
It's a pleasure in Jackson

Teton Village has pizza, Mexican, Japanese, a steakhouse and a number of hotel restaurants. Most people favour the Mangy Moose – good value, good fun. In Jackson there are lots of places to try (but book ahead). The cool art-deco Cadillac Grille does good food. The Range is excellent for trendy American regional cuisine. The Blue Lion is small, cosy and casually stylish. The 'saloons' do hearty meals and good steaks. El Abuelito is 'authentic Mexican, unlike the majority of US so-called Mexicans,' says a reporter who also recommends Antony's Italian and 'for a treat' the Rusty Parrot Lodge. The 'Greek-inspired' food at the cute log-cabin Sweetwater is recommended. A good budget place is the Snake River brew-pub – not to be confused with the expensive Snake River Grill.

APRES-SKI
Amusing saloons

For immediate après-ski at Teton Village, the Mangy Moose is a big, happy, noisy place, often with live music. For a quieter time head for Dietrich's bar at the Alpenhof.

In Jackson there are two famous 'saloons'. The Million Dollar Cowboy Bar features saddles as bar stools and a stuffed grizzly bear, and is usually the liveliest place in town, with live music and dancing some nights. The Silver Dollar around the corner is more subdued; there may be ragtime playing as you count the 2032 silver dollars inlaid into the counter. The Rancher is a huge pool-hall. The Shady Lady saloon sometimes has live country and western. The Virginian saloon is quieter.

For a night out of town, join the local ravers at the Stagecoach Inn at Wilson, especially on Sundays.

OFF THE SLOPES
'Great' outdoor diversions

The famous Yellowstone National Park is 100km/60 miles to the north. You can tour the park by snowcat or snowmobile, but you'll be roaring along the snowy roads in the company of several hundred other snowmobiles – 'more like a Grand Prix than a wilderness', as one reporter puts it. There is much more rewarding snowmobiling to be done elsewhere.

The National Elk Refuge, next to Jackson and across the road from the National Museum of Wildlife Art, has the largest elk herd in the US. In town there are some 40 galleries and museums and a number of outlets for Indian and Western arts and crafts. There is, believe it or not, a branch of Ripley's Believe It or Not® – 'a museum unlike any other', as they say.

A DAY OUT IN GRAND TARGHEE 2440M/8,000FT

We'd recommend any adventurous visitor to make the hour-and-a-half trip over the Teton pass to sample Grand Targhee's fabled powder, especially if there's been a recent big dump. The average snowfall here is over 500 inches – 25% greater than Jackson, and on a par with Utah's best – and the slopes are usually blissfully empty. It is much gentler and easier skiing and boarding than at Jackson. Locals call it Grand Foggee, because there is often low cloud even when it's not snowing.

On the main Fred's Mountain, the 1,500 acres of slopes can all be accessed from a central fast quad. This serves a wide area of open and lightly wooded blue and black runs with a respectable 610m/2,000ft vertical. A long slow double allows you to repeatedly explore a splendid area of tough blues and easy blacks. Lower down a slow quad chair serves an excellent area of short green runs.

Next-door Peaked Mountain offers slopes that are similar in extent, but were previously only accessible by snowcat. For 2001/02 a third of this terrain was accessed by a new high-speed quad. This has a vertical of only 390m/1,280ft and serves four short blue and blue-black trails as well as some wooded terrain. For those (like us) who loved the Targhee snowcat trips, there are still over 1,000 acres kept just for this, mainly great gladed runs in pristine powder.

Daily buses to Targhee pick up from various hotels around town and Teton Village. A combined bus/lift ticket costs $59. The snowcat operation cost $264 a day (including lunch), $199 a half-day last season. You can also stay at Grand Targhee – there's a small, quiet, modern village right at the base.

Sun Valley
1755m/5,750ft

Stylish resort with slopes to flatter its rich and famous guests

WHAT IT COSTS

(((((6)

HOW IT RATES

The slopes

Snow	★★★
Extent	★★★
Experts	★★★
Intermediates	★★★★
Beginners	★★★
Convenience	★★
Queues	★★★★
Restaurants	★★★★

The rest

Scenery	★★★
Resort charm	★★★
Off-slope	★★★

What's new

Sun Valley's owner Earl Holding has invested millions in high-speed lifts, new runs, a huge computer-controlled snowmaking system and plush on-slope restaurant complexes and base lodges. More recently he ploughed money into his new baby, Snowbasin in Utah, which hosted the downhill events in the 2002 Olympics. So development in Sun Valley is on hold.

MOUNTAIN FACTS

For Bald Mountain

Altitude	1755m-2790m
	5,750ft-9,150ft
Lifts	13
Pistes	2,054 acres
Green	36%
Blue	42%
Black	22%
Snowmaking	
	645 acres
Recco detectors used	

SUN VALLEY RESORT

Bald Mountain has mainly intermediate runs at a consistent pitch ➔

- ➕ Luxury resort built around the atmospheric old mining town of Ketchum
- ➕ Ideal intermediate terrain
- ➕ Wonderful luxurious mountain restaurants and base lodges
- ➕ Great restaurants and atmospheric bars for dining out, après-ski, and star-spotting
- ➕ Lots of off-slope diversions

- ➖ Expensive
- ➖ Erratic snow record though extensive snowmaking back up
- ➖ Shuttle-buses between two separate mountains and from most accommodation

Millions of dollars have been pumped into the resort building new facilities – high-speed chair-lifts, a huge computerised snowmaking system, splendid base lodges and mountain restaurants – to maintain Sun Valley's reputation as the US's original luxury purpose-built winter sports resort. For a peaceful, relaxing time, it's hard to beat. For skiing and boarding alone, there are better resorts.

THE RESORT

Sun Valley is based around the old mining village of Ketchum. It was built in the 1930s by Averell Harriman, President of the Union Pacific Railway, and became a favourite with stars such as Clark Gable and Judy Garland. Its current owner has pumped millions of dollars into the mountain to restore it to state-of-the-art luxury and Sun Valley now attracts stars like Clint Eastwood and Arnie Schwarzenegger. The town of Ketchum retains its old-world charm and has atmospheric bars, restaurants and shops. But it's not cheap: 'More expensive than Aspen. I didn't buy, but I enjoyed looking in the high-quality shops,' says a reporter.

Shuttle-buses from most accommodation makes your choice of location less of an issue.

THE MOUNTAINS

There are two separate mountains – Bald Mountain, with the main body of runs, and the smaller Dollar Mountain.

Slopes The main slopes of Bald Mountain (known locally as Baldy) are accessed from one of two luxurious base lodge complexes at River Run and Warm Springs, a shuttle-bus-ride from most accommodation. Of the 13 lifts, seven are high-speed quads. The separate Dollar Mountain has good beginner slopes, three lifts and 13 runs.
Snow reliability The resort has an erratic natural snow record, so it has installed 645 acres of snowmaking, which covers over 70% of the groomable runs.
Experts There are a few tough runs and bowls for experts, but nothing beyond single-black-diamond pitch, including the two most famous mogul runs, Exhibition and Limelight. Heli-skiing is available locally.
Intermediates Most of the terrain is ideal, with lots of runs at a consistent pitch. There are good blue bowl runs with great views from the top ridge as well as groomed cruisers through the trees.

Phone numbers
From distant parts of the US, add the prefix 1 208.
From abroad, add the prefix +1 208.

Central reservations phone number
Call 1 800 634 3347 (toll-free from within the US).

TOURIST OFFICE

Postcode ID 83340
t 786 8259
f 726 4533
ski@sunvalley.com
www.sunvalley.com

Beginners Dollar is the place to be, with gentle, long green runs to progress to. Baldy's greens are tougher.
Snowboarding Snowboarding is now allowed and the chair-lifts make getting about easy. But Sun Valley doesn't have a snowboard culture.
Cross-country 40km/25 miles of prepared trails start at the Nordic Center, with more along the valley.
Queues These are rarely a problem, with Sun Valley's network of high-speed quads whisking people around.
Mountain restaurants The mountain restaurants and base lodges have to be seen to be believed. They are way ahead of most US on-slope facilities, with floor-to-ceiling windows, beautiful wooden decor, heated terraces so snow instantly melts, and marble fittings with gold-plated taps in public restrooms. One reporter enjoyed 'the piano and violin players and people-watching at River Run base' at the end of the day.
Schools and guides We have no reason to believe that the lessons are not up to the usual high standards found in most North American resorts.
Facilities for children The ski school takes children from age three, and children 15 and under stay and ski free during certain periods of the year.

STAYING THERE

How to go There are some wonderful smart hotels to stay in, and there are plenty of cheaper options as well, including motels and self-catering.
Hotels One of our favourite hotels in any resort is the stylish Sun Valley Lodge. As well as magnificent rooms, there is a big outdoor ice rink and a pool, and the corridors are lined with photos of film-star guests. Ernest Hemingway wrote *For Whom the Bell Tolls* here.
Eating out There are over 80 restaurants and Sun Valley was rated number one in the US by readers of *Gourmet* magazine. We had excellent food at the relaxed Evergreen Bistro and a great breakfast at The Knob Hill Inn. A reporter recommends Chandler's, too.
Après-ski Atmospheric places include the Sawtooth Club (popular with locals), Whiskey Jaques for live music and dancing, and the Pioneer Saloon, popular for its prime rib, and Clint Eastwood spotting.
Off the slopes You can have a fine time relaxing off the slopes, including sleigh rides, walking, snowmobiling, ice skating, swimming, fishing, gliding, paragliding and strolling round the galleries and shops. There's a special snow-shoe trail, too.

Bald Mountain
2790m/9,150ft

Seattle Ridge

Lookout

Mayday

Christmas

Challenger

Lookout

Frenchman's

Greyhawk

Roundhouse

Warm Spring

River Run

River Run
1755m/5,750ft

Ketchum

You go to Utah for the deepest snow, to Colorado for the lightest powder and swankiest resorts, to California for the mountains and low prices. You go to New England for ... well, for what? Extreme cold? Rock-hard artificial snow? Mountains too limited to be of interest beyond New Jersey? Yes and no: all of these preconceptions have some basis, but they add up to an incomplete and unfair picture.

Yes, it can be cold: one of our reporters recorded −27°C, with wind chill producing a perceived temperature of −73°C. Early in the season, people wear face masks to prevent frostbite. It can also be warm – another reporter had a whole week of rain that washed away the early-season snow. The thing about New England weather is that it varies. Not as much as in Scotland, maybe, but the locals' favourite expression is: 'If you don't like the weather in New England, wait two minutes.' But we got routine winter weather on both our visits – one in January, one in February.

New England doesn't usually get much super-light powder or deep snow to play in. But the resorts have big snowmaking installations, designed to ensure a long season and to help the slopes to 'recover' after a thaw or spell of rain. They were the pioneers of snowmaking technology; and 'farming' snow, as they put it, is an art form and a way of life – provided the weather is

cold enough. And they make and groom their snow to produce a superb surface. Many of the resorts get impressive amounts of natural snow too – in some seasons.

The mountains are not huge in terms of trail mileage (the largest, Killington, is smaller than all except one of the resorts we feature in western US). But several have verticals of over 800m/2,620ft (on a par with Colorado resorts such as Keystone) and most have over 600m/1,970ft (matching Breckenridge), and are worth considering for a short stay, or even for a week if you like familiar runs. For more novelty, a two- or three-centre trip is the obvious solution.

You won't lack challenge – most of the double-black-diamond runs are seriously steep. And you won't lack space: most Americans visit over weekends, which means deserted slopes on weekdays – except at peak periods such as New Year and during the President's Day holiday, in late

573

AMERICAN SKIING COMPANY /
NATHAN BILOW

Snowmaking is crucial in New England – this is Sunday River ↓

February. It also means the resorts are keen to attract long-stay visitors, so UK package prices are low.

But the big weekend and day-trip trade also means that few New England resorts have developed atmospheric resort villages – just a few condos and a hotel, maybe, with places to stay further out geared to suit car drivers who ski, eat, sleep, ski, go home.

But New England is easy to get to from Britain – a flight to Boston, then perhaps a three-hour drive to your resort. And there are some pretty towns to visit, with their clapboard houses and big churches. You might also like to consider spending a day or two in Boston – one of America's most charming cities. And you could save a lot of money on normal UK prices by having a shopping spree at the factory outlet stores that abound in New England.

We cover four of the most popular resorts on the UK market in the separate chapters that follow. But there are many other small areas, too. And if you are going for a week or more, we recommend renting a car and

visiting a few resorts. In the rest of this introduction, we outline the attractions of the main possibilities.

From Killington (by far the biggest resort), you can go south to a range of smaller resorts. **Okemo** competes with Smugglers' Notch for the family market. Okemo mountain has southern Vermont's biggest vertical (655m/2,150ft) and longest trail (over 7km/4.3 miles). The slopes, on several flanks of a single peak, are largely intermediate or easy – though there are a dozen black runs and a couple of short double-black-diamonds. Boarders are well catered for, with an extensive park leading into a half-pipe. There is almost 100% snowmaking cover – and the product is said to be the best in the east.

Mount Snow is another one-peak resort, with a long row of lifts on the front face serving easy and intermediate runs of just over 500m/ 1,640ft vertical, and a separate area of black runs on the north face – including one short but serious double-black. (The sister resort of **Haystack**, a short drive away, has more steep slopes in its Witches area.) Mount

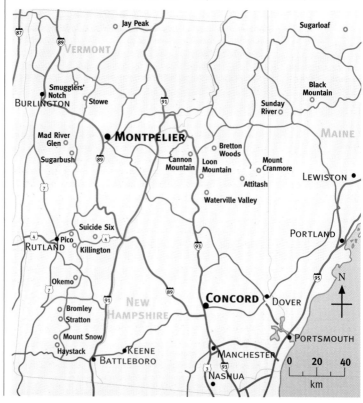

Snow has a huge snowboard park – one of the best in the east.

Stratton offers something like the classic Alpine arrangement of a village at the foot of the lifts. It's a smart, modern development with a pedestrian shopping street. The slopes – mostly easy and intermediate, with some blacks and some short double-black pitches – is spread widely around the flanks of a single peak, served by modern lifts, including a 12-person gondola and four fast six-seat chairs. Stratton calls itself the 'snowboarding capital of the east', with no fewer than six terrain-parks.

You may find more interest in **Sugarbush**, to the north of Killington on the way to Smugglers' Notch. Sugarbush, midway between Killington and Stowe, is a fast-developing resort with one of the larger ski areas. The main sector is an extensive bowl below Lincoln Peak, with lifts up to six points on the rim; a long up-and-over chair-lift links the Mt Ellen area – smaller, but with more altitude and more vertical (808m/2,650ft). The easy skiing is confined to the lower slopes; higher up, the direct runs are seriously steep. There are terrain-parks in both areas. Most of the accommodation is in the historic village of Waitsfield, but a village is developing at the base.

Mad River Glen next door is a cult resort with locals, with some tough ungroomed terrain, a few well-groomed intermediate trails and old-fashioned lifts – it still has a single-person chair-lift. And snowboarding is still banned.

Further north, near the Canadian border, is **Jay Peak**. It gets crowded at weekends (with Canadian as well as American visitors) but is quiet in the week. It has Vermont's only cable-car, which takes you to the summit and to views of four US states plus Canada. It gets a lot of snow for New England and has some good runs for advanced skiers and adventurous intermediates.

Sugarloaf in Maine already has a much better developed village than most small New England resorts. But the mountain is small and a keen piste-basher could ski it out in a day or two. Very popular with day and weekend skiers and boarders, it was very noticeable on our visit how safety conscious the local slope-users were. There was a higher proportion of people wearing protective helmets here than any other resort we have visited. We estimate well over 50% were

helmeted – and these included all age groups, from children to octogenarians. Even teenage and twenty-something skiers and boarders were comfortable in their helmets – a sign of things to come in Europe perhaps? Sugarloaf is another resort that is now owned by the American Skiing Company (Killington, Mount Snow, Sugarbush, Sunday River and Attitash Bear Peak are its other New England resorts).

New Hampshire has several small resorts scattered along the Interstate 93 highway. **Bretton Woods** is one of the smaller areas, 460m/1,510ft vertical on a single mountain face, but it is highly rated, particularly by families, who relish the top-to-bottom easy trails. There is a good mix of terrain, and snowmaking is comprehensive. Snowboarders have a park and a half-pipe. There are a few places to stay near the base, with more five miles away at Twin Mountain.

Cannon is a ski area and nothing more – lifts from two base areas close to I-93 converge on the summit 650m/2,130ft above, serving mainly intermediate slopes; there are quite a few black runs, but no double-blacks and not much that is easy. It's a few minutes' drive to Franconia in one direction and Lincoln in the other.

Loon Mountain Resort is a small, smart, modern resort just outside the sprawling town of Lincoln. The mountain (640m/2,100ft vertical) is mostly intermediate, though some fall-line runs merit their black grading. There is a long snowboard park.

Waterville Valley is a compact area with runs dropping either side of a broad, gentle ridge rising 615m/2,020ft above the lift base. There are a couple of short but genuine double-black-diamond mogul fields, but most of the slopes are intermediate. Boarders are well catered for. The village is a Disneyesque affair a couple of miles away down on the flat valley bottom.

YOU DON'T HAVE TO PAY FOR WHERE TO SKI AND SNOWBOARD

You can get the cost of this book back by booking your next holiday through Ski Solutions – the specialist ski and snowboard travel agent. See page 22.

And you can get the 2004 edition free by sending in a report on this season's holiday. The best 100 earn a free copy. Email and postal addresses at the front of the book.

SKI arrangements.com

Reservations
08700 110565
Bonsall, Matlock, DE4 2AJ

Good slopes, great après-ski, no village (yet)

What's new

The snowmaking capacity has been increased by 30%. A special snowmobile snowcross course for kids will open for 2002/03 – a miniature version of the extreme snowmobile competition courses.

MOUNTAIN FACTS

Altitude	355m-1285m
	1,165ft-4,215ft
Lifts	32
Pistes	1182 acres
Green	30%
Blue	39%
Black	31%
Snowmaking	
	70% of trails

➕ The biggest mountain in the east, matching some Colorado resorts, with terrain to suit everyone

➕ Lively après-ski, with lots of bar-restaurants offering happy hours and late-night action

➕ Excellent nursery slopes

➕ Comprehensive and very effective snowmaking

➕ Good childcare, although it's not a notably child-oriented resort

➖ No resort village: hotels, condos and restaurants are widely spread, mostly along the five-mile access road – a car is almost a necessity

➖ New England weather – highly changeable and can be very cold

➖ The trail network is complex, and there are lots of trail-crossings

➖ Terminally tedious for anyone who is not a skier or boarder

It's difficult to ignore Killington. It claims to have the largest mountain, the largest number of quad chairs, the largest grooming fleet and the longest season in the east and the world's biggest snowmaking installation. (As a result it tries to be the first resort in America to open, in October, but often shuts again shortly after.) It also claims to have America's longest lift and longest trail (a winding 16km/10 miles) and New England's steepest mogul slope (Outer Limits – 800m/0.5 miles long for a drop of 370m/1,210ft). Impressive by local standards. But it also has weekend and public holiday crowds and New England's changeable weather.

For those of us used to resorts with villages at the foot of the slopes, Killington is a bit of a shock. It has been planned to suit car drivers and day or weekend visitors. Most accommodation is away from the slopes on the long approach road. There's no real focus or centre and plans for a slope-side village at the Snowshed lift base have been put on hold. Surprisingly, however there are some lively eating places and nightspots that you have to drive or catch a bus to.

But if we were crossing the Atlantic for a holiday there are plenty of places we'd choose to go to ahead of Killington.

The resort

Killington is an extraordinary resort, especially to European eyes. Most of its hotels and restaurants are spread along a five-mile approach road. The nearest thing you'll find to a focus is the occasional set of traffic lights with a cluster of shops, though there is a concentration of buildings along a two-and-a-half mile stretch of the road. The resort caters mainly for day and weekend visitors who drive in from the east-coast cities (including a lot of New Yorkers). The car is king; provided you have one, getting around isn't that much of a hassle. There's also a good free shuttle-bus service during the day – it costs a dollar after 5pm.

Plans for a new resort village around the Grand Resort hotel at Snowshed have been put on hold. Practically all the other lodgings are a drive from a lift station – either the one at Snowshed or the Skyeship gondola station on the main highway 100, leading past the resort. Staying near the end of the access road is convenient for this and for outings to Pico, a separate little mountain owned by Killington, to be linked one day to Killington's Ram's Head mountain.

The mountains

Runs spread over a series of wooded peaks, all quite close together but giving the resort a basis for claiming to cover six mountains – or seven if you count Pico. A huge number of runs and an impressive number of lifts are crammed into a modest area. The result is a very complex network of runs, and signposting isn't always very clear. To some extent the terrain on its six sectors suits different abilities. But

LIFT PASSES

2001/02 prices in dollars

Killington Mountain Pass
Covers all lifts in the Killington and Pico ski areas.
Beginners See Schools/Guides
Main pass
1-day pass
59 (midweek)
62 (weekend)
6-day pass 288
Senior citizens
Over 64: 6-day pass 168
Children
Under 6: free
6-12: 6-day pass 168
13-18: 6-day pass 258

skiclub.co.uk
0845 45 807 80
skiers@skiclub.co.uk

there are also areas where a mixed ability group would be quite happy, and there are easy runs from top to bottom of each peak. Some runs of all levels are left to form bumps; there is half-and-half grooming on selected trails; and terrain features – ridges, bumps, quarter-pipes – are created.

Killington has also created areas that are called Fusion Zones – thinned-out forest areas, where you pick your own line. These areas are not groomed or patrolled – and they come in blue and single- and double-black-diamond grades. We found them great fun.

The piste map is one of the largest and most fact-packed we've ever come across. But this makes it unwieldy and awkward to handle.

THE SLOPES
Complicated
The Killington Base area has chairs radiating to three of the six peaks – **Snowdon, Killington** (the high-point of the area) and **Skye** – the last also accessible by gondola starting beside US highway 4. Novices and families head for the other main base area, which has two parts: Snowshed, at the foot of the main beginner slope, served by several parallel chairs; and Rams Head, just across the road up to Killington Base, where there's a Family Center at the foot of the entirely gentle **Rams Head** mountain.

The two remaining peaks are behind Skye Peak; they can be reached by trails from Killington and Skye, but each also has a lift base accessible by road. **Bear Mountain** is the expert's

hill, served by two quad chairs from its mid-mountain base area. The sixth 'peak', **Sunrise**, is a slight blip on the mountainside, with a short triple chair up from the Sunrise Village condos area. The area below Sunrise Village is used for snowmobile tours – from the old lift base just off highway 4.

SNOW RELIABILITY
Good if it's cold
Killington has a good snowfall record and a huge snowmaking system. But even that is no good if temperatures are too high to operate it. Bad weather can ruin a holiday even in mid-season. A reporter who had new powder each night in March 1999 went back at the same time in 2000 to find people skiing in shorts and T-shirts on the few runs that were open. A February visitor told of 'everything from frostbite warnings to pouring rain'.

FOR EXPERTS
Some challenges
The main areas that experts head for are Killington Peak, where there is a handful of genuine double-diamond fall-line runs under the two chair-lifts, and Bear Mountain. Most of the slopes here are single blacks but Outer Limits, under the main quad chair, is a double-diamond claimed to be 'the steepest mogul slope in the east'. We suspect there are steeper runs at Stowe and Smugglers' Notch. There are two or three worthwhile blacks on Snowdon, too. The Fusion Zones on Skye and Snowdon are well worth seeking out. But one reporter thought

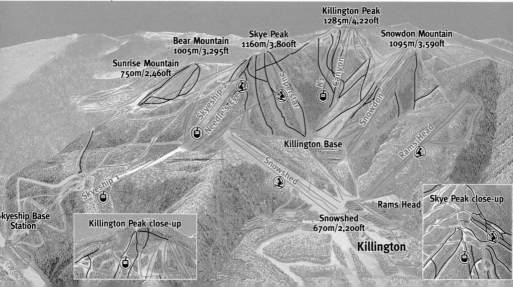

SCHOOLS/GUIDES

2001/02 prices in dollars

Perfect Turn clinics
7 days
2hr from 9.30, 10.15, or 1.30 31
Learn ski clinics
(incl lift pass, equipment and use of Discovery Centre)
1 day 70
3 days 159
Children's classes
Ages: 4 to 6 (incl lift pass)
half day 8.30-12 noon or 12.30-4pm 62
full day 89
Ages: 7 to 12 (excl lift pass)
half day: 9.30-11.30 or 1pm-3pm 93
full day 121
Private lessons
1hr, 2hr, 3hr or full day
85 for 1hr (129 for 2 people), 145 for 2hr (199 for 2 people), 199 for 3hr (285 for 2 people), 349 for full day (445 for 2 people)

CHILDCARE

A Family Center at Rams Head was built a few years ago. The Friendly Penguin nursery takes kids from age six weeks to six years – reservations required. Outside the door is the Snow Play Park, with magic carpet lift and handle tow-lift. There are ski classes for several age groups.

many of the black runs overclassified: 'Some would be red in Europe and comfortably skied by an intermediate.'

FOR INTERMEDIATES
Navigation problems?
There are lots of easy cruising blue and green runs all over the slopes, except on Bear Mountain, where the single blacks present a little more of a challenge for intermediates. Snowdon is a splendid area for those who like to vary their diet. There's a blue-classified Fusion Zone on Rams Head. Finding your way around the complicated network of trails may be tricky, though. One reporter liked Pico a lot but complained that the blue run down was more difficult than some blacks.

FOR BEGINNERS
Splendid
The facilities for complete beginners are excellent. The Snowshed slope is one vast nursery slope served by three chair-lifts and a very slow drag-lift. Rams Head also has excellent gentle slopes. The ski school runs a special, purpose-built Discovery Center just for first-time skiers and boarders – they introduce you to the equipment, show you videos and provide refreshments.

FOR CROSS-COUNTRY
Two main options
Extensive cross-country loops are available at two specialist 'resorts' – Mountain Meadows down on US highway 4, and Mountain Top Ski Touring, just a short drive away at Chittenden.

QUEUES
Weekend crowds
Killington gets a lot of weekend and public holiday business, but at other times the slopes and lifts are likely to be quiet. One New Year reporter told of 'a madhouse with overcrowded slopes, and a 20-minute crawl up the access road', and the gondola to Killington Peak and the Rams Head

chair can get oversubscribed. Overcrowded slopes are more of a problem than lift queues.

MOUNTAIN RESTAURANTS
Bearable base lodges
There are only two real mountain restaurants. We have mixed reports on the one at the top of Killington Peak, in what was the top station of the old gondola. Max's Place, on Sunrise, has table-service burgers, pasta, salad etc, and is highly recommended by a reporter for 'escaping the squalor of the other on-mountain eating places'. Each of the lift base stations has an eatery, of which we found the one at Killington Base Lodge the least dreary and crowded.

SCHOOLS AND GUIDES
In search of the Perfect Turn
The philosophy of the Perfect Turn school is to build on your strengths rather than correct your mistakes, and it seems to work for most people. There is a special Discovery Center for beginners, where you start and finish in a dedicated beginners' building with easy chairs, coffee, videos and help with choosing and fitting your equipment.

FACILITIES FOR CHILDREN
Fine in practice
There is a Family Center at the Rams Head base, which takes kids from six weeks and will introduce them to skiing from age two years. The daughter of one of the editors learned here and approved of it.

Staying there

HOW TO GO
Wide choices
There is a wide choice of places to stay. As well as hotels and condos, there are a few chalets.
Hotels There are a few places near the lifts, but most are a drive or bus-ride away, down Killington Road or on US4.

boarding A cool resort like Killington has to take boarding seriously, and it does. There are three terrain-parks, a super-pipe and a boarder-cross course. And there are terrain features scattered around the area, and parts of the mountain have been reshaped to cut out some of the unpleasant flats on contouring green runs. Several big-name board events are held here. For less competent boarders, there are excellent beginner slopes, and plenty of friendly high-speed (ie slow-loading) chair-lifts – and the Perfect Turn Discovery Center caters just for beginners.

GETTING THERE

Air Boston, transfer 2½hr.

ACTIVITIES

Indoor Killington Grand Resort Hotel has massage, fitness centre, outdoor pool, hot-tub, sauna, aerobics. Cinemas, bowling at Rutland **Outdoor** Skating, snowboarding, sledding, sleigh rides, snow-shoe tours

Central reservations phone number
Call 1 800 621 6867 (toll-free from within the US).

Phone numbers
From distant parts of the US, add the prefix 1 802.
From abroad, add the prefix +1 802.

TOURIST OFFICE

Postcode VT 05751
t 422 3333
f 422 6113
info@killington.com
www.killington.com

(((④ **Cortina Inn** 20 minutes away on US4, near Pico; pool, 'excellent food, but poor soundproofing'.
(((④ **Grand Resort** Swanky resort-owned place at Snowshed, with outdoor pool and health club.
(((④ **Inn of the Six Mountains** Couple of miles down Killington Road; 'spacious rooms, good pool'.
(((③ **Red Rob Inn** Short drive from slopes – 'good restaurant, a cut above the usual motel style'.
(((③ **North Star Lodge** Well down Killington Road; 'good budget accommodation'.

EATING OUT
You name it
There are all sorts of restaurants spread along the Killington Road, from simple pizza or pasta through to 'fine dining' places. They get very crowded at weekends and many don't take reservations. Many of the nightspots mentioned below serve food for at least part of the evening.

The local menu guide is essential reading. Claude's Choices, the Grist Mill, Charity's and the Cortina and Red Rob Inns have been recommended by recent reporters.

APRES-SKI
The beast of the east
Killington has a well-deserved reputation for a vibrant après-ski scene; many of its short-stay visitors are clearly intent on making the most

↑ Killington's powerful lift system means no midweek queues – but on busy weekends it can mean crowded pistes
AMERICAN SKIING COMPANY / NATHAN BILOW

of their few days (or nights) here.

Although there are bars at the base lodges, keen après-skiers head down Killington Road to one of the lively places scattered along its 8km/5 mile length. From 3pm it's cheap drinks and free munchies, then in the early evening it's serious dining time, then later on the real action starts (and admission charges kick in). Most of the places mentioned here would also rate a mention in Eating out.

The train-themed Casey's Caboose is said to have the best 'wings' in town. Charity's is another lively bar, with an interior apparently lifted from a turn-of-the-century Parisian brothel. The Wobbly Barn is a famous live-music place that rivals Jackson's Mangy Moose for the position of America's leading après-ski venue. The Pickle Barrel caters for a younger crowd, with theme nights and loud music. The Outback complex has something for everyone, from pizzas and free massages to disco and live bands.

OFF THE SLOPES
Rent a car
If there is a less amusing resort in which to spend time doing things other than skiing or boarding, we have yet to find it. Make sure you have a car, as well as a book.

Smugglers' Notch   315m/1,030ft

Fine fun for families – but those not saddled with kids should stay away

580

What's new

A new water reservoir has increased the snowmaking capacity by 40%. Five new gladed trails – spread across all three mountains – were added for 2001/02. And a new super-pipe has been built.

There's a new Learn to Ski & Ride Development Center on Morse Mountain offering support and a place to relax for total beginners. The ski school has introduced night classes for beginners. And anyone who buys four days or more of lessons gets an extra day free.

- ➕ Excellent children's facilities
- ➕ Lots of slope-side accommodation
- ➕ Varied slopes with runs for all abilities
- ➕ No queues
- ➕ Great for beginners, with excellent ski school

- ➖ Family orientation may be too much for some child-free visitors
- ➖ New England weather – highly changeable, and can be very cold
- ➖ Limited local slopes
- ➖ No proper mountain restaurants
- ➖ No hotels – condos only
- ➖ Little après-ski atmosphere in the village, and few off-slope diversions

Smuggs hits the family target squarely, with a constant round of early-evening activities, sympathetic instructors, comprehensive childcare, a generally child-friendly layout and some long, quiet, easy runs. There are challenging slopes, too, but mileage-hungry intermediates should go elsewhere.

THE RESORT
Smugglers' Notch is about the nearest thing you'll find in the US to a French-style purpose-built family resort – except that it doesn't look so bad. The village isn't genuinely traffic-free – you may have to tangle with traffic to get to the childcare centre, even – but it comes close, and once installed in your condo you can happily do without a car (much of the accommodation is near to or on the slopes). Those not afflicted with children could find the family orientation of the resort a bit overpowering: you may find it's difficult to get away from Billy Bob Bear and pals.

The resort is energetically managed and produces a constant flow of developments designed to tighten its grip on the family market, on which it is entirely focused. Most years it seems to get voted 'North American family resort of the year' by at least one American skiing publication.

THE MOUNTAIN
Smuggs has varied and satisfying slopes, spread over three hills – Morse, above the village (with the newish Morse Highlands area off to the left), and Madonna and Sterling off to the right, reached by green links. From Sterling you can ski to Stowe (see separate chapter), but the on/off lift pass-sharing arrangement with Stowe is currently off, and the run is classified as a backcountry route.
Slopes There are some real challenges as well as easy cruising, and a worthwhile vertical of 800m/2,610ft. It's blissfully quiet on the mountain except at weekends and holidays. It's undeniably a small area, though.
Snow reliability Snow reliability is good, subject to the inherent variability of New England weather. And the snowmaking has again been improved.
Experts There are challenges for experts. We were impressed by the two or three double-diamond runs on

MOUNTAIN FACTS

Altitude	315m-1110m
	1,030ft-3,640ft
Lifts	8
Pistes	1,000 acres
Green	22%
Blue	53%
Black	25%
Snowmaking	
	141 acres

Central reservations phone number

Call 644 8851.

From the UK ring 0800 169 8219.

Phone numbers

From distant parts of the US, add the prefix 1 802.

From abroad, add the prefix +1 802.

TOURIST OFFICE

Postcode
VT 05464-9537
t 644 8851
f 644 2713
smuggs@smuggs.com
www.smuggs.com

Madonna, and they have recently opened The Black Hole – the only triple-diamond run in the east, they say. You can go off through the trees anywhere within the resort boundary – but these areas are not patrolled.

Intermediates There are intermediate runs of every grade; there just aren't many of them.

Beginners It's a great area for beginners. One of the chair-lifts out of the village runs at half speed, and the runs it accesses are of an ideal gradient. Morse Highlands adds another tailor-made novice area. And the higher lifts take you to long easy runs that even 'never-evers' can tackle during their first week.

Snowboarding Smuggs encourages snowboarding, and has a couple of impressive terrain-parks and a new super-pipe.

Cross-country The 27km/17 miles of trails may be a bit limited for expert skiers.

Queues We encountered no queues, and away from weekends we'd be surprised if anyone else did.

Mountain restaurants There are no real mountain restaurants, but there is a new warming hut with snacks at the top of the Prohibition Park half-pipe and the new lodge at Morse Highlands serves food. Most people go back to base for lunch.

Schools and guides At least one reporter judges the ski school (or 'Snow Sport University') to be 'outstanding', and it has often been

voted the best in North America. Among its bright ideas are private lessons for a parent and child, with the idea that the parent learns how to help the child develop while having fun.

Facilities for children Smuggs aims to be simply the best for children. The mountain is child-friendly, offering excitement with safety – with a special jolly kids' trail map. There's a terrain-park for kids, and little forest glades where even tinies can be taken 'off-piste'. Alice's Wonderland Child Enrichment Center is a comprehensive nursery. The school arrangements are very good, too, with childcare before and after sessions.

STAYING THERE

How to go There are no hotels in the resort itself – though there are some within driving distance.

Self-catering There are lots of comfortable condos on or near the slopes, none very far from the snow.

Eating out There are a couple of restaurants in the resort, including the cosy Hearth and Candle, and others a short drive down the road to the outside world – we and the kids enjoyed an outing to Banditos. Babysitters can be arranged.

Après-ski The adult après-ski possibilities are about the most limited we have come across. We hear good reports of the teen centre.

Off the slopes There is very little to do off the slopes. Organised day trips to Vermont or Montreal are possible.

Smugglers' Notch

581

Madonna Mountain
1110m/3,640ft

Sterling Mountain
925m/3,040ft

Stowe

Mid Station

Morse Mountain
685m/2,250ft

Mid Stations

Morse
Highlands

Smugglers' Notch
315m/1,030ft

Charming Vermont town some way from its small but serious mountain

WHAT IT COSTS

(((((5)

HOW IT RATES

The slopes

Snow	***
Extent	*
Experts	***
Intermediates	****
Beginners	****
Convenience	*
Queues	****
Restaurants	**

The rest

Scenery	***
Resort charm	****
Off-slope	*

What's new

There's a new miniature terrain-park for beginner freestylers (with a special emphasis on learning to ride snowdecks). And there's a new snowboarder-specific resort website: www.ridestowe.com

A 10-year development project is still in the planning phase.

MOUNTAIN FACTS

Altitude	390m-1110m
	1,280ft-3,640ft
Lifts	11
Pistes	480 acres
Green	16%
Blue	59%
Black	25%
Snowmaking	
	350 acres

- ➕ Cute tourist town in classic New England style
- ➕ Some good slopes for all abilities, including serious challenges
- ➕ Few queues
- ➕ Excellent cross-country trails
- ➕ Great children's facilities

- ➖ Town is a shuttle-bus ride or a short drive from the slopes
- ➖ One of the mountains is a short shuttle-bus-ride from the other two
- ➖ New England weather – highly changeable, and can be very cold
- ➖ Limited local slopes
- ➖ Weekend queues
- ➖ No après-ski atmosphere

Stowe is one of New England's cutest little towns, its main street lined with dinky clapboard shops and restaurants; you could find no sharper contrast to the other New England resorts we feature. Its mountain, six miles away, is another New England classic: something for everyone, but not much of it.

THE RESORT

Stowe is a picture-postcard New England town – a real community and a popular spot for tourists year-round, with bijou 'specialty' shops lining its sidewalks and more 3- and 4-diamond hotels and restaurants than any other place in New England except Boston. The slopes of Mount Mansfield, Vermont's snow-capped (though mainly wooded) highest peak, are a 15-minute drive away and much of the resort's accommodation is along the road out to it. There's a good day-time shuttle-bus service but a car is recommended for flexibility.

THE MOUNTAIN

There are three different sectors, two linked by blue runs mid-mountain and green ones at the base, the third (Spruce Peak) a short shuttle-ride away (there are plans for a lift link, but it's not imminent).

Slopes The main sector, served by a trio of chair-lifts from Mansfield Base Lodge, is dominated by the famous Front Four – a row of seriously steep double-black-diamond runs. But there is plenty of easier stuff, too, including long green runs down to the alternative lift base at Toll House.

An eight-seat gondola serves the next sector: easy-intermediate runs with one black alternative – plus the short but very steep Waterfall, under the gondola at the top.

The third area, Spruce Peak, has the main nursery area at the bottom, with

a slow chair-lift to mid-mountain and another beyond that. 'Possibly the slowest chairs in the world,' says a reporter. The old link with Smugglers' Notch, from the top of this sector over the hill, is now a backcountry route. The pass-sharing agreement has also been abandoned.

There are free daily mountain tours with a mountain host.

Snow reliability Snow reliability is helped by snowmaking on practically all the blue (and some black) runs of the main sectors, and on lower Spruce Peak.

Experts The Front Four and their variants on the top half of the main sector present a real challenge – and there are others in this sector. There are various gladed areas, three of them marked on the map.

Intermediates The usual New England reservation applies: the terrain is limited in extent; there's also a severe shortage of ordinary black runs (as opposed to double diamonds).

Beginners The nursery slopes and long green runs are great. 'Spruce Peak is one of the best beginner/early skier areas we've seen,' says a report. Progression to longer green runs means moving over to the main sector, where there are splendid long greens down to Toll House.

Snowboarding Stowe attracts many snowboarders and has two terrain-parks and a half-pipe. Beginners learn on special customised boards at the Burton Method Center on Spruce Peak.

Central reservations phone number
Call 1 877 317 8693 (toll-free from within the US).

From within the UK call 0800 731 9279.

Phone numbers
From distant parts of the US, add the prefix 1 802.
From abroad, add the prefix +1 802.

TOURIST OFFICE
Postcode VT 05672
t 253 3500
f 253 3406
info@stowe.com
www.stowe.com

Cross-country There are excellent cross-country centres scattered around the landscape (including the musically famous Trapp Family Lodge), with lots of connected trails – 35km/22 miles of groomed and 40km/25 miles of back country trails.

Queues The area is largely free of queues mid-week but we've had reports of 25-minute queues at weekends.

Mountain restaurants Cliff House, at the top of the gondola, is a lofty room with table-service and good food and views. Midway Café near the base of the gondola has a BBQ deck and table-service inside. The Octagon Web Café, at the top of the main sector, is a small cafeteria.

Schools and guides A recent reporter was disappointed by the ski school – but this was partly because he had a different instructor every day, which is common in the US.

Facilities for children There are excellent facilities and the nursery takes children from age six months to six years.

STAYING THERE

How to go There are hotels in and around Stowe itself and various points along the road to the slopes, some with Austrian or Scandinavian names and styles.

Hotels 1066 Ye Olde England Inne is recommended by reporters (despite the appalling name). Stowehof Inn and Green Mountain Inn are also recommended. The smart Inn at the Mountain, at the Toll House lift base of Mount Mansfield, is the only slope-side accommodation, with chair-lift access to the main sector of slopes.

Self-catering There is a reasonable range of condos available for rent.

Eating out There are restaurants of every kind. The Cliff House at the top of the gondola is open for dinner.

Après-ski Après-ski is muted – Stowe reportedly goes to bed early. There's a good cinema with new releases.

Off the slopes Stowe is a pleasant town in which to spend time off the slopes – at least if you like shopping. A trip to the Burlington shopping mall is recommended for more serious retail therapy.

Stowe

583

Mount Mansfield

Octagon Web Cafe
1100m/3,610ft

Cliff House
1110m/3,640ft

Smugglers' Notch →

Spruce Peak
1035m/3,390ft

TollRunner

Midway Base Lodge

Gondola Base
475m/1,560ft

Mansfield Base Lodge

Spruce Base Lodge

Toll House

Sunday River 245m/800ft

Quiet slopes and the biggest snowmaking system in New England

WHAT IT COSTS

HOW IT RATES

The slopes

Snow	✱✱✱
Extent	✱✱
Experts	✱✱
Intermediates	✱✱✱✱
Beginners	✱✱✱✱
Convenience	✱✱✱
Queues	✱✱✱✱
Restaurants	✱✱✱

The rest

Scenery	✱✱✱
Resort charm	✱✱
Off-slope	✱

What's new

For 2002/03 yet more snowmaking is planned, as is a new ski adventure trail for families on North Peak. There will be a special deck at the top of Jordan Bowl pointing out the local peaks. And the White Cap Base Lodge will have a new bar.

For 2001/02, free buses were set up between the resort and the village, running until 1am, and a new hi-tech pipecutter was purchased.

➕ Some convenient slope-side accommodation

➕ Some good runs for all abilities

➕ Decent natural snow record with extensive snowmaking back up

➕ Lots of scope for cross-country skiing in the area

➕ No queues

➖ Scattered slope-side developments mean no village atmosphere

➖ Relatively small slopes

➖ No real mountain restaurants

➖ Quiet après-ski scene

➖ Limited off-slope diversions

Sunday River was one of the pioneers of snowmaking, and over 90% of its trails are served by it. So the snow should be as good here as anywhere in the east. The terrain is varied and quite extensive. But it lacks village ambience.

THE RESORT
Sunday River is where the American Skiing Company (which owns several other US resorts) started and where it still has its HQ. Despite this, there isn't really a slope-side village yet – there are various developments scattered around the slopes – so there isn't much village ambience.

The plan is for the area around the Jordan Grand hotel to become the focus of the resort, with shops, bars, restaurants, theatre, nightclub and even a village green and pond. For now, Bethel is the nearest small town, a 10-minute drive away; it's a pleasant place with a few shops and a handful of restaurants and bars. The resort attracts quite a lot of British school groups, especially at half-term and Easter.

THE MOUNTAINS
The slopes range over about 5km/3 miles from east to west and across eight different peaks. It does feel like a reasonably extensive network of trails and glades – 127 at the last count – and there are numerous base areas, parking lots and accommodation units scattered here and there.

Slopes The White Cap base marks the eastern extremity of the system and is handy for the Grand Summit hotel, the half-pipe and other evening activities. The peaks around the main base areas are fairly packed with lifts and trails. The Jordan Grand hotel is at the western limit of the system, and in general the western sector (Aurora, Oz and Jordan Bowl) has far fewer lifts and runs and a more remote and backwoods feel.

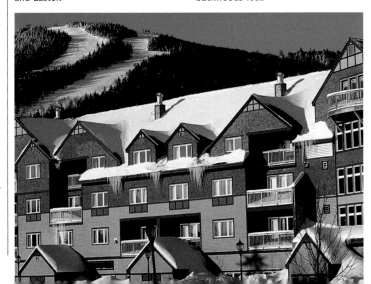

SUNDAY RIVER SKI RESORT

The Jordan Grand at the foot of Jordan Bowl is one of the resort's two widely separated slope-side hotels ➔

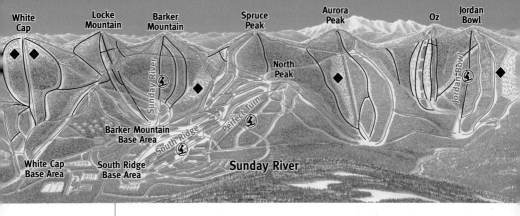

White Cap | Locke Mountain | Barker Mountain | Spruce Peak | Aurora Peak | Oz | Jordan Bowl

North Peak

Barker Mountain Base Area

Sunday River

White Cap Base Area | South Ridge Base Area

Sunday River

MOUNTAIN FACTS

Altitude	245m-955m
	800ft-3,140ft
Lifts	18
Pistes	660 acres
Green	25%
Blue	35%
Black	40%
Snowmaking	
	607 acres

Central reservations phone number
Call 1 800 543 2754 (toll-free from within the US).

Phone numbers
From distant parts of the US, add the prefix 1 207.
From abroad, add the prefix +1 207.

TOURIST OFFICE
Postcode ME 04217
t 824 3000
f 824 5110
info@sundayriver.com
www.sundayriver.com

Snow reliability Snow reliability is good: a decent natural snow record is backed up by a high-capacity, high-tech system for making and grooming man-made stuff.

Experts There are challenging narrow, often mogulled double-blacks on White Cap and Barker Mountain, and there is excellent glade skiing on Aurora, Oz and Jordan Bowl. Indeed, 40% of the trails are classified black.

Intermediates It's generally a good resort for intermediates, who will enjoy cruising around on a series of nice rolling blues (often deserted in mid-week). There are some not too fearsome glades to tempt the bold.

Beginners South Ridge is a well-organised area for beginners, with good, easy runs to progress to.

Snowboarding Boarders will find no fewer than four terrain parks (Rocking Chair, AMEX, Starlight and Who-ville) and a super-pipe, quarter-pipe and mini-pipe.

Cross-country In and around Bethel there are three cross-country centres with a total of around 140km/90 miles of trails.

Queues Mid-week queues are non-existent – indeed most lifts and slopes are deserted. Even on busy weekends you should be okay if you stick to the four high-speed quads.

Mountain restaurants There are none, but there are good, civilised table-service places at the Jordan Grand and Grand Summit hotels, as well as the usual self-service places.

Schools and guides Ski school is not a term they use at Sunday River but there is a series of 'Perfect Turn' clinics available. A reporter who took a group of 40 schoolchildren said the ski instructors were 'overstretched at half-term but still superb, and one even bought his class baseball caps'.

Facilities for children The Grand Summit and South Ridge Centre house the main children's facilities. There are also family entertainment centres called the White Cap and Big Adventure (see Après-ski).

STAYING THERE
There is slope-side accommodation but some people prefer to stay in Bethel – a 10-minute drive from the ski area (with free buses until 1am).

How to go There are numerous inns, lodges, motels and B&Bs in and around Bethel.

Hotels The main slope-side hotels are the Jordan Grand and the Grand Summit. There's a dorm as well as normal rooms at the Snow Cap Inn.

Self-catering The Brookside condos have been recommended. There are plenty of others too.

Eating out As well as options at the slopes (see Mountain Restaurants) there are seven restaurants in Bethel including 'fine-dining', a specialist vegetarian restaurant, a Chinese, and pizza places.

Après-ski Après-ski in Sunday River is quiet. Bumps pub often has live bands. A reporter recommends the Foggy Goggle bar, which also has live music, and the Matterhorn Steak Bar in Bethel (large steaks, local beers, good atmosphere). There's a brew-pub. The White Cap Fun Center has floodlit tubing, sledding and ice skating, while Big Adventure has laser tag and rock climbing. There are guided snow-shoe tours on two evenings a week. There's also a four-screen cinema and a games arcade.

Off the slopes Apart from the likes of snowmobiling, snow-shoeing, tubing, ice-fishing and swimming, there are a few antique and craft shops.

Sunday River

585

We were a bit sceptical about Canadian skiing when it first started to find a place on the British market at the start of the 1990s. Canada seemed to offer very few resorts worthy of international attention, and the main one – Whistler – seemed uncomfortably low. But we were soon converted, once we had experienced the friendly welcome, the spectacular scenery, the impressive terrain, the low prices and – last but certainly not least – the frequent and heavy dumps of snow. It is, you'll agree, a compelling combination. Since our conversion, we've enjoyed many of our best days on skis in western Canada – including some a couple of seasons back, when locals were complaining about snow conditions being the worst in living memory. Basically, people in western Canada don't really know what bad snow conditions are. And when the snow is good – as it was last season – it is phenomenal.

A few seasons ago we drove from Whistler to Banff, calling in at lots of smaller resorts on the way. The whole trip took two weeks and for eight consecutive days in the middle it snowed. It snowed and snowed and snowed. It made driving from resort to resort tricky, as we stuck to our normal scheme of driving at night after getting in a full day on the slopes. But the skiing was spectacular – day after day of dry, light powder. That's a normal winter in western Canada.

In an average year Whistler, for example, gets 360 inches of snow and it snows (or rains, at resort level!) for half the days in the season. That makes for superb conditions on the slopes. Inland at Banff-Lake Louise you might not get quite the same frequency of snow, but it stays in great condition because the air is drier and temperatures are lower. You get a better chance of blue skies there – but also a higher chance of a day or two of very low temperatures (–20°C or less).

So you go to western Canada for the skiing or boarding, not the sunbathing. If you prefer long lunches on sun-drenched mountain restaurant terraces, stick to March in the Alps. If you want a good chance of hitting powder, put Canada high on your list of possible destinations.

If you really want untracked powder and are feeling flush, there is nothing to beat Canada's amazing heli- and snowcat skiing operations. The main difference is that the former is faster paced and more expensive than the latter. But with both, you are taken to the middle of nowhere in a deserted mountain wilderness and then let loose with a guide who takes you down untracked slopes to another spot in the middle of nowhere, where you are picked up and taken to the top of another mountain and another untracked run. And so it goes on! You can do it by the day, but the hedonistic option is to book a few days or a week in a luxury lodge run by the heli-skiing or snowcat operation, eating gourmet dinners and stepping out of the door each morning straight into the chopper or snowcat.

If you can't afford the £3,000 plus a

CANADA

588

week that this would cost, you can always try a day for £200 plus. But if you resist heli-skiing or snowcat heaven, you'll find a holiday in Canada can be very cheap. Package prices start at around £400 for a week to western Canada (though that probably involves sleeping four to a room). These prices are made possible by cheap direct and charter flights to the key airports and the use of accommodation in resorts where winter is low season compared with summer. And once you get there you'll find the cost of meals and drinks very low compared with the Alps. Lift passes fall mid-way between Alpine and American price levels.

Another difference you'll notice compared with the Alps is the people. Not only do they speak English but they are friendly, and have the American service culture – 'the customer is king'. You'll find mountain hosts to show you around the slopes, immaculately groomed runs, civilised lift queues, lots of fast quad chair-lifts, piste maps available at the bottom of most lifts, and cheerful, helpful staff.

In the west you'll also find spectacular scenery (when the clouds clear) to rival that of the Alps and far superior to anything you'll find in the US. You may also find an amazing variety of wildlife, especially in the Rockies and the interior of British Columbia.

For us, the main attraction of eastern Canada is that the resorts are in the heart of the province of Québec, where the French culture is predominant – it makes for a unique ambience. Québec is now attracting a fair number of British winter visitors, including school groups. It also has the attraction of a shorter flight time – but it does have the disadvantage of extremes of weather.

SNOWPIX.COM / CHRIS GILL

One of the minor resorts starting to find its feet on the UK market: Fernie ↓

Western Canada

For international visitors to Canada, the main draw is the west. It has fabulous scenery, good snow and a wonderful sense of the great outdoors. The big names of Whistler, Banff and Lake Louise capture most of the British market at present, but there are lots of worthwhile smaller resorts that more adventurous travellers are now starting to explore. We recommend renting a car and combining two or more of these resorts, perhaps with a couple of days on virgin powder served by helicopters or snowcats as well. You'll have the holiday of a lifetime. Smokers should be warned that BC has banned smoking in all public buildings (ie restaurants etc).

Five of the smaller resorts you're most likely to want to visit for a while now get their own chapters: Big White, BC's highest ski area, and second in size to Whistler; Fernie, with a deserved reputation for great powder and a fast-developing mountain village; Jasper, in the spectacular Jasper National Park, with skiing at nearby Marmot Basin; Panorama, with a big vertical and an attractive new village at the foot of the slopes; and Kicking Horse, the new kid on the block – formerly known as Whitetooth, the mountain has been transformed by the installation of a big gondola.

There are quite a few other resorts that you might want to include in a tour of this area.

Kimberley Alpine Resort is the most accessible – about 90 minutes from Fernie and three hours from Banff. Like Fernie, it's a recent addition to the portfolio of Resorts of the Canadian Rockies, owners of Lake Louise.

At the mountain there are in practice two base areas. The original one is not quite at the bottom of the hill; there are two old chairs and a T-bar here (though they are no longer regularly used), and a range of lodgings including the 'lovely' NorthStar Chalets (condos). On the flat ground below this, a new village is being built, served by a fast quad that is now the resort's staple lift. This set-up may work eventually, but at present it requires everyone using this chair to

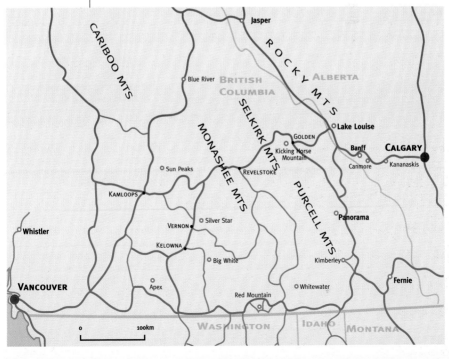

descend a steep, traffic-polished and congested final slope to get back to the lower level. Not ideal.

The new village is at present very limited, but includes the comfortable and very convenient Trickle Creek Residence Inn by Marriott (catchy, eh?), the 'superb' Polaris condos and a couple of restaurants.

The town of Kimberley, about five minutes' drive away, is known for its synthetic and indescribably naff 'Bavarian theme', but is reported to contain some good restaurants.

Kimberley's terrain offers a mix of blue and black runs (plus the occasional green) and a vertical of 750m/2,470ft. In addition to the lifts up the front there are basically two other slow chairs (one is a double discarded from Lake Louise). The runs – all in forest of varying density – are spread over two rather featureless hills. There are only a few short double-diamonds, but grading tends to understate difficulty, and many of the single-diamonds are quite challenging. The resort has a reputation for good powder, although it doesn't get huge amounts by the standards of this region. Further expansion is planned.

There are several resorts clustered around the Okanagan valley, of which the aforementioned Big White is one.

Silver Star, above the town of Vernon, is now in the same ownership as Big White, and helicopter shuttles are offered between the two resorts. It's a recently developed 'gaslight-era' 1890s-style village right on the slopes, now embarking on a programme of expansion; for this season a new fast quad is being installed to open up an additional 600 acres of slopes in the Silver Woods area. At present the wooded mountain has two main linked faces: the south face around the village has mainly easy/intermediate slopes served by a fast quad of 480m/1,570ft vertical, due to be replaced by a six-pack for this season; the back north face is a splendid bowl of easy runs along the rim and black and double-black trails dropping into the middle to meet the 630m/2,070ft-vertical fast quad.

Sun Peaks, near Kamloops, was known as Tod Mountain. Now major investment has created a cute, car-free, Tirolean-style slope-side village and good intermediate and beginner terrain to go with the steeps that used to dominate. The 880m/2,900ft vertical is

claimed to be the biggest in the BC interior; the mountain, open at the top and densely wooded lower down, has a balance of blue and black runs at top and bottom and a couple of areas of genuinely double-black stuff. Novices are safely tucked away on their own hill. The news for 2002/03 is that Mt Morrissey across the valley is to be opened up by construction of a fast quad, taking the resort's lift-served skiable area to an impressive 3,400 acres. Trails were cut on this hill some years back – we skied it by snowcat back in 1998 – and it will be a worthwhile addition to the area. The resort is promising an intriguing new style of slope here: groomed glades.

Probably the least compelling of the Okanagan resorts is **Apex**, a family-oriented place with a modern resort at the foot of its slopes and good views from the top, 610m/2,000ft higher.

Finally, there are a couple of resorts tucked away in the mountains close to the US border.

Red Mountain is up there with Fernie and other cult powder paradises in our estimation. There are green and red runs, but it's the black and double-black stuff that is the real attraction. We loved the terrain here – mostly in trees, and as steep as you can handle. Granite Mountain is a conical peak with more-or-less separate faces of blue, black and double-black steepness, and a total vertical of 880m/2,890ft – all served by a couple of triple chairs. Next-door Red Mountain itself is half the size and has only a lone double chair, but is no less interesting. There's accommodation close to the slopes or a couple of miles away in Rossland, a simple little town that has bred countless Canadian ski racers. No wonder.

Whitewater, not far away, is well worth a look in and an absolute must after a storm. Tucked even further into the ranges than Red Mountain, Whitewater's bottomless powder elicits rave responses from those in the know. Accommodation is found in the charming historic town of Nelson.

Western Canada is also home to the world's most famous **heli-skiing** operations, where you can stay for a week in a luxurious lodge and be whirled up to virgin powder for several runs a day – at a cost of £2,500 or more (plus flights from your starting point). Or you can try heli-skiing for a day from many resorts.

Banff
1385m/4,530ft

A winter wonderland with wildlife

591

WHAT IT COSTS

(((((4)

HOW IT RATES

The slopes

Snow	****
Extent	****
Experts	****
Intermediates	****
Beginners	***
Convenience	*
Queues	****
Restaurants	***

The rest

Scenery	****
Resort charm	***
Off-slope	*****

➕ Spectacular high-mountain scenery – quite unlike the Colorado Rockies

➕ Lots of wildlife around the valley

➕ Lots of touristy shops

➕ Good-value lodging because winter is the area's low season

➕ Local slopes at Norquay limited

➕ Extensive slopes with excellent snow record at Sunshine, but ...

➖ Sunshine is a 20-minute drive or bus-ride away

➖ You'll probably want to take in Lake Louise, too – a 45-minute drive

➖ Can be very cold – and most lifts offer no protection

➖ Banff lacks ski resort atmosphere – though it's not an unattractive town

➖ Resort can seem over-full of Brits

Huge numbers of British skiers and boarders go to Banff. Price has been a key factor in getting us to make the trip, but that's only half the story: most visitors are delighted with what they find, and keen to go back.

It's not difficult to see why. The landscape is one of glaciers, jagged peaks and magnificent views, and the valleys are full of wildlife that you'll never see in Europe. The slopes have something for everyone, from steep couloirs to gentle cruising. The snow is some of the coldest, driest and most reliable you'll find anywhere in the world, and there's a lot of it (at Sunshine Village, at least). And there are the standard Canadian assets of people who are friendly and welcoming, and low prices for meals and other on-the-spot expenses.

For us, these factors count for more than the drawbacks. But then we, luckily, have never encountered the extremely low temperatures (–35°C is not unknown) that have left some early-season reporters feeling less convinced.

What's new

In Sunshine village a sixth quad chair will be in place for 2002/03, replacing the Wawa T-bar on Mount Standish.

The new eight-seater gondola to Sunshine Village is the world's fastest and longest single-cable gondola. It has almost double the capacity of the queue-prone old lift and has cut the journey time from the valley to mid-mountain by over 40% to under 13 minutes.

SKI BANFF/LAKE LOUISE / BILL MARSH

On Goat's Eye you can choose from easy blue on the right through to serious black on the left →

The resort

Banff is a big summer resort that happens to have two separate ski and snowboard areas. Norquay is a small nearby area overlooking the town. Sunshine Village, 20 minutes away, is a bigger mountain; despite the name, it's not a village (nor is it notably sunny) – it has just one small hotel at mid-mountain. Most visitors buy a three-area pass that means they can also spend some time at Lake Louise, 45 minutes away – now covered by a separate chapter.

Banff is spectacularly set, with several towering peaks rising up around its outskirts. There is lots of wildlife around; don't be surprised to find a herd of elk or long-horned sheep outside your hotel (though the town is now trying to keep elk away, for visitors' and their own sakes). In spring there may be bears along the highways.

Banff town has grown substantially since 1990, when it became independent of the Banff National Park authority. But it still consists basically

MOUNTAIN FACTS

For Norquay, Sunshine and Lake Louise, overed by the Tri-area pass

Altitude 1635m-2730m
5,370ft-8,950ft
Lifts 30
Pistes 7,558 acres
Green 25%
Blue 45%
Black 30%
Snowmaking
1,700 acres

For Norquay only

Altitude 1635m-2135m
5,370ft-7,000ft
Lifts 5
Pistes 190 acres
Green 20%
Blue 36%
Black 44%
Snowmaking
90%

For Sunshine only

Altitude 1660m-2730m
5,440ft-8,950ft
Lifts 12
Pistes 3,168 acres
Green 20%
Blue 50%
Black 30%
Snowmaking
none

WESTERN CANADA

592

of one long main street and a small network of side roads built in grid fashion, lined by clothing and souvenir shops (aimed mainly at summer visitors) and a few ski shops. The buildings are low-rise and some are attractively wood-clad. The town is pleasant enough, but it lacks genuine charm; it's a commercial tourist town, not another Aspen or Telluride.

Some of the Banff lodgings (even on the main Banff Avenue) are quite a distance from downtown. A car can be helpful here, especially in cold weather.

Unless you stay mid-mountain on Sunshine (see Staying up the mountain, at the end of the chapter), getting to the slopes means a drive or a bus-ride. Buses are free to Tri-area lift pass holders, frequent, generally reliable, and 'highly organised' – though, depending on the number of pickups, they can take twice as long as advertised. Buses are also arranged to the more distant major resorts of Panorama and Kicking Horse (see separate chapters) and the smaller (and closer) resorts of Nakiska and Fortress, and day-trip heli-skiing and boarding can be organised.

The mountains

The Sunshine Village slopes are set right on the Continental Divide and as a result get a lot of snow. Most of the slopes above the village are above the tree line and can be very cold and bleak during a snowfall or cold snap. Although there is a wooded sector served by the second section of the gondola and a couple of chairs, in bad weather you're better off elsewhere.

Norquay is much smaller. But it's worth a visit, especially in bad weather – it has wooded slopes to suit all abilities and the trails can be delightfully quiet.

THE SLOPES
Lots of variety

The main slopes of **Sunshine Village** are not visible from the base station: you ride a two-stage gondola, first to the base of the recently developed Goat's Eye Mountain, and then on to Sunshine Village itself. The old slow gondola was replaced by a faster and more capacious one last season.

Goat's Eye is served by one lift, a fast quad chair rising 580m/1,900ft. Although there are some blue runs, this is basically a black mountain, with some genuine double-blacks at the extremities. There has been talk of building an additional fast quad up the middle of the slopes to a point more or less on the tree line; this would make the area more useful in bad weather, but the plan is still awaiting approval.

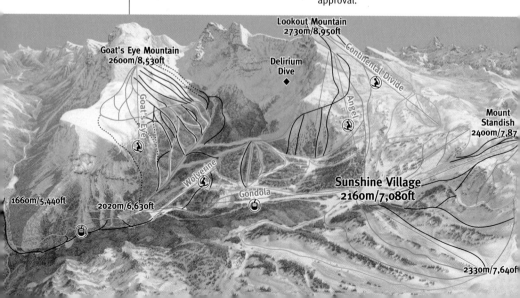

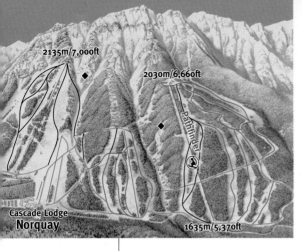

2135m/7,000ft

2030m/6,660ft

Pathfinder

Cascade Lodge
Norquay

1635m/5,370ft

LIFT PASSES

2002/03 prices in
Canadian dollars

Tri-area lift pass
Covers all lifts and
transport between
Banff, Lake Louise,
Norquay and
Sunshine Village,
available for 3 days
or more.
Main pass
3-day pass 186
6-day pass 372
Children
6-12: 6-day pass 128
Beginners First time
ski packages
including rental, pass
and lessons available
Day passes
(2001/02 prices)
Day passes excluding
transport to/from
individual areas (10
return)
Sunshine Village 59
Norquay 49
with reductions for
senior citizens (over
65 at Sunshine, over
55 at Norquay),
teenagers (13-17),
children (6-12). Kids
aged five and under
are free.
Short-term passes
Half-day pass for
individual areas of
Sunshine Village 49
Ski Banff @ Norquay
37 (or hourly rate at
any time of day,
minimum 2hr 26).
Night skiing also
available here on
Friday evenings (free
with tri-area pass).

Lifts fan out in all directions from
Sunshine Village, with short runs back
from Mount Standish and longer ones
from Lookout Mountain. Lookout is
where the Continental Divide is, with
the melting snow flowing in one
direction to the Pacific and in the other
to the Atlantic. From the top here
experts can pass through a gate (you
need an avalanche transceiver to get
through) and hike up to the extreme
terrain of Delirium Dive.

Many people ride the gondola down
at the end of the day. But the
2.5km/1.5 mile green run to the bottom
is a pretty cruise. If you go down while
the lifts are running you can take the
new Jackrabbit chair to cut out a flat
section, but the run gets crowded and
is much more enjoyable if you delay
your descent a bit. The Canyon Trail
provides a fun alternative for more
advanced skiers and riders. Marked
black diamond, it was judged by a
recent reporter 'no more than a blue
and a much more scenic route back'.

The slopes at **Norquay** are served
by a row of five parallel lifts. One trail
is floodlit at weekends.

SNOW RELIABILITY
Excellent
Sunshine Village claims '100% natural
snow', a neat reversal of the usual
snowmaking hype. Certainly, the lack
of snowmaking there has never been a

problem in our experience other than
in the exceptionally poor snow of
2000/01 – when the blues were still
fine but the blacks remained rocky
during our February visit. 'Three times
the snow' is another Sunshine slogan –
a cryptic reference to the fact that the
average snowfall here is 360 to 400
inches (depending on which figures
you believe) – as good as anything in
Colorado – compared with a modest
140 inches at Lake Louise and 120
inches on Norquay. But we're told the
Sunshine figures relate to Lookout, and
that Goat's Eye gets less. There is
snowmaking on 90% of pistes at
Norquay. So all in all, lack of snow is
unlikely to be a problem.

FOR EXPERTS
Pure pleasure
Both areas have satisfying terrain for
good skiers and boarders.

Sunshine has plenty of open runs of
genuine black steepness above the
tree line on Lookout, but Goat's Eye
Mountain makes this area much more
compelling. It has opened up a great
area of expert double-black-diamond
trails and chutes, both above and
below the tree line – one reporter
enjoyed the area so much that he and
his party kept 'going back again and
again'. But the slopes are rocky and
need good cover, and the top can be
windswept. There are short, steep runs
on Mount Standish, too. One particular
novelty is a pitch, near the mid-station,
known as the Waterfall run – because
you do actually ski down over a snow-
covered frozen fall.

Real experts will want to get to
grips with the recently reopened
Delirium Dive on Lookout Mountain's
north face. You are allowed to hike up
to it only if you have a companion, an
avalanche transceiver and a shovel –
and a guide is recommended. ('Book in
advance,' says a disappointed
reporter.) But a local expert says: 'The
patrol neurotically carpet-bombs the
entire cirque and closes Delirium upon
sighting the first tiny fog-bank, making
Delirium about the safest off-piste on

boarding *Boarders will feel at home in Banff. The nearby mountains have
good terrain-parks and half-pipes and some excellent free-riding
terrain for experienced riders. Norquay offers a snowboard park lift ticket for
those wishing to use only the park and pipe. We have had mainly positive reports
about the teaching. Beware green trails, however, as they can be really flat and
require some walking. Banff is quite lively for nightlife.*

SKI BANFF/LAKE LOUISE /
BILL MARSH

Sunshine's Delirium
Dive is something no
expert will want to
miss ↓

the planet. The mandatory transceiver routine is pure theatre.' The area was closed on our 2001 visit, but we did take a look at it, and it is suitably impressive, with pitches over 40°.

Norquay's two main lifts give only 400m/1,300ft vertical, but both serve black slopes and the North American chair accesses a couple of double-diamond runs that justify their grading.

Heli-skiing is available from bases outside the National Park in British Columbia – roughly two hours' drive.

FOR INTERMEDIATES
Ideal runs
Half the runs on Sunshine are classified as intermediate. Wherever you look there are blues and greens – some of the greens as enjoyable (and pretty much as steep) as the blues.

We particularly like the World Cup Downhill run, from the top of Lookout to the mid-mountain base. Don't ignore the Wawa T-Bar, which gives access to the often quiet Wawa Bowl and Tincan Alley. There's a delightful wooded area under the second stage of the gondola served by Jackrabbit and Wolverine chairs. The blue runs down Goat's Eye are good cruises too.

The Pathfinder fast quad at Norquay serves a handful of quite challenging tree-lined blues and a couple of sometimes-groomed blacks – great for a snowy day or a 'first day of the holiday' warm-up.

FOR BEGINNERS
Pretty good terrain
Sunshine has a good area by the mid-mountain base, served by a hand tow. The long Meadow Park Green is a great, long, easy run to progress to.

Norquay has a good small nursery area with a magic carpet and gentle greens served by the Cascade chair.

Banff is not the ideal destination for a mixed party of beginners (who may want to stay in one area) and more experienced friends (who are likely to want to visit other places).

FOR CROSS-COUNTRY
High in quality and quantity
It's a good area for cross-country. There are trails near Banff, around the Bow River, and on the Banff Springs golf course. But the best area is around Lake Louise. Altogether, there are around 80km/50 miles of groomed trails within Banff National Park.

CHILDCARE

Tiny Tigers Daycare at Sunshine Village and Norquay's The Kid's Place take children aged 19 months to 6 years, from 8.30 to 4.30. Children aged 3 or more can take short ski lessons. Reservation is recommended.

GETTING THERE

Air Calgary, transfer 1½hr.

SCHOOLS/GUIDES

2002/03 prices in Canadian dollars

Club Ski and Club Snowboard
3 days of guided tuition of the three areas

Club Program
4½ hr per day
3 full days 186
(incl lunch for Club Junior Program for age 6-12)

Beware of the wildlife though: last season a cross-country skier was killed by a mountain lion.

QUEUES
Should not be a problem
Half the visitors come for the day from cities such as Calgary – so it's fairly quiet during the week. Even on the busiest weekends of the year queues of more than 10 minutes are unlikely.

MOUNTAIN RESTAURANTS
Quite good
Sunshine Village has a choice of eating places at its mid-mountain base. The Day Lodge offers three different styles of food on three floors (table service in the top-floor Lookout Lodge, with great views). Mixed reports of the food but the buffalo stew is recommended. Mad Trapper's Saloon is a jolly western-style place in Old Sunshine Lodge, serving good beer and different food on its two levels (though reporters continue to criticise its disposable plates). The Sunshine Inn hotel has the best food – table-service snacks in the Chimney Corner Lounge or a full lunch in the Eagle's Nest Dining Room. The Java Hut (actually a tent), at the bottom of Goat's Eye Mountain, has had mixed reports.

At the base of Norquay, the big, stylish, timber-framed Cascade Lodge is excellent – it has great views and a table-service restaurant upstairs as well as a self-service cafeteria.

SCHOOLS AND GUIDES
Some great ideas
Both mountains have their own school. But recognising that visitors wanting lessons won't want to be confined to just one mountain, the resorts have organised an excellent Club Ski and Club Snowboard program – three-day courses starting on Mondays and Thursdays that take you to Sunshine, Norquay and Lake Louise on different days, offering a mixture of guiding and instruction and including free video analysis, a fun race and a group photo. We'd recommend this to anyone who wants to see the whole area while improving their technique. Reporters rave about it: 'absolutely brilliant' and 'improved more in three days than in a week anywhere else'. All abilities are catered for, including beginners. We also have a fat file full of praise for the free mountain tours by friendly local volunteer snow hosts.

FACILITIES FOR CHILDREN
Excellent
One reporter who used Sunshine, Norquay and Lake Louise said: 'I'd recommend all three.'

Staying there 🔑

HOW TO GO
Superb-value packages
A huge amount of accommodation is on offer – especially hotels and self-catering, but also a few catered chalets run by British tour operators. We have an enthusiastic report ('wonderful views, excellent food, great hot-tub') on the Timberline Inn, reachable on skis from Norquay and now run as a kind of chalet-hotel by Crystal.
Hotels Summer is the peak season here. Prices halve for the winter – so you can stay in luxury at bargain rates.
((((4 **Banff Springs** (762 2211) A turn-of-the century, castle-style Canadian Pacific property, well outside town. It's virtually a town within itself – it can sleep 2,000 people, has over 40 shops, numerous restaurants and bars, a nightclub and a superb health club and spa (which costs extra).
((((4 **Rimrock** (762 33560) Spectacularly set, out of town, with great views and a smart health club. Luxurious.
(((3 **Inns of Banff** (762 4581) About 20 minutes' walk from town; praised by reporters for large rooms, room service and fitness facilities; 'very large' hot tub the après-ski focus.
(((3 **Banff Park Lodge** (762 4433) Best-quality central hotel, with hot-tub, steam room and indoor pool.
((2 **Banff Caribou Lodge** (762 5887) On the main street, slightly out of town. It has a variety of wood-clad, individually designed rooms, a sauna and hot-tub complex and a good restaurant and bar. Repeatedly recommended by reporters.

Banff

595

ACTIVITIES

Indoor Film theatre, museums, galleries, swimming pools (one with water slides), gym, squash, racquetball, weight training, bowling, hot-tub, sauna, mini-golf, climbing wall

Outdoor Swimming in hot springs, ice skating, heli-skiing, horse-drawn carriage rides, sleigh rides, dog-sled rides, snowmobiles, curling, ice hockey, ice fishing, helicopter tours, night skiing, snow-shoe tours

Phone numbers

From distant parts of Canada, add the prefix 1 403.
From abroad, add the prefix +1 403.

BANFF TOURIST OFFICE

Postcode T1L 1H9
t 762 4561
f 762 8185
info@sblls.com
www.skibig3.com

SUNSHINE VILLAGE

Sunshine Village isn't really a village at all, but you can stay there – the Sunshine Inn is in the background ↓

② **Banff King Edward** (762 2202)
Right in the town centre, set above shops; large rooms and surprisingly quiet for its position.
Self-catering The Banff Rocky Mountain Resort is set in the woods on the edge of town; facilities include indoor pool, squash and hot-tubs. Reporters have also recommended the Douglas Fir resort for families – though 'a bit out of town' – and Woodland Village.

EATING OUT
Lots of choice

Banff boasts over 100 restaurants, from McDonald's to fine dining in the Banff Springs hotel. Many get crowded and don't take bookings. Many places do huge portions that you can share. Recommendations include the new Maple Leaf (Canadian, relatively expensive), Earl's (burgers and ethnic dishes, very popular and lively), Magpie and Stump (Mexican, with Wild West decor), Giorgio's (Italian), Caramba in the Banff Ptarmigan Inn (Mediterranean), Rose & Crown (pub grub), the Keg at Caribou Lodge ('quality steaks', 'lively' second branch downtown), Seoul Country (Korean), Wild Bill's (burgers, grills, Tex Mex, dancing), Melissa's ('good steaks'), Caboose at the train station ('best steak,' 'superb crab'), Bumpers ('big slabs of rib'), Grizzlies ('fondues and fun') and the Spaghetti Factory ('best value, superb staff'). For korma-starved Brits, the Banff Park hotel does a Monday curry buffet.

APRES-SKI
Livens up later on

One of the drawbacks of the area is that tea time après-ski is limited because the resort is a drive from the

slopes. But Mad Trapper's Saloon at the top of the Sunshine Village gondola is popular during the close of play happy hour (with endless free peanuts). In town later in the evening, Wild Bill's has live country and western music and line dancing. The Rose & Crown has live music and gets crowded. The Works and the Barbary Coast nightclubs are popular. And Outabounds attracts a young lively crowd, while Aurora is for more serious clubbing. The St James Gate Irish pub has 'great atmosphere, good-value food and a wide range of beers'.

OFF THE SLOPES
Lots to do

For those who do not intend to hit the slopes, Banff is 'an absolute delight' and one of the best resorts there is: there are so many other things to do and lots of wildlife to see. There are lovely walks, including organised ice canyon walks, and you can go snow-shoeing, dog-sledding, skating and tobogganing. You can go on sightseeing tours and visit natural hot springs as well.

There are museums to visit such as Banff Park Museum, the Whyte Museum of the Canadian Rockies, the Natural History Museum, the Canadian Ski Museum West and the Buffalo Nation's Luxton Museum of the Indians of the Northern Plains.

There are hundreds of shops, aimed at the tourist trade.

STAYING UP THE MOUNTAIN
Worth considering

On the slopes of Sunshine Village, accessible by gondola or snowmobile, the Sunshine Inn (762 6550) is well worth considering. Luggage is transported for you in the gondola while you hit the slopes. Rooms vary in size. Big outdoor hot-pool. Sauna. Good restaurant.

Big White

Big by local standards, white by any standard

WHAT IT COSTS

HOW IT RATES

The slopes

Snow	*****
Extent	***
Experts	****
Intermediates	****
Beginners	****
Convenience	****
Queues	*****
Restaurants	*

The rest

Scenery	***
Resort charm	**
Off-slope	**

Made to Measure Holidays

Custom-made ski holidays to

Big White

☎ **01243 533333**

What's new

Big White has bought Silver Star and a new joint-mountain lift pass and daily bus and helicopter shuttles will allow day trips there (and two-centre holidays) – see western Canada introduction for more on Silver Star. Big White is planning two new terrain-parks, and lots of new lodgings are opening.

BIG WHITE / KLAUS GRETZMACHER

The traffic-free resort centre and excellent care facilities make Big White very child-friendly →

➕ BC's highest ski area, with a good snow record

➕ Mainly fast lifts, with few queues

➕ Extensive, varied slopes, deserted except at weekends and holidays

➕ Convenient, purpose-built village with mainly ski-in/ski-out accommodation and car-free centre

➕ Excellent kids' facilities

➖ Few off-slope diversions – and isolated without a car

➖ Upper mountain is very exposed – and is known for freezing fog

➖ No mountain restaurants

➖ Limited après-ski

'It's the snow,' says the Big White slogan. And as slogans go, it's spot on. If all you want to do is ski or ride, with a fair chance of doing it in deep snow, put Big White high on the shortlist. If other things enter into your holiday equation, the attractions are less clear. That's if you're planning a week-long stay in one place; for anyone planning a tour of BC resorts, Big White should be on your itinerary. And it now owns neighbouring (in Canadian terms) Silver Star, too.

THE RESORT

Big White is a modern, purpose-built resort above the Okanagan valley. It is built on a sloping hillside, slightly above the three main chair-lift bases so that much of the accommodation is ski-in/ski-out. A lot of the resort's business comes from day visitors, who can park near these lift bases or at the more remote base of Westridge, but these days are most likely to park at the newly created Happy Valley activity area, where a powerful new gondola gives access to the village centre. This is a rather piecemeal affair (Intrawest-style urban planning not in evidence) but attractive in wood and stone.

Big White is only 45 minutes from Kelowna airport (but a long drive from bigger gateways). If you are planning a tour, consider Red Mountain (see Western Canada introduction) as well as Silver Star.

THE MOUNTAINS

Much of the terrain is heavily wooded. But the trees thin out towards the summits, leading to almost open slopes in the bowls at the top. There's at least one green option from the top of each lift so beginners need not be intimidated by any one sector. Grooming is excellent.

Slopes Fast chairs run from points below village level to above mid-mountain, serving the main area of wooded beginner and intermediate runs above and beside the village. Slower lifts – a T-bar and two chairs – serve the higher slopes. Quite some way across the mountainside is the Gem Lake fast chair, serving a range of long top-to-bottom runs to its base at Westridge; with its 710m/2,330ft vertical, this lift is in a different league from the others. There are free daily mountain tours and floodlit skiing.

597

MOUNTAIN FACTS

Altitude 1510m-2320m
4,950ft-7,610ft

Lifts	13
Pistes	2,565 acres
Green	18%
Blue	56%
Black	26%
Snowmaking	none
Recco detectors used	

Central reservations
Call 765 8888.
Toll-free number
(from within Canada)
1 800 663 1772.

Phone numbers
From distant parts of
Canada, add the
prefix 1 250. From
abroad, add +1 250.

TOURIST OFFICE

Postcode V1X 4K5
t 765 8888
f 765 1822
bigwhite@bigwhite.com
www.bigwhite.com

Snow reliability Big White has a reputation for great powder; average snowfall is about 300 inches, which is similar to many Colorado resorts. There is no snowmaking.

Experts There is lots to do, especially if you get good snow. The main bowl off the side of the T-bar is of serious double-black pitch. The Sun-Rype bowl at the opposite edge of the ski area is more forgiving. There are some superb long blacks off the Gem Lake chair and several shorter ones off the Powder chair. In most areas there are extensive glades to explore, too.

Intermediates The resort is excellent for cruisers and families with long blues and greens all over the hill.

Beginners There's a good dedicated nursery area in the village and lots of long easy runs to progress to.

Snowboarding There's some excellent free-riding terrain and various terrain-parks and pipes. Novices are well catered for with long, chair-lift-served green runs.

Cross-country There are 25km/15 miles of trails in total.

Queues With four fast quads and few visitors still, queues are pretty rare. However, the Alpine T-bar can be a bottleneck on sunny days.

Mountain restaurants The nearest thing to a mountain restaurant is the Westridge base warming hut.

School and guides We have no reason to believe these are not up to the usual high Canadian standards.

Facilities for children The excellent 'Kids' Centre' takes children from 18 months. And there's a dedicated nursery slope with a magic carpet lift at the Happy Valley area. Evening activities are organised.

STAYING THERE

How to go There's an increasing range of packages to Big White.

Hotels The White Crystal Inn, Coast Resort and Chateau Big White are recommended by readers – all are convenient for the slopes.

Self-catering There's a reasonable choice of accommodation. Grocery shopping is very limited.

Eating out The choice of restaurant is gradually widening. Snowshoe Sam's is good for casual dining. Other options include Powder Keg (Greek), Swiss Bear in the Chateau Big White (Swiss!), China White Wok, Kettle Valley Steakhouse (steaks!) and Coltino's in the Hopfbrauhaus (Italian).

Après-ski The atmospheric Snowshoe Sam's is a focal point, with a DJ, pool tables, live entertainment, dancing and infamous 'gunbarrel coffee'. Raakel's in the Hopfbrauhaus has live music and dancing.

Off the slopes The Happy Valley adventure park features western Canada's largest tubing hills and ice skating, and is the launch pad for snowmobiling, snow-shoeing and dog-sledding. Helicopter tours and the two health spas are also popular.

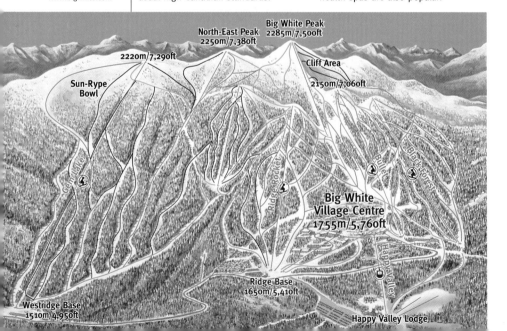

Fernie 1070m/3,500ft

Lots of snow, and lots of steeps

WHAT IT COSTS

((((5)

HOW IT RATES

The slopes

Snow	★★★★★
Extent	★★★
Experts	★★★★★
Intermediates	★★
Beginners	★★★★
Convenience	★★★★
Queues	★★★★
Restaurants	★

The rest

Scenery	★★★★
Resort charm	★★
Off-slope	★★

➕ Good snow record, with less chance of rain than at Whistler (and less chance of Arctic temperatures than at resorts up in the Rockies)

➕ Great terrain for those who like it steep and deep, with lots for confident intermediates too

➕ Snowcat operations nearby

➕ More good on-slope accommodation becoming available but ...

➖ Mountain resort still being built is very limited, and town of Fernie is not particularly appealing either

➖ Lift system still a weakness, especially for experts

➖ After a dump it can take time to make the bowls safe

➖ Little groomed cruising for timid or average intermediates

➖ No decent mountain restaurants

Fernie has long had cult status among Alberta and BC skiers for its steep gladed slopes and superb natural snow. In the last five years there has been a lot of investment in the development of the village at the foot of the slopes – though it still remains small, without many facilities. Some visitors would rather see more investment in the mountain, to cut down the amount of hiking and traversing to the best steep terrain, and to hasten reopening after a serious snowfall. We see their point, but most reports we get are dominated by excitement at Fernie's combination of snow and terrain – 'just like Jackson Hole', to quote two reporters from last year. Progress was interrupted last year by the owning company's financial problems; but these appear to have been resolved, so we look forward to a resumption of investment.

599

What's new

Fernie Lodging Company's new Balsam Lodge will be open for the coming season.

Last year's development of new restaurants, condo-hotels, a couple of shops and a nursery have helped to give the new mountain village more shape and identity.

SNOWPIX.COM / CHRIS GILL

If the primitive Face Lift is working, a traverse across Lizard Bowl is the start of adventures on some seriously steep terrain on the ridge above the village ➔

The resort

Fernie Alpine Resort is set at the lift base a little way up the mountainside from the flat Elk Valley floor and a couple of miles from the little town of Fernie. It has grown considerably from very little in the last few years, but there's still not much there other than convenient accommodation and a few places to eat. It is quiet at night.

The town of Fernie is named after William Fernie – a prospector who discovered coal here and triggered a boom at the turn of the century. Much of the town was destroyed by fire in 1908 but some downtown stone and brick buildings survived and are still there. We thought it a nondescript spot on our first visit three years ago but noticed a few more tourist shops on our 2001 visit. One reporter described it as 'a bit like staying in an industrial estate on the outskirts of Barnsley' – a bit unfair, we thought, but you can't describe it as 'charming'. There are buses between the town and the mountain, but they run at hourly intervals and cost $3 one way.

You're going for the snow, so our advice would be to stay on or close to

Snow

MOUNTAIN FACTS

Altitude 1070m-1925m
3,500ft-6,320ft

Lifts	10
Pistes	2,500 acres
Green	30%
Blue	40%
Black	30%

Snowmaking 25 acres
Recco detectors used

LIFT PASSES

2001/02 prices in
Canadian dollars

Main pass
1-day pass 56
6-day pass 312
Senior citizens
Over 65: 6-day pass
240
Children
13-17: 6-day pass 240
Under 13: 6-day pass
90
Under 6: free pass
Short-term passes
Half-day pass from
noon (adult 45)
Notes
Mighty Moose lift
passes available for
beginners: 15

WESTERN CANADA

600

the hill. But it's cheaper to stay in the town, where there is a wider choice of restaurants, bars and other diversions.

Outings to Kimberley are possible; a coach does the trip every Thursday (there's also a helicopter option).

The mountains

Fernie's 2,500 acres pack in a lot of variety, from superb green terrain at the bottom to ungroomed chutes (that will be satisfyingly steep to anyone but the extreme specialist) and huge numbers of steep runs in the trees. A lot of the runs have the rare quality of consistently steep pure fall lines.

THE SLOPES
Bowl after bowl
What you see when you arrive at the lift base is a trio of impressive mogul slopes towering above you. The Deer chair approaches the foot of these slopes, but goes no further. You get to them by traversing and hiking from the main Lizard Bowl, on the right. This is a broad snowfield reached by a series of lifts: a slow quad (which one reporter found stopped 'on average four times per uplift'); a fast quad; and finally the short Face Lift, a dreadful rope tow. It wasn't working when we were there in February 2001 because lack of snow left it high above the ground – in the same season it also 'shredded' one reporter's gloves. This is also the main way into lift-free Cedar Bowl (where a reporter came across a moose) and to Snake Ridge beyond it. There is a mini-bowl between Lizard and Cedar, served by the 500m/1,500ft vertical Boomerang chair.

The Timber Bowl fast quad chair gives access to Siberia Bowl and the lower part of Timber. But for access to the higher slopes and to Currie Bowl

you must take the White Pass quad. A long traverse from the top gets you to the steeper slopes on the flanks of Currie (our favourite area), which are otherwise reached by hiking from the main Lizard Bowl. From there you have to go right to the bottom, and it takes quite a while to get back for another go.

There are excellent, free, hosted tours of the area in groups of different abilities for two hours twice a day. These may be a good way to get your bearings, as several readers found the signposting 'minimal', and we found both signs and trail map dangerously inadequate – when we tried to find the long black Diamond Back run from the top of the White Pass quad, we failed and ended up in tight trees on a slope of triple-diamond steepness – scary.

SNOW RELIABILITY
A key part of the appeal
Fernie has an excellent snow record – with an average of 350 inches per year, better than practically all of Colorado. Even in the exceptionally poor 2000/01 season, it got 178 inches, which is better than Panorama or Lake Louise in an average year. But the altitude is modest – rain is not unknown, and in warmer weather the lower slopes can suffer. There is very little snowmaking, and reporters found piste maintenance poor in the snow drought season.

FOR EXPERTS
Wonderful – deep and steep
The combination of heavy snowfalls and abundant steep terrain with the shelter of trees makes this a superb mountain for good skiers. There are about a dozen identifiable faces offering genuine black or double-black slopes, each of them with several alternative ways down. Currie and

boarding

Fernie is a fine place for boarders (and there are a lot of local experts here). Lots of natural gullies, hits and endless off-piste opportunities – including some adrenalin-pumping tree-runs and knee-deep powder bowls – will keep free-riders of all abilities grinning from ear to ear. There's also a good terrain-park and half-pipe. Snowcat operators can take you to some excellent untouched powder. There are a couple of decent bars in the town, and Frozen Ocean and Board Stiff are the main board shops.

Timber Bowls both have some serious double-diamonds but mainly have single-diamonds. However, one of our regular reporters says, 'The majority of the single blacks are tough. Some of them are so steep that I can't work out how you could get anything harder without falling off the mountain ... just like Jackson Hole but without the cliffs.' Even where the trail map shows trees to be sparse, expect them to be close enough together, and where there aren't any, expect alder bushes unless there's lots of snow.

There are also backcountry routes you can take with guidance and snowcat operations in other nearby mountain – see feature panel.

FOR INTERMEDIATES
Far from ideal

Although there are intermediate runs both low down and high up, they don't add up to a lot of mileage. Most high runs are not groomed, and one reporter said, 'The blues in all bowls except Timber would be black in most resorts.' Adventurous, strong intermediates willing to give the ungroomed terrain a try will enjoy the area. The blue/green Falling Star run (a short hike up from the top of the

Timber Bowl chair) is often completely deserted and has good snow, although near the bottom it is narrow and it gets a bit flat. But if you want miles of groomed cruising, go elsewhere.

FOR BEGINNERS
Excellent

There's a good nursery area and the lower mountain served by the Deer and Elk chairs has lots of wide, smooth trails to gain confidence on. But most runs from the top of the mountain have tough parts to them.

FOR CROSS-COUNTRY
Some possibilities

There are 14km/9 miles of trails marked out in the forest adjacent to the resort, and the Fernie golf and country club allows enthusiasts on to their white fairways.

QUEUES
Not usually a problem

Unless there is a weekend invasion from Calgary, queues are rare. Poor snow two years ago kept numbers down but in a normal year we guess that the new fast Bear quad chair will lead to queues at the inadequate and atrocious Face Lift tow (if it is

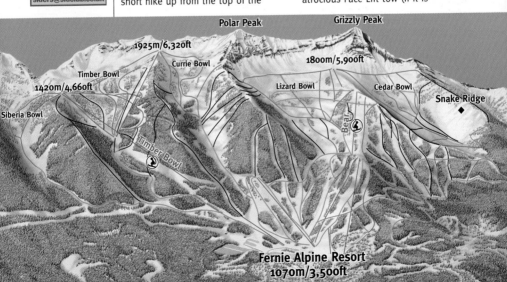

Polar Peak

Grizzly Peak

1925m/6,320ft

Currie Bowl

1800m/5,900ft

Timber Bowl

Lizard Bowl

Cedar Bowl

1420m/4,660ft

Snake Ridge

Siberia Bowl

Bear

Timber Bowl

Fernie Alpine Resort
1070m/3,500ft

ACTIVITIES

Indoor Museum, galleries, aquatic centre, saunas, bowling, fitness centre, ice skating, cinema, curling
Outdoor Sleigh rides, snowmobiling, dog-sledding, snow-shoe excursions, ice fishing

SCHOOLS/GUIDES

2001/02 prices in Canadian dollars
Fernie
Classes
1¹/₄hr: 10am and 1.30
Half day 27
Multi half days 23
Children's classes
Ages 3 to 4 years and 5 to 12 years:
Multi full day 38
Private lessons
2hr 100 (22 for each additional person)

CHILDCARE

The resort day care centre takes children of all ages. It is open daily from 9am to 4pm.

GETTING THERE

Air Calgary, transfer 3¹/₂hr.

Phone numbers
From distant parts of the Canada, add the prefix 1 250.
From abroad, add the prefix +1 250.

Central reservations phone number
For all resort accommodation call 1 800 258 7669 (toll-free from within Canada).

TOURIST OFFICE

Postcode V0B 1M6
t 423 4655
f 423 6644
info@skifernie.com
www.skifernie.com

---

working). If heavy snow keeps part of the mountain closed, there can be queues elsewhere.

MOUNTAIN RESTAURANTS
What mountain restaurants?

Bear's Den at the top of the Elk chair is an open-air fast-food kiosk. So it's back to base for lunch – the ancient Day Lodge is grim but cheap and serves good soups and sandwiches to order. Or see Eating Out.

SCHOOLS AND GUIDES
'Lessons for all abilities'

Reporters have praised the ski school and its small classes. One tried telemarking and described the lessons as 'outstanding' and 'best ever', with only two people in the class. 'First Tracks' gets you up the mountain at 8am for two hours, but when we tried it the instructor didn't know which lifts were open and there was a lot of wasted time.

FACILITIES FOR CHILDREN
New day care centre

There's a new day care centre in the Cornerstone Lodge, which a reporter found 'very well run'. There are also 'Kids' Activity Nights'.

Staying there

HOW TO GO
More packages

Fernie is increasingly easy to find in tour operator brochures.
Chalets Some UK tour operators run chalets.
Hotels and condos As the resort develops, the choice is widening and shifting upmarket.
((((4) **Lizard Creek Lodge** Luxury ski-in, ski-out condo hotel. Spa, outdoor pool and hot-tub. We stayed there and highly recommend it.
(((3) **Cornerstone Lodge** Condo hotel in the village core.
(((3) **Griz Inn** Condo-hotel with good facilities. Pool.
((2) **Wolf's Den Lodge** 'Adequate but uninspiring' with 'simple' rooms say

---

reporters. Indoor hot-tub, games room and small gym. At base of slope.
((2) **Timberline Village** Very comfortable condos a shuttle-ride from the lifts.
((2) **Cedar Lodge** Motel on road to town. 'Comfortable and clean, but not very welcoming,' said reporters.
((2) **Alpine Lodge** New B&B recommended by reporter.

EATING OUT
Not a highlight

At the base, the Lizard Creek Lodge is expensive but serves the best gourmet food in the district (in small portions). Kelsey's (part of a chain) is more casual and offers good food and large servings, with Asian dishes as well as standard burgers, steaks, pasta, The Powderhorn in the Griz Inn does 'good, reasonably priced' food. Gabriella's is cheap but nothing special.
In Fernie, there are quite a few options. The Old Elevator is in a converted grain store and does good grills and pasta. Jamocha's is a coffee house that does meals. Other reader recommendations include the Curry Bowl (various Asian styles), the Royal hotel, Rip n' Richard's Eatery (south-western food and a lively atmosphere). The current favourite, though, is the new Wood bistro and tapas bar.

APRES-SKI
Have a beer

The Grizzly bar in the Day Lodge and the Powderhorn, in the nearby Griz Inn, are quite lively when the lifts close – the latter with live bands sometimes. During the week, the bars are pretty quiet later on, but one reporter recommends Kelsey's. In town, the bar of the Royal hotel is popular with locals. Other recommendations are the Park Place Lodge Pub and the bar in the Grand Central hotel.

OFF THE SLOPES
Get out and about

There is a heritage walking tour of historic Fernie. The old railroad station is now the Art Station. The main diversion is the great outdoors.

Small area of slopes set amid glorious scenery and wildlife

HOW IT RATES

The slopes

Snow	***
Extent	*
Experts	**
Intermediates	**
Beginners	****
Convenience	*
Queues	****
Restaurants	**

The rest

Scenery	***
Resort charm	***
Off-slope	***

What's new

For 2001/02 the new Eagle Ridge quad chair opened up twenty new runs on either side of Eagle Ridge – previously accessible only by taking a long, high traverse from the top of the Knob chair.

This season will bring extensive glading in Eagle East, further increasing the skiable area.

MOUNTAIN FACTS

Altitude	1705m-2600m
	5,590ft-8,530ft
Lifts	8
Pistes	1,500 acres
Green	30%
Blue	30%
Black	40%
Snowmaking	10 acres

➕ Lots of lovely walks and drives in National Park land

➕ Extensive cross-country trails

➕ Spectacular scenery and wildlife

➖ Slopes of Marmot Basin are a long way from town and limited in size, especially for intermediates

➖ Town of Jasper is rather spread out and lacks charm

Set in the middle of Jasper National Park, Jasper appeals more to those keen on scenery and wildlife (and perhaps cross-country skiing) than piste mileage. It could be combined with a stay in Whistler, Banff or Lake Louise.

THE RESORT

Jasper is low-key, low-rise little town that started life as a trapper's staging post and now services visitors to Jasper National Park. It spreads a long way along the side of the trans-continental railway but is only a couple of blocks deep.

Its key attraction is the scenery of the unspoiled National Park land surrounding the town. One of the most beautiful drives in the world is the three-hour trip to Lake Louise on the Columbia Icefields Parkway through the Banff and Jasper National Parks – past glaciers, frozen waterfalls and lakes.

This makes Jasper a good place to stay for a couple of days as part of a two-centre holiday. You can travel from Whistler to Jasper by overnight train from Vancouver and wake up to spectacular Rocky Mountains scenery.

The place is geared to cars: most accommodation is out of town or on the outskirts and the local slopes of Marmot Basin are a 30-minute drive away (there are buses).

THE MOUNTAINS

The slopes are at Marmot Basin, in the heart of the unspoiled National Park.
Slopes A high-speed quad takes you to mid-mountain, with three slow chairs above that and then the new quad to Eagle Ridge. The highest Knob chair ends way below the 2600m/8,530ft peak that the area includes in its claim of almost 900m/2,950ft vertical.
Snow reliability Snowfall is 160in on average – a modest figure by North American standards. Cover has been sparse on both our visits and there is little snowmaking capacity.
Experts There are some decent mogul runs on the top and bottom halves of the mountain, and some entertaining off-piste on the top half. The new Eagle Ridge chair has opened up a lot of expert terrain that was difficult to access. In good conditions, there is now lots to do. But slopes like these can be hazardous or unskiable if snow conditions are not good.
Intermediates Keen piste-bashers will cover all the groomed runs in half a

603

As you go up the hill the forest thins out and gives way to open upper slopes ➔

day and find the area very small unless they are prepared to brave the ungroomed blacks. Less adventurous intermediates will be happy to cruise the greens and blues for a day or two.

Beginners The area around the base is very gentle, and there are greens to progress to from a T-bar and the quad.

Snowboarding There's a terrain-park below Caribou Ridge.

Cross-country Over 300km/185 miles of trails make this one of the best areas in Canada, with good trails near Jasper.

Queues These are rarely a problem.

Mountain restaurants At mid-mountain the Paradise Chalet has a big self-service cafe and the connected Eagle Chalet is a cosy table-service place. At the base the rebuilt Caribou Chalet is another option. Catering is run by the Jasper Park Lodge (see Hotels).

Schools and guides These are doubtless up to the usual high Canadian standards.

Facilities for children The Little Rascals nursery takes children from 19 months.

STAYING THERE

Hotels The Fairmont Jasper Park Lodge (852 3301) is a beautiful collection of luxurious log cabins set 4km/2 miles out of town around a lake in the middle of 1,000 acres of land rich with wildlife. Room service is delivered on bicycles and you may well have to walk around grazing elk to reach the outdoor pool and other facilities. On the edge of town, the Royal Canadian Lodge (852 5644) has some comfortable rooms and indoor pool.

Eating out There's plenty of choice – from fine dining at the Jasper Park Lodge to Cajun, pizza and Japanese. We had good seafood and steak at the Fiddle River.

Après-ski The bar in the base lodge is crowded at the end of the day. In town, try Astoria, O'Shea's and Nick's.

Off the slopes There is lots to do, including beautiful walks, ice skating and snow-shoeing, and there is a fine aquatic centre and indoor sports complex.

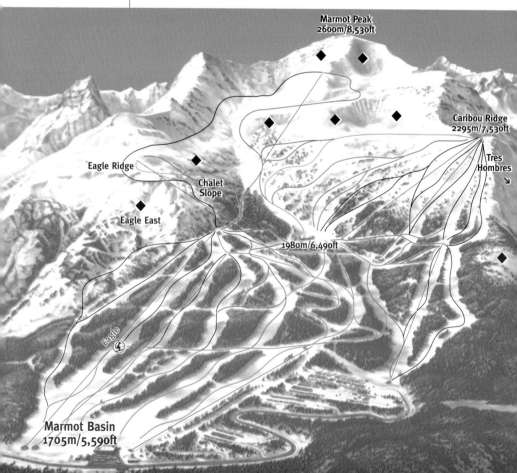

Kicking Horse

Heli-skiing terrain that now has a lift but still has no resort village

WHAT IT COSTS

HOW IT RATES

The slopes

Snow	*****
Extent	***
Experts	****
Intermediates	***
Beginners	***
Convenience	*
Queues	*****
Restaurants	**

The rest

Scenery	***
Resort charm	*
Off-slope	*

➕ A good bet for powder snow

➕ Some great terrain for experts and adventurous intermediates

➕ Big vertical served by one fast lift

➕ Splendid mountaintop restaurant

➖ No resort village yet

➖ Golden, the resort substitute, is neither attractive nor convenient

➖ Single-stage gondola suits summer visitors, not skiers and riders

➖ Few groomed intermediate runs

Three years ago, this was Whitetooth, the local ski hill of the nondescript logging town of Golden: two old lifts, open over the weekend, serving modest wooded slopes beneath high bowls used by the local heli-skiing operation. Enter a Dutch-Canadian consortium, bringing with it vision, capital and a cute name. Within months, in go a new access road, a gondola rising 1150m/3,770ft to the top of the heli-terrain, and smart base lodge and mountaintop restaurant. Soon, in will go a designer mountain village at the lift base, making this a real destination resort. Meanwhile, any competent skier or rider staying in Banff or Lake Louise should give Kicking Horse a shot.

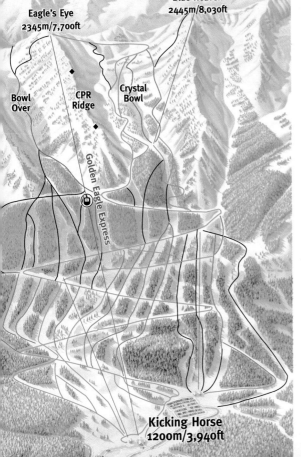

Blue Heaven
2445m/8,030ft

Eagle's Eye
2345m/7,700ft

Bowl Over

CPR Ridge

Crystal Bowl

Golden Eagle Express

Kicking Horse
1200m/3,940ft

THE RESORT

Eight miles from the small logging town of Golden, Kicking Horse is at present simply a lift base station. The first phase of the mountain village promised by the developers has yet to materialise, though road and infrastructure improvements make its eventual arrival more likely.

Golden is a spread-out place beside the transcontinental highway that climbs up into the main Rockies range to the east. It has no real centre – it's the kind of place where you travel from motel to restaurant to shops by car. But the range of places to eat and stay is starting to improve.

THE MOUNTAINS

The lower two-thirds of the hill is wooded, with trails cut in the usual style. The upper third is a mix of open and lightly wooded slopes.

Slopes The only way up to the top of the mountain is by the eight-seater gondola to Eagle's Eye. Despite the serious vertical of 1150m/3,770ft, this lift goes up in a single stage – to give summer sightseeing visitors a quick ascent. In winter, the lack of a mid-station is a real drawback: you have to make the full descent, at least if you opt for Bowl Over – this season there will be a new quad chair-lift from Crystal Bowl to the slightly higher peak of Blue Heaven, so this part of the higher terrain, at least, is skiable without descending to the base. As

What's new

A new quad chair from Crystal Bowl to Blue Heaven is being built for 2002/03, opening 20 marked runs and 150 acres of terrain. A new restaurant is being built at the base of the lift. Capacity on the Golden Eagle Express gondola is being doubled.

MOUNTAIN FACTS

Altitude 1200m-2450m
3,940ft-8,040ft
Lifts 4
Pistes 2,300 acres
Green 26%
Blue 25%
Black 49%
Snowmaking None
Recco detectors used

Phone numbers
From distant parts of Canada, add the prefix 1 250.
From abroad, add the prefix +1 250.

TOURIST OFFICE

Postcode V0A 1H0
t 439 5400
f 439 5401
www.kickinghorse resort.com

---

well as the marked runs there are literally hundreds of ways down through the bowls, chutes and trees. The plan is that hardly any of the terrain will be groomed – making the area a paradise for powder pigs. Two chair-lifts from near the base serve the lower runs that formed the original Whitetooth ski area.

Snow reliability Excellent: it gets an average of 275 inches of snow a year. Although this is not enough to put the area in the very top flight, it's not far off – until recently the top half of the mountain was heli-skiing terrain.

Experts It's advanced skiers and riders who will get the most out of the area. From CPR ridge, drop off to skier's right through trees or to skier's left through chutes – there are endless options. The lower half of the mountain has fine black runs on cleared trails through the trees, some with serious moguls. Do six or seven laps on the gondola in a day and you'll have had a fine time. The new quad chair will open up new possibilities into Crystal Bowl. From the top you can also take off (with guidance) into the next bowl, which is still part of the terrain used by Purcell heli-skiing (in Golden).

Intermediates Adventurous intermediates will have a fine time at Kicking Horse, learning to play in the powder up in Crystal Bowl. But don't expect many groomed runs. Piste-bashers and timid intermediates should go elsewhere. The only easy, groomed way down the mountain is a boring winding road.

Beginners There are some excellent nursery slopes and gentle green trails on the lower mountain.

Snowboarding Free-riders will love this powder paradise. But there's no terrain-park or half-pipe.

Cross-country There are 12km/7 miles of trails at Dawn Mountain and a

---

↑ Eagle's Eye at the top of the gondola is an exceptionally stylish place doing excellent food
SNOWPIX.COM / CHRIS GILL

5km/3 mile loop on the golf course.

Queues We have reports of weekend queues for the gondola, but its capacity is being doubled for this season by the addition of extra cabins.

Mountain restaurants The Eagle's Eye table-service restaurant at the top of the gondola serves excellent food in stylish log-cabin surroundings and has fine views. This season the base lodge is also newly built with logs and beams; its small self-service restaurant struck us as inadequate but it is now being extended.

Schools and guides Surprise, surprise: the school specialises in powder lessons and runs two-hour 'powder tune-up' group lessons.

Facilities for children The school teaches children from the age of three.

STAYING THERE

How to go For the moment, staying here means staying in or near Golden.

Hotels The Prestige Inn (344 7990), a neat, functional hotel with a small pool just off the Trans Canada Highway, is probably the best in town. Sisters and Beans (344 2443) has some well kept rooms – see below. Moberly Mountain Lodge (344 5544) is a luxury B&B that impressed our touring Ozzie editor.

Eating out We enjoyed the cosy Sisters and Beans (pasta, steaks, Asian), but the favourites now are the new Kicking Horse Grill and the out-of-town Cedar House Cafe. Eagle's Eye at the top of the gondola opens some nights.

Après-ski The Mad Trapper is the main drinking spot in town – a lively high-ceilinged pub.

Off the slopes There is lots of local snowmobiling and you can go ice-climbing and dog-sledding. But for someone who isn't going to hit the slopes, Golden is a dire place to stay.

Lake Louise

1645m/5,400ft

Knockout views from Canada's second-biggest mountain

➕ Spectacular high-mountain scenery – the best of any North American resort

➕ Slopes are the largest in the Canadian Rockies

➕ Snowy slopes of Sunshine Village within reach (see Banff chapter)

➕ Lots of wildlife around the valley

➕ Good value for money

➖ Local slopes are a short drive away from the 'village', Banff areas further

➖ Snowfall modest by local standards – though snowmaking is extensive

➖ Can be very cold – and lifts offer no protection

➖ 'Village' is no more than a few hotels and shops dotted around a road junction

➖ Slopes can seem over-populated by British visitors

If you care more for scenery than for après-ski action, Lake Louise is worth considering for a holiday. We've seen a few spectacular mountain views, and the view from the Chateau Lake Louise hotel, of the lake and the Victoria Glacier behind it, is as spectacular as they come; it is simply stunning.

Even if you prefer the more animated base of Banff, you'll want to make expeditions to Lake Louise during your holiday. It can't compete with Sunshine Village for quantity of snow, but it's a big and interesting mountain. And from the slopes you get a distant version of that view.

What's new

The management of Louise has been a bit preoccupied with financial problems of late, so it's good to be able to report that investment has been resumed with the construction for 2002/03 of a new six-pack on the upper mountain, replacing the existing fast quad to the top of the front face.

SNOWPIX.COM / CHRIS GILL

Temple Lodge, where the Ptarmigan area meets the Larch area, is the place for a serious lunch →

The resort

Although it's a small place, Lake Louise is a resort of parts. First, there's the lake itself, in a spectacular mountain setting beneath the Victoria Glacier. Tom Wilson, who discovered it in 1882, declared, 'As God is my judge, I never in all my exploration have seen such a matchless scene.' Neither have we. And it can be appreciated from many of the rooms of the monster Chateau Lake Louise hotel on the shore. Then there's Lake Louise 'village' – a shapeless little collection of hotels, condominiums, petrol station, supermarket, liquor store and a few shops, a couple of miles away on a road junction down in the main valley, close to the railway and highway from Banff to Jasper. Finally, a mile or two across the valley is the lift base station. A car can be helpful, especially in cold weather. Buses to the Lake Louise ski area are frequent, but a lot less so to the Banff areas of Sunshine and Norquay (free to Tri-area lift pass holders). You can also organise trips to the more distant major resorts of Panorama and Kicking Horse and the small resorts of Nakiska and Fortress. Day-trip heli-skiing and boarding can also be arranged.

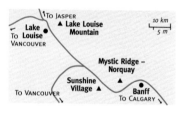

The mountains

MOUNTAIN FACTS

For Sunshine,
Norquay and Lake
Louise, covered by
the Tri-area pass

Altitude 1635m-2730m
5,350ft-8,950ft

Lifts	30
Pistes	7,558 acres
Green	25%
Blue	45%
Black	30%
Snowmaking	
	1,700 acres

For Lake Louise only

Altitude 1645m-2635m
5,400ft-8,650ft

Lifts	12
Pistes	4,200 acres
Green	25%
Blue	45%
Black	30%
Snowmaking	40%

Recco detectors used

The Lake Louise ski area is big, with an excellent mixture of high open slopes, low trails cut through forest and gladed slopes between the two. Reporters are full of praise for the free guided tours of the area given by volunteer 'Ski Friends'.

THE SLOPES
A wide variety

One of two fast quads takes you up the **Front Face** to mid-mountain; from here, a new six-pack will now go to the top of the face. From there, as elsewhere, there's a choice of green, blue or black runs to other lifts. The tree line comes about halfway up the top lift, but there are alternative lifts that stop a bit lower, so you can stay in the trees in bad weather. From mid-mountain, a drag-lift takes you to the high-point of the area, at the shoulder of Mount Whitehorn – there's a stunning view of peaks and glaciers including Canada's uncanny Matterhorn lookalike, Mount Assiniboine.

From either the top chair or the drag you can go over the ridge and into Lake Louise's almost treeless **Back Bowls** – open, predominantly north-facing and mainly steep.

From the bottom of the bowls you can take a lift back to the top again or up to the separate **Larch** area, served by a fast quad chair. With a vertical of

375m/1,230ft it's not huge, but it has pretty wooded runs of all levels. From the bottom you can return to the top of the main mountain via the Ptarmigan chair or take a long green path back to the main base area.

SNOW RELIABILITY
Usually good

Lake Louise gets around 140 inches a year on the front face, which by the standards of western Canada is not a lot. But it is usually enough, and there is snowmaking on 40% of the pistes. The north-facing back bowls hold the snow pretty well.

FOR EXPERTS
Widespread pleasure

There are plenty of steep slopes. On the front face, as well as a score of marked black-diamond trails in and above the trees, there is the alluring West Bowl, reached from the Summit drag – a wide open expanse of snow outside the area boundary. Because this is National Park territory, you can in theory go anywhere. But outside the boundaries there are no patrols and, of

WESTERN CANADA

SNOWPIX.COM / CHRIS GILL

The chutes on Mt Whitehorn, at the far end of the Back Bows, are open only occasionally, and are seriously steep ↓

2635m/8,650ft Back Bowls and Larch ↘

2500m/8,200ft Eagle Ridge

Back Bowls and Larch ↘

Top of the World

Back Bowls and Larch ↘

2435m/7,990ft

Whitehorn Lodge 2055m

2090m

Lake Louise Front Face

Temple Lodge 2015m

Larch →

Glacier / Friendly Giant

Whiskeyjack Lodge 1645m/5,400ft

Lodge of the Ten Peaks

LIFT PASSES

2002/03 prices in Canadian dollars

Tri-area lift pass
Covers all lifts and transport between Banff, Lake Louise and Sunshine Village, available for 3 days or more.

Main pass
3-day pass 186
6-day pass 372

Children
6-12: 6-day pass 128

Beginners First time ski packages including rental, pass and lessons available

Day passes
(2001/02 prices)
Day pass for Lake Louise 59, with reductions for senior citizens (over 65), teenagers (13-17) and students with ID (13-25).

Short-term pass
Half-day pass for Lake Louise 47.

course, no avalanche control. A guide is essential. Inside the boundaries there are also areas permanently closed because of avalanche danger. Going over to the back bowls opens up countless black mogul/powder runs. Try the recently opened avalanche-prone Whitehorn 2 area directly behind the peak (marked 'Occasional Openings' on the trail map). It gave our Ozzie editor what she called 'some of the most exciting in-bounds skiing in North America' – a row of extreme chutes, almost 1km/0.5 miles long.

The Top of the World quad takes you to the very popular Paradise Bowl, served by its own triple chair – one run is marked on the map but there are endless variants. From the Summit drag you can access wide open slopes that take you right away from all signs

of lifts. Again, there are endless variations. The seriously steep slope served by the Ptarmigan quad chair provided many of the logs for the new base lodge, and offers great glade terrain as a result. The Larch area has some steep double-diamond stuff in the trees, and open snowfields at the top for those with the energy to hike up above the lift. Heli-skiing is available from bases outside the National Park in British Columbia – roughly two hours' drive.

FOR INTERMEDIATES
Some good cruising

Almost half the runs are classified as intermediate. But from the top of the Front Face the blue runs down are little more than paths in places, and there are only two blue and two green

609

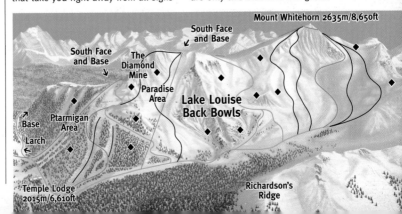

Mount Whitehorn 2635m/8,650ft

South Face and Base

South Face and Base

The Diamond Mine

South Face and Base

Lake Louise Back Bowls

Paradise Area

Base

Ptarmigan Area

Larch

Temple Lodge 2015m/6,610ft

Richardson's Ridge

The best company to
improve your skiing & boarding skills with

* Great range of accommodation - chalets, lodges, hotels and apartments

* Special group deals - up to 1 in 5 travel free, free lift passes for group leaders on selected dates

Call our experts for advice or a brochure

0870 33 33 347
or visit www.neilson.com

Share our passion for the slopes NEILSON

QUEUES
Not unknown

Half of the area's visitors come for the day from nearby cities such as Calgary – so it's fairly quiet during the week, but can have queues at weekends. Any problems at mid-mountain, where one fast quad had to deal with the flow from two similar chairs from the base, should be cured by the six-pack due to be installed for this season. Weekend crowds can form queues for the slow chairs on the back of the mountain.

routes marked in the Back Bowls. Once you get part way down the Front Face the blues are much more interesting. And when groomed, the Men's and Ladies' Downhill black runs are great fast cruises on the lower half of the mountain. Juniper and Juniper Jungle are wonderful cruising runs in the same area. Meadowlark is a beautiful tree-lined run from the top of the Eagle chair to the base area. The Larch area has some short but ideal intermediate runs. And the adventurous should try the blue-classified Boomerang, which starts with a short hike from the top of the Summit drag and some of the ungroomed Back Bowls terrain.

FOR BEGINNERS
Excellent terrain

Louise has a good nursery area near the base, served by a short T-bar; you progress to the gentle, wide Wiwaxy (designated a slow skiing zone) and the slightly more difficult Deer Run or Eagle Meadows on the upper mountain. There are even greens round the back bowls and in the Larch area – worth taking for the views.

FOR CROSS-COUNTRY
High in quality and quantity

It's a very good area for cross-country, with around 80km/50 miles of groomed trails within Banff National Park.There are excellent trails in the local area (and on Lake Louise itself). And Emerald Lake Lodge 40km/25 miles away has some lovely trails and has been highly recommended as a place to stay for a peaceful time.

MOUNTAIN RESTAURANTS
Good base facilities

There's not much choice up the mountain. Temple Lodge, near the bottom of the Larch lift, is the place for a serious lunch – built in rustic style with a big terrace. Sawyer's Nook is its calm table-service restaurant. The self-service cafeteria can get very crowded. Whitehorn Lodge, at mid-mountain on the front face, is a cafeteria doing 'good basic food' with fine views from its balcony. At the base, the Lodge of the Ten Peaks is a hugely impressive, spacious, airy, modern, log-built affair with various eating, drinking and lounging options. The neighbouring, refurbished Whiskeyjack building has the good Northface table-service restaurant and buffet, including a breakfast menu that 'sets you up for the whole day'. Beavertails, at the Gazebo, is popular with reporters for a quick lunch, though it can get very crowded.

SCHOOLS AND GUIDES
Excellent reports

'The best teaching we've encountered' is how a reporter described his 'bumps' lesson at Lake Louise. See the Banff chapter for details on the excellent three-day, three-mountain Club Ski and Club Snowboard Program.

FACILITIES FOR CHILDREN
First-class

A reporter who used Lake Louise, Sunshine and Norquay facilities said: 'I'd recommend all three and advise booking in advance at Lake Louise.'

WESTERN CANADA

610

SCHOOLS/GUIDES

2001/02 prices in Canadian dollars

Club Ski and Club Snowboard
3 days of guided lessons of the three areas
Club Program
4½hr per day
3 full days 169 (incl lunch for Club Junior Program for age 6-12)

CHILDCARE

The nursery at Lake Louise takes children aged 18 days to six years, from 8am to 4.30. Children aged three or more can take short ski lessons.

boarding *Lake Louise is a great mountain for free-riders, with all the challenging terrain in the bowls and glades. The one drag-lift is a tricky one to ride. The resort claims that its terrain-park is now the biggest in Canada, and it's certainly impressive, as is the half-pipe. At the end of the day the bars at the base are lively, but the village is deadly dull at night.*

GETTING THERE

Air Calgary, transfer 1½ hr.

ACTIVITIES

Indoor Mainly hotel-based pools, saunas and hot-tubs
Outdoor Ice-skating, walking, cross-country skiing, ice fishing on the lake, swimming in hot springs, heli-skiing, sleigh rides, dog-sled rides, snowmobiles, helicopter tours, snowshoe tours

Phone numbers
From distant parts of Canada, add the prefix 1 403.
From abroad, add the prefix +1 403.

TOURIST OFFICE

Postcode T1L 1H9
t 762 4561
f 762 8185
info@sblls.com
www.skibig3.com

We arrived at Chateau Lake Louise late at night in falling snow. Next morning, we pulled back the bedroom curtains to find the sun just starting to touch the Victoria Glacier. If there is a more privileged setting for a mountain hotel, we can't imagine it →

HOW TO GO
Superb-value packages

Hotels Summer is the peak season here. Prices halve for the winter – so you can stay in luxury at bargain rates.
((((**Chateau Lake Louise** (522 3511) Isolated position with stunning views over frozen Lake Louise, 500 rooms, lots of shops, groups of tourists (lots of Japanese groups), indoor pool, steam room and hot-tub.
(((**Post Hotel** (522 3989) Small, comfortable Relais & Châteaux place in the village with good restaurant (huge wine list) and pool, hot-tub, sauna.
((**Lake Louise Inn** (522 3791) The cheaper option in the village, with pool, hot-tub and sauna. 'Comfortable rooms' and an efficient shuttle-bus, but 'disappointing restaurants'.
((**Deer Lodge** (522 3747) Charming old hotel next to the Chateau, good restaurant, rooftop hot-tub with amazing views.
Self-catering A limited amount is available.

EATING OUT
Limited choice

The Post hotel has the best cuisine in the Banff region. The Outpost (also in the Post hotel) does good inexpensive pub food. The Station Restaurant is in an atmospheric old station building, but we were disappointed with the food there. The small bakery/coffee shop in the village has had praise from reporters and is good for breakfast.

APRES-SKI
Lively at tea time, quiet later

There are several options at the bottom of the slopes. The Sitzmark Lounge in Whiskeyjack Lodge is a popular – with an open fire and often a live band. The upstairs part of The Lodge of the Ten Peaks has lovely surroundings, an open fire, a couple of bars and a relaxed atmosphere. Beavertails has a good sun terrace. A few times a week there are weekly parties with live music and dancing and an excellent buffet dinner at the mid-mountain Whitehorn Lodge. You ski or ride there as the lifts close and the evening ends with a torchlit descent. It is hugely popular with British visitors, and we loved it.

Later on, things are fairly quiet. For most guests, it's a leisurely dinner followed by bed. But the Glacier Saloon, in Chateau Lake Louise, with traditional Wild West decor, often has live music until late. Explorer's Lounge, in the Lake Louise Inn, has nightly entertainment. The Post hotel's Outpost Pub has been recommended.

OFF THE SLOPES
Beautiful scenery

Lake Louise makes a lovely, peaceful place to stay for someone who does not intend to hit the slopes. The lake itself makes a stunning setting for walks, snow-shoeing, cross-country skiing and ice skating. There are plenty of other things to do and lots of wildlife to see. You can go on organised ice canyon walks, sleigh rides and sightseeing tours, and you can go dog-sledding and tobogganing, and visit natural hot springs.

For a more lively day or for shopping you can visit Banff and all its attractions.

Lake Louise is near one end of the Columbia Icefields Parkway, a three-hour drive to Jasper through National Parks, amidst stunningly beautiful scenery of high peaks and glaciers – one of the world's most beautiful drives.

Lake Louise

611

Panorama

1160m/3,800ft

Developing rapidly and great for a day or two but still too many drawbacks

WHAT IT COSTS

((((5))))

HOW IT RATES

The slopes

Snow	***
Extent	**
Experts	****
Intermediates	***
Beginners	****
Convenience	****
Queues	****
Restaurants	*

The rest

Scenery	***
Resort charm	**
Off-slope	*

MOUNTAIN FACTS

Altitude	1160m-2380m
	3,800ft-7,800ft
Lifts	10
Pistes	2,847 acres
Green	15%
Blue	55%
Black	30%
Snowmaking	40%

Central reservations
1 800 663 2929 (toll-free within Canada).

612

- ⊕ Increasing amount of slope-side accommodation, and the lower village is now linked by lift
- ⊕ Fair-sized area with big vertical and challenging runs for all abilities
- ⊕ Runs are usually deserted
- ⊕ Heli-skiing by the day on hand

- ⊖ May be too challenging for timid intermediates – not many cruisers
- ⊖ Snowfall record not impressive by high local standards
- ⊖ Mainly slow lifts, including T-bars
- ⊖ No real mountain restaurants
- ⊖ No focus to village
- ⊖ Few off-slope diversions

You can expect to hear more and more about Panorama. It is now owned by Intrawest and they have big plans for it. Its vertical of 1220m/4,000ft is one of the biggest in North America, and less than half of the available terrain is in use at present. Like Fernie's, the slopes are less good for the intermediate piste-basher than for the novice and the expert or the confident intermediate. The much-needed slope-side village is still at fledgling stage.

THE RESORT

Panorama is a small, quiet, purpose-built resort above the lakeside town of Invermere in eastern BC, about two hours' scenic drive south-west of Banff. Accommodation is concentrated mainly in two car-free areas. Attractive lodges and a hot-pool compex have recently been built at the foot of the main slopes and, with ski-in, ski-out convenience, this is the best place to stay. But a lot of accommodation is in a 'lower village' which lacks character or life. This is now linked to the 'upper village' and the slopes by a bucket lift. There are also houses spread widely around the hillside and the village as a whole lacks a central focus or hub.

Outings by car are possible to Kimberley, less than two hours south, or to Lake Louise or Kicking Horse, slightly further away to the north. And the resort runs day trips to Lake Louise and Kicking Horse.

THE MOUNTAIN

The slopes basically follow three ridges, joined at top and bottom. At the top, between the left and central ridges, is the double-black-diamond Extreme Dream Zone. Almost all of the terrain is wooded. Daily mountain tours are available.

Slopes From the upper village, a fast quad goes over gentle slopes to mid-mountain. Above this a double-chair followed by successive T-bars opens up intermediate and expert slopes. From the summit there are long runs down the two outer ridges as well as the central one. Those on the right bring you to a triple-chair near the base of the mountain, which also serves its own bunch of runs. Either way, the whole vertical is usable. 2000/01 saw the opening of the new 'Outback' area in Taynton Bowl, off the back of the summit area – 700 acres of lightly wooded expert terrain (previously used for heli-skiing) funnelling down to a long, flat blue run back to the village.

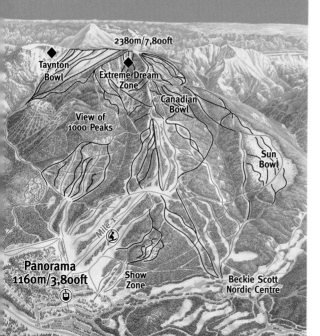

Snow reliability Annual snowfall is low by local standards – less than half the Fernie figure. But snowmaking covers 40% of the area and grooming is good.

Experts There are genuine black runs scattered all over the mountain, and some expert-only areas. At the very top of the mountain and accessed through a gate is the Extreme Dream Zone – seriously steep trails with cliffs as well as tight trees, said to contain the best snow on the mountain. Off the back of the summit, is the Taynton Bowl area with challenging but less extreme terrain – hiking over to the far runs can be worth it for fresh tracks. There are often good bumps on the blacks at mid-mountain. On the extreme right of the mountain is an area of gentler glades, where you can pick the density of trees and steepness of slope to try.

Intermediates For adventurous intermediates the terrain is excellent – there are easy blacks all over the mountain, some of them regularly groomed. The View of 1000 Peaks and Schober's Dream are beautiful and long for North America (up to 3.5km/2 miles). Sun Bowl is a good introduction to a powder bowl and Millennium (black running into blue) is a great roller-coaster. But the less experienced may find all this uncomfortably challenging. The blues in the centre of the area are gentler but they don't add up to a lot. RK Heli-Skiing operates from a base right next to the village and specialises in first-time heli-skiers – well worth a go.

Beginners There are a couple of nursery lifts and access to good, longer runs served by the lower lifts.

Snowboarding The extensive powder bowls and tree runs are ideal for good riders, and there's also the Show Zone terrain-park and pipe (open evenings too). Beginners have several good long green runs to practise on but the main nursery slopes are served by drag-lifts.

Cross-country There are 17km/10 miles of trails out at the Nordic Centre.

Queues There can be queues for the double-chair from mid-mountain and the T-bars above it, though the trails are usually deserted.

Mountain restaurants There are no real mountain restaurants, just two huts offering basic refreshments. But the Ski Tip day lodge at the base is an excellent modern affair.

Schools and guides We have always had glowing reports of the ski school. But this year a reporter found that the advertised Outback Guided Tour and the Free Skiing Camp groups were not in fact being run. They joined an all-day free-skiing group which they found 'didn't live up to the publicity and we were disappointed'. But others were positive about their private lessons.

Facilities for children Wee Wascals is the childcare centre, taking children from 18 months. Snowbirds is for three to five year olds, and the Adventure Club caters for kids from five to fourteen. Evening babysitters are also available.

STAYING THERE

How to go The better places are the newer ones in the upper village.

Hotels Panorama Springs is right on the slopes with a big outdoor hot-pool and sauna facility. Next door Tamarack and Ski Tip have been recommended, too. And the new slope-side stone and timber-clad Taynton Lodge looks impressive. The Pine Inn is a 'high-standard' budget option.

Self-catering There are plenty of condo blocks and town homes. The store is inadequate, so stock up in Invermere.

Eating out Eating out options are mainly in the lodges – the Toby Creek restaurant and the Starbird in the Pine Inn are good. The Heliplex restaurant has great views of the mountain and 'good burgers'. There's a shuttle-bus to the restaurants down in Invermere.

Après-ski Après-ski revolves around the T-bar and Grill in the Pine Inn and the Jackpine pub in the Horsethief Lodge. The Ski Tip Lodge terrace is popular on sunny afternoons. The Glacier is the night club.

Off the slopes The hot-pool facility, with thermal baths, a swimming pool, slides and sauna is excellent, but it gets rather taken over by kids.

Whistler   675m/2,210ft

North America's biggest mountain set in Alpine-style scenery

WHAT IT COSTS

(((((6)

HOW IT RATES

The slopes

Snow	****
Extent	****
Experts	*****
Intermediates	*****
Beginners	***
Convenience	****
Queues	***
Restaurants	**

The rest

Scenery	***
Resort charm	***
Off-slope	**

What's new

Whistler is not planning anything new on mountain this season. The latest change was the two fast quad chairs from the base of Whistler mountain, built a few seasons ago. They provide a good alternative to an often overcrowded gondola.

Longer term it is hoping to open more terrain and has offered to swap some pieces of land with a Provincial Park area to enable it to build a lift. But that is still awaiting approval.

Whistler Creek continues to be developed. New shops and accommodation make it less of an outpost and more a suitable place to stay in its own right.

➕ North America's biggest, both in area and vertical (1610m/5,280ft)

➕ Good slopes for most abilities, with an unrivalled combination of high open bowls and woodland trails

➕ Good snow record

➕ Almost Alpine scenery, unlike the rounded Rockies of Colorado

➕ Attractive modern village at the foot of the slopes, car-free in the centre, with lively après-ski

➕ Good range of restaurants and bars (though not enough of them)

➕ Easy access from the UK – non-stop flights to Vancouver, short transfer

➕ Excellent heli-operation nearby

➖ Proximity to the ocean means a lot of cloudy weather and, with the low altitude, when it's snowing on the mountain it's often raining at resort level

➖ Two separate mountains are linked only at resort level

➖ Some runs get very crowded

➖ Lift queues are often a problem

➖ Mountain restaurants are mostly functional (and overcrowded)

➖ Whistler is in danger of becoming a victim of its own success – attracting more people than the mountain or the village facilities (restaurants in particular) can cope with

Provided you go to Whistler prepared for cloudy skies and rain at the base, you'll love it. Last season our December visit coincided with such typical weather, and huge early snowfalls, but the 2000/01 season was an unusually poor snow year for all of western Canada and meant more blue sky days than usual. Even then, Whistler was a good bet, getting more snow than many places in the area. Whatever the weather, Whistler's combination of wonderful varied and extensive terrain, big vertical, reliable snow and good lifts is unrivalled, and for a purpose-built resort the village is attractive. Most readers love it, though queuing is something of a problem, as are overcrowded runs and restaurants. Extracts from our regular crop of reports: 'Enough terrain to satisfy any expert.' 'Fabulous skiing.' 'Charming, pretty and friendly.' But a touch of scepticism has crept in too: 'Just like Disneyland on snow – highly organised, good at extracting money from you and prone to the odd queue for the best attractions!'

The resort

Whistler Village sits at the foot of its two mountains, Whistler and Blackcomb, a scenic 120km/75-mile drive inland from Vancouver on Canada's west coast. Whistler started as a locals' ski area in 1966 with a few ramshackle buildings in what is now Whistler Creek. Whistler Village was developed in the late 1970s, and a village spread up the lower slopes of Blackcomb Mountain in the 1980s. This village, a 10-minute walk from Whistler, is now known simply as Upper Village.

Both centres are traffic-free. The architecture is varied and, for a purpose-built resort, quite tasteful. There are lots of chalet-style apartments on the hillsides. The centres have individually designed wood and concrete buildings,

blended together in a master plan around pedestrian streets and squares. There are no monstrous high-rise blocks – but there are a lot of large

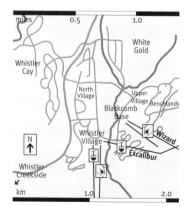

MOUNTAIN FACTS

Altitude	655m-2285m
	2,140ft-7,490ft
Lifts	33
Pistes	7,071 acres
Green	18%
Blue	55%
Black	27%
Snowmaking	
	565 acres
Recco detectors used	

five- or six-storey hotel and apartment buildings. Whistler Village has most of the bars, restaurants and shops, and the two main gondolas (one to each mountain). Whistler North, further from the lifts, is newer and has virtually merged with the original village, making a huge car-free area of streets lined with shops, condos and restaurants. Upper Village is much smaller and quieter. Its huge Fairmont Chateau Whistler hotel dominates the views of the village from the mountain.

Whistler Creek, a 10-minute bus-ride from Whistler Village, is rather out on a limb, with limited bars and restaurants. But it's changing fast – a five-year development project is well under way and more readers are staying there.

There is a free bus between Whistler and Upper Village but it's just as quick to walk. Staying further out means paying for buses or taxis – which are inexpensive.

The most convenient place to stay is Whistler Village as you can access either mountain by gondola. A lot of accommodation is an inconvenient walk or bus-ride from the villages and slopes. Whistler Creek, though convenient for Whistler's slopes, is less so for Blackcomb and is pretty quiet.

Whistler is very cosmopolitan, with many visitors from Japan and Australia as well as Europe and the US. But it is now getting very crowded and some reporters have found the central area around Village Square very noisy in the early hours and complained of rowdy behaviour.

The mountains

The area has acquired a formidable and well-deserved reputation among experts. But both Whistler and Blackcomb also have loads of well-groomed intermediate terrain. Together they have over 200 marked trails, and form the biggest area of slopes, with

boarding *Both mountains are excellent for every level of boarder. All the main lifts are chairs and gondolas and terrain ranges from gentle green runs to wide open bowls and heart-stopping cliff drops and chutes. The Whistler terrain-park and half-pipe is a good place to hone skills before trying the more difficult 26-acre park on Blackcomb. The resort regularly hosts big snowboard events so it's not uncommon to see pro riders. There are T-bars on the glacier, but they're not vicious and any discomfort is worth it for the powder! The resort is popular with snowboarders and known for its summer boarding camps.*

LIFT PASSES

2001/02 prices in
Canadian dollars

**Whistler/Blackcomb
Lift Ticket**
Covers all lifts on
both Whistler and
Blackcomb
mountains.
Main pass
1-day pass 63
6-day pass 360
Senior citizens
Over 65: 6-day pass
295
Children
Age 13-18: 6-day pass
295
Age 7-12: 6-day pass
173
Under 7: free pass
Short-term passes
Half-day pass 47
Notes
Whistler/Blackcomb
pass of 2 days or
over gives one non-
skiing day; 6-day
pass valid for 7 days
with one day non-
skiing. A beginners'
day pass, for the
Magic Chair only, is
available (27).

the longest runs, in North America.

Many reporters enthuse about the
mountain host service and the 'go
slow' patrol – some find the latter
'over zealous', but crowded slopes,
especially on the runs home ('a human
slalom'), mean they're often needed.

THE SLOPES
The best in North America
Whistler Mountain is accessed from
Whistler Village by a two-stage,
10-person gondola that rises over
1100m/3,600ft to Roundhouse Lodge,
the main mid-mountain base. There is
an alternative of two consecutive fast
quads, which take you slightly lower.

Runs back down through the trees
fan out from the gondola – cruises to
the Emerald and Big Red fast chairs,
longer runs to the gondola mid-station.

From Roundhouse you can see the
jewel in Whistler's crown – magnificent
above-the-tree-line bowls, served by
the fast Peak and Harmony quads. The
bowls have groomed trails, but are
mostly go-anywhere terrain for experts.

A six-person gondola from Whistler
Creek also accesses Whistler mountain.

Access to **Blackcomb** from Whistler
Village is by an eight-seater gondola,

followed by a fast quad. From Upper
Village you take two consecutive fast
quads up to the main Rendezvous
restaurant. From the arrival points you
can go left for great cruising terrain
and the Glacier Express quad up to the
Horstman Glacier area, or right for
steeper slopes, the terrain park or the
7th Heaven chair. The 1610m/5,280ft
vertical from the top of this chair to
the base is the largest in North
America (and big even by Alpine
standards). Or you can go into the
glacier area. A T-bar from the Horstman
Glacier brings you (with a very short
hike) to the Blackcomb Glacier in the
next valley – a beautiful run which
takes you away from all lifts.

Fresh Tracks is a deal that allows
you to ride up Whistler mountain (at
extra cost) at 7.30, have a buffet
breakfast and hit the slopes as soon
as they open – very popular with many
of our reporters. A good tip is to hit
the slopes first and breakfast after –
otherwise you may miss the quietest
time on the slopes.

Blackcomb has floodlit beginner
slopes a couple of nights a week. Free
guided tours of each mountain are
offered twice a day.

SNOW RELIABILITY
Excellent at altitude

Snow conditions at the top are usually excellent – the place gets around 360 inches of snow a year, on average. But because the resort is low and close to the Pacific, the bottom slopes can be wet, icy or unskiable. People may 'download' from the mid-stations due to poor snow, especially in late season.

FOR EXPERTS
Few can rival it

Whistler Mountain's bowls are enough to keep experts happy for weeks. Each has endless variations, with chutes and gullies of varied steepness and width. The biggest challenges are around Glacier, Whistler and West Bowls, with runs such as The Cirque and Doom & Gloom – though you can literally go

anywhere in this high, wide area.

Blackcomb has challenging slopes too; not so extensive as Whistler's, but some are more challenging. From the top of the 7th Heaven lift, traverse to Xhiggy's Meadow, for sunny bowl runs.

If you're feeling brave, go in the opposite direction and drop into the extremely steep chutes down towards Glacier Creek, including the infamous 41° Couloir Extreme, which had moguls the size of elephants at the top when we last visited. Or try the also serious, but less frequented, steep bowls reached by hiking up Spanky's Ladder, after taking the Glacier Express lift.

Both mountains have challenging trails through trees. The adventurous can explore the 'Peak to Creek' trails, from below Whistler's West Bowl to Whistler Creek – still outside the area

Whistler

617

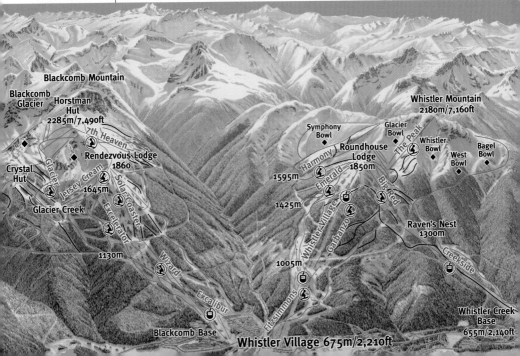

Blackcomb Mountain

Blackcomb Glacier

Horstman Hut 2285m/7,490ft

7th Heaven

Rendezvous Lodge 1860

Crystal Hut

Glacier Creek

1645m

1130m

Blackcomb Base

Whistler Village 675m/2,210ft

Symphony Bowl

Harmony

Roundhouse Lodge 1850m

Glacier Bowl

The Peak

Whistler Bowl

West Bowl

Bagel Bowl

Whistler Mountain 2180m/7,160ft

1595m

1425m

1005m

Raven's Nest 1300m

Creekside

Whistler Creek Base 655m/2,140ft

boundary, so rescues are costly. If all this isn't enough, there's also local heli-skiing available by the day.

FOR INTERMEDIATES
Ideal and extensive terrain

Both mountains are an intermediate's paradise. In good weather, good intermediates will enjoy the less extreme variations in the bowls on both mountains.

One of our favourite intermediate runs is down the Blackcomb Glacier, from the top of the mountain to the bottom of the Excelerator chair over 1000m/3,300ft below. This 5km/3 mile run, away from all lifts, starts with a two-minute walk up from the top of the Showcase T-bar. You drop over the ridge into a wide, wide bowl – not too suddenly or you'll get a short, sharp shock in the very steep double-diamond Blowhole. The further you traverse, the shallower the slope.

You are guaranteed good snow on the Horstman Glacier too, and typically gentle runs. Lower down there are lots of perfect cruising runs through the trees – ideal when the weather is bad.

On Whistler Mountain, there are easy blue pistes in Symphony, Harmony and Glacier bowls. Even early intermediates should try them, since there's always an easy way down. The Saddle run from the top of the Harmony Express lift is a favourite with many of our reporters. The blue Highway 86 path, which skirts West Bowl from the top of the Peak chair, has beautiful views over a steep valley and across to the rather phallic Black Tusk mountain.

Lower down the mountain there is a vast choice of groomed blue runs with a series of efficient fast chairs to bring you back up to the top of the gondola. It's a cruiser's paradise – especially the aptly named Ego Bowl. A great long run is the fabulous Dave Murray Downhill all the way from mid-mountain to the finish at Whistler Creek. Although marked black on the map, it's a wonderful fast and varied cruise when it has been groomed.

FOR BEGINNERS
OK if the sun shines

Whistler has excellent nursery slopes by the mid-station of the gondola, as does Blackcomb, down at the base area. Both have facilities higher up too.

On Whistler, after progressing from the nursery slopes, there are some

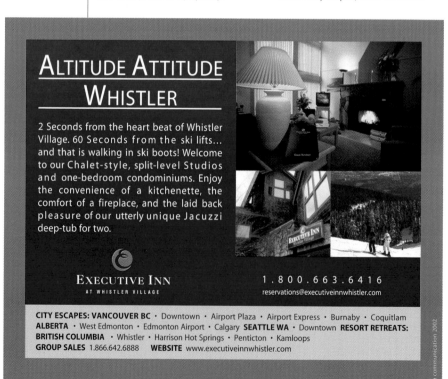

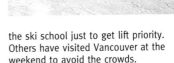

SCHOOLS/GUIDES

2001/02 prices in Canadian dollars

Whistler and Blackcomb
Guided instruction with Ski Esprit course
Classes 3 or 4 days
Full day from 8.45
3 days: 259
4 days: 289
Children's classes
Ages: 3 to 17
5 6hr days including lunch, lift ticket and equipment rental: 519 for 3- to 4-year-olds
Private lessons
Half day: 365
Full day: 545

gentle first runs from the top of the gondola. Their downside is other people speeding past. You can return by various chairs or continue to the base area on greens. Check the latter are in good condition first, and maybe avoid them at the end of the day, when they can get very crowded.

On Blackcomb, Green Line runs from the top of the mountain to the bottom. The top part is particularly gentle, with some steeper pitches lower down. As a recent reporter said, 'A tentative beginner in our group found it hard to move about the resort with confidence because of the varying steepness of green runs.'

Another reservation is – you guessed – the weather. Beginners don't get a lot out of heavy snowfalls, and might be put off by rain and unpredictable conditions.

FOR CROSS-COUNTRY
Picturesque but low
There are over 28km/18 miles of cross-country tracks, starting in the valley by the river, on the path between Whistler and Blackcomb. But it is low altitude here, so conditions can be unreliable. Keen cross-country merchants can catch the train to better areas.

QUEUES
An ever-increasing problem
Whistler is becoming a victim of its own success. Even with 15 fast lifts – more than any other resort in North America – the mountains are queue-prone, especially at weekends when people pour in from Vancouver. There are noticeboards displaying waiting times at different lifts, but most people would prefer shorter queues.

Some reporters have signed up with

the ski school just to get lift priority. Others have visited Vancouver at the weekend to avoid the crowds.

The routes out of Whistler Village in the morning can be busy. Whistler Creek is less of a problem. Some of the chairs higher up both mountains produce long queues – especially Harmony (where even the singles line seems to take ages). Visiting the resort outside peak season may not help – we found some lifts, including the gondola to Blackcomb, were kept closed in an early-December visit.

MOUNTAIN RESTAURANTS
Overcrowded
The main restaurants sell decent, good-value food but are charmless self-service stops with long queues. They're huge, but not huge enough. 'Seat-seekers' are employed to find spaces, but success is not guaranteed.

Past reporters have stressed the need to lunch early. But even that no longer works – 'They're packed by 11.30,' say recent reporters. Late lunches don't work either because the lifts close at 3pm or 3.30, so the answer may be a big breakfast, ski through the day and snack at 3.30.

Blackcomb has the Rendezvous, mainly a big (850-seat) self-service place but also home to Christine's, a table-service restaurant – the best on either mountain. Glacier Creek Lodge, at the bottom of the Glacier Express, is a better self-service place. But even this (1,496 seats) gets incredibly crowded. Whistler has the massive (1,740-seat) Roundhouse Lodge; Steep's Grill is its table-service refuge.

Reporters generally prefer the smaller places – but they're still packed unless you time it right. On

CHILDCARE

Whistler Kids takes non-skiing children aged 3 months to 3 years.

Whistler Kids offers various skiing and snowboarding programmes to children of all ability levels, aged 3 to 17. The Kids' Adventure Camp is a 5-day camp for 3 to 12 year olds. Ride Tribe is a programme for ages 13 to 17.

Après-ski programmes – with a 'Kids' Night Out' – are offered during the season.

Blackcomb, Crystal Hut at the top of the Crystal Ridge chair, and Horstman Hut at the top of the mountain, are tiny Alpine-style huts with great views.

On Whistler, Raven's Nest, at the top of the Creekside gondola, is a small and friendly deli/cafe. And the Chic Pea near the top of the Garbanzo chair-lift is 'funky and rustic' for pizza and barbecue. You can of course descend to the base – the table-service Dusty's at Whistler Creek has good sandwiches and soup and doesn't get too crowded.

SCHOOLS AND GUIDES
A great formula

Ski Esprit and Ride Esprit programmes run for three or four days and combine instruction with showing you around the mountains – with the same instructor daily. Many of our reporters have joined these groups (usually small), and all reports are glowing: 'Big improvement in confidence and skill' is typical. There are specialist clinics and snowboard classes, too.

Extremely Canadian (938 9656) specialise in guiding and coaching adventurous advanced intermediates upwards in Whistler's steep and deep terrain. A lot of their coaches compete in free-ride and skiercross competitions. We have been with them a few times and they really are great! As a reporter said, 'You end up skiing places that other people don't even know about – we were very impressed.' They run two- and four-day clinics and also have their own catered chalet you can stay at.

FACILITIES FOR CHILDREN
Impressive

Blackcomb's base area has a special slow-moving Magic Chair to get children part-way up the mountain. Whistler's gondola mid-station has a splendid kids-only area. A reporter found the staff 'friendly and instilled confidence'. The drawback for young children is the risk of bad weather.

Staying there

HOW TO GO
High quality packages

A lot of British tour operators go to Whistler and some run catered chalets. **Hotels** There is a very wide range.
(((((5) **Fairmont Chateau Whistler** (938 8000) Well run and luxurious at the foot of Blackcomb. Excellent spa with pools and tubs. The Entree Gold floor is expensive and especially cosseting.
(((((5) **Westin Resort & Spa** (905 5000) Luxury all-suite hotel at the foot of Whistler mountain next to the lifts.
(((((4) **Pan Pacific Lodge** (905 2999) Luxury all-suite place at Whistler Village base. Pool/sauna/tub.
((((4) **Lost Lake Lodge** (932 2882) 'Excellent' place: studios and suites, out by the golf course. Pool/tub.
((((4) **Crystal Lodge** (932 2221) 'Comfortable, friendly, convenient', in Whistler Village. Pool/sauna/tub.
(((3) **Glacier Lodge** (932 2882) In Upper Village. Pool/tub.
Self-catering There are plenty of spacious, comfortable condominiums in both chalet and hotel-style blocks.

Selected chalets in Whistler

SKI MIQUEL HOLIDAYS

T 01457 821200 F 01457 821209

THE LOUNGE OF CHALET WHITE WOLF ↑

GETTING THERE

Air Vancouver,
transfer 2hr.

ACTIVITIES

Indoor Ice skating,
museum, tennis, hot-
tubs
Outdoor Flightseeing,
heli-skiing, snow-
shoe excursions,
snowmobiling,
paragliding, fishing,
horse-riding, sleigh
rides, guided tours

Phone numbers
From distant parts of
Canada, add the
prefix 1 604.
From abroad, add the
prefix +1 604.

TOURIST OFFICE

Postcode V0N 1B4
t 932 3928
f 932 7231
reservations@tourism
whistler.com
www.whistler-
blackcomb.com

WHISTLER / LEANNA RATHKELLY

Modern buildings, but
with lots of traditional
elements →

EATING OUT
High quality and plenty of choice

Reporters are enthusiastic about the
range, quality and value of places to
eat, but do book well ahead: there
simply aren't enough restaurant seats
to meet demand. Some cheaper places
won't take bookings for small groups,
meaning long waits. Bars serve decent
food, too. If you've got kids, as one
reporter found, 'Some restaurants
don't allow under-19s in, or even to sit
outside, and we had to wait up to two
hours elsewhere.'

At the top of the market, Umberto's
in Whistler Village has classy Italian
cuisine. The Rimrock Café at Whistler
Creek serves 'the best seafood we
have ever eaten'.

Good mid-market Whistler Village
places include Araxi (Italian/Pacific),
the Keg (steak and seafood), Teppan
Village (Japanese), Mongolie (Asian)
and Kipriaki Norte (Greek). Crab Shack
has good-value seafood. In Village
North: the good-value Brewhouse has
great atmosphere (steaks, burgers),
Caramba has 'good Mediterranean food
at reasonable prices', and the Tandoori
Grill has 'Indian just like at home'. Hy's
Steakhouse has the best steaks. Sushi-
Ya, and Quattro (Italian) are good.

There are plenty of budget places,
including the bars mentioned under
Après-ski. Uli's Flipside and The Old
Spaghetti Factory have been
recommended for pasta.

APRES-SKI
Something for most tastes

With over 50 bars, night-clubs and
restaurants, Whistler is very lively.
Most of the après bars seem to
compete to see who can serve the

biggest dustbin lid of nachos. Popular
at Whistler are the Longhorn, with a
huge terrace, and the Garibaldi Lift
Company. The Dubh Linn Gate Irish pub
has 'great live music and Guinness'.
Black's is good for a quiet drink while
Tapley's seems 'the nearest thing to a
locals' bar'. Merlin's is the focus at
Blackcomb base, and Dusty's at
Whistler Creek – good beer, loud music.

Later on, Buffalo Bills is lively and
loud and the Amsterdam is worth a
look. The Cinnamon Bear in the Delta
Resort hotel is a sports bar with live
music. Tommy Africa's vies with Maxx
Fish, the Savage Beagle, Moe Joe's and
Garfinkel's for the clubbing crowd. Try
the Mallard bar in Chateau Whistler and
the Crystal Lodge piano bar for a
relaxed time.

OFF THE SLOPES
Not ideal

Whistler is a long way to go if you
don't intend to hit the slopes. Meadow
Park Sports Centre has a full range of
fitness facilities. There are also several
luxurious spas. Excursions to Squamish
(famous for its eagles) are easy. A day
trip to Vancouver is recommended.

Whistler

621

For us the main attraction of skiing or riding in eastern Canada is the French culture and language that are predominant in the province of Québec. It really feels like a different country from the rest of Canada – as indeed many of its residents want it to become. It is also only a six-hour flight from the UK, compared with ten for Canada's west. Tremblant is the main destination resort and is one of the cutest purpose-built resorts we've seen (though it is now in danger of being spoilt by expansion). The other main base is Québec city, which dates from the 17th century and is full of atmosphere and Canadian history. The slopes of the main resorts are small both in extent and in vertical drop, and the weather can be perishingly cold in early and mid-winter. But at least this means that the extensive snowmaking systems that all the resorts have can be effective for a long season. Be prepared for variable snow conditions and don't go expecting light, dry powder – if that's what you want, head west.

There are lots of ski and snowboard areas in Ontario – Canada's most populated province – but most of them are tiny and cater just for locals. For people heading on holiday for a week or more, eastern Canada really means the province of Québec. Québec – and its capital, Québec city – are heavily dominated by the French culture and language. Notices, menus, trail maps and so on are usually printed in both French and English. Many ski area workers will be bilingual or just French-speaking. And French cuisine abounds.

The weather is very variable, rather like New England's – but it can get even colder. Hence the snow, though pretty much guaranteed by snowmaking, can vary enormously in quality. When we were there one April we were slush skiing in Tremblant one day and rattling along on a rock hard surface in Mont-Ste-Anne the next. A 2001 reporter visited Mont-Ste-Anne,

Stoneham and Le Massif in late January and experienced mild temperatures and several perfect blue sky days.

The main destination resort is Tremblant (see separate chapter), about 90 minutes' drive from Montreal. Other areas near here popular with locals include **Mont Blanc** (with only 300m/980ft of vertical, hardly a competitor to the Franco-Italian version) and the **Saint-Sauveur** valley (five areas, each with around 200m/660ft of vertical and with interchangeable lift passes).

The other main place to stay for easy access to several ski resorts is **Québec city**. Old Québec, at the city's heart, is North America's only walled city and is a World Heritage site. Within the city walls are narrow, winding streets and 17th and 18th century houses. It is situated right on the banks of the St Lawrence river. In January/February there is a famous

INTRAWEST
Tremblant's modern buildings have a distinctly French-influenced style →

TOURIST OFFICES

Mont Blanc
www.ski-mont-blanc.
com

Saint-Sauveur
www.montsaintauveur.
com

Québec city
www.quebecregion.
com

Mont-Ste-Anne
www.mont-sainte-
anne.com

Stoneham
www.ski-stoneham.
com.

Le Massif
www.lemassif.com

two-week carnival, with an ice castle, snow sculptures, dog-sled and canoe races, night parades and grand balls. But most of the winter is low season for Québec city, with good-value rooms available in big hotels. Because of this, the area is popular with British school groups, especially in late season. Non-skiers, or those who like the option to do other activities, won't be bored whatever time of year they go.

There are several ski and snowboard areas close to Québec city, and a Carte Blanche pass which covers the three main areas: a total of 106 runs, 26 lifts and Canada's largest night skiing area. A car is handy, but there are buses to some areas.

The biggest and most varied area (though easily skied in a day by a good skier) is **Mont-Ste-Anne**, 30 minutes away and with some accommodation of its own. A gondola takes you to the top, and slopes lead down the front (south) and back (north) sides. The views from the front over the ice-flows of the St Lawrence are spectacular. There are intermediate cruising runs on both sides and some steep blacks (including World Cup runs) through the trees on the front among its 63km/39 miles of trails. There are some easy top-to-bottom runs and good nursery slopes at the

base. In the spring you can stop by the Sugar Shack and try fresh maple toffee. The resort has two terrain-parks, including a 600m/1,950ft boarder-cross course. Fifteen trails are floodlit until 10pm seven nights a week (five in January). Over 80% of the runs are covered by snowmaking. It also has the largest cross-country centre in Canada, with 223km/139 miles of trails.

Stoneham is the closest resort to Québec city, around 20 minutes away. It also has its own small village with accommodation and an impressive base lodge with bar, restaurant and big wooden deck. Après-ski in the lodge can be lively, and there is often live music. It is a small area, with only around 30km/20 miles of runs spread between three faces and a vertical of 420m/1,380ft. But it is very sheltered in a sunny setting protected from wind. It suits families well, with mainly intermediate and beginner terrain. It added a new learn to ski area in 2001/02 equipped with a magic carpet moving walkway. Snowboarders, freestylers and freeskiers are attracted to the area by the resort's impressive terrain-park and permanent boarder-cross course, and it now has a 400ft/122m long super-pipe that meets the requirements for international freestyle competitions. A recent reporter raved about how addictive it was. Stoneham also has the biggest night-skiing operation in Canada, with two of the three faces lit top-to-bottom. Some 85% of the area has snowmaking.

Le Massif is around an hour away from Québec city and is a cult area with locals. It is in a UNESCO World Biosphere Reserve, and is just metres from the St Lawrence. The views of the ice-flows are stunning, and you feel you are heading straight down into them when you are on the pretty, tree-lined trails.

The area of slopes, though small, has the largest vertical drop in the east. There are a couple of steep double-black-diamond runs and some good, well-groomed black and blue cruising runs. They have recently added Québec's longest high-speed quad chair and extended their double chair. And sixteen new runs have been added to the area, including beginner and intermediate runs and one designed to meet International Ski Federation World Cup standards.

Introduction

623

Where to Ski and Snowboard is an annual publication – don't rely on an old edition

Resorts change every year as new lifts are built, new slopes are opened up, more snowmaking is installed, ski schools come under new management, hotels, bars and restaurants change hands. We revise the book annually to keep up with these developments.
And the book itself is constantly developing, with new features and new resorts being added.

We publish in late August or early September. To get the latest edition call 01373 835208 or email sales@snow-zone.co.uk

Tremblant 265m/870ft

Charming traffic-free village at foot of surprisingly small area of slopes

WHAT IT COSTS

((((5))))

HOW IT RATES

The slopes

Snow	****
Extent	**
Experts	***
Intermediates	***
Beginners	****
Convenience	****
Queues	***
Restaurants	**

The rest

Scenery	***
Resort charm	****
Off-slope	***

What's new

For 2001/02 a two-acre beginner area was opened by the village with two magic carpet lifts (the longest 128m/420ft). And snowmaking was increased by 33%.

The enlargement of the Sommet des Neiges luxury hotel will be finished for 2002/03. And the new Tremblant-Les-Eaux hotel with outdoor whirlpool will open.

➕ Charming purpose-built core village

➕ Slope-side accommodation

➕ Good snow reliability with extensive artificial back-up

➕ Some good runs for all abilities

➕ Good variety of restaurants and bars

➖ Limited area for keen piste-bashers

➖ Can be perishingly cold in midwinter

➖ Weekend queues and overcrowding

➖ New building on edge not in keeping with cute original style – and huge expansion plans

Tremblant is eastern Canada's main destination resort and attracts quite a lot of Brits. But for keen piste-bashers the limited slopes don't really do justice to the cute and lively little core village, which has been built in traditional style.

THE RESORT

Tremblant has been transformed in recent years from a day or weekend ski area for locals to being eastern Canada's leading ski resort. Intrawest (which also owns Whistler and several other North American resorts) developed a charming purpose-built village in the traditional style of old Québec. Buildings in bright, vibrant colours line narrow, cobbled traffic-free streets and squares, and it has a very French feel to it with lots of galleries, boutiques, patisseries and cafes. But recent development on the edge has been of more modern large hotels and condos which contrast sharply with the original development – and there's a 10-year plan to triple the resort's size.

THE MOUNTAINS

In its small area, Tremblant has a good variety of terrain.

Slopes A heated gondola takes you to the top, from where there are good views over the village and a 14km/9 mile lake on the so-called south side, and over National Park wilderness on the north side. The north side is really north-east facing and gets the morning sun – a high-speed quad brings you back and there are two other chairs to play on. The Edge lift accesses another summit, serving mainly expert terrain. Back on the south side (really south-west facing and so good for the afternoon sun) you can go right back to town on blue or green runs, or use two high-speed quads to explore the top and bottom halves. The Versant Soleil area is more directly south-facing and has one top-to-bottom blue run with all the rest being black runs and tree runs.

Snow reliability Over 50% of the terrain is covered by snowmaking – claimed to be 'the most powerful in North America'.

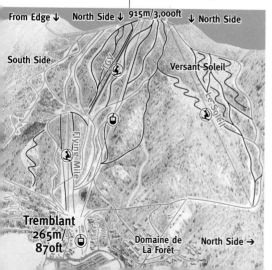

Tremblant
265m/
870ft

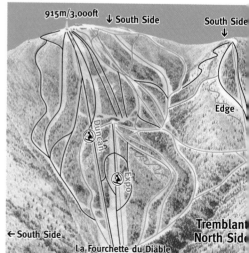

Tremblant
North Side

MOUNTAIN FACTS

Altitude	230m-875m
	750ft-2,870ft
Lifts	13
Pistes	75km
	47 miles
Green	17%
Blue	33%
Black	50%
Snowmaking	
	464 acres

Central reservations phone number
Call 425 8681.

Phone numbers
From distant parts of Canada, add the prefix 1 819.
From abroad, add the prefix +1 819.

TOURIST OFFICE
Postcode JOT 1ZO
t 681 2000
f 681 5990
info_tremblant
@intrawest.com
www.tremblant.ca

Tremblant has more miles of cross-country trails than it has downhill ➔

Experts Half the runs are classified as suitable for advanced skiers and riders. But we found a few of the blacks rather overclassified. There are steep top-to-bottom bump runs on the north side and great tree runs off the Edge lift. The south side has some shorter challenging runs. The Versant Soleil area has more black runs and some tough runs in the trees.

Intermediates Both north and south sides have good cruising and we found the north side rather less crowded. There are blue-classified runs in the trees as well as on groomed trails.

Beginners The new, 2-acre beginner area for 2001/02 is a huge improvement on the previously inadequate facilities. There are long, easy top-to-bottom green runs to progress to on both north and south sides.

Snowboarding The slopes are good, with mostly chairs, and the excellent gravity terrain-park and half-pipe are on the top half of the north side.

Cross-country There are around 100km/60 miles of trails.

Queues At weekends there can be lines but they tend to move quickly. We found crowds on the main run back to the village more of a problem.

Mountain restaurants The main Grand Manitou restaurant has good views back over town and decent food but can get crowded. Many people go back to town for lunch – the Diable was recommended by a reporter for its own micro-brewed beer and huge portions of poutine (a local speciality: chips, melted cheese and gravy).

Schools and guides There's a wide variety of options and a reporter recommends the 90-minute Super

Group 4 (maximum of four people): 'Very impressed with instructors and small group was brilliant.'

Facilities for children Children from age one can be looked after until 9.30pm.

STAYING THERE

How to go There's no shortage of packages from the UK.

Hotels and condos Many reporters stay at the luxurious Fairmont Tremblant and praise it highly. Others have stayed at the Plaza condos – 'central', 'comfortable' and 'well equipped' but warned of 'very limited food shopping – best to have a car'.

Eating out There is a good variety of restaurants.

Après-ski There are several lively bars, and there was live music in the main square when we were there in April. There are floodlit slopes some nights.

Off the slopes There's a £2 million Acquaclub pool complex built to resemble a lake set in a forest. You can go ice climbing, horse-riding, snow-shoeing, ice skating, snowmobiling, dog-sledding and swimming – and visit Montreal.

Tremblant

625

Andorra

- ✚ Excellent choice for beginners and early intermediates, with good instruction, good piste grooming and plenty of gentle slopes
- ✚ Lots of efficient, modern lifts
- ✚ Good combination of altitude and extensive snowmaking with strong southern sunshine
- ✚ Lively nightlife, with cheap duty-free drinks and generous measures
- ✚ Cheap packages in some resorts, competing with those offered in inferior resorts in eastern Europe
- ✚ Resorts close enough to each other – and some are physically linked – so you can sample at least one other during a week

- ➖ Most resorts have little charm
- ➖ Much of the country is often choked with traffic, and Soldeu and Pas de la Casa are on the busy main road through the country
- ➖ Nightlife tends to revolve around bars – not much variety, and some places can get rowdy
- ➖ Potential for a really impressive linked lift network is still not exploited
- ➖ Packages to major resorts no longer the bargain they once were
- ➖ Construction work is still going on
- ➖ Not the place to go if you want to get away from fellow Brits

Andorra is surging in popularity with British visitors. Last season twice as many Brits went to Andorra as to either Switzerland or to Canada and USA combined – and Andorra nearly overtook Italy for numbers of British winter sports visitors.

Andorra used to be seen primarily as a cheap and cheerful holiday aimed mainly at younger singles and couples looking for a good time in the duty-free bars and clubs as well as learning to ski or snowboard. And some of the resorts are still excellent for that market. But there's more to it than that. The ski schools have always been excellent, with lots of native English-speaking instructors. In recent years, some more luxurious hotels have been built. And lots of money has been pumped in to developing powerful lift systems and piste grooming fleets that many well-known Alpine resorts would be proud of; this makes the slopes much more attractive to intermediates as well as beginners.

But there are big differences in the characters of the resorts. Soldeu is the resort that has tried hardest to move up-market; full chapters on Soldeu and the other two major resorts of Arinsal and Pas de la Casa follow.

This introduction includes some comments on the valley towns that are also marketed as ski resorts by some tour operators, and on the excellent out-of-the-way day skiing area of Arcalis.

Andorra has a relatively reliable snow record. Its situation close to both the Atlantic and the Mediterranean oceans, together with the high altitude of its resorts, means it usually gets substantial natural snowfalls. It has also invested heavily in snowmaking. This combination means you can book Andorra months in advance with some confidence. And an early reservation is necessary: late bookers can have difficulty finding an Andorra package.

Package holiday prices vary between resorts; in general, Soldeu is no longer cheap, Arinsal is the cheapest of the mainstream resorts and it and the valley towns such as La Massana and

Encamp can compete with Bulgaria, Romania and Slovenia for those on the tightest budgets. To a degree, prices once you arrive vary between resorts too. But prices for drinks and extras such as instruction and equipment rental are generally lower than in the Alps. Some reporters have found duty-free luxury goods prices not the super-bargains they had expected.

Duty-free prices and large, unmeasured helpings of spirits mean that nightlife can be very lively. If you want to spend your nights in the company of drunken young Brits, you will have no trouble finding places to do it. But in our recent experience you will equally have no trouble avoiding such scenes, and finding more civilised places in which to relax.

The sight of cranes is still common, as hotels and apartments are built to keep up with demand. It is no longer true to say that the resorts resemble giant construction sites, but they all have construction sites within them. Perhaps more irritating is the fact that the Andorrans don't seem to feel any obligation to finish the construction of a hotel in time for the season. On our visit they were still installing lights, or even staircases, in hotels full of guests in mid-season.

Adjacent resorts have linked their slopes together, meaning bigger ski areas and a bit more variety. Arinsal and Pal were linked by a new cable-car for the 2000/01 season – and have had a joint lift pass for some years.

But the biggest nonsense in the ski world still exists in the Pas de la Casa-Soldeu area. The resorts' slopes have been physically linked by lift and piste for a few seasons and form an impressive area of 190km/118 miles, comparable with big-name resorts such as Kitzbühel and Les Deux-Alpes. But because of an ancient feud between the neighbouring communities, there's still no immediate prospect of a joint lift pass; to ski them both in the same day you have to fork out for two separate lift passes.

STAYING DOWN THE VALLEY
Several valley towns can be used as bases, either to use the slopes of one resort or to explore several resorts in the course of a week.

The obviously strong candidate here is **Encamp**, which now has a powerful gondola giving a quick way into the Pas de la Casa slopes. From the top of it you can actually ski into the Soldeu area as well, but you would need to have a day ticket for that area before you set off. Encamp seemed to us the least attractive of the towns (not least because of its situation on the traffic-choked main road), but we can't claim to have examined it closely.

La Massana is a more appealing town, and has the considerable attraction of being quite well placed for access to Arcalis – an excellent but accommodation-free ski area directly to the north, described later in this chapter. La Massana is more often used as a base for Pal and Arinsal, which are much closer – and the hotel-owning mayor is apparently planning a

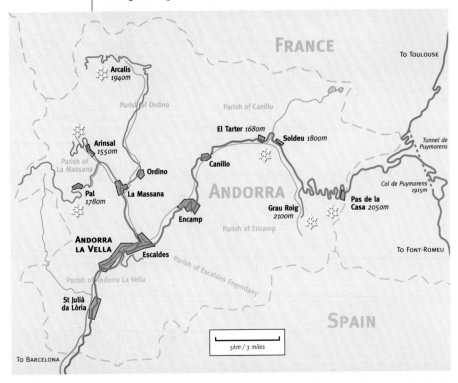

gondola link directly into the Pal slopes at some stage. **Ordino** is slightly nearer Arcalis, and pleasantly rustic.

The capital of **Andorra la Vella** is not far down the valley from Encamp (and the gondola into Pas de la Casa slopes) but is a much more attractive (though still traffic-choked) base,

especially for someone wanting a more rounded holiday. The duty-free shopping could fill a page, but probably the most interesting place is Caldea spa. The interior is laid out in a 'Hanging Gardens of Babylon' style, and the facilities are very impressive – indoor–outdoor pools, with fountains

and waterfalls, saunas, hot-tubs, Turkish baths, hydrotherapy, sunbeds, massage ... even a grapefruit bath!

There are plenty of high-quality, if relatively expensive, hotels. Andorra la Vella is not a big place, and most hotels are within easy walking distance of the centre of the town.

There is plenty of choice when it comes to dining out. Andorrans love seafood, and the traditional Catalan restaurants delight in providing it, which seems odd in the mountains; it is delivered fresh from the coast daily.

Nightlife is also well catered for – there are plenty of bars and nightclubs, and most stay open until 4am. However, the clientele is generally a more sophisticated bunch, mainly Andorrans and Spaniards, and the 'drink-until-you-drop' attitude of the mountain resorts is rare.

Arcalis 1940m/6,36oft

MOUNTAIN FACTS

Altitude 1940m-2640m
6,36oft-8,66oft

Lifts	14
Pistes	26km
	16 miles
Green	24%
Blue	24%
Red	44%
Black	8%
Snowmaking	15km
	9 miles

Recco detectors used – helicopter based

What's new

For 2002/03, 33 new snow-guns will increase snowmaking capacity by over 50%.

For 2001/02, the ski school expanded its weekend timetable. Signposting was expanded and improved.

Phone numbers

From abroad use the prefix +376.

TOURIST OFFICE

t 850121
f 850440
ito@andorra.ad
www.andorra.ad/
comuns/ordino

Arcalis is the most remote resort in Andorra, tucked away at the head of a long valley. But it makes a very worthwhile day trip – the variety of the terrain is greater than in most of the other resorts, and the snow is usually the best you will find. There is no accommodation at the mountain, but increasing amounts along the Vall d'Ordino leading up to it.

THE RESORT

Arcalis resembles some of the smaller New World resorts in having nothing at the lift base apart from a day lodge and a lot of car parking – the resort is very popular with weekenders, both from Andorra and Spain. There are actually two lift bases: Els Planells is up the hill from Arcalis itself, reached by a winding road that provides additional parking.

THE MOUNTAIN

The slopes are made up of two bowls, with lifts meeting at the ridge that separates them. The lower slopes of the main bowl, above the resort base, are lightly wooded, but all the higher slopes are open.

Slopes Chair-lifts from both bases – a fast one from the lower base – cross the main bowl, the Cercle d'Arcalis, to reach the central ridge at 2550m/8,37oft. Long red and black runs come back down. On the left-hand side of this bowl, red and blue runs are served by a chair and several

drags. From the dividing ridge, blue and red runs descend into the bowl, the Cercle de la Coma, which is entirely tree-free (its floor is at 2200m/7,22oft). On the far side of this second bowl, a chair-lift goes up to the area high point at 2640m/8,66oft, with just one red piste back down. From the Cercle de la Coma, there are three ways back to the base: a long red to Arcalis, a long green to Els Planells, or off-piste itineraries off the shoulder of the ridge, reached by a short drag-lift.

Snow reliability This is good. With the expansion for 2002/03, snowmaking will cover over half the pistes. The height of the area, which starts a good 400m/1,300ft higher than Arinsal, also adds to the length of the season.

Experts Of all the resorts in Andorra, Arcalis has the most to offer experts. The black run that leads from the ridge back down towards the base is steep, and often mogulled, while the red run it connects to starts from the top of the main chair, going through a spectacular gully before widening out. There is also plenty of space between runs for off-piste forays, especially in the Cercle de la Coma. We're told there are some good routes down from the chair on the far side of it. Arcalis is well known for heli-skiing.

Intermediates You are well catered for here, with smooth, long blues and reds being the main feature of the slopes in both bowls.

Beginners The beginners' slopes are conveniently located near the upper base lodge, with a couple of drag-lifts leading to some long easy runs.

Snowboarding There is good off-piste but beware flat sections on the easy pistes in the Cercle de la Coma.

Queues There are no problems with queues midweek, when slopes can be deserted. At the weekend the area is much busier and you may encounter a long wait at the base first thing.

Mountain restaurants The base stations have a restaurant and bar. Up the mountain choices are limited; there is a snack bar at the top of the main lift, and a self-service restaurant in the Cercle de la Coma.

Schools and guides We have no reports on the ski school, but it seems well run, with a good range of options.

Facilities for children There is a day nursery for children aged one and over, and a snow playground for 4- to 9-year-olds.

Andorra's bargain basement – much improved by the recent link to Pal

WHAT IT COSTS

HOW IT RATES

The slopes

Snow	★★★
Extent	★
Experts	★
Intermediates	★★
Beginners	★★★
Convenience	★★★
Queues	★★★
Restaurants	★★

The rest

Scenery	★★★
Resort charm	★
Off-slope	★

What's new

2002/03 will see some extra snowmaking and a 'magic carpet' conveyor belt at the El Planell beginners' area.

The main change in recent years was in 2000/01 when the cable-car link between Arinsal and Pal finally opened.

630

MOUNTAIN FACTS

Altitude 1550m-2560m
5,090ft-8,400ft

Lifts		30
Pistes		63km
		39 miles
Green		10%
Blue		39%
Red		39%
Black		12%
Snowmaking		17km
		11 miles

➕ Good value – package prices competitive with eastern Europe

➕ Plenty of lively bars

➕ Ski school geared to British needs

➕ Recent cable-car link with Pal is very good news for non-beginners

➕ Gondola from village centre gives easy access to the slopes

➖ Very confined local slopes

➖ Runs to village need good snow to be open, and don't lead to gondola station

➖ Long, linear and rather dour village, with no focus

➖ Obtrusive construction sites

Arinsal is the most British-dominated resort in Andorra, despite the fact that it is the least attractive. This may be partly because the Spanish and French set their sights higher; but it is also because British tour operators offer packages here at prices that are very tempting, especially for beginners on a budget. Whatever reservations we have, the place is way ahead of Borovets and Poiana Brasov.

Lots of young people come here for the alcohol-fuelled nightlife, and Arinsal does not disappoint. But the village doesn't have many other attractions.

THE RESORT

Arinsal is a long, narrow village of grey, stone-clad buildings, near the head of a steep-sided valley north of Andorra la Vella. Development in recent years has been rapid, and building work continues to spoil the look of the resort.

There is some accommodation at Pal, but it is a bus-ride from the lift base. Staying in Arinsal (preferably close to the gondola station) and accessing the Pal slopes via the recent cable-car link makes better sense for most visitors. Since 1998/99 a gondola from the village centre has given access to the slopes; for most guests, the alternative chair-lift 1km/0.5 miles out of town is now happily irrelevant – though you can stay next to it and ski to the door in good conditions.

There is attractive accommodation in the lower town of La Massana (see the introductory chapter to Andorra). A gondola link from here to Pal's slopes is planned at some stage; La Caubella is 700m/2,300ft above the town.

THE MOUNTAIN

The small local area above Arinsal's gondola is a narrow, east-facing bowl of open slopes. Pal's slopes, in contrast, are the most densely wooded of the Andorran resorts, calling to mind American resorts. They mainly face east; those down to the link with Arinsal face north.

Slopes Arinsal's slopes consist essentially of a single, long, narrow bowl above the upper gondola station at Comallenpla, with runs leading straight back towards that point served by a complex network of chairs and drags. Almost at the top is the cable-car station for the link to Pal. Again, these slopes present a sharp contrast – the runs are widely spread around the mountain, with four main lift bases, all reachable by road. The main one, La Caubella, is at the opposite extreme from the linking cable-car.

Snow reliability With most runs above 1950m/6,400ft, north-easterly orientation and an impressive 350 snow-guns, snow is relatively assured.

Experts These aren't great mountains for experts, but there are short, sharp black slopes at Arinsal, and quite long and challenging reds (and one black) at Pal – where there is also some off-piste scope.

Intermediates Arinsal offers a reasonable range of difficulty, but any confident intermediate is going to want to explore the Pal slopes, which are much more interesting, varied and extensive. There are easy cruises, and a variety of challenges in the central and Seturia sections.

Beginners Almost half the guests here are beginners. Arinsal and Pal both have gentle nursery slopes set apart from the main runs; they can get very crowded at peak times. There are long easy runs to progress to, as well.

Snowboarding It's possible to get around much of the area without using drags. Arinsal has a terrain-park.

Cross-country There isn't any.

Queues Although there is only one lift out of the centre, queues are not a problem on weekdays; however, Spanish weekenders and local children can hit the slopes en masse at times. Most of the higher lifts are drags, keeping the mountain open when it's windy – the cable-car link can easily be closed by wind.

Mountain restaurants These are not a highlight. They are mainly functional self-service places, doing routine snack food, and are often crowded.

Schools and guides Arinsal's ski school is its pride and joy. It offers technically sound, patient instruction, and is geared to the British market – over half the instructors are native English-speakers. Class sizes can, however, be very large in peak season. English speaking is not so widespread in the Pal school.

Facilities for children There is a ski kindergarten for those aged 4 to 8 and a non-skiing nursery for children over one year old.

STAYING THERE

How to go There is a wide choice of packages, using hotel and self-catering accommodation.

Hotels Rooms in the hotel Arinsal (835640) are not large, but it is well run, ideally placed and has a pleasant bar. The Princesa Parc (736500) is a big glossy 4-star place, also close to the gondola, with a swanky spa. The Xalet Verdu (737140) is a smooth little 4-star, a little further from the gondola. The Micolau (835052) is a characterful stone house, close to the centre, with simple rooms and a jolly beamed restaurant. If there is snow to the valley, the Crest (835866), up at the old chair-lift station, has the attraction that you can ski to the door.

Self-catering There is a reasonable choice of places. Aparthotel Sant Andreu (836164) offers simple but comfortable apartments, with a relaxed bar-restaurant on site. There are also apartments attached to the new Princesa Parc hotel.

Eating out There is a fair range of restaurants for a small resort. The Surf disco-pub is a lively spot doing open-fire grills. Cisco's is a central Tex-Mex place in a lovely wood and stone building serving Mexican food. The Rocky Mountain, up at the top of the village, is popular for steaks. The Micolau does very satisfying meals. Borda Callisa does Indian.

Après-ski Arinsal has plenty of animated bars and discos. The Surf, Cisco's and Rocky Mountain, mentioned above, all have lively bars. The liveliest places when we visited are only a short stagger apart – the Quo Vadis (a pub) and El Cau (big, noisy, with disco lights, full of kids). El Derbi was also heaving on karaoke night. If, like us, you prefer something quieter, head for Borda Callisa – out of the way and pleasantly relaxed – or the bar of the hotel Arinsal.

Off the slopes Arinsal has few facilities off the slopes. The main thing to do is to shop in Andorra la Vella, half an hour away by infrequent bus or inexpensive taxi.

Phone numbers
From abroad use the prefix +376.

TOURIST OFFICE
Pal
t 737000
f 835904
Arinsal
t 737020
f 836242
pal@arinsal.ad
www.palarinsal.com

Arinsal

631

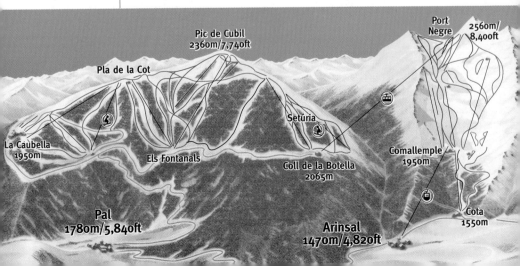

Port Negre 2560m/8,400ft

Pic de Cubil 2360m/7,740ft

Pla de la Cot

Setúria

La Caubella 1950m

Els Fontanals

Comallemple 1950m

Coll de la Botella 2065m

Cota 1550m

Pal 1780m/5,840ft

Arinsal 1470m/4,820ft

Pas de la Casa 2100m/6,890ft

Andorra's biggest ski area and liveliest resort – shame about the lift pass

WHAT IT COSTS

HOW IT RATES

The slopes
Snow	★★★
Extent	★★★
Experts	★
Intermediates	★★★
Beginners	★★★★
Convenience	★★★★
Queues	★★★
Restaurants	★★★

The rest
Scenery	★★
Resort charm	★
Off-slope	★

➕ Slopes to match many mid-sized resorts in the Alps

➕ High altitude means relatively reliable snow

➕ Andorra's liveliest nightlife

➕ Encamp (linked by gondola) is a cheaper but even more dreary base

➕ Grau Roig is a more attractive, quiet base (if you can afford it)

➕ Equally worthwhile Soldeu area is physically linked, but ...

➖ ... still no shared lift pass with Soldeu, although the lifts meet and the runs overlap

➖ Pas is an eyesore – an uncompromisingly commercial frontier town – and the centre suffers from traffic (and fumes)

➖ Very few woodland slopes, and none directly above the village – unpleasant in bad weather

The tour op brochures (and the few readers' reports we get) all say that Pas is Andorra's wildest party resort, and we don't doubt it. Having driven through it and skied down to it, we are quite happy to stay over the hill in Soldeu – or, for ideal access to the Pas slopes, secluded Grau Roig.

What's new

For 2002/03, more snowmaking is planned for the runs back to town and in the beginners' area, which will be expanded and have a new rope-tow.

Two new restaurants are due to open, one in the Pas de la Casa sector and the other in the terrain-park area at Grau Roig.

632

MOUNTAIN FACTS
Altitude	2050m-2640m
	6,730ft-8,660ft
Lifts	31
Pistes	100km
Green	14%
Blue	20%
Red	42%
Black	24%
Snowmaking	29km
	18 miles
Recco detectors used	

THE RESORT

Sited right on the border between Andorra and France, Pas de la Casa owes its development as much to duty-free sales to the French as to skiing. It is a sizeable collection of concrete-box-style apartment blocks and hotels, a product of the rapid development Andorra saw in the late 1960s and early 1970s. Some thought has gone into its layout, if not its appearance, with most accommodation conveniently placed near the lift base and slopes. The town centre boasts plenty of cheap shops and bars, as well as a sports centre. Reporters complain that it's starting to look a little tatty and that the heavy traffic generates fumes.

The resort attracts a lot of French visitors (so beware the February school holidays) and Spanish families, with only a smattering of Brits.

The lift system spreads from Pas over three adjacent valleys. The furthest from Pas has nothing but a lift station, but in the attractively wooded middle one is Grau Roig ('Rosh'). This is a mini-resort that acts as the access point for day visitors arriving by road from central Andorra and Spain, but it also makes a good base.

The road through from France goes on over the Port d'Envalira towards Soldeu and central Andorra. There is accommodation at the pass, which we suggest you avoid.

THE MOUNTAINS

Pas de la Casa boasts the most extensive slopes in Andorra, and has the Soldeu slopes right next door (but no shared lift pass – see right). With the exception of a couple of attractively wooded slopes in the central valley, the slopes are all open, and vulnerable to bad weather. There's floodlit skiing every Wednesday night.

Slopes The treeless local slopes, facing north-east, descend from a high, north–south ridge; lifts go up to it at four points. Runs on the far side of the ridge converge on Grau Roig, where there is some wooded terrain at the head of the valley. And a single lift goes on further west to the bowl of Llac del Cubill, where the Pas area adjoins the Soldeu one. On the far side of this bowl is the arrival station of the 6km/4 mile gondola up from Encamp.

Snow reliability Heavy investment in snowmaking equipment, coupled with the area's height, means a good snow reliability record and a season that often reaches late April.

Experts There are few challenges on-piste – the black runs are rarely of serious steepness, and moguls are rare. But there seem to be plenty of off-piste slopes inviting exploration.

Intermediates The slopes cater for confident intermediates far better, with plenty of top-to-bottom reds and blues on the main ridge, though they do rather lack variety.

LIFT PASS INSANITY

If they could agree on a joint lift pass the Pas de la Casa-Soldeu joint area would rival some of the Alps best-known names for extent and variety. But they can't; so if you want to ski both in a day you need to have two lift passes – one for each area. This insanity is apparently the result of some ancient feud between the families which control the two areas.

Phone numbers
From abroad use the prefix +376.

Central reservations phone number
For all resort accommodation call 801060.

TOURIST OFFICE
t 801060
f 801070
info@pasgrau.com
www.pasgrau.com

Beginners There are beginner slopes in both Pas and Grau Roig. The Pas area is a short but inconvenient bus-ride out of town. Progression to longer runs is easier in Grau Roig, too.

Snowboarding Boarding is popular with the young crowd that Pas de la Casa attracts, and there is a lift-served terrain-park and half-pipe at Grau Roig. Drags are usually avoidable.

Cross-country Although they get very little attention, there are loops totalling 12km/7 miles below Grau Roig.

Queues Queues are rarely serious, now that there are two fast chairs out of Pas – one of them a six-pack. But during French school holidays some bottlenecks can develop.

Mountain restaurants There are routine places at the ridge above Pas and the top of the gondola from Encamp, but the Rifugi dels Llacs dels Pessons at the head of the Grau Roig bowl is far from routine: as well as a bar it has a cosy beamed table-service restaurant with excellent food.

Schools and guides The ski school has an excellent reputation, with good English spoken.

Facilities for children There are ski kindergartens at Pas and Grau Roig, and a non-ski one at the latter.

STAYING THERE

How to go There's a wide choice of apartments and hotels on offer through tour operators, and even a few chalets and chalet hotels.

Hotels Himalaia-Pas is close to the slopes, has a pool and is 'comfortable and recommendable', says a reporter. The Grau Roig hotel is in a league of its own for comfort and seclusion (note that some operators list it under Soldeu).

Self-catering We have no particular recommendations.

Eating out There are doubtless various possibilities, but we rarely get reports on them. 'There are no really good restaurants,' says a reporter.

Après-ski The après-ski is 'very lively' and nightspots 'get very crowded' say reporters. British tour operators take over one bar (the Marseilles). The Billboard is 'by far the best club', and the Milwaukee is one of the most popular bars. The Safari bar is 'a good place to chill out'.

Off the slopes Off-slope activity is limited to shopping ('Electrical goods and perfume are good buys,' says one reporter), visiting the leisure centre or taking a trip to Andorra la Vella for more of the same.

Pas de la Casa

633

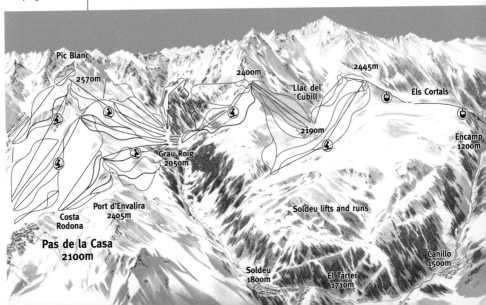

Soldeu

Ideal for beginners and early intermediates, but check where you're staying

WHAT IT COSTS

HOW IT RATES

The slopes

Snow	***
Extent	**
Experts	*
Intermediates	***
Beginners	****
Convenience	***
Queues	***
Restaurants	*

The rest

Scenery	***
Resort charm	*
Off-slope	*

➕ Slopes to match many mid-sized resorts in the Alps

➕ Impressively efficient lift system

➕ Not as rowdy a resort as it once was

➕ Ski school has excellent British-run section for English-speaking visitors

➕ Equally worthwhile Pas de la Casa area is physically linked, but ...

➖ ... still no shared lift pass with Pas de la Casa, although the lifts meet and the runs overlap

➖ Slopes can get very crowded

➖ Village is on the main road through Andorra and suffers heavy traffic

➖ Packages not particularly cheap

➖ Not much to do off the slopes

If we were planning a holiday in Andorra, it would be in Soldeu (or the isolated hotel at Grau Roig, up the road – covered in the Pas de la Casa chapter). Despite the traffic, it is the least unattractive village, and its slopes are the most interestingly varied (though crowded). But we would want to explore the Pas de la Casa slopes, too, even if it meant spending more on lift passes. The alternative bases of El Tarter and Canillo are often sold as Soldeu but are much quieter.

For many people the trickier question is whether to come here or to go somewhere completely different. Soldeu no longer competes on package holiday prices with the bargain basements of eastern Europe, so the alternatives are more likely to be in Austria or Italy. It's easy to find villages there that are a lot prettier than Soldeu, scenery that is more impressive, and off-slope diversions that are more, well, diverting. But you would often have to settle for less extensive and interesting slopes, less carefully organised ski lessons and higher prices for lift passes, lessons and booze.

What's new

For 2001/02 the Soldeu-El Tarter ski pass included the Canillo sector (which opened in 2000/01) for the first time and a new black run opened here. More snow-making was installed and one-third of the pistes are now covered.

The Riba Escorxada beginner area was improved – a new quad and a trail in the woods for children were added. And a new drag-lift was installed in the Espiolets beginner area. The terrain-park was expanded and improved.

The resort

The village is a small, ever-growing ribbon of modern buildings – not pretty, but mainly with traditional stone veneers – on a steep hillside, lining the busy road that runs through Andorra from France to Spain. Most are hotels, apartments or bars, with the occasional shop; for serious shopping or any other off-slope diversions – you have to head down to Canillo (see end of this chapter) or Andorra la Vella.

The steep hillside leads down to the river, and the slopes are on the opposite side. The practicalities of reaching the slopes were transformed a few years back, when a new gondola was built in the heart of Soldeu, and the slopes were extended to the bottom of this new station by a wide bridge across the river, with elevators to take you up to the gondola.

For many years El Tarter, a few miles by road and 200m/66oft vertical down the valley, has offered an alternative way into the slopes. From 2000/01 the same is true of Canillo, another 200m/66oft lower.

The mountain

The main local slopes are on open mountainsides above the woods, though there are runs in the woods back to all of the resort lift bases. At the eastern end the slopes and lifts link with those of Pas de la Casa, but there's no joint lift pass (see later in this chapter). Keen skiers and riders will want to explore the Pas area, and will tailor their pass buying accordingly. There is easy access at Grau Roig, a few miles up the valley..

THE SLOPES
Pleasantly varied

The gondola rises over wooded, north-facing slopes to Espiolets, a broad shelf that is virtually a mini-resort – the ski school is based here, and there are extensive nursery slopes. A gentle run to the east takes you to an area of long, easy runs served by one of Soldeu's three six-packs. And beyond that is an extensive area of more varied slopes, served by a quad and another six-pack, that overlaps with the Pas de la Casa area. Going west

boarding *The excellent school and gentle beginner slopes make this a good place to learn. Intermediates may find the flattish areas of slopes irritating to scoot along. For advanced riders there's a well-equipped terrain-park and half-pipe near Riba Escorxada. Competent free-riders should be among the first in line for the snowcat service when it's running (see Experts).*

MOUNTAIN FACTS

Altitude	1710m-2560m
	5,610ft-8,400ft
Lifts	28
Pistes	90km
	55 miles
Green	24%
Blue	32%
Red	36%
Black	8%
Snowmaking	30km
	14 miles

Recco detectors used
– helicopter based

LIFT PASSES

2002/03 prices in
euros

Soldeu/El Tarter
Covers all lifts in
Soldeu, El Tarter,
Canillo.
Main pass
1-day pass 29.5
6-day pass 138
Children
Under 12: 6-day pass
102
Under 6: free pass
Short-term passes
Half-day pass 21
Alternative passes
The 5-day Ski Andorra
pass covers all five
resorts and costs
around 131 euros. It
allows five days riding
out of six consecutive
days in any one
resort each day.

There are busy mid-
mountain meeting
areas above both
Soldeu and El Tarter

→

from Espiolets takes you to the open bowl of Riba Escorxada and the arrival point of the lift up from El Tarter. From here, the third six-pack serves sunny slopes on Tosa dels Espiolets, while a slow quad leads towards drags serving the high-point of Tossal de la Llosada and the link with the slopes above Canillo. For some reason last season's piste map had a brown background, which made it difficult to read.

SNOW RELIABILITY
Not at all bad
Soldeu enjoys fairly reliable snow. Most slopes are north-facing, with artificial snow on the descents to Soldeu. The snowmaking is expanded each year and grooming is good.

FOR EXPERTS
Hope the snowcat's going
It's a limited area for experts, at least on-piste. The black runs down to Soldeu and El Tarter more or less justify their grading, and the new one at the top of the Canillo sector looked like fun but was short of snow when we visited. The blacks on Tosa dels Espiolets are indistinguishable from the neighbouring (and more direct) red and blue. One intriguing possibility that we were not able to explore on our visit is

that when conditions permit a snowcat takes people up to Pic d'Encampadana whence a range of off-piste routes (dotted on our map) descend to Riba Escorxada. There is plenty of other off-piste potential – notably in the bowl above Riba Escorxada, in the area where Soldeu meets Pas, and above El Forn – given the necessary guidance.

FOR INTERMEDIATES
Pity there's still no joint pass
There is plenty to amuse all but the keenest intermediates. The area east of Espiolets is splendid for building confidence, while those who already have it will be able to explore the whole mountain. Riba Escorxada is a fine section for mixed ability groups and the relatively new link to Canillo/El Forn and newly created runs there allow for more cruising mileage completely free of the crowds that are a drawback on many of the other blue runs. The great frustration for mileage-hungry intermediates is the lack of a joint Soldeu/Pas pass.

FOR BEGINNERS
One of the best
This is an excellent resort for beginners. It is relatively snow-sure, and there are numerous easy pistes to

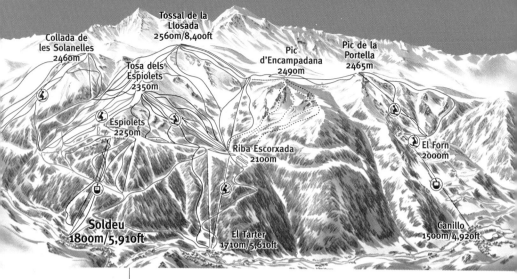

Tossal de la
Llosada
2560m/8,400ft

Collada de
les Solanelles
2460m

Pic
d'Encampadana
2490m

Pic de la
Portella
2465m

Tosa dels
Espiolets
2350m

Espiolets
2250m

Riba Escorxada
2100m

El Forn
2000m

Soldeu
1800m/5,910ft

El Tarter
1710m/5,610ft

Canillo
1500m/4,920ft

LIFT PASS INSANITY

If they could agree on a joint lift pass the Soldeu-Pas de la Casa joint area would rival some of the Alps best-known names for extent and variety. But they can't; so if you want to ski both in a day you need to have two lift passes – one for each area. This insanity is apparently the result of some ancient feud between the communities which control the two areas.

SCHOOLS/GUIDES

2002/03 prices in euros

Soldeu El Tarter school

Classes 5 or 6 days 15hr: 88

Children's classes 15hr: 82

Private lessons 2001/02 prices

Hourly: 28 for 1 or 2 people, 33 for 3 or 4 people.

CHILDCARE

The three nurseries, at Espiolets, Riba Escorxada and El Forn, take children from 3 to 10.

move on to (though the crowds can be off-putting). The Espiolets nursery area is huge and excellent and the ski school top-notch.

FOR CROSS-COUNTRY
Er, what cross-country?

If there is any cross country here we've neither seen it nor heard about it. There is some not far away at Grau Roig (covered in the Pas de la Casa chapter), but Andorra's serious cross-country resort is at La Rabassa, some distance away in the south-west corner of the country, close to Spain – 20km/12 miles of loops at an altitude of 2000m/6,600ft.

QUEUES
Weekends only

The lift system is a mixture of the old and the impressively new and powerful – including three six-packs – which seems to be able to cope. Though there are queues at the morning peak and at weekends for both the gondola out of Soldeu and the chair from El Tarter. More of a problem can be crowds on the blue slopes (even in January when we were there) – the reds and blacks are much quieter.

MOUNTAIN RESTAURANTS
Not a highlight

The mountain restaurants are crowded, not because they stimulate trade but because there aren't enough of them. There is a choice of places at Espiolets, including table-service at crowded refectory-style tables. Reporters favour descending to El Tarter, particularly to the snack bar in the Hotel del Clos.

SCHOOLS AND GUIDES
One of the best for Brits

The ski school is effectively run as two units, the one dealing with English-speaking clients headed by an Englishman and largely staffed by native-English-speaking instructors. 40% of the pupils are beginners, and the school has devised a special 'team teaching' scheme to cope with the challenge of helping this number of beginners to find their feet and sorting them into aptitude groups. The school has an excellent reputation for quality of lessons and friendliness. And we have rarely seen such a high proportion of slope-users in ski school groups as we saw here.

FACILITIES FOR CHILDREN
With altitude

Children are looked after at the mid-mountain stations. There are three nurseries and snow playgrounds at Espiolets, Riba Escoxada and El Forn for children from three to 10 years old.

Staying there

HOW TO GO
Some comfortable hotels

A wide range of UK tour operators offer packages here, mainly in hotels but with some apartments and chalets. **Hotels** The best hotels are very civilised, and far removed from the standards of a decade ago.

《《《4 **Sport Hotel Village** (870500) By far the best in town, with style and space in the public areas – comfortable chairs and sofas, high ceilings, beams and picture windows. Built over the

GETTING THERE

Air Toulouse, transfer
3½hr.

Rail L'Hospitalet-Près-
L'Andorre (25km/16
miles); buses and
taxis to Soldeu

ACTIVITIES

Indoor Ice skating,
swimming, gym,
squash, tennis
Outdoor Thermal
spas, snowmobiling,
tobogganing

Phone numbers
From abroad use the
prefix +376.

**Central reservations
phone number**
Call 890501.

TOURIST OFFICE

t 890500
f 890509
soldeu@soldeu.ad
www.soldeu.ad

gondola station by the family which
sold the land to the lift company.
Sport (870600) Comfortable, with
good lounge areas, a lively bar and a
popular basement disco-bar. But dull
buffet-style food. Not nearly as stylish
as its sister hotel over the road.
Piolets (871787) Pleasant enough,
with a pool and other amenities.
Central.
Himalaia (878515) Recently
refurbished, central.
Self-catering The Edelweiss apartments
(870600) are spacious, pleasant and
well placed opposite the Sport hotel,
the facilities of which are available.

EATING OUT
Some gourmand delights
We enjoyed excellent, satisfying meals
at two cute rustic restaurants – Fat
Albert's in downtown Soldeu and
'Snails and Quails', 3km/2 miles up the
road in Bordes d'Envalira. The
Pussycat and L'Esquirol (Indian) are
recommended by readers.

APRES-SKI
Lively
Although après-ski is lively, it consists
mainly of bars and rep-organised
outings. The bar at Fat Albert's (see
above) has a great atmosphere, with
videos shot on the mountain and often
a live band. The long-established
Pussycat is a good late-night place,
with changing party themes. The
Piccadilly, under the Sport hotel, is
popular. Aspen pub-restaurant is the
main snowboard hang-out. The Naudi
has a quieter locals' bar. The
Avalanche, Villager and Iceberg have
also been recommended. Expect noise
from late-night revellers on the streets
(several reporters this year complained
of 'loutish' and 'unsociable' behaviour
by young Brits).

OFF THE SLOPES
Head downhill
There is little to amuse non-skiers in
Soldeu itself. Down the valley in
Canillo is the smart Palau de Gel (see
below), and in Escaldes (effectively
Andorra la Vella) there are other
diversions, including the impressive
Caldea spa, and some very serious
shopping opportunities. There are
several small museums scattered
around the country. Some of
the bigger hotels have excellent
sports facilities.

El Tarter 1710m/5,610ft

El Tarter has grown over recent years
to the point where it now seems no
smaller than Soldeu; but it is quieter.
There is no shortage of places to stay
here – UK tour operators tend to list it
under Soldeu. Recent reporters
recommend the hotel del Clos ('good
food but up a steep hill') and del
Tarter and the local ski school. But
they complain that the resort is 'dull at
night and has no centre'. The Mosquit
is a recommended pizzeria; a British-
run bar, Peanuts, beneath it seems set
to monopolise the British custom.

Canillo 1500m/4,920ft

If you like the idea of deserted local
slopes and don't mind riding a
gondola down at the end of the day,
you could consider Canillo, which
looked an acceptably pleasant
spot as we repeatedly drove through
it. (Again, UK operators generally
list accommodation here under
Soldeu.) It has the attraction of the
impressive Palau de Gel – an Olympic
ice-rink plus swimming pool, gym and
other amenities.

Soldeu

637

Spain

The Spanish Pyrenees were a popular British budget destination a decade ago, but then Andorra and eastern Europe captured much of the Spanish trade. It's easy to see why this happened. The mass-market resorts often struggled for snow and, even when conditions were good, there was a tendency for high winds to close the lifts. Although prices were low, they were lower elsewhere, and the resorts weren't able to compete with the Alps for quality.

But it's dangerous to generalise about Spanish resorts – which is why we don't provide the lists of ✚ and ✖ points that we do for other second-division countries. There are now some well equipped Pyrenean resorts with fine, snow-sure slopes that compare favourably with mid-sized places in the Alps. Two resorts are certainly not downmarket – Sierra Nevada and Baqueira-Beret are both frequented by the King of Spain. Winter sports are becoming more popular with the prosperous Spanish themselves, and as a result many of the smaller resorts are continually improving.

Furthermore, the general ambience of Spanish resorts is attractive – not unlike that of Italy. There's plenty of animation, with eating, posing and partying taken seriously. Large families often lunch together, creating much merriment while huge amounts of food are consumed. Dinner starts late after such a blowout so, in turn, nightlife doesn't get going before many a British punter has retired, disgruntled at the lack of action.

Sierra Nevada (2100m/6,890ft) in the extreme south of Spain near the Costa del Sol, suffers from extremely unpredictable weather conditions. The much-fêted World Championships in the mid-1990s had to be postponed by a year due to a lack of snow-cover, with high temperatures rendering the resort's state-of-the-art snowmaking installation useless.

The resort's natural snow arrives via completely different weather patterns from those supplying the Alps and the Pyrenees; in 1990, when the Alps were disastrously snowless, Sierra Nevada had the best conditions in Europe.

The mostly beginner and intermediate slopes are very exposed to the elements. When the wind blows, as it does, the slopes close, and the strong sun makes the pistes either icy or soft in late season. On a good day, however, visitors are treated to a fantastic view from the top at Veleta, across the Med, to the Atlas mountains in Morocco (you need the chair from the Laguna area for the view).

The resort is a hotch-potch of building styles but user-friendly, and its restaurants, bars and shops are gathered around a central square at Pradollano (which a recent reporter likens to Whistler). Granada's proximity means good outings but overcrowding at weekends and holidays. Hotels are comfortable and good value; staying in Granada is an option but means a 45 minute drive up on a winding road. You could also add a day or two here to a stay on the coast.

The best of the Pyrenean resorts is Baqueira-Beret (see next chapter).

There is a group of worthwhile resorts in the western Pyrenees, between Pau and Huesca.

Formigal is working hard to improve its standing as a winter resort. There has been recent expansion and a number of lift improvements but the 56km/35 miles of pistes are windswept. When the wind blows, retreat to nearby Panticosa – a charming old village with sheltered but limited slopes that have recently doubled in size to 34km/21 miles of pistes. **Candanchu** and nearby Astún, with almost 100km/62 miles of pistes between them, are popular on the Spanish market. They offer a wide range of lodging set in some of the Pyrenees' most stunning scenery. Candanchu has some tough runs.

The other resorts of international interest are just east of Andorra. The 44km/27 miles of runs at **La Molina** and its purpose-built satellite Supermolina (1700m/5,580ft) are now linked to those of Masella, over the mountain, via a gondola and six-pack. The whole area, called Alp 2500, now extends over 100km/62 miles of mainly intermediate skiing.

TOURIST OFFICES

Sierra Nevada
www.sierranevadaski.com

Formigal
www.formigal.com

Candanchu
www.candanchu.com

La Molina
www.lamolina.com

Baqueira-Beret   1500m/4,920ft

Spain's leading winter resort – fit for their king

WHAT IT COSTS

HOW IT RATES

The slopes

Snow	★★★
Extent	★★★
Experts	★★★
Intermediates	★★★★
Beginners	★★
Convenience	★★★
Queues	★★★
Restaurants	★★

The rest

Scenery	★★★
Resort charm	★★
Off-slope	★

What's new

For 2001/02 some of the slopes were redesigned to avoid flat sections and congestion. The Beret cafeteria was expanded (much to the satisfaction of two female reporters who were delighted with the 'all-new ladies toilets with 24 cubicles'.

MOUNTAIN FACTS

Altitude	1500m-2510m
	4,920ft-8,230ft
Lifts	27
Pistes	87km
	53 miles
Green	8%
Blue	47%
Red	37%
Black	8%
Snowmaking	35km
	22 miles

BAQUEIRA TOURIST OFFICE

Baqueira's lift base is just above the village and its slopes are well-supplied with snowmaking →

- ✚ Compact modern resort
- ✚ Efficient lifts with few queues
- ✚ Reasonable snow reliability
- ✚ Some good off-piste potential
- ✚ Lots of good intermediate slopes
- ✚ Friendly, helpful locals

- ➖ Drab high-rise blocks dominate the main village, though new developments are more attractive
- ➖ Resort is not cleverly laid out, and suffers from traffic around the lift base station
- ➖ Few off-slope diversions

Baqueira is in a different league from other resorts in the Spanish Pyrenees – a smart family-oriented resort with a wide area of north-facing slopes that gives a real feeling of travel. It attracts an almost entirely Spanish clientele (which regularly includes the royal family), so don't count on English being spoken.

THE RESORT

Baqueira was purpose-built in the 1960s and has its fair share of drab, high-rise blocks; these are clustered below the road that runs through to the high pass of Port de la Bonaigua, while the main lift base is just above it. But up the steep hill from the main base are some newer, smaller-scale stone-clad developments. At the very top is an alternative chair-lift into the slopes. The most convenient base is close to the main chair-lift, but the village is small enough for location not to be too much of an issue. There is a lot of accommodation spread down the valley, and a big car park with road-train shuttle up to the lift base.

Ski Miquel has long been the only UK tour operator here. They cater for non-Spanish-speakers by offering their own chalet hotel and tame instructors.

THE MOUNTAINS

There is an extensive area of long, mainly intermediate, runs, practically all of them on open treeless slopes. There are long-term plans to extend the slopes to the sunny side of the Bonaigua pass.

Slopes The slopes are split into three distinct but well-connected areas – Baqueira, Beret and Bonaigua. From the base station at Baqueira, a fast quad which you ride without skis (which fit in slots in the back of the chair in front) takes you up to the nursery slopes at 1800m/5,910ft. Fast chairs go on up to Cap de Baqueira. From here there is a wide variety of long runs, served by chairs and drags. From several points you can descend

into the Argulls valley and the Bonaigua sector, leading over to the summit of the Bonaigua pass. From the opposite extremity at Orri a triple chair takes you off to the Beret sector, where a series of more-or-less parallel chairs serve mainly blue and red runs. A new fast quad and a drag-lift serve a fourth sector across the valley from the Beret slopes, with three blue and a red piste. Beret, Orri and Bonaigua are accessible by road.

Snow reliability Mainly north-west-facing slopes above 1800m/5,910ft and extensive snowmaking make the area fairly snow-sure. But the latitude means strong sun in late season.

Experts Experts will find few on-piste challenges, but there's plenty of off-piste if you hire a guide. The infamous Escornacrabes itinerary, from the top of Cap de Baqueira, is steep and narrow. Cheap heli-lifts are available.

Intermediates It's excellent, with lots of

varied blues and some classic long red runs such as Muntanyo down to Port de la Bonaigua and Mirador above town. Less daring intermediates will enjoy the Beret section and the Argulls valley runs best.

Beginners There are some good nursery runs above town but some of the blues you move on to can be a bit tough. You are better off at Beret (which you have to drive or take a taxi to), where there's an excellent nursery slope and gentle blues.

Snowboarding There's a permanent half-pipe at Argulls. The main nursery slopes are served by drags and some blue runs are a bit tricky for novices.

Cross-country There is 7km/4 miles of trails between Orri and Beret.

Queues The network of modern lifts means few queues most of the time. But at weekends some waits can be 10 minutes. Reporters have commented on how orderly queues are compared to many Alpine resorts.

Mountain restaurants Most have decent good-value food and pleasant terraces. You can get table service at Cap del Port, at the Bonaigua pass, at Baqueira 2200 and at Beret.

Schools and guides The school gets good reports – some spoken English.

Facilities for children The kindergarten takes children from three months but lack of spoken English is a problem. Ski school classes start from age four.

STAYING THERE

How to go There is a reasonable choice of hotels and apartments locally. UK operator Ski Miquel offers packages here. Their chalet-hotel Salana generates good reports, except from people with young children.

Hotels In the main village three hotels have been recommended – the 4-star Montarto (973 639001) with 'pool and wonderful food' and the 3-star Tuc Blanc (973 644350) 'comfortable, with pool', and Val de Ruda (973 645258). The 5-star Tryp Royal Tanau at the top of the resort looks good (973 644446). The Parador (973 640801) down the valley in Arties and the 2-star Vielha (973 640275) further down in Vielha were recommended by 2002 visitors.

Eating out The more interesting restaurants are down the valley in Salardu, Arties and Vielha. Reporters have enjoyed the local tapas bars.

Après-ski There are lots of pubs and discos in the valley. Tiffany's and Pacha are in the main village. They get going very late (ie 1am or 2am).

Off the slopes Pool and spa facilities are available in several hotels, but not much else. Vielha, 15km/9 miles away, has a good sports centre.

Phone numbers
From abroad use the prefix +34.

TOURIST OFFICE
Postcode 25530
t 973 639000
f 973 644488
baqueira@baqueira.es
www.baqueira.es

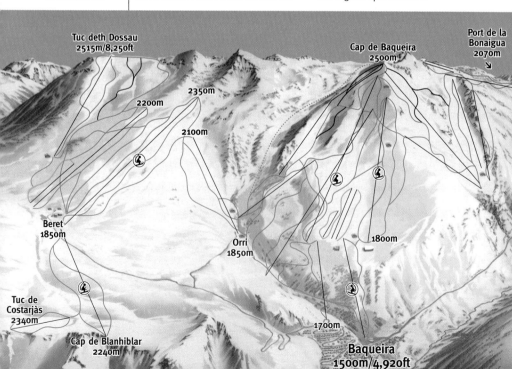

Tuc deth Dossau
2515m/8,25oft

Cap de Baqueira
2500m

Port de la Bonaigua
2070m

2350m

2200m

2100m

Beret
1850m

Orri
1850m

1800m

Tuc de Costarjàs
2340m

Cap de Blanhiblar
2240m

1700m

Baqueira
1500m/4,92oft

Bulgaria

641

WHAT IT COSTS

- ➕ Very cheap
- ➕ A different winter holiday, with the chance to experience a fascinating, although depressed, culture
- ➕ Very friendly, welcoming people
- ➕ Good ski schools

- ➖ Poor snow record and not enough snowmaking
- ➖ Poor piste and lift maintenance
- ➖ Small ski areas
- ➖ Borovets hotels and food poor, and tales of beggars and prostitutes

Bulgaria has traditionally attracted beginners and early intermediates on a tight budget: the basic flight-and-hotel-package, equipment rental, school and lift pass are all very cheap. So is alcohol when you get there. Drawbacks include limited slopes, old lifts, and mountain and hotel food that can have you reaching for the Mars bars. But there are compensations: reporters are struck by the friendliness of the people, the ski schools are excellent, the tour op-organised nightlife is good fun, and from Borovets an excursion to Sofia is recommended.

But keen piste-bashers, gourmets, posers, and those wanting creature comforts should look elsewhere or be prepared for a shock.

The flow of readers' reports has dried up over the last few seasons, but we have trawled the Internet for holiday reports. Most seem extremely positive for Pamporovo, but much more mixed for Borovets, with tales of no snow, long lift queues, poor rental equipment and problems with beggars and prostitutes.

Bulgaria's two main resorts are some way apart, served by different airports, with similarly short transfer times (less than two hours) – assuming everything runs smoothly (which it might well not). They are similar places in that both have good ski schools and a poor selection of quality restaurants, but they suit different levels of ability.

Pamporovo 1650m/5,410ft

THE RESORT
Despite the bus-ride to the lifts, visitors praise Pamporovo. The purpose-built village has 'everything to hand'.

THE MOUNTAIN
Pamporovo is Bulgaria's best bet for beginners and early intermediates, with mostly easy runs. Others are likely to find 17.5km/11 miles of mainly short runs too limited.
Slopes The slopes are pretty and sheltered, with pistes starting at a high point of 1925m/6,320ft and cutting through pine forest.
Snow reliability Late-season snow-cover is unreliable.
Experts Experts will find little to challenge them in this limited ski area.
Intermediates The slopes are too limited for most intermediates.
Beginners Book a 'learn to ski' package through your tour operator,

saving up to 80% on local prices.
Snowboarding The Snow Shack is best for snowboard rental and lessons.
Mountain restaurants The best bets are the Lodge and the Spider restaurant.
Schools and guides The ski schools are repeatedly praised by reporters – instructors are patient, enthusiastic and speak good English, and class sizes are usually quite small.
Facilities for children The English-speaking nursery is well regarded.

STAYING THERE
Hotels The main hotels are in the centre of the handy purpose-built village. Hotel Pamporovo offers the best accommodation in the resort. It's close to the village centre, and facilities include an indoor swimming pool, a hot-tub and a gym. More basic are the Perelik (also with a pool) and Mourgavets – both in the centre.
Eating out The food can be poor. You are best off sticking to local Bulgarian stew dishes, gyuvech and kavarma, which can be delicious. The breakfast buffets offer a fair choice.
Après-ski The nightlife is fairly lively, although limited to a handful of bars and discos – BJ's, the White Hart, Dax and the Havana club are popular.
Off the slopes The organised evening events are recommended by reporters.

Phone numbers
From abroad use the prefix +359.

PAMPOROVO TOURIST OFFICE
Postcode 4870
t 3021 236
f 3021 263
pamporovo@ibox.bsbg.net
www.travel-bulgaria.com

Borovets 1300m/4,270ft

THE RESORT

Borovets is a collection of large, modern hotels, with bars, restaurants and shops housed within them. There is a ramshackle selection of quirkier bars, shops and eating places. The beautiful wooded setting provides a degree of Alpine-style charm, and hides some of the worst architectural excesses. In recent years we have had reports of beggars, ski theft, prostitutes and rip-off exchange dealers, which may cloud your holiday.

THE MOUNTAIN

The 40km/25 miles of piste are spread over three sectors – two loosely linked.
Slopes The two largest sectors have fairly steep and awkward slopes. The gondola rises over 1000m/3,300ft to service both the small, high, easy slopes of Markoudjika (up to 2700m/8,860ft), and the mainly long, steepish Yastrebets pistes. A little drag-lift and path connect the two. The third Baraki sector is accessed by several lifts. Runs are short, with just 550m/1,800ft of vertical drop.
Snow reliability Reliable cover is by no means guaranteed.
Experts There's little of real challenge.
Intermediates The runs are best suited to good intermediates. Less confident skiers may find the mainly tough red runs a bit intimidating.
Beginners The slopes are not particularly suitable for novices. The nursery slopes are inadequate and Markoudjika is good for near beginners, but progress beyond that means going on to reds.

Queues These can be bad – especially for the gondola (down as well as up). Grooming is erratic and signing poor.
Mountain restaurants Mostly basic little snack bars with limited seating, serving large portions of very simple fare.
Schools and guides Repeatedly praised by virtually all reporters.
Facilities for children Reports of the ski kindergarten have been complimentary. The non-ski nursery is in the Rila hotel.

STAYING THERE

Hotels Most reporters stayed at the Rila or the Samokov – both huge and impersonal. Few were impressed (especially with the food or service).
Eating out Reporters recommend Katy's Bar for steaks and the Extreme Pizza Bar for, er, pizza (and beer and full English breakfasts).
Après-ski The nightlife caters well to an 18–30 type crowd. Tour operator reps organise pub crawls, folklore evenings and dinner in a local village. The Black Tiger pub (with karaoke), the Buzz Bar, Titanic and Bonkers are lively.
Off the slopes Excursions to the Rila monastery by coach and to Sofia by coach or helicopter are interesting.

Vitosha 1810m/5,940ft

This is no more than a few widely scattered hotels with very limited, bland runs and a top height of 2290m/7,510ft. The hotels are fairly dour, and most are a bus-ride from the lifts. The resort is just over 20km/12 miles from Sofia, allowing short transfers and easy excursions, but the slopes get overrun at weekends. The slopes are north-facing and have a decent snow record.

BOROVETS TOURIST OFFICE
Postcode 1040
t 2980 5297
f 2981 0114
www.travel-bulgaria.com

VITOSHA TOURIST INFORMATION
www.travel-bulgaria.com

Romania

WHAT IT COSTS

➕ Extremely cheap

➕ Interesting excursions and friendly local people

➕ Good standard of affordable lessons

➖ Primitive facilities

➖ Uninspiring food

➖ Limited slopes with few real challenges

Like Bulgaria, Romania sells mainly on price. On-the-spot prices, in particular, are very, very low. Provided you have correspondingly low expectations – and provided you go to Poiana Brasov and not Sinaia – you'll probably come back content. If you have any interest in good living, and particularly good lunching, stay away. It's a place for beginners and near-beginners – the slopes are limited in extent and challenge, but lessons are good (and cheap, of course).

There is another possible dimension to a holiday here, which is the experience of visiting (and supporting) an interesting and attractive country with a traumatic recent history. Reporters have commented on the friendliness of the people, and most recommend exploring beyond the confines of the resorts. Bucharest is 'not to be missed'.

It's some years since we visited the country. The abiding impression we brought back then was one of resources stretched to their limits. To judge by the few reports we have since received, post-revolutionary Romania has, sadly, not made much progress.

Romania's two main resorts are in the Carpathian mountains, about 120km/75 miles north-west of the capital and arrival airport, Bucharest. They are very different places, but have one or two things in common apart from low prices: patient instruction, with excellent spoken English, and small classes; and very basic mountain restaurants, with extremely primitive toilets that, according to one past reporter, would 'shock the toughest of characters'.

The main resort is **Poiana Brasov** (1030m/3,380ft), near the city of Brasov. It is purpose-built, but not designed for convenience: the hotels are scattered about a pretty, wooded plateau, served by regular buses and cheap taxis. There is nothing resembling a real village – the place has the air of a spacious holiday camp.

The main slopes (approximately 17km/11 miles of pistes in total) consist of decent intermediate tree-lined runs of about 750m/2,460ft vertical, roughly following the line of the main cable-car and gondola, plus an open nursery area at the top. There are also some nursery lifts at village level. A black run takes a less direct route down the mountain, which means that on average it is less steep than the red run under the lifts; it has one steepish pitch towards the end. The more

adventurous would need to seek opportunities to go off-piste. The resort gets weekend business from Brasov and Bucharest, and the main lifts can suffer serious queues then.

The recently refurbished Bradul (068 262252) and Sport (068 262252) hotels are handy for the lower nursery slopes and for one of the cable-cars. The Tirol (068 262460) and the Alpin (068 262343) get good reports. The Ciucas (068 262181) is a 'good, basic' place with satellite TV. Après-ski revolves around the hotel bars and discos and can be quite lively at times. The nightclub puts on cheap cabarets. Off-slope facilities are limited; there is a good-sized pool, and bowling. A trip to the Carpathian Stag in Brasov for an evening of tasting in the wine cellars, dinner and a folklore show has been recommended. An excursion to nearby Bran Castle (Count Dracula's home) is also popular.

You may be offered holidays in **Sinaia** – a small town on the busy road from Bucharest to Brasov. When we visited it some years ago the town seemed to us a rather depressing place, and reporters since have been shocked and saddened by the evident poverty. But there are chalets and a 4-star Holiday Inn (044 310440), which may help to attract your much-needed cash.

643

Phone numbers
From abroad use the prefix +40 and omit the initial 'o' of the phone number.

TOURIST INFORMATION

Poiana Brasov
www.poiana-brasov.com

Slovenia

644

WHAT IT COSTS

+ Good value for money
+ Beautiful scenery
+ Good beginners' slopes and lessons
+ Good off-slope diversions and excursions

− Limited, easy slopes on the whole
− Mainly antiquated lifts
− Uninspiring food

Slovenia offers good value for money 'on the sunny side of the Alps'. A handful of UK tour operators run packages to some of the better-known resorts. An alternative would be to arrange an independent trip to the mountains combined with a break in the vibrant city of Ljubljana.

Kranjska Gora and Bohinj are the best-known resorts, popular with economy-minded British and Dutch visitors, and with visitors from neighbouring Italy and Austria, giving quite a cosmopolitan feel to the resorts.

Slovenia is a small country bordering Italy to the west and Austria to the north. It was the first state to break away from former Yugoslavia and has managed to escape the turmoil that engulfed the Balkans. The economy is improving steadily, and there is a positive feel to the resorts – along with a warm and hospitable welcome.

The main resorts are within two and a half hours' bus-ride of the capital, Ljubljana.

The ski areas are generally small, with fairly antiquated lifts but few queues. The mountain restaurants are mainly unappealing, while the ski schools are of a high standard and cheap, with reputedly good English. Hotel star ratings tend to be a trifle generous, but standards of service and hygiene are high. Snow reliability is not particularly good, but some resorts have snowmaking.

Kranjska Gora (810m/2,660ft), not far from the Austrian and the Italian borders, is the best-known resort on the British market. The pretty village is dominated by the majestic Julian Alps. The Lek, Kompass and Larix hotels – with pools – are the best placed for slope-side convenience.

There are 30km/20 miles of mainly intermediate slopes, rising up to 1625m/5,325ft. The only challenging slopes are a couple of short, demanding runs in the Podkiron area and the World Cup slalom run. For those wanting a change of slopes, trips to Arnoldstein in Austria are available. Snow reliability is not good, despite snowmaking and a northerly exposure. The lift system is rather antiquated (most of the 23 lifts are T-bars), but at

least queues are rare. Mountain restaurants are poor and most people choose to lunch in the village. There are 40km/25 miles of cross-country trails. There is a good selection of bars and discos for Austrian-style après-ski.

Vogel (1540m/5,050ft), in the beautiful Bohinj basin, has the best slopes and conditions in the area. The 36km/22 miles of slopes are reached by a cable-car up from the valley. There's a collection of small hotels and restaurants at the base. Pistes for skiers of varying abilities run from the high point at 1800m/5,910ft back into a central bowl with a small beginner area. When conditions permit, there is a long run to the bottom cable-car station. For a change of scene, **Kobla**, with 23km/14 miles of wooded runs, is a short bus-ride away.

Bled, with its beautiful lake and fairly lively nightlife, is an attractive base. Its local slopes are very limited indeed, but there are free buses to Vogel (about 20km/12 miles) and Kobla (slightly nearer). The Grand Hotel Toplice and the Park are among the best lakeside hotels.

Kanin (2200m/7,220ft), near the village of Bovec, 17km/11 miles from Italy, offers the only high Alpine skiing and boarding – 15km/9 miles of pistes between 980m and 2300m (3,220ft and 7,550ft).

Slovenia's second city, **Maribor** (325m/1,070ft), in the north-east, is 6km/4 miles from its local slopes – the biggest ski area in the country, with 64km/40 miles of runs and 20 lifts. Accommodation is cheap and there are several atmospheric old inns serving good, Hungarian-influenced food.

TOURIST INFORMATION

www.slovenia-tourism.si

Kranjska Gora
www.kranjska-gora.si

Vogel (Bohinj)
www.bohinj.si/vogel

Kobla (Bohinj)
www.bohinj.si/kobla

Bled
www.bled.si

Kanin (Bovec)
www.bovec.si

Maribor
www.maribor.si

Finland

WHAT IT COSTS

((((4))))

- ➕ Peace and quiet
- ➕ Ideal terrain for cross-country and gentle downhilling
- ➕ Reliable late snow
- ➕ Lapp charm

- ➖ Cold
- ➖ Small ski areas
- ➖ Quite expensive
- ➖ Uninspiring food

For skiers with no appetite for the hustle and hassle of Alpine resorts in high season – perhaps especially for families – escape to the white silence of Lapland may be an attractive alternative. Finland has the lion's share of Lapland and has successfully marketed it, not only for day-trip visits to Santa in his home environment but also for ski holidays. With limited downhill slopes but limitless cross-country the resorts compete with the established resorts in Norway, the most important difference being that Finnish resorts lie far to the north. Of half a dozen 'main' resorts only Ruka is south of the Arctic Circle (by 80km/50 miles).

The weather, snow and timing of the season are accordingly different, and ski holidays in Finland have an extra ingredient of folklorish charm, plus a good chance of seeing the Northern Lights (three times in the January week when one reporter visited). Forget Father Christmas, though: Rovaniemi, the capital of the Santa Claus industry, is 200km/125 miles from the main resorts. These are **Levi** and **Ylläs**, respectively 25km/15 miles north and 50km/31 miles west of Kittilä, which has direct charter flights from Britain.

Ylläs mountain has two gateways, of which the major one is Äkäslompolo – a traditional lakeside Lapp settlement, two miles from the lifts. It has a more relaxing atmosphere and longer runs than Levi, whose great appeal is convenience: it is a purpose-built village of hotels and cabins at the foot of the slopes, with more nightlife and commercial development. If you want to buy wine at Äkäslompolo, you have to order it at the post office in the morning, for afternoon delivery.

The Arctic landscape of flat and gently rolling forest punctuated by many lakes and the occasional treeless hill is a paradise for cross-country skiing. Weather permitting, it also offers good beginner and intermediate downhilling, albeit on a small scale. In fine weather it is a land of great beauty, but don't expect drama.

The resorts usually open a few runs in late November. For two months in midwinter, the sun does not rise; at least, not at ground level – even at Christmas (a quiet time) the sun may be visible from the slopes for a period of pale daylight between 10 and 2.

Most of the ski areas have floodlit runs. The mountains do not open fully until mid-February, when a normal skiing day is possible and Finnish schools have holidays that usually coincide with ours – a busy time. Finland comes into its own at the end of the season, with friendlier temperatures and long daylight hours. Understandably, Easter is extremely popular, and the slopes are crowded.

Piste conditions are usually hard-packed powder or fresh snow from the start of the season to the end (usually early May).

The temperature can be extremely variable, yo-yoing between zero and minus 30°C several times in a week. The fine days are the coldest, but usually the best for skiing: because of temperature inversion it may be 10 to 15 degrees warmer on the slopes than at forest level. 'Mild' days of cloud and wind are much worse on the hill. Face masks are helpful and widely sold.

None of the ski areas has significant vertical by alpine standards. Ylläs is the largest in Finland with 463m/1,520ft vertical and, having lifts and pistes on two broad flanks of the mountain (north and south) gives plenty of scope for skiers just off the nursery slopes. Second- and third-week skiers will gain confidence rapidly and conquer the benign black runs by the end of a week.

The staple Finnish lift is the T-bar. Ruka has some chairs, and Levi has Finland's only gondola, which must be a godsend in bitter weather. Pistes are wide, uncomplicated and well maintained, with good nursery slopes and snow fences on the steeper runs

Finland
SUOMI

Do something **Finntastic!**

Whether you want the exhilaration of the traditional winter sports or seek the latest thrilling alternatives, Finland has them all.

Enjoy the excitement of downhill skiing as well as our cross-country variety and the revival of telemarking.
Ride on the cutting edge pleasures of snowboarding and snow-mobiling. Or revel in the exotic delights of the igloo village, reindeer and dog-sled safaris, snow-shoeing – or a cruise on an icebreaker.

Whatever you're after, you'll discover the wonder of winter in Finland.

Find the holiday that suits you from
Emagine UK Ltd, 0870 902 5399;
First Choice, 0870 750 0001;
Headwater Holidays, 01608 813 333;
Inghams, 020 8780 4433;
Inntravel, 01653 628 811;
Norvista, 020 7409 7334;
Scandinavia Freestyle, 020 8846 2666.

**Call 020 7365 2512 today for more
information or visit our website
www.finland-tourism.com/uk**

FINNISH TOURIST
BOARD

to prevent scouring by wind. The Finns are great boarders and consider their terrain-parks far superior to those in the Alps.

The runs are so short that there is no great need for mountain restaurants – on a Finnish piste you are never far from the base lodge, with its shops and self-service restaurant. The ski areas also have shelters or 'kotas' – log-built teepees with an open fire and a smoke hole in the roof – where you can eat a snack or grill some food. Ylläs has a welcoming, snow-encrusted, round restaurant – the highest in the country, at 718m/2,355ft – on the flat top of the mountain, with an open fire, reindeer skins on the benches, and alcohol.

Ski school is good, with English widely spoken. Group lessons are usually in the morning, and in cold weather that may be enough skiing. Afternoon excursions are common – snowmobile safaris, husky sledding, a reindeer sleigh ride and tea with the Lapp drivers in their tent. 'The whole Arctic experience is wonderful,' says an enthusiastic participant. All ski areas have indoor supervised playrooms for small children, but these may not be open at weekends.

Cross-country skiing makes sense of a resort such as Äkäslompolo, transforming it from awkward sprawl to doorstep ski resort of limitless scope. People ski alongside the main road, from their cabins to the hotel or supermarket (pulling children on sledges); up to the base of the lifts where trails fan out around the mountain; across the frozen lake and away through the endless forest for a few kilometres or 50.

Hotels are self-contained resorts, large and practical rather than stylish, typically with a shop, a cafe, a bar with dance floor, and a pool/sauna with outdoor cooling-off area. None matches the best hotels in Norway for cosiness or cuisine. Hotel supper – a rather predictable diet of soups and stews – is served no later than seven, typically, sometimes followed by a children's disco or cheek-to-cheek dancing to a live band. Lapps love to cut a dash on the floor.

Finns usually prefer to stay in cabins, and tour operators offer the compromise of staying in a cabin but taking half-board at a nearby hotel. Cabins vary, but are mostly spacious and well equipped, with a sauna and

heated drying cupboard as standard. The Hillankukka log cabins at Äkäslompolo are exceptionally good, but the ten-minute walk to and from meals at the Äkäs hotel (016 553000) is not to be underestimated. A reporter praises the Äkäs hotel itself – 'beautiful hotel, excellent hydrotherapy pool and under-floor heating'. As well as a big pool and spa, Levi's biggest hotel, Levitunturi (016 646660), has indoor tennis, a golf simulator and a beauty farm.

The southernmost of Finland's resorts, **Ruka** lies 80km/50 miles south of the Arctic Circle, 27km/17 miles from Kuusamo airport and only 25km/15 miles from the Russian border, in a region known for abundant and enduring snow. Finns think nothing of driving the 1000km/620 miles from Helsinki, despite the proximity of Kuusamo airport. The ski area, a mixture of open and forest terrain, has 18 lifts (including four chairs), and 28 runs (22 floodlit, 24 with snowmaking, a mogul run and several black runs, none of them steep), and the vertical range is 200m/690ft. The Freestyle World Championships will be held here in 2005. The cross-country scope is vast: they advertise 500km/310 miles of trails, of which 40km/25 miles are floodlit.

The atmosphere at the resort and on the slopes is upbeat – with live music in the Wunderbar and sun terraces outside Piste, very popular in spring. Hotels include the newly opened Rukahovi (08 85910), only 50m/150ft from the slopes, and the Royal Ruka (08 868 6000), the resort's flagship property; both of these are popular conference venues. Typically for Finland, the best accommodation is in cabins. Good restaurants include Riipinen Riistaravintola, which has bear, boar and capercaillie on the menu, Vanha Karhu, and Kalakeidas, an intimate little fish restaurant.

Pyhä, 150km/93 miles north-east of Rovaniemi, has seven lifts (including two chairs) and 10 runs on a mountain much of which is a National Park. The vertical is only 280m/920ft and there is no steep terrain, but Pyhä enjoys a reputation among young boarders and skiers for good off-piste. The best powder runs are on both sides of a long T-bar on the north slope. The Hotel Pyhätunturi (016 856111) is at mid-mountain, above the base of Pyhä's lifts.

Phone numbers
From abroad use the prefix +358 and omit the initial 'o' of the phone number.

TOURIST OFFICES

Levi
www.levi.fi

Ylläs
www.yllas.fi

Ruka
www.ruka.fi

Pyhä
www.pyha.fi

Norway

➕ Probably the best terrain and facilities in Europe for serious cross-country skiing

➕ The home of telemark – plenty of opportunities to learn and practise

➕ Complete freedom from the glitziness often associated with downhill resorts, and from the ill-mannered lift queues of the Alps

➕ Quiet atmosphere that suits families and older people

➕ Impressive snowboard parks

➕ Usually reliable snow conditions throughout a long season

➖ Very limited downhill areas – small, and mostly with few challenges

➖ Mountain restaurants that are little more than pit stops

➖ Prohibitively high prices (because of high taxes) for alcoholic drinks

➖ Unremarkable scenery – even 'Alpine' Hemsedal resembles the Pennines more than the Alps

➖ Après-ski that is either deadly dull or irritatingly rowdy

➖ Short daylight hours in midwinter

➖ Highly changeable weather

➖ Limited off-slope activities

Norway and its resorts are very different from the Alps, or indeed the Rockies. Some people find the place very much to their taste. For cross-country there is nowhere like it; and for downhillers who dislike the usual ski-resort trappings, and prefer a simpler approach to winter holidays, it could be just the place. For families with young children, in particular, the drawbacks are less pronounced than for others; you'll have no trouble finding junk food for the kids to eat – the mountain restaurants serve little else.

Speaking for ourselves, any one of the first three ➖ points we've listed above would probably be enough to put us off; when these are combined in a single destination – and when you add in the other non-trivial negative points – you can count us out.

From the 1960s to the 1980s, Norway's popularity with British skiers declined steadily, until the country was attracting only 1,500 or so – about one-tenth of the peak number. So in 1988 the tourist agencies launched an initiative to reverse the trend. Aided by the Alpine snow shortages at the turn of the decade and the award of the 1994 Olympic Winter Games to Lillehammer, the campaign has been a success. Bookings from the UK have grown appreciably; according to the Norwegian Tourist Board, the number of UK visitors again increased last season – by 10 per cent – with a sizeable number looking to do cross-country skiing.

There is a traditional friendship between Norway and Britain, and we think of Norwegians as welcoming people, well disposed towards British visitors. We have to say that our visits have left us underwhelmed by the warmth of welcome. But at least English is widely spoken – universally spoken, in our experience.

For the Norwegians and Swedes, skiing is a weekend rather than a special holiday activity, and not an occasion for extravagance. So at lunchtime they tend to haul sandwiches out of their backpacks, and in the evening they cook in their apartments. Don't expect a wide choice of restaurants.

The Norwegians have a problem with alcohol. Walk into an après-ski bar at 5pm on a Saturday and you may find young men already inebriated – and by that we mean not merry but incoherent. And this is despite – or, some say, because of – prohibitively high taxes on booze. Restaurant prices for wine are ludicrous, and shop prices may be irrelevant – Hemsedal has no state-controlled liquor store. Our one attempt at self-catering (well, OK, our one takeaway meal) was an unusually sober affair as a result. Crystal, cutely, offers free wine with dinner in some of its hotels.

Other prices are generally not high by Alpine standards, and those for ski

equipment rental and ski school are relatively low.

Cross-country skiing comes as naturally to Norwegians as walking; and even if you're not that keen, the fact that cross-country is normal, and not a wimp's alternative to 'real' skiing, gives Norway a special appeal. Here, cross-country is both a way of getting about the valleys and a way of exploring the hills. Although you can plod around short valley circuits as you might in an Alpine resort, what distinguishes Norway for the keen cross-country skier is the network of long trails across the gentle uplands, with refuges along the way where backpackers can pause for refreshment or stay overnight. This network of mountain huts offers basic but cheap accommodation which can turn touring into a week-long adventure away from the crowds. Several tour operators now offer ski-touring packages, or they can be arranged on the spot.

More and more Norwegians are taking to telemarking (a bit like cross-country, with a free-heel binding, but with broader skis) for both downhill and backcountry skiing trips.

Snowboarding is very popular, particularly with local youths who swarm on to the slopes and impressive terrain-parks at weekends.

For downhill skiing, the country isn't nearly so attractive. Despite the fact that it is able to hold downhill races, and despite the successes of its Alpine racers during the 1990s, Norway's Alpine areas are of limited appeal.

The most rewarding resort for downhillers is Hemsedal, which we cover in detail in the next chapter.

The site of the 1994 Olympics, the little lakeside town of **Lillehammer** (200m/660ft), is not actually a downhill resort at all. There is plenty of cross-country terrain around, but the nearest downhill runs are 15km/9 miles north at Hafjell (230m/750ft). This is a worthwhile little area, with a vertical of 830m/2,720ft, 11 lifts, and pistes totalling 25km/16 miles with a longest run of 4.5km/2.8 miles. The Olympic slalom events were held here; but the planned women's downhill and super-G races were moved elsewhere after the racers judged the course too easy. They went to Kvitfjell, about 35km/22 miles further north, developed specially for the men's downhill and super-G. It's steeper but a bit smaller – 23km/14 miles of pistes.

Norway's other internationally known resort is **Geilo** (800m/2,620ft) – a small, quiet, unspoiled community on the railway line that links Bergen, on the coast, to Oslo. It provides all the basics of a resort – a handful of cafes and shops clustered around the railway station, 10 hotels more widely spread around the wide valley, children's facilities and a sports centre.

Geilo is a superb cross-country resort. As the Bergen-Oslo railway runs through the town it is possible to go for long tours and return by train.

But Geilo is very limited for downhillers. The 28km/17 miles of piste are spread over two small hills – one, Vestlia, a bus-ride away from Geilo, with a good, informal hotel and restaurant at its foot – offering a maximum vertical of 370m/1,215ft and a longest run of 2km/1.25 miles. None of the runs is really difficult.

Clearly the best hotel, and one of the attractions of staying in Geilo, is the Dr Holms Hotel (call central reservations on 320 95940) – smartly white-painted outside, beautifully furnished and spacious inside. This is the centre for après-ski, but prices are steep. All the other hotels we have seen can be recommended. The resort is quiet at the end of the day, but the main hotels provide live entertainment.

A long way north of the other resorts is **Oppdal** (550m/1,800ft), with more downhill runs than any of its rivals (58km/36 miles). The total vertical is 790m/2,590ft, but this is misleading – most runs are short.

There are almost equally extensive slopes at **Trysil** (460m/1,510ft), off to the east on the border with Sweden, and the runs are longer (up to 4km/2 miles and 685m/2,250ft vertical). The runs here are all around the conical Trysilfjellet, some way from Trysil itself – though there is some accommodation at the hill.

In complete contrast to all of these resorts is **Voss** (50m/160ft), a sizeable lakeside town quite close to the sea. A cable-car links the town to the slopes on Hangur and Slettafjell, with a total of 40km/25 miles of pistes. Snow reliability can be poor. There are plenty of excursion possibilities, in particular the spectacular Flåm railway, which plunges down the side of a mountain to fjord (sea) level. From there you can take a boat trip to link up with a bus back to Voss. Nearby Bergen is a pleasant city that is worth a visit.

Phone numbers
From abroad use the prefix +47.

TOURIST INFORMATION

Lillehammer
www.lillehammerturist.no

Geilo
www.geilo.no

Oppdal
www.oppdal.com

Trysil
www.trysil.com

Voss
www.skiinfo.no/voss/

Hemsedal 650m/2,130ft

The place to go for Alpine skiing in Norway – though we prefer the Alps

WHAT IT COSTS

HOW IT RATES

The slopes

Snow	****
Extent	*
Experts	**
Intermediates	****
Beginners	***
Convenience	**
Queues	****
Restaurants	*

The rest

Scenery	**
Resort charm	**
Off-slope	*

What's new

2001/02 saw the opening of the new Skarsnuten 'mountain village', to one side of the main ski area but linked by a new piste and double chair-lift.

650

SNOWPIX.COM / CHRIS GILL

If the one dreary restaurant is too busy, you can resort to one of the kiosks ↓

➕ Impressive snow reliability because of northerly location

➕ Increasing amounts of convenient slope-side accommodation

➕ Extensive cross-country trails compared to the Alps

➕ Some quite challenging slopes, and mountains with a slightly Alpine feel

➖ Not much of a village

➖ Infrequent shuttle-buses to slopes

➖ Limited slopes

➖ Exposed upper mountain prone to closure because of bad weather

➖ Weekend queues

➖ One abysmal mountain restaurant

➖ No liquor store for miles (though beer available in supermarket)

➖ Après-ski limited during the week and rowdy at weekends

Hemsedal's craggy terrain is reminiscent of a small-but-serious Alpine resort. Most people not resident in Scandinavia would be better advised to go for the real thing, but if you like the sound of Norway, Hemsedal is the place for downhill skiing. Go after the February school holidays, if possible.

THE RESORT

Hemsedal is both an unspoiled valley and a village, also referred to as Trøym and Sentrum ('Centre'), which amounts to very little – a couple of apartment/hotel buildings, a few shops, a bank and a petrol station. Though there has been talk of a lift from Trøym to the slopes, for now the lift base is a mile or two away, across the valley. There are self-catering apartments and houses beside the slopes – with a new development called Skarsnuten linked to the main network by its own lift and piste – and in a separate cluster a walkable distance down the hill from the lifts. A ski-bus links these points, and others in the valley, but the service is inadequate; really, the place is geared to weekend visitors arriving by car or by coach.

THE MOUNTAINS

Hemsedal's slopes pack a lot of variety into a small space. They are shaded in midwinter, and a recent reporter found them 'very cold and very dark'.

Slopes With no fewer than four fast chairs to play on, you can pack a lot of runs into the day. The lift pass also covers smaller Solheisen, a few miles up the valley. A small supplement is required to ski at Geilo, an hour away.

Snow reliability The combination of northerly latitude, reasonable altitude and northerly orientation makes for impressive snow reliability – and there's extensive snowmaking. The season runs until the first weekend in May.

Experts There is quite a bit to amuse experts – two or three black pistes of 450m/1,480ft vertical served by a fast triple chair from the base – one left as a mogul slope – and wide areas of gentler off-piste terrain served by drags above the tree line.

Intermediates Mileage-hungry piste-bashers will find Hemsedal's runs very limited. There are quite a few red and blue runs to play on, but the difference in difficulty is slight.

Beginners There's a gentle new nursery slope for absolute beginners. And there are splendid long green runs (up to 6km/4 miles), but they get a lot of traffic, some of it irresponsibly fast. Some long blues and reds also suit near-beginners.

restaurant doing dreary fast food, plus two or three kiosks with benches.
Schools and guides Our most recent reporter was greatly impressed, not only by the standard of English but by the tuition – 'lots of one-to-one, very encouraging'.
Facilities for children The facilities at the lift base are good, with day care for children over three months, free to parents in ski school. The kids' nursery slope is admirably gentle but not particularly convenient.

STAYING THERE
How to go Most of the accommodation is in apartments, varying widely in convenience. Catered chalets are available through certain UK operators.
Hotels The best hotel is the Skogstad (320 60333) in central Hemsedal – comfortable, but noisy at weekends. Other hotels along the valley are used by UK tour operators.
Self-catering The Alpin apartments, a walk from the lift base, are satisfactory if you don't fill all the beds. The adjacent Tinden ones are quite smart.
Eating out There are half-a-dozen restaurants in the village.
Après-ski It's minimal in the early and middle parts of the week, rowdy at weekends and holidays.
Off the slopes There are some diversions, including sleighs drawn by horses or dogs. The pool at the hotel Skogstad is open to the public.

Snowboarding There's an impressive and 'very well maintained' terrain-park and two half-pipes.
Cross-country By Alpine standards there is lots to do – 90km/56 miles of prepared trails in the valley and forest and (later in the season) 120km/75 miles at altitude. There is a special trail map. Most of the trails are a few miles down the valley at the Gravset centre, served by one bus a day.
Queues Hemsedal is Norway's premier downhill resort, and is only a three-hour drive from Oslo, the capital. Good weekend weather fills the car parks, leading to queues for the main access lifts after mid-morning, and possibly for others. But midweek it is quiet. The upper lifts are very exposed, and are easily closed by bad weather, producing crowds lower down.
Mountain restaurants There's one functional self-service mountain

Hemsedal

651

Totten
1455m/4,770ft

Hamaren
1350m

Røgjin
1325m

Fjellet
1125m

940m

Skarsnuten

Veslestølen

Hemsedal
Skisenter
670m/2,200ft

Hemsedal
650m/2,130ft

Fjellandsby

Sweden

WHAT IT COSTS

- Snow-sure from December to May
- Unspoiled, beautiful landscape
- Uncrowded pistes and lifts
- Vibrant (but regimented) après-ski
- Good range of non-skiing activities

- Limited challenging downhill terrain
- Small areas by Alpine standards
- Lacks the dramatic peaks and vista of the Alps
- Short days during the early season

Sweden's landscape of forests and lakes and miles of unspoiled wilderness is entirely different from the Alps' grandeur and traffic-choked roads. Standards of accommodation, food and service are good and the people welcoming, lively and friendly. There are plenty of off-slope activities, but most of its downhill areas are limited in size and challenge. Sweden is likely to appeal most to those who want an all-round winter holiday in a different environment and culture. Don't be put off by the myths that Sweden is expensive, dark and cold – see below.

Holidaying in Sweden is a completely different experience, culturally as well as physically, from a holiday in the Alps. The language is generally incomprehensible to us and, although virtually everyone speaks good English, the menus and signs are often written only in Swedish. The food is delightful, especially if you like fish and venison.

One of the myths about Sweden is that it is expensive. Sweden is significantly cheaper than neighbouring Norway, especially for alcohol, and prices are pretty much on a par with the main Alpine countries.

Another myth is that it is dark. It is true that the days are very short in December and early January. But from early February the lifts generally work from 9am to 4.30 and by March it is light until 8.30. And most resorts have floodlit pistes for night skiing.

On the down side, downhill slopes are generally limited in both challenge and extent and the lift systems tend to be dominated by T-bars. But there is lots of cross-country and backcountry skiing. Snowboarding is also popular, with parks and pipes in most resorts.

Après-ski is taken very seriously – with live bands from mid- to late-afternoon. But it all stops suddenly, dinner is served and then the nightlife starts and the bands are back. There is plenty to do off the slopes: snowmobile safaris, ice fishing, ice climbing, dog-sled rides, and saunas galore. You can visit a local Sami (the politically correct name for Lapp) village. And resorts are very family-friendly.

The main resort is Åre (see separate chapter). **Sälen** is Scandinavia's largest winter sports area – and is made up of four separate sets of slopes totalling 144km/89 miles of piste. Most slopes are very gentle, suiting beginners and early or timid intermediates best, though there are 31 black runs listed, including the locally notorious 'Wall' in Hundfjället. Lindvalen and Högfjället are vaguely linked by a lift and a long cross-country slog. But you need the unreliable bus service to the others.

Vemdalen has two separate areas of slopes 18km/11 miles apart by road. **Björnrike** is great for families, beginners and early intermediates, with eight lifts and 15km/9 miles of mainly gentle pistes. There is a hotel right on the slopes, built in modern Scandinavian style. **Vemdalsskalet** has more advanced intermediate terrain, which is served by 10 lifts and 13km/8 miles of pistes. The Högfjällshotell at the base is large, dates from 1936 and prides itself on its lively après-ski.

Riksgränsen, 250km/150 miles north of the Arctic Circle, is an area of jagged mountain peaks and narrow fjords. The season starts in mid-February and ends in June – when you can be on the slopes under the midnight sun. There are only six lifts and 21km of piste. But there is some good off-piste and midnight heli-skiing.

Björkliden, also above the Arctic Circle, is famous for its subterranean skiing inside Scandinavia's largest cave system. You need to go with a guide.

Ramundberget is a good, small, quiet family resort with ski-in, ski-out accommodation. It gets large amounts of snow and its 22km/14 miles of pistes are mainly easy or intermediate cruising runs. There is a special children's area with its own lift.

652

TOURIST INFORMATION

www.visit-sweden.com

Sälen
www.malung.se

Vemdalen (Björnrike, Vemdalsskalet)
www.vemdaleninfo.se

Riksgränsen
www.riksgransen.nu

Björkliden
www.bjorkliden.com

Ramundberget
www.ramundberget.se

Åre

Sweden's best slopes strung out along a frozen lake

WHAT IT COSTS

((((4)

HOW IT RATES

The slopes

Snow	★★★
Extent	★★
Experts	★★
Intermediates	★★★★
Beginners	★★★★
Convenience	★★★
Queues	★★★★
Restaurants	★★★

The rest

Scenery	★★★
Resort charm	★★★
Off-slope	★★★

What's new

For 2002/03 a six-pack will be installed next to the main cable-car from town, replacing the slow double chair. This will feed a new 4-seater chair, replacing a T-bar and two double chairs.

The slope-side Sunwing hotel is being renovated and will be called the Tott Hotel & Spa.

Neilson is introducing direct charter flights from Gatwick to Ostersund which cut transfer time to 90 minutes.

For 2001/02 two new red and two new blue slopes (all with snowmaking) were created in the central area above the town.

➕ Cute little town centre

➕ Good snow reliability

➕ Ideal intermediate and beginner runs

➕ Extensive cross-country trails

➕ Excellent children's facilities

➕ Lively après-ski scene

➕ Lots of off-slope diversions

➖ Lots of T-bars

➖ Exposed upper mountain prone to closure because of bad weather

➖ High winds detrimental to snow conditions

➖ Few expert challenges

➖ High season and weekend queues

Åre has the biggest area of linked slopes in Sweden and some of its most challenging terrain. But it suits beginners, intermediates and families best. It has a dinky little town centre and a long area of slopes set along a frozen lake.

THE RESORT

Åre is a small town made up of old, pretty, coloured wooden buildings and some larger, modern additions. When we were there the main square had a roaring open fire to warm up by. As well as accommodation in town, there is lots spread out along the valley, with a concentration in the Duved area. All the slopes and accommodation are set on the shore of a huge, long lake, frozen in the winter months.

THE MOUNTAINS

The terrain is mainly green and blue tree-lined slopes, with a couple of wind-swept bowls above the trees.
Slopes There are two main areas. The largest is accessed by a funicular from the centre of town or by a new six-pack or cable-car a short climb above it. This takes you to the hub of a network of runs and (mainly) T-bars

that stretches for 10km/6 miles from end to end. The cable-car is often shut because it goes to the top of the above-the-tree-line slopes (known as the 'high zone'), which often suffers from howling gales. A gondola also accesses the high zone from a different point. You can get back on-piste right into the town square. A separate area of slopes is above Duved, the other main bed base, now served by a high-speed chair. There are four floodlit slopes, each open on a different night.
Snow reliability Snow reliability is good from November to May. More of a problem is the wind, which can blow fresh snow away. It also means that artificial snow is often deliberately made wet so that it doesn't blow away – it then compacts to a hard, icy surface (and certainly had when we tried the Olympia night skiing area – the top part was sheet ice).

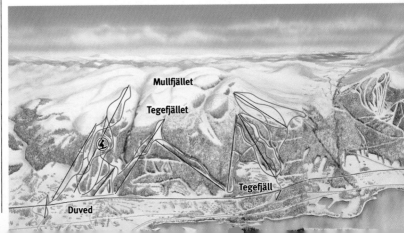

Mullfjället

Tegefjället

Tegefjäll

Duved

MOUNTAIN FACTS

Altitude 380m-1275m
          1,250ft-4,180ft
Lifts   45
Pistes   93km
                   58 miles
Green   12%
Blue   42%
Red   36%
Black   5%
Unpatrolled   5%
Recco detectors used

Experts Experts will find Åre's slopes limited, especially if the 'high zone' is closed. If it is open, there is a lot of off-piste available, including an 8km/5 mile run over the back accessed by a snowcat service in high season. On the main lower area the steepest (and iciest when we were there) pistes are in the Olympia area. There are also steep black and red runs back to town.

Intermediates The slopes are ideal for most intermediates with pretty blue runs through the trees. Because they tend to be more sheltered, the blue runs also often have the best snow. You can get a real sense of travelling on the main area – from hill to hill and valley to valley.

Beginners There are good facilities for beginners, both on the main area and at Duved.

Snowboarding There's a 1.4km/1 mile long boarder and skier-cross course, a half-pipe and terrain-park.

Cross-country The area has an amazing 300km/185 miles of cross-country trails, both on prepared tracks and unprepared trails marked with red crosses. Some trails are floodlit in the evening.

Queues In high season there can be queues for some lifts, especially in the central area immediately above Åre.

Mountain restaurants There are some good mountain restaurants. Our favourite was the rustic Buustamons, tucked away in the woods near Rödkulleomradret.

Schools and guides The ski school has a very good reputation – and this, the easy terrain and excellent childcare facilities make it a good area for families and children.

Facilities for children There are special children's areas and under 11-year-olds

get free lift passes if wearing helmets. There's a kindergarten that takes children from the age of two.

STAYING THERE

How to go A couple of the major UK tour operators offer packages to Åre.

Hotels The main central hotels are the delightful old Åregarden and the simpler Diplomat Ski Lodge. The Renen in Duved is very popular with families.

Self-catering There are plenty of cabins and apartments; reporters have recommended the ones at Åre Fjällby.

Eating out Our favourite restaurant was Sames, with excellent Swedish food. The Bistro is also good and there are plenty of other alternatives.

Après-ski Après-ski is amazingly lively. The Diplomat in town is packed from 3pm onwards and has live bands. Later on, the Diplomat, the Country Club and Bygget all have live bands and there are plenty of bars for a quiet drink. One reporter recommended going to one of the concerts held in igloos by the Tannforsen frozen waterfall.

Off the slopes Lots to do including dog- and reindeer-sled rides, skating, ice fishing, tobogganing, ice driving, ice climbing and snowmobiling.

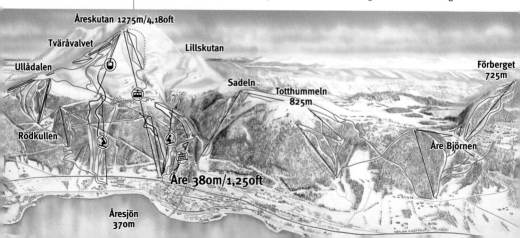

Scotland

What's new

The long-awaited funicular railway at Cairngorm opened in 2001/02.

A joint 5-day lift pass for Nevis Range and Glencoe is now available.

At The Lecht, for 2002/03 an additional ski-tow will be added to the Eagle run and a new day lodge opened.

➕ The resorts are easy to get to from northern Britain

➕ It is possible to experience perfect snow and stirring skiing

➕ Decent, cheap accommodation and good-value packages are on offer

➕ Mid-week it's rarely crowded

➕ Extensive ski-touring possibilities

➕ Few travel hassles

➕ Lots to do off the slopes

➖ Weather is extremely changeable and sometimes vicious

➖ Snowfall is erratic, and piste conditions can be challenging

➖ Slopes are limited; runs tend to be short

➖ Queueing can be a problem – though usually only at peak times and if some lifts are closed

➖ Little ski village ambience and few memorable mountain restaurants

Conditions in Scotland are unpredictable, to say the least. If you are willing to take a chance, or if you live nearby and can go at short notice when things look good, fine. But don't look on it as a replacement for your usual week in the Alps. If you try it, you'll either love it or hate it; but at least you'll know.

FURTHER INFORMATION

The VisitScotland brochure, *Scottish Snow*, has all the information you need to fix up a trip.

t 0131 332 2433

info@visitscotland.com

ski.visitscotland.com

For novices who are really keen to learn, Scotland could make sense, especially if you live nearby. You can book instruction via one of the excellent outdoor centres, many of which also provide accommodation and a wide range of other activities. The ski schools at the resorts themselves are also very good.

Most of the slopes in most of the areas fall around the intermediate level. But all apart from The Lecht offer one or two tough or very tough slopes.

Snowboarding is popular and most of the resorts have some special terrain features, but maintaining these facilities in good nick is problematic. The natural terrain is good for free-riding when the conditions are right.

Cairngorm is the best-known resort, with 16 lifts and 37km/23 miles of runs. Aviemore is the main centre (with a regular shuttle-bus to the slopes) but you can stay in other villages in the Spey valley. The slopes are now accessed by a new funicular from the main car park up to Ptarmigan at 1100m/3,610ft.

Nevis Range is the highest and newest Scottish resort – it opened in 1989. It has 12 lifts and 35km/22 miles of runs on the north-facing slopes of Aonach Mor – Britain's eighth highest peak. You get up to the slopes by means of a long six-seater gondola. There are many B&Bs and hotels in and around Fort William, only 10 minutes away by shuttle-bus.

Glenshee now boasts 25 lifts and 40km/25 miles of runs, spread out over three minor parallel valleys. Glenshee remains primarily a venue for day-trippers, though there are hotels, hostels and B&Bs in the area.

Glencoe's more limited slopes (seven lifts, 20km/12 miles of runs) lie just east of moody Glen Coe itself. You have to ride a double chair-lift and a button lift to get to the main slopes, including the nursery area. The isolated Kings House Hotel is 2km/1 mile away.

The Lecht is largely a beginners' area, with 14 lifts and 20km/12 miles of runs on the gentle slopes beside a high road pass with a series of parallel lifts and runs just above the car parks. With a maximum vertical of only 200m/660ft, runs are short. The village of Tomintoul is 10km/6 miles away.

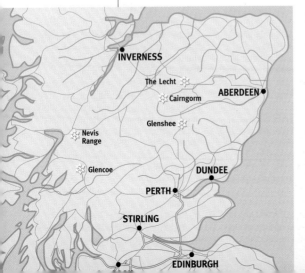

Australia

- Offers skiing and boarding during the European summer
- In one holiday you can also take in a visit to tropical northern Australia
- Some of the resorts are year-round destinations offering upmarket slope-side accommodation

- It's a long way from anywhere except New Zealand and south-east Asia
- Mountains are rather low, and lift/trail networks are small by Alpine standards

Even more than New Zealand, Australia offers resorts that are basically of local interest, but which might amuse people with other reasons to travel there – catching up with those long-lost relatives, say. The mountains are certainly more entertaining than most of the glacier areas that snow-starved Europeans must normally rely on in the summer. Skiing among snow-laden gum trees is also a unique experience for northern hemisphere skiers, plus there is often the chance to see kangaroos, emus, echidnas and wombats.

The major resorts are concentrated in the populous south-east corner of the country, between Sydney and Melbourne, with the largest in New South Wales (NSW) – in the National Park centred on Australia's highest mountain, Mt Kosciusko (2230m/7,320ft), about six hours' drive from Sydney. Skiing has been going on here since the early 1900s – as in the next-door state of Victoria, where there are several resorts within three or four hours' drive of Melbourne.

The Australian ski season generally runs from early June to mid-October, but may be extended at either end if snow conditions allow.

Thredbo, established as long ago as 1955, is a relatively upmarket Alpine village in NSW. It hosted the only World Cup race event held in Australia, thanks to a vertical of 670m/2,200ft.

Thredbo is rather like a small and quite smart French purpose-built resort – user-friendly, and mostly made up of modern apartments, many new luxury ski-in, ski-out chalets and lodges run by clubs. But there are many more bars than you would find in the French equivalent, and the party atmosphere thrives. The Austrian flavour brought by Thredbo's founders is now giving way to modern, casual-elegant restaurants and bars. It's a steep little place, with stiff climbs to get around from one part to another. Road access is easy, but it costs A$15 a day just to enter the park.

The slopes, prettily wooded with gum trees, rise up across the valley from the village, served by a regular shuttle-bus through the resort. The runs are many and varied, and it will take at least a few days until you know your way around, yet the resort as a whole gives the impression of good organisation. The dozen lifts include three fast quad chairs, and the trails include Australia's highest (2037m/

6,680ft) and longest (6km/4 miles). While the blacks are not difficult, they offer some variety, and on the higher lifts there are off-piste variants.

Since 1987 well over A$100 million has been poured into Thredbo by its owners. The result is an abundance of luxury architect-designed apartments, an attractive pedestrian mall with good shopping and some high-class restaurants both on and off the mountain. There is also an impressive modern Australian Institute of Sport training complex open to the public. On the hill a 700m/2,300ft bob-sleigh track for the public is popular all year round. You can take the Crackenback gondola up the mountain for dinner.

On the other side of the mountain range is the **Perisher Blue** resort complex, with a pass covering 51 lifts – more than anywhere else in Australia – but a vertical of less than 400m/1,310ft. The main area is **Perisher/Smiggins**, where lifts and runs – practically all easy or intermediate – range over three lightly wooded sectors. The resort is reachable by road, or by the Skitube, a rack railway that tunnels up from Bullocks Flat and goes on to the second area, **Blue Cow/Guthega**, where the slopes offer more challenges.

Perisher Blue is doing its best to catch up with Thredbo by upgrading hotels and building more facilities, but it remains spread out and does not have the cosy village atmosphere that attracts so many to Thredbo. That said, Perisher Blue has no trouble attracting the crowds, is sponsored by Land Rover and hosts the Australian version of the now world-wide event, the Planet X Winter Games. Perisher Blue also has more ski-in, ski-out accommodation than Thredbo, although it does appeal more to the masses, with its shopping-mall style village terminal centre filled with every manner of shop, bar and fast food restaurant. Its main advantage over Thredbo is its snow, thanks to its position further within the mountain ranges and its altitude: Perisher Blue's lifts start at about the same elevation as Thredbo's mid-station.

Many on a budget choose to stay in the apartments or hotels in the lakeside town of Jindabyne, a half-hour drive from both Thredbo and Perisher, with a lively youth-oriented nightlife scene. There are also some rather upmarket chalets along the Alpine Way, which leads to Thredbo.

From Perisher, a snowcat can take you on an 8km/5 mile ride to the isolated chalets of Australia's highest resort, **Charlotte Pass** (1760m/5,770ft), with five lifts but only 200m/66oft vertical. People visit the Pass more for its charm than for the skiing, although it is a favourite with families. The major hotel is the historic and turreted Kosciusko Chalet, a good spot for romantic weekends (there's no mobile phone reception here!).

In Victoria, resorts are not as high as in NSW but many have good snow since they are set well within the ranges. You're better off flying and coaching to these resorts – most Victorian skifields are approached by tricky winding mountain roads.

Mount Hotham has a reputation for powder snow and some of the steepest runs in Australia. The 11 lifts serve a complete range of runs with plenty of variety. The longest run is 2.5km/1.5 miles and there is more consistently steep terrain here than at any other area in Australia. Mount Hotham is unique among the Australian fields in that the village is built along the top of a ridge, with the slopes below it. The place is also distinguished by its Hotham Heights

Chalets, a nest of multi-storey buildings atop the slopes, the most upmarket of which is fitted out with a tiny DVD theatre, spa, sauna, bar, and spacious lounge areas. The focus of the village is Mount Hotham Central, comprising apartments, shops and eateries including a few excellent restaurants. You can also stay 15 minutes' drive away at Dinner Plain, a group of architect-designed chalets set prettily among gum trees. There are a few restaurants and bars here, many cross-country trails and horse riding.

There is also a 6-minute helicopter link from Mount Hotham to another resort nearby (and covered by the same lift pass), **Falls Creek**, that costs all of A$69. Falls Creek is the most alpine of Australia's resorts, completely snow-bound in winter. Guests not arriving by chopper are taken by snowcat from the car park to their ski-in, ski-out lodge. There are 18 lifts, though the area is smaller than Mount Hotham's and the runs are mostly intermediate. That said, the big attraction at Falls Creek is being able to access Australia's steepest skiing on the adjacent **Mt McKay** – 365m/1,200ft vertical of true black diamond terrain in anyone's language. Guided snowcat trips from Falls Creek to Mt McKay take place twice a day, three hours costing A$69. It's well worth the trip.

The other Victorian resort of note is the isolated peak of **Mt Buller**. This place is to Melbourne what Cape Cod is to Manhattan – a magnet for old money, a place to be seen and with enough quality skiing, hotels, spas and restaurants to make an overseas visitor feel they haven't wasted their time. Big-time entrepreneurs have poured millions into Mt Buller, creating a proper resort village with a luxury hotel, a new pampering spa and even a university campus. Draped around the mountain are 25 lifts – the largest network in Victoria, including 13 chair-lifts. There's also a tubing hill, snow-shoeing, cross-country, telemarking lessons and tobogganing.

Mt Buffalo is worth visiting mainly to stay in the historic Mt Buffalo Chalet, with its dramatic views over the craggy Victorian alps. The Chalet is done up in true 1930s style and offers gourmet dining – the local Angus beef a speciality. The slopes, a short drive away, are in an Alpine basin surrounded by boulders, with five lifts almost purely for beginners.

TOURIST OFFICES

Thredbo
www.thredbo.com.au

Perisher Blue (for Perisher, Smiggins, Blue Cow, Guthega)
www.perisherblue.com.au

Charlotte Pass
www.charlottepass.com.au

Mount Hotham
www.hotham.net.au

Falls Creek
(for Falls Creek and Mt McKay)
www.fallscreek.com.au

Mt Buller
www.mtbuller.com.au

Mt Buffalo
www.mtbuffalochalet.com.au

New Zealand

+ For Europeans, good for a combined holiday to the southern hemisphere and more interesting than summer skiing on glaciers
+ For Australians, conveniently close, with flights from Sydney
+ Huge areas of off-piste terrain accessible by helicopter on the South Island
+ Some spectacular scenery, as seen in *The Lord of the Rings* movies

− It's a long way from anywhere except Australia
− Limited mountain facilities – mountain restaurants are mostly basic pit stops
− Half-hour-plus drives from accommodation up to the ski areas
− Highly changeable weather
− No trees, so skiing in bad weather is virtually impossible

The number of keen skiers and boarders from New Zealand found kicking around the Alps gives a clue that there must be some decent slopes back home – and indeed there are. The resorts here have lifted their game in recent years by adding new lifts and facilities, but even so the slopes are rather different from those of the Alps or the Rockies. The networks of lifts and runs are rather limited by those exalted standards. However desperate you are for snow during the northern summer, we wouldn't advise travelling halfway round the world from Europe or the US just to get access to the likes of Coronet Peak or The Remarkables. But the heli-skiing around the Mt Cook region on the South Island is definitely worth writing home about. For Europeans already spending a lot to travel to New Zealand, the extra cost of a day or two's heli-drops is well worth while. New Zealand's ski resorts could make an interesting part of a wider-ranging visit to the country, and may be the best option you have if you're starting from somewhere nearer.

Whakapapa and Turoa on the North Island still don't have the linking lift that will create arguably the most impressive network in the southern hemisphere. When they do, taken together they will be a match for smaller European resorts.

Skiing at almost every New Zealand ski resort involves at least a half-hour drive from a nearby town – usually below snowline – to the ski field itself. Coach transfers from the hotels and towns to the ski fields are generally very well organised. The ski fields will have a base lodge, usually with a restaurant and a cafeteria, equipment rental and one or two shops as well as the main lifts. The only on-snow accommodation is a few apartments at Cardrona on the South Island, and some private lodges at the base of Whakapapa on the North Island.

There are resorts on both North Island and South Island. The main concentration on South Island is around the scenic lakeside town (and year-round resort) of Queenstown, covered in detail in the chapter after this one. Queenstown is touted as the adrenalin capital of New Zealand – and probably the world – by offering a range of dangerous (or at least thrilling) activities, of which the best

known is bungee jumping. Most are available in winter as well as summer.

In what follows, we describe the most prominent resorts (apart from Queenstown and its two local mountains), but there are a number of other possibilities. The main commercial ones are described briefly in our directory at the back of the book, but there are also other ski fields run by clubs. Don't expect groomed trails or other luxuries: club fields are pretty primitive, involving stiff walks to get to the base and crude rope tows or at best T-bars when you get there. You even have to bring your own food and drink. Craigieburn on the South Island, near Mt Hutt, wins the vote for the most impressive terrain out of the selection.

Any of the major resorts is worth a day or two of your time if you're in the area and the conditions are right. Treble Cone offers the most challenge and interest for advanced skiers. But if your credit card is also in good

Phone numbers
From abroad use the
prefix +64 and omit
the initial 'o' of the
phone number.

WHAKAPAPA MOUNTAIN FACTS

Altitude	1625m-2300m
	5,330ft-7,550ft
Lifts	20
Pistes	1,360 acres
Blue	25%
Red	50%
Black	25%
Snowmaking	some

TOURIST OFFICE

t 07 892 3738
f 07 892 3732
snow@whakapapa.co.nz
www.whakapapa.co.nz

condition, don't miss the heli-skiing; even if you're no expert off-piste, with powder skis it's a doddle, and tremendously satisfying.

We recommend Methven Heliski or Wilderness Heliski. Both operate in the main spine of mountains in the Mt Cook area and offer the longest and most spectacular runs for serious skiers and snowboarders. The cost for about five runs is around NZ$700. There are several other companies operating on South Island. Harris Mts Heli-Ski, operating out of Queenstown and Wanaka, caters mainly for the large Japanese market, and the three-run days are generally very easy skiing with long waits in between lifts. The other major Queenstown operation, Southern Lakes Heli-Ski, is more amenable to exciting skiing. Try to leave the arrangements loose, to cope with the highly changeable weather.

An alternative adventure is to fly by plane to ski 10km/6 miles down the length of the Tasman Glacier. For a gentle schuss the cost is high – about NZ$800-900 for the day. The main draw is the immense grandeur of the place, along with the ski-plane flights over stunning blue ice-flows and the close proximity of Mt Cook. The Tasman is also one of the few glaciers in the world where it is possible to walk through the eery ice-blue glacial caves – quite a surreal experience.

As in the northern hemisphere, the season doesn't really get under way until midwinter – mid or late June; it runs until some time in October. Mount Hutt aims to open first, in mid-May,

and disputes the longest-season title with Whakapapa, which generally stays open until mid-November.

Snowboarding is very popular in New Zealand, and most of the major resorts have special terrain-parks including half-pipes, as well as boarding classes and rental equipment.

Whakapapa (pronounced Fukapapa) is on the slopes of the active volcano Mt Ruapehu, which has occasionally erupted in recent years, leaving the slopes black with volcanic ash. Until the late 1990s the volcano had not caused havoc since the 1950s, when an eruption carried away a bridge.

Mt Ruapehu is in the middle of the North Island and within four hours' drive of both Auckland and Wellington. Whakapapa, New Zealand's largest ski field, is located on the north-facing slopes with a vertical of 675m/2,210ft served by 20 lifts including one fast quad. Terrain is typified by large, wide open cruisers plus challenging off-piste. Next to the base lodge is an extensive beginners' area, Happy Valley, with half a dozen rope tows, a chair-lift that was new last season and snowmaking that allow this particular section to open early in the season. The resort's lifts and runs range across craggy terrain made especially interesting because of the unpredictable twists, turns and drops of the solidified lava on which it sits. There is a mix of deep gullies, superb natural half-pipes for snowboarders and narrow chutes. There is a handful of mountain restaurants and a new cafe at the nearby Turoa ski field.

Introduction

659

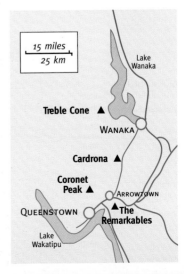

Phone numbers
From abroad use the prefix +64 and omit the initial 'o' of the phone number.

TREBLE CONE MOUNTAIN FACTS

Altitude	1200m-1860m
	3,940ft-6,100ft
Lifts	5
Pistes	1,360 acres
Green	15%
Blue	45%
Black	40%
Snowmaking	
	125 acres

TOURIST OFFICE

t 03 443 7443
f 03 443 8401
tcinfo@treblecone.co.nz
www.treblecone.co.nz

CARDRONA MOUNTAIN FACTS

Altitude	1505m-1895m
	4,940ft-6,220ft
Lifts	7
Pistes	790 acres
Green	20%
Blue	55%
Black	25%
Snowmaking	none

TOURIST OFFICE

t 03 443 7411
f 03 443 8818
info@cardrona.com
www.cardrona.com

MOUNT HUTT MOUNTAIN FACTS

Altitude	1420m-2075m
	4,660ft-6,810ft
Lifts	9
Pistes	900 acres
Green	25%
Blue	50%
Black	25%
Snowmaking	
	103 acres

TOURIST OFFICE

t 03 308 5074
f 03 308 5076
service@nzski.com
www.nzski.com

Views from both resorts are of the surrounding volcanic peaks and wide open fields of tundra – quite surreal.

Accommodation is 6km/4 miles away at Whakapapa village, with the best middle-of-the-road property being a motel named the Skotel. A complete anomaly in this area of rustic lodges is the Chateau, a hotel in the grand style of the 1920s, with overly high ceilings, sweeping drapes over picture windows, a marble foyer and formal dining room with grand piano.

Worth knowing about is the hike to Mt Ruapehu's fizzing Crater Lake. Ask ski patrol for directions or better still talk them into taking you on a guided trip. This involves about a half-hour hike up from the top of the highest T-bar, and then a long traverse across a large flat tundra-like area. A few lefts and rights and you are staring into the mouth of a volcano. Awesome views and neighbouring volcanos give this area an other-worldly feel.

On the south-western slope of Mt Ruapehu is **Turoa** – now under the same ownership as Whakapapa. You can ski both on the same ticket, which cost NZ$56 last season. And there is now a trail that links both – but the snow must be perfect and you must be guided by a ski patroller. Turoa is smaller, but with an impressive 720m/2,360ft vertical – the biggest in Australasia. The longest run is 4km/2.5 miles. There's plenty of off-piste scope away from the gentle intermediate runs, plus the chance to ski on the Mangaehuehu Glacier. Accommodation is 20 minutes away in Ohakune.

The South Island has 15 ski areas, including five club fields. **Mt Hutt**, an hour west of Christchurch in the northern part of the island, has a 670m/2,200ft vertical and some of the country's most impressive, consistently steep, wide-open terrain – all within view of the Pacific Ocean. On a clear day you can even see the sandy beaches in the distance beyond the patchwork Canterbury plains – in fact it often snows on the beaches here. The lift system is half the size of Whakapapa's and a few more fast chair-lifts would not go amiss. The main area is an open bowl with gentle terrain in the centre served by chairs and drags and steeper terrain around the outside, some of which requires a short hike to the top. An impressive big base lodge was built for the 2000 season, including a spacious,

welcoming cafe and brasserie, plus a well-stocked rental shop. Mt Hutt Helicopters offers six-run days in the mountains beyond for NZ$600. The helicopter departs from the heli-pad right in the car park – just wander up to the heli hut and book in. There is no accommodation on-mountain – most people stay in the little town of Methven, where there are several truly comfortable up-market B&Bs as well as motels and apartments. The very British South Island capital of Christchurch, an hour and a half away, is also an option for accommodation.

About six hours' drive south of Christchurch is the quiet lakeside town of Wanaka, which is also 90 minutes from Queenstown, and there are two resorts accessible from here.

Treble Cone, 20km/12 miles from Wanaka, has more advanced slopes than any other NZ ski area, plus the advantage of a better lift system, including the first six-pack in the southern hemisphere. There are two well maintained intermediate trails, one 3.5km/2 miles, the other 2km/1.2 miles. Both on the main flank and off to the side in Saddle Basin there are long natural half-pipes which are great fun when snow is good, as well as smooth, wide runs for cruising. Treble Cone is reached by a long and winding dirt track that adds to the excitement. The ski field offers stunning views across Lake Wanaka, with snowcapped Alpine-style peaks in the distance. There's a revamped cafe at the lift base. The food at Treble Cone and Cardrona is generally far better than the other resorts.

Cardrona, 34km/21 miles from Wanaka, is famous for its dry snow. The terrain is noted for its well-groomed, flattering cruisers. But there are some serious if short chutes, and the middle basin, Arcadia, hosts the New Zealand Extreme Skiing Championships. The total vertical is a modest 390m/1,280ft. Millions have been poured into the resort by its family owners over the past few years, resulting in a large base area focused around an odd clock tower. There's a bar and brasserie-style restaurant, large rental facility and a licensed childcare centre, plus several neat and modern self-contained apartments at the base (but bring all your own supplies). There are four half-pipes for boarders. Learners are looked after well, with three magic carpet lifts.

Queenstown

A lively, action-oriented base for sampling a range of South Island resorts

HOW IT RATES

The slopes

Snow	**
Extent	*
Experts	***
Intermediates	***
Beginners	***
Convenience	*
Queues	***
Restaurants	*

The rest

Scenery	****
Resort charm	**
Off-slope	*****

- ➕ For Europeans, more interesting than summer skiing on glaciers
- ➕ For Australians, conveniently close, with flights from Sydney
- ➕ Huge areas of off-piste terrain accessible by helicopters, with excellent snow at the right time
- ➕ Lots to do off the slopes, especially for adrenalin junkies
- ➕ Lively town, with lots going on and good restaurants
- ➕ Grand views locally, and the spectacular 'fjord' country nearby

- ➖ Slopes (in two separate areas locally) are a drive from town
- ➖ Limited lift-served slopes in each area
- ➖ It's a long way from anywhere except Australia
- ➖ No real mountain restaurants – just pit stops at the lift bases
- ➖ Highly changeable weather
- ➖ No trees, so skiing in bad weather is virtually impossible

If you want a single destination in New Zealand – as opposed to visiting a few different mountains on your travels – Queenstown is probably it, especially if you can cope with the cost of a few heli-drops. Although the resorts of North Island are impressive, the Southern Alps are, in the end, more compelling – and their resorts are free of volcanic interruptions. Mount Hutt may be a slightly more impressive area than either of Queenstown's local fields – Coronet Peak and The Remarkables – but it's a rather isolated field. From Queenstown you have a choice of the two local fields plus the option of an outing to Treble Cone and Cardrona. The best way to take them in would be to plan on a night or two in Wanaka, an hour or two away (see Introduction to New Zealand).

661

The resort

Queenstown is a winter-and-summer resort on the shore of Lake Wakatipu. (There is a map of the area in the introductory chapter.) Although the setting is splendid, with views to the peaks of the aptly named Remarkables range beyond the lake, the town itself is no beauty – it has grown up to meet tourists' needs, and has a very commercial feel. In recent years much effort has been put into smartening up the town, with such additions as the

NZSKI.COM

A magic carpet conveyor-belt now connects the car park at The Remarkables with the main lift station ➔

THE REMARKABLES MOUNTAIN FACTS

Altitude 1620m-1935m
5,310ft-6,350ft

Lifts	5
Pistes	545 acres
Green	30%
Blue	40%
Black	30%
Snowmaking	25 acres

TOURIST OFFICE

t 03 442 4615
f 03 442 4619
service@theremarkables.
co.nz
www.nzski.com

Phone numbers
From abroad use the
prefix +64 and omit
the initial 'o' of the
phone number.

classy new Steamer Wharf complex by the lake and lots of lakeside luxury apartments and hotels. It has a lively, relaxed feel, and makes a satisfactory base, with some good restaurants, plenty of entertaining bars and lots of touristy clothes shops.

The mountains

There are four lift-served mountains – all small by Alpine standards – that you can get to from Queenstown. The two described here – Coronet Peak and The Remarkables – are close by (about a 30-minute drive). The others – Cardrona and Treble Cone – are a more serious drive away (at least 90min), near Wanaka. At each base area you'll find a mini-resort – a ski school, a ski rental shop, a functional self-service restaurant, but no accommodation except at Cardrona.

All these areas have something for all abilities of skier or boarder, with off-piste opportunities as well as prepared and patrolled trails. They use the American green/blue/ black convention for run classification, not the European blue/red/black.

THE SLOPES
Not the height of convenience

The Remarkables, true to their name, are a dramatic range of craggy peaks visible across the lake from some parts of Queenstown. The slopes are tucked in a bowl right behind the largest visible peak, a 45-minute drive from town.

Two chairs go up from the base. The slow Alta lift serves easy runs and accesses the higher Sugar Bowl chair, which serves mainly long, easy runs plus a couple of black chutes. The Shadow Basin chair leads to steeper terrain, including three hike-accessed, expert-only chutes that drop down to Lake Alta, and the Homeward Run – a broad, fairly gentle, unprepared slope down to the resort access road, where a shuttle-truck takes you back to the base. The Remarkables is also home to New Zealand's first snowcat operation, in the bowls behind the main slopes.

Coronet Peak, about 25 minutes' drive from Queenstown, is a far more satisfying resort, especially for intermediates and above. Again, there are three main chair-lifts, one a fast quad that accesses practically all the

boarding Boarding is popular in New Zealand, and although the two mountains close to Queenstown don't seem to have quite such a hold on the boarding market as Cardrona (see New Zealand introduction), they have everything you need, including equipment, tuition and new terrain-parks and half-pipes. You needn't go anywhere near a drag-lift, and there are no flats to worry about except on the lowest green run at The Remarkables.

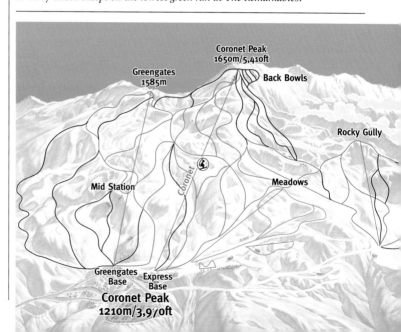

Coronet Peak
1650m/5,410ft

Greengates
1585m

Back Bowls

Rocky Gully

Mid Station

Meadows

Greengates Base

Express Base

Coronet Peak
1210m/3,970ft

CORONET PEAK MOUNTAIN FACTS

Altitude	1210m-1650m
	3,970ft-5,410ft
Lifts	6
Pistes	690 acres
Green	20%
Blue	45%
Black	35%
Snowmaking	
	200 acres

TOURIST OFFICE

t 03 442 4620
f 03 442 4624
service@coronetpeak.
co.nz
www.nzski.com

runs. The main mountainside is a pleasantly varied intermediate slope, full of highly enjoyable rolling terrain that snowboarders adore, though it steepens near the bottom. A fourth lift, a T-bar, serves another mainly intermediate area to one side. There are also drags for beginners. Night skiing runs from July to September on Fridays and Saturdays.

SNOW RELIABILITY
Good overall, but unpredictable

The New Zealand weather is highly variable, so it's difficult to be confident about snow conditions. The South Island resorts are at the same sort of latitude as the Alps, but are much more influenced by the ocean; fortunately, their ocean is a lot colder than ours. Coronet tends to receive sleet and/or rain even when it's snowing in The Remarkables. But Coronet Peak has snowmaking on practically all its intermediate terrain, from top to bottom of the mountain.

FOR EXPERTS
Challenges exist

Both areas have quite a choice of genuinely black slopes. Coronet's Back Bowls is an experts-only area, and there are other black slopes scattered around the mountain. The main enjoyment comes from venturing off-piste all over the place. The Remarkables' Shadow Basin chair serves some excellent slopes. And The Remarkables' hike-up expert chutes are truly world-class.

FOR INTERMEDIATES
Fine, within limits

There's some very enjoyable intermediate skiing in both areas – appreciably more at Coronet, where there are also easy blacks to go on to. But remember: these are very small areas by Alpine standards.

FOR BEGINNERS
Excellent

There are gentle slopes at both areas served by rope tows, and longer green runs served by chairs. And many other diversions if you decide it's a drag.

FOR CROSS-COUNTRY
Unremarkable

There is a short loop around a lake in the middle of The Remarkables area, but the only serious cross-country area is the elevated plateau of Waiorau Snow Farm, near Cardrona.

QUEUES
It depends

Coronet and The Remarkables can suffer a little from high-season crowds – there are certainly enough beds locally to lead to queues at peak times. But they aren't a major worry.

MOUNTAIN RESTAURANTS
Er, what mountain restaurants?

Both areas have a simple cafeteria at the base, and Coronet has a brasserie, but nothing up the mountain. The Remarkables cafeteria has a big sunny deck often visited by the large local mountain parrots, called keas.

GET THAT ADRENALIN RUSH

The streets of Queenstown are lined by agencies offering various artificial thrills.

AJ Hackett's bungee jump at Kawarau Bridge is where this crazy activity got off the ground – you plunge towards the icy river, but are pulled up short by your bungee cord and lowered into an inflatable boat. You can now also jump off a platform near the sightseeing gondola above town, giving you the illusion of leaping out over the lake and Queenstown.

The Shotover Jet Boat experience is less demanding. You get chauffeured at high speed along the rocky river in a boat that can get along in very shallow water, execute high-speed 360° turns and pass very close to cliffs and trees. It's probably more fun in summer than in freezing winter temperatures.

The whitewater rafting is genuinely thrilling – and not as uncomfortable as you'd expect, thanks to the full wet-suit, helmet, boots and gloves, and to the exertion involved. The rivers have some exciting rapids. One route even passes through a tunnel excavated in the gold-mining days, after which comes a small but steep waterfall where your souvenir shots are snapped.

CHILDCARE

At both areas there is a Skiwiland Club for children aged 4 to 6 with morning and afternoon sessions. The Queenstown nursery can take younger children all day. There is a licensed nursery at The Remarkables, taking children from 2 to 4.

Phone numbers
From abroad use the prefix +64 and omit the initial 'o' of the phone number.

SCHOOLS AND GUIDES
All the usual classes
The schools are well organised, with a wide range of options, including 'guaranteed' beginner classes.

FACILITIES FOR CHILDREN
Look good
Childcare looked okay to us. Free lift passes are available for children under 11 at The Remarkables. There is a nursery at Coronet Peak with mini-call pagers for parents.

Staying there

HOW TO GO
Sheer luxury?
There are lots of big, luxury hotels – all either new or refurbished – built to meet the big summer demand for beds in this popular lakeside resort.
Hotels Some hotels are quite some way from central Queenstown – inconvenient for après-ski unless there's a shuttle-bus. They range from the very simple to the glossily pretentious Millennium (03 441 8888). Aim to get a room with a view across Lake Wakatipu and the mountains – the view is worth the extra dollars. Two of the best boutique-style places to stay are the Heritage Hotel (03 442 4988) or the Mercure Grand Hotel St Moritz (03 442 4990).

EATING OUT
Lots of choice
There are over 100 restaurants – Chinese, Italian, Malaysian, Japanese – you name it. The Boardwalk in the Steamer Wharf complex overlooking the lake is the place to go for seafood (Bill Clinton ate there), and the upmarket Copper Club nearby is also excellent. A dining experience with a difference is the Bath House, located in a 1911 Victorian bath house right on the lakeshore. Solero Vino has delicious Mediterranean food and a rustic bar, and McNeill's is an excellent brew-pub with a range of tasty beers, housed in a stone cottage. The Bunker does excellent local cuisine such as Bluff oysters and lamb. Gantley's, a little way out of town, is a classic restaurant in an historic home. At the other end of the scale, pizza-lovers crowd into The Cow, a cosy barn-like place where you sit on logs around a fire waiting for tables or takeaways. Lone Star offers big servings of satisfying American-style food.

APRES-SKI
Lively little town
Queenstown has a good range of bars and clubs that stay open late with disco or live music. A small upmarket casino opened in 1999 in the plush Steamer Wharf, which also holds a classy cigar bar and good duty free.

OFF THE SLOPES
Scare yourself silly
There are lots of scary things to do – see the box on the previous page. Just to the west of Queenstown is New Zealand's spectacularly scenic 'fjord country', and you can go on independent or guided walks. By all reports, the Milford Sound sightseeing flights by plane or helicopter are to be preferred to the slow, lumbering bus-ride from Queenstown – but you should be aware that the weather can ruin your plans.

Arrowtown is interesting for a quick visit – a cute, touristy old mining town where you can kit yourself out to go panning for gold. The Winter Festival, held in mid-July, is an annual 'action-packed week of mayhem on the mountain and in the town'.

Reference section

A classified listing of the names, numbers and addresses you are likely to need.

Tour operators   666

Most people still prefer the convenience of a package holiday, which is what most of the companies listed are set up to provide. But note that we've also included some operators that offer accommodation without travel arrangements.

665

Tour operators

Absolute Ski
Chalet in Méribel
Tel 01788 822100
holiday@absoluteski.com
www.absoluteski.com

Airtours
Mainstream operator
Tel 0800 028 8844
www.airtours.co.uk

Albus Travel
St Anton specialist
Tel 0800 074 7945
info@albustravel.com
www.albustravel.com

Alp Active
Holidays in Les Gets
Tel 01223 568220
info@alpactive.com
www.alpactive.com

Alpine Action
Chalets in Les Trois Vallées
Tel 01903 761986
sales@alpine-action.co.uk
www.alpine-action.co.uk

Alpine Answers Select
Tailor-made holidays
Tel 020 8871 2728
select@alpineanswers.co.uk
www.alpineanswers.co.uk

Alpine Escapes
Catered chalet in Morzine
Tel 01322 616448 / +33 450 747392
alpineescapes@yahoo.com
www.alpine-escapes.com

Alpine Events
Corporate ski specialist
Tel 020 7622 2265
alpine@offsiteevents.com
www.alpineevents.co.uk

Alpine Options
Holidays in the French Alps
Tel 0845 130 0553
info@alpine-options.com
www.alpine-options.com

Alpine Tours
Group holidays in Austria/Italy
Tel 01227 454777
sales@alpinetours.co.uk

Alpine Weekends
Weekends in the Alps
Tel 020 8944 9762
info@alpineweekends.com
www.alpineweekends.com

Alps2Go
Holidays in Morzine
Tel 01908 585548
info@alps2go.com
www.alps2go.com

Altitude Holidays
Catered chalets in Courchevel
Tel 0870 870 7669
info@altitudeholidays.com
www.altitudeholidays.com

AmeriCan Ski
Hotels/B&Bs in North America
Tel 01892 511894
ian.awwt@btconnect.com
www.skiarus.com

American Ski Classics
Major North American resorts
Tel 020 8392 6660
sales@holidayworld.ltd.uk
www.americanskiclassics.com

APT Holidays Ltd
Weekend breaks by coach to France
Tel 01268 783878
apt.holidays@virgin.net
www.apt-holidays.co.uk

Aravis Alpine Retreat
Chalet in St Jean-de-Sixt (La Clusaz)
Tel +33 450 023625
info@aravis-retreat.com
www.aravis-retreat.com

Avant-ski
Mainly holidays in France
Tel 0191 285 8141
sales@avant-ski.com
www.avant-ski.com

Balkan Holidays
Holidays in Bulgaria, Slovenia and Romania
Tel 020 7543 5555
res@balkanholidays.co.uk
www.balkanholidays.co.uk

Barrelli Ski
Chalets in Champagny and Les Houches
Tel 0870 220 1500
whiplash@barrelliski.co.uk
www.barrelliski.co.uk

Beau-mont.com
Flexible breaks in Chamonix, Megève and Cervinia
Tel 0845 070 0203
sales@beau-mont.com
www.beau-mont.com

Bigfoot
Holidays in Chamonix
Tel 0870 300 5874
reservation@bigfoot-travel.co.uk
www.bigfoot-travel.co.uk

Bladon Lines
Chalet arm of Inghams
Tel 020 8780 8800
bladonlines@inghams.co.uk
www.inghams.co.uk

Board and Lodge
Catered snowboarding holidays in Chamonix
Tel 020 7916 2275
info@boardnlodge.com
www.boardnlodge.com

Bonne Neige Ski Holidays
Catered chalets in Méribel
Tel 01270 256966
ukoffice@bonne-neige-ski.com
www.bonne-neige-ski.com

Borderline
Specialist in Barèges
Tel +33 562 926895
info@borderlinehols.com
www.borderlinehols.com

The Chalet Company
Catered chalets in Morzine and Ardent (Avoriaz)
Tel +33 450 796840
moran@thechaletco.com
www.thechaletco.com

The Chalet Group
Chalet holidays in the French Alps
Tel +33 479 013500
kate@chaletgroup.com
www.chaletgroup.com

Chalet Kiana
Chalet in Les Contamines
Tel +33 450 915518 / 01689 838558
chaletkiana@aol.com
www.alpesactives.com

Chalet World
Chalets in big-name resorts
Tel 01952 840462 / 020 7373 2096
sales@chaletworld.co.uk
www.chaletworld.co.uk

Les Chalets de St Martin
Chalets in St-Martin
Tel 01202 473255
les.chalets@virgin.net
www.leschalets.co.uk

Chalets 'Unlimited'
Chalets worldwide
Tel 0191 285 8141
sales@avant-ski.com
www.avant-ski.com

Challenge Activ
Chalets and apartments in Morzine
Tel 0800 328 0513
challenge_activ_morzine@compuserve.com
www.challenge-activ.com

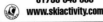
Chamonix Lodge
Chalet in Chamonix
Tel 01525 240357
chamonixlodge@ukonline.co.uk
www.chamonixlodge.com

Chez Jay Ski
Chalet in Les Arcs
Tel 01843 298030
ski@chezjayski.com
www.chezjayski.com

Classic Ski Limited
Holidays for 'mature' skiers/beginners
Tel 01590 623400
info@classicski.co.uk
www.classicski.co.uk

Club Europe
Schools trips to Austria, France and Italy
Tel 020 8699 7788
ski@club-europe.co.uk
www.club-europe.co.uk

Club Med
All-inclusive holidays in 'ski villages'
Tel 08453 676767
admin.uk@clubmed.com
www.clubmed.co.uk

Club Pavilion
Budget holidays
Tel 0870 241 0427
sales@clubpavilion.com
www.clubpavilion.com

Collineige
Chamonix valley specialist
Tel 01276 24262
info@collineige.com
www.collineige.com

Connick Ski
Chalet in Châtel
Tel +33 450 732212
nick@connickski.com
www.connickski.com

Contiki
Coach-travel holidays for 18-35s
Tel 020 8290 6422
travel@contiki.co.uk
www.contiki.com

Cooltip Mountain Holidays
Chalets in Méribel
Tel 01964 563563
ski@cooltip.com
www.cooltip.com

The Corporate Ski Company
Corporate specialists
Tel 020 7627 5500
ski@vantagepoint.co.uk
www.thecorporateskicompany.co.uk

Crystal
Major mainstream operator
Tel 0870 160 6040
skires@crystalholidays.co.uk
www.crystalski.com

CSb Mountain Holidays
Snowboard holidays in France and US
Tel 01235 770002
info@csbmountainholidays.com
www.csbmountainholidays.com

Descent International
Chalets in France and Switzerland
Tel 020 7989 8989
ski@descent.co.uk
www.descent.co.uk

Les Deux Chalets
Chalets in Méribel
Tel 01303 246966
anjid@ukonline.co.uk
www.chalet-de-launey.demon.co.uk

DirectSki.com
Holidays in Austria, France, Italy and Andorra
Tel 00 800 2424 2400
sales@directski.com
www.directski.com

Elegant Resorts
Luxury ski holidays
Tel 01244 897333
enquiries@elegantresorts.co.uk
www.elegantresorts.co.uk

Equity School Ski
School group holidays
Tel 01273 299299
schoolski@equity.co.uk
www.equityschooltravel.co.uk

Equity Ski
All-in holidays
Tel 01273 298298
travel@equity.co.uk
www.equityski.co.uk

Erna Low
Hotel and self-catering holidays, mostly in France and Switzerland
Tel 020 7584 2841
info@ernalow.co.uk
www.ernalow.co.uk

Esprit Ski
Families specialist in Europe and North America
Tel 01252 618300
travel@esprit-holidays.co.uk
www.esprit-holidays.co.uk

Eurotunnel Motoring Holidays
Self-drive holidays to France
Tel 0870 333 2001
ethols@crestahols.co.uk
www.eurotunnel.com

Fairhand Holidays
Ski-drive holidays to France
Tel 01959 702191
sunshine@fairhandholidays.com
www.fairhandholidays.com

The Family Ski Company
Family holidays in France
Tel 01684 540333
enquiries@familyski.co.uk
www.familyski.co.uk

Fantiski – Ski2k
Chalet holidays in France and USA
Tel 01622 862750
fantiski@hotmail.com
www.fantiski.co.uk

Finlays
Mainly chalets in France
Tel 01835 830562
finlayski@aol.com
www.finlayski.com

First Choice Ski
Major mainstream operator
Tel 0870 754 3477
sales@fcski.co.uk
www.fcski.co.uk

FlexiSki
Specialists in flexible breaks
Tel 0870 909 0754
reservations@flexiski.com
www.flexiski.com

Freedom Holidays
Weekends and 'flexible duration' holidays in Châtel
Tel 01798 342034
freedomhols@hotmail.com
www.freedomholidays.co.uk

French Freedom Holidays
Holidays in France
Tel 01724 857108
info@french-freedom.co.uk
www.french-freedom.co.uk

Frontier Ski
Holidays in Canada
Tel 020 8776 8709
info@frontier-travel.co.uk
www.frontier-travel.co.uk

Frosty's Ski and Snowboard Holidays
Chalet in St-Jean-de-Sixt
Tel +33 450 023728
info@frostys.co.uk
www.frostys.co.uk

Haig Ski
Hotels with guiding in Châtel and Morzine
Tel +33 450 811947
sales@haigski.com
www.haigski.com

The Oxford Ski Company
Chalets in Crans-Montana
Tel 07000 785349
info@oxfordski.com
www.oxfordski.com

Panorama Holidays
Budget-oriented holidays in Italy, Andorra and Spain
Tel 08707 505060
panoramaski@phg.co.uk
www.panoramaholidays.co.uk

Peak Ski
Chalets in Verbier
Tel 01442 832629
peakski@which.net
www.peak-ski.co.uk

PGL Ski Europe
Specialist in school group holidays
Tel 01989 768168
ski@pgl.co.uk
www.pgl.co.uk

PGL Teenski
Holidays for teenagers
Tel 01989 767767
holidays@pgl.co.uk
www.pgl.co.uk

Piste Artiste Ltd
Holidays in Champéry
reserve@pisteartiste.com
www.pisteartiste.com

Plus Travel
Specialists in Swiss resorts
Tel 020 7734 0383
plustravel@stlondon.com
www.plustravel.co.uk

Powder Byrne
Small programme of luxury holidays
Tel 020 8246 5300
enquiries@powderbyrne.co.uk
www.powderbyrne.com

Powder Skiing in North America Limited
Heli-skiing holidays in Canada
Tel 020 7736 8191
info@psna.co.uk

Ramblers
Cross-country holidays
Tel 01707 331133
info@ramblersholidays.co.uk
www.ramblersholidays.co.uk

Re-lax Holidays
Hotel holidays in Switzerland
Tel 020 8360 1185
sarah@re-laxholidays.co.uk
www.re-laxholidays.co.uk

Rocketski
All-in holidays online
Tel 01273 262626
info@rocketski.com
www.rocketski.com

Rocky Mountain Adventures
Five or six-month season holidays in the Rockies
Tel 0870 366 5442
seasons@rockymountain.co.uk
www.rockymountain.co.uk

Scott Dunn Latin America
Tailor-made holidays to South America
Tel 020 8682 5030
latin@scottdunn.com
www.scottdunn.com

Scott Dunn Ski
Upmarket holidays
Tel 020 8682 5050
ski@scottdunn.com
www.scottdunn.com

Silver Ski
Chalet holidays in France
Tel 01622 735544
karen@silverski.co.uk
www.silverski.co.uk

Simply Ski
Holidays in big-name resorts
Tel 020 8541 2209
ski@simply-travel.com
www.simplyski.co.uk

Ski 2
Monterosa specialists
Tel 01962 713330
info@ski-2.com
www.ski-2.com

Ski Activity
Holidays in big-name resorts
Tel 01738 840888
sales@skiactivity.com
www.skiactivity.com

Ski Addiction
Chalets and hotels in Châtel and St Anton
Tel 01580 819354
sales@skiaddiction.co.uk
www.skiaddiction.co.uk

Ski All America
US and Canadian holidays
Tel 08701 676 676
sales@skiallamerica.com
www.skiallamerica.com

Ski All Canada
Holidays in Canada
Tel 08705 262 262
mail@all-canada.com
www.all-canada.com

Skialot
Chalet in Chatel
Tel 020 8363 8326
stuey@skialot.com
www.skialot.com

Ski Amis
Chalet holidays in the La Plagne area
Tel 020 7692 0850
info@skiamis.com
www.skiamis.com

Ski Arrangements
Chalets/apartments in Europe and North America
Tel 08700 110565
info@skiarrangements.com
www.skiarrangements.com

SkiAway Holidays
Holidays in the Pyrenees and French Alps
Tel 01903 824823
skiaway@tourplanholidays.com
www.tourplanholidays.com

Ski Balkantours
Holidays in Eastern Europe
Tel 028 9024 6795
mail@balkan.co.uk
www.balkan.co.uk

Ski Barrett-Boyce
Chalet in Megève with tuition
Tel 020 8288 0042
kerry@skibb.com
www.skibb.com

Ski Basics
Chalets in Méribel
Tel 01225 444143
sales@skibasics.co.uk
www.skibasics.co.uk

Ski Beat
Chalets in La Plagne, Val d'Isere and La Tania
Tel 01243 780405
ski@skibeat.co.uk
www.skibeat.co.uk

Ski Blanc
Chalets in Méribel
Tel 020 8502 9082
sales@skiblanc.co.uk
www.skiblanc.co.uk

Ski Bon
Chalets in Méribel
Tel 020 8668 8223
enquiry@skibon.com
www.skibon.com

Reference section

669

SkiBound
Schools division of First Choice
Tel 0870 900 3200
sales@fcski.co.uk
www.fcski.co.uk

Ski Chamois
Holidays in Morzine
Tel 01302 369006
sales@skichamois.co.uk
www.skichamois.co.uk

Ski Club of Great Britain
Holidays for club members
Tel 0845 458 0784
skiers@skiclub.co.uk
www.skiclub.co.uk

The Ski Company
Holidays in France and US
Tel 0870 241 2085
info@theskicompany.co.uk
www.theskicompany.co.uk

The Ski Company Ltd
Luxury chalets in France and Switzerland
Tel 01451 843123
sales@skicompany.co.uk
www.skicompany.co.uk

Ski Cuisine
Chalets in Méribel
Tel 01702 589543
skicuisine@dial.pipex.com
www.skicuisine.co.uk

Ski Deep
Chalets in La Tania and Le Praz
Tel +33 479 081905
info@skideep.com
www.skideep.com

Skiers World
School trips to North America and Europe
Tel 0870 333 3620
info@skiersworld.com
www.skiersworld.com

Ski Etoile
Chalet in Montgenèvre
Tel 01588 640442
ski-etoile@clun25.freeserve.co.uk
www.skietoile.co.uk

Ski Expectations
Mainly hotels and chalets in Europe
Tel 01799 531888
ski.expectations@virgin.net
www.skiexpectations.com

Ski Famille
Family holidays in Les Gets
Tel 01223 363777
info@skifamille.co.uk
www.skifamille.co.uk

Ski France
Chalets and catered apartments
Tel 020 8313 0690
ski@skifrance.co.uk
www.skifrance.co.uk

SkiGower
School and group trips, mainly Switzerland
Tel 01527 851411
linda@gowstrav.demon.co.uk
www.skigower.co.uk

Ski Hame
Catered chalets in the Three Valleys
Tel 01875 320157
powderpigs@skihame.co.uk
www.skihame.co.uk

Ski Hillwood
Austrian, French and Canadian family holidays
Tel 01923 290700
sales@hillwood-holidays.co.uk
www.hillwood-holidays.co.uk

Ski Hiver
Chalets in Peisey (Les Arcs)
Tel 023 9242 8586
skihiver@aol.com
www.skihiver.co.uk

Ski Independence
USA and Canada and self-drive to France and Switzerland
Tel 0870 555 0555
(USA/Canada); 0870 600 1462
(Europe)
ski@ski-independence.co.uk
www.ski-independence.co.uk

Ski La Cote
Chalets in La Chapelle d'Abondance
Tel 01482 668357
adrian@ski-la-cote.karoo.co.uk
www.ski-la-cote.karoo.net

Ski Leisure Direction
Mainly self-catering in France
Tel 020 8324 4042
sales@leisuredirection.co.uk
www.leisuredirection.co.uk

Ski Life
Self-drive holidays to the French Alps
Tel 0870 429 2180
skilife@frenchlife.co.uk
www.skiinglife.co.uk

Ski Line
Holidays in Europe and North America
Tel 020 8650 5900
angus@skiline.co.uk
www.skiline.co.uk

Ski Link
Tel 01983 812883
skilinkuk@aol.com
www.ski-link.co.uk

Ski McNeill
Tailor-made to USA and European weekends
Tel 028 9066 6699
mail@skimcneill.com
www.skimcneill.com

Ski Miquel
Small but eclectic programme
Tel 01457 821200
ski@miquelhols.co.uk
www.miquelhols.co.uk

Ski Morgins Holidays
Chalet holidays in Morgins
Tel 01568 770681
info@skimorgins.com
www.skimorgins.com

Ski Morzine
Holiday accommodation in Morzine
Tel 01372 470104
info@skimorzine.com
www.skimorzine.com

Ski 'n' Action
Chalets in Le Praz (Courchevel)
Tel 01707 251696
info@ski-n-action.com
www.ski-n-action.com

Ski Olympic
Chalet holidays in France
Tel 01302 328820
info@skiolympic.co.uk
www.skiolympic.com

Ski Partners
Schools programme (First Choice group)
Tel 0117 925 3545

Ski Peak
Specialist in Vaujany
Tel 01428 741144
info@skipeak.com
www.skipeak.com

SkiPlan incorporating STS
Schools holidays
Tel 01273 774666
sales@topstravel.co.uk

Ski Rosie
Holidays in Chatel and Morgins
Tel +33 450 813100
rosie@skirosie.com
www.skirosie.com

Ski Safari
Canadian specialist
Tel 01273 223680
info@skisafari.com
www.skisafari.com

Skisafe Travel
Mainly holidays in Scotland
Tel 0141 812 0925
skisafe@osatravel.co.uk
www.osatravel.co.uk

Ski Scott James
Chalets in Argentière
Tel 01845 501139
jamie@skiscottjames.co.uk
www.skiscottjames.co.uk

Ski Solutions
Tailor-made holidays
Tel 020 7471 7777
alc@skisolutions.com
www.skisolutions.com

Ski Success
Group holidays to the USA and Italian Dolomites
Tel 01225 764205
info@success-tours.co.uk
www.success-tours.co.uk

Ski Supreme
Coach and self-drive to France
Tel 01355 260547
info@skisupreme.co.uk
www.skisupreme.co.uk

Ski The American Dream
Major operator to North America
Tel 020 8552 1201
holidays@skidream.com
www.skidream.com

Ski Total
European and US holidays
Tel 08701 633633
sales@skitotal.com
www.skitotal.com

Ski-Val
Holidays in France and Austria
Tel 01822 611200
reservations@skival.co.uk
www.skival.co.uk

Ski Verbier
Specialises in Verbier
Tel 020 7385 8050
info@skiverbier.com
www.skiverbier.com

Ski Weekend
Weekend and ten-day holidays
Tel 01367 241636
sales@skiweekend.com
www.skiweekend.com

Ski Weekends & Board Breaks
3- and 6-day holidays to Les Trois Vallées
Tel 01375 396688
sales@harris-travel.com
www.skiweekends.com / www.boardbreaks.com

Ski Wild
Specialise in Austria and Norway
Tel 0870 746 9668
info@skiwild.co.uk
www.skiwild.co.uk

Ski with Julia
Hotels and catered chalets in Switzerland
Tel 01386 584478
julia@skijulia.co.uk
www.skijulia.co.uk

Skiworld
European and North American programme
Tel 020 8600 1780
sales@skiworld.ltd.uk
www.skiworld.ltd.uk

Ski Yogi
Holidays to the Italian Dolomites
Tel 01799 531886
ski.expectations@virgin.net
www.skiexpectations.com

Sloping Off
Schools and group holidays by coach
Tel 01725 552833
hilary@slopingoff.fsnet.co.uk
www.equity.co.uk

Slovenija & Austrian Pursuits
Accommodation in Slovenija and Austria
Tel 020 220 0201
enquiries@sloveinjapursuits.co.uk
www.slovenijapursuits.co.uk

Snowbizz Vacances
Holidays in Puy-St-Vincent
Tel 01778 341455
wendy@snowbizz.co.uk
www.snowbizz.co.uk

Snowcoach
Holidays to Andorra, Austria and France
Tel 01727 866177
info@snowcoach.co.uk
www.snowcoach.co.uk

The short break specialists
since 1986

TAILOR MADE TO YOUR REQUIREMENTS

Call for a personal quote 01367 241636

Web: www.skiweekend.com
Email: info@skiweekend.com

Snowfocus
Chalet in Châtel with nannies
Tel 01392 479555
action@snowfocus.com
www.snowfocus.com

Snowlife
Holidays in La Clusaz
Tel 01534 863630
snowlife@psilink.co.uk
www.snowlife.co.uk

Snowline
Chalet holidays in France
Tel 020 8870 4807
ski@snowline.co.uk
www.snowline.co.uk

Snowscape
Flexible trips to Austria
Tel 01905 357760
skiandboard@snowscape.co.uk
www.snowscape.co.uk

Solo's
Singles' holidays, ages 25 to 69
Tel 08700 720700
travel@solosholidays.co.uk
www.solosholidays.co.uk

La Source
Luxury chalet in Villard-Reculas (Alpe-d'Huez)
Tel 01707 655988
lasourcefrance@aol.com
www.lasource.f9.co.uk

Stanford Skiing
Megève specialist
Tel 01223 477644
stanskiing@aol.com
www.stanfordskiing.co.uk

St Anton Ski Company
Hotels and chalets in St Anton
Tel +43 676 495 3438
jonathanverney@compuserve.com
www.atlas.co.uk/ski

Susie Ward Alpine Holidays
Flexible holidays to Châtel
Tel 01872 553055
susie@susieward.com
www.susieward.com

Swiss Travel Service
Hotels in Switzerland
Tel 0870 191 7175
swiss@bridge-travel.co.uk
www.swisstravel.co.uk

Thomson Ski & Snowboarding
Major mainstream operator
Tel 0870 606 1470
reservations@thomson-ski.com
www.thomson-ski.com
www.thomson-snowboarding.co.uk

Top Deck
Lively, informal holidays
Tel 020 7370 4555
res@topdecktravel.co.uk
www.topdecktravel.co.uk

Tops Ski Chalets and Club Hotels
Chalets in France
Tel 01273 774666
sales@topstravel.co.uk
www.topstravel.co.uk

Trail Alpine
Chalet in Morzine
Tel 0870 750 6560
info@trailalpine.co.uk
www.trailalpine.co.uk

Trailfinders
Ski Your Way Down Under programme
Tel 0845 050 5900
www.trailfinders.com

United Vacations Ski Freedom USA & Canada
US and Canada programme
Tel 0870 606 2222
uvuk@unitedvacations.com
www.unitedvacations.co.uk

Val d'Isère A La Carte
Specialists in hotels and self-catering holidays
Tel 01481 236800
skialacarte@aol.com
www.skivaldisere.co.uk

Val d'Isère Properties (VIP)
Specialist in Val d'Isère
Tel 020 8875 1957
ski@valdisere.co.uk
www.valdisere.co.uk

Vanilla Ski
Chalet in Seez (near La Rosière and Les Arcs)
Tel 01932 860696
sam@vanillaski.com
www.vanillaski.com

Vertical Reality at Verbier Ltd
Luxury chalet accommodation in Verbier
Tel 01268 452337
verticalr@hotmail.com
www.verticalrealityverbier.com

Virgin Ski
Holidays to America
Tel 0870 990 4210
brochure.requests@virgin holidays.co.uk
www.virginholidays.co.uk

Waymark Holidays
Cross-country skiing holidays
Tel 01753 516477
enquiries@waymarkholidays.com
www.waymarkholidays.com

Weekends in Val d'Isère
Weekends – and not just in Val d'Isère
Tel 020 8944 9762
info@alpineweekends.com
www.val-disere-ski.com

White Roc
Weekends and tailor-made hotel holidays
Tel 020 7792 1188
ski@whiteroc.co.uk
www.whiteroc.co.uk

YSE
Variety of holidays in Val-d'Isère
Tel 020 8871 5117
sales@yseski.co.uk
www.yseski.co.uk

Airlines

Air Canada
Tel 0870 524 7226
www.aircanada.ca

Air France
Tel 0845 0845 111
www.airfrance.com/uk

Air New Zealand
Tel 020 8741 2299
www.airnewzealand.co.uk

Alitalia
Tel 0870 544 8259
www.alitalia.co.uk

American Airlines
Tel 020 8572 5555
www.aa.com
08547 789789 outside London

Austrian Airlines
Tel 0845 601 0948
www.austrianairlines.co.uk

British Airways
Tel 0845 77 333 77
www.british-airways.com
Flight enquiries: 0870 55 111 55; general enquiries: 0845 77 999 77

Buzz
Tel 0870 240 7070
www.buzz.co.uk
Grenoble, Geneva, Chambery

Continental Airlines
Tel 0800 776464
www.continental.com

Delta Airlines
Tel 0800 414767
www.delta.com

EasyJet
Tel 0870 6 000 000
www.easyjet.com
Flights to Geneva, Zurich, Nice

Go
Tel 0870 607 6543
www.go-fly.co.uk

KLM
Tel 08705 074074
www.klmuk.co.uk

Lufthansa
Tel 0845 773 7747
www.lufthansa.com

Qantas
Tel 0845 774 7767
www.qantas.com.au

Ryanair
Tel 0870 1 569 569
www.ryanair.com

Swiss International Air Lines
Tel 0845 601 0956
www.swiss.com

United Airlines
Tel 0845 844 4777
www.unitedairlines.co.uk

Virgin Atlantic Airways
Tel 01293 450 150
www.virgin-atlantic.com

Airports

Aberdeen
Tel 01224 722331
www.baa.co.uk

Belfast
Tel 028 9448 4848
www.bial.co.uk

Birmingham
Tel 0121 767 5511
www.bhx.co.uk

Bournemouth
Tel 01202 364000
www.flybournemouth.com

Bristol
Tel 0870 121 2747
www.bristolairport.co.uk

Cardiff
Tel 01446 711111
www.cial.co.uk

Dublin
Tel +353 1 814 1111
www.dublin-airport.com

East Midlands
Tel 01332 852852
www.eastmidlandsairport.com

Edinburgh
Tel 0131 333 1000
www.baa.co.uk

Exeter
Tel 01392 367433
marketing@exeter-airport.co.uk
www.exeter-airport.co.uk

Glasgow
Tel 0141 887 1111
www.baa.co.uk

Leeds-Bradford
Tel 0113 250 9696
www.lbia.co.uk

London Heathrow
Tel 0870 0000 123
www.baa.co.uk

London Gatwick
Tel 0870 000 2468
www.baa.co.uk

London Luton
Tel 01582 405100
www.london-luton.com

London Stansted
Tel 0870 0000 303
www.baa.co.uk

Manchester
Tel 0161 489 3000
www.manchesterairport.co.uk

Newcastle
Tel 0191 286 0966
www.newcastleairport.com

Teesside
Tel 01325 332811
www.teessideairport.com

Airport transfers

Airport Transfer Service
Tel +33 450 536397
Geneva transfers to Portes du Soleil, Chamonix and Haute Savoie region.

The Alpine Cab Company
Tel +33 450 731938
www.alpinecabco.com

Breakdown insurance

AA Five Star Europe
Tel 0800 444 500
customer.services@theAA.com
www.theAA.com

Autohome
Tel 0800 371280
www.autohome.co.uk

Direct Line Rescue
Tel 0845 246 8999
www.directline.com/rescue

Europ Assistance
Tel 01444 442442
www.europ-assistance.co.uk

First Assist Group
Tel 020 8763 3333
www.firstassist.co.uk

Green Flag Motoring Assistance
www.greenflag.com

Leisurecare Insurance Services
Tel 01793 750150

Mondial Assistance UK
Tel 020 8681 2525
www.mondial-assistance.co.uk

RAC Travel Services
Tel 0800 550055
www.rac.co.uk

Car hire

Alamo Rent A Car
Tel 0870 599 4000
www.alamo.com

Avis Rent A Car
Tel 0870 010 0287
www.avis.co.uk

Budget Car and Van Rental
Tel 08701 565656
www.budget-uk.com

Europcar UK
Tel 0870 6075000
www.europcar.co.uk

Hertz UK Ltd
Tel 08708 484848
www.hertz.co.uk

Holiday Autos International Ltd
Tel 0870 400 4400
www.holidayautos.com

Suncars
Tel 0870 500 5566
www.suncars.com

Car winter equipment

Brindley Chains Ltd
Tel 01925 825555
www.brindley-chains.co.uk
Pewag snowchains

DAP (Cambridge) Ltd
Tel 01223 323488
www.skidrive.co.uk
Thule roof systems, Kar Rite boxes, Skandibox, Konig snowchains

GT Towing Ltd
Tel 01707 652118
www.gttowing.co.uk
Ski boxes and snowchains

Lakeland Roof Box Centre
Tel 08700 766326
www.roofbox.co.uk

Latchmere Motor Spares
Tel 020 7223 5491
Snowchains, roof bars, ski clamps, boxes

Motor Traveller
Tel 01753 833442
www.carbox.co.uk
Thule racks and boxes; Milz snowchains

RUD Chains Ltd
Tel 01227 276611
Snowchains

Snowchains Ltd
Tel 01732 884408
Thule ski boxes, roof bars and ski racks; Weissenfels snowchains

Spikes Spiders
Tel 01706 819365
www.spikesspider.com

The Roof Box Company
Tel 08700 766326
www.roofbox.co.uk

Thule Ltd
Tel 01275 340404
www.thule.co.uk

Cross-Channel travel

Brittany Ferries
Tel 08705 360 360
rwww.brittanyferries.co.uk
Portsmouth-Caen

Eurotunnel
Tel 08705 35 35 35
www.eurotunnel.com
Folkestone-Calais/Coquelles via the Channel Tunnel

Hoverspeed
Tel 0870 524 0241
www.hoverspeed.com
Dover-Calais; Dover-Ostend; Newhaven-Dieppe

Norfolkline
Tel 0870 870 1020
www.norfolkline.com
Dover-Dunkirk

P&O North Sea Ferries
Tel 0870 1296002
www.ponsf.com
Hull-Zeebrugge, Hull-Rotterdam

P&O Portsmouth
Tel 0870 242 4999
www.poportsmouth.com
Portsmouth-Cherbourg; Portsmouth-Le Havre

P&O Stena Line
Tel 0870 600 0600
www.posl.com
Dover-Calais

SeaFrance
Tel 08705 711 711
www.seafrance.com
Dover-Calais

Stena Line
Tel 08705 707070
www.stenaline.co.uk
Harwich-Hook of Holland

Dry ski slopes

SOUTH-WEST ENGLAND

Christchurch Ski Centre
Matchams Lane, Hurn,
Christchurch, Dorset BH23 6AW
Tel 01202 499155
skicentre@lineone.net

Exeter and District Ski Club
Clifton Hill Sports Ground,
Belmont Road, Exeter EX2 2DJ
Tel 01392 211422
exeterclub@ntlworld.com

High Actions' Avon Ski Centre
Lyncombe Drive, Churchill,
North Somerset BS19 5PQ
Tel 01934 852335
www.highaction.co.uk

**John Nike Leisuresport –
Plymouth**
Plymouth Ski Centre, Alpine
Park, Marsh Mills, Plymouth
PL6 8LQ
Tel 01752 600220
www.jnll.co.uk

Torquay Alpine Ski Club
Barton Hall, Kingskerswell
Road, Torquay, Devon TQ2 8JY
Tel 01803 313350
www.skitorquay.co.uk

Warmwell Snow Zone
Warmwell, Dorchester, Dorset
DT2 8JE
Tel 01305 852911

Wellington Sports Centre
Corams Lane, Wellington,
Somerset TA21 8LL
Tel 01823 663010

Yeovil Ski Centre
Addlewell Lane, Nine Springs,
Yeovil, Somerset BA20 1QW
Tel 01935 421702

SOUTH-EAST ENGLAND

Alpine Snowsports Aldershot
Gallwey Road, Aldershot, Hants
GU11 2DD
Tel 01252 325889
www.alpinesnowsports.co.uk

Bishop Reindorp Ski Centre
Larch Avenue, Guildford,
Surrey GU1 1JY
Tel 01483 504988
www.brski.co.uk

Bowles Outdoor Centre
Eridge Green, Tunbridge Wells
TN3 9LW
Tel 01892 665665
www.bowles.ac

Bromley Ski Centre
Sandy Lane, St Paul's Cray,
Orpington, Kent BR5 3HY
Tel 01689 876812

Calshot Activities Centre
Calshot Spit, Fawley,
Southampton SO45 1BR
Tel 023 8089 2077
www.hants.gov.uk/calshot

**Folkestone Sports Centre Ski
Slope**
Radnor Park Avenue,
Folkestone, Kent CT19 5HX
Tel 01303 850333
www.folkestoneski.co.uk

**John Nike Leisuresport –
Bracknell**
Bracknell Ski Centre, Amen
Corner, Bracknell RG12 8TN
Tel 01344 789002
www.jnll.co.uk

**John Nike Leisuresport –
Chatham**
Chatham Ski Centre, Alpine
Park, Capstone Road,
Gillingham, Kent ME7 3JH
Tel 01634 827979
www.jnll.co.uk

Sandown Ski Centre
More Lane, Esher KT10 8AN
Tel 01372 467132
www.sandownsports.co.uk

Southampton Ski Centre
The Sports Centre, Bassett,
Southampton SO16 7AY
Tel 023 8079 0970
ski.centre@southampton.gov.uk

Wycombe Summit
Abbey Barn Lane, High
Wycombe, Bucks HP10 9QQ
Tel 01494 474711
www.wycombesummit.co.uk

MIDDLE ENGLAND

**Gloucester Ski and Snowboard
Centre**
Jarvis Hotel and Country Club,
Robinswood Hill, Matson Lane,
Gloucester GL4 6EA
Tel 01452 414300
www.gloucesterski.com

**John Nike Leisuresport –
Swadlincote**
Swadlincote Ski Centre, Hill
Street, Swadlincote DE11 8LP
Tel 01283 217200
www.jnll.co.uk

Kidsgrove Ski Centre
Bathpool Park, Kidsgrove,
Stoke-on-Trent ST7 4EF
Tel 01782 784908
www.ski-kidsgrove.co.uk

Snozone
Xscape, 602 Marlborough Gate,
Central Milton Keynes MK9 3XS
Tel 01908 230260
www.snozonemk.co.uk

Stoke Ski Centre
Festival Park, Stoke-on-Trent
ST1 5PU
Tel 01782 204159
www.stokeskicentre.co.uk

**Tallington Ski and Snowboard
Centre**
Tallington Lakes Leisure Park,
Barholm Road, Tallington,
Stamford, Lincs PE9 4RJ
Tel 01778 344990
www.waspdirect.com

Tamworth Snowdome
Leisure Island, River Drive,
Tamworth B79 7ND
Tel 08705 000011
www.snowdome.co.uk

Telford Ski Centre
Court Street, Madeley, Telford,
Shropshire TF7 5DZ
Tel 01952 586862
www.telfordleisure.co.uk

The Ackers
Golden Hillock Road, Small
Heath, Birmingham B11 2PY
Tel 0121 772 5111
www.ackers-adventure.co.uk

EASTERN ENGLAND

**Brentwood Park Ski and
Snowboard Centre**
Warley Gap, Brentwood, Essex
CM13 3LG
Tel 01277 211994
www.brentwoodskicentre.co.uk

Gosling Ski Centre
Stanborough Road, Welwyn
Garden City AL8 6XE
Tel 01707 384384
www.goslingsports.co.uk

Hemel Ski Centre
St Albans Hill, Hemel
Hempstead, Herts HP3 9NH
Tel 01442 241321
www.hemel-ski.co.uk

Norfolk Ski Club
Whitlingham Lane, Trowse,
Norwich, Norfolk NR14 8TW
Tel 01603 662781
www.norfolkskiclub.co.uk

Suffolk Ski Centre
Bourne Hill, Wherstead,
Ipswich IP2 8NQ
Tel 01473 602347
www.suffolkskicentre.co.uk

NORTHERN ENGLAND

**Alston Training and Adventure
Centre**
High Plains Lodge, Alston,
Cumbria CA9 3DD
Tel 01434 381886
www.alstontraining.co.uk

Halifax Ski/Snowboard Centre
Sportsman Leisure, Bradford
Old Road, Swalesmoor
Ploughcroft, Halifax HX3 6UG
Tel 01422 340760
www.dryslope.tv

Kendal Ski Club
Canal Head North, Kendal,
Cumbria LA9 7AL
Tel 01539 732948/733031
www.kendalski.co.uk

Pendle Ski Club
Clitheroe Road, Sabden,
Clitheroe, Lancs BB7 9HN
Tel 01200 425222
www.pendleski.org.uk

Runcorn Ski/Snowboard Centre
Town Park, Palace Fields,
Runcorn, Cheshire WA7 2PS
Tel 01928 701965
www.runcornskicentre.co.uk

Sheffield Ski Village
Vale Road, Parkwood Springs,
Sheffield S3 9SJ
Tel 0114 276 9459
www.sheffieldskivillage.co.uk

Ski Rossendale
Haslingden Old Road,
Rawtenstall, Rossendale,
Lancashire BB4 8RR
Tel 01706 226457
www.ski-rossendale.co.uk

**Whickham Thorns Outdoor
Centre**
Market Lane, Dunston NE11
9NX
Tel 0191 460 1193

WALES

Cardiff Ski/Snowboard Centre
Fairwater Park, Fairwater,
Cardiff CF5 3JR
Tel 029 2056 1793
www.skicardiff.com

Dan-yr-Ogof Ski Slopes
Abercrave, Upper Swansea
Valley, Powys SA9 1GJ
Tel 01639 730284

**John Nike Leisuresport –
Llandudno**
Wyddfyd Road, Great Orme,
Llandudno LL30 2QL
Tel 01492 874707
www.jnll.co.uk

Plas y Brenin
Capel Curig, Gwynedd LL24
0ET
Tel 01690 720214

Pontypool Ski Centre
Pontypool Leisure Park,
Pontypool, Gwent NP4 8AT
Tel 01495 756955

Rhiwgoch Ski Centre
Bronaber, Trawsfynydd,
Gwynedd LL41 4UR
Tel 01766 540578
www.logcabins-skiwales.co.uk

Ski Pembrey
Pembrey Country Park, Llanelli,
Carmarthenshire SA16 0EJ
Tel 01554 834443

SCOTLAND

Alford Ski Centre
Greystone Road, Alford,
Aberdeenshire AB33 8TY
Tel 01975 563024

**Ancrum Outdoor Education
Resource Centre**
10 Ancrum Road, Dundee,
Tayside DD2 2HZ
Tel 01382 435911

Bearsden Ski & Board
Stockiemuir Road, Bearsden,
Glasgow G61 3RS
Tel 0141 943 1500
www.skibearsden.co.uk

Firpark Ski Centre
Tillycoultry, Clackmannanshire
FK13 6PL
Tel 01259 751772

Reference section

Glasgow Ski/Snowboard Centre
Bellahouston Park, 16
Dumbreck Road, Glasgow G41
5BW
Tel 0141 427 4991
www.ski-glasgow.org

Glenmore Lodge
Scottish National Sports
Centre, Aviemore, Inverness-
shire PH22 1QU
Tel 01479 861256
www.glenmorelodge.org.uk

**Loch Rannoch Outdoor Activity
Centre**
Kinloch Rannoch, Perthshire
PH16 5PS
Tel 01882 632201

Midlothian Ski Centre
Hillend, Near Edinburgh,
Midlothian EH10 7DU
Tel 0131 445 4433
www.midlothian.gov.uk

Newmilns Ski Slope
High Street, Newmilns KA16
9EB
Tel 01560 322320

Polmonthill Ski Centre
Polmont, Falkirk FK2 0YE
Tel 01324 503835

NORTHERN IRELAND

Craigavon Golf and Ski Centre
Turmoyra Lane, Silverwood,
Lurgan BT66 6NG
Tel 028 3832 6606
www.craigavon.gov.uk

Mount Ober Ski Centre
24 Ballymaconaghy Road,
Knockbracken, Belfast BT8 6SB
Tel 028 9079 5666
mt.ober@ukonline.co.uk

Insurance
companies

ABC Holiday Extras
Tel 0800 171000
www.abctravelinsurance.co.uk

Aon Suretravel
Tel 01883 834033
customer.care@aon.co.uk

Atlas Insurance
Tel 020 7609 5000
www.atlasdirect.net

AUL
Tel 01206 577770
www.aul.co.uk

**Blackwater Travel Indemnity
Limited (BTI)**
Tel 01621 855553
www.blackwater-
insurance.co.uk

**British Activity Holiday
Insurance Services**
Tel 020 7251 6821
www.ansell.co.uk

BUPA Travel Services
Tel 0870 103 2123
www.bupa.co.uk/travel

CGNU
Tel 0800 096 4715
www.norwichunion.co.uk

**Columbus Travel Insurance
Direct**
Tel 020 7375 0011

Direct Line Travel Insurance
Tel 0845 246 8910
www.directline.com/travel

Direct Travel Insurance
Tel 01903 812345
www.direct-travel.co.uk

Douglas Cox Tyrie
Tel 01708 385969

Euclidian Insurance Services
Tel 01784 484601
www.euclidian.co.uk

Europ Assistance
Tel 01444 442442
www.europ-assistance.co.uk

Hamilton Barr
Tel 01483 255666
www.hamiltonbarr.com

JLT Travel Services
Tel 01484 438739

Ketteridge Group
Tel 01277 630770

**Matthew Gerard Travel
Insurance Ltd**
Tel 01483 730900
www.mgtis.co.uk

Perry Gamble
Tel 020 8542 1122

P J Hayman & Company
Tel 023 9241 9010
www.pjhayman.com

Preferential
Tel 01702 423280
www.preferential.co.uk

Primary Insurance Group
Tel 0870 200 0012
www.primaryinsurance.co.uk

Select Travel Insurance
Tel 08707 370870
sxp@inter-group.co.uk

ski-insurance.co.uk
Tel 0870 7556101
www.ski-insurance.co.uk

Snowcard Insurance Services
Tel 01327 262805
www.snowcard.co.uk

Sportscover Direct Ltd
Tel 0117 922 6222
info@sportscover.co.uk
www.sportscover.co.uk

Supreme Travel
Tel 01355 260547
sales@travelinsurance-uk.com
www.travelinsurance-uk.com

Travel Insurance Club Limited
Tel 0800 316 35 60
www.ticdirect.co.uk

Travel Protection Group plc
Tel 028 9032 6585
www.thetravelprotectiongroup.
plc.uk

**World Ski and Snowboard
Association**
Tel 0114 279 7300
www.worldski.co.uk

WorldCover Direct
Tel 0800 365121
www.worldcover.com

**Worldwide Travel Insurance
Services**
Tel 01892 833338
www.worldwideinsure.com

National
tourist offices

Andorran Delegation
Tel 020 8874 4806

Argentine Embassy
Tel 020 7318 1300
www.turismo.gov.ar

Australian Tourist Commission
Tel 09068 633235
www.australia.com

Austrian National Tourist Office
Tel 020 7629 0461
www.austria-tourism.at

Canadian Tourism Commission
Tel 0906 871 5000
www.travelcanada.ca

Chile – Consulate General
Tel 020 7580 1023
cglonduk@congechileuk.demon.
co.uk

Czech Tourist Authority
Tel 09063 640641
www.visitczechia.cz

Finnish Tourist Board
Tel 020 7365 2512
www.finland-tourism.com

French Tourist Office
Tel 09068 244123
www.franceguide.com

Reference section

675

German National Tourist Office
Tel 09001 600100
www.germany-tourism.de

Italian State Tourist Office
Tel 020 7408 1254
www.enit.it

Japan National Tourist Office
Tel 020 7734 9638
www.seejapan.co.uk

Norwegian Tourist Board
Tel 0906 302 2003
www.visitnorway.com

Romanian Tourist Office
Tel 020 7224 3692
www.romaniatourism.com

Scottish Tourist Board
Tel 0131 332 2433
ski.visitscotland.com

Slovenian Tourist Office
Tel 020 7234 7133
www.slovenia-tourism.si

Spanish Tourist Office
Tel 020 7486 8077
www.tourspain.co.uk

Swedish Tourism Council
Tel 00800 3080 3080
www.visit-sweden.com

Switzerland Tourism
Tel 00800 100 200 30
www.MySwitzerland.com

Tourism New Zealand
Tel 09069 10 10 10
www.purenz.com

Turkish Tourist Board
Tel 020 7629 7771
www.gototurkey.co.uk

Visit USA Association
Tel 09069 101020

Railways

Deutsche Bahn
Tel 0870 243 5363
www.bahn.co.uk

Eurostar
Tel 0870 518 6186
www.eurostar.com

Rail Europe
Tel 08705 848 848
www.raileurope.co.uk

Swiss Federal Railways
Tel 020 7292 1550
www.rail.ch

Retailers

SOUTH-WEST ENGLAND

BSB Snowboarding
68 West St, Old Market, Bristol
Tel 0117 955 0779

Christchurch Ski/Leisure Centre
Matchams Lane, Hurn,
Christchurch, Dorset BH23 6AW
Tel 01202 499568

Devon Ski Centre
Oak Place, Newton Abbot,
Devon TQ12 2EX
Tel 01626 351278

Kidski
Unit 7, Romany Centre, Holton
Heath, Poole BH16 6JL
Tel 01929 472540
www.kidski.co.uk

Mission Adventuresport
1 Bank Lane, Brixham, Devon
TQ5 8EX
Tel 01803 855796

Penrose Outdoors
Town Quay, Truro TR1 2HJ
Tel 01872 272116

Skate and Ski
104 High Street, Staple Hill,
Bristol BS16 5HL
Tel 0117 970 1356

Snow & Rock
Units 1-3 Shield Retail Centre,
Gloucester Road North, Filton,
Bristol BS34 7BQ
Tel 0117 914 3000

Two Bare Feet
Fleet Street, Torquay TQ1 1DB
Tel 01803 296060

Westsports
Market House, Marlborough
Rd, Old Town, Swindon
Tel 01793 532588

SOUTH-EAST ENGLAND

Activ (Folkestone)
145 Sandgate Road,
Folkestone, Kent CT20 2DA
Tel 01303 240110

Captain's Cabin
93 High St, Chatham ME4 4DL
Tel 01634 819777

Captain's Cabin
14 St George's Walk, Croydon
CR0 1YG
Tel 020 8680 6968

Captain's Cabin
19 Wincheap, Canterbury, Kent
CT1 3TB
Tel 01227 457906

Country Trails Limited
39 Mount Pleasant, Tunbridge
Wells, Kent TN1 1PN
Tel 01892 539002

Edge 2 Edge
Unit 10, Oakwood Industrial
Park, Gatwick Road, Crawley,
West Sussex RH10 2AZ
Tel 01293 649300

John Pollock
157 High Road, Loughton,
Essex IG10 4LF
Tel 020 8508 6626

John Pollock
67 High Street, Barnet
EN5 5UR
Tel 020 8440 3994

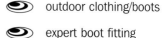

SNOW + ROCK

NEW! Portsmouth Superstore	**0845 100 1000**
Covent Garden	**020 7420 1444**
Kensington	**020 7937 0872**
Holborn	**020 7831 6900**
Surrey Superstore	**01932 566 886**
Hemel Hempstead	**01442 235 305**
Bristol Superstore	**0117 914 3000**
Birmingham	**0121 236 8280**
Sheffield	**0114 275 1700**
Snow+Rock Direct	**0845 100 1000**

Lang & Hunter
12 Thames Street, Kingston-upon-Thames, Surrey KT1 1PE
Tel 020 8546 5427

Snow Boats
8-10 The Street, Wrecclesham, Farnham, Surrey GU10 4PR
Tel 01252 715169

Snow & Rock
188 Kensington High Street, London W8 7RG
Tel 020 7937 0872

Snow & Rock
4 Mercer Street, Covent Garden, London WC2H 9QA
Tel 020 7420 1444

Snow & Rock
150 Holborn, Corner of Grays Inn Road, London EC1N 2LC
Tel 020 7831 6900

Snow & Rock
99 Fordwater Road, Chertsey, Surrey KT16 8HH
Tel 01932 566886

Snow & Rock
The Boardwalk, Port Solent, Portsmouth PO6 4TP
Tel 0845 100 1000

Snowball Ski Company
1 George Street, Richmond, Surrey TW9 1JY
Tel 020 8940 6293

MIDDLE ENGLAND

Active Outdoor & Ski
28 Castle Centre, Banbury, Oxfordshire OX16 5UH
Tel 01295 273700

Attwoolls Ski Shop
Bristol Road, Whitminster, Gloucestershire GL2 7LX
Tel 01452 742200

Beans
86 Sheep Street, Bicester, Oxfordshire OX6 7LP
Tel 01869 246451

BestBuys
Nene Court, 27-31 The Embankment, Wellingborough, Northamptonshire NN8 1LD
Tel 01933 272699

Force Ltd
26 Bakers Lane, Lichfield, Staffordshire WS13 6NG
Tel 01543 411249

Fox's
1 London Road, Amersham HP7 0HE
Tel 01494 431431

High Sports
51-52 Wyle Cop, Shrewsbury, Shropshire SY1 1XJ
Tel 01743 231649

Lockwoods Ski Shop
125-129 Rugby Road, Leamington Spa CV32 6DJ
Tel 01926 339388

Mountain Fever
25 Brunswick Street, Hanley, Stoke-on-Trent ST1 1DR
Tel 01782 266137

Noahs Ark
London Road, Chalford, Stroud, Gloucestershire
Tel 01453 884738

Ski West
9 Draycott Crescent, Cam, Dursley, Glos GL11 5LN
Tel 01453 519084

Snow & Rock
14 Priory Queensway, Birmingham B4 6BS
Tel 0121 236 8280

Solihull Ski Centre
100 Widney Rd, Bentley Heath, Solihull B93 9BN
Tel 01564 774176

EASTERN ENGLAND

Alpine Room
71-73 Main Road, Danbury, Essex CM3 4DJ
Tel 01245 223563

Ski Surf
13 Peartree Centre, Peartree Lane, Stanway, Colchester, Essex CO3 5JN
Tel 01206 502000

Snow & Rock
Hemel Ski Centre, St Albans Hill, Hemel Hempstead, Hertfordshire HP3 9NH
Tel 01442 235305

SnowFit
2 Cucumber Lane, Brundall, Norwich NR13 5QY
Tel 01603 716655

Snowsun
Ski Centre, Bourne Hill, Wherstead, Ipswich IP2 8ND
Tel 01473 713770

NORTHERN ENGLAND

1st Wet & Wild
619 Anlaby Road, Hull HU3 6SU
Tel 01482 354076

BAC Outdoor Leisure
Central Hall, Coronation Street, Elland, Halifax HX5 0DF
Tel 01422 371146

Glide & Slide
5/7 Station Road, Otley LS21 3HX
Tel 01943 461136

Mountain & Marine
159 London Road South, Poynton, Cheshire SK12 1LQ
Tel 01625 859863

Sail & Ski
9 Pepper Street, Grosvenor Shopping Centre, Chester, Cheshire CH1 1EA
Tel 01244 344580

Severn Sports / Boardworx
80 Town Street, Armley, Leeds, West Yorkshire LS12 3AA
Tel 0113 279 1618

Snow & Rock
Sheffield Ski Centre, Vale Road, Parkwood Springs, Sheffield S3 9SJ
Tel 0114 275 1700

WALES

Ski Lodge
Cardiff Road, Barry, Vale of Glamorgan CF63 2QW
Tel 01446 741870

IRELAND

The Great Outdoors
Chatham Street, Dublin 2
Tel +353 1679 4293

Ski organisations

British Association of Snowsport Instructors (BASI)
Tel 01479 861717
www.basi.org.uk

British Ski and Snowboard Federation
Tel 0131 445 7676
www.bssf.co.uk

British Ski Club for the Disabled
Tel 01895 271104
www.bscd.org.uk

British Snowboard Association
Tel 0131 445 2428
www.thebsa.org

English Ski Council
Tel 0121 501 2314
www.englishski.org

Ski Club of Great Britain
Tel 0845 458 0780
www.skiclub.co.uk

Snowsport Scotland
Tel 0131 445 4151
www.snsc.demon.co.uk

Snowsport Wales
Tel 029 2056 1904
www.snowsportwales.net

The Uphill Ski Club
Tel 01479 861272
www.uphillskiclub.co.uk
For people with disabilities

World Ski and Snowboard Association
Tel 0114 279 7300
www.worldski.co.uk

Ski travel agents

Alpine Answers
Tel 020 8871 4656
ski@alpineanswers.co.uk
www.alpineanswers.co.uk

Alps4U.com
Tel 0845 069 9900
www.alps4u.com

Avant-ski
Tel 0191 285 8141
sales@avant-ski.com
www.avant-ski.com

Iglu.com
Tel 020 8542 6658
enquiries@iglu.com
www.iglu.com

Independent Ski Links
Tel 01964 533905
info@ski-links.com
www.ski-links.com

Skiers Travel
Tel 0113 292 0893
sales@skiers-travel.co.uk
www.skiers-travel.co.uk

Ski Expectations
Tel 01799 531888
ski.expectations@virgin.net
www.skiexpectations.com

Ski Line
Tel 020 8650 5900
www.skiline.co.uk

Ski McNeill
Tel 028 9066 6699
mail@skimcneill.com
www.skimcneill.com

Ski Solutions
Tel 020 7471 7700
www.skisolutions.com
A La Carte department:
020 7471 7777

Ski & Surf
Tel 020 8958 2418
janm@skisurf.com
www.skisurf.com

Ski Travel Centre
Tel 0141 649 9696
snow@skitravelcentre.com
www.ski-travel-centre.co.uk

Snow Finders
Tel 01858 466888
sales@snowfinders.com
www.snowfinders.com

Snow Line
Tel 01858 828000
www.snow-line.co.uk

Resort index / directory

This is an index to the resort chapters in the book; you'll find page references for about 400 resorts described elsewhere. But you'll also find brief descriptions here of another 700 resorts, most of them much smaller than those we've covered in full, but often still worth a short visit. We also list here the companies offering package holidays to each resort. To get in touch with one of these tour operators, look them up in the list starting on page 666.

Key

⛄ Lifts
⛷ Pistes
✉ UK tour operators

49 Degrees North USA
Inland area with best snow in Washington State, including 120-acre bowl reserved for powder weekends.
1195m; slopes 1195–1760m
⛄ 5 ⛷ 780 acres

Abetone Italy
Resort in the exposed Appennines, less than two hours from Florence and Pisa.
1390m; slopes 1390–1900m
⛄ 25 ⛷ 50km
✉ Alpine Tours

Abtenau Austria
Sizeable village in Dachstein-West region near Salzburg, on large plain ideal for cross-country.
710m; slopes 710–1260m
⛄ 6 ⛷ 10km
✉ Thomson Ski & Snowboarding

Achenkirch Austria
Unspoiled, low-altitude Tirolean village close to Niederau and Alpbach. Beautiful setting overlooking a lake.
930m; slopes 930–1800m
⛄ 10 ⛷ 25km
✉ Ramblers

Adelboden 415
✉ Interhome, Kuoni, Made to Measure Holidays, Swiss Travel Service

Les Aillons France
Traditional village near Chambéry. Nicely sheltered slopes.
1000m; slopes 1000–1900m
⛄ 24 ⛷ 40km

Alagna 389
Small resort on the western fringe of Monterosa Ski area.
✉ Ski Club of Great Britain, Ski Weekend

Alba Italy
Picturesque Dolomite village with a small, quiet area; access to the Sella Ronda at nearby Canazei.
1515m; slopes 1515–2440m
⛄ 5 ⛷ 10km
✉ Crystal

Alleghe Italy
Dolomite village near Cortina in a pretty lakeside setting close to numerous areas.
980m
⛄ 24 ⛷ 80km

Alpbach 102
✉ Crystal, Equity Ski, Inghams, Interhome, Made to Measure Holidays, Thomson Ski & Snowboarding

Alpe-d'Huez 203
✉ Airtours, Alpine Options, Avant-ski, Chalet World, Chalets 'Unlimited', Club Med, Crystal, Directski.com, Erna Low, Eurotunnel Motoring Holidays, Fairhand Holidays, First Choice Ski, French Freedom Holidays, Independent Ski Links, Inghams, Interhome, Lagrange Holidays, Made to Measure Holidays, Mark Warner, Motours, Neilson, Panorama Holidays, Ski Arrangements, SkiAway Holidays, Ski Club of Great Britain, Ski Expectations, Ski France, Ski Independence, Ski Leisure Direction, Ski Line, Ski Miquel, Ski Supreme, Skiworld, La Source, Thomson Ski & Snowboarding, Tops Ski Chalets and Club Hotels

Alpe-du-Grand-Serre France
Tiny resort near Alpe-d'Huez and Les Deux-Alpes. Good for bad-weather days.
1400m; slopes 1400–2200m
⛄ 20 ⛷ 55km

Alpendorf Austria
Outpost of St Johann im Pongau, at one end of extensive three-valley lift network linking via Wagrain to Flachau – all part of the Salzburger Sportwelt ski pass area that our figures relate to.
850m; slopes 800–2185m
⛄ 100 ⛷ 350km

Alpine Meadows 495
✉ Ski The American Dream, Virgin Ski

Alps Korea
Korea's most northerly, snow-reliable resort, about five hours from Seoul. ⛄ 5

Alta 547
✉ Ski All America, Ski Independence, Ski The American Dream

Altenmarkt Austria
Unspoiled village well placed just off the Salzburg-Villach autobahn for numerous resorts including snow-sure Obertauern and the Salzburger Sportwelt resorts.
855m; slopes 855–2130m
⛄ 23 ⛷ 150km
✉ Made to Measure Holidays, Sloping Off

Alto Campoo Spain
Barren, desolate place with undistinguished slopes, but with magnificent wilderness views.
1650m; slopes 1650–2170m
⛄ 11

Alt St Johann Switzerland
Old cross-country village with Alpine slopes connecting into Unterwasser area near Liechtenstein.
900m; slopes 900–2260m
⛄ 21 ⛷ 50km

Alyeska USA
Alaskan area 60km/35 miles from Anchorage, with luxury hotel. Spring best for weather.
75m; slopes 75–1200m
⛄ 9 ⛷ 785 acres
✉ Inghams

Aminona 423
Resort on the eastern side of the Crans-Montana network.
✉ Lagrange Holidays

Andalo Italy
Atmospheric Dolomite village near Madonna, with low wooded slopes well equipped with snowmakers; best for novices.
1050m; slopes 1035–2125m
⛄ 17 ⛷ 60km
✉ Equity Ski, Rocketski, Sloping Off

Andermatt 417
✉ Made to Measure Holidays, Ski Club of Great Britain, Ski Weekend

Andorra la Vella 626

Angel Fire USA
Intermediate area near Taos, New Mexico. Height usually ensures good snow.
2620m; slopes 2620–3255m
⛄ 6 ⛷ 455 acres

Les Angles France
Attractive resort with one of the best ski areas in the Pyrenees. Pretty, tree-lined, mostly easy skiing.
1600m; slopes 1650–2400m
⛄ 23
✉ Lagrange Holidays

Annaberg-Lungötz Austria
Peaceful village in a pretty setting, sharing a sizeable area with Gosau. Close to Filzmoos.
775m; slopes 775–1620m
⛄ 33 ⛷ 65km

Antagnod Italy
Weekend day-tripper area on the road up to Champoluc, above Aosta valley. No village.
1710m; slopes 1710–2000m
⛄ 4 ⛷ 7km

Anzère Switzerland
Sympathetically designed modern resort on a sunny balcony near Crans-Montana, with slopes suited to leisurely intermediates.
1500m; slopes 1500–2460m
⛄ 13 ⛷ 40km
✉ Interhome, Lagrange Holidays, Made to Measure Holidays

Aosta Italy
Historic valley town with gondola up to mountain resort of Pila; it's an 18-minute ride to the slopes. Aosta is a real working town with people in suits rather than skiwear. It has good-value accommodation, a lot more bars and restaurants than Pila, and a lovely traffic-free centre. Other resorts in the valley are within a day trip and are covered by the lift pass.
1800m; slopes 1550–2710m
⛄ 13 ⛷ 70km

Apex 589
✉ AmeriCan Ski, Frontier Ski, Made to Measure Holidays, Ski Safari

Aprica Italy
Ugly, straggling village between Lake Como and the Brenta Dolomites, with bland slopes and limited facilities.
1180m; slopes 1180–2310m
⛄ 24 ⛷ 40km
✉ Interhome, Thomson Ski & Snowboarding

Arabba 397
Tiny village with the Sella Ronda's highest, steepest skiing.
✉ Independent Ski Links, Inghams, Momentum Ski, Neilson, Ski Yogi

Aragnouet-Piau France
Purpose-built mid-mountain satellite of St-Lary, best suited to families, beginners and early intermediates.
1850m; slopes 1420–2500m
⛄ 32 ⛷ 80km

Arapahoe Basin 522
Small resort a few minutes away from Keystone by road.
✉ Ski The American Dream

Arcalis 626
✉ Snowcoach

679

Les Arcs 211
⊠ *Airtours, Alpine Events, Avant-ski, Chalets 'Unlimited', Chez Jay Ski, Club Med, Crystal, Directski.com, Equity Ski, Erna Low, Esprit Ski, Eurotunnel Motoring Holidays, Fairhand Holidays, First Choice Ski, Independent Ski Links, Inghams, Interhome, Lagrange Holidays, Made to Measure Holidays, Motours, Neilson, Optimum Ski, Rocketski, Ski Activity, Ski Amis, Ski Arrangements, SkiAway Holidays, Ski Beat, Ski Club of Great Britain, Ski France, Ski Independence, Ski Leisure Direction, Ski Life, Ski Line, Ski Olympic, Ski Supreme, Skiworld, Thomson Ski & Snowboarding, Vanilla Ski*

Ardent 217
Quiet hamlet with quick access to Avoriaz and Châtel.
⊠ *The Chalet Company, The Family Ski Company*

Åre 653
⊠ *Neilson*

Arêches-Beaufort France
Secluded little resort accessible only from Mont Blanc region to the north.
1050m; slopes 1050–2300m
🚡 15 🎿 50km

Argentière 221
Unremarkable village beneath Chamonix's Grands Montets.
⊠ *Alpine Answers Select, Bigfoot, Board and Lodge, Chalets 'Unlimited', Collineige, Crystal, Fairhand Holidays, Handmade Holidays, Independent Ski Links, Interhome, Lagrange Holidays, McNab Mountain Sports, Motours, Ski Arrangements, Ski Club of Great Britain, Ski Etoile, Ski Hillwood, Ski Scott James, Ski Weekend, White Roc*

Arinsal 630
⊠ *Airtours, Chalets 'Unlimited', Crystal, Directski.com, First Choice Ski, Inghams, Neilson, Panorama Holidays, Snowcoach, Thomson Ski & Snowboarding, Top Deck*

Arnoldstein/Dreiländereck
Austria
One of several little areas overlooking the town of Villach.
680m; slopes 680–1455m
🚡 8 🎿 12km

Arolla Switzerland
Tiny village in pretty riverside setting south of Sion. Main attraction is heli-skiing. Wonderful descents from 3800m/12,500ft.
2005m; slopes 2005–2890m
🚡 5 🎿 47km

Arosa 419
⊠ *Alpine Events, Interhome, Kuoni, Made to Measure Holidays, Momentum Ski, Plus Travel, Powder Byrne, Ski Weekend, Swiss Travel Service, White Roc*

Artesina Italy
Purpose-built resort lacking character and atmosphere.
1350m; slopes 1320–2100m
🚡 14 🎿 60km

Asiago Italy
Sizeable resort close to Verona, but at low altitude and with limited vertical.
1000m; slopes 1000–1380m 🚡 17
⊠ *Headwater Holidays, Inntravel*

Aspen 504
⊠ *Alpine Answers Select, AmeriCan Ski, American Ski Classics, Chalet World, Chalets 'Unlimited', Crystal, Elegant Resorts, Fantiski-Ski2k, Independent Ski Links, Lotus Supertravel, Made to Measure Holidays, Momentum Ski, Rocky Mountain Adventures, Ski Activity, Ski All America, Ski Expectations, Ski Independence, Ski Line, Ski Safari, Ski The American Dream, Skiworld, Thomson Ski & Snowboarding, United Vacations*

Attitash USA
One of the biggest ski areas in eastern US. Uncrowded slopes. Lodging in nearby North Conway, and other New Hampshire areas close by.
slopes 180–715m
🚡 12 🎿 275 acres
⊠ *Ski Success, Virgin Ski*

Auffach 191
Unexceptional village in the Wildschönau area.

Auris-en-Oisans 203
Quiet hamlet linked across the valley to Alpe-d'Huez.
⊠ *Fairhand Holidays, Lagrange Holidays*

Auron France
Pleasant village with varied, sheltered slopes; a stark contrast to nearby Isola 2000.
1600m; slopes 1165–2450m
🚡 26 🎿 130km

Auronzo di Cadore Italy
Sizeable village that's a cheaper base for visiting Cortina. Its own slopes are of negligible interest.
865m; slopes 865–1585m
🚡 5 🎿 7km

Aussois France
One of many rustic working villages near Modane in the Maurienne valley.
1500m; slopes 1500–2750m
🚡 11 🎿 50km

Autrans France
Major cross-country village, close to Grenoble.
1050m; slopes 1050–1710m
🚡 15 🎿 18km
⊠ *Headwater Holidays, Lagrange Holidays*

Avon USA
Small town close to Beaver Creek. Inexpensive base from which to ski Beaver Creek, Vail and Breckenridge.
⊠ *AmeriCan Ski*

Avoriaz 217
⊠ *Airtours, Chalets 'Unlimited', Club Med, Crystal, Erna Low, Eurotunnel Motoring Holidays, Fairhand Holidays, First Choice Ski, French Freedom Holidays, Independent Ski Links, Lagrange Holidays, Made to Measure Holidays, Motours, Neilson, Ski Arrangements, Ski Independence, Ski Leisure Direction, Ski Life, Thomson Ski & Snowboarding*

Axamer Lizum 119
⊠ *Club Pavilion, Crystal, Equity Ski, Thomson Ski & Snowboarding*

Axams 119
Quiet village in Innsbruck area, below Axamer Lizum ski area
⊠ *Lagrange Holidays*

Ax-les-Thermes France
Sizeable spa village near Font-Romeu and Andorra.
1400m; slopes 1400–2400m
🚡 17 🎿 75km

Bad Gastein 104
⊠ *Airtours, Crystal, Inghams, Made to Measure Holidays, Ski Miquel, Ski Wild*

Badger Pass USA
Base for 560km/350 miles of superb backcountry touring in Yosemite National Park. Spectacular views.
2195m; slopes 2195–2435m
🚡 5 🎿 90 acres

Bad Hofgastein 104
Relaxed spa resort in the Gastein Valley.
⊠ *Airtours, Crystal, First Choice Ski, Inghams, Made to Measure Holidays, Ski Wild*

Bad Kleinkirchheim Austria
Spacious, quiet spa village in south-east Austria spread out along a valley near the Italian and Slovenian borders. Virtually all the slopes are ideal for intermediates, but BKK has little to keep experts interested apart from the beautiful, long Franz Klammer downhill run, which goes from top to bottom away from all the lifts. For beginners there are nursery slopes at BKK and there are easy blue runs to progress to. There are eleven mountain restaurants in the two main sectors. BKK takes cross-country seriously, with 50km/30 miles of tracks. Most of the hotels are comfortable 4-stars and there are lots of gasthofs and self-catering apartments. There are plenty of places for eating out, too. Après-ski is relatively quiet, but there's plenty to do off the slopes – spa facilities are excellent.
1100m; slopes 1100–2010m
🚡 29 🎿 80km
⊠ *Alpine Tours, Crystal, First Choice Ski, Sloping Off, Slovenia & Austrian Pursuits, Solo's*

Banff 591
⊠ *Airtours, Alpine Answers Select, AmeriCan Ski, Crystal, Elegant Resorts, Equity Ski, First Choice Ski, Frontier Ski, Handmade Holidays, Independent Ski Links, Inghams, Lotus Supertravel, Made to Measure Holidays, Neilson, Rocketski, Rocky Mountain Adventures, Ski Activity, Ski All America, Ski All Canada, Ski Club of Great Britain, Ski Independence, Ski Line, Ski Safari, Ski The American Dream, Skiworld, Thomson Ski & Snowboarding, Trailfinders, United Vacations*

Bansko Bulgaria
Old traditional cobbled-street town with two small ski areas 12km/7 miles away.
935m; slopes 1100–2500m
🚡 3 🎿 14km
⊠ *Balkan Holidays*

Baqueira-Beret 639
⊠ *Ski Miquel*

Barboleuse 470
Quiet base from which to ski the Villars and Diablerets slopes.

Bardonecchia Italy
A sizeable old railway town, lacking classic mountain charm but with market-town character and set in a beautiful, wide valley, near the entrance to the Fréjus road tunnel. There are two separate areas of moderately interesting, mainly intermediate slopes either side of town – both a free bus-ride away – which are usually quiet but overcrowded when weekenders pour in from Turin. The snow record isn't particularly good, but there are relatively snow-sure runs above the middle stations. Accommodation is almost all in hotels and there are numerous good-value restaurants and pizzerias, but as a working town, it lacks the usual après-ski. The Three Valleys can be reached via a gondola from Orelle on the French side of the Fréjus tunnel. Off the slopes, trips to Turin are easy.
1310m; slopes 1290–2750m
🚡 24 🎿 140km
⊠ *Alpine Answers Select, Crystal, Equity Ski, Interhome, Motours, Neilson, Rocketski, Ski Arrangements, Thomson Ski & Snowboarding*

Barèges 360
⊠ *Borderline, Fairhand Holidays, Lagrange Holidays, SkiAway Holidays*

Les Barzettes 423
Small base along the road from Crans-Montana.

Bear Mountain USA
Southern California's main area, in the beautiful San Bernardino National Forest region. Full snowmaking.
slopes 2170–2685m
🚡 12 ⛷ 195 acres

Bear's Town Korea
Modern resort with runs cut out of thick forest. Biggest resort near Seoul (only an hour's drive), so it can get very crowded. 🚡 11

Beaulard Italy
Little place just off the road between Sauze d'Oulx and Bardonecchia.
1215m; slopes 1215–2120m
🚡 6 ⛷ 20km

Beaver Creek 511
✉ AmeriCan Ski, Crystal, Elegant Resorts, Handmade Holidays, Made to Measure Holidays, Ski Activity, Ski All America, Ski Independence, Ski Safari, Ski The American Dream, Thomson Ski & Snowboarding, United Vacations

Beaver Mountain USA
Small Utah area north of Salt Lake City, too far from Park City for a day trip.
2195m; slopes 2195–2680m
🚡 3 ⛷ 525 acres

Beitostolen Norway
Small family resort in southern Norway (east of Bergen), with lots of cross-country in the region.
900m 🚡 9 ⛷ 25km
✉ Thomson Ski & Snowboarding

Belleayre Mountain USA
State-owned resort near Albany, New York State. Cheap prices but old lifts and short runs.
775m; slopes 775–1015m
🚡 7 ⛷ 170 acres

Belle-Plagne 297
High-altitude satellite of La Plagne.
✉ Motours

Ben Lomond Australia
Small intermediate/beginner area in Ben Lomond National Park, Tasmania, 260km/160 miles from Hobart.
1570m 🚡 8

Berchtesgaden Germany
Pleasant old town close to Salzburg, known for its Nordic skiing but with several little Alpine areas nearby.
550m; slopes 630–1800m
🚡 21 ⛷ 50km
✉ Moswin Tours

Bergün Switzerland
Traditional, quiet, unspoiled, virtually traffic-free little family resort on the rail route between Davos and St Moritz.
1375m; slopes 1400–2550m
🚡 5 ⛷ 25km

Berthoud Pass 540
Powder heaven on the drive to Winter Park.

Berwang Austria
Unspoiled village nestling in a spacious valley, close to Lermoos.
1335m; slopes 1335–1740m
🚡 13 ⛷ 40km

Bessans France
Old cross-country village near Modane. Well placed for touring Maurienne valley resorts such as Val-Cenis.
1710m; slopes 1740–2200m
🚡 4 ⛷ 5km

Besse France
Charming old village built out of lava, with purpose-built slope-side satellite Super-Besse. Beautiful extinct-volcano scenery.
1050m; slopes 1350–1800m
🚡 21 ⛷ 80km
✉ Lagrange Holidays

Bethel USA
Pleasant, historic town very close to Sunday River, Maine. Attractive alternative to staying in the slope-side resort.
✉ AmeriCan Ski

Le Bettex 267
Small base with links to the Megève network.

Bettmeralp Switzerland
Central village of the sizeable Aletsch area near Brig, perched high above the Rhône valley, amid spectacular glacial scenery. Reached by valley cable-cars.
1955m; slopes 1900–2900m
🚡 32 ⛷ 90km

Beuil-les-Launes France
Alpes-Maritimes resort closest to Nice. Shares area with Valberg.
1400m; slopes 1400–2100m
🚡 26 ⛷ 90km

Bezau Austria
Virtually no slopes of its own but main village lies in low Bregenzwald region north-west of Lech.
650m; slopes 1210–1650m 🚡 2
✉ Inntravel

Biberwier Austria
Limited little village with a small area of its own. Best as a quiet base from which to access the Zugspitz area.
1000m; slopes 1000–1880m
🚡 5 ⛷ 25km

Bichlbach Austria
Smallest of the Zugspitz villages with very limited slopes. Suitable as an unspoiled base for visiting the rest of the area.
1070m; slopes 1070–1620m
🚡 3 ⛷ 7km

Bielmonte Italy
Popular with day-trippers from Milan. Worthwhile on a bad-weather day.
1200m; slopes 1200–1620m
🚡 13 ⛷ 20km

Big Mountain USA
Impressive ski area close to Montana's Glacier National Park, with good snow, a fun town and low prices.
1370m; slopes 1370–2135m
🚡 10 ⛷ 3000 acres
✉ AmeriCan Ski, Inghams, Ski All America, Ski Independence

Big Powderhorn USA
Area with the most 'resort' facilities in south Lake Superior region – and the highest lift capacity too. The area suffers from winds.
370m; slopes 370–560m
🚡 10 ⛷ 250 acres

Big Sky 564
✉ AmeriCan Ski, Ski All America, Ski Independence, Ski The American Dream

Big White 597
✉ AmeriCan Ski, Crystal, Frontier Ski, Made to Measure Holidays, Ski Activity, Ski All Canada, Ski Independence, Ski Line, Ski Safari, Ski The American Dream, Solo's

Bischofshofen Austria
Working town and mountain resort near St Johann im Pongau, with very limited local runs and the main slopes starting nearby at Muhlbach.
545m; slopes 545–1000m
🚡 2 ⛷ 2km

Bivio Switzerland
Quiet village near St Moritz with easy slopes opened up by a few lifts.
1775m; slopes 1780–2600m
🚡 4 ⛷ 40km

Bizau Austria
One of two main areas in the low Bregenzerwald region north-west of Lech.
680m; slopes 680–1700m
🚡 6 ⛷ 24km

Björkliden 652

Björnrike 652

Blackcomb 614
✉ Frontier Ski

Blatten Switzerland
Mountainside hamlet above Naters, beside the Rhône near Brig. Small but tall area in stunning glacial scenery, with larger Aletsch area nearby.
1320m; slopes 1320–3100m
🚡 9 ⛷ 60km

Bled 644
✉ Balkan Holidays, Crystal, Slovenija & Austrian Pursuits, Thomson Ski & Snowboarding

Blue Cow 656

Blue Mountain Canada
Largest area in Ontario, with glorious views of Lake Huron. High-capacity lift system and 100% snowmaking.
230m; slopes 230–450m
🚡 15 ⛷ 275 acres
✉ Ski All Canada

Blue River Canada
Base of world-famous Mike Wiegele heli-ski operation in Cariboo and Monashee mountains.

Bluewood USA
Particularly remote area even by American north-west standards. Worth a visit if you're in Walla Walla.
1355m; slopes 1355–1725m
🚡 3 ⛷ 530 acres

Bogus Basin USA
Sizeable area overlooking Idaho's attractive, interesting capital, Boise.
1760m; slopes 1760–2310m
🚡 8 ⛷ 2600 acres

Bohinj (Vogel) 644
✉ Balkan Holidays, Crystal, Slovenija & Austrian Pursuits, Thomson Ski & Snowboarding

Bois-d'Amont France
One of four resorts that make up Les Rousses area in Jura region.
1050m; slopes 1120–1680m 🚡 40
✉ Lagrange Holidays

Bolognola Italy
Tiny area in Macerata region near the Adriatic Riviera.
1070m; slopes 1070–1845m
🚡 7 ⛷ 5km

Bolton Valley USA
Resort near Stowe with mostly intermediate slopes.
465m; slopes 465–960m
🚡 6 ⛷ 155 acres

Le Bonhomme France
One of several areas with snowmakers near Strasbourg.
830m; slopes 830–1235m
🚡 9 ⛷ 12km

Bonneval-sur-Arc France
Unspoiled, remote old village in the Haute Maurienne valley with many of its slopes at high altitude. Pass to neighbouring Val-d'Isère is closed in winter.
1800m; slopes 1800–3000m
🚡 18 ⛷ 25km
✉ Motours

Bons 251
Rustic, unspoiled old hamlet linked to Les Deux-Alpes' skiing.

Boreal USA
Closest area to north Lake Tahoe town, Truckee. Limited slopes, best for novices.
2195m; slopes 2195–2375m
🚡 9 ⛷ 380 acres

Bormio 366
✉ Airtours, Equity Ski, Inghams, Interhome, Rocketski, Ski Arrangements, Sloping Off

Cavalese Italy
Unspoiled medieval town with its own pretty slopes and close to the Sella Ronda.
1000m; slopes 975–2265m
⛷ 9 ⛷ 70km
✉ *Alpine Tours*

Ceillac France
Tight cluster of rustic old buildings near Serre-Chevalier. Not far from the highest village in Europe, St-Veran.
1600m; slopes 1600–2400m

Celerina 455
Quiet, unpretentious village, with links to St Moritz's slopes.
✉ *Made to Measure Holidays*

Cerler Spain
Very limited, purpose-built resort with a compact ski area similar to that of nearby Andorra's Arinsal.
1500m; slopes 1500–2630m
⛷ 16 ⛷ 45km

Le Cernix France
Hamlet near Megève where Les Saisies' slopes link to those of Crest-Voland. Uncrowded retreat.
1250m; slopes 1150–1950m
⛷ 24 ⛷ 100km

Cerrato Lago Italy
Very limited area near the coastal town of La Spezia.
1270m; slopes 1270–1890m
⛷ 5 ⛷ 3km

Cerro Bayo Argentina
Limited area amid stunning scenery 10km/6 miles from Villa la Angostura, and 90km/56 miles from San Carlos de Bariloche.
slopes 1050–1780m
⛷ 9 ⛷ 20km

Cerro Catedral (Bariloche)
Argentina
The most developed ski and boarding resort in South America, 19 km/12 miles from Bariloche. Lodgings available at the foot of the slopes.
slopes 1040–2050m
⛷ 32 ⛷ 52km
✉ *Scott Dunn Latin America*

Cervinia 368
✉ *Airtours, Alpine Answers Select, Alpine Events, Beau-mont.com, Club Med, Crystal, Elegant Resorts, Equity Ski, Equity Ski, First Choice Ski, Independent Ski Links, Inghams, Interhome, Momentum Ski, Rocketski, Ski Arrangements, Ski Solutions, Ski Weekend, Thomson Ski & Snowboarding*

Cesana Torinese 285
Little Italian village linking the Sauze d'Oulx side of the Milky Way to the Montgenèvre side.

Le Châble 461
Small village below Verbier, linked by gondola.

Chacaltaya Bolivia
Highest lift-served ski area in the world and the only ski area in Bolivia. Reached by four-wheel drive vehicle from La Paz 30km/19 miles away. Only open in summer (too cold in winter).
5190m; slopes 5220–5420m
⛷ 1 ⛷ 2km
✉ *Scott Dunn Latin America*

Chaillol France
Cross-country base on the edge of the beautiful Ecrins National Park, near Gap. Small Alpine area, lots of snowmakers.
1600m; slopes 1450–2000m ⛷ 11

Chamois Italy
A good choice when higher areas are affected by bad weather. Close to Valtournenche and Cervinia.
1815m; slopes 1815–2270m
⛷ 8 ⛷ 20km

Chamonix 221
✉ *Airtours, Alpine Answers Select, Alpine Events, Alpine Options, Avant-ski, Beau-mont.com, Bigfoot, Board and Lodge, Chalets 'Unlimited', Chamonix Lodge, Club Med, Collineige, The Corporate Ski Company, Crystal, Elegant Resorts, Erna Low, Esprit Ski, Eurotunnel Motoring Holidays, Fairhand Holidays, First Choice Ski, French Freedom Holidays, Handmade Holidays, Huski, Independent Ski Links, Inghams, Interhome, Lagrange Holidays, Made to Measure Holidays, Momentum Ski, Motours, Neilson, Rocky Mountain Adventures, Ski Arrangements, Ski Club of Great Britain, Ski Expectations, Ski Independence, Ski Leisure Direction, Ski Life, Ski Line, Ski Solutions, Ski Total, Ski Weekend, Thomson Ski & Snowboarding, White Roc*

Champagny-en-Vanoise 297
Charming village linked to the La Plagne network.
✉ *AmeriCan Ski, Barrelli Ski, Erna Low, Fairhand Holidays, Handmade Holidays, Independent Ski Links, Lagrange Holidays, Made to Measure Holidays, Motours, Ski Expectations, Ski Leisure Direction*

Champéry 421
✉ *Alpine Answers Select, Alpine Events, Made to Measure Holidays, Piste Artiste Ltd, Plus Travel, Ski Weekend, White Roc*

Champex Switzerland
Lakeside hamlet tucked away in the trees above Orsières. A nice quiet, unspoiled base from which to visit Verbier's area.
1470m; slopes 1470–2220m
⛷ 4 ⛷ 8km

Champfér 455
Lakeside hamlet between St Moritz and Silvaplana.
✉ *Made to Measure Holidays*

Champoluc 389
Unspoiled village at one end of the the Monterosa Ski area.
✉ *Chalets 'Unlimited', Crystal, Esprit Ski, Handmade Holidays, Ski 2*

Champoussin 421
Quiet village with links to the rest of the Champéry slopes.

Chamrousse France
Functional family resort near Grenoble, with good, sheltered slopes.
1650m; slopes 1400–2255m
⛷ 26 ⛷ 77km
✉ *Fairhand Holidays, Lagrange Holidays*

Chandolin Switzerland
Picturesque, unspoiled village in the Val d'Anniviers off the Valais, with high, easy open slopes (shared with St Luc) served almost entirely by drags. Valley pass also covers Zinal, Grimentz and Vercorin – 200km/125 miles of runs in total.
1935m; slopes 1660–3025m
⛷ 16 ⛷ 75km

Chantemerle 314
Valley villages with direct access to Serre-Chevalier's slopes.

Chapelco Argentina
Small ski area with full infrastructure of services 19km/12 miles from sizeable town of San Martin de Los Andes. Accommodation in hotels 11km/7 miles from the slopes.
slopes 1250–1980m
⛷ 7 ⛷ 800 acres

La Chapelle-d'Abondance 229
Unspoiled village 5km/3 miles down the valley from Châtel.
✉ *Motours, Ski La Cote*

Charlotte Pass 656

Château d'Oex Switzerland
Pleasant little valley town that is the main French-speaking component of the shared lift-pass area around Gstaad. Local slopes are pleasant and undemanding but low (La Braye, at the top, is at only 1650m/5,400ft), and not connected to any of the Gstaad sectors – though the local railway makes moving around to other resorts painless. This is where Alpine hot-air ballooning first took off, and it's still a local speciality.
970m; slopes 890–3000m
⛷ 67 ⛷ 250km
✉ *Alpine Tours, Crystal*

Châtel 229
✉ *Avant-ski, Chalets 'Unlimited', Connick Ski, Fairhand Holidays, First Choice Ski, Freedom Holidays, Haig Ski, Interhome, Lagrange Holidays, Made to Measure Holidays, Motours, Ski Addiction, Ski Arrangements, SkiAway Holidays, Ski*

Independence, Ski Leisure Direction, Ski Line, Ski Rosie, Skialot, Snowfocus, Susie Ward Alpine Holidays, Tops Ski Chalets and Club Hotels

Le Chatelard France
Small resort in remote Parc des Bauges near Lake Annecy and Chambéry.

Chiesa Italy
Attractive beginners' resort with a fairly high plateau of easy runs above the resort.
1000m; slopes 1700–2335m
⛷ 10 ⛷ 25km

Le Chinaillon 234
Modern, chalet-style village above Le Grand-Bornand.

Chiomonte Italy
Tiny resort on the main road east of Bardonecchia and Sauze d'Oulx. A good half-day trip from either.
745m; slopes 745–2210m
⛷ 6 ⛷ 10km

Chonmasan Korea
Purpose-built resort 30km/20 miles north-east of Seoul. ⛷ 7

Chsea Algeria
Largest of Algeria's skiable areas, 135km/84 miles south-east of coastal town of Alger in the Djur Djur mountains.
1860m; slopes 1860–2510m ⛷ 2

Churwalden Switzerland
Hamlet on fringe of Lenzerheide-Valbella area.
1230m; slopes 1230–2865m
⛷ 35 ⛷ 155km

Clavière 285
Small Italian village linked to Montgenèvre (in France) and the rest of the Milky Way ski area.
✉ *Crystal, Equity Ski, First Choice Ski, Rocketski*

La Clusaz 234
✉ *Aravis Alpine Retreat, Classic Ski Limited, Crystal, Fairhand Holidays, First Choice Ski, Frosty's Ski and Snowboard Holidays, Inghams, Interhome, Lagrange Holidays, The Last Resort, Made to Measure Holidays, Motours, Ski Activity, Ski Arrangements, SkiAway Holidays, Ski Leisure Direction, Ski Weekend, Snowlife*

Les Coches 297
Small, purpose-built village, linked to the La Plagne ski area.
✉ *Crystal, Eurotunnel Motoring Holidays, Fairhand Holidays, Lagrange Holidays, Made to Measure Holidays, Motours, Ski Independence, Ski Leisure Direction, Ski Life*

Cogne Italy
One of Aosta valley's larger villages. Small area worth a short visit from nearby Pila.
1530m; slopes 1530–2245m
⛷ 5 ⛷ 8km
✉ *Inntravel*

Colfosco 397
Sprawling village that makes up part of the Sella Ronda circuit.

Colle di Tenda Italy
Dour, modern resort that shares a good area with much nicer Limone. Not far from Nice.
1400m; slopes 1120–2040m
⬡ 33 ⬆ 80km

Colle Isarco Italy
Brenner Pass area – and the bargain-shopping town of Vipiteno is nearby.
1095m; slopes 1095–2720m
⬡ 5 ⬆ 15km

Le Collet-d'Allevard France
Ski area of sizeable summer spa Allevard-les-Bains in remote region east of Chambéry-Grenoble road.
1450m; slopes 1450–2100m
⬡ 13 ⬆ 35km

Collio Italy
Tiny area of short runs in a remote spot between lakes Garda and d'Iseo.
840m; slopes 840–1715m ⬡ 14

Combelouvière 350
Quiet hamlet tucked away at the foot of Valmorel's slopes.
✉ *Fairhand Holidays, Lagrange Holidays*

Combloux 267
Quiet, unspoiled alternative to linked Megève.
✉ *Lagrange Holidays*

Les Contamines 240
✉ *Chalet Kiana, Chalets 'Unlimited', Classic Ski Limited, Fairhand Holidays, Interhome, Lagrange Holidays, Motours, Ski Arrangements, Ski Expectations, Ski Line, Ski Total*

Copper Mountain 518
✉ *AmeriCan Ski, Made to Measure Holidays, Ski All America, Ski Independence, Ski The American Dream, United Vacations*

Le Corbier France
Purpose-built resort consisting of ugly tower-blocks, with a fair-sized area of slopes shared with La Toussuire, off the Maurienne valley. The resort is compact and conveniently laid out – and very family-friendly, with a sunny car-free central area at the foot of the nursery slopes. The slopes are almost all easy/intermediate, and served by drags and slow chairs. They are low by French standards, and get quite a bit of sun, so snow is not reliable. But they are crowd-free. There are grand plans to build half a dozen new lifts to link this area to the slopes of St Sorlin d'Arves for 2003/04, creating a 220km/137 mile domaine to be known as Sybelles.
1500m; slopes 1300–2265m
⬡ 44 ⬆ 125km
✉ *Equity Ski, Fairhand Holidays, Interhome, Lagrange Holidays, Motours, Rocketski*

Coronet Peak 661

Corrençon-en-Vercors France
Charming, rustic village at foot of Villard-de-Lans ski area. Good cross-country, too.
1160m; slopes 1160–2170m
⬡ 29 ⬆ 130km

Cortina d'Ampezzo 373
✉ *Alpine Answers Select, Alpine Events, Chalets 'Unlimited', Crystal, Elegant Resorts, Inghams, Momentum Ski, Ski Arrangements, Ski Club of Great Britain, Ski Solutions, Ski Weekend, Ski Yogi, White Roc*

Corvara 397
The most animated Sella Ronda village.
✉ *Inghams, Ski Yogi*

Courchevel 242
✉ *Airtours, Alpine Answers Select, Alpine Events, Alpine Weekends, Altitude Holidays, Avant-ski, Bladon Lines, Chalet World, Chalets 'Unlimited', The Corporate Ski Company, Crystal, Elegant Resorts, Erna Low, Esprit Ski, Eurotunnel Motoring Holidays, Fairhand Holidays, Finlays, First Choice Ski, FlexiSki, Independent Ski Links, Inghams, Lagrange Holidays, Le Ski, Lotus Supertravel, Made to Measure Holidays, Mark Warner, Momentum Ski, Motours, Neilson, Powder Byrne, Scott Dunn Ski, Silver Ski, Simply Ski, Ski Activity, Ski Amis, Ski Arrangements, Ski Club of Great Britain, The Ski Company, Ski Expectations, Ski France, Ski Independence, Ski Leisure Direction, Ski Life, Ski Line, Ski Link, Ski 'n' Action, Ski Olympic, Ski Solutions, Ski Weekend, Ski-Val, Skiworld, Thomson Ski & Snowboarding, Tops Ski Chalets and Club Hotels, White Roc*

Courmayeur 378
✉ *Airtours, Alpine Answers Select, Alpine Events, Alpine Weekends, Beau-mont.com, Chalets 'Unlimited', Crystal, First Choice Ski, Independent Ski Links, Inghams, Interski, Mark Warner, Momentum Ski, Ski Arrangements, Ski Expectations, Ski Line, Ski Solutions, Ski Weekend, Thomson Ski & Snowboarding, White Roc*

Cranmore USA
Area in New Hampshire with attractive town/resort of North Conway. Easy skiing. Good for families.
150m; slopes 150–515m
⬡ 8 ⬆ 190 acres
✉ *AmeriCan Ski, Elegant Resorts*

Crans-Montana 423
✉ *Alpine Answers Select, Alpine Events, The Corporate Ski Company, Crystal, Erna Low, First Choice Ski, Independent Ski Links, Inghams, Interhome, Kuoni, Lagrange Holidays, Made to Measure Holidays, Momentum Ski, Motours, The Oxford Ski Company, Plus Travel, Ski Club of Great Britain, Ski Weekend, Swiss Travel Service, Thomson Ski & Snowboarding*

Crested Butte 520
✉ *AmeriCan Ski, Club Med, Made to Measure Holidays, Ski Activity, Ski Independence, Ski Safari, Ski The American Dream, United Vacations*

Crest-Voland France
Attractive, unspoiled traditional village near Megève with wonderfully uncrowded slopes linked to Les Saisies.
1150m; slopes 1230–1650m
⬡ 26 ⬆ 45km
✉ *First Choice Ski, SkiAway Holidays*

Crissolo Italy
Small, remote day-tripper area, south-west of Turin.
1320m; slopes 1745–2340m
⬆ 30km

La Croix-Fry 234
Couple of hotels on the pass close to La Clusaz.

Les Crosets 421
Isolated mini-resort above Champéry.

Crystal Mountain USA
Area in glorious Mt Rainier National Park, near Seattle. Good, varied area given good snow/weather, but both are often wet.
1340m; slopes 1340–2135m
⬡ 10 ⬆ 2300 acres

Cuchara Valley USA
Quiet little family resort in southern Colorado, some way from any other ski area.
2800m; slopes 2800–3285m
⬡ 4 ⬆ 250 acres

Cutigliano Italy
Sizeable village near Abetone in the Appennines. Less than 2 hours from Florence and Pisa.
1125m; slopes 1125–1850m
⬡ 9 ⬆ 13km

Cypress Mountain Canada
Vancouver's most challenging area, 20 minutes from the city and with 40% for experts. Good snowfall record but rain is a problem.
920m; slopes 910–1445m ⬡ 5

Daemyung Korea
One of the less ugly Korean resorts, 75km (47 miles) from Seoul. ⬡ 12

La Daille 338
Ugly apartment complex at the entrance to Val-d'Isère.

Daisen Japan
Western Honshu's main area, four hours from Osaka.
800m; slopes 740–1120m ⬡ 8

Damüls Austria
Scattered but attractive village in Bregenzerwald area close to the German and Swiss borders.
1430m; slopes 1430–2005m
⬡ 8 ⬆ 38km

Davos 428
✉ *Alpine Answers Select, Alpine Events, The Corporate Ski Company, Crystal, FlexiSki, Inghams, Interhome, Kuoni, Made to Measure Holidays, Momentum Ski, Plus Travel, Ski Club of Great Britain, Ski Weekend, SkiGower, Swiss Travel Service, White Roc*

Deer Mountain USA
South Dakota area close to 'Old West' town Deadwood and Mount Rushmore.
1825m; slopes 1825–2085m
⬡ 4 ⬆ 370 acres

Deer Valley 551
✉ *AmeriCan Ski, American Ski Classics, Made to Measure Holidays, Ski All America, Ski Independence, Ski Safari, Ski The American Dream, United Vacations*

Les Deux-Alpes 251
✉ *Airtours, Alpine Options, Avant-ski, Chalet World, Chalets 'Unlimited', Club Med, Crystal, Equity Ski, Erna Low, Fairhand Holidays, First Choice Ski, Independent Ski Links, Inghams, Interhome, Lagrange Holidays, Made to Measure Holidays, Mark Warner, Motours, Neilson, Panorama Holidays, Rocketski, Ski Arrangements, Ski Independence, Ski Leisure Direction, Ski Line, Ski Supreme, Ski Total, Skiworld, Thomson Ski & Snowboarding, Tops Ski Chalets and Club Hotels*

Les Diablerets 470
Spacious chalet resort linked to Villars.
✉ *Crystal, Interhome, Lagrange Holidays, Made to Measure Holidays, Momentum Ski, SkiGower*

Diamond Peak USA
Quiet, pleasant alternative to brash South Lake Tahoe.
slopes 2040–2600m
⬡ 7 ⬆ 755 acres
✉ *Ski The American Dream*

Dienten Austria
Quiet village east of Saalbach at the heart of large, low-altitude Hochkönig area that spreads impressively over four mountains linking Maria Alm to Mühlbach.
1070m; slopes 800–2000m
⬡ 36 ⬆ 150km
✉ *Ski Wild*

Dinner Plain   Australia
Attractive resort best known for
cross-country skiing. Shuttle to
Mt Hotham for Alpine slopes.
4.5 hours from Melbourne.
1520m

Discovery Ski Area   USA
Pleasant intermediate area near
Butte, Montana. Fairmont Hot
Springs (two huge thermal
pools) nearby.
2080m; slopes 2080–2485m
⛷4 ➚ 380 acres

Disentis   Switzerland
Unspoiled old village in a pretty
setting on the Glacier Express
rail route near Andermatt. Scenic
area with long runs.
1135m; slopes 1150–2920m
⛷10 ➚ 60km
✉ Interhome

Dobbiaco   Italy
One of several little resorts near
the Austrian border; a feasible
day out from the Sella Ronda.
1250m; slopes 1250–1610m
⛷5 ➚ 15km
✉ Ramblers, Waymark Holidays

Dodge Ridge   USA
Novice/leisurely intermediate
area north of Yosemite. The
pass from Reno is closed in
winter, preventing crowds.
2010m; slopes 2010–2500m
⛷12 ➚ 815 acres

Dolonne   378
Quiet suburb of Courmayeur.

Dorfgastein   104
Quieter, friendlier alternative to
Bad Gastein and Bad Hofgastein,
with its own ski area.

Dundret   Sweden
Lapland area with floodlit slopes
open through winter when sun
barely rises.
slopes 475–825m
⛷7 ➚ 15km

Durango Mountain Resort   USA
Mountain formerly known as
Purgatory, with good slopes
now accessed by a long six-pack
(the main base is still known as
Purgatory). Durango itself, a half
hour away, is a fun western
town with an historic main
street.
2680m; slopes 2680–3300m
⛷11 ➚ 1200 acres
✉ AmeriCan Ski, Ski
Independence

Eaglecrest   USA
Close to famous Yukon gold
rush town Skagway. Family
resort famous for its ski school.
365m; slopes 365–790m
⛷3 ➚ 640 acres

Eaux-Bonnes-Gourette   France
Most snow-sure resort in the
French Pyrenees. Very popular
with local families, so best
avoided at weekends.
1400m; slopes 1400–2400m
⛷23 ➚ 30km

Eben im Pongau   Austria
Part of Salzburger Sportwelt
Amadé area that includes nearby
St Johann, Wagrain, Flachau and
Zauchensee. Village spoilt by the
autobahn passing through it.
855m; slopes 855–2185m
⛷100 ➚ 350km

Ehrwald   Austria
Friendly, relaxed, pretty village
with several nicely varied areas,
notably the Zugspitz glacier.
Poor bus services, so a car
desirable.
1000m; slopes 1000–3000m
⛷21 ➚ 25km

El Colorado/Farellones   Chile
One of Chile's best ski areas,
40km/25 miles east of Santiago,
and connected to Valle Nevado
ski area. Crowded at weekends.
slopes 2430–3340m
⛷18 ➚ 2500 acres

Eldora Mountain   USA
Varied terrain close to Boulder
City and Denver. Crowded at
weekends.
2795m; slopes 2805–3230m
⛷12 ➚ 680 acres

Elk Meadows   USA
Area south of Salt Lake City,
more than a day trip from Park
City.
2775m; slopes 2745–3170m
⛷6 ➚ 1400 acres

Ellmau   111
✉ Airtours, Crystal, Inghams,
Interhome, Neilson, Ski Wild,
Thomson Ski & Snowboarding

Encamp   626
✉ First Choice Ski, Thomson
Ski & Snowboarding

Enego   Italy
Limited weekend day-trippers'
area near Vicenza and Trento.
1300m; slopes 1300–1445m
⛷7 ➚ 30km

Engelberg   Switzerland
Traditional town resort set amid
spectacular mountains and only
an hour's drive from Lucerne.
The slopes are fragmented: Titlis
is snow-sure – the glacier is
open all year round – but the
Brunni sector is less reliable. For
experts, the attraction is the
famous Laub, which drops
1000m/3,300ft – superb when
conditions are right. Generally
the pistes suit confident
intermediates; there are few
easy slopes and the nursery
slopes involve lift-rides so it's
not ideal for beginners. Cross-
country is good with 39km/24
miles of trails. Mountain
restaurants are plentiful, friendly
and inexpensive by Swiss
standards. Package
accommodation is in hotels,
with chalets and apartments to
rent locally. Eating out is mostly
in hotels and après-ski is good
at weekends. Off the slopes
there are good sports facilities,

a monastery tour, glassworks
and trips to Lucerne and Zürich.
1050m; slopes 1050–3020m
⛷23 ➚ 82km
✉ Alpine Events, The Corporate
Ski Company, Crystal, Inntravel,
Interhome, Kuoni, Made to
Measure Holidays, Plus Travel,
Ski Weekend, SkiGower, Swiss
Travel Service

Entrèves   378
Unremarkable cluster of hotels
at the base of the lift up to
Courmayeur's slopes.

Escaldes   Andorra
Central valley town, effectively
part of Andorra la Vella.

Etna   Italy
Scenic, uncrowded, short-season
area on the volcano's flank, 20
minutes from Nickolossi.
1800m; slopes 1800–2350m
➚ 5km

Evolène   Switzerland
Charming rustic village in
unspoiled, attractive setting
south of Sion. Own little area,
with Verbier's slopes accessed
at nearby Les Masses.
1380m; slopes 1300–3330m
⛷100 ➚ 400km

Faak am See   Austria
Limited area, one of five
overlooking town of Villach.
550m; slopes 840–1045m
⛷2 ➚ 2km

Fairmont Hot Springs   Canada
Major luxury spa complex ideal
for a relaxing holiday with some
gentle skiing thrown in.
⛷2 ➚ 60 acres

Faistenau   Austria
Cross-country area close to
Salzburg and St Wolfgang.
Limited Alpine slopes.
785m; slopes 785–1000m
⛷6 ➚ 3km

Falcade   Italy
Largest of many areas close to
but not part of the Sella Ronda.
1145m; slopes 1145–2170m
⛷11 ➚ 39km
✉ Alpine Tours

Falera   435
Rustic village with access to
area shared by Flims and Laax.

Le Falgoux   France
One of the most beautiful old
villages in France, set in the very
scenic Volcano National Park.
Several ski areas nearby.
930m; slopes 930–1350m

Falkertsee   Austria
Base area rather than a village,
with bleak, open slopes in
contrast to nearby
Badkleinkirchheim.
1690m; slopes 1690–2385m
⛷5 ➚ 15km

Falls Creek   656

La Feclaz   France
One of several little resorts in
the remote Parc des Bauges.

Fernie   599
✉ AmeriCan Ski, Crystal,
Frontier Ski, Handmade
Holidays, Inghams, Made to
Measure Holidays, Ski Activity,
Ski All America, Ski All Canada,
Ski Club of Great Britain, The
Ski Company, Ski
Independence, Ski Safari,
Thomson Ski & Snowboarding

Fieberbrunn   Austria
Atmospheric and friendly,
sprawling Tirolean village with
small, attractive area of wooded
slopes a bus-ride away and best
suited to beginners and leisurely
intermediates. The nursery
slopes are close to the village
centre and graduation to long,
gentle runs is easy. There are
35km/22 miles of good trails for
cross-country skiers. Weekday
queues are rare, but Fieberbrunn
has a reputation for snow and
can be invaded when other
resorts are lacking. There are
some decent mountain
restaurants. Accommodation in
the village is in hotels, and
there is also accommodation at
the lift station. Restaurants are
mainly hotel-based and après-
ski is liveliest at 4pm. Off the
slopes, there's an adventure
pool, skating, sleigh rides,
cleared walks and a toboggan
run, and train excursions are
possible.
800m; slopes 800–2020m
⛷13 ➚ 35km
✉ Snowscape

Fiesch   Switzerland
Traditional Rhône valley resort
close to Brig, with a lift up to
Fiescheralp (2220m/7,280ft) at
one end of the beautiful Aletsch
area extending across the
mountainside via Bettmeralp to
Riederalp.
1060m; slopes 1900–2900m
⛷32 ➚ 90km
✉ SkiGower

Fiescheralp   Switzerland
Mountain outpost of Fiesch,
down in the Rhône valley. At
one end of the beautiful Aletsch
area extending across the
mountainside via Bettmeralp to
Riederalp.
2220m; slopes 1900–2900m
⛷32 ➚ 90km

Filzmoos   Austria
Charming, unspoiled, friendly
village with leisurely slopes that
are ideal for novices. Good snow
record for its height.
1055m; slopes 1055–1645m
⛷12 ➚ 32km
✉ Inghams

Finkenberg   142
Large area between Mayrhofen
and Hintertux.
✉ Crystal, Equity Ski, First
Choice Ski

Fiss Austria
Nicely compact, quiet, traditional village with a sunny area well protected by snowmakers and linked to Serfaus.
1435m; slopes 1200–2540m
⛷ *17* 🚡 *70km*
✉ *Alpine Tours, Interhome*

Flachau Austria
Quiet, spacious village in a pretty setting at one end of extensive three-valley lift network linking via Wagrain to Alpendorf. Flachauwinkl, up the valley, is at the centre of another similarly extensive lift system. All these resorts are covered by the Salzburger Sportwelt ski pass that our figures relate to.
925m; slopes 800–2185m
⛷ *100* 🚡 *350km*
✉ *Interhome, Thomson Ski & Snowboarding*

Flachauwinkl Austria
Tiny ski station beside Tauern autobahn, at centre of extensive three-valley lift network linking Kleinarl to Zauchensee. Flachau, down the valley, is at one end of a similarly extensive lift system. All these resorts are covered by the Salzburger Sportwelt ski pass that our figures relate to.
930m; slopes 800–2185m
⛷ *100* 🚡 *350km*

Flaine 256
✉ *Avant-ski, Classic Ski Limited, Club Med, Crystal, Erna Low, Eurotunnel Motoring Holidays, Fairhand Holidays, First Choice Ski, French Freedom Holidays, Independent Ski Links, Inghams, Lagrange Holidays, Made to Measure Holidays, Motours, Neilson, Ski Arrangements, Ski Club of Great Britain, Ski Independence, Ski Leisure Direction, Ski Life, Ski Weekend, Thomson Ski & Snowboarding*

Flims 435
✉ *Alpine Answers Select, Alpine Events, The Corporate Ski Company, Interhome, Kuoni, Made to Measure Holidays, Momentum Ski, Plus Travel, Powder Byrne, Ski Weekend, Swiss Travel Service, White Roc*

Flumet France
Large resort, well placed for whole Mont Blanc area. Cheap, big-village alternative to Megève.
1000m; slopes 1000–1600m
⛷ *10* 🚡 *40km*

Flumserberg Switzerland
Collective name for the villages sharing a varied area an hour south-east of Zürich.
1220m; slopes 1220–2220m
⛷ *17*

Folgaria Italy
Largest of several resorts east of Trento. Old lift system.
1165m; slopes 1185–2005m
⛷ *38* 🚡 *70km*
✉ *Alpine Tours*

Folgarida 387
Dolomite village, with links to Madonna di Campiglio's area.
✉ *Equity Ski, Rocketski, Sloping Off*

Foncine-le-Haut France
Major cross-country village with extensive trails.
✉ *Headwater Holidays, Lagrange Holidays*

Fonni Gennaragentu Italy
Sardinia's only 'ski area' – and it's tiny.
⛷ *1* 🚡 *5km*

Font-Romeu 360
✉ *Lagrange Holidays, Solo's*

Foppolo Italy
Relatively unattractive but user-friendly village, a short transfer from Bergamo.
1510m; slopes 1610–2160m
⛷ *10* 🚡 *45km*
✉ *Equity Ski*

Forca Canapine Italy
Limited area near the Adriatic and Ascoli Piceno. Popular with weekend day-trippers.
1450m; slopes 1450–1690m
⛷ *11* 🚡 *20km*

Formazza Italy
Cross-country base with some downhill slopes.
1280m; slopes 1275–1755m
🚡 *8km*

Formigal 638

Le Fornet 338
Rustic, old hamlet down the valley from Val-d'Isère.

Forstau Austria
Secluded hamlet above Radstadt-Schladming road. Very limited area with old lifts, but nice and quiet.
930m; slopes 930–1885m
⛷ *7* 🚡 *14km*

Fortress Mountain Canada
Primitive, wild little mountain between Banff and Calgary, renowned for powder snow, dramatic scenery and uncrowded slopes.
2040m; slopes 2040–2370m
⛷ *7* 🚡 *325 acres*

La Foux-d'Allos France
Purpose-built resort that shares a good intermediate area with Pra-Loup.
1800m; slopes 1800–2600m
⛷ *53* 🚡 *230km*
✉ *Fairhand Holidays, Lagrange Holidays*

Frabosa Soprana Italy
One of numerous little areas south of Turin, well placed for combining winter sports with Riviera sightseeing.
850m; slopes 860–1740m
🚡 *40km*

Frisco 513
Small town down the valley from Breckenridge.
✉ *AmeriCan Ski*

Frontignano Italy
Best lift system in the Macerata region, near the Adriatic Riviera.
1340m; slopes 1340–2000m
⛷ *8* 🚡 *10km*

Fügen Austria
Unspoiled Zillertal village with limited area best suited to beginners.
560m; slopes 560–2400m
⛷ *19* 🚡 *48km*

Fulpmes 119
✉ *Crystal*

Furano Japan
Small Hokkaido resort, two hours from Sapporo. One of the few Japanese areas to get reasonable powder.
235m; slopes 235–1065m ⛷ *13*

Fusch Austria
Cheaper, quiet place to stay when visiting Zell am See. Across golf course from Kaprun and Schuttdorf.
805m; slopes 805–1050m
⛷ *2* 🚡 *5km*

Fuschl Austria
Attractive, unspoiled, lakeside village close to St Wolfgang and Salzburg, 30 minutes from its slopes. Best suited to part-time skiers who want to sightsee as well.
670m

Gåla Norway
Base for downhill and cross-country skiing, an hour's drive north of Lillehammer.
930m; slopes 830–1150m
⛷ *7* 🚡 *20km*
✉ *Inntravel*

Gallio Italy
One of several low resorts near Vicenza and Trento. Popular with weekend day-trippers.
1100m; slopes 1100–1550m
⛷ *11* 🚡 *50km*

Galtür 123
Charming traditional village near Ischgl.
✉ *Inghams, Made to Measure Holidays*

Gambarie d'Aspromonte Italy
Italy's second most southerly ski area (after Mt Etna). On the 'toe' of the Italian 'boot' near Reggio di Calabria.
1310m; slopes 1310–1650m ⛷ *3*

Gantschier Austria
No slopes of its own but particularly well placed for visiting all the Montafon areas.
700m

Gargellen 147
✉ *Interhome, Made to Measure Holidays*

Garmisch-Partenkirchen Germany
Large twin resorts; unspoiled, traditional Partenkirchen much the prettier. Superb main area of wooded runs when the unreliable snow cover allows.
720m; slopes 720–2830m
⛷ *38* 🚡 *71km*
✉ *Moswin Tours*

Gaschurn 147

Gaustablikk Norway
Small snow-sure Alpine area on Mt Gausta in southern Norway with plenty of cross-country.
🚡 *15km*

Geilo 648
✉ *Crystal, Headwater Holidays, Inntravel, Neilson, Ski Wild, Solo's, Thomson Ski & Snowboarding, Waymark Holidays*

Gérardmer France
Sizeable resort near Strasbourg with plenty of amenities. Night skiing, too.
665m; slopes 750–1150m
⛷ *20* 🚡 *40km*
✉ *Fairhand Holidays, Lagrange Holidays*

Gerlitzen Alpe Austria
A gondola ride above Villach and with good views. A worthwhile excursion from Badkleinkirchheim.
500m; slopes 1003–1911m
⛷ *14* 🚡 *20km*

Gerlos Austria
One of Austria's few inexpensive but fairly snow-sure resorts, now linked to Zell im Zillertal as well as Königsleiten to form a fair-sized intermediate area.
1250m; slopes 1250–2300m
⛷ *23* 🚡 *70km*
✉ *Interhome*

Les Gets 290
Sprawling chalet resort on low pass near Morzine.
✉ *Alp Active, Avant-ski, Chalets 'Unlimited', Fairhand Holidays, Fantiski-Ski2k, Independent Ski Links, Lagrange Holidays, Made to Measure Holidays, Motours, Ski Activity, SkiAway Holidays, Ski Expectations, Ski Famille, Ski Hillwood, Ski Independence, Ski Total, Ski Weekend, Tops Ski Chalets and Club Hotels*

La Giettaz France
Small resort between La Clusaz and Megève about to be linked in to Megève's Le Jaillet area.

Gitschtal/Weissbriach Austria
One of many little areas near Hermagor in eastern Austria, close to Italian border.
690m; slopes 690–1400m
⛷ *4* 🚡 *5km*

Glaris Switzerland
Hamlet base station for the uncrowded Rinerhorn section of the Davos slopes.
1455m; slopes 1455–2490m
⛷ *5* 🚡 *30km*

Glencoe 655

Glenshee 655
✉ Skisafe Travel

Going 111
Small local ski area near Ellmau, linked to huge Ski Welt area.

Goldegg Austria
Year-round resort famous for its lakeside castle. Limited slopes but Wagrain (Salzburger Sportwelt) and Grossarl (Gastein valley) are nearby.
825m; slopes 825–1250m
⛷4 ✦ 12km

Golden Canada
Small logging town, the place to stay when visiting Kicking Horse resort 15 minutes away. Launch pad for Purcell heli-skiing.

Gore Mountain USA
One of the better areas in New York State. Near Lake Placid, sufficiently far north to avoid worst weekend crowds. Intermediate terrain.
455m; slopes 455–1095m
⛷9 ✦ 290 acres

Göriach Austria
Hamlet with trail connecting into one of longest, most snow-sure cross-country networks in Europe.
1250m

Gortipohl Austria
Traditional village in pretty Montafontal.
920m; slopes 900–2395m
⛷62 ✦ 209km

Gosau Austria
Straggling village with plenty of pretty, if low, runs. Snow-sure Obertauern and Schladming are within reach.
765m; slopes 765–1800m
⛷37 ✦ 65km

Göstling Austria
One of Austria's easternmost resorts, between Salzburg and Vienna. A traditional village in wooded setting.
530m; slopes 530–1800m
⛷12 ✦ 20km

Götzens Austria
Valley village base for Axamer Lizum slopes.
870m

Grächen Switzerland
Charming chalet-village reached by tricky access road off the approach to Zermatt. A small area of open slopes, mainly above the trees and of red-run difficulty, reached by two gondolas – one to Hannigalp (2115m/6,940ft), the main focus of activity with a very impressive children's nursery area. The village has almost a score of hotels, mostly 3-star; most of the accommodation is in chalets and apartments. The sports centre has tennis, badminton, and a natural ice-rink.
1615m; slopes 1615–2890m
⛷13 ✦ 50km
✉ Interhome

Le Grand-Bornand 234
✉ Fairhand Holidays, French Freedom Holidays, Frosty's Ski and Snowboard Holidays, Inntravel, Lagrange Holidays

Grand Targhee 566
Powder skiing paradise an hour from Jackson Hole.
✉ AmeriCan Ski, Lotus Supertravel

Grangesises Italy
Small satellite of Sestriere, with lifts up to the main slopes.

Grau Roig 632
Mini-resort at foot of Pas de la Casa's only woodland runs.
✉ Inghams

La Grave 262
✉ Alpine Answers Select, Interhome, Lagrange Holidays, Motours, Ski Arrangements, Ski Club of Great Britain, Ski Weekend

Gray Rocks Canada
Very popular family resort, 130km/80 miles north of Montreal; renowned for its ski school.
250m; slopes 250–440m
⛷4 ✦ 200 acres

Great Divide USA
Area near Helena, Montana, best for experts. Mostly bowls; plus near-extreme Rawhide Gulch.
1765m; slopes 1765–2195m
⛷6 ✦ 720 acres

Gresse-en-Vercors France
Resort south of Grenoble. Sheltered slopes worth noting for bad-weather days.
1250m; slopes 1250–1800m ⛷16
✉ Interhome, Lagrange Holidays

Gressoney-la-Trinité 389
Village in the central valley of the Monterosa Ski area.
✉ Crystal, Motours, The Ski Company

Gressoney-St-Jean 389
Village in the central valley of the Monterosa Ski area.

Grimentz Switzerland
Exceptionally cute, unspoiled mountainside village with high, varied runs including genuine reds and blacks, mostly on open slopes above the mid-mountain nursery area of Bendolla (2100m/6,890ft). Mostly served by drag-lifts. In the Val d'Anniviers, a side valley near the Valais town of Sierre; valley lift pass also covers St Luc/Chandolin, Vercorin and Zinal – 200km/125 miles of runs in total. Zinal is a short bus-ride up the valley, with a splendid itinerary run back to Grimentz. Grimentz has half a dozen small hotels, 2- and 3-star. There's a public pool and a natural ice-rink.
1570m; slopes 1570–2900m
⛷12 ✦ 50km

Grindelwald 440
✉ Alpine Events, The Corporate Ski Company, Crystal, Elegant Resorts, Independent Ski Links, Inghams, Interhome, Kuoni, Made to Measure Holidays, Momentum Ski, Plus Travel, Powder Byrne, Ski Club of Great Britain, SkiGower, Swiss Travel Service, Thomson Ski & Snowboarding, White Roc

Grossarl 104
Secluded village in the Gastein valley.

Grosskirchheim Austria
Very limited area near Heiligenblut.
1025m; slopes 1025–1400m
⛷2 ✦ 3km

Grouse Mountain Canada
The Vancouver area with the largest lift capacity. Superb city views from mostly easy slopes; night skiing.
880m; slopes 880–1245m
⛷11 ✦ 120 acres

Grünau Austria
Spacious riverside village in a lovely lake-filled part of eastern Austria. Nicely varied area, but very low.
525m; slopes 600–1600m
⛷14 ✦ 40km

Gryon 470
Village below Villars, with which it shares a ski area.

Gstaad 444
✉ Alpine Answers Select, Alpine Events, The Corporate Ski Company, Crystal, Elegant Resorts, Interhome, Made to Measure Holidays, Momentum Ski, Plus Travel, Ski Weekend, SkiGower, White Roc

Gunstock USA
One of the New Hampshire resorts closest to Boston, popular with families. Primarily easy slopes. Gorgeous Lake Winnisquam views. 98% snowmaking.
275m; slopes 275–700m
⛷8 ✦ 220 acres

Guthega 656

Hakuba Happo One Japan
European-style resort four hours from Tokyo. One of Japan's more challenging areas.
750m; slopes 750–1830m ⛷33

Hasliberg Switzerland
Four rustic hamlets on a sunny plateau overlooking Meiringen and Lake Brienz. Two of them are the bottom stations of a varied intermediate area.
1055m; slopes 600–2435m
⛷16 ✦ 60km

Haus in Ennstal 167
Village next to Schladming, with good local slopes connected to the rest of the network.

Haystack 573

Heavenly 490
✉ AmeriCan Ski, American Ski Classics, Crystal, Equity Ski, Independent Ski Links, Neilson,

Rocketski, Ski Activity, Ski All America, Ski Independence, Ski Line, Ski Safari, Ski Success, Ski The American Dream, Skiworld, Trailfinders, United Vacations, Virgin Ski

Hebalm Austria
One of many small areas in Austria's easternmost ski region near Slovenian border. No major resorts in vicinity.
1350m; slopes 1350–1400m
⛷6 ✦ 11km

Heiligenblut Austria
Picturesque village in beautiful surroundings with mostly high terrain. Its remote position west of Bad Gastein ensures that it remains uncrowded.
1300m; slopes 1300–2900m
⛷14 ✦ 55km

Hemlock Resort Canada
Area 55 miles east of Vancouver towards Sun Peaks. Mostly intermediate terrain and with snowfall of 600 inches a year. Lodging is available at the base area.
1000m; slopes 1000–1375m
⛷4 ✦ 350 acres

Hemsedal 650
✉ Crystal, Neilson, Ski Wild

Heremence Switzerland
Quiet village in unspoiled attractive setting south of Sion. Verbier's slopes are accessed a few minutes' drive away at Les Masses.
1250m; slopes 1300–3330m
⛷100 ✦ 400km

Hermagor Austria
Carinthian village below the Sonnenalpe ski area, rated one of the best areas in Austria by the famous Franz Klammer.
600m; slopes 1210–2005m
⛷29 ✦ 101km

Hintersee Austria
Easy slopes very close to Salzburg. Several long top-to-bottom runs and lifts means the size of the area is greatly reduced if the snowline is high.
745m; slopes 750–1470m
⛷9 ✦ 40km

Hinterstoder Austria
A very quiet valley village – neat but not overtly charming – spread along road up the dead-end Stodertal in Upper Austria. The local Höss slopes are pleasantly wooded, less densely at the top, with splendid views. It's a small area, but has a worthwhile vertical of 1250m/4,100ft, and 450m/1,475ft above mid-mountain. A gondola from the main street goes up to the flat-bottomed bowl of Hutererböden (1400m/4,600ft), where there are several restaurants plus the modern 4-star Berghotel, very gentle but undulating nursery slopes and lifts up to higher points. Most of the mountain is of easy red steepness. The run to the valley is a pleasant red with one or

Kals am Grossglockner Austria
Village in remote valley north of Lienz.
1325m; slopes 1325–2305m
⛷7 🚡15km

Kaltenbach Austria
One of the larger, quieter Zillertal areas, with plenty of high-altitude slopes.
560m; slopes 560–2300m
⛷16 🚡60km
✉ *Equity Ski*

Kananaskis Canada
Small area near Calgary, nicely set in woods, with slopes at Nakiska and Fortress Mountain.
slopes 1525–2465m
⛷12 🚡605 acres
✉ *Frontier Ski, Made to Measure Holidays, Ski All Canada*

Kandersteg Switzerland
Good cross-country base set amid beautiful scenery near Interlaken.
1175m; slopes 1175–2000m
⛷7 🚡13km
✉ *Headwater Holidays, Inntravel, Kuoni, Made to Measure Holidays, Waymark Holidays*

Kanin 644

Kaprun 194
Classic Austrian charmer near Zell am See.
✉ *Airtours, Crystal, Directski.com, Esprit Ski, First Choice Ski, Inghams, Made to Measure Holidays, Ski Wild*

Les Karellis France
Resort with slopes that are more scenic, challenging and snow-sure than those of better-known Valloire, nearby.
1600m; slopes 1600–2550m
⛷19 🚡60km

Kastelruth Italy
Charming picturesque village in the south Tirolean Italian Dolomites with good cross-country trails. Near the Sella Ronda circuit.
✉ *Inntravel*

Kasurila Finland
Siilinjarvi ski area popular with boarders. ⛷5

Katschberg Austria
Cute hamlet on road pass from Styria to Carinthia, now by-passed by Tauern motorway through Katschberg tunnel. Non-trivial area of intermediate slopes, linked to lower St Margarethen; lifts include several fast chairs, one a six-pack.
1140m; slopes 1075–2220m
⛷15 🚡80km
✉ *Alpine Tours*

Keystone 522
✉ *AmeriCan Ski, American Ski Classics, Crystal, Handmade Holidays, Neilson, Ski Activity, Ski All America, Ski Independence, Ski Safari, Ski The American Dream, Thomson Ski & Snowboarding, United Vacations*

Kicking Horse
✉ *Airtours, AmeriCan Ski, Crystal, Made to Measure Holidays, Ski All America, Ski Independence, Ski Safari, Ski The American Dream*

Killington 576
✉ *Chalets 'Unlimited', Crystal, Equity Ski, Esprit Ski, First Choice Ski, Independent Ski Links, Inghams, Made to Measure Holidays, Neilson, Rocketski, Ski All America, Ski Arrangements, Ski Independence, Ski Line, Ski Safari, Ski Success, Ski The American Dream, Thomson Ski & Snowboarding, United Vacations, Virgin Ski*

Kimberley 589
✉ *Airtours, AmeriCan Ski, Crystal, Frontier Ski, Inghams, Made to Measure Holidays, Ski Activity, Ski All America, Ski Safari, Ski The American Dream, Thomson Ski & Snowboarding*

Kirchberg 128
Lively little town close to Kitzbühel.
✉ *Beau-mont.com, Directski.com, First Choice Ski, Interhome, Lagrange Holidays, Top Deck*

Kirchdorf 187
Attractive village a bus-ride from St Johann in Tirol.
✉ *Snowcoach, Thomson Ski & Snowboarding*

Kirkwood 495
✉ *AmeriCan Ski*

Kitzbühel 128
✉ *Airtours, Alpine Events, Avant-ski, Beau-mont.com, Bladon Lines, Chalets 'Unlimited', The Corporate Ski Company, Directski.com, Elegant Resorts, First Choice Ski, Independent Ski Links, Inghams, Interhome, Lagrange Holidays, Made to Measure Holidays, Motours, Neilson, Panorama Holidays, Ski Arrangements, Ski Club of Great Britain, Ski Solutions, Ski Wild, Snowscape, Thomson Ski & Snowboarding*

Kleinarl Austria
Secluded traditional village up a pretty side valley from Wagrain, at one end of three-valley lift network linking it via Flachauwinkl to Zauchensee – all part of the Salzburger Sportwelt ski pass area that our figures relate to.
1015m; slopes 800–2185m
⛷100 🚡350km

Klippitztorl Austria
One of many little areas in Austria's easternmost ski region near Slovenian border.
1460m; slopes 1460–1820m
⛷6 🚡25km

Klosters 428
Quiet, affluent chalet village with much-improved access to the huge ski area it shares with Davos.
✉ *Alpine Answers Select, Descent International, Elegant Resorts, FlexiSki, Inghams, Kuoni, Made to Measure Holidays, Momentum Ski, Plus Travel, Powder Byrne, Ski Club of Great Britain, The Ski Company Ltd, Ski Weekend, Ski with Julia, SkiGower, Swiss Travel Service, White Roc*

Kobla 644

Kolsass-Weer Austria
Pair of Inn-side villages with low, inconvenient and limited slopes.
555m; slopes 555–1010m
⛷3 🚡14km

Königsleiten Austria
Quiet, high resort sharing fairly snow-sure area with Gerlos, now also linked to Zell im Zillertal to form a fair-sized area.
1600m; slopes 1245–2300m
⛷25 🚡70km

Kopaonik Serbia
Modern, sympathetically designed family resort in a pretty setting.
1770m; slopes 1110–2015m
⛷21 🚡57km

Koralpe Austria
Largest and steepest of many gentle little areas in Austria's easternmost ski region near the Slovenian border.
1550m; slopes 1550–2050m
⛷10 🚡25km

Kössen Austria
Village near St Johann in Tirol with low, scattered and limited local slopes.
600m; slopes 600–1700m
⛷11 🚡25km

Kötschach-Mauthen Austria
One of many little areas near Hermagor in eastern Austria, close to the Italian border.
710m; slopes 710–1300m
⛷4 🚡6km

Kranjska Gora 644
✉ *Balkan Holidays, Crystal, First Choice Ski, Slovenija & Austrian Pursuits, Solo's, Thomson Ski & Snowboarding*

Krimml Austria
Sunny area, high enough to have good snow usually. Shares regional pass with Wildkogel resorts (Neukirchen).
1075m; slopes 1640–2040m
⛷8 🚡33km

Krispl-Gaissau Austria
Easy slopes very close to Salzburg. Several long top-to-bottom lifts mean the size of the area is greatly reduced if the snowline is high.
925m; slopes 750–1570m
⛷11 🚡40km

Kühtai Austria
A collection of comfortable hotels beside a high road pass only 25km/16 miles from Innsbruck – higher than equally snow-sure Obergurgl or Obertauern, but cheaper than either. Half a dozen drags and two quad chairs serve red cruisers of about 500m/1,650ft vertical on either side of the road, plus some token black runs; not ideal for novices – no easy blues to graduate to. Very quiet in the week, but liable to weekend crowds if lower resorts around Innsbruck are short of snow. One limited mountain hut. Quiet in the evening, but for its size 'a reasonable selection of bars and restaurants', says a report. 3-star Hotel Elizabeth recommended – 'very friendly, excellent food'.
2020m; slopes 2010–2520m
⛷11 🚡40km
✉ *Crystal, Inghams*

Kusatsu Kokusai Japan
Attractive spa village with hot springs, three hours from Tokyo. ⛷13

Laax 435
Old farming community linked to Flims.
✉ *Alpine Answers Select, Made to Measure Holidays*

Ladis Austria
Smaller alternative to Serfaus and Fiss, with lifts that connect into the same varied ski area.
1200m; slopes 1200–2540m
⛷4 🚡18km
✉ *Alpine Tours*

Le Laisinant 338
Tiny hamlet a short bus-ride down the valley from Val-d'Isère.

Lake Louise 607
✉ *Airtours, Alpine Answers Select, AmeriCan Ski, Crystal, Elegant Resorts, Equity Ski, First Choice Ski, Frontier Ski, Independent Ski Links, Inghams, Lotus Supertravel, Made to Measure Holidays, Neilson, Rocketski, Ski Activity, Ski All America, Ski All Canada, Ski Club of Great Britain, Ski Independence, Ski Line, Ski Safari, Ski The American Dream, Thomson Ski & Snowboarding, Trailfinders, United Vacations*

Lake Tahoe 495
✉ *AmeriCan Ski, Equity Ski, Independent Ski Links, Rocky Mountain Adventures, Ski Activity, Ski Independence, Skiworld, Thomson Ski & Snowboarding, Trailfinders, United Vacations, Virgin Ski*

Lanersbach 114
Attractive village and ski area –
the Hintertux glacier is nearby.
✉ *Equity Ski*

Lans-en-Vercors France
Village close to Villard-de-Lans
and near Grenoble. Highest
slopes in region; few
snowmakers.
1020m; slopes 1400–1805m
⛷ 16 ⛷ 24km

Lauterbrunnen 446
Valley town with a funicular and
rail connection up to Mürren.
✉ *Re-lax Holidays, Ski Miquel,
Top Deck*

Le Lavancher 221
Quiet village between Chamonix
and Argentière.

Lavarone Italy
One of several areas east of
Trento, good for a weekend
day-trip.
1195m; slopes 1075–1555m
⛷ 13 ⛷ 12km

Leadville USA
Old mining town full of historic
buildings. Own easy area (Ski
Cooper) plus snowcat operation.
Picturesque inexpensive base for
visiting Copper Mountain, Vail
and Beaver Creek.

Lech 134
✉ *Alpine Events, Avant-ski,
Chalets 'Unlimited', Crystal,
Elegant Resorts, Erna Low,
Fairhand Holidays, FlexiSki,
Inghams, Made to Measure
Holidays, Momentum Ski,
Simply Ski, Ski Expectations,
Ski Solutions, Ski Total, Ski
Weekend, White Roc*

The Lecht 655
✉ *Skisafe Travel*

Lélex France
Family resort with pretty
wooded slopes between Dijon
and Geneva.
900m; slopes 900–1680m
⛷ 29 ⛷ 50km

Las Leñas Argentina
European-style resort, 400km/
250 miles south of Mendoza,
with varied, beautiful terrain.
Lodgings at the foot of the
slopes.
2240m; slopes 2260–3430m
⛷ 11 ⛷ 60km
✉ *Scott Dunn Latin America*

Lenk 415
Traditional village that shares a
sizeable area with Adelboden.
✉ *Made to Measure Holidays,
Swiss Travel Service*

Lenzerheide Switzerland
Spacious village, separated by a
lake from Valbella and sharing a
large intermediate area.
1500m; slopes 1230–2865m
⛷ 35 ⛷ 155km
✉ *Interhome, Made to Measure
Holidays*

Leogang 160
Quiet, spread-out village with
over-the-mountain link to
Saalbach-Hinterglemm.
✉ *Equity Ski, Rocketski*

Lermoos Austria
Pleasant little village with its
own small area of shady
intermediate slopes on
Grubigstein and a pass giving
access to a variety of other
areas in the locality, including
the towering (and glacial)
Zugspitze, on the border with
Germany. Lots of cross-country
trails along the flat valley.
1005m; slopes 1005–2250m
⛷ 10 ⛷ 29km

Lessach Austria
Hamlet with trail connecting into
one of longest, most snow-sure
cross-country networks in
Europe.
1210m

Leukerbad Switzerland
Major spa resort of Roman
origin and recently revamped at
vast expense. The super-neat
towny result is very impressive if
you like that kind of thing. It is
spectacularly set beneath
towering cliffs, which are scaled
by a cable-car up to high-
altitude cross-country trails. The
downhill slopes are on the
opposite side of the valley,
mainly above the tree line,
served by drag-lifts and of red
gradient, though there are a
couple of blacks including a
World Cup downhill course,
which descends from the high,
open slopes into the woods.
There is also a slightly separate
wooded sector served by a
couple of chair-lifts. The spas
have spawned a handful of very
swanky 4-star hotels, but there
are also over a dozen 3-stars,
ranging from cute chalets to the
plainly modern. As well as
fabulous spa facilities, there are
indoor and outdoor ice-rinks,
tennis, squash and badminton
courts and a golf driving range.
1410m; slopes 1410–2700m
⛷ 17 ⛷ 60km
✉ *SkiGower*

Leutasch Austria
Traditional cross-country village
with limited slopes but a
pleasant day trip from nearby
Seefeld or Innsbruck.
1130m; slopes 1130–1605m
⛷ 4 ⛷ 9km
✉ *Headwater Holidays,
Inntravel*

Levi 645
✉ *Bladon Lines, First Choice
Ski, Inghams*

Leysin 470
Large resort near Aigle, with a
good range of facilities.
✉ *Crystal, Plus Travel,
SkiGower*

Lienz Austria
Pleasant town in pretty
surroundings.
675m; slopes 730–2290m
⛷ 12 ⛷ 55km
✉ *Equity Ski*

Lillehammer 648
✉ *Crystal, Ski Wild, Thomson
Ski & Snowboarding*

Limone Italy
Pleasant old town not far from
Turin, with a pretty area, but far
from snow-sure.
1010m; slopes 1030–2050m
⛷ 29 ⛷ 80km

Lincoln USA
New Hampshire town from which
to visit Loon mountain.
✉ *Crystal*

Lindvallen-Högfjället Sweden
Largest ski area (but two
unlinked mountains) in
Scandinavia.
800m; slopes 590–890m
⛷ 46 ⛷ 85km

Le Lioran France
Auvergne village with purpose-
built satellite above. Spectacular
volcanic scenery.
1160m; slopes 1160–1850m
⛷ 24 ⛷ 60km

Livigno 383
✉ *Airtours, Chalets 'Unlimited',
Crystal, First Choice Ski,
Inghams, Interhome, Neilson,
Panorama Holidays, Ski
Arrangements, Thomson Ski &
Snowboarding*

Lizzola Italy
Small base development in
remote region north of Bergamo.
Several other little areas nearby.
1250m; slopes 1250–2070m
⛷ 9 ⛷ 30km

Llaima Chile
Exotic area in central Chile,
around and below a mildly
active volcano.
1500m ⛷ 5

Loch Lomond Canada
Steep, narrow, challenging
slopes near Thunder Bay on the
shores of Lake Superior. Candy
Mountain is nearby.
215m; slopes 215–440m
⛷ 3 ⛷ 90 acres

Lofer Austria
Quiet, traditional village in a
pretty setting north of Saalbach
with a small area of its own, and
Waidring's relatively snow-sure
Steinplatte nearby.
640m; slopes 640–1745m
⛷ 13 ⛷ 46km
✉ *Ski Wild*

Longchamp 350
Dreary resort that shares a ski
area with pretty Valmorel.

Loon Mountain 573
✉ *Equity Ski, Rocketski, Virgin
Ski*

Lost Trail USA
Remote Montana area, open
only Thursday to Sunday and
holidays. Mostly intermediate
slopes.
2005m; slopes 2005–2370m
⛷ 6 ⛷ 800 acres

Loveland USA
High, varied slopes, a day trip
from Keystone and renowned for
snow. Long season, good for all
abilities.
3220m; slopes 3220–3730m
⛷ 11 ⛷ 836 acres

Luchon France
Sizeable village with plenty of
amenities, with gondola (8
minutes) to its ski area and to
purpose-built Superbagnères.
630m; slopes 1440–2260m
⛷ 16 ⛷ 35km
✉ *Lagrange Holidays*

Lurisia Italy
Sizeable spa resort, a good base
for visits to surrounding little ski
areas and to Nice.
750m; slopes 850–1800m
⛷ 30km

Luz-Ardiden France
Spa village below its ski area.
Cauterets and Barèges nearby.
710m; slopes 1730–2450m
⛷ 19 ⛷ 60km

Macugnaga Italy
Pretty, two-part village set amid
stunning scenery. Novice and
intermediate slopes.
1330m; slopes 1330–2970m
⛷ 12 ⛷ 40km
✉ *Interhome, Neilson*

Madesimo Italy
Remote valley village, a mix of
traditional buildings and
piecemeal modern development,
a three-hour drive north from
Bergamo. Great for a weekend,
but for a week it's not ideal:
beginners will not find the
progression to real runs easy,
and others are likely to find the
terrain limited. Experts need the
upper cable-car to be open for
access to the famous Canalone,
a long, sweeping itinerary run
which keeps its snow well. The
village is quite spread out, but
there is a fair choice of good-
value hotels, apartments and
lively restaurants. Après-ski is
otherwise fairly quiet and there's
not much to do off the slopes.
1545m; slopes 1545–2880m
⛷ 15 ⛷ 45km
✉ *Inghams, Ski Arrangements*

Madonna di Campiglio 387
✉ *Alpine Tours, Crystal, Equity
Ski, First Choice Ski, Inghams,
Interhome, Rocketski, Ski
Arrangements, Ski Club of Great
Britain, Ski Yogi, Sloping Off,
Solo's*

Mad River Glen 573

La Magdelaine Italy
Close to Cervinia, and good on
bad-weather days.
1645m; slopes 1645–1870m
⛷ 4 ⛷ 4km

Mont Blanc   622

Montchavin   297
Attractively transformed village on fringe of La Plagne ski area.
☒ *Crystal, Fairhand Holidays, Made to Measure Holidays, Motours*

Mont-de-Lans   251
Low village on the way up to Les Deux-Alpes.

Le Mont-Dore   France
Attractive traditional village, the largest resort in the stunningly beautiful volcanic Auvergne region near Clermont-Ferrand.
1050m; slopes 1350–1850m
⛷ 20 ⛰ 42km
☒ *Lagrange Holidays*

Monte Bondone   Italy
Essentially a Trento weekenders' area (some lifts are closed on weekdays).
slopes 1300–2100m
⛷ 8 ⛰ 13km

Monte Campione   Italy
Tiny purpose-built resort, spread thinly over four mountainsides. 80% snowmaking helps to offset the low altitude.
1100m; slopes 1200–2010m
⛷ 18 ⛰ 100km
☒ *Equity Ski*

Monte Livata   Italy
Closest resort to Rome, popular with weekenders.
1430m; slopes 1430–1750m
⛷ 8 ⛰ 8km

Monte Piselli   Italy
Tiny area with the highest slopes of the many little resorts east of Rome.
2100m; slopes 2100–2690m
⛷ 3 ⛰ 5km

Monte Pora   Italy
Tiny resort near Lake d'Iseo and Bergamo. Several other little areas nearby.
1350m; slopes 1350–1880m
⛷ 8 ⛰ 20km

Monterosa Ski   389
☒ *Crystal, Handmade Holidays, Ski 2, Ski Arrangements, Ski Club of Great Britain, The Ski Company, Ski Weekend, Thomson Ski & Snowboarding*

Mont Gabriel   Canada
Montreal area with runs on four sides of the mountain, though the south-facing sides rarely open. Two short but renowned double-black-diamond bump runs. ⛷ 9

Montgenèvre   285
☒ *Airtours, Crystal, Equity Ski, Erna Low, Fairhand Holidays, Independent Ski Links, Lagrange Holidays, Made to Measure Holidays, Motours, Neilson, Rocketski, Ski Etoile, Thomson Ski & Snowboarding*

Mont Glen   Canada
Least crowded of the Montreal areas, so a good weekend choice.
680m; slopes 680–1035m
⛷ 4 ⛰ 110 acres

Mont Grand Fonds   Canada
Small area sufficiently far from Québec not to get overrun at weekends.
400m; slopes 400–735m ⛷ 4

Mont Habitant   Canada
Very limited area in the Montreal region but with a good base lodge. ⛷ 3

Mont Olympia   Canada
Small, two-mountain area near Montreal, one mostly novice terrain, the other best suited to experts. ⛷ 6

Mont Orford   Canada
Cold, windswept lone peak (there's no resort), worth a trip from nearby Montreal on a fine day.
305m; slopes 305–855m
⛷ 8 ⛰ 180 acres

Mont Ste Anne   622
☒ *Frontier Ski, Inghams, Ski Independence, Ski Safari, The American Dream, Solo's*

Mont St Sauveur   622

Mont Sutton   Canada
Varied area with some of the best glade skiing in eastern Canada, including some for novices. Quaint Sutton village nearby.
⛷ 9 ⛰ 175 acres

Morgins   421
Chalet resort indirectly linked to Champéry.
☒ *Ski Morgins Holidays, Ski Rosie*

Morillon   256
Valley village with link to the Flaine network.
☒ *Fairhand Holidays, Lagrange Holidays, Motours*

Morin Heights   Canada
Area in the Montreal region with 100% snowmaking. Attractive base lodge. ⛷ 6

Morzine   290
☒ *Airtours, Alpine Escapes, Alpine Events, Alpine Weekends, Alps2Go, Avant-ski, Beau-mont.com, Chalets 'Unlimited', Challenge Activ, The Corporate Ski Company, Crystal, CSb Mountain Holidays, Esprit Ski, Fairhand Holidays, First Choice Ski, Haig Ski, Independent Ski Links, Inghams, Lagrange Holidays, Made to Measure Holidays, Momentum Ski, Motours, Mountain Highs, Rocky Mountain Adventures, Ski Activity, Ski Arrangements, SkiAway Holidays, Ski Chamois, Ski Expectations, Ski France, Ski Line, Ski Link, Ski Morzine, Ski Weekend, Snowline, Solo's, The Chalet Company, Thomson Ski & Snowboarding, Trail Alpine, White Roc*

Les Mosses   470
Small resort and area, best for a day trip.

Mottaret   276
Purpose-built but reasonably attractive component of Méribel.
☒ *First Choice Ski, Panorama Holidays, Ski Leisure Direction, Skiworld, Thomson Ski & Snowboarding*

Mottarone   Italy
Closest slopes to Lake Maggiore. No village – just a base area.
1200m; slopes 1200–1490m
⛰ 25km

Les Moulins   Switzerland
Village down the road from Château d'Oex with its own low area of slopes, part of the big Gstaad lift-pass area.
890m; slopes 890–3000m
⛷ 67 ⛰ 250km

Mount Abram   USA
Small, pretty, tree-lined area in Maine, renowned for its easy, immaculately groomed runs.
295m; slopes 295–610m
⛷ 5 ⛰ 170 acres

Mountain High   USA
Best snowfall record and highest lift capacity in Los Angeles vicinity – plus 95% snowmaking. Mostly intermediate cruising.
2010m; slopes 2010–2500m
⛷ 12 ⛰ 220 acres

Mount Ashland   USA
Arty town in Oregon renowned for Shakespeare. Mountain includes glaciated bowl rimmed with steeps. Best for experts.
1935m; slopes 1935–2285m
⛷ 4 ⛰ 200 acres

Mount Bachelor   USA
Extinct volcano in Oregon offering deserted runs on every side served by many fast chairs. Gets a lot of rain. You have to stay in Bend, 25 miles away.
1740m; slopes 1740–2765m
⛷ 13 ⛰ 3680 acres

Mount Baker   USA
Almost on the coast near Seattle, yet averages 600 inches snow a year. Plenty of challenging slopes. Known for spectacular avalanches.
1115m; slopes 1115–1540m
⛷ 9 ⛰ 1000 acres

Mount Baldy   Canada
Tiny area, but a worthwhile excursion from Big White. Gets ultra light snow – great glades/powder chutes.
slopes 1705–2150m
⛷ 2 ⛰ 150 acres

Mount Baldy   USA
Some of the longest and steepest runs in California. Near Los Angeles, but 20% snowmaking and antiquated lifts are major drawbacks.
1980m; slopes 1980–2620m
⛷ 4 ⛰ 400 acres

Mount Baw Baw   Australia
Small but entertaining intermediate area in attractive woodland, with great views. Melbourne 150km/93 miles.
1480m; slopes 1340–1565m
⛷ 8 ⛰ 61 acres

Mount Buffalo   656

Mount Buller   656

Mount Dobson   New Zealand
Mostly intermediate slopes in a wide, treeless basin near Mt Cook, with good snow-cover. Accommodation in Fairlie, 40 minutes away.
1610m; slopes 1610–2010m
⛷ 3 ⛰ 990 acres

Mount Hood Meadows   USA
One of several sizeable areas amid magnificent Oregon scenery. Impressive snowfall record but snow tends to be wet, and weather damp.
1375m; slopes 1375–2535m
⛷ 12 ⛰ 2150 acres

Mount Hood Ski Bowl   USA
Sizeable area set amid magnificent Oregon scenery. Weather can be damp.
1095m; slopes 1095–1540m
⛷ 9 ⛰ 960 acres

Mount Hotham   656

Mount Hutt   658

Mount Lemmon   USA
Southernmost area in North America. close to famous Old West town Tombstone, Arizona. Reasonable snowfall.
2500m; slopes 2500–2790m
⛷ 3 ⛰ 70 acres

Mount McKay   656

Mount Olympos   Greece
Ski mountaineering site with a chain of huts on both faces. Late winter is the best time to visit.
1800m

Mount Pilio   Greece
Pleasant slopes cut out of dense forest, only 15km/10 miles from the holiday resort of Portaria above town of Volos.
1500m ⛷ 3

Mount Rose   USA
Only 22 miles from Reno. Relatively high, with good slopes of its own and well placed for trips to other Tahoe resorts.
2515m; slopes 2515–2955m
⛷ 5 ⛰ 900 acres

Mount Selwyn   Australia
Popular with beginners and families. 6 hours from Sydney. Good lift system.
1520m; slopes 1490–1610m
⛷ 12 ⛰ 111 acres

Mount Snow   573
☒ *Ski Success*

Mount Spokane   USA
Little intermediate area outside Spokane (Washington State).
1160m; slopes 1160–1795m
⛷ 5 ⛰ 350 acres

Mount St Louis / Moonstone   Canada
Premier area in Toronto region, spread over three peaks. Very high-capacity lift system and 100% snowmaking.
⛷ 13 ⛰ 175

Mount Vermio Greece
Oldest ski base in Greece. In central Macedonia 60km/35 miles from Thessaloniki. Barren but interesting slopes.
slopes 1420–2000m 🚡 4

Mount Washington Resort Canada
Scenic area on Vancouver Island with lodging in the base village. Impressive snowfall record but rain is a problem. A reporter in 2002 says: 'Great powder, but they shut the lifts too early (3.30pm). There are plans to add more lifts and runs soon.'
1110m; slopes 1110–1590m 🚡 6 🎿 970 acres
✉ Frontier Ski, Ski Safari

Mount Sunapee USA
Closest area of any size to Boston; intermediate terrain.
375m; slopes 375–835m 🚡 10 🎿 210 acres

Mount Waterman USA
Small Los Angeles area where children ski free. The lack of much snowmaking is a drawback.
2135m; slopes 2135–2440m 🚡 3 🎿 210 acres

Mühlbach Austria
Village east of Saalbach, a short bus-ride from one end of large but low Hochkönig area that spreads over four mountains from Dienten to Maria Alm.
855m; slopes 800–2000m 🚡 36 🎿 150km

Mühltal 191
Small village in the Wildschönau.

Muhr Austria
Village by Katschberg tunnel well placed for visiting St Michael, Badkleinkirchheim, Flachau and Obertauern.
1110m

Muju Korea
Largest area in Korea and with a fair amount of lodging. Though it is the furthest resort from Seoul (some four hours south) it is still overcrowded. 🚡 12

Mürren 446
✉ Alpine Events, Inghams, Kuoni, Made to Measure Holidays, Plus Travel, Ski Club of Great Britain, Ski Solutions, SkiGower, Swiss Travel Service, Thomson Ski & Snowboarding

Mutters 119

Myoko Suginohara Kokusai Japan
A series of small resorts 2-3 hours from Tokyo which together make up an area of extensive slopes, with longer, wider runs than normal for Japan. 🚡 15

Naeba Japan
Fashionable resort with lots of accommodation 2 hours north of Tokyo. Crowded slopes.
900m; slopes 900–1800m 🚡 28

Nakiska Canada
Small area of wooded runs between Banff and Calgary, with state-of-the-art snowmaking.
1524m; slopes 1525–2215m 🚡 5 🎿 230 acres

Nasserein 179
Quiet suburb of St Anton, a short bus ride from the lifts.

Nauders Austria
Spacious, traditionally Tirolean village tucked away only 3km/2 miles from the Swiss border and almost on the Italian one. Its slopes start 2km/1 mile outside the village (free shuttle-bus) and are mainly high and sunny intermediate runs spread over three areas. There is lots of snowmaking. The area is not ideal for experts, though there is a lot of off-piste terrain. It's not ideal for complete beginners either – the village nursery slopes are some way out. There are five cross-country trails amounting to 40km/25 miles in all. Most of the hotels are comfortable 4-stars and many of the eating out possibilities are hotel-based. The après-ski scene has typically Tirolean jollity and there is quite a bit to do off the slopes, including tobogganing, curling, tennis, squash, bowling, and swimming.
1400m; slopes 1400–2850m 🚡 30 🎿 111km
✉ Waymark Holidays

Nax Switzerland
Quiet, sunny village in a balcony setting overlooking the Rhône valley. Own little area and only a short drive from Veysonnaz.
1300m; slopes 1300–3330m 🚡 100 🎿 400km

Nendaz 461
Enormous apartment development offering quiet alternative to Verbier.
✉ Interhome

Neukirchen Austria
Quiet, pretty beginners' resort with a fairly snow-sure plateau at the top of its mountain.
855m; slopes 855–2150m 🚡 14 🎿 35km
✉ Equity Ski

Neustift 119
✉ Alpine Tours, Esprit Ski, Interhome, Made to Measure Holidays

Nevegal Italy
Weekend place near Belluno, south of Cortina.
1030m; slopes 1030–1650m 🚡 14 🎿 28km

Nevis Range 655
✉ Skisafe Travel

Niederau 191
Amorphous chalet-style village in the Wildschönau region.
✉ Airtours, Crystal, First Choice Ski, Inghams, Neilson, Panorama Holidays, Thomson Ski & Snowboarding

Niseko Japan
Town on Hohhaido, three hours from Sopporo and with three ski areas close by. Good snow record and powder. 🎿 28

Nockberge Innerkrems Austria
Area just south of Katschberg tunnel.
1500m; slopes 1500–2300m 🚡 10 🎿 33km

Nordic Valley USA
Utah cross-country area close to Salt Lake City. Powder Mountain and Snowbasin are nearby Alpine areas.
850m; slopes 1000–1090m 🚡 2 🎿 2km

Nordseter Norway
Cluster of hotels in deep forest north of Lillehammer. Some Alpine facilities but best for cross-country.

Norefjell Norway
Norway's toughest run, a very steep 600m/1,970ft drop. 120km/75 miles north-west of Oslo.
185m; slopes 185–1185m 🚡 10 🎿 23km

La Norma France
Traffic-free, purpose-built resort near Modane and Val-Cenis, with mostly easy terrain.
1350m; slopes 1350–2750m 🚡 18 🎿 65km
✉ Erna Low, Fairhand Holidays, Interhome, Lagrange Holidays, Motours

Norquay 591

North Conway USA
Attractive factory-outlet-shopping town in New Hampshire close to Attitash and Cranmore ski areas.
✉ AmeriCan Ski, Virgin Ski

Northstar-at-Tahoe 495
✉ AmeriCan Ski, Ski The American Dream, United Vacations, Virgin Ski

Nôtre-Dame-de-Bellecombe 267
Pleasant village spoiled by the busy Albertville-Megève road. Inexpensive base from which to visit Megève, though it has fair slopes of its own.
✉ Motours

Nova Levante Italy
Little area used mostly by weekend day-trippers.
1180m; slopes 1180–2200m 🚡 14 🎿 20km

Nozawa Onsen Japan
Spa village with good hot springs 3 hours from Tokyo. The runs are cut out of heavy vegetation.
500m; slopes 500–1650m 🚡 24

Nub's Nob USA
One of the most sheltered Great Lakes ski areas (many suffer fierce winds). 100% snowmaking; weekend crowds from Detroit. Wooded slopes suitable for all abilities.
275m; slopes 275–405m 🚡 8 🎿 245 acres

Oberau 191
Very pretty village in the Wildschönau region.
✉ Airtours, First Choice Ski, Inghams, Neilson, Thomson Ski & Snowboarding

Obereggen Italy
Tiny resort used mainly by weekend day-trippers.
1550m; slopes 1550–2200m 🚡 6 🎿 10km

Obergurgl 150
✉ Airtours, Alpine Events, Crystal, Directski.com, Independent Ski Links, Inghams, Made to Measure Holidays, Ski Club of Great Britain, Ski Expectations, Ski Solutions, Thomson Ski & Snowboarding

Oberlech 134
Car- and crowd-free family alternative to Lech.

Oberndorf 187
Quiet hamlet connected to St Johann's undemanding ski area.
✉ Lagrange Holidays

Oberstdorf Germany
Attractive winter-sports town near the Austrian border with three small areas. Famous ski-jumping hill. The Nordic World Ski Championships will be held here in 2005.
815m; slopes 800–2220m 🚡 31 🎿 30km
✉ Moswin Tours

Obertauern 155
✉ Inghams, Made to Measure Holidays, Thomson Ski & Snowboarding

Ochapowace Canada
Main area in Saskatchewan, east of Regina. It doesn't get a huge amount of snow but 75% snowmaking helps.
🚡 4 🎿 100 acres

Oetz Austria
Village at the entrance to the Oetz valley with easy/intermediate ski area of its own and access to the Sölden, Kuhtai and Niederau areas.
820m; slopes 820–2200m 🚡 9 🎿 20km

Ohau New Zealand
Some of NZ's steepest slopes, with great views of Lake Ohau 9km/5 miles away (where you stay). 320km/200 miles south of Christchurch.
1500m; slopes 1425–1825m 🚡 3 🎿 310 acres

Radstadt　　　　Austria
Interesting, unspoiled medieval town near Schladming that has its own small area, with the Salzburger Sportwelt slopes accessed from nearby Zauchensee or Flachau.
855m; slopes 855–2185m
⛷100　🚠350km

Rainbow　　New Zealand
Northernmost ski area on South Island. Wide, treeless area, best for beginners and intermediates. Accommodation at St Arnaud.
1440m; slopes 1440–1760m
⛷5　🚠865 acres

Ramsau am Dachstein Austria
Charming village overlooked by the Dachstein glacier. Renowned for cross-country, it also has Alpine slopes locally, on the glacier and at Schladming.
1200m; slopes 1100–2700m
⛷18　🚠30km

Ramundberget　　652

Rauris　　　　Austria
Old roadside village close to Kaprun and Zell am See, with a long, narrow area that has snowmakers on the lower slopes.
950m; slopes 950–2200m
⛷10　🚠30km
✉ *Crystal*

Ravascletto　　　Italy
Resort in a pretty wooded setting near Austrian border, with most of its terrain high above on open plateau.
920m; slopes 920–1735m
⛷12　🚠40km
✉ *Sloping Off*

Reallon　　　France
Traditional-style village, with splendid views from above Lac de Serre-Ponçon.
1560m; slopes 1560–2115m
⛷6　🚠20km
✉ *Lagrange Holidays*

Red Lodge　　　USA
Picturesque Old West Montana town. Ideal for combined trip with Big Sky or Jackson Hole.
1800m; slopes 2155–2860m
⛷8　🚠1600 acres
✉ *AmeriCan Ski*

Red Mountain　　589
✉ *AmeriCan Ski, Frontier Ski, Ski Safari*

Red River　　　USA
New Mexico western town – complete with stetsons and saloons – with intermediate slopes above.
2665m; slopes 2665–3155m
⛷7　🚠270 acres

Reichenfels　　Austria
One of many small areas in Austria's easternmost ski region near the Slovenian border.
810m; slopes 810–1400m

The Remarkables　　661

Rencurel-les-Coulumes France
One of seven little resorts just west of Grenoble. Unspoiled, inexpensive place to tour. Villard-de-Lans is main resort.

Reutte　　　Austria
500-year old market town with many traditional hotels, and rail links to nearby Lermoos.
855m; slopes 855–1900m
⛷9　🚠18km

Revelstoke　　Canada
Town from which you can heli-ski in Monashees or cat-ski locally at a more reasonable cost than most places.
460m
✉ *Powder Skiing in North America Limited*

Rhêmes-Notre-Dame　Italy
Unspoiled village in the beautiful Rhêmes valley, south of Aosta. Courmayeur and La Thuile within reach.
⛷2　🚠5km

Riederalp　　Switzerland
Pretty, vehicle-free village perched high above the Rhône valley amid the glorious scenery of the Aletsch area. Access by cable-car or gondola from valley village of Mörel near Brig.
1900m; slopes 1900–2900m
⛷32　🚠90km

Rigi-Kaltbad　　Switzerland
Resort on a mountain rising out of Lake Lucerne, with superb all-round views, accessed by the world's first mountain railroad.
1440m; slopes 1195–1795m
⛷9　🚠30km

Riihivuori　　Finland
Finnish area with its 'base' at the top of the mountain. The city of Jyvaskyla is nearby. ⛷5

Riksgränsen　　652

Riscone　　　Italy
Dolomite village sharing a pretty area with San Vigilio. Good snowmaking. Short easy runs.
1200m; slopes 1200–2275m
⛷35　🚠40km

Risoul　　　309
✉ *Airtours, Crystal, Erna Low, Fairhand Holidays, First Choice Ski, Interhome, Lagrange Holidays, Motours, Neilson, Ski Arrangements, Ski Independence, Thomson Ski & Snowboarding*

Rivisondoli　　　Italy
Sizeable mountain retreat east of Rome, with one of the better lift systems in the vicinity.
1350m; slopes 1350–2050m
⛷7　🚠16km

Roccaraso　　　Italy
Largest of the resorts east of Rome – at least when snow-cover is complete.
1280m; slopes 1280–2200m
⛷12　🚠56km

Rohrmoos　　　167
Situated below small mountain next to Schladming.

La Rosière　　　312
✉ *Crystal, Erna Low, Esprit Ski, Interhome, Lagrange Holidays, Motours, Ski Arrangements, Ski Olympic, Ski Supreme, Thomson Ski & Snowboarding, Vanilla Ski*

Rossland　　　Canada
Remote little town 5km/3 miles from cult powder paradise Red Mountain.

Rougemont　　　444
Cute rustic hamlet just over the French/German language border near Gstaad.

Ruka　　　645

Russbach　　　Austria
Secluded village tucked up a side valley and linked into the Gosau-Annaberg-Lungotz area. The slopes are spread over a wide area.
815m; slopes 780–1620m
⛷33　🚠65km

Saalbach-Hinterglemm　160
✉ *Airtours, Crystal, Equity Ski, First Choice Ski, Inghams, Interhome, Made to Measure Holidays, Neilson, Panorama Holidays, Rocketski, Thomson Ski & Snowboarding*

Saalfelden　　　Austria
Town ideally placed for touring eastern Tirol. Extensive lift networks of Maria Alm and Saalbach are nearby.
745m; slopes 745–1550m
⛷3　🚠3km

Saanen　　Switzerland
Cheaper and more convenient alternative to staying in Gstaad – but there's much less going on.
slopes 950–3000m
⛷69　🚠250km
✉ *SkiGower*

Saanenmöser　　444
Small village with local slopes and rail/road links to Gstaad.
✉ *SkiGower*

Saariselkä　　　645

Saas-Almagell　Switzerland
Compact village up the valley from Saas-Grund, with good cross-country trails and walks, and a limited Alpine area.
1670m ⛷6

Saas-Fee　　　450
✉ *Alpine Events, Avant-ski, Crystal, Erna Low, First Choice Ski, Independent Ski Links, Inghams, Interhome, Kuoni, Made to Measure Holidays, Momentum Ski, Plus Travel, Re-lax Holidays, Ski Club of Great Britain, Ski Independence, Ski Solutions, SkiGower, Swiss Travel Service, Thomson Ski & Snowboarding*

Saas-Grund　　Switzerland
Sprawling valley village below Saas-Fee, with a separate, small but high Alpine area.
1560m; slopes 1560–3100m
⛷7　🚠45km
✉ *SkiGower*

Saddleback　　　USA
Small area between Maine's premier resorts. High slopes by local standards.
695m; slopes 695–1255m
⛷5　🚠100 acres

Les Saisies　　　France
Traditional-style cross-country venue in a pretty setting, surrounded by varied four-mountain Alpine slopes.
1650m; slopes 1150–2000m
⛷24　🚠40km
✉ *Classic Ski Limited, Inntravel, Lagrange Holidays, Motours, SkiAway Holidays*

Sälen　　　652

Salt Lake City　　USA
Underrated base from which to ski Utah. 30 minutes from Park City, Deer Valley, The Canyons, Snowbird, Alta, Snowbasin. Cheaper and livelier than the resorts.
✉ *AmeriCan Ski, Club Pavilion*

Salzburg-Stadt　　Austria
A single, long challenging run off the back of Salzburg's local mountain, accessed by a spectacular lift-ride from a suburb of Grodig.
425m

Samedan　　Switzerland
Valley town, just down the road from St Moritz.
1720m; slopes 1740–2570m
⛷3　🚠7km

Samnaun　　　123
Shares large ski area with Ischgl.

Samoëns　　　256
Beautiful village, a bus-ride from lifts into Flaine's skiing.
✉ *Fairhand Holidays, Inntravel, Interhome, Lagrange Holidays, Motours, Ski Life*

San Bernardino　Switzerland
Pretty resort south of the road tunnel, close to Madesimo.
1625m; slopes 1600–2595m
⛷8　🚠35km

San Candido　　　Italy
Austrian border resort on the road to Lienz.
1175m; slopes 1175–1580m
⛷4　🚠15km

San Carlos de Bariloche
　　　　　Argentina
Year-round resort, with five areas nearby.
790m
✉ *Scott Dunn Latin America*

San Cassiano　　397
Pretty village linked to the Sella Ronda.

Sandia Peak USA
World's longest lift-ride ascends from Albuquerque. Mostly gentle slopes; children ski free.
slopes 2645–3165m
⛷7 ↟ 100 acres

San Grée di Viola Italy
Easternmost of resorts south of Turin, surprisingly close to Italian Riviera.
1100m; slopes 1100–1800m
↟ 30km

San Martin de los Andes
Argentina
Sizeable town with accommodation, 19 km/12 miles from Chapelco ski area.
✉ Scott Dunn Latin America

San Martino di Castrozza Italy
Plain village in the southernmost Dolomites with varied slopes in four disjointed areas, none very extensive.
1465m; slopes 1465–2610m
⛷20 ↟ 50km
✉ Interhome, Rocketski

San Pellegrino Italy
Little ski area close to but not part of the Sella Ronda.

Sansicario 392
Modern resort, well placed in Milky Way near Sauze d'Oulx.
✉ Equity Ski, Rocketski

San Simone Italy
Tiny development north of Bergamo, close to unappealing Foppolo area.
2000m; slopes 1105–2300m
⛷9 ↟ 45km

Santa Caterina Italy
Pretty, user-friendly village near Bormio, with a snow-sure novice and intermediate area.
1740m; slopes 1740–2725m
⛷8 ↟ 25km
✉ Airtours, Equity Ski, Rocketski, Thomson Ski & Snowboarding

Santa Cristina 397
Quiet village on the periphery of the Sella Ronda.
✉ Crystal, Inghams

Santa Fe USA
One of America's most attractive and interesting towns. Varied slopes – glades, bowls, cruiser pistes, desert views. Great excursion from Taos.
3145m; slopes 3145–3645m
⛷7 ↟ 600 acres

Santa Maria Maggiore Italy
Resort south of the Simplon Pass from the Rhône valley, and near Lake Maggiore.
820m; slopes 820–1890m
⛷5 ↟ 10km

San Vigilio Italy
Charming Dolomite village with a delightful, sizeable area well covered with snow-guns.
1200m; slopes 1200–2275m
⛷33 ↟ 40km

San Vito di Cadore Italy
Sizeable, alternative place to stay to Cortina. Negligible local slopes, though.
1010m; slopes 1010–1380m
⛷9 ↟ 12km

Sappada Italy
Isolated resort close to the Austrian border below Lienz.
1215m; slopes 1215–2050m
⛷17 ↟ 50km

Sappee Finland
Resort within easy reach of Helsinki, popular with boarders and telemarkers. Lake views. ⛷7

Sarnano Italy
Main resort in the Macerata region near Adriatic Riviera. Valley village with ski slopes accessed by lift.
540m
⛷9 ↟ 11km

Le Sauze France
Fine area near Barcelonnette, sadly remote from airports.
1400m; slopes 1400–2440m
⛷23 ↟ 65km

Sauze d'Oulx 392
✉ Airtours, Avant-ski, Chalets 'Unlimited', Crystal, Equity Ski, First Choice Ski, Independent Ski Links, Inghams, Neilson, Panorama Holidays, Rocketski, Ski Arrangements, Ski Club of Great Britain, Thomson Ski & Snowboarding

Savognin Switzerland
Pretty village with a good mid-sized area; a good base for the nearby resorts of St Moritz, Davos/Klosters and Flims.
1200m; slopes 1200–2715m
⛷17 ↟ 80km

Scheffau Austria
Rustic beauty not far from Söll.
✉ Crystal, Esprit Ski, First Choice Ski, Thomson Ski & Snowboarding

Schia Italy
Very limited area of short runs – the only ski area near Parma. No village.
1245m; slopes 1245–1415m
⛷7 ↟ 15km

Schilpario Italy
One of many little areas near Bergamo.
1125m; slopes 1125–1635m
⛷5 ↟ 15km

Schladming 167
✉ Crystal, Equity Ski, Interhome, Made to Measure Holidays, Rocketski, Sloping Off

Schönried 444
A cheaper and quieter resort alternative to staying in Gstaad.
✉ Interhome

Schoppernau Austria
A scattered farming community, one of two main areas in Bregenzerwald north-west of Lech.
860m; slopes 860–2050m
⛷8 ↟ 37km

Schröcken Austria
Bregenzerwald area village close to the German border.
1260m; slopes 1260–2100m
⛷16 ↟ 60km

Schruns 147
✉ Interhome

Schüttdorf 194
Ordinary dormitory satellite of Zell am See.
✉ Airtours

Schwarzach im Pongau
Austria
Riverside village with rail links. There are limited slopes at Goldegg, and Wagrain (Salzburger Sportwelt) and Grossarl (Gastein valley) are also nearby.
600m

Schwaz Austria
Valley town beside the Inn with a lift into varied terrain shared with village of Pill and its mountain outpost, Hochpillberg.
540m; slopes 540–2030m
⛷6 ↟ 10km

Schweitzer USA
In Idaho but near Spokane (Washington State) and an easy combined trip with Fernie (in Canada). Good snowfall record; uncrowded, varied slopes.
1215m; slopes 1215–1945m
⛷6 ↟ 2350 acres
✉ AmeriCan Ski

Scopello Italy
Low area close to the Aosta valley, worth considering for a day trip in bad weather.
slopes 690–1740m
⛷9 ↟ 26km

Scuol Switzerland
Year-round spa resort close to Austria and Italy, with an impressive range of terrain.
1250m; slopes 1250–2785m
⛷15 ↟ 80km

Searchmont Resort Canada
Ontario area with modern lift system and 95% snowmaking. Fine Lake Superior views.
275m; slopes 275–485m
⛷4 ↟ 65 acres

Sedrun Switzerland
Charming, unspoiled old village on the Glacier Express rail route close to Andermatt, with fine terrain amid glorious scenery.
1440m; slopes 1450–2350m
⛷12 ↟ 50km

Seefeld 119
✉ Airtours, Crystal, Inghams, Interhome, Made to Measure Holidays, Thomson Ski & Snowboarding, Waymark Holidays

Le Seignus-d'Allos France
Close to La Foux-d'Allos (which shares large area with Pra-Loup) and has own little area, too.
1400m; slopes 1400–2425m
⛷13

Sella Nevea Italy
Limited but developing resort in a beautiful setting on the Slovenian border. Summer glacier nearby.
1140m; slopes 1190–1800m
⛷11 ↟ 8km
✉ Sloping Off

Selva/Sella Ronda 397
✉ Avant-ski, Bladon Lines, Chalets 'Unlimited', Crystal, Esprit Ski, First Choice Ski, Independent Ski Links, Inghams, Momentum Ski, Ski Arrangements, Thomson Ski & Snowboarding

Selvino Italy
Closest resort to Bergamo.
960m; slopes 960–1400m
⛷6 ↟ 20km

Semmering Austria
Long-established winter sports resort set in pretty scenery, 100km/62 miles from Vienna, towards Graz. Mostly intermediate terrain.
1000m; slopes 1000–1340m
⛷5 ↟ 14km
✉ Slovenija & Austrian Pursuits

Les Sept-Laux France
Ugly, user-friendly family resort near Grenoble. Pretty slopes for all grades.
1350m; slopes 1350–2400m
⛷25 ↟ 100km
✉ Lagrange Holidays

Serfaus Austria
Charming traffic-free village (with underground people-mover to get you to the lifts) at the foot of a long, narrow, relatively snow-sure ski area, linked to Fiss. There are few challenging slopes for experts, but it is a good area for touring. Most of the area is ideal for intermediates and the nursery slopes are good. The 60km/37 miles of cross-country trails include very pretty loops at altitude. Facilities for children are excellent. Most accommodation is in hotels, and restaurants are mainly hotel-based. Après-ski is lively and traditional, but there's not much to do off the slopes, apart from some beautiful walks.

1430m; slopes 1200–2700m
⛷19 ↟ 80km
✉ Alpine Tours, Interhome, Made to Measure Holidays

Serrada Italy
Very limited area near Trento.
slopes 1250–1605m ⛷ 5
✉ *Alpine Tours, Equity Ski*

Serre-Chevalier 314
✉ *Airtours, Alpine Answers
Select, AmeriCan Ski, Avant-ski,
Bladon Lines, Chalets
'Unlimited', Club Med, Crystal,
Equity Ski, Erna Low, Fairhand
Holidays, First Choice Ski,
Handmade Holidays, Hannibals,
Independent Ski Links,
Inghams, Interhome, Lagrange
Holidays, Made to Measure
Holidays, Motours, Neilson,
Panorama Holidays, Rocketski,
Ski Arrangements, Ski
Expectations, Ski France, Ski
Independence, Ski Leisure
Direction, Ski Miquel, Skiworld,
Sloping Off, Solo's, Thomson
Ski & Snowboarding, Tops Ski
Chalets and Club Hotels*

Sesto Italy
Dolomite village on the road to
Cortina, surrounded by pretty
little areas.
1310m
⛷ 31 ⛷ 50km

Sestola Italy
Appennine village a short drive
from Pisa and Florence with its
pistes, some way above, almost
completely equipped with
snowmakers.
900m; slopes 1280–1975m
⛷ 23 ⛷ 50km

Sestriere 405
✉ *Alpine Answers Select, Club
Med, Crystal, Equity Ski,
Inghams, Interhome,
Momentum Ski, Motours,
Neilson, Rocketski, Ski
Arrangements, Ski Weekend,
Thomson Ski & Snowboarding*

Shames Mountain Canada
Remote spot inland from coastal
town of Prince Rupert and with
impressive snowfall record. Deep
powder.
670m; slopes 670–1195m
⛷ 3 ⛷ 183 acres

Shawnee Peak USA
Small area near Bethel and
Sunday River renowned for its
night skiing. Spectacular views.
Mostly groomed cruising.
185m; slopes 185–580m
⛷ 5 ⛷ 225 acres

Shemshak Iran
Most popular of the three
mountain resorts within easy
reach of Teheran (60km/36
miles). Packed at weekends,
though few go to ski.
3600m

Shiga Kogen Japan
Largest area in Japan, the site of
Nagano's 1998 Olympic skiing
events and including 21
individual resorts.
930m; slopes 1220–2300m
⛷ 73 ⛷ 130km

Showdown USA
Intermediate area in Montana
cut out of forest north of
Bozeman. 50km/30 miles to the
nearest hotel.
2065m; slopes 2065–2490m
⛷ 4 ⛷ 640 acres

Sierra-at-Tahoe 495
✉ *AmeriCan Ski, Ski The
American Dream, Virgin Ski*

Sierra Nevada 638
✉ *Crystal, First Choice Ski,
Independent Ski Links,
Thomson Ski & Snowboarding*

Sierra Summit USA
Sierra Nevada area accessible
only from the west. 100%
snowmaking.
2160m; slopes 2160–2645m
⛷ 8 ⛷ 250 acres

Silbertal 147
Low secluded village in the
Montafon area, linked to
Schruns. A good base for
touring numerous areas.

Sils Maria 455
Pretty lakeside village, linked to
the St Moritz Corvatsch slopes.
✉ *Interhome, Made to Measure
Holidays*

Silvaplana 455
Pretty lakeside village near St
Moritz.
✉ *Interhome, Made to Measure
Holidays*

Silver Creek USA
Child-oriented resort close to
Winter Park. Low snowfall record
for Colorado.
2490m; slopes 2490–2795m
⛷ 5 ⛷ 250 acres

Silver Mountain USA
Northern Idaho area near
delightful resort town of Coeur
d'Alene. Best for experts, but
plenty for intermediates too.
1215m; slopes 1215–1915m
⛷ 6 ⛷ 1500 acres

Silver Star 589
✉ *AmeriCan Ski, Crystal,
Frontier Ski, Made to Measure
Holidays, Ski Activity, Ski All
Canada, Ski Independence, Ski
Line, Ski Safari, Ski The
American Dream*

Silverthorne USA
Factory outlet town on main
road close to Keystone and
Breckenridge. Good budget base
for skiing those resorts plus Vail
and Beaver Creek.
✉ *AmeriCan Ski*

Silverton USA
New expert-only area in
southern Colorado that used to
be heli-ski country. Served by
one lift from 2002. Avalanche
transceiver, shovel and probe
compulsory.
3170m; slopes 3170–3750m ⛷ 1

Sinaia 643

Sipapu USA
Great little New Mexico area that
would be better known if it had
more reliable snow-cover. Mostly
tree-lined runs. Nice day out
from Taos when conditions are
good.
slopes 2500–2765m
⛷ 3 ⛷ 40 acres

Siviez 461
Quiet, cheaper base for skiing
Verbier's Four Valleys circuit.
✉ *Interhome*

Sixt 256
Traditional village near
Samoëns.

Sjusjøen Norway
Cluster of hotels in deep forest
close to Lillehammer. Some
Alpine facilities but better for
cross-country.
885m; slopes 1000–1090m
⛷ 2 ⛷ 2km
✉ *Inntravel, Waymark Holidays*

Ski Apache USA
Apache-owned area south of
Albuquerque noted for groomed
steeps. Panoramic views.
Nearest lodging in charming
Ruidoso.
2925m; slopes 2925–3505m
⛷ 11 ⛷ 750 acres

Ski Cooper USA
Small area close to historic Old
West town of Leadville. Good
ski/sightseeing day out from
nearby Vail, Beaver Creek and
Copper Mountain.
slopes 3200–3565m ⛷ 4

Ski Windham USA
2 hours from New York City and
second only to Hunter for
weekend crowds. Decent slopes
by eastern standards.
485m; slopes 485–940m
⛷ 7 ⛷ 230 acres

Smokovec Slovakia
Spa town with small modern
centre near Poprad, with three
small areas known collectively
as High Tatras. Funicular railway
and snowmaking facilities.
1480m; slopes 1000–1500m
⛷ 6 ⛷ 4km

Smugglers' Notch 580
✉ *Ski The American Dream*

Snowbasin 558
✉ *AmeriCan Ski*

Snowbird 560
✉ *AmeriCan Ski, Crystal, Made
to Measure Holidays, Ski All
America, Ski Independence, Ski
The American Dream, United
Vacations*

Snowbowl (Arizona) USA
One of America's oldest areas,
near Flagstaff, Arizona, atop an
extinct volcano and with
stunning desert views. Good
snowfall record.
2805m; slopes 2805–3505m
⛷ 5 ⛷ 135 acres

Snowbowl (Montana) USA
Montana area renowned for
powder, outside lively town of
Missoula. 700 acres of extreme
slopes. Grizzly Chute is the
ultimate challenge.
1520m; slopes 1520–2315m
⛷ 4 ⛷ 1400 acres

Snowmass 504
Purpose-built village with big
mountain near Aspen.
✉ *Alpine Answers Select,
AmeriCan Ski, Fantiski-Ski2k,
Lotus Supertravel, Made to
Measure Holidays, Ski All
America, Ski Independence, Ski
The American Dream, United
Vacations*

Snow Summit USA
San Bernardino National Forest
ski area near Palm Springs.
Lovely lake views. 100%
snowmaking. High-capacity lift
system for weekend crowds.
2135m; slopes 2135–2500m
⛷ 12 ⛷ 230 acres

Snow Valley USA
Area quite near Palm Springs.
Fine desert views. High-capacity
lift system copes with weekend
crowds better than nearby Big
Bear.
2040m; slopes 2040–2390m
⛷ 11 ⛷ 230 acres

Solda Italy
The other side of the Stelvio
Pass from Bormio. Very long
airport transfers.
1905m; slopes 1905–2625m
⛷ 19 ⛷ 25km
✉ *Inghams*

Sölden 171
✉ *Made to Measure Holidays*

Soldeu 634
✉ *Airtours, Chalets 'Unlimited',
Club Pavilion, Crystal,
Directski.com, First Choice Ski,
Independent Ski Links,
Inghams, Lagrange Holidays,
Neilson, Panorama Holidays,
Ski Club of Great Britain,
Thomson Ski & Snowboarding,
Top Deck*

Solitude 545
✉ *AmeriCan Ski, Ski
Independence, Ski The
American Dream*

Söll 173
✉ *Airtours, Crystal,
Directski.com, First Choice Ski,
Inghams, Interhome, Neilson,
Panorama Holidays, Ski
Hillwood, Ski Wild, Thomson
Ski & Snowboarding*

Sommand France
Purpose-built base that shares
area with Praz-de-Lys.
1420m; slopes 1200–1800m
⛷ 22 ⛷ 50km

Sorenberg Switzerland
Popular weekend retreat
between Berne and Lucerne,
with a high proportion of steep,
low runs.
1165m; slopes 1165–2350m
⛷ 18 ⛷ 50km

South Lake Tahoe 495
Tacky base for skiing Heavenly.

Spital am Pyhrn Austria
Small village near Hinterstoder in Upper Austria, a bus-ride from its limited intermediate slopes at Wurzeralm. From the valley station a 3km/2 mile funicular goes up to a mid-mountain col with several restaurants and nursery slopes. Lifts and runs go off from here in several directions over pleasantly wooded intermediate terrain; the blues are tough, so transition from the nursery slopes is not easy. On the flat Teichlboden (1370m/4,500ft) beyond the col there are cross-country loops. The local lift pass also covers Höss and Bärenalm at Hinterstoder, a short drive away.
650m; slopes 810–1870m
⛷ 10 🚡 18km

Spittal/Drau Austria
Historic Carinthian town with a limited area starting a lift-ride above it. Day trip from Bad Kleinkirchheim or from Slovenia.
555m; slopes 1650–2140m
⛷ 12 🚡 22km

Sportgastein 104
Mountain village with some of the more interesting skiing in the Badgastein valley.

Squaw Valley 495
✉ AmeriCan Ski, Crystal, Ski Activity, Ski All America, Ski Independence, Ski Safari, Ski The American Dream, United Vacations, Virgin Ski

Stafal 389
Tiny, isolated village, with good access to Monterosa Ski area.

St Andrä im Lungau Austria
Valley-junction village ideally placed for one of the longest, most snow-sure cross-country networks in Europe. Close to the Tauern pass and to St Michael.
1045m

St Anton 179
✉ Airtours, Albus Travel, Alpine Answers Select, Alpine Events, Alpine Tours, Avant-ski, Bladon Lines, Chalet World, Chalets 'Unlimited', The Corporate Ski Company, Crystal, Directski.com, Elegant Resorts, First Choice Ski, FlexiSki, Independent Ski Links, Inghams, Lotus Supertravel, Made to Measure Holidays, Mark Warner, Momentum Ski, Neilson, Simply Ski, Ski Activity, Ski Addiction, Ski Arrangements, The Ski Company, Ski Expectations, Ski Line, Ski Solutions, Ski Total, Ski Wild, Ski-Val, Skiworld, St Anton Ski Company, Thomson Ski & Snowboarding, White Roc

St Cergue Switzerland
Limited resort less than an hour from Geneva, good for families with young children.
1045m; slopes 1045–1700m
⛷ 9 🚡 20km

St Christoph 179
Small village on Arlberg pass above St Anton.
✉ Elegant Resorts, Made to Measure Holidays, Powder Byrne, Slovenija & Austrian Pursuits

St-Colomban-des-Villards France
Small resort in next side valley to La Toussuire. Good base for visiting largest areas in vicinity (Valloire and Val-Cenis).

Steamboat 527
✉ Alpine Answers Select, American Ski Classics, Chalets 'Unlimited', Crystal, Inghams, Lotus Supertravel, Made to Measure Holidays, Ski Activity, Ski All America, Ski Independence, Ski Line, Ski Safari, Ski The American Dream, Skiworld, Thomson Ski & Snowboarding, United Vacations

Ste-Foy-Tarentaise 320
✉ Alpine Weekends, Independent Ski Links, Ski Arrangements, Ski Weekend

Steinach Austria
Pleasant village in picturesque surroundings, just off the autobahn near the Brenner Pass. An easy outing from Innsbruck.
1050m; slopes 1050–2205m
⛷ 6 🚡 16km
✉ Alpine Tours

Stevens Pass USA
A day trip from Seattle, and accommodation 60km/35 miles away in Bavarian-style town Leavenworth. Low snowfall and no snowmakers. Mostly intermediate slopes.
1235m; slopes 1235–1785m
⛷ 14 🚡 1125 acres

St-François-Longchamp 350
Sunny, gentle slopes, with a couple of harder runs. Linked to Valmorel.
✉ Lagrange Holidays, Motours, Ski Independence

St Gallenkirch 147

St-Gervais 267
Small town sharing its ski area with Megève and Chamonix.
✉ APT Holidays Ltd, Fairhand Holidays, Interhome, Lagrange Holidays, Snowcoach

St Jakob in Defereggen Austria
Unspoiled traditional village in a pretty, sunny valley close to Lienz and Heiligenblut, and with a good proportion of high-altitude slopes.
1390m; slopes 1390–2520m
⛷ 9 🚡 35km

St Jakob in Haus Austria
Snowy village with its own slopes. Fieberbrunn, Waidring and St Johann are nearby.
855m; slopes 855–1500m
⛷ 7 🚡 22km

St-Jean-de-Sixt 234
Traditional hamlet, a base for La Clusaz and Le Grand-Bornand.

St-Jean-Montclar France
Small village at the foot of thickly forested slopes. Good day out from nearby Pra-Loup.
1300m; slopes 1300–2500m
⛷ 18 🚡 50km
✉ Lagrange Holidays

St Johann im Pongau Austria
Bustling, lively town with a small area of its own. More importantly, an extensive three-valley lift network starts 4km/2.5 miles away at Alpendorf, linking via Wagrain to Flachau – all part of the Salzburger Sportwelt ski pass area that our figures relate to.
650m; slopes 800–2285m
⛷ 100 🚡 350km

St Johann in Tirol 187
✉ Crystal, Directski.com, Ski Wild, Snowscape, Thomson Ski & Snowboarding

St Lary Espiaube 360
✉ Crystal

St-Lary-Soulan 360
✉ Fairhand Holidays, Lagrange Holidays

St Leonhard in Pitztal 157
Village beneath a fine glacier in the Oetz area.

St Luc Switzerland
Quiet, unspoiled rustic village in the Val d'Anniviers on the south side of the Rhône valley, with plenty of high, easy slopes (shared with Chandolin) served almost entirely by drags. Most of the slopes are above the nursery area at Tignousa (2180m/7,150ft), reached by funicular – also the site of an astronomical observatory. Valley pass also covers Zinal, Grimentz and Vercorin – 200km/125 miles of runs in all.
1650m; slopes 1660–3025m
⛷ 16 🚡 75km
✉ Inntravel

St Margarethen Austria
Valley village near Styria/Carinthia border, sharing slopes with higher Katschberg.
1065m; slopes 1075–2220m
⛷ 15 🚡 80km

St Martin bei Lofer Austria
Traditional cross-country village in a lovely setting beneath the impressive Loferer Steinberge massif. Alpine slopes at Lofer.
635m

St-Martin-de-Belleville 322
✉ Beau-mont.com, Equity Ski, Fairhand Holidays, Handmade Holidays, Independent Ski Links, Les Chalets de St Martin, Made to Measure Holidays, Motours, Rocketski, Ski Total, Thomson Ski & Snowboarding

St Martin in Tennengebirge Austria
Highest village in the Dachstein-West region near Salzburg. It has limited slopes of its own but nearby Annaberg has an interesting area.
1000m; slopes 1000–1350m
⛷ 5 🚡 4km

St-Maurice-sur-Moselle France
One of several areas near Strasbourg. No snowmakers.
550m; slopes 900–1250m
⛷ 8 🚡 24km

St Michael im Lungau Austria
Quiet, unspoiled village in the Tauern pass snowpocket with an uncrowded but disjointed intermediate area. Close to Obertauern and Wagrain.
1075m; slopes 1075–2360m
⛷ 25 🚡 60km
✉ Alpine Tours, Equity Ski, Rocketski

St Moritz 455
✉ Alpine Events, Alpine Weekends, Club Med, The Corporate Ski Company, Crystal, Elegant Resorts, FlexiSki, Independent Ski Links, Inghams, Interhome, Kuoni, Made to Measure Holidays, Momentum Ski, Plus Travel, Ski Club of Great Britain, Ski Solutions, Ski Weekend, SkiGower, Swiss Travel Service

St-Nicolas-de-Véroce 267
Small hamlet on the northern fringes of the Megève network.

St-Nizier-du-Moucherotte France
One of seven little resorts just west of Grenoble. Unspoiled, inexpensive place to tour. Villard-de-Lans is main resort.

Stoneham 622
✉ Frontier Ski, Inghams, Ski Safari, Ski The American Dream

Stoos Switzerland
Small, unspoiled village an hour from Zürich. Overcrowded at weekends. Magnificent views of Lake Lucerne.
1300m; slopes 570–1920m ⛷ 7

Storlien Sweden
Small family resort amid magnificent wilderness scenery. One hour from Trondheim, 30 minutes from Åre.
600m; slopes 600–790m
⛷ 7 🚡 15km

Stowe 582
✉ Chalets 'Unlimited', Crystal, Elegant Resorts, Equity Ski, Inghams, Made to Measure Holidays, Neilson, Rocketski, Ski All America, Ski Arrangements, Ski Independence, Ski Line, Ski The American Dream, Solo's, Thomson Ski & Snowboarding, United Vacations, Virgin Ski

St-Pierre-de-Chartreuse France
Locals' weekend place near Grenoble. Unreliable snow.
900m; slopes 900–1800m
⛿ 14 ⛷ 35km

Stratton 573

Strobl Austria
Close to St Wolfgang in a beautiful lakeside setting. There are slopes at nearby St Gilgen and Postalm.
545m; slopes 545–1510m
⛿ 9 ⛷ 12km

St-Sorlin-d'Arves France
Small, traditional village tucked away south of the Maurienne valley, with a fair-sized area of slopes, some reaching a respectable altitude. There are grand plans to build half a dozen new lifts to link this area to the slopes of Le Corbier and La Toussuire for 2003/04, creating a 220km/137 mile domaine to be known as Sybelles.
1500m; slopes 1500–2620m
⛿ 13 ⛷ 90km
✉ *Lagrange Holidays, Motours, Ski Life*

St Stephan Switzerland
Unspoiled old farming village at the foot of the largest sector of slopes in the area around Gstaad.
995m; slopes 950–2155m
⛿ 69 ⛷ 250km

Stuben 134
Small, unspoiled village linked to St Anton.

St Veit im Pongau Austria
Spa resort with limited slopes at Goldegg, but Wagrain (Salzburger Sportwelt) and Grossarl (Gastein) are nearby.
765m

St-Veran France
Said to be the highest 'real' village in Europe, and full of charm. Close to Serre-Chevalier and the Milky Way. Snow-reliable cross-country skiing.
2040m; slopes 2040–2800m
⛿ 15 ⛷ 30km
✉ *Motours*

St Wolfgang Austria
Charming lakeside resort near Salzburg, some way from any slopes, best for a relaxing winter holiday with one or two days on the slopes.
540m; slopes 665–1350m
⛿ 9 ⛷ 17km
✉ *Airtours, Crystal, Inghams, Thomson Ski & Snowboarding*

Sugar Bowl USA
Exposed area north of Lake Tahoe with highest snowfall in California, best for experts. Lodging in Truckee but Squaw Valley nearby. Weekend crowds.
2095m; slopes 2095–2555m
⛿ 8 ⛷ 1500 acres

Sugarbush 573
✉ *Ski Arrangements, Ski Success*

Sugarloaf 573
✉ *First Choice Ski, Ski Success*

Summit at Snoqualmie USA
Four areas – Summit East, Summit Central, Summit West and Alpental – with interlinked lifts. Damp weather and wet snow are major drawbacks.
slopes 915–1645m
⛿ 24 ⛷ 2000 acres

Sun Alpina Japan
Collective name for three ski areas four hours away from Tokyo. ⛿ 20

Sundance 545
✉ *AmeriCan Ski, American Ski Classics, Ski All America, Ski The American Dream*

Sunday River 584
✉ *AmeriCan Ski, Crystal, First Choice Ski, Neilson, Ski Independence, Ski Safari, Ski Success, Ski The American Dream, Virgin Ski*

Sunlight Mountain Resort USA
Quiet little area worth the easy trip from Vail to get away from its crowds for a day. Varied terrain. Good snowboard park.
2405m; slopes 2405–3015m
⛿ 4 ⛷ 460 acres

Sun Peaks 589
✉ *AmeriCan Ski, Frontier Ski, Inghams, Made to Measure Holidays, Ski Activity, Ski All America, Ski All Canada, Ski Club of Great Britain, Ski Independence, Ski Line, Ski Safari, Ski The American Dream*

Sunrise Park USA
Arizona's largest area, operated by Apaches. Slopes are spread over three mountains; best for novices and leisurely intermediates.
2805m; slopes 2805–3500m
⛿ 12 ⛷ 800 acres

Sunshine Village 591
✉ *Ski The American Dream*

Sun Valley 571
✉ *AmeriCan Ski, Ski Activity, Ski All America, Ski Independence*

Suomu Finland
A lodge (no village) right on the Arctic Circle with a few slopes but mostly a ski-touring place.
140m; slopes 140–410m ⛿ 3

Superbagnères France
Little more than a particularly French-dominated Club Med; best for a low-cost, low-effort family trip to the Pyrenees.
1880m; slopes 1440–2260m
⛿ 16 ⛷ 35km
✉ *Lagrange Holidays*

Super-Besse France
Purpose-built resort amid spectacular extinct-volcano scenery. Shares area with Mont-Dore. Limited village.
1350m; slopes 1300–1850m
⛿ 22 ⛷ 45km
✉ *Lagrange Holidays*

Superdévoluy France
Purpose-built but friendly family resort, consisting of a few huge apartment blocks, not far from north-west of Gap, with a sizeable intermediate area shared with La Joue-du-Loup.
1500m; slopes 1500–2510m
⛿ 32 ⛷ 100km
✉ *Fairhand Holidays, Lagrange Holidays, Motours*

Supermolina Spain
Dreary, purpose-built satellite of Pyrenean resort of La Molina, linked to the slopes of Masella to form area called Alp 2500.
1700m; slopes 1600–2535m
⛿ 29 ⛷ 100km

Tahko Finland
Largest resort in southern Finland. Plenty of intermediate slopes in an attractive, wooded, frozen-lake setting. ⛿ 9

Tahoe City 495
Small lakeside base for Alpine Meadows and Squaw Valley.

Talisman Mountain Resort Canada
One of the best areas in the Toronto region, but with a relatively low lift capacity. 100% snowmaking.
235m; slopes 235–420m ⛿ 8

Tamsweg Austria
Large cross-country village with rail links in snowy region close to Tauern Pass and St Michael.
1025m

La Tania 325
✉ *Airtours, Alpine Action, Alpine Options, Avant-ski, Chalet World, Chalets 'Unlimited', Crystal, Erna Low, Eurotunnel Motoring Holidays, Fairhand Holidays, First Choice Ski, French Freedom Holidays, Independent Ski Links, Lagrange Holidays, Le Ski, Made to Measure Holidays, Motours, Neilson, Silver Ski, Ski Amis, Ski Arrangements, Ski Beat, Ski Deep, Ski France, Ski Hame, Ski Independence, Ski Leisure Direction, Ski Life, Ski Weekends & Board Breaks, Snowline, Thomson Ski & Snowboarding*

Taos 563
✉ *AmeriCan Ski, Made to Measure Holidays, Ski Activity, Ski Independence, Ski The American Dream*

Tärnaby-Hemavan Sweden
Twin resorts with own airport. Snow-sure.
slopes 465–1135m
⛿ 13 ⛷ 44km

El Tarter 634
Relatively quiet, convenient alternative to Soldeu.
✉ *Club Pavilion, First Choice Ski, Panorama Holidays, Thomson Ski & Snowboarding, Top Deck*

Tarvisio Italy
Interesting, animated old town bordering Austria and Slovenia. A major cross-country base with fairly limited Alpine slopes.
750m; slopes 750–1860m
⛿ 12 ⛷ 15km

Täsch 478
The final base accessible by road on the way to car-free Zermatt – you take the train the rest of the way.
✉ *Interhome*

Tauplitz Austria
Traditional village at the foot of an interestingly varied area north of Schladming.
900m; slopes 900–2000m
⛿ 18 ⛷ 25km

Telluride 532
✉ *Alpine Answers Select, AmeriCan Ski, American Ski Classics, Made to Measure Holidays, Ski All America, Ski Independence, Ski Safari, Ski The American Dream, Skiworld, United Vacations*

Temu Italy
Sheltered hamlet near Passo Tonale. Worth a visit in bad weather.
1155m; slopes 1155–1955m
⛿ 4 ⛷ 5km

Tengendai Japan
Tiny area three hours by train and bus from Tokyo. One of Japan's best snow records, including occasional powder. ⛿ 5

Termas de Chillan Chile
Ski and spa resort 480km/300 miles south of Santiago. Base village has lodgings and you can stay at Las Trancas a few minutes' drive away.
slopes 1600–2700m
⛿ 9 ⛷ 35km
✉ *Scott Dunn Latin America*

Termignon France
Traditional rustic village with good slopes of its own. A good base for touring Maurienne valley resorts such as Valloire and Val-Cenis.
1300m; slopes 1300–2500m
⛿ 6 ⛷ 35km
✉ *Fairhand Holidays, Lagrange Holidays*

Terminillo Italy
Purpose-built resort 100km/62 miles from Rome with a worthwhile area when its lower runs have snowcover.
1500m; slopes 1500–2210m
⛿ 15 ⛷ 40km

Cedars Lebanon
The largest of Lebanon's ski areas, 130km/80 miles inland from Beirut. Good, open slopes with a surprisingly long season.
1850m; slopes 2100–2700m ⛿ 5

Valmeinier 264
Spread-out resort in the Maurienne valley.
✉ Club Med, Erna Low, Fairhand Holidays, French Freedom Holidays, Lagrange Holidays, Motours, Ski Independence, Ski Leisure Direction, Ski Life, Snowcoach

Valmorel 350
✉ Airtours, Chalets 'Unlimited', Crystal, Erna Low, Fairhand Holidays, Independent Ski Links, Lagrange Holidays, Made to Measure Holidays, Motours, Neilson, Ski Arrangements, Ski Independence, Ski Leisure Direction, Ski Link, Ski Supreme, Thomson Ski & Snowboarding

Val Senales Italy
Top-of-the-mountain hotel, the highest in the Alps, in the Dolomites near Merano.
3250m; slopes 2005–3250m
⛷ 10 ⛏ 24km

Val-Thorens 355
✉ Airtours, Beau-mont.com, Chalet World, Chalets 'Unlimited', Club Med, Crystal, Equity Ski, Erna Low, Eurotunnel Motoring Holidays, Fairhand Holidays, First Choice Ski, French Freedom Holidays, Independent Ski Links, Inghams, Interhome, Lagrange Holidays, Made to Measure Holidays, Motours, Neilson, Panorama Holidays, Rocketski, Silver Ski, Ski Arrangements, Ski Club of Great Britain, Ski Expectations, Ski France, Ski Independence, Ski Life, Ski Line, Ski Supreme, Ski Weekend, Skiworld, Thomson Ski & Snowboarding

Valtournenche 368
Cheaper alternative to Cervinia.
✉ Equity Ski

Vandans 147
Working village well placed for visiting all the Montafon areas.

Vars 309
Large, convenient purpose-built resort linked to Risoul.
✉ Fairhand Holidays, Interhome, Lagrange Holidays, Motours, Tops Ski Chalets and Club Hotels

Vaujany 203
Rustic village with lift accessing the Alpe-d'Huez ski area.
✉ Erna Low, Fairhand Holidays, Lagrange Holidays, Motours, Ski Independence, Ski Peak

Las Vegas Resort USA
Area formerly known as Lee Canyon, cut from forest only 50 minutes' drive from Las Vegas. Height and snowmaking gives fairly reliable snow. Night skiing too.
2590m; slopes 2590–2840m
⛷ 3 ⛏ 200 acres
✉ Virgin Ski

Vemdalen 652
✉ Neilson

Vemdalsskalet 652

Vent Austria
High, remote Oztal village known mainly as a touring base, with just enough lift-served skiing to warrant a day trip from nearby Obergurgl.
1900m; slopes 1900–2680m
⛷ 4 ⛏ 15km

Ventron France
One of several areas near Strasbourg. No snowmakers.
630m; slopes 900–1110m
⛷ 8 ⛏ 15km

Verbier 461
✉ Airtours, Alpine Answers Select, Alpine Events, Alpine Weekends, Avant-ski, Bladon Lines, Chalet World, Chalets 'Unlimited', The Corporate Ski Company, Crystal, Descent International, Elegant Resorts, Erna Low, First Choice Ski, FlexiSki, Independent Ski Links, Inghams, Interhome, Made to Measure Holidays, Momentum Ski, Neilson, Peak Ski, Plus Travel, Simply Ski, Ski Activity, Ski Club of Great Britain, The Ski Company Ltd, Ski Expectations, Ski Independence, Ski Line, Ski Solutions, Ski Verbier, Ski Weekend, Ski with Julia, Skiworld, Swiss Travel Service, Thomson Ski & Snowboarding, Vertical Reality at Verbier Ltd, White Roc

Verchaix France
Charming hamlet in lovely surroundings, next to Morillon, at the foot of the Flaine area.
700m; slopes 700–2560m
⛷ 80 ⛏ 260km

Vercorin Switzerland
Cluster of picture-postcard chalets on a shelf overlooking the Valais, reached by roundabout road or cable-car from near Chalais. Mix of wooded and open intermediate slopes served by a gondola and drags. Valley pass also covers Zinal, Grimentz and St Luc/ Chandolin – 200km/125 miles of runs in total. Natural ice-rink.
1330m; slopes 1330–2400m
⛷ 9 ⛏ 35km

Verditz Austria
One of several small, mostly mountain-top areas overlooking the town of Villach.
675m; slopes 675–2165m
⛷ 5 ⛏ 17km
✉ Sloping Off

Vex Switzerland
Major village in unspoiled, attractive setting south of Sion. Verbier slopes accessed nearby at Mayens-de-l'Ours.
900m; slopes 1300–3330m
⛷ 100 ⛏ 400km

Veysonnaz 461
Little, old village within Verbier's Four Valleys network.

Vic-sur-Mere France
Charming village with fine architecture, beneath Super-Lioran ski area. Beautiful extinct-volcano scenery.
680m; slopes 1250–1850m
⛷ 24 ⛏ 60km

Viehhofen Austria
Cheaper place to stay when visiting Saalbach. It's 3km/2 miles from the Schönleiten gondola, and there is a run back to the village from the Asitz section.
860m

Vigo di Fassa Italy
Best base for the Fassa valley, with Sella Ronda access via nearby Campitello.
1430m; slopes 1465–2060m
⛷ 8 ⛏ 25km

La Villa 397
Quiet Sella Ronda village in pretty setting.

Villacher Alpe-Dobratsch Austria
One of several small, mostly mountain-top areas overlooking the town of Villach.
500m; slopes 980–1700m
⛷ 8 ⛏ 12km

Villar-d'Arêne France
Tiny area on main road between La Grave and Serre-Chevalier. Empty, immaculately groomed runs, plus a couple of hotels.
1650m

Villard-de-Lans France
Unspoiled, lively, traditional village west of Grenoble. Snow-sure, thanks to snowmaking.
1050m; slopes 1160–2170m
⛷ 29 ⛏ 130km
✉ AmeriCan Ski, Equity Ski, Fairhand Holidays, Lagrange Holidays, Rocketski

Villard-Reculas 203
Rustic village on periphery of Alpe-d'Huez ski area.

Villaroger 211
Rustic hamlet with direct links up to Arc 2000.

Villarrica-Pucón Chile
Ski area on side of active volcano in southern Chile, 800km/500 miles south of Santiago. Lodgings are at Pucon village 30 minutes away from the slopes.
1200m; slopes 1200–2080m ⛷ 9

Villars 470
✉ Alpine Events, Club Med, The Corporate Ski Company, Crystal, Erna Low, First Choice Ski, Interhome, Kuoni, Made to Measure Holidays, Momentum Ski, Plus Travel, Powder Byrne, Ski Independence, Ski Weekend, Swiss Travel Service

Vipiteno Italy
Bargain-shopping town close to Brenner Pass.
960m; slopes 960–2100m
⛷ 12 ⛏ 25km

Virgen Austria
Traditional village in a beautiful valley south of the Felbertauern tunnel. Slopes at Matrei.
1200m

Vitosha 641
Vogel 644
Vorderlanersbach 114
Small, satellite village of pretty Lanersbach.

Voss 648
✉ Crystal, Inghams, Ski Wild

Vuokatti Finland
Small mountain in a remarkable setting, surrounded on three sides by lots of little lakes. Good activity base. ⛷ 8

Wagrain Austria
Traditional village at the heart of the intermediate three-valley lift system linking Flachau and Alpendorf. It's pleasant without being notably charming, mainly off the busy road linking the neighbouring resorts; it's a compact place, but the main lift bases are still a good walk apart. The slopes – wooded at the bottom, open higher up – are practically all easy/ intermediate stuff, but cover a huge area almost 15km/9 miles across. Kleinarl, up the valley, is at one end of another similar three-valley system. All these resorts are covered by Salzburger Sportwelt lift-pass that our figures relate to.
900m; slopes 800–2185m
⛷ 100 ⛏ 350km
✉ Thomson Ski & Snowboarding

Waidring 187
Quiet, snowpocket resort near St Johann in Tirol, with good beginner slopes and easy main slopes 4km/2.5 miles away.
✉ Thomson Ski & Snowboarding

Waioru Nordic New Zealand
Specialist cross-country base just over an hour from Queenstown. Spectacular views. Overnight huts.
1600m

Wald im Pinzgau Austria
Cross-country village surrounded by Alpine areas – Gerlos, Krimml and Neukirchen – and with Pass Thurn also nearby.
885m

Wanaka 658
Waterville Valley 573
✉ Virgin Ski

Weinebene Austria
One of many gentle little areas in Austria's easternmost ski region near Slovenia. No major resorts in the vicinity.
1560m; slopes 1560–1835m
⛷ 5 ⛏ 12km

Weissbach bei Lofer Austria
Traditional resort between Lofer and Saalfelden. It has no slopes of its own, but it's well placed for touring the Tirol. Kitzbühel, Saalbach, St Johann and Zell am See are nearby.
665m

Weissensee Naggeralm
Austria
Little area in eastern Austria and the location of Europe's largest frozen lake, which is used for all kinds of ice sports.
930m; slopes 930–1330m
⛷4 ⛇7km

Weisspriach Austria
Hamlet on snowy pass near Obertauern that shares its area with Mauterndorf and St Michael.
1115m; slopes 1115–2050m
⛷7 ⛇20km

Wengen 473
⊠ Alpine Events, Club Med, Crystal, Inghams, Kuoni, Made to Measure Holidays, Plus Travel, Re-lax Holidays, Ski Club of Great Britain, Ski Solutions, SkiGower, Swiss Travel Service, Thomson Ski & Snowboarding

Wentworth Canada
Long-established Nova Scotia area with largest accessible acreage in the Maritime Provinces. Harsh climate ensures good snow despite low altitude.
55m; slopes 55–300m
⛷6 ⛇150 acres

Werfen Austria
Traditional village spoiled by the Tauern autobahn, which runs between it and the slopes. Good touring to the Dachstein West region.
620m

Werfenweng Austria
Hamlet with the advantage over main village Werfen of being away from autobahn and close the slopes. Best for novices.
1000m; slopes 1000–1835m
⛷11 ⛇40km

Westendorf 189
⊠ Inghams, Thomson Ski & Snowboarding

Whakapapa 658

Whistler 614
⊠ Alpine Answers Select, AmeriCan Ski, American Ski Classics, Avant-ski, Chalet World, Chalets 'Unlimited', Club Pavilion, Crystal, Elegant Resorts, Equity Ski, Esprit Ski, First Choice Ski, Frontier Ski, Handmade Holidays, Independent Ski Links, Inghams, Lotus Supertravel, Made to Measure Holidays, Momentum Ski, Neilson, Rocketski, Rocky Mountain Adventures, Simply Ski, Ski Activity, Ski All America, Ski All Canada, Ski Arrangements, Ski Club of Great Britain, The Ski Company, Ski Expectations, Ski

Hillwood, Ski Independence, Ski Line, Ski Miquel, Ski Safari, Ski The American Dream, Ski Total, Skiworld, Solo's, Thomson Ski & Snowboarding, Trailfinders, United Vacations

Whitecap Mountains Resort
USA
Largest, snowiest area in Wisconsin, close enough to Minneapolis to ensure winds and weekend crowds.
435m; slopes 435–555m
⛷7 ⛇500 acres

Whiteface Mountain USA
Varied area in New York State 15km/9 miles from attractive lakeside resort of Lake Placid. 93% snowmaking. Plenty to do off the slopes.
365m; slopes 365–1345m
⛷10 ⛇211 acres

White Pass Village USA
Closest area to Mt St Helens. Remote and uncrowded with a good snowfall record. Mostly intermediate cruising.
1370m; slopes 1370–1825m
⛷6 ⛇635 acres

Whitewater 589
⊠ AmeriCan Ski

Wildcat Mountain USA
New Hampshire area infamous for bad weather, but one of the best areas on a nice day. Lodging in nearby Jackson and North Conway.
slopes 600–1250m
⛷4 ⛇225 acres

Wildhaus Switzerland
Undeveloped farming community in stunning scenery near Liechtenstein; popular with families and serious snowboarders.
1100m; slopes 1100–2075m
⛷9 ⛇50km

Wildschönau 191
⊠ Interhome

Wiler Switzerland
Main village in secluded, picturesque dead-end Lötschental, north of Rhône valley, with small but tall slopes reached by cable-car.
1420m; slopes 1420–2700m⛷6

Willamette Pass USA
US speed skiing training base in national forest near beautiful Crater Lake, Oregon. Small but varied slopes popular with weekenders.
1560m; slopes 1560–2035m
⛷7 ⛇550 acres

Williams USA
Tiny area above the main place to stay for the Grand Canyon.
slopes 2010–2270m
⛷2 ⛇50 acres

Windischgarsten Austria
Large working village in Upper Austria with cross-country trails around and downhill slopes at nearby Hinterstoder and Spital am Pyrhn.
600m

Winter Park 540
⊠ Alpine Answers Select, AmeriCan Ski, American Ski Classics, Chalets 'Unlimited', Crystal, Equity Ski, Lotus Supertravel, Made to Measure Holidays, Neilson, Rocketski, Ski All America, Ski Independence, Ski Miquel, Ski Safari, Ski The American Dream, Skiworld, Thomson Ski & Snowboarding, United Vacations

Wolf Creek USA
Remote area with highest snowfall record in Colorado. Uncrowded; wonderful powder. Great stop en route between Taos and Telluride.
3155m; slopes 3155–3590m
⛷6 ⛇800 acres
⊠ AmeriCan Ski

Xonrupt France
Cross-country venue only 3km/2 miles from nearest Alpine slopes at Gérardmer.
715m; slopes 666–1150m
⛷20 ⛇40km
⊠ Lagrange Holidays

Yangji Pine Korea
Modern resort an hour (60km/37 miles) south of Seoul, with runs cut out of dense forest. Gets very crowded. ⛷7

Ylläs 645
⊠ Bladon Lines, Inghams, Inntravel

Yong Pyeong Korea
Largest resort in Korea, 200km/125 miles east of Seoul, with snowmaking on all its runs.
750m; slopes 750–1460m
⛷16 ⛇20km

Zakopane Poland
An interesting old town 100km/62 miles south of Kraków on the Slovakian border. Mostly intermediate slopes.
830m; slopes 1000–1960m
⛷20 ⛇10km

Zao Japan
Big area with unpredictable weather, 4 hours from Tokyo by train. Known for 'chouoh' – pines frozen into weird shapes.
780m; slopes 780–1660m⛷42

Zauchensee Austria
Purpose-built resort isolated at the head of its valley, at one end of big three-valley lift network linking it to Kleinarl via Flachauwinkl – all part of the Salzburger Sportwelt ski pass area that our figures relate to.
855m; slopes 800–2185m
⛷100 ⛇350km
⊠ Made to Measure Holidays, Ski Hillwood, Sloping Off

Zell am See 194
⊠ Airtours, Alpine Events, Crystal, Directski.com, Equity Ski, First Choice Ski, Inghams, Interhome, Made to Measure Holidays, Neilson, Panorama Holidays, PGL Teenski, Rocketski, Ski Club of Great Britain, Ski Wild, Thomson Ski & Snowboarding

Zell im Zillertal Austria
Sprawling valley town with slopes on two nearby mountains. Now linked to higher Gerlos and Königsleiten to form a fair-sized area.
580m; slopes 930–2410m
⛷22 ⛇47km
⊠ Equity Ski, Thomson Ski & Snowboarding

Zermatt 478
⊠ Alpine Answers Select, Alpine Events, Avant-ski, Bladon Lines, Chalet World, Chalets 'Unlimited', The Corporate Ski Company, Crystal, Elegant Resorts, Erna Low, Independent Ski Links, Inghams, Interhome, Kuoni, Lotus Supertravel, Made to Measure Holidays, Momentum Ski, Motours, Plus Travel, Powder Byrne, Scott Dunn Ski, Simply Ski, Ski Club of Great Britain, The Ski Company Ltd, Ski Expectations, Ski Independence, Ski Solutions, Ski Total, Ski with Julia, SkiGower, Slovenija & Austrian Pursuits, Swiss Travel Service, Thomson Ski & Snowboarding, White Roc

Zinal Switzerland
Pretty, rustic village with some modern development, near the head of the Val d'Anniviers off the Valais. Cable-car up to a high area of open. steepish slopes – most runs are justifiably red or black. Excellent views. There are runs to the valley, including one excellent tough red off which an itinerary links to Grimentz, down the valley. The valley pass covers not only these two resorts but also St Luc/Chandolin across the valley, and Vercorin – 200km/125 miles of runs in total.
1680m; slopes 1680–2895m
⛷9 ⛇70km
⊠ Interhome

Zug 134
Tiny village with Lech's toughest skiing on its doorstep.

Zürs 134
High, smart but soulless village on road to Lech.
⊠ The Corporate Ski Company, Crystal, Elegant Resorts, Made to Measure Holidays, Powder Byrne

Zweisimmen 444
Limited but inexpensive base for slopes around Gstaad.

PUTTING
ACCURACY
FIRST.
Reuters and The European Tour